THE FACTS ON FILE
ENCYCLOPEDIA OF

# WORLD
# MYTHOLOGY
# AND LEGEND

SECOND EDITION

THE FACTS ON FILE
ENCYCLOPEDIA OF

# WORLD
# MYTHOLOGY
# AND LEGEND

SECOND EDITION

ANTHONY S. MERCATANTE
REVISED BY JAMES R. DOW

VOLUME I
A–L

☑®
Facts On File, Inc.

*Dedicated to all my family*
*—J...*

# THE FACTS ON FILE ENCYCLOPEDIA OF WORLD MYTHOLOGY AND LEGEND, SECOND EDITION

Facts On File, Inc.
132 West 31st Street
New York NY 10001

## LIBRARY OF CONGRESS CATALOGING-IN-PUBLICATION DATA

Mercatante, Anthony S.
    The Facts On File encyclopedia of world mythology and legend / Anthony S. Mercatante; revised by James R. Dow—2nd ed.
      p. cm.
    Includes bibliographical references and index.
    ISBN 0-8160-4708-1 (set: alk. paper) ISBN 0-8160-5780-X (volume I) ISBN 0-8160-5781-8 (volume II)
    1. Mythology—Dictionaries. 2. Folklore—Dictionaries. I. Dow, James R. II. Title.

BL303.M45 2003
291.1'3'03—dc21

2003040262

Facts On File books are available at special discounts when purchased in bulk quantities for businesses, associations, institutions, or sales promotions. Please call our Special Sales Department in New York at (212) 967-8800 or (800) 322-8755.

You can find Facts On File on the World Wide Web at http://www.factsonfile.com

Text design by Erika K. Arroyo
Cover design by Cathy Rincon

Printed in the United States of America

VB Logidec 10 9 8 7 6 5 4 3 2

This book is printed on acid-free paper.

# CONTENTS

# AUTHOR'S PREFACE AND USERS' GUIDE

Revision of an 800-page volume written by someone I did not know personally was the assignment I accepted in the late summer of 2000. While I was comfortable with some of the ethnic and cultural areas covered in the book, particularly the European and American, and most particularly the Germanic regions, it was still a formidable task to read through and evaluate encyclopedia entries that dealt with Asia, Africa, Oceania, and many other regions of the world. My proposal was to have professional colleagues help with specific areas, and so they did, particularly with the Greek and Roman, Slavic, and Egyptian entries. The task became more and more interesting as I worked my way through all 3,000 plus entries, and soon I could see the value of having one person responsible for the final revision. It was difficult but still possible to establish a system of cross-references across cul-

tures. After consulting with colleagues and using my own experience with myth, legend, and bibliographical work, I was able to produce a completely revised version of the original. Many new entries have been added, from the Nordic "Aesir-Vanir War" to the American "Work Projects Administration." Perhaps most useful in this revision is the addition of cross-referenced terms following most entries.

The encyclopedia is organized as an A–Z volume, accompanied by a General Index, a Cultural and Ethnic Index, and an updated annotated Bibliography. All entries are numbered, and the two indexes refer to these entry numbers, not to page numbers. The entry number appears above the entry itself, not as part of the text. The entry texts have been somewhat restructured. The headword appears at the very beginning of an entry, followed by variant

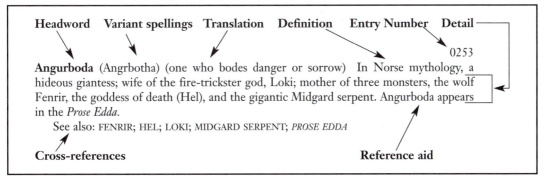

Headword    Variant spellings    Translation    Definition    Entry Number    Detail

0253

**Angurboda** (Angrbotha) (one who bodes danger or sorrow)  In Norse mythology, a hideous giantess; wife of the fire-trickster god, Loki; mother of three monsters, the wolf Fenrir, the goddess of death (Hel), and the gigantic Midgard serpent. Angurboda appears in the *Prose Edda*.

See also: FENRIR; HEL; LOKI; MIDGARD SERPENT; *PROSE EDDA*

Cross-references                                              Reference aid spellings in parentheses. The translations of the entries have been updated or revised when new or more accurate information is known. The most commonly accepted meaning of a name is included when available. The reader, however, must bear in mind that many translations of ancient names are merely scholarly conjectures or folk etymologies. Following the translation of the entry name is a concise definition. Only after all this is the encyclopedic detail offered. As an additional reference aid, citations of relevant art, music, films, and literature have been included. Cross-references follow and relate primarily to the entry itself, but there are also many references to other items; for example, the "Adam and Eve" entry now contains cross-references to figures from many cultures who represent the parents of humanity. These cross-references follow the entry and are listed after the phrase *See also*.

Finally, there is an extensive bibliography, with many new titles, all of which include a brief annotation. In two cases the reader should be aware that the encyclopedia entry itself makes reference to the bibliography. Under the terms *Motif* and *Tale Type*, there is reference to the standard classification reference works found in the Bibliography: the *Tale Type Index of the Folktale* and the *Motif Index of Folk Literature*.

In the first edition, Anthony Mercatante thanked the following, "who read and commented on various entries when in manuscript form": Robert S. Bianchi, Ph.D., Associate Curator of Egyptian, Classical, and Ancient Middle Eastern Art, Brooklyn Museum, Brooklyn, New York; Alexander Carlson (deceased), Late Art Curator, Nicholas H. Morely Collection, Florida; John Charlot, Ph.D., Curator, John Charlot Collection, Hamilton Library, University of Hawaii at Monoa; Roger Corless, Ph.D., Associate Professor of Religion, Duke University, Durham, North Carolina; Daniel Davila, M.A., Chief Librarian and Professor, Queensborough Community College, New York; Rachel M. Gallagher, Assistant to the Director, Department of Film, Museum of Modern Art, New York; Edgar Gregersen, Ph.D., Professor of Anthropology, Queens College and Graduate Center, CUNY; Gary Gisondi, Rogers and Hammerstein Archives of Recorded Sound, New York Public Library, Lincoln Center, New York; James J. Greene, Ph.D., Professor of English, City College of New York, CUNY; John A. Grim, Ph.D., Assistant Professor, Elizabeth Seton College, Yonkers, New York; Linda Hobson, music; Salvatore J. Iacone, Ph.D., St. John's University, New York; Rev. James Proud, Priest, Episcopal Diocese of New York; and Ronald Suter, M.A., Fairleigh Dickinson University, Rutherford, New Jersey.

I would like to add my words of thanks to the following colleagues who assisted me in revising the manuscript: James S. Ruebel, Classicist and Dean of the Honors College at Ball State University; Zora Zimmerman, English Professor, Slavicist and Associate Dean of the College of Liberal Arts and Sciences at Iowa State University; and Christine Shea, Classicist at Ball State University. I am also most grateful to Anne Savarese, formerly an editor at Facts On File, who initially asked if I would be willing to take on the task of revising this encyclopedia and convinced me to do so. Finally I want to thank my wife, Susan, for not only allowing me to spend almost all of my free time for the last year working on this book, even during our annual vacation to the primeval forests of Wisconsin, but also encouraging me to do so. Without her constant encouragement, I doubt if I would have been able to work so efficiently. To my entire family, who knew that I was working very hard, so that I can retire someday, I am also most grateful.

-— James R. Dow
Iowa State University
Ames, Iowa
January 2, 2003

# INTRODUCTION

*Homo narans*. As far back as we can trace our human history, including through prehistorical evidence gained from archaeology, we are aware that the human (homo) community has always participated in the narrating (narans) of stories. Today we are aware that there are many kinds of stories, some ancient and some newly created as part of our daily lives. In everyday speech we use a plethora of terms for these stories, including *myth*, *legend*, *folktale*, and *fable*, but the usage is not very precise. Our curiosity has led us to seek sources for many of these narratives, particularly those that we conceive to be the oldest, through historical and comparative studies, through philological and psychological research, and through insistent attempts at symbolic readings. In the scholarly world we have also long felt the need to classify the different types of stories. Through the classification of narratives, which basically means associating stories with similar plots as well as similar genres, we have long felt that we might gain some insight into the actual works themselves. Source seeking and classification, however, are not the purpose of this volume, for here we are interested in the stories themselves. Two main types of stories, two genres if you will, receive the most attention—myths and legends—but it will be quite apparent to users of this book that there are other kinds of closely related tales, for example, the folktale

and the fable. Thus, this encyclopedia includes all of these genres, and this edition has been expanded to include characters, motifs, and references to other closely related expressive forms. Brief definitions will help us understand the different types of stories that are found in this volume.

**Myth** is certainly the most complex of the genres. Definitions frequently emphasize the anonymous nature of myths, and all too often include imprecise terms like *traditional* or *in oral tradition*, and state that they are "passed from one generation to the next." Some scholars have spoken of "sacred narratives" and have tried to locate them in a "remote past," while others have suggested that the narrators believed the story to be "literally true." There are, it seems, as many definitions of myth as there are those who are interested in them. Most convincing in this array of inherent components of a myth is the suggestion that myths discuss preternatural topics, that is they present and ponder (discuss) in narrative form topics that are beyond (preter) the natural or the normal, not really miracles, but still strange and inexplicable. For too long now there has been an assumption that myths are in fact primarily attempts to explain the origin of natural phenomena or cultural rituals among social groups. It is, however, distinctly possible that myths are never really intended to explain anything, but are rather poetic devices that give concrete images to unexplainable phenomena, both natural and social. The ancient Greeks could not explain the passage of the sun across the sky in astronomical terms, nor could the Japanese explain smoke rising from a particular mountain, at least not in terms of vulcanology. There is, however, sufficient textual evidence in the numerous bodies of mythology from around the world to suggest that ancient peoples, sometimes referred to as "primitives," used poetic devices to describe Apollo's sun chariot on its passage through the sky, or the smoke rising from a volcanic Mount Fujiyama as the fiery passion of an emperor who sought to follow his beloved into heaven from a mountain top. When we create such stories today we call these images simply "metaphors."

For centuries major attempts have been undertaken to understand myths and myth making. In the 19th century there was an attempt to trace all myths back to an Indic source, thus implying what is referred to as the "monogenesis" of such stories. This resulted in competing schools of thought, ranging from sun and moon mythologists to those who sought a ritualistic source for the tales. Countertheories of the "polygenesis" of myths, soon developed, based to some degree on our rapidly expanding collections of the mythologies of people from around the world, but also based on our increasing knowledge of depth psychology. By the 20th century Sigmund Freud seemed to offer a way through this maze of theories. He believed that mythology was "psychology projected into the external world." For him and others, such as Carl G. Jung, it was clear that all human societies go through the same stages of intellectual and cultural development, that nature and the psyche are the same in all human beings, and the psychological processes are then manifested in the same way in all individuals, including in their expressive behavior—for our purposes, in their mythology. Such an approach would help us understand why the biblical flood myth and the

virgin birth story are found in many societies, not just in the Christian tradition.

Alas, all such theories yielded little reliable information on the sources and origins of these tales, and only limited useful information about their spread. Still, most theories of myth, with the possible exception of psychological approaches, have at least one thing in common, and that is the idea that evil, disorder, and chaos come from the outside. In the past and today, in spite of all scientific knowledge to the contrary, we still do not want to believe that evil is inherent to the human condition. This assertion helps us understand why so many myths account for the source of negatives in the world. It is almost always an evil god or goddess, a disorderly figure, or something other than our own human condition that brings on all of the bad things that happen to us. In summary, we don't really know, nor does it seem that we can know, where the plots and the contents of our stories come from. We can know, however, that humans have continually attempted to deal with, but not necessarily explain, the unknown.

Finally in regard to myth, there is a negative use of the word that needs some clarification. In the early years of Christianity in Europe there was a persistent attempt to discredit competing beliefs still surviving among the newly converted populace. Other beliefs were referred to as "false mythologies," while Christian beliefs were treated as "the true religion." We can still see this kind of cultural bias in the modern-day German word for superstition, *Aberglaube*, used in Germany since the 15th century to single out those whose belief (*Glaube*) was other than Christian (*Aber*, meaning here "un-Christian"). This use of myth as something "false" or as something in opposition to the "true" religion, carried over into the secular world. In common usage today, particularly in newspapers or magazines, *myth* is most often used to refer to something that many assert as fact but that can be shown through scientific analysis to be false. We read about the "myth of easy cancer cures" or the "myth of Kentucky Fried Rats." This usage has little to do with the mythologies of the world presented in this volume but sometimes reflects legends current in a modern and more urban setting.

*Legend* may have been even more misused than the word *myth* to describe stories, tales, narratives of various kinds. For the most part legend too has been described as "anonymous" and "traditional," but definitions of legend also usually include a statement to the effect that a legend is "*believed* to be true" and has as its main characters "*historical* personages." More recent scholarly attempts to define legend have refined these terms and focused on the legend's monoepisodic and localized characteristics, which are presented in a conversational mode. The descriptive term *historical* has been replaced by the new term, *historicized*, but there continue to be statements to the effect that such tales are "told as believable." Even with these refined terms, some clarification still seems necessary.

In contrast to myths, legends almost always focus on a single episode, which is then often presented as miraculous, uncanny, bizarre, and sometimes even embarrassing. Legends are indeed set in historical time, as we know it, and they frequently make reference to specific people and places. The full identity of such people and places is seldom directly addressed in the narrative itself, but the narrator assumes that they are known to the audience, and in this way the legend becomes historicized, that is, the story is associated with something or someone who can be factually identified. Most important in the telling of a legend, however, is the question of truth, for a legend places information before a listener who thus must decide whether this particular narrative is to be regarded as false or true, or partly false and partly true. Scholars now think of legends as a negotiation of truth and add that legends never ask for the suspension of disbelief. The result is a story whose truth is worthy of deliberation. Even if this "truth" if finally rejected, the question of truth

must be entertained. Did the Pied Piper of Hamelin really lead the children of the village into the depths of a mountain? After all, there is historical evidence to document the disappearance of 130 children on June 26, 1284. Is there really a mysterious weeping woman, *la llorona*, who seeks her dead children along the river banks and arroyos of the American Southwest? There have been thousands of reports of encounters with her. When these stories are told or even read, the audience immediately seems to divide into believers and doubters, and a negotiation of the truth follows. Legends then, in contrast to myths, have at their very core the question of believability and truth. The question, however, is rarely settled to the satisfaction of all participants of the storytelling event.

*Folktale* has frequently been used as a term to describe many forms of oral narratives, from jokes and anecdotes to lengthy adventure tales. As a result of the collections published by Charles Perrault in 1697, the Brothers Grimm between 1812 and 1815, and Hans Christian Andersen in 1872, we now think of folktales as wonder tales and sometimes use the German term *Märchen* to group them together. These stories were long conceived to be of European origin, and when they were found elsewhere, for example in the Western Hemisphere or even in Africa or Asia, their presence was most often attributed to diffusion. These tales are clearly fictional and ahistorical, as we can see by the opening and closing formulas like "Once upon a time" and "They lived happily ever after."

Again, however, there were generalizations about their "anonymous" nature, or their "being passed on from one generation to another." For most of the latter half of the 19th century and the first half of the 20th, there were enormous scholarly undertakings to record the many variants of the folktales, particularly those of Europe. Monogenesis was assumed, and an elaborate methodology was developed to trace individual tales historically through time, in order to document their antiquity and continuity, and geographically through space, in order to document the diffusion of such tales. Maps were used to create an atlas of the variants, which included the primary tale as well as subtypes or variants. The entire concept of the variant, grew out of these endeavors. Unfortunately, collectors and scholars failed to take into account some variants of the tales by editing or censoring out from truly oral versions those elements that might be considered as obscene or offensive. Both Perrault and the Brothers Grimm were guilty of manipulating their recorded stories. Oral versions of Little Red Riding Hood, for example, include vivid scenes of cannibalism, eating the body and drinking the blood of the grandmother, a virtual striptease, disrobing and burning of her clothes at the command of the wolf, and defecating in bed by the young girl, but all these motifs have been completely suppressed, and only those who use both oral and written sources to try to understand the tales are aware of these variant motifs.

With the flood of information in the form of "collected," published, or archived texts, folklorists were consumed for more than a century and a half with establishing what they conceived to be a core story, which they referred to as a "tale type," and with classifying the thousands of motifs found in these same narratives. Based on this work it seemed that it might indeed be possible to document whether a tale had a single origin or arose in widely separated regions of the world. This might then give us an answer to the questions of monogenesis versus polygenesis. Source seeking set scholars off on a centuries-long quest that left us with intriguing theories and extensive compendia for comparing the various tales but otherwise produced far too little information to give us answers to our continuing quest for sources. Scholars today are more interested in the historical, social, and contextual settings of the storytelling event itself.

What then is a folktale, and perhaps of more interest, does it still exist as an oral form like the myth and the legend? In contrast to the myth,

which may have and still does serve the purpose of depicting natural and social phenomena, as we have seen, and the legend, which laces our conversations with stories that we must decipher as true or false, the folktale is pure fantasy, exceptionally free-flowing, and has the effect of removing its topic from any constraints of reality. Folktales, or wonder tales, however, are seldom a part of our active storytelling repertoire. Still, the stories themselves are sometimes told by professional storytellers, and there are continuing publications of them, both through new translations of older collections and through selections of individual tales and more unified collections.

**Fable** is usually defined simply as an animal tale with a moral. Are fables too "anonymous" like the other narrative forms above? Perhaps, but what about the collections by Aesop or Gotthold Ephraim Lessing, or the modern versions by James Thurber? Have they been passed on from one generation to another, orally? Some have been, but others are purely literary in nature. Are they believed in any sense? Do they really teach a moral? Many conclude with a brief statement, which has often been described as a moral. Are talking animals always the main characters in the fables? Fables are more complex than this kind of generalization would suggest.

They do indeed seem to be oral tales that eventually are written down, and some of the collections have come down to us. Some scholars prefer an ancient Greek definition that captures the fable's essentially rhetorical genius: "a fictitious story picturing a truth." Perhaps more useful would be to describe fables as stories with human, animal, or inanimate objects as their characters. Most important, however, would be an emphasis on fables as stories that teach worldly wisdom and shrewdness, not moral values or good conduct. The many Aesopic fables about foxes and lions, the Joel Chandler Harris stories about Br'er Rabbit and Br'er Fox, James Thurber's tale about the "Unicorn in the Garden," and George Orwell's *Animal Farm* are all good examples of animals and humans exemplifying their shrewd nature, hardly their moral virtues.

The stories included in this volume, even though the collection is quite extensive, represent only a small selection from the world of mythology, legend, folktale, and fable. In the first edition Anthony Mercatante suggested that we enjoy these works because they hold our attention. He went on to say that they are "about us, our hopes, fears, joys and tragedies. Even in our scientific age, when we supposedly have cast aside so many relics from the past, we find these works still vibrant and vital, because they are about us." I would add that they are narrative forms that we learn, teach, and use, many times, during face-to-face interactions. We think of them as traditional because they are based on known models or because they serve as evidence of continuities through time and space in human knowledge, thought, belief, and feeling.

Together we say, What more can we ask?

# A

**Aa** (A, Anunit, Aya)  In Near Eastern mythology (Babylonian-Assyrian), consort of the sun god Shamash, sometimes called Makkatu (mistress; queen). Originally Aa may have been a local male sun god whose gender was changed when the worship of the major sun god, Shamash, took precedence, the minor god becoming the female consort of Shamash. Her attendants were Kittu (truth) and Misharu (righteousness).

See also: SHAMASH

0001

*Aaron*

**Aaron**  In the Bible, O.T., son of Amram and Jochebed and elder brother of Moses and Miriam; married Elisheba; father of four sons. He was a leader of the Exodus.

0002

Aaron, a Levite, is first mentioned in the book of Exodus (4:14). He was appointed by Yahweh (a cult name of the Hebrew god) to be the interpreter of his brother Moses, who was "slow of speech" (Exod. 4:16). Aaron is the instrument of many of the miracles associated with the Exodus from Egypt, such as when he caused the rivers of Egypt to turn to blood (Exod. 7:20) and when he brought on Egypt a plague of frogs (Exod. 8:5). But Aaron was not as strong a personality as Moses. When his brother went up to the mountain to converse with Yahweh, Aaron gave in to the demands of the people and fashioned a golden calf for them to worship (Exod. 32). When Moses descended from Mount Sinai, he found the people worshiping their new god (based on Egyptian deities) and in anger destroyed the tables of stone containing the Ten Commandments that Yahweh had given him on the sacred mountain. Then he burned the golden calf, ground it to powder, mixed it with water, and forced the worshipers to drink it. Yahweh intended to destroy Aaron for his sin, but Moses intervened and prayed for his brother (Deut. 9:20).

Aaron was then consecrated High Priest of Yahweh by Moses. From that time the legend of Aaron turns almost entirely to his priestly functions. One tells of the rebellion of the sons of Korah (Num. 16:1–35). Korah, a Levite, with Dathan and Abiram, questioned Aaron's right to the priesthood. Moses then challenged them to offer incense to Yahweh (a rite only to be done by the priests). As a punishment Yahweh had the earth open up and swallow Korah and his men.

Aaron was the keeper of the tribal rod, an official talisman that each of the Twelve Tribes possessed. At Yahweh's command Moses ordered each of the 12 to bring its rod to the Tabernacle. When the rods were left in front of the Ark, Aaron's rod miraculously budded, bearing almonds (Num. 17:5–11) and was seen as Yahweh's approval of Aaron's role as priest. Aaron died at Mount Hor at 123 years of age after transference of his priestly robes and office to Eleazar (Num. 20:28). Jewish folk tradition not included in the Bible says that at Aaron's death the cave on the mountain was obliterated by God, but the people claimed that Moses had killed his brother out of jealousy for his popularity. To prove the people wrong, God produced a vision of Aaron on a couch, floating in midair.

In Islamic legend Aaron is called Harun. In the Koran (sura 19) Moses and Aaron went up to the mountain together, knowing that one was about to die but not knowing which. They found a coffin that did not fit Moses but fit Aaron. Moses then told Aaron to rest in it, and Aaron was taken up to heaven. Jewish folk tradition records that Aaron is in Paradise seated beneath the Tree of Life, where he instructs priests in their duty. Christian writers during the Middle Ages looked on Aaron as a prefiguration of Christ. Thus, just as Aaron was a high priest of the Old Testament, so Jesus was the high priest of the New Testament. Some of the cult objects associated with Aaron in the Old Testament were viewed as prefigurations of the vestments worn by Christian priests and bishops. This, however, is not the actual case; the vestments were based on secular Roman dress of the early Christian era.

Western art frequently pictures Aaron in paintings of Moses. Often Aaron holds a censer and a flowering wand or rod. Sometimes he appears in full priestly vestments, which are de-

scribed in detail in Exodus (chap. 28). He may wear a turban or a crown that resembles the papal crown of later Christian art. His robe may have bells, which he used to frighten off demons. Tintoretto painted *Worship of the Golden Calf*, and Felix Chretien painted *Moses before the Pharaoh*; the latter portrays Aaron and his magic rod and the transformation of the snakes, as told in the Bible. In music, Rossini's opera *Mosè in Egitto* (Moses in Egypt) and Arnold Schoenberg's opera *Moses und Aron* (Moses and Aaron) both contain roles for Aaron.

In Christian folklore the name "Aaron's beard" is applied to several wild plants, such as St. John's wort, the ivy-leaved toadflax, and meadowsweet. The name is derived from the mention of Aaron's beard in Psalm 133, which also inspired a poem by the 17th-century English poet George Herbert.

"Aaron's rod" is a name given to various plants, including the great mullein and the goldenrod. It is also a name for the divining rod or magic wand used by magicians. The expression "Aaron's serpent" refers to the biblical legend that his rod turned into a serpent and swallowed up the serpents of the Egyptian priests (Exod. 8:10–12).

See also: MARS; MOSES; YAHWEH

*Korah*

**Aba** (above)    In North American Indian mythology (Choctaw of Bayou Lacomb, St. Tammany Parish, Louisiana), good spirit, creator, heaven. At first there was a mountain, Nane Chaha (high hills), that had a passage from the top to caverns under the earth. From these caverns emerged the first Choctaws, along with ants. The Choctaws killed the ants' mother, and they called on Aba, who closed the mountain exit, locking in the remaining people and later transforming them into ants.

**Abaris** (boatless one)    In Greek mythology, a sage who traveled with a magic arrow given him by the god Apollo. Abaris also used the arrow to invoke oracles and later gave it to Pythagoras in exchange for lessons in the latter's philosophy. It was believed that Abaris never ate.

See also: APOLLO

**Abderus** (son of battle)    In Greek mythology, a son of Hermes and Opus. A male lover of Heracles, the hero sent Abderus to guard the man-eating mares of the Bistonian king Diomedes. When Heracles discovered the lad had been eaten by the mares, he built the city of Abdera in his lover's memory.

See also: DIOMEDES; HERACLES; HERMES

**Abdiel** (servant of God)    In medieval Jewish folklore, an angel appearing in *The Book of the Angel Raziel*. Milton's *Paradise Lost* (book 5:805–808, 896) makes Abdiel the angel who opposes Satan's plans to overthrow God's rule. Milton may have borrowed the name Abdiel from 1 Chronicles (5:15) where it is given as the name of the son of Guni and the father of Ahi in the genealogy of Gad. Or Milton may have known the medieval Jewish work since he was well read in rabbinical writings.

**Abel** (meadow? breath?)    In the Bible, O.T., a shepherd, the second son of Adam and Eve. Abel was killed by his brother Cain (Gen. 4:2–8). Yahweh (a cult name for the Hebrew god) favored Abel's offering over Cain's, though the reason is not stated exactly in the Bible. In the New Testament Jesus speaks of Abel as the first martyr (Matt. 23:35), and he was considered so by the writers in the early Church. In the Koran (sura 5) Abel is called Habil. Albrecht Dürer and William Blake are among the artists who have portrayed Abel's death.

Abelites were a fourth-century Christian sect mentioned by St. Augustine. They married but had no children except by adoption. Since no children of Abel are mentioned in the Bible, Abelites assumed he had none and followed his lead.

See also: ADAM AND EVE; AUGUSTINE, ST.

**Abenamar and King Don Juan**    Late medieval Spanish-Moorish historical ballad. In 1431 King Juan II of Castile besieged the Moorish stronghold of Granada. After defeating the Moors the king placed the Moorish Infante Abenalmao on the throne. The ballad tells in part how the king questions a Moorish slave, Abenamar, on the condition of the city. The Moorish lad replies with a description of its beauties. The king then says:

> If thou art willing, O Granada
> I will woo thee for my bride,
> Cordova shall be thy dowry,
> And Sevilla by its side.

The answer, however, is

> I'm no widow, good King John,
> I am still a wedded wife;
> And the Moor, who is my husband,
> Loves me better than his life (James Young
>     Gibson translation).

Arabic poets, from whom this ballad stems, often used the term *husband* or *spouse* to refer to the lord of a region or city; the city is often spoken of as a bride.

See also: BALLAD; DON JUAN

**0009**

**Abe no Seimei** (Kamo Yasunari, Kamo Hogon, Abe no Yasunari) In Japanese folklore, hero-magician, son of the poet Abe no Yasuna and Kuzunoha, a white fox. Abe no Seimei was the court astrologer and is sometimes portrayed with his fox mother, Kuzunoha, who holds a writing brush in her mouth. Abe no Seimei once cured the Emperor Toba of a grave illness when he showed that the emperor's favorite mistress, Tamamo no Maye, was actually a nine-tailed fox who had bewitched him. Sometimes he is portrayed in a wizard's competition, conjuring white mice from an empty box.

See also: ABE NO YASUNA

**0010**

**Abe no Yasuna** In Japanese mythology, poet-hero who married a beautiful woman, Kuzunoha, who originally was a white fox. One day as Abe no Yasuna was walking in the gardens of the temple of the rice god, Inari, reciting his poems aloud, a party of nobles passed by in pursuit of a fox. They were after the fox for its liver, which was used in medicine. The fox ran into the temple gardens, stopping near Abe, who caught the animal and hid it in the folds of his kimono. The pursuers gave up the chase and left the area, and Abe freed the fox. A year later Abe fell in love with a beautiful woman, Kuzunoha, who gave birth to a boy, Abe no Seimei, noted in Japanese legend as a magician. Soon after his birth she died of a fever. Three days later she appeared to her husband in a dream, telling him not to weep, as she was the fox he had saved earlier.

See also: ABE NO SEIMEI; INARI

**0011**

**Abere** In Melanesian mythology, a wild woman, seducer and often slayer of men.

See also: MESEDE

**0012**

**Abezi-thibod** (the father who is devoid of counsel) In Jewish mythology, an evil spirit who fought against Moses but was finally drowned with the Egyptians in the Red Sea, where he is kept a prisoner under a pillar.

See also: MOSES

**0013**

**Abgar** In Christian legend, a king of Edessa who corresponded with Jesus. Jesus left no written records, but Christian legend has supplied them in the form of a correspondence with Abgar. In one letter Abgar asks "Jesus the good Savior" to come to heal him because "it is reported that you cause the blind to see, the lame to walk, do both cleanse lepers, and cast out unclean spirits and devils." Abgar's letter is answered by Jesus saying he must "fulfill all the ends" of his mission but will send after his Ascension to heaven one of his disciples "who will cure" the king's disease.

These unhistorical letters are reproduced in Eusebius' *Ecclesiastical History*, written in the fourth century. In a later addition to the letters there is one in which Jesus sends a portrait of himself on a cloth used to wipe his face. Upon touching the portrait, Abgar is cured of his illness. As fantastic as the letters are, some clergymen, both Catholic and Protestant, have defended them as genuine. Up to the middle of the 19th century it was common in some English homes to have the letters framed with a portrait of Christ.

See also: JESUS CHRIST

**0014**

**Abhinna** In Buddhism, supernatural knowledge or insight, possessed by the Buddha and those who have been enlightened. One Buddhist text tells of the Buddha and a disciple discussing Abhinna. The disciple asked: "Can an humble monk, by sanctifying himself, acquire the talents of supernatural wisdom called Abhinna and the supernatural powers called Iddhi?" The Buddha then asked: "Which are the Abhinnas?" The disciple replied: "There are six Abhinnas: (1) the celestial eye; (2) the celestial ear; (3) the body at will or the power of transformation; (4) the knowledge of the destiny of former dwellings; so as to know former states of existence; (5) the faculty of reading the thoughts of others; and (6) the knowledge of comprehending the finality of the stream of life." The sixth Abhinna is possessed only by enlightened beings. Spiritually advanced beings may possess the other five.

See also: BUDDHA, THE

0015

**Abigail** (a father's joy)   In the Bible, O.T., a beautiful woman; wife of Nabal (the fool), a wealthy sheep owner. She supported David with food and drink during his exile from King Saul, when her husband refused him help. When Nabal died, David married Abigail (1 Sam. 25:2–42). The name Abigail is used in Elizabethan writings to signify a lady's maid and is found in works of Christopher Marlowe, Beaumont, and Fletcher. In the neoclassic age, Pope, Swift, and Fielding also used the name, but their use may partly derive from Abigail Hill (Mrs. Masham), waiting woman to Queen Anne. Rubens painted an *Abigail*.

See also: DAVID; SAUL

0016

**Ab Kin Xoc**   In Mayan mythology, god of poetry, also known as Ppiz Hiu Tec.

0017

**Abomination of Desolation**   In the Bible, a phrase used by Jesus (Matt. 24:15) as a sign of the approaching destruction of Jerusalem. It probably refers to the statue set up in the Temple by

either heathens or Romans. Reference is found in the Book of Daniel (9:27, 11:31, 12:11) in the Old Testament. The term is now used for something that is destructive or hateful.

0018

**Abore**   In the mythology of the Warau Indians of the Guianas of South America, a culture hero. The evil frog woman Wowta made Abore her slave when he was a young boy, but when he grew up, she wished to marry him. Abore lured Wowta toward a hollow tree that he had filled with honey, Wowta's favorite food. When she saw the honey, she became so excited that she got stuck in the hollow tree. Abore then fled in a canoe, reaching the land of the white man, to whom he taught the arts of civilization. Wowta eventually escaped from the tree by turning herself into a small frog.

0019

**Abracadabra**   A medieval kabalistic charm said to be made up of the Hebrew words *ab* (father), *ben* (son), and *ruach acadsch* (holy spirit). The charm was first used in the second century as a powerful antidote against ague, flux, toothache, and numerous other ailments. The word was written on parchment and suspended from the neck by a linen thread.

See also: ABRAXAS

*Abraham*

0020

**Abraham** (father of a multitude?)   In the Bible, O.T. (Gen. 11:26–17:4), the first Patriach, the founder of the Hebrew people, who was at first called Abram; son of Terah; father of Isaac. Abraham was brought up worshiping many gods; then Yahweh, the Hebrew cult god, revealed himself to Abraham. As a young man Abraham married his half-sister Sara, later called Sarah, and then, under the direction of Yahweh, moved from Ur to Haran. He was driven by famine to Egypt and was accompanied by his nephew Lot. In Egypt he told Sarah to pretend she was his full sister and not his wife, for he feared he would be killed. Pharaoh took Sarah into his harem, and Yahweh sent a plague on Egypt. When Pharaoh discovered he had taken Abraham's wife, he sent Abraham and his wife back to Canaan (Genesis repeats this tale at the court of King Abimelech). Abraham settled in Mamre, and Lot moved to Sodom. Sarah, who had been barren, gave her maid Hagar to Abraham for childbearing, so she could claim the child as her own. When Hagar bore Ishmael to Abraham, the child became a source of contention between Sarah and Hagar. At one point Hagar and Ishmael were sent into the desert to die, but they were saved by an angel of Yahweh. The Lord blessed Abraham, appearing to him one day with two companions (often portrayed in art as three angels). One of the men told him that Sarah would bear a child. She laughed at that because she was too old to bear children. However, a child was born and named Isaac. To test Abraham's faith, Yahweh commanded him to sacrifice his son Isaac, but an angel of Yahweh stopped him at the last moment. When Sarah died at 127 years of age, Abraham bought a cave for her resting place at Machpelah. At the end of his life Abraham gave all of his possessions to Isaac. Then Abraham "died in a good old age, an old man, and full of years; and was gathered to his people" (Gen. 25:8). Nonbiblical works that deal with Abraham are *The Apocalypse of Abraham*, which tells of his youth and his journey to heaven escorted by the angel Jaoel, and *The Testament of Abraham*, which tells of Abraham's death. In the latter the archangel Michael is sent to fetch Abraham to heaven. Abraham, who does not want to die, is shown heaven and the judgment of the dead and then returned to earth. There he is tricked into giving his hand to the Angel of Death.

In medieval Christian belief Abraham was looked on as a prefiguration of Christ. His meeting with the high priest Melchizedek (Gen. 14:18–24), who blessed bread and wine, was seen as a prefiguration of the Last Supper of Jesus and the institution of the Holy Eucharist. Abraham's meeting with the three young men (Gen. 18:1–19) was seen as a symbol of the Christian Trinity and the sacrifice of Isaac as a symbol of the Crucifixion of Jesus, God the Father sacrificing his only Son. In Islamic tradition Abraham's sacrifice took place on the site of the Mosque of Omar at Jerusalem. In Islam, Abraham is called Khalilu'illah (the friend of Allah). In Christian art, Abraham is portrayed as a patriarch with a full beard, and sometimes carrying a knife, alluding to the sacrifice of Isaac. Dierick Bouts's *Abraham Being Blessed by Melchizedek* portrays the patriarch in rich medieval garb.

See also: ISAAC; ISHMAEL; MELCHIZEDEK; SARAH; SODOM

0021

**Abraxas**   Name of a god or demon found on Gnostic gems and amulets from the second century C.E. Abraxas's name was used in various magical rites. The name denoted the Supreme Being, the source of 365 emanations, the sum of the numbers represented by the Greek letters to which numerical equivalents had been assigned. The god appears on amulets with the head of a cock or a lion and the body of a man with legs that terminate in scorpions, holding in his right hand a club or flail and in his left a round or oval shield. The word *abracadabra*, according to some scholars, is derived from Abraxas. He appears in *The Book of the Angel Raziel*, a mystical work. In Hermann Hesse's novel *Demian* (1917), Abraxas is used as a symbolic representation of the realm "beyond good and evil."

See also: ABRACADABRA; GNOSTICISM

*Absalom*

other accounts say Absyrtus was not killed by Medea but arrived safely in Illyrium. Ovid's *Tristia* (3.9) tells the tale of Medea and Absyrtus, which is alluded to in Shakespeare's *Henry VI, Part II* (5.2.59). Other works dealing with the tale include Apollonius Rhodius's *Argonautica* (4.3303—482) and Apollordorus's *Bibliotheca* (*Library*) (1.9.24).

See also: JASON; MEDEA

0024

**Abuk and Garang**   In African mythology (Dinka of Eastern Sudan), the first woman and man; they were tiny and made of clay. When a pot in which they were placed was opened, they grew larger. The Great Being allotted them one grain of corn each day, but Abuk became selfish and planted more. While doing this, she struck the supreme god on the toe. As a result he retreated and cut the rope that connected heaven and earth. The Dinka associate Abuk with produce, gardens, grain, and waters. She is also the patron of all women. Her symbol is a snake.

See also: ADAM AND EVE; ASK AND EMBLA; SNAKE

0022

**Absalom** (father is peace, prosperity)   In the Bible, O.T., King David's third son, known for his physical beauty. He plotted against his father and "stole the hearts of the men of Israel" (2 Sam. 15:6). Riding on a mule in the decisive battle at Ephraim, Absalom was caught by his long hair in an oak tree. He was found by one of David's men, who killed him even though David did not want him killed. David lamented his death: "O my son Absalom, O Absalom, my son, my son!" (2 Sam. 19:4). William Faulkner picked up the lament for the title of his novel *Absalom, Absalom!* The English poet Dryden gave the name Absalom to the duke of Monmouth, Charles II's natural son, in his satire *Absalom and Achitopel* (1681), which attacks Puritan attempts to exclude the duke of York from the throne of England because, although the legitimate heir, he was a Roman Catholic.

See also: DAVID

0025

**Acamas** (untiring)   In Greek mythology, son of Theseus and Phaedra; brought up with his brother Demophon by Elephenor, king of Euboea. He was sent with Diomedes as ambassador to Troy to persuade King Priam to send Helen back in peace. After the destruction of Troy, he and his brother restored Theseus to the Attica throne. They then led a colony from Athens to Cyprus, where Acamas died. Acamas was one of the Greeks inside the wooden horse during the siege of Troy. Acamas also is the name of a son of Antenor mentioned in Homer's *Iliad* (book 11), as well as the name of a captain of the Thracians, Trojan allies who were killed by Ajax, according to Homer's *Iliad* (book 11).

See also: AJAX; ANTENOR; DIOMEDES; HELEN OF TROY; *ILIAD, THE*; THESEUS

0023

**Absyrtus**   In Greek mythology, son of King Aeetes of Colchis; brother of Medea. In her flight from Colchis with her lover Jason, Medea cut Absyrtus into pieces and threw them one by one into the sea, so that Aeetes, stopping to pick them up, would be delayed in his pursuit of the lovers. Some variant accounts say Medea killed Absyrtus in Colchis, others, near Istria. Still

**Acantha** (thorn)    In Greek mythology, a nymph who was loved by Apollo and was transformed into the acanthus flower.

See also: APOLLO

**Acanthus**    A large-leafed plant common in the Mediterranean region. In Greek legend the Athenian architect and sculptor Callimachus one day happened to pass a tomb, near which he saw an acanthus plant enfolding both a tile and a basket. He was inspired by the sight to design a capital for a column, since known as the Corinthian order. According to an earlier Greek legend, a young girl died, and her devoted nurse collected her trinkets and ornaments and placed them in a basket near her tomb and covered them with a tile. The nurse set the basket down on an acanthus root, whose stalks and leaves grew up enfolding the basket. It was this tomb that Callimachus saw. In medieval Christian symbolism, the acanthus signified "the awareness and the pain of sin" as well as heaven.

**Acarnan** (a fish, probably the labrax) **and Amphoterus** (both)    In Greek mythology, sons of Alcmaeon and Callirrhoë. When their mother heard of their father's murder by Phegeus and his sons, she prayed to Zeus (who was her lover) to let her sons grow up at once into men to avenge his death. Her prayer was granted, and her two sons killed Phegeus and his sons. Acarnan and Amphoterus then took the jewels of Harmonia and offered them at the shrine at Delphi. Later the two founded a kingdom called Acarnania, named after the elder brother, Acarnan.

See also: ALCMAEON; CALLIRRHOË; DELPHI; HARMONIA; ZEUS

**Acastus** (maplewood)    In Greek mythology, king of Iolcus, a son of Pelias and Anaxibia; Acastus was one of the Argonauts and a member of the Calydonian boar hunt. His sisters were persuaded by Medea, who was a witch, to cut up their father, Pelias, and boil him to make him young again. They followed Medea's advice, which was a trick to murder Pelias. When Acastus discovered this, he drove Medea and her lover, Jason, from the land and instituted funeral games in honor of his murdered father. During these games Hippolyte (or Astydameia), wife of Acastus, fell in love with her husband's friend, Peleus. When Peleus ignored her sexual advances, she accused him of attempting to rape her. Soon afterward, while Acastus and Peleus were hunting on Mount Pelion, Acastus took Peleus's sword after he had fallen asleep. As a result, Peleus, unable to defend himself, was nearly killed by the centaurs. He was saved by either Chiron or Hermes (ancient accounts differ). Peleus later returned and killed Acastus and his wife. Acastus is the father of Laodameia and is mentioned in Ovid's *Metamorphoses* (book 8).

See also: ARGONAUTS; CENTAUR; HERMES; HIPPOLYTE; JASON; MEDEA; PELEUS

**Acca Larentia**    In Roman mythology, an ancient Italian earth goddess whose feast was celebrated on 23 December; mother of the Lares. Roman accounts vary. In some she is said to have been the nurse of Romulus and Remus; in others, the mistress of Heracles and the wife of a rich Etruscan called Tarutius. She was believed to have left great possessions either to Romulus or to the Roman people. Acca Larentia also is said to have had 12 sons, called the Arval Brothers, one of whom was sacrificed each year. She may be connected with Larunda, a Sabine goddess whose feast and sacrifices also were made on

23 December. Acca Larentia is also the name of a companion of Camilla in Vergil's *Aeneid*.

See also: *AENEID, THE;* HERACLES; ROMULUS AND REMUS

0031
**Accolon of Gaul**   In Arthurian legend, a knight loved by Morgan le Fay, sister and enemy of King Arthur. Morgan le Fay gave Accolon the scabbard of King Arthur's sword, which protected its owner from bleeding, no matter how severely wounded. Despite this, however, King Arthur eventually killed Accolon.

See also: ARTHUR; MORGAN LE FAY

0032
**Acestes** (healer)   In Greek and Roman mythology, a king of Eryx; son of the Sicilian river god Crimisus and a Trojan woman, Egesta (or Segesta) who was sent by her father to Sicily to escape from monsters menacing the area around Troy. Acestes founded the town of Segesta. There he hospitably received the Trojan hero Aeneas after he fled from Troy. Acestes helped Aeneas bury his father on Mount Eryx, and in commemoration of this deed Aeneas built a city there called Acesta. The story of Acestes is told in Vergil's *Aeneid* (book 5).

See also: AENEAS

0033
**Achates** (agate)   In Roman mythology, the faithful friend of the hero Aeneas in Vergil's *Aeneid*. His devotion to Aeneas was so great that the term *fidus Achates* (faithful Achates) became synonymous with loyalty.

0034
**Acheflour**   In some Arthurian legends, mother of Perceval and sister of King Arthur. She was married to Bliocadrans, one of the 12 knights of Wales, who was killed in a tournament. Not wishing their son Perceval to follow in his father's footsteps, after his death, Acheflour pretended to go on a pilgrimage to St. Brandan in Scotland, but left instead for the Waste Forest. There she brought up her son without any knowledge of fighting. She warned Perceval that men in armor were devils and must be avoided.

See also: ARTHUR; PERCEVAL

0035
**Achelous** (he who drives away grief?)   In Greek mythology, the oldest of the river gods, son of Oceanus and Tethys; also the name of the river in northwestern Greece that forms part of the boundary between Aetolia and Acarnania. Achelous was the eldest of the 3,000 sons of Oceanus and Tethys and was the father of the Sirens. As a water god, Achelous was capable of metamorphosis and could turn himself into a serpent or an ox. In the form of an ox, when fighting with Heracles for the possession of Deianira, he lost one horn, which was later returned in exchange for the horn of Amalthea. Achelous was worshiped all over Greece and its colonies, especially Rhodes, Italy, and Sicily. At Dodona the oracle's answers always contained an injunction to sacrifice to Achelous. Ovid's *Metamorphoses* (book 8) tells of the god. Milton refers to the horn of Achelous in his *Animadversions Upon the Remonstrant's Defence*, in which he writes: "Repair the Acheloian horn of your dilemma how you can." Rubens portrays the god in his painting *The Feast of Achelous*.

See also: AMALTHEA; DEIANIRA; HERACLES; OCEANUS; SIRENS

0036
**Acheron** (woeful)   In Greek mythology, river believed to lead to the underworld. Homer, Vergil, and other ancient poets made Acheron the principal river of Hades. The rivers Cocytus, Phlegethon, and Styx were believed to be its tributaries. In Dante's *Divine Comedy*, Acheron forms the boundary of hell, and on its shore all of those who have died in the wrath of God wait to be ferried across by Charon. The origin of the river is explained to Dante by the poet Vergil.

Shakespeare's *Macbeth* (3.5.15) alludes to "the pit of Acheron," in *Titus Andronicus* (4.3.44) it is a "burning lake," and in *A Midsummer Night's Dream* (3.2.357) the heaven is carved "with drooping fog as black as Acheron." Milton's *Paradise Lost* (2.578) makes Acheron one of the four infernal rivers, calling it "sad Acheron of sorrow, black and deep." Acheron, according to some European poets, stands for hell itself.

See also: CHARON; HADES; PHLEGETHON; STYX

0037

**Achilles** (possibly, bane of the army)    In Greek mythology, hero, demigod, son of Peleus and the Nereid Thetis; married to Deidamia; father of Neoptolemus (Pyrrhus); father of Caistrus by Penthesilea; originally called Ligyron.

According to Homer, Achilles was brought up by his mother, Thetis, together with his older cousin, Patroclus. Achilles was taught both war and eloquence by Phoenix and the art of healing by the centaur Chiron, his mother's grandfather.

*The embassy to Achilles (John Flaxman)*

Accounts written after Homer added numerous details to Achilles' youth. According to one ancient account, Thetis, in an effort to make Achilles immortal, anointed him with ambrosia by day and held him in a fire at night to destroy whatever mortal element he had derived from his father, Peleus. One night Peleus saw the boy over the fire and made an outcry. Thetis, angry at the intrusion, left her son and husband and returned to the Nereids. Peleus then took the

motherless boy to Chiron on Mount Pelion. There the boy was fed on the entrails of wild animals. At the age of six, he was so strong and swift that he killed wild boars and lions and caught stags without a net or hounds. In a later variation of the myth, Thetis dipped the child Achilles into the river Styx, making him invulnerable except for the heel by which she held him, the spot in which he later receives his death blow—thus, the expression "Achilles heel."

*Thetis entreating Zeus to honor Achilles (John Flaxman)*

In another version, Thetis, alarmed by the prophecy of Calchas that Troy could not be taken without the help of Achilles and knowing that he would die in the effort, took the nine-year-old boy to the island of Scyros, where, in female dress, he grew up among the daughters of King Lycomedes. Calchas betrayed his whereabouts, and Odysseus and Diomedes unmasked the hero. Disguised as a merchant, Odysseus spread out female ornaments before the maidens, as well as a shield and a spear. Suddenly, a trumpet sounded the call to battle. The girls fled, but Achilles clutched the arms and said he was ready to fight.

During the first nine years of the Trojan War Achilles led the Greeks on plundering excursions around Troy, destroying 11 inland and 12 seacoast towns.

Angered when Agamemnon took the young girl Briseis, Achilles' mistress, Achilles drew back from the fight, and as a result the Trojans took the Greeks' camp and set their ships on fire. Achilles then relented to the extent of allowing Patroclus, wearing the armor of Peleus, to lead the Myrmidons into battle. Although Patroclus drove the Trojans back, he was killed by Hector, who took Peleus's arms from Patroclus's dead body. Grief for his male lover Patroclus and thirst for vengeance at last overcame Achilles' hatred for Agamemnon, and he reentered the Trojan War. Furnished with new arms by the smith god Hephaestus, Achilles went out against Hector, the Trojan hero, and eventually killed him. Homer's *Iliad* ends with the burial of Hector and leaves the ultimate fate of Achilles untold.

According to some accounts, Achilles' fate was one he had chosen himself: an early death with undying fame rather than a long but inglorious life. Near the Seasean Gate he was struck by the shaft of Paris, which was guided by Apollo. In a variant account the shaft struck Achilles in his one vulnerable heel. After Achilles' death the Greeks and Trojans fought over his body until Zeus sent down a storm to end the fight. In Homer's *Odyssey*, Achilles' spirit descended to the underworld, where he later met Odysseus, who was journeying to the land of the dead. In non-Homeric variant accounts, Thetis snatched her son's body out of its burning pyre and carried it to the island of Leuke at the mouth of the Danube, where the transfigured hero lives on, sovereign of the Pontus and husband of Iphigenia. Other myths place Achilles in Elysium with Medea or Helen as his wife. Greeks worshiped Achilles at his tomb on the Hellespont, where, according to another account, he appeared to Homer in the full blaze of his armor and struck the poet blind.

Dante's *Divine Comedy* places Achilles in the Second Circle of Hell, among those who met their death through love. The Italian poet says of him, alluding to popular medieval myth, that "he fought with love at the last." This refers to the widespread medieval legend that Achilles was killed by the treachery of Paris in the temple of Apollo Thymbraeus in Troy. Achilles had been lured there by the promise of a meeting with Polyxena, with whom he was in love and whom the Trojans offered to him if he would desert to their cause. Instead of meeting Polyxena he was killed by Paris. Lully's opera *Achille et Polyxène* (1687) is based on this medieval variation of the Achilles myth.

In addition to *Troilus and Cressida*, where Achilles is a main character, Shakespeare mentions him three times. In *Love's Labour's Lost* (5.2.635) and the narrative poem *The Rape of Lucrece* (1424), Achilles is one of the figures in the painting of Troy. In the play *Henry VI, Part II* (5.1.100), Achilles' spear is mentioned:

> That gold must round engirt these brows of
>     mine,
> Whose smile and frown, like to Achilles'
>     spear,
> Is able with the change to kill and cure.

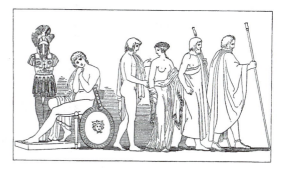

*Briseis leaving Achilles' tent (John Flaxman)*

This magic spear had wounded King Telephus, who learned from the oracle that only Achilles, who had inflicted the wound, could cure him. Shakespeare's source was probably Arthur Golding's translation of Ovid's *Metamorphoses* (book 12), which says: "I did wound King Teleph with his speare, and when he lay upon the ground, / I was intreated with the speare to heale him safe and sound."

Chaucer, in The Squire's Tale, part of *The Canterbury Tales*, also refers to the power of the spear of Achilles, both to kill and to cure. The plant Achillea (milfoil), named after the hero, is supposed to have the power to heal.

The Greek philosopher Zeno told a paradox, titled *Achilles and the Tortoise*, in which Achilles and a tortoise have a race. The hero runs 10 times as fast as the tortoise, which has a 100-yard start. Achilles, however, can never overtake the tortoise because in the time it takes him to cover the 100 yards to where the tortoise started, the tortoise has covered 10 yards; while Achilles is covering those 10 yards, the tortoise has gained another yard, and so on.

More then 50 operas have been written of the subject of Achilles. Notable among them are Pietro Mestastasio's libretto *Achilles in Scyros* (1736) and Hugo von Hofmannsthal's libretto *Achilles auf Skyros*, which was set to music by E. Wellesz in 1929. Paintings depicting Achilles include *Achilles at the Court of Scyros* by Nicolas Poussin and Peter Paul Rubens's *Thetis Dips Achilles in the Styx* and *Achilles Kills Hector*.

See also: AGAMEMMNON; CALCHAS; CENTAUR; DEIDAMIA; DIOMEDES; HOMER; ODYSSEUS; *ODYSSSEY, THE*; PATROCLES; PELEUS; PENTHESILEA; STYX; THETIS; ZEUS

*Achilles contending with the rivers (John Flaxman)*

0038

**Acidalia**   In Greek and Roman mythology, name given to Aphrodite (Venus), goddess of love, after she had washed in the same fountain as the Graces in Boeotia, a district in central Greece bordering on Attica. Both Vergil's *Aeneid* (book 1) and Ovid's *Fasti* (book 5) mention Acidalia.

See also: APHRODITE; VENUS

0039

**Acontius of Cea** (spear-man)   In Greek mythology, a poor young man who fell in love with Cydippe, daughter of a rich Athenian nobleman. Acontius carved an oath on an apple (or orange or quince). He gave the fruit to Cydippe, and she read out the oath, which said, "I swear by Artemis's Temple that I will marry no one but Acontius." Alarmed at the prospect of a poor match for their daughter, her parents went to the Delphic oracle for guidance and were told to let the lovers marry. Acontius's story is in one of Ovid's *Heroides* (21), verse letters from women of both myth and history to their absent lovers and husbands.

See also: ARTEMIS; DELPHI

0040

**Acrisius** (lacking judgment)   In Greek mythology, king of Argos, son of Abas and Aglaia; great-grandson of Danaus; and brother of Proteus. After an oracle told Acrisius that a son of his daughter Danaë would kill him, Acrisius shut her up in a tower, but Zeus came to her as a shower of gold (urine), and she bore a son named Perseus. When Perseus grew up, he went with his mother to seek Acrisius, who had fled from Argos, fearing the truth of the oracle. Perseus found Acrisius at Larissa in Thessaly and killed him unawares with a discus. His tale is told in Ovid's *Metamorphoses* (book 4).

See also: AGLAIA; DANAË; PERSEUS; PROTEUS; OVID; ZEUS

**Actaeus** (of the coast)   In Greek mythology, first king of Attica and father of Agraulos. Agraulos married Cecrops, whom the Athenians called their first king, though Actaeus ruled before him.

See also: CECROPS

**Actis** (beam of light)   In Greek mythology, son of Helios and Rhode; brother of Candalus, Cercaphus, Macar, Ochimus, Tenages, and Triopas. Actis and his brothers were the first to sacrifice to Athena. He founded Heliopolis in Egypt. The Colossus of Rhodes was erected in his honor.

See also: ATHENA; HELIOS; COLOSSUS OF RHODES

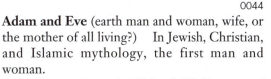

*Adam and Eve*

**Adachigahara**   In Japanese folklore, a cannibalistic woman spirit, portrayed with a kitchen knife, sometimes preparing to kill a child.

According to one legend, she was a woman of high rank attached to the court of a prince who suffered from a strange disease. The remedy required obtaining the blood of a child born during a certain month. Adachigahara, a faithful servant, killed various children in order to cure her master. When the cure was successful she confessed her guilt but was pardoned.

Another legend tells how one winter evening a pilgrim came to the door of her hut and asked permission to spend the night in her kitchen. Adachigahara at first refused but finally consented. After a few minutes she went out, forbidding her guest to look in a certain room. However, the pilgrim was inquisitive, opened the door, and found the room full of human bones and spattered with blood. Taking his hat and staff, he fled while Adachigahara was returning to her goblin shape.

See also: BLUEBEARD

**Adam and Eve** (earth man and woman, wife, or the mother of all living?)   In Jewish, Christian, and Islamic mythology, the first man and woman.

In Genesis (2:4–4:26) Yahweh Elohim, one of the names of God, forms Adam (man) from the earth and gives him life by breathing into him the breath of life. Yahweh forms Eve from the rib of the sleeping Adam. Both are placed in the Garden of Eden and told not to eat fruit from the Forbidden Tree. The couple do so and are cast out of the Garden of Eden. Suffering and death enter the world as a result of their sin. Medieval Christian belief held Adam to be a prefiguration of Christ, Jesus being the first spiritual man as Adam had been the first physical man. According to medieval Christian belief, Eve, the first mother, foreshadowed the Virgin Mary or the Church. The Temptation and Fall were seen by Christians as the foreshadowing of the Annunciation to the Virgin Mary that she would be the mother of Jesus.

In Islamic mythology Allah sent the angels Gabriel, Michael, and Israfel, one after the other, to fetch seven handfuls of earth from different depths and of different colors for the creation of Adam. The angels returned empty-handed because Earth foresaw that the new creature would rebel against Allah and draw down a curse on Earth. Allah then sent a fourth angel, Azrael, who accomplished the mission. Thereafter Azrael was appointed to separate the souls of men from their bodies at death. The earth taken by Azrael was carried to Arabia to a place between Mecca and Tayef, where it was kneaded by the angels and fashioned into human form by Allah. The clay was left to dry for either 40 days or 40 years; then Adam was born. (Forty is a mystical number in Jewish, Christian, and Islamic belief.)

Adam's apple is a folk name for the laryngeal cartilage because, according to folk tradition, the Forbidden Fruit got stuck in Adam's throat. Adam's ale is water, and Old Adam means man in sin without redemption, according to Christian belief.

Adam and Eve, with the serpent who tempted them, frequently appear in Western art. Dürer's *Adam and Eve* is one of the best-known works.

In Africa the original pair is called Abuk and Garang; in Norse mythology they are called Ask and Embla; and in Slavic they are called Khadau and Mamaldi.

See also: ABUK AND GARANG; ALLAH; ASK AND EMBLA; AZRAEL; GABRIEL; ISRAFEL; KHADAU AND MAMALDI; MICHAEL; VIRGIN MARY

0045
**Adamanthaea**    In Greek mythology, a Cretan nurse of Zeus who suspended his cradle from a tree so that he was neither on earth nor heaven nor the sea. She had drums and cymbals sounded around the tree to drown out his cries. All of this was done to protect Zeus from the anger of his father, Cronus, who wished to swallow his son to prevent Zeus from replacing him as ruler.

See also: ZEUS

0046
**Adam Bell** (redness)    In medieval British legend, hero who appears in a ballad of the same name. He lived in Englewood Forest, near Carlisle. Clym of the Clough and William of Cloudesly were his companions. When William was captured and being taken to his execution for robbery, Adam and Clym saved him. All three then went to London to ask the king's pardon, which was granted at the queen's request. To show their appreciation they all demonstrated their skill in archery. The king was so impressed that he named William a "gentleman of fe" and the other two, yeomen of the bedchamber.

See also: CLYM OF THE CLOUGH

0047
**Adapa** (man)    In Near Eastern mythology, Babylonian hero who lost the gift of immortality for humankind through a trick of the gods.

The myth of Adapa is found in various texts, all incomplete, the earliest dating from the 14th century B.C.E. and found at El-Amarna, Egypt. Adapa was "wise like one of the gods," being under the special protection of his father, the god Ea. Ea gave Adapa "intelligence enough to comprehend the design of the world: but he made him a dying man." One day Adapa went fishing. While he was in the middle of the sea, a storm caused by the south wind capsized Adapa's boat. In a fit of rage Adapa cursed the south wind.

"O south wind," he cried out, "you have overwhelmed me with your cruelty. I will break your wings." (The south wind is often pictured as a winged bird or monster in Babylonian art.)

As Adapa finished his curse, the wings of the south wind were destroyed. For seven days (a number to indicate a rather long though indefinite period) the wind did not blow over the sea or earth. When Anu, the god of heaven, discovered this, he called his god Illabrat to see why the south wind did not blow.

"Why has the south wind not blown for seven days across the land?" the god asked Illabrat.

"My lord, Adapa, the son of Ea, has broken the wings of the south wind," Illabrat replied.

Anu commanded Adapa to appear before him, and Ea prepared his son Adapa for the questioning from the god.

"When you come before Anu, you will be offered the food of death," he said. "Do not eat it. You will also be offered the waters of death. Do not drink. You will be offered a garment. Put it on. You will be offered oil. Anoint yourself. Do not forget now what I have told you."

When Adapa appeared before Anu, he did as his father had told him and refused the food and drink offered, even though Anu said to him it was the food of life and the water of life.

Anu looked at Adapa after he refused and said, "Why did you not eat and not drink? Now you cannot live forever, for you refused the food and water of everlasting life."

"Ea, my lord," replied Adapa, "commanded me not to eat and not to drink."

Then Anu laughed, for Ea had tricked his own son, Adapa, keeping for the gods the gift of immortality.

See also: ANU; EA

0048

**Adaro**   In Melanesian mythology, sun spirits who move about in waterspouts, cross from place to place using rainbows as bridges, or come to earth during sun showers. They are part fish, part human. Their chief is Nyorieru. An Adaro spirit may shoot a man with a flying fish, causing him to become unconscious. Only if a special offering is made in time will the victim recover.

0049

**Addanc of the Lake**   In the medieval Welsh *Mabinogion*, a monster slain by Peredur, who uses a magic stone that makes him invisible to the monster.

See also: *MABINOGION, THE*

0050

**Adder**   A common European viper, often said to be deaf in world mythology and folklore.

Psalm 58:4–5 reads: "Their poison is like the poison of a serpent: they are like the deaf adder that stoppeth her ear." For medieval Christianity this signified those people who would not listen to the Gospel. A 12th-century bestiary by Phillippe de Thaon says that the adder is "sly and aware of evil: when it perceives people who want to enchant it and capture it, it will stop up its ears." St. Augustine equated the adder with the devil.

See also: AUGUSTINE, ST.; BASILISK

0051

**Adharma** (unrighteousness)   In Hindu mythology, a son of the god Brahma. He personified unrighteousness or vice, being called "the destroyer of all things."

See also: BRAHMA

0052

**Adi**   In Hindu mythology, a son of Adharma. He tried to avenge his father's death at the hands of Shiva by transforming himself into a snake and entering Shiva's abode. He then transformed himself into the beautiful Uma, but Shiva was not deceived and killed him. In some texts Adi is a form of the great goddess Devi, the wife of Shiva, who, when angry with her husband, took on the demonic form.

See also: DEVI; SHIVA; UMA

0053

**Adi-Buddha** (first enlightened one)   In Mahayana Buddhism, the primordial Buddha who "was before all," infinite, omniscient, self-existing, without beginning and without end. He is not, however, a creator god, nor equivalent to the Western concept of God. One myth tells how all was void when the mystic sound Om became manifest, from which at his own will Adi-Buddha was produced. When the world was created, he revealed himself as a flame issuing from a lotus flower. In Buddhist art of Nepal he is often portrayed in this form. From Adi-

Buddha came five Dhyani-Buddhas (Buddhas of Mediation) who are Vairocana, Askhobhya, Amitabha, Amoghasiddhi, and Ratnasambhava.

See also: AMITABHA; AMOGHASIDDHI; DHYANI-BUDDHAS; MAHAYAHNA; OM; VAIROCANA

0054

**Adiri**   In Melanesian mythology, the land of the dead, located in the west.

0055

**Aditi** (free, unbounded?)   In Hindu mythology, a goddess, the "mother of the world," who, according to some Hindu texts, is the mother of both Indra and Vishnu. Aditi's descendants, the Adityas, are listed as 12, corresponding to the months of the year. In the Rig-Veda, Aditya is one of the names of the sun.

See also: INDRA; RIG-VEDA; VISHNU

0056

**Admetus** (untamed)   In Greek mythology, an Argonaut, son of Pheres and Periclymene (or Clymene) and husband of Alcestis; father of Eumelus and Perimele. Admetus took part in the Calydonian boar hunt and the voyage of the Argo. Apollo served Admetus for a time as a shepherd, either from love as a reward for his piety or to expiate a capital crime. Admetus wooed Alcestis, the daughter of Pelias, but her father would give her only to one who could yoke lions and boars to a chariot. Admetus accomplished the task with Apollo's aid. Apollo then prevailed on the Moirai (Fates) to release Admetus from death, provided that someone would volunteer to die in his place. When Admetus was about to die after being seized by a sickness, his parents refused to die in his place. Finally, his wife, Alcestis, died for her husband. Alcestis was, however, sent back to the upper world by Persephone, goddess of death, or, according to a variant myth, was rescued out of Hades by Heracles. Euripides' *Alcestis* deals with the tale. The time that Apollo spent with Ad-

metus is the subject of George Meredith's poem "Phoebus with Admetus."

See also: ALCESTIS; APOLLO; ARGO; ARGONAUTS; CALYDONIAN BOAR HUNT; HADES; HERACLES; PERSEPHONE

0057

**Adno-artina**   In Australian mythology, the gecko lizard that challenged Marindi, a dog, to a fight. Marindi was killed, and his blood dyed the rocks red.

See also: MARINDI

0058

**Adrammelech** (Adramelech, Adramelek) (the lordship of Melech, the king)   In Near Eastern mythology, a god worshiped by the people of Sepharvaim.

According to 2 Kings (17:31), the "Sepharvites burnt their children in fire to Adrammelech and Anammelech, the gods of Sepharvaim." In later Jewish folklore Adrammelech was turned into one of the 10 archdemons, who often appeared in animal forms such as that of a peacock, mule, horse, or lion. In Milton's *Paradise Lost* (book 6:365) the good angels Uriel and Raphael vanquish Adrammelech. The German poet Klopstock, in his epic poem *The Messiah*, calls Adrammelech "the enemy of God, greater in malice, ambition, and mischief than Satan, a

*Altar of the god Moloch*

fiend more curst, a deeper hypocrite." Adrammelech may be derived from the Babylonian god Anu and the Ammonite god Moloch, to whom children were sacrificed.

The name is also used for a son of Sennacherib in 2 Kings (19:37), who with Sharezer, his brother, murdered his father in the temple of the god Nisroch after they learned their father planned to sacrifice them to the god. The name appears in Josephus's *Antiquities of the Jews* (book 16, chapter 8) as Andromachos and in Greek sources as Adramelos and Ardumuzan.

See also: ANU; HORSE; LION; PEACOCK; RAPHAEL; SENNACHERIB; URIEL

0059

**Adrasteia** (inescapable)   In Greek mythology, a Cretan nymph who was a nursemaid of Zeus; daughter of Melisseus; sister of Ida. Also a country near Troy named for Adrastus, who built a temple to Nemesis. The name also is given to a daughter of Zeus and Necessity, who is identified in some accounts as Nemesis, who is called Adrasteia in Plato's *Republic*.

See also: NEMESIS; NYMPHS; ZEUS

0060

**Adrastus** (he who stands his ground)   In Greek mythology, a king of Argos; son of Talaus and Lysimache (or Eurynome or Lysianassa); married to Amphithea; father of Argeia, Aegialeia, Aegialeus, Cyanippus, Deipyle, and Hippodameia. Adrastus led the "Seven against Thebes" in an ill-fated expedition to restore Polynices, son of Oedipus, to the throne of Thebes. In a fight between the three ruling houses in Argos—the Biantidae, Melampodidae, and Proetidae—Adrastus was driven out by Amphiaraus. Adrastus fled to his maternal grandfather, King Polybus of Cicyoun, and later inherited his kingdom. Adrastus was reconciled to Amphiaraus, to whom he gave his sister Eriphyle. He later returned and ruled over Argos, where one stormy night a great scuffle was heard outside the palace. Two fugitives, Polynices and Tydeus (one

wrapped in a lion's skin, the other in a boar's skin), had sought refuge in the front court and were fighting for a night's lodging. Adrastus recognized this as the fulfillment of an oracle that had told him to marry his daughters to a lion and a boar. Adrastus gave his daughter Argeia to Polynices and Deipyle to Tydeus. He promised to conduct the two exiles to Thebes and install Polynices on the throne. This is the subject of Aeschylus's play *Seven Against Thebes*. In the ensuing war only Adrastus escaped destruction by fleeing on his winged horse Arion. Ten years later, with the sons (called the Epigoni) of the slain warriors of this ill-fated expedition and his son Aegialeus, Adrastus marched on Thebes. He took the city but lost his son and died of grief on his way home.

See also: AMPHIARAUS; ARGEIA; OEDIPUS

0061

**Adrian, St.** (the man from Adria)   Fourth century. In Christian legend, a military saint in northern Europe during the Middle Ages. Patron of Flemish brewers. Feast, 8 September.

The life of St. Adrian is found in *The Golden Legend*, a collection of saints' lives written in the 13th century by Jacobus de Voragine. Adrian was a pagan officer at the imperial Roman court at Nicomedia. When some Christians were arrested he witnessed their strength and was converted, saying he was to be accounted with them. When the emperor heard this he had Adrian thrown into prison. His wife, Natalie, who secretly was a Christian, ran to prison and "kissed the chains that her husband was bound with," according to *The Golden Legend*. She often visited her husband in prison, urging him on to martyrdom. When the emperor heard that women were entering the prison, he ordered the practice stopped. But "when Natalie heard that, she shaved her head and took the habit of a man, and served the saints in prison and made the other women do so."

This state of affairs, however, could not continue. The saint was eventually martyred in the most gruesome way. The prison guards "hewed off his legs and thighs, and Natalie prayed them that they would smite off his hands, and that he should be like to the other saints that had suffered more than he, and when they had hewn them off he gave up his spirit to God." Natalie took her husband's remains and fled the city, settling in Argyropolis, where she died in peace, though she is included among Christian martyrs in the Roman church calendar of saints.

In Christian art St. Adrian is portrayed with an anvil in his hand or at his feet. Sometimes a sword or ax is beside him. His sword was kept as a relic at Walbeck in Saxony, Germany. Emperor Henry II used it when preparing to go against the Turks and Hungarians.

See also: GOLDEN LEGEND, THE

0062

**Adu Ogyinae**    In African mythology (Ashanti of Ghana), the first man. The Ashanti tell several myths concerning the origin of man. One states that on Monday night the first man, Adu Ogyinae, came to the surface of the earth through holes bored in the ground by a worm. Adu Ogyinae was the leader of a small group of seven men and a few women, as well as a leopard and a dog. Of the entire group, only Adu Ogyinae was not frightened by the new things he saw on the surface of the earth. By Tuesday he managed to calm the others, but they did not begin to build homes until Wednesday. Adu was killed when a tree fell on him. Then the dog was sent in search of fire. Meat was cooked with the flame he brought back and was fed to him to test whether it was safe. When the dog showed no signs of illness, all of the others began to eat. The god of creation then came upon one of the members of the group and made him his assistant. Each year the Ashanti hold ceremonies in the woods to commemorate the first human beings.

See also: ABUK AND GARANG; ADAM AND EVE; ASK AND EMBLA

0063

**Advent** (coming)    In Christian ritual, first season of liturgical or church year. Its development over the centuries in the Western church was gradual, but by the 13th century it had come to encompass the four Sundays before Christmas. Advent was retained in *The Book of Common Prayer* (1549) of the Church of England but was rejected by the Calvinists and some other Reformers. Two basic motifs, or themes, developed over the centuries. The first is that of joyous preparation for the Feast of the Nativity, or Christmas. But parallel to this joyous note is the second motif of Advent: preparation for the Second Coming of Christ when he will judge the world. Thus, the traditional color for Advent is purple, stressing the penitential character of the season. During the Middle Ages a fast was observed, with weddings, amusements, and conjugal relations forbidden. The Advent wreath is the principal symbol of the season. It was generally assumed that the Advent wreath originated in Lutheran Germany a few hundred years ago, but recent scholarship suggests a 19th-century origin. Advent and the Advent wreath have been adopted by many other Christian churches. It consists of a wreath, an ancient symbol of glory and victory, and four candles, one for each Sunday in Advent. Three of the candles are purple; the fourth is rose for *Gaudete* Sunday. Sometimes the center of the wreath has a Christ candle. On the first Sunday of Advent the first candle is lit, on the second Sunday, the second is lit, and so on until all four are lit. The wreath is removed at the Feast of Christmas.

See also: CHRISTMAS

0064

**Aeacus** (bewailing)    In Greek mythology, first king of Aegina; son of Zeus by Aegina, a daughter of the river god Asopus in Philius. Zeus, in the form of an eagle, had taken Aegina and carried her off to the island named after her, where Aeacus was born. As king of Aegina, Aeacus ruled the Myrmidons, people whom Zeus had transformed from ants to populate the island. Aeacus was loved by the gods for his piety, and when a drought desolated Greece, his intercession obtained rain from Zeus. The Greeks built Aeacus a temple enclosed with a marble wall. The poet Pindar says that Aeacus helped Poseidon and Apollo construct the walls of Troy.

Because Aeacus was noted for his justice, he was made one of the judges over the dead, along with Minos and Rhadamanthys. At Aegina and Athens he was worshiped as a demigod. His sons by Chiron's daughter Endeis were Telamon and Peleus, the fathers of Ajax and Achilles. Another son, Phocus, by the Nereid Psamathe was killed by his half-brothers, who were then banished by their father for the crime. Ovid's *Metamorphoses* (book 7) and Hesiod's *Theogony* (1003–5) tell of Aeacus.

See also: ACHILLES; AJAX; APOLLO; ASOPUS; MINOS; MYRMIDONS; OVID; PELEUS; POSEIDON; RHADAMANTHYS; ZEUS

0065

**Aeaea**    In Greek mythology, a female hunter who was changed by the gods into an island of the same name to help her escape the pursuit of Phasis, a river god. Odysseus stayed on Aeaea with Circe for a year according to Homer's *Odyssey*. The poet, however, does not identify the location of the island. Later writers have placed it off the western coast of Italy. Cape Cicero, which is south of Rome and was once an island, has also been cited as the original Aeaea.

See also: HOMER; ODYSSEUS; *ODYSSEY, THE*

0066

**Aëdon** (nightingale, songstress)    In Greek mythology, daughter of Pandareos, wife of the Theban king, Zethus; and mother of Itylus, whom she killed and fed to her husband.

Envious of her sister-in-law Niobe for having six sons, Aëdon tried to kill the oldest but by mistake killed one of her own. She was changed into a nightingale by Zeus and forever bewailed her fate.

In a later variant myth Aëdon is the wife of Polytechnus at Colophon in Lydia. She angered the goddess Hera by boasting that she lived more happily with her husband than Hera with Zeus. Hera sent Eris (strife) to set a wager between Aëdon and Polytechnus that whoever finished first the piece of work they had in hand (he a chair, she a garment) should be given by the other the present of a slave girl as a prize. With Hera's aid Aëdon won. In anger Polytechnus fetched Aëdon's sister Chelidonis on a false pretext from her father's house and subdued her. He then presented her to his wife as her slave. Aëdon did not recognize her sister dressed in slave garments. One day Aëdon overheard Chelidonis lamenting her fate and helped her plot to kill Aëdon's son Itylus, cook him, and feed him to his father, Polytechnus. Learning the fate of his son, Polytechnus pursued Chelidonis to her home. But the gods, wishing to prevent more bloodshed, turned them all into birds: Pandareos became an osprey; his wife, a kingfisher; Polytechnus, a pelican; Chelidonis, a swallow; and Aëdon, a nightingale.

See also: HERA; NIOBE; ZEUS

0067

**Aegeus** (goatish?)    In Greek mythology, king of Athens; father of the hero Theseus, son of Pandion and Pylia; brother of Lycus, Nisus, and Pallas. With the help of his brothers Aegeus took Attica from the sons of his uncle Metion, who had earlier driven out their father, Pandion. Then, dethroned by Pallas and his sons, Aegeus was rescued and restored to power by his son Theseus. Aegeus then slew Androgeos, son of Minos, and to punish Aegeus, Minos forced him to send seven boys and seven girls to Crete every nine years as victims of the Minotaur. When Theseus set out to free his country from this tribute, he told his father he would change the black sail of his ship to a white sail if he succeeded. But he forgot to switch the sail, and seeing the black sail on the returning vessel, Aegeus believed Theseus had been killed. He threw himself into the Aegean Sea, which, according to some accounts, is named after him.

Aegeus had a shrine at Athens where he introduced the worship of Aphrodite, who had left him childless until he honored her. Plutarch's *Life of Theseus* and Mary Renault's novels *The King Must Die* and *The Bull from the Sea* have Aegeus as part of the narrative. Ovid's *Metamorphoses* (book 7) also tells the tale.

See also: APHRODITE; MINOS; MINOTAUR; PALLAS; THESEUS

0068
**Aegialeia**　In Greek mythology, daughter of Adrastus of Argos and Amphithea; wife of Diomedes, sister of Argeia, Aegialeus, Cyanippus, Deipyle, and Hippodameia. In her husband's absence during the Trojan War, Aegialeia prostituted herself to her servants, chiefly Cometes, whom the king had left master of the house. When Diomedes learned of Aegialeia's unfaithfulness, he settled in Daunia.

See also: ADRASTUS; ARGEIA; DIOMEDES

0069
**Aeginetan Sculptures**　The marble pediments of Athena's temple at Aegina, portraying combat between the Greeks and Trojans. They were rediscovered by the modern world in 1811 and removed to Munich. Athena is seen in the center as the protector of the Greeks. Of the figures in the sculpture, 10 in the west pediment, representing the contest for the body of Patroclus, are complete.

See also: ATHENA; PATROCLUS

0070
**Aegir** (the sea)　In Norse mythology, a host of the gods, the sea god, brother of Kari, the air, and Loki, the fire-trickster god; married to Ran, his sister, father of nine daughters, the waves, or wave maidens. Like his brothers Kari and Loki, Aegir belonged to a primeval order of gods, older than the Aesir, the Vanir giants, dwarfs, or elves.

Aegir was portrayed as a gaunt old man with long white hair and beard and ever-clutching, claw-like fingers. Whenever he appeared above the waters, it was to destroy ships and take the men and cargo to his underground kingdom. Aegir's servants were Elde and Funfeng, who waited on guests in his banquet hall under the sea. In Anglo-Saxon mythology Aegir was called Eagor. Whenever an unusually large wave came thundering toward a ship, its sailors would cry, "Look out, Eagor is coming!" In ancient Saxon times one of every 10 prisoners was sacrificed to Aegir to ensure that the raiders would return safely. A ship was referred to by the kenning "Aegir's horse." Aegir also was known as Hlér or Ler (the shelterer) and Gymir (the concealer). In the *Prose Edda* he is said to be "well skilled in magic." Aegir and Ran appear in William Morris's *Sigurd the Volsung and the Fall of the Niblungs*.

See also: AESIR; KENNING; LOKI; RAN; VANIR

0071
**Aegis** (goatskin)　In Greek mythology, the shield forged by Hephaestus that had on it the Gorgon Medusa's head. When Zeus shook the aegis, thunder ripped through the heavens. It was used not only by Zeus but also by Athena and Apollo. Since the word means goatskin, the aegis was said in later myth to be the skin of the goat that had suckled Zeus in his infancy. When the aegis became part of the iconography of Athena, it was portrayed as a shaggy or scaly skin with a fringe of snakes and the Gorgon's head in the middle. Vergil's *Aeneid* (book 8), Ovid's *Fasti* (book 3), and Milton's *Comus* (447) are among the literary works that refer to the shield.

See also: APOLLO; ATHENA; GORGONS; HEPHAESTUS; ZEUS

0072
**Aegisthus** (goat strength)　In Greek mythology, lover of Clytemnestra and murderer of Agamemnon; the son of Thyestes by his daughter Pelopia. He was suckled by a goat (thus his name) and brought up by Atreus, who had mar-

ried Pelopia. When Atreus's son Agamemnon left for Troy, Aegisthus became the lover of Clytemnestra, wife of Agamemnon. The two later killed Agamemnon and in turn were killed by Orestes, Agamemnon's son. Aegisthus is one the the main characters in Aeschylus's *Oresteia*, three plays dealing with the myth. He also appears in Sophocles' *Electra* and Seneca's *Agamemnon*.

See also: AGAMEMNON; ATREUS; ORESTES

0073

**Aegle** (dazzling light)   In Greek mythology, one of the Hesperides, who guarded the Golden Apples. The name is also that of the youngest daughter of Asclepius and Epine (or Lampetia); a sister of Phaethon, who was transformed into a poplar; and beloved of Theseus when he abandoned Ariadne.

See also: ARIADNE; ASCLEPIUS; GOLDEN APPLES OF THE HESPERIDES; HESPERIDES; PHAETHON; THESEUS

0074

**Aegyptus** (Greek form of Het-Ka-Ptah, an ancient city near Egyptian Memphis)   In Greek mythology, son of Belus and Anchinoë; twin brother of Danaus. Aegyptus conquered the land of Melampodes (black-feet) and named it after himself (Egypt). He fathered 50 sons and compelled Danaus's 50 daughters, against their will, to marry them. He went to Argos, where his sons had pursued their brides, and died there of grief on learning of their deaths at the hands of their wives on their wedding night. A variant of the myth says Aegyptus's only surviving son reconciled him to his brother Danaus, who was the father of the 50 wives. Apollodorus's *Bibliotheca* (Library) (2.1.4–5) tells his tale.

See also: APOLLODORUS

0075

**Aeneas** (praiseworthy)   In Greek and Roman mythology, Trojan hero appearing in the Latin epic poem the *Aeneid*. Aeneas was the son of An-

*Aeneas*

chises and the goddess Aphrodite, the brother of Lyrus. He was born on the mountains of Ida and brought up until his fifth year by his brother-in-law Alcathous or, according to a variant myth, by the nymphs of Ida. Though he was a close relative of King Priam of Troy, Aeneas did not enter the war until his cattle had been stolen by the Greek hero Achilles. Priam did not love Aeneas because he knew that Aeneas and his descendants would be the future rulers of the Trojans. At Troy he was highly esteemed for his piety ("pious Aeneas" he is called in *The Aeneid*), prudence, and valor. Often the gods came to his assistance. Thus, Aphrodite and Apollo shielded him when his life was threatened by Diomed, and Poseidon snatched him out of combat with Achilles.

His escape from Troy is told in several variations. In one he makes his way through the enemy to Ida. In another Aeneas was spared by the Greeks because he had always sought peace and the return of Helen to Greece. A third variation tells how he made his escape during the confusion following the fall of the city. In yet another he is said to have formed a new kingdom out of the wreck of the people and handed it down to his progeny. Several cities on Ida claimed Aeneas as their founder. The myth of Aeneas's emigrating and founding a new kingdom beyond the seas is post-Homeric. His tale, as it is known in Western art and literature, is told in Vergil's *Aeneid*. Dante, in *The Divine Comedy*, regards Aeneas as the founder of the Roman Empire. Aeneas is placed by Dante in limbo in company with his ancestress Electra, as well as Hector and Julius Caesar. In British mythology Brutus, the first king of Britain, is the great-grandson of Aeneas. In Shakespeare's *Troilus and Cressida*, the character of Aeneas is not developed, but in *Julius Caesar* (1.2.112) and *Henry VI, Part II* (5.2.62) reference is made to Aeneas's bearing his father, Anchises, on his shoulders. In *Cymbeline* (3.4.60) the hero is "false Aeneas," referring to his desertion of Dido.

See also: ACHILLES; *AENEID, THE*; ALCANTHOUS; APHRODITE; APOLLO; HELEN OF TROY; POSEIDON; PRIAM

0076

***Aeneid, The***   The Latin epic poem by the Roman poet Vergil (70–19 B.C.E.) in dactylic hexameters, telling of Aeneas and the founding of a new home for the Trojans. The poem was left unfinished at Vergil's death. In his will he asked that the work be destroyed, but the emperor Augustus intervened, and so the poem survived. It is the most influential work of Latin literature and is one of the cornerstones of world literature.

*The Aeneid* is written in 12 books, or sections. The translation by John Dryden opens with the well-known lines from book 1:

Arms, and the man I sing, who forc'd by fate,
And haughty Juno's unrelenting hate,
Expell'd and exil'd, left the Trojan shore.
Long labors, both by sea and land, he bore,
And in the doubtful war, before he won
The Latian realm, and built the destin'd town'
His banish'd gods restor'd to rites divine,
And settled sure succession in his line,
From whence the race of Alban fathers come,
And the long glories of majestic Rome.
O Muse! the causes and the crimes relate;
What goddess was provok'd, and whence her hate;
For what offense the Queen of Heav'n began
To persecute so brave, so just a man;
Involv'd his anxious life in endless cares,
Expos'd to wants, and hurried into wars!
Can heav'nly minds such high resentment show,
Or exercise the spite in human woe?

*Book 1*: Fate sends Aeneas to Latium to found Rome, but the goddess Juno's hostility delays his success. Juno, seeing him and his Trojans in sight of Italy, bribes Aeolus to raise a storm for their destruction. One Trojan ship is already lost when Neptune learns of the plot and calms the storm. Aeneas escapes, lands in Libya, and rallies his men. Venus appeals to Jupiter, who tells her that Aeneas will be great in Italy. Aeneas's son will found Alba, and his son's sons will found Rome. Juno will eventually relent, and Rome under Augustus will rule the world.

Mercury is sent to secure from Dido, Queen of Libya, a welcome for Aeneas. Meanwhile Aeneas and Achates meet Venus in the forest, where she is disguised as a nymph. Venus tells them Dido's story. Aeneas in reply bewails his own troubles, but Venus interrupts him with promises for success. She then changes before their eyes from nymph into goddess and vanishes. Hidden in a magic mist, Aeneas and Achates approach Carthage. They reach the citadel unobserved and are encouraged when they see scenes from the Trojan War depicted on the city walls. Dido appears and takes her throne. Trojan leaders who Aeneas believed to have died in a storm come to her as suppliants. Ilioneus, their spokesman, tells the story of the storm and asks for help. "If only Aeneas were here!" he says.

Dido echoes his words. The mist scatters and Aeneas appears. He thanks Dido and greets Ilioneus. Dido welcomes Aeneas to Carthage and prepares a festival in his honor. Aeneas sends Achates to summon his son Ascanius and to bring gifts for Dido. Cupid, persuaded by Venus to impersonate Ascanius and inspire Dido with love for Aeneas, arrives with the gifts while the real Ascanius is carried away to Idalia. The night is passed in feasting. After the feast Iopas sings the wonders of the firmament. Dido, bewitched by Cupid, begs Aeneas to tell her his tale of adventure.

*Book 2*: Aeneas tells his tale. The Greeks, baffled in battle, built a huge wooden horse in which their leaders hide. Pretending to abandon the wooden horse, their fleet sails for Tenedos. The Trojans take the horse into Troy as a trophy, believing the Greeks have given up the war. Sinon, a Greek, brought before King Priam, feigns righteous recriminations against the Greeks. The Trojans sympathize and believe his lies of the wrongs done him by Ulysses (Odysseus in Greek).

Sinon says, "When Greek plans of flight had often been foiled by storms, oracles foretold that only a human sacrifice could purchase their escape."

Chosen for the victim, Sinon had fled. He swears before the Trojans that the wooden horse is an offering to the goddess Pallas (Athena). "Destroy it and you are lost," he says. "Preserve it in your citadel and your revenge is assured."

Most of the Trojans believe the lying Sinon. Laocoön, a priest, does not, however, and is destroyed when a monster rises from the sea, killing him and his sons. This is taken as a sign by the Trojans that they should take the wooden horse into the city. Cassandra warns them against doing so, but though she was gifted with prophecy, she was also cursed with never being believed.

While Troy sleeps the Greek fleet returns, and Sinon releases the Greeks from the wooden

*Poseidon's serpents strangling Laocoön*

horse. The spirit of the dead Hector warns Aeneas in a dream to flee with the sacred vessels and images of the gods. Panthus then brings news of Sinon's treachery. The city is set aflame by the Greeks. Aeneas heads a group who wish to escape. He and his followers exchange armor with Greeks slain in the night. The ruse succeeds until they are taken for enemies by their friends. The Greeks rally, and the Trojans scatter. At Priam's palace a last stand is made, but Pyrrhus forces the great gates and the defenders are massacred. When Aeneas sees the headless body of Priam, he thinks of his father. Aeneas hastens home, but his father, Anchises, refuses to flee. Anchises, seeing a halo about the head of Aeneas's son Ascanius, takes it as an omen and relents. During the escape Creusa, the wife of Aeneas, is lost. He seeks her. Her dead spirit appears to him and tells him to flee.

*Book 3*: In obedience to oracles the Trojans build a fleet and sail to Thrace. Seeking to found a city, they are warned away by the ghost of Polydorus and visit Anius in Ortygia. Apollo promises Aeneas and his descendants worldwide empire if they return to "the ancient motherland" of Troy, which Anchises says is Crete. The Trojans reach Crete only to be thwarted again. Drought and plague interrupt this second attempt to found a city. On the point of returning to ask Apollo for a clearer sign, Aeneas is told by the gods of Troy in a dream that the true home of the Trojans is Italy. Landing in the Strophades, the Trojans unwittingly wrong the Harpies, whose queen, Celaeno, threatens them with a famine. Panic-stricken, the Trojans coast along to Actium, where they celebrate their national games. They go to Buthrotum, and on a voyage from Dyrrhachium they get their first glimpse of Italy. They land and make offering to Juno, then travel along the coast until they see Mount Aetna. The book ends with the death of Anchises at Drepanum.

*Book 4*: Dido has fallen in love with Aeneas. She opens her heart to her sister Anna. Dido would yield except for her promised loyalty to her dead husband, Sychaeus. Anna pleads for Aeneas, and Dido, half yielding, sacrifices to the marriage gods. Venus reappears and lies to Juno (goddess of marriage) that she will let Aeneas marry Dido, and he will be made king of Carthage. At a hunt Juno sends a storm, and the lovers shelter in a cave where they make love and exchange vows. Jupiter sends Mercury to remind Aeneas of his mission to found a new home for the Trojans in Italy. Aeneas, terrified by the message, prepares to leave. Dido pleads with him, but he says he must obey the gods. In utter misery Dido, on pretext of burning all of Aeneas's love gifts, prepares a pyre and summons a sorceress. Her preparations complete, she utters a lament. Mercury repeats his warning to Aeneas, who sets sail. Daybreak reveals his flight, and Dido, cursing her betrayer, stabs herself.

*Book 5*: Aeneas, unaware of Dido's suicide, sails away to Acestes in Sicily. He prepares funeral games to mark Anchises' death. Offerings are paid to the spirit of his dead father. Sicilians and Trojans assemble for the first contest, a boat race. Juno schemes to destroy the Trojan fleet while the games are being held. She inflicts madness on the Trojan matrons, who are not allowed to be present at the games, and they set the ships aflame. Jupiter sends rain and saves all but four of the ships, and the Trojans depart. Venus prevails on Neptune, god of the sea, to grant the Trojans a safe journey in return for the death of the helmsman, Palinurus, who is drowned.

*Book 6*: The Trojans arrive at Cumae. Aeneas visits the Sibyl's shrine. After prayer and sacrifice to Apollo, he asks permission to enter the underworld to visit his father. He must first pluck the Golden Bough. Vergil writes (MacKay's translation):

O sprung of gods' blood, child of Anchises of Troy, easy is the descent into hell; all night and day the gate of dark Dis stands open; but to recall thy steps and issue to upper air, this is the task, this the burden. Some few of gods' lineage have availed, such as Jupiter's gracious favor or virtue's ardor had upborne to heaven. Midway all is muffled in forest, and the black sliding coils of Cocytus circle it round. Yet if thy soul is so passionate and so desirous twice to float across the Stygian lake, twice to see dark Tartarus, and thy pleasure is to plunge into the mad task, learn what must first be accomplished. Hidden in a shady tree is a bough with leafage and pliant shoot all of gold, consecrate to nether Juno, wrapped in the depth of woodland and shut in by dim dusky vales. But to him only who first has plucked the golden-tressed fruitage from the tree is it given to enter the hidden places of the earth. This has beautiful Proserpine ordained to be borne to her for her proper gift. The first torn away, a second fills the place with gold, and the spray burgeons with even such ore again. So let thine eyes trace it home, and thine hand pluck it duly when found; for lightly and unreluctant will it follow if thine is fate's summons; else will no strength of thine avail to conquer it nor hard steel to cut it away.

Aeneas sees all of the sights of the underworld and visits his father, Anchises, who explains to him the mystery of the Transmigration of Souls; and the book closes with the revelation to Aeneas of the future greatness of Rome. Aeneas then leaves through the Ivory Gate and sails to Caieta.

*Book 7*: Passing Caieta and Circeii, Aeneas sails up the Tiber. An embassy is sent to the Latin capital by the Trojans. Latinus offers peace to the Trojans, and to Aeneas his daughter's hand. (All of this was to fulfill the oracles.) Juno again intervenes and summons the demon Alecto, who first excites Amata then Turnus against the peace. War begins. On the side of the Latins are the hero Turnus and the heroine Camilla.

*Book 8*: The war now started, Turnus sends to Diomedes for help, while Aeneas goes to ask aid of Evander and the Tuscans. Evander receives him kindly, furnishes him with men, and sends his son Pallas with him. Vulcan, at the request of Venus, makes arms for her son Aeneas that portray the future greatness of Rome.

*Book 9*: Turnus takes advantage of Aeneas's absence to set some ships on fire, but they turn into sea nymphs. Turnus then attacks the Trojan camp. Nisus and Euryalus are sent to recall Aeneas.

*Book 10*: Jupiter calls a council of the gods and forbids them to enter into the battle. Aeneas returns, and the fighting becomes bitter. Turnus kills Pallas; Aeneas kills Lausus and Mezentius.

*Book 11*: Aeneas erects a trophy of the spoils of Mezentius. A truce is granted for the burying of the dead. The body of Pallas is sent home. Latinus then calls a council to offer peace to Aeneas. Turnus says he will meet Aeneas in single combat. Camilla is killed. The Latins are defeated, and Turnus, learning of the news, hurries to the city, closely followed by Aeneas.

*Book 12*: Turnus realizes that he must now redeem his promise to meet Aeneas in single combat. The challenge is sent, and the two make ready. Juno tells the nymph Juturna to aid her brother Turnus in the battle. The truce is broken; Aeneas is wounded but is healed by Venus. In the ensuing combat Aeneas kills Turnus:

> He rais'd his arm aloft, and, at the word,
> Deep in his bosom drove the shining sword.
> The streaming blood distained his arms
>  around,
> And the disdainful soul came rushing thro'
>  the wound.

Vergil's great poem was read during the Middle Ages and was consulted as a book of magic, because the poet had the reputation of being a magician. Dante chose Vergil as his guide through hell and purgatory in *The Divine Comedy*. *The Aeneid* influenced Spenser, Tasso, and Milton. The translation by John Dryden was published in 1697 and has become an English classic. The first translation of *The Aeneid* into English verse was by Gavin Douglas, Bishop of Dunkeld in Scotland, published in 1553. Henry, earl of Surrey, published his version in 1557, and William Morris's, version appeared in 1876.

In musical settings of *The Aeneid*, the English composer Henry Purcell wrote *Dido and Aeneas* (1689/90) for performance in a girls' school. In 1782 German composer Joseph Martin Kraus (1756–1792) wrote *Aeneaus i Carthago*, which was performed in 1799, some years after the composer's death. The most important operatic version is that of the French Romantic composer Hector Berlioz, which was completed in 1858 in two parts and called *The Trojans*.

Though *The Aeneid* has generally been respected, the English Romantics disliked the work. Samuel Taylor Coleridge wrote: "If you take from Vergil his diction and metre, what do you leave him?" Percy Bysshe Shelley preferred Lucan, and Lord Byron hated Vergil's work intensely.

See also: AENAS; AEOLUS; ASCANIUS; DIDO; HECTOR; JUNO; JUPITER; LAOCOÖN; MERCURY; NEPTUNE; NYMPHS; PALLAS; PRIAM; SINON; VENUS

0077

**Aengus og** (Angus, Oengus)   In Celtic mythology, son of Dagda, god of love and beauty, who had a golden harp. His kisses became birds that hovered invisibly over young men and women, whispering thoughts of love in their ears. Aengus og drank the Ale of Immortality, and four swans circled over him when he traveled. In James Joyce's novel *Ulysses* the god is called Aengus of the Birds.

See also: DAGDA

0078

**Aeolus** (earth destroyer?)   In Greek mythology, the god of the winds; son of Hellen and the nymph Ortheis; married to Enarete; father of seven sons, Athamas, Cretheus, Deion, Macareus, Perieres, Salmoneus, and Sisyphus, and seven daughters, Alcyone, Arne, Calyce, Canale, Peisidice, Perimele, and Tanagra; brother of Xuthus and Dorus. In Homer's *Odyssey* (book 10) Aeolus gives Odysseus the contrary winds tied up in a bag, but the sailors let them out, and the ship is blown off course. On his Aeolian island, floating in the far west, its steep cliff encircled by a brazen wall, Aeolus lived in unbroken bliss with his wife and his sons and daughters, whom he wedded to one another. Aeolus also appears in Vergil's *Aeneid* (book 1) and Ovid's *Metamorphoses* (book 11). Aeolus is called Hippotades in some accounts.

See also: *AENEID, THE*; NYMPHS; ODYSSEUS; *ODYSSEY, THE*; OVID; SISYPHUS

0079

**Aequalitas** (fairness)   In Roman mythology, the personification of equity or fairness, as opposed to justice by the letter of the law. Aequalitas was often portrayed as a young woman holding a pair of scales in her left hand.

0080

**Aerope** (sky-face)   In Greek mythology, wife of Atreus; daughter of Catreus of Crete. She was given by her father to Nauplius to be sold abroad. She married Atreus and bore him Agamemnon and Menelaus, and possibly Anaxibia and Pleisthenes. Aerope was thrown into the sea by Atreus for her adultery with his brother Thyestes.

See also: AGAMEMNON; ATREUS; CATREUS; MENELAUS

0081

**Aesacus** (myrtle branch)   In Greek mythology, son of King Priam of Troy and Arisbe (or Alexiroe); he learned the art of interpreting dreams from his maternal grandfather, Merops. Priam consulted Aesacus about Hecuba's bad dreams prior to the birth of Paris. Aesacus's advice was to have the child killed because he would bring about the destruction of Troy. Aesacus married the nymph Asterope (or Hesperia). When he pursued her, she threw herself into the sea and was changed into a bird. In despair Aesacus also threw himself into the sea and was changed into a diver bird (cormorant). Ovid's *Metamorphoses* (book 11) and Apollodorus's *Bibliotheca* (Library) (3.12.5) tell the story.

See also: HECUBA; OVID; PARIS; PRIAM

0082

**Aeshma** (Aeshm)   In Persian mythology, archdemon who is the spirit of anger, violence, and devastation, "occasioning trouble by contests, and causing an increase in slaughter." He is the same as the demon Asmodeus who appears in the Book of Tobit (3:8) in the Old Testament Apocrypha.

See also: AHURA MAZDA; ASMODEUS

0083

**Aesir** (god)   In Norse mythology, a race of gods and goddesses under the leadership of Odin and opposed to the Vanir. The name may come from the Indo-European *áss*, meaning breath, life, or life-giving forces. They were Balder, Baugi, Bragi, Forseti, Frey, Heimdal, Hodur,

Hoenir, Loki, Njord, Thor, Vilur, Vili, and Vidar. Another group of deities, called Vanir, predated the Aesir. The Vanir group included Boda, Bil, Eir, Fimila, Fjorgyn, Freya, Frigga, Frimla, Fulla, Gefjon, Gerda, Gna, Hnossa, Horn, Jord, Nanna, Saga, Sit, Siguna, Skadi, and Vanadis. The two groups fought but settled their disagreements, all creating the dwarf Kvasir, from whose blood mead was made. The Icelandic historian Snorri Sturluson (13th century) suggests that the Aesir were "men of Asia" and that to the east there was a land known as Ásaland.

See also: BALDER; BAUGI; BRAGI; FREYA; FRIGGA; HOENIR; KVASIR; LOKI; NJORD; ODIN; THOR; VANIR; VILI

0084

**Aesir-Vanir War**   In Germanic mythology, a war fought at the beginning of time that was concluded by a truce that joined the two warring entities into a single unified group of gods. The war was precipitated when a mysterious figure named Gullveig, sometimes called Heid and other times Freyja, came to the hall of Odin. There she was attacked but could not be killed and went on performing *seid*, a form of magic or divination. Accounts of the war place more emphasis on the final settlement than on the details of the battle, and the symbol of the truce, the mixed spittle Odhrerir, became a symbol for wisdom, the mead of poetry. The Vanir are usually viewed as fertility gods who may have been overrun by a more warlike cult, the Aesir. Some scholars have tried to associate the Aesir with the invading Indo-European tribes, but recent scholarship does not accept this interpretation, since war in a myth does not have to have a historical origin.

See also: AESIR; ODHRERIR; ODIN; SEID; VANIR

0085

**Aesopic fables**   Short didactic tales, often with animal characters. Other definitions include "an animal tale with a moral," and a popular Greek definition, "a fictitious story picturing a truth."

*The Frogs Desiring a King*

For the most part these stories depict human failings, particularly in regard to pride, arrogance, greed, and folly. Although not all fables include animals, most do, and they are often in pairs: the mouse and the lion, the tortoise and the birds, and so on. Over 350 such fables have been ascribed to Aesop, a Thracian slave who lived in the sixth century B.C.E.

Whether Aesop actually lived is still debated by some scholars, though he is mentioned in the works of Herodotus, Aristophanes, and Plato. He is believed to have been the slave of a man named Iadmon. Tradition says he was a hunchback, born dumb but given the gift of speech by the goddess Isis for his great devotion to her cult. His ability to tell tales or fables won him his freedom, and according to various accounts, he became counselor to Solon and Croesus. His good fortune, however, was short-lived. He was falsely accused and convicted of theft by the citizens of Delphi, who as punishment threw him over a cliff to his death. A plague immediately swept over the city. The citizens, realizing their guilt, offered "blood money" to atone for the murder. Herodotus, in his *History of the Persian Wars* (book 2), says that Iadmon, grandson of the former Iadmon, "received the compensation. Aesop therefore must certainly have been the former Iadmon's slave."

However, the fame of Aesop continued. Tradition says he returned to life to fight at the battle of Thermopylae. A statue was erected to him in Athens some 200 years after his death. It was placed before the statues of the Seven Sages. One Attic vase from about 450 B.C.E. portrays the fabulist listening to a fox.

One of the most interesting legends in the life of Aesop concerns his telling of the fable *The Frogs Desiring a King* to a mob that was threatening to kill the tyrant Pisistratus, the moral of the fable being "Let well enough alone!" The populace knew the evils of Pisistratus but did not know how evil his successor would be. The fable is typical in that one of the main ingredients of many fables is their conservative nature. Often the moral is one of leaving well enough alone or supporting the status quo. This is somewhat ironic because in early times the fable was used to castigate ruling authorities. About 300 B.C.E. Demetrius Phalereus collected all of the fables he could find under the title of *Assemblies of Aesopic Tales*. This collection, running to about 200 fables, was used as the basis for a version in Latin verse by Phaedrus or Phaeder in the first century C.E. Like Aesop, Phaedrus also was a slave, freed during the reign of Augustus or Tiberius. Under Tiberius he published two books of his fables. His style was ironic, ridiculing the emperor and his minister, Sejanus. After the death of Sejanus, Phaedrus published a third book of fables, and a fourth and fifth were added in his later years. Phaedrus added many fables of his own to the Aesopic collection, as well as others collected from various sources.

Babrius, believed to have lived in the second century C.E., wrote ten books in Greek called *Aesop's Fables in Verse*. They were lost, however, until 1842, when 123 of the fables were discovered in the monastery at Mount Athos. An additional 95 were added in 1857, though scholars have debated how genuine the fables actually were. The Latin version of Phaedrus, therefore, was the one that was popular during the Middle Ages, although it was not credited to Phaedrus, but to a fictional person named Romulus. By the time *Romulus' Aesop* was in circulation, many tales from various sources, such as those from the East, had come to be credited to Aesop.

The power of the fables to hold the attention of audiences throughout the ages attests to their universal appeal. They are simple, direct, and well told. These characteristics have made them particularly popular with illustrators. The first English edition of Aesop, translated by Caxton from a French version, was published in 1484. By the end of the 15th century there were more than 20 different illustrated editions in Europe. Among the most famous are those of Mondovi, Ulm, and Verona, all published between 1476 and 1479. Among the best known later illustrators are Thomas Bewick (1784), Gustave Doré (1868), Walter Crane (1886), Richard Heighway (1894), Arthur Rackham (1916), Alexander Calder (1931), Antonio Frasconi (1953), and Joseph Low (1963).

Although the fables would seem to be ideal for dramatic musical settings, very few composers have attempted to deal with them. John Whitaker wrote music for English versions of Aesop's fables, and another English composer, W. H. Reed, wrote an orchestral work, *Aesop's Fables*. In 1931 the German composer Werner Egk composed *Der Löwe und die Maus* (*The Lion and the Mouse*) for narrator, chorus, and orchestra. It was written especially for radio. Egk also wrote *Moralities*, using three Aesop fables, with a text by W. H. Auden. James Thurber's *Fables for Our Times* (1940) and George Orwell's *Animal Farm* (1945) are modern adaptations of fables. In 1990 Jim Weiss produced *Animal Tales*, a tape featuring many of Aesop's fables. Boris Karloff has also performed fables on audiocassette, and Mary Carter Smith has performed, recorded, and published collections of the fables. American oral tradition has converted many of the fables into proverbial expressions, including sour grapes, the goose that laid the golden egg, the lion's share, and don't count your chickens before they hatch.

See also: DELPHI; DEMOPHON; ISIS; SEVEN SAGES; THESEUS

*Aethra and Theseus*

**Aethra** (bright sky)    In Greek mythology, mother of Theseus by Aegeus or, according to another account, by Poseidon. Homer mentions her as a servant to Helen at Troy, but later Greek myth adds that when the Dioscuri took Aphidnae and set free their sister, whom Theseus had carried off, they brought Aethra to Sparta as a slave. She then accompanied Helen to Troy. When the city fell, she brought her grandsons Acamas and Demophon back to Athens. Hyginus's *Fabulae* (myths, 37) tells her story.

See also: AEGEUS; DIOSCURI; HELEN OF TROY; POSEIDON; THESEUS

0087

**Afanasiev, Alexander Nikolaievitch** (Afanasyeu, Afanasyeff)    1826–1871. Russian folklorist, compiler of *Russian Folktales* (1855–1863), published in eight parts. Afanasiev's work, which has achieved the status of a Russian classic, was influenced by the Grimms' collection of German folktales. Based partly on oral sources, Afanasiev's work also depended on published sources, so many present-day scholars dismiss his work as being "too literary" and lacking research from primary sources. Aside from this major collection, Afanasiev also published *Russian Popular Legends* (1860), which was banned by the Russian

Orthodox Church as well as the government because it used "vulgar" words and was critical of both church and state. His work was also banned by the Soviets for the same reasons.

0088

**Af and Hemah** (anger and wrath)    In Jewish folklore, two angels created at the beginning of the world to execute God's will.

0089

**Afra, St.** (dust)    Fourth century? In Christian legend, martyr, patron saint of Augsburg, Germany. Invoked by penitent women. Feast, 5 August.

Afra was a common whore who ran a house of pleasure, even though she was the daughter of St. Hilaria. She was assisted in her work by three girls, Digna, Eunomia, and Eutropia. One day Narcissus, a Christian priest fleeing from the pagan authorities, came to her house for protection. He talked with the girls and converted them to Christianity. When the police came, all of them were arrested. Afra, who was brought before a judge who had once bought her favors, was sentenced to death by burning. As she prayed, angels bore her soul to heaven.

Medieval Christian art portrays St. Afra in a boiling caldron or surrounded by flames. Sometimes she is suspended from a tree and beaten or bound to a tree and burned.

0090

**Agama**    In Mahayana Buddhism, a term used for the collection of sacred writings, roughly equivalent to the Nikaya collection of Theravada Buddhism, containing the discourses of Buddha on general topics. Because Buddha's doctrines were often abstruse and mysterious, he decided to preach his sermons in accordance with the intellectual capacity of his audience. He then divided them into five categories, with the Agamas devoted to the doctrine of substantiality.

See also: MAHAYANA

0091

**Agamemnon** (very resolute)    In Greek mythology, king of Mycenae and Argos; son of Atreus and Aerope; married to Clytemnestra; father of Chrysothemis, Electra, Iphigeneia, Iphianassa, and Orestes, father of Chryses by his slave Chryseis, and father of Pelops and Teledamas by Cassandra; and brother of Menelaus. Agamemnon was commander of the Greek forces in the Trojan War. Driven from Mycenae after the murder of Atreus by Atreus's brother Thyestes, Agamemnon and Menelaus fled to Sparta, where King Tynadaeos gave them his daughters: Clytemnestra to Agamemnon and Helen to Menelaus. Menelaus inherited Tynadaeos's kingdom, and Agamemnon drove out his uncle Thyestes from Mycenae; as king he extended the country's boundaries. According to Homer's *Iliad*, Agamemnon, though vain and arrogant, was chosen to lead the Greek expedition to rescue his sister-in-law Helen, who had been abducted by Paris. The expedition was stalled at Aulis because Agamemnon had offended Artemis. Calchas, a soothsayer, told Agamemnon that the goddess could be appeased only by the sacrifice of Agamemnon's daughter Iphigenia (or Iphianassa). Agamemnon tricked his wife, Clytemnestra, into sending Iphigenia to Aulis by telling her that Iphigenia was to be married to Achilles. But at Aulis Iphigenia was sacrificed despite the protest of Clytemnestra. Some accounts say that Artemis spared Iphigenia when the goddess beheld the girl's innocence.

Agamemnon displayed further arrogance and invited another plague on the expedition when he refused to accept a ransom from a priest of Apollo, Chryses, who wanted to redeem his daughter Chryseis, who had been given to Agamemnon as a war prize. Agamemnon then took Briseis, Achilles' mistress. In response Achilles laid down his arms and withdrew from the war, though he eventually relented and became the major hero of the Trojan War.

After the Greek victory at Troy, Agamemnon brought home his spoils, including the captive princess Cassandra, who had warned him that he would be killed by his wife. True to the curse of Cassandra (to be always right and never believed), he ignored her warning. His wife, Clytemnestra, prepared a welcoming bath of purification. When he stepped from the bath, she wrapped him in a binding garment, and her lover, Aegisthus, stabbed Agamemnon while Clytemnestra killed Cassandra.

Agamemnon was worshiped by the Greeks as a hero. He appears in Homer's *Iliad* and *Odyssey* (book 4); Aeschylus's *Agamemnon* and *Choephoroe*, Euripides' *Electra*, *Iphigenia in Aulis*, *Iphigenia in Tauris*, and *Orestes*; Sophocles' *Electra* and *Ajax*; Vergil's *Aeneid* (book 6); Ovid's *Metamorphoses* (book 12); Seneca's *Agamemnon*; and a host of modern works such as T. S. Eliot's *The Family Reunion*, based on the Greek plays; Eugene O'Neill's *Mourning Becomes Electra*; Sartre's *Les Mouches* (The Flies); and works by Giraudoux, Robinson Jeffers, Hofmannsthal, Racine, Shakespeare, and Tennyson.

See also: ARTEMIS; ATREUS; CALCHAS; CASSANDRA; ELECTRA; HELEN OF TROY; *ILIAD, THE*; IPHIGENEIA; ORESTES; PARIS; PELOPS

0092

**Agaran**    In Arthurian legend, nephew of a hermit encountered by Lancelot in his quest for the Holy Grail.

See also: HOLY GRAIL; LANCELOT OF THE LAKE

0093

**Agastya** (mountain thrower)    Legendary Indian sage, author of several hymns in the Rig-Veda, the sacred collection of hymns.

In the Hindu epic poem *The Ramayana*, Agastya lived in a hermitage on Mount Kunjara, situated in a most beautiful country to the south of the Vindhya Mountains. He was the chief of the hermits of the South, keeping the Rakshasas, demonic beings who infested the region, under control. Once he was challenged by a Rakshasa named Vatapi, who had taken the form of a ram. Agastya attacked him and ate him up. When

Vatapi's brother Ilvala tried to avenge the death, he too was killed by Agastya.

Rama, the hero of *The Ramayana*, visited Agastya with his wife, Sita. The sage received them with great kindness, becoming Rama's friend, adviser, and protector. He gave Rama the bow of the god Vishnu, which the hero used in regaining his kingdom. When Rama was restored, Agastya accompanied him to his capital, Ayodhya.

The longer Hindu epic poem, *The Mahabharata*, relates the legend of the creation of Agastya's wife, Lopamudra. Once Agastya saw a vision of his ancestors suspended by their heels in a pit. He was told by them that they could only be rescued if he had a son. The problem was that Agastya was not married and had no mistress. He then formed a girl out of the most graceful parts of various animals. He took her secretly into the palace of the king of Vidarbha, where she grew up as the daughter of the king. When she came of age, Agastya asked for her in marriage. The king granted the wish even though he disliked Agastya.

Agastya is sometimes called "Ocean Drinker" in reference to the legend that he once drank an entire ocean after it offended him. Another explanation for the title is that he offered his aid to the gods in their battle with the Daityas (giants), who had taken refuge in the ocean.

See also: DAITYS; *MAHABHARATA, THE*; RAKSHASAS; RAMA; *RAMAYANA, THE*; RIG-VEDA; VISHNU

0094

**Agatha, St.** (good woman)   Third century? In Christian legend, martyr, patron saint of bell founders, girdlers, jewelers, malsters, wet nurses, weavers, and shepherdesses. Invoked against earthquake, fire, lightning, storm, sterility, wolves, and diseases of the breast. Feast, 5 February.

There are many accounts of the saint's life in both Latin and Greek; these influenced the version in *The Golden Legend*, a collection of saints'

lives written in the 13th century by Jacobus de Voragine.

Agatha was loved by the Roman consul Quintian, but she wanted to remain a virgin. When Quintian found out she was a Christian, he brought her up on charges. She was handed over to a courtesan, Aphrodisia (or Frondisia), who ran a brothel with her six daughters. All of Aphrodisia's attempts to turn Agatha into a whore failed. When she reported her failure to Quintian, he became so angry that he had Agatha tortured. Her breasts were crushed and then cut off. At night, however, St. Peter and an angel visited her in prison and healed her wounds with "celestial ointment" and then "vanished from her sight."

The next day, when Quintian saw that Agatha's wounds were healed, he ordered that the girl be rolled over hot coals. When this was done, an earthquake shook the city (Catania, in Sicily), and the people blamed it on Quintian for mistreating Agatha. Finally, after more gruesome torture the saint asked God to free her spirit, and God answered her plea.

The cult of St. Agatha goes back to the first centuries of Christianity. Her name occurs on a calendar of saints in Carthage written about the sixth century, and she is named in the old Latin Mass. Venantius Fortunatus, the early Christian poet, wrote a hymn in her honor. In Christian art she is shown in the procession of saints at Sant' Apollinare Nuovo in Ravenna, Italy. One of her attributes, her breasts (during the Middle Ages there were at least six breasts claimed as relics by various churches), were mistaken for loaves of bread in some art works, resulting in the blessing of bread on her feast day. In Sicily she is invoked against the outbreak of fire because, according to her legend, she saved Catania from destruction when Mount Etna erupted. The people took the veil that covered her body and carried it on a spear in procession. As a result of the rite the flames from the eruption stopped spreading.

Sebastiano del Piombo, the 16th-century Italian artist, painted *The Martyrdom of St. Agatha*, taking the removal of her breasts by pincers for his subject. However, the artist seems to be more concerned with the erotic connotations of the exposed breasts than with the saint's martyrdom.

See also: AGNES, ST.; *GOLDEN LEGEND, THE*; PETER, ST.

0095

**Agathodaemon** (good demon)    In Greek mythology, a good spirit of the cornfields and vineyards. Libations of unmixed wine were made to the spirit at meals. In Greek art Agathodaemon was portrayed as a youth holding a horn of plenty and a bowl in one hand, and in the other a poppy and ears of corn.

0096

**Agenor** (heroic)    In Greek mythology, a hero, son of Antenor by Theano, a priestess of Athena; brother of Acamas, Achelous, Coon, Crino, Demolem, Glaucus, Helicaon, Iphidamas, Laocoön, Laodamas, Lycam, Polybus, and Polydamas; half-brother of Pedaeus; father of Echeclus. Agenor was one of the bravest heroes of Troy. In Homer's *Iliad* (book 11) he leads the Trojans in storming the Greek entrenchments and rescues Hector when he is thrown down by Ajax. When he enters into battle with Achilles, he is saved by Apollo. In post-Homeric myth Agenor is killed by Neoptolemus, the son of Achilles. Agenor is also the name of a son of the sea god Poseidon and Libya; king of Phoenicia; twin brother of Belus; married to Telephassa (or Argiore); and father of Cadmus, Cilix, Demodoce, Electra, Europa, Phineus, Phoenix, and Thasus.

See also: ACHILLES; AJAX; ANTENOR; APOLLO; ATHENA; ELECTRA; HECTOR; LAOCOÖN; *ILIAD, THE*; POSEIDON

0097

**Aglaea** (splendor)    In Greek mythology, daughter of Zeus and Eurynome; one of the three Graces. The others were Euphrosyne (joy) and Thalia (abundance). In some accounts Aglaia is said to be the wife of Hephaestus.

See also: AGLAIA; EUPHROSYNE; HEPHAESTUS; ZEUS

0098

**Aglookik**    In Eskimo mythology, beneficent spirit who lives under the ice and helps hunters find game.

0099

**Agnes, St.** (pure, chaste)    Fourth century. In Christian legend, martyr. One of the Four Great Virgin Martyrs of the Latin, or Western, church; patron saint of betrothed couples, gardeners, and virgins. Invoked to preserve chastity. Feast, 21 January.

Agnes is one of the most popular saints in Christian legend. Her life is discussed by St. Ambrose, who wrote a hymn in her honor, and by St. Augustine, who wrote that she died a virgin martyr at the age of 13. The main source of her legend, however, comes from the early Christian poet Prudentius. *The Golden Legend*, a collection of saints' lives written in the 13th century by Jacobus de Voragine used Prudentius, among others, as a source.

Agnes was loved by a pagan Roman, whose advances she blocked by telling him she was in love with another (Christ) who was better than he. Out of jealousy the young man denounced Agnes as a Christian, and she was sent to a brothel as punishment. When she arrived, her clothes were removed, but God "gave her such grace that the hairs of her head became so long that they covered her body to the feet, so that her body was not seen," according to *The Golden Legend*. God sent an angel who defended her chastity against all assaults from customers of the house. When one man tried to rape her, the angel "took him by the throat and strangled him" and he fell dead.

In the end Agnes was raped and finally martyred, but the various accounts do not agree on how she met her death. *The Golden Legend* says a "sword was put in her body." St. Ambrose, however, says she "bent her neck," meaning she was decapitated. Pope Damascus says she was burned alive. In Rome on her feast day two white lambs are offered at the sanctuary rails in her church while a hymn is sung in her honor. The wool from the lambs is used to weave the pallium, part of the vestments worn by archbishops in the Latin Church. The custom may have been derived from the folk etymology of her name; lamb in Latin is *agnus.*

It is believed that on St. Agnes's Eve if you take a row of pins and stick them in your sleeve one after the other, while saying a paternoster, you will dream of the one you will marry. Taking this folk belief John Keats wrote a magnificent poem, *The Eve of St. Agnes* (1819), a work rich in romantic celebration of erotic love and fantasy. Alfred Lord Tennyson also used the saint in his poem *St. Agnes Eve*, though he attempted to treat the subject in a different manner. José de Ribera, the 17th century Spanish artist, painted his *St. Agnes*, showing a young girl on her knees, crossing her breasts in modesty, while her long hair and drapery, held by an angel, cover the rest of her body.

See also: AMBROSE, ST.; AUGUSTINE, ST.; *GOLDEN LEGEND, THE*

0100
**Agnes of Montepulciano, St.** (pure, chaste) 1268–1317. In Christian legend, Dominican abbess. Feast, 20 April.

Agnes was placed in a nunnery at the age of nine and was made abbess of a new convent at Procino when she was 15 years old. For 15 years she slept on the ground, using a stone pillow, and lived on bread and water until she nearly died and had to "diminish her austerities on account of her health," according to one account. The citizens of her town, Montepulciano, promised to build a convent for Agnes if she would return to them. They tore down some brothels and constructed the convent. When Agnes arrived, she was made the prioress, a position she held until

her death. Numerous miracles are recorded in her later life. One tells of how she had a vision in which an angel held her under an olive tree and offered her a cup, saying, "Drink this chalice, spouse of Christ: the Lord Jesus drank it for you." At 49 she died, after telling her nuns she was going to her "spouse," Jesus Christ.

Another saint, Catherine of Siena, visited her tomb, as did Emperor Charles IV. When St. Catherine visited the shrine she stooped to kiss the feet of the "incorrupt body," and the foot "lifted itself to meet her lips," according to legend.

In Christian art the scene of the foot rising is often portrayed. When St. Agnes is shown alone, she is dressed as a Dominican abbess, with white habit and black mantle and with a lamb (for her purity), a lily and a book. Often she is shown gazing on the cross, since she was devoted to the Passion of Christ.

See also: CATHERINE OF SIENA, ST.

0101
**Agneyastra** In Hindu mythology, a fire weapon given to Agnivesa, the son of Agni, the fire god. He then gives the weapon to Drona.

See also: AGNI; DRONA

*Agni*

0102
**Agni** (fire) In Hindu mythology, the fire god. Fire and its relation to sacrifice was a dominant feature of the fire cult during Vedic times. The flames and the aroma of the sacrifice rose into

the sky and were thus assumed to be the most effective way to reach the all-powerful beings. In the sacred Indian collection of hymns the Rig-Veda, Agni has more hymns addressed to him than has any other god except the storm god, Indra. Agni is called the messenger and mediator between heaven and earth, announcing to the gods the hymns sung to them and conveying offerings of their worshipers. He invited the worshipers by his crackling flames, bringing fire down on the sacrifice.

The Hindu epic poem *The Mahabharata* tells how Agni, having devoured too many offerings, lost his power. To regain his strength he wanted to consume a whole forest. At first Indra prevented him, but eventually Agni tricked Indra and accomplished his task. In another Hindu epic, *The Ramayama*, Agni is the father of Nila, who aids the hero Rama.

Agni is portrayed as a red man with three legs, seven arms, and dark eyes, eyebrows, and hair. He rides a ram and wears a *yajñopavita* (a Brahmanical thread) and a garland of fruit. Fire issues from his mouth, and seven streams of glory radiate from his body.

Gustav Holst wrote *Hymn to Agni*, based on a hymn in the Rig-Veda. The work is scored for male chorus and orchestra.

Agni is also called Vahni (he who receives the burnt offerings); Brihaspati (lord of sacred speech) in his role as creative force; Vitihotra (he who sanctifies the worshiper); Dhananjaya (he who destroys riches); Kivalana (he who burns); Dhumektu (he whose sign is smoke); Chagaratha (he who rides on a ram), referring to his mount; Saptajihva (he who has seven tongues); Pavaka (the purifier); and Grihapati, when referring to household fire.

Associated with Agni are the Bhrigus (roasters or consumers), spirits who nourish a fire and are the makers of chariots. Also associated with Agni is Kravyad, the fire that consumes bodies on a funeral pyre. In Hindu folklore today a *kravyad* is a flesh-eating goblin or any carnivorous animal.

See also: INDRA; KRAVYAD; *MAHABHARATA, THE*; RAMA; *RAMAYANA, THE*; RIG-VEDA

0103
**Agove Minoire**　　In Haitian voodoo, a female loa (deified spirit of the dead) who guards groves; symbolized by a phallus carved from wood. Sometimes her symbol is a mirror.

See also: LOA

0104
**Agramante**　　In the Charlemagne cycle of legends, a king of Africa who invaded France to avenge the death of his father, Troyano. He besieged Paris but was defeated and later killed by Roland (Orlando). He appears in Boilardo's *Orlando Innamorato* and Ariosto's *Orlando Furioso*.

See also: CHARLEMAGNE; ROLAND

0105
**Agrat bat Mahalath**　　In Jewish mythology, demoness queen who travels about in a chariot causing harm. Her evil actions are confined to the eve of the Sabbath and Wednesdays. Medieval Jewish legend held that she would be destroyed when the era of the Messiah arrived.

0106
**Agretes**　　In Arthurian legend associated with the Holy Grail, a king of Camelot who pretended to be a Christian but persecuted his people when they were converted to Christianity. As punishment he went insane and died.

See also: CAMELOT; HOLY GRAIL

0107
**Agwé** (Agoué, Agoueh R Oyo, Aguet)　　In Haitian voodoo, sea god, married to Erzulie, who as his wife is called La Sirène and is portrayed as a mermaid. Agwé's *vévé*, or symbol, is a large sailboat, and his sacred colors are blue and white. With the blending of voodoo and Christian mythologies in Haiti, Agwé is often identified with St. Ulrich, a 10th-century bishop whose symbol is a fish. The Barque d'Agwé is a specially constructed raft on which offerings to Agwé are placed and then sent out to sea. Agwé's home,

Zilet en bas de l'eau (island below the sea), is where the souls of the dead live. Voodoo cultists send down ships filled with gifts to his palace below the sea.

See also: ERZULIE; MERMAID; ULRICH, ST.

0108

**Aharaigichi**   In the mythology of the Abipone Indians of South America, principal god, identified with the Pleiades.

Martin Dobrizhoffer, a Jesuit priest in the 18th century, spent 18 years as a missionary in Paraguay. He wrote of the beliefs of the Abipone in his book *History of the Abipones*, which both praises and condemns the Indians.

I said that the Abipones were commendable for their wit and strength of mind, but ashamed of my too hasty praise, I retract my words and pronounce them fools, idiots, and madmen. Lo! this is the proof of their insanity! They are unacquainted with God, and with the very name of God, yet they affectionately salute the evil spirit, whom they call *Aharaigichi*, or *Queevet*, with the title of grandfather, *Groaperikie*. Him they declare to be their grandfather, and that of the Spaniards, but with this difference, that to the latter he gives gold and silver and fine clothes, but to them he transmits valour.

Dobrizhoffer then goes on to inform his readers that the constellation Pleiades is believed to be closely connected with Aharaigichi, and when it "disappears at certain periods from the sky of South America . . . they [the Indians] suppose that their grandfather is sick" and is going to die. When the stars return again in May, the Indians "with joyful shouts, and the festive sound of pipes and trumpets," congratulate him on the "recovery of his health."

See also: PLEIADES

0109

**Ahasuerus**   In medieval Christian legend, one of the names given to the Wandering Jew. The name is derived from the king of the Medes and Persians mentioned in the Old Testament book of Esther, who in turn is derived from Xerxes I (485–464 B.C.E.).

See also: WANDERING JEW

0110

**Ahl-at-tral**   In Arabic and Islamic mythology, demons who live beneath the Sahara Desert and appear as whirling sandstorms, drying up the wells before caravans arrive.

0111

**Ahmad**   In Islamic legend, the name Jesus Christ called Muhammad when he foretold the Prophet's coming. The Koran (sura 61) says: "And remember when Jesus the son of Mary said, 'O children of Israel! of a truth I am God's Apostle to you to confirm the law which was given before me, and to announce an apostle that shall come after me, whoso name shall be Ahmad.'"

See also: KORAN, THE; MUHAMMAD

0112

**Ahoeitu** (day god)   In Polynesian mythology, Tongan culture hero, son of the sky god Eitumatupua and his wife, the worm Ilaheva. Born on the the earth, Ahoeitu decided to ascend to the sky to visit his father. However, his heavenly brothers murdered him, cutting him into pieces and eating them. When his father, Eitumatupua, learned what had happened, he ordered his sons to vomit up Ahoeitu. They obeyed, and Eitumatupua restored his son to life with some magic herbs and sent him to rule Tonga.

0113

**Ah Puch** (Ahpuch, Ahal Puh, Ah-Puchah) (to melt, to dissolve, to spoil)   In Mayan mythology, god of death, the destroyer, ruler of the lowest of the nine underworlds (Hunhau), where he is chief demon. Ah Puch was the patron god of the number 10, the horrible Mitnal. He was associated with three Mayan symbols of death: the dog, the Moan bird, and the owl. In ancient Mayan mythology Ah Puch was associated with the god of war. Sometimes Ah Puch is identified by scholars with A of the Mayan letter gods. Today Ah Puch is known in the folklore of the Mayans as Yum Cimil (lord of death). He is believed to prowl about, causing sickness and death. In Mayan art Ah Puch is portrayed as a skeleton and often a bloated body with decaying flesh. He holds in his hands a skull, symbol of death.

**Ah Raxá Lac** (the lord of the green plate)   In Mayan mythology, an earth god, mentioned in the *Popol Vuh*, sacred book of the ancient Quiché Maya of Guatemala.

See also: *POPOL VUH*

0115

**Ah Raxa Tzel** (the lord of the green gourd or blue bowl)   In Mayan mythology, a sky god or personification of the sky, mentioned in the sacred book *Popol Vuh* of the ancient Quiché Maya of Guatemala. The name of the god reflects the belief that the sky was an inverted bowl or gourd.

See also: *POPOL VUH*

0116

**Ahriman** (Angra Mainyu, Anra Mainyu, Aharman)   In Persian mythology, the evil spirit, opposed to the good creator god, Ahura Mazda; in the end Ahriman will be destroyed by the forces of good.

Though the prophet Zarathustra raised Ahura Mazda to the major rank of god and made Ahriman a lesser deity, in earlier Persian mythology both gods were equals and brothers, sons of the great god of time-space, Zurvan. When the two were conceived, Zurvan decided that whichever

*Ahriman*

came to him first would be made king. When the evil Ahriman heard this in his mother's womb, he ripped it open, emerged, and approached his father.

"Who are you?" Zurvan asked.

"I am your son, Ahura Mazda," the evil Ahriman replied.

"Ahura Mazda is light, and you are black and stinking," Zurvan declared.

While they were speaking, Ahura Mazda came out of his mother's womb. Zurvan immediately recognized him and made him king.

"Did you not vow that to whichever of your sons should come first you would give the kingdom?" Ahriman complained.

"You false and wicked one," Zurvan replied, "the kingdom shall be given to you for nine thousand years, but Ahura Mazda is nevertheless king over you and will triumph after that time."

Ahura Mazda then created the heavens and the earth and all beautiful things, but Ahriman created demons, snakes, and all evil.

Ahriman is identified with Iblis, the devil in Islamic mythology. In some works Ahriman, rather than the snake of biblical lore, is pictured as an old man offering Adam and Eve the fatal fruit. One early Persian sculpture portrays Ahura Mazda riding on horseback trampling on Ahriman's snake-covered head.

See also: AHURA MAZDA; IBLIS; ZARATHUSTRA; ZURVAN

0117

**Ahtoltecat**   In Mayan mythology, silversmith god of the Quiché Maya of Guatemala, patron of the Toltecs, skilled silversmiths.

0118

**Ahulane**   In Mayan mythology, archer god, portrayed holding an arrow. Ahulane was worshiped on the island of Cozumel, where his cult was connected with warfare, as were those of Ah Chuy Kay, the fire destroyer; Hun Pic Tok, who carried 8,000 spears; Kac-u-Pacat, who carried a shield of fire; and Ah Cun Can, the serpent charmer. Many of these names may have a purely symbolic connection with war and may not be the names of separate deities.

0119

**Ahura Mazda** (Ahura Mazdah, Auhar Mazd) In Persian mythology, good creator god, the wise lord, later called Ohrmazd (Ormuzd). Ahura Mazda is continually battling the evil spirit Ahriman; in the end Ahura Mazda and the forces of goodness will prevail over Ahriman.

In the beginning Ahura Mazda may have been connected with Mithra, before he was elevated to the role of supreme being in Persian religion. According to the prophet Zarathustra, Ahura Mazda created cosmic order. He created both the moral and material worlds and is the sovereign, omniscient god of order. Creator of all things, Ahura Mazda is himself uncreated and eternal. One of the hymns ascribed to Zarathustra says:

O Ahura Mazda, this I ask of thee: speak to me truly!
How should I pray, when I wish to pray to one like you?
May one like you, O Mazda, who is friendly, teach one like me?
And may you give us supporting aids through friendly Justice,
And tell how you may come to use with Good Disposition?

A rock inscription placed by King Darius I has these lines to the god:

There is one God, omnipotent Ahura Mazda,
It is He who has created the earth here;
It is He who has created the heaven there;
It is He who has created mortal man.

In Persian art Ahura Mazda is sometimes portrayed as a bearded man emerging from a winged creature. He is often described as wearing a star-decked robe, and the "swift-horsed sun" is said to be his eye. His throne is in the highest heaven, where he holds court as his angels minister to him.

See also: AESHMA; AHRIMAN; ZARATHUSTRA

0120

**Ahurani**   In Persian mythology, water goddess who watches over rainfall as well as standing water; invoked for health and healing, for prosperity and growth.

0121

**Aido Quedo**   In Haitian voodoo, a female loa (deified spirit of the dead) who determines man's fate. She is often compared to the Virgin Mary in Christian symbolism.

See also: LOA; VIRGIN MARY

0122

**Aijeke**   In Lapland mythology, a wooden god worshiped as late as the 17th century, even though the country was nominally Lutheran. John Scheffer, a professor at the University of Uppsala, in his book *Lapponia*, says the image of Aijeke was always made of birch wood. "Of this wood,' he writes, "they make so many idols as they have sacrifices and, when they have done, they keep them in a cave by some hillside. The shape of them is very rude; at the top they are made to represent a man's head." Aijeke's rude shape had two spikes in its head to strike fire with. He was often identified with the Norse god Thor. Aijeke was also called Murona Jubmel (wooden god).

See also: ASK AND EMBLA; THOR

0123

**Aino** (peerless, splendid)   In the Finnish epic poem *The Kalevala* (runes 3–5), a Lapp maiden who was to marry the culture hero Vainamoinen but was drowned instead.

To ransom his life, her brother, the evil Joukahainen, offered Aino to Vainamoinen as a wife. The parents of the girl were happy about the match, but she was not because Vainamoinen was an old man. After Aino met Vainamoinen in the forest while gathering birch shoots for brooms, she was even more determined not to marry. Her mother, however, bribed her with gifts. Aino, dressed in her wedding garments, then wandered out into the fields, wishing she were dead. Stealing down to the river bank, she laid aside her garments and ornaments and swam to a neighboring rock. No sooner did she sit on the rock than it toppled, drowning her. The animals sent a message of Aino's death, by way of the hare, to her mother, who lamented her daughter's death, saying that mothers should not force their "unwilling daughters" to take bridegrooms "that they love not."

Vainamoinen then went fishing for Aino in the rivers. He caught a fish, which he was about to kill when he discovered it was Aino. Not giving up his quest, he asked her to become his wife, but she refused.

The sad fate of Aino inspired the Finnish composer and conductor Robert Kajanus to compose his *Aino* Symphony in 1885 for chorus and orchestra. The Finnish painter Akseli Gallen-Kallela portrayed the fate of Aino in a triptych.

See also: JOUKAHAINEN; *KALEVALA, THE*; LÖNNROT, ELIAS; VAINAMOINEN

0124

**Aiomun Kondi**   In the mythology of the Arawak Indians of the Guianas, the dweller-on-high. Aiomun Kondi destroyed the earth twice because of the disobedience of humankind. Once he used fire; the second time, water. He saved one good man, Marerewana, and his family from destruction.

0125

**Aipalookvik**   In Eskimo mythology, evil spirit who lives in the sea and attempts to destroy boatmen.

0126

**Airyaman**   In Persian mythology, god of healing, invoked against disease, sorcerers, and demons. The good god, Ahura Mazda, called on Airyaman to help expel disease. The god was so successful that he caused 99,999 diseases to cease. In the *Bundahishn*, a sacred Persian book of the Zoroastrians, Airyaman is called he "who gives the world healing of all pains."

See also: AHURA MAZDA

0127

**Aiwel**   In African mythology (Dinka of Eastern Sudan), hero, founder of a group of men who perform political and religious functions as members of a hereditary priesthood, the spear masters. Aiwel was born to a woman whose husband had been killed when a lion, desiring the man's bracelet, bit off his thumb to get it. The stubborn man had refused to give it up. The woman had wanted a son and was able to bear one through the aid of a water spirit. Aiwel was born with a full set of teeth and was able to drink a full gourd of milk at a time. When his mother discovered that it was Aiwel, not his older sister, who was drinking all of the milk, she became very upset. Aiwel told her not to tell anyone or else she would die. Nevertheless, she spoke and died.

Aiwel then joined his father, the water spirit. Returning from the river, he took the form of a man and a multicolored ox, named Longar. As it is the Dinka custom to name a person after the characteristics of his ox, Aiwel was called Aiwel Longar. A drought came and only Aiwel's cattle remained fat. Aiwel then left for a promised land of plenty, asking the people to follow him. At first they refused, and when they later tried to follow, he grew angry and killed some of them with his fishing spear. A man called Agothyathik saved some of the people by fighting with Aiwel, and in time Aiwel surrendered.

Aiwel gave fishing spears to the first group of people to cross the river and thus founded the spear-master clans. Those who came later were given war spears, and they founded the warrior clans. Aiwel left his people, saying that he would return only in time of need.

See also: DENG

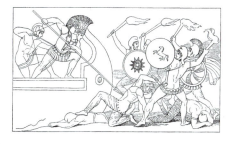

*Ajax*

0128
**Ajax** (of the earth?)    In Greek and Latin mythology, Latin form of the Greek Aias, a great hero of the Trojan War. Ajax was the son of Telamon of Salamis and Periboea (or Erioboea), and half-brother of Teucer. He was called Great Ajax be-

cause he was taller than the other Greek heroes. Ajax brought 12 ships to Troy, where he proved himself second only to Achilles in strength and bravery, though he is portrayed as rather stupid by Homer in the *Iliad*.

In later mythology Ajax goes mad when the armor of the dead Achilles is offered as a prize to Odysseus for his cunning and not to Ajax for his bravery. Ajax, according to this version, killed himself by falling on the sword given him by Hector. Out of his blood sprang the purple lily, and on its petals could be traced the first letters of his name, *Ai*. His death is the subject of Sophocles' play *Ajax*, he is described in detail in Ovid's *Metamorphoses* (book 13), and he appears in Horace's *Odes* (II, IV, 5).

A statue and temple to Ajax were erected at Salamis, and a yearly festival, the Aianteia, was held in his honor. He was also worshiped at Athens, where the tribe Aiantis was named after him. In later Greek mythology he was supposed to linger with Achilles in the island of Leuce.

Another Ajax in Greek mythology was the son of the Locrian king Oileus and was called Locrian or Lesser Ajax to avoid confusion with the Great Ajax. He took 40 ships to Troy. Though he was small, he distinguished himself beside his larger namesake. He was renowned for hurling the spear and was the swiftest runner next to Achilles. On his voyage home, to appease the anger of Athena, he suffered shipwreck on the Gyraean Rocks off the island of Myconos or, according to a variant myth, on the southernmost point of Euboea. Poseidon rescued him, but when Ajax boasted that he had escaped against the will of the gods, Poseidon took his trident and struck off the rock on which Ajax sat, and he sank into the sea.

Other accounts say that Athena's anger fell upon Ajax because when Cassandra had sought refuge at Athena's altar during the taking of Troy. Ajax tore her away by force, causing the sacred image of Athena, which Cassandra was holding, to fall. Though Agamemnon took Cassandra from Ajax, the Greeks left the crime of sacrilege unpunished, and the goddess vented her anger on the whole fleet with shipwrecks and high winds on the way home.

Along with other heroes of the Trojan War, Ajax was believed to live with Achilles in the island of Leuce. The Locrians worshiped him as a hero. A vacant place was left for him in the line when their troops formed for battle.

See also: ACHILLES; ATHENA; CASSANDRA; HECTOR; *ILIAD, THE*; ODYSSEUS; OVID

**Ajy** In Siberian mythology, a term meaning creator, birth-giving, life-giving, or nourishing. It is often used in conjunction with the names of various gods and goddesses.

0130

**Ajyset** (Ajysyt) (birth giver) In Siberian mythology, mother goddess worshiped by the Yakut, a Turkish people living near the Lena River. She presided over birth and brought souls from heaven to the newly born. She owned the Golden Book of Fate, which contained the names and fates of every human being, living or yet to be born. In prayers she was often addressed as Ajy-Khotun (birth-giving mistress) and Ajysyt-Ijaksit-Khotun (birth-giving nourishing mother). Ajyset is similar to another Siberian goddess, Yakut-Kubai-Khotun, worshiped by the Buriat, who lived in the Tree of Life or under its roots. She was considered the mother of men and animals.

See also: TREE OF LIFE

0131

**Akhenaton** (Ikhnaton) (glory of Aten) 1372–1355 B.C.E. In Egyptian history, the name chosen by Amenhotep IV when he adopted the worship of Aten. The son of Amenhotep III and his commoner wife, Tiye, Amenhotep IV was raised in a court of luxury and peace. Debate still rages as to whether or not he was a co-ruler with his father. In any event, when he ruled as pharaoh in his own right, he changed his name to Akhenaton and moved the capital of Egypt from Thebes to Amarna, a virtually virgin tract of land in middle Egypt. There he dedicated himself to the worship of the sun disk, or Aten, at the expense of the priesthood of Amun at Thebes. Aten was divorced from all anthropological associations and was regarded as a kindly creative force. Akhenaton's own hymn to Aten is close to certain hymns in the Old Testament, although we know that other deities continued to be worshiped alongside Aten. So pervasive was the influence of this new religion that the art of the period underwent a transformation that stressed naturalism in a way unparalleled in earlier periods of Egyptian art. Akhenaton forms the main character in Agatha Christie's play *Akhenaton*, Mika Waltari's novel *The Egyptian*, and Philip Glass's opera *Akhenaton*.

See also: ATEN

0132

**Akhtar** In Persian mythology, zodiacal constellation that makes up the army of the good god, Ahura Mazda.

See also: AHURA MAZDA

0133

**Akkruva** (Avfruvva, Havfru) In Finno-Ugric mythology, fish goddess worshiped in Lapland. Akkruva appeared as a mermaid, the upper part of her body human, her head covered with long hair, and her lower portion that of a fish. She was believed to rise from the sea combing her hair. When the goddess was in a beneficent mood she helped men catch fish, but she could also be destructive.

See also: MERMAID

0134

**Akshobhya** In Mahayana Buddhism, one of the five Dhyani-Buddhas. Called the Immovable, his symbol is the thunderbolt and his mount an elephant.

See also: DHAYANI-BUDDHAS; MAHAYANA

0135

**Akubo**   In Japanese No plays, the character of a wicked priest who wears a coarse beard and carries a halberd.

See also: NO

0136

**Akuma**   In Japanese folklore, an evil spirit who carries a sword and a huge head with flaming eyes. One day a nobleman saw an akuma with a naked sword floating toward him in the sky. Frightened by the hideous sight, the nobleman hid himself under a mat and looking out, saw the akuma enter the house next door. Hearing a terrible uproar, he went to see what had happened and found that his neighbor, in trying to kill the akuma, had accidentally killed his wife, children, and servants. *Variant terms*: ma, toori akuma.

0137

**Akupera** (tortoise, turtle)   In Hindu mythology, the name of the tortoise on which the earth is sometimes said to be supported.

0138

**Ala**   In African mythology (Ibo of Eastern Nigeria), daughter of Chuku (the great god), mother earth, goddess of the underworld, ruler of men, guardian of the harvest, and dispenser of fertility to people and animals. Ala is worshiped all over Ibo country with shrines and special houses, called Mbari, which are square and contain vividly colored mud figures. Ala is portrayed in the center of the house with a wide variety of animals, men, and other gods surrounding her. As ruler of the underworld, Ala receives the dead into her womb or pocket.

0139

**Ala**   In Russian mythology, daughter of Volos, god of beasts and flocks. Serge Prokofiev's ballet *Ala and Lolli* (1914–1915) deals with the myth. In the ballet Ala is taken prisoner by the enemy god and freed by the hero, Lolli, with the help of

Volos. Prokofiev used the ballet score for his orchestral *Scythian Suite*.

See also: VOLOS

0140

**Al Aaraaf** (Al Arg) (the partition)   In Islamic mythology, the region between paradise and Djahannam, or hell, presided over by the beautiful maiden Nesace. Al Aaraaf is the place for those persons who are morally neither good nor bad, such as infants, lunatics, and idiots, as well as those whose life is a balance of good and evil.

Edgar Allan Poe was fascinated by the idea and wrote in a letter to Isaac Lea that Al Aaraaf "is a medium between Heaven and Hell where men suffer no punishment but yet do not attain that tranquil or even happiness which they suppose to be characteristic of heavenly enjoyment." In Poe's poem "Al Aaraaf" it is a wondrous star surrounded by four suns. A youth, Angelo, is brought there with the hope of entering heaven, but an earthly love prevents him from hearing the call of Nesace.

See also: HADES; HEAVEN AND HELL

0141

**Aladdin** (Alaeddin)   Hero in the tale "Aladdin and the Enchanted Lamp" from *The Thousand and One Nights*. The tale is not included in any manuscript copy of the work. It first appeared in the French translation of the *Nights* (1704–1715) by Galland, who heard the tale from a Christian Syrian, Youhenna Diab.

Aladdin is a good-for-nothing son of a poor tailor in China. After his father's death he takes to the streets and turns up at his mother's house only for meals. One day a man pretending to be his uncle gains Aladdin's confidence and takes him to a high and barren mountain. The man then builds a fire and pours on it some perfumes, muttering incantations at the same time. Suddenly the earth quakes and opens, revealing an alabaster slab. Prodded by the sorcerer disguised as his uncle, Aladdin removes the slab and descends into a vault below. It is filled with silver and gold.

"Above the dais," the sorcerer tells Aladdin, "thou wilt find a lamp hung up; take it and pour out the oil that is therein and put it in thy sleeve; and fear not for thy clothes therefrom, for it is not oil. And as thou returnest, thou mayest pluck from the trees what thou wilt, for that is thine as long as the lamp is in thy hand." The sorcerer then gives Aladdin a ring that will protect him from all evil.

Then, as Aladdin is trying to climb out of the vault, the sorcerer closes the marble slab over him. Aladdin calls upon Allah for help and at the same time accidentally rubs the lamp, whereupon one of the marids, the most powerful of the djinn (genies), appears. "Here am I, thy slave," announces the marid. "Ask what thou wilt, for I am his slave who hath the ring in hand, the ring of my lord." Aladdin asks to be freed and the marid obeys his wish. By means of the magic lamp Aladdin obtains wealth, has a palace built, and marries Bardroulboudour. When the sorcerer finds that Aladdin has escaped, he sets out to recover the magic lamp. After buying a number of lamps from a coppersmith, the sorcerer goes about the streets, crying: "Who will barter an old lamp for a new?" All the town thinks he is crazy, but Bardroulboudour exchanges the magic lamp for a new copper one. Immediately the sorcerer rubs the lamp, conjures the marid, and orders Aladdin's palace and all his goods transported to Africa, the sorcerer's home.

Aladdin is out hunting while this happens and, rubbing his ring to return to the palace, he is transported to Africa. Later, with the aid of his wife, Aladdin drugs the sorcerer and cuts off his head. After some more adventures (for the sorcerer has an evil brother) Aladdin and his wife live happily until death, the destroyer of delights, separates them.

Aladdin's story has been set to music by many composers (although none of the operas is still performed), and it has been a favorite movie subject.

The palace built by the marid of the lamp had a room with 24 windows, all but one set with precious stones. The last was left for the sultan to finish, but his monetary resources were unequal to the task; thus the phrase, "to finish Aladdin's window," which means to attempt to complete something begun by a master hand or genius. Longfellow's poem on Hawthorne's death concludes:

Ah! who shall lift that wand of magic power
And the lost clue regain?
The unfinished window in Aladdin's tower
Unfinished must remain!

See also: ALLAH; *THOUSAND AND ONE NIGHTS, THE*

0142

**Alains le Gros** (rock, noble?)   In medieval legend connected with the Holy Grail, the first fisher king. Alains was told by Josephus, keeper of the Holy Grail, to take a net from the table on which the Grail stood and cast it into a lake. One fish was caught, and Alains's men laughed at him for believing the single fish could feed all of them. But Alains prayed over the fish, and it multiplied enough for all of the men to eat. He was then called the "fisher king" or "rich fisher." Afterward all keepers of the Holy Grail were called fisher kings.

See also: HOLY GRAIL

0143

**Alastor** (avenger)   In Greek mythology, the name for an avenging demon who follows the footsteps of criminals according to Aeschylus's *Agamemnon*. Shelley used the name for *Alastor, or The Spirit of Solitude* (1816); his first important work, the poem is a condemnation of self-centered idealism. The name Alastor is also borne by a son of Neleus and brother of Nestor, married to Harpalyce.

See also: AGAMEMNON; NESTOR

0144

**Alban, St.** (man from Alba)    Fourth century. In Christian legend, proto-martyr of England. Feast, 22 June.

St. Bede records the life of the saint in his *Ecclesiastical History of the English People*. When the persecution of the Christians in England was ordered by the emperor Diocletian, Alban, though a pagan, hid a Christian priest. For his crime he was condemned to death. He was first tortured and then led to the place of execution. On the way it was necessary to cross the river Coln. A great crowd had gathered, and the bridge was too narrow for the many people to pass. When St. Alban "drew near the stream," it "was immediately dried up, and he perceived that the water had departed and made way for him to pass," according to Bede's account. When they reached the hill of execution, Alban prayed for water to quench his thirst. A spring suddenly gushed out at his feet. Finally, the saint was beheaded, and the executioner's eyes "dropped to the ground together with the blessed martyr's head."

St. Alban's burial place was forgotten and then rediscovered by King Offic in 793 after the king had seen in a vision where the remains of the saint could be found. A church was built over the spot, and nearby the great Benedictine monastery and the town of St. Alban's in Hertfordshire, England, were built.

The saint is variously portrayed: as a warrior with a cross and sword, crowned with a laurel, with a peer's coronet and cross, with his head cut off, with his head in a holly bush, spreading his cloak with the sun above, and in a scene with the executioner's eyes dropping out. He is often depicted as carrying his head in his hands, a conventional symbol adopted by artists to show that the martyr had been beheaded.

See also: BEDE THE VENERABLE, ST.; DENIS OF FRANCE, ST.

0145

**Albania**    In medieval British legend, name for Scotland, derived from Albanact, son of Brute,

the first king of Britain. At the death of Brut, Britain was divided by his sons: Locrin got England; Albanact got Albania (Scotland); and Kambler got Cambria (Wales). Albania later became Albany, as in Shakespeare's *King Lear*, in which the Duke of Albany is a Scotsman, although not specifically mentioned in the play.

See also: BRUT; LEAR, KING

0146

**Albertus Magnus, St.** (Albert the Great) 1193–1280. In Christian legend, bishop and Doctor of the Church, responsible for the introduction of Aristotelian methods and principles to the study of Christian theology. Feast, 15 November. Albert was considered one of the greatest Christian thinkers of the Middle Ages. He was a Dominican friar and later bishop of Ratisbon. The saint is often portrayed with his student St. Thomas Aquinas in works by the Dominican painter Fra Angelico.

See also: THOMAS AQUINAS, ST.

0147

**Albion** (white)    In medieval British legend, name for England, possibly based on the White (Latin *albus*) Cliffs of Dover that face France. Albion is also the name of a giant who conquered the island and named it after himself. Legend offers other origins for the name. A giant son of Neptune was named Albion. He is said to have discovered the country and ruled it for 44 years. According to another story, 55 daughters of the king of Syria, the eldest of whom was Albion, were all married on the same day and murdered their husbands on their wedding night. They were packed onto a ship and set adrift. They landed in England, went ashore, and married natives.

0148

**Albiorix**    In Celtic mythology, a war god worshiped by the continental Celts at Avignon,

France. Ancient Roman writers identified Albiorix with their war god, Mars.

See also: MARS

0149

**Alcathous** (swift aid)    In Greek mythology, king of Megara, the son of Pelops and Hippodameia; brother of Astydameia, Atreus, Chrysippus, Copreus, Lysidice, Nicippe, Piltheus, Troezen, and Thyestes; husband of Euaechme. He slew the Cithaeron lion that had torn Euippus, the son of Megareus, to pieces. As a reward he was given Euaechma, the daughter of Megareus, as well as the throne. With Apollo as his friend and helper, he rebuilt the city walls and one of two fortresses, Alcathoe, that had temples to Apollo and Artemis. A singing stone in the fortress was said to be the one on which Apollo laid down his lyre when at work. Alcathous's eldest son, Ischepolis, was killed in the Calydonian boar hunt. His second son, Callipolis, running with the news to his father when Alcathous was sacrificing to Apollo, scattered the altar fire. Alcathous then struck his son dead, believing the boy had committed sacrilege. By his daughters Automedusa and Periboea, the wives of Iphicles and Telamon, Alcathous was the grandfather of Iolaus and Ajax.

See also: AJAX; APOLLO; CALYDONIAN BOAR HUNT; PELOPS

0150

**Alcestis** (might of the home)    In Greek mythology, daughter of Pelias and Anaxibia (or Phylomache); wife of Admetus, king of Pherae in Thessaly. When Admetus, in order to achieve immortality, had to find someone to die in his place, all refused, including his parents; only Alcestis volunteered and gave her life for his. She was later brought back from the underworld by Heracles. She appears in Euripides' play *Alcestis*, in which Admetus is portrayed as being a selfish husband. Many later writers have based their characterizations of Alcestis on Euripides. William Morris wrote "The Love of Alcestis" in

1868, and Robert Browning in *Balaustion's Adventure* (1871) has a translation of Euripides' play in the poem. In medieval tradition Alcestis was the model wife, appearing in Chaucer's *Legend of Good Women*. She is called Celia in T. S. Eliot's play *The Cocktail Party*. In the play Celia prefers to return to the land of the dead because for her it is a greater reality. Milton cites Alcestis in his "Sonnet 23," and Rilke wrote a poem "Alcestis." The best known operatic setting is *Alceste* (1767) by Gluck, based on Euripides' play. In the opera Apollo, not Heracles, brings back Alcestis. A modern operatic version is *Alkestis* (1922) by Rutland Boughton in Gilbert Murray's English translation of Euripides' play. There is also *Alkestis* (1924) by Egon Wellesz with a libretto by Hugo von Hofmannsthal.

See also: ADMETUS; ALCESTIS; CHAUCER; HERACLES

0151

**Alcina** (sea maiden)    In the Charlemagne cycle of legends, a powerful enchantress, the embodiment of carnal pleasure. Alcina was the sister of Logistilla (reason) and Morgana (lasciviousness). When she grew tired of her sexual conquests, she changed her lovers into trees, fountains, and rocks. The hero Astolpho fell in love with Alcina, and she changed him into a myrtle tree. He was later disenchanted by Melissa, who by means of a magic ring made Alcina's real senility and ugliness appear. Alcina appears in Boiardo's *Orlando Innamorato* and Ariosto's *Orlando Furioso*, as well as in Handel's opera *Alcina*.

See also: ASTOLPHO; CHARLEMAGNE; MYRTLE

0152

**Alcinous** (mighty mind)    In Greek mythology, king of the Phaeacians; husband of Arete; father of Nausicaa; the king with whom Odysseus finds shelter and aid. Alcinous appears in Homer's *Odyssey* (books 6, 7, 8).

See also: ODYSSEUS; *ODYSSEY, THE*; NAUSICAA

**Alcithoe** (swift might)   In Greek mythology, daughter of Minyas; sister of Arsippe and Leucippe. She and her sisters were changed into bats for refusing to join the other women of Boeotia in the worship of Dionysus. Ovid's *Metamorphoses* (book 4) tells her tale.

See also: DIONYSUS; OVID

0153

**Alcmaeon** (strong youth)   In Greek mythology, son of Amphiaraus and Eriphyle and brother of Amphilochus. Alcmaeon took part in the expedition of the Epigoni against Thebes. On his return home he killed his mother at the instigation of his father, and as punishment he was driven mad and haunted by the Erinyes. Alcmaeon went to Phegeus, in Psophis, to be purified by Phegeus and was then given Phegeus's daughter Arsinoe (or Alphesiboea). He gave her the jewels of Harmonia, which he had brought from Argos. In a short time the crops failed, and he again went mad. Wandering, he eventually arrived at the mouth of the Achelous River. There he found an island that had not been there when his mother cursed him, and he was cured of his madness. He then married Achelous's daughter Callirrhoë and had two sons, Acarnan and Amphoterus. Unable to resist his wife's entreaties that she have Harmonia's necklace and robe, he went to Phegeus in Arcadia and took them, pretending they would be dedicated at Delphi for the healing of his madness. When Phegeus learned he had been deceived, Alcmaeon was killed. His death was avenged by his two sons. He was worshiped at a sanctuary at Thebes that was said to contain his tomb. Alcmaeon is cited in Dante's *Divine Comedy* (Purgatory, canto 12; Paradise, canto 4).

See also: ACARNAN AND AMPHOTERUS; AMPHIARAUS; AMPHILOCHUS; CALLIRRHOË; DELPHI; HARMONIA

0154

**Alcmene** (steadfast strength)   In Greek mythology, daughter of King Electryon of Argos and Anaxo; wife of Amphitryon; mother of Heracles by Zeus. When she died at a great age, Zeus sent Hermes to take her body from its coffin and bring Alcmene to the Elysian Fields. In this heaven Alcmene married Rhadamanthys. When Hermes stole the body of Alcmene, he substituted a large stone, which was placed in a sacred grove in Thebes and worshiped. Alcmene also had an altar in the temple of Heracles at Athens. Ovid's *Metamorphoses* (book 9) tells her tale.

See also: ALCMENE; HERMES.; HERACLES; OVID; RHADAMANTHYS; ZEUS

0155

**Alcyone** (kingfisher)   In Greek mythology, wife of Ceyx; daughter of Aeolus and Enarete. When she learned that her husband, Ceyx, had been drowned on his way to consult an oracle, Alcyone threw herself into the sea, and she and Ceyx both were changed into birds. As long as they built and tended their nest, the Aegean was calm. The term "halcyon days" comes from her name, also rendered Halcyone. Her tale is told in Ovid's *Metamorphoses* (book 11) and in Chaucer's *Book of the Duchess*.

See also: AEOLUS; CHAUCER; OVID

0156

**Alcyoneus** (kingfisher)   In Greek mythology, son of Uranus, whose blood touched Gaea, the earth; eldest and mightiest of the Titans. Alcyoneus could not be overtaken by death in his own country. In the war with the Titans, Heracles had to drag Alcyoneus away from Pallene before he could kill him. The hero lifted him from the earth, his mother, and killed him. Alcyoneus also is the name of a giant who stole the oxen of Helios from the island of Erytheia. As Heracles was crossing the Thracian isthmus of Pallene, Alcyoneus crushed 12 of his wagons and 25 of his men with a huge piece of rock. When

0157

the giant hurled it at Heracles, the hero struck it back with his club and killed Alcyoneus with the same blow.

See also: GAEA; HERACLES; TITANS; URANUS

**0158**

**Aldinger, Sir**    In medieval British legend, a knight who appears in a ballad. Aldinger is steward to Queen Eleanor, wife of King Henry II. He impeaches her fidelity and submits to a combat to substantiate his charge. However, an angel in the shape of a child establishes the queen's innocence.

*A Fury*

**0159**

**Alecto** (Allecto) (the enticer)    In Greek and Roman mythology, one of the three Furies, or Erinyes. The others were Megaera and Tisiphone. Alecto is cited in Vergil's *Aeneid* (book 7), in Dante's *Divine Comedy* (Inferno, canto 9) as "she who wails," and in Shakespeare's *Henry IV, Part II* (5.5.39).

See also: *AENEID, THE*

**0160**

**Alectryon** (rooster, cock)    In Greek mythology, a youth who was to watch for the approach of the sun when Ares was making love to

Aphrodite so that they would not be discovered by her husband, Hephaestus. Alectryon fell asleep, and the two lovers were discovered. In anger Ares turned Alectryon into a cock, which still heralds the dawn.

See also: APHRODITE; ARES; COCK; HEPHAESTUS

**0161**

**Aleine**    In Arthurian legend, the niece of Gwain. She persuaded Perceval to enter the Easter tournament at King Arthur's court, giving him a suit of red armor. He entered the lists unknown and won a vacant seat at the Round Table.

See also: ARTHUR; EASTER; GWAIN; PERCEVAL; ROUND TABLE

**0162**

**Alexander Nevsky**    1220–1263. In Russian legend, prince-saint who defended Russia against foreign invaders. The heroic personality Alexander Nevsky, the first prince of Novgorod and (after 1252) great prince of Vladimir and all Russia, is one of the heroes of both Imperial and Soviet Russia. His most famous exploit was the Russian defense of Novgorod in 1242 against the invading Knights of the Teutonic Order. Called to save his country, Prince Alexander, through the power of his personality alone, gathered together an enormous army and met the enemy on a frozen lake. There he and his army dealt them a humiliating defeat. When the prince was laid out for burial, the Metropolitan Archbishop Cyril wanted to place in the prince's hand a "charter with prayers asking for the remission of sins." Alexander, "as if he were alive, extended his hand and took the charter from the hand of the Metropolitan Archbishop," according to one Russian legend.

The famous Russian movie director Sergei Eisenstein used the legend of Alexander for his first sound film, *Alexander Nevsky*. Made one year before the Soviet-Nazi pact, the movie portrays the Germans as complete barbarians. Prokofiev's music for the film was later adapted by the composer for his cantata *Alexander Nevsky* for mezzo-soprano, chorus, and orchestra.

See also: VLADIMIR, ST.

**Alexander the Great** (he who wards off men) 356–323 B.C.E. In Greek history and legend, king of Macedonia, son of Philip II and Olympias. He was educated by Aristotle. The story of Alexander is a combination of history and legend. His life appears in Greek, medieval Christian, Jewish, and Islamic legends. One legend illustrating his early life and his relationship with his father is told in Plutarch's *Parallel Lives.* Philip had a beautiful white horse, Bucephalus, which could not be tamed. When Alexander succeeded in breaking the horse, Philip is said to have told him that he, Alexander, must seek a larger kingdom because Macedonia was not large enough to reflect his greatness. Alexander's compassion is the subject of another legend in Plutarch's work. It tells of a matron of Thebes who had been raped by one of Alexander's captains after Alexander had sacked that city. She told her captor that she kept her jewels at the bottom of a well. When the officer went to fetch them, she pushed him in. Alexander did not punish the woman because he said she did the right thing. Plutarch also tells the tale of the Gordian knot. During his war against the Persian king Darius, Alexander entered the Phrygian city of Gordium. Here there was a chariot bound with cords in a knot so complex that whoever could untie it would be the ruler of the world. Alexander cut the knot with his sword and took the city. When Alexander became ill, no one would treat him for fear of the consequences if they failed. His friend Philip, however, agreed to procure him medicine. Alexander had just received a letter from one of his generals, Parmenio, that said Philip would murder him. To show his trust in Philip, he showed him the letter while he took the medicine.

Other legends portray Alexander's generosity. After his victory over Darius he treated Darius's family kindly. When Darius was killed by his own men, he gave his last message to Alexander and asked him to care for his family, which Alexander did.

Painters, especially those of the 17th century, frequently portrayed Alexander's marriage to Roxana. She was the daughter of a chieftain of Sogdiana, one of the conquered territories of Asia. There are also stories of her cruelty after his death. Cassander is said to have put her to death.

Alexander reached Egypt in the autumn of 332 B.C.E. According to one legend, he consulted the oracle of Zeus-Amen (Ammon) (a composite god made up of the Greek god Zeus and the Egyptian god Amen) in the Siwa oasis. Amen recognized Alexander as his son and promised him control over the entire world. A short time later Alexander was crowned king of Egypt in the temple of Ptah at Memphis. On his way to the shrine of Zeus-Amen, Alexander made a stop at Rhacotia, a small fishing village and former frontier post of the pharaohs. Realizing the advantages of the site, Alexander decided to build a new city, to be called Alexandria. The layout of the city was geometric, with wide streets on a rectangular grid. The plan was drawn up by Deinocrates, an architect from Rhodes, and by Cleomenes of Naucratis, who was in charge of the project. According to one legend, the city was in the shape of a Greek garment. The perimeter was laid out by dropping seeds, which birds promptly ate. This seemingly bad omen was interpreted as a good sign by Alexander. Later he left Alexandria and died in Asia. Ptolemy, one of Alexander's generals, was responsible for returning his body to Egypt, and he erected a magnificent tomb for his leader in Alexandria. When Julius Caesar was in Egypt, he asked to see the tomb of Alexander. The emperor Caracalla is reported to have stolen Alexander's sword from his body. Despite these persistent legends, the burial places of Alexander and the Ptolemies have not been discovered.

The *Alexander Romance* (second century B.C.E.) added numerous mythical episodes to the life of Alexander, such as a trip to the heavens. Most medieval legends of Alexander were influenced by this work. Alexander appears among the Nine Worthies, or Men of Worth, a grouping popular during the Middle Ages. The Latin poem *Alexandreis* (12th century) was very popular, as well as the long French work *Roman d'Alexandre*. Alexander appears in one of Racine's early plays, as well as in Dryden's poem *Alexander's Feast*, and he is the subject of a novel, *Fire from Heaven*, by Mary Renault. In art there is Pinturicchio's *Triumph of Alexander*, Jordaens's tapestries, Aldorfer's *Alexander's Victory* (one of Napoleon's favorite artworks), and Veronese's *The Family of Darius Before Alexander*. There are more than 100 operas based on episodes from Alexander's life, though none are currently popular.

See also: AMEN; ARISTOTLE; GORDIAN KNOT; NINE WORTHIES; PTAH; ZEUS

0164

**Alf** (elf)   In Norse mythology, a dwarf mentioned in the *Voluspa*, a poem in the *Poetic Edda* that tells of the creation and destruction of the world. The name Alf is used also for a number of other dwarfs and other characters. From it comes, through Old English, the word *elf*.

See also: ELVES; *PROSE EDDA*

0165

**Alfadir** (Alfadur) (all-father)   In Norse mythology, a title for Odin, chief of the gods, and often used in Christian times for God. In the *Prose Edda* the Alfadir is said to have existed "from all ages." He formed "heaven and earth, and the air, and all things thereunto belonging." Also in the *Prose Edda* it is said: "Odin is the foremost and eldest of the aesir; he rules all things, and as powerful as the other gods are, they serve him as children do a father. . . . Odin is called Alfadir." He is credited with the creation of man and is said to have "given him a soul which shall live and never perish though the body shall have moldered away, or have been burnt to ashes. And all that are righteous shall dwell with him in a place called Gimli, or Vingolf; but the wicked

shall go to Hel, and thence to Niflheim, which is below, in the ninth world."

See also: ODIN; HEL; NIFLHEIM; *PROSE EDDA*

0166

**Alfar** (elves or dwarfs)   In Norse mythology, the elves or dwarfs ruled over by the god Frey. The *Prose Edda* gives an account of their origin:

Then the gods, seating themselves upon their thrones, distributed justice, and bethought them how the dwarfs had been bred in the mould of the earth, just as worms are in a dead body. It was, in fact, in Ymir's flesh that the dwarfs were engendered, and began to move and live. At first they were only maggots, but by the will of the gods they at length partook both of human shape and understanding, although they always dwell in rocks and caverns. Modsognir and Durin are the principal ones.

From Alfar are derived all small creatures, such as alvors, elves, brownies, and ras found in northern myths and legends. Two groups of Alfar are cited, the *liosalfar* (light elves) who live in Alfheim, and the *dockalfar* (dark elves) who live underground and are mostly of an evil nature. Other names used are *huldu folk* (hidden folk) and *liufliger* (darlings).

The dark dwarfs were so ugly, with their dark skin, green eyes, large heads, short legs, and crows' feet, that the gods forced them, under penalty of being turned to stone, to live underground and never show themselves during the daytime. Although less powerful than the gods, the dwarfs were far more powerful than men.

In northern folklore and legends, dwarfs transport themselves easily from one place to another. They wear red capes that can make them invisible. They like to hide behind rocks and mischievously repeat the last words of every conversation they overhear. Echoes are therefore called "dwarfs' talk." In various countries of northern Europe their ruler is called Andvari,

Alberich, Elbegast, Gondemar, Laurin, or Oberon.

Generally, dwarfs in northern legends and tales are kind and helpful. Sometimes they knead bread, grind flour, brew beer, and perform countless other tasks. If ill-treated, however, or laughed at, they will leave a house. When Christianity replaced the northern gods, the dwarfs, in anger, left forever to punish the people for their lack of belief in the old gods.

According to some northern legends, dwarfs envied man's taller stature and often tried to increase their race's height by marrying human wives or stealing unbaptized children and substituting their own offspring for the human mother to nurse. These dwarf babies were known as changelings. To recover the true child and rid herself of the changeling, a woman had either to brew beer in eggshells or to grease the soles of the changeling's feet and hold them so near the flames that, attracted by their babies' cries, the dwarf parents would come to claim their own child and bring back the human child.

Female dwarfs were believed able to change themselves into maras (or nightmares). If a victim succeeded in plugging the hole through which a mara made her entrance into his room, she was then at his mercy—he could even marry her. She would be his faithful wife as long as the hole by which she had entered was plugged. If it was open, she would escape.

The *Prose Edda* gives an account of the origin of the Alfar. Offerings of milk, honey, or a small animal was made to the Alfar.

See also: ALFHEIM; ANDVARI; FREY; *PROSE EDDA*

0167

**Alfasem**   In Arthurian legend, the king of Terre Foraine, converted and baptized by Alains, keeper of the Holy Grail. Alfasem was wounded in both thighs by an angel for sleeping where the Grail had rested. He later died of the wounds.

See also: HOLY GRAIL

0168

**Alfheim** (elf home)   In Norse mythology, home of the light elves or dwarfs, as well as of the god Frey. It was located in the air between heaven and earth. In the *Prose Edda* Snorri Sturluson makes a distinction between light and dark elves: "There is yet that place, which is called Álfheim; there lives that people, who are called the light-elves, but the dark-elves dwell down in the earth, . . . The light-elves are fairer than the sun in appearance, but the dark-elves are blacker than pitch." Sir Walter Scott, in his poem "Thomas the Rhymer," in *Contributions to the Minstrelsy of the Scottish Border: Imitations of the Ancient Ballad*, uses the words *Elfland* and *Elflyn land*.

See also: ALF; FREY; *PROSE EDDA*

0169

**Ali**   600?–661. In Islamic legend, husband of Fatima, one of Muhammad's daughters; fourth caliph (656–661). Numerous legends collected around Ali, as both saint and warrior. He is credited with many miracles, such as raising a man from the dead. Persian Muslims speak of more than 1,000 miracles, although only 60 are recorded. Some Muslim sects believe that Allah became incarnate in the person of Ali by "indwelling." The Nusairi sects regard Ali as the first of the three persons of the Trinity.

As a warrior Ali is said to have killed 523 men in one day. His sword cut them from their horses with such speed that half of each body remained on the horse while the other half fell to the ground. Ali is famous in Persian poetry for his beautiful eyes. The expression *Ayn Hali* (the eyes of Ali) is a term of praise for a person's beauty. Ali was assassinated in 661 by being struck on the forehead with a poisoned saber.

See also: ALLAH; FATIMA; MUHAMMAD

0170

**Ali Baba**   Hero of the tale "Ali Baba and the Forty Thieves" included in *The Thousand and One Nights* but not in any manuscript copy of the

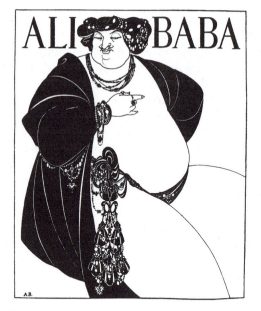

*Ali Baba (Aubrey Beardsley)*

jars. One of the men hears her approach and asks if it is time to come out. She replies, "Not yet." Deciding that they must be robbers, she fills a caldron from the single jar that contains oil and pours the oil over the thieves, killing all of them. Ali, in gratitude, then marries Morgiana to his nephew, or in some versions to his son.

The tale of Ali Baba is one of the most popular in the entire collection. It was made into an opera seven times and was filmed in 1902, 1919, 1943, 1952, and 1962. Comic variations, with Eddie Cantor in 1938 (*Ali Baba Goes to Town*) and Fernandel in 1954, also have been filmed. Hidden treasure is a common legend motif.

See also: MOTIF; *THOUSAND AND ONE NIGHTS, THE*

work. It first appeared in the French translation of the *Nights* by Galland, who heard the tale from a Christian Syrian, Youhenna Diab.

Ali Baba and his brother Kassim live in Persia. One day Ali Baba, while collecting wood in the forest, sees 40 thieves enter a cave after saying: "Open, Sesame!" At the first opportunity Ali goes to the cave and says the magic words. It opens, and he discovers that the cave is filled with gold and treasure. He takes some of it home, and in a short time his brother also discovers the secret. Kassim enters the cave but forgets the magic words needed to get out. The thieves return, kill Kassim, cut him into quarters, and hang him in the cave.

Ali goes in search of his brother and, finding the body, takes it to a cobbler who can sew it back together so that Kassim's death will appear natural. Through the cobbler, the thieves come in search of Ali in order to kill him too. The head thief poses as an oil merchant and enters Ali's house. He asks Ali if he may store his oil jars in the shed, and Ali agrees. A thief is hiding in each of the jars except one, waiting to kill Ali. The maid, Morgiana, needing some oil, goes to the

0171

**Aliosha Popovich** (Aljosa Popovic)   11th century C.E.. In Russian legend, *bogatyr* (epic hero) who appears in the *bylini* (epic songs) and in folktales. Aliosha was one of seven legendary *bogatyri* and the son of a priest, a "mighty hero" who grew as much in one day as other babies did in a week, and he achieved a year's growth in one week. When he was fully grown, he asked his father if he could "try his luck in the field of battle." His father agreed if he would take along Maryshko Parnov's son to be his servant. Both set out and journeyed to the realm of Prince Vladimir, who welcomed them. At the same time the evil Turgarin Zmeevich, "a mighty champion, invaded and scourged Prince Vladimir's kingdom," entering the palace and eating everything in sight. Aliosha challenged him to a duel. The next day, when the two were to fight, Aliosha saw Turgarin Zmeevich flying through the air on his horse. Aliosha called on the Holy Mother of God to send a black cloud to "wet Turgarin's paper wings." The prayer was answered, and the evil one fell to earth. In the ensuing battle Turgarin's head was cut off and carried on a spear to Prince Vladimir.

See also: VALDIMIR, ST.

**Alisaunder**   In Arthurian legend, son of Prince Boudwin and Anglides. His father was killed by King Mark, and when Alisaunder grew up, his mother handed him his father's doublet, covered with blood. "Avenge your father!" she told the youth. King Mark, however, had Alisaunder slain instead.

**Al Jassasa** (Al Jassaca) (the spy)   In Islamic mythology, the name of the beast or monster in the Koran (sura 27) that will appear at the Last Judgment. According to folklore, he or she (accounts vary) will have a bull head, hog eyes, elephant ears, stag horns, ostrich neck, lion breasts, tiger color, a back like a cat, camel legs, the voice of an ass, and the tail of a ram. The beast will mark those who are saved and those who are damned.

See also: KORAN, THE

**Alkha**   In Siberian mythology, the personification of the darkness of the sky, a dragonlike monster who causes eclipses of the sun and moon. In one Buriat myth Alkha swallowed the sun and moon, plunging the earth into utter darkness. The gods became angry and cut his body into two pieces, one part falling to the earth and the forepart remaining in heaven. As a result, although the monster continually tries to swallow the moon and sun, each time they fall out of his back.

In some myths Alkha is called Arakho. In one of these, told by the Buriat, Arakho lived on the earth eating the hairs off people's bodies. This made God angry because hair was needed for man's protection. As a result God cut Arakho into two parts. Yet the monster still tried to swallow the sun and moon. The gashes made by Alkha's fangs are visible on the surface of the moon.

In a variant myth Arakho drank from a cup prepared by the sun and moon that contained the Water of Life. By drinking from the cup Arakho dirtied it, and God cut him in two as a punishment. But Arakho's forepart became immortal. Arakho still chases the moon, leaving his monstrous marks, which are called moon spots.

See also: WATER OF LIFE

**Al-Khadir** (Al-Khidr, El Khizr) (the green one)   In Islamic legend, a saint who found the Waters of Immortality or Fountain of Life. He is believed to appear clad in green robes to Muslims in distress. The green symbolizes his unfading youth.

The legend of Al-Khadir appears in various Islamic works, such as *The Thousand and One Nights*, and is partly told in the Koran (sura 18). When Moses, or Musa to use his Arabic name, was preaching to the people, they admired his knowledge and eloquence so much that they asked him if there was any man in the world wiser than he. Musa answered no. Allah was not satisfied with Musa's answer and told the prophet that there was a man who was wiser than he, and the man's name was Al-Khadir. Musa was told to go in search of Al-Khadir and to take along his servant (who was Joshua) and a fish. When they arrived at a certain rock where "two seas" met, the fish disappeared. There are different explanations for this: that the fish, being roasted, jumped out of the basket into the sea, or that Joshua accidentally sprinkled on it some water from the Fountain of Life (for though they did not know it, they had arrived at their destination). The Koran says the "fish took its way in the sea at will."

Suddenly a stranger appeared. It was Al-Khadir, but neither Musa nor Joshua was aware of his identity. Musa said he would like to follow the stranger, but the man replied that Musa would complain about what he was going to do. Musa promised not to complain, and they all set out. When the stranger scuttled a boat and Musa complained, the stranger reminded Musa of his promise. As they continued on their way and the stranger murdered a boy, Musa was horrified. They then reached a city that refused them hospitality. In it was a wall ready to crumble, but the stranger fixed it. Musa said he should be paid for such services.

The stranger told Musa he would at last explain his actions. "As to the vessel," he said, "it belonged to a poor man who toiled upon the sea. I was minded to damage it, for in their rear was a king who seized every ship by force. As to the youth, his parents were believers and we feared lest he should trouble them by error and infidelity. And we desired that their Lord might give them in his place a child better than he in virtue and nearer in filial piety. And as to the wall, it belonged to two orphan youths in the city, and beneath it was their treasure; and their father was a righteous man; and the Lord desired that they should reach the age of strength, and take forth their treasure the mercy of thy Lord. And not of mine own will have I done this. This is the interpretation of that which thou couldst not bear with patience."

According to some Islamic traditions, Al-Khadir is thought to be Phineas, Elias, and St. George in one because his soul passed by metempsychosis successively through all three. Al-Khadir is sometimes identified with Khwadja Khidr, who presides over the Fountain of Immortality in Indian Islamic belief. Khwadja Khidr, however, is identified in many parts of India with a river god or with the fish avatar of the god Vishnu. Some Indian Muslims offer prayers to Khwadja Khidr at the first shaving of a boy. Part of the ceremony also consists of launching a small boat. Along the Indus, Khwadja Khidr is often identified with the river and is seen as an old man clothed in green. When a man escapes drowning, he is said to have evaded Khwadja's domain.

See also: AVATAR; GEORGE, ST.; JOSHUA; KORAN, THE; VISHNU; WATER OF LIFE

0176

**Allah**   In Islam, the proper name of God. The origin of the name Allah goes back before

Muhammad, who found that the Meccans worshiped a supreme deity whom they called Allah. Along with Allah, however, they also worshiped a host of lesser gods and "daughters of Allah." When Muhammad set down the first article of Islam (submission), "There is no God save Allah," he attacked belief in any other gods the Meccans worshiped besides Allah, who was the true God. The best summation of the Islamic concept of Allah is found in part of the opening sura of the Koran, called Al-fataih:

> In the Name of Allah, the Compassionate, the Merciful. Praise be to Allah, Lord of the worlds; The Compassionate, the Merciful! Thee only do we worship, and to Thee do we cry for help. Guide Thou us on the straight path; The path of those to whom thou hast been gracious.

The Al-fataih is recited several times in each of the five daily prayers, and on many other occasions, such as when concluding a bargain. The *Basmala*, "In the Name of Allah, the Compassionate, the Merciful," has become part of the rubric at the head of every sura except the ninth in the Koran. Allah is also addressed as Al-Hayn (the living), Al-Alim (the knowing), Al-Murid (the purposer), As-Sam (the hearer), Al-Basir (the seer), and Al-Mutakallim (the speaker).

See also: MUHAMMAD

0177

**Allallu**   In the Babylonian epic poem *Gilgamesh*, a fantastic bird destroyed by the goddess Ishtar. The goddess at one time loved the bird, but she destroyed him as she did all of her lovers. The bird then lamented his fate, saying, "O my pinions!"

See also: GILGAMESH

0178

**Allan-a-Dale** (Allin-a-Dale, Allen-a-Dale) (rock, noble)   In British legend, a minstrel in the Robin Hood ballads. Robin Hood aided Allan-a-Dale when the minstrel carried off his sweetheart before she could be forced to marry a rich old knight. Allan-a-Dale also appears in Walter Scott's novel *Ivanhoe*.

See also: ROBIN HOOD

0179

**Allen, Ethan**   1738–1789. In American history and folklore, hero of Vermont during the American Revolution who organized the Green Mountain Boys. Legend says that when he demanded from the British the surrender of Fort Ticonderoga he asked it "in the name of the Great Jehovah and the Continental Congress." In actuality, he is believed to have said, "Come out of there, you damned old rat!" Allen told his own story in his *Narrative of Ethan Allen's Captivity* and appears in Daniel Pierce Thompson's novel *The Greene Mountain Boys* and Van de Water's novel *Reluctant Rebel*.

0180

**Allison, Robert Clay**   1840–1887. In American history and folklore, a gunfighter who was kind when sober and a devil when drunk. Born in Tennessee, he left his father's farm to join the Confederate army. When the war was lost, Allison went West. One account describes him as over six feet tall, with blue eyes, a long mustache, and hair down to his shoulders. He had a melancholy look and was slightly crippled from having accidentally shot himself in the instep. His changing moods were described by a contemporary: "He was a whale of a fellow, and considerate of his companions; but throw a drink into him, and he was hell turned loose, rearin' for a chance to shoot—in self defense." Another account tells how he challenged a man to fight in an open grave; the winner was to bury the loser.

According to one report, he led a lynching mob that hanged a man named Charles Kennedy, an accused murderer. He cut Kennedy's head off and put it on a pole outside the saloon. He led yet another mob that hanged

Cruz Vega; then he tied a rope to Vega and dragged his body through the rocks and brush. Another tale tells how Bill Chunk met his death in 1873 when he tried to draw a gun from under a dinner table. The barrel of his revolver struck the edge of the table, and Allison fired at Chunk. Chunk's head fell on the table and into a plate. Clay coolly replaced his gun and went on with his meal, demanding that the other guests at the table do likewise. Allison died when he fell from a wagon and one of its rear wheels passed over his back.

0181

**All Saints' Day**   Christian feast celebrated on 1 November to commemorate all of the saints. Sometime in the early part of the seventh century, Pope Boniface IV obtained permission from the emperor Phocas to turn the Pantheon in Rome, an old pagan temple to all of the gods and unused since the fifth century, into a place of Christian worship. On 13 May the pope dedicated the pagan temple to St. Mary and All Martyrs. Pope Gregory III (731–741) dedicated a chapel to All Saints in St. Peter's in Rome on 1 November, thus changing the date of commemorating all saints. Some scholars say the date was changed to coincide with a pagan Germanic festival that honored all of the gods, though some Christian scholars (such as Francis X. Weiser in his *Handbook of Christian Feasts and Customs*) say the date was changed because the "many pilgrims who came to Rome for the Feast of the Pantheon could be fed more easily after the harvest than in the spring."

In the 15th century Pope Sixtus made All Saints a holy day of obligation for the entire Western, or Latin, church. The feast was retained in *The Book of Common Prayer* of the Church of England. All Hallows' Eve, or Halloween, is celebrated the night before All Saints' Day and is now a secular celebration.

See also: ALL SOULS' DAY

0182

**All Souls' Day**    Christian feast celebrated on 2 November to commemorate all of the dead. In the 10th century St. Odilo, Abbot of Cluny—who, according to Christian legend, had heard from a pilgrim to the Holy Land that there was an island where the groans of the souls in Purgatory could be heard asking for prayers to release them—issued a decree that all monasteries of the congregation of Cluny were to keep 2 November as a "day of all the departed ones." On 1 November, All Saints' Day, after vespers or evening prayer the bell was to be tolled and the office of the dead recited. On the next day three masses were to be said for the souls in Purgatory. By the 13th century the feast was established in the Latin, or Western, church.

The Christian feast of All Souls is an adaptation of the custom of setting aside part of the year to remember the dead, found in numerous cultures, from ancient Babylonia and China to the Romans. The Buddhist feast of the dead takes place on the anniversary of the death of Buddha, 15 April; the Romans celebrated their feast of the dead during the Parentalia, 13 to 21 February, the end of the Roman year. In some Roman Catholic countries food is left at grave sites for the dead, recalling old pagan rites. In the Philippines tomb niches and crosses are repainted, hedges trimmed, flowers planted, and all weeds removed from the graves. In Poland paper sheets with black borders, called, *Wypominki* (naming), with the names of the family dead written on them, are used in religious devotions during the month of November. In the Polish custom it is said that the souls of the departed appear on All Souls' Day as a great light from the parish church. When the light is seen, the parishioners know they are to pray for the dead. In Austria the souls of the dead are said to wander about through the forests, sighing and praying for their release from Purgatory. Children are told to pray aloud when they walk through forests and cemeteries so that the dead know they are praying for their release.

The mixture of Christian and ancient religious rites (mainly from the Druids) is found in Halloween, or as it was earlier called, All Hallows' Eve or All Saints' Eve. During this time it is believed that demons, witches, and evil spirits roam about the earth and must be appeased by offerings such as sweet cakes. This recalls the belief that the dead must be placated so as not to disturb the living. The demons today, however, have become the popular jack-o'-lanterns—pumpkins with candles or electric lights inside—and children wearing mass-produced costumes of witches and demons.

See also: ALL SAINTS' DAY; DRUIDS.

0183

**Almond**    A nut tree found in warm, temperate countries. In world mythology and folklore the almond is often a symbol of the womb. In Christian art the *mandorla* (Italian for almond) often surrounds figures of Christ, representing the womb of the Virgin enclosing her son. In Genesis (43:11) the almond is among the "best fruits in the land." When Aaron's rod blossomed, it bore almonds overnight. His staff, which in folklore became the magician's wand, plays an important part in the Exodus narrative. After the Exodus from Egypt, Aaron's rod was placed with the rods of the other tribes in the tabernacle; it then "budded, and brought forth buds, and bloomed blossoms, and yielded almonds" (Num. 17:8). This was a sign that Yahweh gave Aaron and his tribe of Levi the exclusive right to the Hebrew priesthood. In Chinese symbolism the almond signifies feminine beauty, fortitude in sorrow, and watchfulness. The tale given to the Grimms by Philip Otto Runge and generally translated in English as "The Juniper Tree" was originally called "Vom Machandelbom," which means the "Almond Tree."

See also: AARON; HATIM; JUNIPER; YAHWEH

0184

**Aloadae** (children of the threshing floor)    In Greek mythology, sons of Poseidon by

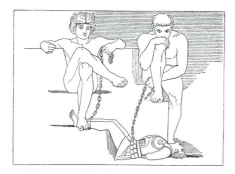

*Otus and Ephialtes holding Ares captive (John Flaxman)*

Iphimedia, the wife of Aloeus. Aloeus was the son of Canace and Poseidon. The Aloadae's names were Ephialtes and Otus, and they grew every year an ell in breadth and a fathom in length. In nine years time they were 36 feet high. Their strength was such that they chained up the god Ares and kept him in a brazen cask for 13 months, until their stepmother, Erioboea, told Hermes, who came and freed his brother. The Aloadae threatened to storm heaven by piling Mount Ossa on Olympus and Mount Pelion on Ossa. Homer's *Odyssey* (book 11) says they would have accomplished this feat if Apollo had not slain them with his arrows before their beards had grown, symbols of their strength. A later myth tells of Ephialtes' love for Hera, the wife of Zeus, and Otus's love for Artemis. Still another variation says they were slain by Artemis on the island of Naxos when she appeared as a hind, which they attempted to kill. Instead their spears killed one another by mistake. According to another myth they were bound with snakes to a pillar, back to back, while tormented by the screeching of an owl in the underworld. The two were worshiped as heroes on Naxos and in the Boeotian Ascra, where they were regarded as founders of the city. Both Homer's *Iliad* (book 5) and *Odyssey* (book 11) and Vergil's *Aeneid* (book 6) allude to them.

See also: AENEID, THE; ARES; ARTEMIS; CANACE; HERA; HERMES; *ILIAD, THE*; IPHIMEDIA; *ODYSSEY, THE*; POSEIDON; ZEUS

0185

**Alonzo de Aguilar, Don**   15th century. Spanish hero in the reconquest of Spain from the Moors and the subject of various ballads. One ballad, *The Death of Don Alonzo de Aguilar*, tells of his last mission. King Ferdinand of Aragon, husband of Isabella, desires to rid the Sierra of Alpuxarra, mountains not far from Granada, of Moors who refuse to accept the Christian faith. He chooses Don Alonzo to lead his forces. With a thousand men Alonzo reaches Nevada, but before he can reach the ravine, he and his men are detected by the Moors, who hurl rocks at them. Alonzo escapes into the field. The ballad continues:

> There, like a lion, stands at bay, in vain
>    besought to yield;
> A thousand foes around are seen, but none
>    draws near to fight;
> Afar, with bolt and javelin, they pierce the
>    steadfast knight (John Gibson Lockhart
>    translation).

The Moors then come down from their hiding place and take the body. Washington Irving's *The Conquest of Granada* includes "The Legend of the Death of Don Alonzo de Aguilar" at the end of the book.

See also: BALLAD

0186

**Alope** (vixen)   In Greek mythology, daughter of Cercyon of Eleusis and, by Poseidon, mother of Hippothoon. After Hippothoon's birth she exposed him in the woods to die. When Alope's father learned of this, he planned to kill her, but Poseidon saved her by changing her into a fountain. Hippothoon was saved by some shepherds and was placed by Theseus on his grandfather's throne.

See also: POSEIDON; THESEUS

**Alpha and Omega** (A Ω)    In the Bible, N.T., the first and last letters of the Greek alphabet, used in the Book of Revelation (22:13) as a symbol of God: "I am Alpha and Omega, the beginning and the end, the first and the last." Earlier in the same book (1:3) is the verse "I am Alpha and Omega, the beginning and the ending, saith the Lord," symbolizing the beginning of a new era.

The use of the first and last letters of an alphabet to signify totality was used by many cultures, including the Hebraic. The idea is expressed in a passage in Isaiah (44:6): "Thus saith the Lord the King of Israel, And his Redeemer the Lord of hosts; I am the first, and I am the last; And beside me there is no God."

The early Christians naturally applied the Greek letters to Christ in his role as God-Redeemer. The symbol appears on frescoes, monuments, lamps, etc., as early as the third century C.E. in Rome and was known throughout most of Europe by the early Middle Ages.

Often the Greek letters were combined with other symbolic devices. As a symbol of Christ, they were sometimes used with the cross. Other times they were combined with a wreath (Christian symbol of victory over death), a triangle (symbol of the Christian Trinity), or a circle (symbol of eternity). In some symbolism alpha resembles a compass and omega, a torch, with God both creator (the compass) and destroyer (fire).

See also: BIBLE (REVELATION)

0188

**Alphege, St.** (successor)    11th century. In Christian legend, archbishop of Canterbury. Feast, 19 April. He was made archbishop in 1006; six years later the Danes took the city and the cathedral of Canterbury, killing the people and burning the city. Alphege was kept in prison for seven months, then he was stoned to death because he refused to pay a large ransom for his life. Ten years after his death his body was found

"entire and incorrupt," according to medieval Christian legend.

0189

**Alphesiboea** (bringing many oxen, much-courted)    In Greek mythology, daughter of Phegeus and first wife of Alcmaeon as Arsinoe. Though Alcmaeon was unfaithful to her, she continued to love him and was angry when her brothers killed him. Her brothers shut her up in a box and brought her to Agapenor, king of Tegea, pretending that she had killed her husband. Eventually she died, but not before she had her brothers killed by the son of Alcmaeon.

See also: ALCMAEON

0190

**Als**    In Persian mythology, demonic beings, found also in later Persian-Islamic, Christian, and Armenian myths and legends. Als are half human, half animal, of both sexes, who live in watery and sandy places. One Christian Armenian legend tells of an encounter St. Peter and St. Paul had with an Al.

One day Sts. Peter and Paul were traveling and came to a roadside where a man was sitting in the sand. His hair was made of snakes, his eyebrows of brass, his eyes of glass, and his teeth of iron; his face was as white as snow, and he had a tusk like a wild boar.

"What are you, you ugly, unclean, beast?" the saints asked him.

"I am the wicked Al. I sit upon the childbearing mother, I scorch her ears and pull out her liver. I strangle both mother and child. Our food is the flesh of little children. We steal unborn infants of eight months and bring them to our demon king. The abyss, the corners of houses, and stables are our abode."

To prevent the Al from doing its evil work, sabers and other weapons are placed under a woman's pillow. After the child's birth the mother is kept awake so that the Als do not have the opportunity to catch her off guard.

See also: PAUL, ST.; PETER, ST.

0191

**Al-Safa and Al-Marwa**   Two mounds at Mecca that lie opposite each other. Muslims perform a rite called *sa'y* between the two mounds. The rite is in memory of Hagar (in Arabic, Hadjar), who, according to Islamic legend, ran seven times between al-Safa and al-Marwa to find water for her thirsty son Ishmael.

In another legend Isaf and Na'ila were guilty of indecent conduct in the Kaaba, which is located near al-Safa and al-Marwa. As a result of their sin they were turned into stone statues. Isaf was placed on al-Safa and Na'ila on al-Marwa. In time pagan Arabs began to worship the two as gods.

In another tradition the hills were once the home of night-shrieking demons. They were removed when Muhammad took Mecca from the pagans.

See also: ISHMAEL

0192

**Altis** (grove)   In Greek cult, a grove sacred to Zeus near Olympia in which the Olympic Games were celebrated. Statues of the champions were placed in the grove.

See also: ZEUS

0193

**Altjira** (him none made)   In Australian mythology, self- existent creator god of the Arunta (Aranda), conceived of as a large man with reddish skin, long hair, and the feet of an emu. His sons also have emu-feet, but his daughters have the feet of dogs. After creation Altjira grew bored with the world and its people and returned to the sky, where he displays little concern for the affairs of humankind.

0194

**Aluluei**   In Micronesian mythology, god of seafaring. He was killed by his jealous brothers but restored to life by his father, who set numerous eyes in his head to protect him from further harm. His eyes became the stars in heaven and are used by sailors to navigate.

0195

**Al-Uzza** (the strong, the powerful)   In Arabian mythology, goddess whose shrine was destroyed by order of Muhammad. Al-Uzza, along with Manat, or Manah, the goddess of fate and death, and al-Lat, or Allat, the sun, formed a trinity. Al-Uzza's shrine was located in the valley of Nakhla on the road from Taif to Mecca. It consisted of three *samura*, or acacia trees. There was also a cave where animals were sacrificed to her. The three goddesses, al-Uzza, Manat, and al-Lat, were held in such high regard by the Arabs that Allah once consented to recognize them as intercessors with him. He changed his mind, however, and ordered them wiped out (suras 53, 22).

The pagan Arabs also worshiped another trinity: Shamshu, the sun (a female divinity), and two male divinities, Athtar (the planet Venus) and Shahar (the moon).

See also: MUHAMMAD

0196

**Amadis of Gaul** (love-god)   In late medieval Spanish legend, hero who appears in an anonymous prose romance, *Amadis of Gaul*, first published in 1508 in four books. Numerous additional books by various authors were added later. Amadis, also called the Lion Knight, from the device on his shield, and Beltenbros (darkly beautiful), from his physical appearance, was the illegitimate son of Perion, king of Gaula (Wales) and Elizena, princess of Brittany. At his birth his mother, anxious to conceal the boy, placed him in an ark and launched him in a stream, which carried him to the Scottish coast. He was then found by the knight Gandales and called "child of the sea." A parchment roll, which Gandales found around the child's neck, declared the boy to be the son of a king and eventually helped to identify him. Amadis loved Oriana (Oriane), and in one episode in the legend the lovers came to Firm Island, once ruled by King Apolidon, whose fantastic palace contained the Arch of True Lovers and the Forbidden Chamber, both used to test Amadis's love for Oriana. Eventually, the two were married and had a son, Esplandian. Numerous operas have been written about Amadis of Gaul, among them Jean Baptiste Lully's *Amadis de Gaule*; Johann Christian Bach's *Amadis de Gaule*; Handel's *Amadigi di Gaula*, sometimes called *Oriana*; and Jules Massenet's *Amadis*. The English poet Robert Southey published an abridged English version of the first four books of *Amadis of Gaul* in 1803.

0197

**Amaethon** (great plowman)    In Celtic mythology, culture hero, a god of agriculture and labor in early Welsh narrative; son of Don; brother of Gwydion. He stole a dog, lapwing, and roebuck from Arawn, god of the dead, causing a war called the Battle of Cath Godeau, or Battle of the Trees, in which Gwydion transformed trees into fighting men. Amaethon and Gwydion, along with Llaw, defeated the underworld deities.

See also: GWYDION

0198

**Amalthea** (tender)    In Greek mythology, a goat nymph or goat who suckled the newborn Zeus. According to one account, Amalthea was the daughter of the Cretan king Melisseus, and she brought up the infant Zeus on the milk of a goat, while her sister Melissa (a bee) offered him honey. The horn of the goat was given to her by Zeus, with the promise that she would always find in it whatever she wished. From Amalthea the cornucopia passed to the river god Achelous, who was happy to exchange for it his own horn, which Heracles had broken off. The cornucopia is a common attribute of Dionysus, Plutus, and other deities associated with the earth. In a variant myth, Amalthea was later transformed into the star Capella. Amalthea was the patron of shepherds and frequently appears in 18th-century grottoes, such as the Queen's Dairy at Versailles.

She appears as a goat in an early work of the Italian sculptor Bernini and in two paintings by the French painter Poussin. Milton's *Paradise Regained* (book 2.355) refers to her horn, and Keats's *Endymion* (II.448) refers to her role as nurse to Zeus.

See also: ACHELOUS; DIONYSUS; HERACLES; NYMPHS; PLUTUS; ZEUS

0199

**Amangons**    In Arthurian legend, the king of Logres. In the wells and springs of Logres lived damsels who fed the wayfarers with meat and bread. One day, Amangons wronged a damsel, carrying off her golden cup. Later, subjects of the king followed his example; the damsels never again appeared, and the land became desolate.

See also: ARTHUR

0200

**Ama-no-hashidate** (heavenly stairs) (Ama-no-uki-hasi [floating bridge of heaven], Ame-no-iha-fune [heavenly rocking boat])    In Japanese mythology, bridge or stairway between heaven and earth. On it the primeval creator couple, Izanagi and Izanami, stood while forming the earth. One day the bridge collapsed into the sea, forming an elongated isthmus situated to the west of Kyoto in the province of Tamba.

See also: IZANAGI AND IZANAMI

0201

**Ama-no-Kawa.** (Ama-no-yase-kawa, Ame-no-yasu-no-kawa, Yasu)    In Japanese mythology, the river of heaven, identified with the Milky Way or the rainbow.

0202

**Ama-no-Minaka-Nushi**    In Japanese Shinto mythology, primeval god, mentioned in the *Kojiki* (records of ancient matters), who stood motionless in the center of the cosmos. In the *Nihongi* (chronicles of Japan), written later than the *Kojiki*, he is called Kuni-Toko-Tachi-No-

Mikoto. He is the ancestor of the primeval creator couple, Izanagi and Izanami.

See also: IZANAGI AND IZANAMI; *KOJIKI*; *NIHONGI*

0203
**Amant, Sir**   In Arthurian legend, a knight at the court of King Arthur, slain by King Mark of Cornwall. Amant is mentioned in Malory's *Morte d'Arthur*.

See also: ARTHUR

0204
**Amareswara** (lord of the immortals)   Title often applied to the Hindu gods Vishnu, Shiva, and Indra. The term is also used for the 12 great *lingas* (phalluses) worshiped as forms of the god Shiva.

See also: INDRA; LINGAM; SHIVA; VISHNU

0205
**Amario** (Amaryu)   In Japanese mythology, the rain dragon.

0206
**Amaterasu Omikami** (heaven-shining great goddess)   In Japanese Shinto mythology, sun goddess, born from the left eye of Izanagi, the great primeval creator god. She taught her people to plant rice and weave cloth.

One of the main myths contained in the *Kojiki* (records of ancient matters) tells of the conflict between Amaterasu and her brother Susano, the storm god. One day Susano asked his father, Izanagi, for permission to visit his sister Amaterasu. But as the text says, Susano

. . . so greatly mortified his august sister Amaterasu Omikami, that she hid herself in a cave, whereupon both heaven and earth became dark; and to entice her forth, the eight million spirits of the Plain of Heaven assembled trees before the cave, bedecked with jewels, lighted bonfires, and laughed aloud with such uproar an obscene dance

performed by a spirit-female named Uzume that the goddess in her cave, becoming curious, opened the door to peek out. They held a mirror before her, the first she had ever seen: she was drawn out, and the world again was light. (Based on Basil H. Chamberlain translation)

After the world was restored to light, Susano was exiled and fled to the earth, to Izumo (Japan). His descendants gradually took possession of the land that had given them hospitality. However, Amaterasu later regained possession of her domains. It was then that her grandson Ninigi no Mikoto came in person to rule the land and married the goddess of Mount Fuji. Ninigi was the great grandfather of Jimmu Tenno, the first historical emperor of Japan; thus, the royal house claimed Amaterasu as its first ancestor. The sakaki tree, identified as *Eura ochnacea* and *Cleyera japonica*, is sacred to the goddess. Combs are made from it for the deity. The tree grows around shrines of the goddess, and sprigs of it are used as offerings.

The goddess is worshiped at her great shrine at Ise. She is sometimes called Ohirume, Shimmei, or Tenshoko Daijin.

See also: IZANAGI AND IZANAMI; JIMMU TENNO; *KOJIKI*; SUSANO

0207
**Ama-tsu-kami and Kuni-tsu-kami** (Ama-tsu-Koyane)   In Japanese mythology, terms for "heavenly gods" and "earthly gods." However, the distinction between the Ama-tsu-kami, who inhabit the vast region called the Milky Way, and the Kuni-tsu-kami, who inhabit mountains, rivers, and trees of the earth, is not absolute: some of the heavenly gods descend to earth, and some of the earthly gods ascend to the heavens.

0208
**Amazons** (without breast)   In Greek mythology, tribe of female warriors who lived in Cappadocia in Asia Minor. They had only one

*An Amazon*

*Theseus capturing Hippolyte*

loins and bows and arrows in their hands, with which they killed seven or eight Spaniards." Amazons are mentioned or cited in Vergil's *Aeneid* (book 5), Apollodorus's *Bibliotheca* (Library, book 2), Herodotus's *Histories* (book 4), and Pausanias's *Description of Greece* (book 7).

See also: *AENEID, THE;* ANTIOPE; BELLEROPHON; HERACLES; PENTHESILEA; THESEUS

breast, one having been removed in youth so that they could more freely shoot their bows. No men were allowed in the tribe. Mating took place at certain seasons with men of another race, and only girl babies were kept. If boys were born, they were killed, maimed, or given to their fathers. The Amazons appear in myths relating to Bellerophon, Heracles, Perseus, and Theseus, all of whom fought against them. Theseus kidnapped the Amazon queen Hippolyte (Antiope). Another Amazon queen, Penthesilea, aided the Trojans and was killed by Achilles during the Trojan War. In Greek art the Amazons are portrayed as manly women with two breasts. Usually they are portrayed on horseback, sometimes in Scythian dress—a tight fur tunic with a cloak and a kind of Phrygian cap—though sometimes they are portrayed wearing a Dorian tunic tucked up, the right shoulder bare. The most famous statues of Amazons were by Phidias, Polyclitus, and Cresilas. The Greeks often cited the conquest of the Amazons as a triumph of civilization over barbarism. When the Spanish came to the New World, they reported that there was a race of Amazons in Brazil. One Spanish clergyman described them as "very tall, robust, fair, with long hair twisted over their heads, skins around their

0209
**Ambapali** Fifth century B.C.E. In Buddhist legend, a courtesan of the city of Vaishaili who offered her house to the Buddha for his use as a meeting place. Buddha said of her, "This woman moves in worldly circles and is a favorite of kings and princes; yet is her heart composed and quieted. Young in years, rich, surrounded by pleasures, she is thoughtful and steadfast. This, indeed, is rare in the world."

0210
**Ambrose, St.** (immortal) 339–397. In Christian legend, Doctor of the Church, patron saint of beekeepers, bakers of honey-bread, domestic animals, geese, and wax refiners. Feast, 4 April.

Born in Gaul and trained as a lawyer, Ambrose was elected bishop of Milan when he was 35 years old, although at the time he was not even baptized. When this was remedied, he took office and became noted for his strict discipline. He was a close friend of St. Augustine, whose conversion he was partly responsible for, with the help of Augustine's mother, Monica. In 384 he introduced the Ambrosian Chant from the Eastern Church, which was used until Pope Gregory the Great introduced the Gregorian Chant two centuries later.

As recorded in numerous sources, such as *The Golden Legend*, a series of saints' lives written in the 13th century by Jacobus de Voragine, the most famous episode in the life of St. Ambrose concerns his treatment of the Roman emperor Theodosius. The emperor had killed some 7,000 men, women, and children as punishment for a small uprising in Thessalonica, where some of his soldiers were injured. St. Ambrose refused to let the ruler enter his church and excommunicated him. After eight months Ambrose consented to relent on two conditions: first, that the emperor should publish an edict by which no capital punishment could be executed until 30 days after conviction of a crime, and second, that the emperor should perform public penance. Theodosius consented to the arrangement and did public penance in the bishop's church. The scene was sometimes painted to symbolize the authority of the church over secular powers, one of the key issues during the Middle Ages.

According to another legend, when Ambrose was an infant, a swarm of bees alighted on his mouth without harming him. This was taken as a sign that he would be noted for his eloquence. The same tale is told of Plato and numerous Christian saints. Another legend tells how a prefect, Macedonius, closed his doors to the pleas of a poor criminal. When he heard of it, St. Ambrose said to Macedonius, "Thou, even thou, shalt fly to the church for refuge, and shalt not enter." A short time afterward, Macedonius was pursued by some of his enemies and fled for sanctuary to the church. Even though the doors were wide open, he could not find the entrance but walked around as a blind man until he was slain.

In Christian art St. Ambrose is often portrayed as a bishop with miter and crosier. He sometimes holds a book or a pen with the inscription *In carne vivere preter carnem angelicam et non humanam* (to be nourished by food, but rather the food of angels, not of mortals).

See also: AUGUSTINE, ST.; *GOLDEN LEGEND, THE;* MONICA

0211
**Ambrosia** (immortal)    In Greek mythology, the honey-flavored food of the gods, as nectar was their drink. Doves daily brought ambrosia from the far west to Zeus and the other gods. Ambrosia was also the name given to anointing oil, which was believed to preserve the dead from decay. Homer's *Iliad* (books 1, 14, 16, 24), Vergil's *Aeneid* (book 1), and Ovid's *Metamorphoses* (book 2) all cite the magic food.

See also: *AENEID, THE; ILIAD, THE;* ZEUS

0212
**Amburbium** (around the city)    In Roman cult, the name for a solemn procession of the people, led by the pontifex and various orders of priests, three times around the boundaries of Rome. It was performed at times of national distress. A hog, a ram, and a bull were sacrificed, with special prayers. The rite was adopted by the Christian church as Rogation Days, which are set aside for the harvest and generally are observed on the three days before Ascension Day.

0213
**Amenhotep** (Amenophis)    In Egyptian history and legend, sage and minister of Amenhotep III, invoked as an intercessor by the people in times of trouble or need. He was known for his wisdom and for the beautiful temples he had built. Some of the architectural features he introduced remained standard for 1,500 years. In Egyptian art Amenhotep is usually portrayed as a scribe with a roll of papyrus on his knees.

0214
**Amesha Spentas** (Ameshospends, Amshaspands)    In Persian mythology, seven "immortal bounteous ones," or archangels, created by the

good god, Ahura Mazda, and manifestations of himself. They are

Vohu Manah—the firstborn of Ahura Mazda, who sits at his right hand. He protects animals and appeared to the prophet Zarathustra. Vohu Manah keeps a record of men's thoughts, words, and deeds and acts as a recording angel. Vohu Manah is also known as Bahman.

Asha—truth, the most beautiful of Ahura Mazda's creations. She represents divine law and moral order. Asha is also known as Asha-Vahista or Ardabhisht. The faithful in Zoroastrian belief are called Ashavans, followers of the truth of Ahura Mazda.

Kshathra Vairya—a personification of god's might, majesty, dominion, and power. He helps the poor and weak overcome all evil, protects metals, and is the enemy of the demon Savar, who is responsible for misgovernment. Kshathra Vairya is also known as Shahrevar.

Armaiti—devotion, the daughter of Ahura Mazda who sits at his left hand, presiding over the earth and giving pasture to cattle. She is the personification of faithful obedience, harmony, and religious worship.

Haurvatat—integrity, a personification of salvation, the spirit of health, and protector of water and vegetation. Haurvatat is also known as Khurdad.

Ameretat—immortality or deathlessness. Ameretat, like Haurvatat, is associated with water and vegetation.

Sraosha—obedience, the guardian of the world, who feeds the poor and will later help judge the world.

The Amesha Spentas are the cause of considerable debate among scholars in Persian mythology. Some scholars believe them to be based on the ancient gods of the Indo-Iranian hierarchy, some of which are also found in Hindu mythology. Others see the seven as manifestations of the one god, Ahura Mazda, similar to the archangels in Christian mythology. Some scholars, in fact, believe the concept of angels in Jewish-Christian mythology is derived in part from the Amesha Spentas.

See also: AHURA MAZDA; ZARATHUSTRA

0215

**Amfortas**  In Arthurian legend, the most famous fisher king, keeper of the Holy Grail. In early medieval French works his title is rich fisher, and eventually it became fisher king. In one legend he meets Perceval while he is fishing and invites him to his castle. Perceval is afterward informed that because Amfortas is wounded he is unable to mount his horse; therefore, his only solace is fishing. Amfortas is also called the Maimed King, referring to his condition. He appears in T. S. Eliot's poem *The Waste Land* as well as in Wagner's last stage work, *Parsifal*. In Wagner's opera Amfortas's wound is caused when the king had been enticed into the garden of Klingsor, the evil magician. Klingsor had determined to secure the Holy Grail, the cup used by Jesus at the Last Supper, as well as the spear that had pierced Jesus' side. Wrestling the spear from Amfortas, Klingsor wounded the king in the process. The wound then could only be healed by a guileless fool, who in Wagner's music drama is Parsifal.

See also: HOLY GRAIL; LONGINUS, ST. PERCEVAL

0216

**Amitabha** (Buddha of Infinite Light)  In Buddhism, one of the five Dhyani-Buddhas issuing from the Adi-Buddha, the primordial Buddha. In Pure Land Buddhism he is the Supreme Buddha, and Vairocana is not mentioned. In China and Japan he is also known as Amitayus. In Tibet, Amitayus is a subsidiary emanation of Amitabha.

See also: ADI-BUDDHA; AVALOKITESHVARA; DHYANI-BUDDHAS; VAIROCANA

0217

**Amnon of Mainz**  Tenth century. In Jewish legend, a martyr who refused to be converted to Christianity by force under the archbishop of

*Amitabha*

Mainz. When Amnon refused, his limbs were cut off and he was taken to the synagogue reciting a fragment of a prayer. After he died he appeared in a dream to another Jew and taught him the complete prayer.

**Amoghasiddhi**   In Mahayana Buddhism, one of the five Dhyani-Buddhas. He is the Buddha of Infallible Magic, whose symbol is the double-thunderbolt and whose mount is a dwarf.
   See also: DHYANI-BUDDHAS; MAHAYANA

0218

**Amor** (love)   In Roman mythology, a name given to Cupid, the god of love, son of Venus and Mars; called Eros in Greek mythology.
   See also: EROS; MARS; VENUS

0219

**Amphiaraus** (Amphiorax) (doubly cursed)   In Greek mythology, a hero, son of Oicleus and Hypermnestra; married Eriphyle; father of Alcmeon, Amphilocus, Demonassa, and Eurydice; great-grandson of the seer Melampus. Homer says Amphiaraus was a favorite of Zeus and Apollo and was both a hero and a seer, taking part in the Calydonian boar hunt, the voyage of the Argonauts, and the expedition of the Seven against Thebes. Amphiaraus fought with Adrastus, but the quarrel was settled when he married Adrastus's sister Eriphyle. He agreed that any future difference between Adrastus and himself would be settled by Eriphyle. But Eriphyle, bribed by Polynices with the fatal necklace of Polynices' ancestress Harmonia, insisted that her husband, Amphiaraus, join in the war against Thebes. Amphiaraus knew that he would die, and he told his youthful sons Alcmeon and Amphilocus to avenge his coming death. He warned the other chiefs of the coming disaster but was forced into a final battle with Tydeus. In the fight, just as Amphiaraus was about to die, Zeus opened the earth with his thunderbolt and swallowed up Amphiaraus and Baton, his charioteer.

0220

   Amphiaraus was worshiped at Oropus on the frontier of Attica and Boeotis, where he had a temple and an oracle for the interpretation of dreams. Games were also celebrated in his honor.
   See also: ADRASTUS; ALCMAEON; AMPHILOCHUS; ARGONAUTS; CALYDONIAN BOAR HUNT; EURYDICE; HARMONIA; ZEUS

**Amphilochus** (double ambush)   In Greek mythology, son of the Argive seer Amphiaraus and Eriphyle; Alcmaeon's brother. Amphilochus also was a seer and according to some accounts took part in the war of the Epigoni, or Seven, against Thebes, and the murder of his mother. Amphilochus was believed to have founded the Amphilochian Argos near Neckhori in Acarnania. Later myths say he took part in the Trojan

0221

War. After the fall of Troy he went with Mopsus and founded the oracle at Mallus. However, the two fought and killed one another for the possession of the shrine. After the funeral pyre had consumed their bodies, their spirits, or ghosts, became close friends. As a result, an oracle was established in their honor. The supplicants would write their questions on wax tablets, and the spirits would answer them in a dream.

See also: ALCMAEON; AMPHIARAUS

*Amphion and Zethus*

0222

**Amphion and Zethus**   In Greek mythology, the Boeotian Dioscuri, twin sons of Antiope by Zeus. A variant account says Zethus was the son of Epopeus. The two infants were exposed to die on Mount Cithaeron and were rescued and reared by a shepherd. When they grew up, they found their mother, who had fled from imprisonment at Thebes, where she had been mistreated by Dirce, the wife of Lycus, who governed Thebes as guardian to Laius. They avenged their mother by tying Dirce to the horns of a bull that dragged her to her death. They then threw Dirce's corpse into a spring near Thebes, which was later renamed after her. They killed Lycus and assumed his throne, or according to a variant account, it was given to them by Lycus when the god Hermes told him to abdicate. They fortified Thebes with walls and towers. Zethus brought up the stones, while Amphion, a harper, fit them together by the music of his lyre. Zethus married Thebe, the daughter of Asopus or, according to a variant account, Aëdon, daughter of Pandareos. Amphion married Niobe. After the destruction of his family by Apollo and Artemis as punishment for a boast by Niobe, Amphion killed himself. In a variant myth, Amphion was killed by Apollo for attacking Apollo's priests in revenge for the god's murder of his children. Both brothers were said to be buried in one grave.

See also: ANTIOPE; APOLLO; DIOSCURI; LAIUS; NIOBE; ZEUS

0223

**Amphisbaena** (both ways, to go)   Fantastic two-headed poisonous serpent with legs. It could stick one of its heads into the mouth of the other, forming a loop, which enabled it to roll down a road. Aeschylus' play *Agamemnon* compares Clytemnestra, the wife and murderess of Agamemnon, to the animal. During the Christian Middle Ages the bestiaries portrayed the animal as a symbol of the devil. In Milton's *Paradise Lost* (book 10) Satan's followers are turned into scorpions, asps, and "Amphisbaena dire."

0224

**Amphitrite** (the third one who encircles, i.e., the sea)   In Greek mythology, a sea goddess, daughter of Nereus and Doris (or Oceanus and Tethys); wife of Poseidon; mother of Albion, Benthesicyme, Charybdis, Rhode, and Triton. Poseidon saw Amphitrite dancing with the Nereids on the island of Naxos and carried her off. According to a variant account, she fled from Poseidon to Atlas, but Poseidon's dolphin saw her and brought her to the god. Homer does not call her Poseidon's wife but a sea goddess who beats the billows against the rocks. Amphitrite had no separate worship or cult. She was often portrayed with a net confining her hair, with crabs' claws on the crown of her head, being carried by Tritons or by dolphins and other marine animals, or drawn by them in a chariot of shells. The Romans identified her with Salacia, their goddess of the salt waves. Amphitrite appears in Ovid's *Metamorphoses* (book 1) and Keats's *Endymion* (II.108) She appears in Poussin's painting *The Triumph of Neptune and Amphitrite.*

See also: ATLAS; DOLPHIN; DORIS; NERIDS; OVID; POSEIDON; SALACIA; TRITON

0225
**Amphitryon** (harassing on either side)   In Greek mythology, king of Tiryns, son of Alcaeus and Astydameia, Hipponome, or Laonome; first husband of Alcmena; father of Iphicles; grandson of Perseus. His father's brother, Electryon, king of Mycenae, went to war against Pterelaus, king of the Taphians and Teleboans, because their sons had carried off his cattle and slain Electryon's eight sons except Licymnius. Electryon left Amphitryon in charge of his kingdom and gave him his daughter Alcmena to be his wife. On Electryon's return Amphitryon killed him in a quarrel (or by accident). Amphitryon fled with his future wife and her brother Licymnius to Creon, king of Thebes. Creon was a brother of Amphitryon's mother. Creon purged Amphitryon of his blood guilt for slaying Electryon and offered him aid against Pterelaus if Amphitryon first would render harmless the Taumessian fox. Alcmena would not wed Amphitryon unless her brothers' deaths were avenged. Having rendered the fox harmless with the help of Cephalus, Amphitryon marched against the Taphians, accompanied by Creon, Cephalus, and other heroes and conquered their country. While Amphitryon was away at war, Zeus assumed his likeness for the purpose of seducing Alcmena. Later the same night, Amphitryon himself slept with Alcmena. Two children were conceived that night, Hera-

cles and Iphicles. Amphitryon was told by a seer what Zeus had done, and he accepted both children as his sons. According to a variant myth, he put two harmless snakes in their crib to see which son was his and which belonged to Zeus. Heracles seized both snakes and killed them. Amphitryon knew then that Iphicles was his son and Heracles belonged to the god. In a variant account, it was Hera, the wife of Zeus, who placed the snakes in the crib, and they were poisonous and meant to kill Heracles. Amphitryon was killed in a war with Erginus, the Minyan king of Orchomenus.

The seduction of Alcmena by Zeus has had special appeal to playwrights, such as the Roman Plautus, the Frenchman Molière, and the Englishman John Dryden, with music of Henry Purcell. Jean Giraudoux wrote *Amphitryon 38*, saying it was the 38th version of the story.

See also: ALCMENA; FOX; HERA; HERACLES; IPHICLES; PERSEUS; ZEUS

0226
**Amrita** (immortal)   Water of life in Hindu mythology, often identified with Soma juice, a sacrificial libation offered to the gods, though drunk by the officiating priests. The Soma juice was derived from a plant. The Amrita was produced at the churning of the ocean, when the gods and demons, at odds with one another, brought it forth. In some texts Amrita is called Nir-jara and Piyusha.

0227
**Amun** (Amen, Aman, Ammon, Amon, Hammon) (the invisible one)   In Egyptian mythology, a god whose presence could be sensed in temples when pennants attached to the flagstaves in front of the pylons fluttered. Amun and his wife Amunet were part of a group of eight primeval gods who were known as the Ogdoad of Hermopolis. Sometimes Amun and the sun god Ra were combined to form the composite god Amun-Ra. At first Amun was merely a god of local importance. However, after the princes of

Thebes gained sovereignty over Egypt, making their city the new capital of the country, Amun became a prominent god in Upper Egypt and was looked upon as "King of the Gods." At that time Amun's sanctuary at Karnak was a comparatively small building consisting of a shrine surrounded by a few small chambers and a forecourt with a colonnade on two sides. When the Theban princes became kings of Egypt, their priests declared their god Amun not only another form of the great Amun creator sun god who was worshiped under such names as Ra and Khepera, but they gave him all the attributes that were ascribed to the sun gods and proclaimed him the greatest of them all. When Amun was coupled with Ra, forming the composite god Amun-Ra in the Eighteenth Dynasty, he became the mysterious creative power that was the Amun-Ra source of all life in heaven, earth, and the underworld. Eventually the priests of Amun claimed that there was no other god like Amun, who was the "one one" and had "no second."

In Egyptian art Amun-Ra is usually portrayed as a bearded man with a headdress of double plumes, various sections of which are colored alternately red and green or red and blue. Around his neck he wears a broad collar or necklace, and his close-fitting kilt or tunic is supported by elaborately worked shoulder straps. His arms and wrists are decked with armlets and bracelets. In his right hand is the ankh, symbol of life, and in his left, the scepter. The tail of a lion or bull hangs from his tunic. Sometimes Amun-Ra is given a hawk's head surmounted by the solar disk encircled by a serpent. When Amun appears with his wife, Amunet, he is often portrayed as a frog-headed man and she as a uraeus-headed woman. When Amun is shown with the uraeus, Amunet is depicted with the head of a cat.

See also: ANKH; KHEPERA; KHONSU; MUT; RA; URAEUS

0228

**Amycus** (without bellowing)  In Greek mythology, a giant son of Poseidon and Melië, a nymph. Amycus would force everyone who landed on the Bithynian coast to box with him. When the Argonauts wished to draw water from a spring in his country, he forbade them. He was killed in a match with Polydeuces. Ovid's *Metamorphoses* (book 12) and Apollonius Rhodius's *Argonautica* (book 2) tell the tale.

See also: ARGONAUTS; OVID; POSEIDON

0229

**Anael** (Haniel, Hamiel, Onoel)  In Jewish and Christian folklore, angel. In Henry Wadsworth Longfellow's dramatic poem *The Golden Legend* (not to be confused with the 13th century book of saints' lives) Anael is one of the seven angels that bear the star of Bethlehem. In the Old Testament Apocrypha Book of Tobit (1:22) Anael is the name of Tobit's brother. His son Ahikar served as Sennacherib's cupbearer, accountant, and chief administrator. Ahikar appears in many Oriental tales as an ancient wise man.

See also: ANGEL

0230

**Anahita** (Anaitis, Aredvi Sura Anahita)  In Persian mythology, water and fertility goddess who cleaned the seed of the male, blessed the womb of the female, and purified the milk in a mother's breast. According to the Greek historian Strabo, writing in the early part of the first century C.E., the daughters of noble families had to serve in the temple of the goddess at Anatolia as prostitutes before their marriage. The cult of Anahita was found in Armenia under the name of Anahit, the "great queen," the "one born of gold," "the golden mother," who, though a fertility goddess, was not connected with water, as in Persia. In Greece, Anahita often was equated with the goddesses Artemis and Aphrodite.

In Persian art, Anahita is portrayed as a beautiful, strong woman, wearing a golden crown with eight rays and surrounded by a hundred stars. She also wears a golden necklace and a dress.

See also: APHRODITE; ARTEMIS

0231

**Anakims** (Rephaim) (long-necked)   In the Bible, O.T., race of pre-Israelites in the Holy Land. The term was originally an appellative, "people of the neck" or "necklace."

In the Old Testament the Anakims are described as a tall people, whose gigantic size terrified the Hebrews (Num. 13:28). In Jewish folklore they are considered the offspring of fallen angels and mortal women, alluding to a belief in Genesis (6:2): "That the sons of God [angels] saw the daughters of men that they were fair; and they took them wives of all which they chose." The mystical Zohar says the "Hebrews were like grasshoppers in comparison with the Anakims." Erich Von Däniken's *Chariots of the Gods* argues that the Genesis text illustrates that intelligent space travelers visited earth during man's early years on the planet, becoming prototypes of "gods" in many ancient mythologies.

See also: ZOHAR

0232

**Ananda** (bliss)   Fifth century B.C.E. In Buddhist legend, one of the foremost disciples of the Buddha; noted for his faith and devotion and for his ability to remember all of the sutras, or spoken words, of the Buddha. According to some accounts he compiled the Buddhist writings. In Buddhist art Ananda is portrayed as a monk. In Chinese Buddhist artworks he is often shown with Kasyapa, another disciple of the Buddha.

See also: BUDDHA, THE; KASYAPA; SUTRA

0233

**Anansi**   In African mythology, trickster who was originally credited with the creation of the world and who can transform himself into a spider. Anansi's exploits are presented as puzzles, rituals, and dilemmas common to human interaction. He is known by such names as Gizo, Kwaku Ananse, Nansi, and Miss Nancy. Anansi appears in West African folktales and is also known in the West Indies. One of the most famous tales connected with Anansi was the source for the black American folktale of Br'er Rabbit and the Tar Baby. In Sierra Leone he has a similar encounter with a Wax Girl, and elsewhere in Africa he gets stuck to a gum man. Anansi's son is called Ntikuma or Tacuma.

See also: BR'ER FOX; BR'ER RABBIT; COYOTE; TRICKSTER; UNCLE REMUS

0234

**Anatapindaka** (one who gives alms to the unprotected)   Fifth century B.C.E. In Buddhist legend, a wealthy layman friend of the Buddha. When Anatapindaka asked the Buddha if he should give up his wealth, the Buddha replied: "I say unto thee, remain in thy station of life and apply thyself with diligence to thy enterprises. It is not life and wealth and power that enslave men but the cleaving to life and wealth and power."

0235

**Anath** (Anat, Anata, Hanata)   In Near Eastern mythology (Canaanite), war goddess, queen of heaven, mistress of the gods. In one myth Anath obtained the help of the great god Baal to conquer the mountains of Lebanon and build a temple in his and her honor. She did this by making a feast and destroying all of Baal's enemies when they attended. Part of her cult consisted in sacrifices of young men. One myth reveals the goddess's demonic nature. Aqhat was the son of King Danel (or Daniel) and had a magnificent bow that the goddess wished to possess. She tried every ploy in an unsuccessful effort to trick Aqhat into giving her the bow and finally had him killed. At his death, however, the earth became sterile. Eventually, he was restored to life (though this part is missing from the myth), but the bow and arrows were lost or broken. Anath was portrayed with a helmet, shield, and spear in her right hand, a battle ax or club in her left. The lion was her sacred animal.

See also: AQHAT; BAAL; DANIEL

0236

**Anchises** (living close by)    In Greek and Roman mythology, father of Aeneas; king of the Dardania; loved by Aphrodite; son of Capys and Themiste. Aphrodite loved him for his beauty and bore him Aeneas. When Anchises boasted of her favor, he was either paralyzed, killed, or struck blind by the lightning of Zeus; accounts differ. Vergil's *Aeneid* (book 2) portrays Anchises as being borne out of the burning city of Troy on Aeneas's shoulders and sharing in his wanderings over the sea until they reached Drepanum in Sicily, where Anchises died at age 80 and was buried on Mount Eryx. Aeneas carrying his father is the subject of an early work of the Italian sculptor Bernini, as well as the subject of a painting by Raphael.

See also: AENEAS; APHRODITE; ZEUS

0237

**Ancient of Days**    In the Bible, O.T., title applied to Yahweh, the Hebrew god, in the Book of Daniel (7:9) in the King James Version of the Bible.

Daniel describes a vision: the "Ancient of days did sit, whose garment was white as snow, and the hair on his head like the pure wool; his throne was like the fiery flame, and his wheels as burning fire" (Dan. 7:9). William Blake, the English poet, used the term *Ancient of Days* for Urizen, his poetical creation who filled the role of Yahweh in his personal mythology. There is a well-known watercolor by the poet depicting the figure. A popular hymn begins with:

Ancient of Days, who sittest throned in glory;
    To thee all knees are bent.

Other translations of Ancient of Days are "a primeval Being" (Moffatt), "a Venerable One" (American Translation), "One . . . crowned with age" (Knox).

Some medieval Jewish commentators found the application of the term to God as too anthropomorphic and explained the title as referring to the angel of Yahweh. Other commentators see the concept going back to the figure of the Persian good god Ahura-Mazda. The popular Christian image of God the Father as an old man wearing white is derived from Daniel's image of the Ancient of Days.

See also: AHURA-MAZDA; YAHWEH

0238

**Ancile**    In ancient Roman ritual, a small, oval, sacred shield, curved inward on either side, believed to have fallen from heaven during the reign of Numa. There was a prophecy that the stability of Rome depended on the ancile; Numa had 11 others made exactly like it so that the real one could not be stolen. The set was sacred to the god Mars and was entrusted to the Salii, Roman priests who had to carry them through the city of Rome once a year.

See also: MARS

0239

**Andersen, Hans Christian**    1805–1875. Danish author of literary folktales, often based on European folk sources; best remembered for his *Eventyr*. Andersen was noted for his sensitive portrayal of people. Even though he is best known for his tales, he was also a playwright, a novelist and a writer of travel books. In his autobiography, *The Fairy Tale of My Life*, he wrote: "I had experienced what it was to be poor and lonely, and to move in luxurious surroundings; I had experienced being scorned and honored." In 1872, after 37 years of writing, his collected works were published in six volumes called *Fairy Tales and Stories*. Some of the many operas based on his fairy tales are Alfred Bruneau's *Le Jardin du paradis*, August Enna's *The Princess and the Pea*, Niels-Erich Fougstedt's opera for radio *The Tinderbox*, Ebke Hamerik's *The Traveling Companion*, Douglas Moore's *The Emperor's New Clothes*, and Stravinsky's *The Em-*

*peror's Nightingale*. *The Red Shoes* was made into a British film of the same title in 1948. Danny Kaye played the role of Hans Christian Andersen in a movie by that name in 1952.

0240

**Andhaka** (blind)   In Hindu mythology, a demon killed by the god Shiva. Andhaka had 1,000 arms and heads and 2,000 eyes and feet. Despite all of this physical equipment, or because of it, Andhaka walked as if he were a blind man (symbolic of spiritual blindness). When he tried to steal the Parijata Tree, which perfumed the whole world with its blossoms, he was killed by Shiva. From this feat Shiva earned the title *Andhaka-ripu* (foe of Andhaka).

See also: SHIVA

0241

**Andrew, St.** (manly)   First century. In the Bible, N.T., one of the Twelve Apostles of Jesus; patron saint of Russia and Scotland; protector of fishermen, fishmongers, and sailors. Invoked against gout and stiff neck. Feast, 30 November.

In the New Testament Andrew was the brother of St. Peter. He was one of the first two disciples of Jesus and is considered in Christian tradition to be the first missionary because he brought his brother Peter to meet Jesus. In Mark's Gospel (1:16) both Andrew and Peter immediately "forsook their nets" and followed Jesus when he called them to give up their trade as fishermen. We know nothing further of Andrew after the Resurrection of Jesus. An *Acts of St. Andrew*, which no longer survives complete, was written in the early part of the third century. It depicts St. Andrew as imprisoned at Patras and describes his death by crucifixion, though the type of cross is not mentioned, and scholars have debated as to its form. The one that appears most frequently in Christian art is the X-shaped cross, called the *crux decussata*. The cross of St. Andrew appears on the British Union Jack, along with the crosses of St. George and St. Patrick, repre-senting, respectively, Scotland, England, and Ireland.

According to legend, Achaius, king of the Scots, and Hungus, king of the Pics, saw St. Andrew's cross in the sky before their battle with Athelstane, which they won. They therefore adopted the cross of the saint as the national emblem.

*Andreas*, a narrative poem in Old English, formerly attributed to the poet Cynewulf, is based on an early Greek work *Acts of Andrew and Matthias*. The poem tells of St. Andrew's mission to the Mermedonians, Ethiopian savages who had imprisoned Matthias.

According to *The Golden Legend*, a series of saints' lives written in the 13th century in which numerous earlier sources were combined, Andrew made missionary journeys to Scythian Russia, Asia Minor, and Greece, preaching the gospel. At Nicaea he saved the inhabitants from seven demons that plagued them in the shape of dogs. Later, on another journey, a dead boy was brought to the saint. Andrew asked what had happened and was told "seven dogs came and strangled him." Andrew said these were the seven he had driven out in Nicaea.

"What wilt thou give to me if I raise him?" he said to the father.

"I have nothing so dear as him; I shall give him to thee," the father replied.

Andrew then raised the boy to life, and he became a disciple of the saint.

Other episodes tell how St. Andrew, dressed as a pilgrim, saved a bishop from yielding to the charms of a courtesan, who in actuality was the devil. Another episode tells how he cured Maximilla, wife of the Roman governor Egeas. When she became a Christian, Maximilla discontinued sexual relations with her husband. This was too much for the man to bear, and St. Andrew was imprisoned and finally crucified as a result.

Luther, in his *Table Talk*, tells of the custom of young girls stripping themselves naked and reciting prayers to St. Andrew on the eve of his feast day, to see "what manner of man it is that shall lead" them to the altar.

In Christian art St. Andrew is usually portrayed as an old man with a white beard, holding his cross or on his knees gazing at it. Perhaps the greatest tribute to the saint is Bernini's magnificent church of Sant' Andrea al Quirinale in Rome (1658–1670). It took the artist 12 years to complete the oval building. Behind the altar is a painting of St. Andrew's martyrdom on the cross. Above the altar is a statue of the saint gesturing toward heaven, which is symbolized by the skylighted opening in the gold dome.

See also: CROSS; GEORGE, ST.; *GOLDEN LEGEND, THE*; JESUS CHRIST; PATRICK, ST.; PETER, ST.

0242

**Androcles and the Lion**   Medieval European legend of a runaway slave who was saved by a lion. The story may be a fable that has grown into a Christian satire of martyrdom and fanaticism. Androcles fled from his evil master and hid in a cave, where he encountered a lion that had a thorn in its paw. Androcles removed it. Later he was recaptured and thrown to the lions in the arena. The lion he had helped was among them and protected Androcles from the other beasts. When the crowd saw this, they demanded Androcles' freedom. The legend is told in *Noctes Atticae* (Attic nights) by Aulus Gellius and inspired George Bernard Shaw's play *Androcles and the Lion* (1951). Shaw's play caricatures the hypersensitive male with these lines:

Did um get an awful thorn into um's tootsums wootsums? Has it made um too sick to eat a nice little Christian man for um's breakfast? Oh, a nice little Christian man will get um's thorn out for um; and then um shall eat the nice Christian man and the nice Christian man's nice big tender wifey pifey.

0243

**Androgeos** (man of the earth)   In Greek mythology, son of Pasiphae and Minos, king of Crete. He visited Athens at the first celebration of the Panathenaea and won victories over all of the champions. Out of jealousy, King Aegeus sent him to fight the bull of Marathon, which killed him. According to a variant account, Androgeos was killed in an ambush. Minos avenged his son's death by making the Athenians send seven young men and seven young girls every nine years as victims to his Minotaur. Funeral games were held in the Ceramicus at Athens in honor of Androgeus, who was then named Eurygyes. The cult is mentioned in Vergil's *Aeneid* (book 6), Apollodorus's *Bibliotheca* (3.15.7), and Pausanias's *Description of Greece* (1.27.9–10).

See also: AEGEUS; *AENEID, THE*; APOLLODORUS; MINOS; MINOTAUR; PANATHENAEA; PASIPHAE

*Andromache fainting after her son is hurled from the wall (John Flaxman)*

0244

**Andromache** (battle of men)   In Greek mythology, wife of Hector and daughter of King Eetion of Cilician Thebes. In Homer's *Iliad* she is considered one of the most moving characters, especially in her parting scene from Hector and when she mourns his death. In later, non-Homeric myth Achilles kills Andromache's father and seven brothers. When Troy is taken, her one son, Astyanax (or Scamander), is hurled from the walls to his death. As part of the spoils after the Trojan War, Andromache was given as the prize to Greek hero Neoptolemus, who first took her to Epirus, then surrendered her to Hector's brother Helenus. After Helenus's death Andromache returned to Asia with Pergamus, her son by Neoptolemus, and there she died. In the myth as told by Euripides in his play *Andromache* and by Vergil in *The Aeneid* (book 3), Hermione, the wife of Neoptolemus, hated Andromache because she knew her husband cared for the woman. The theme of Racine's play *Andromaque* is the jealousy of Hermione. The neoclassical French painter David painted *Andromache Mourning Hector*. There are more than 20 operas based on Andromache's tale, among them one by Martin y Soler (1754–1806) and one by Paisiello (1741–1816), both called *Andromaca*.

See also: *AENEID, THE;* ASTYANAX; HECTOR; *ILIAD, THE*

**0245**

**Andromeda** (ruler of men)   In Greek mythology, heroine saved by Perseus; daughter of the Ethiopian king Cepheus, a son of Belus by Cassiopeia; wife of Perseus; mother of Alcaeus, Electryon, Heleus, Nestor, Perses, Sthemelus, and Gorgophone. Cassiopeia had boasted of being more beautiful than any of the Nereids, and Poseidon, to punish her arrogance, sent a flood and a sea monster. An oracle promised an end to the plague that resulted only if Andromeda were to be exposed to the monster, so Cepheus chained his daughter to a rock in the sea. Andromeda was saved by the hero Perseus and promised to him in marriage. At the wedding a violent quarrel arose between the king's brother Phineus (who previously had been betrothed to Andromeda) and Perseus. The hero turned his rival into stone by showing him the Gorgon's head. Andromeda followed Perseus to Argos and became the ancestress of the Perseidae. Athena set Andromeda among the stars at her death. Milton makes reference to this in *Paradise Lost* (book 3.559). There are numerous paintings of the rescue scene, among the most famous being *Perseus and Andromeda* by Peter Paul Rubens. Other works are by Titian, Piero di Cosimo, and Ingres, as well as an earlier fresco at Pompeii. There are some 20 operas about Andromeda,

one by the brother of Franz Joseph Haydn, J. M. Haydn (1737–1806) called *Andromeda e Perseo*.

See also: ATHENA; CASSIOPEIA; GORGON; NEREIDS; NESTOR; PERSEUS

**0246**

**Andvaranaut** (Andvari's ring)   In Norse mythology, a magic ring belonging to the dwarf Andvari, stolen by the fire-trickster god, Loki. The ring was given to Hreidmar, king of the dwarfs, in part restitution for the murder by Loki of Hreidmar's son Otter. Andvari, however, cursed the ring so that it would destroy all who came in contact with it. In Germanic mythology and in Richard Wagner's works, the ring belongs to Alberich, another name for Andvari. Alberich appears in Wagner's music dramas *Der Ring des Nibelungen*, which have to do with the magic ring and the tragedy it brings on all who possess it. He also is portrayed by Arthur Rackham in his illustrations for Wagner's Ring Cycle.

See also: ANDVARI; LOKI; *RING DES NIBELUNGEN, DER*

**0247**

**Andvari**   In Norse mythology, a dwarf who is robbed of his wealth by Loki, the fire-trickster god. He is called Alberich (elf rule) by Wagner in *Der Ring des Nibelungen*. Once the gods Odin, Hoenir, and Loki came down to earth in human guise to test the hearts of various people. They came to the land where Hreidmar, the king of the dwarfs (or elves), lived. The gods had not gone far when Loki saw an otter basking in the sun. Up to his evil tricks, Loki killed the otter, which happened to be Hreidmar's son Otter. He flung the lifeless body over his shoulder, thinking it would make a good meal.

Following his companions, Loki came at last to Hreidmar's house with the dead otter, which he flung on the floor. When Hreidmar saw his dead son, he flew into a rage. Before the gods could act, they were bound and told they could not be freed unless they paid for Otter's death with gold enough to cover his skin, inside and out. The otter skin had the magical property of stretching itself to any size, so no ordinary treasure would suffice. Loki was appointed to find enough gold. He ran to a waterfall where the dwarf Andvari lived.

Loki did not find Andvari but instead saw a salmon in the water, which he knew to be Andvari in disguise. Loki caught the salmon in a net and said he would not free him unless he gave Loki his treasures, including the Helmet of Dread and his hoard of gold. Only his magic ring, Andvaranaut, was Andvari to be allowed to keep. The ring worked like magic, collecting rich ore. But then Loki, greedy as usual, also took the ring. Andvari cursed it, saying anyone who possessed the ring would be destroyed. In the *Poetic Edda* Andvari says:

That gold which the dwarf possessed shall to two brothers be cause of death, and to eight princes, of dissension. From my wealth no one shall good derive.

Loki nevertheless took the ring. It was given in the payment to Hreidmar, who gloated over his new treasure. One night his son Fafnir killed him and took the treasure.

The myth, which is the basis of Richard Wagner's *Der Ring des Nibelungen*, is found in the *Poetic Edda* and the *Volsunga Saga*, which also influenced William Morris's epic poem *Sigurd the Volsung and the Fall of the Niblungs*. Andvari (Alberich) is portrayed by Arthur Rackham in his illustrations for Wagner's Ring Cycle.

See also: ANDVARANAUT; FAFNIR; HOENIR; LOKI; ODIN; *PROSE EDDA*; *RING DES NIBELUNGEN, DER*

men. After a series of adventures, in which he is called the "Dumb Youth" or the "Young Mute," he appears at court but is so changed by his ordeals that he goes unrecognized. Angarad, not knowing it is Peredur, is so moved that she says she loves him above all men. Peredur is then released from his vow.

See also: ARTHUR; ROUND TABLE

*Angels taking soul to heaven*

**0248**

**Angarad of the Golden Hand**  In Arthurian legend, a lady at the court of King Arthur who is loved by Sir Peredur, a knight of the Round Table. She, however, scorns Peredur, and he vows never to speak until she loves him above all

**0249**

**Angel** (messenger)  In Jewish, Christian, and Islamic mythology, supernatural being who acts as an intermediary between God and man. The seven holy angels are Michael, Gabriel, Raphael, Uriel, Chamuel, Jophiel, and Zodkiel. Only Michael and Gabriel are mentioned in the Bible. Raphael is mentioned in the Apocrypha, and the others are in the apocryphal book Enoch. The

Old Testament contains numerous references to angels. Sometimes, however, when the expression "angel of the Lord" or "angel of Yahweh" is used, it refers to God himself, particularly in the earlier books of the Bible (for example Gen. 22:11–12). In later books, such as the Book of Daniel, angels are separate from God. The angel Michael is called a "prince" of Israel. By New Testament times belief in good and evil angels was accepted in both Christian and Jewish belief.

Angels multiplied at such a rate in the writings of both Jews and Christians that it was felt necessary to put them into some order. Various early Church writers attempted this. Dionysius the Areopagite, a mystical theologian of the fifth century, divided the heavenly host into nine orders: seraphim, cherubim, and thrones in the first circle; dominions, virtues, and powers in the second circle; and principalities, archangels, and angels in the third circle. Other writers, both Christian and Jewish, such as St. Ambrose, St. Gregory the Great, and St. Jerome, also made up different lists, some with nine orders, some with seven. Dante's list contains nine orders of angels, whereas Moses Maimonides' list contains 10.

The Koran based its angelology in part on Jewish and Christian writings. It frequently mentions angels, or *malaika*, who bear witness to Allah (sura 3). The righteous must also believe in angels (sura 2). A succinct account of belief in angels is given in sura 13, subtitled "Thunder": "Each hath a succession of angels before him, who watch over him by God's behest."

The Koranic statement reflects the belief, held also in Judaism and Christianity, that individuals and also countries have guardian angels. St. Basil of Caesarea believed each nation had a guardian angel, and in Jewish belief each nation has either a demon or an angel watching over it. The English writer Robert Burton, in his *The Anatomy of Melancholy*, written in the 17th century, says, "Every man has a good and bad angel attending him in particular, all his life long." His statement reflects the Roman Catholic belief found in the Feast of the Holy Guardian Angels, observed on 2 October, which has as its collect:

"God, who in thy transcendent providence deignest to send thy holy angels to watch over us, grant our humble petition that we may ever be safe under their protection, and may rejoice in their companionship through all eternity." Popular prints portraying an angel guiding a child are still sold today with an appropriate prayer:

Guardian angel, my guardian dear
To whom God's love commits me here,
Ever this day be at my side,
To rule and guide,
To guide and rule,
Amen.

In Christian art angels first appeared as young men without wings. By the fourth century winged angels with long hair and flowing robes, derived from copies of Greek and Roman victory statues, occur in some works. During the fifth century, winged angels with halos, robed in white, appear in scenes taken from the New Testament, as in the mosaic of the *Annunciation* in Santa Maria Maggiore in Rome. Yet when angels appeared in Old Testament scenes, they were usually wingless. By the ninth century the winged angels had finally taken the field. Rembrandt, in his painting *Manoah's Sacrifice*, returned to the old usage and omitted wings on his angel, though he often painted winged angels. Dante Gabriel Rossetti, in his painting the *Annunciation*, has a wingless angel confront a rather frightened Virgin Mary. Islamic art does not allow the depiction of human beings nor of angels, but Persian art, when it treats Islamic themes, shows angels as delicate creatures with multicolored wings, as in *The Angel Gabriel Appearing to Muhammed* in a manuscript of Jai'al-Tawarikh.

Angels are not confined to canvases and books but also appear in numerous movies, such as the early silent film *Intolerance*. In 1936 *Green Pastures* featured an angel, and in 1941 *Here Comes Mr. Jordan* told the story of a boxer in a plane crash who died before his time was up, so an angel, played by Claude Rains, was assigned the task of finding him a new body. In *Heaven Only Knows* an angel comes to earth to reform a Western badman, and in *The Bishop's Wife* Cary Grant played an angel who comes to earth to aid in the lives of various people.

See also: ALLAH; AMBROSE, ST.; BASIL, ST.; CHERUBIM; GREGORY THE GREAT, ST.; JEROME, ST.; MICHAEL; SERAPHIM; VIRGIN MARY; YAHWEH

0250

**Angelica** (angel, messenger)    In the Charlemagne cycle of legends, the heroine who appears in Italian versions of the tale of Orlando (Roland). Angelica was "the fairest of her sex." Daughter of Galafhron, king of Cathay (China), she was sent to Paris to sow discord among the Christians. Orlando fell in love with her, but Angelica did not return his love. Instead, she was passionately in love with Rinaldo. He, however, hated her. But when Angelica and Rinaldo drank from a magic fountain, he fell in love with her, and she began to despise him. In Ariosto's *Orlando Furioso*, Charlemagne sends Angelica to the duke of Bavaria, but she escapes from the castle, only to be seized and bound naked to a rock guarded by a sea monster. Later she is freed by Rogero. Eventually, Angelica marries Medoro, a young Moor, and returns to Cathay, where Medoro succeeds to the throne of her father.

See also: CHARLEMAGNE; RINALDO; ROLAND

0251

**Angel of Hadley**    In American history and folklore, popular name given to General William Goffe (died c. 1679), an English Puritan who hid from Royalist forces in the American colonies. Having signed the death warrant of King Charles I (1649), Goffe fled England when the Royalists returned to power. He disappeared from sight, then reappeared in Hadley, Massachusetts, when the village was being attacked by a band of Indians.

According to legend, a tall man, of stern look, wearing elkskin garments and carrying a sword and gun, appeared. "Men and brethren," he said to the people, "why sink your hearts? and why are you thus disquieted? Fear ye that the God we serve will give you up to yonder heathen dogs? Follow me; and ye shall see that this day there is a captain in Israel." Spurred on by these heroic words, the people fought off the Indians. When they wished to thank the stranger who had saved them, he replied: "Not unto me be the glory. I am but the implement frail as yourselves in the hand of Him who is strong to deliver." Then as suddenly as he appeared, he disappeared.

In Sir Walter Scott's novel *Peveril of the Peak* one of the characters, Bridgenorth, narrates the incident. It also appears in James Fenimore Cooper's novel *Wept of Wish-ton-Wish*, but its most striking use is made by Hawthorne in his short story "The Gray Champion," part of *Twice Told Tales*, in which the name and locale are changed but the basic legend maintained. The Angel of Hadley is a good example of a revenant, someone who returns from the dead.

See also: REVENANT

0252

**Angry Acrobat, The**    Moral fable by the Persian poet Sadi, in his *The Gulistan* (chapter 2, story 43). A holy man saw an acrobat in a great dudgeon, full of wrath and foaming at the mouth. "What is the matter with this fellow?" the holy man asked. "Someone has insulted him," a bystander replied. "This poor fellow is able to lift hundreds of pounds and hasn't the power to bear one word," the holy man said.

See also: *GULISTAN, THE*

0253

**Angurboda** (Angrbotha) (one who bodes danger or sorrow)    In Norse mythology, a hideous giantess; wife of the fire-trickster god, Loki; mother of three monsters, the wolf Fenrir, the goddess of death (Hel), and the gigantic Midgard serpent. Angurboda appears in the *Prose Edda*.

See also: FENRIR; HEL; LOKI; MIDGARD SERPENT; *PROSE EDDA*

**Anhanga**   In the mythology of the Amazonian Indians of Brazil, a name for the devil, used along with Korupira, who was the demon of the forest and also was equated with the devil. Anhanga is formless, living in a person's dream life. He loves to play pranks, often stealing children. In a short tale, "The Yara," by the Brazilian journalist and historian Alfonso Arinhos de Melo Franco, he is described as having a "fearful voice" and scattering "upon the grass and the leaves of the bushes the seeds of the sorrows that kill."

See also: KORUPIRA

*Animal Farm*   Novel published in 1945 by George Orwell, a satire of Stalinism and the Russian Revolution. The story, which resembles a modern fable and takes place on a farm somewhere in England, is told in the third person.

The oldest pig on the farm, Old Major, calls a secret meeting and tells the other animals about his dream of a revolution against the farmer, Mr. Jones. Major dies, but two other pigs, Napoleon and Snowball, take up his dream. Napoleon is big but not articulate; Snowball is a better speaker. Together with another pig, called Squealer, they promote their theory of "Animalism." They begin a rebellion when Mr. Jones comes home drunk one night and forgets to feed the animals. They go to the house where the food is stored, but Mr. Jones tries to frighten them with his shotgun. The animals, however, drive him off the farm and destroy all of the whips, nose rings, reins, and the other instruments that have been used to suppress them. The same day the animals celebrate by making up seven commandments, which they post above the door of the big barn.

1. Whatever goes upon two legs is an enemy.
2. Whatever goes upon four legs or has wings is a friend.
3. No animal shall wear clothes.
4. No animal shall sleep in a bed.
5. No animal shall drink alcohol.
6. No animal shall kill another animal.
7. All animals are equal.

The animals also agree that no animal shall have contact with humans.

After a while, Jones comes back with some other men from the village to recapture the farm. The animals fight bravely, and Snowball and Boxer receive medals for defending the farm. But Napoleon, who did not fight at all, also receives a medal. When Snowball decides to build a windmill to produce electricity, Napoleon calls nine strong dogs. The dogs drive Snowball from the farm, and Napoleon says Snowball had been cooperating with Mr. Jones. The animals then start building the windmill, but in time the work increases and the food ration declines. The common animals do not have enough food, but the pigs get fatter and fatter. They then tell the other animals that they have begun trade with the neighbors, which is disturbing to the common animals since they had been told that no animal should trade with humans. Then the pigs move into the farm house, and the other animals remember that they had been forbidden to sleep in beds. The fourth commandment on the barn door has been changed to read: "No animal shall sleep in a bed with sheets." Other commandments have also been changed. When the windmill is damaged by a storm, Napoleon accuses Snowball.

Once again Jones attacks the farm, and the windmill is destroyed. While they are rebuilding the mill, Boxer breaks down and is sold to a butcher. Napoleon says that Boxer had been brought to a hospital where he died. When the mill is finished and the farm restored, Napoleon invites the neighbors to their farm, where they celebrate its efficiency. During the celebration all the other animals gather at the window of the farm, and when they look inside they can not distinguish between man and animal.

**Animisha**   In Hindu mythology, epithet often applied to various gods, such as Vishnu, Shiva, and Indra, meaning "who does not wink." All of the gods are said to have nonblinking eyes as one of their characteristics. That is how they can be spotted as gods when they assume human form.

See also: INDRA; SHIVA; VISHNU

0257

**Anius** (grievous, troublesome)   In Greek mythology, son of Apollo by Rhoeo (or Creusa). Rhoeo's father, Staphylus of Naxos, a son of Dionysus and Ariadne, put Rhoeo to sea in a box. Rhoeo was carried to Delos and there gave birth to her son Anius. Apollo taught Anius divination and made him priest-king over Delos. Because they were descendants of Dionysus, the daughters of Anius by the nymph Dorippe—called Oeno, Spermo, and Elais—had the gift of turning anything they pleased into wine, corn, or oil. When Agamemnon set sail for the Trojan War, he wished to take the three women to help supply his troops with food. They complained to Dionysus, who transformed them into doves. Vergil's *Aeneid* (book 3) and Ovid's *Metamorphoses* (book 13) tell the story.

See also: *AENEID, THE*; AGAMEMNON; ANIUS; APOLLO; ARIADNE; DIONYSUS; NYMPHS

*Ankh*

0258

**Ankh**   Egyptian hieroglyph for "life," a stylization of a sandal strap, later identified with the Greek tau cross and the Christian *crux ansata*. The tau cross is often identified with the Egyp-

tian hermit St. Anthony the Abbot and was worn by the Knights of St. Anthony, established in 1352.

See also: AMUN; ISIS; MUT; NEITH; NUT; RA; TEM; THOTH; WENENUT

0259

**Anna** (grace, favor) **and Joachim** (the Lord will establish), **Sts.**   First century. In Christian legend, parents of the Virgin Mary. Feasts, 26 July for Anna and 20 March for Joachim. Neither Anna nor Joachim is mentioned in the New Testament. Their legend is found in various early apocryphal writings that circulated within the early Church. One of the major sources is *The Gospel of the Birth of Mary*, once ascribed to St. Matthew and translated from Greek into Latin in the fourth century by St. Jerome.

Joachim was from Nazareth and Anna from Bethlehem; both were of the royal house of King David. The couple was rich but also childless. One day, when Joachim brought his offering to the temple, it was refused by the high priest, Issachar, because Joachim had no children. Joachim was afraid to return home, but an angel appeared to him telling him he would be a father. Afterward the angel appeared to Anna, his wife, saying: "Fear not, neither think that which you see is a spirit. For I am that angel who hath offered up your prayers and alms before God, and now sent to you, that I may inform you, a daughter will be born unto you, who shall be called Mary, and shall be blessed above all women."

As foretold by the angel, the two met at the Golden Gate. Anna embraced her husband, "hanging about his neck," according to another apocryphal account, *The Protevangelion*. She said, "Now I know that the Lord had greatly blessed me. For behold, I who was a widow am no longer a widow, and I who was barren shall conceive." Then they returned home together. Anna gave birth to a girl, who was called Mary, which in Hebrew is Miriam.

The Franciscans were not satisfied with the apocryphal accounts of Mary's birth and added to the legend. They believed that Mary was conceived when Anna and Joachim kissed at the Golden Gate in Jerusalem. This part of the legend is one of the most popular subjects in Christian art. The whole legend forms part of a series of frescoes done by Giotto.

St. Anna is one of the most popular saints in the Roman Catholic church. About 550 the emperor Justinian I built a church in her honor at Constantinople, and her relics were removed there from Palestine in 710.

See also: JEROME, ST.; MATTHEW, ST.; VIRGIN MARY

**0260**

**Anna Perenna**    In Roman mythology, an ancient Italian goddess believed to be associated with the revolving year. Every month she renewed her youth and was therefore regarded as a goddess who bestowed long life. On the Ides (15th) of March (then the first month of the year) the Romans held a feast in her honor at the first milestone on the Flaminian Way. In Vergil's *Aeneid* (book 2) Anna Perenna is identified as Dido's sister. According to a later account, she fled to Aeneas in Italy after the death of her sister Dido. Lavinia, Aeneas's wife, was jealous of her, however, and plotted her ruin. In despair Anna Perenna threw herself into the Numicius, becoming a nymph or goddess of the river. Ovid's *Fasti* (3) tells of the goddess and her feast.

See also: AENEAS; *AENEID, THE*; DIDO; LAVINIA; NYMPHS; OVID

**0261**

**Annie Christmas**    In American folklore, legendary whore of New Orleans, from the pen of Lyle Saxon, Louisiana local color writer. She is found in *Fabulous New Orleans* (1930) and also in the Louisiana collection assembled and published under the auspices of the Works Progress Administration, *Gumbo ya ya* (1945). She was six feet eight inches tall, and could outdrink any man. She could walk a gangplank with a barrel of flour under each arm, and one on her head. Annie ran a floating brothel aboard a ship. She dressed in red satin and wore a red turkey feather in her hat, a badge of honor of the river champions. She had a 30-foot necklace with beads made of the eyes she had gouged out in fights or of ears or noses she had chewed off. Mother of 12 sons, each seven feet tall, she killed herself when she fell in love with a man who did not return her love.

See also: FAKELORE; PAUL BUNYAN; PECOS BILL; MIKE FINK; JOE MAGARAC

**0262**

**Anpetu wi and Hanhepi wi**    In North American Indian mythology (Sioux), the sun and the moon.

**0263**

**Anshar** (Assors, Shar) (the totality of what is above)    In Near Eastern mythology (Sumero-Akkadian), a primeval sky god who sent out the god Ea, and later his son Anu, to conquer the primeval monster of chaos, Tiamat. In some ancient texts Anshar was regarded as the father of the gods, though his role was later assumed by his son Anu. In some myths he is credited with being the father of Tiamat and is also connected with the primeval god Kishar.

See also: ANU; EA

**0264**

**Ant**    A small, wingless insect, often a symbol of industry in world folklore. Both the biblical book of Proverbs (6:6–7) and the Aesop fable "The Ant and the Grasshopper" use the ant as a symbol of industry. The Japanese represent ant in their writing by using the word *insect* combined with the characters that represent unselfishness, justice, and courtesy. In contrast, the Pueblo Indians of North America consider the ant to be vindictive and the cause of disease. In West African belief ant nests are looked upon as homes for demons and evil spirits. In Hindu folklore the ant symbolizes the pettiness of all things. There are numerous motifs associated with ants in the *Motif Index of Folk Literature*.

See also: AESOPIC FABLES; THE ANT AND THE GRASSHOPPER

0265

**Antaeus** (besought with prayers, rival)    In Greek mythology, a Libyan giant son of Poseidon and Gaea (the earth); brother of Charybdis and Ogyges. Antaeus grew stronger every time he touched his mother, the earth. He forced all strangers who ventured into his country to wrestle with him, and being powerfully strong, he killed them. Heracles, on his journey to fetch the apples of the Hesperides, was challenged to wrestle with Antaeus. Heracles lifted him off the ground and held him aloft—away from his mother—until he died. Antaeus's tomb was near Tingis in Mauretania. One of the most striking representations of Heracles wrestling Antaeus is the statue by Pollaiuolo, *Hercules and Antaeus*, an Italian Renaissance work. There is also a painting by Hans Baldung Grien (1484/85–1545) titled *Hercules and Antaeus*. Antaeus is also the name given to a friend of Turnus killed by Aeneas in Vergil's *Aeneid* (book 10).

See also: *AENEID, THE*; GAEA; HERACLES; HESPERIDS; POSEIDON

0266

**Ant and the Grasshopper, The**    Aesopic fable, derived from the medieval prose version by Phaedrus.

One frosty autumn day an ant was busily storing away some of the kernels of wheat he had gathered during the summer to eat throughout the coming winter. A grasshopper, half perishing from hunger, came limping by. Seeing what the industrious ant was doing, he asked for a morsel from the ant's store to save his life.

"What were you doing all during the summer while I was busy harvesting?" inquired the ant.

"Oh," replied the grasshopper, "I was not idle. I was singing and chirping all day long."

"Well," said the ant, smiling grimly as he locked his granary door, "it looks as though you will have to dance all winter."

*Moral: It is thrifty to prepare today for the wants of tomorrow.*

The ant is nearly always used as an example of hard work, as in Proverbs (6:6) in the Old Testament. La Fontaine's first fable deals with this subject. It forms the basis for three French operas, all called *La Cigale et la Fourmi*, written in the 19th century. The fable also influenced some North American Indian fables, which derived the story from European versions.

See also: AESOPIC FABLES

0267

**Antar** (Antarah)    fl. 600. In Arabian legend, warrior and poet; subject of *The Romance of Antar*, a popular narrative that developed over the centuries. At the time *The Romance* opens, the most powerful and best governed of the Bedouin tribes are those of the Absians and the Adnamians. King Zoheir, chief of the Absians, is firmly established on the throne, and the kings of other tribes pay him tribute. The whole of Arabia is subject to the Absians, and all of the inhabitants of the desert dread their power and depredations.

Several chieftains (among whom is Shedad, son of Zoheir) secede from the Absian tribe and set out to seek adventures, to attack other tribes, and to carry off cattle and treasure. These chieftains fight against a tribe called the Djezila, whom they defeat and whose city they pillage. Among the booty is a black woman of extraordinary beauty, the mother of two children. Her name is Zebiba, her eldest son is Djaris, and her youngest Shidoub. Shedad is so taken by the beauty of Zebiba that he gives up all of his booty just to possess her. They live together, and she bears him a son, Antar, who is born tawny as an elephant. His eyes are bleared, his head thick with hair, his features hard and fixed. Antar grows up strong and becomes a protector of women, falling in love with one named Ibla.

Antar becomes known as a brave warrior who possesses a fabulous horse, Abjer, and a fantastic sword, Djamy. Every time he goes into battle or returns from combat, he intones: "I am the lover of Ibla." After many adventures, in which he fights for the woman he loves, Antar finally marries her. At one point in his heroic life he is given the title of Alboufauris (the father of horsemen) because of his skill with the animal.

Rimsky-Korsakov's second symphony, *Antar*, depicts a rather melancholy hero who is dissatisfied with women and love. The composer revised the score in 1875 and in 1897, when it was termed a symphonic suite.

0268

**Antelope**   Plant-eating, cud-chewing mammal resembling a deer; it has permanent hollow horns that molt annually. In Egyptian mythology the antelope is associated with Anubis, Set, Osiris, and Horus; in Roman mythology, Minerva, goddess of wisdom, has the antelope as one of her animals because it was believed to have very sharp eyes. In Hindu mythology the animal is associated with Shiva, Soma, and Chandra. In the Rig-Veda antelopelike animals are the steeds of the Maruts, the wind gods. In medieval Christianity the antelope was symbolic of man armed with two horns, one representing the Old Testament and the other the New Testament.

See also: ANUBIS; CHANDRA; HORUS; MARUTS; MINERVA; OSIRIS; *RIG-VEDA*; SET; SHIVA; SOMA

0269

**Antenor** (opponent)   In Greek and Roman mythology, a Trojan, counselor to King Priam of Troy; son of Aesyetes and Cleomestra; husband of Athena's priestess Theano, who was the sister of Hecuba; father of 14 sons—Coon, Demoleon, Iphidamas, Polydamas, Laodamas, Polybus, Acamas, Agenor, Archelous, Glaucus, Helicaon, Laocoön, Lycaon, Pedaeus (by a different mother), and one daughter, Crino. When Menelaus and Odysseus came to demand the surrender of Helen from the Trojans, Antenor received them hospitably, protected them from Paris, and then advised them to seek peace. Because of this, later Greek mythology said he betrayed the Trojans by opening the gates to the Greeks, and as a result, when the Greeks took the city, they spared his house and his friends. Some accounts say he told the Greeks to steal the Palladium, a sacred statue that protected Troy, and that he advised making the Trojan horse. One myth says his ship sailed with Menelaus but was driven off course to Cyrene. He settled there, and his descendants, the Antenoridae, were worshiped as heroes. Another myth tells of his leading the Veneti, driven out of Paphlagonia, taking them by way of Thrace and Illyria to the Adriatic and then on to the mouth of the Paudus (Po), where he founded Patavium (Padua), the city of the Veneti. Antenor appears in Homer's *Iliad* (book 3), Vergil's *Aeneid* (book 1), and Ovid's *Metamorphoses* (book 13).

See also: ATHENA; HECUBA; HELEN OF TROY; *ILIAD, THE*; MENELAUS; ODYSSEUS; OVID; PALLADIUM; PRIAM

0270

**Anteros** (love-for-love)   In Greek mythology, god of passion, mutual love, and tenderness; son of Aphrodite and Ares; brother of Eros, Delmos, Enyo, Harmmia, Pallor, and Phobos. Aphrodite was told by Themis that her son Eros would grow only if he had another brother. As soon as Anteros was born, Eros began to grow, and his strength increased, but whenever Eros found himself at a distance from Anteros, he returned to his baby form. Often Anteros and Eros were portrayed striving to seize a palm tree from one another, to symbolize that true love endeavors to overcome by kindness and gratitude. Anteros and Eros were always portrayed in Greek academies as a symbol that students should love their teachers. Anteros is cited in Pausanias's *Description of Greece*.

See also: APHRODITE; ARES; EROS; THEMIS

0271

**Antero Vipunen** (Wipunen)    In the Finnish epic poem *The Kalevala* (rune 17), primeval giant who gave charms to the culture hero Vaina-moinen.

Once, wanting to build a boat, Vainamoinen asked Tapio, the forest god, to supply him with the necessary woods. But all of the trees except the oak refused to offer themselves. Vaina-moinen began to construct the boat but discov-ered he lacked the necessary magic words to complete the project. After vainly seeking the words among birds and animals, he journeyed to Tuonela, the land of the dead. He was told the magic words were possessed by the giant Antero Vipunen, and Vainamoinen went to seek him. Awaking Antero Vipunen from his long sleep underground, Vainamoinen opened the giant's mouth, forcing him to speak, but in the effort he slipped into the giant's mouth. Not wishing to remain the giant's guest, Vainomoinen set up a forge, which caused intense pain to Antero Vipunen. When the culture hero demanded the magic words as payment for stopping the forge, the giant supplied them and let him out. With the magic words Vainamoinen finished the boat, which was self-propelled. It carried him to Poh-jola, the Northland, where he wooed the Maiden of Pohjola, who refused his advances.

The name Antero is derived from St. An-dreus, or Andrew, and Vipunen signifies the cross of the saint, revealing the Christian influ-ence on the final form of the Finnish epic poem.

See also: ANDREW, ST.; *KALEVALA, THE*; LÖNN-ROT, ELIAS; TAPIO; VAINAMOINEN

0272

**Anthony of Padua, St.** (praiseworthy, priceless) 1195–1231. In Christian legend, Doctor of the Church. Invoked to find lost property. Feast, 13 June.

Born in Portugal, Anthony wished to become a missionary. He went to Italy, where he became a follower of St. Francis of Assisi. He was noted for his preaching and knowledge of the Bible.

There are numerous legends associated with him, some contained in *The Little Flowers of St. Francis*, a collection of medieval tales and legends of St. Francis and his companions. According to that source, one day as Anthony was preaching before the pope and cardinals, he spoke so elo-quently, "so sweetly, so clearly, and in a manner so efficacious and so learned, that all those who were in the Consistory, though they spoke dif-ferent languages, understood what he said as per-fectly as if he had spoken the language of each."

Another legend in the same collection tells how he preached to the fishes in Rimini after some heretics had refused to listen to him. He went to the seashore and placed himself on a bank and "began to speak to the fishes . . . who kept their heads out of the water" and looked at-tentively at the saint. When the townspeople heard what was happening, they came to see, and the heretics among them were converted by An-thony's preaching.

Once the saint preached at the funeral of a very rich and avaricious man. He condemned the man, syaing his heart would be found in his treasure chest. The man's relatives discovered that his heart was missing from his body.

Another legend tells how the saint was asked by a heretic to prove that Christ was really pres-ent in the Holy Eucharist. The man's mule bowed down as Anthony carried out the Sacra-ment and remained so until he passed. A 17th-century legend tells of the Christ Child appearing to the saint, standing on a book.

In Christian art St. Anthony of Padua is por-trayed as a young Franciscan, often with a lily or crucifix in his hand, or in later paintings, with the Christ Child standing on a book or carried by the saint in his arms.

See also: FRANCIS OF ASSISI, ST.

0273

**Anthony the Abbot, St.** (praiseworthy, price-less)    251–356. In Christian legend, patron saint of basket makers. Invoked against erysipelas

*St. Anthony the Abbot*

(or St. Anthony's fire), an acute local inflamation of the skin. Feast, 17 January.

St. Anthony was among the first "desert fathers" of the Christian Church. The list includes such saints as Pachomius, Simeon Stylites, Hilarion, and Jerome. His life, written in the fourth century by St. Athanasius, bishop of Alexandria, is believed to be the first example of an extended, or full-length, biography of a saint. It set the style for the saints' lives that were written later. It tells of numerous miracles and the proverbial combat with the devil, which became a standard literary device in writing about the lives of the saints.

Born in Alexandria, Anthony was an orphan. He divided his inheritance with his sister, sold his portion, and went to live among the hermits in the desert. But as St. Athanasius writes, "the devil, the envier and enemy of all good, could not bear to see such a purpose in so young a man" and sent many temptations to the saint. The devil "would assume by night the form and imitate the deportment of a woman, to tempt Anthony." The saint, however, overcame all of the sensual assaults. The devil then assumed the forms of various monsters, serpents, and poisonous animals to torment Anthony. Again, the saint overcame them.

After Anthony had lived for 75 years in the desert, he had a vision of St. Paul the Hermit, who had been living in penance for 90 years. So Anthony set out across the desert. After journeying several days and meeting on the way a centaur and a satyr, he came at last to a cave of rocks where St. Paul the Hermit lived beside a stream and a palm tree. The two men embraced. While they were talking, a raven came, bringing a loaf of bread in its beak. St. Paul said the raven had come every day for the last 60 years, but that day the portion of bread was doubled. St. Paul asked Anthony to fetch a special cloak, for he was about to die and wished to be buried in it. Anthony set out to get the cloak (it was in a monastery some distance away), but as he went he had a vision of St. Paul ascending to heaven. When he returned to the cave, he found St. Paul dead. Anthony had no strength to dig a grave, but two lions came and helped him. St. Anthony died 14 years later and was buried secretly, according to his wish.

St. Anthony is portrayed as a very old man, in his monk's habit, often with a crutch and an asperges or a bell to exorcise demons; a pig, the ancient symbol of the Egyptian gods Osiris and Set; and a Tau cross. Perhaps the most striking paintings of the saint's life were done by Mathias Grünewald in his Isenheim altarpiece. In *The Temptation of St. Anthony*, one of the panels of the altarpiece, the saint is shown assaulted by demons and with the rotted body of a man suffering from St. Anthony's fire. Another panel of the altarpiece, *The Meeting of St. Anthony and St. Paul the Hermit*, portrays the saints awaiting the arrival of the raven with the bread in its beak. The Isenheim altarpiece inspired Paul Hindemith's opera *Mathis der Maler*, based on the life of Mathias Grünewald. The music from the opera was used by the composer in a symphonic suite, made up of "The Concert of the Angels," "The Entombment," and "The Temptation of Saint Anthony." Gustave Flaubert wrote *La Tentation de Sainte Antoine*, a prose poem based on the legend of the saint.

See also: ATHANASIUS, ST.; CENTAUR; JEROME, ST.; OSIRIS; SATRY; SET; SIMEON STYLITES

0274

**Antigone** (in place of a mother)    In Greek mythology, daughter of Oedipus and his mother, Jocasta (or Euryganeia); sister of Eteocles, Esmene, and Polynices. Antigone accompanied her blind father into exile in Attica, and after his death, she returned to Thebes. In defiance of her uncle Creon, she attempted to bury the body of her brother Polynices, which Creon had cast outside the walls of the city because Polynices had died trying to usurp his brother Eteocles' throne. Creon sentenced her to be entombed alive.

Sophocles, in his play *Antigone*, pictures her as defiant in defending her ministrations to her dead brother. Sophocles has her say, "And what law of heaven have I transgressed? . . . if these things are pleasing to the gods [to be punished for ministering to her dead brother], when I have suffered my doom, I shall come to know my sin; but if the sin is with my judges, I could wish them no fuller measure of evil than they, on their part do wrongfully to me." Antigone then hangs herself, while her betrothed, Haemon, the son of Creon, stabs himself beside her body.

In a variant myth Antigone and Argeia, the widow of Polynices, try to bury Polynices and are seized by Creon's guards. They are handed over to Haemon for execution, but Haemon hides Antigone in a shepherd's hut, and the two live together secretly for years. Antigone bears a son who, when he grows up, engages in some funeral games in Thebes and is recognized by a birthmark peculiar to the family. He is revealed to be the child of Antigone and Haemon, who were secretly among the spectators. Creon orders them put to death. To escape Creon's vengeance, Haemon kills Antigone and himself.

In addition to Sophocles' play, Antigone has inspired numerous others, including those of Cocteau, Anouilh, and Brecht. Cocteau's play (1922) forms the basis for Honegger's opera *Antigone* (1927). Carlos Chávez's Symphony Number 1 (1933) is subtitled *Sinfonia de Antigona* and is based on incidental music to Cocteau's version of Sophocles' play. A German translation of Sophocles is used by Carl Orff for his "tragic play with music" *Antigono* (1948), and the earlier opera *Antigono* (1756) by Gluck uses an Italian translation of the Greek play.

See also: JOCASTA; OEDIPUS

0275

**Antilochus** (lying in ambush against)    In Greek mythology, a hero, the eldest son of Nestor and Anaxiba (or Eurydice); brother of Aretus, Echephron, Paeon, Peisidice, Peisistratus, Perseus, Polycaste, Stratius and Thrasymedes; possibly the father, not brother, of Paeon. Antilochus accompanied his father to the Trojan War and was distinguished for his beauty and bravery. Homer, in *The Iliad*, calls him a favorite of Zeus and Poseidon. After Patroclus he was closest to Achilles. Antilochus was chosen by the Greeks to tell Achilles that Patroclus had been slain by Hector. In later myth, when Memnon attacked the elderly Nestor, Antilochus threw himself in the way and was killed as a result. His death was avenged by Achilles. The ashes of Antilochus, Patroclus, and Achilles were laid together in the same grave. In the underworld Odysseus saw the three heroes pacing the asphodel meadow. Sacrifices were offered to all three as semidivine beings.

See also: ACHILLES; HECTOR; *ILIAD, THE*; NESTOR; PATROCLUS; POSEIDON; ZEUS

0276

**Antinous** (hostile mind)    c. 110 C.E. In Roman history and legend, the emperor Hadrian's male lover, drowned in the Nile. Whether Antinous drowned himself or was murdered is not known. Hadrian had his lover deified and founded the city of Antinoöpolis at the site of his death. Coins and statues of Antinous as a handsome youth also were produced, one of the most beautiful statues being the Farnese Antinous. Marguerite Yourcenar's novel *Memoirs of Hadrian* deals in part with Hadrian's love for Antinous.

**Antiope** (with face confronting)   In Greek mythology, the daughter of the Boetian river god Asopus and Metope, or of Nycteus of Thebes and Polyxo; mistress of Zeus, by whom she was the mother of Amphion and Zethus. When her father discovered that Zeus, in the form of a satyr, had seduced Antiope, he threatened to punish her. Antiope fled her father and went to Epopeus of Sicyon, but he had been killed by her uncle Lycus. The girl was brought back and bore twin sons, Amphion and Zethus. Nycteus ordered the boys exposed on a mountain to die, but the babies were saved by a shepherd. In the meantime Antiope was kept a prisoner by Dirce, the wife of Lycus. Eventually Antiope escaped, found her sons, and took her revenge on Dirce by having her tied to the tail of a wild bull, which dragged her until she died. Antiope's seduction by Zeus has for centuries fascinated European artists, among them Pinturicchio, Correggio, Titian, and Watteau.

Another Antiope, also called Melanippe, was the sister of Hippolyte, queen of the Amazons. She was given as a prize to Theseus and bore him a son, Hippolytus; she was killed by Theseus when he wanted to marry Phaedra. In a variant account she was given to Pirithous.

See also: AMPHION AND ZETHUS; SATYR; ZEUS

**Anu** (wealth, abundance)   In Celtic mythology, principal figure of pre-Christian Ireland. She is the goddess of prosperity and abundance who appears in Celtic folklore as Aine, a powerful fairy, queen of South Munster. Two breast-shaped promitories located near Killarney, called The Paps, were once called the Paps of Anu.

**Anu** (An, Ana, Anos, Dana, Danu, Nanu) (lofty, sky)   In Near Eastern mythology (Sumero-Akkadian), sky god, head of a triad of gods made up of Anu, Enlil, and Ea. Anu's wife was Antum; his daughter the goddess Bau. In the Babylonian creation epic poem *Enuma Elish*, Anu is the son of the primeval god Anshar. In Hittite mythology Anu is called Anus. In one myth he ousted his father, Alalus, from the throne. He was in turn dethroned by his son Kumarbi, who emasculated Anus by a single bite of his penis. Kumarbi then spit out the penis and three gods: Teshub, the storm god; Tasmisus, the god's attendant; and a river god. Teshub in turn dethroned Kumarbi and was father of the giant Ullikummi, who was destroyed by the god Ea. Anu's symbols are a horned cap and star.

See also: ANSHAR; ANU; BAU; EA; ENLIL

*Anubis*

**Anubis** (Anpu)   In Egyptian mythology, Greek name for the jackal-headed god of the dead, called Anpu by the Egyptians. Although the jackal was known to prowl the ancient cemeteries as a scavenger, the early Egyptians turned him into a god who protected rather than pillaged tombs. According to one myth, Anubis was the son of the goddess Nephthys, who had tricked her brother, the god Osiris, into adulterously sleeping with her. Nephthys abandoned Anubis at birth, and he was found and raised by Osiris's sister-wife, the goddess Isis. He accompanied Osiris on his conquest of the world, and when Osiris was murdered and dismembered, Anubis helped find his body and then embalmed it so well it resisted the influences of time and decay. Thus, it was said, the burial rites were invented. In another story, the wicked god Seth, disguised as a leopard, approached the body of Osiris. Anubis seized him and branded him all over with a hot iron. According to this myth, this is how the leopard got its spots.

Subsequently, Anubis presided over funerals and guided the dead through the underworld into the kingdom of Osiris. In his function as guide of the dead he assimilated the character of the earlier Egyptian god Wepwawet (he who opens the ways). Anubis's cult continued during Greek and Roman times. According to Plutarch, the Egyptian jackal god was common to both the celestial and infernal regions. This dual role was reinforced in Roman times by Apuleius's Latin novel *The Golden Ass* (book 11), which describes a procession of the goddess Isis in which Anubis appears with his dog's head and neck, a "messenger between heaven and hell, displaying alternately a face black as night and golden as day."

See also: ISIS; NEPHTHYS: OSIRIS; SET

0281
**Anunnaki** (Anunna, Anunnake, Ennuki)    In Near Eastern mythology (Babylonian), gods or spirits of the underworld, opposed to the Igigi, the heavenly gods. In the ancient narrative poem *Inanna's Journey to the Underworld* the Anunnaki are the seven judges of the underworld. Sometimes, however, they are listed as gods. In the *Enuma Elish*, the epic of creation, they are the defeated rebel gods who build the city of Babylon for the hero god Marduk.

0282
**Anuruddha**    Fifth century B.C.E. In Buddhist legend, a disciple of the Buddha who was present at his death. He is mentioned in the Pali sacred writings. Physically blind, Anuruddha was fa-

mous for his spiritual insight. He was considered to be an example of unity.

0283
**Apauk-kyit Lok**    In Burmese mythology, an old man responsible for bringing death into the world. Though old, Apauk-kyit Lok had renewed his life nine times because there was no death in the world. One day he went fishing and saw an animal (either a monkey or squirrel) that had fallen asleep on a branch and was floating in the river. He placed the animal in a basket and covered it with his clothes; then he disappeared. It was announced (though the myth does not tell us how) that he was dead. All of his neighbors came to see, but no one dared remove the coverings. When the lord of the sun heard what had happened, he sent some messengers to investigate. They took the form of dancers at the funeral. As they danced, they removed the clothes that covered the basket, revealing the fraud. Because of this the lord of the sun caused Apauk-kyit Lok to die, and people have been dying ever since.

0284
**Ape or Monkey**    Any mammal of the primates except humans, seen as a symbol of both beneficence and evil. In ancient Egypt a dog-headed ape assisted the god Thoth when the soul of a deceased person was weighed on the scales. Apes were embalmed when they died. In Hindu mythology Hanuman, who helps the hero Rama, is an ape or monkey god. In China a whole cycle of monkey tales developed around the adventures of a seventh-century Buddhist monk who traveled from China to India with his companion monkey and brought back sacred books.

In contrast to the beneficent aspect of the ape or monkey, the ancient Jewish rabbis said that if one saw a monkey it was a sign of bad luck. One Jewish tale says three classes of men built the Tower of Babel, one of which turned into apes as punishment from God. Some Moslems still believe that the ancient Jews who lived in Elath on the Red Sea were turned into monkeys or apes as a punishment from Allah for having fished on the Sabbath. In medieval Christian folklore the monkey was seen as shameless and lustful. One bestiary of the 12th century says that while the monkey's whole physical being is "disgraceful, yet their bottoms really are excessively disgraceful and horrible." The proverbial saying "Hear no evil, see no evil, speak no evil" became associated with monkeys when travelers to China and Japan saw three carved Koshin monkey-deities on pedestals alongside the road, with their ears, eyes, and mouths covered up.

See also: HANUMAN; RAMA; TOWER OF BABEL

*Aphrodite (Venus)*

0285

**Aphrodite** (foam-born)   In Greek mythology, one of the 12 Olympian gods; a form of the Great Mother goddess; the goddess of sensual love; daughter of Zeus and Dione; or born of the foam of the sea when the severed genitals of Uranus were cast into the sea; still other accounts say Eileithyia was her mother; identified by the Romans with Venus. Aphrodite often appears as the wife of Hephaestus, the smith god.

Her erotic adventures with Ares produced Eros, Anteros, and Harmonia, wife of Cadmus, as well as Deimos and Phobos (fear and alarm), attendants to their father, Ares. By the mortal Anchises, Aphrodite was the mother of Aeneas, the Trojan hero. A passage in the Homeric Hymns (not by the poet Homer) describes Aphrodite's encounter with Anchises. Zeus himself inspired Aphrodite with the desire to lie in the arms of a mortal man so that she might be practiced in the art of "mingling goddesses in love with mortal men."

By Hermes she bore Hermaphroditus; by Poseidon she bore Eryx; by Dionysus she bore Priapus; and by Adonis a boy and a girl. Aphrodite's main adherents were in Paphos, Amathus, and Idalion (all in Cyprus), in Cindus in Dorian Asia Minor, in Corinth, on the island of Cythera, and in Eryx in Sicily. As mother of Harmonia, Aphrodite was the guardian deity of Thebes. Among plants, the myrtle, the rose, and the apple were sacred to her as goddess of love; among animals the ram, he-goat, hare, dove, and sparrow; as sea goddess, the swan, mussels, and dolphin; as Urania, the tortoise. The goddess appears in Homer, Hesiod, Ovid, Vergil, Pausanias, and Euripides, among other ancient authors.

The best-known statue of Aphrodite in the ancient world was the Aphrodite of Cnidos by Praxiteles, made about 350 B.C.E. It is known to us by Roman copies. Other works are the Capitoline Venus in Rome and the Aphrodite of Melos, called the Venus di Milo.

In Western literature and art the name Aphrodite rarely appears; the more common Roman form, Venus, is used. However, Pierre Louÿs wrote a novel *Aphrodite*, which was made into a five-act opera by Erlanger, published in 1906.

There is a ballet *Aphrodite* (1930) by Nikolay Nabokov; a setting for women's chorus and orchestra of *Sappho's Ode to Aphrodite* (1946) by Albert Moeschinger; and a symphonic poem, *Aphrodite* (1910), by the American composer George Chadwick.

Aphrodite had many epithets, among them Aphrodite Acrae (of the height), Doritis (bountiful), Epistrophia (she who turns men to love), Euploia (fair voyage), Limenia (of the harbor), Pontia (of the deep sea), Area (warlike), Aphrodite Migonitis (uniter), Aphrodite Nymphaea (bridal), Aphrodite Melaenis (black), Scotia (dark one), Androphonos (man slayer), Epitymbria (of the tombs), Pandemos (common to all), Aphrodite Urania (heavenly), Pasiphae (shining one), Asteria (starry), Apostrophia (rejecter), and Aphrodite Morpho (shapely).

See also: AERES; ANTEROS; CADMUS; GREAT GODDESS; HEPHAESTUS; HERMAPHRODITUS; HESIOD; HOMER; OVID; PAUSANIAS; POSEIDON; PRIAPUS; URANUS; VENUS; ZEUS

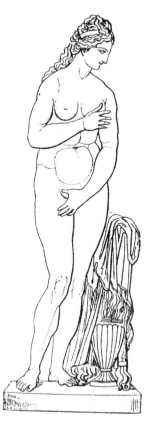

*(Aphrodite) Venus*

**Apis**   In Egyptian mythology, Greek name for the sacred bull, Hapi, associated with the god Ptah of Memphis and regarded as his earthly manifestation during the Ramesside period (1320–1085 B.C.E.). When an Apis bull died, it was given great honors similar to those for a dead pharaoh. The animal was buried at Memphis in the Serapeum, a vast system of catacombs cut into the limestone beneath the desert sands. A committee of priests was then appointed to search throughout Egypt for another Apis bull to replace the dead one. The replacement had to have 29 marks, the most important being a rich black coat intermingled with white patches and a triangular blaze on the forehead. Once chosen, the new Apis was enthroned in his own palace, or *sikos*, located to the south of the temple of Ptah at Memphis.

Apis was also associated with Osiris, the major god of the dead. In one myth Apis assisted Isis, Osiris's wife, in searching for the body of Osiris. It was believed by the ancient Egyptians that the bull's fecundity and generative powers could be transferred to the deceased, ensuring him or her rebirth in the next life. In another myth, the Apis was stabbed to death by the invading Persian king Cambyses. After the bull was killed, its corpse was thrown out of the temple, but no carrion eaters would approach the body except for dogs. After devouring the body of the bull, dogs lost their place of honor in Egyptian religion.

See also: ISIS; OSIRIS; PTAH

**Apis** (far off)   In Greek mythology, a son of Phoroneus and the nymph Teledice, or of Apollo. Apis was credited with driving monsters, plagues, and snakes from Argos and was given the power to heal illness by Apollo. St. Augustine, in commenting on the tale, believed Apis went to Egypt and founded a colony of Greeks who later worshiped Apis as the god Serapis.

See also: APOLLO; AUGUSTINE, ST.; SERAPIS

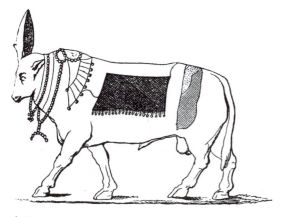

*Apis*

**Apizteotl** (hungry god)  In Aztec mythology, god of famine. When a sacrifice was offered and human flesh eaten as part of the rite, those who did not then wash in a fresh-running river or spring were said to be "addicted to the god of famine," according to Fray Diego Durán in his book *The Ancient Calendar*, which describes Aztec feasts and festivals.

0289
**Apocatequil** (chief of the followers of the moon) In the mythology of the Huamachuco Indians of Peru, god of night, twin brother of the god Piguero (white bird), who represents day. Apocatequil was the son of Guamansuri, the first man to descend to earth. Guamansuri came down and lived underground with a people called Guachimines. He seduced their sister and as a result was killed along with the girl. Their offspring, born from two eggs, survived and were the twins Apocatequil and Piguerao. Apocatequil, with the aid of a creator god, Atagudu, brought his mother back to life and killed the other Guachimines. With a golden spade he made an aperture in the earth through which the race of Peruvians emerged and took possession of the land. Apocatequil was called Prince of Evil, though this title may stem from his association with night.

0290
**Apoiaueue**  In the mythology of the Tupi Indians of Brazil, rain spirits who cause rain when the land is dry.

0291
**Apollo** (destroyer, apple man)  In Greek mythology, one of the Olympian gods; god of prophecy, healing, archery, music, youth, plastic arts, science, and philosophy; son of Leto and Zeus and brother of Artemis. Apollo was also the protector of flocks and herds and patron of the founding of cities and colonies.

The *Hymn to Apollo* (one of the Homeric Hymns falsely ascribed to Homer) describes how the island of Delos was raised up out of the sea by Zeus for the special purpose of becoming the birthplace of Apollo. Leto, Apollo's mother, says:

Delos, would that thou were minded to be the seat of my Son, Phoebus Apollo, and to let him build therein a rich temple! No other God will touch thee, nor none will honor thee, for I think thou art not to be well seen in cattle or in sheep, in fruit or grain, nor wilt thou grow plants unnumbered. But were thou to possess a temple of Apollo the Far-darter; then would all men bring thee hecatombs, gathering to thee, and ever will thou have savor of sacrifice . . . from others' hands, although thy soil is poor. (Andrew Lang translation)

The island then speaks directly to Leto, lamenting its bleak and barren terrain and fearing that Apollo, who will be lord over men and the grain-giver (earth), will disdain Delos and cause a tidal wave to wipe out the island. Delos therefore asks Leto to promise that Apollo will build a temple on the island so that it would be forevermore sacred to Apollo and thus protected from destruction. Leto gives her oath: "Bear witness, Earth, and the wide heaven above, and dropping water of Styx—the greatest oath and the most dread among the blessed Gods— that verily here shall ever be the fragrant altar and the portion of Apollo, and thee will he honor above all." Apollo had numerous love affairs with both men and women. Among the most famous (and the offspring they produced) are the following: Acacallis (Amphithemis and Miletus); Arsinoe (Erioris); Calliope (Orpheus); Calaeno (Delphus); Chione (Philammon); Chrysorthe (Coronus); Coronis or Arsinoe (Asclepius); Cyrene (Autychus, Idom, and Aristaeus); Dryope (Amphissus); Evadne (Iamus); Hecuba (Troilus, possibly); Ocyrrhoe (Phasis); Parthenone (Lycomedes); Pythia (Dorus, Laodocus, and Polypoetes); Procleia (Tenes); Psamathe (Linus); Rhoeo (Anius); Stilbe (Centaurus and Lapithus); Syllis (Zeuxippus); Thyia (Delphus); Thyria (Cycnus and Phylius). Other lovers included Acantha, Bolina, Clymene, Daphne, Issa, and Leucothoe. His favorite male lover was Hyacinthus.

Numerous symbols were attached to Apollo. The most common were the lyre and the bow, symbols of his role as god of song and as the far-hitting archer. In his role as Pythian Apollo, he is portrayed with the tripod, which was also the favorite offering at his altars. Laurel trees were planted around his temples since the leaf of the laurel, the bay leaf, was used for expiation of sins. Bay leaves were plaited into garlands of victory at the Pythian Games. The palm tree was also sacred to Apollo, for it was under the palm tree that he was born in Delos.

Among animals sacred to Apollo were the wolf, the dolphin, and the snow-white and musical swans. The hawk, raven, crow, and snake were symbols of Apollo as prophet.

In ancient art he was portrayed as a handsome youth. The Apollo Belvedere is a marble copy of a Hellenistic bronze found in Rome in the late 15th century; it is now in the Vatican Museum. The German artist Dürer based his proportions for the "ideal male" on the statue. Lord Byron wrote of it in *Childe Harold's Pilgrimage*:

The God of life, and poesy, and light— The Sun in human limbs array'd and brow All radiant from his triumph in the fight. . . .

Apollo appears in numerous paintings from ancient times to the 19th century. During the Middle Ages he was portrayed as a doctor or scholar in contemporary medieval dress. During the Renaissance he appears as a handsome youth. The Galérie d'Apollon in the Louvre was painted by Le Brun for Louis XIV, whose emblem was Apollo, le Roi Soleil.

In music and dance the best-known ballet about Apollo is Stravinsky's *Apollon Musagète* (1928), which is sometimes called simply *Apollo*. The ballet depicts Apollo, leader of the Muses, preparing himself for his duties as a god. Supported by the Muses, he ascends Olympus to drive his sun chariot across the heavens. There are also more than 20 operas with Apollo as the subject.

In English literature, Shelley's "Hymn to Apollo" reflects the poet's view of the god:

I am the eye with which the Universe
Beholds itself and knows itself divine;
All harmony of instrument or verse,
All prophecy, all medicine are mine,
All light of art or nature — to my song
Victory and praise in their own right belong.

Swinburne, in his poem "The Last Oracle," sees Apollo as the god who triumphs over the Christian god.

Apollo had many epithets; among them, in his role as god of healing, Alexicarus (averter of evil) and Paean (healer); before setting out on a journey, Apollo Embasius (Apollo of embarkations); in his role of removing a plague of locusts from Attica, Apollo Parnopius (locust god). In his role as seer Apollo was called Loxias (crooked, ambiguous) because many of his oracles were difficult to understand. As god of music, poetry, and dance he was called Musagetes (leader of the

*Apollo Musagetes*

Muses). He was also Phoebus (bright or pure god).

   See also: ARTEMIS; ASCLEPIUS; CALLIOPE; DELOS; HYACINTHUS; LETO; OLYMPIAN GODS; STYX; ZEUS

0292
**Apollodorus** (gift of Apollo)   c. 140–115 B.C.E. Greek writer on mythology, history, and grammar whose best-known work is the *Bibliotheca* (Library), which presents the deities and myths of the Greeks. The extant works of the book belong to the first or second century of our era. James G. Frazer, who translated it into English, wrote, "It is a history of the world as it was conceived by the Greeks."

0293
**Apollonia, St.** (of Apollo)   Third century. In Christian legend, patron of dentists and their patients. Feast, 9 February.

   The life of the saint is recorded in *The Golden Legend*, a collection of saints' lives written in the 13th century by Jacobus de Voragine. Apollonia was the daughter of rich parents in Alexandria, Egypt. She was a virgin "far advanced in years" and noted for her "chastity, purity, piety and charity." All of these virtues, however, did not deter a pagan mob from attacking her house because it was a refuge for Christians. Apollonia was dragged out, and the mob began "tearing out all her teeth." When that was done the saint was burned. In a variant account of her life she was killed with a sword.

   In Christian art St. Apollonia is usually shown with a pair of pincers, occasionally holding a tooth. One work, ascribed to Piero della Francesca, portrays the saint holding her symbol and looking quite determined if not angry.

   See also: *GOLDEN LEGEND, THE*

0294
**Apollyon** (destroyer)   In the Bible, N.T., angel of the bottomless pit (Revelation 9:11). Apollyon is a Greek translation of the Hebrew word *Abaddon*, a poetic name for the land of the dead in the Old Testament. Milton uses the name in his *Paradise Regained*: "In all her gates Abaddon rues the bold attempt" (IV, 624). In early Christian literature Apollyon is a name for the devil. John Bunyan's *Pilgrim's Progress* calls Apollyon an evil monster, "hideous to behold," with "scales like a fish," "wings like a dragon," bear's feet, and a lion's mouth. Christian, the hero of Bunyan's work, battles Apollyon and wounds the monster with his two-edged sword. In later Christian writings Apollyon is often identified as the angel of death.

0295
**Apophis**   In Egyptian mythology, Greek name of the Egyptian Apep, or Aaapef, giant serpent,

sometimes a crocodile, and night demon. According to some ancient accounts, Apophis was a form of Set, god of evil and darkness. Each night Apophis battled with the sun god Ra, whose spells and flames eventually destroyed the serpent. This nightly combat took place right before Ra's ascension from Duat, the underworld. In the ancient Egyptian ritual text *Books of the Overthrowing of Apophis*, a rite was to be recited in the temple of the sun god, cataloging in great detail the destruction that was to befall Apophis. The monster's statue or representation was to be speared and gashed and every bone of his body cut by knives. His head, legs, and tail were to be scorched, singed, and roasted until the whole was consumed by fire. The same fate awaited Apophis's monstrous helpers, Sebau and Nak, as well as other shadows and offspring of night. Another myth explained that Apophis sprang from the saliva of the goddess Neith while she was still living in the primeval waters. The idea of the Apophis snake may derive from the African python, which can open its mouth wide enough to swallow a human.

See also: DUAT; NEITH; RA; SET

0296

**Apostle** (ambassador, messenger, envoy)   In the Bible, N.T., title given to the 12 chief disciples of Jesus. The names given in the Gospels and Acts vary, a fact often explained by the custom of calling the same person by different names; thus, Peter is also known as Simon Peter or just Simon, and Bartholomew is sometimes called Nathanael. In general, the Twelve Apostles are Simon, called Peter or Cephas (rock); Andrew; James the Greater (or Elder or Major); John; James the Less (or Younger or Minor); Jude, also called Thaddaeus; Philip; Bartholomew, also called Nathanael; Matthew, surnamed Levi; Thomas, surnamed Didymus or the Twin; Simon, the Cananean or Zealot; Judas, surnamed Iscariot.

After the suicide of Judas, his place was taken by Matthias, who was then called Apostle. The term also was applied to St. Paul, who is the Apostle to the Gentiles, and to saints who in legend are responsible for the conversion of countries to Christianity. Thus, St. Patrick is the Apostle to Ireland, and Sts. Cyril and Methodius are Apostles to the Slavs.

The earliest paintings of the Twelve Apostles are in the Roman catacombs of Domitilla (fourth century). They are pictured seated in a semicircle around Christ. In two Ravenna baptisteries of the mid-fifth century and early sixth century they are seen walking in procession around the cupola of the building. Sometimes the Apostles are portrayed as 12 lambs around Christ, the Good Shepherd, as in St. Clement's Church in Rome (12th century). Sets of the 12 Apostles in later Christian art were painted by Raphael and engraved by Marc Antonio, Lucas van Leyden, Parmigiano, El Greco, and Albert Dürer. However, not all of the Dürer set survive.

Edward Elgar, the English composer, planned a sequence of oratorios dealing with the calling of the apostles and their mission to convert the world. The first part of the project was called *The Apostles* and the second part, *The Kingdom*; the third part was never finished.

See also: BARTHOLOMEW, ST.; CYRIL AND METHODIUS; JAMES THE GREATER, ST.; JAMES THE LESSER, ST.; JUDAS ISCARIOT; JUDE, ST.; MATTHEW, ST.; PATRICK, ST.; PETER, ST.; SIMON, ST.; THOMAS, ST.

0297

**Apple**   A fruit tree common throughout the temperate regions of the world; in world mythology and folklore, a symbol of fertility and love. In Christian folklore the apple is often identified as the fruit eaten by Adam and Eve, though the actual fruit is not named in Genesis. Thomas Otway, in his play *The Orphan*, tells of how Eve "for an apple damned mankind." Often a golden apple is a prize; in Greek mythology it was cast into a gathering of the gods to cause dissension among them. It was to be awarded to the goddess who won the love of the youth Paris, and Aphrodite, the goddess of sexual love, won it. In Greek custom, tossing an apple to the object of one's desire was an invitation to sexual intercourse. The apple or apple tree was sacred to Nemesis, Artemis, and Apollo. In Aristophanes' play *The Clouds* young men are told not to frequent houses of dancing girls where "while they are gaping at some cute strumpet, she might get them involved by tossing an apple at them." In one of Lucian's dialogues, *Conversations of the Courtesans*, a courtesan complains that her lover is not paying attention to her, but "throwing apples" at another girl. In Norse mythology the Aesir goddess Iduna is known for her magic apples. In present-day custom boys and girls dunk for apples at Halloween. Sometimes they twirl them by the stem, with each twist accompanied by a letter of the alphabet, which indicates the first letter in the name of a future mate. According to European folklore, apples could induce pregnancy.

See also: ADAM AND EVE; IDUNA

0298

**Apple of Discord**   In Greek mythology, a golden apple with the inscription "For the fairest." Eris, the goddess of discord, threw it into an assembly of the gods at the wedding of Thetis and Peleus because she alone of the immortals had not been invited. Aphrodite, Hera, and Athena each claimed the apple. None of the gods could decide who should have it, so Zeus chose Paris of Troy to be the judge. Paris gave the apple to Aphrodite, who then promised him Helen, the most beautiful woman in the world. Helen was already the wife of Menelaus, king of Sparta, and brother Agamemnon, king of Argos. The seduction and removal of Helen from Greece led directly to the Trojan War. The event is frequently painted as *The Judgment of Paris* and was popular with artists from the Middle Ages to the 19th century.

See also: AGAMEMNON; APHRODITE; HELEN OF TROY; HERA; MENELAUS; PARIS; PELEUS; THETIS; ZEUS

0299

**Appomattox Apple Tree**   In American history and folklore of the Civil War, tree under which General Lee surrendered to General Grant. According to legend, General Lee mistook General Grant (who was far from neat) for an orderly and handed him his sword to clean, thus surrendering by mistake. Afterwards the tree was quickly sliced up and stripped clean by enterprising soldiers until only a gigantic hole was left. The bark was enshrined as an heirloom and handed down from one generation to the next. In actuality, nothing took place under the Appomattox Apple Tree; the surrender was made at the house of Major Wilmer McLean on 9 April 1865.

0300

**Apricot**   A tree that bears fruit similar to the peach. In European folklore the apricot was believed to be a stimulant to sexual activity. In Shakespeare's *Midsummer Night's Dream* (3.1), when Titania fell in love with Bottom, the weaver turned into an ass, and she ordered her elves to feed him "apricocks." In English folklore, to dream of an apricot means good luck, health, and pleasure. In Chinese belief, however, the apricot symbolizes death and timidity.

0301

**Apsu** (Absu, Apason, Apsu-Rishtu) (sweet water ocean)   In Near Eastern mythology (Babylonian), primordial god of fresh water, husband of Tiamat, or chaos. In the Babylonian epic of creation *Enuma Elish*, Apsu's nature is described:

> There was a time when above the heaven was
>     not named Below, the earth bore no name.
> Apsu was there from the first, the source
>     of both. And raging Tiamat the mother of
>     heaven and earth. But Apsu and Tiamat
>     were gathered together in a mass.

Apsu represents the male and Tiamat the female principle of the primeval universe. In the poem, however, Ea, the son of Apsu, castrates his father and takes over his role as god of fresh water. The worship of Ea as god of fresh water was even found in the temple of King Solomon, where water jars stood near the great altar in the large court. The great basin in the court was called Apsu.

See also: EA; SOLOMON

0302

**Aqhat**   In Near Eastern mythology, a Canaanite hero restored to life. Aqhat was the son of Daniel. He had been given to his father as a gift by the god El for the father's prayers. Aqhat was perfect in all things. One day Daniel gave Aqhat a bow made by the divine smith of the gods. However, the war goddess, Anath, coveted the boy and made an offer to Aqhat. "Ask for everlasting life and I will give it to you," the goddess said to Aqhat. "How can a mortal live forever?" Aqhat asked. His question so angered the goddess that she sent a hired killer, Yatpan, to murder Aqhat. After his death Aqhat was restored to life by the goddess, who felt remorse for her evil deed. This ending, however, is only conjectural, because the myth, found on tablets from the ancient city of Ugarit in 1930 and 1931, is not complete.

See also: ANATH; EL

0303

**Aquarius** (water bearer)   The eleventh sign of the Zodiac. Aquarius rises 20 January and sets in February. Aquarius is the water-bearer constellation said to represent Ganymede, the young boy lover and cupbearer of the Greek god Zeus. Other accounts say it represents Deucalion or Cecrops.

See also: DEUCALION; GANYMEDE; ZODIAC

0304

**Ara**   In Armenian mythology, a handsome hero who died in battle and was restored to life. An evil queen, Semiramis, heard how handsome Ara was and sent messengers to propose that he marry her. Ara rejected the offer because he was married to Nvard, whom he deeply loved. Semiramis, upset by the refusal, sent an army against the hero, and he was killed in battle. His lifeless body was taken to Semiramis and placed in an upper chamber, where she prayed to her gods to restore it to life.

0305

**Arachne** (spider)   In Greek mythology, daughter of the Lydian cloth dyer Idmon and Colophon. Arachne challenged Athena to a weaving match in which she wove a tapestry portraying the erotic activities of the gods. Athena was offended by the work and destroyed it. Arachne then hanged herself, and Athena changed her into a spider. The myth is told in detail in Ovid's *Metamorphoses* (book 6) and by the English poet Spenser in *Muiopotmos*. A magnificent painting depicting the weaving contest is *The Competition between Arachne and Pallas Athene* or *The Spinners* by Velasquez.

See also: ATHENA; OVID; SPIDER

0306

**Arae** (altars)   In Roman mythology, rocks in the Mediterranean between Africa and Sardinia. Vergil's *Aeneid* (book 1) tells how Aeneas lost most of his fleet there. It is also the place where Aeneas and the Africans ratified a treaty.

See also: *AENEID, THE*

0307

**Aralu** (Arallu, Irkalla)   In Near Eastern mythology, the Babylonian land of the dead, ruled over by the goddess Ereshkigal and her husband, the god Nergal. Aralu was pictured as a vast place, dark and gloomy. Sometimes it was called a land, sometimes a great house. It was difficult to approach because it lay in the lowest part of a mountain. Aralu was surrounded by seven walls and guarded so that no living persons could enter it. If they did, they would never come out. A second name for the land of the dead in Babylonian mythology was Ekur (the bright mountain house), a third was Shalu (to ask), and a fourth was Ganzir, a name whose meaning is uncertain. In numerous incantations used in cultic rites the names of the dead were avoided and the place was often described as "land of no return," "dark dwelling," or "great city."

See also: ERESHKIGAL; NERGAL

**Aram**   In Armenian folklore, hero who conquered Barshamina, the giant. Barshamina ruled a great land, which Aram conquered; Aram made himself king and forced the people to learn Armenian. Some scholars believe that Aram was originally an Armenian war god, Aremenius; and the giant Barshamina was none other than the Syrian god Ba'al Shamin, the lord of heaven, imported into Armenian mythology and demoted into a giant in later legend.

See also: BAAL

0309

**Aramazd**   In Armenian mythology, supreme god, derived in part from the Persian good god, Ahura Mazda. Aramazd was the giver of prosperity, abundance, and fatness to the land. He made the fields fertile and may therefore have been a rain god. He was the father of the gods Anahita, Nane, and Mihr.

See also: AHURA; ANAHITA; MAZDA; MIHR; NANE

0310

**Arcadia** (bear-country)   In Greek mythology, a mountainous region in the Peloponnesus, the central district of Greece, associated with pastoral life in much poetry and art; named after Arcas, king of the Arcadians. Ancient authors such as Theocritus and Vergil used Arcadia to portray

an ideal state, and it has been used by poets and artists ever since. One of the most popular works was *Arcadia* (1481) by the Italian Sannazaro, a collection of poetic eclogues connected by prose passages. Other works in literature are Spenser's *Shepherd's Calendar* and Sir Philip Sidney's prose romance *Arcadia*. The use of Arcadia to denote a pastoral state that never existed except among the poets was attacked by the English poet William Cowper in his poem "Hope":

> The poor, inured to drudgery and distress,
> Act without air, think little, and feel less,
> And no where, but in feign'd Arcadian scenes
> Taste happiness, or know what pleasure
>    means.

The saying *Et in Arcadia ego* (even in Arcadia I am found) refers to death and was used by Poussin as the title for a painting of Arcadian shepherds looking at a skull and tomb. Often, however, the lines are mistranslated as "I too have lived in Arcadia."

0311

**Arcas** (bear)   In Greek mythology, a culture hero, king of Arcadia; a son of Zeus and Callisto; married the Dryad Erato; father of Azan, Apheidas, Elatus, Hyperippe, and the illegitimate Autolaus. Arcas taught the Arcadians agriculture and the art of spinning wool. He was turned into a star, the Little Bear (Arcturus), located behind his mother, Callisto, who was turned into the Great Bear by Zeus. Arcas is cited in Apollodorus's *Bibliotheca* (3), and Pausanias's *Description of Greece*.

See also: APOLLODORUS; ARCADIA; CALLISTO; DRYADS; ZEUS

0312

**Archangels**   In Jewish, Christian, and Islamic mythology, order of angels.

In the Old Testament Apocrypha Book of Tobit (12:15) the archangel Raphael says he is "one of the seven holy angels, which present the prayers of the saints, and which go in and out before the glory of the Holy One." Influenced by this verse, the author of the Book of Revelation (8:2) has seven angels who stand before God. However, the names of the seven are not given in either text. Judaeo-Christian tradition has supplied a list: Michael (who is like unto God), Raphael (God has healed), Gabriel (God is my strength), Uriel (the light of God), Chamuel (he who seeks God), Zophiel (the beauty of God), and Zadkiel (the righteousness of God). There are numerous variant spellings of the names, often making it difficult to know which angel is spoken of in a particular text. The first three on the list, however, are most often represented in Western medieval art and literature.

Islam does not have seven archangels but four. They are Michael, Gabriel, Azazel (the angel of death), and Israfel (the angel who will sound the trumpet on the Last Day when everyone will be judged by Allah). Michael and Gabriel are named directly in the Koran; the other two names are not given but are supplied by Islamic tradition.

See also: AZAZEL; BIBLE (REVELATION); CHAMUEL; GABRIEL; ISRAFEL; KORAN, THE; MICHAEL; RAPHAEL; URIEL; ZADKIEL; ZOPHIEL

0313
**Ardhananari** In Hindu mythology, epithet of the god Shiva, meaning half man. Often it signifies Shiva as an androygne or as a composite god made up of his male element, Shiva, and his female form, Parvati. This androgynous figure is depicted as a female on the left and a male on the right side.

See also: SHIVA

0314
**Ares** (male-warrior) In Greek mythology, one of the 12 Olympian gods, the war god, son of Zeus and Hera; lover of Aphrodite; father of Deimos and Phobos (or Pavor) (gods of tumult and terror), Enyo (goddess of battle), and Eris (goddess of discord); equated by the Romans with their god Mars.

*Diomedes casting his spears against Ares (John Flaxman)*

Ares was "the blood-stained bane of mortals," according to Homer in *The Iliad* (book 5). He was hated by the other gods and even disliked by his parents, Zeus and Hera, as demonstrated in a passage from Homer's *Iliad* (book 5) in which the god is wounded. Zeus says to Ares, "You are to me the most hateful of the gods who dwell upon Olympus. For dear to you always are strife and wars and battles. You have your mother Hera's intolerable, unyielding spirit. Hardly can I restrain her with words. Therefore I think that it is at her prompting that you suffer thus. But still I will not long endure that you suffer pain, for you are my offspring and your mother bore you to me. If you had been born so insolent of any other of the gods, long ago would you have been lower than the sons of heaven" (translated by Chase and Perry).

The *Hymn to Ares*, one of the Homeric Hymns (works ascribed to Homer but not by the poet), gives a contrasting image of the god and portrays Ares as a benign protector as well as a patron of bravery:

. . . O defence of Olympus, father of warlike Victory, ally of Themis, stern governor of the rebellious, leader of righteous men, sceptred King of manliness. . . . helper of men, giver of dauntless youth! Shed down a kindly ray from above upon my life, and strength of war, that I may be able to drive away bitter cowardice from my head and crush down the deceitful impulses of my soul. . . . O blessed one, give you me boldness to abide within the harmless laws of peace, avoiding strife and hatred and the violent fiends of death. (Translated by Hugh G. Evelyn-White)

Among his many loves (and the offspring produced) were Aerope (Aeropus); Agraulos (Alcippe); Althaea (Meleager); Astynome (Calydon); Astyoche (Ascalaphus and Ialmenus), Atlanta (Parthenopapaeus); Asterope or Harpina (Oenomaus); Chryse or Dotis (Phlegyas); Cyrene or Asterie (Diomedes); Demonice or Alcippe (Evenus, Molus, Oeneus, Pylus, and Thestius); Otrera (Antiope, Hippolyte, and Penthesilea); Pelopia or Pyrene (Cycnus); and Protogeneia (Oxylus).

Ares was worshiped by the Spartans, who sacrificed dogs to him. The vulture also was sacred to Ares. He had sanctuaries under the name of Enyalius in several places. The Spartans also called him Theritas (wild beast). Among his other names were Gradivus (leader of armies) and Ares Gynaecotheonas (he who entertains women), the latter because, according to one myth, the women of Tegea armed themselves and drove out the Spartans who had attacked them. The god was also called Aphneius (abundant), referring to the myth of Aerope, a daughter of Cepheus. Ares loved her, but she died giving birth to a child, who clung to her breast even after she was dead. Through the power of Ares, the child still sucked great amounts of milk from its mother's breasts. The Areopagus (hill of Mars), northwest of the Acropolis in ancient Athens, was the meeting place for elders, who tried treason and homicide cases. Ares was the first to be tried by the Areopagitae, the court, for the murder of Halirrhotius, son of Poseidon, who had raped Ares' daughter Alcippe. Orestes was also tried at this court. The Areopagus is the "Mars Hill" cited in Acts (17:22) from which St. Paul tried to convince the Athenians of the merits of Christianity over their pagan gods.

Ares appears in Homer's *Iliad* and *Odyssey* (he sides with the Trojans), Vergil's *Aeneid* (book 8), Hesiod's *Theogony*, the Homeric Hymns, and Apollodorus's *Bibliotheca* (Library), among other works.

In ancient works of art Ares is portrayed as a young and handsome man. One of the best-known statues of him portrays him seated with his son Eros at his feet.

See also: AEROPE; APHRODITE; HALIRRHOTIUS; HESIOD; *ILIAD, THE;* MARS; *ODYSSEY, THE;* OLYMPIAN GODS; THEMIS

0315

**Arethusa** (the waterer?)   The name of several springs, notably one in Ithaca and one in Syracuse. In Greek mythology, the latter was a nymph of Elis (or Achaed); daughter of Oceanus. Arethusa was a follower of Artemis, who turned her into a fountain. One day she bathed in the stream of the river god Alpheus, who fell in love with her. She fled his sexual advances and was transformed by Artemis into a spring on the island of Ortygia near Syracuse. But Alpheus, following under the sea, was united with the fountain. Ovid's *Metamorphoses* (book 5) and Shelley's poem "Arethusa" (1824), as well as *Arethusa*, a "Symphonic Myth" by Alex Voormolen, all deal with the myth. The Fontana Arethusa still exists today, though it is now a saltwater stream.

See also: ARTEMIS; NYMPHS; OCEANUS; OVID

0316

**Aretos**   In Greek mythology, a hero; the name of a son of Nestor mentioned in Homer's *Odyssey* (book 3), as well as the name of a son of Priam killed by Automedon, according to Homer's *Iliad* (book 17). Aretos was also the name of a warrior who used as his weapon an iron club. He was slain by Lycurgus, king of Arcadia, according to Pausanias's *Description of Greece*.

See also: AUTOMEDON; *ODYSSEY, THE;* PRIAM

0317

**Arge** (brightness)   In Greek mythology, a female hunter who was transformed into a stag by Apollo. Arge is also the name of one of the Cyclopes according to Hesiod's *Work and Days*, as well as the name of a daughter of Heracles by Thespius and of a nymph daughter of Zeus and Hera, sister of Ares, Elleithyia, Hebe, Eris, and Hephaestus, according to Apollodorus's *Bibliotheca* (Library).

See also: APOLLO; APOLLODORUS; ARES; HEPHAESTUA; HERA; HESIOD; THESPIUS; ZEUS

0318

**Argeia** (brilliant)   In Greek mythology, daughter of Adrastus and Amphithea; sister of Aegialeia, Aegialeus, Deipyle, Cyanippus, and Hippodameia; mother of Thersander and another Adrastus. Argeia was the wife of Polynices, whom she loved very dearly. Together with Antigone, she tried to bury Polynices' body, and Creon had her killed for the deed. Theseus, in turn, killed Creon. The name Argeia is also given to the mother of Argos, who built the first ship, *Argo*, for the hero Jason.

See also: ADRASTUS; ANTIGONE; JASON

0319

**Argives**   The ancient inhabitants of Argos and Argolis. Homer and other early poets called the people of Greece by local tribe names, including Argives. Homer's *Iliad* does not use the term *Greek*, but *Argives, Achaeans,* or *Danaans*. Later Greek writings use *Hellenes* (descendants of Hellen), while Romans used *Greek* to cover all tribes.

See also: DANAANS; HOMER; *ILIAD, THE*

0320

*Argo* (bright)   In Greek mythology, the 50-oared ship in which the Argonauts sailed with Jason to Colchis to capture the Golden Fleece. The *Argo* was built by Argus, son of Argeia. Its prow contained magic wood, given by Athena, from the sacred talking oak of Dodona. While at sea, sometimes the beam would speak oracles to the crew. The *Argo*, according to some accounts, was the first ship. It appears in Apollonius

Rhodius's epic *Argonautica* and William Morris's *Life and Death of Jason*.

See also: ARBEIA; ARGONAUTS; ARGUS; ATHENA; DODONA; GOLDEN FLEECE; JASON

*The building of the* Argo

0321

**Argonauts**   In Greek mythology, the name given to Jason and his 55 companions who sailed the *Argo* to capture the Golden Fleece. The list of heroes varies from source to source. The Argonauts according to Apollonius Rhodius's epic poem *Argonautica* are

Acastus, son of King
Pelias of Iolcus
Admetus, prince of Pherae, son of Pheres
Aethalides, son of Hermes
Amphidamas, son of Alcus, from Arcadia
Amphion, son of Hyperasius, from Pellene
Ancaeus, son of Lycurgus, from Arcadia
Ancacus, a steersman, son of Poseidon, from
   Tegea
Areus, a son of Bias
Argus, builder of the *Argo*
Asterion, son of Cometes
Asterius, brother of Amphion
Augeas, son of Helius, from Elis
Butes, son of Teleon, from Athens
Canthus, son of Canethus, from Euboea
Calais, winged son of Boreas and Orithyia

Castor, one of the Dioscuri, from Sparta

Cepheus, son of Aleus, from Arcadia

Clytius, son of Eurytus, from Oechalia

Coronus, son of Caenus, a Lapith from Thessaly

Echion, herald of the Argonauts, son of Hermes

Erginus, son of Poseidon, from Orchomenus

Eribotes, son of Teleon, from Athens

Erytus, brother of Echion, from Alope

Euphemus, son of Poseidon, from Taenarus

Eurydamas, son of Ctimenus, a Dolopian

Eurytion, son of Irus

Heracles, son of Zeus, from Tiryns

Hylas, squire of Heracles

Idas, son of Aphareus, from Arene

Idmon, a seer, son of Apollo, from Argos

Iphiclus, son of Thestius, from Aetolia

Iphiclus, son of Phylacus, from Phylace

Iphitus, brother of Clytius

Iphitus, son of Naubolus, from Phocis

Jason, son of Aeson, captain of the expedition

Laocoön, uncle of Meleager

Leodocus, brother of Areus

Lynceus, brother of Idas

Meleager, son of Oeneus, from Calydon

Menoetius, son of Actor

Mopsus, son of Ampycus, a Lapith

Nauplius, son of Clytonaeus, from Argos

Oileus, father of Ajax the Lesser, from locris

Orpheus, the musician and poet, from Thrace

Palaemonius, lame son of Hephaestus, from Actolia

Peleus, father of Achilles, from Phthia

Periclymenus, son of Nestor, from Pylus

Phalerus, archer from Athens

Phlias, from Araethyrea

Polydeuces, one of the Dioscuri, from Sparta

Polyphemus, son of Elatus, from Arcadia

Tacnarus, son of Poseidon

Talaus, brother of Areus

Telamon, father of Great Ajax, from Salamis

Tiphys, the steersman, son of Hagnias, from Boeotia

Zetes, winged brother of Calais

Others sometimes listed as Argonauts include

Actor, son of Deion, from Phocis

Amphiaraus, the seer, from Argos

Ascalaphus, son of Ares, from Orchomenus

Atalanta, the virgin huntress, from Calydon

Caeneus, the Lapith, father of Coronus

Euryalus, son of Mecisteus, one of the Epigoni

Iphitus, from Mycenae

Laertes, son of Acrisius, from Argos

Melampus, son of Poseidon, from Pylos

Peneleus, son of Hippalcimus, from Boeotia

Phanus, son of Dionysus, from Crete

Poeas, father of Philoctetes

Staphylus, brother of Phanus.

The myth of the Argonauts, which predates Homer, has inspired numerous ancient and modern works in addition to the *Argonautica*, including Euripides' play *Medea* and Pindar's *Pythian Ode*. Chaucer tells the tale in his *Legend of Good Women*. The longest reworking of the myth is found in William Morris's *Life and Death of Jason* (1867), a poem of 7,500 lines. Robert Graves wrote a novel on the theme called *Heracles, My Shipmate* (1944). Other versions of the tale include Hawthorne's *Tanglewood Tales* (1851) and *The Heroes* (1855) by Charles Kingsley; both were written for children and reflect more of the 19th century than of ancient Greece.

See also: ACASTUS; ARGO; BOREAS; CHAUCER; DIOSCURI; GOLDEN FLEECE; HOMER; JASON

0322

**Argus** (bright)   In Greek mythology, the name of the 100-eyed giant who guarded Io on the orders of Hera. The myth is told by Ovid in the *Metamorphoses* (book 1). Argus is also the name of Odysseus's dog in Homer's *Odyssey* (book 17), as well as the name of the builder of the ship *Argo* used by Jason to capture the Golden Fleece. Others in Greek mythology with the same name are a king of Argos who reigned for 70 years; a son of Agenor; a son of Zeus and Niobe (Zeus's first child by a mortal); one of the dogs of Actaeon; a son of Jason and Medea; and a grandson of Aeëtes, king of Colchis.

See also: HERA; IO; JASON; MEDEA; NIOBE; OVID; ZEUS

0323

**Arhat** (worth)   In Theravada Buddhism, one who has reached the end of the Eightfold Path. Their number varies in Buddhist works from 16 to 500. Often they are portrayed as dignified, bald, and with a certain severity, seated along the eastern and western walls of the principal hall in a Buddhist temple. An arhat is often seen in contrast to the Bodhisattva of Mahayan Buddhism, in which the Enlightened One delays entrance into Nirvana to teach the way to others. In China the term *lohan* is used; in Japan, *rakan*. In Pali the term is Romanized as *arahat*.

See also: BODHISATTVA; MAHAYANA; NIRVANA

*Ariadne*

0324

**Ariadne** (very pure, guiltless)   In Greek mythology, daughter of Minos and Pasiphae; sister of Acacallis, Andiogeus, Catreus, Deucalion, Euryale, Glaucus, Lycastus, Phaedra, and Xenodice. Ariadne fell in love with Theseus when he came to Crete to kill the Minotaur. She gave him yarn to mark his path into the labyrinth so

that he could find his way back after slaying the Minotaur. Ariadne then eloped with Theseus. Homer's *Odyssey* (book 11) says Ariadne was killed by the goddess Artemis in the Island of Dia, near Crete, at the request of Dionysus. Later, post-Homeric myth shifts the scene to the Island of Naxos, where the slumbering Ariadne is deserted by Theseus. Waking up, she is on the brink of despair, when Dionysus comes and makes her his wife. Zeus grants her immortality and sets her bridal gift, a crown, among the stars.

Ariadne was accorded godlike honors. At Naxos her festivals portrayed her life. At Athens in the autumn a festival in honor of Dionysus and Ariadne was celebrated. In Italy Dionysus was identified with the ancient Italian wine god Liber, and Ariadne with the wine goddess Libera.

Ariadne's abandonment by Theseus inspired a poem by the Roman poet Catullus. She is also the subject of one of Ovid's *Metamorphoses* (book 8) and *Heroides*, and appears in Chaucer's *Legend of Good Women*. Tintoretto, Raphael, Titian, and Poussin all deal with the subject in paintings. Richard Strauss's opera *Ariadne auf Naxos* (1912) has a libretto by Hugo von Hofmannsthal. An earlier opera, *Ariadne auf Naxos* by Georg Benda, was much admired by Mozart.

See also: ARTEMIS; CHAUCER; DEUCALION; DIONYSUS; MINOTAUR; *ODYSSEY, THE*; OVID; PHAEDRA; THESEUS; ZEUS

0325

**Arianrhod** (silver circle)   In Celtic mythology, a goddess married to the British king and magician Gwydion. Their sons were Lleu Llaw Gyffes, the culture hero, and the sea god Dylan, who at birth plunged into the sea.

See also: CASWALLAWN; DYLAN; GWYDION; LLEU LLAW GYFFES

0326

**Ariel** (lion of God or hearth of God)   In the Bible, O.T., symbolic name for Jerusalem in Isaiah (29:1–2). In occult medieval literature, the name of a water spirit under the leadership of the arch-angel Michael.

Ariel figures rather prominently in English literature. In *The Tempest* Shakespeare lists Ariel as an "airy spirit," who is rescued by Prospero from imprisonment in a cloven pine and becomes a servant of the magician. At Prospero's bidding he causes the storm and shipwreck. He lures Ferdinand to a meeting with Miranda, singing "Come unto these yellow sands." He also awakens Gonzalo in time to frustrate the murder of the king. At the end of the play, after Ariel has provided a calm sea and a good wind for a voyage to Milan, Prospero frees the spirit.

Whereas Shakespeare's Ariel is airy and mis-chievous, Milton's Ariel in *Paradise Lost* is part of the "atheist crew" of fallen angels. The mischie-vous Ariel returns in Pope's brilliant poem *The Rape of the Lock*, in which Ariel is a sylph assigned to protect Belinda, the heroine, as long as she does not let love for a man enter her heart. Ariel is chief of the "light Militia of the lower Sky," a place inhabited by other sylphs. He rules over other fairies like an epic hero and takes the most dangerous position, guarding Belinda's lapdog. Although he is brave, loyal, and heroic, he can-not help Belinda once she falls in love.

Percy Bysshe Shelley, the English Romantic poet, often called himself Ariel. One biography of Shelley, written by André Maurois, is titled *Ariel*. In music, Ariel is depicted in Tchai-kovsky's symphonic poem *The Tempest* and in Sibelius's incidental music for Shakespeare's *The Tempest*.

See also: MICHAEL

**Arimaspi**    In Greek mythology, a fantastic one-eyed people of Scythia, according to Herodotus's *History* (book 4). They were said to be constantly fighting with griffins for the gold the griffins guarded. Milton in *Paradise Lost* (book 2.943-5) cites them.

See also: GRIFFIN

0327

**Arinna** (Arinniti)    In Near Eastern mythology (Hittite), sun goddess and goddess of fecundity. Arinna was the most important deity in the Hit-tite pantheon, being addressed in masculine terms as "sun god of heaven." Her symbols were the lion and the dove.

0328

**Arioch** (fierce lion)    In the Bible, O.T., name given in the Book of Daniel (2:14) for one of the fallen angels; also used in Milton's *Paradise Lost* for a fallen angel.

0329

**Aristaeus** (the best)    In Greek mythology, god of beekeeping and protector of fruit trees; a son of Apollo and a Lapith girl, Cyrene; half-brother of Orpheus. Though he was married to Autonoe, daughter of Cadmus, he fell in love with his sis-ter-in-law Eurydice and pursued her. When he accidentally caused her death by snakebite, the gods punished him by killing his bees. His mother advised him to sacrifice cattle to placate the gods. Nine days after the sacrifice he found swarms of bees in the cattle carcasses. He disap-peared near Mount Haemus. Vergil's *Fourth Ge-orgic* tells the tale, and it is his version of Eurydice's death that Niccolo dell'Abbate fol-lowed in his painting *The Story of Aristaeus*.

See also: APOLLO; AUTONOE; CADMUS; EURY-DICE; ORPHEUS

0330

**Arjuna** (white, bright, silvery)    In the Hindu epic poem *The Mahabharata*, a hero, third of the five Pandu princes/brothers. The diverse ac-counts of his life suggest that he is a composite figure representing several legendary heroes, or that the accounts are regional and relate to a sin-gle figure.

Arjuna's father was the storm god, Indra, and he was taught the use of arms by Drona. His skill was so great that he won the girl Draupadi at her

0331

*svayamvara* (self-choice), a contest of arms at which a girl chose her husband. However, Arjuna's mother, Kunti, not knowing Arjuna had just acquired a bride, commanded him to share his acquisition with his brothers. Thus, Draupadi became the joint wife of all five Pandu brothers. They all agreed that when one of them was making love with Draupadi no other brother was to enter the room. One day, Arjuna, looking for some weapons, walked into the room when his brother Yudhi-shthira and Draupadi were making love. As a punishment Arjuna went into exile. (At the same time, however, Arjuna kept an entire harem.)

While in exile Arjuna experienced many adventures, among which was winning as a gift from the fire god, Agni, the magic bow, Gandiva. Arjuna's exile over, he returned home, only to find that his brother Yudhi-shthira had lost the kingdom in a gambling match. As a result all five Pandu brothers had to go into exile for 13 years. At one time during the long exile Arjuna went on a pilgrimage to the Himalayas to ask the gods to give him celestial weapons to use against the enemy, the Kauravas. At another time Arjuna took a journey to the heaven of his father, Indra.

In the great battle with the Kauravas, Arjuna obtained the help of Krishna (an incarnation of the god Vishnu), who acted as his charioteer. Their great dialogue, which has been inserted into *The Mahabharata*, is called the Bhagavad-Gita.

On the 10th day of the great battle Arjuna wounded the hero Bhishma; on the 12th day he defeated Susarman and his four brothers; on the 14th day he killed Jayadratha; on the 17th, he argued with his brother Yudhi-shthira and would have killed him had it not been for the interference of Krishna, who stopped the fight. Finally, Arjuna and the other Pandavas were victorious over the Kauravas.

Numerous other adventures as well as love affairs of Arjuna are narrated in the epic. In the end he retired to the Himalayas.

In the epic Arjuna is called Aindri because his father was Indra; also Bibhatsu (supercilious);

Dhananjaya (wealth-winning); Gudakesa (tufted hair); Jishu (victorious); Kapidhvaja (ape standard) because his flag bore an ape as a symbol; Kiritin (diademed); Paka-sasana (punisher of the demon Paka); Partha (descent of Pritha); Phalguna because he was born in the month of Phalguna; Savya-sachin (ambidextrous); and Sveta-vahana (white-vehicled).

See also: AGNI; BHAGAVAD-GITA; DRAUPADI; DRONA; INDRA; KRISHNA; *MAHABHARATA, THE;* VISHNU

*Ark of the Covenant*

0332

**Ark of the Covenant or Testimony**    In the Bible, O.T. (Exod. 25:10–22), a chest some 3 feet, 9 inches long, 27 inches broad and deep, made of acacia wood overlaid with gold, and fitted with staves and rings for handles. It was covered with a golden lid called the Mercy Seat, which bore the figures of two cherubim, griffin-like beings derived from Near Eastern mythology. The Ark was a fetish and may have originally contained a live snake god, then an image of a snake, and later the Ten Commandments. It was placed in the Holy of Holies in the temple but later disappeared. It may have been carried away or destroyed as an idol. In medieval Christian symbolism the Ark symbolized the Virgin Mary, who bore, or sheltered, Christ. Many medieval statues of the Virgin would open to show the infant Christ or the crucified Christ inside. The Hollywood movie *Raiders of the Lost Ark* (1981) tells of an attempt to find the ark.

See also: CHERUBIM; GRIFFIN; VIRGIN MARY

0333

**Armageddon** (the mount or city of Megiddo) In the Bible, N.T., name given in the Book of Revelation (16:16) to the site of the last battle between Good and Evil before the Day of Judgment. The word is now used for any great battle.

See also: BIBLE (REVELATION)

0334

**Armida**   In the Charlemagne cycle in medieval legend, a beautiful sorceress. In Torquato Tasso's poem *Jerusalem Delivered* Rinaldo falls in love with Armida and wastes his time in voluptuous pleasure. After his escape from her, Armida followed him and, unable to lure him back, set fire to her palace. She then rushed into the midst of a battle and was killed. When she made love, she wore an enchanted girdle, which "in price and beauty" surpassed all of her other ornaments.

In 1806, when Frederick William of Prussia declared war on Napoleon, his young queen rode about in military costume to arouse popular support. When Napoleon was told, he said, "She is Armida, in her distraction setting fire to her own palace." Armida is the central character of Gluck's opera *Armide*, Haydn's opera *Armida*, Rossini's opera *Armida*, and Dvořák's last opera, *Armida*. She appears in Anthony Van Dyck's *Rinaldo and Armida*, one of his most erotic paintings.

See also: CHARLEMAGNE; RINALDO

0335

**Armilus**   In Jewish legend, false Messiah, offspring of Satan and a beautiful marble statue of a woman in Rome. Armilus will claim to be the Messiah, gaining some followers, but he will be defeated by God or the true Davidic Messiah. In one medieval text he is described as bald, leprous, deaf in one ear, and maimed in his right arm.

0336

**Army of the Dead**   In American folklore of the Civil War, ghosts of Confederate soldiers who still march through certain streets of Charleston, South Carolina. It was believed they were the souls of those dead who could not find rest. This folk belief was fostered by the Ku Klux Klan to frighten blacks, who were told that the white-hooded figures were the spirits of the dead.

See also: GHOST RIDERS

0337

**Arne** (ewe lamb)   In Greek mythology, daughter of Aeolus, king of Magnesia in Thessaly, and Thea, daughter of Chiron the centaur. Poseidon transformed himself into a bull in order to have sexual intercourse with her. On discovering she was pregnant, her keeper Desmontes blinded and placed her in prison. Arne bore two sons, Aeolus and Boeotus. Ovid's *Metamorphoses* (book 6) tells the tale.

See also: AEOLUS; CENTAUR; OVID; POSEIDON

0338

**Aroteh and Tovapod** (Aricoute, Timondonar) In the mythology of the Tupi Indians of Brazil, two primeval magicians who brought the first men and women up from under the earth.

In the beginning there were no men or women on the face of the earth, for they all lived underground. They had long canine teeth like a wild boar's. Their hands and feet were webbed like a duck's. There was little food underground for them to eat. One day the men and women discovered a way out to the upper earth. Aboveground they found two primeval magicians, Aroteh and Tovapod, and stole peanuts and maize from them. At first the magicians believed some animal had taken the food, but when they followed the tracks, they found the hole where the people had come up. They began digging around it and heard screams from the underground. As people emerged from the hole, the two magicians snapped off their tusks and shaped their hands and feet, making them look as humans look today.

Though many men and women came to the earth's surface, some remained underground. When the descendants of all those who came up have died, the underground people, the *kinno*, will then come up and repopulate the earth.

0339

**Aroundight**  In Arthurian legend, the sword of Lancelot of the Lake. Longfellow wrote, "It is the sword of a good knight."

See also: LANCELOT OF THE LAKE

0340

**Artemis** (slayer?, protector?)  In Greek mythology, one of the 12 Olympian gods; goddess of the moon, hunting, and childbirth and patroness of chastity and unmarried girls; daughter of Zeus and Leto and twin sister of Apollo. The Romans equated her with their goddess Diana.

One of the Homeric Hymns (works ascribed to Homer but not written by him) praises her role as female twin to Apollo:

. . . Goddess of the loud chase, a maiden revered, the slayer of stags, the archer, very sister of Apollo of the golden blade. She through the shadowy hills and the windy headlands rejoicing in the chase draws her golden bow, sending forth shafts of sorrow. Then tremble the crests of the lofty mountains, and terribly the dark woodland rings with din of beasts, and the earth

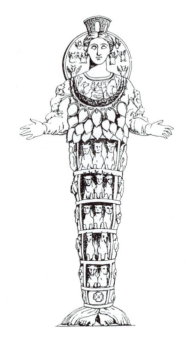

*Artemis*

shudders, and teeming sea. (Translated by Andrew Lang)

The various epithets of the goddess reflect her many roles. She was called Orthia (upright) and Lygodesma (willow bound) because of an image of the goddess that was said to have been found in a thicket of willows and was held upright by willow fronds that twined around it. Artemis was Agrotera (huntress), Coryphaea (of the peak), Limnaea and Limatis (of the lake), Daphnaea (of the laurel), Lyceia or Lycea (wolfish), Aeginaea (goat goddess), Caryatis (of the walnut tree), Ariste (best), Calliste (fairest). Her most famous title was Artemis Plymastus (many-breasted); she appeared in this form at Ephesus. In the New Testament Artemis is called Diana. In Acts 19 the famous temple of Diana of the Ephesians is the great Artemisium at Ephesus, one of the Seven Wonders of the Ancient World. Most literary allusions to the goddess use her Roman name, Diana.

See also: APOLLO; DIANA; LETO; OLYMPIAN GODS; SEVEN WONDERS OF THE ANCIENT WORLD; ZEUS

ARTHUR AND GUENEVERE KISS BEFORE ALL THE PEOPLE

*King Arthur and Guenever*

0341

**Arthur** (bear, hero)   In medieval legend, king of Britain. According to various medieval sources, King Uther Pendragon and Igraine were the parents of King Arthur. Merlin, the magician, built a beautiful castle for Uther Pendragon and placed in it the Round Table, in imitation of the one Joseph of Arimathea had once instituted. The table had places for many knights (the number varies) and a special place was reserved for the Holy Grail, the cup that Christ used at the Last Supper. The Holy Grail had disappeared from Britain because of the sinfulness of the people.

A great festival was announced for the institution of the Round Table. All of the knights came to Carduel (Carlisle), accompanied by their wives. Among the latter was Igraine, wife of Gorlois, lord of Tintagel in Cornwall. When Uther Pendragon saw Igraine he fell in love with her. Igraine already had three or four daughters, famous in Arthurian legends as mothers of the knights Gwain, Gravain, and Ywaine. One of the king's counselors, Ulfin, told of Uther's passion for Igraine, and she told her husband. Indignant at the insult, Gorlois left the court, locked up his wife in the fortress at Tintagel, and gathered an army to fight Uther Pendragon.

The day before the battle Merlin used his magic to change Uther Pendragon into the form of Gorlois. Merlin also transformed himself and Ulfin into the squires of the duke of Cornwall. In this guise the three went to Tintagel, where Igraine opened the gates and received Uther, thinking he was her husband.

The next morning the battle took place. Gorlois was killed. Not long afterward Uther married Igraine, who never suspected that the child soon to be born was not the son of Gorlois. When Arthur was born, he was given to Merlin, who entrusted him to Sir Hector, who brought up Arthur with his own son, Sir Kay. Sir Hector, however, had no idea whose son Arthur was because Merlin never informed him.

Two years later Uther died. His noblemen, not knowing whom to choose as his successor, consulted Merlin, promising to abide by his decision. By Merlin's advice they all assembled in St. Stephen's Church in London on Christmas Day. When Mass was over, they saw a large stone that had mysteriously appeared in the churchyard. The stone was surmounted by an anvil in which the blade of a sword was deeply sunk. Drawing near to examine the sight, they read an inscription on the jeweled hilt. It said that the man who could withdraw the sword was the rightful king. All of those present attempted to pull the sword from the stone, but all failed.

Several years had passed when Sir Hector came to London with his son Sir Kay and his foster son Arthur. Sir Kay, who was to take part in his first tournament, discovered that he had forgotten to bring his sword. Arthur volunteered to ride home to fetch the sword; however, he found the house closed. So he went to the churchyard of St. Stephen, saw the stone with the sword in it, and easily drew it from the anvil.

This mysterious sword was given to Sir Kay by Arthur. Sir Hector, however, recognized the sword and asked Arthur how he had obtained it. At first he refused to believe that Arthur had removed it by himself, but after Sir Hector witnessed Arthur place the sword back in the stone and then withdraw it, he believed.

Because Merlin was known to be an enchanter, rumors spread that Arthur was not Uther Pendragon's son but a child from the sea who had been brought up on the ninth wave and cast ashore at Merlin's feet. Many people, therefore, mistrusted Arthur at first and refused to give him their allegiance. Among the unbelievers were some of the king's own family, notably his four nephews, Gwain, Gaharin, Agravaine, and Garath. Arthur was forced to declare war against them. Although Gwain's strength increased from 9:00 to 12:00 in the morning, and from 3:00 to 6:00 in the afternoon, Arthur succeeded in defeating him by taking advantage of his weak moments, as Merlin advised.

With Merlin's aid Arthur ruled over the land and established peace and justice. But one day, having drawn his blade on Sir Pellinore without reason, the sword suddenly failed and broke. Left without any means of defense, Arthur would have perished had not Merlin used his magic to put Sir Pellinore to sleep and remove Arthur to a safe place.

Deprived of his magic sword, Arthur was at a loss as to what to do. While standing by a lake, he saw a white-draped hand and arm rise out of the water, holding aloft a jeweled sword that the Lady of the Lake, who appeared beside Arthur, told him was intended for his use.

Arthur rowed out to the middle of the lake and secured the sword, which was known as Excalibur. He was then told by the Lady of the

Lake that the sword possessed magic powers. As long as the scabbard remained in Arthur's possession he would not be defeated by anyone.

Thus armed, Arthur went back to his palace and defeated the Saxons who had invaded his land. Arthur then came to the aid of Leodegraunce, King of Scotland, who was threatened by his evil brother Ryance, King of Ireland. Ryance was determined to complete a mantle furred with the beards of kings and wanted to secure Leodegraunce's for the last one. Arthur not only killed Ryance but took the mantle and carried it away as a trophy.

Later Arthur returned to Leodegraunce's court and fell in love with Guinever, the king's daughter. Merlin objected to the marriage unless Arthur first had a successful campaign in Brittany. When the king returned in triumph a wedding was celebrated at Camelot (Winchester) at Pentecost. Arthur received the Round Table as a gift. Earlier Arthur had successfully defeated the 12 kings who had revolted against him. Their remains had been interred at Camelot by his order. There Merlin erected a castle containing a special hall for the reception of the Round Table. The hall was adorned with lifelike statues of all of the conquered kings, each holding a burning taper that Merlin said would burn brightly until the Holy Grail should appear.

The variant legends range from 12 (the mystical number of Christ's Apostles) to more than 100 knights of the Round Table. Among the many knights connected with the Round Table, Lancelot was the handsomest. He fell in love with Guinever, and the queen returned his love. In time the queen was accused of adultery, and Lancelot, who had disappeared for some time, returned to the court to defend her honor, then left for Brittany. Arthur pursued Lancelot, leaving Guinever in the care of Mordred, his nephew, or as some accounts say, his son.

Mordred immediately took advantage of Arthur's absence and seized the throne, saying that Arthur had been killed. He then tried to force Guinever to marry him. At first she refused but finally consented for fear of her life. However,

*Sir Mordred (H. J. Ford)*

she asked Mordred permission to go to London to buy some wedding garments. When the queen arrived in the city she went to the Tower and sent word to Arthur of what had happened. Without delay Arthur abandoned the siege of Lancelot's castle and, crossing the channel, encountered Mordred's army near Dover.

Negotiations took place, and it was agreed that Arthur and a certain number of knights should meet Mordred with an equal number to discuss peace terms. No weapons were to be drawn. A serpent, however, was lurking in the grass when the knights met, and one of them drew his sword to kill it. His drawn sword was taken as a signal to begin the battle. On both sides the slaughter was terrible, and nearly all of the knights were slain. Arthur then encountered Mordred. Summoning all of his strength, the ex-

hausted king finally slew the usurper, but not before Mordred dealt Arthur a mortal blow.

This never would have happened if Morgan le Fay, Arthur's evil sister, had not stolen his magic scabbard and substituted another. All of the enemy's army had perished, and of Arthur's knights only one man remained alive, Sir Bedivere. He hastened to Arthur's side, and Arthur, giving him his sword, asked him to cast it into the lake. At first Bedivere refused but finally did as Arthur asked. As the magic sword touched the waters, Sir Bedivere saw a hand and arm rise up from the depths of the water to seize it, brandish it three times, and disappear.

Arthur gave a sigh of relief when he heard this report. He then told his faithful knight that Merlin had said Arthur would not die. He asked Sir Bedivere to place him on a barge hung with black. Sir Bedivere obeyed, then seeing Arthur about to leave him, he asked permission to accompany him. However, Arthur could not grant the wish because he had to go to Avalon to be cured of his wound and wait to return one day to his sorrowing people.

King Arthur's legend is one of the high points of medieval imagination, representing a portrait of the ideal Christian hero, whose life and deeds often parallel those of his master, Jesus. Some of the analogies to Jesus' life that run through the complex legend are Arthur's birth under mysterious circumstances; his betrayal by a loved one, Guinever; his death at the hands of his enemies; his triumph over death, when he is taken to Avalon, the land of bliss; and finally, the belief that he will return when Britain is in most need.

Around this thread medieval imagination wove a rich tapestry of legends that are still potent today, as witnessed by the success of T. H. White's novel *The Once and Future King* and Lerner and Lowe's Broadway musical *Camelot,* both dealing with Arthur and his legend.

Did King Arthur actually exist? Scholars disagree. Some medievalists believe that King Arthur's legend is based on Artorius, a British war chief, leader of the Romanized Britons against

Saxon war bands that invaded Britain from about 450 onward.

The *Cambrian Annals*, written in the 10th century, say Arthur defeated the Saxons at Mount Badon in 516. According to the same work, he fell in battle with Mordred in 537. In 1113 a medieval chronicle mentions a quarrel between a Cornishman and some French monks about whether King Arthur actually existed at all. But in 1125 the historian William of Malmesbury defended the belief in the historical Arthur. In the first half of the same century, on a portal of the cathedral of Modeno in Italy, masons portrayed a siege of a castle by Arthur and his Knights of the Round Table.

An entire literature, both prose and poetry, grew up in medieval Europe around King Arthur. One of the first accounts is in Geoffrey of Monmouth's Latin work *History of the Kings of Britain*, written in the 12th century, which inspired an account by Wace, a French poet, who turned the chronicle of Geoffrey into some 14,000 lines of French verse. This version was used by Layamon, a priest, for his version of Arthur and British legends, running to some 32,000 lines of alliterative verse. Additions were made by successive writers.

Chrétien de Troyes, who lived in the 12th century at the court of the countess of Champagne in Troyes, based his poem about Arthur (so he said) on earlier written texts, which have not survived. In Geoffrey of Monmouth's telling of Arthur's legend the emphasis is on the hero, but in Chrétien's poems Arthur recedes into the background, and the adventures of Gwain, Yvain, Erec, Lancelot, and Perceval are told.

Chrétien also tells of the love affair between Lancelot and Guinever, King Arthur's wife, and how Arthur was cuckolded. Arthur as the duped husband figures in many later tellings of the legends. The work of Chrétien was followed by Robert de Borron's *Merlin*, written about 1200, in which Arthur's birth, his upbringing, and the drawing of the sword are narrated. The poem *Mort Artu* (Arthur's Death) tells of the disappearance of Arthur's sword, Excalibur, into a magic lake when Arthur is carried away to Avalon.

Sir Thomas Malory's *Morte d'Arthur*, though having a French title, is a masterpiece of English prose of the 15th century in which all of the previous legends were used.

Malory's work was not the last to deal with the King Arthur legends. Tennyson's *Idylls of the King* owes much to Malory's work, but his approach is different. The poet makes the adultery of Lancelot and Guinever the evil cause of the failure of the Round Table. Arthur tends to be more a symbolic figure in Tennyson than a flesh-and-blood creation. Other 19th-century poets, such as William Morris, Swinburne, and Matthew Arnold, also treat the legends. In the 20th century the best versions are those of the American poet Edwin Arlington Robinson, whose *Tristram, Merlin,* and *Lancelot* form a trilogy on Arthurian legends. Mark Twain's *Connecticut Yankee in King Arthur's Court* treats the legends in a less than respectful manner.

See also: AVALON; BEDIVERE, SIR; CAMELOT; EXCALIBUR; GUINEVER; GWAIN; HOLY GRAIL; IGRAINE; LADY OF THE LAKE; MERLIN; MORGAN LE FAY; ROUND TABLE; TINTAGEL; UTHER PENDRAGON

0342

**Aruru**   In Near Eastern mythology (Babylonian-Assyrian), a creator goddess, perhaps a later manifestation of the Great Goddess. Together with the hero god Marduk, she made man. In the Babylonian epic poem *Gilgamesh* she creates Gilgamesh's rival and companion, Enkidu, by washing her hands and taking a bit of clay, which she throws on the ground. In a variant tradition the god Ea is credited with the creation of mankind.

See also: EA; ENKIDU; GILGAMESH; GREAT GODDESS; MARDUK

0343

**Asanga**   In Indian legend, author of some hymns in the Rig-Veda, a collection of hymns to the gods. As a result of a curse by the gods, Asanga was changed into a woman but recovered his form after repenting.

See also: RIG-VEDA

**Ascanius** (tentless)   In Roman mythology, the son of Aeneas and his wife, Creusa. He escaped with his parents and his grandfather, Anchises, from burning Troy. Later Roman mythology makes him the son of Lavinia, a Latin princess. Ascanius succeeded his father as second king and moved the kingdom from Lavinium to Alba Longa, where he and his descendants reigned for 420 years, until the reign of Numitor, son of the Alban king Procas. Ascanius was also called Iulus or Ilus, as well as Julus. The family of Julius Caesar claimed descent from him. Vergil's *Aeneid* (book 1) tells part of his tale.

See also: AENEAS; *AENEID, THE*; LAVINIA

0344

0345

**Asclepius** (Asklepios) (unceasingly gentle?)   In Greek mythology, god of healing and medicine, son of Apollo and Coronis, who was the daughter of a Thessalian prince Phlegyas (or Arsinoe). The wife of Asclepius was Epione (soother), and his most celebrated daughters were Hygieia (fullness bringer), goddess of recovery, Acesis (remedy), Aegle, Iaso (cure), Janisais, and Panacea (all-healing). In Roman religion and mythology he was called Aesculapius. One of his titles was Paean (healer).

Coronis was killed by Artemis for unfaithfulness. Her body, pregnant with Asclepius, was about to be burned on a pyre when Apollo snatched the boy out of her womb and handed him over to the wise centaur Chiron. The centaur instructed Asclepius in all of the healing arts. In a variant myth Coronis accompanied her father on a campaign to the Peloponnesus and bore the child secretly. She exposed it on a mountain to die, but Asclepius was nursed by a herd of goats. When he grew up, his fame as a healer spread. He even brought the dead back to

*Asclepius*

life. Zeus killed Asclepius with a thunderbolt either in fear of his setting men free from death or on a complaint from Hades, god of death. In revenge Apollo slew all of the Cyclopes who forged the thunderbolts. For this insult to Zeus, Apollo had to serve Admetus for a time as a shepherd.

In Homer and Pindar, Asclepius is only a hero doctor and the father of two heroes, Machaon and Podalerius. Asclepius had a widespread cult in the ancient world. Cocks were sacrificed to him. Plato has Socrates say, as his last words, that he owes a cock to Asclepius, the sacrifice for a cure. It was Socrates' ironic way of saying death was the supreme "cure" for life. Asclepius was worshiped as god of healing in groves, beside medicinal springs, and on mountains. The seats of his worship served also as places of cure, where patients left thank offerings and votive tablets describing their complaints and the manner of the cure. Often the cure was effected through the dreams of the patients, who were required to sleep in the sacred building, in which there sometimes stood a statue of Sleep or Dreaming. Asclepius's worship extended all over Greece and its islands and colonies.

At Rome the worship of the god was under the name Aesculapius. His cult was introduced by order of the Sibylline books when a plague in 293 B.C.E. devastated the area. The god was brought from Epidaurus in the shape of a snake. The animal was sacred to the god, and snakes were kept in his temples.

In later times Asclepius was confused with the Egyptian composite god Serapis. He appears in art as a bearded man holding a staff with a serpent coiled around it.

See also: ADMETUS; APOLLO; ARTEMIS; ASCLEPIUS; CENTAUR; COCK; HADES; PHLEGYAS; SERAPIS; ZEUS

0346

**Asgard** (home of the gods)    In Norse mythology, home of the Aesir gods. Asgard was surrounded by an enormous wall and consisted of many palaces, such as Valaskjalf, a hall roofed with silver in which the god Odin lived. Valaskjalf contained a room, Valhalla, the hall of the slain, where those who had died in battle were feasted by the gods. Asgard was encircled by a wall built by the giant Hrim-thurs to protect it from the frost giants. Heimdall was the watchman at the gate to Asgard, which could be reached only by crossing Bifrost Bridge. It was believed that Asgard would be destroyed at the

end of the world, Ragnarok, but finally restored to even greater glory.

See also: AESIR; BIFROST; HEIMDALL; ODIN; RAGNAROK; VALHALLA; VALKYRIES

0347

**Asgardreia**    In northern folklore, a name for the Wild Hunt, also known as Woden's Hunt, which people believed was the souls of the dead let loose during a storm.

See also: WILD HUNT

0348

**Asgaya Gigagei** (red man)    In North American Indian mythology (Cherokee), bisexual deity, either the Red Man or the Red Woman. Believed originally to have been a thunder deity, Asgaya Gigagei is invoked by the medicine man to cure sickness. The sex of the deity varies with the sex of the supplicant.

0349

**Ash**    A tree of the olive family. In world mythology, the ash tree is often the Cosmic Tree or World Tree; in Nordic mythology it is called Yggdrasil. In Hesiod's *Work and Days* the poet tells how Zeus created the "third generation of men" (that is, the Bronze Age) "from ash spears." In North American Indian mythology the Algonquins believed that the creator god shot an arrow into an ash tree, from which the first human beings emerged.

See also: YGGDRASILL; ZEUS

0350

**Asherah**    In Near Eastern mythology (Canaanite), sea goddess, mother of the gods; her son was Ashtar, a Ugaritic god. At ancient Ugarit, Asherah was the mother-goddess, consort of El, and mother of 70 gods, including Baal. She appears as a rival of Yahweh, the Hebrew god, in the Old Testament. She was represented by a plain pole, a carved pole, a triangle on a staff, a cross, a double ax, a tree, a tree stump, a headdress for priests, and a wooden image. Asherah is seen in some texts to be a variant of the Great Mother goddess Ishtar.

See also: BAAL; EL; ISHTAR; YAHWEH

**Ashta-mangala**  0351  In Buddhism, the Eight Glorious Emblems. They are found in numerous Oriental art works. They are the Wheel of the Dharma, the Conch Shell, the Umbrella, the Canopy, the Lotus, the Vase, the Paired Fish, and the Entrails, or Endless Knot. Sometimes a bell is substituted for the Wheel of the Dharma. In Chinese the Eight Glorious Emblems are called *Pa Chi-hsiang*.

See also: DHARMA

**Ashtavakra** (eight crooked limbs)  0352  In Hindu legend, a priest who was cursed by his father before birth and was born deformed.

Kahoda, the father of Ashtavakra, paid so little attention to his wife and her pregnancy that the still unborn child, Ashtavakra, rebuked him for his neglect. Kahoda, angry at the child's impertinence, condemned him to be born deformed. Despite this, when his father was killed, Ashtavakra went to seek vengeance on the sage who had committed the crime. When he got the better of the sage and was ready to throw him into a river (his father had been drowned), the sage told him that he was the son of the god of the waters and had thrown people into the water in order to obtain priests for the cult. Then Ashtavakra was told by the sage to bathe in the waters and he would be healed. He did, and his deformity disappeared.

In a variant of the legend Ashtavakra was standing in water performing penances when he was seen by some Apsaras, water nymphs, who worshiped him. He was so pleased that he told them to ask him for any gift. They asked for the best of men as husbands. Ashtavakra came out of the water and offered himself. When they saw his crooked body, they laughed at him. He was

angry but could not recall the blessing he had given them. He did say, however, that after obtaining the blessing they should fall into the hands of some thieves. The story was told by Vyasa to Arjuna to console him for the loss of the women he had loved.

See also: ARJUNA

**Ashur** (Ashir, Ahshur, Asir, Asshur, Asur)  0353  In Near Eastern mythology (Assyrian), war god married to the chief goddess, Ishtar. Ashur was the patron god of the city of Ashur, a military city situated on the Tigris. It is believed to have been the first city to employ cavalry, horse-drawn chariots, and siege machinery. Ashur was symbolized by a winged disk that enclosed a human figure shooting an arrow. Sometimes he appeared eagle-headed. Other animals associated with Ashur were the bull, the ox, and the lion. His standard was carried into battle to indicate his presence among his faithful followers.

See also: ISHTAR

**Ashva-medha**  0354  In ancient Hindu ritual, a horse sacrifice performed in Vedic times.

In the Hindu epic poem *The Mahabharata*, the Ashva-medha is given great importance. It was performed only by kings, and its performance indicated that a king was a great conqueror. One hundred Ashva-medhas would enable a mortal king to overthrow the throne of Indra, making the mortal the ruler of the entire universe.

During the rite a horse of a particular color was consecrated by the priests, then allowed to wander at will for a year. The king or his representative followed the horse with an army. When the horse entered a foreign country, the ruler of the country was bound either to fight with the invading army or submit. If the king who followed the horse conquered all other kings whose territory he entered, he would return in triumph, ordering a great festival, at which the horse was sacrificed. In some cases, however, the horse was only symbolically sacrificed.

See also: INDRA; *MAHABHARATA, THE*

0355

**Ash Wednesday**   In Christianity, the seventh Wednesday before Easter, the day after "fat Tuesday," or mardi gras. The first day of Lent in the Western church, observed since the sixth century. It is said that the custom was introduced by St. Gregory the Great. The name comes from the ceremony of placing blessed ashes in the form of a cross on the foreheads of the faithful. The priest pronounces the words *Memento homo quia pulvis es et in pulverem reverteris* (Remember, man, that thou art dust, and to dust thou shalt return.) The ashes used in the ceremony are obtained from burning the palms used on the previous Palm Sunday.

Originally, the service was connected with public penance. Sinners would approach the priest shortly before Lent and accuse themselves. The priest then would bring them before the bishop. The sinners, dressed in sackcloth, were assigned acts of penance. Afterward they went into the church and had the ashes imposed on them. The sinners were not allowed to reenter the church until Holy Thursday, when they were reconciled. As part of their penance they had to go barefoot, sleep on straw, and not bathe or cut their hair.

By the end of the 11th century the rite of public penance had been adopted by many of the faithful. Medieval ritual was done away with at the time of the Protestant Reformation, but the Church of England, by special proclamations in 1538 and 1550, continued its use. However, the Puritans objected to any ritual that seemed pagan, and in time it was dropped. *The Book of Common Prayer*, therefore, had no service for the imposing of ashes until the revision of the American prayer book in 1977. The prayer said when ashes are imposed: "Almighty God, you have created us out of the dust of the earth: Grant that these ashes may be to us a sign of our mortality and penitence, that we may remember that it is only by your gracious gift that we are given everlasting life; through Jesus Christ our Savior. Amen."

The ashes are imposed, the celebrant saying: "Remember that you are dust, and to dust you shall return."

Eastern Orthodox churches do not observe Ash Wednesday. Their Lent begins on Monday before Ash Wednesday, which is called Clean Monday. The name refers not only to the cleansing of souls but also to the washing and scrubbing of cooking utensils to remove for the season any trace of meat or fat, which is not allowed to be eaten.

During the Middle Ages in England, France, and Germany a Lenten cloth was used at the altar during Lent. It was made of a large piece of white or purple cloth decorated with crosses or other symbols of the Passion of Christ. Suspended in front of the sanctuary, it was parted in the middle to symbolize the casting out of the penitent congregation from the sight of the altar and was was drawn apart only during the main part of the mass. It was removed during the reading of the Passion on Wednesday of Holy Week.

T. S. Eliot's "Ash Wednesday" (1930) is an example of his Anglican High Church beliefs, stressing the joy found in traditional Christianity.

See also: EASTER; GREGORY THE GREAT, ST.

0356

**Ashwins** (Ashwin) (horsemen)   In Hindu mythology, twin brother gods who preceded Ushas, the dawn. They are young and handsome, bright with golden hair, and ride in a golden chariot drawn by horses or birds. In the Rig-Veda they are "destroyers of foes" and "send adorable light from heaven to men." Some Hindu texts, however, make them into day and night or physicians to the gods. In their role as physicians they are called Dasras and Nasatyas. According to some accounts their mother was Saranyu (fleet runner), who bore them to her husband Vivaswat and then fled, leaving in her place another woman who looked just like her. In a variant account Saranyu took the form of a mare and was mated by Vivaswat, who took the form of a horse. In their haste, however, Vivaswat's semen fell to the ground. Saranyu smelled it, and from the act of smelling it the Ashwins were born.

See also: RIG-VEDA

0357

**Asita**    In Buddhist legend, a hermit sage who told the father of the Buddha that the child born to him would "bring deliverance to the whole world."

0358

**Ask and Embla** (ash and elm)    In Norse mythology, the first man and woman. Odin, Vili, and Ve (or as a variant account lists them, Odin, Hoenir, and Lodehur) were walking along a beach when they found "two stems of wood, out of which they shaped a man and woman," according to the account in the *Prose Edda*. Odin infused them with life and spirit; Vili, with reason and the power of motion; and Ve, with speech and features, hearing and vision.

In another version the dwarfs make human forms of earth, but the gods endow them with life: one gives spirit and life, the second mind and movement, the third appearance, speech, hearing, and vision. From Ask and Embla descended the whole human race. Ask and Embla (the latter also spelled Emla or Emola) appear in the *Poetic Edda*.

See also: HOENIR; ODIN; *POETIC EDDA*; *PROSE EDDA*; VILI

0359

**Asmodeus** (destroyer)    In Jewish and Christian mythology, demon of lust, sometimes identified with the Persian demon Aeshma, "friend of the wounding spear."

Asmodeus is not mentioned in the Hebrew Scriptures, but he is found in many Jewish folktales and the Old Testament apocryphal Book of Tobit. In Tobit he is in love with Sarah, daughter of Raguel. She had been given seven husbands and "the evil Asmodeus had slain each of them before he had been with her as a wife" (Tobit 2:8 RSV). Tobias wished to marry Sarah and, aided by the archangel Raphael, "took the live ashes of incense and put the heart and liver of the fish upon them and made a smoke." When Asmodeus smelled the odor he fled to the remotest part of Egypt, where Raphael made him a prisoner.

The Latin translation of the Book of Tobit adds the fact that Tobias and Sarah defeated the demon because, aside from using the fish spell, they remained chaste for the first three nights of their marriage. "Tobias nights" later became a custom in some parts of Europe. The husband and wife were not allowed to have sexual intercourse for three nights after the wedding. In medieval France, however, the church allowed husbands to buy a license to disregard the custom.

According to various Jewish sources, Asmodeus was the son of Naamah, a mortal woman by either a fallen angel or by Adam before Yahweh had created Eve. Asmodeus was responsible for the drunkenness of Noah in one Jewish tale and the construction of the Temple of Solomon in another. By the use of his magic ring King Solomon forced Asmodeus and his devil cohort to work on the massive undertaking. Asmodeus was not happy, and he devised a plan to get the better of Solomon. One day Solomon foolishly allowed the demon to seize his magic ring. The devil hurled the ring into the bottom of the sea, sent the king into exile, and then ruled in his place. However, Solomon recovered the ring when he found it in the belly of a fish. As punishment for his evil deed, Asmodeus was imprisoned with his demons in a large jar.

In a romance by Le Sage, *Le Diable Boiteux* (The Lame Devil), Asmodeus is released from his bottle or jar by Don Cleofas Zambullo. As a reward for his release, Asmodeus lets his master see into the various lives of people by lifting off the rooftops of their homes. At the end of the romance Don Cleofas marries Serafina with the help of the demon. Le Sage's romance was continued in English by W. Comb in *The Devil upon Two Sticks in England.*

The *Lemegeton*, a textbook of ceremonial magic and conjuration written in the 17th century and often called the *Lesser Key to Solomon*, says that when Asmodeus appears to humans, he rides a dragon, carries a spear, and has three heads: a ram's, a bull's, and a man's. All three, of course, are noted for lechery.

See also: ADAM AND EVE; AESHMA; ANGEL; NOAH; RAPHAEL; SOLOMON

0360
**Asoka** (Ashoka)    Third century B.C.E. King of the Mauryan empire in North India, perhaps converted to Buddhism. In Buddhist works he is portrayed as a king who wished to spread Buddhism throughout his empire, including Ceylon. He is said to have had 64,000 Buddhist monks in his palace and to have had more than 80,000 Buddhist shrines constructed.

0361
**Asopus** (never silent)    In Greek mythology, a river god, son of Poseidon or of Oceanus and Tethys. His wife was Metope, daughter of Ladon. Their children included Pelagon, Pelagus, and Ismenus, and many daughters, who were often abducted and raped by the gods; among them Aegina, Antiope, Cleone, Corcyra, Plataea, Salamis, and Thebe. When his daughter Aegina was carried off by Zeus, Asopus was determined to have his revenge. Asopus chased Zeus and found him in a forest. Zeus, not armed with his thunderbolts, changed himself into a huge stone, and Asopus lost him. Zeus then went to Olympus, where he hurled thunderbolts at Asopus, wounding and laming the river god. According to the ancient Greeks, the reason the Asopus

River flowed so slowly was that the thunderbolts hurled by Zeus left charcoal in the riverbed.

See also: ANTIOPE; LADON; POSEIDON; ZEUS

0362
**Aspen**    A poplar tree with quivering leaves, popularly known as a quaking aspen. In Christian folklore the aspen trembles because it refused to bend to the Christ when the Holy Family made the flight into Egypt. The child Jesus, according to one medieval text, looked at the tree in such a way that "she trembles evermore." In a variant account the aspen was used to make the True Cross, the cross on which Jesus was crucified, and has trembled ever since.

See also: CROSS

0363
**Asphodel Fields**    In Greek mythology, the meadow of the dead. According to Homer's *Odyssey* (book 14), Odysseus saw the dead heroes Achilles, Patroclus, and others in the Asphodel Fields. The asphodel was the flower of the underworld (or Hades).

See also: ACHILLES; HADES; ODYSSEUS; *ODYSSEY, THE*; PATROCLUS

0364
**Ass**    Horselike mammal with large ears, erect mane, and dark stripe along the back. Noted for its stupidity, obstinancy, lewdness, and patience, the ass appears in world folklore and mythology. In Egyptian mythology the ass is associated with the evil god Set. Greek mythology associates the animal with Dionysus, Typhon, Priapus, and Cronos. In the Old Testament, as in Aesop's fables, asses talk (Num. 22:4–24:25). Yahweh, the Hebrew god, talks through the ass to Balaam, a Midianite magician who had set out to curse the Israelites but ended by blessing them. The biblical account does not say what happened to the speaking asses. According to later Jewish legend, an angel slew the animal to make sure the Hebrews would not be tempted to worship it as they

had earlier worshiped the golden calf. Ancient Roman authors accused the Jews of worshiping an ass-headed god, and the Jesuits in the 17th century accused the Masons of the same crime. One medieval bestiary equates the ass with the devil because the ass "brays about the place night and day, hour by hour, seeking its prey." During the Middle Ages, however, at the Feast of Fools, the ass on which Jesus made his triumphal entry into Jerusalem was honored. The congregation, upon reaching the end of each prayer, would bray instead of saying "Amen." The dark stripe running down the back of an ass is crossed by another at the shoulder. According to legend this cross was left on the ass when Jesus rode it into Jerusalem. There are numerous motifs associated with the ass in the *Motif Index of Folk Literature*.

See also: AESOPIC FABLES; BALAAM; DIONYSUS; FOOLS, FEAST OF; PRIAPUS; SET; TYPHON; YAHWEH

0365

**Ass in the Lion's Skin, The**   Aesopic fable found throughout the world.

Once upon a time an ass found a lion's skin and put it on. In this disguise he roamed about, frightening all the silly animals he met. When a fox came along, the ass in the lion's skin tried to frighten him too. But the fox, having heard his voice, said: "If you really want to frighten me, you will have to disguise your bray."

Moral: *Clothes may disguise a fool, but his words will give him away.*

The fable is found in the *Jatakas, or Birth-Stories of the Former Lives of the Buddha.* The ass in the *jataka* is dressed every morning by his master in the lion's skin, so as to obtain free pasturage by frightening away the villagers. The same story is told of a hare in South Africa, and Thackeray includes a reference to it in the prologue to his novel *The Newcomers*.

See also: AESOPIC FABLES; *JATAKA*

0366

**Ass's Brains**   Aesopic fable found in various collections throughout the world.

A lion and a fox went hunting together. The lion, on the advice of the fox, sent a message to the ass, proposing to make an alliance between their two families. The ass came to the place of meeting, overjoyed at the prospect of a royal alliance. But when he arrived the lion simply pounced on the ass and said to the fox: "Here is our dinner for today. Watch you here while I go and have a nap. Woe betide you if you touch my prey."

The lion went away and the fox waited. Finding that his master did not return, he ventured to take out the brains of the ass and eat them. When the lion came back, he soon noticed the absence of the brains. He asked the fox, "What have you done with the brains?"

"Brains, Your Majesty! It had none, or it would never have fallen into your trap."

Moral: *Wit always has an answer ready.*

The fable appears in the great Indian collection *The Panchatantra*, as well as in a rabbinic commentary on Exodus. In both the Indian version and the Greek original the animal loses its heart, which was regarded as the seat of intelligence.

See also: AESOPIC FABLES; *PANCHATANTRA*

0367

**Astarotte**   In the Charlemagne cycle of legends, a friend who by magic conducts Rinaldo from Egypt to Roncesvalles in just a few hours. He appears in Pulci's epic *Il Morgante Maggiore*.

See also: CHARLEMAGNE; MORGANTE; RINALDO

0368

**Astarte** (Aserah, Asherah, Asherat, Ashtart, Ashtoreth)   In Near Eastern mythology, Great Mother goddess worshiped throughout the ancient Near East, identical with the goddess Ishtar.

Astarte was one of the most popular goddesses in the entire pantheon of the Near East; in the

Old Testament she was the great rival of Yahweh, the Hebrew deity, in the affections of the people. The Book of Judges (2:12) tells how the Jews "forsook the Lord God of their fathers, which brought them out of the land of Egypt, and followed other gods, of the gods of people that were round about them, and bowed themselves unto them . . ." Of these many strange gods, often connected with fertility rites, Astarte was the leading female deity. King Solomon built "high places" or sanctuaries "on the right hand of the mountain of corruption . . . for Ashtoreth [a variant of her name] the abomination of the Zidonians" (2 Kings 23:13). Later we are told how the evil King Ahab and his wife, Jezebel, were devoted to the goddess, maintaining some 400 prophets in her honor.

The rivalry between Astarte and Yahweh was in part due to the goddess's role as promoter of fertility in plants, animals, and men. Part of her cult consisted of male and female prostitution. Astarte was so popular that her worship spread to Rome, where it was eagerly accepted. The Roman writer Apuleius, in his novel *The Golden Ass*, cynically describes the priests of Astarte with "their faces daubed with rouge and their eye sockets painted to bring out the brightness of their eyes." Ironically, during the Middle Ages the Christians turned the goddess into a male demon, Astaroth, and connected him with the archdemon Asmodeus. In 1637 Madame de Montespan sacrificed children to Astarte and Asmodeus, "princes of amity," in her attempt to maintain her hold on the affection of Louis XIV.

The goddess has appealed to poets. Milton in his *Ode on the Morning of Christ's Nativity* makes reference to:

. . . mooned Ashtaroth,
Heaven's Queen and Mother both . . .

In *Paradise Lost* (book 1) he again mentions the goddess, spelling her name differently:

With these in troop
Came Astoreth, whom the Phoenicians called

Astarte, Queen of Heaven with Crescent horns.

Milton believed the "crescent horns" referred to the goddess in her role as moon deity, though some scholars associate the horns with the cow, as a symbol of fertility.

Byron, in his poetic drama *Manfred*, gives the name Astarte to the beloved of the suffering hero, Manfred. D. G. Rossetti, the English poet-artist, painted *Astarte Syriaca*, in which the goddess has all of the decking of a pre-Raphaelite beauty—heavy lips and long, waving hair.

The oldest known image of Astarte, at Paphos, portrayed the goddess in the form of a white conical stone. In Canaan and Phoenicia she assumed the form of a cow or had the head of a cow or bull. Later she was symbolized by a star. In later art she was portrayed as the Queen of Heaven, and the lion was her symbol. One statue from Mesopotamia (c. 2000 B.C.E.) portrays a nude woman with a horned headdress wearing earrings and necklace. Cypress groves were sacred to the goddess.

See also: ASMODEUS; ISHTAR; JEZEBEL; SOLOMON; YAHWEH

0369

**Asteria** (heavenly)   In Greek mythology, a daughter of Ceus (Coeus) and Phoebe, both Titans. Asteria was the mother of Hecate by Perses and sister of Leto. (In some accounts Hecate is another form of Artemis.) Asteria was pursued by Zeus against her will; she transformed herself into a quail and leaped into the sea to escape his sexual advances. She then turned into an island, Ortygia. The island later became the birthplace of Apollo and Artemis when Leto, their mother, sought refuge there. Four pillars arose from the sea; the island became anchored and was then called Delos (Asteria). Asteria's fate is narrated in Ovid's *Metamorphoses* (book 6).

See also: APOLLO; ARTEMIS; HECATE; LETO; OVID; ZEUS

0370

**Astolat**   In Arthurian legend, a town identified in Malory's *Morte d'Arthur* as Guildford in Surrey. The Fair Maid of Astolat was Elaine le Blank, who died for love of Lancelot. Tennyson's early poem "The Lady of Shalott" and his longer poem *Lancelot and Elaine* tell the tale. Edward MacDowell's symphonic poem *Lancelot and Elaine* is based on Tennyson's poem.

See also: ELAINE

0371

**Astolpho**   In the Charlemagne cycle of legends, one of the 12 Paladins of Charlemagne. Astolpho was an English duke who joined Charlemagne in his struggle with the Saracens (Muslims). He was a great braggart but very generous, courteous, and handsome. In Ariosto's *Orlando Furioso* he is carried to Alcina's magic isle on the back of a whale. When the enchantress becomes bored with him sexually, she transforms him into a myrtle tree. Astolpho is later disenchanted by Melissa. He also descends to the underworld and takes a trip to the moon to find the wits, or brains, of Orlando (Roland), bringing them back in a vial to cure Orlando of his madness. Logistilla gives Astolpho a book called *Astolpho's Book*, which will direct him on his journeys. He also has a horn, another gift from Logistilla. Whenever it is sounded, any human or animal within hearing distance is seized with panic and becomes an easy prey of Astolpho.

See also: CHARLEMAGNE; MYRTLE; PALADINS, THE TWELVE; ROLAND

0372

**Astraea** (starry)   In Roman mythology, goddess of justice; daughter of Zeus and Themis; sister of the Moerae and the Horae; sometimes called Dike; she lived on earth during the Golden Age but fled when men became wicked. She was placed among the constellations of the Zodiac as Virgo. Vergil refers to the goddess in his *Fourth Eclogue*: "Now returns the Virgin, too, the Golden Age returns." Dryden, the English poet, wrote *Astraea Redux* (1660) to celebrate the return of Charles II after the harsh rule of Cromwell. Alexander Pope also used the image in his poem *Messiah*, which deals with the coming of Christ. Pope used the name directly in *Imitations of Horace* (First Epistle, Second Book) when he writes:

> The stage how loosely does Astraea tread,
> Who fairly puts all characters to bed.

The lines refer to Mrs. Aphra Behn, who used the *nom de plume* Astraea. She wrote plays in which women often had to resort to sex to win their ends. In *The Faerie Queene* by Spenser the knight of Justice, Artegall, is brought up by Astraea.

See also: THEMIS; ZEUS

0373

**Astraeus** (starry)   In Greek mythology, a Titan, son of Crius and Eurybia; brother of Pallas and Perses. He was the father by Eos, the goddess of dawn, of the stars, and of the winds—Boreas, Hesperus, Notus, Phosphorus, Zephyrus, and, according to some accounts, Aura. He was also an enemy of Zeus.

See also: BOREAS; HESPERUS; PALLAS; TITANS; ZEPHYRUS; ZEUS

0374

**Astyanax** (king of the city)   In Greek mythology, a young son of Hector and Andromache. He was saved from burning Troy by his mother, only to be thrown from its towers by the Greeks, who feared he would grow up to avenge the death of his father, Hector. Odysseus advised that the child be killed. In some variant accounts Menelaus is said to have killed the boy or Achilles' son Pyrrhus (Neoptolemus). Astyanax appears in Homer's *Iliad* (book 6), Vergil's *Aeneid* (book 2), and Ovid's *Metamorphoses* (book 13). Astyanax was also known as Scamandrius.

See also: ANDROMACHE; HECTOR; *ILIAD, THE;* MENELAUS; ODYSSEUS; OVID

0375

**Asuras** (divine beings)    In Hindu mythology, demons often in combat with the gods. In the epic myths contained in the *Puranas* and other late Hindu writings, the Asuras are powerful evil beings. In the earlier Vedas, however, the name Asuras is often applied to the gods themselves, rather than to their enemies, the demons.

See also: *PURANAS; VEDAS*

0376

**Ataensic**    In North American Indian mythology (Iroquois), sky woman, creator goddess, mother of twin brothers, Hah-gweh-di-yu (sapling) and Hah-gweh-da-et-gah (flint), one good and one evil.

Long ago there grew one stately tree that branched beyond the range of vision. Perpetually laden with fruit and blossoms, the air was fragrant with the tree's perfume. People gathered under its shade when councils were held. One day the Great Ruler said to his people: "We will make a new place where another people may grow. Under our council tree is a great cloud sea that calls for our help. It is lonesome. It knows no rest and calls for light. We will talk to it. The roots of our council tree point to it and will show the way."

Having commanded that the tree be uprooted, the Great Ruler peered into the depths where the roots had grown. He then summoned Ataensic, the sky woman, who was with child, and asked her to look down. She saw nothing. The Great Ruler, however, knew that the sea voice was calling and bidding Ataensic to carry light to it. He wrapped a great ray of light around Ataensic and sent her down to the cloud sea.

When the animals saw the blinding light they became frightened.

"If it falls, we will be destroyed," they said.

"Where can it rest?" asked Duck.

"Only the *oeh-da* [earth] can hold it," said Beaver, "the *oeh-da*, which lies at the bottom of our waters. I will bring it up."

The beaver went down but never returned. Then Duck ventured, but soon his dead body floated to the surface.

Many other divers also failed. Then Muskrat, knowing the way, volunteered. He soon returned bearing a small portion of mud in his paw. "But it is heavy and will grow fast," he said. "Who will bear it?"

Turtle was willing, and *oeh-da* was placed on his hard shell. Hah-nu-nah, the turtle, then became the earth bearer. The *oeh-da* grew, and Ataensic, hearing the voices under her heart, one soft and soothing, the other loud and contentious, knew that her mission to people the island was nearing. Inside Ataensic were the twin brothers Hah-gweh-di-yu, who was good, and Hah-gweh-da-et-gah, who was evil. Hah-gweh-da-et-gah, discovering that there was some light coming from his mother's armpit, thrust himself through it, causing Ataensic's death. Hah-gweh-di-yu, however, was born in the natural manner. Foreknowing their power, each claimed dominion over the other. Hah-gweh-di-yu claimed the right to beautify the land, whereas Hah-gweh-da-et-gah was determined to destroy it.

Hah-gweh-di-yu shaped the sky with the palm of his hand and created the sun from the face of his dead mother, saying, "You shall rule here where your face will shine forever." But the evil brother set darkness in the western sky to drive the sun down before it. The good brother then drew forth the moon and the stars from the breast of his mother and led them to the sun as its sisters who would guard the night sky. He gave to the earth her body, its Great Mother, from whom was to spring all life.

The two then created all that is on the earth. Hah-gweh-di-yu created mountains, valleys, forests, fruit-bearing trees, and good animals, such as the deer. Hah-gweh-da-et-gah, the evil one, created monsters that dwell in the sea, hurricanes, tempests, wild beasts that devour, grim flying creatures that steal life from helpless victims, and creeping poisonous reptiles.

When the earth was completed, Hah-gweh-di-yu bestowed a protecting spirit on each of his creations. He then asked his evil brother to make peace, but Hah-gweh-da-et-gah refused and challenged Hah-gweh-di-yu to combat, the victor to be ruler of the earth.

Hah-gweh-da-et-gah proposed weapons that he could control—poisonous roots strong as flint, monster's teeth, and fangs of serpents. But these Hah-gweh-di-yu refused, selecting the thorns of the giant crabapple tree, which were arrow pointed and strong.

They fought with the thorns, and Hah-gweh-da-et-gah was defeated. Hah-gweh-di-yu, having become ruler of the earth, banished his brother to a pit under the earth, whence he cannot return. But he still retains servers, half human and half beasts, whom he sends to continue his destructive work. They can assume any shape or form. Hah-gweh-di-yu the good, however, is continually creating and protecting.

See also: EARTH DIVER: GLUSKAP AND MALSUM; IOUSKEHA AND TAWISCARON

**0377**

**Atago-Gongen**    In Japanese Buddhist mythology, god worshiped on Mount Atago in the province of Yamashiro; he is the patron god of fire. His temple, built in the eighth century C.E., became popular with the military caste, and numerous warriors came to pray to the god, who is portrayed as a Chinese warrior on horseback.

**0378**

**Atai**    In African mythology (Efik of Nigeria), wife of the sky god Abassi who sent death into the world. Abassi placed the first couple on earth but forbade them to work or produce children for fear they would become more powerful than he. But the couple produced food and children, provoking Abassi to ask his wife Atai to punish them. She sent death and discord into the world to plague humankind.

See also: ABUK AND GARANG; ADAM AND EVE; ASK AND EMBLA

**0379**

**Atalanta** (equal in weight, unswaying)    In Greek mythology, two women: Atalanta of Arcadia, a virgin huntress, daughter of Iasus and Clymene; and Atalanta of Boeotia, daughter of Schoeneus, king of Scyros. Some scholars, however, regard the two as one person.

Atalanta of Arcadia was the supposed daughter of Iasus of Arcadia, though her real father was Zeus. Iasus wanted a son, and when Atalanta was born he exposed the girl on a mountain to die. (It was a common practice of the Greeks to let their female infants die.) Artemis, however, protected the child by sending a she-bear to nurse Atalanta until the child was found by a band of hunters, who rescued her and brought her up. Atalanta was told that if she married she would be unhappy, so she avoided men. She devoted her time to hunting and became so skilled that she killed two centaurs who had attempted to rape her. Some ancient accounts say Atalanta was with the Argonauts in the quest for the Golden Fleece.

Meleager of Calydon fell in love with her and invited her to join the Calydonian boar hunt. The men, however, objected. Meleager said he would leave if Atalanta was not accepted, and the men reluctantly accepted her. Atalanta was the first to draw blood from the boar. Ancaeus, another hunter, said he would teach her how to kill a boar. He attacked the boar and was disemboweled by the boar's tusks. Meleager then struck the fatal blow and presented Atalanta with the boar's hide and tusks. The men of the hunt were insulted by his presenting the prize to a woman.

According to some accounts, Atalanta and Meleager had a son, Parthenopaeus, who was exposed by his mother on a mountain to die. She then pretended she had never married and was a virgin. Atalanta returned home and was welcomed by her father, who now wished to see her married. She remembered the oracle that said she would be unhappily married and devised a means to defeat her father's schemes. She informed her suitors that whoever wanted to marry her must first beat her in a foot race, but whoever lost to her in the race must die. Many suitors died as a result, but they still came. One, Hippomenes (or Melanion), prayed to Aphrodite, goddess of love, to help him win Atalanta. The goddess brought three golden apples from her garden on the island of Cyprus and gave them to Hippomenes with directions for their proper use. The race was begun, and Atalanta was about to pass Hippomenes when he dropped one of the golden apples. Atalanta slowed down to pick it up. Hippomenes then dropped the second and third apples and won the race. At first Atalanta did not want to honor her bargain, but eventually she did. The two were so happy that they forgot to thank Aphrodite. The goddess then made them offend Zeus or Cybele by causing them to make love in the deity's temple. Because of the sacrilege, Atalanta was transformed into a lioness and Hippomenes into a lion. The two were then yoked to Cybele's chariot to draw it for eternity. The other Atalanta, of Boeotia (or perhaps the same one), was the daughter of the king of Scyros. She married Hippomenes (or Melanion).

Atalanta's myth is told in Ovid's *Metamorphoses* (book 10), in which Venus narrates the tale to Adonis. This was the version painted by Poussin. The tale is also told in *The Earthly Paradise* by William Morris and in Swinburne's play *Atalanta in Calydon*.

See also: APHRODITE; ARGONAUTS; ARTEMIS; CALYDONIAN BOAR HUNT; CENTAUR; GOLDEN FLEECE; MELEAGER; OVID; VENUS; ZEUS

0380
**Atar** (Ataro)   In Persian mythology, fire god, protector against demons; son of the good god, Ahura Mazda. Atar watched over pregnant women and bitches and blessed those who brought him dry wood for the fire sacrifice. One myth records his battle with the demon Azhi Dahaka. The demon tried to seize the Divine Glory by rushing toward it and trying to extinguish it. (It would seem to be some form of fire or light.) However, Atar cursed Azhi Dahaka, saying he would burn his "hinder part" if he did

not give in. Threatened with such violence to his person, the demon relented.

See also: AHURA MAZDA; AZHI DAHAKA

0381
**Atargatis** (Atarate, Atargate, Atharate)   In Near Eastern mythology (Hittite), mother goddess, associated with the moon and fertility; called Dea Suria in Roman mythology.

Atargatis was born from an egg that the sacred fishes found in the Euphrates and pushed ashore. Her shrine at Ascalon had a pool near her temple that contained sacred fish. The Old Testament Apocrypha book 2 Maccabees (12:26) tells how Judas Maccabeus "marched forth to Carnion, and to the temple of Atargatis, and there he slew five and twenty thousand persons." A marginal note to the King James Version says in reference to Atargatis, "That is, Venus."

Atargatis's cult was very popular in the Near East, and she was known under various names. The Phoenicians called her Dereto, and some scholars believe the goddess Atheh, worshiped at Tarsus, was another version of the goddess. The Greeks identified her with Aphrodite.

In art Atargatis was sometimes portrayed as half woman and half fish. Doves were sacred to her, and fish were used in her worship.

See also: APHRODITE; ATHEH

0382
**Atchet** (the nurse?)   In Egyptian mythology, goddess associated with the sun god Ra and in some texts considered the female counterpart of the sun god. Atchet may have been a deity associated with nursing children.

See also: RA

0383
**Ate** (reckless guilt, ruin)   In Greek mythology, a goddess of discord, evil, mischief, and infatuation and the personification of moral blindness; daughter of Zeus and Eris; identified by the Romans with their goddess Discordia. Ate was cast

out of heaven by Zeus because she had misled him. One day, according to Homer's *Iliad* (book 19), Zeus, tricked by Ate, boasted among the gods that on that day a man should be born, mightiest of his race, who should rule over many. Hera saw an opportunity to deceive Zeus, who was waiting for the birth of Heracles by one of Hera's female rivals. After getting Zeus to make an oath that he would keep his word, Hera persuaded the goddess of childbirth to delay Heracles' birth and hasten that of Eurystheus, who then had power even over Heracles. Ate was not invited to the marriage of Peleus and Thetis. Angry, she wrote "For the fairest" on the Golden Apple and rolled it into the midst of the gathering. The goddesses all claimed it. Zeus refused to make judgment, and the matter was given to Paris. His choice of Aphrodite caused the Trojan War. Behind Ate go the Litai (prayers), the lame, wrinkled, squinting daughters of Zeus. They can heal the evils of Ate, but they bring new evils upon the stubborn. Hesiod's *Theogony* mentions the goddess.

See also: APHRODITE; HERA; HERACLES; HESIOD; *ILIAD, THE*; PELEUS; THETIS

0384

**Atea and Papa** (sky and flat)   In Polynesian mythology, the sky and the earth, who were later made into gods. In one myth the couple held themselves in such a tight sexual embrace that none of their children could free themselves. Finally, the children conspired to kill their mother and father, but one of the children, Tane, suggested that the two be separated. This was done, forming the sky and earth.

See also: TANE

0385

**Aten** (Aton, Adon, Eton)   In Egyptian mythology, the sun disk worshiped by Akhenaton (1372–1355 B.C.E.). Surviving hymns to Aten emphasize his role as a benevolent creator. He is said to have "made everything according to his

heart" when he was alone. One hymn to Aten by the pharaoh has been preserved. It opens:

Thy rising is beautiful in the horizon of heaven, O thou Aten, who hadst thine existence in primeval time. When thou riseth in the eastern horizon thou fillest every land with thy beauties. Thou art beautiful to see, and art great, and art like crystal, and art high above the earth. Thy beams of light embrace the land, even every land which thou hast made. Thou art as Ra, and thou bringest thyself unto each of them, And thou bindest them with thy love. Thou art remote, but thy beams are upon the earth.

Although this extract from the hymn gives some idea of Akhenaton's views and those of his followers concerning the Aten, it is still impossible to gather precise information about the details of cult and belief. Incense was burned several times a day, and hymns were sung to the Aten, accompanied by harps and other instruments. Offerings to the deity consisted of fruits and flowers, with no animal sacrifice. Worship was joyous. Mika Waltari's novel *The Egyptian* deals with the failure of Akhenaton to convince the priests to worship the Aten over other gods.

See also: AKHENATON

0386

**Athaliah** (Yahweh has shown his sublimity)   In the Bible, O.T., queen, the daughter of Ahab and Jezebel and the wife of Joram, king of Judah. After Joram's death, Athaliah's son Ahaziah took the throne after killing the princes of King David's house. Athaliah ruled for six years. When Joash, who had escaped massacre, was proclaimed rightful king, Athaliah entered the temple, where she was killed by the mob (2 Kings 11). Jean Racine's play *Athalie* uses the biblical legend. Mendelssohn wrote incidental music for the play.

See also: DAVID; JEZEBEL

**Athamas** (reaper on high)    In Greek mythology, a king of Achaea, Orchomenus, Phthiotis, or Thebes (ancient accounts vary); son of Aeolus and Enarete; husband of Nephele; father of Phryxus and Helle. Anthamas later married Ino, daughter of Cadmus, and the couple had two sons, Learchus and Melicertes. His children fled to Colchis on a golden ram to escape the wrath of their jealous stepmother, Ino, who resented Athamas's preference of them over her own children. Athamas accidentally killed his son Learchus, mistaking him for a stag.

See also: AEOLUS; CADMUS

0388

**Athanasius, St.** (immortal)    c. 296–373. In Christian legend, bishop of Alexandria; one of the Greek Doctors of the Church. Feast, 2 May.

A pupil of St. Anthony the Abbot, Athanasius wrote what is considered the first full-length biography of a saint. He is best known for the Athanasian Creed, which scholars now say was not composed by the saint, though the saint was a staunch defender of orthodoxy over Arianism, a heresy of the early church. The Athanasian Creed is one of three creeds accepted by the Roman and the Anglican Churches. In Christian art he is portrayed as old, bald, and with a long white beard, wearing vestments of the Greek church.

See also: ANTHONY THE ABBOT, ST.; DOCTORS OF THE CHURCH

0389

**Atheh**    In Near Eastern mythology, goddess worshiped at Taraus, portrayed wearing a veil and seated on a lion. Some scholars believe Atheh to be another version of the Hittite mother goddess, Atargatis.

See also: ATARGATIS

0390

**Athena** (Athene) (queen of heaven)    In Greek mythology, one of the 12 Olympian gods; goddess of wisdom, skill, and warfare; identified with Minerva by the Romans. Athena was born, full grown, out of the head of Zeus, who had swallowed his first wife Metis (counsel) for fear that she would bear a son superior to himself. Hephaestus (or Prometheus) opened Zeus's head with an ax, and Athena sprang forth clad in armor. Her ancient epithet Tritogeneia (born of Triton or the roaring flood) would seem to indicate that she was the daughter of the ocean. Oceanus, according to Homer, was the origin of all things, all gods and goddesses.

*Athena repressing the fury of Achilles (John Flaxman)*

Athena had a prominent place in ancient Greek religion. When solemn oaths were to be taken, her name was invoked along with those of Zeus and Apollo. Athens, named for her, was the most important seat of her worship. The names of Athena's earliest priestesses, the daughters of Cecrops—Aglaurus, Pandrosus, and Herse—signify the bright air, the dew, and the rain.

Athena was important in agriculture. The sowing season was opened in Attica by three sacred rites of plowing, two of which honored Athena as inventor of the plow. It was Athena who taught man to attach oxen to the yoke, and it was she who gave man the olive tree. Her chief feast was the Panathenaea, which was originally a harvest festival but later became a festival to honor the intellectual gifts of Athena.

Athena's birth story influenced Milton's *Paradise Lost* (book 2), in which the poet describes the birth of Sin from the head of Satan.

Among artworks inspired by Athena, one of the best-known statues was the Palladium, an image that was believed to have fallen from heaven. A priestly family in Athens had charge of the sacred image. It was believed that as long as the statue was safe, the city of Athens was safe. The Trojans had the statue earlier, and the fall of Troy is sometimes attributed to its removal, either by Odysseus and Diomedes or by Aeneas when he left the city. Athens, Argos, and Rome all claimed to have the real statue. Matthew Arnold's poem "Palladium" contains the lines:

And when it fails, fight as we will, we die;
And while it lasts, we cannot wholly end.

Another famous image, contained in the Parthenon, was the gold-and-ivory statue by Phidias, of which we have only small copies. Another statue by Phidias, a 30-foot bronze of Athena the warrior, stood by the Propylaea, the great marble gateway at the west end of the Acropolis.

*Athena (Minerva)*

In works of art Athena is usually portrayed with a shield and a spear and holding the bleeding head of Medusa. The olive, the cock, the owl (late classical times), the crow, and the serpent were sacred to her. Among Athena's epithets were Athena Polias (of the city), Poliatas (keeper of the city), Ergane (worker) as patroness of workers in the decorative arts, Athena Leitis (goddess of beauty), Paeonia (healer), Athena Zosteria (girder) when she armed for battle, Athena Anemotis (of the winds) as goddess of winds and rains, Promachorma (protector of the anchorage), Pronaea (of the foretemple), Pronoia (forethought), Xenia (hospitable), Larisaea (of Larisa), Ophthalmitis (of the eye), Cissaea (ivy phasium), Aeantis (Ajacian), Aethyia (Gannet), Agoraea (of Hippola), Athena Nike (victory) for her special temple on the Acropolis at Athens, Parthenon (virgin or maiden), and Athena Promachus (champion), which inspired the statue by Phidias. Among the myths associated with Athena are the giving of the magic bridle to Bellerophon, helping Perseus kill Medusa, teaching Argus to build the ship *Argo*, teaching Epeius to build the wooden horse (she sided with the Greeks), giving dragon's teeth to Cadmus and Aeetes, and helping Heracles, Diomedes, Odysseus, and Tydeus. Athena appears in Homer, Vergil, the Homeric Hymns, Pausanias, Ovid, Aeschylus, Sophocles, and in English literature often, though generally under the Roman form of her name, Minerva.

See also: AENEAS; DIOMEDES; METIS; MINERVA; OCEANUS; ODYSSEUS; OLYMPIAN GODS; PALLADIUM; PROMETHEUS

0391

**Atlacamanc**   In Aztec mythology, a storm god, often identified as the male counterpart of Chalchihuitlicue, the Aztec storm goddess.
See also: CHALCHIHUITLICUE

0392

**Atlantes**   In the Charlemagne cycle of legends, a wizard who educated Ruggiero in all of the manly arts. He appears in Ariosto's *Orlando Furioso*.

See also: CHARLEMAGNE; ROLAND

0393

**Atlantis**   In European legend, an island that was destroyed by a tidal wave. It is possible that the legend of Atlantis was a recollection of the destruction of the island of Thera, now Santorina, which had a volcanic eruption about 1450 B.C.E. and destroyed Knossos, as well as leaving ash on eastern Crete. Supposedly, the island of Atlantis had attempted to enslave its neighbors but was defeated by Athens and then destroyed by a tidal wave. The idea of an ideal island still fascinates many, and Atlantis is popular in contemporary folklore. Plato, in his *Timaeus*, says the story was told to Solon in Egypt. Seneca's *Medea* also cites Atlantis in a chorus, though he does not use the name.

0394

**Atlas** (he who dares or suffers)   In Greek mythology, son of the Titan Iapetus and Clymene (or Aisa); brother of Menoetius, Prometheus, and Epimetheus. Atlas was a Titan who sided with the Titans against Zeus and was condemned by Zeus to stand in the west holding up the sky on his shoulders. His burden was relieved by Heracles while Atlas fetched for Heracles the Golden Apples of the Hesperides. In one early myth Atlas was visited by Perseus and was inhospitable. Perseus turned him into stone by showing him the Gorgon's head. The stone became Mount Atlas in northwestern Africa. Homer makes Atlas the father of Calypso. Other accounts say the Pleiades are his daughters. Because he was associated with the sky, it was believed during the Middle Ages that Atlas had taught man astrology. A book of maps is called an atlas because the figure of Atlas with the world on his shoulders was used by the 16th-century mapmaker Mercator on the title page of his book.

Atlantiades (offspring of Atlas) was a patronymic of Hermes, the Pleiades, and the Hesperides. The seven daughters of Atlas, the Pleiades, were Alcyone, Celaeno, Electra, Maia, Merope, Sterope or Asterope, and Taygete. Atlas appears or is mentioned in Vergil's *Aeneid* (book 4), Hesiod's *Theogony*, and Ovid's *Metamorphoses* (book 4). Heinrich Heine's poem on Atlas was set to music by Franz Schubert. The Titan also appears in Rockefeller Center, New York, in a rather gross statue.

See also: AENEID, THE; ALCYONE; CALYPSO; CELAENO; ELECTRA; GOLDEN APPLES OF THE HESPERIDES; GORGON; HERACLES; MAIA; OVID; PERSEUS; PLEIADES; PROMETHEUS; TITAN

0395

**Atlatonan**   In Aztec mythology, goddess "of the leprous and maimed," according to Fray Diego Durán in his *Book of the Gods and Rites* (c. 1576), dealing with Aztec mythology and ritual. She was one of the wives of Tezcatlipoca.

See also: TEZCATLIPOCA

0396

**Atlaua** (master of waters)   In Aztec mythology, a water god, also associated with arrows. Armed with reed arrows he emerges as a Quetzal bird, the Aztec symbol of regeneration.

See also: PHOENIX

0397

**Atman** (Sanskrit root *an*, "to breathe")   In Hinduism, the essence of life, often translated as soul, spirit, ego, world spirit, or world soul.

0398

**Atnatu**   In Australian mythology, self-created god who punished some of his children by casting them out of heaven through a hole in the sky.

0399

**Atreus** (fearless)   In Greek mythology, king of Mycenae; son of Pelops and Hippodameia; brother of Alcathous, Astydameia, Chrysippus,

Copreus, Lysidice, Nicippe, Pittheus, Thyestes, and Troezen; married to Aerope; father of Agamemnon, Menelaus, and Anaxibia; grandson of Tantalus.

Atreus, with the help of his brother Thyestes, murdered his step-brother Chrysippus. To escape the wrath of their father, the two took refuge with their brother-in-law Sthenelus, king of Mycenae, who gave them the kingdom of Media. Eurystheus, the brother of Sthenelus, was killed in a battle, and his kingdom, Argos, was taken over by Atreus, who ruled with the scepter made by the god Hephaestus and given him by his father, Pelops. Atreus's first wife was Cleola, who died in childbirth after delivering a son, Plisthenes. Atreus then married Aerope. Their children were Agamemnon, Menelaus, and Anaxibia. Hermes had given Atreus a horned lamb with a golden fleece which was to be sacrificed to Artemis. Instead Atreus killed the lamb and had it stuffed and mounted. He proclaimed that whoever possessed the golden lamb possessed the right to the throne. Thyestes, with the aide of Aerope, conspired against Atreus and stole the lamb. Thyestes was thereupon acknowledged king. Atreus then made a bargain with Thyestes that if he, Atreus, could cause the sun to reverse its path in the heavens, his throne would be restored to him. With the aid of Zeus and Eris the feat was accomplished, and Atreus was restored. This, however, did not please Thyestes, and he arranged for the murder of Plisthenes, Atreus's son. To avenge Plisthenes' death, Atreus killed one of Thyestes' sons and invited Thyestes to a banquet. After he had eaten, Atreus told him he had eaten the flesh of his own child. Thyestes then placed a curse on the house of Atreus and went into exile, where he met and raped Pelopia, not knowing she was his daughter. A famine in the kingdom had followed Thyestes' curse, and and an oracle told Atreus he must bring back Thyestes in order to end it. Atreus cast the unfaithful Aerope into the sea and went in search of Thyestes. He came upon Pelopia at about the time she was to deliver Thyestes' son, Aegisthus, whom she exposed to die on a mountain. Atreus rescued Aegisthus and brought him up as his own son. Years later Atreus succeeded in bringing Thyestes back and putting him in prison. He then instructed Aegisthus to kill Thyestes. When Thyestes discovered that Aegisthus was the son of Pelopia, he knew that he was the boy's father. He revealed his identity to his son, and the two plotted against and killed Atreus.

The tale of the House of Atreus, made of the stories of Agamemnon, Menelaus, Clytemnestra, Helen, Aegisthus, Orestes, Electra, and Iphigenia, inspired eight of the 33 surviving Greek tragedies and also inspired modern dramatists and poets such as Eugene O'Neill and T. S. Eliot.

See also: AEGISTHUS; AEROPE; AGAMEMNON; ATREUS; HEPHAESTUS; HERMES; MENELAUS; PELOPS; ZEUS

0400

**Attila** (little father)   404–453. In medieval history and legend, king of the Huns, known as the Scourge of God, who was stopped by Pope Leo I. Attila and his army ravaged the eastern Roman Empire for several years, then made peace with Emperor Theodosius. The Hun then turned toward the western empire and was defeated by Aetius, the Roman general, in 451. Undaunted, Attila then invaded northern Italy as far as the Po River. He was met by Pope Leo I, who came to plead with the invader to spare Rome from destruction. To the amazement of everyone, Attila removed his army. When asked why, he said, "While Pope Leo was speaking, I distinctly saw two shining beings of venerable aspect, and manifestly not of this earth, standing by his side. They had flaming swords in their hands, and menaced me with death if I refused to withdraw the army." The two beings, according to the account of Damasus in his *Lives of the Popes*, were St. Peter and St. Paul. But the truth is that Attila agreed to leave Italy in return for the Princess Honoria and her vast dowry, according to Gibbon in his *Decline and Fall of the Roman Empire.*

Tradition has it that he was murdered by his German wife on their wedding night. The medieval legend inspired Raphael's fresco in the Stanza d'Eliodoro in the Vatican Museum, *The Encounter of Attila and Leo I*, Delacroix's mural *Attila Tramples Italy and the Arts*, and William von Kaulbach's *Hunnenschlacht* (The Battle of the Huns), which in turn inspired Franz Liszt's symphonic poem of the same name. Attila appears in Corneille's play *Attila* and Verdi's opera *Attila*. He also appears as the character Etzel in the medieval epic *Nibelungenlied*, in which he is married to Kriemhild and assists her in taking revenge on her family for murdering her husband Siegfried. He also appears in the earlier work, *Volsunga Saga*, in which he is called Atli.

See also: SAINTS; *NIEBELUNGENLIED*; *VOLSUNGA SAGA*

0401

**Attis** (Atys, Attes) (luckless)   Phrygian god of death and resurrection, annually mourned and rejoiced over at a festival in spring. Attis was a handsome young shepherd who was loved by the goddess Cybele, mother of the gods. Cybele's chief shrine was at Phrygia, the name given to a large area in ancient Asia Minor. Some myths say Attis was the son of Cybele, though most texts give Nana, a virgin, as his mother. She conceived him by putting a ripe almond or pomegranate in her bosom. His death, however, was the major motif of his myth. In one account he was killed by a boar. According to a variant text, Attis castrated himself under a pine tree and bled to death on the spot. Worship of Attis and Cybele spread to Rome in the second century B.C.E. Attis, in the form of a pine log covered with violets, was annually mourned, as were Tammuz and Adonis, at a spring festival, part of which consisted of self-mutilation of Cybele's priests. The Roman poet Catullus, in his *Carmina*, tells of one priest, named after the god, who castrated himself and then lamented his rash act. Catullus reflects the rites in such a way that the priest of the poem is literally possessed with a religious frenzy of un-

bridled proportions, which is so strong that it compels him to commit the castration. It is only after the heat of the moment has sufficiently subsided that the priest realizes the effect of his actions.

See also: ALMOND; POMEGRANATE; TAMMUZ

0402

**Audhumla** (Audhumbla, Audumla) (rich, hornless cow)   In Norse mythology, the primeval cow at creation, formed from vapors. She fed the primeval giant Ymir and lived by licking the salt from stones. On the first day she licked the stones the hairs of a man appeared. On the second day a human head appeared. On the third day "an entire man appeared, who was endowed with beauty, agility and power," according to the *Prose Edda*. The man was Bur, father of Bor, who married the giantess Bestla; she bore three gods, Odin, Vili, and Ve. A similar pattern is found in Tacitus's *Germania* (98 C.E.), where he traces the origin of the Germans to an earth-born god Tuisco and his son Mannus, who then had three sons.

See also: *PROSE EDDA*; YMIR

0403

**Auge** (Auga, Augea) (radiance)   In Greek mythology, a goddess of childbirth, an Arcadian princess, priestess of Athena; daughter of Aleus, king of Tegea, and Naera. She was raped by Heracles and bore him a son, Telephus. Auge's father, Aleus, did not believe Heracles to be the father of her child and ordered Nauplius to drown Auge and expose the baby on Mount Parthenius to die. Instead of drowning Auge, Nauplius sold her to King Teuthras, who adopted her as his daughter. Telephus was rescued by a shepherd and reached manhood. When King Teuthras's kingdom of Mysia was invaded, it was Telephus, directed to Mysia by an oracle, who drove out the invaders. His mother's identity was then made known to him by Heracles.

See also: ATHENA; HERACLES

0404

**Augeas** (bright ray)   In Greek mythology, son of Helios (or Phorbas) and Hyramina; brother of Actor and Tiphys; the king of the Epeians in Elis and one of the Argonauts. He possessed 3,000 sheep and oxen, among which were 12 white bulls consecrated to the sun. The cattle were blessed by the gods and never sickened or died of disease, and they were extremely fertile. They were kept in a stable that had not been cleaned for 30 years. Heracles' sixth labor, given him by Eurystheus, was to clean the stable. Augeas agreed to pay Heracles one-tenth of his herd if he fulfilled the task in one day. Heracles diverted the Rivers Alpheus and Peneus to wash away the dirt, but Augeas refused to pay, so Heracles killed him and all of his sons, except for Phyleus, whom he made ruler of the kingdom. The term "Augean stables" is now applied to anything filthy.

See also: ARGONAUTS; HELIOS; HERACLES

0405

**Augures** (watchers of birds)   In ancient Roman cult, a group of priests established, according to tradition, by Romulus. Their function, important in Roman life, was not to predict the future but, by observing natural signs, to determine if the gods approved of a specific action. They wore a state dress with a purple border and carried a staff without knots and curled at the top. Roman augury was based chiefly on written works such as the *Libri Augurales*, a book on the techniques of augury, and the *Commentarii Augurales*, a collection of answers given to inquiries of the Roman senate. Magistrates would commission augurs to provide answers to specific questions by observing omens of birds. They would consecrate the observation place with the following rite: Immediately after midnight or at dawn, the augur, in the presence of the magistrate, selected an elevated spot with a view as wide as possible. Taking his station, he drew with his staff two straight lines crossing one another—one north to south, the other east to west. He then enclosed this cross in a rectangle, forming four smaller rectangles. The augur then spoke the ritual words consecrating the marked space. This space within the rectangle as well as the space upward to the sky was called the *templum*. At the point of the intersection in the center of the rectangle was erected the *tabernaculum*, which was a square tent with its entrance looking south. Here the augur, facing south, sat down, asked the gods for a sign according to a prescribed formula, and waited for an answer. Complete quiet, a clear sky, and an absence of wind were necessary conditions for the rite. The least noise was sufficient to disturb it, unless noise was an omen of terror, called *diroe*.

The Romans regarded signs on the left side as propitious omens, signs on the right side as unlucky. The east was the region of light, and the west was that of darkness. The reverse was the case in ancient Greece, where the observer looked northward.

The augur watched the birds for omens. Eagles and vultures gave signs by their manner of flying; ravens, owls, and crows by their cry as well as their flight. Some bird species were held sacred to particular gods, and the appearance of those birds were omens of good or evil. The augur's report was expressed in the words "the birds allow it" or "on another day," meaning postponement

See also: CROW; RAVEN; OWL; ROMULUS AND REMUS

0406

**Augustine, St.** (venerable)   354–430. In Christian legend, bishop of Hippo in Africa; Doctor of the Church; author of *The City of God*, a defense of Christianity against pagan philosophy, and an autobiography, *The Confessions*. Feast, 28 August.

Augustine's father was a pagan, but his mother, Monica, was a Christian. As a young man Augustine devoted his life to the pursuit of pleasure (he had numerous mistresses) and the study of philosophy. As he was interested only in some heretical sects, his mother prayed for his

*St. Augustine*

conversion to Catholic Christianity. Eventually, her prayers were answered; Augustine was baptized by St. Ambrose, bishop of Milan.

The most famous legend regarding the saint is called the vision of St. Augustine and is frequently portrayed in art. While Augustine was busy writing his *Discourse on the Trinity*, he wandered along the seashore lost in meditation. Suddenly he saw a child who had dug a hole in the sand and was bringing water from the sea to fill it. Augustine stopped and asked the boy what he was doing. The boy replied that he wanted to empty into the hole all of the water of the sea.

"Impossible," the saint replied to the child.

"Not more impossible than for thee, O Augustine, to explain the mystery of the Trinity," the child answered.

St. Augustine is often portrayed in his episcopal vestments carrying a book and a heart, symbol of his love and learning. Sometimes he is shown as a young man, before his conversion, reading or disputing with his mother, St. Monica. He is also sometimes painted in the

black habit of the Augustinian Order, which legend credits him with founding.

See also: AMBROSE, ST.; MONICA, ST.

0407
**Augustine of Canterbury, St.** (venerable) Died 605. In Christian legend, first archbishop of Canterbury. Feast, 26 May.

The legend of St. Augustine of Canterbury is told in St. Bede's *Ecclesiastical History of the English People*. Augustine was sent by Pope St. Gregory the Great as a missionary to Kent in England. The queen, Bertha, was already a Christian, but her husband, Ethelbert, was not. However, Ethelbert permitted Augustine and his followers to enter Canterbury, which they did, singing praises and carrying an image of Christ. The king was so moved that he consented to be baptized along with his people. The saint then wished to speak with others on the island, the Britons, who had been converted to Christianity earlier but followed different customs from those of the Roman Church. A meeting was held during which they debated the date of Easter and some other customs. To prove that God was on his side in the matter, a blind man was brought in and immediately "received sight, and Augustine was by all declared the preacher of the Divine Truth." However, the Celtics, or Britons, said they had to get the "consent and leave of their people," and they asked for a second conference. This was arranged, and seven Celtic bishops arrived.

"If he is a man of God, follow him," a holy man said.

"How shall we know that?" the bishops asked.

"If at your approach he shall rise up to you," he said, "hear him submissively, being assured that he is the servant of Christ; but if he shall despise you, and not rise up to you, whereas you are more in number, let him also be despised by you."

When they arrived, Augustine remained in his chair, and the conference fell apart. Augustine, however, had the last word. He cursed the group, saying they would fall under the judgment of death. This prediction came true after St. Augustine's death, for some 2,000 monks who followed the Celtic church were killed by Ethilfrid, king of the pagan Northern English.

In Christian art Augustine is shown either as a Benedictine with a staff or as a bishop with a pallium, cope, and miter.

See also: BEDE THE VENERABLE, ST.; EASTER; GREGORY THE GREAT

0408

**Augustus** (magnified, sanctified)   Honorary Latin title given in 27 B.C.E. to Octavian, great nephew and adopted son of Julius Caesar. The title was not hereditary but was taken by succeeding emperors as bestowed by the senate. The title of Augustus was reserved exclusively for the emperor, but the corresponding feminine style of Augusta was assumed by great ladies of the imperial house. The title was used by Christian emperors of the Holy Roman Empire. The Greek translation of the title was Sebastos, holy.

0409

**Aunyain-á**   In the mythology of the Tupi Indians of Brazil, an evil magician who fed on children. From his body iguanas, lizards, and other animals were produced. Aunyain-á had tusks like a boar's. The people, wishing to rid the land of him, climbed up a creeper vine to heaven, knowing he would follow. When Aunyain-á began climbing, a parrot flew ahead of him and gnawed through the vine, so that Aunyain-á fell back to earth. From his arms and legs caymans (a kind of alligator) and iguanas grew; from his fingers and toes, other lizards. What was left of his body was then eaten by vultures.

0410

**Aurora** (dawn)   In Roman mythology, the dawn; daughter of Hyperion and Thia (or Thea); married to Astraeus; mother of the wind and the stars; called Eos by the Greeks. Aurora's chariot,

drawn by white horses, raced across the heavens and caused the constellations to disappear at her approach. The subject is found frequently in Baroque paintings, including works of Carracci, Guercino, and Guido Reni. In literature, Shakespeare refers to the dawn in *A Midsummer Night's Dream* as "Aurora's harbinger," (3.2.380), and Spenser in *The Faerie Queene* (book 1) writes: "And fayre Aurora from the deawy bed / Of aged Thitone gan herselfe to reare." Thitone is Spenser's spelling of Tithonus, the old lover of the goddess. Ancient references are found in Homer's *Odyssey* (book 10), Vergil's *Aeneid* (book 6), and Ovid's *Metamorphoses* (book 3).

See also: *AENEID, THE*; ASTRAEUS; *ODYSSEY, THE*; OVID

0411

**Ausonia**   An ancient name for Italy, derived from Auson, a son of the Greek hero Odysseus and Calypso. In Vergil's *Aeneid* (book 3) Aeneas speaks of Ausonia.

See also: AENEAS; *AENEID, THE*; CALYPSO; ODYSSEUS

0412

**Auster**   In Roman mythology, the southwest wind; called Notus in Greek mythology.

0413

**Autolycus** (very wolf)   In Greek mythology, a son of Hermes and Chione or Philonis; father of Anticleia; maternal grandfather of Odysseus. Autolycus was a noted thief, having the gift of being able to change his form and that of his stolen goods at will. Autolycus stole the cattle of Sisyphus, who, after he found the cattle, raped Anticlea, Autolycus's daughter. Autolycus also stole the cattle of Eurytus of Oechalia. After changing their color, he sold them to Heracles. In *The Winter's Tale* Shakespeare uses the name Autolycus for the rogue in the play. Autolycus is also the name of one of the Argonauts, cited in

Homer's *Odyssey* (book 14) and Ovid's *Metamorphoses* (book 1).

See also: HERMES; HERACLES; ODYSSEUS; *ODYSSEY, THE*; SISYPHUS

0414
**Automedon** (independent ruler)    In Greek mythology, a hero, son of Diores; he sailed for Troy with 10 ships. He was Achilles' charioteer and later Pyrrhus's. Automedon is mentioned in Homer's *Iliad* (book 9) and Vergil's *Aeneid* (book 2).

See also: ACHILLES; *AENEID, THE*; *ILIAD, THE*

0415
**Autonoe** (with mind of her own)    In Greek mythology, daughter of Cadmus and Harmonia; sister of Agave, Illyrius, Ino, Polydorus, and Semele. She was the wife of Aristaeus and mother of Actaeon and Macris. Autonoe was driven insane, along with her other sisters, for their ill treatment of Semele. Ovid's *Metamorphoses* (book 3) tells the tale.

See also: ARISTAEUS; CADMUS; HARMONIA; OVID

0416
**Av** (Ab)    Fifth month in the cultic calendar of the ancient Babylonians. Av corresponds to parts of July and August. The month is also sacred in Judaism, often being called Menahem (comforter). As comfort must arise from despair, according to Jewish tradition, so in the ninth month, during which the Temple was destroyed by the Babylonians under Nebuchadnezzar in 586 B.C.E. and the Second Temple under the Roman Titus in 70 C.E., the Messiah will be born. On that date a fast is held, ornaments are removed from synagogues, and the Book of Lamentations is read. The commemoration has been used in recent times in memory of the Jews killed by the Nazis.

See also: NEBUCHADNEZZAR

0417
**Avalokiteshvara** (Avalokita) (he who hears the groanings of the world)    In Buddhism the Bodhisattva who appears in any appropriate form to help suffering beings. In China and Japan he has many female forms. In Mahayana Buddhism he is either one of the five Dhyani-Bodhisattvas who is noted for his compassion or a Bodhisattva in his own right.

Avalokiteshvara appears in numerous forms throughout Buddhism. In the form of the Bodhisattva of Infinite Compassion with 11 heads and 8 or 1,000 arms, he looks in every direction to save all creatures. The nine heads in three tiers have a benign expression, the 10th head shows anger, and the 11th is that of Amitabha, the father of Avalokiteshvara, shown with a *cintamani*, a sacred pearl. Some of his hands are in prayer; others hold a lotus, a vase of ambrosia, a rosary, a bow, and the *cakra*, Wheel of the Dharma. One hand, the lower right, is the *mudra* gesture of charity.

Another well-known icon is that of Avalokiteshvara as the Four-Armed Bodhisattva of Infinite Compassion. One pair of hands is in the gesture of prayer. The upper right hand holds a rosary; the upper left, a lotus. The top of the head is surmounted by a representation of Amitabha, his spiritual father. An antelope skin drapes the left shoulder.

See also: AMBROSIA; AMITABHA; BODHISATTVA; DALAI LAMA; DHYANI-BODHISATTVAS; KUAN-YIN; LOTUS; MAHAYANA; MUDRA

0418
**Avalon** (island of apples)    In Arthurian legend Elysium, where, according to some accounts, King Arthur still lives. He was transported there by Morgan le Fay. Ogier the Dane and Oberon also held their courts on Avalon. Some scholars believe Avalon is derived from Yns Afallach (Avallon's Island), the realm of the Celtic god Avallach and land of the blessed dead.

See also: ARTHUR; OBERON; OGIER THE DANE

0419

**Avaricious and Envious, The**   Aesopic fable found in various collections throughout the world.

Two neighbors came before Zeus and asked him to grant their hearts' desire. One was full of avarice, and the other was eaten up with envy. To punish them both, Zeus granted that each might have whatever he wished for himself, but only on condition that his neighbor had twice as much. The avaricious man prayed to have a room full of gold. No sooner said than done, but all of his joy was turned to grief when he found that his neighbor had two rooms full of the precious metal. Then came the turn of the envious man, who could not bear to think that his neighbor had any joy at all. So he prayed that he might have one of his own eyes put out, by which means his neighbor would be made totally blind.

Moral: *Vices are their own punishment.*

This is one of the most popular Aesopic fables. It occurs in the Indian collection *The Panchatantra* and in various collections of the Middle Ages. It is told by Hans Sachs, the German poet and dramatist of the 16th century, and by John Gower, the English poet and friend of Chaucer, in his *Confessio Amantis* (book 2:2).

See also: AESOPIC FABLES; *PANCHATANTRA*; ZEUS

0420

**Avatar** (a descent)   In Hindu mythology, the incarnation of a god in some form, often applied to Vishnu.

See also: VISHNU

0421

**Avernus** (without birds?)   In Greek and Roman mythology, a deep sulfurous lake northwest of Roman Puteoli (Pozzouli), believed by the ancients to be one of the entrances to the underworld, the land of the dead. No birds were ever seen in its area. Vergil's *Aeneid* (book 6) tells how the hero Aeneas was told by the Sibyl of Cumae to enter the underworld through Avernus. It is still called Lago Averno today.

See also: AENEAS; *AENEID, THE*; SIBYL

0422

*Avesta*   (knowledge, wisdom, or injunction) Sacred book of ancient Persia (Iran), containing the teachings of the prophet Zarathustra as well as pre-Zoroastrian myths from Persian mythology.

The *Avesta* proper consists of the following:

*Gathas*, a collection of hymns, some ascribed to the prophet Zarathustra and others believed to have been written earlier and adapted for the work.

*Yashts*, hymns to the individual gods, as well as some material on earlier Persian mythology.

*Yasna*, liturgical texts in prose and verse.

*Vendidad*, a miscellaneous collection of writings in prose.

The original *Avesta* is believed to have been lost during the time of Alexander the Great (fourth century B.C.E.). From the third century to the sixth century C.E. magi (Zoroastrian priests) compiled a collection of sacred writings consisting of some 21 *nasks*, or books, of which only a small part contained material from the original *Avesta*. The *Zend Avesta*, the term usually applied to the sacred writings of Persia, is actually a zend (commentary) on the parts of the original *Avesta*, containing quotes from the original lost text.

See also: ZARATHUSTRA

0423

**Awonawilona** (maker and container of all)   In North American Indian mythology (Zuni), bisexual creator deity. In the beginning Awonawilona was alone in a dark void, "though outward in space," according to *Report of the Bureau of American Ethology* (Cushing), "whereby mists of increase, steams potent of growth, were evolved and uplifted. Then Awonawilona became the sun and mist formed creating Awitelin Tsita (four-fold containing Mother-earth) and Apoyan Ta'chu (all-covering Father-sky)."

The two then had sexual intercourse and "terrestrial life was conceived; whence began all beings of earth, men and the creatures." The first humans on earth were strange beings. They had adapted to life within the womb and thus had scales, short tales, huge owl eyes, large ears, and webbed hands and feet. They only adjusted to life on earth very slowly. Among the first humans was Poshaiyangkyo, who led the people from the darkness to the light.

See also: MAWU LISA; YIN AND YANG

**0424**
**Ayesha** c. 610–677. In Islamic legend, favorite wife of Muhammad, married to the prophet when she was a child. At one time she was suspected of being unfaithful to Muhammad, but the prophet defended her honor. He ultimately died in her arms. At his death she helped her father, Abu-Bakr, to become the first caliph, and he reigned for two years. She was defeated in 656, when she tried to gain more power from Ali.

See also: ALI; MUHAMMAD

**0425**
**Ayida** In Haitian voodoo, the rainbow snake, female counterpart of Danbhalah Houé-Do. A form of the goddess Erzulie Ayida is also called Aida Wédo.

**0426**
**Aymon, The Four Sons of** In medieval French legend, the sons of Aymon: Renaud (Rinaldo), Alard, Guichard, and Richard, all of whom were knighted by Charlemagne. They appear in the medieval French romance *The Four Sons of Aymon* as well as Boilardo's *Orlando Innamorato*, Ariosto's *Orlando Furioso*, Tasso's *Rinaldo*, and *Jerusalem Delivered*. Their story also formed the basis for many chapbooks.

See also: CHAPBOOK; CHARLEMAGNE; RINALDO; ROLAND

**0427**
**Aynia** In Celtic folklore, the most powerful fairy in Ulster, Ireland, thought to be derived from Anu, the goddess who presided over prosperity and abundance. There are many stories about Aynia. The best known is about Maurice, the Earl of Desmond, who fell in love with her by seizing her cloak and making her his bride. Their son was Gerald, who still lives, according to legend, in the waters of Lough Gur. He reappears every seven years to ride around it on a shining white horse. Sometimes he appears as a goose swimming on the lake.

See also: ANU

**0428**
**Azaca Mede** In Haitian voodoo, the loa (deified spirit of the dead) of gardens and mountains, who is offered goats in sacrifice. Often the goats are black.

See also: LOA

**0429**
**Azadovskii, Mark Konstantinovich** 1888–1945. Russian folklorist whose expeditions in 1913–1915 took him to the Amur and Lena Rivers in Siberia, where he gathered materials on folk narratives from the local peasants. He is best known for his collection of tales told by Natalia Osipovna Vinokurova, which he published and also described in a 1926 German publication called *Eine sibirische Märchenerzählerin*. This study of a Siberian tale teller has been repeatedly praised by folktale scholars as a pioneering and exemplary work. Azadovskii saw storytelling as a complex act that cannot be fully appreciated on the basis of the study of written records or "texts" of orally transmitted tales. He viewed tales as expressive manifestations of the personalities of the communicators and the surroundings within which the narrators learn and continue to practice their art. He speaks of determining "those formative forces which govern the generation of a folktale," and discovering the underlying "artistic purpose" of storytelling. Thus,

for him the study of narrative traditions was "inseparably bound up with the study of the creative individuality of the narrator." To demonstrate his ideas, Azadovskii focused on the tales told to him by his primary informant, N. O. Vinokurova. Later he became particularly interested in the interrelations between oral and written traditions. Unfortunately, his work remains largely unknown outside the Russian-speaking world.

0430

**Azariel** (God has helped)   In Jewish folklore, angel of the earth waters, invoked by fishermen to obtain a good catch.

0431

**Azazel**   In the Bible, O.T., a scapegoat, an evil spirit or demon. In Leviticus (16:8) the high priest Aaron casts lots "upon two goats, one lot for the Lord and the other lot for Azazel." The one chosen for the Lord was sacrificed as an offering for sins, and Azazel was driven into the desert. Originally, Azazel was a Semitic satyr or god of flocks who was incorporated into Hebrew ritual.

In medieval Jewish folklore Azazel is credited with being one of the angels who came down from heaven to have intercourse with the daughters of men, teaching men witchcraft and warfare.

In Islam, Elbis (the equivalent of Satan) is considered to be a form of Azazel. In Islamic legend, Azazel is a *jenin* (supernatural being) of the desert. When God commanded him to worship Adam, Azazel replied "Why should the son of fire fall down before the son of clay?" God then cast him from heaven and changed his name to Elbis, which means "despair."

In *Paradise Lost* (book 1:534) Milton describes Azazel as a "Cherub Tall" who holds the "glittering staff" of the fallen angels. In Collin de Plancy's *Dictionnaire Infernal*, Azazel is portrayed as a fat, naked man with horns holding a pitchfork-type banner on which a frog is shown. In his

other hand he holds a goat. The English Pre-Raphaelite artist William Holman Hunt painted *The Scapegoat*, which portrays the goat with photographic accuracy.

See also: IBLIS; SATAN; SATYR

0432

**Azeto**   In Haitian voodoo, an evil loa (deified spirit of the dead), either a male or female werewolf or vampire.

See also: LOA; VAMPIRE; WERWOLF

0433

**Azhi Dahaka** (Asi Dahak, Az-i Dahak, Dahhak)   In Persian mythology, archdemon with three heads, six eyes, and three jaws, who is defeated by the hero Traetaona.

Azhi Dahaka is under the control of the evil spirit, Ahriman. His greatest battle was with the hero Traetaona. The two fought in Varena (the heavens). Traetaona clubbed Azhi Dahaka in the head, neck, and heart, but the demon refused to die. Finally, Traetaona took a sword and plunged it into the monster's breast. Out of the wound came a host of ugly animals: snakes, toads, scorpions, lizards, and frogs. Frightened that more of such animals were inside the demon, Traetaona took the body and imprisoned it in Mount Demavend. Here the demon is to stay for a time, then he will escape to cause havoc in the world until he is slain by the hero Keresaspa, who will usher in a new world order.

In Firdusi's epic poem *Shah Namah* the character of the evil king, Zahhak, is modeled on that of Azhi Dahaka.

See also: AHRIMAN; KERESASPA

0434

**Azrael** (Izrail) (whom God helps)   In Jewish and Islamic mythology, angel of death, often identified with Gabriel in Jewish writings and with Raphael in Islamic works. He will be the last to die.

Azrael keeps a roll containing the name of every person born in the world. The time of death and whether the person is saved or damned is not known to Azrael. When the day of death approaches, Allah lets a leaf inscribed with the person's name drop from his majestic throne. Azrael reads the name and within 40 days must separate the soul from the body. If the person makes a struggle, Azrael flies back to the throne of Allah and informs him. Then Allah gives him an apple from paradise on which the *basmala*, the Name of God, "the merciful and compassionate," is written. When the person reads the Name of God, he then gives up his life to the angel of death.

However, if the person is an unbeliever and lost, Azrael tears the soul from the body in a rough manner. The gate of heaven closes, and the person is cast into hell.

Azrael is variously described in Islamic writings. In general he has some 70,000 feet and 4,000 wings. He has four faces and as many eyes and tongues as there are men in the world.

Longfellow, in one of his metrical poems included in *Tales of a Wayside Inn*, has a Spanish Jew tell a tale of Azrael and King Solomon. The king is entertaining a "learned man" who is a rajah. As they walk, a white figure in the twilight air is gazing intently at the man. The rajah asks Solomon:

What is yon shape, that, pallid as the dead,
Is watching me, as if he sought to trace
In the dim light the features of my face?

The king calmly tells his guest that it is the angel of death, Azrael. The man then asks Solomon to get him as far away from Azrael as possible. The king, with his magic ring, sends him off to India. The angel of death asks Solomon who the man was who left so suddenly. The king gives Azrael the name, and Azrael thanks the king for sending the man off to India, since he was on his way "to seek him there."

See also: ALLAH; GABRIEL; RAPHAEL; SOLOMON

# B

**Ba** (soul)   In Egyptian mythology, the soul, or that part of a person that had eternal existence after death, represented as a human-headed bird. The *ba* was closely associated with the *ka*, a person's double, and the *ib*, or heart, and constituted one of the principles of a person's life. After death the *ba* was believed to visit its body in the tomb. In the pyramids of Meroë openings were left in the stone covering the apex so that the *ba* might enter, and a ledge was placed beneath each opening for the *ba* to stand on. A small figure of the *ba* made of gold and inlaid with some precious stones was placed on the breast of the mummy in the hope of preserving it from decay, because the ancient Egyptians believed there was to be a final union of all souls with their bodies.

See also: KA

**Baal** (Ba'al, Ball) (lord, owner, possessor)   In Near Eastern mythology, generic name for numerous gods of rain, agriculture, and fertility.

Many Baals or Baalim, as the Old Testament calls them, were worshiped in the ancient Near East. Usually a god was called Baal when his worshipers had taken "possession" or "ownership" of land by settling it. Many place names in the Old Testament indicate that a local form of Baal was worshiped in the land, thus Baal-peor (Num. 25:3) and Baal-hermon (Judg. 3:3). The influence of Baal worship, with its fertility rites, left its mark on the worship of the Hebrew deity Yahweh since at one time the two gods were worshiped together. Yahweh, however, eclipsed the worship of Baal, and the latter was denounced by the later Hebrew prophets. Yet the titles assigned to Baal were often also assigned to Yahweh. Baal was "he who mounts the clouds," whereas Yahweh, the god of Jerusalem, was he "who rideth upon the heaven" (Deut. 33:26). Among the most famous Baals worshiped in the Near East were Baal Berith, Baal-hermon, Baal-macod, Baal-peor, Baalsamin, Baalzebub, and Baal-zephon.

See also: YAHWEH

**Baba Yaga** (Baba Jaga) (old woman)   In Russian folklore, cannibalistic ogress who kidnaps children, then cooks and eats them. She is the best known of all Slavic legendary characters. She is mostly malevolent, but sometimes she is a benefactress. She is never portrayed as a goddess, but in her earliest form she shows similarity to the Great Goddess, the patron goddess to women. Since the Christian era she has been downgraded to witch status.

Baba Yaga usually lives in a hut that stands on hens' legs. Sometimes it faces the forest, sometimes the path, and sometimes it moves about from place to place. In some Russian folktales Baba Yaga's hut is surrounded by a railing made of sticks surmounted by human skulls, which glow at night from candles placed inside them.

One Russian folktale, simply titled "Baba Yaga," tells of an evil stepmother who attempted to have her daughter eaten by Baba Yaga. The girl was saved when a magic comb thrown in Baba Yaga's path made it impossible for the ogress to catch the girl as she escaped. In a variant tale, however, the girl was broken into little pieces and placed in a basket.

Anatol Liadov's short symphonic poem *Baba Yaga* deals with the ogress, as does one section of Modest Moussorgsky's *Pictures at an Exhibition*, also titled "Baba Yaga," originally written for piano and transcribed for orchestra by Maurice Ravel in 1923.

See also: GREAT GODDESS

0438

**Babe, the Blue Ox**   In American folklore, a giant ox, companion of Paul Bunyan. He created Lake Michigan when he sank knee-deep into solid rock. He died when he accidentally ate a stove instead of the batch of hotcakes on it.

See also: PAUL BUNYAN; FAKELORE

*Tower of Babel*

0439

**Babel, Tower of** (confusion)   In the Bible, O.T., a ziggurat erected on the plains of Shinar by the descendants of Noah when they reached Babylonia. Genesis (11:1–9) says the plan was to build a tower that would reach to heaven. Yahweh, the Hebrew cult god, said "Go to, let us go down, and there confound their language, that they may not understand one another's speech" (Gen. 11:7). This accounts for the variety of languages in the world. The ziggurat is believed to have been of the god Marduk's temple in Babylon, which consisted of six square stages, one on top of the other, the last with a small room for the god. Numerous paintings on the subject exist. One of the most famous is by Brueghel; another is by Marten van Valckorborch.

See also: MARDUK; YAHWEH

0440

**Babes in the Wood**   Popular title of the English ballad "Children in the Wood," found in Percy's *Reliques*. The master of Wyland Hall, Norfolk, leaves a little son and daughter to the care of his wife's brother. Both children were to inherit money, but if they died, the money would go to the uncle. After 12 months the uncle hired two men to murder the children. One of the murderers relented and killed his fellow, leaving the children in the wood. They died during the night and were covered with leaves by Robin Redbreast. The uncle eventually died after seeing his children die and his wealth destroyed. After seven years the murderer was caught and confessed. A play by Robert Farrington (1599) tells the tale. The phrase "babes in the wood" is often used for simple, trusting people, never suspicious and easily fooled.

0441

**Baboon**   A large monkey of Arabia and Africa, with a short tail and doglike muzzle. In Egyptian mythology the baboon was sacred to the moon god Thoth, who was sometimes portrayed as a baboon. In the Egyptian *Book of the Dead* the dead person's heart is shown placed on a scale, on top of which sits a baboon. The baboon was to report to Thoth when the pointer was in the middle, indicating a balance of the person's deeds so he or she could be judged. Sacred baboons were kept in various Egyptian temples that were dedicated to moon gods. The baboons were believed to be the spirits of the dawn who had been transformed into baboons as soon as the sun arose when they sang a hymn in the sun's honor.

See also: *BOOK OF THE DEAD*; THOTH

0442
**Baca, Elfego**  1865–1945. In American history and folklore, Mexican-American hero. When Baca, at 19, was told that a band of Texans had publicly castrated a Mexican and used another for target practice, he borrowed a lawman's badge and set out for Frisco (now Reserve), New Mexico. When he got there, some cowboys were still causing trouble, and Baca promptly arrested one who had shot off Baca's hat. The next day some 80 cowboys arrived to teach Baca a lesson; a gunfight ensued in which some 4,000 rounds of ammunition were fired during a 36-hour period. At the end, four Texas cowboys were dead. Baca was brought to trial but acquitted. He became a lawyer, and later the deputy of Socorro County, New Mexico, and finally the owner of a detective agency. His business card read: "Discreet Shadowing Done." He was known as hero of the people, and his legend continued in his lifetime.

0443
**Bacabs** (erected, set up)  In Mayan mythology, four giant brothers who supported the four corners of the heavens, blowing the winds from the four cardinal points. They kept the sky in place after it had fallen following a great flood. Each was identified with a particular color and cardinal point, thus Kan (belly) was associated with the south and the color yellow. The remaining three were Chac, who was red and assigned to the east; Zac, who was white, to the north; and Ed, who was black, to the west. The winds and rains were said to be under the control of these Bacabs.

As each year in the Mayan calendar was supposed to be under the influence of one of the brothers, one Bacab was said to die at the close of each year. After the nameless or intercalary days had passed, the next Bacab would come alive. Each computation of the year began on the day Imix, which was the third before the close of the Mayan week; this was said to be figuratively the day of death of the Bacab of that year. It was not until three or four days later that a new year began, with another Bacab, who was said to have died and risen again. *The Ritual of the Bacabs*, an ancient Mayan book containing incantations, was so named because of its frequent mention of the Bacabs.

See also: CHAC

0444
**Bacalou**  In Haitian voodoo, an evil loa (deified spirit of the dead), represented by a skull and crossbones.

See also: LOA

*Bacchants*

0445
**Bacchants** (Bacchantes, Bacchae)  In Greco-Roman cult, women who followed the god Dionysus, who was also called Bacchus. His fol-

lowers, also called Maenads, were said to become mad with frenzy, to tear human flesh, and even eat their own children. The cult was banned as the source of a political conspiracy by the Roman Senate in 186 B.C.E. Euripides' play *The Bacchae* deals with the cult. Numerous paintings depict the Bacchanalia, the festival held in honor of the god. Among the most famous are those by Rubens and Poussin. Picasso "repainted" the Poussin work. The poet Keats wrote of the Bacchants:

We follow Bacchus! Bacchus on the wing, A conquering! Bacchus, young Bacchus! good or ill betide, We dance before him through kingdoms wide.

In "Drinking Song" Longfellow wrote:

Round about him fair Bacchantes, Bearing Cymbals, flutes, and thyrses.

See also: DIONYSUS

*Priest of Bacchus*

0446

**Bacchus**    In Greek and Roman mythology, a title for Dionysus, son of Zeus and Semele, who was a daughter of Cadmus; also called Liber. Numerous art and music works identify the god Dionysus as Bacchus, such as *The Young Bacchus* by Caravaggio, which portrays one of the artist's male lovers; Titian's great *Bacchus and Ariadne*, depicting the god jumping from his chariot; and Roussel's two-act ballet, *Bacchus et Ariane* (1930). Ovid's *Fasti* (book 3) supplied most of the imagery for the paintings.

See also: ARIADNE; CADMUS; DIONYSUS; OVID; SEMELE; ZEUS

0447

**Bachúe** (she of the large breasts)    In the mythology of the Chibcha Indians of Colombia, mother goddess and protector of crops. After the supreme god Chiminigagua had created light, the goddess Bachúe emerged from a mountain lake with a three-year-old child. She went to live in a nearby village, Iguaque, and brought up the child. When he was of age, she married him and bore four or six children, who populated the land. With her task finished, Bachúe and her husband left for the mountains and finally reentered the sacred lake as snakes. In some accounts the name of the goddess is given as Fura-chogue, "the beneficent female."

See also: CHIMINIGAGUA

0448

**Bacon, Roger**    1214–1292. In medieval history and legend, English monk, believed to be a wizard. Bacon did numerous scientific experiments, which earned for him a reputation as being in league with Satan. One legend, commonly found in early romances, tells of the Brazen Head. The monk had a head made of bronze, which he often consulted. He had his attendant Miles watch the Brazen Head while he slept. Once, while Miles was watching the head, it spoke to him. "Time is," it said. A half hour later it said, "Time was." In another half hour it said,

"Time's past." Then the Brazen Head fell to the ground and broke to pieces. Byron in his mock epic poem *Don Juan* (book 1), uses the lines:

Like Friar Bacon's brazen head, I've spoken
"Time is," "Time was," "Time's past."

Earlier the English poet Alexander Pope had written in his mock epic *The Dunciad* (book 3): "Bacon trembled for his brazen head." The monk is the subject of a play by Robert Greene, *Friar Bacon and Friar Bungay* (1594).

See also: SATAN.

0449
**Badal** (Abdal) (substitute, double)   In Islamic folklore, spirit of a man. The badal are known only to Allah. The number of badals varied. Some Islamic accounts give 40, some 30, others just 7. It is believed that when a holy man or saint dies, his badals, or "substitute," immediately fills his place. Some Islamic writers explain badal as "one who, when he departs from a place, has the power to leave his double behind him." Others say the badal is "one who has experienced a spiritual transformation."

See also: ALLAH

0450
**Badessy**   In Haitian voodoo, loa (deified spirit of the dead) of the winds.

See also: LOA

0451
**Badi** (mischiefs)   In Malayan mythology, demons that inhabit animate and inanimate objects. Various accounts are given of their origin. One says they sprang from three drops of blood spilled by Adam on the ground; another account says they are the offspring of the djinn; still another credits their origin to the yellow glow at sunset. There is disagreement on their total, which is either 190 or 193. Various charms and ceremonies are used in Malaya to cast out badi from people, animals, plants, and objects.

See also: ADAM AND EVE; DJINN

0452
**Bagadjimbiri**   In Australian mythology, twin culture heroes of the Karadjeri in northwestern Australia. At first they appeared in the form of dingos; they created water holes and sexual organs for humankind and instituted the rite of circumcision. The two brothers were killed when, having become gigantic men, they annoyed the cat man, Ngariman, with their loud laughter. He gathered together his relatives, and they speared the twins to death. Distraught at this, Dilga, their mother, the earth goddess, caused milk to flow from her breasts, which drowned the killers and revived her sons. When the Bagadjimbiri decided to leave earth, their dead bodies became water snakes, and their spirits ascended to the sky.

0453
**Baginis**   In Australian mythology, half-human and half-animal female beings who have lovely faces but claws instead of fingers and toenails. They capture men and rape them. After they are satisfied, the men are freed.

0454
**Bahram Fire** (Berezisauanh)   In Persian mythology, sacred fire that represents all fires and shoots up before the good god, Ahura Mazda. It is composed of 16 different kinds of fire and is the earthly representative of divine fire.

See also: AHURA MAZDA

0455
**Bahram Gur** (Bahramgor, Bahram Gor)   In Persian mythology, a hero king appearing in the epic poem *Shah Namah* by Firdusi, as well as in the poem *Haft Paykar* (seven portraits) by another Persian poet, Nizami.

Bahram Gur is encountered frequently in Persian poetry and legend. He is credited with the invention of Persian poetry and appears in many tales as a "great hunter." In Firdusi's epic Bahram Gur married seven princesses, daughters of the king of the Seven Climates, each of whom told him a story at night before retiring. Each night Bahram Gur slept with a different wife and heard a different tale.

Often Bahram Gur is depicted in Persian art hunting with his mistress Azada. One scene often portrayed is that of the hero meeting a shepherd who has hung his dog on a tree because the dog let the wolf steal lambs from his flock.

Some scholars believe Bahram Gur is a portrait of a Sassanian king of Persia who lived in the fifth century C.E.

See also: SHAH NAMAH

0456

**Baiame**    In Australian mythology, the totemic ancestor of the Kamilaron tribe of New South Wales who taught the people customs and sacred rites. His wives are Cunnembeille, who bore him children, and his favorite, Birrahgnooloo, who did not. Birrahgnooloo, however, sends floods upon the earth; Baiame is invoked for rain.

See also: BUNJIL

0457

**Bailiff's Daughter of Islington**    English ballad found in Percy's *Reliques*. A squire's son loved the bailiff's daughter, but she gave him no encouragement. His friends sent him to London, "an apprentice for to binde." After seven years, the bailiff's daughter, "in ragged attire," set out to walk to London, "her true love to inquire." The young man, on horseback, met her but did not recognize her. When he asked after the bailiff's daughter of Islington, she at first said she was dead but later told the truth, revealing her identity.

0458

**Bajang** (Badjang)    In Malayan mythology, an evil spirit whose presence foretells disaster and brings illness. Generally, it takes the form of a polecat and disrupts the household by mewing like a great cat.

The *bajang* is considered very dangerous to children, who are sometimes provided with amulets of black silk threads, called bajang bracelets, which are supposed to protect them against the evil influence of the *bajang*. In Perak and some other parts of the Malay Peninsula, the *bajang* is regarded as one of several kinds of demons that can be enslaved by man and become familiar spirits.

Such familiars are handed down in certain families as heirlooms. The master of the familiar is said to keep it imprisoned in a *tabong*, a vessel made from a joint of bamboo closed by a stopper made from leaves. Both the case and the stopper are prepared by certain magic arts before they can be used. The familiar is fed with eggs and milk. When its master wishes to make use of it, he sends it forth to possess and prey on the vitals of anyone whom his malice may select as victim. The victim is at once seized by a deadly and unaccountable ailment that can be cured only by magic. If the *bajang* is neglected by its keeper and is not fed regularly, it will turn on its owner, who will thereupon fall victim to the *bajang*.

0459

**Baka** (Babako)    In Haitian voodoo, a very evil loa (deified spirit of the dead). Black roosters and black goats are sacrificed to appease his anger. Sometimes instead of the blood sacrifice he will accept a virgin girl for sexual intercourse. His symbol is two broken crosses.

See also: LOA

0460

**Bakemono**    In Japanese folklore, a generic name for evil spirits or ghosts. They are often portrayed without feet and with long straight hair.

*Balaam*

**Balaam**   In the Bible, O.T., a Midian prophet   0461
or seer, called on to curse the Hebrews by Balak,
king of Moab (Num. 22–23). On his journey an
angel of Yahweh, the Hebrew god, invisible to
Balaam, barred the way, causing his ass to turn
aside (the ass could see the angel). Balaam then
beat his ass, and the animal spoke to him, asking
him why he was doing it since an angel was in the
way. In medieval Christian belief the conversion
of Balaam by the angel was regarded as a prefiguration of the appearance of the risen Christ to
the Apostle Thomas. The theme is often found
in Romanesque and Gothic church decorations.
Medieval Christians believed that the ass Jesus
rode into Jerusalem was a direct descendant of
Balaam's ass and that after Jesus' death it was
taken to Verona, Italy, and died later of old age.
Its bones were set aside as relics and preserved in
the city's cathedral. Rembrandt painted the subject.

See also: THOMAS, ST.; YAHWEH

**Balam-Quitzé** (smiling jaguar)   In Mayan   0462
mythology, first man and a culture hero in the
*Popol Vuh*, the sacred book of the ancient Quiché
Maya of Guatemala.

Balam-Quitzé was the first man, created by
Hurakán from the flour of white and yellow
maize. He was followed by Balam-Agag (nocturnal tiger), Mahucutan (famous name), and Iqui-

Balam (moon tiger). These four were the
ancestors of the Quiché, providing them with
skills and knowledge.

The *Popol Vuh* tells how Balam-Quitzé provided fire for his people. One day the god Tohil
appeared to Balam-Quitzé, who took the god
and "put him on his back" in a wooden chest he
carried. As yet there was no fire, and the hero
asked Tohil to provide him with it. The god gave
Balam-Quitzé fire, which the culture hero then
took to his people.

After the four men had completed their task
of educating the people, they departed from the
land and disappeared on Mount Hacavitz. Before
the departure Balam-Quitzé left behind the Pi-
zom-Gagal, a package that "was wrapped up and
could not be unwrapped; the seam did not show
because it was not seen when they wrapped it
up." The mysterious package was never opened.
It was called the Bundle of Greatness.

See also: HACAVITZ; *POPOL VUH*

**Balan and Balin**   In Arthurian legend, two   0463
brothers: Balan, the wiser and more even-
tempered, and Balin, the hot-tempered.
Through some mistake the two meet in battle,
and both are killed. They are the subject of Tennyson's narrative poem "Balin and Balan" in
*Idylls of the King*. Balan is also the name of a
strong and courageous giant in many old romances.

**Balarama** (he who delights in power)   In   0464
Hindu mythology, brother of Krishna. He is
often regarded as an avatar or incarnation of the
god Vishnu.

The Hindu epic poem *The Mahabharata* tells
how the god Vishnu took two hairs, one black
and one white, and they became Krishna and
Balarama. Krishna was of dark complexion and
Balarama light. Once when Balarama was drunk,
he called on the Yamuna River to come to him
that he might bathe himself. The river did not

listen to him, so he dragged its waters until they assumed a human form and asked Balarama for forgiveness. This action gained for Balarama the title Yamuna-bhid (breaker; dragger of the Yamuna).

Another important episode in the life of Balarama tells how he killed the demon Dhenuka. As boys Krishna and Balarama picked some fruit from a grove belonging to the demon. Dhenuka took the form of an ass and began to kick Balarama. The young hero seized Dhenuka by the heels, whirled him around till he was dead, and then threw his body on top of a palm tree. Several other demons came to the assistance of Dhenuka, but they were also thrown to the top of palm trees until "the trees were laden with dead asses."

Balarama also fought an apelike demon, Dwivida, who had stolen Balarama's plowshare. Dwivida was thrown to the earth, and "the crest of the mountain on which he fell was splintered into a hundred pieces by the weight of his body."

In Indian art Balarama is portrayed with a fair complexion. His weapons are a club, plowshare, and pestle, and his emblem is the palm tree.

See also: AVATAR; KRISHNA; *MAHABHARATA, THE*; VISHNU

**0465**

**Baldak Borisievich**   In Russian folklore, a hero who defeated the Turkish sultan. One day Baldak Borisievich, with 29 other young men, went directly to the Turkish sultan to "take from him his steed with the golden mane." They accomplished the deed, and in the process they killed the sultan's cat, spat in the sultan's face, and hanged the sultan with a silken noose, his favorite pasha with a hempen noose, and his youngest daughter with a bast (rope of tree bark) noose.

**0466**

**Baldur** (Balder, Baldr, Balldr) (lord)   In Norse mythology, god of light, the sun, who always spoke the truth; son of Odin and Frigga; husband

*Baldur (W. G. Collingwood)*

of Nanna; father of Forseti. Baldur's myth, told in the *Prose Edda*, is one of the most complete in Norse mythology. Baldur was tormented by terrible dreams, indicating that he was to die. He told the gods of his evil dreams, and they resolved to "conjure all things to avert from him the threatened danger." Frigga exacted an oath from fire, water, iron, metals, stones, earths, diseases, beasts, birds, poisons, and creeping things so that none of them would harm Baldur. When this was done the gods passed their time hurling darts, swords, and battle-axes at Baldur, knowing he could not be harmed. When the evil god Loki saw that Baldur remained unhurt, he transformed himself into a woman and went to Frigga's home, Fensalir. Loki, in disguise, asked Frigga why the gods were throwing stones at Baldur.

She replied that he could not come to any harm. "Neither metal nor wood can hurt Baldur," she said, "for I have exacted an oath from all of them."

"What!" exclaimed Loki. "Have all things sworn to spare Baldur?"

"All things," replied Frigga, "except one little shrub that grows on the eastern side of Valhalla. It is called mistletoe, and I thought it too young and feeble to ask an oath from it."

As soon as Loki heard this he went away. Resuming his natural shape, he cut off a twig of mistletoe and went to the assembly hall of the gods. Hodur, the blind god, was asked by Loki why he was not throwing anything at Baldur.

"Because I'm blind," Hodur said, "and can't see where Baldur is standing. Also, I haven't anything to throw at him."

"Come then," said Loki, "do as the rest of the gods. Show honor to Baldur and throw this twig at him. I'll direct your arm toward the right place."

Hodur took the mistletoe and under Loki's guidance hurled it at Baldur, who was pierced through and fell dead to the ground. The gods were stunned and began to lament. Frigga then said she would give all of her love to anyone who would ride to Hel to find Baldur and offer Hela, goddess of death, a ransom for the god's return to Asgard. Hermod volunteered. He arrived in Hel and found Baldur occupying the most distinguished seat in the hall of the dead. He then asked Hela to let Baldur ride home with him, saying that the whole world was lamenting the god's death.

"If all things in the world both living and lifeless weep for him, then I will let him return," she said, "but if any one thing speak against him or refuse to weep, he shall be kept in Hel."

The gods then sent messengers throughout the world asking everything to weep for Baldur. All things complied. As the messengers were returning, believing their mission a success, they found an old hag named Thaukt sitting in a cavern. They asked her to weep for Baldur so the god could return. She refused.

The *Prose Edda* ends the account with "It was strongly suspected that this hag was no other than Loki himself who never ceased to work evil among the gods."

Baldur's myth was the inspiration for Matthew Arnold's long narrative poem *Balder Dead*.

See also: ASGARD; FRIGGA; HERMOD; HODUR; LOKI; *PROSE EDDA*

0467
**Balmung**  In Norse mythology, a magical sword forged by Völund the Smith (Wayland the Smith). Balmung appears in the sagas relating to the adventures of the Norse Sigmund, called Siegfried in Germanic myth. The sword was placed in the Branstock tree by Odin, chief of the gods. Odin said that the weapon would belong only to the warrior who could pull it out of the tree. The sword then would assure its owner victory in battle. Nine Volsung princes and others tried to remove the sword and failed. Sigmund, the 10th and youngest, laid a firm hand on the sword's hilt and easily removed it from the Branstock tree. The episode is vividly recreated in William Morris's narrative poem *Sigurd the Volsung and the Fall of the Niblungs*. According to other sources, Balmung was later destroyed by Odin, restored, and used by Sigurd (Siegfried) to kill the dragon Fafnir.

See also: *NIBELUNGENLIED*; ODIN; SIEGFRIED; SIGMUND; SIGURD; WAYLAND THE SMITH

0468
**Balor**  In Celtic mythology, a god-king of the Fomorians, a group of deities connected with darkness and evil; grandson of Net; son of Buarainech; husband of Cathlionn. Balor had one eye, poisoned in his youth, but it retained the power of striking dead anyone it looked at. He never opened it except on the battlefield with the aid of four men who lifted the eyelid. In the war with the beneficent gods Balor slew Nuada but was killed by the god Lugh, his grandson, who finally destroyed his fatal eye with a magic missile. In James Joyce's novel *Ulysses*, the god is called Balor of the Evil Eye.

See also: ETHNE; FOMORIANS

0469
**Bamapama**  In Australian mythology, trickster of the Murngin in northern Australia, often called the "crazy man" because he violates various taboos, especially those involving clan incest.

See also: TRICKSTER

**0470**

**Bamboo**   A plant with hollow reeds that grows in tropical and semitropical regions. In Chinese mythology, the bamboo is a symbol of longevity because of its durable, evergreen qualities. In the Philippine Islands, Christian crosses made of bamboo are set up in the fields to ensure that the crops will grow. The Aka-Bo of the Andaman Islands believed that the first man, called Jutpu, came to life inside a large bamboo.

**0471**

**Bana** (arrow)   In Hindu mythology, a demon giant with 1,000 arms who was a friend of the god Shiva and an enemy of the god Vishnu. Bana is sometimes called Vairochi. In the Rig-Veda Bana referred to Indra's thousand-feathered and hundred-barbed arrows.

See also: SHIVA; VISHNU

**0472**

**Banaidja**   In Australian mythology, ancestral figure, son of Laindjung. He taught the Arnhem Landers their totems and sacred rituals. One of his enemies, Muru, said "He has made a charm so that women follow him as the eye of a snake follows a bird. He must die." One day when Banaidja left camp and walked through the grass, a spear was thrust into his back, followed by a rain of spears. Muru and his companion hid the body, but his spirit entered a paperbark tree. When people celebrate Laindjung and Banaidja, they tie bundles and beat them while they dance.

See also: LAINDJUNG

**0473**

**Banba**   In Celtic mythology, a goddess representing Ireland, as well as one of the three ancient names for the country (the other names were Eriu and Fodla). Banba is cited in James Joyce's novel *Ulysses*, in which the novelist writes: "Wail, Banba, with your wind. . . ." In a variant myth influenced by Christianity, Banba was said to be a daughter of Cain who lived in Ireland before the Flood recorded in Genesis (6:5–8:22).

See also: CAIN AND ABEL

**0474**

**Ba-neb-djet** (Ba-neb-Tatau, Ba-neb-Tet, Benedbdetet) (soul, lord of Busiris)   In Egyptian mythology, ram god of Mendes, portrayed as a ram with flat, branching horns surmounted by a uraeus. He was the northern equivalent of the god Khnum. As with the Apis bull, a live ram was used in worship and believed to have within him the soul of a god. Ba-neb-djet was believed to have the souls of Ra, Osiris, Geb, and Shu. The ancient Greeks identified the Egyptian deity with their Priapus and Pan.

See also: APIS; GEB; KHNUM; OSIRIS; PAN; PRIAPUS; RA; SHU; URAEUS

**0475**

**Banjo**   In American folklore, a guitar-like stringed instrument said to have been invented by Ham, a son of Noah, when the family was on the Ark. President Thomas Jefferson added this footnote to his *Notes on Virginia*: "The instrument proper for them [the slaves] is the banjar, which they brought hither from Africa." Reverend Jonathan Boucher, a British Loyalist who lived in America prior to the Revolutionary War, wrote of the banjo in his dictionary: "The body was a large hollow gourd with a long handle attached to it, strung with catgut, and played on with the fingers." It is also said that the gift of making music on the banjo is granted to those who meet the devil at a crossroads "where men are hanged and suicides buried."

**0476**

**Bannik** (bath spirit)   In Slavic folklore, bathhouse (banya) spirit, portrayed as a small old man with a large head and lots of disheveled hair. Bannik is either beneficent or demonic, depending on his mood. He guards the entrance to the bathhouse and allows three groups of bathers to

Bannik (I. Bilibin)

enter unharmed, but the fourth group is his to do with as he wishes. If he is angry, he pours scalding water over a bather's head or, even worse, strangles the bather to death. Sometimes he invites devils and forest spirits into the bathhouse. To pacify him, peasants leave some water for him to bathe in. If one wishes to discover the future, Bannik gives the answer, but only if he is in the right mood. Before entering one has to put his naked back through a half-open door of the bathhouse. If Bannik touches the person with his claws, it is a bad omen, but if he touches the person with the soft part of his hand, it is a good omen.

mense black coach mounted with a coffin and drawn by headless horses. If this funeral entourage arrives at a house and the householder opens the door, a basin of blood will be thrown in his or her face. A banshee's attention to a family was considered to be a mark of high station, especially in Ireland, and many families boasted of their own banshee. Various tales of the banshee are found in William Butler Yeats's collection of *Irish Folk Stories and Fairy Tales*.

Baphomet

0477

**Banshee** (Bean-sidhe) (woman fairy)  In Celtic folklore, an attendant fairy that follows a family and wails, foretelling but not causing the death of one of its members. The Caoine, the funeral cry of the Irish peasants, is said to be an imitation of the cry of the banshee. When more than one banshee is present and they wail and sing in chorus, it is for the death of some very holy or great person. An omen that sometimes accompanies the banshee is the Coach-a-bower, an im-

0478

**Baphomet**  In medieval Christianity, idol said to have been worshiped by the Order of Knights Templar. Some scholars believe that Baphomet is a corruption of the medieval French spelling of Mahomet, who was accused of being a devil by the Christians. The Order of Knights Templar were said to worship the idol Baphomet and were charged with both heresy and homosexuality by King Philip IV in 1307. Whether the charges were true or false is still debated by historians.

Baphomet's idol was a small figure with two heads, one male and one female. The body was that of a woman.

See also: KNIGHTS TEMPLAR, ORDER OF

0479

**Baphyra** In Greek mythology, the name assumed by the Helicon River when it refused to wash away the blood the Bacchants (or Maenads) had spilled when they tore Orpheus limb from limb. To avoid complicity in the crime, the river submerged itself and reemerged miles away, taking the name Baphyra.

See also: ORPHEUS

0480

**Baptism** (to dip or to dunk) In Christian ritual, sacrament of initiation by immersion in or sprinkling with water. It was one of the seven sacraments of Christianity during the Middle Ages.

The rite of baptism was not originally connected with the followers of Jesus but with those of St. John the Baptist. When Jesus' followers absorbed those of John, the rite was taken over into Christianity. In John's baptism the sinner was made aware of his sinfulness, but in Christian baptism the sinner was cleansed from Original Sin, the mark of Adam, which, according to Christian dogma, had descended on all men and women. Thus, the Church Council of Orange, held in 529, decreed: "With the grace received through baptism aiding and cooperating, all those are baptized in Christ can and ought, if they will strive faithfully, to fulfill what pertains to the salvation of the soul." Part of the medieval rite of baptism contained an exorcism. The priest would say over the person or child to be baptized:

I exorcise you, unclean spirit, in the name of the Father, and of the Son, and of the Holy Spirit. Come out and leave this servant of God [name]. Accursed and damned spirit, hear the command of God Himself, he who

walked upon the sea and extended his right hand to Peter as he was sinking. Therefore, accursed Devil, acknowledge your condemnation; pay homage to the true and living God; pay homage to Jesus Christ, his Son, and to the Holy Spirit, and depart from this servant of God, [name], for Jesus Christ, Our Lord and God, has called [him/her] to his holy grace and blessing, and to the font of Baptism.

This formula is still used today in the English versions of the Roman rite of baptism.

A medieval baptismal rite used in northern countries contained the following recitation by priest and candidate:

Q Forsaketh thou the Devil?
A I forsake the Devil!
Q And all the Devil guilds.
A And all Devil guilds.
Q And all Devil works?
A And I forsake all Devil works, and words. Thor and Woden and Saxenote [pagan Norse gods] . . . and all the evil ones that are his companions.

This formula took for granted that the northern pagan gods actually existed and were devils.

See also: JESUS CHRIST; JOHN THE BAPTIST, ST.

0481

**Barabbas** (son of Abba) In the Bible, N.T., the robber and insurrectionary leader whom Pilate freed from prison instead of Jesus (Matt. 27, Mark 15:7, Luke 23:18, John 18:40). The incident, which has no historical basis, is an attempt to place the blame for Jesus' death on the Jews instead of the Romans, who were responsible for his trial and execution. A novel, *Barabbas*, by Par Lagerkvist, tells the story of what happened after the Crucifixion.

0482

**Barada, Antoine** 1807–1885. In American history and folklore, son of an Indian woman named Laughing Buffalo, a member of the Omaha tribe, and of Parisian count Michael

Barada, who was employed as interpreter. In Missouri according to the Prairie du Chien Treaty of 1830 a "Half Breed Tract" of land was given to outcast "half-breeds," progeny of Indians and French trappers. Antoine Barada received 320 acres in 1856. According to legend, he once stuck a post into the ground, which caused a geyser to shoot 50 feet into the air. In order to stop it, he sat on it. Antoine was later referred to as the "mighty Paul Bunyan" of the area.

0483
**Barbara, St.** (strange, foreign)   Third century. In Christian legend, martyr. Patron saint of architects, builders, and fireworks makers. Invoked against thunder and lightning and all accidents arising from explosions of gunpowder. Feast, 4 December.

One of the most popular saints during the Middle Ages, St. Barbara's life is told in *The Golden Legend*, a collection of saints' lives written in the 13th century by Jacobus de Voragine. Barbara was the daughter of Dioscorus, a rich pagan nobleman. He loved her dearly but did not want her to be married, so he shut her up in a solitary tower. There she began to contemplate the meaning of life and came to the realization that the gods worshiped by her father—the sun, moon, and stars—were false. Seeking some answer to the mystery of life, she called upon Origen, the Christian writer, to instruct her in the Christian faith. Origen sent her one of his disciples disguised as a physician. Barbara was taught and was baptized a Christian.

One day, before Dioscorus left on a journey, he "sent skillful architects to construct within the tower a bath-chamber of wonderful splendor. One day Saint Barbara descended from her turret to view the progress of the workmen." She saw they were constructing two windows and ordered that they make three instead. When her father returned, he asked why she had changed his orders.

"Know, my father," said Barbara, "that through three windows doth the soul receive light, the Father, the Son and the Holy Ghost; and the Three are One."

Dioscorus was not at all pleased by his daughter's theological explanation of the three windows. In a fit of anger he "drew his sword to kill her," but she fled and was hidden by angels. A shepherd betrayed her by pointing silently to the place of her concealment. Her father dragged her by the hair, beat her, and shut her up in a dungeon. After she had been tortured by the proconsul Marcian, her father "carried her to a certain mountain near the city, drew his sword, and cut off her head with his own hands." As he descended from the mountain, a "most fearful tempest, with thunder and lightning, and fire fell upon this cruel father and consumed him utterly, so that not a vestige of him remained."

This gruesome tale found great acceptance during the Middle Ages, when statues of St. Barbara were frequently placed in churches and at shrines. In some sections of central Europe it is the custom to break a branch off a cherry tree on St. Barbara's feast day, place it in a pot of water in the kitchen, and keep it warm. When the twig bursts into bloom at Christmastime, it is used for decoration. The girl who tends the twig, according to the belief, will find a good husband within the year if she succeeded in producing the bloom exactly on Christmas Eve.

In medieval Christian art St. Barbara is often portrayed with her tower. Sometimes she is shown holding a feather in her hand. This refers to an old medieval German legend that when she was scourged by her father, angels changed the rods into feathers.

As the patron saint connected with firearms, an effigy of St. Barbara is often found on shields, great guns, and fieldpieces. During World War I, however, St. Joan of Arc was considered the patron of firearms among the French.

See also: *GOLDEN LEGEND, THE*

0484

**Barbara Frietchie**   In American folklore, a heroine of John Greenleaf Whittier's poem of the same title, published in 1864, that tells how Barbara Frietchie raised the Union flag when the Confederate general Stonewall Jackson entered Frederick, Maryland, during Lee's Antietam campaign on 6 September 1862. Barbara says in the poem:

Shoot if you must, this old gray head,
But spare your country's flag, she said.

Touched by her bravery, a Confederate officer saluted "To you, madam, not your flag." Whittier, however, confused the facts. A Mrs. Mary S. Quantrell waved the Union flag at the Confederate general. Barbara waved the Union flag when General Burnside, a Union officer, came into the town after Jackson's men left. Frietchie was a local legend; she had met George Washington, and the story was attached to her.

0485

**Barbarossa**   The Grimm Brothers include the legend of Friedrich Barbarossa at Mt. Kyffhausen in their collection of German folklore. The Emperor Barbarossa drowned in 1190 C.E. while on a crusade. Legend has it that he did not die but sits on a bench at a round stone table, resting his head in his hand, sleeping. Some say his beard has grown long, right through the stone table; others say it has grown around the table, and when it has encircled the table three times, he will awaken. He will return when his country needs him again.

One story from 1669 tells of a peasant transporting grain from the village of Reblingen to Nordhausen. He was stopped along the way by a dwarf and led into the mountain. There he was told to empty his sacks and fill them with gold. He saw the emperor sitting there motionless.

In another story a shepherd was also led into the mountain by a dwarf. The emperor asked him, "Are the ravens still flying around the mountain?" The shepherd assured him that they were, to which he replied, "Now I am going to have to sleep for another hundred years."

See also: ARTHUR; CHARLEMAGNE; MÁTYÁS; MERLIN; OGIER THE DANE; RÁKÓCZI, FERENC; SOLOMON

0486

*Bardo Thodol*   In Buddhism, the Tibetan *Book of the Dead*, or the "After-Death Experiences of the Bardo Plane, according to Lama Kazi Dawa-Samdup's English rendering." Published in English translation in 1927, compiled and edited by W. Y. Evans-Wentz, it is a guide for a dying man to pass through death and rebirth. In his second preface the editor writes that the message of the work is "that the Art of Dying is quite as important as the Art of Living . . . of which it is the complement and summation; that the future of being is dependent, perhaps entirely, upon a rightly controlled death. . . ." Traditionally composed by Padmasambhava, its full Tibetan title literally means "the Dharma that liberates the hearer in the Bardo just by being heard." The *Bardo* is any intermediate state of confusion, not necessarily that between lives. The version of Evans-Wentz is considered inaccurate, and that of Francesca Fremantle and Chogyam Trungpa is preferred. In this work there is much in common with the Egyptian *Book of the Dead*.

See also: *BOOK OF THE DEAD*; DHARMA; PADMASAMBHAVA

0487

**Bariaus**   In Melanesian mythology, spirits who inhabit old tree trunks. They are often shy and run away when approached by people.

0488

**Barlaam and Josaphat**   Eighth-century Christian tale by St. John of Damascus, a Syrian monk. It tells how Barlaam, a monk living in the Sinai, converted Josaphat, the son of a Hindu king, to Christianity. The basis for the legend is the life of Buddha, which filtered into medieval Christian sources from the East. The work contains the tale of the three caskets, which was used by Shakespeare in *The Merchant of Venice*.

See also: BUDDHA

*St. Barnabas*

0489
**Barnabas, St.** (son of consolation)   First century. In the Bible, N.T., companion of St. Paul who, according to Christian tradition, was martyred either by burning or being stoned to death. He is invoked against hailstorms and as a peacemaker. Feast, 11 June. His symbol is a rake because 11 June is the time for the hay harvest.

See also: PAUL, ST.

0490
**Barnum, Phineas Taylor**   1810–1891. In American history and folklore, a showman who was called the "Prince of Humbug." In 1835 he exhibited a black female slave, Joice Heth, who he claimed was 161 years old and had been George Washington's nurse. Actually, she was only 80 years old. In 1881 he merged his circus with that of his rival, James A. Bailey, forming the circus company Barnum and Bailey. He introduced to America General Tom Thumb, a midget, and Jenny Lind, the Swedish soprano. He also displayed a replica of the petrified remains of the Cardiff Giant, discovered on a farm in Cardiff, New York, in October 1869. On his deathbed he is reported to have asked how much money the circus pulled in that day. He is credited with saying, "A sucker is born every minute," but it is believed he said, "The American people like to be humbugged." The American composer Douglas Moore's symphonic work *Pageant of P. T. Barnum* tries to capture Barnum's spirit.

See also: CARDIFF GIANT

0491
**Baron Samedi**   In Haitian voodoo, a loa (deified spirit of the dead), lord of the cemeteries and god of the crossroads. Baron Samedi is also known as Baron Cimitière.

See also: LOA

0492
**Barsisa**   In Islamic legend, a man who bargains with the devil and loses. There are various versions of the legend, which is based on a verse in sura 59 of the Koran.

A monk or devotee, living in a cell for some 60 years, is continually tempted by the devil. To win the monk the devil brings a girl (who is variously described as a shepherdess, a neighbor's daughter, a princess) to the monk. The monk has intercourse with the girl, and she becomes pregnant. To cover his sin, he kills the girl and buries the body. Of course, the devil makes the crime known, and the man is arrested and sentenced to die. The devil reveals himself to the monk, offers to save him, and gives his condition: the monk must worship him. The monk agrees, but the devil, in an ironic tone, quotes a verse in sura 59 of the Koran: "Verily, I am clear of thee! I fear Allah the Lord of the Worlds!"

A more elaborate version of the tale is found in the 15th-century Turkish collection *History of the Forty Viziers*. From the Turkish collection the tale passed into European literature, finding its best-known Western expression in Matthew Gregory Lewis's Gothic novel *Ambrosio, or The Monk*. The novel was so popular that it earned the author the nickname "Monk Lewis."

Ambrosio, the superior of the Capuchins in Madrid, is known for his holy life. Matilda, a young noblewoman (who is actually a demon in disguise), enters the monastery dressed as a young novice. She entices Ambrosio, and the two go from one crime to another (described with relish by the author), including the seduction and murder of a young girl by the monk. The crimes are brought to light, and Ambrosio is tried before the Inquisition. He bargains with the devil to free him, and the devil agrees, releasing Ambrosio in a desert waste. When the lost monk realizes what he has done and wants to repent, the devil dashes him to pieces against a rock.

See also: FAUST; KORAN, THE

0493

**Bartek and Pies**   In Polish folklore, a king and his jester who exchange places in order to discover a person's true feelings. One day King Bartek, in the clothes of his jester, with the jester in royal robes, went to meet the king's prospective bride, Bialka, and her sister Spiewna. Of course Bialka thought the jester, Pies, was the king and fawned over him, but Spiewna showed she cared for Bartek even though she did not know he was the king. The tale ends with the marriage of Spiewna to the king and her sister Bialka married to an old organist.

0494

**Bartholomew, St.** (son of Tolmai)   First century. In the Bible, N.T., one of the Twelve Apostles of Jesus. Patron saint of Florentine salt and cheese merchants, bookbinders, butchers, corn chandlers, dyers, furriers, leather workers, shoemakers, tailors, and vine growers. Invoked against nervous diseases and twitching. Feast, 24 August.

Bartholomew's name appears on all four lists of the Twelve Apostles given in the Gospels. Some scholars believe he and Nathanael, mentioned in the Gospel According to Saint John, to be one and the same person. Bartholomew, they contend, is the patronymic, or surname, by which Nathanael is specified as the son, or *bar*, of Tolmai or possibly Ptolemy.

In an early Christian legend (not included in the New Testament), Bartholomew was the son of Prince Ptolomeus (a corruption of Tolmai or possibly Ptolemy). After the Ascension of Christ, according to that legend, Bartholomew preached the gospel in India and Armenia.

He was martyred, but the accounts of his death do not agree. In the Middle Ages various accounts circulated. *The Golden Legend*, a collection of saints' lives written in the 13th century, says that "some say he was crucified and was taken down ere he died, and for to have greater torment he was flayed and at the last beheaded." *The Golden Legend* always tried to reconcile differing accounts and may have combined three different legends that variously said Bartholomew was crucified, flayed, or beheaded.

Medieval Christian art often portrays the saint carrying a large knife, symbol of one form of his martyrdom. Sometimes St. Bartholomew is portrayed with his skin hanging over his arm, as in Michelangelo's *Last Judgment*, in which the saint defiantly holds a knife in one hand and his flayed skin in the other.

See also: APOSTLE; *GOLDEN LEGEND, THE*

0495

**Basilisk** (little king)   Fantastic lizardlike creature believed to be able to kill with its look or breath; often equated with the cockatrice. Pliny's *Historia Naturalis* recounts the myth of the basilisk, saying it is hatched from the egg laid by a

*Basilisk*

0496
**Basil the Great, St.** (kingly)   328–379. In Christian legend, one of the Four Doctors of the Greek church. Feast, 14 June.

Basil was made bishop of Caesarea in 370 and came into conflict with the emperor Valens, who was an Arian Christian. Though threatened with death by the emperor, Basil remained steadfast and later even gained some concessions for the Catholics. Robert Southey took a legend from the saint's life and used it for one of his narrative poems, *All for Love or A Sinner Well Saved*. Elëemon, a freedman, makes a compact with Satan that if he can marry his master's daughter, Cyra, he will give Satan his soul. The compact is agreed on and the devil delivers the girl to Elëemon; the two stay married for 12 years. Then the ghost of Cyra's father reveals the compact. Elëemon flees to St. Basil, who imposes penance on the sinner. When Satan comes to collect Elëemon, the saint enters into a debate with Satan, proving that the deal is no longer valid.

In Christian art St. Basil is often pictured with the Four Doctors of the Greek Church.

See also: DOCTORS OF THE CHURCH; FAUST

toad or a cock. To avoid being killed by the animal, travelers were advised to carry a mirror with them or a cock or a weasel, two mortal enemies of the beast. It was believed that if the basilisk saw its own reflection in the glass it would instantly die. Early Christian belief saw the basilisk as a symbol of the devil or of the Antichrist. A statue in the cathedral at Amiens, France, portrays Christ treading on a basilisk, referring to Psalm 91:13: "thou shalt tread upon the adder and the basilisk, and trample under foot the lion and the dragon" (Douay version). Chaucer, Spenser, and Shakespeare all refer to the fantastic creature. When Richard III attempts to woo Ann, Edward's widow, he cites the beauty of her eyes. She replies, "Would they were basilisks to strike you dead." In *Romeo and Juliet* (3:2) Shakespeare uses the word cockatrice, meaning basilisk:

. . . say thou but "I," And that bare vowel "I"
    shall poison more
Than the death-darting eye of cockatrice.

See also: ADDER; CHAUCER; DRAGON; LION; WEASEL

0497
**Bass, Sam**   1851–1878. In American history and folklore, a bandit who started out as a deputy sheriff and became a criminal who rode about the state of Texas robbing banks and sending the law on wild goose chases. According to legend, he often gave his stolen money to the poor. He was killed at Round Rock by one of his own men, who informed the Texas Rangers of a projected bank robbery. Stories of his death abound. Some are found in the Works Progress Administration files in the Library of Congress. The folk song "The Ballad of Sam Bass" makes him into a Robin Hood. For years a legend persisted about gold he had hidden and never recovered.

See also: WPA

*Bast*

**Bast** (Bastet, Pasht)   In Egyptian mythology, cat goddess worshiped at Bubastis in the eastern delta. She was looked upon as a manifestation of the solar eye and was even referred to as "the Eye of Ra who protects her father Ra." Bast, who loved music and dance, was the protector of pregnant women and also protected men against disease and evil spirits. Generally, she was considered the personification of the beneficial, fertilizing power of the sun, whereas her counterpart, Sekhmet, the lion goddess, represented the fierce, destructive power of the sun.

Bast became an important national deity about 950 B.C.E., and her festival was among the most popular in Egypt. According to Herodotus's *History* (book 2), vast numbers of men and women came to her festival by barge, singing and dancing, clapping their hands, and playing the castanets. On their way the women would shout abuses and even expose themselves to those along the shore. At Bubastis the feast was cele-brated with abundant sacrifices and festivities. Dead cats were carefully mummified and buried. It was said that more than 700,000 devotees attended Bast's yearly festival and that more wine was consumed than in all of the rest of the year besides.

In the Bible the Hebrew prophet Ezekiel (30:17) refers to Bast's city, which he calls Phibeseth, and says of Bast's worshipers that the young men will "fall by the sword" for their worship of her.

Egyptian art usually portrays Bast as a woman with the head of a cat. She holds in her right hand a sistrum for her music and in her left a shield with the head of a cat or lioness at the top.

See also: CAT; EZEKIEL

**Bat**   Any nocturnal flying mammal having modified forelimbs that serve as wings; symbol of both good and evil in world mythology and folklore. In ancient China and Japan the bat was a symbol of good fortune. Five bats in Chinese belief are symbolic of the five blessings: wealth, health, old age, love of virtue, and a natural death. It is said the Chinese eat bats to ensure all of these blessings. In contrast, the bat was considered a demonic creature during the Christian Middle Ages, being identified with witches and the devil. This belief in part stems from the Old Testament, where the prophet Isaiah (2:20) tells of a time when sinners will cast their idols "to the moles and to the bats." The animal is also listed among the unclean ones in the Old Testament. Some cultures believe that bats contain the souls of the dead. There are numerous motifs associated with bats in the *Motif Index of Folk Liter-*

*Bat*

*ature.* In popular movies and comicbooks the heroes Batman and Robin seem to see the animal as a beneficent symbol.

**Batara Guru** (Betara Guru)   0500   Name of the Hindu god Shiva used in the Malay Peninsula, Bali, Java, and Sumatra. Batara Guru is often identified with the spirit or god of the sea, Si Ray or Madu-Ray. The god rules over the sea from the low-water mark (at the river's mouth) to midocean. His home is in Pusat Tassek, the navel of the lake. In this mysterious home lives a gigantic crab. When the crab goes out for food at certain times during the day, he displaces the water in Pusat Tassek, causing the ebb and flow of the tides. From the center of Pusat Tassek springs a gigantic magic tree, Pauh Jangi, in whose boughs perches the roc, a large bird able to lift an elephant (found also in *The Thousand and One Nights* in the story of Sinbad the Sailor). Batara Guru has a wife, Madu-ruti, and two children, Wa' Ranai and Si Kekas (the scratcher).

See also: SHIVA; SINBAD THE SAILOR; *THOUSAND AND ONE NIGHTS, THE*

**Bato Kanzeon** (horse-headed Kanzeon)   0501   In Japanese Buddhist mythology, a form of Avalokitesvara, the Bodhisattva of compassion, guardian of horses, farm animals, and travelers. Usually Bato Kanzeon is portrayed wearing a crown or hat on which is a small horse's head. Some Japanese artworks portray him with three faces, each having three eyes. Most images portray him seated, though some show him on a horse. Often his image is placed beside roads and near mountain passes.

See also: AVALOKITESVARA; BODHISATTVA

**Battus** (stammer)   0502   In Greek mythology, a shepherd of Pylos who saw Hermes steal the cattle of Apollo. Battus promised not to divulge the theft but broke his promise and was turned into stone. The story of Battus's transformation is told in Ovid's *Metamorphoses* (book 2). The name is also borne by a king of Cyrene, son of Polymnestus, a Theraean noble, and Phronime, daughter of Etearchus. That Battus founded Cyrene in Libya and was cured of his stammer when he was frightened by a lion.

See also: APOLLO; HERMES; OVID

**Batu Herem**   0503   In Malayan mythology, the stone pillar that holds up the sky.

**Bau**   0504   In Near Eastern mythology (Babylonian), goddess of abundance and fertility worshiped in Babylon before 2300 B.C.E. In various inscriptions Bau is called the chief daughter of Anu, the god of heaven. Among her titles, the one most frequently given is that of "good lady." She was the mother who fixed the destinies of men and provided abundance for the tillers of the soil. On the feast of Zag-Muk (New Year), bridegrooms offered presents to their prospective brides in honor of Bau.

See also: ANU; ZAG-MUK

**Baucis and Philemon** (over-modest and   0505   friendly slinger)   In Greek mythology, an old couple rewarded for their hospitality to Zeus and Hermes.

Zeus and Hermes, in human form, found themselves in Baucis and Philemon's country, Bithynia, without shelter for the night. They sought lodging at every house, but it was late, and the householders refused to accommodate the travelers. At last they came to the house of Baucis and Philemon, a poor couple who had grown old together. Baucis and Philemon welcomed the travelers, raked up the coals into a fire, and prepared food. When the wine was poured out for the visitors, the couple saw that its level in the pitcher had not gone down, but the wine had replenished itself. They realized that their visitors were gods and, becoming fearful, apologized for the poor quality of their hospitality. But Zeus said: "We are gods. This inhospitable village shall pay the penalty of its impiety; you alone shall go free from the chastisement. Quit your house, and come with us to the top of yonder hill."

They hastened to obey, and staff in hand, labored up the steep ascent. When they turned and looked back down at their village, they saw that it had been submerged in a lake, with only their own house standing on a small island of dry ground. Suddenly, before their eyes, their house was transformed into a magnificent temple. Their reward for their hospitality to the gods was to become priest and priestess in the temple for the rest of their lives. Their final prayer to the gods was that when the time came for them to die, they should both die at the same hour so that they should never be without each other.

Ovid's *Metamorphoses* (book 8) tells the myth, which was also translated into French by La Fontaine and into English by Dryden, who translated part of the entire *Metamorphoses*. The myth was used by Rembrandt for his *Philemon and Baucis*, in which he portrays the couple and the gods at dinner. Rubens also painted the scene. There are some 10 operas on the subject. One, *Philémon et Baucis* (1860), is by Charles Gounod, the composer of *Faust*.

See also: HERMES; OVID; ZEUS

0506

**Baugi** In Norse mythology, an evil giant; brother of Suttung; killed by Odin, chief of the gods. Baugi had attempted to kill Odin, but the god overpowered him. In the legend, Odin sets out to obtain the sacred mead Odhrerir, which Suttung controls. When Suttung refuses to give Odin a single drop of the mead, Odin asks Baugi for help. They drill a hole into the mountain where the mead is kept, but when Odin blows into the hole, the dust comes back, and Odin

knows that Baugi is trying to deceive him. They drill again, and Odin transforms himself into a snake and crawls inside. Baugi tries to strike him, but Odin is already inside and takes a drink of the mead. Odin married Baugi's daughter Gunlod. She bore Odin a child, Bragi, the god of poetry and eloquence. Baugi appears in the *Prose Edda*.

See also: BRAGI; GUNLOD, ODHRERIR; SUTTUNG; *PROSE EDDA*

0507

**Bavon, St.** Seventh century. In Christian legend, patron saint of falconers and of the cities of Ghent and Haarlem. Feast, 1 October.

Born a nobleman, Bavon was converted to Christianity by St. Amand of Belgium, first bishop of Maestricht. This happened when Bavon was nearly 50 years old, a widower who had led a life of considerable dissipation, spending most of his time hunting with his falcon. After his conversion he gave all of his possessions to the poor and was placed in a monastery by St. Amand in Ghent. Not satisfied with the way the monastery was ruled, Bavon decided to live alone as a hermit in the forest. He found a tree with a large opening and set up house, living off herbs. One legend says that when he became a Christian he was so guilt-ridden because of his past life that he asked a former slave to beat him and then cast him into prison. The servant refused the second part of the wish, but he did beat the saint.

In Christian art Bavon appears with his falcon. Sometimes he is portrayed as a hermit living in a tree, other times as a well-dressed prince holding the falcon. In Hieronymus Bosch's *The Last Judgment* the saint is shown with a falcon on his left hand, while his right hand reaches for money to distribute to the poor. Bavon is also known as Allowin.

0508

**Bayard** (ruddy, red-haired) In the Charlemagne cycle of legends, a horse of incredible swiftness given by Charlemagne to the four sons of Aymon. If only one of the sons mounted, the horse was of ordinary size. But if all four mounted, its body became elongated to accommodate the extra riders. It appears in Boiardo's epic *Orlando Innamorato* and Ariosto's *Orlando Furioso*. Legend says that it is still alive and can be heard neighing in the Ardennes on Midsummer Day.

See also: AYMON, THE FOUR SONS OF; CHARLEMAGNE; ROLAND

0509
**Bean** A legume. The bean was sacred to the Egyptians, who therefore did not eat it. The Greek philosopher Pythagoras was said to believe that the souls of the dead were lodged within beans, and ancient Roman legend held that ghosts of the dead, *lemures*, threw beans at houses at night and brought bad luck to the inhabitants. To placate these ghosts the Romans held festivals in which beans were placed or burned on graves. Bean festivals are common in world mythology and tradition. Native American Hopi and Iroquois both celebrate the bean in ritual, and bean festivals in Europe celebrated Epiphany, or Twelfth Night, at which a king and queen were chosen. The king, Rey de Habas, was elevated three times in honor of the Trinity and then held up to the ceiling while he made crosses on the rafters with chalk to protect the house from evil. Bean cakes were baked for the feast and portioned out: one for God, one for the Virgin, one for each member of the family, and one for the poor.

See also: JACK AND THE BEANSTALK

0510
**Bean, Judge Roy** 1825–1904. In American history and folklore, self-proclaimed "law west of the Pecos." Roy Bean (really Isaac Parker of Fort Smith, Arkansas) ran a saloon and courtroom in Langtry, Texas, where he meted out his type of justice. He kept a pet bear in court and had a reputation for bragging, dueling, and gambling on cockfights. He was known as the "Hanging Judge" and was famous for saying: "Hang 'em

first, try 'em later," but there is no evidence to prove that he had anyone hanged. When a man was accused of killing a Chinese worker, Bean let the man go free because he could not find in his law book "any place where it is named an offense for a white man to kill a Chinaman." In another case, in which he acted as the town coroner, he fined a dead man for having a concealed weapon on his person.

Bean also owned a saloon. It was the custom in those days for a beer salesman to buy drinks for the whole crowd present; the empty bottles then were counted and paid up. Bean always added old empties to the lot. One day a salesman questioned him about the large amount he was being charged and the fact that some of the beer bottles did not look freshly emptied. Bean replied, "It does look fairly dry, but it's the way of drinking that some of the boys has. They don't often get good beer, and when they do, they not only drink the bottle dry but they sop it out. Purty good vouch for yore beer, son."

Bean named a saloon and town after the love of his life, Lily Langtry, a British actress he had never met. Bean was not gunned down by a Mexican outlaw, as some believe, but got drunk and died in his own bed. Lily Langtry came to visit 10 months later and listened to the stories of the man who worshiped her. Hollywood and the television industry have dealt with the legend several times. Walter Brennan received an Academy Award in 1936 for his portrayal of Bean, in 1956 there was a TV series starring Edgar Buchanan, and in 1972 the film *The Life and Times of Judge Roy Bean* featured Paul Newman and Ava Gardner.

0511
**Bear** A large mammal with massive body and heavy fur; symbol of both good and evil in world mythology and folklore. American Indians regard the bear with awe and respect. When an Indian killed a bear, he would beg its pardon and often smoke a peace pipe so that the bear's spirit would not be angry. This respectful approach re-

flects the belief that the bear possessed curative powers, and American Indian shamans in some tribes would imitate the bear in order to possess those powers. It was believed by many American Indian tribes that shamans could transform themselves into bears and that when they died they went to the heaven of bears. The Nordic *berserk* is derived from the words for bear and *sekr* (cloak), and was used to describe warriors who clothed themselves in bear skins in order to frighten the enemy during battle. In Greek mythology the bear was sacred to the goddess Artemis. At her shrine in Arcadia girls between five and ten years, called "brown bears," would dance in honor of the goddess.

In the Old Testament the bear is a symbol of evil and cruelty, representing the kingdom of Persia in the Book of Daniel (7:5). Medieval Christians believed that a bear was born as a shapeless white lump of flesh, a little larger than a mouse, without eyes or hair, and that the mother bear would lick this mass into shape, eventually forming a bear cub. The legend was seen as a symbol of the Christian church converting the unbeliever to the "true faith." In today's American popular symbolism, the bear is both good, as in Smokey the Bear, and demonic, as the symbol of Soviet Russia. There are numerous motifs associated with the bear in the *Motif Index of Folk Literature*.

See also: ARTEMIS; BERSERK

*Bear*

**Beast Epic**   In European medieval literature, a series of linked tales grouped about animal characters. The tales are often used to make satirical comment on the church or the court. The best-known beast epic is the *Roman de Renart*, about Reynard the Fox. An excellent example of the beast epic in English is found in Chaucer's *Canterbury Tales* in *The Nun's Priest's Tale*.

See also: AESOPIC FABLES; CHAUCER; REYNARD THE FOX

**Beatrix** (bestower of the blessings)   In medieval legend, a nun devoted to the cult of the Virgin Mary, to whom she offered daily prayers. One day a clerk spotted her and wanted her for his mistress. He tempted her until the "old serpent enkindled her breast so vehemently that she could not bear the flames of love," according to one medieval account. Beatrix went to the statue of the Virgin and said, "Mistress, I have served thee as devoutly as I could; behold, I resign thy keys to thee. I cannot longer withstand the temptations of the flesh." She then left the convent to live with her lover, but he abandoned her after a few days. Ashamed to return to the convent, she became a whore for some 15 years.

One day she returned to her convent and asked the doorkeeper, "Did you know Beatrix, formerly custodian of this oratory?"

The man replied, "I know her well. For she is an honest and holy woman, and from infancy even to the present day has remained in this convent without fault."

When Beatrix heard this, she wanted to run away. Suddenly, the Virgin Mary appeared to her. "During the fifteen years of thy absence, I have performed thy task: now return to thy place and do penance; for no one knows of thy departure." There are various medieval retellings of the legend, the most famous being a Dutch version.

See also: VIRGIN MARY

**Beaver**    Gnawing mammal with a broad, flat, naked tail and webbed hind feet. In ancient Roman folk belief, as recorded in Pliny's *Historia Naturalis*, the beaver would castrate itself when pursued by a hunter, knowing that the hunter only wanted its testicles, which contained a magical medicine. Medieval Christians who read Pliny's work took up the belief and gave it symbolic meaning. For them the beaver symbolized the sinner who should cut off his sinfulness (testicles) and throw them at the devil (the hunter).

*St. Bede*

**Bede the Venerable, St.** (prayer)    673–735. In Christian legend, Doctor of the Church. Author of the *Ecclesiastical History of the English People*, a record of the conversion of England to Christianity as well as a secular history of the island. Feast, 27 May.

In the conclusion to his major work (he also wrote saints' lives and commentaries on the Bible) Bede says he was a "priest of the monastery of the blessed apostles, Peter and Paul, which is at Wearmouth [now Monkwearmouth] and Jarrow." He was born in the neighborhood of the monastery and was sent there to live at the age of seven. He "wholly applied" himself to study of the Bible and "took delight in learning, teaching, and writing." When he was 19 years old he was made a deacon and became a priest when he was 30 years old. In his *Vita sancti Cuthberti* Bede tells the story of how Cuthbert saved monks from drowning. He describes how the legend circulated orally for generations among the local populace before Bede heard it in a live performance.

According to legend, Bede died while dictating the last words of his translation of the Gospel According to St. John. His title "Venerable" is a term of respect often bestowed on members of religious orders in his time. There is a legend, however, with a different accounting for the title. A priest, wishing to put an inscription on his tomb, left out a word, since he could not find a suitable one. At night an angel came and wrote *venerabilis* (venerable). In *The Divine Comedy* (Heaven, canto 10) Dante places St. Bede, together with St. Isidore of Seville and St. Richard, among the great Doctors of the Church in the Heaven of the Sun.

In Christian art St. Bede is portrayed as an old monk writing at his desk with a quill.

See also: CUTHBERT, ST.; DOCTORS OF THE CHURCH; PETER, ST.; PAUL, ST.

**Bedivere, Sir** (birch hero)    In Arthurian legend, a knight of the Round Table, the butler and staunch supporter of King Arthur. He was present at the last battle between King Arthur and Mordred. At the request of the dying king, Bedivere threw the sword Excalibur into the lake. Afterward he bore the king's body to the three fairy queens, who set it on a barge for Avalon.

See also: ARTHUR; AVALON; EXCALIBUR; ROUND TABLE

**Bee**    Any of a large group of four-winged insects, usually with a sting, sacred to many gods and goddesses in world mythology. In Greek mythology Zeus, the sky god, was sometimes called Melissaios (bee-man) in the myth that he had a son by a nymph, who, fleeing the wrath of Hera, Zeus's wife, hid their child in the wood, where his father sent him food by bees. The bee was also sacred to the Greek goddess Artemis in her role as orgiastic nymph. It was identified with Demeter in Greek mythology and with

Cybele in Roman mythology as a sign of productivity. Vishnu, Krishna, and Indra in Hindu mythology are called Madhava (nectar-born ones) and are often portrayed with a bee resting on a lotus flower. Karma, the Hindu god of love, has a bowstring made of bees. Christianity also adopted the bee as a symbol. St. John Chrysostom (golden-mouthed) was born, according to legend, with a swarm of bees hovering around his mouth to symbolize the sweetness of his preaching. The same legend is told of St. Ambrose and St. Bernard of Clairvaux, both noted preachers. The bee was the emblem of Napoleon I.

Various accounts are given of the bee's origin in world folklore. Medieval German Christians believed that bees were created by God to supply wax for church candles. In a Breton belief, bees were created from the tears of Christ on the cross. The most common story, however, given in Vergil's *Fourth Georgic*, is that bees are produced from decaying oxen. This belief, also expressed by Aristotle, arose because the rib cage of a dead ox provided a perfect natural frame for a beehive.

Another common belief is that bees had to be informed of the death of their keeper or they would leave or die. In Mark Twain's *Huckleberry Finn* Jim tells Huck: "If a man owned a beehive and the man died, the bees must be told it before sun-up next morning, or else the bees would all weaken down and quit work and die." This belief may stem from the ancient belief that bees were the messengers of the gods, announcing the arrival of the dead in the underworld. There are numerous motifs associated with bees in the *Motif Index of Folk Literature*.

See also: AMBROSE, ST.; ARTEMIS; BERNARD OF CLAIRVAUX; DEMETER; HERA; INDRA; JOHN CHRYSOSTOM, ST.; KARMA; VISHNU; ZEUS

0518

**Beetle**    An insect having hard, horny front wings that cover the membranous flight wings. In Egyptian mythology, the beetle, or scarab, is a common symbol of spontaneous creation and re-generation, often associated with the great god Ra and his various manifestations. In Christian belief, the beetle has often been identified with the devil. Irish Christians, for example, see the darbhodaol, a species of long black beetle, as a devil that has eaten the souls of sinners.

See also: RA

0519

**Befana**    In medieval Italian folklore, a good fairy who gives gifts to children on Epiphany, 6 January, or Twelfth Night. Her name is a corruption of the word *Epiphany*. According to legend, Befana was too busy with house affairs to look after the Magi when they passed on their way to visit the Christ Child. She said she would wait for their return, but they went another way. Every Twelfth Night she watches, hoping to see them. In accordance with folkloric custom, on Twelfth Night after the children are in bed, someone enters their rooms, leaving the gifts, and the children say, "*Ecco la Beffana.*"

See also: MAGI

0520

**Begochiddy** (one who grabs breasts)    In North American Indian mythology (Navaho), great creator god. He was put in charge of game and domesticated animals. He has intercourse with everything, giving birth to monsters. His name comes from his practice of sneaking up on young girls and grabbing them by the breasts, shouting "be'go be'go." He is also known for grabbing hunters by the testicles just as they are about to shoot an animal.

0521

**Bego Tanutanu** (Bego the maker)    In Melanesian mythology, creator god and culture hero who formed the land and taught various arts. Bego's wife put limits to the sea, but when she was seen by her grandsons, she caused a flood.

**Behdety** (he [i.e., Horus] of Behdet)  In Egyptian mythology, the winged sun disk, combining the sun with the falcon as the two highest soaring bodies known to the ancient Egyptians. Later assimilated with the god Horus, the winged sun disk is a frequent motif found at the top of funerary stelae. The cult was localized in the district of Edfu, called Apollinolis Magna by the ancient Greeks, who equated this disk with their god Apollo.

See also: APOLLO; HORUS

**Bel** (lord, master)  In Near Eastern mythology (Babylonian-Assyrian), earth god; a form of the title Baal (lord) applied to various gods, especially to Enlil, the lord of the underworld, and to Marduk, the patron god of Babylon.

Bel, as god of the earth, was associated with Anu, as god of heaven, and Ea, as god of the watery deep, forming a triad that embraced the whole universe. When the three gods were invoked, it was equivalent to naming all of the powers that influenced the fate of man. Bel's wife was the goddess Belit.

The tale of *Bel and the Dragon*, which is part of the Old Testament Apocrypha, tells how the Hebrew prophet Daniel proved to King Cyrus of Persia that a statue of Bel could not possibly eat the food provided for it.

Every day, according to the tale, the statue of the god was provided with "twelve great measures of fine flour, and forty sheep, and six vessels of wine." The king would come to the temple and worship the idol. One day he said to Daniel, "Why dost not thou worship Bel?"

Daniel replied: "Because I may not worship idols made with hands, but the living God, who hath created the heaven and the earth, and hath sovereignty over all flesh."

"Thinkest thou not that Bel is a living god?" said the king. "Seest thou not how much he eateth and drinketh every day?"

Then Daniel laughed, saying the king was deceived, that the idol did not eat any food because it was made of clay and brass. The king then got angry and called his priests.

"If ye tell me not who this is that devoureth these expenses, ye shall die. But if ye can certify me that Bel devoureth them, then Daniel shall die; for he hath spoken blasphemy against Bel."

The priests and Daniel agreed to a contest. Food and wine were brought to the chamber. The priests, however, had a private entrance under the table by which each night they entered with their wives and children, eating all of the food. Daniel knew of this and asked that his servants bring ashes and strew them throughout all of the temple in the presence of the king alone before the room was sealed. When they went out, the door was sealed with the king's signet.

That night the priests came with their wives and children and ate the food. When the king and Daniel returned the next morning they opened the seal. The king looked at the table and said, "Great art thou, O Bel, and with thee is no deceit at all."

Then Daniel said to the king: "Behold now the pavement, and mark well whose footsteps are these."

"I see the footsteps of men, women, and children," the king replied.

Angry at being deceived by his priests, "the king slew them, and delivered Bel into Daniel's power, who destroyed him and his temple."

According to ancient historians, however, it was not Daniel, the Hebrew prophet, but King Xerxes, a pagan, who destroyed Bel's temple.

See also: BAAL; BELIT; DANIEL; EA; ENLIL; MARDUK

**Belial** (worthless, useless)  In the Bible, O.T., a good-for-nothing or scoundrel is called a "man of Belial" (1 Sam. 20:1, 30:22). In the New Testament, however, the term is used for the opponent of Christ, or the devil (2 Cor. 6:15).

*Belial*

St. Paul in 2 Corinthians (6:15) writes: "And what concord hath Christ with Belial." Most biblical commentators assume the reference to Belial to be another name for Satan, since various apocryphal books use Belial as the name of a demon or the name of the Antichrist. In *Das Buch Belial* by Jacobus de Theramo, Belial is the official lawyer of the devils. He appears before God and demands that the deeds of Christ be investigated. King Solomon, who was noted for his wisdom, is chosen by God to be the judge of the case. Moses is chosen by Jesus as the lawyer to defend him. Belial accuses Jesus of tampering with the infernal machinery of the world, usurping the powers of the devil, since not only hell but the seas, the earth, and "all beings that inhabit it" are under his control now. To influence his case Belial does a dance for King Solomon. The king, unmoved, favors Jesus. Belial does not give up; he appeals the case, and with Joseph, the patriarch of the Old Testament, as judge, Christ is found guiltless, but Belial is given power over the damned on Judgment Day.

In Milton's *Paradise Lost* (book 1:490–492) Belial is a "lewd" spirit who loves "vice for it self." Victor Hugo, in his novel *The Toilers of the Sea*, credits Belial with being hell's ambassador to Turkey.

See also: MOSES; PAUL, ST.; SATAN; SOLOMON

0525

**Belin** (bright?)   In medieval British legend, the 21st of the mythical kings of Britain. Belin fought with his brother Brennius over the inheritance of the kingdom, but their mother, Conwenna, persuaded them to join forces to fight against the Romans. Belin is credited with building the Tower of London. His ashes are said to have been placed in a golden urn at the top of the tower.

See also: CONWENNA

0526

**Belinus** (Belenos) (bright)   In Celtic mythology, a British sun god whose cult reached from Italy to the British Isles; son of Ana; husband of Don; father of Caswallacon, Llevelys, Lludd, and Nynnyan; who in later medieval legend is called King Belinus and appears in Geoffrey of Monmouth's *History of the Kings of Britain*. Belinus may be a variant of Bile, a Celtic god of the dead, to whom human sacrifices were made. Some ancient commentators linked him with Apollo

See also: APOLLO; BELTAINE; LLUDD; NUDD

0527

**Belisama**   In Celtic mythology, among the British Celts, tutelary goddess of the river Ribble. The name was given to the goddess by ancient Roman writers, who identified her with their goddess Minerva.

See also: MINERVA

0528

**Belisarius**   Sixth century C.E. In Eastern history and legend, general of the emperor Justinian who defended the Roman Empire against Vandals and Goths. He was charged by his enemies with conspiracy, imprisoned, and later freed. Legend, however, says that he died blind and a beggar. David's painting *Give Belisarius a Penny* is based on this legend. Robert Graves's novel *Count Belisarius* also deals with the general.

**Belit**   In Near Eastern mythology 0529
(Babylonian-Assyrian), wife of the great god Bel.
Among her many titles were Nin-khar-sag (lady
of the high or great mountain), referring to the
mountain of the gods; Nin-lil (mistress of the
lower world); Nunbar-Segunnu, goddess of
agricultural fertility; Nisaba, goddess of wisdom;
and Haya, goddess of direction. Belit was often
equated with Ishtar.

See also: BEL; ISHTAR

**Bellerophon** (he who slays the monster)   In 0530
Greek mythology, a hero, son of Glaucus of Corinth or Poseidon and Eurymede; brother of De-
liades; grandson of Sisyphus; married Philinoe;
father of Deidameia, Hippolochus, Islander, and
Laodameia.

Bellerophon was a virtuous man who was betrayed by a spurned love. According to Homer's
*Iliad* (book 6), Antaea, wife of King Proteus, had
a mad passion for Bellerophon, but Bellerophon,
being a man of honor, would not have an affair
with another man's wife. Antaea, furious at the
rejection, told her husband lies about Bellerophon, that he had attempted to rape her, and
begged the king to have Bellerophon killed. Proteus, who abhorred violence, demurred, but to
placate Antaea, he agreed to send Bellerophon to
her father, king of Lycia, to be dealt with. Bellerophon was sent to Lycia with sealed letters to
the king telling of his alleged crime and begging
Antaea's father to see to his punishment. Accordingly, Bellerophon was sent out to slay the
Chimera, a fire-breathing monster— lion in
front, serpent behind, and goat in the middle.
Bellerophon succeeded with the aid of his
winged horse, Pegasus. He then went on to conquer the Solymi and the Amazons. Later he married Philline and had children. Pindar adds to the
Homeric account by telling how Bellerophon,
proud of his feats, wanted to mount to heaven on
Pegasus, but Zeus drove the horse insane with a
gadfly and Bellerophon fell to earth and died.

Bellerophon appears in Edward Young's
*Night Thoughts*, William Morris's "Earthly Para-
dise," and George Meredith's "Bellerophon." In
*Paradise Lost* (book 7) Milton asks his Muse Ura-
nia, who has helped him soar "above the flight of
Pegasean wing," to descend again:

. . . up led by thee
Into the Heav'n of Heav'ns I have presum'd
An earthlie Guest, and drawn Empyreal Aire,
Thy tempring; with like safeties guided down
Return me to my Native element:
Lest from this flying Steed unrein'd, (as once
Bellerophon, though from a lower Clime)
Dismounted, on th' Aleian Field I fall
Erroneous, there to wander and forlorne.

The phrase "letters of Bellerophon" is
sometimes applied to documents that are
dangerous or prejudicial to the bearer.

See also: AMAZONS; CHIMERA; DEIDAMEIA;
GLAUCUS; *ILIAD, THE*; LAODAMEIA; PEGASUS; POSEI-
DON; PROTEUS; SISYPHUS; ZEUS

**Belle Starr**   1848–1889. In American history 0531
and folklore, popular name of Myra Belle Shirley, the Queen of the Bandits and Petticoat of
the Plains. Her father, John Shirley, married Eliza Pennington of the Hatfield family (from the
Hatfield-McCoy feud). The leader of a band of
cattle rustlers, horse thieves, and bank robbers,
she rode the Owlhoot Trail, where she was ambushed and killed. Her boyfriend was Cole
Younger, a member of Jesse James's gang of robbers. The chorus of a ballad about her concludes
with:

Belle Starr, Belle Star, with a bullet in your
back
Are you lyin' there a-wishin' that you'd never
joined that pack?

Her life and legend appeared in Richard E.
Fox's *Belle Starr, the Bandit Queen: Or, the Female*

*Jesse James*, as well as a Hollywood movie, *Belle Starr*, with Gene Tierney, which presents a laundered version of her life.

See also: HATFIELDS AND MCCOYS; JESSE JAMES

0532

**Bellona** (war)    In Roman mythology, ancient Italian war goddess, wife or sister of Mars (or Quirinus), identified by the Greeks with Enyo. Bellona's temple, which was situated on the Campus Martius, was used for meetings of the senate when it dealt with foreign ambassadors or Roman generals who claimed a triumph (a festal procession, the highest honor accorded a commander) on their return from war. Without permission the generals were not allowed to enter the city. The Columna Bellica (pillar of war) stood nearby. It was from near Bellona's temple that the Fetialis threw his lance when declaring war. The cult of the war goddess Bellona, however, seems to have been confused with another Bellona, a goddess brought from Comana in Cappadocia towards the beginning of the first century B.C.E. This goddess was worshiped in a different locality and with a service conducted by Cappadocian priests and priestesses. During the festivals of the goddess these Bellondrii moved through the city in procession, dressed in black and shedding their blood by wounding themselves in the arms and loins with a two-edged ax. Drums and trumpets were part of the ritual. Her festival date was 3 June. Bellona appears in Vergil's *Aeneid* (book 8).

See also: *AENEID, THE*; MARS

0533

**Belly and Its Members, The**    Aesopic fable found in various collections of fables throughout the world.

It is said that in former times the various members of the human body did not work together as amicably as they do now. On one occasion the members began to be critical of the belly for spending an idle life of luxury while they had

to spend all of their time laboring for its support and ministering to its wants and pleasures.

The members went so far as to decide to cut off the belly's food supplies for the future. The hands were no longer to carry food to the mouth, nor the mouth to receive it, nor the teeth to chew it.

But, lo and behold, it was only a short time after they had agreed on this course of starving the belly into subjection that they all began, one by one, to fail and flop, and the whole body started to waste away. In the end the members became convinced that the belly also, cumbersome and useless as it seemed, had an important function of its own and that they could no more exist without it than it could do without them.

*Moral: As in the body, so in the state, each member in his proper sphere must work for the common good.*

The fable occurs in Plutarch's life of Coriolanus and is important in the second scene of Shakespeare's play *Coriolanus*, based on Plutarch. Similar fables occur in Egypt and India (in the great epic poem *The Mahabharata*), in Buddhistic sources, and in Jewish ones, where it is told in a rabbinic commentary on Psalm 39. St. Paul may have had a similar fable in mind when he wrote 1 Corinthians, in which he compares the church to the body of Christ (12;12–26).

See also: AESOPIC FABLES; *MAHABHARATA*

0534

**Belshazzar** (may Bel protect the king)    In the Bible, O.T., last Babylonian king, killed in the sack of the city by Cyrus II in 539 B.C.E. Belshazzar gave a great feast (Dan. 5) for his court, using golden vessels that his father, Nebuchadnezzar, had taken from the temple in Jerusalem. As the party progressed, a hand wrote on the wall: *Mene, mene, tekel, upharsin.* Wanting to know what these words meant, the king called his astrologers, magicians, and soothsayers. None of them could translate the words. Then Daniel, the Hebrew prophet, was called in. He told Belshazzar the words meant that he was "weighed in the balances and art found wanting" (Dan. 5:27), and his kingdom would be destroyed. That night the Medes invaded the city, killing Belshazzar, and Darius the Persian came to the throne. Our common expression "the writing on the wall" comes from this passage. The legend inspired Rembrandt's painting *Belshazzar's Feast*, Handel's oratorio *Belshazzar*, and William Walton's *Belshazzar's Feast*. In modern German, a *Menetekel* is a warning sign, a portent.

See also: NEBUCHADNEZZAR

0535
**Beltaine** (Beltane, Baltein, Bealtuinn, Beltan) In Celtic mythology, a feast held at the spring equinox in early May, which may or may not derive from the veneration of Belinus. Part of the rituals associated with the day consisted of bonfires and the sacrifice of a man who represented the Oak King. In Ireland the feast was called Samradh or Cetsamain; in Wales it was Cytenfyn.

See also: BELINUS

0536
**Bendis** In Greek mythology, a Thracian goddess of the moon, identified by the Greeks with Artemis, Hecate, and Persephone. Bendis's worship was introduced into Attica by Thracians and was very popular during Plato's time. A public festival called the Bendideia was held annually at which there were torch races and a solemn procession of Athenians and Thracians at the Piraeus, a promontory outside Athens.

See also: ARTEMIS; HECATE; PERSEPHONE

0537
**Benedict, St.** (blessed)   480–543. In Christian legend, father of Western monasticism. Patron saint of coppersmiths and schoolchildren. Invoked against fever, gallstones, nettle rash, poison, and witchcraft, by servants who have broken their employer's possessions, and by the dying. Feast, 21 March.

Benedict was born of a noble family in Spoleto and sent to study in Rome, where he showed great scholarly promise. However, he was disgusted by the life of the clergy, who lived in debauchery. To escape he became a hermit at the age of 15. His nurse, Cyrilla, who was always with him, tried to follow, but Benedict escaped, hiding in the wilderness of Subiaco. Here, according to numerous legends, he underwent many temptations from the devil. Once the devil tried to distract him with the vision of a beautiful woman, but the saint, to avoid falling into sin, threw himself on a thicket of briars and arose "bleeding, but calm." Another time the devil transformed himself into a blackbird and began to flutter around Benedict. Although the saint was hungry, he did not reach out for the bird. In fact, he was suspicious of the creature and made the sign of the cross. The bird instantly disappeared.

Despite the annoyances from the devil, the saint founded 12 monasteries with the help of St. Maurus and St. Placidus, sons of Roman senators. Both afterward became famous. St. Maurus introduced the Benedictine rule in France; St. Placidus brought it to Sicily, where his sister St. Flavis joined him and was martyred with him. His sister, St. Scholastica, founded a similar order for nuns.

St. Gregory the Great, in his *Dialogues* (book 2), records a legend about Mount Cassino (destroyed in World War II by Allied bombers because it was a Nazi stronghold). The devil, since he could not get anywhere tempting the flesh of St. Benedict, decided he would obstruct his efforts to build a monastery on the site of the temple of Apollo. One day the builders went to carry a stone prepared for a certain part of Mount Cassino, but when they attempted to lift it, they found it was too heavy. They went to Benedict, who immediately saw that the devil was holding the stone down. He made the sign of the cross over the stone and picked it up all by himself. The stone, St. Gregory informs his readers, can still be seen at the monastery.

Another legend recorded by St. Gregory tells how a novice, in clearing the banks of a lake, accidentally lost his ax head, which flew off its handle and into the water. Benedict went at once to the lake and held the wooden handle in the water; the iron ax head rose to the surface and fitted itself firmly onto the handle. The miracle is similar to that of Elisha in the Old testament (2 Kings 6:5–7).

A much later legend tells how he healed Bruno, later Pope Leo IX, of toad poison by touching the boy's lips with a crucifix.

In Christian art St. Benedict is usually shown bearded, generally in a black Benedictine habit but sometimes the white one of the reformed order. He holds an asperges for sprinkling holy water on people possessed by demons, or a pastoral staff, signifying his position as an abbot. Sometimes a raven is shown, referring to the legend, or a piece of crockery, which the saint miraculously put together after it had accidentally been broken by a servant.

See also: ELISHA; GREGORY THE GREAT, ST.

0538

**Benini**   In Near Eastern mythology (Babylonian), a monster with the face of a bird or raven. Benini, along with his evil mother, Melinni, and a host of demonic birds once attacked Babylon. They were finally defeated when the proper prayers were said and the proper sacrifices offered to the gods.

*Benjamin*

0539

**Benjamin** (child of fortune or son of the right) In the Bible, O.T. (Gen. 35ff), youngest son of Jacob and Rachel, who died giving him birth; brother of Joseph. Benjamin's descendants became the tribe of Benjamin. Saul, the first king of Israel, and St. Paul both descended from the tribe.

See also: JACOB; JOSEPH; PAUL; SAUL

0540

**Benkei**   12th century C.E. In Japanese folklore, a hero, often called Oniwaka (young demon). Benkei was the son of a priest of Kumano in Kii. Because of his boisterous nature he gained the nickname Oniwaka. When he was 17 years old, he became a wandering priest and is sometimes portrayed with his head partly shaven and wearing a hexagonal cap. Often he is shown blowing on a huge conch shell or inside a conch shell drinking sake. His most common form in Japanese art, however, is fighting the Yamabushis (mountain warrior-priests) or capturing a huge fish in a waterfall. Benkei was said to be eight feet tall and as strong as 100 men.

0541

**Benten** (Bensaiten, Benten Sama, Dai Bensaiten)   In Japanese Shinto-Buddhist mythology, the only female among the gods of luck. She is the goddess of love, beauty, music, and other arts; one of the Shichi Fukujin, gods of good luck or fortune. Benten was originally derived from the Hindu goddess Sarasvati, who was also associated with love, but when her cult reached Japan, her nature was somewhat changed. Benten is frequently portrayed with a Hakuja, a white serpent, and is known as the White Snake Lady. The snake, aside from being a symbol of fertility and sexuality, is also one of the symbols of the sea and thus connects Benten's worship with rivers, seas, and water in general. Belief in the existence of serpent-people in the oceans around Japan was common. The goddess is also invoked for the growth of rice.

Her main seat of worship is a shrine on Eno-shima, near Kamakura, and at Itsukushima, on Miyajima near Hiroshima.

Benten is portrayed with four or eight hands, two of which are folded in prayer. Each remaining hand holds a different symbol, such as a sword, wheel, ax, rope, bow and arrow, tama (symbolic jewel of purity), and key. Her crown varies. Sometimes it has a phoenix on top, sometimes three flaming jewels or a coiled white snake with the face of an old man. Often the goddess is shown playing a *biwa*, a Sino-Japanese instrument resembling a lute. Benten is also called Kotokuten (goddess of meritorious works) and Ako Myo-on-ten (goddess of the marvelous voice). She is also the mother of 15 sons, the Ji-ugo Doki.

See also: SHICHI FUKUJIN

*Beowulf (H. J. Ford)*

**0542**

**Benu** (rise and shine) In Egyptian mythology, bird identified by the Greeks with the phoenix. The benu was said to be the oldest living creature. It created itself from fire that burned at the top of the sacred persea tree of Heliopolis. Its cry was the first sound ever heard and represented the point at which time began. It was essentially a sun bird, symbol of both the rising sun and the dead sun god, Osiris, from whose heart, in one account, the bird sprang. The benu not only signified the rebirth of the sun each morning but became a symbol of the resurrection of man. *The Book of the Dead* provides a formula for enabling the deceased to take the form of the benu. After Egyptian kings had ruled for 30 years, they asked the benu for renewed strength and vitality. According to the Greek historian Herodotus (book 2), the benu made its appearance once every 500 years. Its plumage was partly golden and partly red, and in size and form it resembled an eagle. It came from Arabia and brought with it the body of its father (which it had enclosed in an egg of myrrh) to bury at the temple of the sun.

See also: *BOOK OF THE DEAD, THE*; OSIRIS; PHOENIX

**0543**

**Beowulf** (wolf-of-croft, bear's son; Anglo Saxon corn god Beow) In medieval British legend, hero of the epic poem *Beowulf*, recorded by an unknown monk of Northumbria early in the eighth century, combining pagan and Christian myths and legends. In the poem Heorot, the palace of Hrothgar, king of the Danes, is visited nightly by a monster named Grendel, who devours the king's thanes as they sleep. Beowulf, the nephew of Hygelac, king of the Geats (a tribe in southern Sweden or, according to some scholars, the Jutes), comes across the sea with 14 followers to free the Danes from this scourge. After a cordial welcome by Hrothgar and his court the visitors are left alone in the hall for the night. As they sleep, Grendel enters and devours one of the Geats. Though invulnerable to weapons, Grendel is seized by Beowulf and held in a mighty grip, from which he breaks away only with the loss of his arm, and he flees to his cavern beneath the lake to die.

There is great rejoicing in Heorot at Grendel's death. The minstrels sing lays to honor Beowulf, and the king loads him with gifts. But another monster, Grendel's mother, still lives, and she comes to the hall that night to avenge her son's death. She finds Hrothgar's followers asleep and carries off one of them, Aeschere, and eats him. Beowulf pursues the monster to the depths of the lake. She grapples with Beowulf and drags him into the cavern beneath the water. A desperate struggle ensues, in which Beowulf loses his sword, but the hero finds a magic sword in the cave and kills Grendel's mother. Beowulf cuts off her head and returns to the shore. Again he is thanked by Hrothgar, and after many ceremonial speeches, he returns to the palace of Hygelac.

A long interval ensues, in the course of which Hygelac and his son Heardred are killed in battle, leaving the kingdom to Beowulf, who rules it for 50 years. Then a dragon with a fiery breath devastates the kingdom. Going out with 12 followers to kill the monster, Beowulf is wounded and deserted by all but one of his comrades. He finally kills the dragon but at the cost of his own life. His body is burned by the Geats on a funeral pyre, and the ashes are enclosed in a barrow.

The burial of Beowulf inspired American composer Howard Hanson's *Lament for Beowulf* for chorus and orchestra. Hanson used the translation of William Morris, the 19th-century English poet.

0544
**Berenice**    Third century B.C.E. In Roman history and legend, wife of Ptolemy III. (There were in fact numerous other Ptolemaic princesses named Berenice.) She dedicated a lock of her hair to ensure her husband's safe return from a war in Syria. The lock then disappeared. It was later seen as a group of stars by the royal astronomer. The "lock of Berenice" is referred to by Catullus (poem 66) and inspired Pope's mock epic *The Rape of the Lock*, in which the heroine's curl of hair is also made into a star at the poem's conclusion. Berenice also is the name of a daughter of Herod Agrippa, born 28 C.E., who married her uncle and lived incestuously with her brother. Later she became mistress to Titus, Emperor Vespasian's son. When Titus became emperor, he dismissed her. Berenice appears in the Acts of the Apostles at St. Paul's trial (chap. 25) as Bernice, in Corneille's *Tite et Berenice*, and in Racine's *Berenice*.

0545
**Bergelmir** (Bergelmer) (mountain old, that is, the old man of the mountain)    In Norse mythology, a giant from whom all the frost giants descended. After the original giants were destroyed at the death of the primeval giant Ymir, whose blood flooded the earth, only Bergelmir survived. He and his wife climbed up to his boat made of a hollow tree trunk, according to the *Prose Edda*. Matthew Arnold refers to the incident in his narrative poem *Balder Dead*, saying that Bergelmir "on shipboard fled."

See also: *PROSE EDDA*; YMIR

0546
**Bernardino of Siena, St.** (bear-brave) 1380–1444. In Christian legend, patron saint of wool weavers. Invoked against diseases of chest and lungs. Feast, 20 May.

One of the most notable preachers of the 15th century, St. Bernardino held aloft a tablet with the carved monogram IHS (a contraction of the Greek IHϵουσ, or Jesus) encircled by rays when he preached. The *Life of St. Bernardino* by his contemporary, Barnaby of Siena, tells how the saint walked on water. Bernardino had to cross a river to reach Mantua, where he was to preach. He did not have the money for the crossing, and the ferryman refused to take him. The saint took his cloak, cast it on the water, and sailed away. In

*St. Bernardino of Siena*

Christian art St. Bernardino is usually shown with the IHS monogram, as in El Greco's painting of the saint. Bernardino is a form of the name Bernard.

0547

**Bernardo del Carpio**   In medieval Spanish legend, hero who fought against Charlemagne, appearing in many Spanish ballads.

Bernardo del Carpio was the illegitimate son of Doña Ximena, sister of King Alfonso II, who came to the Visigoth throne about 795. The king, known as the Chaste because he did not have intercourse with his wife, had Ximena locked up in a convent for giving birth illegitimately, and the father of her son, Sancho Diaz, count of Saldana, was imprisoned and blinded. (Some Spanish chroniclers gloss over the cruel incident, alleging that a private marriage took place between the lovers.)

When Bernardo was grown, Alfonso, according to the Spanish chronicles, invited the emperor Charlemagne into Spain to eventually become king of Spain, Alfonso being childless. The Spanish nobility, headed by Bernardo, opposed the alliance, and the king finally gave in to their wishes. Charlemagne, however, came to Spain to expel the Moors and found that Alfonso had united with the Moors against him. A battle took place at Roncesvalles in which the French were defeated and the hero Roland was slain. The victory, which in the *Chanson de Roland* is credited to the Moors, was chiefly due to Bernardo del Carpio.

A Spanish ballad, *The March of Bernardo del Carpio*, describes the enthusiasm among his men when Bernardo first raised the standard to oppose Charlemagne's army.

> "Free were we born,—" 'tis thus they cry—
>    "though to our King we own
> The homage and the fealty behind his crest
>    to go;
> By God's behest our aid he shares, but God
>    did ne'er command
> That we should leave our children heirs of an
>    enslaved land" (John Gibson Lockhart
>    translation).

Another Spanish ballad, *The Complaint of the Count of Saldana*, narrates the imprisonment of Don Sancho, Bernardo's father; another, *The Funeral of the Count of Saldana*, narrates the gruesome death of Don Sancho, who was mounted on his horse after his death and sent to his son, who did not know his father had been killed at the orders of King Alfonso. When Bernardo saw his father he cried out:

> "Go up, go up, thou blessed ghost, into the
>    hands of God;
> Go, fear not lest revenge be lost, when
>    Carpio's blood hath flowed;
> The steel that drank the blood of France, the

arm thy foe that shielded,
Still, father, thirsts that burning lance, and
  still thy son can wield it" (John Gibson
  Lockhart translation).

A ballad titled *Bernardo and Alfonso* recounts
events taking place after the funeral of
Bernardo's father. Bernardo argues with King
Alfonso and leaves the court, going over to the
Moors. The actual end of Bernardo del Carpio,
however, is not known. Bernardo de Balbuena
wrote an epic poem, *El Bernardo, la Victoria de
Roncesvalles*, in which Bernardo is the main hero.
The poem is an imitation of Ariosto's *Orlando
Furioso*. Balbuena was born in Spain but went to
Mexico as a child. He was made bishop of Puerto
Rico in 1620.

See also: CHARLEMAGNE

0548

**Bernard of Clairvaux, St.** (bear brave)
1090–1153. In Christian legend, patron saint of
beekeepers and wax melters. Doctor of the
Church. Feast, 20 August.

Born of noble parents near Dijon, Bernard
studied at the University of Paris and entered the
Benedictine monastery of Citeaux when he was
20 years old. A few years later, at the abbot's bidding, he set out with 12 monks and founded
another monastery at Clairvaux. He became one
of the most important preachers of the age. He
was in part responsible for the Second Crusade,
which killed more European Jews than Muslims
in the Holy Land. He was known to have had a
fierce debate with Abelard, whom he hated intensely. Among his numerous works, *On the Love
of God* and his *Commentary on the Song of Songs* are
the best known.

According to legend, when he was writing his
commentary on the Song of Songs in praise of
the Virgin Mary, to whom he was dedicated, she
appeared to him. She moistened his lips with
milk from her bosom, and from that day he had a
supernatural eloquence. Legend also says the

white habit of the Cistercians was chosen by the
Virgin Mary herself.

In Christian art St. Bernard is shown in the
white habit of the Cistercians carrying a book or
writing one. Sometimes he is shown presenting
his works to the Virgin Mary or being inspired
by her to write them, as in Fra Filippo Lippi's
painting *The Vision of St. Bernard*.

See also: BENEDICT, ST.; VIRGIN MARY

0549

**Berserks** (bear-shirt)  In northern countries,
warriors who wore bear-skin garments (*serkr*)
and became possessed during the fury of battle.
The Viennese Mythological School of the 1930s
and 1940s interpreted them as part of ancient
Germanic ecstatic cults. They were dedicated to
the god Odin and believed to be under his control. They would enter battle, seemingly imper-
vious to wounds and danger. One medieval
Nordic source says they "went without mail-
coats, and were frantic as dogs or wolves; they bit
their shields and were as strong as bears or boars;
they slew men, but neither fire nor iron could
harm them." This behavior was known as "running berserk." In Scandinavian society berserks
were viewed as holy because they were sacred to
Odin. However, the god would at his will desert
them in battle. For this reason Odin was often
called the Arch-Deceiver.

See also: ODIN

0550

**Bertha** (bright)  In Germanic folklore, one of
the names by which the Norse goddess Frigga is
known. Bertha, sometimes called Brechta (the
white lady) or Perchta, is said to live in the hollow of a mountain in Thuringia, where she keeps
watch over the souls of unbaptized children. She
also watches over plants. She is said to be the
ancestor of numerous European noble families.
Charlemagne's mother was called Berthe aux
grande pieds (Bertha with the large feet) because
the continual working of the foot-treadle on her
spinning wheel caused her feet to flatten, accord-

ing to medieval legend. She appears in a 13th-century *chanson de geste* by Adenet le Roi.

Bertha is believed to appear as a wild woman with shaggy hair before the death or misfortune of a family. At Christmastime Bertha is said to pass through village streets during the 12 nights between Christmas and Epiphany to see whether spinning is being done. She rewards some with golden threads or a distaff of extra-fine flax, but she befouls the dresses of young girls who do not finish spinning all their flax on the last day of the year.

Many people eat dumplings or herring on this day and believe that if they do not, Bertha will cut their stomachs open, take out the contents, and fill them with straw. She sews up her incisions with a plowshare and a chain instead of a needle and thread.

See also: FRIGGA; TWELVE NIGHTS

*Bes*

0551

**Bertoldo** In Italian legend, a clown whose life is told in *Vita di Bertoldo* by Giulio Caesare Croce, written in the 16th century. His antics and those of his son Bertoldina and his grandson Cacasenno frequently appear in Italian tales.

0552

**Bes** In Egyptian mythology, a patron god of art, music, and childbirth as well as a god of war and a strangler of antelopes, bears, lions, and serpents; derived from a lion deity. He was a kind of divine exorcist, driving away evil by dancing and banging a drum or tambourine. The dual nature of Bes in Egyptian belief is reflected in the various images of the god. Usually he is portrayed as a dwarf with a huge bearded head, protruding tongue, flat nose, shaggy eyebrows and hair, large projecting ears, long thick arms, and bowed legs. Around his body he wears an animal skin whose tail hangs down, usually touching the ground behind him. On his head he wears a tiara of feathers, which suggests his primitive nature. In later Egyptian art, however, Bes is given a handsome body because he absorbed the charac-

ter of the sun god and became identified with Horus the Child as well as Ra and Temu. As Horus he wore a lock of hair on the right side of his head, which is the symbol of youth. All of these images suggest the various phases of the sun during the day. Bes was frequently portrayed on steles, vases, and amulets, often in ithyphallic form. His image was hung over headrests as a charm to keep away evil spirits. His female counterpart was Beset.

See also: HORUS; RA; TEM

0553

**Bestiary** (Bestials) A book of beasts, popular during the Middle Ages, containing natural history and lore. The bestiary in one form or another is found in major languages: Old English, Arabic, Armenian, English, Ethiopic, French, German, Icelandic, Provençal, and Spanish. For medieval man a bestiary was a serious work of natural history, not a collection of myths and legends. What information it contained was believed to be factually true. Yet the medieval mind was not satisfied with mere facts. They had to be interpreted. Thus, bestiaries contain symbolic meanings. In Guillaume's *Le Bestiaire Divin* we have an excellent example:

The unicorn represents Jesus Christ, who took on him our nature in the Virgin's womb, was betrayed by the Jews, and delivered into the hands of Pontius Pilate. Its one horn signifies the Gospel truth, that Christ is one with the Father.

The legendary lore of animals often served as texts for devotional homilies.

**0554**

**Bestla** In Norse mythology, giantess, wife of Bor; daughter of the giant Bolturon; mother of the gods Odin, Vili, and Ve. Odin was thus descended from a giantess on his mother's side, which means that the killing of Ymir by Odin was a killing within the family. Bestla appears in the *Prose Edda*.

See also: ODIN; VILI; *PROSE EDDA*

**0555**

**Bevis of Hampton** (dear son) In medieval legend, an English hero who converts his pagan wife, Josian, to Christianity, defeats a host of enemies, and converts the giant Ascapart (Asclopard) to Christianity. The tale is slightly connected to the Charlemagne cycle. Bevis's magic sword is called Morglay. His tale is told in the 14th-century English romance *Bevis of Hampton* and in Samuel Drayton's *Poly-olbion*.

See also: CHARLEMAGNE

**0556**

**Bhaga** In Hindu mythology, a god who bestows wealth and presides over marriage. Bhaga is mentioned in the sacred Vedas, though her personality and powers are rather indistinct.

See also: VEDAS

**0557**

**Bhagavad-Gita** (song of the divine one) A dialogue between the hero Arjuna and the god Krishna, forming part of the Hindu epic poem *The Mahabharata*.

Though part of a vast epic poem, the longest in the world, the Bhagavad-Gita is frequently found in separate editions. It is the most popular sacred book of India, even though it is not part of *shruti*, or revealed writings, but belongs to *smriti*, or traditional works. The main theme of the dialogue between Arjuna and his charioteer, Krishna (who is an incarnation of the god Vishnu), concerns the role Arjuna must play in the coming battle with the Kauravas, his enemies but also his relatives. Krishna assures Arjuna that he should not hesitate to slay his foes because he is just killing their bodies, which does not affect the vital principle that inhabits the body. Throughout the dialogue Krishna touches on various Hindu beliefs, often found expressed in the Upanishads. Arjuna, as a member of the warrior caste, must fulfill his role in the world, since God himself is tirelessly engaged in works in order to keep the universe going. The Gita also declares that the ancient faith in sacrifice as the sole means of liberation is no longer valid.

One of the most important sections of the poem is that in which Arjuna asks Krishna to reveal himself. There takes place a transfiguration of All-Form-Vision (book 9), in which Krishna displays his true, godlike nature.

"In him was the whole universe centered in one," says the Bhagavad-Gita. "Endowed with countless eyes and numberless mouths, and innumerable faces turned in every quarter, and blazing with the glory of a thousand arms, with celestial ornaments and fierce weapons; with many hands, feet, and organs, with countless stomachs and fierce and fearful tusks terrible to behold."

Arjuna then sees the Kauravas, his enemies, in Krishna's mouths, with their hands crushed to powder. Krishna tells Arjuna to worship him by fixing his heart and thought on Krishna. At the conclusion of the work (book 18) Arjuna says:

Trouble and ignorance are gone! The Light
Hath come unto me, by Thy favor, Lord!
Now am I fixed! My doubt is fled away!
According to Thy word, so will I do!
(Edwin Arnold translation)

There is a version of the Bhagavad-Gita in
which the name Ganesha, the elephant-headed
god of wisdom and good fortune, is substituted
for that of Krishna. It is called Ganesha-Gita and
is used by the Ganapatyas (worshipers of
Ganesha), who see their god as the supreme
being.

See also: ARJUNA; GANESHA; KRISHNA; *MAHAB-
HARATA, THE*; UPANISHADS; VISHNU

**Bhakti** (be devoted to)    In Hinduism the love
existing between the human soul and the divine.
Bhakti yoga is one of the ways of achieving this
union. Bhakti is associated with the doctrine of
liberation by faith, as opposed to the Vedic doctrine of liberation through works or knowledge.

0558

**Bharata**    In Hindu mythology, the name of an
Aryan tribal group prominent in early vedic
times; also a king devoted to the worship of the
god Vishnu. He abdicated his throne to continue
in constant meditation on the god.

0559

While Bharata was at his forest retreat, he
went to bathe in the river and saw a pregnant doe
frightened by a lion. Her fawn, which was born
suddenly, fell into the water, and Bharata rescued
it. He brought up the animal, becoming very
fond of it and forgetting his worship of Vishnu.
When Bharata died, he was transformed into a
deer, with the faculty of remembering his former
life as a punishment for forgetting to honor
Vishnu. Bharata continued in his deer form and
atoned for his sin, being born again as a priest
who was ungainly and looked as if he were a
madman. In his new life he constantly worshiped
Vishnu and as a result was exempt from future
births.

Another Bharata is the ancestor of the warring
sides, the Pandavas and Kauravas, in the Hindu
epic poem *The Mahabharata*.

See also: *MAHABHARATA, THE*; VISHNU

**Bhavacakra**    In Buddhism, the Wheel of Life
or Existence, used to bring before the mind the
nature of existence. The wheel is portrayed as
being whirled around by a monster, who symbolizes the limitations of human existence. Outside
the wheel the Buddha is portrayed to show the
release. In some versions the Buddha is also portrayed within the wheel, symbolizing the accessi-
bility of Buddhist teachings to all beings. The
segments of the wheel depict the levels of rebirth
as a human, an animal, a god, or other form of
life.

0560

**Bhikkhu** (Bhikshu)    In Buddhism, one who has
devoted his life to the following of the Eightfold
Path by renunciation and relies for his livelihood
on gifts of lay disciples, in return for which he
preaches and gives counsel. Often the
term—*bhikku* in Pali and *bhikshu* in Sanskrit—is
translated into English as monk, mendicant,
friar, or priest. The female equivalent is *bhikk-
huni* or *bhikshuni*.

0561

**Bhima** (the terrible)    In the Hindu epic poem
*The Mahabharata*, a hero, second of the five
Pandu brothers. Bhima, the son of Vayu, the
wind god, had great strength but was of a fierce
and often cruel nature. His coarse manners
earned for him the title Vrikodara (wolf's belly)
because he ate more food than all of his brothers
combined. One episode in *The Mahabharata* tells
how his cousin Dur-yodhana, jealous of his great
strength, poisoned him and threw his body in the
Ganges. He was bitten by the Nagas, but the poison in his blood neutralized their venom and he
recovered. The Nagas then gave him eight jars of

0562

nectar, which he drank, giving him great strength. Bhima then kicked the head of his prostrate enemy, Dur-yodhana, earning him the title Jihma-yodhin (the unfair fighter).

See also: DUR-YODHANA; *MAHABHARATA, THE*; VAYU

---

0563

**Bhishma** (the terrible)   In the Hindu epic poem *The Mahabharata*, a hero, commander-in-chief of the Kauravas in the war with the Pandavas. Bhishma taught the children of both sides, the Kauravas and Pandavas, but when the war broke out between the two sides, he took the part of the Kauravas. He laid down some rules for mitigating the horrors of the war, stipulating that he should not be called on to fight Arjuna, the Pandu prince and main hero of the poem. However, Bhishma was goaded by one of the Kauravas to fight against Arjuna; their encounter took place on the 10th day of battle. Bhishma was pierced with so many arrows that there was no space for a finger's breadth. When he fell from his chariot, he was held up from the ground by the arrows in his body. He lived for some 58 days more because he had determined the hour of his death. During that time he delivered several long didactic discourses, which make up part of the epic poem. Bhishma is also called Tala-ketu (palm banner), referring to his banner symbol.

See also: ARJUNA; *MAHABHARATA, THE*

---

0564

**Bhrigu**   In Hindu mythology, a Prajapati, a son of the god Brahma, sent by the priests to test the characters of various gods. Bhrigu could not get to see Shiva because the god was making love to his wife. As a result, Bhrigu, "finding him, therefore to consist of the property of darkness," sentenced Shiva "to take the form of the Linga (phallus) and pronounced that he should have no offerings presented to him, nor receive worship of the pious and respectable." Bhrigu's next visit was to his father, Brahma, whom he saw sur-

rounded by sages and so much inflated by his own importance as not to pay any attention to Bhrigu. Brahma was therefore excluded from worship by the priests. Next Bhrigu went to Vishnu and found the god asleep. Bhrigu stamped on Vishnu's chest with his left foot and awoke the god. Instead of being offended, Vishnu gently pressed Bhrigu's foot and said he was honored. Bhrigu, pleased by the god's humility, proclaimed Vishnu the only being to be worshiped by men or gods.

See also: BRAHMA; LINGAM; SHIVA; VISHNU

---

0565

**Bhuta**   In Hindu mythology, a ghost, imp, or goblin. Bhutas are malignant and haunt crematoria, lurk in trees, animate dead bodies, and delude and devour humans. According to the *Vishnu Purana*, a text in honor of the god Vishnu, they are "fierce beings and eaters of flesh" who were created when the Creator was angry. In another text their mother is said to have been Krodha (anger). The Bhutas are attendants on the god Shiva, their lord. The term *Bhutesa* (lord of beings; lord of created things) is applied to the gods Vishnu, Brahma, and Krishna (an incarnation of Vishnu).

See also: KRISHNA; SHIVA; VISHNU

---

0566

**Bible, The**   In Christianity, sacred writings compiled from the Hebrew Scriptures and various early Christian works. The word *bible* is derived from the Greek *biblos*, part of an ancient plant used in making books. The Greek word *biblia*, meaning "the books," referred to the Scriptures. The Greek *biblia* (plural) became the Latin *biblia* (feminine singular), from which came the English word *bible*.

The Catholic Church in the third century took the Hebrew Scriptures, both the Hebrew books accepted by all Jews and those written in Greek and used by some Jews in various parts of the world, then added various Christian works, forming the Bible.

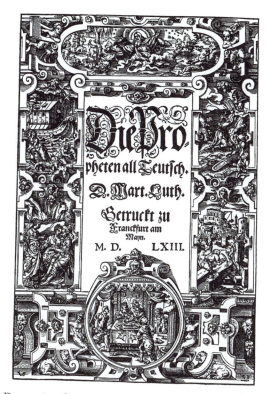

*Decoration from a 1563 edition of the Bible*

The King James, or Authorized, Version, completed in 1611, is the best-known translation of the Bible into English, though numerous other versions exist. During the Middle Ages the common Bible was the Latin translation called the Vulgate, made by St. Jerome in the fourth century. It contained books later rejected by Protestants at the Reformation and placed in the Apocrypha.

Translations of the Vulgate into some European languages were made during the Middle Ages. One of the first is ascribed to Caedmon about 650. St. Bede the Venerable made a translation of the Gospel According to St. John about 735. In 825 Anglo-Saxon glosses (marginal annotations) were made of the Vulgate Gospels and psalters. Between 890 and 900 King Alfred made various translations of selected passages of the Bible. In the year 1000 the earliest extant English translation of the four Gospels appeared. In 1320

William of Shoreham made an English translation of the Psalms, and Richard Rolle made an English translation of the Psalms in 1340. The first Wycliffe translation of the whole Bible appeared in 1384 but was condemned by the church. A revised version by John Purvey was made about 1396. Numerous English versions followed the Reformation, the most famous, because of its influence on English literature and life, being the King James Version of 1611.

In Germany the Bible was translated by Martin Luther between 1522 and 1534. There had been several prior translations into German; some were literal translations of the Latin Vulgate and were thus not very readable. Luther's Bible was not only closer to the Hebrew and Greek originals, but also could be read in both major dialect regions of Germany. As a result of the recently developed movable type procedure, it was possible to produce many copies of the Bible for sale and distribution. Some records suggest that as many as 100,000 copies appeared during Luther's time.

The Bible has two major divisions, the Old Testament, containing the pre-Christian Jewish Scripture, and the New Testament, containing writings of the early Christian era. Each division of the Bible consists of many different books, written by various authors over a long period of history. In the King James Version the Old Testament consists of 39 books, the New Testament, 27. Roman Catholic Bibles contain the Apocrypha within the Old Testament. For example, the Catholic New American Bible contains 46 books within the Old Testament and the same New Testament books found in the King James Version.

The following books of the Bible are found in the King James Version:

*Genesis* (in the beginning) is the first book of the Bible, narrating the myths and legends of the ancient Hebrews from the Creation to the story of Joseph in Egypt. Genesis forms the first part of the Law, or Torah or Pentateuch (five-volume document), which consists of the first five books of the Bible. The major themes of Genesis are primeval legends and myths of humankind (1–11:19) and accounts of the patriarchs (11:28–50:26), including the legends of Abraham (11:26–25:10), Isaac (25:11–26:35), Jacob (27–36), and Joseph (37–50).

*Exodus* (going out) continues the tales, legends, myths, and history of the Hebrews. The main themes of Exodus are oppression and deliverance (1–18), including Moses' call (2–4), escape from Egypt (5–14), and the wilderness (14–18); imposing the law through delivering the Ten Commandments (20); forming the Covenant between God and Israel (21 and 23) and giving details and specific laws of the tribes; the Tabernacle at Sinai and the construction of the Ark (24–40).

*Leviticus* consists of ritual laws; its title comes from the tribe of Levi, the hereditary priests.

*Numbers* is so named because of the two numberings of the people. It focuses on Moses, the leader and prophet. The book narrates the legends of the Hebrews from their second year in the wilderness to the arrival on the borders of Moab, close to the Promised Land.

*Deuteronomy* (second law) is the last book of the Pentateuch; the title refers to the repetition by Moses of Yahweh's commandments. The book consists almost entirely of discourses ascribed to Moses by later Hebrew legend. It narrates a résumé of the wilderness events (1–4), the Decalogue and other laws (5–26), the written law (27–28), Moses' farewell speech and his charge to Joshua (29:1–31:13), and Moses' last days and death (31:14–34:12).

*Joshua at Jericho*

*Joshua*, the last of the first six books of the Bible, called the Hexateuch, is named for the successor of Moses, who led the Israelites into Canaan. Its main themes are the conquest of Canaan (1–12), division of the land (13–22), and Joshua's last speech and death (23–24).

*Judges* deals with the activities of the "Judges," or tribal leaders, who ruled between the entry into Canaan and the establishment of the monarchy. Its main divisions are introduction (1–2:5); the legends of the judges (2:6–16:31), telling of Othniel, Ehud, Deborah, Gideon, Abimelech (antihero), Tola, Jair, Jephtah, Ibzan, Elon, Abdon, and Samson; the conquest of Laish by the Danites, who renamed it Dan; and the sexual abuse of a Levite's concubine by Benjamites of Gibeah, resulting in her death and the subsequent war of vengeance by the rest of the tribes of Israel (17–21).

*Ruth* tells a story of the days of the Judges concerning the family of a man of Bethlehem who was forced by a famine to migrate to Moab; his Moabite daughter-in-law Ruth became the ancestress of King David and, according to New Testament accounts, also of Jesus.

*1 Samuel* records the events leading to the establishment of the kingdom of Israel and the reign of Saul, the first king. Its main themes are legends of Samuel (1–12) and the reign of Saul (12–31), telling of the conflict of David, who later became king, and ending with the killing of Saul and his sons at Gilboa by the Philistines.

*2 Samuel* continues the narrative, telling of David, who became first king of Judah and later of all Israel. Its main themes are David's attainment of the monarchy (1–10), David and Bathsheba (11–12), David and his rebel son Absalom (13–19), and the last events in David's life (20–24).

*1 Kings* tells of the death of David and the succession and reign of his son Solomon (1–11); then of the legends, history, and myths of Israel and Judah (12–22) after the split of Israel. Important figures are Ahab, Elijah, and Elisha.

*2 Kings* continues 1 Kings, narrating the end of the northern kingdom, the reign of Hezekiah in Judah, and legends and tales of Elisha. The book ends with the destruction of the southern kingdom and tells of Josiah and the conquest of Judah by Babylon.

*1 and 2 Chronicles* recapitulate previous books, often contradicting information in them.

*Ezra* tells of Ezra and Nehemiah, who came back from Babylon with the Jews to rebuild the Temple.

*Nehemiah* continues the legends recorded in 1 and 2 Chronicles as well as in Ezra.

*Esther* is a folktale about the Jewess Esther who married Xerxes, king of Persia, and saved the Jews from a pogrom. The Jewish feast of Purim was established to celebrate this deliverance. The next major division of the Bible consists of the five poetical books, Job, Psalms, Proverbs, Ecclesiastes, and the Song of Solomon or Song of Songs.

*Job*

*Job* tells of a man punished by God, though he is guilty of no sin. The book explores the question "Why do the righteous suffer?" but produces no answers.

*Psalms* is a collection of prayers, poems, and hymns recited and sung in both Jewish and Christian worship.

*Proverbs* is a book of sayings illustrating general truths, using pithy and colorful language. It was traditionally ascribed to Solomon but is written by many other hands.

*Ecclesiastes* is filled with skepticism and pessimism about the world and its creator. After it was included in the Bible, it was edited to soften its

harsh message. The next major division of the Old Testament contains the Major and Minor Prophets.

*Isaiah* is named for a prophet who warned Israel of its sin and promised a messiah to deliver her from her enemies. Isaiah also was a preacher who used parables, as Jesus did much later. Jesus was probably greatly influenced by Isaiah and his preaching, since Christians consider the central message of his prophecy to be the coming of Jesus. Much of the text of Handel's *Messiah* was taken from the Book of Isaiah. It is now agreed by scholars that Isaiah wrote only part of the book; his followers wrote some sections.

*Jeremiah* is named after the prophet. It includes his prophecies as well as considerable biographical material.

*Lamentations* consists of five poems that have been ascribed to Jeremiah but were not written by him. They tell of the siege of Jerusalem by the Babylonians and are used extensively in Christian liturgy.

*Ezekiel* is a long, often tedious work, but it contains some passages of greatness. Ezekiel claimed he was commanded to warn Israel about its rebellion against God. Much of his prophecy he received through visions, the best known being his vision of the fiery wheels.

*Daniel*

*Daniel* contains legends about the prophet for whom it is named. Daniel was an Israelite in the land of Persia and came into conflict with Persian officials when he refused to worship Persian idols. He was cast into a lion's den for his refusal, but the God of Israel protected Daniel, and he emerged unharmed. It was also Daniel who correctly interpreted the "writing on the wall" for King Belshazzar, which predicted the king's destruction.

*Hosea*, the 28th book and the first of the Minor Prophets, uses symbolic language, telling of Hosea's marriage to a whore, who represents faithless Israel.

*Joel*, the second of the Minor Prophets, consists of only three chapters in three discourses. It contains no Bible stories in the usual sense but is largely a series of exhortations for Israel to repent its sins.

*Amos* is the first prophetical book compiled. It denounces wealth and luxury.

*Obadiah* is only 21 verses long. It is a violent attack on Edom, Israel's enemy.

*Jonah* is a short folktale about the prophet, in which Jonah causes a tempest at sea when he flees from God in a boat. When he confesses he is the cause of the tempest, the mariners cast him overboard, and he is swallowed by a giant fish. After Jonah repents, the fish vomits him out on dry land, and Jonah fulfills his promise to God and becomes a prophet.

*Micah* is ascribed to the prophet Micah, a contemporary of Isaiah in Judah. Micah laments the degeneracy of the house of Jacob and warns against false prophets.

*Nahum* is a collection of oracles written by Nahum, the Elkoshite about 700 B.C.E. He warns of punishment for Nineveh for the sins of its people and predicts that God will rout the enemies of Israel.

*Habakkuk* concerns the threat of the Babylonians to Judah's security. The prophet rebukes the Chaldeans for their sins.

*Zephaniah* speaks of the sins of Judah and predicts God's severe punishment. He ends with a vision of the dispersed people of Judah returning to their own land.

*Haggai* is the prophet chosen by God to encourage the rebuilding of the Temple. He tells the people that sin impedes their work.

*Zechariah* stresses temple worship. He warns the people of Jerusalem of their possible destruction and of the vengeance of God against the enemies of the city.

*Malachi* is the last of the Old Testament prophets. He tells of a time when the prophet Elijah will return.

The next section of the Bible, which is often omitted, contains the Apocrypha, those books rejected by Protestants as not belonging in the Hebrew Bible because they were written in Greek and used by Greek-speaking Jews, not by the Jews in Jerusalem. All the books influenced Christian art, which has used many of their legends and tales.

The 15 books of the Apocrypha are the following:

*1* and *2 Esdras* is a Greek reworking of the books of Ezra and Nehemiah.

*Tobit* is a tale beloved by Martin Luther that tells of a demon who possesses various people and of how the angel of the Lord frees them.

*Judith* is a short novel of a Jewess who destroys the enemy by cutting off the head of their leader.

*The Rest of Esther* consists of additions to the Hebrew Book of Esther in the Bible, giving more details and dwelling on God and Israel. The Hebrew Book of Esther never mentions God.

*Wisdom of Solomon* is a collection of proverbs, similar to the Book of Proverbs in the Old Testament. *Ecclesiasticus* is another wisdom book.

*Baruch* is a short book ascribed to the secretary of the prophet Jeremiah.

*Letter of Jeremiah*, a short letter ascribed to the prophet, ridicules idolatry.

*Prayer of Azariah and the Song of the Three Young Men* gives their prayer, which is not found in the biblical Book of Daniel.

*Susanna* is a short folk tale of a woman vindicated by the prophet Daniel.

*Bel and the Dragon* is a short tale of Daniel in which he shows that idols are not really gods.

*Prayer of Manasseh*, a short prayer, is still used in the Anglican church.

*Susanna*

*1* and *2 Maccabees* are two books of legends and history of the Jews.

The next major division in the King James Bible is the New Testament, which consists of 27 books, all accepted by Christians today. The first four books are called the Gospels (good news) and are the Early Church's view of the person of Jesus as Messiah and the Son of God. They are not concerned with history but with faith, and they rearrange information to suit the needs of the believing Christians at the time they were compiled. The four Gospels are Matthew, Mark, Luke, and John.

*Matthew*, the first but not the oldest Gospel, is arranged as a teaching manual. Matthew mentions many Jewish customs and stresses that Jesus is the Jewish Messiah. The main divisions of his account are as follows: Jesus' birth and childhood (1–2); Jesus' baptism (3); Jesus' temptation (4:1–11); the beginning of Jesus' work in Galilee (4:12–25); the Galilean ministry (5–13), including the Sermon on the Mount; miracles and teachings (14–20), journey to Jerusalem (21–25); and the trial, passion, death, and Resurrection (26–28).

*Mark*, the second Gospel but the earliest, is very short. It was used by Matthew and Luke when they compiled their own accounts. It breaks down as follows: Jesus' baptism and temptation (1:1–13); Galilean ministry (1:14–6:6); ministry outside Galilee (6:7–8:21); labors and instructions (8:22–13:37); and passion and Resurrection (14–16).

*Luke*, the third Gospel, is written in better Greek than that of either Matthew or Mark. It gives more details but softens harsh aspects of the legend. It breaks down as follows: introduction (1:1–4); birth and childhood of Jesus (1–2); baptism and temptation (3:1–4:13); Galilean ministry (4:14–9:50); journey to Jerusalem (9:51–21:38); and trial, passion, death, Resurrection, and Ascension (22–24). These first three Gospels are called synoptic because they often use the same material, though they shift it about for different emphasis.

*John*, the last Gospel, is completely different in character. In it Jesus speaks like a Greek philosopher, and little is told of the historical Jesus. It breaks down as follows: prologue (1:1–18); narrative demonstrating the Incarnation (1:19–12:11); and trial, passion and Resurrection (12:12–21;25.

*Acts of the Apostles*, written by the author of Luke's Gospel, tells the history of the Early Church and the lives of St. Peter and St. Paul.

The next division of the New Testament contains Epistles, or letters, the majority ascribed to St. Paul. They are *Romans*, *1* and *2 Corinthians*, *Galatians*, *Ephesians*, *Philippians*, *Colossians*, *1* and *2 Thessalonians*, *1* and *2 Timothy*, *Titus*, and *Philemon*. *Hebrews*, ascribed to St. Paul in the King James Version, was not written by him. The other letters are *James*, which contradicts St. Paul's teaching regarding faith and works; *1* and *2 Peter*; *1*, *2*, and *3 John*, and *Jude*. The last book of the Bible is *Revelation*, the only prophetic book in the New Testament. It deals with the end of the world, the punishment of sinners, and the vindication of the righteous.

See also: BEDE THE VENERABLE, ST.; DAVID; JEROME, ST.; SAUL; SOLOMON; YAHWEH

**0567**

**Bicorn and Chichevache**   In medieval French folklore, two animals, one fat and the other thin. Chichevache (lean cow) lived on patient wives and was therefore very thin, whereas Bicorn lived on patient husbands and was well fed. Chaucer's clerk mentions Chichevache in the conclusion of his story in *The Canterbury Tales*. Bi-corn (two horns) is an allusion to the horned cuckold.

See also: CHAUCER

**0568**

**Bidental** (struck by lightning)   In Roman cult, a consecrated spot where lightning had passed into the ground, where it was forbidden to walk.

**0569**

**Bifrost** (Bilrost, Bif-raust) (rainbow or quivering roadway)   In Norse mythology, rainbow bridge, made of fire, water, and air, that led from Asgard, home of the Aesir gods, to the well of Urd. The *Prose Edda* tells how the gods made "a bridge from earth to heaven . . . constructed with more art than any other work. But, strong though it be, it will be broken to pieces when the sons of Muspell [the frost giants]), after having traversed great rivers, shall ride over it." To delay as much as possible the end of their existence and that of the world, the gods ordered the god Heimdall to be a watchman and inform them when the frost giants were on their way. It is here that Surt and the Aesir will do battle at Ragnarok.

See also: ASGARD; HEIMDALL; MUSPELL; RAG-NAROK; SURT; URD; *PROSE EDDA*

**0570**

**Big Foot**   In North American folklore, the traditional wild man figure, named for the large footprints the creature purportedly leaves. He is called Sasquatch in Canada, an anglicization of a Salish Indian term. The legends are best known in the Pacific Northwest, both among lumber-men and Native Americans. The creature may derive from European legends of a wild man that have become fused with Native American beliefs in an oversized and hairy humanoid. Descriptions are always similar: he is large and has hairy, apelike features and an overpowering stench. Sightings are usually at the edge of a forest or crossing a road and come from almost all U.S. states. The wild man figure is also known elsewhere. The best known is the Yeti, the Abominable Snowman of the Himalayas.

**0571**

**Biggarro**   In Australian mythology, the wombat snake who aids man to the spirit land, the Land of Perfection. He is the opposite of the evil carpet snake, Goonnear.

See also: GOONNEAR

**0572**

**Big Harpe**   In American folklore, a sadistic outlaw who killed men, women, and children for pleasure, including his wife and child. He threw his child against a tree because he was crying. According to legend, his father was a British sympathizer during the Revolutionary War. The brothers Micajah and Wiley Harpe, Big and Little Harpe, ran away and joined a band of renegade Cherokee. They were accused of horse stealing and murdering. They filled one man with stones and pushed him into the river and tied another man to his horse and drove him over a cliff. Harpe was captured by a posse, and when one man grabbed his hair and proceeded to cut off his head, Harpe cried out: "You're a damned rough butcher, but cut on and be damned." Big Harpe's head was then stuck in the fork of a tree near Red Bank on the Ohio River.

**0573**

**Bik'eguidinde** (according to whom there is life) In North American Indian mythology (Mescalero Apache), creator god.

0574

**Bil and Hjuki**   In Norse mythology, the waxing and the waning moon. The *Prose Edda* says, "One day he [the moon] carried off from the earth two children, named Bil and Hjuki, as they were returning from the spring called Byrgir, carrying between them the bucket called Saegr, on the pole Simul. Vidfinn was the father of these children, who always follow Mani [the moon], as we may easily observe even from the earth." The image of Bil and Hjuki, holding their pails, was said to be darkly outlined on the moon.

0575

**Billy Blin**   In English and Scottish folklore, a household spirit who protects the family. He appears in some Scottish ballads and also is called Billy Blind, Belly Blin, and Blind Barlow.

0576

**Billy Potts**   In American folklore, a murderer and robber, said to be a member of the Cave-in-Rock gang in the Ohio and Mississippi River area. The gang consisted of Billy, his mother, and his father. Billy Potts was really Isaiah Potts, the owner of Potts's Inn. He had spotters to tell him who had money so that his robberies were worthwhile. After one killing, Potts's father told him to flee and hide out for a time. When he returned, he was shot by his father, who did not recognize him with his new beard and added weight.

0577

**Billy the Kid**   1859–1881. In American history and folklore, bandit; popular name of Henry McCarty, alias Kid Antrim, and William H. Bonney. Born in New York City, his family moved to Kansas and then to New Mexico when he was a child. By the time he was 16 he was credited with killing 16 men, and at his death the total was past 20. His personality affected people differently. To some, he was "a nondescript, adenoidal, weasel-eyed, narrow-chested, stoop-shouldered, repulsive looking creature with all the outward appearance of a cretin," whereas others called him "the darling of the common people." Pat Garrett, the sheriff who finally killed Billy on 14 July, 1881 at Old Fort Sumner, wrote in his *Authentic Life of Billy the Kid* that "the Kid had a lurking devil in him. It was a good-humored, jovial imp, or a cruel and blood-thirsty fiend, as circumstances prompted. Circumstances favored the worser angel, and the Kid fell." One ballad says:

> There's many a man with face fine and fair
> Who starts out in life with a chance to be
>   square.
> But just like poor Billy, he wanders astray
> And loses his life in the very same way.

Although he was no angel, folklore tends to see Billy the Kid in a kind light. Two Hollywood films, both called *Billy the Kid*, present romanticized views of the murderer. Other movies are *Dirty Little Billy* and *Pat Garrett and Billy the Kid*. Aaron Copland's one-act ballet *Billy the Kid* presents the life of Billy the Kid against the ongoing push of the pioneers, who had to put down Billy's lawlessness to achieve civilization.

0578

**Bimbo**   In Japanese legend, a poor farmer who was given a son by Raiden, the thunder god. After 20 years of toil Bimbo owned barely three-quarters of an acre of land. He had no son and wished to adopt one. One day, as he was leaving the field, a storm broke, and the lightning dazzled him. After many invocations to the gods he started home, then he noticed a little rosy boy lying on the ground. He picked up the child and took him to his wife. They called the child Raitaro in honor of Raiden, the god of thunder, who had given them this gift. Prosperity followed their adoption of the child. When Raitaro was 18 years old, he took the shape of a dragon and flew away to a castle formed of clouds, above the hills. When Bimbo and his wife died, their grave was marked with the shape of a dragon.

See also: RAIDEN

**Birch**    A hardwood tree with thin, layered bark. According to one Slavic legend, the birch tree was used to placate forest spirits. The celebrants would gather in the forest, cut down a small birch, form a circle, each in turn stepping on the stump of the tree, and call upon the spirit. The spirit indicated its presence through the trembling of the birch leaves. In ancient Rome birch bundles wrapped around an ax were symbols of authority. The birch was sacred to the Nordic god Thor and was later associated with the switches used to scourge Christ during his Passion. In Scandinavia a birch branch protected against the evil eye, lightning, gout, and barrenness. In Victorian England the birch symbolized grace and meekness.

See also: THOR

**Bird**    Warm-blooded vertebrate having a body covered with feathers and forelimbs modified into wings. Because birds fly they have often been symbols of the soul leaving the body at death. In ancient Egyptian mythology the *ba* (soul) was portrayed as a bird with the head of a human being. Bird features were also assumed by various gods: the hawk was associated with Horus, Ra, and other sun deities; the ibis with the god Thoth; the goose with Geb; and the swallow with Isis. The *ba* abandoned the body at death and hovered over the mummy to protect it from decay until it reentered the body. In Hindu mythology birds are also symbols of the soul or contain the souls of humans. In Jewish folklore the hoyl bird was believed to be the only creature that refused to eat the forbidden fruit when Adam gave it to all the animals after he and Eve had eaten it. The hoyl, therefore, does not know death but like the phoenix goes to sleep, a divine fire consuming it and its nest. All that remains is

an egg, which miraculously hatches a new, full-grown hoyl.

One of the most persistent motifs regarding birds in nearly all mythologies and folklore is their ability to speak and to be understood by humans. In Christian legend St. Rose of Lima sang to the birds, and they answered her. In Norse mythology Sigurd tastes dragon's blood and then understands the language of birds. In the Grimm folktale The White Snake a servant eats a part of the king's supper and then is able to understand the language of birds and other animals. There are numerous motifs associated with birds in the *Motif Index of Folk Literature*.

See also: ADAM AND EVE; BA; FAFNIR; GEB; HORUS; ISIS; PHOENIX; SIGURD; THOTH

**Bisan**    In Malayan mythology, the female spirit of camphor, who assumes the form of a cicada.

**Bishamon**    In Japanese Buddhist mythology, war god and a god of riches; one of the Shichi Fukujin, seven gods of good luck or fortune. Often he is portrayed dressed in armor and carrying a pagoda in his left hand and a scepter, lance, or three-pointed halberd in his right hand. He is one of the Jiu No O, 12 Japanese Buddhist gods and goddesses adopted from Hindu mythology. Bishamon is derived from the war god Skanda or Vaiśrávana.

See also: JIU NO O; SHICHI FUKUJIN; SKANDA

**Bith and Birren**    In Celtic mythology, husband and wife in the myth of the Great Flood. Bith was the apocryphal son of Noah who was denied entry into the ark. With the counsel of his daughter Cesara he built an idol who then commanded him to build a ship and take refuge in it. Bith, his wife, Birren, their daughter Cesara and her husband, Fintaan, with their son Lara and his wife, Balma, sailed in this ship for seven years before they reached Ireland. There were 50 women but only three men. Bith took one of Cesara's companions as well as 16 other women and settled in the north. He died before the Flood. A short time later, the moon, blood red, broke into hundreds of pieces, killing the whole family.

See also: DYLAN; NOAH

0584

**Biton and Cleobis** (wild ox and famous life) In Greek mythology, two heroes of Argos. They were sons of Cydippe, a priestess of the goddess Hera. When no oxen could be found to draw their mother's chariot, they pulled it several miles to the temple of the goddess. There Cydippe prayed that they receive the best possible gift as a reward for their filial duty. In response the goddess let them die in her temple, indicating that death is the only truly happy event for humankind.

See also: HERA

0585

**Black Bart**    1829–1888? In American history and folklore, popular name of Charles E. Boles, the bane of Wells Fargo bank. Black Bart was a Union soldier and a schoolteacher before he took up stealing. He is credited with more than 30 robberies without ever firing a shot. He was said to be very polite, always telling his victims: "Please throw down the box!" His trademark was to leave a signed poem as a reminder of his visit, such as:

I'll start out to-morrow with another empty
  sack.
From Wells Fargo I will borrow
But I'll never pay it back.

The poems were signed: "Black Bart, Po. 8."

When he was released after four years in San Quentin, the warden asked him if he was finished with a life of crime. Black Bart replied he was.

"What are you going to do then, Bart?" the warden asked. "Are you going to write poetry for a living?"

"Warden," Bart replied, "didn't I tell you I wasn't going to commit any more crimes."

When he was old, Bart was given a pension of $200 a month not to rob Wells Fargo. All he had to do was report every week to the authorities to let them know his whereabouts. He was seen for the last time in San Francisco on 28 February 1888 at the Nevada House. The next day he was gone, leaving all his belongings behind. He appears in the Hollywood movie *Black Bart*, in which Lola Montes falls in love with him.

0586

**Blackbeard**    d. 1718. In American history and folklore, popular name of the sadistic English pirate Edward Teach, who wore black, braided whiskers. His name originally was Edward Drummond, and he began his career as an honest seaman, sailing out of his home port of Bristol, England. He is seldom known by that name, for after he became a pirate he called himself Edward Teach. It was under this name that the people of his generation knew him, "a swaggering, merciless brute." Preying on ships and coastal towns from the West Indies to the Atlantic coast of North America, Blackbeard's activities were overlooked by the governor of North Carolina, who shared in his booty. But eventually the British sent troops from Virginia to capture the pirate. When he was beheaded, according to legend, his headless corpse swam around the ship three times before it sank, and his skull was later made into a drinking cup.

0587

**Bladud**    In British mythology, the 10th king of Britain, father of King Lear. Bladud built Bath "and fashioned hot baths therein, meet for the needs of men, in which he placed under the guardianship of the deity Minerva," according to Geoffrey of Monmouth's *History of the Kings of Britain*. Bladud practiced sorcery and attempted to fly with artificial wings but fell on the Temple of Apollo and was dashed to pieces.

See also: APOLLO; LEAR, KING; MINERVA

**0588**
**Blain** (Ymir's bones?)    In Norse mythology, a giant, often identified with Ymir, the great giant from whose body the earth was formed. The name appears in the *Prose Edda*.

See also: *PROSE EDDA*; YMIR

*St. Blaise*

**0589**
**Blaise, St.** (crippled, stammering)    Fourth century. In Christian legend, bishop, patron saint of physicians, wax chandlers, and wool combers. Invoked against throat infections. Feast, 3 February.

Blaise was a physician before he became a bishop in Armenia. He suffered beheading after his flesh was torn with iron combs used for carding wool. One legend tells that while the bishop was in prison awaiting his martyrdom, he miraculously cured a little boy who nearly died because a fishbone was stuck in his throat.

During the Middle Ages, St. Blaise was one of the most popular saints. In central Europe and in Latin countries people are still given *pan bendito* (St. Blaise sticks), which they eat when they have a sore throat. One of the most popular customs of the Roman church is the blessing of throats, held on St. Blaise's feast day. A priest holds crossed candles against the head or throat of a person, saying: "Through the intercession of St. Blaise, bishop and martyr, may the Lord free you

from evils of the throat and from any other evil." In certain parts of Italy priests touch the throats with a wick that has been dipped into blessed oil.

**0590**
**Blanchefleur** (white flower)    In medieval French legend, a Moorish slave girl rescued by a Christian prince from the harem of the emir of Babylon. The heroine appears in a French metrical romance, *Flore et Blanchefleur*. She also appears in Boccaccio's *Il Filocopo* and Chaucer's *Dorigen and Aurelius*.

See also: CHAUCER

**0591**
**Blánik**    In Czech legend, name of a hillside where a troop of sleeping Hussites wait to answer the call of their country in its time of need. The 15th-century legend inspired Smetana's symphonic poem *Blánik*, last in his cycle of six symphonic poems included in *Má Vlast* (My Country). Smetana uses the old Hussite hymn "Ye Are the Warriors of God" in the work to express, according to the composer, "the resurrection of the Czech people."

**0592**
**Blathnat** (Blathine) (little flower)    In Celtic mythology, daughter of Mider, king of the Gaelic underworld. She becomes the lover of the hero Cuchulain, who first meets her on a raid to the Otherworld, where her husband, Curoi Mac Daire, is guarding the magic caldron. With Curoi's aid, Cuchulain carries off the magic caldron, three cows, and Blathnat. Curoi subsequently recovers them and then humiliates Cuchulain by burying him in the earth up to his armpits and shaving his head. A year later Cuchulain meets with Blathnat, and they take Curoi unawares and kill him. The murder is revenged when Curoi's poet, Ferchertne, sees Blathnat standing at the edge of a steep cliff. He rushes to her, places his arms around her, and plunges to the beach below. Her counterpart in Welsh leg-

end is Blouderwedd (flower maiden), who also betrayed her husband and as a punishment was changed into an owl.

See also: CUCHULAIN

0593

**Blood Libel Legend**    Roman writers accused Christians of drinking blood in orgies of incest, sodomy, infanticide, and ritual cannibalism. Similar accusations were frequently made during the Middle Ages against Jews, who already were said to have the blood of Christ on their hands and were then persecuted for similar bloody offenses. The first case involving Jews accused of the ritual murder of Christian children for their blood was in the city of Fulda, Germany, in 1235, where 34 Jews were executed. The legend has been amazingly persistent through time and is still often reported when a child is gruesomely slain. The Website Snopes.com repeatedly documents cases of the legend around the world.

0594

**Bluebeard**    In European folktales, a villain who marries, one after the other, three or seven women, killing each of them, but he himself is killed by his last wife. Bluebeard may appear as a king, merchant, or sorcerer. In the story, the villain Bluebeard gives his wife the keys to his castle or house, telling her not to open one certain door. Of course, the wife opens the door and discovers either a number of dead wives or a basin of blood. When Bluebeard returns, he either kills his wife or locks her in a dungeon to eat only human flesh. This happens to all of his wives except the last, the youngest, who either kills Bluebeard with a saber or is saved by a young man; in some variants she outwits Bluebeard and has her brothers kill him. The most famous telling of the tale is Charles Perrault's version in his *Contes de ma mère, l'oye'* (1697), often translated as *Tales of Mother Goose*. The story of Bluebeard is also found in the early collections by the Brothers Grimm, but it was left out in later editions, possibly because the same tale type was found in their

*Bluebeard*

collection under the titles "The Virgin Mary's Child" and "Fitcher's Bird." Béla Bartók's *Prince Bluebeard's Castle* is an operatic version of the folktale.

See also: BROTHERS GRIMM; MOTHER GOOSE; TALE TYPE

0595

**Blunderbore**    In British legend, a giant who is tricked by Jack the Giant Killer into cutting open his own stomach. Blunderbore offered Jack the Giant Killer a bed for the night, hoping to club him to death while he slept. Jack, suspicious, placed logs under the bed covers and crept underneath the bed. Blunderbore came into the room and thoroughly pounded the bed with his club. Next morning Jack appeared at breakfast, and the giant was thoroughly surprised, believing he had killed Jack the night before. As they ate their breakfast of hasty pudding, Jack seemed to be consuming vast quantities of it, but in reality he was surreptitiously stuffing the pudding into a bag hidden underneath his clothing. The giant, trying to keep up with Jack, stuffed himself with more and more pudding. Jack then put a knife into the bag and let out some of the pudding. The giant, seeing this, put a knife into his stomach, killing himself.

0596

**Boabdil**    Died c. 1533. In Spanish history and legend, last Moorish king of Granada, subject of numerous Spanish ballads. Boabdil, also called El Chico (the young one), dethroned his father but was later forced to give up his throne and city to King Ferdinand of Spain. The Spanish ballad *The Flight from Granada* tells the legend of his escape. José Zorrilla y Moral's literary ballad *Boabdil* tells the legend of the king's love for a Christian lady to whom he would give all Granada, and Washington Irving's *The Conquest of Granada* deals with Boabdil's history and legend.

See also: BALLAD

0597

**Boadicea** (Boudicca) (victorious)    First century C.E. British queen who led a revolt against the Romans, failed, and poisoned herself.

Boadicea was the wife of Prasutagus, king of the Iceni. On his death the Romans seized the territory, and according to Tacitus in *Annals* (book 14), "Boadicea was flogged and her daughters raped." However, she rallied and appeared riding in a chariot with her daughters in front of her. She cried out: "We British are used to woman commanders in war. I am descended from mighty men! But I am not fighting for my kingdom and wealth now. I am fighting as an ordinary person for my lost freedom, my bruised body, and my outraged daughters."

Boadicea raised a revolt and burned Camulodunum and Londinium (Colchester and London), but eventually lost. Rather than fall into the hands of the Romans, she poisoned herself. Her story forms the theme for a play, *Bonduca* (Boadicea), by John Fletcher, produced in 1619; a literary ballad by William Cowper, *Boadicéa: An Ode*; and Tennyson's poem *Boädicea*. John Milton, in his *History of Britain*, rejects the legend, saying it was written to prove that "in Britain women were men, and men women."

0598

**Boann** (goddess of the white cow)    In Celtic mythology, water goddess, wife of Nechtan or Ecmar, mistress of the god Dagda, and mother of Aengus og, god of love and beauty. After her affair with Daga, she attempted to prove she was chaste by walking around Connla's well or Nechtan's well. But three waves arose. One took off her thigh, another a hand, and the third an eye. Boann fled and was drowned by the pursuing waves, which became the river Bogne. Near it lived the magic Salmon of Knowledge, who was fed by nuts dropped from the nine hazel trees at the water's edge.

See also: AENGUS OG; DAGDA

0599

**Bochica**    In the mythology of the ancient Chibcha Indians of Colombia, chief god and culture hero. He came from the east, traveling across the country disguised as a bearded old man, teaching moral laws and arts to man. In one myth Bochica saved the people when a flood inundated the plain of Bogotá. He appeared and cleaved the mountains with his golden scepter, opening a passage for the waters into the valley below. Bochica's wife was Cuchaviva, the rainbow goddess, who watched over women in childbirth and made the fields fertile. Bochica was sometimes worshiped as Zuhe (sun) or Xue (lord) or was identified with the culture hero Nemterequeteba or Chimizapagua.

See also: NEMTEREQUETEBA

**Bodhi**   0600

In Buddhism, term meaning enlightenment or awakening. *Buddha* means "one who has attained *Bodhi*."

**Bodhidharma**   0601

Fifth century C.E. In Buddhism, sage who introduced Buddhism to China, where he is called P'u-T'i-Ta-Mo, often abbreviated Ta-Mo. In Japanese legend he is called Daruma. According to legend Bodhidharma crossed the Yangtze River and went to the Wei kingdom. There he practiced wall contemplation, sitting in meditation before a wall, for nine years. A young monk named Shen-kuang came and asked him for instruction. Bodhidharma paid no attention to him until the monk cut off his arm to prove his sincerity. Bodhidharma then instructed him.

**Bodhisattva** (Bodhisatta)   0602

In Buddhism, one who aspires to *Bodhi* (enlightenment), a potential Buddha, a Buddha-to-be. When a Mahayana Bodhisattva has achieved stage seven on the Path and is entitled to enter lesser Nirvana, he refuses, renouncing it in favor of greater enlightenment. In the Avatamsaka Sutra the reason is stated: "Forasmuch as there is the will that all sentient beings should be altogether made free, I will not forsake my fellow creatures." There are, according to the Lotus of the Good Law (chapter 20), "hundreds of thousands of myriads of Bodhisattvas who equal in number the atoms contained in the thousand worlds. . . ."

In Buddhist art the Bodhisattvas are portrayed crowned and loaded with jewels, whereas the Buddha himself, who is in the center, is simply adorned. Among the best-known Mahayana Bodhisattvas are Avalokiteshvara, Manjushri, Samantabhadra, Kshitigarbha, and Mahasthamaprapta. The Sanskrit term *Bodhisattva* also is used in the Pali texts (*Bodhisatta*) for the Buddha before he reached his Enlightenment, and the term is applied in the Jatakas, folktales of the former existences of the Buddha.

See also: AVALOKITESSHVARA; BODHI; BUDDHA, THE; JATAKA; MAHASTHAMAPRAPTA; MAHAYANA; MANJUSHRI; NIRVANA; SAMANTABHADRA

**Bodhi-Tree**   0603

In Buddhism, tree under which the Buddha gained Enlightenment. The tale of the tree is told in the *Mahabodhi-Vamsa* (The Great Bodhi Chronicle), written in the 11th century and ascribed to Upatissa. The tale tells of the various fortunes of the tree from before the time of the Buddha and after his Enlightenment. The tree is a specific example of the *pipal*, or sacred fig, a very common species in India, sacred to Hindus as a source of fertility and/or gnosis.

**Bogy**   0604

In English and Scottish folklore, a person or object of terror, a hobgoblin. The word appeared in use in the early 19th century and may be related to the Scottish word *bogle* and with the obsolete word *bug*.

**Bomazi**   0605

In African mythology (Bushongo of the Congo), lord of Bushongo, father of the male twins Woto and Moelo. Once the fair-skinned Bomazi told an old couple that they would bear a child. In time they had a daughter, whom Bomazi married. She bore him five sons, two of whom were the twins Woto and Moelo. Woto later became the founder of the Bushongo people.

**Bona Dea** (the good goddess)   0606

In Roman mythology, the ancient Italian goddess, also called Fauna, who was patron of chastity and fruitfulness; married to Faunus, who was the only being who saw her after their marriage. Her worship was conducted by vestal virgins. The festival of the founding of her temple was held on

1 May. Prayers were then offered for the averting of earthquakes. During the nights of 4 and 5 December each year, select married women celebrated secret rites on behalf of the whole people under the supervision of the Vestal Virgins. The ceremony was held in the house of a major magistrate, often the Urban Praetor (who was always in the city). The magistrate had to sleep elsewhere this night, for no male creature was allowed to witness the rites. The mistress of the house presided over the rites. After offering a sacrifice of suckling pigs, the women performed a dance accompanied by stringed and wind instruments.

In Roman art Bona Dea was portrayed with a scepter in her left hand, a wreath of vine leaves on her head, and a jar of wine at her side. Near her image was a consecrated serpent. Tame serpents were kept in her temple, located on the slope of the Aventine in Rome, and healing plants were preserved at her shrine, which no men were allowed to enter. Cicero gave details of the rites when he wrote about his political archenemy, Clodius, who was indicted for sacrilege when he attempted to witness the secret rites dressed as a woman. Ovid's *Ars Amoris* also cites the goddess.

See also: FAUNUS; OVID; VESTAL VIRGINS

0607
**Bonaventura, St.** (good fortune)    1221–1274. In Christian legend, the Seraphic Doctor. Feast, 14 July.

Born Giovanni Fidanga in Tuscany, he was so ill as a child that his mother took him to St. Francis of Assisi to be healed. When St. Francis saw him he said, "*O, buona venturai,*" (Oh, good fortune). His mother then named the child Bonaventura and dedicated him to God. At 22 he became a Franciscan and went to Paris to study theology.

Legend says that when he did not come to receive Holy Communion, feeling himself unworthy, an angel brought it to him. Though he was known for his humility, he was greatly hon-

ored by St. Louis, king of France, and made general of the Franciscan order in 1256. Some years later he was made cardinal and bishop of Albano.

According to legend, when two nuncios came from Pope Gregory X to present him with the cardinal's hat, they found him in the garden of a convent near Florence washing his plate after dinner. He told them to hang the hat on a tree until he had finished. The great council at Lyons (1274) held to reconcile the Greek and Latin churches, in which he took part, exhausted the saint, and he died shortly afterward. Some claim, however, that he was poisoned. He was buried in the Church of the Franciscans at Lyons. In 1562 Calvinists broke open his shrine and threw his ashes into the Saône.

In Christian art St. Bonaventura is shown in a Franciscan habit, sometimes wearing a miter or cardinal's hat, or with one hanging on a tree. Often he carries the Host (communion wafer), or an angel is giving one to him.

*St. Boniface*

0608
**Boniface, St.** (of good fate)    c. 675–754. In Christian legend, Apostle of Germany. Patron saint of brewers and tailors. Feast, 5 June.

Born Winfred in Devonshire, England, he taught in a Benedictine abbey near Winchester. In his middle age he had a great desire to preach the Gospel in Germany and went to Rome to gain the support of Pope Gregory II. Here he changed his name to Boniface. He then started on his mission, visiting Thuringia, Bavaria, and Saxony. In 732 he was made primate of all Germany and soon afterward first bishop of Mainz. When he was 74, he was sent out on another missionary journey, carrying a copy of St. Ambrose's *De Bono Mortis* under his cloak. He got as far as Friesland, where he was murdered by some pagans. For centuries his bloodstained book was exhibited as a relic in Fulda, where he supposedly lies buried.

In Christian art he is portrayed as a bishop— in one hand, a crosier and in the other, a book pierced by a sword. Sometimes he is shown baptizing a convert, with one foot on a fallen oak, the symbol of Druidism, which he overthrew by his preaching.

See also: AMBROSE, ST.; BENEDICT, ST.; DRUIDS

0609

**Bonten**   In Japanese Buddhist mythology, a god derived from the Hindu god Brahma, in art portrayed standing on a lotus leaf. He has three heads of equal size with three eyes each, surmounted by a smaller head with two eyes only. One hand holds a lotus; another, a trident; and a third, a drinking vessel. The fourth and last one is directed downward with open palm and fingers extended in the *mudra*, or gesture, of charity. He is one of the Jiu No O, 12 Japanese gods and goddesses adopted from Hindu mythology.

See also: BRAHMA; JIU NO O; LOTUS; MUDRA

0610

*Book of the Dead, The*   Popular title given to a collection of ancient Egyptian funerary texts composed for the benefit of the dead. The collection consists of incantations, hymns, prayers, and magic words and formulas that were found cut or painted on the walls of pyramids and tombs and on rolls of papyrus. The texts do not form a connected work, nor do they belong to any one period. They are miscellaneous in character and tell nothing of the lives or works of the dead with whom they are buried. The Egyptians possessed many funerary works, but none of them bore a name that could be translated *The Book of the Dead*. This title was given in the early

The Book of the Dead

19th century by tomb robbers, who discovered buried with the mummies rolls of papyrus, which they called *Kitâb al-Mayyit* (book of the dead man) or *Kitâb al-Mayyitun* (book of the dead). The robbers, however, knew nothing of the contents of the rolls; they were merely saying that what they found in the coffin was a "dead man's book."

See also: BENU; BUTO; COFFIN TEXTS; ISIS; MAAT; NEPHTHYS; OSIRIS; PYRAMID TEXTS; TEM; THOTH; UTCHAT

0611

**Boone, Daniel**   1734–1820. In American history and folklore, a frontiersman. Boone began his life as a backwoods trailblazer, an agent for the Transylvania Company in Kentucky. He became a land speculator but lost many of his holdings and later moved westward to Missouri. His fame in American folklore began with the publication of John Filson's *Discovery, Settlement* *and Present State of Kentucke*, which was a supposedly autobiographical account of Boone's life.

One legend says that in later years Boone kept a coffin under his bed, and when the mood came upon him, he would try it on for size. According to another legend, he died alone in the wilderness. In reality he died with his family around him. The state legislature of Missouri even wore mourning crepe for 20 days after his death.

In art, a lithograph published by Currier & Ives portrayed Boone defending his family against an Indian attack. Charles F. Wimar's *The Abduction of Daniel Boone's Daughter* portrays his daughter Jemina being abducted by Chief Hanging Maw. Hollywood has used Boone's legend in *Daniel Boone, Young Daniel Boone*, and *Daniel Boone, Trail Blazer*, and television had a long-running series, *Daniel Boone*, which began in 1964.

0612
**Boorala**   In Australian mythology, tribal name for a creator god. Those who are good go to Boorala's home when they die.

0613
**Borak** (Al Burak, Alborac, Al-borach, Al-Buraq) (lightning)   In Islamic mythology, fabulous animal brought by Gabriel that carried the prophet Muhammad mounted on the night of his ascension to the seventh heaven. The Koran (sura 17) tells of a vision the prophet had in which he was borne from Mecca to Jerusalem and then on to the various heavens. The animal that carried him is neither described nor named in the text. Islamic legend, however, has embellished the story, and *The Ascension of Muhammad* tells of the prophet's journey to the heavens. Borak is described as "smaller than a mule and larger than an ass, his face was like that of a human being, while his tail and hoofs were like those of a cow." (In another telling the tail and hoofs resembled a goat's.) "He had the rump of a horse, and carried an emerald green saddle, a

harness of pearls, and turquoise stirrups." When Borak took a stride, it "was as far as the eye could reach."

In Islamic art the fabulous animal is often portrayed with the head of a veiled woman and a peacock's tail. His saddle is shown to pilgrims in the mosque of al-Sakhra in Jerusalem.

See also: KORAN, THE; MUHAMMAD

0614
**Borden, Lizzie**   1860–1927. In American history and legend, a woman accused of murdering her father and stepmother on 4 August 1892 in Fall River, Massachusetts. When Lizzie was brought to trial, she displayed little or no emotion over the event, but she was found innocent of the crime. However, a popular American ballad, *Lizzie Borden*, finds her guilty:

Lizzie Borden took an ax
And gave her mother forty whacks;
When she saw what she had done,
She gave her father forty-one.

Morton Gould's ballet *Fall River Legend* deals with the story in flashbacks, finally ending with Lizzie's hanging for murder. The distinguished actress Lillian Gish portrayed Lizzie in a 1934 play, *Nine Pine Street*, although her character was renamed Effie Holden and Effie used a flatiron and a heavy walking stick as her weapons. In 1995, Lizzie was the subject of an episode of Arts & Entertainment's *Biography*, and she was "tried" (and found innocent) in a mock trial on C-SPAN.

0615
**Boreas** (north wind, devouring)   In Greek mythology, the North Wind; son of Astraea and Eos, brother of the Winds, Zephyrus, Eurus, and Notus; called Aquilo in Roman mythology. His home was in the Thracian Salmydessus on the Black Sea. He carried off and raped Orithyia after her father Erechtheus, king of Athens, had refused to give her to Boreas in marriage. Their

*Boreas carrying off Orithyia*

children were Calais and Zetes, the Boreadae; Cleopatra, the wife of Phineus; and Chione, the beloved of Poseidon. Vergil's *Aeneid* (books 10, 12) cite Boreas, as does Shakespeare's *Troilus and Cressida* (1.3.37). In Western Renaissance art, Boreas appears in allegories of the Four Seasons as the personification of Winter. He is shown as an old man with flowing gray locks and wings.

See also: *AENEID, THE*; POSEIDON; ZEPHYRUS

0616

**Bori**   In Australian mythology, invisible spirit who kills his victims by injecting them with incurable diseases.

0617

**Boris and Gleb, Sts.** (fight)   11th century. In Christian legend, martyrs. In Russia patrons of brotherly love and devotion. Feast, 24 July.

They were the sons of St. Vladimir, ruler of Kiev. At Vladmir's death the throne was to be divided among them and their elder brother, Sviatopolk. The elder brother, however, decided he wanted the throne for himself and planned the murder of both of his brothers. As the *Primary Chronicle* or *The Tale of Bygone Years*, compiled by various hands from about 1040 to 1118,

tells it, Sviatopolk "was filled with lawlessness," and he hired men to kill Boris. Boris was attacked and wrapped in a canvas, loaded into a wagon, and dragged off, though "he was still alive." A knife was then plunged into his heart. His brother Gleb was attacked by Sviatopolk's men, but Gleb's cook, fearful he would be killed, murdered Gleb to appease the assassins.

From about 1200 the two saints were honored in the Cathedral of St. Sophia at Constantinople, where their icon stood to the right of the altar at which the Byzantine emperors were consecrated. In Russia the saints were extremely popular and frequently painted on icons. In a 13th-century icon of the Moscow school, the two saints hold swords, crosses, and emblems of their rank. The two are usually dressed alike but in different colors.

See also: VLADIMIR, ST.

0618

**Boris Godunov**   1552–1605. Czar of Russia who became part of Russian legend because of his supposed murder of Ivan IV's younger son, Dmitri. Boris came to the throne in 1598, having been regent since 1584. Ivan IV's son Dmitri had been banished to the upper Volga, where he died. It was believed he had been murdered by order of Boris. A pretender, claiming to be Dmitri, said he had escaped the assassins and was the rightful heir to the throne. Supported by an advancing army, Dmitri was crowned in 1605, but Boris died suddenly, avoiding a dethronement.

Influenced by the legend of Boris and by his reading of Shakespeare, Pushkin wrote a dramatic play, *Boris Godunov*, which was later used by Moussorgsky for his opera *Boris Godunov*. The opera is considered one of the cornerstones of Russian and modern opera and is performed in numerous musical arrangements, the best-known being Rimsky-Korsakov's 1908 version.

0619

**Borvo** (Bormo) (boil, seethe)   In Celtic mythology, a god who presided over healing hot springs and health resorts in central France. He was identified by ancient Roman writers with their god Apollo; he was called Bormanus in Provence and Bormanious in Portugal. Borve, the king in Celtic mythology whose children were turned into swans by his evil second wife, Aeife, is believed to be derived from the god.

See also: APOLLO; BELINUS

0620

**Boyde, Rebel Belle**   1844–1900. In American history and Civil War folklore, a Southern woman whose charm captivated the Yankees. When she killed a Yankee soldier who, she said, was attacking her mother, the Yankee captain not only thought what she did was honorable but also gave her a small revolver so she could better protect her mother and herself in the future. Belle was courted by Union soldiers but spied on them. She finally was arrested in 1862 and escorted to jail by nearly 400 Union troops. In prison she gained the friendship of all of the jailers and was out in a month. She wrote *Belle Boyde in Camp and Prison* and gave lectures on her Civil War adventures.

0621

**Bragi** (to shine, leader)   In Norse mythology, Aesir god of eloquence and poetry; son of Odin and Gunlod; married to Iduna; considered to be the first skald. Some scholars believe that Bragi might be a deified ninth-century poet named Bragi Boddason or merely another name for Odin, chief of the gods, since both Odin and Bragi are called Long-Bearded. Both are associated with the cult of the dead. When a king died, a feast was held, and a cup, called Bragarfull (cup of Bragi), was drunk from in his honor. Each guest pledged some great deed at the time. Some connect Bragi's name with the English "to brag." Northern poets were often called Braga-men and priestesses Braga-women. Bragi was portrayed as an elderly man with a long white beard, holding a harp. At the sound of his music

trees bloomed. Bragi greeted the slain heroes in Valhalla.

See also: AESIR; IDUNA; ODIN; SKALD; VALHALLA

*Brahma*

0622

**Brahma**   In Hinduism, creator god in the triad of deities called Trimorti, including Vishnu and Shiva.

Brahma in present-day Hinduism is often called the first of the gods, the framer of the universe, and the guardian of the world. In the ancient Vedas, however, he is not named; there the creator is called Hiranya-garbha (the golden egg) or Prajapati (lord of creatures). Prajapati was later used as a title for Brahma and also for his sons, who in Hindu mythology are progenitors of the human race.

Various accounts, which differ considerably, are given of Brahma's origin. In the Hindu epic poem *The Mahabharata* Brahma is said to have issued from the lotus that sprang from the navel of the god Vishnu. In another text Brahma is said to have lived in a cosmic egg for 1,000 years and then burst out. Seeing that the earth was sunk beneath the waters, Brahma assumed the form of a boar (in later Hindu writings the role is assigned to Vishnu in one of his avatars, or incarnations) and diving, raised the earth on his tusks. After this Brahma continued the work of creation. Concerning this role as supreme creator of the universe, Ralph Waldo Emerson wrote in his poem "Brahma":

If the red slayer think he slays,
Or if the slain think he is slain,
They know not well the subtle ways
I keep, and pass, and turn again.
Far or forgot to me is near;
Shadow and sunlight are the same;
The vanished gods to me appear;
And one to me are shame and fame.
They reckon ill who leave me out;
When me they fly, I am the wings;
I am the doubter and the doubt,
And I the hymn the Brahmin sings.
The strong gods pine for my abode,
And pine in vain the sacred Seven;
But thou, meek lover of the good!
Find me, and turn thy back on heaven.

Emerson was questioned about the meaning of his poem because many readers were upset by the imagery and reference to an alien god. He said to his daughter: "Tell them to say Jehovah instead of Brahma."

Numerous myths are told of the god in various Hindu texts. Once Brahma, as Apava (who sports in the waters), formed two beings from his body, a male, Viraj, and a female, Shatarupa (the hundred-formed). After creating Shatarupa, Brahma lusted for her. "How beautiful you are," he said to his daughter.

Shatarupa turned to avoid Brahma's lustful look, but the god sprouted a second head. As she passed to the left, two other heads appeared. At last Shatarupa sprang up to the sky, and Brahma grew yet another head to view her. Shatarupa then came down, and the two made love, producing offspring that later populated the earth. She was then made Brahma's wife.

Brahma, however, did not keep his fifth head, for it was cut off by the god Shiva. Once when the holy sages were assembled at Brahma-pura, the heavenly city of Brahma on Mount Meru, they asked Brahma to display his true nature. Brahma, influenced by delusion brought on him by a demon and obscured by spiritual darkness (both gods and people in Hindu mythology often share the same virtues and faults), said: "I am the womb of the universe, without the beginning or end, and the sole and self-existent lord; and he who does not worship me shall never attain beatitude."

On hearing this reply Kratus (a form of the god Vishnu) smiled and said: "Had thou not been misled by ignorance, thou would not have made an assertion contrary to truth; for I am the framer of the universe, the source of life, the unborn, eternal and supreme. Had I not willed it, creation would not have taken place."

The two gods then fought, finally agreeing to let the sacred writings, the Vedas, decide the issue. The Vedas declared that Shiva was the creator, preserver, and destroyer. Shiva then appeared and Brahma's fifth head asked Shiva to worship him. Shiva then assumed a horrible form and cut off Brahma's fifth head with the thumb of his left hand.

Brahma is also called Srashtri (creator), Ka (who), Dhatri and Bidhatri (sustainer), Pitamaha (the great father), Lokesa (lord of the world), Parameshta (supreme in heaven), Adikavi (the first poet), Drughana (the ax, the mallet), and Hiranya-garbha (the golden egg), referring to the myth that Brahma "continued a year in the egg" and then "divided it into two parts by his mere thought, and with these two shells he formed the heavens and the earth."

The four mind-born sons of Brahma are Sanaka (the ancient), Sananda (joyous), Sanatana (eternal), and Sanatkumara (eternally a youth).

See also: AVATAR; *MAHABHARATA, THE* ; SANAKA; SANANDA; SANATANA; SANATKUMARA; SHATARUPA; SHIVA; VISHNU; VEDAS

**Brahman**   A term used in Hinduism for ultimate reality, as well as for the priestly caste.
Brahman is a neuter term (the masculine form is
Brahma, which is also the name of the Hindu
god but is distinct from the term *Brahma*). It refers to the sacred powers implicit in and created
through sacrificial ritual by the priests who are
called Brahmans. A Brahman is believed to be a
god. In the sacred book *Satapatha Brahmana* a
Brahman is defined thus: "There are two kinds of
gods; first the gods, then those who are Brahmans, and have learnt the *Veda* and repeat it: they
are human gods." Of course, this sentence was
written by a Brahman and was used to reinforce
his authority and position in Indian society.
Some Hindu texts equate the terms *Brahman* and
*Atman*, both being used for "ultimate reality" or
"world spirit."

The term *Brahmin* in English and American
literature has come to mean a socially exclusive
person who considers himself better than those
not of his own class. It was applied to many rich
families in New England during the 19th century, and the term *Boston Brahmin* is still occasionally heard.

See also: ATMAN; BRAHMA; VEDAS

0624

**Bran**   In Celtic mythology, god who presided
over poetry and, according to some scholars, was
lord of the underworld in Welsh mythology because his totem was a crow or raven, both connected with death. Bran, according to myth,
invaded Ireland to redress a wrong done by King
Matholwch, who was married to Branwen, sister
of Bran and goddess of love. When he and his
host of men were defeated, his head was cut off,
carried to White Tower Hill in London, and
buried with the eyes looking toward France as a
spell against foreign invasion. King Arthur, according to medieval legend, unearthed the head,
which was called Uther Ben (wonderful head),
saying Britain would remain a power by virtue of
her own strength. In some medieval Christian le-

gends Bran is transformed into Bran the Blessed
and credited with bringing Christianity to Britain. Bran appears under various names in medieval lore, among them Brandegore, Sir Brandel,
and Ban of Belwik Leodegrance.

See also: ARTHUR; BRANWEN; UTHER BEN

0625

**Branwen** (white raven)   In Celtic mythology,
goddess of love, wife of King Matholwch, and
sister of Bran, god of poetry.

See also: BRAN; CASWALLAWN

0626

**Breidalblick** (Breithablik) (broad blink, wide
glancing)   In Norse mythology, the palace of
the god Baldur, where nothing impure and the
fewest evils were found. Even so, Baldur was
murdered by a scheme of the evil god Loki. Matthew Arnold, in his narrative poem *Balder Dead*,
describes the palace where engraved on the columns were "enchantments that recall the dead
to life."

See also: BALDUR; LOKI

0627

**Brendan, St.** (stinking hair)   Sixth century. In
Christian legend, patron saint of seafarers and
travelers. Feast, 16 May.

The best-known legend of St. Brendan concerns his fantastic voyage to find the Earthly
Paradise, narrated in the *Navigatio Sancti Bren-
dani*. The work, which appeared in numerous
European languages during the Middle Ages, is
filled with adventures, many based on earlier
Irish pagan sagas, such as *The Voyage of Bran*.
Before St. Brendan reaches the Earthly Paradise,
which is an island in the middle of the Atlantic,
he encounters on his way the arch-traitor Judas
on a lonely rock on Christmas night. Here Judas
is allowed to cool himself on certain feast days
for the one kind act he performed during his life.

The episode inspired Matthew Arnold's poem
"St. Brendan", in which the poet changes the

rock to an iceberg and Judas's relief to but one hour annually at Christmas. Dante is believed to have read one version of the voyages of the saint before writing *The Divine Comedy*. Alfred Lord Tennyson, in his *Voyage of Maelduce*, says: "And we came to the Isle of a saint who had sailed with Brendan of yore, he had lived ever since on the Isle and his winters were fifteen score." Maps as late as the 18th century marked St. Brendan's Island, or the Earthly Paradise, to the west of Ireland, inspiring many Spanish and Portuguese expeditions to go in search of the island.

See also: JUDAS ISCARIOT

0628

**Br'er Fox**   In American folklore, the wily fox of Joel Chandler Harris's *Uncle Remus: His Songs and His Sayings*. One fable tells how Br'er Fox outwitted and ate Ole Sis Goose. Br'er Fox caught Ole Sis Goose sailing on his lake and said he would take her to court and then eat her. She protested. But when they arrived at court, the sheriff, the judge, and all of the jury were foxes. "And they tried Ole Sis Goose and convicted her and executed her and they picked her bones," the fable ends. Br'er Fox appears in Walt Disney's movie *Song of the South* (1947), which combines live actors and cartoon animation.

See also: BR'ER RABBIT; UNCLE REMUS; TRICKSTER

0629

**Br'er Rabbit**   In American folklore, the trickster rabbit of Joel Chandler Harris's *Uncle Remus: His Songs and His Sayings*. In Harris's tales Br'er Rabbit always outwits Br'er Fox and most of the other dull-witted animals. The most famous tale, variants of which are found in African folklore, is that of the tar baby with which Br'er Fox traps Br'er Rabbit by molding a life-size doll out of tar and placing it in Br'er Rabbit's way. When the tar baby does not answer Br'er Rabbit's greeting, he becomes annoyed and slaps the creature. His hand sticks to the tar baby, and in his effort to free himself by kicking and hitting it,

he becomes completely entangled. Br'er Fox, pondering the cruelest fate for his captive, is begged by Br'er Rabbit to do anything to him except "please don't throw me in the briar patch." Br'er Fox then tosses Br'er Rabbit into the briar patch, thinking it the fate Br'er Rabbit dreads most. As Br'er Rabbit scampers away to freedom he calls back to Br'er Fox, "I was born and raised in the briar patch." Br'er Rabbit appears in Walt Disney's movie *Song of the South* (1947), which combines live actors and cartoon animation.

See also: BR'ER FOX; UNCLE REMUS; TRICKSTER

0630

**Bress** (beautiful)   In Celtic mythology, a sun god; son of Fomer and Eri, air goddess; married to Brigit; king of the Tuatha de Danann, the good people descended from the goddess Danu (Anu). Though handsome, he was disliked because he neglected his responsibilities and oppressed his people with labor and high taxes. Eventually he was murdered.

See also: DANU; FOMORIANS; TUATHA DE DANANN

0631

**Brewins**   In Australian mythology, invisible evil spirits who cause disease. They can be driven away by a medicine man, who uses foul language against them and sucks the parts of the victim's body that have been attacked.

0632

**Brian** (strong)   In Celtic mythology, a wind god or god of knowledge, son of Tuirenn and Danu or Buan Ann, brother of Iuchon and Iuchurba. The three brothers married three princesses, Banba, Eriu, and Fodla.

See also: BANBA; DANU; TUATHA DE DANANN

0633

**Bridget of Sweden, St.** (the high one, strength) Died 1373. In Christian legend, mystical writer, founder of Brigittine Order. Feast, 8 October.

*St. Bridget (Dürer)*

Daughter of a wealthy family in Sweden, she married at 13 (not uncommon for the time) and had eight children. She made a journey to the shrine of St. James at Compostela with her husband. At his death she founded a monastery at Wastein for 60 nuns and 24 monks under the rule of St. Augustine. In 1349 she went to Rome to obtain confirmation for her order from the pope. She also traveled to the Holy Land. Her most famous work, *Revelations*, about the birth and Passion of Christ, had a deep influence on Christian symbolism and art.

In Christian art she is shown as an abbess holding a crosier. She may have a pilgrim's staff with wallet in reference to her journeys to the Holy Land or a book and pen for her mystical writings. Sometimes she is shown with a candle, which according to legend she let drip on her hand to imitate the wounds of Christ.

See also: AUGUSTINE, ST.

0634

**Brigit** (Brigid, Brid, Bride, Bridget, Brigindo) (high one, strength)   In Celtic mythology, goddess of knowledge, fire, the hearth, and poetry. Brigit is a culture goddess, her name being found in various forms throughout Britain as well as the Continent. When the Irish became Christian, Brigit was, according to some scholars, metamorphosed into Saint Brigit. Her sacred shrine at Kildare was guarded by 19 nuns, and men were not permitted to enter. One legend about her tells how she converted a pagan on his deathbed while holding a cross made from rushes on the floor. Crosses of St. Brigit, made of rushes, are still common in Ireland. Among some of the variant names by which the goddess was known in Celtic mythology are Berecyntia, Briganta, and Brigindo.

0635

**Brigit, St.** (the high one, strength)   Seventh century. In Christian legend, abbess of Kildare. Feast, 1 February.

Brigit was born at Faughart, near Dundalk, a few years after St. Patrick arrived on his mission to convert the Irish. One day, after milking the cows, Brigit gave the contents of her pail to some poor people who were passing. Then realizing that her mother would be angry at her for giving away the milk, Brigit asked God to make good the loss. On reaching home Brigit's milk pail was found to be full.

According to another medieval legend, she once sat with a blind nun, Dara. They talked and the night passed and the sun rose. Brigit passed her hands over the eyes of Dara, and the nun gained her sight. The nun looked around and then said to Brigit, "Close my eyes again, dear Mother, for when the world is so visible, God is seen less clearly to the soul."

Brigit was called the Mary of Gael because one monk said he had seen a vision of the Virgin Mary, who said she would appear to him again the next day. When he happened to see Brigit, he called out that she was the woman he had seen in his vision.

Some legends attached to the saint derive from her namesake, Brigit, the pagan Celtic goddess of knowledge, fire, the hearth, and poetry. When the Irish became Christian, they transferred some of the tales of the goddess to the saint. St. Brigit's shrine at Kildare was guarded by 19 nuns who would never allow a man to enter. This stems from the earlier practice relating to the goddess Brigit.

See also: BRIGIT (CELTIC); PATRICK, ST.; VIRGIN MARY

**0636**

**Brihaspati** (lord of sacred speech)   In Hindu mythology, originally an epithet of Indra, or Agni. It later evolved into a separate god who instructed the other gods; he is equated with the planet Jupiter. A myth records how his wife, Tara, was kidnapped and raped by the moon god Soma and later bore a son, Budha (wise), who is the planet Mercury.

See also: AGNI; INDRA; MERCURY

**0637**

**Brimir** (the bloody moisture)   In Norse mythology, a giant, sometimes believed to be identical with the primeval giant Ymir, whose blood flooded the earth when he was slain. In the *Grimnismal*, one of the poems of the *Poetic Edda*, Brimir is the name of a sword.

See also: *PROSE EDDA*; YMIR

**0638**

**Britomartis** (sweet maid?)   In Greek mythology, a Cretan goddess, daughter of Zeus and Carme (or Charme or Leto). Britomartis was often identified with the goddess Artemis, patroness of hunters, fishermen, and sailors, and she also was goddess of birth and chastity. In her role as sea goddess Britomartis was called Dictynna (lady of the net?). Minos loved her and pursued her for nine months. Britomartis leaped into the sea from a high rock to avoid his advances. According to one myth she was saved by Artemis, who caught her in a net. Artemis then made Britomartis a goddess. In Aegina she was known as Aphaea. In Spenser's *Faerie Queene*, Britomart is Chastity.

See also: ARTEMIS; CARME; MINOS; ZEUS

**0639**

**Brizo** (charmer, soother)   In Greek mythology, a goddess worshiped at Delos and honored by women as the protector of mariners. Food offerings (no fish) were set before the goddess in little boats. Brizo presided over an oracle that was consulted on matters relating to navigation and fishing. The answers were given in dreams.

See also: DELOS

**0640**

**Brok** (Brokk) (hunchback)   In Norse mythology, dwarf, brother of Eitri. Brok blew the bellows for the dwarf sons of Sindri, who were the gold workers. Eitri made a boar with golden bristles, then the ring Draupnir, and finally Thor's hammer, Mjolnir. Loki, the evil god, tormented him by taking the form of a fly and buzzing around him. The fly bit him between his eyes, causing blood to flow into them. Brok appears in the *Prose Edda*.

See also: LOKI; *PROSE EDDA*

**0641**

**Brontes** (thunder)   In Greek and Roman mythology, son of Uranus and Gaea; one of the three Cyclopes, the other two being Arges (the lightning bolt) and Steropes (the lightning flash).

See also: GAEA; URANUS

**0642**

**Brown, John**   1800–1859. In American history and folklore, father of 20 children and an abolitionist. The most famous episode in Brown's life is his raid on Harper's Ferry, now in West Virginia, on 16 October 1859 when he and 21 followers crossed the Potomac and captured the U.S. Arsenal. Eventually Brown was caught and hanged on 2 December 1859. His courage and devotion to freeing the slaves had great impact on American folklore. One of the most popular Civil War ballads was "John Brown's Body," which is also the title of Stephen Vincent Benét's long narrative poem. Whittier's poem "John Brown of Osawatomie" also deals with the man, as does Edmund Stedman's "How Old Brown Took Harper's Ferry" and Leonard Ehrlich's novel *God's Angry Man.*

0643

**Brownie** (little brown man)   In Celtic mythology, a Scottish goblin who may have earlier been some Celtic god. At night he is supposed to busy himself on little jobs for the family over which he presides. He also assists in childbirth. If he is criticized he may take revenge by breaking dishes, spilling milk, or driving cows away. Brownies are brown or tawny spirits. In England they are called Robin Goodfellow or Puck. They have much in common with the kobold in Germanic folklore.

See also: KOBOLD

0644

**Bruce, Robert**   1272–1329. In Scottish history and legend, national hero, crowned Robert I at Scone in 1306. He died of leprosy. He appears in numerous legends as a hero. The most famous tale deals with a spider. While lying concealed from the English on the island of Rathlin, Bruce one day watched a spider making repeated attempts to attach its web to a ceiling beam. At last the spider succeeded in its task. Encouraged by this example, Bruce left the island in 1307, landed at Carrick with some followers, and drove the English from Scotland. His life is told in the epic poem *The Brus* by John Barbour, written about 1375.

See also: STONE OF SCONE

0645

**Bruno, St.** (brown)   c. 1033–1101. In Christian legend, founder of the order of Carthusians. Invoked against carbuncles. Feast, 6 October.

Born in Cologne, St. Bruno became chancellor of the diocese of Rheims but left after denouncing the archbishop for simony. With six companions he opted for the solitude of La Chartreuse in the mountains near Grenoble, where he founded the first Carthusian community. St. Bruno was never formally canonized, but his feast was extended to the whole Latin church in 1674.

Though his life was not filled with miracles, Bruno has been painted frequently. Some scenes portray the death of Raymond Diocres, Bruno's teacher, who said on his deathbed, "By the justice of God, I am condemned." This statement, according to various accounts, made a deep impression on the saint. Other scenes portray St. Bruno praying in the desert of the Grande Chartreuse, refusing a bishopric, and dying surrounded by monks of his order.

0646

**Brut**   In British mythology, the first king of the Britons, son of Sylvins, grandson of Ascanius and great-grandson of Aeneas, the Trojan hero. The name Britain is derived from Brut (Brute). At 15, according to the myth, Brut accidentally killed his father with an arrow while out hunting. Banished from his home, he sought refuge in Greece with a band of Trojan exiles. After several encounters with the Greeks, Brut captured the Greek king. In exchange for his freedom the Greek king offered Brut his daughter Imogen. After the marriage Brut and his men set sail, arriving at a deserted island, where Brut saw the ruins of the Temple of Diana and called on her for guidance. She answered him, telling him there was an island past the realms of Gaul in which he was to settle with his people. The island was Britain, which Brut and his army settled. Brut had Trojanova (new Troy) built, which later became London. He was the progenitor of a host of kings—Bladud, Gorboduc, Ferrex, Porrex, Lud, Cymbeline, Coel (Cole), Vortigern, and Arthur. Brut's myth is told in Layamon's *The Brut*, written between 1189 and 1205.

See also: AENEAS; ALBANIA; ARTHUR; BRUT; DIANA

**Brutus, Lucius Junius**  Fifth century B.C.E. In Roman history and legend, the first consul of Rome, who is said to have held office in 509 B.C.E. Brutus condemned to death his own sons for joining a conspiracy to restore the banished Tarquin to the throne. Brutus was, according to James Thomson in his poem, *Winter* (1726–1730):

The public father who the private quelled,
And on the dread tribunal sternly sat.

The Italian dramatist Alfieri wrote a play on the subject in 1783, and Rembrandt painted the scene, as did David in his neoclassical style.

See also: JUDAS ISCARIOT

**Brutus, Marcus Junius**  85–42 B.C.E. In Roman history and legend, Julius Caesar's friend, sometimes said to be but almost certainly not his natural son; Caesar had, however, a long-standing affair with Brutus's mother. Brutus joined the conspiracy to murder Caesar. He committed suicide after his defeat in battle at Philippi. Shakespeare, in *Julius Caesar*, calls Brutus "the noblest Roman of them all." Dante, seeing Brutus differently, placed him, along with Cassius and Judas Iscariot, in the lowest circle of Hell in *The Divine Comedy* (Inferno, canto 34).

*Brynhild*

**Brynhild** (Brünnhilde, Brunhild, Brunhilda) (warrior in coat of mail)   In Norse mythology, a Valkyrie, daughter of Odin. Brynhild appears in numerous northern legends and myths. In the *Volsunga Saga* she is chief of the Valkyries. When she disobeyed Odin by siding with Sigmund (Sigurd's father), Odin punished her by putting her to sleep with a sleep thorn and surrounded her with a ring of fire. Only a hero brave enough to ride through the flames could awaken her, a feat accomplished by Sigurd. On waking she fell in love with the hero, and he gave her a magic ring. Sigurd then rode off to the land of the Nibelungs. Here he was given a magic drink that made him forget his love for Brynhild, and he married Gudrun. In time he urged his brother-in-law Gunnar to seek the hand of Brynhild. Gunnar made two attempts but failed to break through the circle of fire. Sigurd, disguised with the Tarnkappe (camouflage cloak) as Gunnar, rode again through the fire and received from Brynhild the magic ring he had previously given her. Thinking it was Gunnar who had broken the ring of fire to reach her, she married him and plotted Sigurd's death. After his death, however, she was overcome with remorse, killed herself, and was burned on Sigurd's funeral pyre.

The Germanic *Nibelungenlied*, in which she is called Brunhild, recounts her story differently. Gudrun is called Kriemhild, Gunnar is known as Gunther, and Sigurd is called Siegfried. The events are more elaborately drawn out, and the tragic elements form an important part of the work.

Richard Wagner, in his four music dramas *Der Ring des Nibelungen* for the most part uses the names in the *Nibelungenlied*. However, he generally follows the plot of the *Volsunga Saga*. Arthur Rackham portrays Brynhild in his illustrations for Wagner's Ring Cycle.

See also: *NIBELUNGENLIED*; *RING DES NIBELUNGEN, DER*; SIGMUND; SIGURD; TARNKAPPE; VALKYRIE

0650

**Bucephalus** (ox-headed)    In Greek history and legend, the horse of Alexander the Great. Plutarch, in his *Parallel Lives*, tells the legend of how the horse was given to Alexander by his father, Philip of Macedon, because the boy was the only person who could tame the animal. Bucephalus died after the battle of Hydaspes (326 B.C.E.) and was buried with honors. The city of Bucephala (modern-day Jhelum in Pakistan) was named after the horse.

See also: ALEXANDER THE GREAT

0651

**Buchis** (Bacis, Bkha)   In Egyptian mythology, the sacred bull worshiped at Hermonthis, believed to be an incarnation of the war god Menthu.

See also: APIS; MENTHU

*The Buddha*

0652

**Buddha, The** (enlightened one, awakened one) c. 566–486 B.C.E. Title of Siddhartha Gautama (he whose aim is accomplished; of the lineage of Gotama), founder of Buddhism.

Most scholars accept the fact that Siddhartha Gautama was a historical person, and, as in the case of Jesus, that many mystical and legendary events have been attached to the historical being, making it impossible to disentangle history from myth and legend. The events in the Buddha's life are usually arranged in a set order, as depicted in literature and art.

The first event is Maya's Dream. Maya was the mother of the future Buddha. She is portrayed as a woman asleep on a couch, with a small white elephant, sometimes ridden by a child, coming down to impregnate her.

The next event is the Buddha's birth. When Maya was ready to give birth, she asked her husband, Shuddhodana, "to send her home to her parents; and Shuddhodana, anxious about his wife and the child she would bear him, willingly granted her request. While she passed through the gardens of Lumbini, the hour arrived; her couch was placed under a lofty satin-tree and the child came forth from the womb like the rising sun, bright and perfect."

This event is usually portrayed in Buddhist art as a woman standing with one hand against a tree trunk, while an attendant receives the child from Maya's side. Sometimes accompanying the Buddha's birth is his bath, in which the Nagas make a screen for the child's back. Occasionally the scene will show a small bathtub or fountain near the child.

The next event is the Buddha's First Seven Steps. This scene portrays the infant pacing forward to each of the cardinal points to which he had announced the end of birth, old age, sickness, and death. Each place is marked by a lotus flower. Being a prince, the future Buddha had to marry when he became a young man. For his wife he chose Yashodhara, his cousin. Their union produced a son, Rahula.

The Four Encounters are the next episode often portrayed in Buddhist art and literature. All the happiness one could expect was enjoyed by the prince. "All sorrowful sights, all misery, and all knowledge of misery were kept away from Siddhartha, and he knew not that was evil in the world," according to the Buddhist texts. But the prince ventured out on four occasions to meet for the first time old age (a man leaning on a staff), sickness (a man lying in a bed), death (a man in a shroud), and finally poverty (a man shorn and shaved carrying an alms bowl). These encounters changed his outlook. He said, "I see everywhere the impression of change; therefore, my heart is heavy. Men grow old, sicken, and die. This is enough to take away the zest of life."

The next main event in the Buddha's life is called the Great Renunciation. Buddhist art often portrays this as the prince mounted on his horse, Kantaka, riding away from the city with his servant Chandaka. "Thus," say the Buddhist texts, "the prince renounced worldly pleasures, gave up his kingdom, severed all ties, and went into homelessness." Sometimes Buddhist art portrays the scene of the future Buddha sending his horse or his servant back to his home at Kapilavastu. The horse is often shown kneeling before the future Buddha.

*Buddha preaching the law*

The future Buddha then went in search of a system to free himself. He practiced intense mortification but found it futile. He then sat himself underneath the Bodhi Tree and was at-tacked by Mara, who was supreme god of desire and thus evil for one seeking release from desire. The scene portrays the future Buddha seated under the Bodhi Tree with demons on either side of him. Along with the demons are beautiful women, meant to seduce the future Buddha from his aim; however, he remains unmoved. Often the future Buddha is portrayed in the *bhumisparsa mudra*, or the earth-touching gesture. It shows his arm fully extended, his hand palm downward with the tips of the fingers just touching the earth. It symbolizes the call to witness of the earth goddess of the future Buddha's right to sit under the Bodhi Tree, the Tree of Wisdom.

Having defeated Mara, the future Buddha became a Buddha, an Enlightened One. He saw the Four Noble Truths: (1) existence is unhappiness; (2) unhappiness is caused by desire; (3) desire and craving can be overcome by (4) following the Eightfold Path.

The Eightfold Path is (1) right understanding; (2) right purpose; (3) right speech; (4) right acts; (5) right way of earning a livelihood; (6) right efforts; (7) right thoughts; (8) right concentration or the right state of a peaceful mind.

The Buddha then went out to make disciples for his belief. The next episode in the Buddha's life is called Preaching the Law or the Sermon in the Deer Park at Benares. Gathered around him were men who at first came to laugh at the Buddha. But as they listened to his discourse, they were converted. In traditional Buddhist texts the following are examples from the sermon:

The spokes of the wheel are the rules of pure conduct; justice is the uniformity of their length; wisdom is the tire; modesty and thoughtfulness are the hub in which the immovable axle of truth is fixed. . . .

He who recognizes the existence of suffering, its cause, its remedy, and its cessation has fathomed the four noble truths. He will walk in the right path. . . .

Right views will be the torch to light his way. Right aims will be his guide. Right words will be his dwelling-place on the road.

His gait will be straight, for it is right behavior. . . .

Whatsoever is originated will be dissolved again. All worry about the self is vain; the ego is like a mirage, and all the tribulations that touch it will pass away. They will vanish like a nightmare when the sleeper awakes. . . .

He who has awakened is freed from fear; he has become Buddha; he knows the vanity of all his cares, his ambitions, and also of his pains. . . .

Happy is he who has overcome all selfishness; happy is he who has attained peace; happy is he who has found the truth. . . .

The truth is noble and sweet; the truth can deliver you from evil. There is no savior in the world except the truth.

*Buddha's death*

In Buddhist art the Preaching of the Law (Dharma) usually portrays the Buddha seated with his hands in the *dharmacakra mudra*. The hands are together before the breast; the index finger of the left hand touches the right hand, the finger and thumb of which are joined at the tip.

Sometimes called "Turning the Wheel of the Law," the gesture is symbolic of the Buddha's preaching. The Buddha may be seated on a lotus throne or supported by lions. There also may be a pair of deer, symbolic of the Deer Park.

The last scene or episode in the Buddha's life often is that of the *Parinirvana* (complete disappearance). It portrays the Buddha apparently asleep, sometimes with mourning figures around him. After the Buddha's death his body was burned, and the relics were recovered for his followers. An ordinary person's cremation is believed to leave only ashes. A holy person's, according to Buddhist belief, leaves spherical crystalline objects, *sharira* (body), suitable for veneration.

The historical Buddha (anyone who follows the Eightfold Path can become a Buddha) is often called Shakyamuni (The Holy One of the Shakyas)—his clan name plus *muni*, which means holy man or monk. One of the few titles applied by the Buddha to himself was Bhagavat (the Blessed One).

See also: BODHI TREE; DHARMA; KANTAKA; LOTUS; MARA; MAYA; MUDRA; NAGA; YASHODHARA

0653

**Buddhas** (enlightened ones)   In Buddhism, those who have achieved *Bodhi* (Enlightenment). Aside from the historical Buddha, Gotama, there are, according to Theravadins, numerous other Buddhas who existed before the historical Buddha and Buddhas who will come. The Mahayanists believe in an infinite number of Buddhas. The *Aparimita-Dharani* says, "The Buddhas who have been, are, and will be, are more numerous than the grains of sand on the banks of the Ganges." In Nepal, for example, there was a system where some 1,000 Buddhas were honored. However, the number is greatly reduced in some other Buddhist mythologies. There is a group of 25, beginning with Dipankara Buddha and ending with the historical Buddha, Gotama. Sometimes the last 7 of the 25 are recognized as the Principal Buddhas, with the Buddha Maitreya (the Buddha of the Future) as number 8, a sacred number of the Buddhists. All Buddhists believe in the existence of numerous Buddhas. Theravadins hold that there is only one Buddha at a time; Mahayanists hold to the simultaneous existence of many Buddhas in different world systems.

See also: BODHI; MAHAYANA; MAITREYA

**Bue**    0654    In Micronesian mythology, culture hero of the Gilbert Islands who ascended to the sky and brought back fire to humankind. Bue also taught people how to construct boats and houses and to sing and dance.

**Buffalo Bill**    0655    1846–1917. In American history and folklore, the popular name of William Frederick Cody, scout and showman. Born in Iowa, Buffalo Bill's family moved West, where he had various jobs as "herder, hunter, pony express rider, stage driver, wagon master in the quartermaster's department, and scout of the army," to quote from his press agent. In 1867 Cody took up the trade that gave him his nickname, hunting buffalo to feed the construction crews of the Kansas Pacific Railroad. By his own count, he killed 4,280 head of buffalo in 17 months. It is said that he won the name "Buffalo Bill" in an eight-hour shooting match with a man named William Comstock, to determine which of the two Buffalo Bill's deserved the title. In 1883 he organized Buffalo Bill's Wild West show, which increased his reputation, as did a series of dime novels by Prentise Ingraham and Ned Buntline (pen name for the writer E. Z. C. Judson). More a product of publicity than of folklore, the hero appears in two Hollywood films, *Buffalo Bill* and *Buffalo Bill and the Indians, or Sitting Bull's History Lesson*, in which Buffalo Bill and his friends discuss his legend and life.

See also: ANNIE OAKLEY

**Buga** (god)    0656    In Siberian mythology, creator god among the Transbaikal Tungus. Buga took materials from the four quarters of the earth. The east supplied him with iron; the south, with fire; the west, with water; and the north, with earth. Out of the earth he created flesh and bones for the first two people; out of the iron, the heart; out of the water, blood; and out of fire, warmth.

**Bulla** (bubble)    0657    In Roman cult, a round or heart-shaped box containing an amulet, worn around the neck by freeborn Roman male children. To wear a golden *bulla* was originally a privilege of the patricians but later was extended to rich and distinguished nonpatrician families. Leather *bullae* were worn by children of poor families and of freedmen (former slaves). Boys ceased to wear the *bulla* when they assumed the *toga virilis* at age 16 or 17. The *bulla* was then dedicated to the Lares, household gods, and hung up over the hearth. Girls did not wear the *bulla* at marriage. It was sometimes worn by adults on special occasions as a protection against the evil eye.

See also: LARES

**Bumba**    0658    In African mythology (Bushong of the Congo), creator god; a gigantic white being in human form. Bumba existed alone in the universe when there was nothing but water. One day he felt severe internal stomach pains and vomited up the sun, moon, and stars, thus giving light to the world. The heat from the sun's rays dried up the water, and sand banks began to appear. Bumba then vomited up eight living creatures: a leopard, a crested eagle, a crocodile, a small fish, a tortoise, a white heron, a beetle, and a goat. Then Bumba created humankind, among whom were three of his sons. The human race was given laws and customs to follow as well as rulers. When Bumba felt he had finished his work, he left for his home in the sky. Now he communicates with men through dreams and visions.

**Bunjil**    In Australian mythology, creator sky god and culture hero. According to one version of the creation myth, Bunjil formed rivers, trees, plants, and hills from the bare land. At first there were only animals, then Bunjil created the first men out of clay. His brother, the Bat, created woman from the mud in the depths of the water. After the creation, Bunjil taught the people the sacred rites and customs, then left for his home in the sky. In Australian ground reliefs Bunjil is portrayed as a man with a large phallus and a mouth filled with a quartz crystal. Though Bunjil is one of the most common names for the creator god in Australia, other names also are assigned to him, such as Daramulum, Baiame, Nurrundere, or Ngurunderi. As Daramulum, he is said to be the son of Baiame and the husband of Ngalalbal. In Daramulum's creation myth he leaves the earth after a great flood and returns to the sky.

See also: BAIAME; EARTH DIVER; NGALALBAL

0660

**Bunyip**    In Australian mythology, an evil water monster who lives in mud at the bottoms of lakes. Also called Moolgewanke, he pulls his victims down and drowns them. He is depicted as half man, half fish, and has a crop of reeds in his hair.

See also: GOIN

0661

**Buri**    In Germanic mythology, the first of the Aesir, father of Bur who with the giantess Bestla was the father of Odin, Vili, and Ve. He is part of the creation story, being licked from a salt block by the cow Audhumla. The pattern of a single father whose son then has three sons is also found in Tacitus's *Germania* (98 C.E.), where the god Tuisto bore a son named Mannus who himself had three sons, from whose names derive those

of the three Germanic tribes: those nearest the ocean are called the Ingaevones, those in the center are the Herminones, and the rest are the Istaevones.

See also: AESIR; AUDHUMLA; BESTLA; ODIN, VILI

0662

**Burkhan** (Burkhan-Bakshi)    In Siberian mythology, a creator god in a myth told by the Buriat. Burkhan created a man completely covered by hair but in need of a soul or spirit to bring him to life. Burkhan left a dog to guard the body while he went off to heaven to fetch the soul. The dog, tricked by Shulman, the devil, let the devil remove all of the hair from the man's body except for certain parts. If the devil had not touched man, he would never get sick.

0663

**Busiris** (grave of Osiris)    In Greek mythology, a king of Egypt, the son of Poseidon and Lysianassa, a daughter of Epaphus. According to one myth, Busiris's country had been in the midst of a nine-year series of crop failures when Phrasius of Cyprus, a prophet, told Busiris to sacrifice a stranger every year to Zeus. The king made Phrasius the first sacrificial victim. When Heracles came to Egypt during his quest for the apples of the Hesperides, he allowed himself to be bound and taken to the altar as a victim. Then he broke his bonds and killed Busiris, as well as the king's son Amphidamas and all of his followers.

See also: HERACLES; HESPERIDES; POSEIDON; ZEUS

0664

**Bussumarus** (the large-lipped)    In Celtic mythology, a god worshiped by the continental Celts, identified by ancient Roman writers with their god Jupiter.

0665
***Bustan, The*** (*Bostan*) (the orchard)   Didactic poem, consisting of numerous fables, by the Persian poet Sadi, written in 1257.

*The Bustan* is a mystical book by a Sufi poet consisting of "dissertations of Justice, good government, beneficence, earthly and mystic love, humility, submissiveness, contentment and other excellencies." It was translated into Latin and became known in Europe. Jeremy Taylor, an Anglican divine who lived in the 17th century, retold a fable from *The Bustan* in one of his works. Benjamin Franklin came upon the fable in Taylor's work and, as a hoax, passed it off as a missing chapter from the Book of Genesis in the Old Testament.

Three fables bring out the mystical element in the work. "The Moth and the Flame" is one of the best known.

One night a moth, flying near a burning candle, said, "Ah, my beloved, I am your lover and weep with desire, and burn with pleasure; that is expected of me, but why do I see you weeping."

"The honey of my life melts from my brow," the flame answered. "You fly near my naked flame, desiring, yet afraid of your desire, but I consume, exhale, glow, and expire."

A man then came and put out the flame.

"Look, lover," the dying flame said. "Love now ends. Dying thou gainest love's best ecstasy!"

"The Sufi and the Slanderer" brings out the wisdom of a Sufi.

One day a man said to a Sufi, "You do not even know how they talk behind your back."

"Silence," said the Sufi. "It is best not to know what your enemies say behind your back." Sadi's moral is:

A talebearer gives to old war a fresh life,
And urges a good, gentle person to strife.
Fly away from that comrade, while strength
   in you lies! (Davie translation).

"The Tale of the Pearl" has an almost New Testament cast to it.

A droplet of rain descended from a cloud to the sea, but it was ashamed when it saw how vast the sea was.

"Who may I be," the droplet said, "when the sea is so vast. If the sea has existence, then I have none."

But Sadi adds the moral conclusion:

Since in its own eyes the drop humble
   appeared,
In its bosom, a shell with its life the drop
   reared;
The sky brought the work with success to a
   close,
And a famed royal pearl from the raindrop
   arose.
Because it was humble it excellence gained;
Patiently waiting till success was obtained
   (Davie translation).

See also: *SHAH NAMAH*

0666
**Butch Cassidy**   1866–1911? In American history and legend, assumed name of Robert Leroy Parker, leader of the Wild Bunch, an outlaw gang consisting of Kid Curry, Harry Longbaugh (the Sundance Kid), Ben Kilpatrick (the Tall Texan), Harry Tracy, Elza Lay, Deaf Charley Hanks, and other criminals. When the railroads hired the Pinkerton Agency to chase down Cassidy, he and Harry Longbaugh, along with Etta Place (who was likely a girl named Ann Bassett), fled to South America and purchased a ranch in Argentina. After a few years of trying to make it as ranchers, the pair again turned to their previous method of obtaining money, robbery. According to one account, Butch Cassidy and the Sundance Kid were killed by Bolivian troops in 1911 in the village of San Vicente. But legend says they both escaped death. Cassidy is said to have returned to the United States and died in 1937, and the Sundance Kid is said to have lived to 1957. Their romantic legend as thieves was used in the Hollywood movie *Butch Cassidy and*

*the Sundance Kid*, starring Paul Newman and Robert Redford.

0667

**Butes** (herdsman)    In Greek mythology, a Thracian, the son of Boreas. His brother Lycurgus, whom he had tried to murder, banished him, and he settled on the island of Strongyle (or Naxos). Finding no women there to marry, he went to Thessaly and carried off some of the women while they were celebrating a sacrifice to Dionysus. One of these, Coronis, whom he raped and forced to be his wife, prayed to Dionysus for vengeance. In retaliation Dionysus drove him mad, and Butes threw himself into a well. Butes is also the name of an Athenian hero, son of the Athenians Pandion and Zeuxippe. He was a tiller of the soil and a priest of Athena and Poseidon. He was believed to be the ancestor of the priestly caste of the Butadae and Eteobutadae. He was worshiped at an altar in Erechtheum with Poseidon and Hephaestus. Variant myths say he was the son of Teleon and Zeuxippe and took part in the expedition of the Argonauts. Another Butes, a Sicilian hero, was also on the *Argo*. He was enticed by the Sirens' song and leaped into the sea but was rescued and brought to Lilybaeum in Sicily by Aphrodite. He became the father of Eryx by Aphrodite.

See also: APHRODITE; ARGO; ARGONAUTS; ATHENA; BOREAS; DIONYSUS; HEPHAESTUS; POSEIDON

0668

**Buto** (Bouto)    In Egyptian mythology, Greek name for the cobra, or uraeus, goddess Utachet (Wadjet, Inadjet, Edjo), protector of Lower Egypt. Her twin sister, Nekhebet the vulture, was the goddess of Upper Egypt.

Buto helped the goddess Isis hide from the demonic god Set, the murderer of Isis's brother-husband, Osiris. Isis retreated to the papyrus swamps to give birth to her son Horus, who would in time avenge his father's death. Set never succeeded in finding her hiding place be-cause Buto caused the papyrus and other plants to screen Isis from view. She further helped to camouflage Horus by shaking her hair over him.

In *The Book of the Dead* Utachet generally plays the part of destroyer of the foes of the deceased. During the ceremonies connected with embalming, the priest addresses the mummy, saying, "The goddess Utachet [Buto] cometh unto thee in the form of the living uraeus, to anoint thy head."

Egyptian art portrays Buto as a woman wearing on her head the crown of Lower Egypt. In one hand she holds the papyrus scepter, around which is sometimes twined a snake. In some pictures she bears the crown of Lower Egypt in her right hand, about to place it on the head of the king. Occasionally, she appears as a winged serpent with the crown of the north, or Lower Egypt, on her head.

See also: *BOOK OF THE DEAD, THE*; HORUS; ISIS; OSIRIS; NEKHEBET; PYRAMID TEXTS; SET; URAEUS; UTACHET

0669

**Butterfly**    Any of numerous diurnal insects with a slender body and broad, often brightly colored wings. In Christian symbolism the butterfly is a sign of the Resurrection of Christ, based on its natural order of caterpillar, chrysalis, and then butterfly—life, death, and resurrection. However, some ancient mystical groups, such as the Gnostics, saw the butterfly as a symbol of corrupt flesh. The Angel of Death in Gnostic artworks was portrayed crushing a butterfly. In Slavic countries it was believed that butterflies were symbols of the soul, issued from the mouths of witches to invade living bodies when the true soul was absent.

See also: GNOSTICISM

0670

**Buurt-kuuruk**    In Australian mythology, an evil spirit in the form of a woman as tall as a gum tree, which can range to 50 feet in five years.

**Byelobog and Chernobog** (Byelbog, Cernobog, Zcernoboch) (white god and black god) In Slavic mythology, one white and one black god, representing the dual nature of good and evil in the world. Byelobog went about in daytime helping lost travelers find their way out of the dark forest. He also bestowed wealth and fertility and helped with the harvest. In White Russian popular legends, he was called Belun (Byelun) and was portrayed as an old man dressed in white with a white beard. His evil counterpart, Chernobog, represented darkness and evil. Chernobog was particularly feared in northern Russia, where darkness prevailed for long periods each year. In western Slavic folklore, which had contact with Christianity, Chernobog acquired many of the traits of the Christians' devil.

**Byggvir** (barley?) In Norse mythology, the personification of the barley god, husband of Beyla; servant of Frey. He appears in the *Prose Edda* in the poem *Loki Asena* (Loki's mocking).

See also: FREY; LOKI; *PROSE EDDA*

**Byleipt** (raging fire) In Norse mythology, brother to the fire-trickster god Loki, or merely another name for the god. One kenning for Loki is "Byleipt's brother." He appears in the *Prose Edda*.

See also: KENNING; LOKI; *PROSE EDDA*

**Bylina** (pl.: *bylini*) (true story) In medieval Russia, an oral heroic song or poem, originally sung by court minstrels and in recent centuries by *skaziteli*, peasant bards.

The *bylini* are usually about 300 lines long. They are in verse and are intended to be sung or chanted. The earliest *bylini* came from the 10th or 11th century, but the content is much older. Many tell of the exploits of the *bogatyrs*, or epic heroes, such as Ilya Muromets, Potok-Mikhailo-Ivanovich, Syyatogor, Volkh, Mikula, and Aliosha Popovich. All of these *bogatyrs* were men of superhuman strength who used their physical power as well as their cunning to defend Russia from the "infidels" and foreign invaders. Their adventures usually took place around the city of Kiev, under the rule of Prince Vladimir, sometime in the 11th or 12th century. Another cycle of *bylini*, centering around the city of Novgorod, tell of the merchant *bogatyr* Sadko. They are dated somewhat later, perhaps the 13th to the 15th century, though scholars differ.

The *bylina* "Why There Are No More Bogatyrs in Holy Russia" tells how, after a successful battle one of the *bogatyrs*, Ilya Muromets pridefully said he could conquer any enemy. God first sent two men who, when sliced in half, multiplied into four, and so on until they became a large army and attacked Ilya Muromets. The battle lasted "for three days, three hours and three brief minutes." Out of fear the *bogatyrs* fled to a mountain, where they were all turned to stone.

See also: ALIOSHA POPOVICH; ILYA MUROMETS; MIKULA; POTOK-MIKHAILO-IVANOVICH; SADKO; SVYATOGOR; VLADIMIR, ST.; VOLKH

# C

**Cabauil** Among the Quiché Maya of Guatemala, generic name for god, sometimes erroneously translated as "idol."

**Cabbage** A plant of the mustard family that forms a head and is eaten as a vegetable. In one European folk belief babies are found under cabbage leaves. In Irish folklore cabbage stalks serve fairy spirits as steeds. One folktale tells of a farmer near Cork who was believed to be under the control of fairies in his garden. For a long time he suffered from the "falling sickness" (epilepsy) owing to the long journeys he was forced to make with the fairy folk, night after night, on one of his own cabbage stalks.

**Cabeiri** (great, mighty?) In Greek and Roman mythology, ancient deities worshiped with secret rites especially in Boeotia and at Lemnos and Samothrace along the coast of the Aegean Sea and on the Aegean islands. Cabeiri is also the name of the children of Uranus, according to some accounts the first people; or children of Camillus, son of Cabeiro, who had three daughters, called Caberides, and three sons, Cabeiri; or

sons of Zeus and Calliope, called the Cabeiri of Samothrace.

See also: CALLIOPE; URANUS; ZEUS

**Caca** (excrement?) In Roman mythology, ancient Italian goddess of the hearth whose cult was supplanted by Vesta, also a Roman hearth goddess. Caca was the daughter of Vulcan and Medusa and the sister of Cacus, a fire-breathing giant with three heads who lived in a cave on Mount Palatine in Rome. He was killed by Heracles. Caca was also said to be the goddess of excrement, and the word is sometimes used in present-day vulgar Italian for excrement.

See also: HERACLES; VESTA; VULCAN

**Cacce-jielle and Cacce-jienne** In Lapland mythology, water gods. Cacce-jielle appeared in various forms—an old man, a beautiful woman, a naked child, or a fish. When he appeared as a fish in a piece of bread, a coin or brandy was offered to appease his evil spirit. His companion, Cacce-jienne, the water mother, appeared as a naked woman emerging from the water to comb her hair, often enticing men to fall in love with her and then drowning them. Other water spirits were Jengk-tongk, Vit-khan, Vu-murt, Kul, Vasa, Vut-oza, Vut-kuguza, Vut-kuva, Ved-eraj,

Vesta-erag, Veeneiu or Mereneiu, and Vete-
hinen.

See also: LORELEI

0680

**Cachimana**   In the mythology of the Orinoco
Indians of South America, the great spirit who
regulated the seasons and harvests. He was opposed by an evil spirit, Iolokiamo, who was less
powerful but cleverer and more active than Cachimana. He is the trickster of the region.

See also: TRICKSTER

0681

**Cacus**   In Roman mythology, a fire-spitting
giant, son of Vulcan and Medusa; brother of
Caca, who was goddess of excrement.

When Heracles, with the cattle of Geryon,
wandered into the vicinity of Cacus's cave, Cacus
stole some of the cattle while Heracles was sleeping. Cacus dragged them backward into his cave
so that their hoof prints would seem to be going
in the opposite direction. He then closed the entrance to the cave with a rock so heavy that 10
pairs of oxen could not budge it. The lowing of
the cattle in the cave guided Heracles to their
hiding place. He moved the rock, opened the
cave, and killed Cacus with his club. At the site of
the cave Heracles then built an altar to Jupiter,
under the title Pater Inventor (the discoverer).
He then sacrificed one of the cows on the altar.

Vergil's *Aeneid* (book 8) locates the cave of
Cacus on the Aventine in Rome. Medieval
Christian writers saw Heracles' triumph over the
giant Cacus as a symbol of the forces of evil being
vanquished by those of good. The French artist
Poussin painted the scene, as did Domenichino.
There is an engraving by Dürer on the subject.
In literature Cacus was the standard for thievery.
Cervantes wrote: "There you will find the Lord
Rinaldo of Montalban, with his friends and com-
panions, all of them greater thieves than Cacus."
The English novelist Sir Walter Scott wrote:
"Our hero, feeling his curiosity considerably ex-
cited by the idea of visiting the den of an High-

land Cacus, took however, the precaution to
inquire if his guide might be trusted."

See also: *AENEID, THE;* CACA; HERACLES; JUPITER

*Europa*

0682

**Cadmus** (spear, shield)   In Greek mythology,
culture hero, king of Thebes; son of Agenor of
Phoenicia and Argiore (or Telephassa); brother
of Cilix, Electra, Demodoce, Phineus, Thasus,
Europa, and Phoenix; married Harmonia; father
of Agave, Autonoe, Illyrius, Ino, Polydorus, and
Semele. Cadmus's sister Europa was carried off
and raped by Zeus. Cadmus and his brothers
Phoenix and Cilix were sent out with the command to find Europa. They were forbidden to
return to Phoenicia without their sister. In the
course of their wanderings they arrived in
Thrace, where Cadmus's mother, who had accompanied him so far, died. Cadmus then asked
the Delphic oracle what he should do. He was
told to cease his search for Europa and follow a
certain cow and to establish a city on the spot
where the cow would lie down. The cow met
Cadmus in Phocis and led him to the site that
was to become Boeotia. Cadmus wanted to sacrifice the cow to Athena, so he sent his companions to a nearby spring to bring water for the
rites. The spring was guarded by a dragon-
serpent, the offspring of Ares and the Erinys Til-
phosa. When the men did not return in a short
time, Cadmus went in search of them. He found
the dragon-serpent feeding on their flesh, and he
killed the monster. (Medieval European paintings show the beast with wings.) Athena then advised Cadmus to sow the teeth of the dragon like

seeds. He did so, and immediately a crop of armed warriors sprang up. Cadmus then flung a stone into their midst. A battle broke out, and all but five of the men killed each other. The five were called Spartoi (sown men). They were Echion (snake man), Udaeus (ground man), Chthonius (earth man), Hyperenor (superman or overbearing), and Pelorus (monster).

The price Cadmus had to pay for killing the dragon of Ares was to serve the god for an "eternal" year—about eight years, the period of banishment for a homicide. Afterward Athena made him ruler of Thebes. Zeus gave Harmonia, the daughter of Aphrodite and Ares, to Cadmus as his wife. Cadmus gave Harmonia an outer robe or cloak and a necklace made by the craft god Hephaestus.

As further punishment for killing Ares' dragon-serpent, many of the children of Cadmus and Harmonia died. Childless, the couple left Thebes and settled in the country of the Enchelians. The people received them kindly, making Cadmus their king. One day Cadmus said, "If a serpent's life is so dear to the gods, I would I were myself a serpent." No sooner had Cadmus uttered the words than he began to change into a snake. When Harmonia saw him, she asked the gods to grant her the same. The two became serpents. When they died, they went to Elysium.

Later Greek mythology credits Cadmus with the invention of the Greek alphabet and the art of mining and with the introduction of the worship of Dionysus. Lord Byron refers to the belief that Cadmus invented the alphabet:

> You have the letters Cadmus gave
> Think you he meant them for a slave?

In *Paradise Lost* (book 9.503–506) Milton refers to the changing of Cadmus and Harmonia into serpents:

> . . . pleasing was his shape,
> And lovely: never since of serpent kind
> Lovelier; not those that in Illyria changed
> Hermione and Cadmus. . . .

(Milton confused Hermione with Harmonia.)

Matthew Arnold's play *Empedocles on Aetna* refers to Harmonia and Cadmus's tale:

> . . . Two bright and aged snakes
> Who once were Cadmus and Harmonia,
> Back in the glens or on the warm sea shore,
> In breathless quiet after all their ills.

Ovid's *Metamorphoses* (book 3), Chaucer's *Knight's Tale*, and Alexander Pope's *Thebais* all refer to the myth.

See also: AGENOR; APHRODITE; AREAS; ATHENA; CHAUCER; CULTURE HERO; DELPHI; DIONYSUS; ELECTRA; ELYSIUM; HARMONIA; OVID; ZEUS

0683

**Caduceus** (herald staff)    In Greek and Roman mythology, a magic wand consisting of a rod topped by wings and intertwined by two snakes; called *kery keionin* in Greek. The caduceus was carried by Hermes in Greek myths and Mercury in Roman mythology. Originally, the caduceus was represented as a simple staff wound about with two white ribbons. It was a symbol of authority and inviolability and protected the herald who carried it. In Homer's *Iliad* and *Odyssey* the caduceus is often mentioned as a type of magic wand by which Hermes opened and closed the eyes of mortals. It was therefore connected with death and the journey through the underworld. Later myth says Hermes once threw his magic wand at two snakes fighting on the ground. The snakes became entangled in the magic wand and have been attached to it ever since. The wings at the top were added in later Greek and Roman art. In Vergil's *Aeneid* (book 4) the caduceus is said to have been given to Mercury by Apollo in exchange for the lyre. Milton, calling it Hermes' "opiate rod" in *Paradise Lost* (book 11.133), refers to the belief that the caduceus can induce sleep. Today the caduceus is associated with medicine because it was one of the symbols of Asclepius, the god of medicine for the ancients. Le Sage, in *Gil Blas* (1715) writes: "I did not think the post of Mercury-in-chief quite so honorable as it was called . . . and resolved to abandon the Caduceus [give up the medical profession] for ever."

See also: *AENEID, THE*; APOLLO; ASCLEPIUS; CADMUS; HERMES; *ILIAD, THE*; MERCURY; *ODYSSEY, THE*

0684

**Caeculus**  In Roman mythology, a son of Vulcan and the sister of the Frates Delpidii; ally of Turnus in the war against the Trojans. Caeculus's mother became impregnated by Vulcan when a spark from heaven fell into her bosom. Her son Caeculus, however, became a robber. In time he built the city of Praeneste and wanted to find citizens to inhabit it, but no one would consent to live there. Caeculus then prayed to Vulcan, asking him to show the gathered crowd that the god was his father. A flame suddenly shot up, and the mob, moved by the miracle, consented to become citizens of Praeneste. Vergil's *Aeneid* (book 7) says Caeculus was born among herds in the country, exposed by his mother to die, and later found near the hearth at a shrine of Jupiter.

See also: *AENEID, THE*; JUPITER; VULCAN

0685

**Caeneus** (new)  In Greek mythology, a Lapith chieftain who was born a girl, Caenis, daughter of the Thessalian king Elatus and Hippea, and later transformed into a man. He was the father of Coronus and the brother of Polyphemus and Ischys. As a girl, Caeneus was very beautiful and caught the eye of Poseidon, who raped her. The god then offered to grant her any wish. She chose to be turned into a man so she could not be raped again. The god granted her request. Caeneus then became the leader of the Lapiths. When the Lapiths and centaurs had their great battle at the wedding of Peirithous and Hippodameia, Caeneus killed several of the foe. However, he offended Zeus and was beaten on the head with fir trees or else buried beneath a pile of them. Ovid's *Metamorphoses* (book 12) says Caeneus was finally changed into a bird.

See also: CENTAURS; OVID; POLYPHEMUS; POSEIDON; ZEUS

0686

**Cagn**  In African mythology (Bushman), creator god who often appears as a mantis or caterpillar. His wife, Coti, bore him two sons, Gogaz and Gowi, both culture heroes, who taught the people how to make digging tools with sharp stone points. Cagn's mysterious power was believed to reside in his tooth, which he sometimes lent to others who wanted added strength. After he created the world, Cagn became annoyed with man's stupidity and left. No one knows where he went. The northern Bushmen call him Cagn or Kang, and the southern Bushmen call him Thora.

0687

**Cahá-Paluna** (standing water falling from above?)  In Mayan mythology, wife of the first man and culture hero, Balam-Quitzé, of the Quiché Maya of Guatemala. Cahá-Paluna is called a "distinguished woman" in the *Popol Vuh*, the sacred book of the Quiché.

See also: BALAM QUITZÉ; *POPOL VUH*

0688

**Caicas**  In Greek mythology, the northeast wind, son of Eos and Astraeus.

0689

**Cain and Abel** (smith and meadow? breath?)  In Jewish, Christian, and Islamic mythology, first children of Adam and Eve.

In the Old Testament (Gen. 4:1–15) Cain murdered his brother Abel (the reason is not given) and became a "fugitive and a vagabond" on the earth (Gen. 4:12). God marked Cain with a sign to protect him from the vengeance of others for the murder, though the term "mark of Cain" has come to signify a stigma for an outlaw

*Cain and Abel*

(Gen. 4:15). In medieval Christian belief Abel was the first martyr, a prefiguration of Christ because he suffered an unjust death.

In Islamic legend, Cain and Abel are called Kabil and Habil. Kabil (Cain) and Habil (Abel) each had a twin sister. Kabil's twin sister was Aclima, and Habil's twin was Jumella. Adam wanted Kabil to marry Jumella and Habil to marry Aclima. Kabil, however, rejected the idea. Adam then said God would be asked through a sacrifice to decide. Sacrifice was made, and Kabil's offering was rejected, signifying that God did not approve of Kabil's rejection of the marriage. In a fit of anger Kabil killed Habil. For some time Kabil carried around the dead body of his brother, until he saw a raven scratch a hole in the ground to bury a dead bird. Kabil took the hint and buried Habil in the ground.

Medieval Christian belief held that Cain had a yellowish or sandy-red beard, which then became a symbol of murder and treason and was used in medieval art to depict Cain, Judas, and the Jews. (Yellow became a color for anti-Semitic propaganda.) Shakespeare in *The Merry Wives of Windsor* (act 1, sc. 4, line 22), writes: "He hath but a little wee face, with a little yellow beard, a Cain-colored beard."

The biblical account inspired Samuel Taylor Coleridge's prose poem *The Wanderings of Cain* and Lord Byron's poetic drama *Cain, A Mystery,* in which Cain's wife is called Adah (adornment).

See also: ADAM AND EVE; BANBA; JUDAS IS-CARIOT

**0690**
**Calais** (green-blue gemstone)    In Greek mythology, an Argonaut; son of Boreas and Orithyia; twin brother of Zetes (searcher). Calais and Zetes aided Jason as Argonauts. Both were given wings for recovering Phineus from the Harpies in Bithynia. When they were killed, they were transformed into birds. Ovid's *Metamorphoses* (book 8) gives the myth.

See also: ARGONAUTS; BOREAS; HARPIES; JASON; OVID; ZETES

**0691**
**Calamity Jane**    1848–1903. In American history and folklore, popular name for Martha Jane Canary, noted for her marksmanship, who dressed as a man. She got her nickname in 1872 in a peculiar way. She was at that time at Goose Creek Camp, South Dakota, where Captain Egan, commander of the post at Goose Creek (now Sheridan), Wyoming, and a small body of men were stationed. In a battle with the Indians Captain Egan and his men were surrounded and had to fight desperately for their lives. Captain Egan was wounded and had fallen off his horse. Suddenly, it is said, a woman rode into the center of the trouble, dismounted, lifted the captain in front of her on her saddle, and rode away. When he recovered, Captain Egan laughingly spoke of Miss Canary as "Calamity Jane," and the name clung to her.

Some accounts allege that she was a lesbian and that her affair with Wild Bill Hickok was a coverup, because he was said to be homosexual as well. But Hollywood's movie *Calamity Jane,* starring Doris Day and Howard Keel, tells how Calamity Jane wins the love of Hickok. It was from her that Bret Harte took his famous character of Cherokee Sal in "The Luck of Roaring Camp."

**0692**
**Calchas** (brazen)    In Greek mythology, a soothsayer, son of Thestor and Megaera; brother of Alcmeon, Leucippe, and Theonoe; father of

Cressida. Calchas was an Argonaut who accompanied Agamemnon's army in the Trojan War. Homer, in the *Iliad* (book 1), says that Calchas was the "most excellent of augurs, who knew of things that were and that should be and that had been before." In post-Homeric myth, it was Calchas whose predictions demanded the sacrifice of Iphigenia as well as the building of the wooden horse. He died when he met another soothsayer, Mopsus, who beat him at guessing how many figs were in the branches of a certain fig tree. Some accounts say he died of grief; others say he took his own life. Another myth tells that he died laughing when, as he raised a cup of wine, someone said he would never live to drink it.

See also: AGAMEMNON; ARGONAUTS; *ILIAD, THE*

0693

**Caleuche**   In the folklore of the Araucanian Indians of Chile, a witch boat, seen illuminated at night, carrying fishermen to the treasure stores at the bottom of the sea.

0694

**Callidice** (fair justice)   In Greek mythology, queen of Thesprotia and a wife of Odysseus after the Trojan War. According to some accounts, when Odysseus was returning to Ithaca, he stopped off at Thesprotia and married Callidice, who bore him a son, Polypoetes. When Callidice died, Odysseus continued on his journey and left the kingdom to Polypoetes.

See also: ODYSSEUS

0695

**Calliope** (beautiful voice, fair face)   In Greek mythology, one of the nine Muses, the Muse of epic or heroic poetry; daughter of Zeus and Mnemosyne; mother of Orpheus and Linus by the Thracian king Oeagrus (or by Apollo). She is portrayed in Western art with a tablet and stylus or a trumpet. Often she holds a laurel crown. In 17th-century paintings, books such as the *Iliad*,

*Odyssey*, and *Aeneid* are shown as part of her attributes.

See also: *AENEID, THE*; *ILIAD, THE*; APOLLO; MUSE; *ODYSSEY, THE*; ORPHEUS

0696

**Callirrhoë** (fair flowing)   In Greek mythology, daughter of the river god Achelous; sister of Castalia and Peirene; unwittingly sent her husband Alcmaeon to his death by persuading him to obtain Harmonia's necklace and robe from Alphesiboea. When Alphesiboea's brothers discovered the attempt, they murdered him. Callirrhoë is also the name of a daughter of Oceanus and Tethys and the mother of the three-headed cowherd Geryon, Cerberus, and Echidna, according to some accounts. The name is also that of a daughter of the Trojan river god Scamander; she was married to Tros and mother of Assaracus, Cleopatra, Ilus, and Ganymede. She killed herself, and a fountain in Attica is named after her.

See also: ACHELOUS; ALCMAEON; ALPHESIBOEA; CASTALIA; GANYMEDE; GERYON; HARMONIA; OCEANUS

0697

**Callisto** (fairest)   In Greek mythology, an Arcadian nymph, follower of Artemis; daughter of Lycam and Cyllene (or Nycteus or Cereus); sister of Pallas; mother of Arcas by Zeus. Callisto was transformed into a bear and placed in the heavens as the Great Bear along with her son Arcas as the Little Bear.

Callisto was a follower of Artemis and had taken a vow of chastity. Zeus, ever lustful, saw her one day resting alone in the woods. Disguising himself as the goddess Artemis, he began caressing Callisto. Before the girl was fully aware of what was happening, he raped her. In order to keep his adultery a secret from his wife, Hera, the god changed Callisto into a bear. A variant account says Artemis discovered the girl was pregnant and metamorphosed her into a bear.

Another account says that Hera changed the girl into a bear when she discovered Zeus's infidelity.

The story's ending also varies considerably in the ancient accounts. In some versions Artemis shoots Callisto while she is out hunting with Hera, who points out the bear. Zeus sends Hermes to save the baby Arcas, who is then brought up by Maia, Hermes' mother. Another story is that Arcas, when grown up, saw the bear in the woods and, not knowing the bear was his mother, killed it. Still another variation tells how the bear wandered into the sacred shrine of Zeus Lycaeus and was killed for sacrilege.

The fate of Callisto, however, finds all of the accounts in agreement. Zeus transported her to the stars as the constellation Arctos, the Great Bear. Either at the same time or later he placed their son Arcas as the nearby constellation Arctophylax, which appears to be guarding the Great Bear. Hera, however, was not at all happy at this and appealed to Tethys, the sea goddess and Hera's old nurse. She asked that Tethys and her husband Oceanus never permit Callisto to enter their realm. They agreed, and that is why the Great Bear is doomed to revolve ceaselessly about the North Star. The ancient Arcadians showed visitors a tomb of Callisto on a hill, the top of which contained a sanctuary of Artemis Calliste, indicating that Callisto was another form of the goddess Artemis. The she-bear was the animal associated with the cult of Artemis Calliste.

Sources for the myth of Callisto are Ovid's *Metamorphoses* (book 2), Hyginus's *Fabulae* and *Poetica Astronomica*, and Apollodorus's *Bibliotheca* (Library).

The rape of Callisto is the theme of the painting *Jupiter and Callisto* by François Boucher, the French artist. He shows Jupiter in his female disguise as Artemis. Titian painted *Diana and Callisto*, portraying the goddess discovering that Callisto is pregnant.

See also: ARCADIA; ARCAS; ARTEMIS; HERA; HERACLES; MAIA; NYMPHS; OCEANUS; PALLAS; TETHYS

**Calydon**   In Greek mythology, son of Thestius, accidentally killed by his father; also the name of the son of Aetolus and Pronoe; the brother of Pleuron; husband of Aeolia; and father of Epicasta and Protogeneia. Calydon is also the name of a son of Ares and Astynome, turned into stone for seeing the goddess Artemis bathe. Finally, Calydon is the city of Aetolla, Greece, founded by Calydon and Pleuron, the setting for the Calydonian boar hunt.

See also: ARES; ARTEMIS; CALYDONIAN BOAR HUNT

**Calydonian Boar Hunt**   In Greek mythology, the Calydonian boar was sent by Artemis to ravage the territory of King Oeneus of Calydon because Oeneus had offended Artemis by not offering proper sacrifice. Meleager, the son of

*Meleager*

Oeneus, was sent to kill the boar. Heralds were sent all over Greece summoning sport- and adventure-loving heroes to aid in the task. Castor and Polydeuces came from Sparta, and Idas and Lynceus came from Messene. Theseus of Athens, his friend Peirithous, and Jason and his cousin Admetus came. Peleus, the father of Achilles, and Telamon, the father of Ajax, also responded to the summons. From the royal family of Arcadia came Ancaeus and Atalanta. Atalanta was the only woman in the hunt. These heroes and others were entertained for nine days by King Oeneus before the hunt began. It was his son Meleager who finally killed the wild boar after it had been first wounded by Atalanta.

The prize—the boar's skin—became the object of a quarrel after Meleager had given it to Atalanta. A battle ensued in which, according to some accounts, Meleager was the victor. In a later myth, Meleager died after the hunt because of the anger of his mother, Althaea. When Meleager was born, the two Fates predicted he would be a brave warrior but that he would die when a stick, in a fire burning at the time of his birth, was consumed. Althaea, Meleager's mother, hid the stick, but when Meleager killed her brothers in the battle over the boar's skin, she took the stick and had it burned. Meleager then died agonizingly in the fighting when the Curetes attacked the Calydonians after the boar had been killed. After his death he was changed into a guinea fowl by Artemis.

The myth is told in Ovid's *Metamorphoses* (books 8, 10), William Morris's *Earthly Paradise*, and Swinburne's poetic drama *Atalanta in Calydon*.

A late Roman sarcophagus in the Capitoline Museum, Rome, portrays the hunt. Meleager stands in the center of the piece thrusting his spear into the boar. To his right is Atalanta with her bow. Poussin based his painting on Ovid's account.

See also: ACHILLES; ADMETUS; AJAX; ARCADIA; ARTEMIS; ATALANTA; CASTOR AND POLYDEUCES; MELEAGEER; OVID; PELEUS; THESEUS

0700
**Calypso** (hider)   In Greek mythology, daughter of Atlas and Pleione or of Oceanus and Tethys; sister of Hyas, the Hyades, the Hesperides, Maia, and the Pleiades. Calypso received Odysseus on her island, entertained him, became his mistress, and bore him two children, Nausinous (cunning sailor) and Nauisithous (in the service of the sea goddess). Odysseus remained with Calypso for seven years. Calypso at last received the command of Zeus to dismiss him. Hermes brought the message to Calypso and found her in her grotto. With much reluctance, Calypso obeyed the command of Zeus. She supplied Odysseus with means for constructing a raft, provisions, and a favorable wind.

Fénelon, the French writer, in his romance *Telemachus*, which tells of the adventures of Odysseus's son, has Telemachus visit the island of Calypso. As with his father, she offered him immortality (it is believed she was originally a goddess connected with death), but the lad refused. Minerva (Fénelon uses the Latin names of the Greek gods), in the shape of Mentor, Telemachus's friend, escaped with Telemachus by leaping from a cliff into the sea. They both reached a boat offshore. Lord Byron, in his long poem *Childe Harold*, alludes to this incident when he writes: "But not in silence pass Calypso's isles." Goza is sometimes identified as the isle of the goddess.

See also: ATLAS; HESPERIDES; MAIA; MINERVA; ODYSSEUS; OCEANUS; TELEMACHUS; TETHYS

0701
**Camahueto**   In the folklore of the Araucanian Indians of Chile, a sea monster who wrecks large boats.

0702
**Camazotz** (Camalotz)   In Mayan mythology, vampire-bat god of the Quiché Maya of Guatemala. He is often portrayed with large teeth and claws and a sacrificial flint knife in one hand and his victim in the other. He slew

Hanahpú when he and his brother came to Hanahpú's domain, as one of many tests.

See also: HANAHPÚ

0703

**Camel**   A large ruminant found in desert countries and used as a beast of burden. In medieval Christianity the camel was a symbol of temperance because it could go without water for long periods. It was also a symbol of humility because, as Christ carried the burden of the world's sins, the camel carried man's physical burdens. St. John the Baptist "was clothed with camel's hair, and with a girdle of a skin about his loins." (Mark 1:6) as a sign of penitence. In artworks of the Christian Middle Ages and the Renaissance the camel is shown in paintings of Joseph and his brothers, Rebecca at the well, the Exodus from Egypt, and the Adoration of the Magi.

In Islam the Camel of Seleh is one of the 10 animals admitted into heaven. Another of the 10 was Muhammad's camel Al Adah, who made the entire journey from Jerusalem to Mecca in four bounds. Other animals in heaven were Al Borak, Balaam's ass, Tobit's dog, and the dog of the Seven Sleepers. The camel also had its detractors. Aristotle wrote that camels spend nearly the whole day copulating, and Leviticus (11:4) calls the camel an unclean animal.

See also: BALAAM; BORAK; JOHN THE BAPTIST, ST.; JOSEPH; REBECCA; SEVEN SLEEPERS OF EPHESUS, THE

0704

**Camelot**   In Arthurian legend, the home of King Arthur and his knights. It has been variously identified as Caerleon-upon-Usk in Wales, Camelford in Cornwall, and by Malory in *Morte d'Arthur* as Winchester, England. Large entrenchments at South Cadbury (Cadbury Castle) are still called King Arthurs's Palace by local inhabitants. Lerner and Lowe's Broadway musical about King Arthur is titled *Camelot*.

See also: ARTHUR

0705

**Camilla** (feminine form of Camillus)   In Roman mythology, a virgin queen of the Volsci (Volscians) and a daughter of Metabus and Casmilla; she fought against Aeneas. Camilla was dedicated to the goddess Diana and fought with one breast exposed to give greater freedom to her bow arm. Camilla was killed by Aruns's spear in an ambush, according to Vergil's *Aeneid* (book 7).

See also: AENEAS; *AENEID, THE*; DIANA

0706

**Camillus**   In Roman cult, the Latin name for the boys and girls who served the priests and priestesses during the performance of their religious functions. The children had to be below the age of puberty with both parents living. The name was used as a cognomen by the Roman hero Marcus Furius Camillus, who engineered the capture of Veii in 396 B.C.E. and saved Rome from the Gauls in 390.

See also: CAMILLA

0707

**Camillus, Marcus Furius**   In Roman history and legend, conqueror of the Gauls. Camillus cast them out of Rome in 387 B.C.E. He was noted for his sense of justice. One legend tells how he reprimanded a schoolteacher. When the Romans were attacking Falerii, the local schoolteacher brought the children in his charge to Camillus and offered them as hostages. Shocked at the schoolteacher's treachery, Camillus sent the children back but not before he had the schoolmaster whipped in front of them. Poussin's *Camillus and the Schoolmaster of Falerii* depicts the legend. Both Livy's *History of Rome* and Plutarch's *Parallel Lives* have biographies of him with legendary material.

See also: LIVY

0708

**Campus Martius** (field of Mars)   A plain lying to the north of Rome, outside the Pomerium, between the Tiber, the Quirinal, and the Capitoline Hills. The Campus Martius was dedicated to Mars, the god of war. Roman youths performed exercises in its field. It is the site of Pompey's Theater, constructed in 52 B.C.E., the Theater of Marcellus, the Pantheon, the Stadium of Domitian (now the Piazza Navonna), and many other famous monuments, as well as the voting stalls where elections for major magistrates were held. Roman generals who could not reenter the city (cross the Pomerium) without laying down their command, or who held special commands or appointments with military power, often resided in the Campus Martius until their command expired. Caesar was assassinated in Pompey's Theater in the Campus Martius.

See also: MARS

0709

**Camulos** (Camulus) (powerful)   In Celtic mythology, a war god worshiped in Colchester, England, who possessed an invincible sword; also called Camolundunum. The ancient Romans equated him with Mars. In some places he is depicted with a ram-horned head. Some scholars believe he is the original for the King Cole who figures in children's nursery rhymes.

0710

**Canace** (barking)   In Greek mythology, daughter of Aeolus and Enarete; she committed incest with her brother Marcareus, had a child, and then killed herself at her father's command. Marcareus also committed suicide. In variant accounts Canace is the mother of Hopleus, Nireus, Epopeus, Aloeüs, and Tripoas by Poseidon. Canace is one of the heroines in Ovid's *Heroides* (11).

See also: AEOLUS; OVID; POSEIDON

0711

**Cancer** (crab)   One of the 12 signs of the Zodiac. Cancer is called the Crab. It appears when the sun has reached its highest northern limit and begins to go backward toward the south. Like a crab, the return is sideways. The dates generally are 21 June to 23 July. In Greek mythology Hera sent Cancer against her enemy Heracles when he fought the Hydra. Cancer bit Heracles' foot, but the hero killed the animal. However, Hera rewarded the crab by making it the constellation of Cancer.

See also: HERA; HERACLES; HYDRA; ZODIAC

0712

**Candlemas Day** (Candlemass)   Christian feast celebrated on 2 February, also called the Feast of the Purification of the Virgin Mary, or Presentation of Our Lord. Candlemas begins four days after Christmas, initiating the 40-day period of isolation that Hebrew law required for mothers and their infants. Since Christ's birthday is given as 25 December, Mary and her newborn son would be presented at the Temple for purification on 2 February. During the Middle Ages candles that were to be used during the church year were consecrated on this day, symbolizing Jesus Christ, "the light of the World." The feast is still observed in Roman and Anglican churches. The ceremony of the candles may stem from the pagan Roman custom of carrying lighted torches to honor Juno Februata. An old Scottish proverb for the feast day of Candlemas went:

If Candlemass Day be fair and bright,
Winter will have another flight.
If Candlemass Day be shower and rain,
Winter is gone and will not come again.

In German tradition, the badger peeps out of his hole on Candlemas Day. If he finds snow, he walks abroad, but if he sees the sun shining he draws back into his hole. In secular custom today, we have Groundhog Day on 2 February.

See also: BLAISE, ST.; BRIGIT, ST.; JESUS CHRIST; VIRGIN MARY

0713

**Canens** (singer)   In Roman mythology, a nymph, the daughter of Janus and Venilia. She pined away when her husband, Picus, was lost. Picus was a handsome youth and Canens a nymph who attracted trees and rocks by her voice, soothed wild beasts, detained the birds, and halted rivers in their courses. One day Circe made sexual advances toward Picus. The youth refused, and the angry Circe turned him into a woodpecker. Canens searched for Picus for six days and nights. At last, melting with grief, she pined away and by degrees vanished into the air. Ovid's *Metamorphoses* (book 14) tells the tragic tale of Canens and Picus.

See also: JANUS; NYMPHS; OVID; PICUS

0714

**Capaneus** (charioteer)   In Greek mythology, one of the Seven against Thebes; son of Hipponous and Astynome, married to Evadne, and father of Sthenelus. Capaneus boasted that not even Zeus could stop him from entering Thebes. The god, of course, sent a thunderbolt and killed Capaneus. Some accounts say Asclepius, the god of medicine, resurrected Capaneus. Other accounts say he was the inventor of the scaling ladder.

See also: ASCLEPIUS; ZEUS

0715

**Caphaurus** (Cephalion) (camphor)   In Greek mythology, a Libyan shepherd, son of Amphithemis and Tritonis; brother of Nasamon; he killed the Argonauts Canthus and Eribotes for attempting to steal his sheep. He was in turn killed by other Argonauts. Cape Capharus is a rocky promontory in southeast Euboea, where

Nauplius lit beacons to lure returning Greek ships to their doom on the rocks.

See also: ARGONAUTS

0716

**Capitol**   The southern summit of the Capitoline Hill at Rome, separated from the northern summit by a saddle. On the highest point of the southern tip was the temple of Jupiter Optimus Maximus, begun by the Tarquins but not finished until the first year of the republic in 509 B.C.E. In 83 B.C.E. the whole temple burned down to the vaults where the Sibylline books and other consecrated objects were preserved. A new temple was consecrated in 69 B.C.E. A statue of Jupiter in ivory and gold, on the model of the Olympian Zeus of Apollonius, was substituted for the old terra-cotta image of the god. One hundred years later the temple again burned. Vespasian restored it, but the new structure was destroyed by fire in 80 C.E. In 82 C.E. a new temple was erected by Domitian that survived until the fifth century C.E. It was gradually destroyed by the Christians and Barbarians during the Middle Ages.

0717

**Capricorn** (goat's horn)   The goat, the tenth sign of the Zodiac, which the sun enters on 22 December. Capricorn's form combines the upper half of a goat with the lower half of a fish. According to some ancient texts, it represents Aegipan, son of Zeus and Aex (Aega), a nymph, or of Boetis, a goat. In Greek mythology Aegipan was immortalized by Zeus for helping the god recover his stolen sinews, which the evil Typhon had severed and hidden with the monster Delphyne. Aegipan also taught the Greek gods to change their shapes into animal forms to escape from Typhon. Many Greek texts identify Aegipan as a form of the goat god Pan. Other accounts say the goat is Amalthea, who fed Zeus with her milk when he was an infant.

See also: PAN; TYPHON; ZODIAC

0718

**Captain Kidd**    1645–1701. In British and American history and folklore, popular name of William Kidd, privateer. Born in Scotland, Kidd came to New York City, where he ran a thriving ship business. He worked for the British government in their fight against French privateers, but in 1697 he turned pirate himself. Two months later he refused to attack a Dutch ship, which nearly brought his crew to mutiny, and in an angry exchange Kidd mortally wounded his gunner, William Moore. Kidd returned to Boston in the hope of being pardoned but was sent to England, where he was tried for murder and piracy, found guilty, and hanged.

After his death various ballads were circulated, such as "Dialogue Between the Ghost of Capt. Kidd and the Kidnaper." Legend grew up around his life and about where he had hidden his vast treasure, inspiring various hoaxes about the burial site. According to legend, his spirit hovers over his treasure. Captain Kidd's treasure appears in Edgar Allan Poe's tale "The Gold Bug," set on Sullivan's Island near Charleston, South Carolina. Poe's tale influenced Robert Louis Stevenson's novel *Treasure Island*. Hollywood's *Captain Kidd*, starring Charles Laughton, deals with the legend.

0719

**Capys** (breath)    In Greek and Roman mythology, son of Assaracus and Hieromneme; father of Anchises and Laocoön by his cousin Themiste. Capys is also the name of a Trojan hero who warned against bringing in the wooden horse. He advised casting it into the sea, but his advice was not heeded. When Troy fell, Capys fled with Aeneas. He founded Capua in Italy with Aeneas after the Trojan War.

See also: AENEAS; LAOCOÖN

0720

**Caractacus** (Caradoc)    First century C.E. In British history and legend, son of Cymbeline. Caractacus was a king who fought against Rome for nine years but was betrayed by Carthismandu, queen of the Brigantes, and captured by the Romans. Edward Elgar's cantata *Caractacus* deals with the legend.

See also: CYMBELINE

0721

**Carausius**    Third century. In British history and legend, a hero who fought successfully against Rome, became ruler of Britain with full Roman approval, and later was murdered. MacPherson's Ossianic poem "Caros," the name he gives Carausius, tells the legend.

See also: OSSIAN

0722

**Cardea** (hinge)    In Roman mythology, tutelary virgin goddess of thresholds and door pivots. Cardea warded off evil spirits, especially the Strigoe, who were believed to suck the blood of children by night.

See also: VAMPIRE

0723

**Cardiff Giant**    "America's Greatest Hoax" was a scheme by George Hull, a cigarmaker from Binghamton, New York. Hull's hoax was based on the biblical passage, "There were giants in the earth in those days" (Genesis 6:4). In 1868 Hull journeyed to Ft. Dodge, Iowa, and ordered a five-ton block of gypsum in order to create a "piece of patriotic statuary." The massive block was delivered to a stonecutter named Edward Burghardt in Chicago. Burghardt and his assistants carved the figure, which is 10 feet tall and weighs 3,000 pounds. Hull then crated the giant and shipped him to Union, near Binghamton, and later to Cardiff, a village just south of Syracuse. Hull returned, and Stub Newell, his brother-in-law, dug a pit in a marshy area. The crate was opened, the giant was placed in the grave, and the site was then planted in clover.

On Saturday, 16 October 1869, Newell hired two workmen to dig a well. He showed them where to dig. One of the workers struck the giant's foot three feet down. Word of a petrified man spread quickly. A tent was placed over the pit, and a 50-cent admission was charged to view the giant. Newell took in a fortune. Scientific experts came to see the giant and offered theories of his origin. Dr. John F. Boynton, scientific lecturer, declared that no evidence existed for the petrification of flesh. Instead, he suggested that the giant was a statue created by a Jesuit priest during the 17th century to impress local Indian tribes. State geologist James Hall was likewise convinced that the giant was an ancient statue. A third group said it was of recent origin.

Soon the hoax began to unravel. Reporters looked into Newell's and Hull's activities, and farmers remembered seeing a large crate travel toward Cardiff a year earlier. A Yale paleontologist, Othniel C. March, pointed out fresh tool marks and declared the giant a "decided humbug of recent origin." Hull was forced to admit the fabrication to the press, but the giant continued to be of interest to a curious public. A national tour was booked with P.T. Barnum, who tried to buy the giant for $60,000 but failed and had his own carved from wood. Interest in the giant waned, but he was brought out of storage and exhibited at the 1901 Pan-American Exposition in Buffalo.

Between 1913 and the mid-1930s, the giant was exhibited in Syracuse, New York, and in Ft. Dodge, Iowa, where the original stone was quarried. In 1947 the giant was sold to the Farmers' Museum in Cooperstown, New York. He is still on display at the museum in a tent that duplicates the original one erected after his discovery at Stub Newell's farm.

See also: BARNUM, PHINEAS TAYLOR

0724
**Carlos, Don**   1545–1568. In Spanish history and legend, son of Philip II of Spain by his wife, Maria of Portugal. The historical picture of Don Carlos varies widely from the legendary one. According to most historical accounts, he plotted the death of his father, Philip II, was arrested, and died in prison. He is described in numerous contemporary accounts as brutal, intolerable, devilish, ill-tempered, vicious, and vindictive. One source tells how he roasted a rabbit alive; in another he forced a shoemaker to eat a pair of shoes. But the legend says Don Carlos was a handsome prince (he was actually short and ugly), who died in the cause of freedom, fighting against the dictatorship of his father, Philip II. To add to his charm he was also supposed to be in love with his father's intended wife, Elisabeth of Valois. The most famous play treating the legend is Schiller's *Don Carlos*, which was used as the basis for Verdi's opera *Don Carlo*.

0725
**Carme**   In Greek mythology, a nymph, daughter of Eubulus and the mother of Britomartis by Zeus. Carme was an attendant of the virgin goddess Artemis and was nursemaid to Scylla.

See also: ARTEMIS; BRITOMARTIS; NYMPHS; SCYLLA AND CHARYBDIS; ZEUS

0726
**Carmenta** (singer, spellbinder)   In Roman mythology, one of the Camenae, goddesses and water deities identified with the Muses. Carmenta was an ancient Italian goddess of prophecy who protected women in childbirth. In Rome she had a priest attached to her cult and a shrine near one of the gates of Rome, the Porta Carmentalis, near the capitol. On this spot Roman women celebrated the festival of Carmentalia in her honor. She was worshiped along with her sisters, Porrima (or Antevorta) and Postvorta. According to Roman myth, Carmenta was the prophetic mother, by Mercury, of the Arcadian stranger Evander. Other accounts say she was Evander's wife. Carmenta was the Roman counterpart of the Greek Themis and also was known as Nicostrata.

See also: EVANDER; MERCURY; THEMIS

**Carna** (flesh)   In Roman mythology, goddess of hearts and other body organs. She had a shrine on the Caelian Hill in Rome. Her festival, at which the worshipers ate beans and bacon and made offerings of them to the goddess, was held on 1 June.

0727

**Carnation**   A large white, pink, yellow, or red flower with fringed petals; a symbol of Mother's Day, celebrated in the United States on the second Sunday in May. In Christian legend the carnation is associated with the Virgin Mary; when she witnessed her son carrying the cross, she shed tears that turned into carnations when they touched the ground. Indians in Mexico call the carnation the "flower of the dead" and mass the flowers around corpses in preparation for burial. In Korean legend a cluster of three carnations is placed on the hair; if the top flower withers first, the last years of life with be difficult; if the second, one will suffer in youth. In the Victorian language of flowers the carnation symbolized admiration.

See also: VIRGIN MARY

0728

**Carpo** (fruit)   In Greek mythology, goddess of autumn, daughter of Zeus and Themis, and one of the Horae, who were goddesses of the seasons.

See also: HORAE; THEMIS; ZEUS

0729

**Cartwright, Peter**   1785–1872. In American history and folklore, a Methodist circuit rider in the South and Middle West who preached against drunkenness and slavery.

Cartwright thought he would demonstrate the danger of strong drink. He placed a worm in a glass of wine. It wriggled. He transferred it to a glass of whiskey. It curled up and died. "There," Cartwright said. "What does that tell you?"

0730

A man replied, "It shows that if you drink whiskey you won't have worms."

One legend says Cartwright held a man under water for advocating slavery, saying he would let him go free if the man recited the Lord's Prayer every morning and night and attended every sermon delivered anywhere within five miles. Cartwright also made the man promise to give free rides on his ferry to Methodist ministers. In his *Autobiography* he recounts many of his adventures, including a story that he had fought the legendary boatman Mike Fink, which place him more in the realm of legend than history.

See also: MIKE FINK

**Carya** (nut tree)   In Greek mythology, a girl loved by the god Dionysus. After her death she was turned into a walnut tree, and a city in Laconia was named after her. Artemis, who reported the death of Carya, was called Caryatis (of the walnut tree).

See also: ARTEMIS; DIONYSUS

0731

**Caryatis** (of the walnut tree)   In Greek mythology, Carya, a girl loved by Artemis who died and was transformed into a walnut tree. Artemis repented Carya's death and was given the epithet Caryatis. Caryatids, female-form statues used for support, are said to be based on Caryatis. In a variant myth Caria, a Greek state, supported the Persians in their war against the Greeks. When the Persians were defeated, the Greeks killed off all the Carian men and enslaved the women. Greek builders' use of statues of the women as building supports was symbolic punishment. Examples of caryatids are found in the ruins of Cnidos and Siphnos at Delphi. The *salle des Caryatides*, a 16th-century room in the Louvre, Paris, also uses the motif.

See also: ARTEMIS; CARYA; DELPHI

0732

**Casey at the Bat**   American literary ballad, published in 1888 by Ernest Lawrence Thayer, under his nickname "Phin" in the *San Francisco Examiner*. The ballad tells how the mighty Casey of the Mudville baseball team strikes out and loses the game. William Schuman's opera *The Mighty Casey* deals with the hero.

**Casey Jones**   In American history and legend, the popular name of John Luther Jones (1864–1900), a train engineer believed to be responsible for one of the worst train wrecks in history. The ballad "Casey Jones" was written by Wallace Saunders, an African-American engine wiper who had been a close friend of the famous engineer, published in 1909. It opens:

Come all you rounders for I want you to hear
The story told of a brave engineer;
Casey Jones was the rounder's name
On a heavy six-eight wheeler he rode to fame.

The ballad then goes on in detail, telling how Casey stayed on the train, even though warned that a wreck was about to take place. In 1948, a "Mrs. Casey Jones" was interviewed about her late husband. She said: "He was a lovable lad—6 feet 4½ inches in height, dark-haired and gray-eyed. Always he was in good humor and his Irish heart was as big as his body. All the railroaders were fond of Casey. . . ." Aside from the ballad, Casey Jones appears in a play by Robert Ardrey.

**Casilda, St.**   Eleventh century. In Christian legend, Spanish saint of Moorish descent invoked against bad luck, hemorrhage, and sterility. Daughter of a Moorish king, she secretly sympathized with Christian captives. She took bread to the starving prisoners, which then turned to roses at the approach of the guards. She is portrayed by Francisco de Zurbarán as an elegant Spanish woman holding roses.

**Casimir of Poland, St.** (proclamation of peace) Died 1483. In Christian legend, prince often portrayed in ecstasy with a lily and crown nearby; a patron saint of Poland and Lithuania. Feast, 4 March.

**Cassandra** (she who entangles men)   In Greek mythology, prophetess, daughter of King Priam and Queen Hecuba; sister of Aesacus, Creusa, Hector, Helenus, Paris, Polyxena, and Troilus, among others. Cassandra is sometimes called Alexandra.

According to some ancient accounts, Cassandra and Helenus, her twin, as children fell asleep in a temple of Apollo while their parents were taking part in the sacred rites. Sacred serpents, kept in the temple, licked the ears of the children while they were asleep. When Hecuba saw this, she screamed, and the serpents fled. However, since the serpent was sacred to Apollo, the children were given the gift of prophecy from the archer god.

In a variant account Apollo fell in love with Cassandra. He promised her the gift of prophecy if she returned his love. Cassandra, who was the most beautiful of all King Priam's daughters, agreed. However, when it came time for her to return Apollo's love, she refused. In anger Apollo, who could not take back his gift, cursed Cassandra: she would tell the future correctly, but no one would ever believe what she said.

Cassandra warned the Trojans about the wooden horse but was silenced. When the Greeks took the city, Cassandra was given as a prize to Agamemnon. She warned him that he would be killed by his wife, but this prophecy, like all her prophecies, was ignored. Both Cassandra and Agamemnon as well as their sons were killed by Clytemnestra and her lover.

Cassandra appears in Homer's *Iliad* (books 6, 13) and *Odyssey* (book 4); she is a character in Vergil's *Aeneid*, Ovid's *Metamorphoses*, Chaucer's narrative poem *Troilus and Crisyde*, Byron's *Don*

*Juan*, Shakespeare's play *Troilus and Cressida*, Meredith's poem "Cassandra," Dante Gabriel Rossetti's poem "Cassandra," Schiller's poem "Kassandra," Tennyson's *Oenone*, and Robinson Jeffers's "Cassandra."

See also: *AENEID, THE*; AESACUS; AGAMEMNON; APOLLO; HECTOR; HECUBA; *ILIAD, THE*; PARIS; POLYXENA; PRIAM

### 0738

**Cassiopea** (Cassipea, Cassiope, Cassiopeia) (cassia juice)   In Greek mythology, the wife of Cepheus, king of Ethiopia; mother of Andromeda and of Atymnius by Zeus. Cassiopea boasted that she and her daughter were more beautiful than the Nereids. This angered the sea god Poseidon, who sent a monster to devastate the land. To appease the god an oracle had demanded that Andromeda be placed on a rock in the sea, exposed to the monster. After being tied to the rock by her father, the girl was freed by the hero Perseus, whom she then agreed to marry. Cassiopea, however, objected to Andromeda marrying Perseus and broke in on the wedding festivities. Perseus then turned Cassiopea and Phineus (whom Cassiopea wanted Andromeda to marry) into stone by showing them the head of Medusa. For further revenge Poseidon placed Cassiopea in the heavens as a constellation where at certain times she appears to be hanging upside down. Cassiopea is a northern constellation containing 13 stars. Five of the brightest resemble a chair and have been given the name Cassiopea's Chair. Ovid's *Metamorphoses* (book 4) tells the myth.

See also: ADROMEDA; NEREIDS; OVID; PERSEUS; POSEIDON

### 0739

**Castalia**   In Greek mythology, daughter of the river god Achelous and sister of Callirrhoë and Peirene. Castalia was chased by Apollo and turned into a spring at Mount Parnassus at Delphi. The spring, called Castalia, then became sacred to Apollo and the Muses. Castalides was an epithet applied to the Muses because of their connection with the sacred spring.

See also: ACHELOUS; APOLLO; CALLIRRHOË; DELPHI

### 0740

**Castor and Polydeuces** (beaver and much sweet wine)   In Greek mythology, twin brothers, sons of Leda and Tyndareus; often called Dioscuri (sons of Zeus); brothers of Phoebe, Philonoe, Timanda, and Clytemnestra; half-brothers of Helen.

The myths of Castor and Polydeuces (called Pollux in Latin) vary. In Homer, they are said to be the sons of Leda and King Tyndareos and are called Tyndaridae (sons of Tyndareos). They died sometime between the rape of Helen and the Trojan War and were buried in Lacedaemon. But even in death they were said to live because Zeus, the king of the gods, honored them. Thus, it was believed that they lived and died on alternate days—the day Castor was on earth, Pollydeuces was in the underworld. Their positions were reversed the following day.

In a later variant myth only Polydeuces is said to be a son of Zeus. Polydeuces was born after Zeus, disguised as a swan, raped Leda. In the later account they freed their sister Helen, whom Theseus had abducted. They also took part in the Argonauts' search for the Golden Fleece. Castor, in the later myth, died in a contest with Idas and Lynceus, the sons of their paternal uncle Aphareus. The fight arose in a quarrel over some cattle that Castor and Polydeuces had carried off. In a variant myth, the quarrel was about the rape by Castor and Polydeuces of two daughters of another uncle, Leucippus, who were betrothed to the sons of Aphareus. When Castor died, Polydeuces, the immortal one of the pair, prayed to Zeus to let him die also. Zeus permitted Polydeuces to spend one day among the gods, the other in the underworld with his beloved brother.

According to another variant myth, Zeus rewarded the two for their brotherly love by placing them in the heavens as the constellation Gemini (the twins). They never appear together; when one rises, the other sets. The sun enters the constellation 21 May. The pair was worshiped at Sparta and Olympia, along with Heracles and other heroes. At Athens they were honored as gods under the title Anakes (lords or protectors). They were also regarded as gods of the sea. When sailors saw a flame at the masthead of a vessel, they believed Castor and Polydeuces were present. White lambs were sacrificed to the two.

Roman cult also honored Castor and Polydeuces. A temple was built in their honor in the Roman Forum in 484 B.C.E. in honor of their help during the battle of Lake Regillus 12 years earlier. Macaulay's *Lays of Ancient Rome* tells of the battle. On 15 July Roman *equites* (cavalry divisions) passed in solemn review in honor of the battle. Castor's and Pollux's images were found on the oldest Roman coins. They were also regarded as patrons of horses, their horses being Xanthus (Yellow) and Cyllarus.

They are cited in Vergil's *Aeneid* (book 6), Ovid's *Metamorphoses* (book 6), Euripides' *Helen*, the Homeric Hymns, and Spenser's "Prothalamion." In the New Testament (Acts 28:11) Saint Paul sails from Malta in a ship "whose sign was Castor and Pollux." They are the subject of Rameau's opera *Castor et Pollux*.

See also: *AENEID, THE*; ARGONAUTS; DIOSCURI; GOLDEN FLEECE; HELEN OF TROY; HERACLES; LEDA; LEUCIPPUS; SWAN; XANTHUS; ZEUS

0741

**Caswallawn** (Cassibellawn, Cassivelaonus) (war king)   In Celtic mythology, a war god who conquers Britain, righting the wrongs of Brenwen; son of Beli; brother of Penardon, Llevelys, Lludd, Nynnyaw, and Peiban. He was noted for his cloak, which made him invisible. Caswallawn reigned when Julius Caesar first invaded Britain.

See also: ARIANRHOD; BRENWEN; LLUDD

*Cat*

0742

**Cat**   A domesticated carnivore, associated in many mythologies with female goddesses and witches. In ancient Egypt the people were forbidden on pain of death to harm a cat. When a cat died, the bereaved family would shave off their eyebrows as a mark of mourning. The cat was then mummified, and a grand funeral procession took place. With weeping and lamentation the cat, along with its favorite toys and saucers of food, was placed in a tomb. This ceremony was the rule, not the exception. Many cats were brought to Europe by Roman soldiers returning from Egypt, even though Julius Caesar hated the animal intensely. But his dislike in no way affected the beliefs of the people. Bast, the Egyptian goddess, as well as the Greek goddesses Demeter and Artemis, were identified with the cat.

The cat population of Europe increased during the Christian Middle Ages when Crusaders returned with them from their pillage of the Holy Land. During the 15th century there was a resurgence of the cult of the Norse goddess Freya, whose chariot was drawn by black cats. In Christian Europe the church made an effort to suppress witchcraft, and the cat came to be identified with witches. Many women were killed along with their cats. Cats, as demons, were burned, usually in a rite on Shrove Tuesday, the day before Ash Wednesday.

The ancient Jews disliked cats. Only one mention of a cat is given in the Epistle of Jeremy (v.22), part of the Old Testament Apocrypha but not included in the Jewish Scriptures today. The Arabs, along with the Jews, disliked cats, but Muhammed was said to have had a cat named Muezza. If a cat enters a mosque, it is considered a sign of good fortune even today.

In Buddhist folklore the cat is disliked. One tale tells that when the Buddha was sick a rat was sent to obtain medicine to cure him, but a cat captured the rat and ate him. In Thailand and Burma the soul of a person who at death has attained a degree of spiritual enlightment enters the body of a cat. The soul is believed to stay with the cat until the animal dies, and then the soul proceeds to heaven. In an ancient Thai burial custom, when a member of the royal family died, a live cat was buried along with the body. Small holes were strategically placed in the burial site so the cat could eventually get out. When the cat escaped, the temple priests declared that the soul of the dead person had passed into the cat. There are numerous motifs associated with cats in the *Motif Index of Folk Literature*.

See also: ARTEMIS; ASH WEDNESDAY; BAST; BUDDHA, THE; DEMETER; FREYA;

**Catequil** (Choke Illa)   In Inca mythology, thunder and lightning god, attendant on Inti, the sun, and Mama Quilla, the moon, and portrayed

0743

as carrying a sling and a mace. Children were sacrificed to Catequil.

See also: INTI; MAMA QUILLA

*St. Catherine of Alexandria*

0744

**Catherine of Alexandria, St.** (pure, clean) Third century. In Christian legend, patron saint of theologians, philosophers, saddlers, spinsters, students, and rope-makers. Invoked against diseases of the tongue. Feast, 25 November.

The life of St. Catherine of Alexandria is found in a collection of saints' lives written in the 13th century by Jacobus de Voragine. Catherine was the daughter of Costis, a brother of Emperor Constantine the Great, and of Sabinella, daughter of the king of Egypt. At 15 Catherine was conversant with the works of Plato and was considered wiser than the Seven Wisest Men of her day. Her father died at this time, and she was made queen. Nevertheless, she continued to study, even though her people objected. Finally, she refused to marry until a prince possessing all of the virtues should woo her.

A vision then appeared to an old hermit in the desert near Alexandria in which the Virgin Mary told him to go to Catherine and tell her that the Savior of the world would come to be her bridegroom. That same night Christ appeared to Catherine and placed a wedding ring on her finger.

While Catherine was busy with her spiritual life, Maxentius came to the throne and started a persecution of Christians. Catherine argued so forcibly with him that he called together 50 of the most learned philosophers, promising them great rewards if they could refute her arguments. One by one they renounced their belief and accepted Christianity. Maxentius had them all burned to death, but he saved Catherine, who was beautiful, for himself. She, however, could not be moved. When she was locked in prison, her steadfastness so impressed the empress and a minion of the emperor that they both became Christians. The emperor then ordered Catherine bound on the sharp points of four revolving wheels, which when turned would tear her to pieces. The saint went gladly to her death, but an angel came and broke the wheels, the fragments of which killed many of the onlookers. Catherine was then carried outside the city, tortured, and finally beheaded. Angels came and carried her body to the top of Mount Sinai.

In medieval Christian art St. Catherine has proved an almost inexhaustible subject. She is usually shown as a young, beautiful girl with a palm, book, or sword in her hand. Her most distinguishing attribute is her spiked wheel, often shown broken. In pictures of the Mystical Marriage of St. Catherine, Christ is portrayed as a child in the lap of his mother, the Virgin. This convention arose from the reluctance of medieval Christians to portray an adult Christ placing the wedding band on the finger of the female saint. The term *Catherine wheel* is now used for a kind of firework in the shape of a wheel, driven around by the explosions, and for a rose-wheel shaped window in a cathedral.

See also: CATHERINE OF SIENA, ST.; *GOLDEN LEGEND, THE* ; VIRGIN MARY

0745

**Catherine of Siena, St.** (pure, clean) 1347–1380. In Christian legend, mystical author, patron saint of Italy. Feast, 30 April.

Catherine was the youngest child of a rich dyer of Siena. At an early age she displayed an intense religious sensibility, often causing her to go into a trancelike state. Her family was displeased with her and attempted to have her married off, but the girl had taken a vow of virginity. In her teens she sought admission to the Daughters of Penance of St. Dominic's Order of Preachers. Since she did not have to live in a convent, she chose a room in her father's house, where she stayed for three years suffering from great temptation. Finally, she had a vision of Christ, who set a ring on her finger and married her.

"Behold," he said to her, "I hereby espouse thee to myself in faith, which shall adorn thee from this time forward evermore . . . until . . . thou shalt celebrate with me in heaven the eternal wedding feast."

Catherine left her room and entered the world of political and religious intrigue, fighting to force the pope into leaving his residence at Avignon and returning to Rome. In 1375, according to legend, she received the stigmata, the wounds of Christ. They did not show on her body, however, until after her death. She died in Rome and was buried in the Minerva Church. Her head was removed and carried to Siena, where it is venerated as a sacred relic.

Among her writings, the *Dialogue*, dedicated in 1378, is considered a masterpiece of mystical writing, whereas her letters display another side to her complex personality.

In medieval Christian art St. Catherine of Siena is portrayed in the habit of her order, with the stigmata, holding a lily or crown of thorns.

See also: CATHERINE OF ALEXANDRIA, ST.

0746

**Cat Maiden, The** Aesopic fable found in various collections throughout the world.

A beautiful cat fell in love with a young man. Naturally, the young man did not return the cat's affections, so she prayed to Venus, the goddess of love and beauty, for help. The goddess, taking compassion on her plight, changed her into a fair damsel.

No sooner had the young man set eyes on the maiden than he became enamored of her beauty and in due time led her home as his bride. One evening a short time later, as the young couple were sitting in their chamber, the notion came to Venus to discover whether in changing the cat's form she had also changed her nature. So she set down a mouse before the beautiful damsel. The girl, reverting completely to her former character, started from her seat and pounced on the mouse as if she would eat it on the spot, while her husband watched her in dismay.

The goddess, provoked by such clear evidence that the girl had revealed her true nature, turned her into a cat again.

Moral: *What is bred in the bone will never be absent in the flesh.*

A similar fable is told in the great Indian collection *The Panchatantra.* A Brahmin saves a mouse and turns it into a girl, whom he determines to marry to the most powerful being in the world. The mouse maiden objects to the sun as a husband, as being too hot; to the clouds, which can obscure the sun, as being too cold; to the wind, which can drive the clouds, as too unsteady; to the mountain, which can withstand the wind, as inferior to mice, which can bore into its entrails. So the Brahmin goes with her to the mouse king. The mouse maiden says: "Papa, make me into a mouse, and give me to him as a wife."

See also: AESOPIC FABLES; VENUS; *PANCHATANTRA*

---

0747
**Cato the Younger, Marcus Porcius**  95–46 B.C.E. In Roman history and legend, great-grandson of Cato the Elder and supporter of Pompey. Cato committed suicide at Utica rather than consent to live under a tyrant when he learned Caesar had defeated Pompey. Lucan's epic *Pharsalia* pictures him as a hero. Dante's *Divine Comedy* makes Cato guardian of the approach to Mount Purgatory because of Cato's devotion to liberty. One of Plutarch's *Parallel Lives* and Joseph Addison's tragedy *Cato* deal with the Roman hero.

---

0748
**Catreus** (pheasant)  In Greek mythology, son of King Minos of Crete and Pasiphae; brother of Acacallis, Androgeus, Ariadne, Deucalion, Euryale, Glaucas, Lycastrus, Phaedra, and Xenodice. Catreus was the father of three daughters, Aerope (the mother of Agamemnon and Menelaus), Clymene, and Apemosyne. Catreus had one son, Althaemenes, who, an oracle predicted, would kill his father. Many years later when Catreus went to Rhodes to visit him, Althaemenes mistook him for a pirate and killed him.

See also: AGAMEMNON; ANDROGEUS; ARIADNE; DEUCALION AND PYRRHA; MENELAUS; PHAEDRA

---

0749
**Cattle of the Sun**  In Greek mythology, cattle living on the island of Thrinacia that were sacred to Apollo. Odysseus warned his men not to eat the cattle, but they paid no attention. As a result, Apollo sank their ship, and all of the men drowned except Odysseus. The episode is in Homer's *Odyssey* (book 12).

See also: APOLLO; ODYSSEUS; *ODYSSEY, THE*

---

0750
**Caucasus**  Mountain range where the Greek god Zeus chained Prometheus as a punishment. Each day Prometheus's liver was devoured by an eagle or a vulture. Vergil's *Aeneid* (book 4) says that Mount Caucasus burned when Phaethon's chariot came too close to earth.

See also: *AENEID, THE*; PHAETON; PROMETHEUS; ZEUS

---

0751
**Caunus and Biblis**  In Greek and Roman mythology, brother and sister, children of Miletus and Cyanee. Biblis fell in love with her brother and wrote him a letter telling of her sexual passion. Caunus fled in horror to Caria. Biblis followed him, but eventually she wearied of the chase, dissolved in her tears, and changed

into a fountain. Ovid's *Metamorphoses* (book 9) tells the tale.

See also: OVID

**Cavall**    In Arthurian legend, the dog of King Arthur. In Tennyson's poem "Enid," part of *Idylls of the King*, he is described as "King Arthur's hound of deepest mouth."

**Cecilia, St.** (blind)    Third century. In Christian legend, patron saint of the blind, music, and musicians. Feast, 22 November. One of the most popular saints in Christianity.

In *The Canterbury Tales* Chaucer has the Second Nun narrate the life of the saint. The poet based his telling on *The Golden Legend*, a collection of saints' lives written in the 13th century by Jacobus de Voragine.

Cecilia was born blind of noble Roman parents during the reign of the emperor Severus. Both parents were Christian, and the girl was brought up in that faith. She always carried a copy of the Gospels concealed in her robe, and she pledged herself to Christ and chastity. She was noted for her gift of music. She composed and sang hymns so sweetly that angels came down from heaven to listen to her. Because the instruments employed in secular music were insufficient for the music of her soul, she invented the organ, according to legend.

Her parents wanted her to marry a young Roman noble, Valerian, when she was about 16 years old. She persuaded the young man to respect her vows of chastity and even converted him to Christianity. The young man went to St. Urban in the catacombs and was baptized by him. When he returned, he found Cecilia with an angel, who crowned them both with roses from Paradise. Valerian, in response to the angel's offer to grant any request of him, asked that his brother Tiburtius might also be converted to Christ. Soon after Tiburtius came in and noticed the scent of roses, though he could not see them.

When he was converted by the words of Cecilia, he too saw the roses. The two men and Cecilia then went about doing good among the poor and sick. This came to the notice of the authorities, who had the two men arrested and executed for being Christians. Cecilia buried their bodies and was also arrested. Thrown into a boiling bath, she emerged alive. She was then given three wounds in the neck and breast and was left for dead. After three days she died.

When the Academy of Music was founded at Rome in 1584 Cecilia was adopted as the patroness of church music. Ironically, the patronage arises from a medieval misunderstanding that associated her with the invention of the organ. Actually, the earliest known organ was the *hydraulos*, built by the ancient Greeks about 250 B.C.E. Both John Dryden and Alexander Pope wrote odes in honor of St. Cecilia. Dryden's work, *Ode for St. Cecilia's Day*, was set to music by Handel in 1739. Liszt composed a legend for chorus and orchestra, *Die heilige Cäcilia*. On St. Cecelia's Day the Worshipful Company of Musicians meet and go in procession to St. Paul's Cathedral in London. In Christian art St. Cecilia is portrayed with a palm; sometimes she is crowned with roses. She is easily distinguished from other virgin martyr saints by her organ or other musical instrument or roll of music.

See also: CHAUCER; *GOLDEN LEGEND, THE*

**Cecrops** (face with a tail)    In Greek mythology, a culture hero, son of Gaea; married Agraulos; father of Erisichthon, Herse, and Pandrosus. Cecrops was half man, half serpent with the torso of a man and the lower body of a serpent.

According to some accounts, Cecrops was the first king of Attica, which was called Cecropia in his honor. He built temples, established the worship of the gods, abolished human sacrifice, and introduced the art of writing.

When Poseidon and Athena were contending for possession of the land, Poseidon struck the

*Cecrops*

**Cedalion** (he who takes charge of sailors)   In Greek mythology, a man sent by Hephaestus to carry the blind Orion from Lemnos to the sun, where Apollo restored Orion's sight.

See also: APOLLO; ORION

**Cedar**   A fragrant evergreen tree; in world mythology and folklore, often a symbol of fidelity, manly strength, and fatherhood. In Near Eastern mythology the hero king was often represented by the cedar. In Assyria the cedar was under the protection of the god Ea, who personally watched over the fortunes of the sacred king. In Ezekiel (31) the cedar is used in a messianic allegory and represents strength and greatness. In Christian writing the cedar is often used as a symbol for Christ.

See also: EA; EZEKIEL

rock of the Acropolis with his trident, and water (or, according to a variant myth, a horse) sprang forth. Athena, however, planted the first olive tree. Cecrops, who had to decide which god would have the land, conferred the honor on Athena because the olive branch was a sign of peace, whereas the horse was a symbol of war. Pandrosos (all dewy), his daughter, was the first priestess of Athena and had a shrine of her own, the Pandroseum, in the temple of Erechtheus on the Acropolis. She was invoked in time of drought. In her temple stood the sacred olive tree that Athena had created.

Cecropia was the original name for Athens, in honor of Cecrops. The word was used for Attica, and Athenians were called Cecropidae (descendants of Cecrops).

See also: ATHENA; GAEA; POSEIDON

**Ceiuci**   In the mythology of the Tupi Indians of Brazil, a cannibalistic witch.

One legend recounted by José Viera Couto de Magalhaes in his *O Selvagen* (1874), tells how Ceiuci caught a young man to eat. One day Ceiuci came to fish and saw a young man's shadow near the water. She cast her line into the water and saw the young man laugh. She looked up and said, "Descend," but the young fellow refused. She then sent biting ants after him. When he jumped into the water, she caught him and took him home, intending to eat him. While she was fetching wood, her daughter came upon the captive. He persuaded her to hide him. When Ceiuci returned, the two fled, dropping palm branches on the way; these were transformed into animals that the witch stopped to eat. Eventually, the young man reached the hut of an old woman, who was his mother. By this time he was an old man himself.

0758

**Celaeno** (swarthy)    In Greek mythology, one of the seven Pleiades (a constellation), daughter of Atlas and Pleione. Celaeno was the mother of Lycus and Chimaereusc by Poseidon and, according to some accounts, the mother of Delphus by Apollo. Celaeno is also the the name of one of the Danaides (the 50 daughters of King Danaus), the name of a daughter of Poseidon and Ergea, and the name of one of the Harpies.

See also: APOLLO; ATLAS; HARPIES; PLEIADES; POSEIDON

0759

**Cenn Cruaich** (lord of the mound)    In Celtic mythology, chief idol worshiped in pre-Christian Ireland by the sacrifice of firstlings, both human and animal, on Samh'in. According to ancient accounts, his image was made of gold surrounded by 12 stones, and stood on the plain of Mag Slecht in Ulster. When St. Patrick came to Ireland, according to Christian accounts, the Idol of Cenn Cruaich bent down to honor the saint and was called Cromcruaich (the bowed-one Cruaich).

See also: PATRICK, ST.; SAMH'IN

0760

**Centaur** (wounder, stabber)    In Greek mythology, a half-man, half-horse creature living principally in Thessaly; offspring of either Ixion and Nephele, a cloud, or Apollo's son Centaurus and Silbia, or Centaurus and the mare Magnesian. Centaurs, noted as rapists and drunkards, came to the marriage of Hippodameia and Pirithous, king of the Lapiths, as invited guests and attempted to rape the women and kill the men. Pirithous and his friend Theseus killed many centaurs at the wedding and drove the rest out of Thessaly. But not all centaurs were lascivious drunkards. The centaur Chiron, son of Cronus and an Oceanid, was a friend of man, teaching him the arts of healing, hunting, and music. He was the tutor of Asclepius, the god of medicine, and also of Jason, Achilles, and Heracles. During a fight with some other centaurs one of Heracles' poisoned arrows accidentally struck Chiron, who was immortal. To avoid suffering from the wound for eternity, Chiron asked Zeus to let him die. Zeus then presented his immortality to Prometheus and out of pity placed Chiron in the heavens as the constellation Sagittarius, the archer, the ninth sign of the Zodiac. In general, the Greeks used centaurs in their art and literature to represent barbaric civilization. They are often portrayed on vases and appear on the metope of the Parthenon and as sculptures on the west pediment of the temple of Zeus at Olympia. In Roman art they are portrayed in Pompeii at the House of the Centaur. In medieval Christian art they represent man's animal nature. For example, a centaur is portrayed on one of the capitals of Winchester Cathedral in England. Vergil's *Aeneid* (book 6.618) and Ovid's *Metamorphoses* (book 12), which describes the battle of the Lapiths and centaurs, inspired

*The centaur Chiron*

*Sagittarius*

Spenser's *Faerie Queene* (4.1.23), which tells of the battle of the centaurs with Heracles as well as the Lapith-centaur battle.

See also: ACHILLES; APOLLO; ASCLEPIUS; HERACLES; IXION; JASON; PROMETHEUS; THESEUS; ZODIAC

**0761**
**Ceridwen** (Cerridwen, Keridwen) (white, blessed)  In Celtic mythology, a British fertility goddess; the shape-shifting daughter of Ogyrven; wife of Tegid the Bold; mother of Crerwy, the most beautiful girl in the world, and Avagdu, the ugliest boy. She possessed a magic caldron called Amen which she kept at the bottom of Bala Lake (Wales). The caldron contained a magic drink called greal, made from six plants. When the greal was drunk, it gave inspiration and knowledge. When three drops of the caldron intended for her son Avagdu fell instead on Gwion, giving him wisdom and insight, Ceridwen pursued him. He first changed into a hare and she into a greyhound; he became a fish and she an otter; he became a bird and she a hawk; he became a grain of corn and she a hen—and finally she ate him. She then gave birth to him and

threw him into the sea, and he became the bard Taliesin.

**0762**
**Cernunnos** (the horned one)  In Celtic mythology, the "lord of animals"; he was portrayed horned, sitting cross-legged, and flanked by various animals. Cernunnos was associated with fertility and prosperity, causing ancient Roman writers to equate him with Mercury, their god of commerce and leader of the souls of the dead. In later medieval Christian legend Cernunnos became a symbol of the Antichrist. His posture has been compared to Buddha's.

See also: BUDDHA; MERCURY

**0763**
**Cessair**  In Celtic mythology, one of the tribal goddesses of the peoples who preceded the Celts in Ireland. In medieval legend Cessair was regarded as a daughter of Bith, son of the biblical Noah and the first person to set foot in Ireland. Another version makes her the daughter of Banba.

See also: BANBA; BITH AND BIRREN; NOAH

**0764**
**Chabriel** (dryness)  In medieval Jewish folklore, the angel credited with drying up the waters of the flood mentioned in Genesis (8:13). In the biblical account, however, Yahweh, the Hebrew God, is responsible.

See also: YAHWEH

**0765**
**Chac** (Chaac)  In Mayan mythology, four-part god of rain and thunder, patron of the number 13. Chac is the Mayan equivalent of the Aztec deity Tlaloc. At his festival babies and young children were sacrificed, cooked, and eaten by his priests. Each part of Chac was connected with a cardinal point and a color. They were Chac Xib Chac (the red man), Chac of the east; Sac Xib Chac (the white man), Chac of the

north; Ek Xib Chac (the black man), Chac of the west; and Kan Xib Chac (the yellow man), Chac of the south. In Mayan art Chac appears more frequently than any other god. He is portrayed with a long truncated nose and two curling fangs protruding downward out of his mouth. Paul Schellhas, when classifying the gods in some Mayan codices, gave Chac the letter *B*, and the god is sometimes referred to as God B.

0766

**Chachalmeca**   In Aztec ritual, high-ranking priest in charge of sacrifices. Aztec priests were not allowed to marry, and they lived in a cloister-like compound. As part of their initiation they were castrated and blood was drawn from their penises, ears, and tongues by a *chaichiutzli*, a ritual stone.

0767

**Chad, St.** (battle)   Seventh century. In Christian legend, bishop of Lichfield, England. Feast, 2 March.

Chad became abbot of the priory of Lastingham in 659, which had been founded by his brother, St. Cedd. King Oswy then appointed Chad to the see of York, but he was removed by St. Theodore in favor of St. Wilfrid. Theodore was impressed by Chad, however, and arranged for him to be bishop of Mercia. Chad moved the episcopal seat from Repton to Lichfield, "the field of the dead." He built a church and lodging. After some two years he had a vision in which he was warned of his approaching death. He saw his brother, St. Cedd, with a troop of angels. They sang and called him to follow them to God as they ascended to heaven. Shortly afterward Chad died. In art he is shown holding a model of the cathedral of Lichfield.

0768

**Chagan-Shukuty**   In Siberian mythology, a creator god who formed the earth with the aid of Otshirvani, another creator god. The creation is similar to the Earth Diver myth found in many cultures. The two companions one day descended from heaven. They saw a frog or turtle diving into the water. Chagan-Shukuty raised the animal and placed it on the water. Otshirvani then sat on the animal's stomach. Otshirvani asked Chagan-Shukuty to dive to the bottom of the water and bring up what he found. On the second try Chagan-Shukuty came up with a piece of dirt, which was sprinkled on the stomach of the animal. By now both gods were sitting on the animal. The animal then sank out of sight, and only the earth remained visible on the surface of the waters. The two gods fell asleep, and the devil decided to drown them. But when he attempted to seize the edge of the earth he no longer saw the water, for the earth kept growing. He then seized the two gods under his arm and began to run toward the shore, but the earth kept ahead of him. Realizing he could not accomplish his task, he dropped the gods and escaped.

See also: EARTH DIVER; OTSHIRVANI

0769

**Chalchihuitlicue** (Chalchiuhtliycue, Chalchiuhcihuatl, Chalchiuhtlicue) (lady of the turquoise skirt)   Aztec storm goddess, personification of whirlpools and youthful beauty; wife of her brother Tlaloc, the god of rain and water.

According to Fray Bernardino de Sahagún in his *Historia general de las cosas de Nueva España*, the goddess "had power over the sea and the rivers, and could drown those who navigated on the waters, causing tempests and whirlwinds that would flood the boats and barges and other vessels happening to be on the water." However, Lewis Spence, the Scottish anthropologist, observed that Sahagún's description "appears inexact" since the "Mexicans were not a seafaring people." In art Chalchihuitlicue was portrayed as a bare-breasted woman wearing a coronet of blue paper surmounted by green feathers. Her dress was of a green-blue tint. In her left hand she carried a large water plant, in the right a vase surmounted by a cross, symbol of the four points of the compass, from which the rain comes. She was of great significance for rituals, but she plays little part in Aztec narratives.

**Chalmecaciuatl**   In Aztec mythology, paradise for children who died before they reached the age of reason. The concept is similar to the Christian limbo and may merely be an Aztec reworking of the Christian belief prompted by Spanish missionaries.

0770

**Chamalcán**   In the mythology of the Cakchiquel Indians, a bat god, mentioned in the *Popol Vuh*, the sacred book of the ancient Quiché Maya of Guatemala.

See also: *POPOL VUH*

0771

**Chamuel** (Camael, Camial, Camniel, Cancel, Chamael, Kemuel, Khamael) (he who seeks God)   In Jewish and Christian folklore, one of the seven archangels. In Jewish folklore Chamuel is the name given to the angel who wrestled with Jacob (Gen. 32:24–32) but who is not named in the biblical text. In Christian folklore Chamuel is name of the angel who comforted Jesus in the Garden of Gethsemane (Luke 22:43) but is not named in the text.

See also: JACOB

0772

**Chandra** (moon)   In Hindu mythology, moon god, source of fertility, often identified with the magic drink of the gods, Amrita or Soma. Chandra was the ancestor of the Chandra-vansa, the lunar race, which was divided into two branches, the Yadavas and the Pauravas. Krishna (an incarnation of the god Vishnu) was descended from the Yadavas.

Wilkie Collins, the English writer, in his novel *The Moonstone*, tells of the Chandra-kanta

0773

(the moonstone), an enormous diamond placed in the head of a statue of Chandra. The moonstone is guarded by three priests who are killed by an Englishman, John Herncastle. The novel then traces the life of the gem and the evil it brings on each person who comes into contact with it.

Another magic gem in Hindu lore, the Chinta-mani (the wish gem) grants the owner all he or she desires. It belongs to the god Brahma, who is sometimes called by its name. Other traditions ascribe it to Indra as part of his crown, or say it is the third eye of a snake god.

See also: AMRITA; BRAHMA; INDRA; KRISHNA; SOMA; VISHNU

**Chang Chiu**   In Chinese legend, a deified Taoist sage who wore thin, unlined clothes, even in the depths of winter. Once Chang Chiu was invited to the emperor's court to exhibit his magical powers. He cut his clothes into small pieces and transformed them into butterflies. They resumed their original shape when he clapped his hands.

0774

*Chang Hsien*

**Chang Hsien** (Chang the immortal)   In Chinese mythology, a deified mortal, patron god of

0775

childbearing, often portrayed as an old man. He holds in his hand a bow and arrow, with which he shoots at the Dog Star.

**Chang Kuo-lao**    Eighth century C.E.? In Chinese Taoist mythology, one of the Pa-Hsien, the Eight Immortals. He was a noted magician who could become invisible. He rode a magic mule that, when not in use, was folded up and put in his wallet. When the mule was needed, water was poured into Chang Kuo-lao's wallet, and the mule reappeared. He is portrayed often with a bamboo tube drum, carried in either arm; its sounds announced his arrival in a community. In Japanese legend Chang Kuo-lao is called Chokaro.

See also: PA-HSIEN

0777

**Channa**    In Buddhist legend, the faithful charioteer of the Buddha who accompanied him when he went out to see the world. He does not appear in Buddhist legend, however, as a convert to Buddhism.

See also: BUDDHA, THE

0778

**Chanson de geste** (song of deeds)    Old French epic, often telling of the deeds of such heroes as Charlemagne, Roland, and Huon de Bordeaux. The most famous chanson de geste is the 11th-century *Chanson de Roland*.

See also: CHARLEMAGNE; ROLAND

0779

**Chanticleer** (sing clear?)    In medieval folklore, a clever rooster, always pursued by the fox. Chaucer's The Nun's Priest's Tale, part of *The Canterbury Tales*, narrates one of the tales associated with the cock. One day the fox, Dan Russell, came to the poultry yard and told Master Chanticleer he could not resist Chanticleer's singing. Flattered by the fox, Chanticleer closed

his eyes and began to sing. The fox immediately seized Chanticleer and ran off. "I would recommend you eat me at once for I think I can hear your pursuers," Chanticleer said to the fox. When the fox opened his mouth to reply, Chanticleer flew out. Edmund Rostand wrote a play with the title *Chantecler* (1910).

See also: CHAUCER; COCK; REYNARD THE FOX

0780

**Chapbook** (German *Volksbuch*)    Following the development of movable type and the printing press by Johannes Gutenberg in Germany in the mid 15th century, small unbound books were printed and sold at markets by peddlers who obtained their wares from printshops. The name derives from the Old English *ceapman*, meaning merchant. The books were small, only 3.5 by 5.5 inches, and normally consisted of 24 pages. They often included woodcuts. The chapbook trade flourished until the late 19th century. For the most part these small books were condensed and illustrated versions of well-known works, particularly of local legends and folktales, such as Robin Hood, Dr. Faustus, Reynard the Fox, and Sleeping Beauty. Religious societies also distributed large numbers of chapbooks that dealt with moral topics. Some of the chapbooks clearly present long-lived oral traditions, while others suggest written materials that entered oral tradition by being read aloud. Only a few collections of these chapbooks still survive, for example in the British Library, the Harvard College Library, and the New York Public Library.

See also: FAUST; REYNARD THE FOX; ROBIN HOOD

0781

**Charivari**    A superstitious custom observed by many primitive peoples in which a loud racket was made by beating drums, pots, or other objects to keep evil spirits away from newlyweds. These evil spirits were always very jealous, and if allowed to enter the newlywed's abode they would bring harm to the pair. Noise, however, frightened the evil spirits away. Charivari was once a widespread custom in central Europe, but it degenerated into coarse horseplay intended to annoy the bride and groom on their wedding night. Sometimes the nuptial bed was "fixed" so that it would collapse when the couple got in, or cowbells were attached to the springs, and a crowd would wait just outside the window, listening or even offering suggestions. When the crowd had caused enough disruption, it was expected that the husband would come to the door and invite the revelers in for food and drink, at which time many toasts were offered, especially to the bride.

0782

**Charlemagne** (Charles the great, Karl der Grosse)   c. 742–814. In medieval history and legend, king of the Franks, first Holy Roman Emperor, who appears in medieval legends and French *chansons de gestes*.

Charlemagne was the son of Pepin the Short and Bertha the Largefooted. Pepin died in 768, and his Frankish kingdom was willed to his sons Carloman and Charles. Three years after the accession of the brothers Carloman died, and Charles took possession of his dominions. During his long reign of nearly half a century Charlemagne extended his boundaries until they embraced the larger part of western Europe. He conducted more than 50 military campaigns, among which were those against the Lombards, the Saracens, and the Saxons. He was crowned by the pope in 800 as emperor of the Romans.

His rule as emperor lasted 14 years and established what would become the Holy Roman Empire. During that time he called synods, or councils, of the clergy in his dominions, presided at these meetings, and addressed words of admonition to abbots and bishops. Education was important to Charlemagne. In his old age he tried to learn to write but found it beyond his powers. Distressed by the ignorance of his people, he established schools and had numerous manuscripts copied. He invited Alcuin, one of the finest scholars of his day, to come from England to his court and help him organize a palace school. Numerous legends grew about his person, forming an important part of medieval folklore.

In one legend Charlemagne, having built for his own use a new castle overlooking the Rhine, was awakened from his sleep during the first night he spent there by the touch of an angel. The heavenly messenger told Charlemagne to go out into the night and steal something. So the ruler saddled his horse and rode off. He had not gone far when he met a knight unknown to him. A challenge ensued, and Charlemagne unhorsed his opponent. When he learned that he had disarmed Elbegast (Alberich), the notorious highwayman, he promised to let him go free if he would only help him steal something that night.

Guided by Elbegast, Charlemagne secretly went to the castle of one of his ministers. With Elbegast's aid he got into the bedroom of his minister unseen. There, crouching in the dark, Charlemagne overheard his minister confide to his wife about a plot to murder the emperor the next day. Patiently biding his time until they were sound asleep, Charlemagne took a worthless trifle and noiselessly made his way out, returning to his castle unseen. The next day he foiled the plot and later forgave the conspirators when they swore allegiance to him. Elbegast was so impressed by Charlemagne that he renounced his dishonest profession and joined the emperor's service.

Grateful to the angel, Charlemagne named his new castle Ingelheim (angel home). This episode is often alluded to in later legends of chivalry, in which knights, called on to justify their unlawful appropriation of another's property, disrespectfully remind the emperor that he too was once a thief.

When Charlemagne's third wife died, he married a beautiful Eastern princess, Frastrada, who with a magic ring soon won Charlemagne's complete devotion. The new queen, however, did not long enjoy her power, for a dangerous illness overcame her. At the point of death, she feared the ring might be worn by another, and she slipped it into her mouth and died. Solemn preparations were made to bury her in the cathedral of Mayence (Mainz), but the emperor refused to part with her body. Neglectful of all matters of state, he remained in the mortuary chamber day after day. Turpin, his archbishop and adviser, slipped into the room while the emperor, exhausted with fasting and weeping, was asleep. After carefully searching for the magic ring, Turpin discovered it in the queen's mouth. The archbishop slipped on the ring and was about to leave the room when Charlemagne awoke. The emperor flung himself on Turpin's neck, saying he needed him to be near. Taking advantage of the ring's magic power, Turpin told Charlemagne to eat and drink and after the funeral to resume his affairs of state.

Although old, Turpin was now forced by the magic ring (which he never took off for fear it would fall into the wrong hands) to accompany Charlemagne everywhere. One moonlit night he stole noiselessly out of the emperor's tent and wandered alone in the woods, thinking how he could get rid of the ring without exposing Charlemagne to danger. As he walked, he came to a glade in the forest and saw a deep pool. He cast the ring into the pool and went back to his tent. The next day he was delighted to see that the magic spell of love was broken and that Charlemagne had returned to his own self. Charlemagne, however, seemed restless and soon went out to hunt. He lost his way and came to the pool where Turpin had thrown the ring. He was so charmed by the spot that he gave orders later that a castle should be erected there. The castle was to become Aix-la-Chapelle (Aachen).

Charlemagne gathered around him 12 paladins, among them Roland (his nephew), Rinaldo, Namo, Salomon, Astolpho of England, Florismart, Malagigi, Ganelon (the traitor), Ogier the Dane, Fierambras, Oliver, and Archbishop Turpin. (Other names given in various legends are Ivon, Ivory, Otton, Berengier, Anseis, Gerin, Guarinos, Engelier, Samson, and Gerard.)

Another legend tells how St. James the Greater appeared to Charlemagne, telling him to free Spain from the Moors. The emperor went to Spain with a large army and attacked Pamplona. For two months they were beaten back; then they prayed for God's help, and the walls of the city fell like those of Jericho. All of the Moors who converted to Christianity were spared, but the remainder were slaughtered. Afterward the emperor went to the shrine of St. James at Santiago de Compostela to pay his devotions and later returned to France.

Once Charlemagne was challenged to single combat by Ferracute, a giant. Although Charlemagne is described as 20 feet tall in most legends, the emperor felt himself no match for the giant, so he sent Ogier the Dane to fight him. Ogier failed, as did Renaud de Montauban, and finally Roland took the field. The two fought, with Roland trying to convert Ferracute to Christianity. With heavenly aid, Roland dealt a death blow. The giant fell, calling on Muhammad, while Roland laughed.

Later Roland was killed at the battle of Roncesvalles, the subject of *The Song of Roland*. The defeat was the result of Ganelon's betrayal of Charlemagne's forces. On his return Ganelon was convicted of treason and sentenced to be drawn and quartered.

Another legend, which sometimes appears in European art, relates to St. Giles. Charlemagne had an unconfessed sin (perhaps an incestuous relationship with his sister). One day Giles was celebrating mass in the emperor's presence when an angel appeared above the altar bearing a scroll on which the sin of the emperor was written. Charlemagne then confessed his sin and was given absolution by the saint.

When Charlemagne is portrayed as a devotional figure in Christian art, he often stands next to Constantine the Great. He generally wears armor and a cloak lined with ermine. He also wears the Iron Crown of Lombardy and holds an orb and scepter, a book, or a model of a cathedral, signifying Aix-la-Chapelle, where his relics lie. His cult as a saint was advanced by Frederick Barbarossa and the antipope Paschal III in 1166. Though he was not officially canonized as a saint, he was given the title "Blessed" by Pope Benedict XIV. His feast day is 28 January. In 1475 his feast was made obligatory in France, but today it is observed only in Aix-la-Chapelle and two Swiss abbeys.

See also: ASTOLPHO; BARBAROSSA; FIERAMBRAS; GANELON; GILES, ST.; IRON CROWN OF LOMBARDY; JAMES THE GREATER, ST.; OGIER THE DANE; OLIVER; PALADINS, THE TWELVE; RINALDO; ROLAND

**Charm**   0783
An incantation that is used to work some kind of magic. Today the term is also applied to an object that brings good luck or averts bad luck, or even a motion, such as touching or knocking on wood to bring good luck. Sometimes mere avoidance is considered a charm, such as not using the number 13, or two people not going around a post on opposite sides. Charms are used to propitiate beneficent powers or placate evil ones. Many charms, however, still exist in verbal and even rhymed forms, such as "Rain, rain, go away, come again another day," "Step on a crack, break your mother's back," and "Find a penny, pick it up." Evidence of such charms reaches into antiquity, when charms were used to ward off bees, heal a broken bone, and control enemies captured in battle. Two such charms from the beginning of the ninth century in Germany are the Merseburg Charms.

Mark Twain uses an entire series of charms in his *The Adventures of Tom Sawyer*, where Tom and his friend Huck Finn debate which charm best removes warts. They decide you have to go to the woods where there's a rotten stump with "spunk water" in it, just about midnight, back up to the stump, jam your hand in, and say:

Barley-corn, Barley-corn, injun-meal shorts,
Spunk-water, spunk-water, swaller these warts.

Then you walk away 11 steps with your eyes shut, turn around three times, and walk home without saying anything. The importance of the verbal as well as the active is emphasized in Twain's charms.

See also: MERSEBURG CHARMS

**Charon** (fierce brightness)   0784
In Greek mythology, ferryman of the Styx who carried the dead to the underworld. The dead were buried with a coin in the mouth.

See also: STYX

**Charter Oak**   0785
In American history and folklore, a large tree once standing near Hartford, Connecticut. Supposedly, the oak was the place where the colonial charter of 1687 was hidden when it was demanded by the royal governor Sir Edmund Andros. King James II had appointed Andros governor over all New England, with the intent of declaring all the previous royal charters void. When Andros demanded the Connecticut charter at a Colonial Assembly meeting where it was displayed, its members held him off for a long debate. It continued into the night, and candles had to be lit. Then suddenly all of the candles went out; when they were relit, the charter had disappeared. According to legend, it was hidden in the oak by Captain Joseph Wadsworth. The tree lived until 1856, when it was destroyed by a storm.

**Chasca**   0786
In Inca mythology, the planet Venus, known as the "youth with the long and curling locks." Chasca was worshiped as a page of the sun (Inti), whom he attended in his rising and setting. He was sometimes mistakenly thought to be a goddess.

See also: INTI

**Chaucer, Geoffrey**   0787
1344?–1400. English poet whose work *Canterbury Tales* is one of the best records of stories and storytelling from the

English Middle Ages. The work was begun in 1387 but had not been completed at his death. The tale of a group of pilgrims on their way to the tomb of St. Thomas à Becket in Canterbury provides the frame for their stories. The pilgrims borrow from Boccaccio and Dante, but they also relate several popular English tales of the period. Chaucer himself, in the person of a pilgrim, alludes to the Arthurian tales. Some of the narrators speak in their regional dialects. The collection by Chaucer is thus a sample of popular narratives during his time and a study in when and how stories came to be told.

See also: ARTHUR; FRAME TALE; THOMAS À BECKET, ST.

0788

**Chay**   In the mythology of the Cakchiquel Maya, obsidian stone from which they made their cutting tools and ornaments; worshiped as a god. *The Annals of the Cakchiquels*, written at the end of the 16th century, tells how the Indians "gave homage to the Obsidian Stone" and how it spoke to them, telling them where to settle for a happy and good life.

0789

**Chelm Goat, The**   Jewish folktale about how the disciples of the rabbi of Chelm were tricked by an innkeeper.

Once the rabbi of Chelm became ill. He was told that only goat's milk could cure him, so his disciples went to another town to buy a nanny goat. On their way home they stopped at an inn. The innkeeper switched his billy goat for the nanny goat while the men drank. When they arrived home and tried to milk the goat they discovered it was a billy goat. They returned to the trader, thinking he had tricked them, and again they stopped at the inn for a drink. The innkeeper again switched the goats, so they arrived at the trader with the nanny goat and complained that it was a billy goat. The trader demonstrated that the goat was indeed a nanny capable of giving milk. The rabbi of Chelm asked the disciples

to get a certificate from Rabbi Shmul in the trader's town, warranting that they were sold a nanny goat. They obtained the document and returned to Chelm, but the goats were once again switched at the inn, and they arrived with the billy goat. They now believed they had been bewitched. The rabbi of Chelm replied, "Rabbi Shmul is a wise and upright man. He never writes anything that is not true. If he tells us that the goat is a nanny, you can believe that it is not a billy. Now you will ask: how is it that the goat he says is a nanny turns out to be a billy goat? A good question. The answer is simple. The goat he saw was a nanny, but we have such bad luck in Chelm that by the time the goat reached our town it was turned into a billy goat."

This folktale was used by Sholom Aleichem in his Yiddish short story "The Enchanted Tailor," included in his book *The Old Country* (1946).

0790

**Chemosh**   In Near Eastern mythology (Moabite), a god of Moab; enemy of Yahweh, the Hebrew god, in the Old Testament. Nothing specific is known about the cult of Chemosh, though King Solomon, beguiled by his foreign wives, built "an high place for Chemosh, the abomination of Moab, in the hill that is before Jerusalem" (2 Kings 11:7). This shrine to the god was destroyed by the religious reforms of King Josiah (2 Kings 23:13). In Milton's *Paradise Lost* (book 1), Chemos is a fallen angel listed in a catalog of demons enumerated by the poet. Milton's line "Next Chemos, th' obscene dread of Moab's sons," indicates that Milton believed that human sacrifices of young men were made to Chemos. St. Jerome, commenting on some biblical verses that mention Chemosh, equated the name with Baal-peor, another Moabite god, whom the Israelites adopted in their worship of foreign gods and goddesses.

See also: BAAL; JEROME, ST.; SOLOMON; YAHWEH

**Cheng San-kung**   In Chinese legend, a deified mortal honored as patron god of fishermen. Cheng San-kung, Hou Erh-kung, and Keng Ch'i-kung all fished together, as sworn brothers. One day they saw a yellow rock protruding out of the water. A spirit told them it was made of gold. They rowed to the rock and tried to pick it up, but it was too heavy to move. Then they prayed to Buddha, promising to build a temple in exchange for the golden rock. Their prayers were answered: the rock became light, and they took it home. In return, they built a temple to Buddha.

See also: BUDDHA, THE

**Ch'en Nan**   In Chinese legend, a sage who had the power to cause rain; he lived 1,350 years, mostly on dogs' flesh. Once, passing through a village, he found people praying for rain. Detecting a dragon (maker of rain) hidden in the mud, he forced the animal to come out, which made it rain. Ch'en Nan is often portrayed in Chinese and Japanese art evoking a dragon from a gourd or bowl or sailing on a large hat, which he used once to cross a river when there was no one to ferry him. In Japanese legend, Ch'en Nan is called Chinnan.

**Chenuke**   In the mythology of the Ona Indians of Tierra del Fuego, the personification of evil. The hero hunter Kwanyip fought and defeated him.

**Che Puteh Jambai**   In Malayan legend, a poor man who was told in a dream to murder his wife if he wished to get rich.

Che Puteh Jambai and his wife were so poor they could not afford clothes for both of them. When one left the house, the other stayed at home naked. In a dream Che Puteh was told to kill his wife and he would then be rich, so the man told his wife to prepare for death. She, being a faithful wife according to Oriental beliefs, just asked permission to go down to the river to wash herself with some lime juice. At the river she divided the limes with her knife, cutting herself in the process, and blood dripped onto the rocks and into the river. As each drop was carried away by the current, a large jar immediately rose to the surface and floated upstream. When each jar reached her, Che Puteh's wife tapped it with her knife and pulled it in to the edge of the rocks. When she found the jars full of gold, the ever-faithful wife went in search of her husband. He kept the gold and decided it was best to keep his wife as well.

They lived happily together for many years, and a beautiful daughter was born to them. All the rajahs and chiefs wanted her for a wife. The couple, however, hid all of their gold and disappeared. They have not been seen since, nor has their treasure ever been found.

**Cheron, St.** (dear one?)   Third century. In Christian legend, bishop of Chartres, France. On his way to visit his teacher, St. Denis, Cheron was attacked by robbers who struck off his head. Taking his head into his hand, he continued his journey from Chartres to Paris. One of the windows in the cathedral of Chartres portrays the legend of the saint.

See also: DENIS, ST.

**Cherruve**   In the folklore of the Araucanian Indians of Chile, the spirits of shooting stars.

**Cherry**   A fruit tree; in world mythology and folklore, often a symbol of female sexuality. In the Finnish epic poem *The Kalevala* (rune 50), the Maiden of the Air, Marjatta, swallows a cherry and becomes pregnant. In China the cherry is identified with female beauty and female power. In Japanese folklore, the cherry symbolizes prosperity and riches. In an American folksong the cherry appears in the following verse:

I gave my love a cherry without a stone;
I gave my love a chicken without a bone;
I gave my love a ring without an end;
I gave my love a baby with no crying.

This riddle song concludes with these answers:

A cherry, when it's blooming, it has no stone;
A chicken, when it's pipping, it has no bone;
A ring, when it's rolling, it has no end;
A baby, when it's sleeping, has no crying.

In English folklore, dreaming of a cherry tree means ill fortune is on the way. In Germany it was considered inadvisable to eat cherries with princes because the ruler might use the pits to gouge out one's eyes; no reason can be traced for this outrage. The "magic cherry" ( D981.4) is a common motif in folk literature.

See also: *KALEVALA, THE;* MOTIF

0798

**Cherubim** (intercessor)    In Jewish, Christian, and Islamic mythology, an order of beings or angels derived from griffinlike monsters in Near Eastern mythology. In western European art they are usually portrayed as chubby-faced babes with small wings.

In the Old Testament cherubim are spirits in the service of Yahweh (a Hebrew cult name of God). They are not, strictly speaking, angels, since they do not deliver any messages from Yahweh. In Genesis (3:24), for example, they stand guard over the way to the Tree of Life, guard the Ark of the Covenant (Exod. 25:18–20), and serve as the mount of Yahweh (2 Sam. 22:11).

In medieval Jewish folklore cherubim were thought of as beautiful men. Christianity in the Baroque age reduced them to chubby-faced chil-

dren, who often appear in paintings such as those by Rubens. The singular of cherubim is cherub.

See also: ANGEL; ARK OF THE COVENANT; GRIFFIN; SERAPHIM; YAHWEH

0799

**Chia-Lan**    In Chinese Buddhism, generic name for tutelary gods who protect monasteries.

0800

**Chibcachum** (Chicchechum)    In the mythology of the Chibcha Indians of Colombia, patron god of laborers and merchants. Once Chibcachum became angry with the people and sent a flood over the land. They called on Bochica, chief of the gods, to save them. He appeared as a rainbow near the town of Soacha. As the sun, he dried the waters, then with his staff he opened a deep chasm in the rocks so that the flood waters could recede. From this the great waterfall Tequendama was formed. Chibcachum went underground, and from that time he has supported the earth. Earthquakes occur when Chibcachum shifts his burden from one shoulder to another.

See also: BOCHICA

0801

**Chiconquiahuitl** (seven rain)    In Aztec ritual, a god who was impersonated by a slave during the feast of the god Xolotl Huetzi, the lord of the evening star. The slave who represented Chiconquiahuitl and slaves who represented other gods, such as Yacatecutli (he who goes first), Cauhtlaxayanh (eagle face), Coatlinahual (weresnake), and the goddess Chachalmecacihuatl (lady of the Chachalmec people), were "honored as if they had been the gods themselves," according to Fray Diego Durán in his *Book of the Gods and Rites* (c. 1576), describing Aztec ritual. On the feast day the impersonators were "cast alive into the fire" and pulled out "half-roasted." Their chests were then opened.

See also: YACATECUTLI; XOLOTL HUETZI

**Ch'ih Ching-tzu** (son of red essence, red spirit) 0802
In Chinese mythology, the spirit of fire, who made himself clothes from red leaves. He is one of the Wu Lao, the five spirits of natural forces.

See also: WU LAO

**Chih Nu** In Chinese mythology, the goddess 0803
of weavers.

**Ch'i Ku-tzu** In Chinese mythology, seven 0804
deified young women, invoked in times of drought, flood, and other natural disasters.

**Chimaera** (she-goat) In Greek mythology, a 0805
fantastic fire-breathing creature with the head of a lion, the body of a goat, and the tail of a serpent or dragon; offspring of Typhon and Echidna. Homer's *Iliad* (book 6), Vergil's *Aeneid* (book 6), the visit to the underworld, and Ovid's *Metamorphoses* (book 9.647) describe the beast. Spenser's *Faerie Queene* (6.1.8) makes the Chimaera and Cerebus the parents of the Blatant Beast, the evil monster of the poem. Milton's *Paradise Lost* (book 2.624–8) places Chimaeras in hell. In Greek mythology the hero Bellerophon destroyed the Chimaera by mounting his winged horse, Pegasus, and shooting the monster with his arrows. There is a famous fifth-century B.C.E. Etruscan bronze Chimaera which is now housed in Florence.

See also: *AENEID, THE;* BELLEROPHON; ECHIDNA; *ILIAD, THE;* OVID; PEGASUS; TYPHON

**Chiminigagua** (Chimizigagua) In the myth- 0806
ology of the Chibcha Indians of Colombia, a creator god. Chiminigagua held light inside his being. When it burst forth, creation began. He first made gigantic black birds that covered the mountain, bringing light. Chiminigagua's cult

was unimportant among the Chibcha because they considered the sun (Zuhe) and the moon (Chia) more beautiful and therefore more deserving of honor and worship.

See also: BACHUÉ; NEMTEREQUETEBA

**Chin** In the mythology of the Muysca Indians 0807
of Bogotá, Colombia, moon goddess representing the power of female destructiveness. In one myth she was credited with flooding the earth when she was displeased. In order to pacify her, men would dress up in women's clothes and perform women's duties in the hope that the goddess would not punish them for being men.

**Ching Tu** (the pure land) In Chinese Bud- 0808
dhism, the dwelling place of those liberated who have prayed to A-mi-t'o Fo, the Buddha of Infinite Light. Sometimes it is called Hsi fang chi-lo-shih-chieh (the paradise in the west).

See also: BUDDHA, THE

**Ch'in-kuang wang** In Chinese mythology, 0809
ruler of the first hell of Ti Yü, the underworld.

See also: TI YÜ

**Chinvat** (Chinvad, Kinvad) In Persian myth- 0810
ology, a bridge over which all souls of the dead must pass on their way to heaven or hell. According to one Zoroastrian text, Chinvat "is like a beam of many sides, of whose edges there are some which are broad, and there are some which are thin and sharp; its broad sides are so large that its width is twenty-seven reeds, and its sharp sides are so contracted that in thinness it is like the edge of a razor." Both the good and the wicked come to the bridge, but it "becomes a narrow bridge for the wicked, even unto a resemblance to the edge of a razor. . . . He who is of the wicked, as he places a footstep on the bridge . . .

falls from the middle of the bridge, and rolls over head-foremost" to hell. The good, however, pass over the bridge easily.

See also: ZARATHUSTRA

0811

**Chipiripa**    In the mythology of the Indians living in the Isthmus of Panama, a rain god.

0812

**Chiu-t'ien Lei Kung**    In Chinese mythology, a thunder god, invoked against disasters.

0813

**Chonchon**    In the folklore of the Araucanian Indians of Chile, a vampire with a human head and huge ears. It uses its large ears for wings to fly about seeking its prey.

0814

**Christina the Astonishing, St.** (I anoint, the anointed)    1150–1224. In Christian legend, patron saint of psychotherapists. Feast, 24 July.

Born at Brusthem in the diocese of Liège, Christina at 15 was left an orphan with her two elder sisters. At the age of 22 she had a seizure and was pronounced dead. Her coffin was carried to the church and a requiem mass was begun. Suddenly, after the *Agnus Dei*, Christina sat up in her coffin and soared to the beams of the ceiling "like a bird," according to one account, and perched there. The congregation, except for her elder sister, who stayed for the end of the mass, fled from the church. The priest then called Christina to come down from the beams. She cried out that she was up in the beams because she could not stand the smell of sinful human flesh. She then said she had died, gone down to hell, visited Purgatory, and had a trip to heaven. God had offered her the choice of staying in heaven or returning to earth to help the poor souls in Purgatory by her prayers. Christina decided to come back to life and help the dead. She said that by the time the *Agnus Dei*

had been said the third time, her soul had been restored to her body.

After Christina came back to life, her day-to-day activities became abnormal. She would flee to remote places, climb trees, towers, and rocks, and crawl into ovens to escape the smell of human flesh. She would handle fire, rush into a river in the depth of winter, or jump into a mill-race and be carried away unharmed under the wheel. She liked to pray by balancing herself on the top of a hurdle or curled up on the ground looking like a ball.

Though the medieval mind was understanding of many oddities, her actions made some accuse her of being possessed by devils. Attempts were made to confine her, but she always broke loose. One time a man attacked her, broke her leg, and tied her up. A doctor came to mend the leg but chained her to a pillar for safety. No sooner had he left than Christina escaped. Another time a priest refused to give her Holy Communion, and she jumped into the Meuse river and swam away. She kept herself alive by begging. She dressed in rags, frightening the populace. However, when she sat in water blessed for baptism, "her way of living was more conformed to that of men, she was quieter, and better able to bear the smell of human beings," writes her Dominican biographer, Thoma de Cantimpré, who had known her personally. Christina's last years were spent in the convent of St. Catherine at Saint-Trond, where many nobles came to her for advice.

0815

**Christmas** (Christ's Mass)    Feast of the Nativity of Jesus, celebrated on 25 December. The date of Christmas was chosen in 440 to coincide with the winter solstice and a pagan festival in honor of the sun god. The actual birth date of Jesus is not known, and the early Church paid little attention to the matter. St. Leo, however, writing in the fifth century, describes the importance of Christmas: "When adoring the Birth of Our Savior, we are celebrating our own true origin. For indeed this generation of Christ in time is the source of the Christian People, and the birth of the Head is, too, that of his Mystical Body."

Numerous legends arose during the Middle Ages regarding the Christmas season. At 12 midnight, the time of Jesus' birth (the Gospels do not mention this, but tradition assigned the time), all of the animals in the stables, such as cattle, and deer in the field kneel down to honor Christ. Bees were believed to awake from sleep and hum a song in praise of the Child, but the song could be heard only by those chosen by Jesus. The birds were believed to sing all night at Christmas. In addition to kneeling in adoration of the Christ Child, the animals were gifted with speech on the sacred eve. One French medieval play portrays the belief. The animals, it seems, preferred to speak in Latin.

CROW: *Christus natus est* (Christ is born)
OX: *Ubi?* (Where?)
LAMB: *Bethlehem*
ASS: *Eamus* (Let us go).

Central Europeans believed, and some still do, that the animals also discuss the virtues and faults of various people since they hear all conversations during the year.

People of medieval times believed in a host of devils, ghosts, witches, and assorted malignant spirits, and it was believed that their power was suspended during the Christmas season. Since the Christ Child was present, no harm could be worked by the demons of darkness. Shakespeare in *Hamlet* (act 1, sc.1, lines 158–164) alludes to this belief:

Some say that ever 'gainst that season comes
Wherein our savior's birth is celebrated,
The bird of dawning singeth all night long:
And then, they say, no spirit dare stir abroad!
The nights are wholesome; then no planets
    strike,

No fairy tales, no witch has power to charm,
So hallow'd and so gracious is the time.

If you were lucky enough to die at midnight on Christmas, you could enter heaven at once. Children born on Christmas were blessed with the power of seeing spirits and even controlling them, according to some medieval accounts. But in some other accounts a child born on Christmas was cursed because it was born at the same time as Jesus.

One legend that constantly reappeared in different guises during the Middle Ages relates to the Christmas Angel. Every year the Virgin Mary selected a number of angels and sent them out from heaven into different parts of the world. Each angel awakened a little child from its first sleep and carried it to heaven to sing a carol to the Christ Child. When the children returned to earth, not everyone would believe their story, but those blessed by God would know that the children had been specially chosen.

The first hymns in honor of Christmas were written in the fifth century, soon after the Christmas Feast was established in the medieval church. The birthplace of the Christmas carol was Italy. In the 13th century St. Francis of Assisi wrote a hymn in Latin, "Psalmus in Nativitate." Franciscans then composed hymns in Italian, among them, one that opens:

In Bethlehem is born the Holy Child,
On hay and straw in the winter wild
O, my heart is full of mirth
At Jesus' birth

From Italy the carol spread to other European countries, such as France, Spain, Germany, and England. The earliest English carol was written at the beginning of the 15th century.

One of the most important folk customs of Christmas is that of the crèche, which portrays the Christ Child, the Virgin Mary, St. Joseph, and the Wise Men, or Magi. Legend also credits it to St. Francis of Assisi. His biographer,

Thomas of Celano, writes of how the custom came about:

It should be recorded and held in reverent memory what Blessed Francis did near the town of Greccio, on the Feast Day of the Nativity of Our Lord Jesus Christ, three years before his glorious death. In that town lived a certain man by the name of John (Messer Giovanni Velitta) who stood in high esteem, and whose life was even better than his reputation. Blessed Francis loved him with a special affection because, being very noble and much honored, he despised the nobility of the flesh and strove after the nobility of the soul.

Blessed Francis often saw this man. He now called him about two weeks before Christmas and said to him: "If you desire that we should celebrate this year's Christmas together at Greccio, go quickly and prepare what I tell you; for I want to enact the memory of the Infant who was born at Bethlehem, and how He was deprived of all the comforts babies enjoy; how He was bedded in the manger on hay, between an ass and an ox. For once I want to see all this with my own eyes." When the good and faithful man had heard this, he departed quickly and prepared in the above mentioned place everything that the Saint had told him.

The joyful day approached. The brethren (Franciscans) were called from many communities. The men and women of the neighborhood, as best they could, prepared candles and torches to brighten the night. Finally the Saint of God arrived, found everything prepared, saw it and rejoiced. The crib was made ready, hay was brought, the ox and ass were led to the spot. . . . Greccio became a new Bethlehem. The crowds drew near and rejoiced in the novelty of the celebration.

Also associated with Christmas was the Yule log, believed to be derived from pagan Northern ritual. The log was burned in an open hearth during the Christmas season. Its unburned parts were put away until the following year, when they were used to light the new Yule log. Closely connected with the Yule log is the Christmas tree. It is believed to be in part derived from the pagan Yule log and the paradise tree, which appeared in medieval miracle plays about Adam and Eve. The tradition may be related to the Roman feast of Saturn, held in December, during which the temples were decorated with green branches. The paradise tree had apples and wafers—later candy—hung from it, and it signified both the Tree of Sin and Death and the Tree of Life, the wafers representing the Holy Eucharist. The modern Christmas tree is, however, credited to Martin Luther, the Protestant reformer, who saw a fir tree in the forest lit by stars and was inspired to bring it home and decorate it as a reminder of the coming spring. The custom of Christmas trees decorated with candles and hung with presents came to England following the marriage of Queen Victoria to Prince Albert of Saxe-Coburg in 1840, when there was a craze for things German.

The custom of giving gifts during the Christmas season derives from an old pagan Roman custom called *strenae* when the people gave gifts of pastry, lamps, precious stones, and coins as tokens of good wishes for the new year. The giver of the gifts for Christmas varies from one Christian country to another. In Italy it is Lady Befana, a fairy queen or witch, who gives the gifts on Epiphany (6 January), when the Magi were believed to have given their gifts to the Christ Child. Her name, Befana, is actually a corruption of the word Epiphany. In Russia Babushka (grandmother) gives the gifts. The most famous gift giver in European folklore, however, is Santa Claus, who is derived in part from St. Nicholas and the pagan god Thor. When the Protestants abolished the feast of St. Nicholas (5 December), who was the patron saint of children, a composite figure, made up of the bishop saint and the pagan god, emerged and was responsible for giving gifts.

Christmas was not just one day during the Middle Ages but a season that consisted of 12 days, from Christmas to Twelfth Night, or Epiphany. It was a time of rest for domestic animals, horses, and most servants, who often celebrated various feasts such as one dedicated to fools that had a Bishop of Fools and a Pope of Fools. All of this was abolished by the Reformation, since few of the reformers had any sense of humor or fun. In the United States Christmas was outlawed in Boston during a large part of the 19th century. Schools and businesses were open, and people were fired if they refused to work.

See also: ADVENT; BEFANA; FRANCIS OF ASSISI, ST.; JESUS CHRIST; JOSEPH, ST.; MAGI; NICHOLAS, ST.; THOR; YULE

*St. Christopher*

0816
**Christopher, St.** (Christ bearer)    Third century? In Christian legend, patron saint of travelers. Feast, 25 July.

Although officially removed in the 1960s from the Roman Catholic calendar of saints, St. Christopher still maintains his popularity with the faithful. His legend, based on Eastern sources, came to Western Europe about the ninth century. One tradition says that before his conversion to Christianity he had the head of a dog (he is sometimes portrayed with one in Eastern art); others say he was a prince who, through the intercession of the Virgin Mary, was born to a heathen king. Some sources say he was born in Syria; others, Canaan; and still others, Arabia. His name before his conversion is given as Offerus, Offro, Adokimus, Reprobus, or Reprebus.

According to *The Golden Legend*, a series of saints' lives written in the 13th century, St. Christopher was called Reprobus and was a Canaanite. He was of "prodigious size, being twelve cubits in height, and fearful of aspect." He was so proud of his size and strength that he swore he would enter the service of the most powerful monarch in the world. So he went searching and came to the court of a great king. He served that monarch until he noticed that the king made the sign of the cross at the mention of the devil. He therefore went in search of Satan, assuming that he must be more powerful than the king. He found Satan and his host of followers, but in their travels he noticed that Satan trembled when they came upon a wayside cross. Christopher asked the devil why he was afraid. He was told that the cross symbolizes Christ. Christopher then went in search of Christ, who was an even greater king than the devil.

Christopher found a hermit who instructed him in the Christian faith, but the saint refused to be bound by prayers and fastings. So the hermit told him that if he could not worship in the acceptable manner he could serve Christ another way. He sent him to a certain river where there was a ford and told him to carry over on his shoulders all who wished to cross. Christopher uprooted a palm tree for a staff. Day and night he carried across all who came to the river.

After many days, as he slept in his hut, he heard a child's voice calling him and saying, "Christopher, come out and carry me across the river."

He ran out of his hut and found no one, so he returned. But again he heard the child's voice, and again no one was outside. At the third call he went out and found a child who asked to be ferried across the water. Christopher took the child on his shoulders and, taking his staff, set out. Little by little, the child grew heavier, until Christopher thought he would fall into the stream.

"Child, why have you put me in dire peril? You weigh so heavily on me that if I had borne the whole world on my shoulders, it could not have burdened me more heavily."

"Wonder not," said the child, "for you have not only borne the world on your shoulders but him who created the world. For I am Christ the King."

The Christ Child then told Christopher to plant his staff, and the next morning it was filled with flowers and fruits. After many adventures Christopher was finally beheaded as a martyr.

In Christian art St. Christopher is portrayed as a very tall and strong man fording a river with his huge staff in his hand carrying the Christ Child on his shoulders. Sometimes the hermit's hut is seen in the distance. Often found near his image is the inscription: "Whoever shall behold the image of St. Christopher shall not faint nor fail on that day." Liszt composed *Sankt Christoph*, a legend for baritone, female chorus, piano, harmonica, and harp, but the work remains unpublished.

See also: *GOLDEN LEGEND, THE*; VIRGIN MARY

0817

**Chthonian Gods** (earth gods)  In Greek mythology, deities who ruled under the earth or were connected with Hades, the underworld, such as Hades, Pluto, Persephone, Demeter, Dionysus, Hecate, and Hermes.

See also: DEMETER; DIONYSUS; HADES; HECATES; HERMES; PERSEPHONE; PLUTO

0818

**Chuang Tzu** (Kwuangze) (Master Chuang) c.399–295 B.C.E. Title given Chuang Chou, Chinese Taoist philosopher, whose work contains fables, parables, and anecdotes.

Chuang Tzu's basic premise in his work is that the Tao is the universal way of everything, pervading the entire universe. One becomes free only when one identifies with the Tao. There is no right or wrong because such concepts always stem from a point of view. For example, life is good and desirable and death is evil only from the point of view of the living. How does one know that the reverse is not true?

One of the most famous episodes in his work is the account of his mourning for his wife. When Chuang Tzu's wife died, Hui Tzu went to console him. He found the widower sitting on the ground with his legs spread out at a right angle, singing and beating time on a bowl.

"To live with your wife," said Hui Tzu, "and see your eldest son grow up to be a man, and then not to shed a tear over her corpse—this would be bad enough. But to drum on a bowl and sing; surely this is going too far."

"Not at all," replied Chuang Tzu. "When she died, I could not help being affected by her death. Soon, however, I remembered that she had already existed in a previous state before birth, without form, or even substance; that while in that unconditioned condition, substance was added to spirit; that this substance then assumed form; and that the next stage was birth. And now, by virtue of further change, she is dead, passing from one phase to another like the sequence of spring, summer, autumn, and winter. And while she is thus lying asleep in eternity, for me to go about weeping and wailing would be to proclaim myself ignorant of these natural laws. Therefore I refrain."

0819

**Chu Jung**  In Chinese legend, a deified mortal, nicknamed Ch'ih Ti (the red emperor), honored as the god of fire, which he taught men how to use. He is also regarded as the spirit of the Southern Sea. He helped break the link between heaven and earth and was appointed to keep men in their right positions in the established order. He is sometimes portrayed seated on or riding a tiger, or as an animal with a three-eyed human face, the extra eye in the center of his forehead. He is surrounded by his servants and fire symbols, a fiery serpent and a fire wheel—plus a pen and pad to list the places he intends to burn. He is invoked both to prevent and to cause fire.

0820

**Chu-ko Liang**   Third century C.E. In Chinese legend, a deified mortal, who in life was noted for his wisdom. Chu-ko Liang, who was eight feet tall, was called by the emperor to be his general. At the time human sacrifices were made to the gods, but Chu-ko Liang put an end to the practice by substituting clay figures. When he saw his death approaching, he lit 49 candles, which burned for seven days on a heap of rice. When he was informed of the defeat of an enemy, he accidentally kicked over the candles and fell dead. Before dying, however, he ordered that seven grains of rice should be put in his mouth so that his body might be kept unchanged forever. He also asked that his body be placed on the battlefield with two pigeons sewed into his sleeves. When the enemy saw the sleeves of Chu-ko Liang's garment moving, they assumed he had come back to life and fled in terror. In Japanese legend, Chu-ko Liang is called Komei.

0821

**Chu-lin Chi'i-Hsien** (seven immortals of bamboo grove)   In Chinese legend, seven men who drank and conversed together in a bamboo grove, or in a place called Bamboo Grove, about 275 B.C.E. They are called the Seven Immortals and were known for getting drunk and challenging Confucian beliefs. They are Juan Chi and his nephew, Juan Hsien; Liu Ling; Hsiang Hsiu; Wang Jung; Shan T'ao; and Hai K'ang.

See also: JUAN CHI; HAI K'ANG; LIU LING; SHAN T'AO; WANG JUNG

0822

**Chunda**   In Buddhist legend, a smith who invited the Buddha to his house and offered him a meal. It was the last meal eaten by the Buddha.

0823

**Chung-li Ch'üan** (Chang Liang)   Second century B.C.E. In Chinese Taoist mythology, one of the Pa-Hsien, the Eight Immortals. In one legend he was forced by an old man to pick up a shoe that had fallen, and in another he is said to have done it of his own free will. In art he is often portrayed as an extremely fat person, with a bare stomach, carrying a peach, symbol of immortality, and a fan, by which he revives the dead. He is believed to have found the elixir of life. In Japanese legend he is called Chorio.

0824

**Chun T'i**   In Chinese mythology, goddess of dawn and light, protector against war; she is portrayed with eight arms, two of which hold the sun and moon.

0825

**Churinga** (Tjuringa)   In Australian mythology, sacred objects of stone or wood in which the spirits of ancestors come to dwell; also, a mnemonic device for storytelling. These churingas are ritually decorated, they have high totemic significance, and they are guarded with great secrecy. They are also a symbol of the individual possessor's eternal identity.

0826

**Churning of the Ocean**   In Hindu mythology, term used for the cosmic struggle between the demons and gods over the Amrita, the water of life, often identified with Soma juice.

Durvasas (ill-clothed), a Hindu sage and an incarnation of the god Shiva, offered Indra a garland as a gift, which Indra ignored. Because of this affront, Durvasas cursed Indra, saying that "his sovereignty over the three worlds should be subverted." Under the curse Indra and the gods grew weak and were on their way to destruction. The Asuras, or demons, seeing an opportunity, used all of their powers to finish off the gods and gain control of the three worlds.

In desperation some of the gods fled to Brahma, asking him for protection. He advised them to seek the aid of Vishnu.

"I will restore your strength," Vishnu replied, "but you must do as I command you. Cast into the Milky Sea some magic herbs, then take Mount Mandara for a churning stick, the serpent Shesha for a rope, and churn the ocean to obtain the Amrita, the water of life. To do this you will need the help of the Asuras. Promise them some of the Amrita, but I will make sure they have no share of it. "

The gods listened to Vishnu and entered into an alliance with the Asuras, the demons, to set about the task of obtaining the Amrita. They cast the magic herbs and took Mount Mandara for a churning stick and Shesha the serpent for a rope. (In India a churning stick is a stick with a long rope twisted around it. The rope, held at both ends, keeps the stick in a vertical position, while the turning caused by pulling the rope accomplishes the churning.) The gods grabbed the serpent's tail while the Asuras pulled its head. Vishnu took the form of Kurma, a tortoise, his second avatar or incarnation, and became a pivot as the mountain twirled around.

Vishnu was also present but unseen among the gods and demons pulling the serpent back and forth, as well as present on top of the mountain. Vishnu thus sustained the gods with his powerful energy. When the venom from the serpent Shesha burned the faces of the Asuras, Vishnu protected the gods from the same fate by sending up clouds with rain that drifted toward the serpent.

First, the wish-bestowing cow, Surabhi, arose from the sea. Next came the goddess of wine, Varuni, with rolling eyes. Suddenly the magic tree Parijata appeared. It was "the delight of the nymphs of heaven, perfuming the world with its blossoms." (Later the tree was kept in Indra's heaven and was the pride of one of his wives, Sachi. When Krishna visited Indra he carried away the tree, causing a war between the two, which Indra lost. After Krishna's death, however, the tree was returned to Indra.) After the appearance of the Parijata there came the Apsaras, water nymphs, then the moon, which Shiva took and placed on his brow. Next came a draft of deadly poison, which Shiva drank lest it should destroy the world. The bitter poison turned the god's throat blue, earning for him the epithet Nilakantha (blue throat). Next came Dhanvantari, physician of the gods, holding in his hands a cup of the Amrita. Then the goddess Sri appeared seated on an open lotus. She came to the god Vishnu's breast to rest. A fabulous jewel, Kaustubha, also appeared, which Vishnu placed on his breast.

The demons now took the opportunity to steal the cup from Dhanvantari and were ready to drink the water of life. Vishnu then appeared as a ravishing woman, Mohini (the enchantress), which made the demons so lustful that they forgot to protect the cup of Amrita. While they disagreed among themselves, Vishnu took the cup and gave it to the gods.

The Amrita, or Soma, as it is identified in some tellings of the myth, has been interpreted as the life-giving genital semen produced by the rubbing of the snake (phallus) at the base of the mountain.

See also: AMRITA; ASURAS; AVATAR; BRAHMA; DHANVANTARI; INDRA; SHESHA; SHIVA; SOMA

0827

**Chyavana**   In Hindu legend, a sage, opponent of Indra, restored to youth by the twin gods, the Aswins.

The Rig-Veda, the ancient collection of hymns to the gods, tells how Chyavana was restored to his youth, "making him acceptable to his wife, and the husband of maidens," by the twin gods, the Aswins. This miracle made Chyavana devoted to the Aswins and, according to the Hindu epic poem *The Mahabharata*, he asked Indra to allow them to drink the magic Soma juice.

Indra objected, however, and Chyavana began a sacrifice that found acceptance before the gods. In a rage Indra rushed at Chyavana with a mountain in one hand and a thunderbolt in the other, but Chyavana stopped the god by sprinkling him with water. He then "created a fearful open-mouthed monster called Mada, having teeth and grinders of portentous length, and jaws one of which enclosed the earth, the other the sky; and the gods, including Indra, are said to have been at the root of his tongue like fishes in the mouth of a sea monster."

In this predicament "Indra granted the demand of Chyavana, who was thus the cause of the Aswins becoming drinkers of the Soma."

See also: ASWINS; INDRA; *MAHABHARATA, THE*; RIG-VEDA; SOMA

0828
**Cid, El** (lord, master)   In medieval Spanish legend, a hero, Rodrigo Díaz de Bivar (1040–1099), whose victories over the Moors inspired ballads, chronicles, and the national epic poem, *Poema del Cid* (*Cantar de mio Cid*). There are some 200 Spanish ballads that treat El Cid's legend, forming, as it were, an introduction to the epic.

Rodrigo, also called El Campeador (the champion), was a young man when he avenged an insult to his father, Don Diego Laynez, by Don Gómez. The young hero challenged Don Gómez and killed him, cutting off his head and presenting it to his father as proof that the wrong had been avenged. Don Diego then took his son to court, but the young man did not please King Ferdinand, who banished him from his presence. Rodrigo then left with 300 knights, encountered the Moors, who were invading Castile, and defeated them, taking five of their kings prisoner. He released them only after they promised to pay him tribute and refrain from further warfare. They were so grateful for their liberty that they pledged themselves to his will, calling him El Cid. After Rodrigo had delivered the land from the Moors, King Ferdinand restored him to favor at the court.

Shortly after this, Doña Ximena, daughter of Don Gómez, the man El Cid had killed, demanded vengeance for the murder of her father. When her pleas to the king came to no avail, she asked that the king order El Cid to marry her instead. To win Doña Ximena's love El Cid said he would not rest until he had won five battles for her. Before he left he went on a pilgrimage to Santiago de Compostela, the shrine of St. James the Greater, where he had a vision of Lazarus, the leper beggar (Luke 16:19–31) and as a result established a leper house in St. Lazarus's honor.

When King Ferdinand died, his relatives fought over the succession. Finally Don Alfonso came to the throne, but the king hated El Cid. *The Poema del Cid* opens with King Alfonso's banishment of El Cid from court. El Cid was given nine days to leave Castile. He and his men left and were supported by admirers to whom El Cid was a hero. Once again El Cid went into battle against the Moors and again defeated them. The king restored El Cid to favor, but the reconciliation was not to last. There was a misunderstanding between El Cid and the king. El Cid left the court again, and during his absence the Moors took Valencia. Hearing of this, El Cid promptly returned, captured the city, and established his headquarters there. He asked King Alfonso to send his wife and daughters. As master of Valencia, El Cid was enormously rich, and therefore his daughters Doña Elvira and Doña Sol were much sought after as brides. Among the suitors were the counts of Carrion, whose proposals were warmly encouraged by King Alfonso. El Cid, in obedience to the king, had his daughters married to the counts, but the results were not happy.

Once a lion broke loose from El Cid's private menagerie. It entered the hall where he was sleeping while his guests were playing chess. His sons-in-law fled, one falling into an empty vat, the other hiding behind El Cid's couch. Awakened by the noise, El Cid seized his sword, twisted his cloak around his arm, and, grasping the lion by its mane, thrust it back into its cage. He then calmly returned to his palace. The two men, however, were angered by the humiliation of their cowardly behavior and asked to leave with their wives. After traveling some time with their brides and an escort named Felez Muñoz, the counts of Carrion camped near Douro. Early the next day they sent all of their suites ahead, and being left alone with their wives, stripped them of their garments, lashed them with thorns, kicked them with spurs, and finally left them for dead on the bloodstained ground. They then rode on. The brides were rescued by Felez Muñoz and taken home. El Cid demanded vengeance, and the king summoned the counts. A battle was arranged, and the counts of Carrion were defeated and banished. The daughters were then married to counts from Navarre.

The *Poema del Cid* ends here with a statement of El Cid's death. Ballads continue the tale. In one the Moors, under the leadership of Cucar, king of Morocco, returned to besiege Valencia. El Cid was preparing to do battle when he had a vision of St. Peter. The saint predicted his death within 30 days but assured him that, even though he would be dead, he would still triumph over the enemy.

El Cid then prepared to die. He appointed a successor, gave instructions, and directed that his body be embalmed, set on his horse, Babieca, with the sword Tizona in his hand, and sent into battle. When these instructions had all been given, he died at the appointed time. The successor and El Cid's wife, Ximena, carried out his wishes. A sortie was planned against the Moors, and El Cid, fastened onto his warhorse, rode in the van. Such terror was created by his presence that the Moors fled.

King Alfonso ordered El Cid's body placed in the church of San Pedro de Cardena, where it remained for 10 years seated in a chair of state in plain view of all. Such respect was paid the body that no one dared touch it, except one person who, remembering El Cid's proud boast that no man had ever dared lay a hand on his beard, attempted to do so. Before he could touch the beard, however, El Cid's lifeless hand clasped the hilt of Tizona, his sword, and drew it a few inches out of its scabbard. The man fled.

The legend of El Cid inspired the two-part play by Guillén de Castro, *Las Mocedades del Cid* (the youth of the Cid), which in the first part centers around his wedding. The French playwright Corneille used part 1 of the Spanish drama for his play *Le Cid*, which in turn was made into an opera by Jules Massenet. The English poet Leigh Hunt wrote a verse play, *A Father Avenged*, based on El Cid and his father. A movie starring Charlton Heston as El Cid and Sophia Loren as his wife, Doña Ximena, was also based on the legends.

See also: BALLAD; JAMES THE GREATER, ST.; LAZARUS

0829

**Cigouaves**  In Haitian voodoo, a demon who comes at night and castrates men. To avoid this, genital organs of animals are offered to the demon.

0830

**Cihuateteo** (Cihuapipiltin)  In Aztec mythology, the spirits of women who died in childbirth. They would leave their paradise of the West, called Tamoanchan, coming back to bring disease to children. On the days that the Cihuateteo were believed to descend, parents would not allow their children outdoors. To placate the evil spirits, temples were built at crossroads, and offerings of bread, sometimes in the form of butterflies, were made. The Cihuateteo were portrayed with blanched white faces, and their hands, arms, and legs were whitened with powder. To die in childbirth, however, was considered honorable and good by the Aztecs.

0831

**Cincinnatus, Lucius Quinctius**  Named dictator in 458 B.C.E. In Roman history and legend, a hero who left his farm and aided the Roman army, which was besieged in the Apennines by the Aequi. Cincinnatus was elected dictator but resigned his office and returned to his farm after 16 days. Livy's *History of Rome* (book 3) tells the tale as an example of old-fashioned Roman virtue.

See also: LIVY

0832

**Citipati**   In Mahayana Buddhism, two skeletons, one of a man and one of a woman, often portrayed with arms and legs interlaced, dancing on two corpses. According to Buddhist legend, they were two ascetics who were deep in meditation and did not notice that a thief had cut off their heads and thrown them into the dust. Because of this they are the enemies of thieves. Often they carry a scepter topped by a skull.

See also: BUDDHA, THE

*St. Clare*

0833

**Clare, St.** (bright, illustrious)   1194–1253? In Christian legend, founder of the Order of Poor Clares. Feast, 12 August.

Clare, the oldest daughter of a noble family of Assisi, wanted to devote herself to a religious life. Her parents objected, but Clare fled from her father's house to the Chapel of the Porzioncula one Palm Sunday. There she met St. Francis of Assisi and placed herself under his care. In vain her parents tried to win her back. They also lost another daughter, Agnes, to religious life. The order of the Poor Clares was founded in 1212 by St. Francis for Clare. (The order is also called

Clarisses, Minoresses, or Nuns of the Order of St. Francis.)

Legend credits St. Clare with stopping the Moors when they overran Assisi. They approached her convent when the saint was bedridden. She rose up and, taking the pyx (the vessel that contains the consecrated Host from the Mass), placed it on the threshold of the doorway. Upon seeing the pyx, the enemy fled.

Medieval Christian art portrays St. Clare as a nun in a gray habit with a cord holding a cross or a lily. Her distinctive attribute is the pyx. The great Italian artist Giotto portrayed the saint in frescoes in the Santa Croce in Florence and in the Upper Church of St. Francis in Assisi.

See also: AGNES, ST.; FRANCIS OF ASSISI, ST.

0834

**Clement, St.** (merciful)   First century. In Christian legend, third bishop of Rome. Feast, 23 November.

According to legend, St. Clement was a disciple of St. Peter and St. Paul. During the reign of Trajan he was banished, together with other Christians, to an island where there was no water. St. Clement prayed, and a lamb appeared to him on a hill. He dug a hole where the lamb stood, and a stream flowed from it. As a punishment for providing water to the Christians he was thrown into the sea with an anchor around his neck. But the waters drew back for three miles, and the people could then see a ruined temple that the sea had covered. In it was found the body of the saint with the anchor around his neck. For many years at the anniversary of his death the sea retreated for seven days, and pilgrimages were made to his tomb. Once a woman came with her child to pray at the tomb. The baby fell asleep, and the woman became absorbed in prayer. Suddenly the waters arose, and the woman fled, forgetting her child. The next year, when she returned to the tomb when the waters had retreated, she found her child sleeping safely.

The Church of San Clemente in Rome contains his supposed relics as well as scenes illustrating his life.

See also: PAUL, ST.; PETER, ST.

**Clootie** (one division of a cleft hoof)   In Scottish folklore, one of the names of the devil. It was a custom to leave an untilled section of land, or one that could not be tilled, as a gift to Old Cloots or Auld Clootie, representing the devil. In contrast, Erksine Caldwell's Southern Gothic novel *God's Little Acre* tells of a protagonist who dedicates an acre of his farmland to God. Any crop produced on God's Little Acre is to be sold and given to the church. The protagonist, who is obsessed with finding a buried treasure, never bothers to plant anything on God's Little Acre. When he begins to suspect that the treasure might be buried there, he deftly shifts God's Little Acre to another spot. He never finds the treasure—or much of anything else.

**Clotilda, St.** (loud battle)   Sixth century. In Christian legend, wife of Clovis, king of France. Feast, 3 June.

When in danger of defeat by the Huns, King Clovis, who was a pagan, asked his queen, Clotilda, to pray to her god to bring him victory. When he defeated the Huns in battle, he ascribed it to the Christian god and was baptized by St. Rémy. At the king's baptism, according to legend, the oil was brought from heaven by a dove, and an angel came down bearing three lilies, which he gave to St. Rémy. The saint in turn gave them to Clotilda, who then changed the arms of France from the three toads, or *crapauds*, to the fleurs-de-lis, emblems of purity and regeneration.

In Christian art St. Clotilda is portrayed in royal robes, with a long white veil and jeweled crown, either kneeling in prayer or bestowing alms. Sometimes she is attended by an angel holding a shield bearing the three fleurs-de-lis.

See also: RÉMY, ST.

**Clover**   A forage plant with trifoliate leaves. In Christian symbolism, the clover is used to explain the Trinity (three leaves yet one clover; three persons yet one God). St. Patrick is said to have converted the pagan Irish with this explanation when confronted by King Leoghaire. In Druid belief the clover was a sacred plant, sign of both good and evil. In English folklore, if one dreams of a clover, it means a happy marriage filled with wealth and prosperity. According to the Victorian language of flowers the clover is a symbol of fertility. Finding a four-leaf clover is still today viewed as a sign of good luck.

See also: DRUIDS; PATRICK, ST.

**Cluricane** (Cluralan, Cluricaune)   In Celtic folklore, an elf who often appeared as a wrinkled old man. He is one of three kinds of solitary fairies in Ireland; the other two are the Leprechaun and Far Darria. Cluricane was noted for his ability to find hidden treasure. He likes to enter a rich man's wine cellar and drain all the casks. When outside he will often harness a sheep dog and ride it for his amusement, leaving the dog mud-covered. A spirit taking food from the table or a cupboard is a well know motif in folk literature.

See also: FAR DARRIA; LEPRECHAUN; MOTIF

**Clym of the Clough** (Clement of the cliff)   In British legend, an outlaw hero who was supposed to have lived shortly before Robin Hood. He appears in ballads in Percy's *Reliques*, along with Adam Bell and William of Cloudesly. They were as famous in the North of England as Robin

Hood was in the Midlands. Clym is mentioned in Ben Jonson's play *The Alchemist*.

See also: ADAM BELL

0840

**Coachman Legends**   In Hungarian folklore, a series of tales around the figure of a coachman endowed with supernatural knowledge and powers. Often the coachman is in the service of some country squire, and there is a younger coachman who wishes to discover how the older man can perform all of his duties seemingly without doing any work. The younger coachman often achieves the knowledge by performing some magical rite or is told the secret by the older coachman, who cannot die unless he passes on his knowledge. The older coachman's powers are ascribed to an evil spirit with whom he has had contact.

0841

**Coal-Oil Johnnie**   In 19th-century American history and folklore, popular name of John W. Steel, who inherited oil money on his 21st birthday. He left his wife, job, and child and spent lavishly. Stories tell of him scattering 10-dollar bills in all directions, and buying teams of horses in Philadelphia on one day, only to give them to his coachmen on the next. He built an opera house in Cincinnati, but he ended his career as its doorkeeper. When he had used up all of his cash, he returned home to his wife and family.

0842

**Coatlicue** (Ciuacoatl, Civocoatl, Cihuacoatl, Coatlantona, Conteotl) (the serpent lady, robe of serpent)   In Aztec mythology, mother of the Sun as well as his wife and sister, appearing in numerous forms throughout Aztec mythology as both beneficent and demonic. She was also the mother of Quetzalcoatl.

According to Fray Bernardino Sahagún in his *Historia general de las cosas de Nueva España*, Coatlicue was responsible for giving people "poverty, mental depression, and sorrows." She would often appear in the marketplace dressed as a lady of rank and leave a cradle in which was found a lance point later used in human sacrifices.

Fray Diego Durán in his *Historia de las Indias de Nueva España e islas de tierra firme* relates that Montezuma II sent representatives to find the origin of his ancestors. They discovered a hill containing seven caves. A priest appeared and introduced them to an old woman, ugly and dirty, whose "face was so black and covered with filth that she looked like something straight out of Hell." The woman was Coatlicue. She welcomed the ambassadors and said she was the mother of the god Huitzilopochtli. She had been fasting since the day the god left and not washing or combing her hair, waiting for his return from the Aztec land. As the messengers prepared to leave, she called to them, telling them that in her land no one grew old. She then told them to watch as one of her servants ran down a hill and became younger as he reached the bottom. The ambassadors watched the man become younger as he descended and old again when he ascended the hill.

One of the most prominent manifestations of Coatlicue was as the deity of grain, in which role she would appear in both male and female forms under the name of Centeotl. Centeotl was often portrayed as a frog with numerous breasts, symbolic of the wet earth, according to some commentators. Her face was painted yellow, the color of corn. During her festivals the priests wore phallic emblems in the hope of inducing Centeotl to provide crops for the coming year.

Another important manifestation was as an earth goddess. She appeared with a huge open mouth and ferocious teeth, and was dressed all in white. Durán says that when the Aztecs won a great victory under the leadership of Montezuma II, Prince Cihuacoatl, who was named after the goddess, "attired himself in the garb of the goddess Cihuacoatl." These were the female clothes that were called "eagle garments."

An Aztec statue of Coatlicue in the Mexican Anthropological Museum portrays the cosmic aspects of the goddess as the great mother, who brings life and death.

Coatlicue was also known as and identified with Tonantzin (our mother), Ilamatecuhtli (old goddess), Tlatecutli (earth toad swallowing stone knife), Temazalteci (grandmother of the sweat bath), Itzpapalotl (obsidian butterfly), and as goddess of fate, portrayed as a beautiful woman with the symbols of death on her face.

See also: HUITZILOPOCHTLI; MONTEZUMA II; QUETZALCOATL

0843

**Cock**    A male bird, usually the domestic rooster. The shrill crow of the cock in world mythology and folklore is often a symbol of the rising sun. The Greeks identified the bird with Apollo in his role as sun god, but it was also associated with Demeter and her daughter Persephone as a symbol of fertility. Cocks were often used as sacrifices to various deities. In Aztec ceremonies a cock could often be substituted for a human victim. Cocks were sacrificed by the Romans and were sacred to Mars, the god of war, because of their fighting nature. But along with the snake they were also sacred to Asklepius, the god of medicine, for their believed curative properties.

According to Islamic legend the Prophet found a cock of enormous size in the first heaven, so large that its crest touched the second heaven. The crowing of this bird awakens every living creature except man.

In Christian mythology the cock is associated with St. Peter's denial of Jesus as narrated in the Gospels. Jesus said: "Before the cock crow, thou shalt deny me thrice" (Matt. 26:75). But the cock is also a symbol of Christ's Resurrection and placed on the top of churches. When the cock ceases to crow, the day of judgment will be at hand. Shakespeare's *Hamlet* (1.1) alludes to the belief that the cock crows all night on Christmas Eve so as to drive away every malignant spirit and evil influence. There are numerous motifs associated with the cock in the *Motif Index of Folk Literature*.

See also: APOLLO; BASILISK; DEMETER; MARS; PERSEPHONE

0844

**Cockaigne, Land of** (Cocagne, Cockayne)    In medieval European folklore, an imaginary land of pleasure, wealth, luxury, and idleness. In Germany the same land is called the *Schlaraffenland* and became widely know through the works of Hans Sachs. The 13th century Middle English poem *The Land of Cockayne* describes it as having houses made of barley sugar and cakes, streets paved with pastry, and shops with an unending supply of goods. In the satiric novel *Jurgen* by American writer James Branch Cabell, the hero visits Cockaigne, which is described as a land of curious delights. Edward Elgar's *Cockaigne Overture* is a musical description of London, which in some accounts was identified as the land of Cockaigne.

See also: SACHS, HANS

0845

**Cock and the Pearl, The**    Aesopic fable found in various European collections such as those of Luther, La Fontaine, Lessing, and Krilof.

A cock was strutting up and down the farmyard among the hens when suddenly he saw something shining amid the straw.

"Ho! ho!" he said. "That's for me." He soon rooted it out from beneath the straw. The shiny object turned out to be a pearl that by some chance had been lost in the yard. "You may be a treasure," said Master Cock, "to men that prize you, but for me I would rather have a single barleycorn than a peck of pearls."

Moral: *Precious things are for those who can prize them.*

The fable is quoted by Rabelais, Bacon in his *Essays* (13), and R. L. Stevenson in *Catriona*, his sequel to *Kidnapped*.

See also: AESOPIC FABLES; BACON, ROGER; LA FONTAINE, JEAN DE; LESSING, GOTTHOLD

0846

**Coffee** (Turkish *qahwah*)    A bean used to brew a strong caffeinic drink. Various world legends account for the origin of coffee. In an Ethiopian tale the bean was discovered by a goatherd named Kaldi. He kept noticing that his charges were especially lively after they had eaten berries from a certain bush. Curious about their behavior, Kaldi ate some of the berries himself and found them stimulating. Excited by his discovery, he took some of the beans to his religious leader (he was a Muslim), who decided that this might be an ideal way of keeping the faithful awake during the long evening prayers. In European versions of the tale the shepherd is a monk and the goats are sheep. Various forms of the tale are found in South America.

**0847**

**Coffin Texts**   In ancient Egypt, magic formulas found inside wooden coffins of the Middle Kingdom. They were derived from spells used during the Old Kingdom to guarantee the deceased king's entry into the hereafter and were first carved into the walls of the pyramids at Saqqara. The right to use these texts or spells, known collectively as the Pyramid Texts, in time was granted to individuals of nonroyal status. During the time of the Middle Kingdom, these Coffin Texts, loosely based on the Pyramid Texts, began to appear inside coffins. In the New Kingdom a somewhat modified form of these texts became known as *The Book of the Dead*.

See also: *BOOK OF THE DEAD, THE*; PYRAMID TEXTS

**0848**

**Colbumatuan-kurrk**   In Australian mythology, an evil female spirit who kills people by throwing tree limbs at them.

**0849**

**Colossus of Rhodes**   One of the Seven Wonders of the World, completed c. 280 B.C.E. It was a statue of the sun god Helios and was erected to commemorate the successful defense of Rhodes against Demetrius Poliorcetes in 304 B.C.E. A 16th-century legend said that it was built so large that its spread legs reached across the harbor and that ships could pass full sail beneath it. There is no evidence to support this legend, however. In *Julius Caesar* (I, ii) Shakespeare says, "He doth bestride the narrow world like a Colossus."

See also: SEVEN WONDERS OF THE WORLD

**0850**

**Columba, St.** (dove)   521–597. In Christian legend, Apostle of Scotland, abbot of Iona. Feast, 9 June.

Born the son of Feidilmid, an Ulster chief, Columba with 12 companions landed on the island of Iona in 563, having made the passage in a wicker boat covered with hides. The Druids who occupied the island tried to prevent the Christians from forming a community, but Columba persisted and built a monastery on Iona, of which he was made the abbot. The members of Columba's community were not bound by celibacy or poverty, only obedience. They were allowed to marry, though their wives were not allowed to live with them but had special quarters on an adjacent property, called Eilen nam ban (Woman's Island). The monks, however, were allowed to visit their wives from time to time.

The followers of Columba's rule were called Culdees. Thomas Campbell, the Scottish poet, alludes to them in his *Reullura*:

. . . The pure Culdees
Were Albyn's earliest priests of God,
Ere yet an island of her seas
By foot of Saxon monk was trod,
Long ere her churchmen by bigotry
Were barred from holy wedlock's tie.

The Irish poet Thomas Moore, in his *Irish Melodies*, tells the legend of St. Senanus and a lady who sought shelter on the holy island but were told to leave. The relics of St. Columba were transferred to Ireland in 878 but were destroyed by the pagan Danes in the 12th century.

See also: DRUIDS

*Confucius*

Shang-ti (the emperor above). In the *Analects* (3:12) he counseled the worship of spirits as if they were present but made no decision on whether or not they existed. The emphasis is on the value of ceremony, which for Confucius was not separable from morality. Proper ceremony is morally edifying; proper morals are expressed in ceremony. Thus, for him it was not important whether the spirits existed, but it was essential that they be worshiped. Later, therefore, the worship of Confucius' spirit does not necessarily imply that he was regarded as having a spirit that could be worshiped. Traditionally, the mandarins have been skeptical or agnostic and have regarded religion as an affair of the peasants.

See also: SHANG-TI; SHEN

0851

**Confucius** (K'ung Fu-Tzu) (Master K'ung) 551–479 B.C.E. Chinese philosopher. Confucius, the Latinized form of his name in Chinese, K'ung Fu-Tzu, was born of a poor family, but he received a good education. He married at the age of 19 and had a son. Deeply interested in the Chinese past, he acquired an extensive knowledge of the ancient traditions and worked as a teacher, passing this knowledge on to his followers. Though he did some government work, at which he failed, most of his life was nomadic.

According to legend, he was raised to the status of a shen (spirit) in 195 B.C.E., when the emperor of China offered animal sacrifice at his tomb. In 555 C.E. separate temples for worship of Confucius were ordered at the capital of every prefecture in China. Even in 1914 the worship of Confucius was continued by Yuan Shih'iai, the first president of the Republic of China.

This is ironic because the attitude of Confucius himself toward deities and spirits is uncertain. He constantly referred to heaven as if it were a semipersonal moral overseer but only once used the more distinctly personal title

0852

**Coniraya**   In the mythology of the Huarochiri (Warachiri) Indians of the western side of the coastal cordillera of Peru, a creator god, the all-wise god who knew the thoughts of both men and gods. It is possible that Cun (Con) was another version of Coniraya or an aspect of the god. Coniraya's myths are told by Francisco de Ávila, a Roman Catholic priest, in his *A Narrative of the Errors, False Gods, and Other Superstitions and Diabolical Rites . . . [of] the Indians* (1608). Coniraya once appeared dressed as an old beggar. He fell in love with the virgin Cavillaca, who sat weaving under a lucma tree. The god dropped a ripe fruit containing his seed near the girl, and she ate the fruit and became pregnant. Determined to find out who was responsible for fathering the child, she called together the "principal idols of the land" and watched as her child crawled to Coniraya, who was still disguised as a beggar. Disgusted at seeing who the father of her child was, she took the baby and fled to the sea. Coniraya now dropped his disguise. He "put on magnificent golden robes, and leaving the astonished assembly of the gods" ran after her, crying out: "O my lady Cavillaca, turn your eyes and see how handsome and gallant am I."

However, the girl continued her flight and jumped into the sea. When Coniraya came to the coast he found that Cavillaca and her son had "turned to stone."

Coniraya then met two daughters of Pachacamac, the supreme god of the Incas. Since their mother, Ursihuachac, was away, "Coniraya had intercourse with the elder daughter and wished to do the same with the other, but she turned into a pigeon and flew away."

Coniraya then went to Cuzco, taking with him the Inca monarch Huayna Capac. He told the king to send a commission to the lowlands of the west. The commission was made up of descendants of the condor, the falcon, and the swallow. "After five days one of the descendants of the swallow reached his journey's end. There he was given a coffer with instructions that it was to be opened by the Inca in person." Of course, the coffer was opened by the messenger, who found "inside a radiantly beautiful woman with hair like gold and dressed as a queen." This vision disappeared.

When Coniraya arrived before Huayna Capac, the monarch "spared his life because he was descended from the swallow and sent him back to the highlands. This time he brought the coffer intact into the hands of the Inca, but before the latter could open it Coniraya said to him: 'Inca, we must both leave this world. I go to [the] other world and you shall go to another in the company of my sister. We shall not see each other again.' When the coffer was opened an immediate splendor covered the world. The Inca determined not to return to Cuzco. 'Here I will stay with my princess,' he said, and sent back one of his relations to Cuzco in his place with the command: 'Go thou to Cuzco and say that your are Huayna Capac.' In that moment the Inca disappeared with his spouse, as did Coniraya."

See also: CUN; PACHACAMAC

0853

**Constans**   In British mythology, an early king, eldest of the three sons of the emperor Constantine. His two brothers were Aurelius Ambrosius and Uther Pendragon, who was the father of King Arthur. Constans was a monk, but at the death of his father he laid aside the cowl for the crown. Vortigern, however, had him assassinated and then took the throne. Aurelius Ambrosius succeeded Vortigern, and he was followed by Uther Pendragon.

See also: ARTHUR; UTHER PENDRAGON; VORTIGERN

0854

**Constantine the Great** (firm, constant, persevering)   c. 280–337. Roman emperor (306–337) who granted toleration to the Christians.

The historical Constantine bears little resemblance to the legendary one found in such works as Eusebius' *Life of Constantine* and the *Vita Beati Silvestri*. According to legend, Constantine had a dream in which he was told he would be victorious over his rival, Maxentius, if he would adopt the sign of the cross. He saw in the sky a luminous cross with the words *In hoc signo vinces* (By this sign thou shalt conquer). The emperor, after defeating Maxentius in the Battle of Saxa Rubra (312), then adopted the standard, the *chi-rho* monogram, to replace the imperial eagles.

Another legend is that while Constantine was a pagan he suffered from leprosy. His priests said he should bathe in the blood of some 3,000 children and he would be cured of his disease. The children were rounded up, but after hearing the pleas of their mothers, the emperor decided against the sacrifice.

"Far better it is that I should die, than cause the death of these innocents," he said.

That night St. Peter and St. Paul appeared to him and told him that Christ had sent them to him because he had spared the innocent children. They told him to send for Sylvester, the bishop of Rome, who would show him a pool in which he could wash and be healed of his sickness. When this happened, he should then stop his persecution of the Christians and adopt the faith of Jesus Christ.

Sylvester was found hiding in a cave near Monte Calvo when the emperor's men came for him. He had hidden there in fear of his life. When he appeared before Constantine the ruler asked him who were the two gods he had seen in a vision the night before. Sylvester said they were not gods but the Apostles of Jesus Christ, the only true God. Constantine then asked to see an image of the Apostles to see if they were the same as the two men in his vision. When the images agreed with what he had seen, he asked to be baptized. Bishop Sylvester performed the rite.

The historical Constantine, however, was not baptized by Sylvester, as the legend says, but by an Arian bishop of Nicomedia as he lay on his deathbed. Sylvester had been dead some 18 months before the event.

When Helena, the mother of Constantine (who later went in search of the True Cross), heard that her son had become a Christian, she said she would rather be a follower of the Jewish god than the Christian one. Constantine then asked his mother to bring all of the most learned Jewish rabbis to debate with his bishop. One hundred forty rabbis came and debated with Sylvester, who defeated them all in argument except for Zambri, a magician. Zambri said he could whisper the secret name of God into a bull's ear, and the animal would die. A bull was brought forth, the magician whispered into its ear, and the animal fell dead. Sylvester, not flustered, said he would raise the bull to life. He called on Christ, the god of the living, and the bull arose.

Later legend says that Constantine was so impressed by Sylvester that he gave him and his successors (the popes) the territory of central Italy as well as primacy over all other bishops in the church. The *Donation of Constantine*, as the document proving Constantine's gift was called, was proved a forgery by Lorenzo Valla, a 15th-century Italian scholar, though it had been used by the Roman church to support its claims for secular authority.

In art Constantine and St. Sylvester are sometimes portrayed together. Sylvester is seen receiving the deed from the emperor. When Sylvester is portrayed alone, he is seen with a bull. He is easily distinguished from St. Luke, who is also portrayed with a bull, by his rich pontifical robes. Piero della Francesca painted the *Dream of Constantine*, which portrays the emperor asleep with the angel hovering overhead, as well as the *Victory of Constantine over Maxentius* for the choir of the Church of San Francesco in Arezzo, Italy. Rubens also painted the victory of the emperor.

See also: APOSTLE; CROSS; LUKE, ST.; PAUL, ST.; PETER, ST.

0855

**Conwenna**   In British mythology, the wife of King Dunwallo, the first king to wear a gold crown. In William Blake's poem "Jerusalem" she appears and "shines a triple form over the north with pearly beams, gorgeous and terrible."

0856

**Cooper, D. B.**   In American folklore, a man who gave his name as Dan Cooper, boarded a Northwest Airlines flight from Portland to Seattle on November 24, 1971, hijacked the aircraft, and demanded and received a $200,000 ransom on landing at the Seattle airport. When the plane took off again, this time headed toward Mexico, the highjacker parachuted at 10,000 feet from the rear door of the aircraft into the forest below and was never seen again.

The disappearance of Dan "D. B." Cooper has led to numerous legends, ballads, and even an otherwise forgettable movie about the heist starring Robert Duvall. Posters, T shirts, and other items also appeared after the heist. Seattle playwright John Orlock wrote a play about it, a restaurant in Salt Lake City is called D. B. Cooper's, and the town of Ariel, Washington, near the spot where Cooper is believed to have jumped, has a yearly D. B. Cooper festival during Thanksgiving week (a tradition that dates back to 1976). As many as 300 to 500 people show up each year from as far away as Japan.

0857

**Cophetua**   In British mythology, a mythical king of Africa who fell in love with a beggar maid, Penelophon, and married her. She is mentioned as Zenelophon in Shakespeare's *Love's Labour's Lost*, Tennyson's poem "The Beggar Maid," and in a ballad, "King Cophetua and the Beggar Maid," included in Percy's *Reliques*. The subject was used by Edward Burne-Jones, the 19th-century painter and designer.

0858

**Corey, Giles**   c. 1619–1692. In American history and legend, one of the victims of the Salem witchcraft trials, he was accused by Ann Putnam, Mercy Lewis, and Abigail Williams of witchcraft. Ann Putnam claimed that on April 13 the specter of Giles Corey visited her and asked her to write in the Devil's book. Later, Putnam claimed that a ghost appeared before her to announce that it had been murdered by Corey. Other girls described Corey as "a dreadful wizard" and recounted stories of assaults by his specter. He was pressed to death under heavy weights. Hundreds were tried and 19 executed, including Corey's wife.

In legend Corey is said to reappear before times of disaster in Salem. Corey appears in a good light in Robert Calef's *More Wonders of the Invisible World*, which attacks Cotton Mather, whose writings were in part responsible for the trials. Longfellow's poetical play *Giles Corey of Salem Farms*, part of his *New England Tragedies*, has Corey as a hero, as does Arthur Miller's play *The Crucible*, which was used as the basis of Robert Ward's opera *The Crucible*.

See also: REVENANT

0859

**Corn**   In Europe, seed of any cereal grass used for food (wheat, oats, maize, barley), and in the Americas, Indian corn, *Zea Maya*, native to the American continent. In European folklore corn is often personified as the corn mother or corn maiden. In Germany peasants would cry out as the grain waved in the wind: "There comes the corn mother" or "The corn mother is running over the field." Children were told not to pull cornflowers or red poppies in the field because the corn mother was sitting in the corn and would catch them. Sometimes the last sheaf of grain was called the harvest mother, great mother, or grandmother. In Germany the last sheaf was dressed as a woman, and harvesters danced around it. It was believed that whoever got the last sheaf would be married by the following year, though the spouse would be old. If a woman got it, she would marry a widower; if a man, an old crone. The North American Ojibwa Indians have a myth about Mondamin, who came to earth and battled a hero. He was defeated and buried, and from his body the corn grew—a gift to man. The tale is told in Longfellow's poem *The Song of Hiawatha*.

*The Holy Eucharist*

0860

**Corpus Christi** (Christ's body)   Medieval Christian feast of the Holy Eucharist, celebrated on the Thursday after Pentecost; instituted by Pope Urban IV in 1264. The feast was first suggested by St. Juliana (13th century), who was the prioress of Mont Cornillion in Liege, Belgium. She said she frequently had visions in which the full moon appeared to her in a brilliant light, except for one spot, which was black. The dark spot, she said Christ told her, was the lack of a feast in honor of the Holy Eucharist. One man who supported Juliana in her efforts to institute the feast was Jacques Pantaleon, the archdeacon of Liege, who later became Pope Urban IV.

Thomas Aquinas's hymn, "Adoro Te Supples, Latens Dietas," "Godhead here in hiding, whom I do adore," was written for the feast. Other hymns he composed for the feast were *Lauda, Sion* and *Pangue Lingua*. Part of the celebration consisted of miracle plays, which were performed in York, Coventry, and Chester in England until the Reformation, when they were banned. In Spain *autos sacramentales* (sacramental act), one-act verse plays, were performed. Calderón wrote more than 70 such plays.

Two English colleges, one at Cambridge and one at Oxford, are named after the feast. Corpus Christi, Texas, and Sacramento, California, also are named in honor of the Holy Eucharist.

See also: THOMAS AQUINAS

0861

**Corydon**    In Roman mythology, common name given to Arcadian shepherds. Vergil's second *Eclogue* tells of the love of Corydon for his faithless male lover, Alexis. André Gide's dialogue *Corydon* uses the shepherd's name in his defense of homosexuality.

See also: ARCADIA

0862

**Cosmas and Damian, Sts.** (order, tamed, tamer)    Third century. In Christian legend, patron saints of barbers, apothecaries, and physicians. Feast, 27 September.

Their legend, from the East, became a part of Western Christian lore in the early ages of the Church. Cosmas and Damian were brothers born in Cilicia. Their father died when they were young, and their mother, Theodora, brought them up as Christians. They became physicians to help the sick, whether rich or poor, and to help animals. They were eventually arrested for being Christian and thrown into prison. At first

they were to be drowned at sea, but an angel saved them. Then they were to be burned to death, but the fire refused to consume them. They were then bound to two crosses and stoned, but the stones, instead of pelting them, fell on those who threw them. The proconsul, believing them to be enchanters, then had them beheaded.

One tale in *The Golden Legend*, a collection of saints' lives written in the 13th century by Jacobus de Voragine, tells how the saints replaced the diseased leg of a patient. They took the black leg of a dead Moor and used "celestial ointment" to attach it to the white man. The operation was a success.

Among Greek Christians the saints displaced the worship of Aesculapius, the Greek god of medicine. They were called Anargyres (without fees), since it was as rare then as now for a doctor not to charge for his services.

In Christian art the two are portrayed in loose dark robes trimmed with fur. In *The Canterbury Tales* Chaucer describes the dress of a physician of his time as a "scarlet gown, furred well." Often they hold a box of ointment in one hand and a lancet or some surgical instruments in the other. Sometimes they hold a pestle and mortar.

Stravinsky's *Les Noces* (The Wedding), a piece for dancers and chorus with various Russian texts, invokes the names of Sts. Cosmas and Damian because they are recognized in Russia as wedding saints who watch over the fertility of the couple.

See also: ASCLEPIUS; CHAUCER; *GOLDEN LEGEND, THE*

0863

**Cow**    Female ruminant, symbol of the Great Mother and creation in world mythology. The cow was sacred to Hathor and Isis in Egyptian mythology. In Nordic mythology, as told in the *Prose Edda* and the *Poetic Edda*, Audhumla, a cow, licked the salt of the earth and created the first man.

See also: AUDHUMLA; HATHOR; ISIS

**Coyolxauhqui** (golden bells) In Aztec mythology, goddess, the moon lady, sister of the god Tezcatlipoca, who cut off her head, which now lives in the sky.

0864

**Coyote** A carnivorous wolflike mammal of western North America that frequently appears in American Indian tales as a trickster and creator. In one myth Coyote prevented the creator god from turning some wooden dummies into animals. In anger the creator god left, and Coyote took the wooden dummies, planted them, and the first Indians sprouted up. In another myth Coyote plants some bird feathers that sprout into humans. Sometimes, however, he is a victim, as when Coyote's entire family is killed by Porcupine because he had cheated the animal out of his share of some buffalo meat.

See also: TRICKSTER

0865

**Crab** A crustacean having a short, broad, flattened body. In Greek mythology the crab obstructs Heracles in his battle with the nine-headed monster, the Hydra of Lerna. In Japanese folklore the facelike form or imprint on the back of a crab is that of the Heiki, a family of warriors who in the 12th century engaged in a massive battle with another Japanese family, the Genji. The Heiki lost and committed mass suicide by throwing themselves into the sea, where they were turned into crabs. Their faces were impressed on the backs of the crab shells. In Siamese folklore the crab is a symbol of sleeplike death. As one of the signs of the Zodiac, Cancer, the crab signifies the oblique, sideways movements of the sun during the summer solstice.

See also: CANCER; HEIKI; HERACLES; HYDRA; ZODIAC

0866

**Cradlemont** In Arthurian legend, king of Wales, subdued by King Arthur, mentioned in Tennyson's "The Coming of Arthur," one of the *Idylls of the King*.

See also: ARTHUR

0867

**Cradock** In Arthurian legend, the only knight who could carve the boar's head that no cuckold could cut, or drink from a bowl that no cuckold could drink from without spilling. His lady was the only one in King Arthur's court who could wear the mantle of chastity.

See also: ARTHUR

0868

*Crane*

**Crane** A long-necked, long-legged bird. The crane is often a messenger of the gods in Chinese, Japanese, and Greek mythologies. In medieval Christianity the crane is a symbol of vigilance, loyalty, and good works.

0869

**Credne** (Creidne) (craftsman) In Celtic mythology, culture hero and bronze worker who aided the Tuatha de Danann (the good people of the goddess Danu) with weapons in their fight against the evil Fomorians.

See also: DANU; FOMORIANS; TUATHA DE DANANN

0870

0871

**Crispin and Crispinian, Sts.** (Latin *crepida*: sandal)    Third century. In Christian legend, patron saints of shoemakers. Feast, 25 October.

The saints were brothers who went with St. Denis from Rome to preach in France. They supported themselves by making shoes. According to one legend, angels supplied them with leather to make shoes for the poor. This upset the Roman authorities, who had the two beheaded at Soissons.

According to a Provençal legend, St. Crispin is responsible for the practice of the craft of shoemaking by cripples and hunchbacks: The saint was so pleased with his first feast day that he asked that God grant the shoemakers a glimpse of paradise. A ladder was lowered from heaven, and some of the shoemakers mounted it. When they reached heaven, there was a celebration for St. Peter, and everyone was singing the *Sursum corda*. St. Paul, who was deaf, mistook the words that were sung and cut the rope holding the ladder. The shoemakers fell to earth, causing many of them to become cripples.

St. Crispin's Day, 25 October, is the anniversary of the transfer of the relics of the two saints from Soissons to Rome in the ninth century. The date is the same as that of the battle of Agincourt. Shakespeare makes Crispin and his brother Crispinian into one person, Crispin Crispian, in *Henry V*.

See also: DENIS, ST.; PAUL, ST.; PETER, ST.

0872

**Crockett, Davy**    1786–1836. In American history and folklore, Tennessee-born frontiersman. Crockett served as a scout under Andrew Jackson in the Creek Indian War. He entered political life and was elected three times as a U.S. Congressman. His motto was, "Be always sure you are right, then go ahead." Known as the "Coonskin Congressman," Crockett opposed the policies of President Jackson and eventually lost his seat. He left for Texas, where he died defending the Alamo.

His legend, partly of his own making, began during his lifetime and told how he spoke the language of animals, whipped wildcats, and killed as many as 100 bears in less than nine months. *A Narrative of the Life of David Crockett*, attributed to him, helped spread his legend, as did the *Crockett Almanacs*, which began to appear about 1835 and were published long after his death. An example from one of the almanacs says: "Friends, fellow citizens, brothers and sisters! Jackson is a hero and Crockett is a horse! They accuse me of adultery; its a lie—I never ran away with any man's wife that was not willing, in my life." His tombstone reads: "Davy Crockett, Pioneer, Patriot, Soldier, Trapper, Explorer, State Legislator, Congressman, Martyred at The Alamo. 1786–1836." A popular television series based on his life and legend was later made into a Walt Disney movie, *Davy Crockett*.

0873

**Crocodile**    An amphibious reptile, both beneficent and demonic in world mythology; the crocodile is identified with Sebek, Set, and Horus in Egyptian mythology. A sacred, tamed crocodile was kept in an artificial lake by Egyptian priests and fed cakes, meat, and wine. Some of the priests would open its mouth while others put in cakes and other food. The meal would end with a mixture of milk and honey. In the Middle Ages in some Arab countries, accused criminals were thrown into a lake of crocodiles. If the crocodiles ate the accused, he was pronounced guilty; if not, innocent. In West African belief crocodiles are reincarnations of murder victims, and in Hindu mythology they are the reincarnations of murdered Brahmins. In European folklore the crocodile is best known for the tears it is supposed to shed over its victims. Shakespeare's *Othello* (4:2) cites the belief, and the English poet Robert Herrick in his poem "To Mistress Ann Potter" refers to the belief that the beast has no tongue: "True love is tongueless like a crocodile."

See also: SEBEK; SET; HORUS

*Christ on the Cross*

0874
**Cross**   Major symbol of the Christian faith, but found in many other cultures. Runic crosses were used as boundary markers by Scandinavians. Cicero in his *De Divinatione* (11, 27, 80, and 81) tells us that an augur's staff used to mark the heavens was a cross. The Egyptians used the cross as a sacred symbol. It was also a sacred symbol among the Aztecs: It was an emblem of Quetzalcoatl, representing the four winds that blow. In Cozumel it was an object of worship, and it is found in Tabasco and Palenque.

Numerous references are made to the cross in the writings of the early Christian Church. The legend of the True Cross, as it was known in the Middle Ages, was one of the most popular in Western art and literature. It was frescoed on the choir walls of the Church of Santa Croce in Florence by Agnolo Gaddi and by Piero della Francesca in the Chapel of the Bacci, Church of San Francesco in Arezzo.

The tale is told in *The Golden Legend* by Jacobus de Voragine, source of much of the lore surrounding saints' lives and Christian festivals. When Adam was banished from the Garden of Eden, he lived a life of penitence, toiling day and night and praying to God. When he reached old age and felt death approaching, he called his son Seth.

"Go, my son," he said, "to the Garden of Eden and ask the Archangel who keeps the gate to give me a balsam that will save me from death. You will easily find the way, for my footsteps scorched the soil as I left the garden."

And Seth went to carry out his father's command. As he drew near, he saw the flaming sword in the hand of the archangel guarding the gate, and his wings were spread to block entrance to the garden. Seth prostrated himself before him, unable to utter a word.

"The time of pardon is not yet come," said the archangel. "Four thousand years must roll away ere the Redeemer shall open the gate to Adam which was closed by his disobedience. But as a token of future pardon, the wood on which redemption shall be won shall grow from the tomb of your father Adam.

"I will give you three seeds from this tree. When Adam is dead, place them in his mouth and bury him."

Seth took the seeds and in the course of time did as the archangel instructed. Three trees grew at his father's grave—a cedar, a cypress, and a pine. They touched and mingled with one another, finally becoming a single trunk. It was beneath this great tree that King David sat when he bewailed his sins.

King Solomon attempted to use this tree in the building of his palace, but the tree would not cooperate, so he cast it out where it would be trampled. The Queen of Sheba found it and caused its trunk to be buried on the spot near where the pool of Bethesda would be placed, and the tree acquired miraculous properties.

When the time of the crucifixion of Christ drew near, the wood rose to the surface and was brought out of the water. The executioners, seeking a suitable beam for his cross, found it there. After the crucifixion, the wood was buried on Calvary, but according to legend was uncovered on 3 May 328 by the empress Helena, mother of Constantine the Great. The cross was carried away by Chosroes, King of Persia, at the destruction of Jerusalem but recovered in the year 615, on 14 September, a day that has since remained in the Christian calendar as the Feast of the Exaltation of the Cross.

See also: CEDAR; CONSTANTINE THE GREAT; *GOLDEN LEGEND, THE*; HELENA, ST.; PINE; QUETZALCOATL

0875

**Crow** A large bird having lustrous black plumage, often associated with the devil in Christian symbolism. English folklore says the crow visits hell in midsummer each year and makes payment to the devil by giving its feathers. The birds do molt in midsummer, and since they are usually absent from their regular haunts during that time it was easy for people ignorant of bird migrations to believe. Plutarch, the Greek author, uses the crow in one of his essays dealing with chastity. The crow is cited for its faithfulness to its mate because, according to Plutarch, it does not remarry for nine human generations. "Can Penelope match that?" Plutarch asks. There are numerous motifs associated with the crow in the *Motif Index of Folk Literature*.

See also: RAVEN

0876

**Cuchulain** (the hound of Cullan) In Celtic mythology, greatest hero in early Irish literature. Cuchulain, who is believed to have lived in the first century C.E., was the son of the sun god, Lugh, and Dectera, though his reputed father was Sualtam. As a child he was called Setanta (the little); he received the name Cuchulain (the hound of Cullan) when he killed the watchdog of the smith Cullan and compensated the owner by undertaking to guard his house in the dog's place. Later, when the men of Ulster asked Cuchulain to take a wife, he said he loved Emer, daughter of Forgall. He set out in his chariot for Forgall's home, only to learn that Emer would not marry him until he had slain hundreds of men. Cuchulain went to the war goddess Skatha for advice and lived with her for a year and a day,

learning how to use the Gae Bolg, a magic deadly weapon.

Skatha then made war with Aifa, the strongest woman in the world. However, the goddess did not wish Cuchulain to enter the battle because he was very young. She therefore gave him a sleeping potion that was to last 24 hours. However, he awoke one hour later and attacked the enemy, causing havoc and death. Finally, Aifa incited Skatha to single combat. Cuchulain accepted the challenge for himself and by his victory made an end of the war. Aifa then became his friend and lover. Before he left her, Cuchulain gave Aifa a ring to give their son if a child should be born of their union. A son called Connla was born; however, he did not know his real father and was later killed by Cuchulain, who learned too late that he had killed his own son.

Cuchulain then fought the sons of Nechtan, whom he slew, fastening their heads to his chariot's rim. He returned to battle with 16 swans and 2 stags also yoked to his chariot. Cuchulain then went to fight Forgall and his men, all of whom he defeated, thus winning Emer as his wife. When Cuchulain was born, the Druid priest Morann had said: "His praise will be in the mouths of all men. Charioteers and warriors, kings and sages will recount his deeds. He will win the love of many."

The most famous deed of the hero is contained in the saga *Táin Bó Cualgne* (The Cattle Raid of Cooley), written in the eighth or ninth century. The epic opens with Queen Maev (Medb) of Connacht and her henpecked husband, Ailill, arguing over who had greater possessions. The queen discovers she has possessions equal to those of her husband, except for one bull owned by Ailill, the White Horned Bull of Connacht. Maev determines to correct this imbalance by obtaining the bull from the Donn of Cooley. She asks Daire, a chief of Ulster, to lend her the bull. He refuses, and she then sends an army to invade Ulster. The warriors of Ulster, however, are under a curse; only Cuchulain is free of it. All alone he withstands the enemy.

Once during the various battles Cuchulain is compelled to fight his dear friend Ferdiad, who made a bold challenge to him while drunk. For three days they fight, until Cuchulain finally kills Ferdiad. Eventually a truce is made between Cuchulain and Queen Maev, but she breaks it, sending her men to steal the bull. They are defeated, and the White Horned Bull of Connacht is killed by the Donn of Cooley, who later dies when his heart bursts.

According to other accounts, Queen Maev waited for her time to avenge herself on Cuchulain for his victory. Maev sent the posthumous three sons of the three daughters of the wizard Catlin against Cuchulain. He became ill and was tended in his despondency in a solitary glen by Niam, the wife of Connel, and other princesses. Then Bave, Catlin's daughter, took the form of Niam and beckoned him forth to battle. At the touch of his lips, the wine that his mother, Dectera, gave him turned to blood. When he reached the ford on the plain of Emania, he saw a maiden weeping and washing bloody garments and arms—they were his own. Then breaking his geis, or taboo, Cuchulain ate the roasted dog offered him by Catlin's three daughters and went forth again to battle. He bound himself with his belt to a pillar so that he might die standing. Cuchulain was killed by Curoi's son, whose father had earlier been killed by Cuchulain. The age of the hero was 27.

Cuchulain's legends were used by W. B. Yeats in "The Death of Cuchulain," as well as in another poem, "Cuchulain's Fight with the Sea." Lady Gregory compiled the legends and myths in *Cuchulain of Muirthemne.*

See also: MAEV

**Cuckoo**   Slender-bodied, long-tailed bird with downcurved beak and pointed wings. In Greek and Hindu mythology the cuckoo is noted for its sexual appetite. Both the Greek sky god Zeus and the Hindu sky god Indra at one time transformed themselves into cuckoos in order to take advan-

0877

tage of some maiden. The ancient Romans called an adulterer a cuckoo. Shakespeare's song in *Love's Labour's Lost* (5.2) expresses the European belief:

The cuckoo then on every tree,
Mocks married men; for thus sings he,
"Cuckoo! Cuckoo, cuckoo! O word of fear,
Unpleasing to the married ear!"

In European folk belief a man's fancy turns toward love in springtime, and the cuckoo is popularly known as the herald of spring. Delius' symphonic poem *On Hearing the First Cuckoo in Spring* captures the mood of springtime.

See also: INDRA; ZEUS

0878

**Cun** (Con)   In the mythology of the Quechua Andes Indians near Lake Titicaca, a thunder god who lived in the mountains high above the snow peaks. He had no bones, muscles, or members, though he was as swift as the wind. His nature was irritable, and he was not interested in human affairs.

0879

**Cupay** (Supay, Supai)   In Inca mythology, an evil spirit, equated with the devil by Christian Indians of Peru and Bolivia today. W. H. Prescott, in *The History of the Conquest of Peru*, wrote that no sacrifices were made to Cupay. He "seems to have been only a shadowy personification of sin, that exercised little influence over the daily lives of the people." But Max Fauconnet, in his discussion of Cupay in the *New Larousse Encyclopedia of Mythology*, wrote that he was "a god of death . . . who lived inside the earth." He was a "dreary and greedy god, always longing to increase the number of his subjects, so he must be placated, even at the cost of painful sacrifices. Thus, every year a hundred children were sacrificed to him."

0880

**Cupid**   In Roman mythology, the god of love, passion, and desire. He is the son of Venus and

Mercury, and he is identified with the Greek Eros. In art he is usually depicted as a beautiful, naked, winged boy carrying a bow and arrow. With his arrows he could make mortals fall in love with each other, or in some cases refute the advances of another. According to legend he would whet the grindstone on which he sharpened his arrows with blood. He was also a mischievous god who played tricks on mortals and even on immortals.

See also: EROS; MERCURY; VENUS

0881

**Curtana** (short)    The Sword of Mercy in England borne before English kings at their coronation. The sword, according to medieval legend, belonged to St. Edward the Confessor. Curtana has no point, hence "shortened," and thus symbolizes mercy. Dryden's *The Hind and the Panther* contains these lines:

But when Curtana will no do the deed
You lay the pointless clery-weapon by,
And to the laws, your sword of justice fly.

*Curtius riding into the pit*

0882

**Curtius, Marcus**    Fourth century B.C.E. In Roman legend, a hero who killed himself to close a chasm. According to the legend, a gigantic chasm opened and could be closed only if Rome's greatest treasure were cast into the pit. Mounting his horse, Curtius leaped in, and the chasm closed.

0883

**Cuthbert, St.** (famous, bright)    Died 687. In Christian legend, patron saint of shepherds and seafarers. Invoked against plague. Feast, 20 March.

The legends of the saint were written by St. Bede as *The Life and Miracles of St. Cuthbert, Bishop of Lindisfarne*, in the seventh century. Cuthbert was a young shepherd in the valley of Tweed. One day an angel appeared to him and told him to lead a holy and pious life. He therefore went to be instructed at the monastery of Melrose near his home, which was run by St. Aidan. One night, as Cuthbert tended his flocks, he saw a dazzling light and, looking up, beheld angels bearing St. Aidan to heaven. He then entered the monastery and became abbot. He was noted for his preaching as he wandered among the mountainous regions. Later he went to live on an island off the coast of Northumberland, one of the Farne Islands, called Lindisfarne (Holy Island). Numerous miracles are recorded by Bede in his life of the saint. For example, one night when the saint lay on the cold shore, exhausted by his penance, two otters licked him and revived his benumbed limbs.

His main attribute, however, is the head of King St. Oswald, which was buried in the tomb of St. Cuthbert when the king was slain in battle.

See also: BEDE THE VENERABLE, ST.; OSWALD, ST.

0884

**Cuthman, St.** (famous)    Died c. 900. In Christian legend, builder of the first Christian church in Sussex, England. Feast, 8 February.

Cuthman lived with his mother at Steyning in Sussex. One medieval legend concerns the Devil's Dyke at Brighton. One day St. Cuthman was walking over the South Downs thinking of how he had saved the whole country from paganism. Suddenly, the devil appeared.

"Ha, ha," said the devil, "so you think that by building churches and convents you can stop me. Poor fool! Why, this night I will flood the whole land and destroy all the churches and convents."

"Forewarned is forearmed," said St. Cuthman to himself as he calmly left the devil to his ranting. Cuthman went to his sister Cecilia, mother superior of a convent that stood on the present site of Dyke's House.

"Sister," said the saint, "I love you very much. This night, for the grace of God, keep lights burning at the convent windows from midnight to daybreak, and let Masses be said."

At sundown the devil came with a pickax, spade, mattock, and shovel and set to work to let the sea flow into the downs. But the sound of the nuns' singing at Mass made it impossible for the devil to continue his work, and he became paralyzed. When the candles were lit by the nuns, the cock, thinking it was morning, began to sing, and the devil, who could only work at night, fled as fast as he could. Before he fled, however, he had dug a small hole, which is called Devil's Dyke to this day.

0885

**Cuycha**   In Inca mythology, rainbow god who attended the sun, Inti, and the moon, Mama Quilla.

See also: INTI; MAMA QUILLA

0886

**Cyhiraeth**   In Celtic mythology, a goddess of streams who appears in Welsh folklore as a species of spectral female, haunting woodland brooks. Her blood-freezing shriek foretells a death. She is depicted as invisible and bodiless and is heard groaning before death, especially before deaths caused by a disaster or an epidemic.

See also: BANSHEE; LA LLORONA

0887

**Cymbeline**   In British legend, a king who reigned for 35 years under Roman rule. In Holinshed's *Chronicles* he is said to have been "brought up in Rome, and there made a knight by Augustus Caesar." He had two sons, Guiderius and Arviragus. Shakespeare used the reference to Cymbeline in *Chronicles* as well as the story of Imogen from Boccaccio's *Decameron* for the plot of his play *Cymbeline*. In some accounts, Cymbeline is identified with King Cunobeline, after whom the city of Camalodunum, or Colchester, is named.

0888

**Cyril and Methodius, Sts.** (lord)   Ninth century. In Christian legend, Apostles of the Slavs. St. Cyril's feast, 9 March in the Greek church; St. Methodius, 11 May. In the Latin church both are honored on 9 March.

Cyril was a philosopher and Methodius an artist; both belonged to the order of St. Basil. They were sent by the patriarch of Constantinople as Christian missionaries to the people who lived on the borders of the Danube. One legend tells how Bogaris, the king of Bulgaria, asked Methodius to paint a picture in his palace hall that would impress his subjects. Methodius painted the Last Judgment with Christ enthroned and surrounded by angels and also panels portraying the punishment of hell and the rewards of heaven. Impressed by the work, Bogaris became a Christian and adopted the religion for his country. Cyril and Methodius then went among the surrounding nations preaching the gospel. St. Cyril, according to legend, invented the Cyrillic alphabet and translated parts of the Gospels.

The two saints are portrayed together in most icons. St. Cyril holds a book, and St. Methodius has a tablet on which he is painting.

See also: BASIL, ST.

# D

**Da** In African mythology (Fon of Benin), serpent god, who symbolizes life and movement. Dako, chief of the Fon nation, murdered a sovereign prince who was on a friendly visit in honor of one of his festivals. This was a violation of the sacred law of hospitality. He then attacked Da, the king of Abomey, laid siege to his capital, and put Da to death by cutting open his belly. He then placed Da's body at the foundation of the palace he built in Abomey, which he called Dahomey. The word derives from Da, the unfortunate victim, and Homy, his belly—that is, a house built on Da's belly.

**Dabaiba** In the mythology of the Indians of the Isthmus of Panama, a rain goddess and mother of the creator god. Dabaiba was worshiped near a river of the same name. Human sacrifices were made to her, perhaps in the hope that she would never again send a drought such as a previous one that nearly destroyed the population. In a myth of the Antioquians, Dabaiba appears as the goddess Dabeciba, and her son is Abira, the creator god.

**Dadak** In Tibetan Buddhism, a guardian deity, associated with the hero and founder of Buddhism in Tibet, Padmasambhava.

See also: PADMASAMBHAVA

**Dadhyanch** (Dadhica, Dadhicha) In Hindu mythology, a sage who was taught certain sciences by Indra but was not allowed to pass on his knowledge to anyone else without punishment. However, Dadhyanch gave some of the knowledge to the Aswins, the twin gods. When Indra discovered this he set out to cut off Dadhyanch's head. The Aswins, however, removed Dadhyanch's head and replaced it with a horse's head. When Indra cut off Dadhyanch's horse head, the Aswins then replaced it with Dadhyanch's real head.

See also: ASWINS; INDRA

**Daedala** (derived from the name Daedalus) In ancient Greek cult, a festival in honor of Hera by the Boetians. It commemorated the myth about Hera leaving Zeus and hiding. The god said he would then marry another and had a wooden image dressed up as his bride. When Hera believed Zeus was to marry another, she reappeared and attacked the "bride," only to discover it was a wooden statue. Part of the rites of the festival consisted of dressing a statue and offering a goat to Zeus and a cow to Hera.

See also: HERA; ZEUS

**Daedalion** (little Daedalus)   In Greek mythology, a young man, son of Phosphorus; brother of Ceyx; father of Chione (Philonis). He was loved by the gods Apollo and Hermes. His daughter Chione slept with both Apollo and Hermes and gave birth to twins. When she was turned into a hawk by Artemis for rejecting her love, Daedalion jumped from the summit of Mount Parnassus. Apollo then changed him into a hawk. The myth is told in Ovid's *Metamorphoses* (book 11).

See also: APOLLO; ARTEMIS DAEDALUS; HERMES; OVID

**Daedalus** (bright, cunningly wrought)   In Greek mythology, a culture hero, son of Eupalamus (or Metion) and Alcippe (or Merope); brother of Perdix and Sicyan; father of Icarus. Instructed by the goddess Athena, Daedalus was inventor of the ax, awl, and level. He was exiled from Athens after he murdered his nephew, Talus (sufferer?), whom Daedalus envied because Talus showed promise of becoming as great as Daedalus. He escaped to Crete, where he built the famous labyrinth with a thousand turnings for King Minos. Inside the labyrinth lived the Minotaur, the offspring of Minos's wife, Pasiphaë, and the Cretan bull. Daedalus, along with his son Icarus, was imprisoned in the maze as punishment for giving Ariadne directions for guiding Theseus out of the maze. To escape, Daedalus fashioned wings out of wax and feathers for himself and Icarus. During their escape Icarus flew too close to the sun, the wax in his wings melted, and he fell onto the island of Icaria. Daedalus flew to Sicily. The Sicilian king Cacalus refused a request to return Daedalus to Crete.

The scene of the fall of Icarus is frequently found in paintings. Daedalus and Icarus are a motif in the writings of James Joyce, whose hero is Stephen Daedalus. Ovid's *Metamorphoses* (book 8) tells the myth of Daedalus and Icarus. Socrates claimed descent from Daedalus (Plato, *Alcibiades* 1). English poets borrowed from Greek the adjective *daedal*, which means "cunningly wrought." Both Keats and Shelley use the word. Other English poets who mention Daedalus are Chaucer, Shakespeare, and Auden.

See also: ARIADNE; CULTURE HERO: MINOS; OVID; PASIPHAË; PERDIX; TALUS

**Daemon** (spirit)   In Greek mythology, a supernatural being, part god and part man. Daemons were believed to be guiding spirits of people assigned to them by Zeus. Agathodaemas (good demon) was the name of the good spirit of rural prosperity and of vineyards. The Romans called the male individual spirit Genius (procreator), the female Juno (youth). The word is the source for the English word *demon*.

See also: AGATHODAEMON; GENIUS; JUNO

**Daena** (Din, Dino)   In Persian mythology, an angel, the personification of Zoroastrian law and religion, who presides over the 24th day of the month.

See also: ZARATHUSTRA

**Dagda** (Daghda) (good god?)   In Celtic mythology, Irish god of fertility, husband of Brigit or a goddess with three names—Breg (lie), Meng (guile), and Meabel (disgrace)—who bore him a daughter named Bridgit, and Bodb the Red, Ceacht, Midir, and Ogma. He possessed a magic caldron, Undry, that could feed the whole earth. Sometimes he is called the Lord of Great Knowledge because he possessed all wisdom. He was forced from his throne as king of the Tuatha de Danann (people of the goddess Danu) by his son Oengus. Dagda was portrayed holding a large club or fork, so great it had to be dragged on wheels, the symbol of his dominion over the food supply.

See also: AENGUS OG; BOANN; BRIGIT; DANU; TUATHA DE DANNAN

0899

**Dagon** (corn, grain)    In Near Eastern mythology (Canaanite), vegetation god worshiped by the Philistines.

The Old Testament records three incidents that portray the encounter between the worship of Dagon and of the Hebrew deity Yahweh. The first (Judg. 16:29–30) tells how the hero Samson destroyed the temple of Dagon by taking "hold of the two middle pillars upon which the house stood, and on which it was borne up, of the one with his right hand, and of the other with his left. . . . And he bowed himself with all his might; and the house fell upon the lords, and upon all the people that were therein."

The second episode (1 Sam. 5:3–4) tells how the Philistines at Ashdod were killed when the Ark of God, which contained the tablets of the law, was taken into the temple of Dagon and placed by Dagon's image.

"And when they of Ashdod arose early on the morrow, behold, Dagon was fallen upon his face to the earth before the ark of the Lord. And they took Dagon, and set him in his place again. And when they arose early on the morrow morning, behold, Dagon was fallen upon his face to the ground before the ark of the Lord; and the head of Dagon and both the palms of his hands were cut off upon the threshold; only the stump of Dagon was left to him."

In *Paradise Lost* (book 1) Milton refers to this biblical episode when he turns Dagon into a fallen angel:

. . . Next came one
Who mourn'd in earnest, when the captive
  Ark

Maim'd his brute image, head and hands lopt
  off
In his own Temple, on the grunsel edge,
Where he fell flat, and sham'd his
  Worshipers:
Dagon his Name, Sea Monster, upward Man
And downward Fish: . . .

Milton's description of Dagon as half fish, half man is incorrect. The poet may have borrowed it from an earlier work by Alexander Ross called *Pansebeia, or A View of All Religions of the World*, which gives such a description. Modern scholars, however, discredit this image of the god, which goes back to St. Jerome, who believed the word *Dagon* was related to "fish," not "grain," as is now known.

First Chronicles (10:10) supplies the last Old Testament episode. It tells how King Saul was killed at Mount Gilboa and his head fastened "in the temple of Dagon."

See also: ARK OF THE COVENANT; JEROME, ST.; SAUL; SOLOMON; YAHWEH

0900

**Dagonet**    In Arthurian legend, King Arthur's fool. One day Sir Dagonet came to Cornwall with two squires. As they drew near a well, Sir Tristram soused them and made them mount their horses and amid jeers ride off dripping wet. Malory in *Morte d'Arthur* writes that "King Arthur loved Sir Dagonet passing well, and made him a knight, with his own hands; and at every tournament he made King Arthur laugh." Tennyson, however, in "The Last Tournament," one of the *Idylls of the King*, says Sir Gwain made Dagonet "mock-knight of Arthur's Table Round."

See also: ARTHUR; GWAIN; ROUND TABLE

0901

**Dagr** (day)    In Norse mythology, the day, son of Nott (night) and Delling (dayspring). Dagr's horse is Skinfaxi. Dagr and Nott had a horse and carriage that went around the earth once a day. Dagr appears in the *Prose Edda*.

See also: NOTT; *PROSE EDDA*; SKINFAXI

*Amida Buddha*

0902

**Daibutsu** (great Buddha) In Japanese Buddhist art, name given to several large bronze images of the Buddhas; the most famous, Amida Buddha, some 49 feet, 7 inches in height, located at Kamakura. The work was erected in 1252 and housed in a temple. The temple has been destroyed twice; after the second destruction it was not rebuilt.

See also: BUDDHAS

0903

**Daikoku** In Japanese Shinto-Buddhist mythology, god of wealth, portrayed as a short, stout man standing or sitting on two bales of rice, with a large wooden mallet in his right hand and a bag with a nonvegetable treasure slung over his left

shoulder. The god's "lucky mallet" is capable of bestowing wealth with one stroke. Daikoku is the guardian of farmers and is always good-natured and cheerful. He is one of the Shichi Fukujin, the seven gods of good luck or fortune.

See also: SHICHI FUKUJIN

0904

**Dai Mokuren** In Japanese mythology, one of the disciples of the Buddha. Seeing the soul of his mother in the Hell of Hungry Spirits, Dai Mokuren sent her some food, which became transformed into flames and blazing embers as she lifted it to her lips. He asked the Buddha for an explanation and was told that in her previous life his mother had refused food to a wandering mendicant priest. The only way to obtain her release from perpetual hunger was to feed, on the tenth day of the seventh month, the souls of all of the great priests of all countries. Notwithstanding the difficulty of this undertaking, Dai Mokuren succeeded, and in his joy at seeing his mother relieved, he started to dance. This performance is said to be the origin of the Japanese *Bon Odori*, dances that take place during the Festival of the Dead, variously scheduled in different regions but usually mid-July and mid-August.

0905

**Daisy** (day's eye, from O.E. *daeges eaye*) A small wildflower with white and yellow blossoms. The flower closes its lashes and goes to sleep when the sun sets, only to awaken, opening its eyes, in the morning. In Roman mythology, the daisy was formed when the nymph Belides escaped being raped by Vertumnus, god of orchards, by being transformed into a daisy. In Christian legend St. Mary Magdalene, repenting her sinful life, shed tears that fell to earth and became daisies. In European folk medicine the daisy was used to cure ulcers, madness, and chest wounds. The daisy root, according to legend, will stunt growth.

See also: MARY MAGDALENE; VERTUMNUS

*Daisy (Walter Crane)*

0906

**Daityas**   In Hindu mythology, giants who inhabit Patala, the lowest region of the underworld. They warred against the gods and interfered with sacrifices.

See also: DITI

0907

**Dajoji**   In North American Indian mythology (Iroquois), the panther, god of the west wind; his snarl makes even the sun hide its face.

0908

**Dakhma** (Dahkma)   Tower of Silence in Zoroastrian funeral rites, where the bodies of the dead are left to be eaten by vultures. A corpse is regarded as unclean and therefore not fit to be buried in the earth, which it would defile, or burned in fire, which would also be defiled.

See also: ZARATHUSTRA

0909

**Dakinis** (sky goer)   In Tibetan Buddhism, eight goddess assistants who are probably metamorphoses of the "eight mothers." They encircle the heavens and appear in many of the magic circles. They are Lasya, of white complexion, holding a mirror in a coquettish attitude; Mala, of yellow color, holding a rosary, called *pren-ba-ma*; Git, of red color, holding a lyre; Gar-ma, of green color, dancing; Pushpa, of white color, holding a flower, also called Me-tog-ma; Dhupa, of yellow color, holding an incense vase, also called bDug-spos ma; Dipa, of red color, holding a lamp; Gandha, of green color, holding a shell vase of perfume, also called Dri-ch'a-ma.

0910

**Daksha** (able)   In Hindu mythology, a Prajapati, one of the sons of the god Brahma; he sprang from his father's right thumb. Daksha's first attempt at populating the world was unsuccessful. A thousand sons were born to him by his wife, Asikni, but they did not produce any offspring. Another thousand sons, by the same wife, also did not produce any offspring. In all, 5,000 children were born, called Haryaswas. With Asikni he also had 24, 50, or 60 daughters. He gave 13 to Kasyapa, who then became the mother of the gods, demons, men, birds, serpents, and all living things.

In Indian art Daksha is portrayed with a goat head. One day, according to one account, he insulted the god Shiva, who was his son-in-law. Shiva, in anger, changed Daksha's head to that of a goat, a perpetual sign of stupidity. Ironically, Daksha's name means "able," "competent," or "intelligent."

See also: BRAHMA; KASYAPA; SHIVA

0911

**Dalai Lama** (great ocean Lama)   In Tibetan Buddhism, the spiritual and temporal head, who is regarded as an incarnation of Avalokiteshvara, one of the five Dhyani-Bodhisattvas. He is called in Tibet Gyal-wa Rin-po-che'e (the gem of majesty; victory). The Panchen Lama (learned Lama) ranks second after the Dalai Lama and is considered an incarnation of Amitabha, the Buddha of Infinite Light. The Panchen Lama, being a Buddha, is spiritually superior to the Dalai Lama. But since a Buddha is not involved in the temporal process, but a Bodhisattva is, the Dalai Lama is temporally superior to the Panchen Lama. Together, each has the superiority of *primus inter pares*, as did the kings of old Tibet.

See also: AVALOKITESHVARA; AMITABHA; DHYANI-BODHISATTVAS

0912

**Dambhodbhava**    In the Hindu epic poem *The Mahabharata*, a king who was punished for his pride. Dambhodbhava had an overweening conceit about his own powers. He was told, however, by his priests that he was no match for two sages, Nara and Narayana, who were living as ascetics on the Gandha-madana Mountain. Puffed up with pride, the king went with his army and challenged Nara and Narayana. Nara at first tried to dissuade Dambhodbhava, but the king insisted on fighting. Nara then took a handful of straws and, using them as missiles, sent them through the air, penetrating the eyes, ears, and noses of the king's army. Defeated, Dambhodbhava fell at Nara's feet and begged him for peace.

See also: *MAHABHARATA, THE*

0913

**Damkina** (Dauke, Dawkina) (rightful wife)    In Near Eastern mythology (Babylonian-Assyrian), earth goddess married to Enki, lord of the good place. She was probably one of the manifestations of the Great Goddess.

See also: ENKI; GREAT GODDESS

0914

**Damon and Pythias** (tamer and discoverer)    Fourth century B.C.E. In Greek legend, two male lovers, believed to be Pythagorean philosophers. Pythias plotted against the Sicilian tyrant Dionysius and was condemned to death. He was allowed to return home first to arrange his affairs. Damon then offered to take his place as a hostage, even to suffer death if necessary. Dionysius was so moved by this offer that he pardoned the two men.

See also: DIONYSIUS

0915

**Danaans**    In Greek mythology and legend, name given to the subjects of King Danaus of Argos. The name was then applied to all Greeks. Homer never uses the word *Greek* in his writings but calls the people Achaeans, Argives, and Danaans. Sometimes Ovid and Vergil use *Danai* for Greeks.

See also: ARGIVES; OVID

0916

**Danaë** (laurel, bay)    In Greek mythology, mother of the hero Perseus; daughter of King Acrisius of Argos and Eurydice; sister of Evarete. Acrisius had been told by an oracle that one day his daughter would bear a son who would kill him. Acrisius locked Danaë in a bronze chamber, either in a tower or underground. Zeus, always ready to sleep with a beautiful young girl, came to Danaë in the form of a golden shower (urine) and fathered Perseus. The king, however, refused to believe his daughter's son was fathered by Zeus. He shut Danaë and the boy in a chest and had it cast into the sea. It floated safely to the island of Seriphus and was found by Dictys, a fisherman. He took care of Perseus until the lad was grown. Polydectes, brother of Dictys and king of the island, fell in love with Danaë, who did not return his love. To more easily pursue Danaë, Polydectes sent Perseus to fetch the head of Medusa, hoping the young man would be killed. Danaë went into hiding until Perseus returned with Medusa's head. In anger at being sent on the expedition, Perseus showed the head to Polydectes and his guests at a banquet, and they all turned to stone. He then took his mother back to Argos. Homer's *Iliad* (book 14), Vergil's *Aeneid* (book 7), and Ovid's *Metamorphoses* (book 10) all cite the myth. Numerous Renaissance paintings portray Danaë and the Golden Shower as an opportunity to be both erotic and learned. Among the artists who treated the subject are Titian, Correggio, Tintoretto, and Rembrandt. Richard Strauss's opera *Die Liebe der Danaë* also deals with the myth.

See also: *AENEID, THE*; ACRISIUS; DANAË; EURYDICE; *ILIAD, THE*; OVID; PERSEUS; ZEUS

**0917**

**Danaidae**    In Greek mythology, the 50 daughters of Danaus who married the 50 sons of Aegyptus, Danaus's brother. Among the women were Calaeno, Exato, Eurydice, Glauce, and Hypermnestra. On their wedding night, 49 of the women killed their husbands. As punishment they were condemned to draw water with a sieve in Hades. Only one, Hypermnestra, saved her husband, Lynceus. Aeschylus's *The Suppliant Maidens* and Chaucer's *Legend of Good Women* draw on the myth.

See also: AEGYPTUS; CHAUCER; HADES

**0918**

**Danavas**    In Hindu mythology, giants who warred against the gods. They are descendants of Danu by the sage Kasyapa, and they live in Patala, the lowest region of the underworld.

See also: KASYAPA

**0919**

**Danbhalah Houé-Do** (Damballa, Damballah, Damballa Wédo, Dan-Gbe)    In Haitian voodoo, major serpent god, the oldest of the loas (deified spirits of the dead). His symbol is a snake, arched in the path of the sun as it travels across the sky. Sometimes half of the arch is made up of his female counterpart, Ayida, the rainbow. He has his origin in the West African divine python or Rainbow Snake Dan Ayido Hwedo. He is often identified in Haitian voodoo belief with St. Patrick of Christian legend because the saint is often pictured with a snake at his feet. He is one of the most powerful of the

loa, and he governs snakes and floods. He can also afflict people with disease or cure them.

See also: AYIDA; LOA; PATRICK, ST.; RAINBOW SNAKE

*Dance of Death*

**0920**

**Dance of Death** (French: *Danse macabre*; German: *Totentanz*)    A medieval series of woodcuts or paintings depicting Death claiming his victims. The series portrays Death taking people from all walks of life, from peasant to pope. The theme became popular in the late 15th century in Germany and spread to other European countries. A series of woodcuts by Hans Holbein the Younger was published in 1538. Liszt's *Totentanz* (dance of death) is a work for piano and orchestra that uses the medieval sequence "Dies Irae" as its theme. Saint-Saëns's symphonic poem *Danse Macabre* is a short work dealing with the subject. An Ingmar Bergman film, *The Seventh Seal*, also used the motif.

**0921**

**Danh**    In Haitian voodoo, a loa (deified spirit of the dead) who brings good fortune and money; symbolized by a horned and coiled snake.

See also: LOA

0922

**Daniel** (God is my judge)   In the Bible, O.T., one of the Four Major Prophets, the others being Isaiah, Jeremiah, and Ezekiel; title of one of the books of the Bible, placed among the Hagiographa (sacred writings) in Hebrew Scriptures but among the prophets in the King James Version.

Daniel was a captive at the court of Nebuchadnezzar and was called Belshazzar. He interpreted Nebuchadnezzar's dream by telling the king that the great beast of gold, silver, brass, iron, and clay in the dream represented the gradual disintegration of the kingdoms to come after him. Interpreting another dream, Daniel told Nebuchadnezzar of his future madness. Through his skill Daniel, as well as his friends Shadrach, Meshach, and Abednego, rose in power in the court. Because they were Jews, they refused to worship Nebuchadnezzar's golden idol, and Daniel's three young friends were cast into the fiery furnace but were not consumed by the flames. Later Daniel interpreted the writing on the wall for King Belshazzar, Nebuchadnezzar's son, in which the king's death was predicted. The king's successor, Darius, gave Daniel a high position in his court. Other courtiers, jealous of Daniel, persuaded Darius to have Daniel thrown into the lion's den, but God closed the mouth of the lion, and Daniel remained unharmed. Daniel also appears in the Old Testament Apocrypha in the tales of Bel and the Dragon and Susanna. In Christian art Daniel is seen as the prophet of justice. Daniel also had visions, which are recounted in the second half of the Book of Daniel. Rembrandt painted *The Vision of Daniel*.

See also: BELSHAZZAR; EZEKIEL; ISAIAH; JEREMIAH; NEBUCHADNEZZAR

0923

**Danu**   In Celtic mythology, mother goddess, sometimes identified with the goddess Anu (Ana) among the Irish Celts. Danu was the daughter of King Dagda and ancestress of the Tuatha de Da-nann, the people and gods of the goddess Danu. In British Celtic mythology Danu is known as Don, her children as the Children of Don. When she is identified with the goddess Anu (scholars do not agree on whether the two are the same goddess), she is known as a goddess of prosperity and abundance to whom human sacrifices were made. The name Anu clings to two breast-shaped mountains near Killarney, Ireland, which are called the Paps of Anu, indicating her role as a mother goddess.

See also: ANU; DAGDA; TUATHA DE DANANN

0924

**Daphne** (bay, laurel)   In Greek mythology, a mountain nymph, daughter of the river god Peneus (or Ladon). She was dedicated to Artemis, the virgin goddess, and spurned all men. Apollo fell in love with her, pursued her, and lost her when she cried for help, and her father transformed her into a laurel. Embracing its trunk, Apollo said its leaves would be ever green, and later he wore laurel leaves as a crown. The myth is told in Ovid's *Metamorphoses* (book 1), alluded to by Chaucer and Milton, painted by Giorgione, Pollaivolo, Poussin, and Tiepolo, and sculpted by Bernini. Richard Strauss also told the story in his opera *Daphne*.

See also: APOLLO; ARTEMIS; CHAUCER; LADON; LAUREL; NYMPHS

0925

**Daphnis** (laurel)   In Greek mythology, inventor of bucolic poetry; a son of Hermes by a Sicilian nymph. He was exposed to die but was saved by shepherds and taught by Pan to play the flute and sing. Daphnis fell in love with Piplea (variant names for the naiad are Lyce, Nais, Nomia, and Xenea), entered a contest to win her hand, and was about to lose when Heracles killed his rival, Lityerses. In a variant myth, Daphnis promised Piplea he would never fall in love with another woman. Daphnis broke his promise and was punished by the Muses with blindness. He died when he refused to eat after his five hunting dogs died. He has no connection with the myth of Daphnis and Chloe.

See also: DAPHNIS AND CLOE; HERMES; HERAQ-CLES; NYMPHS; PAN

0926

**Daphnis and Chlöe** (laurel and bright green) In Greek and Latin mythology, a romance by Longus (third century C.E.) of Daphnis, a young shepherd, and Chlöe, a shepherdess. They lived on the island of Lesbos. The tale is a pastoral story about the maturing of love. The theme was a favorite in 17th- and 18th-century France and England and inspired Ravel's ballet *Daphnis and Chlöe (1910)*. Daphnis is also the name of a Sicilian shepherd in pastoral poetry, credited with the invention of the genre. He was blinded by the Muses and later died for love. He appears in Theocritus and in Vergil's *Eclogues*. Daphnis is also the name of a shepherd on Mount Ida transformed to stone by a jealous nymph. Ovid's *Metamorphoses* (book 4) tells the tale.

0927

**Darana**   In Australian mythology, the rainmaker who causes rain to fall by singing. Once when Darana sang, so much rain fell that the earth was flooded. He placed his throwing stick in the waters, and they receded. As a result of the rainfall, flowers and witchetty grubs bloomed in the desert. Darana picked them, placed them in bags, and hung them on trees. Finished with his work, he went on a journey. But two youths, the Dara-ulu, spotted the bags and threw their boomerangs at them, causing them to break and scatter to the winds. Dust seemed to cover the whole earth and obscure the sun. When the Muramura spirits saw what was happening, they came down and killed the two boys. Darana restored the youths to life, only to have them killed a second time and transformed into heart-shaped stones. Heart-shaped stones are still used in rainmaking ceremonies. It is believed that if these stones are destroyed the earth would be covered with red dust.

0928

**Dardanus** (burner-up)   In Greek mythology, prime ancestor of the Trojans, son of Zeus and Electra; brother of Iasim; married to Chryse and after her death to Bateia (Arisbe); father of Erichthonius and Ilus and of Herophile by Neso. He founded Dardania, which later became Troy, at the foot of Mount Ida. He is mentioned in Vergil's *Aeneid* (book 5) and Homer's *Iliad* (book 20). The mares of Dardanus are mares from which Boreas, who changed himself into a horse, later fathered 12 steeds that could not be overtaken.

See also: *AENEID, THE;* BOREAS; ELECTRA; *ILIAD, THE;* ZEUS

0929

**David** (well beloved)   c. 1085–1015 B.C.E. In the Bible, O.T., second king of Israel, youngest son of Jesse, of the tribe of Judah, settled in or near Bethlehem.

David was a handsome youth who was chosen by Yahweh (the Hebrew cult god) to replace King Saul, with whom Yahweh was displeased. Samuel the prophet anointed David with his horn of oil in the midst of his other brothers. David first won a place at Saul's court by playing the harp to ease Saul, who was being tormented by an evil spirit sent by Yahweh. Later, David killed the giant Goliath with a single stone from his slingshot. After cutting off the giant's head, David brought it to Saul as a trophy. When Jonathan, Saul's son, saw David, he fell in love with him and defended him when Saul wanted to have him murdered. David fled and gathered a following of men after Saul himself tried to murder him with a javelin. David's wife, Michal, one of Saul's daughters, let David out through the window of their house. She put a pillow of goat's hair in the bed and pretended David was sick. Fleeing to the fields, he met Jonathan, who warned him he must flee for his life. The two men parted, promising love and friendship forever. From then until Saul's death, David lived the life of an outlaw. Three times David had the opportunity to kill

Saul but refused. Saul was "the anointed king of God." (This passage was used by later Christian kings as authority against any form of sedition.) Finally, Saul and his son Jonathan were killed by the Philistines, and David lamented their deaths, saying, "I am distressed for thee, my brother Jonathan: very pleasant hast thou been unto me: thy love to me was wonderful, passing the love of woman" (2 Sam. 1:26). David then recaptured the Ark (in which Yahweh lived) and brought it to Jerusalem amid shouts of great joy. David even danced before the Ark, which upset his wife, Michal, whom he then had locked up, never sleeping with her again. One of David's hero warriors, Uriah the Hittite, had a wife, Bathsheba, whom David saw bathing from his rooftop. David lusted after her and committed adultery with her. He then caused her husband's death by sending him into battle and then took Bathsheba as one of his wives. As punishment for David's sin, Yahweh caused the first child of David and Bathsheba to die. After David's penitence, a second child was born and was named Solomon. When David grew old and was no longer able to have sexual intercourse, a successor was sought, and after much court intrigue, Solomon was chosen.

Medieval Christianity took the various incidents from David's life and tied them into Christian belief. David was viewed as a type of prefiguration of Christ, who descended from David. Various events in David's life were given a Christian interpretation. David's slaying of the lion and bear (1 Sam. 17:32–37) was seen as a prefiguration of Christ's victory over Satan. David's slaying of Goliath (1 Sam. 17:38–51) was a prefiguration of Christ's temptation in the desert by the devil, and the triumph of David after Goliath's defeat (1 Sam. 18:6–7) was viewed as a prefiguration of Christ's entry into Jerusalem. Even the episode of David and Bathsheba (2 Samuel 11:4, 5) was seen as a prefiguration of Christ (David) and the Church (Bathsheba).

Medieval art usually portrayed David playing the harp. Among some famous works are Michelangelo's statue, Caravaggio's *David with the Head of Goliath*, Rembrandt's *David Playing the Harp for Saul*, and Honegger's cantata *Le Roi David*, a popular musical setting of part of David's legend. In Islamic legend David is called Dawvd, the king to whom Allah revealed the Zabur, or Book of Psalms.

See also: GOLIATH; JONATHAN; SAMUEL; SAUL; SOLOMON; YAHWEH

*David and Bathsheba*

0930
**David, St.** (beloved of Yahweh)    Sixth century. In Christian legend, patron saint of Wales. Feast, 1 March.

David was the son of Xantus, prince of Cereticu (Cardiganshire), but he was brought up a priest and became an ascetic on the Isle of Wight. He established a strict rule, founded some 12 monasteries, and even visited Jerusalem. He was a defender of the Catholic faith against the monk Pelagius, who denied Original Sin and said men could be good without grace from God. Various legends surround the saint. One is that when the blind priest who baptized David was touched with some of the baptismal water, which David splashed in his eyes, the priest regained his sight. Another tells how a hill on which he stood rose so that all of the crowds could hear him preach. A white dove is said to have appeared on his shoulder. He lived on leeks and water and was called "the waterman." Geoffrey of Monmouth, in his *History of the Kings of Britain*, writes that David was the uncle of King Arthur. David's name is also given as Dewi Sant.

See also: ARTHUR

0931

**David of Sassoun**   Armenian epic poem compiled in the 19th century from oral and written
sources. The epic consists of four cycles.

*Sanassar and Baghdassar*: Once King Senakerim besieged the city of Jerusalem, but his troops
were killed by angels sent by God to punish the
pagan king. He vowed that if he could safely escape the city, he would sacrifice his own sons
when he reached his native land. Senakerim's
wife, who was secretly a Christian, learned of the
vow and warned her two sons, Sanassar and
Baghdassar. They fled the country disguised as
servants. They found a place to stay with the king
of Kraput-Koch. One day, to test the young
men, the king asked them to fight his soldiers.
Accepting the challenge, Sanassar and Baghdassar defeated the men, and as a result they were
told to leave the land. They would not leave unless the king granted them land and workmen to
build a city. The wish was granted, and they built
Sassoun. The king also gave his daughter as a
wife to Sanassar.

The god of King Senakerim, however, would
not let the king forget his vow of sacrificing his
two sons. Each night the god appeared to the
king in his sleep in the form of a goat. Knowing
what the king would do, Baghdassar decided to
return home. When he arrived, his father took
him to the idol of the god to sacrifice him. Baghdassar asked Senakerim to show him how to bow
to the god. Complying, the king knelt down,
whereupon the son cut off his head. Baghdassar
was then crowned king.

*David of Sassoun*: The main hero of the poem,
David of Sassoun, is one of the sons of King
Baghdassar. He is noted for his strength and for
the oaken stick with which he performs many
feats.

David, along with a friend, took care of the
calves. One day the devs, half-demon, half-men
monsters, came and drove away the calves. David
followed their tracks to the entrance of a cave
and paused. He cried out with so loud a voice
that the devs became frightened and "were as full

of fear as is the devil when Christ's voice is heard
in hell."

When the leader of the devs heard the voice,
he said: "That is surely David, the son of Baghdassar. Go receive him with honor, else he will
strike us dead."

They went out, one by one, and David struck
them with his oak cudgel as they passed, so that
their heads fell off. He then cut off the ears of all
40 devs and buried them at the mouth of the
cave. When he entered the cave, he found heaps
of gold and silver.

Numerous other exploits of the hero are narrated. David was killed by one of the illegitimate
children of his father, Baghdassar, a girl who was
not a Christian but a Muslim.

*Lion-Mher*: This cycle tells of the hero Lion-
Mher, who fought single-handed against the
Turks.

*Davith-Mher*: This cycle contains the tale of
Davith-Mher, who married the queen of Egypt
and had a son, Misra-Malik.

See also: DEVS AND HAMBARUS; GOAT

0932

**Dayunsi** (beaver's grandchild)   In North
American Indian mythology (Cherokee), the little water beetle that helped form the earth. The
earth was a great island floating in a sea of water.
It was suspended at each of the four cardinal
points by a cord hanging down from the sky
vault, which was of solid rock. When all was water, the animals were above, in Galunlati, beyond
the arch. But it was very crowded, and there was
no more room. They wondered what was below
the water. At last Dayunsi offered to go and see
what he could learn. He darted in every direction
over the surface of the water but could find no
firm place to rest. Then he dived to the bottom
and came up with some soft mud, which began to
grow and spread on every side until it became an
island that is now the earth. It was afterward fastened to the sky with four cords.

See also: EARTH DIVER

0933

**Dazhbog** (Dazbog, Dazdbog) (giving god)   In Slavic mythology, sun god, son of Swarog, the sky god, and brother of Svarogich, the fire god.

According to one myth, Svarog became tired of reigning over the universe and passed on his power to his sons, Dazhbog and Svarogich. Dazhbog lived in the East, the land of eternal summer, in a golden palace from which he emerged every day in a chariot drawn by white horses that breathed fire. Some accounts say the chariot was drawn by three horses, others say 12. The chariot is described as golden with diamonds, and the horses as white with golden manes.

Among the Serbians, Dazhbog was believed to be a handsome young king who ruled over the 12 kingdoms of the Zodiac and lived with two beautiful maidens, the Zoyra. One maiden was the Aurora of the Dawn; the other, the Aurora of the Evening. In some myths the two sisters were accompanied by two stars—the morning star, Zvezda Dennitsa, and the evening star, Vechernyaya Zvezda—who help the Zorya in tending the horses of the sun god. In the Russian epic poem *The Lay of Igor's Army*, Prince Vladimir and the Russians call themselves the "grandchildren of Dazhbog." In other Slavic folklore, however, Dabog or Dajbog, variants of Dazhbog, are names applied to a devil-like creature that opposes God. In 933, when Vladimir married Anna and became Christian, the huge statue of Dazhbog was thrown into the river along with other pagan deities. Sometimes Dazhbog is identified with Chors, a Russian sun god.

See also: AURORA; *LAY OF IGOR'S ARMY, THE*; SVAROGICH; VLADIMIR, ST.

0934

**Deborah** (a bee)   In the Bible, O.T., a Hebrew prophetess and judge of Israel (Judges 4:4), wife of Lapidoth. She called Barak to fight against King Jabin, prophesied success, and accompanied him in the battle against Sisera, captain of Jabin's army. Her triumphant song (Judges 5) is

one of the oldest writings in the Bible. Handel's oratorio *Deborah* deals with the prophet.

0935

**Decius Mus**   Fourth century B.C.E. In Roman history and legend, general who sacrificed his life to save his army. Decius dreamed that to win a battle the general of one army had to kill himself. To save his army he went into battle alone and was killed. Livy's *History of Rome* (book 8) tells the tale. Rubens left a series of oil sketches of the legend.

See also: LIVY

0936

**Deert**   In Australian mythology, the moon god, who punished animals with death. Only he, Deert, would be able to die and return to life again.

0937

**Deianira**   In Greek mythology, second wife of Heracles; daughter of Dionysus (or Oeneus) and Althaea; half-sister of Gorge, Meleager, and Toxeus; mother of Ctesippus, Hyllus, and Macaria. She accidentally killed Heracles when she sent him, by the centaur Nessus, a garment soaked in poisoned blood, which she believed would renew Heracles' love for her. Ovid's *Metamorphoses* (book 9) and Chaucer's The Monk's Tale, part of *The Canterbury Tales*, all refer to the myth.

See also: CENTAURS; CHAUCER; DIONYSUS; HERACLES; OVID

0938

**Deidamia** (taker of spoil)   In Greek mythology, mistress of Achilles; daughter of Lycomedes, king of Scyros; mother of Neoptolemus (Pyrrhus). She was seduced by Achilles when he hid on the island of Scyros disguised as a woman. A second Deidamia was the daughter of Bellerophon and Philonoe; sister of Hippolochus, Isander, and Laodameia; married to Evander;

and mother of Dyna, Pallantia, Pallas, Roma, and Sarpedon II. A third bearing the name was a daughter of Amyntor and Cleobule; sister of Crantor and Phoenix.

See also: ACHILLES; EVANDER; PALLAS; SARPEDON

0939

**Deino** (terrible)    In Greek mythology, daughter of Phorcys and Ceto; one of the three Graeae—the others being Enyo and Pephredo—who were guardians of the Gorgons. They had one eye and one tooth among the three of them.

See also: GRAEAE; GORGONS

0940

**Deirdre** (Deidrie, Deidra, Deidre, Dierdrie) (diminutive of *der*, daughter)    In Celtic mythology, a great heroine. The many retellings of the story have made her one of the best-known figures from Celtic mythology around the world.

Felim, a lord of Ulster, invited King Conor (Conchuber) to a feast. During the festivities a messenger brought word of the birth of a daughter to Felim. Then Cathbad, the king's Druid, said: "The infant shall be fairest among the women of Erin and shall wed a king, but because of her, death and ruin shall come on the prince of Ulster."

King Conor sought to avert the doom by sending the child, called Deirdre, with her nurse, Lavarcam, to a solitary place in the wood. Here she was visited by the king, who intended to wed her when she was of marriageable age. The girl saw no other except the Druid, Cathbad.

One winter's day, however, near the bridal day, Deirdre saw upon the white snow the blood of a newly slain calf and a raven lapping it. She told her nurse that she wished to wed a man with hair as black as the raven's wing, a cheek as red as the calf's blood, and skin as white as the snow. Her description fit Naisi (Naois), a member of the Red, or Ulster, branch of King Conor's household. The nurse then, upon the pleading of Deirdre, took the girl to meet Naisi. Deirdre's

beauty so overwhelmed Naisi that he fled with her to Scotland. Naisi then took service with the king of the Picts. However, after seeing Deirdre, the king wanted her for himself. Therefore, Deirdre, Naisi, his two brothers, Arden and Allen, and the nurse fled to shelter in Glen Etive.

Years passed, and King Conor, promising not to avenge the wrong done to him, invited Naisi, his brothers, and Deirdre to return. With misgivings, Deirdre came. Naisi and his two brothers were killed by Owen, who cut off their heads. Deirdre was then taken by the king to live at Emain Macha. A year passed, and the king asked Deirdre what she hated most.

"Thou thyself and Owen," she replied. So King Conor sent Deirdre to Owen for a year, but on the way she threw herself from the chariot against a rock and died.

In one variant of the myth, Deirdre sees the bodies of the three dead brothers being buried. She sits on the edge of the grave, constantly asking the grave diggers to dig the pit wide and free. When the bodies are put in the grave, she says:

Come over hither, Naisi, my love,
Let Arden close to Allen lie;
If the dead had any sense to feel,
Ye would have made a place for Deirdre.

The men do as she asks them. She then jumps into the grave and dies.

Two great Irish playwrights took up the myth of Deirdre. William Butler Yeats wrote a tragedy, *Deirdre*, about the last day in the life of the lovers, and John Millington Synge wrote *Deirdre of the Sorrows*. Black, white, and red symbolism is a well-known motif in folk literature.

See also: DRUIDS; MOTIF

0941

**Dekanawida** (two river currents flowing together)    16th century. In North American Indian history and legend, hero, one of the founders of the Iroquois Confederacy with Hiawatha, credited with supernatural powers.

According to legend he was born of a virgin mother. Warned before his birth that he would bring ruin upon her people, the Hurons, Dekanawida's mother tried to drown her child. She threw the child through a hole in the ice three times, but the morning after each attempt, she found him lying next to her, safe and sound. Dekanawida grew to manhood quickly and left home. Before he left, he placed an otter skin on the wall, hanging by its tail. He told his mother that if he died a violent death the skin would vomit blood.

Hiawatha enlisted Dekanawida's help in his plan for the unity of Indian nations, known as the "League of the Long House," and the two worked until it was achieved. In some accounts Dekanawida is credited with the idea and became the confederacy's law-giver.

See also: HIAWATHA

**0942**

**Delilah** (languishing)   In the Bible, O.T., a Philistine woman who seduced Samson into revealing the secret of his strength, which lay in his hair. She cut his hair so that he could be captured by the Philistines (Judges 16). Delilah appears in Rembrandt's painting of Samson as well as in Saint-Saëns' opera *Samson et Dalila*.

See also: SAMSON

**0943**

**Delos** (clear)   In Greek legend, a small island in the Cyclades, where Apollo and Artemis were born on Mount Cynthos. Poseidon raised it from the sea as a place of refuge for their mother, Leto, to escape the wrath of Hera, the ever-jealous wife of Zeus. Referring to their birthplace, Apollo was sometimes called Delius, and Artemis was called Delia. Delos's king was Anius.

See also: ANIUS; APOLLO; ARTEMIS; HERA; LETO; POSEIDON; ZEUS

**0944**

**Delphi** (from Delphus, a son of Apollo; dolphin?)   In Greek history and mythology, a town of Phocis at the foot of Mount Parnassus. Delphi was famous for its oracle and temple to Apollo. Delphi was believed to be the center of the earth. The *omphalos* (navel stone) was kept there. At Apollo's temple was the inscription "know thyself and honor the god" which came to mean seek self-understanding, though originally it meant: "Know that I, Apollo, am immortal, and you are mortal and must die." According to Greek myth, Apollo killed Python, the Chthonic deity who guarded the site, and then set up a shrine to himself. The name Pytho is popularly derived from *pythein*, "to rot," but was more likely itself derived from the process of aquiring information from the oracle, as seen in the verb *pynthanein*, "to discover by inquiry." The Delphic oracle was the most authoritative in the ancient Mediterranean world. It is believed that the various buildings of Delphi were destroyed by Alaric and the Goths in 396 C.E.

The Homeric *Hymn to Apollo* (a work ascribed to Homer but not by him) describes the contest between Apollo and Python. Pausanias's *Description of Greece* (book 10) describes the site. Often in English poetry Delphi is confused with Delos, the smallest island of the Cyclades, sacred to Apollo, who was born there along with his sister Artemis. Milton's *Ode on the Morning of Christ's Nativity* compounds Delphi and Delos into Delphos. This was a common mistake of writers of the Middle Ages and passed on to later writers.

See also: APOLLO; ARTEMIS; CHTHONIAN GODS; DELOS; HOMER; OMPHALE; PAUSANIAS

**0945**

**Dem Chog**   In Tibetan Buddhism, a tutelary deity, the chief of happiness, also known as Samvara. In general, the terms devil and demon are products of early Western misunderstanding of the wrathful aspect of Tibetan deities, an obverse of their pacific aspect.

*Demeter (Ceres)*

0946

**Demeter** (barley?-mother)    In Greek mythology, Great Mother goddess, one of the 12 Olympian deities, daughter of Cronus and Rhea; mother of Plutus by Iasim and mother of Persephone by her brother Zeus; called Ceres by the Romans. Demeter was worshiped as provider of harvest and fertility. Her daughter Persephone was raped by Hades and brought to the underworld as his bride. Demeter, not knowing Persephone's fate, went in search of her. She searched for nine days before she was told by Helius, the all-seeing sun god, that Hades had abducted Persephone. Furious with Zeus for allowing the rape, Demeter, disguised as an old woman, left Olympus to seek Persephone. When she arrived at Eleusis, she was welcomed by Queen Metanira and King Celeus and tended their son Demophon. One night she held the child over a fire in order to give him immortality but was surprised in the act by the king. She then revealed her identity and commanded King Celeus to build a

temple in her honor. In the meantime, Zeus sent Iris to ask Demeter to return, but she refused. Finally, Zeus sent Hermes to the underworld to fetch Persephone, but already the girl had eaten four pomegranate seeds (fruit of the underworld), so she was allowed to spend only eight months of the year in the upper world. Returning to Olympus, Demeter left the gift of corn and the holy mysteries at Eleusis with King Celeus. She sent Triptolemus, Celeus's son, around the world to spread the knowledge of agriculture and cult. Fall and winter came to represent the time of the year when Demeter, grief-stricken over the absence of her daughter, let plant life wither. The mysteries of Eleusis were dedicated to Demeter.

Demeter appears in Hesiod, the Homeric Hymn to Demeter, Vergil's *Aeneid* (book 1), and Ovid's *Fasti* (book 4) and *Metamorphoses* (book 5). Among English poets, Tennyson's "Demeter and Persephone" is best known, but Pope, Spenser, Shakespeare, Milton, Keats, Shelley, Arnold, and Swinburne all cite the goddess, often under her Latin name, Ceres.

In Greek and Roman art, Demeter was always portrayed as a mature, clothed woman, often drawn in her chariot by serpents. The honeycomb, fruit, cow, and sow were sacred to her. Other attributes were poppies, symbolizing sleep and death; ears of corn; wheat; a basket of fruit; a torch; or a serpent shedding its skin, symbol of rebirth.

See also: *AENEID, THE;* DEMOPHON; GREAT GODDESS; HADES; IRIS; OVID; PERSEPHONE; PLUTUS; ZEUS

0947

**Demophon** (voice of the people)    In Greek mythology, joint king of Melos; son of Theseus and Phaedra or of Theseus's mistress, Antiope; half-brother or brother of Acamas; and in some accounts father of Munitus by Laodice, a daughter of King Priam. Demophon was one of the Greeks hidden in the wooden horse, and he helped steal the Palladium from Troy. After

*Priestess of Demeter*

Troy's fall he fell in love with Laodice, but on the way home from Troy he visited Thrace and fell in love with Phyllis, daughter of the king of Thrace. When he deserted her to live in Athens, she either hanged herself or was turned into an almond tree by Athena. Ovid's *Heroides* (book 2) and Chaucer's *Legend of Good Women* deal with her sad fate.

See also: ANTIOPE; ATHENA; CHAUCER; LAODICE; OVID; PHAEDRA; PHYLLIS; PRIAM; THESEUS

0948

**Dendan** In Arabic legend, a monstrous fish that dies when it eats human flesh or hears a human voice. In the tale "Abdallah the Fisherman and Abdallah the Merman" in *The Thousand and One Nights* (nights 940–946), the fat from a dendan is made into an ointment to cover Abdallah the Fisherman's body so he can live under the water when he visits his friend Abdallah the Merman. While they are undersea, a black dendan, bigger than a camel, comes near Abdallah the Fisherman, whose immediate shout in his human voice causes the monstrous fish to die instantly.

See also: *THOUSAND AND ONE NIGHTS, THE*

0949

**Deng** In African mythology (Dinka of Eastern Sudan), sky god, ancestor of the Dinka. Deng, the son of god, mediates between man and the universal spirit. The Dinka believe that in the beginning the sky was very low, so low that man had to be extremely careful when hoeing or pounding grain so as not to hit the sky. One day the greedy woman Abuk pounded more grain than she was allotted, using an especially long pestle. Deng was so angered by this that he cursed mankind, saying people would have to work harder for the fruits of the earth and in the end would also have to die.

Lightning is Deng's club, and rain and birth are manifestations of his presence. If one is struck by lightning, one is not to be mourned because it is believed that Deng has taken that person directly to himself.

See also: ABUK AND GARANG; AIWEL

0950

**Denis of France, St.** (lame god, Dionysos) Third century? In Christian legend, patron saint of Paris, along with St. Geneviève. Invoked against frenzy, headache, and strife. Feast, 9 October.

St. Denis of France is often confused with Dionysius the Areopagite, a follower of St. Paul, and Pseudo-Dionysius, a mystical writer whose dates are unknown. His legend therefore combines three personalities into one.

Dionysius was an Athenian philosopher who went to study astrology in Egypt. While he was at Heiliopolis, Christ was crucified, and he witnessed the darkness over the face of the land for three hours. He went to inquire why this had happened and eventually was converted to Christianity by St. Paul. (The time sequence in the legend makes no actual sense.) According to legend, he was present at the death of the Virgin Mary in Jerusalem as well as the martyrdom of St. Paul in Rome.

From Rome he was sent by Pope Clement to preach the gospel in France. He left with two deacons, Rusticus and Eleutherius. When he arrived in France, his name was changed to Denis. (Here again the legend tries to connect the three men.) After preaching for some time and winning many converts he was arrested along with his two deacons. At the place of execution all three were beheaded, but St. Denis took his severed head and walked all the way to Montmartre (Mount of Martyrs). Angels sang as the saint held his head. Later he was buried by St. Geneviève.

In Christian art he is portrayed as a bishop holding his severed head in his hand.

See also: ALBAN, ST.; CHERON, ST.; CRISPIN AND CRISPINIAN, STS.; PAUL, ST.; VIRGIN MARY

**Deohako**   In North American Indian mythology (Seneca), three sisters, spirits of corn, beans, and squash. They all lived on one hill. One day Onatah, the corn spirit, left in search of moisture but was attacked by the evil spirit Haghwehdaetgah, who took her to the underground. He then sent winds to destroy the two remaining sisters, who also fled. Finally, the sun saved Onatah, but she must now stand in the field, through rain and drought, never to leave again.

**Dervish and the King, The**   Moral fable by the Persian mystic poet Sadi, in *The Gulistan* (chapter 1, story 28).

A solitary dervish (holy man) was sitting in a corner of the desert when a king passed by, but he took no notice of the king. The king became angry, saying to his prime minister, "This tribe of rag weavers resembles beasts."

The prime minister went to the dervish. "The king has passed near you," he told the dervish. "Why haven't you shown him homage and respect?"

"Tell the king," the dervish replied, "to look for homage from a man who expects to benefit

from him. Kings exist for protecting subjects. Subjects do not exist for obeying kings."

See also: GULISTAN, THE

**Deucalion and Pyrrha** (new-wine sailor and fiery red)   In Greek mythology, hero and heroine of the Deluge, or Flood. Deucalion was the son of Prometheus and Hesione; married Pyrrha; father of Amphictyon, Hellen, Pandora, Protogeneia, and Thyia. Hellen was the ancestor of the Hellenes, or Greeks. Deucalion and his wife, Pyrrha, survived the world flood. They repeopled the earth by casting stones behind them that were transformed into people. Ovid's *Metamorphoses* (book 1) tells the myth. Reference is made to the myth in Giles Fletcher's *Christs Victorie and Triumph*, Milton's *Paradise Lost* (book 11), and Spenser's *Faerie Queene* (book 5).

See also: AMPHICTYON; HESIONE; OVID; PANDORA

**Deva**   In Hindu and Buddhist mythology, a term for a deity or divine being, from the Sanskrit root *div*, to shine. They are 33 in number, 11 for each of three worlds.

**Devadasi** (female slaves of the gods)   In Hinduism, dancers and courtesans who are connected with various ceremonies devoted to images of the gods, such as singing, dancing before the god when he is carried in procession, and purifying the temple floor with cow dung and water. They are considered married to the god. Every temple, based on its size, had eight or more dancers.

**Devadatta**   Fifth century B.C.E. In Buddhist legend, cousin of the Buddha, who at first was converted by the Buddha but later became his archrival. Devadatta attempted to kill the Buddha numerous times.

See also: BUDDHA, THE

0957

**Devak**  In Hindu folklore, a guardian deity or spirit, such as an animal, tree, or implement of trade. Those people having the same *devak* cannot marry, possibly suggesting that once the *devak* was a totem of a clan.

0958

**Devala**  In Hindu mythology, the personification of music as a female. The name also is used for several sages who, legend says, composed hymns for the Rig-Veda, the ancient collection of hymns to the gods.

See also: RIG-VEDA

0959

**Devarshis**  In Hinduism, sages or holy men who have attained perfection on earth and have been exalted to demigods. They live in the region of the gods.

0960

**Devils**  Demons and evil spirits, which abound in medieval Jewish, Christian, and Islamic mythology.

In the Hebrew Old Testament, Satan is not the devil. He is the "adversary," part of God's heavenly host. This is shown in the Book of Job. Satan tempts Job, destroying his family and goods, but only with the permission of God. When Job cries out for justice, he does not condemn Satan, but God himself (Job 9:21–24). As Judaism developed, coming into contact with many pagan cults, Satan took on more of the attributes we know as belonging to the devil. By the time of the New Testament, Satan was generally regarded as an evil demon or ruler of demons (Matt. 12:24–28). He not only controls the body but also has power over spiritual nature, being called "prince of the world" (John 16:11) and

even "god of the world" (2 Cor. 4:4). All of these New Testament quotes reflect the Jewish belief of that time.

In Christianity the belief in the corporeal existence of the devil assumed its greatest force during the Middle Ages. St. Thomas Aquinas believed in devils, witches, incubi, and succubi. When he wrote a commentary on the Book of Job, he identified the monster Behemoth as the devil and concluded that the devil could have intercourse with humans. When the devil assumed a female form (succubus), he seduced men. When he assumed a male form (incubus), he impregnated women. The result of this sexual union produced, according to Aquinas, a human being, though the child would be more cunning than children of an ordinary human couple.

Aquinas's many explanations of Christian doctrines find their full expression in Dante's *The Divine Comedy.* In this massive work the entire universe is ordered according to Scholastic teaching. The poem, divided into three sections—Hell, Purgatory, and Heaven—contains many descriptions of demons and, of course, Satan. Dante describes the three-faced Satan as a parody of the Christian Trinity and portrays him chewing on three sinners: Judas Iscariot, who betrayed Jesus, and Brutus and Cassius, who betrayed Julius Caesar. Dante leaves out Pontius Pilate because, to placate the Roman Empire, Christianity forgave Pilate's part in the murder of Jesus. In fact, one branch of the Eastern Orthodox church lists Pilate among its saints.

The medieval belief in demons passed on to the Protestant Reformation. Luther, like Aquinas, believed in the devil's evil power to assist wizards and witches. Following St. Augustine's authority, Luther had come to believe in incubi and succubi, since Satan in the form of a handsome man loves to decoy young girls. Luther also believed in changelings, children of the devil who replace human children.

Islam, which is in part based on Jewish and Christian beliefs, calls Satan Iblis. He is mentioned in the Koran, as are the djinn (plural of genie), his offspring.

Djinn are divided into different categories, although Islamic folklore is not always clear in its distinctions, many names being just different words for a demonic being. The orders are jann, the lowest and weakest; the djinn proper, who often appear in animal form; the shaitan or sayatin; ifrits; and the marida, djinn of the most powerful class. In all there are some 40 troops of 600,000 djinn, according to one count.

When King Solomon (who often appears in Islamic legend) first saw the djinn, he was horrified at how ugly they were. He used his magic ring to gain mastery over them, forcing them to help build his great temple. A modern Islamic tale tells of a family so tormented by djinn, which appeared in various animal shapes, that the family went into the desert, the home of the djinn, and killed all of the animals they could capture. This so reduced the population of djinn that Allah (who wanted to maintain a balance in his order of nature) had to intervene, and a truce was made to ensure that the djinn would not be wiped out entirely.

The Koran (sura 6) tells that the djinn "in their ignorance" believed Allah had "sons and daughters." Some, however, were later converted by Muhammad to Islam and are diligent followers of its rites. These djinn often appear as "household serpents" who protect the family, much in the manner of the *genii* in Roman mythology.

The shaitans are a more dangerous breed of spirit than the djinn proper. Allah created al-Shaitan, perhaps another name for Iblis, who then produced eggs from which other demons were hatched. In a variant legend, Allah created not only al-Shaitan, but a wife, who produced three eggs. When hatched, the children were all ugly, having hoofs instead of feet. Shaitans are even uglier in their eating habits. They like excrement and other dirt and waste and prefer the shade to sunlight. It is believed that every man has a personal shaitan or demon, just as he has a personal guardian angel. Sometimes the shaitan is considered the muse of poetic inspiration.

Ifrits, or afrits, are an even more dangerous group than the shaitans. Originally the word may have meant one who overcomes an antagonist and rolls him in the dust. In time the term was applied to a very powerful and always malicious djinn. The Koran (sura 27) makes brief mention of the spirit as an "ifrit, one of the djinn," and Islamic legend has added to this brief Koranic mention. In Egypt, ifrit has come to mean the ghost of a murdered man or one who died a violent death. Yet the female version of the ifrit, the ifriteh mentioned in *The Thousand and One Nights*, is a benevolent djinn. In fact, in The Second Old Man's Story (night 2) a pious woman is turned into an ifriteh and carries the hero to an island to save his life. In the morning she returns and says: "I have paid thee my debt, for it is I who bore thee up out of the sea and saved thee from death, by permission of Allah. Know that I am of the djinn who believe in Allah and his Prophet."

Of the other demons in Arabic and Islamic folklore, perhaps the most dreaded is the Ahl-at-Tral, who live below the Sahara desert and appear as whirling sandstorms, drying up the wells before caravans arrive.

There are numerous variant spellings of the demons in Islamic mythology. Djinn sometimes appears as jinn and jinniyeh (feminine). Ifrit is also spelled efreet, alfrit, afrit and for the female, ifriteh and afriteh.

See also: AHL-AT-TRAL; ALLAH; AUGUSTINE, ST.; JOB; BRUTUS; IBLIS; IFRITS; JUDAS ISCARIOT; KORAN, THE; MOHAMMAD; PILATE, PONTIUS; SATAN; SHAITAN; SOLOMON; THOMAS OF ACQUINAS, ST.; *THOUSAND AND ONE NIGHTS*

0961

**Devi or Mahadeve** (the goddess and the great goddess)   In Hindu mythology, the great goddess, sometimes regarded as the wife of Shiva. She has both a gentle and a fierce nature.

Devi is one of the most ancient deities worshiped in present-day Hinduism. Traces of her worship date back to prehistoric times. She was taken into the Hindu pantheon and wedded to

*Devi (Kali)*

the god Shiva, being made his *shakti*, or female energy. Among the many roles she assumes in Hindu mythology are the following:

*Sati* (the good woman), daughter of Daksha. She married the god Shiva, even though her father opposed the match. To prove her love for Shiva she burned herself alive at Jwala-mukhi (mouth of fire), a volcano in the lower Himalayas, north of Punjab. Today the place is a pilgrimage site. When Shiva embraced the body of his wife, it took the god Vishnu to cut her out of Shiva's hold. Fifty pieces of her bodily remains were then scattered, each becoming a place of worship for the *yoni* (womb), the female organ, along with Shiva's *linga* (phallus).

*Parvati* (the mountain girl). Devi is the constant companion and loving wife of Shiva, often engaging in lovemaking. On one occasion Shiva reproached Parvati for the darkness of her skin. She was so upset by the reproach that she went to live alone in the forest, where she performed austerities. The god Brahma said he would grant her any wish as reward for her austerities. Parvati asked that her complexion be golden. She was then called Gauri (yellow, or brilliant) and became regarded as the goddess of crops (the

harvest bride) or Uma (mother), the golden goddess, personification of light and beauty; as Sandhya (joint) she is viewed as twilight personified. In some texts Sandhya is believed to be the daughter of the god Brahma.

*Jaganmata* (the mother of the world), the goddess as the great mother. This name recalls early worship of her.

*Durga* (the inaccessible), one of the most popular manifestations of the goddess. The title was given her when she fought the great buffalo demon, Mahisha. The demon, having performed penance, obtained great power and took control of the three worlds, dethroning Indra as well as sending the other gods fleeing to Brahma for help.

At a meeting of the gods, their united energies produced a woman, Durga, "more dangerous than all the gods and demons." (In a variant account Durga already existed as the wife of Shiva and came to the aid of the gods.) Durga now set out to destroy the buffalo demon. At first she sent Kalaratri (dark night), a female whose beauty bewitched the three worlds. Mahisha, even though moved by her charms, came after Kalaratri, who, of course, was a form of Durga, but "she took the unassailable form of fire." When the demon in the form of a buffalo saw her standing before him, blazing with her great magic power of illusion, he made himself as large as Mount Meru. He sent an army, but it was reduced to ashes by the fire.

Mahisha then sent 30,000 giants, and they made Kalaratri rush to Durga (the goddess can be in two places at the same time as well as be two beings). The demon's troops hurled arrows as thick as raindrops in a storm at Durga as she sat on Mount Vindhya. In return Durga threw weapons that carried away the arms of many of the giants. Mahisha then hurled a flaming dart at the goddess, which she turned aside. He sent another, and she stopped it by 100 arrows. His next arrow was aimed at Durga's heart, but this was also stopped. At last the two came together, and Durga seized Mahisha, setting her foot on his chest. However, he managed to disengage himself and renew the battle.

The battle continued for some time, until Durga pierced Mahisha with her trident. He reeled to and fro and again assumed his original form, that of a giant with 1,000 arms, a weapon in each. He approached Durga, who seized him by his arms and carried him through the air. She then threw him to the ground. Seeing that the fall did not kill him, she pierced him in the chest with an arrow. Blood began to flow from his mouth, and he died.

In Indian art Durga is often portrayed as a golden-colored woman with 10 arms, called Dashabhuja (ten-armed). In one hand she often holds a spear, which is piercing Mahisha. With another hand she holds the tail of a serpent, with another the hair of Mahisha, whose chest the snake is biting. Her other hands are filled with weapons, and a lion, tiger, leopard, or other large cat leans against her right leg.

Durga's battle with Mahisha is but one of many fought by the goddess against various demons. Often she gained the title or name of the demon because of her encounter with him. One epic myth describes such an incident: "From the forehead of the goddess contracted with wrathful frowns, sprang swiftly forth a goddess of black and formidable aspect, armed with a scimitar and noose, robed in the hide of an elephant, dry and withered and hideous, with yawning mouth, and lolling tongue, and bloodshot eyes, and filling the regions with shouts." When the goddess in this form killed the two demons Chandra and Munda, she returned to herself and was called by a contraction of the two demon's names, Chamunda.

Devi is also known as Kali (the black woman). Devi was sent to earth to destroy a host of demons, but in her rampage of death and destruction she also killed men and women. The gods, horrified and fearing that if she was not stopped all life would cease, pleaded with her but to no avail. Finally Shiva, her husband, threw himself down amid the bodies of the dead. When Kali realized she was trampling on her husband, she regained her senses. As a sign of shame she stuck out her tongue. Kali is often portrayed in this manner in Indian art. Another account says that she fought a demon who could restore himself from a drop of blood that hit the ground; Kali therefore stuck out her tongue from her many heads to lick up the blood.

Other attributes of Kali are fanged teeth, matted hair, red eyes, and four eyes. In two arms she holds the symbols of death: a noose to strangle her victims and a hook to drag them. In her other hands she holds the symbols of life, a prayer book and prayer beads. Kali also wears a necklace of skulls and corpse earrings and is surrounded by serpents, showing her mastery over the male, according to some interpretations.

Calcutta, India, receives its name from Kalighat (the steps of Kali), where her worshipers descend into the sacred Ganges. In earlier times human sacrifices were made to the goddess. Today black goats are sacrificed to her. Thugs (a Hindi word that has passed into English) robbed and strangled their victims before sacrificing them to the goddess.

See also: BRAHMA; CHANDRA; DAKSHA; LINGAM; SHIVA; UMA

0962

**Devs and Hambarus**   In Armenian mythology and folklore, demonic spirits. The Devs are male and female spirits, often appearing as humans, such as old women, or in animal guise. One Armenian folktale, "The Sheep Brother," tells how a girl encountered a Dev. She stepped into a cavern and saw a thousand-year-old Dev lying in a corner.

The Dev said, "Neither the feathered birds nor the crawling serpent can make their way in here; how then hast thou, maiden, dared to enter?"

The girl thought quickly and said, "For love of you I came here, dear grandmother."

The Dev then took a liking to the girl and rewarded her with golden hair and a golden dress.

The Hambarus, cousins to the Devs, are spirits who live in desert places and also reward or punish at will. For a passage in Isaiah (13:21) in which the King James Version of the Bible reads "satyrs" and "owls," the Armenian translation uses "Hambarus" and "Devs."

See also: OWL; SATYRS

**0963**

**Dhammacakka**   In Buddhism, the Wheel of the Dharma, which was set into motion when the Buddha preached his first sermon in the Deer Park near Benares.

See also: BUDDHA, THE; DHARMA

**0964**

**Dhammapada, The** (verses on Dhamma)   A Buddhist sacred book in 26 divisions, consisting of 423 verses attributed to the Buddha. Each aphorism is encapsulated in a legendary incident, which is told in the *Dhammapadattha-katha* (Dhammapada commentary) collected in the fifth century C.E. Another version exists in Chinese, translated from the Sanskrit, and a partial manuscript of still another version, in Gandhari (a language related to Sanskrit), has been recovered.

See also: BUDDHA, THE

**0965**

**Dhanvantari** (moving in a curve)   In Hindu mythology, physician of the gods who was produced at the Churning of the Ocean when the gods and demons fought for the Amrita, the water of life.

See also: AMRITA; CHURNING OF THE OCEAN

**0966**

**Dharma** (Dhamma)   Term in Hindu and Buddhist works (*Dharma* in Sanskrit, *Dhamma* in Pali), variously translated as truth, law, religion, doctrine, righteousness, virtue, or force-factor. For Buddhism it often means the doctrine of the Buddha as found in the sacred writings and a mo-

mentary, irreducible component of the perceived universe. It is the Buddhist term for Buddhism.

**0967**

**Dharmapala** (Dharma protector)   In Mahayana Buddhism, the Eight Terrible Ones, defenders of the Dharma, who wage war against demons and enemies of Buddhism. They are Lha-mo, a female goddess, portrayed on a mule with a sword and mace; Ts'angs-pa Dkar-po, often portrayed on a white horse, with a sword, and sometimes carrying a banner; Beg-Ts'e, god of war and protector of horses, carrying a sword with a shrimp-shaped handle and wearing Mongolian boots; Yama, the Hindu god of the dead, who is also found among the Buddhists; Kubera, god of wealth and guardian of the North, borrowed from Hindu mythology, among whose symbols are a mongoose vomiting jewels, a trident, a banner, and an elephant or lion; Mahakala, the great black one, often portrayed with a trident, possibly derived from the Greek god Poseidon or a variant of Kubera or Shiva; Hayagriva, the horse-necked one, also derived from Hindu mythology, portrayed with a bull's head and his symbols, a chopper and skull cap.

See also: DHARMA; HAYA-GRIVA; KUBERA; MAHAYANA; POSEIDON; SHIVA

**0968**

**Dhyani-Bodhisattvas**   In Mahayana Buddhism, five Bodhisattvas emanating from the five Dhyani-Buddhas. They are Samantabhadra, Vajrapani, Ratnapani, Avalokiteshvara, and Vishvapani. Also, there are eight Bodhisattvas who act as protectors. They are Samantabhadra, Vajrapani, Avalokiteshvara, Manjushri, Maitreya, Akashagarbha, Kshitigarbha, and Sarvanivaranavishkambhin.

See also: AVALOKITESHVARA; BODHISATTVA; DHYANI-BUDDHAS; MAHAYANA; MAITREYA; MANJUSHRI; RATNAPANI; SAMANTABHADRA; VAJRAPANI

*Avalokiteshvara*

0969

**Dhyani-Buddhas** (Buddhas emanated by meditation)    In Mahayana Buddhism, five Buddhas who came from Adi-Buddha, the primordial Buddha. They are Vairocana, Akshobhya, Ratnasambhava, Amitabha, and Amoghasiddhi. They have in turn five Dhyani-Bodhisattvas who are Samantabhadra, Vajrapani, Ratnapani, Avalokitesvara, and Vishvapani.

See also: ADI-BUDDHA; AKSHOBHYA; AMITABHA; DHYANI-BODHISATTVAS; MAHAYANA; RATNAPANI; SAMANTABHADRA; VAJRAPANI; VISHVAPANI

0970

**Diab**    In Haitian voodoo, a male demon who controls sexual passions in men. He is symbolized by a penis.

0971

**Diablesse**    In Haitian voodoo, a female demon who controls sexual passions in women. She is symbolized by a vagina.

0972

**Diamond Jim Brady**    1856–1917. In American history and legend, popular name of James Buchanan Brady, American financier and philanthropist, noted for his passion for diamonds. He wore them on his fingers, cuffs, and shirt fronts and is believed to have had some diamonds in his bridgework. He was also noted for his immense appetite for food. Brady's usual evening meal began with an appetizer of two or three dozen oysters, six crabs, and a few servings of green turtle soup. The main course was two whole ducks, six or seven lobsters, a sirloin steak, two servings of terrapin, and a variety of vegetables. He topped it off with a platter of pastries and often a two-pound box of candy. He was particularly fond of confectionery delights. His stomach, so legend goes, was replaced by that of an elephant by doctors at Johns Hopkins Hospital in Baltimore. He did give money to the institution in 1912 to found the James Buchanan Brady Urological Institute. A Hollywood movie, *Diamond Jim*, starring Edward Arnold and Jean Arthur, deals with his love for Lillian Russell.

0973

**Diana** (belonging to the divine)    In Roman mythology, an ancient Italian goddess honored in central Italy; identified with the Greek goddesses Artemis and Selene. The Italian Diana was the guardian of those treaties by which peaceful relations were begun. In her sacred grove at Aricia she presided over the league of Latin cities. Her worship moved to Rome when it became the center for treaties. Diana also was the patron goddess of women and their protector in childbirth. Diana was often associated with Apollo, and during the reign of Augustus the two deities became patron gods of the new imperial residence on the Palatine during a special festival. During the Christian Middle Ages the name Diana was often used for the leader of the witches, along with Hecate. In George Meredith's novel *Diana of the Crossways* (1875) the heroine

*Diana*

complains of her "pagan" name, saying, "to me the name is ominous of mischance."

See also: APOLLO; ARTEMIS; HECATE; NYMPHS; SELENE

0974

**Diancecht** (swift in power)   In Celtic mythology, god of medicine and healing. He is able to heal all but those who are decapitated. At the battle of Magtured he sat by a stream that possessed magic healing properties. There he bathed the mortally wounded, hence his association with healing wells. In Christian medieval legend he appears as an enchanter. Today, Diancecht porridge is a cure for colds, sore throats, and worms. It is made of hazelnuts, dandelions, woodsorrel, chickweed, and oatmeal.

0975

**Dido**   In Roman mythology, queen of Carthage, mistress of the Trojan hero Aeneas;

daughter of Mutto or Belus, a king of Tyre; or of Agenor; sister of Anna and Pygmalion. Dido's husband, Acherbas, Acerbas, or Sychaeus, was murdered by his brother Pygmalion. Dido (also called Elissa of Belus) fled to North Africa, where she was allowed to buy as much land as a bull's hide could cover. The hide was cut into thin strips and used to outline a large section of land. On that site Dido founded Carthage and became its queen. When Aeneas landed in Carthage, she entertained him, and the two fel' in love. When Mercury reminded Aeneas of his mission to found a new city for the Trojans, pious Aeneas deserted Dido. In complete despair she committed suicide. Some variants of the myth, however, say her sister Anna killed herself for love of Aeneas.

Vergil was apparently the first to synchronize the legends of Dido and Aeneas and make them lovers in the *Aeneid* (book 4); later, in book 6 the hero visits the underworld, sees Dido, and calls out to her, but she turns her back on him and does not answer. Aside from Vergil's *Aeneid*, Dido appears in Ovid's *Heroides* (7); Dante's *Divine Comedy* (Inferno, canto 5), in which she is the one who died for love; Chaucer's *Legend of Good Women*, in which the tale is based on Vergil and Ovid; Marlowe's play *Dido, Queen of Carthage* (1689); Shakespeare's *The Merchant of Venice* (5.1.9–12), which alludes to Dido's death; Purcell's one-act opera *Dido and Aeneas* (1689), which contains the great aria, "When I Am Laid in Earth"; and Berlioz's *Les Troyans* (1858), based on Vergil. Liberale de Veroan's painting *Dido's Suicide* portrays the queen on a the funeral pyre about to stab herself to death.

See also: AENEAS; *AENEID, THE*; AGENOR; MERCURY; PYGMALION

0976

**Diego de Alcalá, St.** (James)   1400–1463. In Christian legend, patron saint of cooks. Feast, 13 November.

Diego was a cook in a monastery. One day he was caught giving away some bread to the poor and was reprimanded by his religious superior. But when he opened his tunic, the hidden bread had turned into roses. He was canonized at the request of King Philip II of Spain, who believed that his son Don Carlos had been healed of a serious wound by the prayers of the saint. About 1600 a wealthy Spaniard living in Rome dedicated a chapel to the saint in the Church of San Giacomo degli Spagnoli. Frescoes were painted by Annibal Caracci and Albano, his pupil. Diego's name is also given as Diadacus or Didace.

0977

**Dietrich of Bern**   In medieval legend, hero of numerous poems, ballads, and chronicles, identified with Theodoric the Great (c. 454–526), king of the Ostrogoths.

Dietrich's name is spelled at least 85 different ways in various medieval manuscripts. He was the son of Dietmar and Odilia, the heiress of the conquered duke of Verona.

As a child he was gentle and generous when things went his way, but when he was angry, flames would shoot out of his mouth and consume any flammable object nearby. When Dietrich was five, his training was entrusted to Hildebrand, son of Herbrand, one of the Volsung race. In a short time Dietrich was an accomplished fighter and a close friend of Hildebrand. In one of their first adventures the two went out to seek the giant Grim and the giantess Hilde. On their way they came to a forest and met a dwarf, Alberich (Alferich, Alpris, or Elbegast; the name varies). They bound the dwarf and told him they would free him only when he told them where the giants lived.

The dwarf not only told them where the giants lived but gave Dietrich the magic sword Nagelring, which alone could pierce the giants' skin. The giants' hiding place was found, and after an intense battle Grim was killed by Dietrich with the magic sword. But Hilde, though cut in half, was still not defeated because her body knit together again. To prevent this the next time, Dietrich cut her in two and placed his sword between the severed parts, knowing that the magic steel would annul any magic of the giantess.

The two men returned home, Dietrich with his magic sword, Nagelring, and with Hildegrim, a magic helmet he had taken from the giants. But though Dietrich believed he had undone all of the giants, he was mistaken. More battles ensued. One giant, Sigenot, would have defeated Dietrich had it not been for Hildebrand's coming to his rescue.

Alberich appears again later in legends of Dietrich. Dietlieb, a close companion of Dietrich, went to his master to inform him that his only sister, Kunhild (Similde or Similt), had been carried away by Alberich, who now kept her a prisoner in the Tyrolean mountains, not far from his rose garden. This garden was surrounded by a silken thread and guarded by Alberich, who exacted the left foot and the right hand of any knight venturing to enter or breaking a single flower from its stem.

As soon as Dietrich heard the tale, he set out to rescue Kunhild. He was accompanied by Dietlieb, Hildebrand, Wittich, and Wolfhart. As they came to the rose garden, all of the men except Dietrich and Hildebrand began to trample on the flowers and break the silken thread. Alberich put on his shining girdle of power, which gave him the strength of 12 men, and brandished a sword that had been tempered in dragon's blood and could cut through iron and stone. He also put on his ring of victory and the Tarnkappe (Helkappe), which allowed its wearer to work magic.

Dietrich, following Hildebrand's instructions, struck off Alberich's cap and took his girdle and ring. The dwarf promised to return Kunhild unless she wished to stay as his wife. An agreement was made, and the knights were treated to a supper. Alberich had drugged the wine, and soon they all fell asleep and were bound and cast into a prison. When Dietrich awoke at midnight and saw his condition, he opened his mouth, and his fiery breath burned all the ropes. He then released Kunhild. Noiselessly, she brought them all back to the great hall, where they took their arms and were given magic rings made by the dwarfs. These rings enabled them to see their tiny foes, who otherwise were invisible to the naked eye.

A terrible battle ensued in which Dietrich's men were the victors. Now Kunhild pleaded for Alberich's life, asking Dietrich to set the dwarf free if he promised to be good. Of course Alberich agreed. The two were then married and went to live in the rose garden and the underground palace. In his old age Dietrich, weary of his life and his various wives, ceased to have any pleasure except in hunting. One day while he was bathing in a stream, his servant came to tell him that there was a stag in sight. Dietrich immediately called for his horse, and as it did not arrive quickly, he jumped on a coal-black steed standing nearby and was quickly borne off.

Numerous other adventures are recorded of the hero in other Middle High German poems, such as *Das Heldenbuch* (book of heroes). He also appears in *The Nibelungenlied* as a liegeman of King Etzel.

See also: ATTILA; *HILDEBRANDSLIED*; *NIEBELUN-GENLIED*

0978
**Dilmun** In Near Eastern mythology (Sumerian), paradise, the place where the sun rises and the land of the living. At one time Dilmun lacked fresh water, which was supplied by Enki, the water god. Eaki ordered Utu, the sun god, to fill the land with fresh water taken from the earth. Dilmun was then turned into a divine garden. Dilmun appears in the epic poem *Gilgamesh* as the home of Utnapishtim and his wife, who were granted immortality after the great flood. Some scholars locate Dilmun in the Persian Gulf.

See also: GILGAMESH; UTNAPISHTIM

0979
**Dilwica** (Diana?) In Slavic mythology, Serbian goddess of the hunt, portrayed as a young girl mounted on a swift horse and accompanied by steeds and hounds. She galloped through the forests with her retinue. To meet Dilwica in the forest would mean almost certain death, sometimes being torn to death by her hounds. Dilwica was called Devana by the Czechs and Dziewona by the Poles, indicating that her myth may have been derived from that of the Roman goddess Diana. Others suggest that Dilwica was one aspect of the Great Goddess common to many cultures. Areas of her worship came into contact with Teutonic races, who had absorbed some Greek and Roman mythology in their religious beliefs.

See also: DIANA; GREAT GODDESS

0980
**Dimbulans** In Australian mythology, large, strong creatures who approach women in a friendly way but later rape them. They then allow their victims to return home.

0981
**Dinah** (judged) In the Bible, O.T. (Gen. 34:1–31), daughter of Jacob and Leah, who married Shechem, a Hivite, the man who had raped her. Dinah's brothers were so incensed that they killed Shechem and all of his men and destroyed their city.

See also: JACOB; LEAH

0982
**Diomedes** (godlike ruler) In Greek mythology, hero, king of Argos, son of Tydeus and Deipyle; companion to Achilles in the siege of Troy. He was a favorite of Athena, who constantly protected him, especially since he wounded both Ares and Aphrodite (Venus), who sided with the Trojans. He entered Troy in the wooden horse. Diomedes appears in Homer's *Iliad* (books 2, 5, 6, 10, 23), Vergil's *Aeneid* (book

1), Ovid's *Metamorphoses* (book 14), and Dante's *Divine Comedy* (Inferno), in which he is placed, along with Ulysses (Odysseus), as one of the "counselors of fraud" in the Eighth Circle of Hell. Ingres's *Venus Wounded by Diomedes* deals with one episode of his life.

See also: ACHILLES; *AENEID, THE*; ARES; ATHENA; *ILIAD, THE*; OVID; TROY; VENUS

*Reception of Dionysus (Bacchus)*

0983

**Dionysus** (lame god)  In Greek mythology, one of the 12 Olympian gods; god of fertility, ecstasy, and wine; son of Zeus and Semele; called Bacchus by the Romans. Zeus's wife, Hera, angry that her husband had another mistress, persuaded Semele to let Zeus appear to her in all his splendor. When Zeus appeared with thunder and lightning, Semele was burned to ashes by the splendor of the vision. Before she was completely consumed, Zeus seized her unborn child, Dionysus, and implanted the child in his own thigh until the child was ready to be born; thus, Dionysus is sometimes called *Dithyrambus* (twice born). The young god was taken to Mount Nysa in India, where he was raised by Ino, his mother's sister, and by nymphs. The uses of wine were taught to him by Silenus, a son of Pan, and by the satyrs. He was also taught the mystery of ivy, a mild intoxicant when chewed and a symbol of everlasting life. Always angry with him, Hera drove Dionysus mad, sending him wandering around the world. The god was restored to his senses by the earth goddess Rhea. Dionysus then went on to teach humankind the cultivation of the vine and the uses of wine. Once during his travels he was captured by sailors who wanted to sell him into slavery in Egypt. During the voyage to Egypt, Dionysus had vines grow up out of the sea, entwining the mast of the ship. Then the god appeared in all his splendor, surrounded by wild beasts and crowned with ivy. All of the sailors except Acetes, who had befriended Dionysus, were transformed into dolphins. Acetes piloted the ship to Naxos, where Dionysus found Ariadne, who had been deserted by Theseus. Dionysus fell in love with her and asked Zeus to grant her immortality. Ariadne's wedding gift, a golden crown, appears in the constellation of Taurus and is called the Corona Borealis.

Dionysus's cult was one of the most important in Greece and later in Rome, where at first it was forbidden because its ceremonies sometimes culminated in the ritual killing of animals or even human victims. One myth tells how King Pentheus opposed the worship of the god, and Dionysus had him torn to pieces by his own mother when the king attempted to stop the Dionysian rites on Mount Cithaeron. In another myth, when King Lycurgus of Thrace opposed worship of the god, Dionysus drove the king mad, having him kill his own son, who the king believed was a vine in need of pruning.

*Bacchanalian reclining on a couch*

Dionysus was closely associated with Demeter as a season divinity; his festivals were celebrated in winter (when the god was believed to suffer) and in spring (when the god arose from his deathlike sleep). Often the celebrations took the form of orgiastic rites, but these were somewhat tamed down when Dionysus's cult was accepted by Apollo at Delphi. Greek drama stems from the Athenian spring festival, the Great Dionysia, held in honor of the god, who was a patron of the drama in association with Apollo and the Muses. The first tragedy was composed by Thespis under commission from the Athenian tyrant Pisistratus in 534 B.C.E. to inaugurate the Great Dionysia. Comedies and tragedies were played at the theater of Dionysus in Athens. Plato's *Ion* has Socrates say that "all good poets, epic as well as lyric, compose their poems not by art, but because they are inspired and possessed by a god," namely Dionysus. The release of powerful irrational impulses through ritual drama was seen as a necessary catharsis, according to Aristotle's analysis of the effect of tragedy in his *Poetics*.

In Greek art Dionysus appears as a handsome, strong man, crowned with ivy leaves and holding a bunch of grapes in one hand and a cup in the other. Often surrounding him are tigers, panthers, and other wild animals. His staff, thyrsus, is tipped with a pinecone.

Dionysus's female followers are called Maenads, Bacchantes, or Bassairds. The term *Dionysian* is now generally used to express sensual and irrational impulses in man, as opposed to Apollonian, the rational, according to Nietzsche in his discussion of the Greeks.

Dionysus appears in the Homeric *Hymn to Dionysus*, which tells the myth of the sailors; in Ovid's *Metamorphoses* (book 3); and in Euripides' *Bacchae*, which tells of the killing of Pentheus. He also appears in various English and American poems, including Spenser's *Shepheardes Calendar*; Milton's *Paradise Lost* (book 7.31–33), in which the poet condemns the god; Keats's *Ode to a Nightingale*, which rejects the irrational power of the god, and also *Endymion* (book 4.193–267), in which the poet describes a Bacchanalian procession; Matthew Arnold's "Bacchanalia: or, The New Age"; Ralph Waldo Emerson's "Bacchus"; Shelley's "Ode to the West Wind" (20–23), which describes the Maenads; Swinburne's *Atalanta in Calydon*, in which the female devotees of the god are described; and Albert Noyes's "Bacchus and the Pirates." In music Richard Strauss's opera *Ariadne auf Naxos* and Albert Roussel's ballet *Bacchus et Ariadne* deal with the god. In art Michelangelo's statue of *Bacchus*; Titian's *Bacchus and Ariadne*; Correggio's *Bacchus*; Piero di Cosimo's *Discovery of Wine*; Poussin's *Bacchanalian Revel*; the frieze in the Villa dei Misteri at Pompeii, which shows scenes from the mystery cult of the god; and the reclining Dionysus of the Elgin Marbles are some of the artworks inspired by Dionysus.

See also: ACETES; DOLPHIN; HERA; NYMPHS; OLYMPIAN GODS; PAN; SEMELE; SATYRS; ZEUS

0984

**Dioscuri**    In Greek and Roman mythology, the Heavenly Twins, Castor and Polydeuces (Pollux to the Romans). Polydeuces was said to have been the son of Zeus and Leda and was thus immortal, while Castor was fathered by Tyndareus, Leda's husband. The conceptions took place simultaneously. In Sparta, where there were also often dual kings, Castor and Polydeuces were worshiped in the form of a wooden structure shaped like a capital H. They were famous as athletes, Castor as a rider and Polydeuces as a boxer. Polydeuces displayed his skills during the voyage of the Argonauts. The two seem to have close links with other Indo-European deities, such as the Ashwins in Hindu mythology and Hengist and Horsa in Anglo-Saxon mythology.

See also: ARGONAUTS; ASHWINS; CASTOR AND POLYDEUCES; HENGIST AND HORSA; LEDA; ZEUS

0985

**Dipankara Buddha** (light-bringer)    In Buddhism, the Buddha of Fixed Light, who is portrayed in the *mudra* of "blessing of fearlessness"

and that of charity and love. Dipankara lived some 100,000 years on earth, some 3,000 years before anyone was found worthy to hear his message. When he was born there was a miracle—a large number of lamps were suddenly lit—thus his name. In Tibet he is called Mar-me-mdsad; in China, Ting-kuang-fo. The life that was to become Buddha Shakyamuni made his definite Bodhisattva resolves under Dipamkara, in the form of the Brahmin Megha (i.e., Megha became Sakyamuni.)

See also: MUDRA

**0986**
**Dirona** (Sirona)   In Celtic mythology, a mother goddess who appears to be identical with the goddess known elsewhere as Divona. She is depicted with a dog on her lap, a diadem (implying high status), three eggs (a fertility symbol), and a snake wrapped around her arm. The ancient Roman writers associated her with the consort of their god Mercury.

See also: MERCURY

**0987**
**Dismas** (Dysmas, Dimas)   In medieval Christian legend, the name usually given to the Penitent Thief who suffered with Christ at the Crucifixion. He is, however, not named in the Gospels. His relics are claimed by Bologna, and he is commemorated on 25 March. The impenitent thief is usually called Gesmas or Gestas.

**0988**
**Diti**   In Hindu mythology, mother of the Dityas, a race of demon giants, and the Maruts, the wind gods. Diti was married to the sage Kasyapa and through him was the mother of the Dityas. Indra, however, objected to the demons and cast them down into the ocean depths. Upset by the loss of her children, Diti asked her husband, Kasyapa, for a child who would destroy Indra. The wish was granted but with one condition.

"If, with thoughts wholly pious and person entirely pure," her husband said, "you carefully carry the babe in your womb for a hundred years." Following this condition, Diti went through 99 years. In the last year, she went to bed one night without washing her feet, which was a ritual necessity. Indra then cast a thunderbolt into Diti's womb, dividing the unborn child into seven. The children then began to cry. Indra said, "*Ma rodih*" (weep not), but this was to no avail. Indra divided each of the seven into another seven, thus creating 49 Maruts.

Another explanation for the origin of the Maruts is that 49 lumps of flesh were made into boys by the god Shiva at the request of his wife, Parvati. In this telling they are called Rudras because Rudra has come to be another name for the god Shiva.

See also: INDRA; KASYAPA; MARUTS; RUDRA; SHIVA

**0989**
**Divali**   A Hindu festival celebrated for five days in October and November. Originally, Divali was a fertility festival, and up to the end of the 19th century farmers would go to dung heaps and worship them by placing flowers, fruit, other offerings, and lights on them. Today it is a sort of All Fools' Day, when servants are allowed to play practical jokes on their masters, and people joyfully throw water, colored powder, and excrement at each other.

See also: ALL SOULS' DAY

**0990**
**Dives** (rich)   In medieval Christian legend, the name given to the unnamed rich man in Jesus' parable of the rich man and Lazarus (Luke 16:19–31). *Dives* is Latin for "rich" and appears in the Vulgate translation of the Bible.

**0991**
**Divji Moz** (wild men)   In Slovenian folklore, wild men who inhabit the forest. They have

enormous strength, the peasants are generally fearful of them, but often the Divji Moz help by offering advice on how to work in the forest. In return the peasants offer them food. Sometimes, when not in a good mood, the Divji Moz cause peasants to lose their way in the forests or, worse, tickle them to death.

**Djanbun**   In Australian mythology, a human being who turned into a platypus. One day a man named Djanbun came out of Washington Creek and was traveling alone across great mountains. He was carrying a fire stick and trying to get it to burst into flame. As he blew and blew on the sparking end, some glowing chars fell from it and turned into gold. But still the stick would not turn to flame. As he blew harder, he felt that his mouth was growing larger. Djanbun threw the stick down to the ground and jumped into the water. As soon as he did, he turned into a platypus. To this day natives warn of blowing too hard on fire sticks for fear that, like Djanbun, one just might turn into a platypus.

**Djanggawul**   In Australian mythology, primeval beings, two sisters and a brother and their companion Bralbral, who traveled across the earth. The Djanggawul brother is depicted as coming ashore on Arnhem Land, his face covered with sea foam. Always pregnant by their brother, the two sisters peopled the land, teaching various rituals and customs to the people. At first the two sisters had elongated genitals, embodying both male and female aspects. However, their brother cut off the "excess," making them proper women according to the myth. This belief is used to explain why men now control the sacred ceremonies that were once believed to have been the property of women alone.

**Djinn** (Jinn, Jinni, Jinnee; in English confused with genie)   In Arabic mythology, one of a class of supernatural beings subject to magic control. According to myth they were created from fire two millennia before Adam and are governed by a race of kings named Syleyman, one of whom built the pyramids. They take on different shapes, as serpents, dogs, cats, monsters, and also as humans. The evil djinn are exceptionally ugly, and the good ones are exquisitely beautiful.

See also: ALADDIN; DEVILS; HAFAZA; HARUT AND MARUT; HOURI; IBLIS; RUH; SAKHAR; SANG GALA RAJA; SHAITANS

**Djokhrane**   In Islamic legend, Berber folk hero who fought against the Romans. Djokhrane led a rebellion against Rome, finally ending in hand-to-hand combat with one Roman soldier. He was losing the battle when a jaybird flew down and pecked out the eyes of the Roman soldier. Djokhrane told his children: "As long as you live, never eat this bird. If anyone brings you one to eat, buy it and set it free." The Romans had a similar legend concerning a raven. Marcus Valerius, a Roman hero, was fighting a Gallic warrior when a raven swooped down and pecked out the eyes of Marcus's adversary.

See also: RAVEN

**Dockalfar** (dark elves)   In Norse mythology, the dark elves or dwarfs who live underground. They tend to be evil by nature but often can be appeased.

See also: ALFAR; ALFHEIM; NINE WORLDS

**Doctors of the Church**   In Christianity, title used since the Middle Ages for certain Christian writers noted for their theological works, which are considered the foundation of most Christian theology. In the Western church the Four Doctors are St. Jerome, St. Ambrose, St. Augustine, and St. Gregory the Great. In the Eastern church the Four Doctors are St. John Chrysostom, St. Basil the Great, St. Athanasius, and St. Gregory Nazianzen. In medieval Western art the Four Western, or Latin, Doctors are often grouped around the Virgin and Child. The Eastern, or Greek, Doctors are rarely found in Western medieval art. However, they appear, in the central dome of the baptistery of St. Mark's in Venice, the work having been done by Greek artists of the 12th and 13th centuries. The term Fathers of the Church is also used for Doctors of the Church.

During the Middle Ages the Schoolmen, theologians who lectured in the cloisters and cathedral schools, also were called doctors. Many of them became known under special titles such as Angelic Doctor for St. Thomas Aquinas, Mellifluous Doctor for St. Bernard, and Seraphic Doctor for St. Bonaventura.

See also: AMBROSE, ST.; ATHANASIUS, ST.; AUGUSTINE, ST.; BASIL, ST.; BONAVENTURA, ST.; GREGORY, ST.; JEROME, ST.; JOHN CHRYSOSTOM, ST.; THOMAS ACQUINAS

0998

**Dodona**   In Greek cult, the site of the oracle of Zeus, built by Deucalion after the deluge and located in northwestern Greece. At Dodona there were priestesses called Peleiades (pigeons) who made known the will of Zeus. A large oak, sacred to Zeus, was the home of the real pigeons, and the god revealed himself by the rustling or markings of the leaves and the murmuring of a nearby brook. The priests of the shrine were called Selloi according to Homer's *Iliad* (16). In later times oracles were taken from lots and the ringing of a gong or basin. In front of the gong was an iron statue of a boy with a whip made of three chains, from which hung some buttons that touched the gong. If the whip moved in the breeze, the buttons sounded against the gong. The shrine of Zeus gave way to that of Delphi,

dedicated to Apollo, though it continued until about the fourth century C.E.

See also: APOLLO; DELPHI; DEUCALION; *ILIAD, THE*; PELEIADES; ZEUS

0999

**Dog**   A domesticated carnivorous mammal; in world mythology and folklore, symbol of both demonic and beneficent forces. In the Buddhist hell, dogs inflict punishments, and the Hindu god of death, Yama, has two dogs that are sent out to bring back wandering souls. A red dog was sacrificed by the Aztecs to help carry the soul of the dead king across a stream or to announce his arrival in the other world. The dog is referred to some 40 times in the Bible. Deuteronomy (23:18) sums up the Hebrew attitude: "Thou shalt not bring the hire of a whore, or the price of a dog, into the house of the Lord thy God for any vow: for even both are abomination unto the Lord thy God." "Dog" was a term used for a male homosexual dedicated to pagan gods who took part in sexual rites. In the book of Tobit (5:16), part of the Old Testament Apocrypha and not included in the Hebrew or Protestant Bible, there is a positive mention of Tobit's dog, reflecting a different attitude.

In many ancient and modern tales dogs help solve crimes. Plutarch, the Greek writer, reports a tale of how King Pyrrhus came upon a dog on the road guarding the body of a dead man. The dog was taken back to the king's palace, fed, and made comfortable. One day while the king was reviewing his troops, the dog began to growl and bark at some soldiers. The men were arrested, questioned, and found guilty of the murder of the dog's master.

European medieval legend tells of Aubry of Montdidier, who was murdered in 1371. His dog, Dragon, always snarled and went for the throat of a man named Richard of Macaire. Years later Richard was condemned to judicial combat with the dog. He lost, and with his dying breath Richard admitted he had killed Aubry. Based on tales of this type, medieval Christianity saw the dog as a symbol of conscience. Francis Thompson's ode "The Hound of Heaven" portrays the soul's flight from God and God's unrelenting houndlike pursuit. In Goethe's *Faust*, Mephistopheles makes his first appearance disguised as a dog. Walt Disney's Pluto combines the beneficent aspect of the dog with a demonic name, since Pluto is the Latin form of Hades, the god of the underworld, whose dog was Cerberus. Snoopy, of the *Peanuts* cartoon, is also beneficent. In fact, he often sounds like a Midwestern preacher. There are numerous motifs associated with dogs in the *Motif Index of Folk Literature*.

See also: FAUST; HADES; MEPHISTOPHELES; PLUTO; SEVEN SLEEPERS OF EPHESUS, THE; YAMA

1000
**Dog and His Shadow, The**  Aesopic fable found in various European and Oriental collections.

A dog stole a piece of meat from a butcher shop. On his way to a safe place where he could eat it without interruption he had to cross a footbridge over a clear stream. Looking down, he saw his own reflection in the water. Thinking that the reflection was another dog with another piece of meat, and being a greedy dog, he made up his mind to have that also. So he snarled and made a grab for the other dog's meat. As his greedy mouth opened, out dropped the piece of meat, which fell into the stream and was lost.

Moral: *Grasp at the shadow and lose the substance.*

In one Indian version of the fable, the tale is somewhat expanded. An unfaithful wife eloping with her lover arrives at the bank of a stream. There the lover persuades her to strip herself so that he may carry her clothes across the stream. He does so but never returns. The god Indra, seeing the woman's plight, changes himself into a jackal bearing a piece of flesh in his mouth and goes down to the bank of the stream. When the god, transformed into a jackal, sees the fish sporting in the water, he lays aside the meat, and plunges in after them. A vulture hovering nearby

seizes the meat and bears it off. The jackal, returning unsuccessfully from his fishing, is taunted by the woman, who cries out:

"The fish swims in the waters still, the vulture is off with the meat. Deprived of both fish and meat, Mistress jackal [here the god is addressed as a woman], whither away?"

The jackal replies:

"Great as is my wisdom, thine is twice as great. No husband, no lover, no clothes, lady, whither away?"

Thus, in the Indian version the loss of the meat is a deliberate plan of the god Indra to read a lesson to the unfaithful wife.

Juan Ruiz, the archpriest of Hita, in his *El Libro de Buen Amor* (The Book of Good Love), also tells the fable, with the moral: "The same thing happens every day to the servant of cupidity. He expects to realize a profit with your help, and he loses his capital. From this evil root springs all evil; cupidity is truly a deadly sin. Man should never abandon goods of great value, already secure, and held free and clear, for an empty dream; he who abandons what he has strikes a very bad bargain" (translated by Rigo Mignani and Marie A. Di Cesare).

See also: AESOPIC FABLES; INDRA

1001
**Dolphin**  A marine mammal resembling a small whale with an elongated head; in world mythology and folklore, often appearing as a friend of man. One Greek myth tells how Arion, a poet of the sixth century B.C.E., was saved by dolphins when he was cast overboard from a ship. In a similar myth Telemachus, son of the Greek hero Odysseus, was saved from drowning by a helpful band of dolphins that carried him safely to shore. In gratitude Odysseus engraved a dolphin on his ring and emblazoned one on his

shield. The Roman emperor Titus had a portrait of a dolphin twisted around an anchor to symbolize the mean between the dolphin's swiftness and the anchor's heaviness. Many early Christian paintings and carvings portray a dolphin swallowing Jonah. In later European heraldry the device of a dolphin was often used with the motto *Festina lente* (hasten slowly). In medieval Christian folklore the dolphin was believed to carry the souls of the blessed to the isle of the dead.

See also: JONAH; ODYSSEUS; TELEMACHUS

**Domitilla, Nereus, and Achilleus, Sts.**    First century. In Christian legend, martyrs. Feast, 12 May.

*The Golden Legend*, a collection of saints' lives written in the 13th century by Jacobus de Voragine, contains the lives of the Roman martyrs. The two men were chamberlains to Flavia Domitilla, a rich woman. They not only converted her to Christianity but made her take a vow of chastity. When her betrothed, Aurelian, heard of her vow, he ordered her servants to sacrifice to the Roman gods, knowing they would refuse and be executed. They refused, and their heads were "smitten off." Aurelian then decided he would marry Domitilla. He sent two men and two women to obtain her consent by magic, but she converted them also. When he realized that his scheme had failed, he came to her room, asking "the enchanters to sing, and commanded the others to dance with him as he would defoul Domitilla, but the jugglers left singing, and the others dancing, and he himself ceased not to dance two days continually, unto the time that he expired and died."

When Aurelian's brother Luxurius heard what had happened, he set fire to the palace and burned all of the Christians, Domitilla among them. Rubens painted *St. Domitilla, St. Nereus and St. Achilleus* as part of a triptych for the Oratorians of the Chiesa Nuova in Rome. The Oratorians rejected the first version of the work but accepted the second, which portrays Domi-

tilla richly dressed, holding a palm, with the two male saints on either side.

See also: *GOLDEN LEGEND, THE*

**Domnu** (abyss, deep sea)    In Celtic mythology, a goddess of the Fomorians, the evil deities who were defeated and replaced by the Tuatha de Danann, people of the goddess Danu.

See also: DANU; FOMORIANS; TUATHA DE DANANN

**Domovoi** (Domoule, Domovik, Domovoj, Domovoy) (house spirit)    In Slavic folklore, a house spirit, often called grandfather or master of the house. It is also called *dedushka* (granddad) or *chelovek* (fellow) in Russian.

According to one myth, when Svarog created the heavens and the earth, one group of spirits revolted against him. God cast out the rebellious spirits from heaven; some fell into the water or forests, and others fell onto housetops or in backyards. Those that fell onto housetops or in backyards became good because of their contact with humans; the others remained wicked. It is believed by some Russians that when someone is about to die in a house, the Domovoi will cry. Domovoi likes living near the stove in a house, while his wife, Domovikha, likes to live in the basement. Some accounts say his wife is Kikimora. Every time the master of the house left, his wife would cover the mouth of the stove so that Domovoi would not leave as well.

Variant names for the house spirit in Slavic folklore are Iskrzychi (Galicia and Poland), Syenovik (Montenegro), Tsmok (White Russia), and Djadek (Czech and Slovak).

See also: KIKIMORA

**Donato of Arezzo, St.** (given)    Fourth century. In Christian legend, bishop and martyr. Feast, 7 August.

Born of a noble family, Donato studied with his companion, Emperor Julian. When Julian gave up Christianity and became known as Julian the Apostate, he put Donato's father to death for being a Christian. Donato fled from Rome to Arezzo along with his companion, the monk Hilarion. They preached and performed many miracles.

One legend tells how he helped find hidden money. A tax collector went on a journey and left money with his wife, Euphrosina. She died suddenly, having told no one where she had hidden the money. When the tax collector returned, he was afraid he would be thought a thief. He called Donato to help him. They went to Euphrosina's tomb and called to her, and her voice told them where the money was hidden. Since many others were present at the miracle, a vast number of people were converted. Donato was made bishop of Arezzo. Once when he was saying Mass, the chalice of wine (which was made of glass) was broken by some idolaters. Donato prayed over it, and it was restored with not one drop spilled. Again, because it was witnessed by so many people, many pagans were converted. This caused the authorities to arrest Donato and Hilarion. Donato was beheaded, and Hilarion was scourged to death.

Their bodies lie under the high altar of the cathedral of Arezzo, where their shrine has sculptures by Giovanni di Francesco of Arezzo and Betto di Francesco of Florence, completed in the 14th century.

1006

**Don Juan Tenorio**  14th century. In late medieval legend, libertine Spanish nobleman who is taken off to hell for his sins. Don Juan, the son of a leading family in Seville, killed the commandant of Ulloa after seducing his daughter. To put an end to his debaucheries the Franciscans enticed him to their monastery and killed him, telling the people that he had been carried off to hell by the statue of the commandant, who was buried on their monastery grounds.

The legend of Don Juan is believed to have originated in various Spanish ballads in which insult to the dead and invitation to join the living at a banquet frequently appear. Don Juan first appears on the stage in Tirso de Molina's play *El burlador de Sevilla y convidado de piedra* (The Playboy of Seville and the Stone Guest). The French took up the subject with plays by Dorimon, De Villiers, and Molière. The German and Swiss writers Grabbe and Frisch also wrote plays about Don Juan, the former on Don Juan and Faust, while the latter wrote a comedy in which Don Juan flees from his wedding, only to meet his bride in a park, to which she had also fled in fear of marriage.

The most important opera on the theme is Mozart's *Don Giovanni*, with a libretto by Da Ponte. Other musical works are Dargomijsky's *Kamjennyi Gost* (The Stone Guest) with a Pushkin text, Gluck's ballet *Don Juan*, and Richard Strauss's tone poem *Don Juan*. Later plays on the subject are Zorrilla's *Don Juan Tenorio*, in which the don is saved, and Shaw's *Man and Superman*. Byron's long narrative poem *Don Juan* recasts the Don into an agreeable young man, passively amoral rather than actively evil.

See also: BALLAD; FAUST

1007

**Doodang**  In American folklore, a mythical creature who wished to swim and then fly and was never satisfied. Finally, given wings, he flew, failed, and died.

See also: UNCLE REMUS

1008

**Doris** (bountiful)  In Greek mythology, a sea goddess, daughter of Oceanus and Tethys; sister of Eidyia, Electra, Clymene, Meliboea, Metis, Perseis, Pleione, Proteus, Styk, Europa, Clytia, and Callirrhoë, the rivers and fountains; wife of the sea-god Nereus; mother of 50 daughters, called Nereids or Dorides, and in some myths mother of Amphitrite, Galatea, and Thetis.

See also: AMPHITRITE; CALLIRRHOË; ELECTRA; GALATEA; NEREIDS; OCEANUS; THETIS

*St. Dorothy*

**Dorothy, St.** (Dorothea) (gift of God)    Third century? In Christian legend, patron saint of brewers, brides, florists, gardeners, midwives, and newly married couples. Feast, 6 February.

Her life is contained in *The Golden Legend*, a collection of saints' lives written in the 13th century by Jacobus de Voragine. Dorothy was tortured by Fabricius, governor of Caesarea, Cappadocia, for refusing to marry and to worship idols. As she was on her way to execution a young lawyer, Theophilus, mocked her: "Send me some of the fruit and flowers from that garden you speak of," he said, "where you are going to your bridegroom!" "Thy request is granted," the young saint replied.

When she was about to die, an angel or the Christ Child appeared to her with a basket of three apples and three roses. She then asked that they be carried to Theophilus as she had pro-

1009

mised. The angel or the Christ Child appeared to Theophilus and gave him the basket. Theophilus then became a Christian and later met his death for being one. In Christian art St. Dorothy is portrayed with the Christ Child and the basket of fruit and flowers, as in Francesco di Giorgio's charming painting of the subject. The story forms the basis for Philip Massinger's tragedy *The Virgin Martyr* (1620).

See also: *GOLDEN LEGEND, THE*

1010

**Dosojin** (earth ancestor god, road ancestor god) In Japanese Shinto mythology, phallic god, protector of roads and travelers, invoked to ensure abundance in agriculture and human reproduction. One of his most popular forms is as Sarutahiko (monkey rice field prince).

1011

**Douban**    Physician who killed King Younan in the "Story of the Physician Douban," a tale in *The Thousand and One Nights* (nights 4, 5, and 6, with interruptions from other tales in the collection).

A physician named Douban cured a Persian king, Younan, of leprosy. But because of the whispers of a vizier, the king suspected that the physician wished to kill him. When he ordered the death of the physician, the man pleaded for some time to straighten out his home and books, many of which were valuable. The king agreed. The next day, after the amirs and viziers and chamberlains had gathered at the court, the physician entered, "bearing an old book, and a small pot full of powder." He told the king that when his head was cut off it would speak to the king if the king placed the head on the powder to stop the bleeding. The king should then open the book and read from where the head directed him. The king took the book and gave the signal to the executioner, "who rose and struck off the physician's head and set it on the dish, pressing it down on the powder." The blood immediately ceased to flow. The head opened its eyes and said: "Open the book, O King!"

Younan opened the book and found the leaves stuck together, so he put his finger to his mouth, taking his "spittle and loosened them therewith and turned over the pages in this manner, one after another." Eventually, he cried out that there was nothing there to see. The head said: "Open more leaves." The king wet his finger and continued. The leaves of the book were poisoned and before long the poison began to work upon the king. He fell back in convulsions crying out: "I am poisoned!"

See also: THOUSAND AND ONE NIGHTS, THE

*Dove*

**Dove**    1012

A small bird resembling a pigeon, often used as a symbol of peace (secular) or the Holy Spirit (religious). The Near Eastern goddess Astarte and the Greek goddess Aphrodite had doves sacrificed to them in their temples. One Greek myth tells of the origin of the doves that drew Aphrodite's chariot. Eros and Aphrodite were picking flowers in a contest to see who could pick the most. Eros was winning when two nymphs began to aid the goddess. Indignant, Eros changed the nymphs into doves. Aphrodite then had them draw her chariot as a reward.

In early Christian legend a dove descended on the staff of St. Joseph to indicate that he was to be the husband of Mary. In another early Christian legend Joachim and Anna, parents of the Virgin, dreamed of a dove before her birth. In the Gospel According to Mark (1:9–11) a dove descends to Jesus when he is baptized, and the dove is the Holy Spirit. As symbol of the Holy Spirit the dove is often seen in art portraying saints noted for their spiritual writings. It also appears in paintings of the Annunciation to the Blessed Virgin. In Moslem folklore the dove is also a symbol of the Holy Spirit. According to one legend, a dove used to feed out of the ear of Muhammed. His followers said it was the Holy Spirit giving the prophet advice. Shakespeare's *Henry VI, Part I* (1.2) refers to this belief in a mocking tone: "Was Mahomet inspired with a dove?" There are numerous motifs associated with the dove in the *Motif Index of Folk Literature*.

See also: APHRODITE; ASTARTE; EROS; JOSEPH, ST.; MUHAMMAD

**Drac**    1013

In French folklore, a spirit in human form who lives in the caverns of rivers. Sometimes *dracs* will float like golden cups along a stream to entice bathers, but when the bather attempts to catch one, the *drac* draws him under water.

**Dracula**    1014

c. 1431–1476. In eastern European history and legend, popular name of Vlad the Impaler, a Romanian tyrant who is known in folklore and literature as a vampire.

Various theories have been advanced about the truth of Vlad the Impaler, or Vlad Tepes, who lived in Walachia, a region south of Transylvania. An official Romanian Communist government tourist agency claimed: "The real Dracula fought for the cause of the Romanian people." Older legend has credited this "hero" of the people with the most horrendous deeds. In German, Russian, Hungarian, and Italian folklore, the deeds of Dracula are copiously recorded, though no mention is made of his vampirism.

A few of the legends surrounding the sadistic tyrant tell how he punished those who in any way offended him. For example, when a group of Turkish envoys did not remove their turbans in his presence, he had their turbans nailed to their heads. Dracula often dined outdoors amid the screams of his impaled victims, hung on stakes around the dinner table. Once a guest complained of the stench of the decaying bodies. Dracula had the guest impaled on a stake much higher than the other victims, so that he might die out of the range of their stench. Another tale tells how Dracula invited some beggars into his castle, fed them, and told them he could end all of their troubles if they wished. They agreed, and he had them shut indoors and burned alive.

However, in modern folklore Dracula is noted for his vampirism, tales of which stem from Bram Stoker's novel *Dracula*. Stoker's novel was used as the basis of numerous films, beginning with a silent film, *Nosferatu*, and continuing through many versions, including the classic *Dracula* starring Bela Lugosi, who became identified with the role in movies. *The Fearless Vampire Killers* by the Polish director Roman Polanski gives Dracula the name Count Von Krolock, but he retains all of the characteristics of the old vampire count. Recently Norine Dresser published a study called *American Vampires*.

See also: VAMPIRE

*Dragon*

**1015**

**Dragon** A fantastic beast that appears in world mythology and folklore as either demonic or beneficent. In most European mythologies the dragon is viewed as a demonic beast, usually a winged crocodile with a serpent's tail. In Christian symbolism the dragon is the devil, as in the Book of Revelation (20:2), where Satan is referred to as the "Great Dragon." The Christian devil is derived from the dragon in the Old Testament, who in turn is derived from Tiamet, the Babylonian female dragon monster. The most famous encounter between a Christian and dragon is that of St. George and the dragon. He slays the dragon or tames the animal and frees the maiden. In Norse mythology the dragon appears as Fafnir, a giant who changed himself into a dragon to guard the gold that he had stolen.

In Oriental mythologies the dragon is seen as a beneficent animal. In China the emperor's throne was referred to as the Dragon's Throne and his face as the Dragon's Face. At the emperor's death it was said he ascended to heaven like a dragon. As a dragon ascends to heaven, the pressure of its feet on the clouds causes rain. Lung Wang is the Chinese dragon-king and supernatural rainmaker. One of the most common motifs in Chinese art is the dragon with its claws outstretched, reaching for a disk. Some explain the disk as the sun, which the dragon tries to swallow; being a watery creature, it wishes to drown the heat of the day. Others see the disk as a pearl or the moon. The dragon is one of the four constellations in Chinese astronomy. There are numerous motifs associated with dragons in the *Motif Index of Folk Literature.*

See also: BIBLE (REVELATION); FAFNIR; GEORGE, ST.; LUNG WANG; UTHER PENDRAGON

**Draupadi**   1016   In the Hindu epic poem *The Mahabharata,* the common wife of the five Pandu princes.

Draupadi, daughter of King Draupada of Panchala, was of dark complexion and great beauty, "as radiant and graceful as if she had descended from the city of the gods." (In a former existence she had been the daughter of a sage.) She performed a most severe penance in order that she might have a husband. The god Shiva, pleased with her devotion, said: "You shall have five husbands; for five times you said, 'Give me a husband.' " Her father, King Draupada, held a *svayamvara,* a tournament in which the princess would choose for herself a husband from among the contestants. Arjuna was selected from among the many suitors on account of his skill in archery.

When he and his four brothers returned home, they told their mother, Kunti, that they had made a great acquisition. Kunti replied that they should share it among themselves. The command of a mother could not be opposed, so the sage Vyasa settled the matter by having Draupadi "become the wife of all of the brethren." It was arranged that she should stay two days in the house of each brother, and no other brother should enter that house while she was there. Although she was shared by all the brothers, Draupadi loved Arjuna and displayed jealousy when he married Su-bhadra.

See also: ARJUNA; *MAHABHARATA, THE*; SHIVA; SU-BHADRA

**Dreamtime**   1017   In Australian mythology, the primeval past when spirits, gods, and ancestors walked on earth. A person's "dreaming" is his or her share of the myths, rites, and historical traditions of the "eternal" dreamtime.

**Drithelm, St.**   1018   Died c. 700. In Christian legend, monk. Feast, 1 September. Drithelm was seized with a fatal illness and died in 693, but before he was buried he arose from the dead and told his wife and children he had visited hell, Purgatory, and heaven. He then left his family and went to live as a monk. St. Bede tells his tale in his *History of the English People.*

See also: BEDE THE VENERABLE, ST.

**Drona** (a bucket)   1019   In the Hindu epic poem *The Mahabharata,* a priest who was generated in a bucket by his father, Bharadwaja. Drona taught archery to both the Pandavas and the Kauravas. When the great war broke out, however, Drona sided with the Kauravas, eventually becoming commander-in-chief. When he received news that his son had been killed, he was so upset that an enemy cut off his head while he was distracted with grief.

See also: *MAHABHARATA, THE*

**Drugaskan**   1020   In Persian mythology, section of hell filled with darkness and evil. Located "at the bottom of the gloomy existence," it is the lowest section of hell. Drugaskan is also the name of the son of the evil spirit, Ahriman, in Persian mythology.

See also: AHRIMAN

**Druids** (wise men of the woods)   1021   Priests of Druidism, the name given to the religion of the ancient Celts as practiced in Gaul and Britain. It is said that the Druids ate acorns to make themselves ready for prophecy.

The function of a Druid was described by Julius Caesar in *The Gallic Wars* (book 6). He wrote that Gallic society had two main classes: the warriors, or knights, and the Druids. The Druids "officiate at divine worship, regulate sacrifices public and private, and expound questions of ritual. Numbers of young men resort to them for study and hold them in high respect. They are judges in nearly all disputes, whether public or private, and in cases of crimes or murders or disputes about inheritances or boundaries, they settle the matter and fix awards and penalties. And those who do not abide by their decision, whether an individual or a tribe, they excommunicate, and this is their severest penalty.... As a rule Druids keep aloof from war, and do not pay taxes with the rest. They are exempt from military service and all obligation."

They had many gods, but Dis Pater was the father god from whom the Gauls claimed descent. The Druids observed two festivals each year. One, Beltaine (fire of god), was in honor of the sun and was held at the beginning of May; at the other, Samh'in (fire of peace), at the beginning of November, judicial functions were dealt with.

The concept of the Druids in literature and music has very little to do with any of the known facts culled from ancient sources. During the 18th century Druidism was greatly romanticized, with some English writers claiming that the Druids were descendants of Ashkenaz, eldest son of Gomer and great grandson of the biblical Noah. Others believed that the Druids were one of the 10 lost tribes of Israel. William Blake, the English poet and painter, found many of these ideas congenial to his own mythmaking. He wrote in "Jerusalem" that Adam, Noah, and other patriarchs were actually Druids, with Britain being "the Primitive Seat of the Patriarchal Religion," to which the Druid temples and oak groves in Britain were a "witness to this day." In the same poem Blake credits the Druids with inventing "female chastity." This concept of Druid vestal virgins is best known through the Italian opera *Norma* (1821) by Vincenzo Bellini with a libretto by Felice Romani. The work tells how Norma, the high priestess of the Druid temple of Esus, breaks her vow of virginity by bearing the Roman soldier Pollione two sons. At the end Norma confesses her sin to her people, saying she must be sacrificed. Both Norma and Pollione then enter the funeral pyre. In modern literature James Joyce mentions the Druids several times in his novel *Ulysses*.

See also: BELTAINE; OSSIAN; SAMH'IN

1022

**Dryads** (oak nymphs)  In Greek mythology, wood nymphs who lived in trees; also called hamadryads. They died when the tree died. Pope's *Moral Essays* (book 4.94) and Keats's "Ode to a Nightingale" cite the dryads.

1023

**Dryope** (oaken face)  In Greek mythology, a name for various women. According to the *Homeric Hymn to Pan* (attributed to Homer but not by him), one, a nymph of Arcadia, was the mother of Pan by Hermes. In Ovid's *Metamorphoses* (book 9) Dryope was a woman married to Andraemon, and she was raped by Apollo. The god first appeared as a turtle that Dryope picked up, but suddenly it was transformed into a serpent, which frightened the hamadryads who were companions of Dryope. Apollo then appeared in his human form and seduced Dryope. Their child was Amphisusus. When a year old the child was transformed, along with Dryope, into a lotus as a punishment for picking flowers from a tree that was the name of the nymph Lotis. Another Dryope was a nymph, mother of Tarquitus by Faunus in Vergil's *Aeneid* (book 10). Dryope was also the name of a woman of Lemnos whose shape the goddess Aphrodite assumed to persuade the women on the island to murder all of the men.

See also: *AENEID, THE*; APOLLO; HERMES; LOTUS; OVID; PAN

**Dsajaga**    In Siberian mythology, spirit who rules over the fate of the individual. It is closely connected with the sky god Tengri, who also watches over the fate of man. In *The Chronicle of Ssangang Ssetsen* Ghengis Khan is said to have been born through "the Dsajaga of the blue, eternal sky." Not only rulers were born under Dsajaga, however, but peasants as well. In laws written by Mongolian rulers, the phrase "by the Dsajaga of the eternal sky" is used, instead of the formula "by the Grace of God," so often found in Western documents. Each person is believed to have a special ruler over his life, called Dzajagatsi. Often the term Dzajagatsi Tengri is used.

See also: TENGRI

**Duat** (Tuat)    In Egyptian mythology, the underworld or other world. Originally, Duat signified the place through which the sun god Ra passed each evening after his setting, or death, on his journey to that portion of the sky where he would appear the next morning. Although generally called the underworld, Duat was not believed to be situated under the earth but rather away from the earth, in a part of the sky where the gods resided. It was the realm of the great god Osiris, who reigned over all other gods of the dead as well as the dead themselves. Duat was separated from the world by a range of mountains that surrounded it, forming a great valley. On one side the mountains separated the valley from the earth and on the other side, the valley from the heavens. Through Duat ran a river that was the counterpart of the Nile in Egypt and of the celestial Nile in heaven, and on each bank of this river lived a vast number of beasts and devils who were hostile to any being that invaded the valley. Duat was further divided into 12 sections, or *nomes*, each of which corresponded to one of the hours of the night.

According to one Egyptian text, *The Book of Pylons*, Duat is a long, narrow valley with sandy slopes, divided into two equal parts by a river on which the boat of the sun sails. Each of the 12 sections, or *nomes*, of the valley has its own demons, or ordeals, that the deceased has to pass in order to be worthy of life with Osiris. The same concept is used in Mozart's opera *The Magic Flute*, in which the hero, Tamino, undergoes a series of ordeals instituted by the high priest Sarastro in order to be worthy to praise Isis and Osiris.

Duat is sometimes called Ta-dchesert (the holy land), Neter-khertet, or Khert Neter (divine subterranean place).

See also: ISIS; OSIRIS; RA

**Dudugera**    In Melanesian mythology, the sun, according to a myth from New Guinea. Once a woman played with a fish that rubbed itself against her leg. In time her leg swelled, and when it was cut open, a baby, Dudugera, appeared. The young Dudugera did not get along with his playmates, so one day his great fish father came and took him away. Before he left, he told his mother and relatives to hide under a big rock because he was going to climb up to the sky on a plant and become the sun. They did as he asked. When Dudugera became the sun, his heat rays were destroying all plant and animal life until his mother threw some lime juice in his face. From that day clouds appeared, relieving the earth from the sun's heat.

**Dugong**    In Islamic mythology, herbivorous aquatic man of the Red Sea, the Indian Ocean, and the waters around Australia. In Malay mythology it is believed to have sprung from the remains of a pig on which Muhammad himself had dined before he pronounced pork to be cursed. It was cast into the sea by the prophet but revived and took the shape of the dugong. The tears of the dugong are believed to be a strong love charm. The dugong is also called a sea cow and may be an origin of mermaids in mythology.

See also: MUHAMMAD

**1028**

**Dumah** (Douma) (silence?)    In Jewish folklore, an angel of death to whom one has to give account. Isaac Bashevis Singer, in his short story "Short Friday," tells of a husband and a wife who discover they have died and are thinking about what is going to happen to the Sabbath meal they have just prepared. They realize, however, that they have to wait for the angel Dumah "with his fiery staff" and "give an account" of themselves to him. In their stillness they hear "the flapping of wings" and a "quiet singing" as they are taken to paradise. In Genesis (25:14) Dumah is a son of Ishmael and the presumed ancestor of an Arabian tribe. Dumah is also the name given to the guardian of the 14th gate, through which the goddess Ishtar passed on her journey to the underworld in Babylonian mythology.

See also: ISHMAEL; ISHTAR

**1029**

**Dun Cow**    In British legend, a fantastic cow slain by Sir Guy of Warwick on Dunsmore Heath. The Dun Cow was kept by a giant in Mitchel Fold (middle fold), Shropshire. Its milk was inexhaustible. One day an old woman who had filled her pail with its milk wanted to fill her sieve also, but this so enraged the cow that it broke away and wandered to Dunsmore, where it was killed. A huge tusk, probably from an elephant, is still shown at Harwick Castle as one of the horns of the Dun Cow.

See also: GUY OF WARWICK, SIR

**1030**

**Duns Scotus, Joannes**    1265–1308? In Christian legend, Franciscan theologian who supported the doctrine of the Immaculate Conception (that the Virgin Mary was born without Original Sin) against St. Thomas Aquinas, who opposed the doctrine. His followers were called Dunsers or Dunsmen. Tyndal says when they saw the new theology developing, "the old barking curs raged in every pulpit" against the new notions. The name for his fol-

lowers passed into the language as *dunce* because so much time was spent in his scholastic philosophy on "nonsense." Duns Scotus is also known as Doctor Subtilis.

See also: THOMAS AQUINAS, ST.; VIRGIN MARY

**1031**

**Dunstan, St.** (hill stone)    In Christian legend, archbishop of Canterbury, patron saint of blacksmiths, armorers, goldsmiths, locksmiths, musicians, and the blind. Feast, 19 May.

A monk of Glastonbury, Dunstan was a noted scholar, musician, painter (his self-portrait at the foot of Christ is still preserved at the Bodleian Library, Oxford), and metalworker. As a young man he was a great favorite of King Edmund, who admired his musical talents. He had such a strong influence over the king that he was accused of sorcery and driven from the court. One day, as the king was stag hunting, his dogs leaped over a precipice. The king thought he would be unable to rein his horse and would also fall. He prayed and thought of his ill treatment of Dunstan, and the horse stopped on the brink. The king then begged Dunstan to return to his court.

One legend tells how the devil asked St. Dunstan to shoe his "single hoof." He realized who his customer was, tied him to the wall, and proceeded. He caused the devil so much pain that he cried out for mercy. Dunstan agreed, but on the condition that the devil would never enter a place where a horseshoe was displayed. Another legend tells how Dunstan outwitted the devil. He was making a chalice to use at Mass when the devil suddenly appeared before him. The saint, however, was not afraid. He took the pincers out of the fire and seized the nose of the devil, who ran off howling and never again bothered the saint. An old poem commemorates the event:

St. Dunstan, as the story goes,
Once pulled the devil by the nose
With red-hot tongs, which made him roar
That he was heard three miles or more.

In Christian art St. Dunstan is portrayed as a bishop holding a pair of tongs.

1032

**Duppies**   In Haitian voodoo, evil spirits of the dead.

1033

**Durán, Fray Diego**   c. 1537—1588. Spanish historian who did missionary work in Latin America. Author of three works dealing with Aztec history and mythology: *Book of the Gods and Rites*, giving a detailed description of Aztec gods; *The Ancient Calendar*, a guide to the Mesoamerican system of counting time; and *Historia de las Indias de Nueva España y islas de tierra firme*, which tells the history of the Aztecs from their beginnings to their fall in 1521 at the hands of the Spanish. The *Historia* also contains numerous references to the religious and mythological beliefs of the Aztecs.

1034

**Duranki** (the bond that unites heaven and earth) Ancient name for Nippur, a Sumerian city sacred to the god Enlil. According to myth, Enlil split the earth's crust with his pickax at Nippur so that the first man could break through to the upper earth.

See also: ENLIL

1035

**Dur-yodhana** (hard to conquer)   In the Hindu epic poem *The Mahabharata*, a leader of the Kauravas against their enemies, the Pandavas. Dur-yodhana battled Bhima, one of the five Pandu princes. Bhima kicked Dur-yodhana in the head and left him mortally wounded. Dur-yodhana then asked his men to slay all of the Pandavas and bring Bhima's head to him before he died. Some Kauravas entered the Pandava camp and killed five young sons of the Pandavas. Their heads were brought to Dur-yodhana, who was told they were the five Pandu princes. In the

twilight Dur-yodhana was unable to tell the difference. When he asked for Bhima's head, one of the children's heads was given to him, and he crushed it. Because it was so easily crushed, he knew it could not be the head of Bhima. He cried out: "My enmity was against the Pandavas, not against these innocents." Dur-yodhana died shortly afterward of the wound inflicted by Bhima. Dur-yodhana was also called Su-yodhana (good fighter).

See also: BHIMA; *MAHABHARATA, THE*

1036

**Dushan the Mighty**   c.1308–1355. In Serbian legend, emperor crowned in 1346. Stefan Dushan ruled medieval Serbia at the peak of its power, consolidating and expanding the realm to include Albania, Bulgaria, Epirus, Macedonia, and northern Greece. Author of the Law Code (1349 and 1354), Stefan also became an important folk hero in Serbian heroic epic ballads. Noteworthy is *The Wedding of Stefan Dushan*, first collected by Vuk Stefanovich Karadzich in 1815.

See also: KARADZICH, VUK STEFANOVICH

1037

**Dustin, Hannah**   1657–after 1729. In American history and folklore, New England pioneer woman captured, along with her young son, by Indians in 1697. Eventually she and her son escaped after having killed and scalped ten of their captors. In Robert P. Tristram Coffin's ballad "The Lady of the Tomahawk" she scalps 20 braves.

1038

**Dvalin**   In Norse mythology, a dwarf who gave to the dwarfs magic runes that made them skillful in crafts. The kenning for poetry is "Dvalin's drink" because the mead of poetry was in the possession of the dwarfs. Dvalin, along with Alfrigga, Berling, and Grerr, possessed the magic necklace of the Brislings, which the goddess

Freyja wanted. She agreed to sleep one night with each dwarf to gain the necklace. In some accounts Dvalin is said to be the father of the Norns, who dispense fate. Dvalin is also the name of one of the harts at the foot of the world or cosmic tree, Yggdrasill.

See also: KENNING; NORNS; YGGDRASILL

**1039**

**Dwyvan and Dwyvach**   In Celtic mythology, the man and woman who built the ark *Nefyed Nevion* in the Welsh account of the flood. The flood was caused by the monster Addanc.

See also: BITH AND BIRREN; CESSAIR: NOAH

**1040**

**Dyaus and Prithivi** (shine and broad)   In early Hindu mythology, the sky god and the earth goddess; Dyaus is often called the "vigorous god" and Prithivi, "the heroic female." In many texts they are represented as the universal parents, not only of men but of the gods. Among their offspring were the storm god, Indra; Ushas, the dawn; and Agni, the fire god. One text asks: "Which of these two was first and which last? How have they been produced? Who knows?"

See also: AGNI; INDRA

**1041**

**Dybbuk** (attachment)   In Jewish folklore, the disembodied spirit of a dead person who cannot find rest, often owing to his sin. The most famous dramatic work on the subject is *The Dybbuk* by S. Ansky. In it a rabbinical student, Khonnon, turns into a dybbuk when he dies because he invoked Satan in order to win his love, Leye. He had been forbidden by her father, Sender, to marry her because he did not possess wealth. At the end of the play Leye, who has been possessed by Khonnon's spirit, is freed; she dies, and her spirit joins Khonnon's. A ballet by Leonard Bernstein titled *The Dybbuk* also deals with the folkloric spirit.

See also: SATAN

**1042**

**Dylan** (son of the wave)   In Celtic mythology, a sea god, son of Gwydion and Arianrhod, twin brother of Llewllaw. Dylan was slain by his uncle, Govannon, and a loud lament was made for him by the waves, his burial place being where their murmur sounds sullenly along the seacoast. Legend has it that Arianrhod gave birth immediately after stepping over Gwydion's magic wand.

See also: ARIANRHOD; GWYDION; LLEW LLAW GYFFES

**1043**

**Dzelarhons**   In North American Indian mythology (North Pacific Coast Indians), heroine who, accompanied by six canoes filled with people during their migrations across the Aleutian Islands, came to marry and settle with Kaiti, the bear god, chief of the Grizzlies. However, her husband did not have sexual intercourse with her for the first four nights of their marriage. When her uncle Githawn (salmon eater) was told of this, he made war on Kaiti and his tribe. When Githawn searched for Dzelarhons, all he found was a stone statue of her. Dzelarhons is called the Copper Woman, Volcano Woman, Frog Woman, or Copper Frog, depending on which tribe tells the story.

**1044**

**Dziady** (ancestors)   In Slavic folklore, ancestor spirits. The White Russians honor the Dziady four times a year, at home or at churchyard ceremonies. The autumn celebration is connected with the harvest and the spring celebration with Easter, when eggs (symbols of resurrection) are rolled and Christian priests bless the graves. In Bulgaria the ancestor spirits are called Zadusnica.

See also: EASTER

**1045**

**Dziwozony** (wild women)   In Polish folklore, wild women who have cold hearts but are extremely passionate. They are tall with thin faces and long disheveled hair. They fling their breasts over their shoulders in order to run. If they come upon an adult in the forest, the Dziwozony usually tickle the person to death. Younger people are often made their lovers. The Diva-ta-Zena in Bulgarian folklore is similar to the Polish version. She, however, throws her breasts over her shoulders to nurse her children. Sometimes the Dziwozony will substitute a *premien*, or changeling, for a human child.

1046

**Dzoavits** In North American Indian mythology (Shoshonean), an evil monster and a cannibal giant. Dzoavits stole two of Dove's children.

With the aid of Eagle, Dove saved the two, but Dzoavits would not give up and continued to pursue the group. Dzoavits was close upon them when Badger intervened. He dug two holes and had Dove and his children hide in one. When Dzoavits asked Badger where Dove and his children were, Badger pointed to the other hole. The monster quickly went into the hole, and just as quickly, Badger threw in some hot rocks and then sealed the hole with a stone.

# E

1047
**Ea** (Hea, Hoa)    In Near Eastern mythology (Sumero-Akkadian), god of sweet waters, earth, and wisdom; patron of the arts; one of the creators of humankind; also called Enki.

In the Babylonian epic poem *Enuma Elish*, Ea is given credit for creation:

Who but Ea created things?
And Ea knoweth everything.

In a much later text the myth of Ea's appearance to help mankind is told. The god appeared as "an animal endowed with reason," having a body "like that of a fish; and had under a fish's head another head, and also feet below, similar to those of men, subjoined to the fish's tail." This mysterious animal was "articulate" and spoke like a human, teaching men "every kind of art. He taught them to construct houses, to found temples, and to compile laws and explained to them principles of geometrical knowledge." Ea also taught mankind how to till the earth and "how to collect fruits . . . he instructed them in everything which could tend to soften manners and humanize mankind."

Ea's chief seat of worship was at Eridu, an old Sumerian city at the top of the Persian Gulf. His wife was the goddess Damkina, and his son was Marduk. In art his symbol was either a ram's or a goat's head, with the body of a fish. Copper was his metal. Ea was also known an Enki, "lord of the world," and Oannes.

See also: DAMKINA; MARDUK

*Eagle*

1048
**Eagle**    A large bird of prey noted for its strength and vision, often associated with sky gods. In Greek mythology the eagle was sacred to the sky god Zeus, who often took eagle form in his sexual adventures. When Zeus fell in love with the Trojan boy Ganymede he took the form of an eagle, swooped down, and abducted the boy. The eagle was also adopted as a symbol of the Roman sky god Jupiter, or Jove. The eagle as an imperial symbol appeared on Austrian and

Russian heraldic devices. When the United States chose the bald eagle for the new nation's symbol, Benjamin Franklin disagreed with the choice. He wrote to his daughter that the bird was a "rank coward" and had a "bad moral character; he does not get his living honestly." Franklin wanted the turkey to be chosen instead. The eagle is also a symbol of the Aztec god Tonatiuh and the Norse god Odin.

In Christian symbolism the eagle is often a symbol of Christ. Dante's *The Divine Comedy* calls the eagle the bird of God. St. John the Evangelist is often portrayed as an eagle or with an eagle companion because his Gospel account was considered by the Church Fathers the most elevated and spiritual of all four accounts. Nietzsche, the 19th-century German philosopher and despiser of Christianity, chose the eagle as one of the animal companions of the Solitary Sage in *Thus Spake Zarathustra*. The other animal companion is the snake. Nietzsche calls the eagle and the snake the "proudest and the shrewdest among animals." Both animals appear on the Mexican flag. There are numerous motifs associated with the eagle in the *Motif Index of Folk Literature*.

See also: GANYMEDE; JOHN THE EVANGELIST, ST.; JOVE; ODIN; TONATIUH; ZEUS

1049

**Eagle and the Arrow, The**   Aesopic fable found in various collections throughout the world, possibly of Eastern origin.

One day a bowman saw an eagle soaring lazily in the sky. Quickly, he notched an arrow and sent it whizzing after the bird. It found its mark, and the eagle felt itself wounded to death. As it slowly fluttered down to earth, it saw that the haft of the arrow that had pierced its breast was fitted with one of its own feathers.

Moral: *How often do we supply our enemies with the means of our own destruction!*

George Gordon Byron, in his *English Bards and Scotch Reviewers*, a satirical poem in heroic couplets that lambastes such poets as Southey,

Scott, Wordsworth, and Coleridge and praises Pope and Dryden, has an allusion to the fable of *The Eagle and the Arrow*:

> So the struck eagle, stretch'd upon the plain,
> No more through rolling clouds to soar
>   again,
> View'd his own feather on the fatal dart,
> And wing'd the shaft that quiver'd in his
>   heart.

Byron got the idea from Edmund Waller's poem *To a Lady Singing a Song of His Composing*. The fable is also told in La Fontaine's collection.

See also: AESOPIC FABLES; LA FONTAINE, JEAN DE

1050

**Earth Diver**   In North American Indian mythology, an account of the origin of the world. The culture hero dives repeatedly into primeval waters, or flood waters, to obtain mud or sand from which the earth is to be formed. Various aquatic animals are sent down into the waters that completely cover the earth. Each one fails, but the last one, either a beaver, hell diver, crawfish, or mink, succeeds, floating half dead to the surface. He has a little sand or mud under his claws. The mud is then placed on the surface of the water and magically expands to become the world as we know it. The Earth Diver myth is one of eight myths among North American Indians that have counterparts in Europe and Asia and were brought to the New World by people migrating to North America via northeastern Asia and Alaska, or from southeastern Asia by way of the Pacific islands to Meso-America. These creation myths treat the origin of the world, its inhabitants, the emergence of humans, the spider as creator, and so on.

See also: ATAENSIC; BUNJIL; DAYUNSI; HURA-KÁN; KUMOKUMS

**Earthly Paradise, The**   In medieval mythology, a land or island where everything was beautiful and restful, where death and decay were unknown. The Earthly Paradise was usually located far away to the east. William Morris's long poem *The Earthly Paradise* tells how a party of adventurers leave a Scandinavian port during a pestilence to search for the Earthly Paradise. After many adventures the remnant of the band discovers the land.

See also: SCHLARAFFENLAND

**Easter**   In Christianity, feast celebrating the Resurrection of Christ from the dead. The English name *Easter* was explained by St. Bede the Venerable as coming from the Anglo-Saxon goddess Eostre, who was associated with the season of new birth. Some modern scholars, however, contend that St. Bede misread the Anglo-Saxon word for spring, thinking it was an ancient pagan goddess.

Easter falls on the first Sunday after the full moon that occurs on the day of the vernal equinox (21 March) or on any of the next 28 days. Easter Day cannot be earlier than 22 March or later than 25 April. The date for Easter was fixed by the Council of Nicaea in 325, though various Christian groups still celebrate it at different times. Until the Roman church made headway in Britain during the Middle Ages, the Celtic church celebrated Easter at a time different from that of the Roman observance. Numerous battles were fought over the proper date, but eventually the stronger Roman position (it was backed by the pope and the rest of Western Christendom) won out.

Medieval documents often mention Easter as the beginning of the new year, especially in France, where it was so until 1563. At Easter time the Roman emperors, starting with Valentinian in 367, released nondangerous criminals from prison. This custom was followed by medieval popes, emperors, and kings for centuries.

The preparation for Easter season, beginning on Ash Wednesday and continuing for a week after Easter Day, was filled with pagan customs that had been revised in the light of Christianity. Germanic nations, for example, set bonfires in spring. This custom was frowned on by the Church, which tried to suppress it. But when Irish monks in the sixth and seventh centuries came to Germany, they brought their earlier pagan rites and would bless bonfires outside the church building on Holy Saturday. The custom spread to France, and eventually it was incorporated into the Easter liturgy of Rome in the ninth century. Even today the blessing of the new fire is part of the Vigil of Easter.

It was a custom during Easter celebration in the Middle Ages to raise the Host, or the cross, from the shrine of the sepulcher during the night of Holy Saturday. A figure of the dead Christ was also kept in the church from Holy Thursday until Holy Saturday, and the faithful would sit with it as at a wake.

Medieval celebrations of Easter began at dawn. According to one old legend, the sun dances on Easter morning or makes three jumps at the moment of its rising in honor of Christ's Resurrection. The rays of light penetrating the clouds were believed to be angels dancing for joy.

Part of the medieval Easter rites consisted of the sequence *Victimae Paschali Laudes* (Praise to the Paschal Victim), written by Wipo, a priest who about 1030 was court chaplain of the emperor Conrad. The poem, which was placed in the Latin Mass for Easter, is believed to have been the inspiration for miracle plays that developed from the 10th century on. (However, scholars still debate the origin of medieval drama.) In time plays dealing with Christmas, Epiphany, and other Christian feasts were written.

Some Easter folk traditions that have survived today are the Easter egg, rabbit, and lamb. During medieval times it was a tradition to give eggs at Easter to servants. King Edward I of England had 450 eggs boiled before Easter and dyed or covered with gold leaf. He then gave them to members of the royal household on Easter day. Eating of eggs was forbidden during Lent but allowed again on Easter Day. The egg was an earlier pagan symbol of rebirth and was presented at the spring equinox, the beginning of the pagan new year.

The Easter rabbit is first mentioned in a German book of 1572 and also was a pagan fertility symbol. The Easter lamb goes back to the Middle Ages; the lamb, holding a flag with a red cross on a white field, represented the resurrected Christ. A prayer for blessing lambs can be traced to the seventh century in Italy. In the ninth century Rome adopted the prayer, and a roasted lamb was part of the pope's dinner for Easter. It was believed lucky to meet a lamb during Easter time because the devil could assume any animal shape but one, the lamb, for the lamb was a symbol of Christ. Medieval Easter week was one long celebration. One Spanish missal of the ninth century has Mass texts for three masses each day of the Easter Octave. Gradually, however, the church reduced the celebration to three days. Since many people were baptized on Holy Saturday, they wore new white garments, from which we still have the custom of new clothes for Easter.

Monday and Tuesday of Easter week in northern countries were the traditional days of "drenching" and "switching," customs based on pagan fertility rites. The drenching custom consisted of the boys dousing the girls with buckets or bottles of water. In the switching ceremony the boys switched the women with pussy willow or leaved branches.

See also: ASH WEDNESDAY; BEDE THE VENERABLE, ST.; BONIFACE, ST.

---

**1053**

**Ebba of Codingham, St.** (boar protection) Ninth century. In Christian legend, martyr, abbess. Feast, 2 April. When the Danes invaded her land, Ebba, fearful that all of her nuns would be raped, cut off her nose and upper lip to make herself unattractive. Her nuns followed her example and also cut off their noses and disfigured themselves. When the Danes arrived and saw the noseless nuns, their anger flared, and they set the convent on fire, burning the nuns inside.

---

**1054**

**Ebisu** In Japanese Shinto-Buddhist mythology, god of daily food who was born deformed, having no legs and also being deaf. He is the god of honest dealing and is portrayed with a beard, wearing a two-pointed hat, laughing, and holding a fishing pole and a *tai*, a sea bream. He is the patron of tradesmen and fishermen. Sometimes he is called Hiruko. He is one of the Shichi Fukujin, the seven gods of good luck or fortune.

See also: SHICHI FUKUJIN

---

**1055**

**Echidna** (she-viper) In Greek mythology, half-woman, half-serpent monster, child of Chrysaor and Callirrhoë, the daughter of Oceanus (or Phorcys and Ceto). Echidna was the mother, by the monster Typhon, of Orthus, Geryon's hound, Cerberus, the Hydra, and the Chimaera. By Orthus she was the mother of the Sphinx and the Nemean Lion. According to Herodotus's *Histories* (book 3) the hero Heracles had three children by her, Agathyrsus, Gelonus, and Scytha. Echidna appears in Hesiod's *Theogony* (295 ff.) and Ovid's *Metamorphoses* (book 9).

See also: CALLIRRHOË; GERYON; HYDRA; OCEANUS; OVID; TYPHON

---

**1056**

**Echo** (ring, resound) In Greek mythology, a nymph of Mount Helicon; daughter of Gaea. Echo was deprived of speech by the ever-jealous Hera because she was a confidant of Zeus's many love affairs. She wasted away when Narcissus, whom she loved, did not return her love. Ovid's *Metamorphoses* (book 3) tells the tale. Juliet in Shakespeare's *Romeo and Juliet* (2.2) says:

Else would I tear the cave where Echo lies,
And make her airy tongue more hoarse than
    mine,
With repetition of my Romeo's name.
    (2.2.163–5)

English poets who have used or referred to
the tale of Echo are Chaucer, Spenser, Marlowe,
Milton, Shelley, and Keats.
   See also: CHAUCER; ECHO; GAEA; HERA; NARCIS-
SUS; NYMPHS; OVID; ZEUS

1057

**Edith of Wilton, St.** (prosperous war)    In
Christian legend, daughter of King Edgar of
England. Feast, 16 September.
   Edith's mother was a beautiful nun, Wilfrida,
who was taken by the king to be his mistress. As
soon as she could, Wilfrida escaped and returned
to her nunnery, but she bore a child, Edith. The
girl stayed with her mother in the convent but
spent most of her time dressing up in costly array. St. Ethelwold, who often visited the convent, rebuked the girl for her dress. She replied,
"Pride may exist under the garb of wretchedness
and a mind may be pure under these rich garments as under tattered ones."

1058

**Edmund, St.** (prosperity, guardian)    841–870.
King and martyr, invoked against plague. Feast,
20 November. When the Danes invaded East
Anglia in 870, they slew King Edward, who had
been crowned king of the East Angles in 855.
The king was shot with arrows and then beheaded. According to legend, when his followers
sought his body, they found a huge gray wolf
reverently watching over it. They bore it away,
the wolf quietly following, and interred the saint
in a town now known as Bury St. Edmund's. In
Christian art St. Edmund is portrayed with an
arrow in his hand. Sometimes a gray wolf
crouches at his feet.

1059

**Edyrn**    In Arthurian legend, son of Nudd, who
ousted Yniol from his earldom and tried to win
Enid, the earl's daughter. He was overthrown by
Geraint and sent to the court of King Arthur,
where he became a gentle person. He appears in
Tennyson's narrative "Marriage of Geraint,"
one of the *Idylls of the King*, and in *Geraint* in
Lady Charlotte Guest's translation of the Welsh
collection of tales *The Mabinogion*.
   See also: ARTHUR; *MABINOGION, THE*

1060

**Efé**    In African mythology (Pygmy), the first
man who God created. After God created Efé, he
wanted him to return to heaven so that he could
hunt for Him. Efé served God well in heaven,
but in time he wanted to return to earth. All of
the Pygmies came out to greet him on his return,
but because he had been away so long, no one
was able to recognize him, not even his brother.
When asked if God was still alive in the sky, Efé
said that he was, and as presents he gave the people three spears he had used for hunting in
heaven.
   See also: ABUK AND GARANG

1061

**Egeria** (of the black poplar)    In Roman mythology, protector of unborn babies; wife of Numa
Pompilius, second king of Rome. She melted
into tears when Numa died and was transformed
into a fountain by the goddess Diana. Ovid's
*Metamorphoses* (book 15) tells her tale.
   See also: OVID

1062

**Egil**    In Germanic mythology, peasant whom
the god Thor visited several times. Thor would
often leave his goats and chariot for the night.
Once he saw that Egil's family had no food and
told them to kill the goats but to make sure they
put the bones back into the skin when they had
finished. The evil god Loki, however, convinced

Egil's son Thialfi to break one of the bones and eat its marrow. When Thor returned, he brought the goats back to life, but one of them was missing a leg. To appease the god, Egil gave Thialfi and his sister Roskova as gifts to the god. Egil is also the name of a hero who, along with his two brothers Slagfin and Volund, married three Valkyries by stealing their swans after bathing. After nine years of marriage, however, the women returned to their swan shapes. The myth is told in the *Poetic Edda* in the *Song of Volund*.

See also: LOKI; *POETIC EDDA*; THOR; VALKYRIES

1063

**Ehecatl**  In Aztec mythology, wind god, a manifestation of the god Quetzalcoatl. One day Ehecatl realized that besides the fruits of the earth man also needed sexual love. He therefore went in search of a maiden, Mayahuel, who was in the underworld under the guardianship of Tzitzimitl. The maiden agreed to go with Ehecatl to the upper world, the earth, and there they had sexual intercourse. As the two touched the ground, a beautiful tree with two great branches shot up. One branch was known as "precious willow" and belonged to Ehecatl, the other was covered with flowers and belonged to Mayahuel. The sound of the wind in the trees was feared by the ancient Mexicans, who offered sacrifices to Ehecatl, going so far in some cases as to "bleed" the genital organ "by passing cords as long as fifteen to twenty yards through it," according to Fray Diego Durán in his *Book of the Gods and Rites*.

See also: MAYAUEL; QUETZALCOATL

1064

**Eikthyrnir** (oak-encircler)  In Norse mythology, the hart or stag that eats from the branches of the cosmic or world tree, Yggdrasill. The *Prose Edda* states that "whilst he is feeding so many drops fall from his antlers down into Hvergelmir that they furnish sufficient water for the

rivers that issuing thence flow through the celestial bodies."

See also: *PROSE EDDA*; YGGDRASIL

1065

**Einherjar**  In Germanic mythology, the warriors chosen by Odin. They reside at Valhalla and await the last great battle, Ragnarok. In the *Prose Edda* (c. 1220 C.E.) by Snorri Sturluson, these warriors are described as "all those men who have fallen in battle since the beginning of the world." It also says that they will be sent out against the forces of chaos during the last battle. One assumption is that the myth is based on an Odin cult, which included young warrior men who feasted endlessly with Odin.

See also: ODIN; *PROSE EDDA*; RAGNAROK; VALHALLA

1066

**Eirene** (peace)  In Greek mythology, goddess of peace and wealth, daughter of Zeus and Themis; called Pax by the Romans. In Greek art she was portrayed as a young woman with the infant Plutus, god of wealth, in her arms. Other attributes are the cornucopia, the olive branch, Hermes' staff, and ears of corn on her head.

See also: HERMES; PAX; THEMIS; ZEUS

1067

**Eka Abassi**  In African mythology (Ibibios of southern Nigeria), wife of Obumo, the thunder god; in some accounts she is said also to be the mother of Obumo. She is believed to be the mother of God and is regarded as the divine creatress. She is also believed to have conceived Obumo, her first-born, without the aid of a husband.

See also: OBUMO; VIRGIN MARY

1068

**Ek Balam** (Equebalam) (black jaguar?)  In the mythology of the ancient Indians of Yucatán, a god who may have been worshiped as a jaguar.

1069

**Ek Chauah** (Ekahau)    In Mayan mythology, a god of war, of cacao, and of traveling merchants; he is portrayed with a lance in one hand or in combat with another war god. In his role as god of traveling merchants, Ek Chauah is portrayed with a bundle of merchandise on his back. Paul Schellhas, when classifying the gods in some Mayan codices, gave Ek Chauah the letter *M*, and Ek Chauah is sometimes referred to as God M.

1070

**Ekkekko** (Ekeko, Ekako, Eq'eq'o)    In the mythology of the Peruvian highland Indians, domestic god of good luck. Ekkekko is portrayed as a small figure with a pot belly; he is covered with toy household utensils. To this day *alacitas* (fairs) in Bolivia sell objects in miniature in his honor. Thus, a woman will buy a miniature house in the hope that she will obtain a husband and a house of her own.

1071

**El**    In Near Eastern mythology, basic Semitic word for a god, often used to designate a supernatural power. Among the Canaanites and Phoenicians, El was the king of the gods, "creator of creation," the all-wise judge of humankind. In the Old Testament El and Elohim are often used to designate a god or the Hebrew god. Among the most frequent titles found in the Old Testament are the following: El Shadday (God, the one of mountains), translated as God Almighty in the King James Version; El Elyon (Exalted One, Most High); Melchizedek (Gen. 14:18), a priest of the "most high God"; El Olam (God of Eternity), originally a title of a Canaanite god worshiped at Beer-sheba and later applied to the Hebrew god, Yahweh, translated as "the Lord, the everlasting God" in the King James Version; El-Bethel (God of Bethel), the god who revealed himself to Jacob (Gen. 35:7); El Berith (God of the Covenant), appearing in Judges (9:46); El Elohe-Israel (God the God of Israel), the god to whom Jacob (Gen. 33:19– 20) built an altar in Shechem; and Elchim (god or gods), often appearing in the Old Testament. In Genesis, the King James translators substitute God for Elohim.

See also: MELCHIZEDEK; YAHWEH

*Elaine (A. Beardsley)*

1072

**Elaine** (the bright one, the shining one)    In Arthurian legend, the name of two women, both of whom were in love with Lancelot. The first Elaine was the daughter of King Pelles and the mother of Galahad by Lancelot. When Lancelot refused to marry her, Elaine used magic and assumed the form of Queen Guinever, who was loved by Lancelot. Through this deception, the first Elaine became the mother of Galahad. The second Elaine was known as the Lily of Astolat. Lancelot did not return her love, and she died. By her request her body was placed on a barge.

In her right hand was a lily and a letter avowing her love for Lancelot. An old servant rowed the barge until it reached the palace of King Arthur, where the king asked that the letter be read and then commanded the woman be buried as a queen. She is the subject of Tennyson's poem "The Lady of Shalott."

See also: ARTHUR; ASTOLAT; GALAHAD; GUINEVER; LANCELOT OF THE LAKE

**El Dorado** (the gilded man)   In Central and South American legends, a fantastic city and its king. The earliest form of the legend tells of a priest-king who once a year covered his body with oil and gold dust and bathed in a river, offering the gold to the river spirits. When the Spaniards came to the New World, the Indians told them of the city where the king lived (it was called Omagua, Manoa, Paytiti, or Enim). They usually located it far from their own cities, in the hope that the Spanish greed for gold would encourage the conquistadores to move on. The legend was probably based on a religious rite performed on Lake Guatavita.

In 1530 a German knight, Ambros von Alfinger, went in search of El Dorado, chaining his native carriers to one another and cutting off the heads of any who died, to avoid having to break the chains. This sadist was eventually killed by an arrow shot into his neck. Others who sought the city were Diego de Ordaz (1531), Philip von Hutten (1540–1541), and Sir Walter Raleigh (1595). One of the most interesting was a group under the leadership of Don Pedro de Ursúa that set out from Peru in 1559. Though Don Pedro was a gentleman, his men were a band of cutthroats. By the end of the journey most of them had been killed by the others. Another seeker, Lope de Aguirre, proclaimed himself prince and king of Tierre Firme; he was murdered by one of his men. His name continues in Venezuelan folklore, in which the phosphorescence of a swamp is called *fuego de Aguirre* (Aguirre's fire).

The term *El Dorado* has come to be a metaphor for any place that offers unrealistic hope of quick riches. Voltaire, in his satirical book *Candide*, had the hero discover the country of El Dorado. Candide is told by a 172-year-old man that El Dorado was the ancient country of the Incas, "who left it very indiscreetly, in order to conquer one part of the world; instead of doing which, they themselves were all destroyed by the Spaniards." He tells Candide that "the Spaniards have some confused idea of this country and have called it El Dorado." Candide and his associate Cacambo are entertained in the kingdom, given gold (which is of no value to the inhabitants), and then placed on a specially constructed machine that carries them out of the country. Edgar Allan Poe's poem *Eldorado* also invokes the legend.

See also: GUATAVITA LAKE

**Electra** (amber)   In Greek mythology, daughter of Agamemnon and Clytemnestra; sister of Orestes, Iphigenia, and Chrysothemis. Electra convinced her brother Orestes to murder their mother, Clytemnestra, and Aegisthus, their mother's lover, in retaliation for the murder of their father, Agamemnon. In later life she married Pylades and was mother of Medon and Strophius. Electra is also known as Laodice. Electra appears in Sophocles' *Electra*, Euripides' play *Electra*, Richard Strauss's one-act opera *Electra* (1909), Giraudoux's *Electre* (1939), Eugene O'Neill's *Mourning Becomes Electra* (1931), which later was filmed, and Cacoyannis's film *Electra*. The term *Electra complex* is sometimes used to describe the pathological relationship of a woman with men, based on her unresolved conflicts with her father.

See also: AGAMEMNON; IPHIGENIA; LAODICE; ORESTES

**El El**   In the mythology of the Puelcho Indians of the Patagonian pampas in South America, El

*Electra mourning for Orestes*

or lives of the Buddha, tells how the future Buddha gave away his father's white elephant to bring rainfall to a nearby country suffering from drought and famine. The king's subjects felt betrayed and forced the future Buddha into exile. Buddha's birth is connected with a white elephant. Buddha's mother, Queen Maya, had a dream of a white elephant who entered her body. When she told her dream to the soothsayers, they said she would bear a son who would either rule the world or save it. She bore the latter, the Buddha.

In Chinese folklore the elephant is a symbol of sagacity and prudence, as well as strength. In Roman belief the elephant was said to be a religious animal, one who worshiped the sun and stars. In medieval Christian folklore it was believed the elephant could not bend its knees and had to lean against a tree to sleep. If the tree broke, the elephant would fall and could never get up. In modern folklore Dumbo and Babar, both children's book characters, portray the elephant as a sweet, lovable animal.

See also: BUDDHA, THE; GANESHA; *JATAKA*

El is the leader of a host of demons, called Quezubu, who are bent on destroying mankind.

1076

**Elephant**    A large mammal with large floppy ears, ivory tusks, and flexible trunk found in India and Africa. In Hindu mythology the elephant is a manifestation of Ganesha, the friendly god who brings good luck to his worshipers. No venture or undertaking is begun without prayers being offered to the elephant deity. In Hindu folklore it is also believed that white elephants attract white clouds and thus cause rain. If a ruler did away with a white elephant, his people would feel betrayed. In Buddhist folklore one tale in the *Jataka*, a collection of tales on the previous births

1077

**Eleusinian Mysteries**    In ancient Greece, sacred rites initiated by Eumolpus and Celeus in honor of the goddess Demeter and her daughter Persephone; held at Eleusis, a city 14 miles west of Athens, near the Isthmus of Corinth. Celebrated in February and September, the rites consisted of purifications, fasts, and dramas, but the exact particulars of each are not known. Their purpose was to ensure rebirth and immortality. Because such rites conflicted with Christianity, they were abolished by Emperor Theodosius at the end of the fourth century. Swinburne's "At Eleusis," Shelley's "Song of Proserpine, While Gathering Flowers on the Plain of Enna," Tennyson's "Demeter and Persephone," and George Meredith's "The Appeasement of Demeter" all deal with Demeter and Persephone.

See also: DEMETER; PERSEPHONE

**Elfthryth**   In medieval British legend, a queen noted for her beauty. King Edgar sent Aethelwald, his friend, to ascertain if Elfthryth was really as beautiful as she was reported to be. When Aethelwald saw Elfthryth, he fell in love with her. Reporting to the king, he said she was not beautiful enough for the king but was rich enough to make an eligible wife for himself. The king agreed to the match and became godfather to the first child, Edgar. One day the king told his friend he intended to pay him a visit to see his wife for the first time. Aethelwald then told his wife the truth and begged her to make herself as ugly as possible. Indignant, she appeared in all her beauty. When the king saw her, he fell in love with her, slew his friend Aethelwald, and married Elfthryth. A similar tale is told in the *Histories* of the Greek writer Herodotus, with Prexaspes as the name of the woman and Kambyses that of the king.

**Elgin Marbles**   Popular name given to Greek sculptures from the Parthenon at Athens portraying Theseus, Lapiths, Centaurs, three Fates, Iris, and others. They were removed from the ruins by the seventh earl of Elgin in 1801–1803. The sculptures, displayed in the British Museum as the "Parthenon Sculptures," are the work of Phidias (c. 490–415 B.C.E.) or his studio and pupils.

See also: CENTAUR; LAPITHS; IRIS; THESEUS

**Elidure**   In British mythology, a king who was placed on the throne three times. He first came to the throne when he believed his brother Artegal (Arthgallo) was dead. At the return of Artegal he stepped down. Ten years later Artegal died, and Elidure again was made king. Shortly afterward he was deposed by two younger brothers. Finally, they both died, and he was made king for the third time. He appears in Geoffrey of Monmouth's *History of the Kings of Britain*, in the poet Milton's *History of Britain*, and in William Wordsworth's poem *Artegal and Elidure*, which was inspired by Milton's and Monmouth's accounts of the king.

**Elijah** (my god is Yahweh)   Ninth century B.C.E. In the Bible, O.T., prophet taken up to heaven in a chariot of fire. Elijah prophesied during the reigns of Ahab and Jezebel. One of his major battles was against the worship of Baal as instituted by Jezebel. In a competition on Mount Carmel, Elijah called on Yahweh, the Hebrew god, to set fire to the altar sacrifice, winning the contest when Baal's priests could not muster their god to do the same. Though he won, Elijah had to flee from Jezebel. He went to Mount Horab (Mount Carmel), where he was fed by an angel, as earlier at Cherith he had been fed by ravens. While on the mountain he heard or felt the presence of Yahweh in "a still small voice"(1 Kings 2:11). As he was being taken to heaven, his mantle fell on his successor, Elisha (2 Kings 2:13). In the New Testament, Elijah appears at

*Elijah*

the Transfiguration of Jesus, along with Moses. A place for the prophet is set aside at every Passover meal. The Carmelite religious order claims Elijah as its founder because he lived a solitary life in a cave on Mount Carmel. Dieric Bouts (c. 1415–1475) painted an *Elijah Comforted by an Angel*, and Giovanni Battista Piazzetta (1682–1754) painted *Elijah Taken Up to Heaven in a Chariot of Fire*. Mendelssohn's oratorio *Elijah* also deals with the prophet. Elias is the Greek form of his name.

See also: ELISHA; JEZEBEL; YAHWEH

*Elisha*

**1082**

**Elisha** (God is salvation)    Ninth century B.C.E. In the Bible, O.T., attendant and disciple of the prophet Elijah. Among his miracles, the influence of which can be seen in New Testament writings, are the purification of Jericho springs (2 Kings 2:19–22), the multiplication of the widow's oil (2 Kings 4:1–7), returning a woman's son to life (2 Kings 4:8–37), increasing loaves (2 Kings 4:42–44), and the cleansing of Naaman, army chief of the king of Syria (2 Kings 5:1–14).

See also: ELIJAH

**1083**

**Elivagar** (rivers whipped by passing showers) In Norse mythology, a river located at the outer reaches of the mythological world, filled with venom that froze over the icy banks of Ginnun-

gagap, the abyss from which the primeval giant Ymir was born. Elivagar is mentioned in the *Prose Edda*.

See also: GINNUNGAGAP; *PROSE EDDA*; YMIR

**1084**

**Elizabeth, St.** (God swearer)    In the New Testament, mother of John the Baptist, wife of Zacharias, and cousin of the Virgin Mary (Luke 1:11–13). Feast, 5 November. Although an old woman, she bore John the Baptist. When Mary knew she was pregnant by the Holy Spirit, she went to visit Elizabeth, who greeted her with "Whence is this to me, that the mother of my Lord should come to me?" (Luke 1:43). This scene, called the Visitation, is frequently painted in Christian art.

See also: JOHN THE BAPTIST, ST.; VIRGIN MARY

**1085**

**Elizabeth of Portugal, St.** (God has sworn) 1271–1336. In Christian legend, patron saint of peacemakers. Feast, 8 July.

Unhappily married to King Denis of Portugal, Elizabeth devoted her time to negotiating peace between rival elements in her society, such as Ferdinand IV of Castile and his cousin and Ferdinand and James II of Aragon. After the death of her husband she retired to a convent and became a Poor Clare. Schiller's poem *Fridolin* recounts a legend in which St. Elizabeth saved her servant from being murdered by her husband. In the poem, however, the setting is Germany, and the saint is called *Die Gräfin von Savern* (The Countess of Savern). In Spanish her name is Santa Isabel de Paz.

See also: CLARE, ST.

**1086**

**El-lal**    In the mythology of the Tehuelche Indians of the Patagonian pampas in South America, a creator-hero god.

El-lal's father, Nosjthe, wanted to eat his son and snatched him from his mother's womb. A rodent saved the child and carried him to a cave that Nosjthe was unable to enter. The rodent taught El-lal the secrets of plants and the different paths in the mountains. El-lal then invented the bow and arrow, and with these he learned how to hunt wild animals. El-lal did not hold a grudge against his father but taught him all he knew, and Nosjthe acted "as master of it" even while still plotting to kill his son. He followed El-lal across the Andes, but when he was about to kill him a dense forest arose between the two, saving El-lal. The hero descended to the plain, which in the meantime had become populated with men and women. Among the group was also a giant, Goshy-e, who liked to eat children. El-lal fought against the giant, but his arrows were useless. He then transformed himself into a gadfly and, entering the stomach of the giant, wounded Goshy-e fatally with his sting. After numerous other heroic feats El-lal wanted to marry the daughter of the sun, but she refused. El-lal left the earth, borne on the wings of a swan, and found eternal rest "in the verdant island that rose among the waves at the place where arrows shot by him had fallen on the surface of the water," according to Ramón Lista in *Los Indios Tehuelches*.

---

### Ellora
1087

**Ellora**   Site in Maharashtra, India, associated with the deeds of many gods and heroes, as well as with ancient blood sacrifices. There are numerous Hindu, Jain, and Buddhist cave temples in the area.

---

### Eloy of Noyon, St.
1088

**Eloy of Noyon, St.**   588–659. In Christian legend, patron saint of metalworkers, goldsmiths, farriers, and horses. Feast, 1 December.

Eloy was a goldsmith of Limoges who went into the service of King Clotaire II in Paris. The king asked him to make a throne for him, and Eloy was supplied with gold and jewels for the work. After making the throne, there was so much precious metal and so many stones left over that Eloy made a second throne for the king rather than pocket the leftover materials. The king was so pleased with the work and with Eloy's honesty that he took him into his confidence. Clotaire's successor, King Dagobert, made Eloy the master of the mint. He cast the dies for the coinage of the realm (13 are known to bear his name). When King Dagobert died, Eloy was made bishop of Noyon.

He was sent to preach in Belgium and, legend says, he went as far as Sweden and Denmark. Before his consecration as bishop, he was tempted by the devil. One day a horse was brought to him to be shod. The animal was possessed by a devil. Eloy cut off the leg of the horse and quietly put on the shoe. When he was done he made the sign of the cross over the leg, and it attached itself to the horse. The greatest oath of Chaucer's prioress in *The Canterbury Tales* is "By Seint Eloy."

In Christian art St. Eloy of Noyon is portrayed either as a bishop or a smith. In either case he holds his smith's tools, tongs, hammer, or bellows. The miracle of the horse is portrayed on the exterior of Or-San-Michele at Florence by Nanni di Banco.

*Elves*

---

### Elves
1089

**Elves**   In Norse mythology the elves are often associated with the Aesir. The English translation of *Alfar* is elves. It also can be translated as "dwarfs."

See also: AESIR; ALF; ALFAR; ALFHEIM; NIBELUNGS; NINE WORLDS

1090

**Elysium**   In Greek and Roman mythology, the home of blessed dead. In early Greek mythology it was said to be situated in the Islands of the Blessed in some remote part of the earth. In later Greek and Roman mythology the location of the Elysian Fields (another name) was in the underworld. Vergil's *Aeneid* (book 6) tells how the hero Aeneas meets his dead father, Anchises, in the Elysian fields. Elysium is used in Shakespeare's *Two Gentlemen of Verona* (2.7.37), *Henry VI, Part III* (1.2.30), and *Twelfth Night* (1.2.3); Milton's *Comus* (257); Cowper's *Progress of Error*; Andrew Lang's *The Fortunate Islands*; Schiller's *Elysium*; Shelley's "Ode to Naples" (30); and Swinburne's "Garden of Proserpine." The Champs Elysées in Paris is named after the Greek myth.

See also: *AENEID, THE*

1091

**Emma Ten**   In Japanese Buddhist mythology, a god based on the Hindu god of death, Yama, portrayed sometimes as a youth with three eyes, carrying in his right hand a scepter terminating in a small Bodhisattva head. He is one of the Jiu No O, 12 Japanese Buddhist gods and goddesses adopted from Hindu mythology.

See also: BODHISATTVA; JIU NO O; YAMA

1092

**Enceladus** (clear-voiced)   In Greek and Roman mythology, a giant, son of Titan and Gaea. Enceladus fled from Phlegra to Sicily pursued by Zeus, who hurled a thunderbolt to destroy him. Mount Aetna was then placed above his body. When Enceladus turns over, an earthquake results. When the giant hisses and thrusts out his fiery tongue, Mount Etna erupts. Vergil's *Aeneid* (book 3) cites the myth. In variant myths he was killed by Heracles or by Athena, who placed Mount Aetna over his body.

See also: *AENEID, THE*; ATHENA; GAEA; HERACLES; TITANS; ZEUS

1093

**Enchanted Horse, The**   Tale in *The Thousand and One Nights* (nights 357–371). A Persian inventor constructed a mechanical horse for Sabour, king of the Persians, and as a reward the king offered the old man his daughter. However, the girl did not want to marry the old man and asked her brother to help her. The young prince went to the old man and asked him about the mechanical horse, which could soar into the sky. The inventor, aware of the prince's hatred for him, taught the prince how to mount the horse, and how to let it fly—but he didn't tell him how to get the horse down again.

The young man ascended to the heavens and then realized that he did not know how to get down. After thinking about it for some time and calling upon Allah, he discovered the peg to let the horse down. The prince came to a city where he found a beautiful princess. After many adventures he finally married her and returned home. His father, the king, then destroyed the magic horse.

See also: ALLAH; *THOUSAND AND ONE NIGHTS, THE*

1094

**Endicott, John**   1588–1666. In American history and folklore, colonial administrator, and acting governor of Massachusetts Bay Colony until 1630. An intolerant Puritan, Endicott persecuted the Quakers and high-church Anglicans who did not follow his narrow views of Christianity. Hawthorne's short story "Endicott and the Red Cross," included in *Twice Told Tales*, tells the legend of Endicott's cutting the red cross, symbol of St. George, patron saint of England, from the English flag. Hawthorne has Endicott say: "Before God and man, I will avouch the deed. . . . Beat the flourish, drummers!—shout, soldiers and people!—in honor of the ensign of New England. Neither Pope nor Tyrant hath part in it now." Longfellow's play *John Endicott*, part of his *New England Tragedies*, deals with Endicott's persecution of Quakers in Boston.

**Endo Morito** (Mongaku Shonin, Endo Musha Morito)   12th century C.E. In Japanese legend, a hero, a warrior who killed the woman he loved, and later a monk.

Endo Morito was a captain living in Kyoto who fell in love with Kesa, the wife of a samurai, Watanabe Wataru. When Kesa resisted his advances, Endo Morito vowed to kill her family unless she allowed him to murder her husband and agreed to become his wife. She made an appointment to receive him in her house at night, when he would find her husband asleep alone in a room and could kill him. Endo came and cut off the head of the person he found sleeping in the appointed room, only to discover that it was Kesa herself. Her husband being on a journey, she had dressed herself in some of his clothes and sacrificed herself to save her honor. Endo was overcome with grief, shaved his head, and became a monk, calling himself Mongaku. He retired to the district of Oki and for 21 days remained naked, holding in his teeth the *vajra*-shaped handle of his bell, counting his beads, and praying under a waterfall. In Japanese art Endo Morito is often portrayed doing his penance.

**Endymion** (weighing on the mind)   In Greek mythology, handsome youth, son of Acthlius or of Zeus and Calyce. Endymion was the king of Elis. In some accounts Zeus gave him the choice of death or immortal sleep. The king chose sleep. Endymion was loved by the moon goddess Selene (or Artemis), who saw him naked. Artemis (or Selene) made love to Endymion while he was asleep and bore him 50 daughters. To preserve his beauty Artemis made him sleep everlastingly. Shakespeare's *The Merchant of Venice* (5.1) has Portia explain a moonless night by saying, "the moon sleeps with Endymion, / And would not be awak'd." Endymion appears in Spenser's *Epithalamium* (372 ff.), John Lyly's play *Endymion, the Man in the Moon* (1606), Michael Drayton's *Endymion and Phoebe* (1595), and Keats's narra-

tive poem *Endymion*. Endymion was painted by Tintoretto, Van Dyke, and Rubens.

See also: ARTEMIS; SELENE; ZEUS

**Enkidu** (Eabani, Endimdu, Engidu, Enkita) (land of the good place)   In the Babylonian epic poem *Gilgamesh*, rival and companion to Gilgamesh. He was molded of clay by Aruru, goddess of creation, in the image of "the essence of Anu," the sky god, and of Ninurta, the war god. Enkidu is the archetypal wild or "natural" man in contrast to the sophisticated Gilgamesh. In Babylonian religion he became the patron god of animals because in the poem he is credited with many animal-like qualities until he tastes sex with a harlot. He then becomes a man, an enemy in the eyes of the animals.

See also: ANU; ARURU; GILGAMESH; NINURTA

**Enlil** (Bel Enlil, Eilil, Illillos) (storm god)   In Near Eastern mythology (Sumero-Akkadian), creator god, storm god, god of earth and air; he was also called father of the gods and king of heaven and earth, as well as the king of all lands, patron god of the city of Nippur, and lord of the underworld. Often Enlil was called Bel (lord) in other Near Eastern mythologies.

In one myth, titled *Enlil and the Creation of the Pickax*, Enlil separates Ansar (the upper heavens) and Kisar (the earth), taking earth as his portion. He then brings up "the seed of the land" from the earth and discovers the pickax, which he teaches man to use. In a variant myth Enlil is responsible for the creation of trees and grains, as well as for appointing the seasons.

Another myth tells how Enlil was banished to the underworld for rape. Before man was created, Enlil lived in the city of Nippur with the goddess Ninlil and her mother, Nunbarshegunu. One day the mother told her daughter to bathe in the river so "the bright-eyed Enlil" would see her and then marry her. Enlil saw Ninlil and wanted to have sexual intercourse with her, but the girl said:

"My vagina is too small, it does not know how to copulate.
My lips are too small, they do not know how to kiss. . . ."

Enlil paid no attention and raped Ninlil. The gods in anger banished him to the underworld. Ninlil became pregnant and followed Enlil to the underworld, giving birth to the moon god Sin.

See also: BEL; SIN

1099

**Ennead** (nine)   In Egyptian mythology, nine deities whose characteristics symbolize the elemental-primal forces in the universe. The Great Ennead revolved around the mythology of Heliopolis, a suburb of modern Cairo, and consisted of Atum the sole creator, his offspring Shu (air) and Tefnut (water), and their children Geb (earth), Nut (sky), Isis, Osiris, Seth, and Nephthys. As time passed, other cult centers developed their own enneads, and therefore the numbers varied. The ennead at Thebes consisted of 15 deities, and that of Hermopolis consisted of 8. The latter became so famous that it is called the Ogdoad of Hermopolis (the eight deities of that site). They were Nun and Naunet, Huh and Hauhet, Kuk and Kauket, Amen and Amunet. The four male gods were portrayed as frog-headed; the females were shown as snake-headed.

See also: AMUN; ATEN; GEB; ISIS; OSIRIS; NEPHTHYS; NUT; SET; SHU; TEFNUT

1100

**Enoch** (dedicated)   In the Bible, O.T., father of Methuselah; he "walked with God: and he was not; for God took him"(Gen. 5:24). This is generally understood to mean he did not die but was taken to heaven like the prophet Elijah. In the New Testament the Epistle of Jude (chap. 14)

describes Enoch as "the seventh from Adam." In medieval Jewish folklore Aupiel, the tallest angel, is credited with taking Enoch to heaven.

See also: ELIJAH; METHUSELAH

1101

**Ephialtes** (he who leaps upon)   In Greek mythology, a giant, son of Poseidon (or Aloeus and Iphimedeia or Uranus and Gaea), twin brother of Otus. When the war between the Titans (giants) and the gods took place, Ephialtes was nine years old and had grown nine inches every month. Ephialtes was killed by Apollo, according to some accounts, or by Apollo and Heracles, each of whom shot an arrow into each eye of the giant.

See also: APOLLO; GAEA; HERACLES; POSEIDON; TITANS; URANUS

1102

**Ephraim ben Sancho and the Parable of the Two Gems**   Jewish folktale from *Liber Shebet Yehuda* (The Book of the Rod of Judah) by Solomon ibn Verga, written in the 16th century.

Often Christian kings would invite Jews to debate with Christians the various merits of their faiths. One day Nicholas of Valencia, who hated the Jews, asked Don Pedro, king of Aragon, to bring Ephraim ben Sancho to court to ask him which faith was superior, Judaism or Christianity.

When Ephraim was brought to court he asked the king for three days to come back with an answer. When he returned he had a sad look.

"What is wrong?" asked the king.

"A month ago," replied Ephraim, "a neighbor who is a jeweler went on a journey. Before he left he gave me instructions to keep the peace between his two sons, both of whom he had given precious gems. They came to me asking which gem was the superior of the two. I told them their father was the only man who could answer that and they beat me."

"They have mistreated you," the king replied, "and should be punished."

"O king," replied Ephraim, "may your ears hear what your mouth has said. The two brothers were Esau and Jacob [the twin sons of Isaac in the Old Testament]. Each received from God a priceless gem. You have asked me which religion is superior. How can I answer; only our Father in heaven can tell us."

When the king heard the wise reply, he rebuked his counselor, Nicholas of Valencia, and praised Ephraim for his wisdom.

See also: ESAU; ISAAC; JACOB

**Epimenides**   1103   In Greek mythology, a culture hero and a shepherd of Crete. He wrote poetry, taught the worship of the gods, and built the first temples. One day he fell asleep while searching for lost sheep and slept for 57 years.

**Epona** (the great mare)   1104   In Roman mythology, a Celtic goddess, daughter of a man and a mare; she protected cattle, oxen, and horses. Epona was worshiped in Roman Gaul, from Spain to the Balkans and from northern Britain to Italy. In art she was portrayed riding on a horse or seated and surrounded by mares. Juvenal's *Eighth Satire* (157) mentions the goddess.

**Erato** (sexual passion)   1105   In Greek mythology, one of the nine Muses; Muse of love or erotic poetry, lyrics, and marriage songs; daughter of Zeus and Mnemosyne. Her symbol was a lyre. The Muses are invoked at the beginning of Homer's *Iliad* and *Odyssey*, Spenser's *Teares of the Muses* and *The Fairie Queene* (Prologue, 2), Shakespeare's *Sonnet XXXVIII*, Gray's *Progress of Poesy* (2.3), Milton's *Paradise Lost* (book 7.1), Byron's *Childe Harold* (1.62), Wordsworth's "Ode" (1816), and Matthew Arnold's "Consolation" and *Empedocles on Etna*.

See also: *ILIAD, THE; ODYSSEY, THE; ZEUS*

*Erato*

**Erda** (earth)   1106   In Germanic mythology, earth goddess, the protector of secret treasures, but especially known as the giver of strength and nourishment for plants, animals, and humans. She is almost always viewed as a motherly goddess. She is known in Norse mythology as Jord. She appears in Richard Wagner's *Der Ring des Nibelungen*. In his *Das Rhinegold* the goddess warns Wotan (Odin) to give up the ring.

Yield it, Wotan! Yield it!
Flee the ring's dread curse!
Awful
And utter disaster
It will doom thee to.

The god does not listen to Erda's plea and as a result eventually brings about the destruction of all of the gods and humankind. During the Middle Ages plows were carried in Christian Shrovetide processions to bless the earth, an indiction that the goddess may still have been worshiped. Erda is portrayed by Arthur Rackham in his illustrations for Wagner's Ring Cycle. Erda is also known as Hertha or Aertha.

See also: NERTHUS; TUISTO; *RING DES NIBELUN-GEN, DER*

1107
**Eremon** ( Herimon)    In Celtic mythology, the first Milesian king of Ireland. Eremon was said to be a contemporary of King David of the Bible. He was the elder of two brothers, but after the victory of the Milesians over the Danaans, the original inhabitants of the land, Eber, his brother, refused to obey Eremon. A war ensued in which Eber was killed, but the feud was continued by their descendants.

See also: DAVID, KING

1108
**Ereshkigal** (queen of the great below)    In Near Eastern mythology (Babylonian-Assyrian), goddess of the underworld, married to the war god Nergal.

Once the gods made a feast and sent a message to Ereshkigal saying that, though they could go down to her realm of the dead, she could not come up to their home, and therefore it would be best if she sent a messenger to fetch the food set aside for her. Ereshkigal sent a messenger. When he arrived, all of the gods stood up to receive him, except for Nergal, who did not show the proper respect.

When the messenger returned to Ereshkigal, he told her what had happened. The goddess then asked that the delinquent be sent to her so that she could kill him. The gods discussed the matter and decided to send the culprit to the vengeful goddess. When Nergal arrived in the underworld, he grabbed Ereshkigal by her hair and dragged her from her throne.

"Do not kill me, my brother," cried the goddess. "Let me speak with you. You shall be my husband and I will be your wife. I will make you to rule the whole earth. I will place the Tablet of Wisdom in your hand. You shall be Lord and I will be Lady."

Nergal kissed the goddess, wiping away her tears.

"Whatever you have asked me in the past will now be yours," Nergal replied. The two were then married.

In many texts Ereshkigal is called Allatu.

See also: NERGAL

1109
**Erh-shih-ssu Hsiao** (24 examples of filial piety)    In Chinese folklore, 24 individuals who exemplify the important virtues. They are

1. Emperor Shun, 2317–2207 B.C.E. Though mistreated by his father, Shun maintained the proper respect for him. Eventually Emperor Yao chose Shun to succeed him, even passing over his own son. In art Shun is often portrayed plowing a field with the aid of an elephant, which helped him do the work given him by his evil father.

2. Tseng Shen, 505–347 B.C.E. A disciple of Confucius. When he was gathering fuel in the woods, his mother at home, in her anxiety to see him, bit her finger. At once he knew his mother wished to see him because the sympathy between the two was so strong.

3. Emperor Wen, 179–156 B.C.E. He stayed with his mother for three years during her illness, never leaving her room or changing his clothes.

4. Min Sun, sixth century B.C.E. A pupil of Confucius. His father remarried, and the step-mother disliked the boy. When the father discovered this, he wished to divorce his wife, but Min Sun pleaded with his father, saying it would leave her two sons without a mother.

5. Chung Yu, 543–480 B.C.E. A disciple of Confucius. He carried rice bags on his back to

support his poor parents. He is said to have been originally the son of the thunder god. He is also called Tze Lu and in Japanese legend is known as Chiuyu.

6. T'ung Yung, second century C.E. He had no money to bury his parents, so he sold himself to raise the money. When he returned home he met a young woman who offered to marry him, releasing him from his bondage. His owner demanded 300 pieces of silk, which the girl wove in a month. She was Chih N'u', the Weaving Damsel, sent by heaven to reward T'ung Yung for his devotion. In Japanese legend he is called Tovei.

7. Yen Tz'u (Chou dynasty?). His parents wanted doe's milk, which he procured by dressing in deer skins and mingling with the herd. In Japanese he is called Enshi.

8. Chiang Ko (Kiang Keh), 500 C.E. When his mother was captured by robbers, he asked the robber chief permission to take her away. He then carried her a long distance on his back.

9. Lu Hsü (Lu Sü), first century C.E. He was released from jail on account of his devotion to his mother. When he was six years old, he was invited to the house of a rich neighbor, Yüan Chou, and was given some oranges to eat. As he was taking leave, his host saw two oranges fall from his dress. Yüan Chou asked the boy why he hadn't eaten the oranges. Lu Hsü replied that his mother was very fond of oranges, and he had not eaten them so he could give them to her. In Japanese legend Lu Hsü is called Rikuzoku.

10. T'ang Fu-jen or Ts'ui Shih (Ts'ui She), the only woman on the list. She gave milk from her own breasts to her mother-in-law, who had lost her teeth.

11. Wu Mêng, fifth century C.E. He allowed himself to be bitten by mosquitoes, rather than brush them off, for fear they might annoy his parents, who were in the same room sleeping. Sometimes Wu Mêng is portrayed crossing a river on a feather fan, which he waves over the boisterous waters. Other times he is shown with a fan in his hand, driving through the heavens in a chariot drawn by two stags. He is credited with

slaying a giant snake. In Japanese legend he is called Gomo.

12. Wang Hsiang (Wang Siang), 185–269 C.E. To satisfy his stepmother's desire for fish during winter, he lay down naked on the ice pond until a hole melted, out of which jumped two carp.

13. Kuo Chu (Kwoh Ku), second century C.E. Not having enough food to feed his mother, Kuo Chu proposed that he and his wife kill their son so that there would be enough food to go around, saying that they could have another child but not another mother. When they were about to bury the child alive, they found a bar of gold on which it was written that it was a gift of the gods. Kuo Chu is often portrayed with his wife and son in a garden.

14. Yang Hsiang (Yang Hiang), Han dynasty. He jumped in front of a tiger to save his father's life, thus losing his own.

15. Chu Shou-ch'ang (Cho Show-Chiang), 1031–1102 C.E. He searched for 50 years to find out the identity of his true mother. When he did, he served her the rest of his life.

16. Yu Ch'ien-lou (Yü K'ien-low), sixth century C.E.. He left his government post after 10 days to take care of his sick father.

17. Ta'i Shun (Tseng Shên), first century C.E. He gave his mother ripe berries while he ate only green ones.

18. Lao Lai-tsu. At 70 years of age he still dressed as a child to entertain his senile parents. In Japanese legend he is called Roraishi.

19. Huang Hsiang (Huang Hiang). He lost his mother when he was a child and grieved so much that he became as thin as a skeleton. He devoted the rest of his life to his father, fanning him in the summer and in winter lying in his father's bed to warm it.

20. Chiang Shih (Kiang She), Han dynasty. In conjunction with his wife he devoted himself to waiting on his aged mother. To gratify her he went everyday to a pond to draw drinking water and obtain fresh fish for her table. The devotion was rewarded by a miracle. A spring burst forth close by his home, and a pair of carp were daily produced for his mother.

21. Wang P'ou (Wang Ngai), third century C.E. He sat beside a pine tree weeping for his dead father so long and devotedly that he caused the tree to rot.

22. Ting Lan, first century C.E. After his mother's death he preserved a wooden image of her to which he offered the same respect he had offered her during her life. One day, while he was absent from home, his neighbor Chang Shu came to borrow some household articles. Ting Lan's wife inquired by divining slips whether the image mother would consent to lend the articles. She received a negative reply. The neighbor then struck the image. When Ting Lan returned home, he saw the image of his mother had an expression of displeasure. He then went to beat the neighbor who had insulted his mother.

23. Men Tsung (Men Sung), third century C.E. One cold winter day Men Tsung's mother expressed a craving to eat stewed bamboo shoots. Weeping because such a delicacy could not be gotten so early in the year, Men Tsung still went out to search the snow. He found under the snow a fresh-grown shoot of unequaled succulence, which he then brought his mother. In Japanese legend Men Tsung is called Moso or Kobu.

24. Huang T'ing-chien (Hwang T'ing-kien), 1050–1110. One of the four great scholars of the Sung dynasty, who was deeply devoted to his parents, taking care of his sick mother.

Paul Carus, commenting on the series in his book *Chinese Thought*, wrote: "Some of the stories seem silly to us. . . . Still, it will be wise for us whose habits of life suffer from the opposite extreme . . . to recognize that all of them are pervaded with a noble spirit of respect for parents, which though exaggerated is none the less touching and ought to command our admiration."

See also: CHIH NU; CONFUCIUS

1110

**Erichthonius** (much earth)    In Greek mythology, culture hero, fourth king of Athens, who had serpent's tails for legs. Erichthonius was the son of Hephaestus, the lame god, whose sperm fell on the ground when he attempted to rape Athena. Athena placed Erichthonius in a basket with a serpent, and she then gave the basket to the Cecrops daughters, telling them not to look inside. Aglauros, one of the sisters, opened the basket and was punished by Athena, who made her insane or killed her. Erichthonius reigned for 50 years and invented chariots. Athena gave Erichthonius two drops of blood from the Gorgon. One was poisoned, but the other healed. Ovid's *Metamorphoses* (book 2) and Apollodorus's *Bibliotheca* (Library) tell his story.

See also: APOLLODORUS; ATHENA; CECROPS; GORGONS; HEPHAESTUS; OVID

1111

**Erigone** (plentiful offspring)    In Greek mythology, daughter of Icarius of Athens. She was raped by Dionysus, who transformed himself into a grape. When her father was murdered, she hanged herself and was transformed into the constellation Virgo. Ovid's *Metamorphoses* (book 6) tells the tale. A second Erigone was the daughter of Aegisthus and Clytemnestra, sister of Aletes. She had an adulterous affair with Orestes and bore Penthilus and, according to variant accounts, Tisamenus. She killed herself when Orestes was acquitted for the murder of Clytemnestra, their mother.

See also: AEGISTHUS; DIONYSUS; ORESTES; OVID

1112

**Erisichthon** (wool of the earth, much earth) In Greek mythology, a sacrilegious person, son of Triopas and Hiscilla of Thessaly; brother of Iphimedeia, Messene, and Phorbas; father of Mestra. Mestra could take any beast form, which was a gift from her lover, Poseidon. Erisichthon would sell Mestra in one form of animal, and she would return in another. When Erisichthon cut down a sacred grove belonging to the goddess Demeter, she cursed him with an insatiable hunger, so he ate his own legs and eventually his whole body. Ovid's *Metamorphoses* (book 8) tells of his fate.

See also: DEMETER; OVID; POSEIDON; SHAPE-SHIFTER

1113
**Erlik** (Irlek) (first life)   In Siberian mythology, the devil, also known as Shulman.

Various myths are told of the origin of Erlik. In some he was originally a man who helped the creator god Ulgen make the earth, though later he turned against Ulgen. In a variant myth Erlik is said to have been originally some mud in human form to which Ulgen gave life as it floated on the ocean.

In another variant, when Ulgen ran out of mud and left the people to dry, he left a huge dog as guard. Erlik saw the people and tried to bribe the dog to let him have them. The dog refused, and Erlik spat on them, covering them with saliva. Upon Ulgen's return he saw this and turned the people inside out. To this day humans are dry on the outside and foul and wet on the inside.

These myths agree that Erlik will be destroyed at the end of the world. In myths told by the Torgot, Erlik is called Shulman. In one, Shulman created three suns in order to burn the earth, which had been newly created by Burkhan-Bakshi, a creator god. But Burkhan, taking the form of the hero Erkhe-Mergen, shot down the extra two suns, letting them fall into the sea, so that only one remained. In a variant myth Burkhan-Bakshi covered the uninhabited earth with water and destroyed the extra suns. Erlik is also called Erlik-Khan (great man), meaning that he is lord of the dead. He sends out his fellow evil spirits to seize the souls of those who have sinned.

See also: BURKHAN; EARTH DIVER; ULMEN

1114
**Erl-King**   In Germanic legend, king of the elves or dwarfs. He was believed to be a malevolent goblin of the Black Forest in Germany who lured children to their deaths. He appears in Goethe's literary ballad "Der Erlkönig," which was translated by Sir Walter Scott as "The Erl-King" and set to music in the original German by Schubert. The name comes from the Danish *el-verkonge* (elf king), but was misunderstood as *Erl* and has since been referred to that way. The ballad depicts a father riding with his child. The child sees "the Erl-King with his crown and his shroud" waiting for him. The Erl-King then calls the boy to come with him. The father attempts to save the boy, the Erl-King wins, and the boy is dead in his father's arms. Sir Walter Scott's note says, "To be read by a candle particularly long in the snuff."

1115
**Ermine**   A weasel having a white winter coat, often used as a symbol of chastity and purity in medieval and Renaissance folklore. It was believed that if the ermine was surrounded by mud it would prefer to be captured rather than dirty its white coat trying to escape. In Christian art St. Mary Magdalene's cloak is sometimes made of ermine to indicate that the former prostitute had reformed her ways. Ermine was often used to line royal garments in the Middle Ages and Renaissance. In some Renaissance art works the Roman goddess of wisdom, Minerva, is portrayed with an ermine to represent virtue.

See also: MARY MAGDALENE, ST.; MINERVA

1116
**Eros** (sexual desire)   In Greek mythology, god of love, son of Aphrodite and Ares, or of Chaos with Gaea or Tartarus, or of Aphrodite and Hephaestus; brother of Anteros, Deimos, Enyo, Harmmia, Pallor, and Phobus; married to Psyche; father of Delight; called Cupid by the Romans. Erotica, a festival in Eros's honor, was celebrated with sports and games every fifth year by the Thespians. Associated with Eros was his brother Anteros, god of mutual love; Peithos, goddess of persuasion; Himeros, god of desire; Pothos, god of longing; and the Muses and

*Eros (Cupid) shooting an arrow*

Graces. In art, especially as the Roman Cupid, he is often portrayed as a small baby with wings, though he is a youth in the famous statue in Piccadilly Circus in London, and a handsome youth in Apuleius's story of Cupid and Psyche. Eros appears in Vergil's *Aeneid* (book 1), Ovid's *Metamorphoses* (book 1), Apuleius's *The Golden Ass*, Keats's *Endymion* and "Ode to Psyche," and Robert Bridges' *Eros* and *Psyche*.

See also: *AENEID, THE*; ANTEROS; APHRODITE; ARES; GAEA; HEPHAESTUS; PSYCHE; TARTARUS

**1117**
**Erulus** (little lord)    In Roman mythology, a king of Italy, son of Feronia, goddess of the orchard and woods. He had three arms and three lives and had to be killed three times the same day by Evander. Vergil's *Aeneid* (book 8) records his fate.

See also: *AENEID, THE*; EVANDER; FERONIA

**1118**
**Eruncha**    In Australian mythology, devils who turn people into medicine men. In some accounts, however, the Eruncha are said to eat medicine men.

**1119**
**Erymanthian Boar**    In Greek mythology, the boar captured by Heracles as his fourth labor; it lived on Mount Erymanthus in Arcadia. Erymanthus is also the name of a son of Apollo who was blinded by Aphrodite because he had seen the goddess bathing. In retaliation Apollo transformed himself into a boar and killed Admis, the young lover of Aphrodite.

See also: APHRODITE; APOLLO; ARCADIA; HERACLES

**1120**
**Erytheis** (crimson)    In Greek mythology, one of the Hesperides who guarded the Golden Apples in the garden of the Hesperides.

See also: GOLDEN APPLES OF THE HESPERIDES; HESPERIDES

**1121**
**Erzulie** (Erzilie, Erzulia)    In Haitian voodoo, mother goddess, wife of Agwé. She represents jealousy, vengeance, and discord but also love, perpetual help, goodwill, health, beauty, and fortune. In her demonic role she is called Marinette-Bois Chèche, Erzulie Toho, Erzulie Zandor, and Erzulie Mapiangueh, and in that aspect she causes the people she mounts or possesses to twist in fantastic convulsions. In her beneficent aspect she is called Tsilah Wédo and Ayida. Her symbol is often a heart pierced by swords, the same as that of the Virgin Mary in Christian symbolism.

See also: AGWÉ; AYIDA; VIRGIN MARY

**1122**
**Esau** (hairy)    In the Bible, O.T., Isaac's oldest son and twin brother of Jacob. Esau sold his

birthright to Jacob for some pottage (lentils) (Gen. 25:24–34). Esau was an ancestor of the Edomites.

See also: JACOB

---

1123

**Eshu**   In African mythology (Yoruba of southwestern Nigeria), a trickster who acts as mediator between Olorun, the sky god, and the people. He also is a judge who mediates between the benevolent and malevolent supernatural powers. Eshu, who knows all languages, brings down the messages of Olorun to the people and brings up the people's sacrifices to the sky god. He also presides over chance, accidents, and unpredictability, and he lurks in highways, crossroads, and gateways to trick people. Once he had an argument with Shango, the thunder god, over which of them was more powerful. Eshu, who could change shape and size at will, made his penis grow to an enormous size, frightening the other god, who admitted Eshu was the greater of the two. Another time Eshu deliberately brought chaos into the home of a man who was living comfortably with his two wives. Disguising himself as a merchant, Eshu sold a beautiful hat to one of the wives, which made the other very jealous. The second wife bought an even more beautiful hat, until at last rivalry and despair characterized the man's life and household. Eshu is sometimes called Elegbara.

See also: LEGBA; OLORUN; ORISHA; SHANGO; TRICKSTER

---

1124

**Esmun** (Ashmun, Eshmoun, Eshmun, Esmoun, Esmounos)   In Near Eastern mythology (Syro-Phoenician), sun god of vital force and healing, worshiped at his patron city of Carthage. He was loved by the goddess Astronoe, but when she was about to capture him, he cut off his genitals with an ax. He was then turned into a god of generative heat. Esmun was combined with the goddess

Astarte, forming a composite male and female deity, Esmun-Astarte.

See also: ASTARTE

---

1125

**Essus** (Esus, Hesus) (lord)   In Celtic mythology, god of vegetation and war, mentioned by ancient Roman writers and identified with Mars or Mercury. Human sacrifices were made to Essus with the victims suspended from trees and ritually wounded. The priests then read omens from the way the blood ran from their wounds.

See also: MARS; MERCURY

*Esther*

---

1126

**Esther** (a form of Ishtar, goddess of sexual love) In the Bible, O.T., a Jewish heroine. In Hebrew her name is Hadassah (myrtle). Esther was chosen to replace Queen Vashti, wife of King Ahasuerus (Xerxes), after the queen insulted the king. Esther did not tell the king she was a Jewess. On the advice of her uncle Mordecai she helped destroy Haman, who wished to massacre the Jews. This deliverance is celebrated by Jews today at the Feast of Purim.

The Old Testament Book of Esther never once mentions God. Martin Luther hated the Book of Esther, saying it would have been better if it had been left out of the Old Testament. Jean Racine's *Esther* is based on the Book of Esther in the Vulgate Latin translation of the Bible, which contains passages not found in the King James translation of the Hebrew text. Artemesia Gentileschi painted *Esther before Ahasuerus*, and Rembrandt painted *Haman Begging Esther for Forgiveness*. An epic poem, *Esther*, by Jean Desmarets de Saint-Sorlin is based on the biblical tale. Handel's oratorio *Esther* also deals with the heroine.

See also: AHASUERUS; ISHTAR; MYRTLE

1127

**Estmere**   In medieval English legend, a king who defeated a Moorish king and won the daughter of King Adland. The happy-go-lucky Estmere was advised by Adler (either a bosom friend or his brother, depending on which account of the legend is followed) to seek a wife. The two set out for King Adland's palace. He welcomed them after he had determined they were Christians. They asked to see his daughter, and he informed them that a Moor, King Bremor, had wanted his daughter's hand in marriage but he had refused because Bremor was not a Christian. Bremor threatened to return. When the princess was introduced to Estmere, she fell in love with him. When Bremor returned, Estmere defeated him, and King Adland allowed Estmere to marry his daughter. An English ballad tells one version of the tale. It was set to music by Gustav Holst for chorus and orchestra.

1128

**Estrildis**   In British mythology, the daughter of a German king and mistress to King Humber of Britain. When Humber was drowned in the river that bears his name, Locrine fell in love with Estrildis and would have married her had he not been betrothed already to Guendoloena. However, the two became lovers, and Estrildis bore a daughter named Sabrina.

1129

**Estsanatlehi** (woman who changes)   In North American Indian mythology (Navaho), mother earth, who renews youth with the seasons, brings

female rain, and has power over all reproduction on earth. She helped create light for the world through the use of her white shell and turquoise beads and by using a magic crystal. She left the earth to live with her husband beyond the waters. She is also called Whiteshell Woman, Ashonnutli, and Changing Woman.

1130

**Etana** (Etanna) (strong)   In Near Eastern mythology (Babylonian), hero who ascended to the heavens on the back of an eagle only to fall back to earth.

The myth of Etana is found in fragmentary form. It has been pieced together by scholars. One section tells how Etana prayed to the sun god, Shamash, to give a son to his wife by revealing to him the place where the "plant of life" was to be found. How the "plant of life" was found by the hero, however, is missing in the fragment.

Another part of the myth tells of the miraculous journey Etana made to the heavens on the back of an eagle. The eagle kept taking the hero higher and higher, past the abode of the gods Anu, Bel, and Ea, to where the great goddess Ishtar lived. But Etana, not able to bear the journey, fell to the earth, taking the eagle with him.

The character of Etana also appears in the Babylonian epic poem *Gilgamesh*, in which he is said to have founded a kingdom.

See also: ANU; BEL; EA; EAGLE; GILGAMESH; ISHTAR; SHAMASH

1131

**Eteocles and Polynices** (true glory and much strife)   In Greek mythology, sons of Oedipus and Jocasta (or Euryganeia); brothers of Antigone and Ismene. Both sons had insulted their blind father, Oedipus, by giving him a cup that had once belonged to Laius and by giving him a portion of meat not fit for a king. Oedipus cursed both sons. They were to rule jointly after their father's death. Eteocles refused to surrender the throne when his brother's turn came. In the ensuing war both brothers were killed in one-to-one combat. Aeschylus's *Seven against Thebes* and Euripides' *The Phoenician Woman* deal with the tragic tale.

See also: ETEOCLES AND POLYNICES; JOCASTA; OEDIPUS

**1132**
**Ethne** (Ethlinn, Ethna, Eithne, Ethnee, Ethnea, Aithne) (little fire)   In Celtic mythology, the daughter of the god-king of Balor, who was informed by a Druid that his daughter would have a child who would kill him. King Balor therefore imprisoned Ethne in a tower on Tory Island in the charge of 12 matrons who were forbidden to tell her that men existed. Earlier Balor had stolen a magic cow belonging to Kian, who now avenged himself on the king by disguising himself as a woman and entering the tower. From Ethne and Kian's intercourse three children were born, whom Balor ordered drowned. But one, Lugh, was accidentally spared and later killed Balor.

See also: BALOR

**1133**
**Etna** (Aetna, Etna)   In Greek and Roman history and mythology, volcanic mountain on the eastern coast of Sicily where the forge of Hephaestus, god of fire, was located and where Zeus confined the giants. The volcano is said to be named after Aetna, daughter of Briareus (or Uranus) and mother, by Hephaestus, of the two Palici volcanoes.

See also: HEPHAESTUS; URANUS; ZEUS

**1134**
**Etzel** (little father)   Name given in Germanic legend to Attila the Hun. In the epic poem the *Nibelungenlied*, Etzel marries Kriemhild, the widow of Siegfried. She is called Gudrun in the *Volsunga Saga*, where Attila is given the name Atli.

See also: KRIEMHILD; *NIBELUNGENLIED*; SIEG-FRIED; *VOLSUNGA SAGA*

**1135**
**Eudora** (generous)   In Greek mythology, one of the Nereids, the 50 daughters of Nereus and Doris who attended Poseidon. Homer's *Iliad* (book 18), Hesiod's *Theogony*, and Ovid's *Metamorphoses* all mention the Nereids.

See also: DORIS; HESIOD; *ILIAD, THE*; NEREIDS; OVID; POSEIDON

**1136**
**Euhemerus** (spending days cheerfully) Fourth century B.C.E. Greek writer on mythology whose book *Sacred History* theorizes that the gods were originally humans who were later deified.

**1137**
**Eunomia** (good government)   In Greek mythology, one of the Horae; goddess of order and legislation, daughter of Zeus and Themis. Her sisters were Eirene (peace) and Dice (justice).

See also: EIRENE; HORAE; THEMIS; ZEUS

**1138**
**Euphrosyne** (good cheer)   In Greek mythology, one of the three Graces. The others were Aglaea (splendor) and Thalia (abundance). They were all daughters of Zeus and Eurynome.

See also: AGLAEA; THALIA; ZEUS

**1139**
**Eurydice** (wide justice)   In Greek mythology, a dryad, wife of Orpheus, who died of a snakebite as she fled from Aristaeus. Orpheus went to the underworld in search of her. He was given permission to return Eurydice to life if he would not look back before he reached the upper earth. Orpheus did and lost Eurydice forever. The myth is told in Vergil's *Georgics IV*, Ovid's *Metamorphoses* (book 10), Milton's "L'Allegro," and Landor's *Orpheus and Eurydice*. The many operas on the subject include Monteverdi's *La Favola d'Orfeo* (1607), Gluck's *Orfeo ed Euridice*, and Offen-

bach's comic opera *Orphee aux enfers* (Orpheus in the Underworld) (1858).

See also: ARISTAEUS; ORPHEUS; OVID

**Eurytion** (full-flowing little one)    In Greek mythology, a centaur who caused the fight at the wedding of Pirithous and Hippodameia. Ovid's *Metamorphoses* (book 12) tells the tale. The same name is born by the herdsman of Geryon, king of Erythia. Both he and his dog Orthus were killed by Heracles during his 10th labor. The name is also held by a companion of Aeneas in Italy who was a great archer.

See also: AENEAS; CENTAURS; GERYON; HERACLES; OVID

**Eustace, St.** (plentiful harvest)    Second century. In Christian legend, patron saint of hunters. Feast, 20 September. His legend is similar to St. Hubert's, and the two are often confused in legend and art. Eustace's life is found in *The Golden Legend*, a collection of saints' lives written in the 13th century by Jacobus de Voragine.

Eustace, whose Roman name was Placidus, was a Roman soldier under the Emperor Trajan. He had a wife and two sons. One day, while hunting in the forest, he saw a white stag of "marvelous beauty" and pursued it. The stag fled and ascended a high rock. Then Placidus, looking up, beheld "between the horns of the stag, a cross of radiant light, and on it the image of the crucified Redeemer." He was dazzled by the vision and fell to his knees. A voice cried out: "Placidus? Why dost thou pursue me? I am Christ, whom thou hast hitherto served without knowing me. Dost thou now believe?"

"Lord, I believe," Placidus said.

Placidus went home, converted his wife and sons, and in a short time was arrested for being a Christian. The family was asked to sacrifice to the Roman gods. They refused and were placed in a brazen, or bronze, bull and roasted to death.

See also: *GOLDEN LEGEND, THE*; HUBERT, ST.

**Evander** (good man)    In Roman mythology, culture hero, son of the nymph Carmenta and the god Hermes (or Sarpedon and Laodameia), married Deidamia; father of Pallantia, Pallas, Dyna, Roma, and Sarpedon II. He settled near Rome after the Trojan War. Evander introduced the Greek alphabet and worship of the gods, and he built Pallanteum on the Palatine Hill outside Rome. He was honored by the Romans as a god and worshiped at an altar built on Mount Aventine. Evander appears in Vergil's *Aeneid* (book 8), where he kills Erulus three times in one day.

See also: *ANEID, THE*; CARMENTA; HERMES

**Evangeline**    In American literary folklore, name given Emmeline Labiche by Henry W. Longfellow in his narrative *Evangeline*, in dactylic hexamters. The basis for the legend was told by the Reverend Horace Lorenzo Connolly, an Episcopal priest, to Nathaniel Hawthorne, with the view that the author would use it for a novel, but Hawthorne said, "The story is not in my vein," and offered it to Longfellow.

The legend tells how Emmeline Labiche was raised in the French village of St. Gabriel in Acadia, now Nova Scotia. She was to be married to Louis Arceneau, a childhood sweetheart. When the British dispersed the colony, Emmeline and Louis were separated, only to meet years later when he was about to marry another woman. Emmeline went insane and died a few years later.

Longfellow took the bare facts and wove them into an American literary legend in 1847. In his poem the lovers are separated, and Gabriel (the name given to Louis) and his father make their way to Louisiana. Evangeline continues to seek them. After years of wandering she settles in Philadelphia, becoming a Sister of Mercy. There, during a plague, she sees a dying old man. Realizing it is Gabriel, she dies of shock, and the two are buried in a Catholic cemetery. Longfellow's poem, one of the most popular in American literature, was used as the basis for three operas.

In Louisiana, the story was transformed by the French Creole educator and writer Madame Sidonie de la Houssaye into the French novel *Pouponne et Balthazar* (1888), in which Evangeline and Gabriel were depicted as upper-class French Creoles who frowned on their Acadian neighbors. The story serves as a source of ethnic pride and has taken on mythological status among upper classes. Among the working class the subject is viewed with apathy or even derision, as we see in the lyrics of a Cajun song: "Gabriel, il etait pas beau [Gabriel wasn't good-looking], / Evangeline ne se valait pas mieux [Evangeline wasn't any better]." Statues of the heroine have been erected in Grand Pré, Nova Scotia, and St. Martinville, Louisiana.

See also: FAKELORE

*Eve*

**Evangelists, The Four** (publishers of glad tidings)   In Christian tradition, Matthew, Mark, Luke, and John, credited with the authorship of the four Gospels in the New Testament. During the Middle Ages Matthew was portrayed as a man with an angel nearby, or a winged man; Mark as a lion; Luke as an ox; John as an eagle. St. Jerome set down the generally accepted interpretation of the symbolism. Matthew was given the angel or human semblance because he begins his account with the human generation of Christ; Mark has the lion because he tells the royal dignity of Christ; Luke has an ox because he dwells on the sacrifice of Christ; and John has the eagle because he dwells on the divinity of Christ.

See also: JEROME, ST.; JOHN THE EVANGELIST, ST.; LUKE, ST.; MARK, ST.; MATTHEW, ST.

1144

1145

**Eve** (the mother of all living?)   In the Bible, O.T., first woman, wife of Adam, mother of Cain, Abel, and Seth. (Gen. 3:1–24).

See also: ABUK AND GARANG; ADAM AND EVE; ASK AND EMBLA; CAIN AND ABEL; KHADAU AND MAMALDI

1146

**Exaltation of the Holy Cross**   Medieval Christian feast, celebrated 14 September, often called Holy Cross Day. The feast commemorates the return to Jerusalem in 630 of a relic of the true cross. The tale is told in *The Golden Legend* by Jacobus de Voragine. The emperor Heraclius (c. 575–641) defeated King Chrosröes (Khrosrow II) of the Persians, who had taken a piece of the true cross and used it to make up part of his throne. For his impiety Heraclius had Chrosröes killed and took back the part of the true cross. As he was entering Jerusalem through the gate through which Jesus came, stones fell, barring his entrance. An angel appeared, telling

*The Cross (Dürer)*

Heraclius that Jesus entered on a donkey, not dressed in royal garb. The king then stripped himself to his shirt and carried in the relic, as the stones miraculously moved out of his way.

See also: GOLDEN LEGEND, THE

**Excalibur** (to free from the stone?)   In Arthurian legend, the sword of King Arthur. The sword was given to Arthur by the Lady of the Lake, according to some accounts. When Arthur lay dying he commanded Sir Bedivere to return Excalibur to the Lady of the Lake. Sir Bedivere threw the sword into the waters, and an arm clothed in white samite appeared to receive it. Arthur's sword is sometimes called Caliburn and Caledvwlch.

See also: ARTHUR; BEDIVERE, SIR; LADY OF THE LAKE

*Sir Bedivere casts Excalibur into the lake (A. Beardsley)*

**Exemplum** (Latin, *exempla*, plural)   A tale told to illustrate an ethical or theological point and usually attributed to a religious specialist. The sources for these tales are the Bible, lives of the saints, books of miracles, history, legend, and descriptions of natural happenings. The golden age for the exemplum was from the 13th to the 15th century, during which time the most famous of all collections appeared, the *Gesta Romanorum*, published in England around 1300.

**Exodus** (a going out)   In the Bible, Greek title of the Old Testament book telling of the escape by the Israelites from their bondage in Egypt. The book is the second part of the Pentateuch, or Torah, giving the account of Moses' birth, the Israelites' departure from Egypt, and their journey to Palestine. The Ten Commandments are found in chapter 20, verses 1–18. Handel's oratorio *Israel in Egypt* uses the book as a basis for its libretto.

**Exorcism**   The expelling of evil spirits or demons by prayers, incantations, and rites, practiced in all religions that admit the existence of demonic forces in the world.

Pagan, Jewish, Christian, and Islamic religions all believed in demonic possession. Lucian, writing in the second century C.E., tells of a professional exorcist:

> . . . everyone already knows this remarkable man who in the case of people falling down at the sight of the moon, rolling their eyes and foaming at the mouth . . . sends them home free from their infirmity, for which he charges a large sum each time. When he is with sick persons he asks them how the devil entered into them; the patient remains silent, but the devil replies, in Greek or a barbarian tongue . . . how he has entered into the man's body.

In the Hebrew Old Testament demons are sent directly by God. When King Saul is

*Exodus*

tormented (1 Sam. 16:14–16), it is God who is the instigator:

But the Spirit of the Lord departed from Saul, and an evil spirit from the Lord troubled him. And Saul's servants said unto him, "Behold now, an evil spirit from god troubleth thee. Let our lord now command thy servants, which are before thee, to seek out a man, who is a cunning player on an harp: and it shall come to pass, when the evil spirit from God is upon thee, that he shall play with his hand, and thou shalt be well."

King Saul is freed of his evil spirit by David, the future king.

Medieval Jews also believed in demonic possession and exorcism. In a typical example a woman was possessed by the spirit of a drunken Jew "who died without prayer and impenitent." His spirit wandered about for a long time and was allowed to enter the woman's body when she was blaspheming against God. From the moment of possession the woman became a hysteric. A Jewish exorcist was called in. He forced the demon to reveal his true name and then, using the secret name of God, forced the demon out "by the little toe of the possessed."

Christianity is filled with tales of possession, beginning with accounts in the New Testament in which Jesus acts as an exorcist. St. Zeno of Verona wrote in the fourth century of demonic possession:

. . . we cannot so much lay claim that the souls of the dead live as rather prove it by manifest facts. For the impure spirits of both sexes which prowl hither and thither, make their way by deceitful flatteries or by violence into the bodies of living men. . . . His face is suddenly deprived of colour, his body rises up of itself, the eyes in madness roll in their sockets and squint horribly, the teeth, covered with a horrible foam, grind between blue-white lips; the limbs twisted in all directions are given over to trembling; he sighs, he weeps; he fears the appointed day of Judgment and complains that he is driven out; he confesses his sex, the time and place he entered into the man, he makes known his name and the date of his death, or shows by manifest signs who he is; so that we generally learn that there are many of these who, according to our own memory, persisting in the worship of idols, have recently died a violent death.

Belief in demonic possession can still be found in major Christian churches. The Roman Catholic church has a whole section devoted to exorcism in *The Roman Ritual*, the introduction to which begins "That there is a world of demons is a teaching of revealed religion which is perfectly clear to all who know Sacred Scripture and respect and accept its word as inspired of God. It is part of the whole Christian-Judaeo heritage."

The rite, which consists of prayers and psalms, opens with this passage: "I cast you out, unclean spirit, along with every satanic power of the enemy, every spectre from hell, and all your fell companions; in the name of our Lord Jesus Christ. Begone and stay far from this creature of God."

See also: DAVID; SAUL

1151

**Ezekiel** (may God make the child strong?) Sixth century B.C.E. In the Bible, Hebrew prophet and title of a book in the Old Testament. Ezekiel was taken captive by the Babylonians and moved from Judah to the banks of the Chebar River in Babylonia (Ezek. 1:1). His book, filled with lurid visions, divides as follows: Ezekiel's call (1:1–3:27), prophecies of doom of Jerusalem (4:1–24:27), God's judgment on the nations (25:1–32:32), God's promises (33:1–37:28), prophecy against God (38:1–39:29), and a vision of the future temple and land (40:1–48:35).

In Islamic legend, Hizqil is the name given to Ezekiel. He is believed to be referred to in the Koran (sura 2), although not by name.

The prophet appears in Duccio di Buoninsegna's The Nativity with prophets Ezekiel and Isaiah. He sometimes appears with a scroll in Western art with the Latin form of one of his sayings: *Porta haec clausa erit; non aperietar* (this gate shall be shut, it shall not be opened, and no man shall enter in by it) (Ezek. 44:2) Medieval writers made the text refer to the perpetual virginity of St. Mary.

See also: ISAIAH; KORAN, THE

1152

**Ezra** (help)   In the Bible, O.T., a Jewish priest who led the Jews back to Jerusalem from their captivity in Babylon, about 300 B.C.E. The Book of Ezra, a sequel to Chronicles, tells his story. He is called Esdras in the Apocrypha. In Islamic legend his name is Uzair. He is mentioned in the Koran (sura 9), which says, "The Jews say Uzair is a son of God."

See also: KORAN, THE

# F

**Fa**  In African cult, a system of divination taken from the Yoruba of southwestern Nigeria and practiced by the Fon of Benin. When the supreme god Mawu completed the creation of the world, two messengers named Koda and Chada were sent to the earth to tell man that each person must have his own Fa. Fa can be loosely defined as the knowledge or destiny given by God to each man whereby he may come to know how to perform the will of the Creator. It is a system by which one comes to learn the kind of behavior expected of him. One man was selected to contact the oracle by manipulation of nuts from a special palm tree. If the nuts of the palm tree were handled properly, the eyes of Fa would be opened and man would be able to gain a glimpse of the future. This complicated method of divination would permit man to foretell his destiny. A selected group of heavenly messengers were taught how to work the oracle. The nuts of the palm tree were thrown from one hand to the other. A pattern resulted when one counted the number of nuts left over from the throw. Often this pattern was carved on the skin of a calabash, which was placed in a bag so that the secret of one's future could remain hidden from those who might use this information against one.

See also: ESHU; LEGBA; MAWU LISA

**Fabiola, St.** (bean grower)    Died 399. In Christian legend, friend of St. Jerome. Feast, 27 December. Fabiola had divorced her drunken husband and remarried. After her second husband's death she devoted her life to works of charity, establishing the first Christian hospital in the West. When she told St. Jerome she wished to settle in Bethlehem, he advised her against it, saying she was too lively. Thousands attended her funeral when she died in Rome.

See also: JEROME, ST.

**Fafnir**  In Norse mythology, a dragon guardian of gold, son of Hreidmar and brother of Regin and Otter. He was slain by the hero Sigurd, who then bathed in his blood, making himself invulnerable, except for one spot between his shoulders, where a linden leaf, sticking fast, prevented the blood from touching.

In the *Volsunga Saga* Fafnir, in his lust for gold, slays his father, Hreidmar, and steals the skin of his dead brother, Otter, which contains a gold treasure. To guard his treasure Fafnir transforms himself into a dragon. Sigurd comes to slay the dragon Fafnir and obtain the treasure. He kills Fafnir by a ruse.

According to the *Volsunga Saga*, Fafnir engages in a long discussion with Sigurd to discover who his murderer is, then dies. In *Der Ring des Nibelungen* Richard Wagner makes Fafner (Fafnir) one of the giants who built Valhalla for Wotan (Odin). Fafner and his brother Fasolt accept Alberich's ring in place of the beautiful goddess Freyja, the price originally agreed on. Fafner kills Fasolt and changes himself into a dragon to guard his gold hoard. He is eventually killed by Siegfried (Sigurd). Fafnir is portrayed in Arthur Rackham's illustrations for Wagner's Ring Cycle.

See also: KRIEMHILD; *NIBELUNGENLIED*; *RING DES NIBELUNGEN, DER*; SIEGFRIED

**1156**

**Faith, Hope, and Charity, Sts.**    Second century? In medieval Christian legend, the three saints were believed to be the children of Saint Sophia (holy wisdom). They were said to have been martyred in Rome under the emperor Hadrian. In medieval Gothic art St. Faith is often portrayed as a woman holding a cross or chalice. Feast, 1 August. The English Puritans introduced the English words Faith, Hope, and Charity as given names in the 16th century.

**1157**

**Fakelore**    In American folklore, a term coined by Richard Dorson in 1950 to describe "the presentation of spurious and synthetic writings under the claim that they are genuine folklore." According to Dorson, fakelore is the product of writers, not of the anonymous folk or what he referred to as the "folk process." Dorson's term was offered as a response to Benjamin Botkin's *A Treasury of American Folklore* (1944), which was widely and positively acclaimed, but which was little more than an "uncritical encomium" that was intended for the marketplace. In Europe a similar term arose, *Folklorismus*, but this term sought to legitimize scholarly investigation of the commercialization of folklore for the mass market and for tourism.

See also: JOE MAGARAC; PAUL BUNYAN; PECOS BILL

**1158**

**Falcon and the Owls, The**    Moral fable by the Persian Sufi mystic and poet Rumi, in *The Masnavi* (book 2, story 4).

A certain falcon lost his way and found himself in a foul place inhabited by owls. The owls suspected that the falcon had come to seize their nests. They all surrounded him to kill him. The falcon assured them that he had no such design because he lived on the wrist of the king and had no desire to live in their foul place. The owls replied that he was trying to deceive them, since such a strange bird as he was could not possibly be the king's favorite.

"It is true," the falcon replied, "I am not the same as the king, but yet the king's light is reflected in me, the same as water and earth that nourish plants are part of the plant. I am, as it were, the dust beneath the king's feet. If you become like me in this respect, you will be exalted as I am. Copy the outward form you behold in me, and perchance you will reach the real substance of the king."

See also: *MASNAVI, THE*

*Fama eluding her follower*

**1159**

**Fama** (reputation, report)    In Roman mythology, goddess of fame; equivalent to the Greek goddess Pheme. She was sometimes portrayed blowing a trumpet.

**Fan-Wang**    In Chinese mythology, a creator god who hatched the universe from a cosmic egg. Fan-Wang is also found in Chinese Buddhist mythology, not, however, as a creator god (which Buddhism does not have) but as a deity inferior to anyone who is on his way to Buddhahood.

1160

**Faran**    In African mythology (Songhai of the upper Niger), hero who fought the water spirit Zin-Kibaru. Each night Zin-Kibaru would play his guitar, enticing fish to eat the rice that grew in Faran's pond. Faran was angered, and the two decided to fight. During the battle each one cast a spell on the other, but Faran's spell was stronger. Zin-Kibaru lost, leaving all of his magical instruments and spirit followers to Faran.

See also: ZIN

1161

**Farbauti** (cruel striker)    In Norse mythology, the father of Loki, the fire-trickster god. Loki's mother was the giantess Laufey, or Nal. Farbauti appears in the *Prose Edda*.

See also: LOKI; *PROSE EDDA*

1162

**Far Darria**    In Irish folklore, a fairy who wears a red cap and coat and spends his time at practical joking, especially of a gruesome kind. There are numerous motifs associated with Far Darria: red fairy; fairy tricks mortals; mortals as captives in fairyland.

See also: MOTIF

1163

**Faridun** (Feridoun, Feridun, Freydun)    In the Persian epic poem *Shah Namah*, by Firdusi, a hero who defeats the evil king Zahhak.

Firdusi's portrait of Faridun is derived from Traetaona, a hero of Persian mythology who had fought with a demon, Azhi Dahaka. In Firdusi's

1164

epic Azhi Dahaka is transformed into the evil king Zahhak, and Traetaona is called Faridun. These changes were made to make the poem acceptable to an Islamic audience that did not want the ancient gods and heroes mentioned in works by Islamic poets. (When Islam conquered Persia, it all but wiped out earlier beliefs.)

One night, according to *Shah Namah*, King Zahhak dreamed that a young man hit him on the head with a mace. When he awoke from his dream, he asked his courtiers what the dream signified, but they refused to give him an answer. When they could no longer avoid answering the king, they said it was an apparition of Faridun, the hero who was "destined to smite" the king on his head.

"But why," demanded the king, "does the youth wish to injure me?"

"Because his father's blood will be spilled by you, and he will have to avenge his father's death," the courtiers replied.

As the courtiers had predicted, Zahhak had Abtin, the father of Faridun, killed, but Faranuk, Faridun's mother, and her newborn child escaped. As she fled, she came upon a cow named Pur'maieh, which yielded milk in abundance. Because of the murder of her husband, Faranuk's milk had dried up, and the cow now fed her little son, Faridun. The boy was placed in the care of shepherds by his mother. After some time his hiding place was discovered by King Zahhak, and the shepherds who had protected the lad were killed, but Faridun eluded the slaughterers.

When he was 16, his mother told him the story of his father's death at the hands of the evil king, and Faridun resolved to avenge the death. After numerous adventures Faridun succeeded in his task and was made king. His reign is described in *Shah Namah* by an envoy to another court:

He who has never seen the spring
Would see it when he looked upon the king.
A spring of Paradise, 'twas to behold,
Its dust of amber and its bricks of gold.
Upon his palace heav'n found resting place

With Paradise e'er smiling on its face
(Alexander Rogers translation).

Faridun had three sons, Silim, Tur, and Irij.
Silim continually prodded his brother Tur to
have Irij put to death, so that the kingdom would
pass to Tur. One day Tur attacked Irij and cut off
his head. Irij's murder was later avenged by
Minuchihr, who was Faridun's grandson.

See also: AZHI DAHAKA; MINUCHIHR; *SHAH
NAMAH*; ZAHHAK

1165
**Fasces** (bundles)    In ancient Roman ritual,
birch or elm rods held together by a red thong.
Fasces were carried by lictors as the symbol of
authority of a Roman major magistrate. An ax
was added to the fasces to signify that not only
whipping but also death was within his power.
Italian Fascists adopted the symbol as well as the
name for their party, which was nominally intended to restore the ancient power of Rome.

1166
**Fatima**    606?–632. In Islamic legend, daughter
of Muhammad by his first wife, Khadijah. Fatima
was the wife of Ali, a saint and warrior in Islam.
She was one of the four "perfect women." (The
others were Khadija; Mary, daughter of Imran;
and Asiyah [Asia], wife of the pharaoh drowned
in the Red Sea.) In Islamic tradition Fatima is
called bright-blooming, which means one who
has never menstruated. In actuality, she had
three sons by Ali.

In the town of Fátima, near Leiria, Portugal,
the Virgin Mary appeared to three children in
1917. The shrine, built in 1944, is called Our
Lady of the Rosary of Fátima. Some Roman
Catholic writings explain the appearance at the
small town as an indication that one day devotion
to the Virgin Mary will bring Islam under the
banner of Christianity.

Fatima is also the name of a holy woman in
the story of Aladdin in *The Thousand and One
Nights*. She is slain by the necromancer, brother

of the sorcerer. Dressed in Fatima's clothes, he
makes his way into Aladdin's house, but Aladdin
discovers the disguise and kills the necromancer.
The name is also that of the last wife of Bluebeard in the well-known fairy tale.

See also: ALADDIN; ALI; BLUEBEARD; MUHAM-
MAD; *THOUSAND AND ONE NIGHTS*; VIRGIN MARY

1167
**Faunus** (he who favors)    In Roman mythology,
an early Italian god of agriculture, shepherds,
woods, and pastures; equivalent of the Greek
Pan. In art Faunus was portrayed as a goat-
legged half-human creature similar to a Greek
satyr. Fauns as the followers of Bacchus appear in
Vergil's *Aeneid* (book 7). Debussy's tone poem
*Prelude a l'Apres-Midi d'un faune* (Prelude to
"The Afternoon of a Faun"), inspired by Mal-
larmé's poem about Faunus and used as a ballet
by Diaghilev's company in 1912, also deals with
the god.

See also: *AENEID, THE*; PAN; SATYRS

*Faust*

1168
**Faust** (fortunate)    16th century. In European
history and legend, Dr. John Faustus, a professional magician in Germany who, according to
legend, sold his soul to the devil. The idea of
making a pact with the devil for worldly gain may
be Jewish in origin and date back to the time of
Christ. The Faust legend is a conglomerate of
anonymous folk traditions largely of medieval

origin. One of the first books dealing with the legend, *The History of the Damnable Life and Deserved Death of Dr. John Faustus*, has a deep Protestant cast. Mephistopheles, the devil, wears a Franciscan robe, and Faust, with his freethinking and love of the ancients, is condemned for opposing all authority, both state and church. Among the most famous works dealing with the subject are Marlowe's play *Dr. Faustus* (1589) and Goethe's epic drama *Faust* (Part 1, 1808; Part 2, 1832), which inspired numerous musical settings, among them Schumann's *Scenes from Goethe's Faust*, Berlioz's *La Damnation de Faust*, and Gounod's opera *Faust*. Other works include Thomas Mann's novel *Dr. Faustus* and Busoni's opera *Doktor Faust*, based on the European puppet plays of Faust.

See also: MEPHISTOPHELES

**Fear-Gorta** (man of hunger)   1169   In Irish folklore, the "man of hunger" who appears as an emaciated phantom going through the land in famine time, begging alms and bringing good luck to the giver. It is said that he is so weak he can barely lift his alms cup, and he has few clothes to cover himself, even in winter.

**Feathertop**   1170   In American literary folklore, scarecrow given life by the witch Mother Rigby in Nathaniel Hawthorne's short story "Feathertop," included in *Mosses from an Old Manse*. Mother Rigby creates a Lord Ravensbane from a scarecrow to get revenge on her former lover, Justice Merton, but Merton's daughter Rachel falls in love with the mirage. When Feathertop and Rachel look in a glass, however, his true identity is revealed. Fleeing, he returns to Mother Rigby, casts away the magic pipe that made him seem a human, and returns to being a scarecrow. Mother Rigby says, "Poor fellow! My poor, dear, pretty Feathertop! There are thousands upon thousands of coxcombs and charlatans in the world, made up of just such a mumble of worn-out, forgotten, and good-for-nothing trash as he was! Yet they live in fair repute, and never see themselves for what they are. And why should my poor puppet be the only one to know himself and perish for it." The tale was dramatized by Percy MacKaye as *The Scarecrow*, which was made into the silent film *Puritan Passions*.

**Febold Feboldson**   1171   In American folklore, hero of the Great Plains who could influence weather conditions. Once when it was dry, he hypnotized some frogs into croaking, telling them it was raining. When the Indian rain god heard all the croaking, he got a headache and sent down rain to shut up the frogs. Febold Feboldson appears in Paul R. Beath's *Legends of Febold Feboldson*, a pamphlet written for the Federal Writers' Project in Nebraska, and in a later book *Febold Feboldson: Tall Tales from the Great Plains*. How much of Feboldson's legend is Beath's invention and how much is folklore is still debated.

See also: FAKELORE; JOE MAGARAC; MIKE FINK; PAUL BUNYAN; PECOS BILL; WPA

**Februata** (Februus)   1172   In Roman mythology, god of purification, whose name derives from *februa*, or rituals of purification, for which the month of February is named. The Feralia was the Roman All Souls Day (21 February), last of the dies Parentales (which began at noon 13 February), when the family made offerings at the graves of their dead. The feast is mentioned in Ovid's *Fasti* (book 2).

See also: OVID

**Felicitas and Her Seven Sons, St.** (lucky)   1173   Second century. In Christian legend, martyrs. Invoked by women who want sons. Feast, 10 July. Coming from a rich Roman family, Felicitas was widowed and brought up her seven sons as Christians. She was arrested, and they were killed one by one in front of her. Finally, she was beheaded or placed in a boiling caldron. Medieval art portrays her as a veiled widow with a martyr's palm surrounded by her seven sons.

**1174**

**Feng-huang**   In Chinese mythology, the phoenix; the male, *feng*; the female, *huang*. The phoenix is the emperor of birds as the unicorn is the emperor of quadrupeds. In Chinese belief the unicorn does not prey on living creatures and symbolizes peace and prosperity. The pair of the male and female phoenix is inseparable and symbolizes conjugal fidelity. In Japanese the phoenix is called Ho-o.

See also: PHOENIX; UNICORN

**1175**

**Feng Po**   In Chinese mythology, god of winds, often portrayed as an old man with a white beard, yellow cloak, and blue and red cap. In his hands he holds a sack that contains the winds.

*Feng-huang*

*Fenrir the Wolf*

**1176**

**Fenrir** (Fenris) (from the swamp)   In Norse mythology, a giant wolf, son of the evil fire-trickster god, Loki; brother of Hela. When Fenrir opened his mouth one jaw touched the earth and the other reached to heaven. Fenrir is best known as the wolf who bit off the god Tyr's hand. "When the gods tried to persuade the wolf Fenrir to allow the fetter Gleipnir to be placed on him, he did not believe that they would free him until they put Tyr's hand in his mouth as a pledge. Then, when the Aesir would not loose him, he bit off the hand at the place now known as the 'wolf joint.' [So Tyr] is one-handed and he is not called a peace-maker." Fenrir was expected to swallow the god Odin at the day of doom when gods, giants, people, and the world would be destroyed. Fenrir appears in the *Poetic Edda*, the *Prose Edda*, and a dramatic poem, *Fenris the Wolf*, by Percy MacKay (1875–1956).

See also: ANGURBODA; HEL; NIFELHEIM; RAGNAROK; TYR; VIDAR

**1177**

**Ferdinand III of Castile, St.** (peace)   Died 1252. In Christian legend, king of Castile when he was 18, Ferdinand spent almost his entire life fighting the Moors. In one battle he was aided by St. James the Apostle, who helped his army kill thousands of Moors. Only one Christian died in the battle. He is buried in the cathedral at Se-

**Fig 1182** 343

ville, having been canonized in 1668 at the request of Philip IV. Feast, 30 May.

See also: JAMES THE MAJOR, ST.

1178

**Feronia** In Roman mythology, early Italian goddess of groves, woods, orchards, and fountains; patroness of ex-slaves; mother of Erulus, a king of Italy who had three lives and had to be slain by Evander three times before he died. Feronia had a temple in Feronia near Mount Soracte. A yearly sacrifice was made to her. To wash one's face and hands in her sacred fountain near her temple was one of her rites. Those worshipers whom the goddess filled with her spirit were believed able to walk barefoot over burning coals. Feronia is cited in Vergil's *Aeneid* (book 7).

See also: *AENEID, THE;* ERULUS; EVANDER

1179

**Fiacre, St.** Seventh century. In Christian legend, abbot of Breuil; patron saint of gardeners, florists, trellis makers, box makers, brass beaters, coppersmiths, lead founders, needle makers, hosiers, tile makers, potters, and cab drivers. Invoked against venereal disease, sterility, fistula, colic, tumors, and headache. Protector of field and garden fruits. Feast, 1 September.

Fiacre was born in Ireland and sailed to France to devote himself completely to God. Arriving at Meaux, he was given a forest dwelling called Breuil by St. Faro, the local bishop. St. Faro offered St. Fiacre as much land as he could turn up in a day. Instead of driving his furrow with a plow, St. Fiacre turned the top of the soil with the point of his staff. He cleared the ground of trees and constructed a cell with a garden. He also made a chapel to the Virgin Mary, and a hospice for travelers later developed near it. Known throughout the area for his healing powers, many faithful often consulted the saint, but he would not allow any women near his hermitage or the chapel. If a woman attempted to break in, she was stopped by some supernatural power. Some died on the spot. After St. Fiacre's death

numerous miracles were claimed for his relics at Meaux. Louis XIII was restored to health by invoking the saint, as was Louis XIV.

St. Fiacre is the patron saint of Parisian cab drivers because the first establishment to allow coaches on hire in the 17th century was in the rue Saint-Martin, near the Hotel Saint-Fiacre, in Paris. French cabs are called *fiacres*, and the word is still widely used in Europe for a horse-drawn carriage.

See also: VIRGIN MARY

1180

**Fides** (loyalty, trust) In Roman mythology, goddess of oaths, honesty, and faith. Numa Pompilius, second king of Rome, was the first to worship Fides. Her feast day was 1 October.

1181

**Fierabras, Sir** (Ferumbras) In the Charlemagne cycle of legends, one of the paladins. He was the son of Balan, king of Spain. Physically he was noted for his stature, breadth of shoulder, and hardness of muscle. He controlled all of Babylon to the Red Sea and was seigneur of Russia, lord of Cologne, and master of Jerusalem and even of the Holy Sepulcher. He carried away the crown of thorns and the balsam used to embalm the body of Jesus, one drop of which would cure any sickness or heal any wound. One of his major feats was the slaying of the "fearful, huge giant that guarded the bridge Mantible." The bridge was noted for its 30 arches of black marble. Fierabras was at first a Saracen knight. He fought with the Christian knight Oliver, was defeated, and converted. He was then accepted by Charlemagne as a paladin. He died "meek as a lamb and humble as a chidden slave."

See also: CHARLEMAGNE; OLIVER; PALADINS, THE TWELVE

1182

**Fig** A fruit tree. The fig is often cited in European folklore as the fruit eaten by Adam and Eve in the Garden of Eden, as the biblical account in Genesis has the first couple covering "their nakedness" with fig leaves. Thus the fig has come to be connected in Jewish and Christian tradition with lust as well as fertility, but when shown on its tree in art, it signifies peace and plenty. An insulting sexual gesture, called "making a fig," is made by inserting the thumb between the index and middle fingers, indicating the vulva and the penis. Sicilian legend says that Judas hanged himself on a fig tree, and therefore the leaves of the tree house evil spirits. Another Sicilian legend says that if a man rests under a fig tree in the heat of summer a woman dressed as a nun will come and ask whether he will grasp the knife she is holding by the handle or by the blade. If he grasps the blade, the nun will stab him to death. If he grasps the handle, she will help him in all of his endeavors. Fig Sunday is an old name for Palm Sunday, because figs were eaten on that day to commemorate Jesus' blasting of the barren fig tree.

In India the god Vishnu is sometimes worshiped in the form of a fig tree, where, it is believed, his spirit hovers. A sacred fig with roots in heaven and branches and fruit on earth is a symbol of the cosmic tree in many mythologies.

The fig is sacred to Buddha because he was seated underneath the bo or pipal tree when he received the perfect knowledge and enlightenment of Nirvana.

See also: ADAM AND EVE; BUDDHA; JUDAS ISCARIOT; NIRVANA; VISHNU

1183
**Finn**    In Celtic mythology, hero who was the son of Cumhal, a king of the Tuatha de Danann, people of the goddess Danu. As a child Finn studied with a magician of the same name, who once caught the Salmon of Knowledge. Touching the salmon, Finn burned his finger, which he

then sucked to ease the pain. As a result he became the possessor of all knowledge.

See also: DANU; SALMON OF KNOWLEDGE; SIEGFRIED; TUATHA DE DANANN; *NIBELUNGENLIED*; *RING DES NIBELUNGEN*

1184
**Fintaan** (Fintan)    In Celtic mythology, a name borne by many figures in early Ireland, both secular and ecclesiastical, including 74 saints and pseudo-saints. The best known is Fintan mac Bóchra, the only Irishman to survive the Biblical flood. In one story he was 15 years old when the flood came, but he survived another 5,500 years. During this time he witnessed the exploits of Cuchulain, the coming of Christianity, and the entire history of the Western world.

See also: BITH AND BIRREN; CUCHULAIN

1185
**Firebird, The**    In Russian folklore, magical bird with golden wings and crystal eyes. The Firebird appears in many Russian folktales. One of the best known is "Prince Ivan, the Firebird, and the Gray Wolf." One day the Firebird visited the king's garden and plucked golden apples from its magical tree. Ivan, the king's son, was told by his father to capture the Firebird when it returned. After some nights of waiting Ivan caught the bird, but it struggled and escaped. All that remained was a feather from its tail "so wonderful and bright that when carried into a dark chamber it shone as if a great multitude of tapers were lighting the place." Not satisfied, the king sent Ivan and his two brothers, Dmitri and Vassily, to capture the Firebird.

Along the way Ivan met a gray wolf, which aided him in all sorts of difficulties and helped him capture the Firebird. As part of Ivan's adventure's the gray wolf made him fall in love with a beautiful girl, Yelena. On their way home Ivan and Yelena stopped to rest, and Ivan's two brothers attacked the couple. Ivan was killed by Dmitri, and Yelena was taken back with the brothers to the king's palace. Ivan remained dead for some

30 days. After the gray wolf, using *mertvaya voda* (dead water) and *shivaya voda* (living water), restored him to life, Ivan went to his father's palace, claimed his due, and married Yelena. Igor Stravinsky's ballet *L'Oiseau de feu* (The Firebird) uses the well-known folktale, adding to it the evil Kostchei. The Firebird is frequently found on lacquered boxes (*shatulki*).

See also: KOSTCHEI

1186

**Fish**   In excavations of ancient Egypt mummified fish have been found. A fish cult existed in the city of Oxyrhynchus, where the mormyrus fish was worshiped. It was believed to have swallowed the phallus of Osiris, god of the dead, when his evil brother Set hacked his body to pieces. In Greek mythology the fish was sacred to Aphrodite, goddess of love, and to Poseidon, god of the sea. In the worship of Adonis a fish was offered to the dead. In Roman mythology the fish was sacred to Venus and to Neptune. In Norse mythology the fish was sacred to Frigga as goddess of love and fertility. In Sumero-Semitic rites the fish was sacrificed to Ishtar, Adapa, Ea, and Thammuz. In Hindu mythology the fish is one of the mounts of Vishnu as savior of the world when he came as a fish to aid Manu. In Christianity the fish is a symbol of Jesus Christ because the first letters of *Iesous Christos Theou Huios Soter* (Jesus Christ, Son of God, Savior) spell *ichthus*, the Greek word for fish. In Buddhist belief a fish is symbolic of the footprint of the Buddha, indicating freedom from desires and attachments.

See also: ADAPA-EA; APHRODITE; BUDDHA, THE; FRIGGA; ISHTAR; MANU; NEPTUNE; OSIRIS; POSEIDON; SET; VENUS; VISHNU

1187

**Flamen Dialis**   In Roman ritual, a priest serving Jupiter. A Flamen Dialis could be married only once, could not be divorced, and had to resign his office if his wife died. His person could not touch a horse, flour, dogs, she-goats, beans,

or raw meat. He was forbidden to have any knots on his clothing. His headdress was the apex, a conical hat wrapped with a strip of white wool. If the headdress fell off during some ritual, he had to resign office. The Flamen Martialis (Mars) and the Flamen Quirinalis (Quirinus) came from the patrician class; other flamines (of a group of 12 to 15) came from the plebeian class and had fewer restrictions on their persons.

See also: MARS

1188

**Flaming Angel**   In Jewish and Christian mythology, angel often identified with Gabriel, Uriel, or Madiel.

The Flaming, or, as he is sometimes called, the Fiery, Angel is mentioned several times in Jewish and Christian literature. His exact identification is not known because the name assigned to him varies from work to work or is omitted entirely. In the New Testament Book of Revelation (14:18) he is identified as the angel "which had power over fire." In the Jewish-Christian work *Fourth Book of Maccabees* he appears as an adversary of the high priest Aaron, who defeats him. From the two texts it appears that the Flaming Angel is a demonic creature.

The Russian composer Prokofiev used the demonic aspect of the angel for his opera *The Flaming Angel*, giving the creature the name Madiel. The opera is based on a work (*Ognennyy Angel*) of the Russian poet, critic, and novelist Valery Yakovlevich Bryusov. Set in 16th-century Germany, the opera tells of a young girl, Renata, who had seen in her childhood a vision of Madiel, the Flaming Angel, and had fallen in love with him. The angel told her that if she wished to love him as a human being, she must meet him in his human form. The opera deals with the girl's quest to find the angel incarnate among the men she meets. Ultimately, however, she is destroyed. Prokofiev's opera was not produced until 1955. Some of its music was used by the composer in 1928 for the Third Symphony because he believed the work would never be produced on stage.

A painting by Marc Chagall entitled *Descent of the Red Angel* portrays the Flaming Angel descending to earth amid a burst of color.

See also: GABRIEL; URIEL

**1189**
**Flidais** (deer)    In Celtic mythology, an Irish woodland goddess, reputed to drive a chariot drawn by deer, wife of Ailill, mother of Fand, connected with hunting and protection of wild animals. Flidais had a magic cow that could produce milk for 300 men in one night, similar to the seven kine of Mananaan. She is better known for a lusty affair with Fergus, whose sexual appetite only she could satisfy; otherwise he needed seven women.

See also: MANANAAN

**1190**
**Flora** (flower, bloom)    In Roman mythology, goddess of flowering and blossoming plants; married to Zephyrus, who gave her perpetual youth; equivalent to the Greek goddess Chloris. Flora's festival, *Floralia*, was held between 28 April and 1 May; it consisted of games and indecent farces. Ovid's *Fasti* (book 5) tells of the goddess, and Robert Herrick's poem "Corinna's Going a-Maying" also cites her.

See also: OVID; ZEPHYRUS

**1191**
**Florian, St.** (flourishing)    Fourth century. In Christian legend, one of the patron saints of Austria and Poland; patron of brewers, coopers, chimney sweeps, and soap boilers. Invoked against bad harvests, battles, fires, floods, and storms. Feast, 4 May.

Florian was a Roman soldier who, because he was a Christian, had a millstone tied around his neck and was thrown into the river Enns, near Lorch (about 230). One of his many miracles was to put out a large city fire with a single pitcher of

*Flora*

water. His image often appears on fountains and pumps in Austria. In medieval Christian art he is portrayed as a young man in armor with a palm in his hand and a burning torch under his feet. Sometimes an eagle is shown near his dead body because legend says such a bird protected his body.

**1192**
**Fly**    Any of numerous two-winged insects. In Near Eastern mythology Beelzebub (Matt. 12:24), the Syrian god, was called Lord of the Flies. In Greek mythology Zeus was the god who warded off flies. In Jewish and Christian folklore, the fly is often identified with the devil.

See also: BEELZEBUB; ZEUS

1193

**Flying Dutchman, The**   Later medieval legend of a ship's captain condemned by God to wander about until the Last Judgment.

According to one account, the Flying Dutchman was a captain who persisted in trying to round the Cape of Good Hope in spite of the violence of a storm and the protests of his passengers and crew. Eventually, a form appeared (some accounts say it was God, others an angel of God) on the deck to warn the captain. Without warning the captain fired on the form and cursed it. As a punishment the Dutchman was condemned to sail and to be the torment of sailors until Judgment Day. Thus, he commands a spectral ship that perpetually rounds the Cape of Good Hope, luring other vessels to their doom.

Wagner's opera *Der Fliegende Holländer* uses his own version of the legend. Captain Frederik Marryat's novel *The Phantom Ship* (1839) is about Philip Vanderedecken's disastrous search for his father, the captain of the ship.

1194

**Fo**   In Chinese Buddhism, the name of the Buddha, though it is applied to any person who has attained Buddhahood. *Fo* is an abbreviated Chinese transliteration of Buddha. In full, it is *Fo-t'o*, originally pronounced "but-da"; in Japan, pronounced "butsu-da"; in Vietnam, "phat."

See also: BUDDHA, THE

1195

**Foma Berennikov**   In Russian folklore, hero who said he had killed 12 mighty heroes but in actuality had killed 12 gadflies. His boasting and cleverness enabled him to defeat various other heroes. He finally married the daughter of the king of Prussia.

1196

**Fomorians** (under, giant)   In Celtic mythology, the gods of the original population in Ireland. They were regarded by the later Celtic inhabitants as hurtful, evil gods, each having only one eye, one arm, and one leg. They were in opposition to the Tuatha de Danann, the gods and the people, or descendants, of the goddess Danu, who represented light and goodness. They were said to be wantonly cruel, cutting the noses off those who would not pay them tribute. W. B. Yeats often spoke of Fomorians. In *The Shadowy Waters* (1905) his sorceress Orchid is a Fomorian.

See also: BALOR; DANU; TUATHA DE DANANN

1197

**Fools, Feast of**   In medieval Christianity, a festival in honor of the ass on which Jesus made his triumphant entry into Jerusalem on Palm Sunday. Its origin was the "feast of the subdeacons," when members of the lower clergy switched places with their superiors. The subdeacon chosen as "king for a day" would read the Biblical verse "He has put down the mighty from their seats and exalted them of low degree" (Luke 1: 52). The verse referred to God's exaltation of the Virgin Mary, but it was used by the lower clergy to temporarily unseat their superiors.

The feast was held on 1 January, which is also the day of the Feast of the Circumcision of Jesus. The daily offices were chanted but in travesty. A procession was formed, and all the town indulged in a fools parade. An ass was part of the feast, and instead of saying "Amen" at the end of prayers the congregation would bray.

Part of the celebration consisted of "fools" being "ordained" as priests and bishops. Dice would be played on the altar, or food eaten, such as puddings, cakes, or sausages. Shoes would be burned as incense, men would often dress as women, and masks would be worn. The Feast of Fools died out by the 16th century under pressure from Protestant reformers, who disliked any kind of fun, and the Roman church no longer wanted to be identified with it. Scholars have traced the festival to the Roman Festa Stultorum and Saturnalia. The feast persists in popular imagination through Victor Hugo's *Notre Dame de Paris* and the film *The Hunchback of Notre Dame*.

**Formula**    Traditional expression tends to be formularized (not formalized). Formulas begin and end tales and indicate what kind of story is about to be told. "Once upon a time" clearly indicates fantasy, a fairy tale, while "I heard" suggests a legend, and "Have you heard the one about . . ." is the opening formula for a joke. These may be set or fixed phrases, patterns of repetition, closing devices, or even extended passages that often include stereotypes. There are also nonverbal formulas, such as hand gestures, designs, and stereotyped habits. In some cases formulas can even distinguish between folklore of the same genre but from different countries. English and American ballads, for example, have different formulas and on occasion present the performer and the listener with difficulty in understanding. In the famous ballad known in America as the "Cowboy's Lament," and in the United Kingdom as "The Bad Girl's Lament," the American version of the refrain includes the line: "So beat your drum lowly and play you fife slowly." Cowboys were certainly never buried to drum beat and fife playing, but since the ballad came with immigrants and was varied to suit its new home, this formulaic line survived and is still sung.

See also: ORAL THEORY

**Fornax** (oven)    In Roman mythology, goddess who presided over bread baking. Her festivals, called Fornacalia, were first instituted by Numa Pompilius, second king of Rome. Ovid's *Fasti* (book 2) tells of the feast, which was held 17 February or earlier.

See also: OVID

**Forseti** (Forsete) (he who sits in the front seat; chairman)    In Norse mythology, god of justice and conciliation; son of Baldur and Nanna, whose home was Glitnier. The kenning for Baldur is "Forseti's father." According to the *Prose Edda*, "all disputants at law who bring their cases before him go away perfectly reconciled." The term *forseti* is still in use today as the title for the president of Iceland.

See also: BALDUR; KENNING; NANNA; *PROSE EDDA*

*Fortuna*

**Fortuna** (fortune)    In Roman mythology, goddess of fortune, chance, and luck; identified with the Greek goddess Tyche. Originally, Fortuna was an ancient Italian goddess of increase and fertility, but she became goddess of fortune, thus the wheel of fortune. She was invoked by young Roman married women to grant fertility or a safe delivery. Her feast was 11 June according to Ovid's *Fasti* (6.569). The goddess continued to play a prominent role during the Christian Middle Ages, appearing in the 13th-century collection of songs in Latin, German, and French known as *Carmina burana*. Some of the texts were set by Carl Orff. Fortuna was also known as Fors or Fors Fortuna.

See also: OVID

**Four Horsemen of the Apocalypse**   1202   In the Bible, N. T., four figures in the Book of Revelation symbolizing the evils that will come to pass at the end of the world. The figure who represents conquest rides a white horse, war rides a red horse, famine a black horse, and pestilence a pale horse. The best known representation is in a woodcut by the German artist Albrecht Dürer (1471–1528), with the angels looking down from above while three of the horsemen trample men and women and Death treads upon a bishop falling into the gaping jaws of the Dragon of Hell.

See also: BIBLE (REVELATION)

**Fourteen Holy Helpers, The**   1203   In Christian legend, a group of saints honored during the Middle Ages in Germany, Bohemia, Moravia, Hungary, Italy, and France. Feast, 8 August.

The names of the 14 Holy Helpers vary, but the most common are the following:

*Achatius* (feast, 22 June).

*Barbara* (feast, 4 December). Invoked against lightning, fire, explosion, sudden and unprepared death; patron of architects, builders, and fireworks makers.

*Blaise* (feast, 3 February). Invoked against throat infections; patron of physicians, wax chandlers, and wool combers.

*Catherine of Alexandria* (feast, 25 November). Invoked by philosophers, saddlers, spinsters, students, and rope makers.

*Christopher* (feast, 25 July). Invoked against storms and for a safe journey; patron of navigators, sailors, and travelers.

*Cyriacus* (feast, 8 August). Invoked against demonic possession.

*Denis* (feast, 9 October). Invoked against frenzy, headache, rabies, and strife.

*Erasmus* (feast, 2 June). Invoked against birth pangs, colic, cattle pest, and danger at sea; patron of sailors.

*Eustace* (feast, 20 September). Patron of huntsmen.

*George* (feast, 23 April). Patron of calvarymen, chivalry, and soldiers.

*Giles* (feast, 1 September). Invoked against epilepsy, insanity, and sterility.

*Margaret* (feast, 20 July). Invoked in childbirth and against barrenness or lack of milk; patron of women (virgins), nurses, and peasants.

*Pantaleon* (feast, 27 July). Invoked against phthisis.

*Vitus* (feast, 15 June). Invoked against epilepsy and St. Vitus dance. Other saints sometimes included in the list are Dorothy (feast, 6 February), Leonard of Noblac (feast, 6 November), Oswald (feast, 5 August), and Nicholas (feast, 6 December).

The Feast of the Fourteen Holy Helpers is still observed in some parts of Germany. A church in Baltimore, Maryland, is dedicated to the group.

See also: BARBARA, ST.; BLAISE, ST.; CATHERINE OF ALEXANDRIA, ST.; CHRISTOPHER, ST.; DENIS, ST.; DOROTHY, ST.; EUSTACE, ST.; GEORGE, ST.; GILES, ST.; LEONARD, ST.; MARGARET, ST.; OSWALD, ST.; NICHOLAS, ST.; VITUS, ST.

**Fox**   1204   A small wild animal of the dog family; in European mythologies often a symbol of cunning; in Oriental mythologies women often turn into foxes and are beneficent creatures. Often equated with the devil in Christian symbolism, the fox is noted for his maliciousness, pious fraudulence, revengefulness, and thievery. In numerous Aesop fables and fables based on Aesop, the fox is presented as an evil, clever being, out to destroy. In Dante's *Inferno*, the spirit of Guido de Montefeltro, a famous warrior, says that his deeds were not those of a lion but of a fox. He used crafty, secretive ways to achieve his ends. Machiavelli's *The Prince* advises rulers to imitate two animals: the lion and the fox. The strength of the lion, Machiavelli says, is not sufficient for a ruler; he must also have the deceit of a fox.

Oriental mythologies often take a different approach. Japanese and Chinese tales abound with stories of fox transformations—women turned into foxes or foxes into women. In Oriental tales the appearance of a dog always forces the fox maiden into revealing her true nature. In Japanese folklore a fox maiden can be recognized by a spurt of flame flickering over her human head. The fox also has a strong sexual significance in Chinese and Japanese art and literature. The final panel of a four-panel Japanese screen portrays some merchants engaged in various sexual activities with different women. In the next panel the women have turned into vixens and the men into peasants. Janácek's opera *The Cunning Little Vixen* deals with a Czech legend of a woman turned into a fox. There are numerous motifs associated with the fox in the *Motif Index of Folk Literature*.

See also: AESOPIC FABLES; FOX AND THE CROW, THE; FOX AND THE GRAPES, THE; FOX AND THE MOSQUITOES, THE; REYNARD THE FOX

1205

**Fox and the Crow, The**   Aesopic fable, probably of Indian origin because some of the *Jatakas, or Birth-Stories of the Former Lives of the Buddha*, have the same moral.

A crow who had stolen a piece of cheese was flying toward the top of a tall tree, where he hoped to enjoy his prize, when a fox spied him.

*The Fox and the Crow*

"If I plan this right," said the fox to himself, "I shall have cheese for supper."

So, as he sat under the tree, he began to speak in his politest tones: "Good day, Mistress Crow, how well you are looking today! How glossy your wings, and your breast is the breast of an eagle. And your claws—I beg pardon—your talons are as are strong as steel. I have not heard your voice, but I am certain that it must surpass that of any other bird just as your beauty does."

The vain crow was pleased by all this flattery. She believed every word of it and waggled her tail and flapped her wings to show her pleasure. She liked especially what friend fox said about her voice, for she had sometimes been told that her caw was a bit rusty. So, chuckling to think how she was going to surprise the fox with her most beautiful caw, she opened her mouth wide.

Down dropped the piece of cheese! The wily fox snatched it before it touched the ground, and as he walked away, licking his chops, he offered these words of advice to the silly crow: "The next time someone praises your beauty be sure to hold your tongue."

Moral: *Flatterers are not to be trusted.*

There is an English proverb, "The fox praises the meat out of the crow's mouth." The fable is pictured on the Bayeux tapestry, and Thackeray makes use of it in his potpourri of fables in the Prologue to *The Newcomers*. In De Gubernatis' *Zoological Mythology*, he explains it: "The fox (the spring aurora) takes the cheese (the moon) from the crow (the winter night) by making it sing!" This explanation, however, is as fanciful as the fable itself and has been discredited by modern scholars.

See also: AESOPIC FABLES; *JATAKA*

*The Fox and the Grapes*

1206

**Fox and the Grapes, The** Aesopic fable found in numerous European collections such as Phaedrus, Babrius, and La Fontaine.

Mister Fox was just about famished, and thirsty too, when he stole into a vineyard where the sun-ripened grapes were hanging on a trellis too high for him to reach. He took a run and a jump, snapping at the nearest bunch, but missed. Again and again he jumped, only to miss the luscious prize. At last, worn out with his efforts, he retreated, muttering: "Well, I never really wanted those grapes anyway. I am sure they are sour."

Moral: *Any fool can despise what he cannot get.*

In La Fontaine's version the fox is something of an aristocrat. He says the grapes were only "fit for peasants." The expression "sour grapes," used when someone belittles something he or she once wanted but was unable to obtain, is derived from this fable. A modern retelling of the

fable, called *The Mookse and the Gripes*, is found in Joyce's *Finnegans Wake*.

See also: AESOPIC FABLES; LA FONTAINE, JEAN DE

1207

**Fox and the Mosquitoes, The** Aesopic fable found in various European collections.

A fox, after crossing a river, got its tail entangled in a bush and could not move. A number of mosquitoes, seeing its plight, settled on it and enjoyed a good meal undisturbed by its tail. A hedgehog strolling by took pity on the fox and went up to him. "You are in a bad way, neighbor," said the hedgehog. "Shall I relieve you by driving off those mosquitoes that are sucking your blood?"

"Thank you, Master Hedgehog," said the fox, "but I would rather not."

"Why, how is that?" asked the hedgehog.

"Well, you see," the fox answered, "these mosquitoes have had their fill; if you drive these away, others will come with fresh appetite and bleed me to death."

Moral: *Be satisfied with what you have, something new may be worse.*

Aristotle credits Aesop with the authorship of this fable, and Joseph Jacobs in his edition of *The Fables of Aesop* says it is "the only fable which can be traced with any plausibility to Aesop." Of course, his argument assumes that Aesop was a real person. Roman emperors, Jacobs writes, had a special liking for this fable since they used it to console provincial officials when they were mistreated by proconsuls or procurators.

See also: AESOPIC FABLES; ARISTOTLE

1208

**Frame Tale** A tale that holds several other tales together. Chaucer's *Canterbury Tales* were told as entertainment while pilgrims were on their way to the tomb of Thomas à Becket. In *The Thousand and One Nights* Princess Shahrazad marries a king who has the habit of each day killing his bride to marry another. The princess tells the king a story on their wedding night, always stopping at a most interesting point, whereupon the king decides each time to postpone the execution until he has heard the ending of the story. By telling a new tale every night, she is able to forestall her death. The frame is the story of Shahrazad; the individual tales are told within this frame.

See also: CHAUCER; *THOUSAND AND ONE NIGHTS, THE*

1209

**Francesca da Rimini**   13th century. In medieval history and legend, daughter of Guido da Polenta, lord of Ravenna. She was married to Malatesta, lord of Rimini, but her love for his younger brother, Paolo, was discovered by her husband, and the lovers were murdered by Malatesta in about 1289. In Dante's *The Divine Comedy* (Inferno, canto 5) she appears along with Paolo in Circle 2 of hell, where sins concerned with carnal love are punished. In Dante's work Francesca tells her own sad tale. Dante's poem inspired Tchaikovsky's fantasy for orchestra *Francesca da Rimini*, Rachmaninoff's opera *Francesca da Rimini*, and Zandonai's opera *Francesca da Rimini*.

1210

**Francesca Romana, St.** (a Frank)   1384–1440. In Christian legend, patron saint of Roman housewives. Feast, 9 March.

Francesca Romana was married to a rich nobleman, Lorenzo Ponziano, but spent most of her time in prayer. After his death she devoted what time was left to more prayer and works of charity. Once when she was praying she was called away four times at the same verse. The fifth time she found the verse written in golden light on the page of her prayer book by her guardian angel. She is credited with raising a dead child to life, stopping an epidemic by her prayers, and multiplying bread to feed the poor. In medieval Christian art she is often portrayed with her deacon (her guardian angel) by her side

and holding a book. Sometimes she is portrayed receiving the Christ Child from the Virgin Mary.

1211

**Francis of Assisi, St.** (the Frenchman)   1181?– 1226. Patron saint of animals, founder of Fratre Minori, known as the Franciscans, one of the three mendicant orders of Friars. Feast, 4 October. The order of Franciscan nuns was founded in 1212 by St. Clare.

Francis's father, Pietro Bernardone, was a rich merchant. Originally, Francis was named Giovanni, but he was called Francisco (the Frenchman) after his father had him trained in the French language in preparation for a business career. In his early years Francis was known for his passionate nature as well as for his love of all of the pleasures of life. In a quarrel between the people of Assisi and those of Perugia, Francis was taken prisoner and held for a year in the fortress of Perugia. After his release he was ill for many months. During this illness he spent time reflecting on the wasteful life he had led. Soon after his recovery, he met a beggar, whom he recognized as a man who had formerly been rich. Francis exchanged garments with the poor man, giving his rich cloak to the beggar and putting on the man's tattered garments. That night, in a vision, Francis saw himself in a beautiful apartment filled with all kinds of arms, rich jewels, and handsome garments—all of them marked with the sign of the cross. In the midst of the riches stood Jesus, who said to Francis: "These are the riches reserved for my servants and the weapons wherewith I arm those who fight for my cause." Francis took this to mean that he should become a soldier. After the vision Francis went to pray in the half-ruined church of San Damiano. As he knelt to pray a voice said to him, "Francis, repair my church, which falleth to ruin."

Taking the command literally, Francis sold some merchandise and gave the money to the priests of San Damiano to repair the church. His father was so angry that Francis hid in a cave for some days to escape his wrath. When Francis returned to the city, he was so tired and ragged that he was not recognized. Believing him insane, Francis's father had him confined, but his mother set him free, begging him at the same time to obey his father and to stop his strange conduct. His father took him to the bishop, and when they were in the presence of the bishop, Francis took off his fine clothes and threw them at his father, saying, "Henceforth I recognize no father but Him who is in heaven." The bishop took a poor man's cloak and covered Francis's naked body. Francis was at that time 25 years of age. He then began taking care of lepers; he begged, wandered about the mountains, and later lived in a cell near the chapel of Santa Maria degli Angeli. Soon he was joined by disciples, who also wished to follow his simple life.

Numerous legends grew about his holy life. One, contained in *Fioretti di San Francisco* (The Little Flowers of St. Francis) tells of a journey to Siena during which he met "three maidens in poor raiment, and exactly resembling each other in age and appearance, who saluted him with the words, 'Welcome, Lady Poverty!' and suddenly disappeared. The brethren not irrationally concluded that this apparition imported some mystery pertaining to St. Francis, and that by the three poor maidens were signified Chastity, Obedience, and Poverty, the beauty and sum of evangelical perfection; all of which shone with equal and consummate luster in the man of God, though he made his chief glory the privilege of Poverty."

In time Francis went to Rome to obtain confirmation of his religious order. At first Pope Innocent III thought Francis was insane, but in a dream the pope saw the Church tottering and kept from falling only by the support of Francis. He immediately sent for Francis and approved his right to preach. Francis's following grew, and missionaries were sent to Muslim countries. Francis even went himself, reaching Damietta (Egypt), where he was taken before the sultan. The sultan would not let Francis preach but also would not let him be martyred, and he was sent back to Italy. A few years later Pope Honorius confirmed his order. Francis resigned as its head and went to live in a cave on Mount Alverna. There he experienced many visions, the most famous being the one in which he received the stigmata, the wounds of Jesus, earning him the title of "the Seraphic." Following is the description from *The Little Flowers of St. Francis:*

After having fasted for fifty days in his solitary cell on Mt. Alverna, and passed the time in all the fervor of prayer and ecstatic contemplation, transported almost to heaven by the ardor of his desires; then he beheld as it were a seraph with six shining wings, bearing down upon him from above, and between his wings was the form of a man crucified. By this he understood to be figured a heavenly and immortal intelligence, subject to death and humiliation. And it was manifested to him that he was to be transformed into a resemblance to Christ, not by the martyrdom of the flesh, but by the might and fire of Divine love. When the vision had disappeared and he had recovered a little from its effect, it was seen that in his hands, his feet, and side he carried the wounds of our Savior.

Various legends are associated with Francis's love of animals. He preached to the birds about God's love. The most famous legend is that of the Wolf of Gubbio, who had been ravaging the countryside until Francis spoke to him. He told the wolf that food would be provided by the town, provided that he no longer attacked any of its inhabitants. The wolf obeyed the saint and became a friend of the people. Francis is known as the author of some poetry, among which the *Canticle of the Sun* is best known. His prayer, "Lord make me an instrument of your peace," has now been included in the American Book of Common Prayer of the Episcopal church.

Giotto's frescoes are the best known portrayals of the saint. Other artists who have painted Francis are El Greco, Dürer, and Rubens. Paul

Hindemith used episodes from the saint's life for a ballet. In literature, Laurance Houseman's short plays, *Little Plays of St. Francis* (1922) deal with the saint.

See also: CLARE, ST.

1212

**Francis Xavier, St.** (a Frank)   1506–1610. In Christian legend, missionary. Born of a noble family at his father's castle in the Pyrenees, Francis went to Paris to study theology and there became a friend and associate of St. Ignatius Loyola, the founder of the Jesuits. He joined the community and was sent as a missionary to Goa in India. He spent the rest of his life in the East and died while on a journey to China.

There are numerous legends of the saint recounted by Cardinal de Monte in his speech before Pope Gregory IX on the canonization of Francis Xavier. One is the tale of the crab that brought Francis Xavier his crucifix. As Francis was sailing from Ambionum, a city of the Molucca Islands, to Baranula the ship was overtaken by a storm, which threatened to wreck the vessel. Xavier took his crucifix from his neck and held it in the raging sea in order to still the billows. But suddenly the vessel lurched, and the crucifix dropped into the water. The ship arrived safely the next day at Baranula. When Xavier went ashore, a great crab leaped out of the sea carrying the crucifix "devoutly, and in an upright direction between its fins." The crab made its way to Francis, delivered the crucifix, and returned to the sea.

The cardinal also told the canonization commission how Francis Xavier had the gift of tongues. As soon as Francis came into any of the strange countries where he preached, he spoke the language of the people instinctively, without any accent.

When Xavier died, his body was laid in a coffin filled with pure lime to consume the flesh. Four months afterward, when the coffin was opened, it was found that the grave clothes were entirely intact and his flesh was as fresh as if the body had just died. No stench came from the body, but instead a sweet perfume. The body was put back into the coffin and taken to Malacca, which at the time was suffering from a plague. The moment the coffin arrived the plague ceased. A new coffin was made, but it was too small, and the body had to be forced into it, causing blood to spill out and stain the shroud. The coffin was buried in the churchyard of Our Blessed Lady and was opened again in nine months. Again, the body was fresh and the blood moist on the shroud. The body was now laid in a sumptuous coffin and carried to the Indies. It was received at Goa with great pomp, the viceroy himself taking part in the ceremony. No ointment, spices, or balm had been used, but his body "had a ravishing fragrance" and was laid on the right side of the high altar. Today, however, the body is nearly completely decayed.

Francis Xavier is often shown as a young bearded Jesuit with torch, flame, cross, and lily. Sometimes he is shown with St. Ignatius Loyola holding a cross.

See also: IGNATIUS LOYOLA, ST.

1213

**Frankie and Johnny**   American folk ballad, dating to the 19th century and first printed in 1912. It tells how Johnny, a St. Louis black procurer, was killed by his mistress, Frankie, a prostitute, when he went with another woman. There are more than 300 variants of the verses and music. Plays by Mae West and John Huston are based on the ballad, as well as the ballet *Frankie and Johnny*, with music by Jerome Moross. Hollywood's *Frankie and Johnny* (1966) uses the ballad for the tale of a Mississippi riverboat's gambling singer and his mistress, starring Elvis Presley.

See also: VARIANT

1214

**Franklin, Benjamin**   1706–1790. In American history and folklore, statesman, printer, scientist, and writer, the American self-made man. He was noted in folklore for his great love of women, especially in old age. According to one legend, when he was in France, numerous ladies swarmed around the old man, each asking him if he loved her the most. Franklin's reply was, "Yes, when you are closest to me—because of the force of attraction." Aside from his *Autobiography*, Franklin's most famous work was *Poor Richard's Almanack*, issued from 1732 to 1757. Filled with maxims, some by Franklin but most based on folk sayings and world literature, the work was extremely popular with the public. Among some of its most famous maxims are Make haste slowly; God helps them that help themselves; Early to bed and early to rise / Makes a man healthy, wealthy, and wise; Nothing but money is sweeter than honey; Approve not of him who commends all you say. Franklin was known during his lifetime as Ben the Magician because of his electrical experiments with the lightning rod. The famous legend of the kite is dim and mystifying in fact. Franklin himself did not write the story of this most dramatic of his experiments. All that we know about what happened on that day, of no known date, is found in Joseph Priestley's account, published 15 years later, but it was read in manuscript by Franklin, who evidently gave Priestley the familiar details. He invented the Franklin stove and bifocal spectacles.

1215

**Fraus** (deceit)    In Roman mythology, goddess of treachery, daughter of Orcus (Dis, Hades, Pluto) and Night (Nox).

See also: HADES; NOX; ORCUS; PLUTO

1216

**Fravashis**    In Persian mythology, spiritual primeval images of men, preexistent souls. They watch over procreation, do battle, are invoked against danger, and guard the seed of the prophet Zarathustra, which will later be planted in future saviors: Hushedar, Hushedar-man, and Soshyant.

The *Zend Avesta*, which is the *Avesta* with a commentary, writes of the Fravashis, "which have existed from of old" and are found in houses, villages, communities, and provinces, that they "hold the heaven in its place apart, and the water, land and cattle, which hold the children in the wombs safely enclosed apart so they do not miscarry."

See also: *AVESTA*; HUSHEDAR; HUSHEDAR-MAN; SOSHYANT; ZARATHUSTRA

1217

**Freki and Geri** (greedy and ravenous)    In Norse mythology, two wolves who sit by Odin, chief of the gods, when he feasts. Odin gives them all of the food set before him and drinks only wine, since food and wine are the same to the god. They appear in the *Poetic Edda* and the *Prose Edda*.

See also: ODIN; *POETIC EDDA*; *PROSE EDDA*

1218

**Frenchy Aucoin**    In American folklore, a lumberman who turned into a Canada jay after his death, only to be stripped of his feathers and thrown out into the cold night to return to hell. Harry N. Lundmark picks up the theme in 2001 in *The Curse of the Gorby* where a small gray, gull-like bird, also known as the Moosebird or Gorby, is waiting to steal the soul of a dying woodsman. This bird must never be harmed, under any circumstance, for the culprit would suffer a fate of unutterable horror.

1219

**Frey** (lord, master)    In Norse mythology one of the Vanir; god of fertility, peace, and wealth; son of Njord and patron god of Sweden and Iceland. Frey's wife was Gerda, daughter of mountain giants Gymir and his wife Aurboda. When Frey first saw Gerda he immediately fell in love with her and sent his messenger Skirnir to her, telling him, "Go, and ask her hand for me, and bring her to me whether her father be willing or

*Frey*

not, and I will amply reward you." Skirnir was willing to undertake the mission, provided he was given Frey's wonderful sword, which Frey then gave him. Eventually he returns with Gerda's promise that within nine nights she would come to a place called Barey and there marry Frey.

The *Prose Edda* describes Frey as "one of the most celebrated of the gods. He presided over rain and sunshine, and all the fruits of the earth, and should be invoked in order to obtain good harvests and also peace. He moreover dispenses wealth among men." Among Frey's treasures were Blodighofi (bloody-hoof), his magical horse; Gullinbursti (gold-bristled), a golden boar or a chariot drawn by a boar; and Skidbladnir (wooden-bladed), a magic ship that could be folded up like a tent. Frey's boar reflects the cult of the boar associated with the god. On the eve of

the Yule festival a sacrifice called *sónargöltr* (atonement boar) was offered to make Frey favorable to the New Year. The ancient pagan cult still survives in Sweden in the cakes baked at Yule (now Christmas) in the form of a boar. Frey was sometimes called Ingvi-Frey or Ingunar-Frey (Frey of Ingun). Edward Burne-Jones's 19th-century painting of Frey portrays him seated with an olive branch and a boar at his feet.

See also: GERDA; NJORD; SKIRNIR; VANIR; YULE

1220

**Freyja** (Frea, Frija, Freya, Foige) (the lady)    In Norse mythology, the only named Vanir goddess; goddess of youth, beauty, and sexual love; sister of the god Frey; married to Odur. Friday was sacred to the goddess and named after her. In northern mythology Freyja and Frigga are often confused for the same deity. Freyja, in some accounts, was married to Odur, and their daughter was called Hnossa. But Odur left Freyja in order to travel around the world. Since that time Freyja continually weeps, and her tears are drops of gold. Freyja, according to the *Prose Edda*, rides into battlefields asserting "her right to one-half of the slain, the other half belonging to Odin." Her most famous possession is her necklace, Brising (necklace of the dwarfs?), given her by the dwarfs. One day while Freyja was in the underground kingdom of the dwarfs, she saw them fashion a necklace. She asked the dwarfs to give it to her. They refused at first, but eventually gave it to the goddess on condition she have sexual intercourse with them. Brising was later worn by the god Thor when he impersonated the goddess in order to trick the giants. The necklace was once stolen by the evil god Loki but recovered by Heimdall. Freyja, according to the *Prose Edda*, lends a very favorable ear to those who sue to her for assistance: "She is very fond of love ditties, and all lovers would do well to invoke her."

Often in the myths Freyja is accused of having sexual intercourse with many men and gods. The goddess is called a "she goat" that leaps after goats. The giantess Hyndla taunts the goddess by saying that "many have stolen under thy girdle." Freyja's home is in Folkvang (field of folks), in which her hall, Sessrumnir (love, which supports the idea of the Vanir as a fertility cult), is located. Each day she leaves her mansion in a chariot drawn by two cats. Freyja is also called Mardoll (shining over the sea), Horn, Gefn, Syr, and Vanadjs.

See also: AESIR-VANIR WAR; DVALIN; FREY; FRIGGA; HNOSSA; RAGNAROK; SEID; THOR; VANIR;

1221

**Frigga** (Frigg, Frija, Fri) (lady, mistress, bearer?) In Norse mythology, an Aesir goddess, wife of Odin, mother of Baldur. She presides over marriage. In the *Prose Edda* she is in the front rank of the goddesses. Her home was Fensalir (sea hall), and she dressed in the plumage of falcons and hawks. Frigga has 11 maidservants: Fulla, Hlin, Gna, Lofn, Vjofn, Syn, Gefjon, Snotra, Eira, Vara, and Vor, who help the goddess preside over marriage and justice. She is called upon in the ninth-century German "Merseburg Charms" to help cure a broken leg on Baldur's horse. She appears in Richard Wagner's *Der Ring des Nibelungen* as Fricka. Friday is dedicated to the goddess and is named for her. Frigg is part of many Scandinavian place names. Sometimes Frigga is confused with Freya in Germanic mythology.

See also: AESIR; BALDUR; MERSEBURG CHARMS; ODIN; *RING DES NIBELUNGEN, DER*

1222

*Frithjof's Saga*  Thirteenth-century Icelandic saga believed to have originated in the eighth century. Frithjof (peace maker) was the son of Thane Thorsten, the friend of King Bele of Norway. He played with the little princess Ingebjorg and was sent with her to learn wisdom from the sage Hilding. When King Bele and Thorsten died, Princes Helgi and Halfdon assumed the throne. Frithjof inherited from his father a wonder-working sword, Angurvadel, with strange runes that dulled in peace and flamed in war; the

arm ring of Wayland the Smith; and *Ellide*, the dragon ship. After the death feast of his father, Frithjof went to the land of Helgi and Halfdon to ask for the hand of Ingebjorg, their sister, in marriage. Helgi sneered at the idea. Another suitor, King Ring, an old widower, was also rejected and returned to make war on Helgi and Halfdon. Ingebjorg was then locked up in Baldur's temple. Frithjof entered the sacred temple, having no fear that he profaned it. He offered to help Ingebjorg's brothers, but they refused his aid. Defaming Baldur's temple was a crime, and on pain of perpetual exile Frithjof was forced to wrest from Yarl Angantyr the tribute due to the sons of King Bele.

Unable to persuade Ingebjorg to go with him, he set sail for an island ruled over by Yarl Angantyr. His dragon ship made a safe voyage, even though Helgi caused a storm to be raised by the sea-witches Heyd and Ham. Before reaching the castle he overcame the Viking Atli but spared his life because of Atli's fearlessness; the two became friends. Frithjof was welcomed by Yarl Angantyr, his father's friend, who had given presents, not tribute, to King Bele and had been rewarded with a purse of gold. Remaining with Yarl Angantyr until spring, Frithjof then sailed for seven days to Framnas, only to find that it had been burned and was in ruins. He learned from Hilding that King Ring had married Ingebjorg.

Angry at the turn of events, Frithjof went to the temple of Baldur during a midsummer feast and fought with Helgi in single combat. When he noticed that Ingebjorg's armlet was on the image of the god Baldur, he pulled it off, causing the god's statue to fall into the fire. The temple caught fire, and the surrounding area was set ablaze. Frithjof fled, chased by Helgi with 10 warships. Bjorn, however, had bored holes in the ships the previous night, and all aboard were drowned except for Helgi.

Frithjof became a pirate for three years. On his return he dressed as a beggar and appeared at the Yuletide feast of King Ring. When a soldier made fun of Frithjof, he caught him and turned him head over heels. King Ring asked the beggar to take off his disguise but did not seem to recognize Frithjof, though Ingebjorg did. Twice Frithjof had his enemy's life in his hands. But the old king had recognized him from the first. Finally, King Ring plunged a sword into his own chest. Before Frithjof married Ingebjorg, he went to seek forgiveness from the god Baldur. He made a temple to the god, and the wedding took place.

This medieval saga inspired the 19th-century narrative poem *Frithiof-Saga* or *Lay of Frithiof* by Esaias Tegnér, bishop of Vaxjo, Sweden. The work was known to Henry Wadsworth Longfellow, who translated the bishop's narrative poem, "The Children of the Lord's Supper."

See also: BALDUR; WAYLAND THE SMITH

1223

**Frode**   In Danish legend, a king who had a magic millstone that ground out gold for him. When he demanded more and more gold, the two giant maidens Frenja and Menja ground out salt. This killed Frode and brought famine to the land.

1224

**Frog**   A tailless amphibian having long hind legs used for jumping. In Egyptian mythology the frog goddess was Heket, and the four male primeval gods of the Ogdoad, which formed a group of eight deities who created the world, were portrayed as frog-headed. In Greek and Roman mythology the frog was associated with Aphrodite and Venus, as goddesses of sex and love.

In Christianity the frog is often a symbol of evil. But often the frog and toad are confused in Christian symbolism. Shakespeare's King Richard III is called "this poisonous hunchback'd toad" (1.3), and in Milton's *Paradise Lost* Satan takes the form of a toad to squat at the ear of the sleeping Eve and distill poison into her blood. This recalls the European belief that toads are venomous creatures whose blood, if drunk, would kill instantly. The antidote for toad poi-

son is a jewel found in the toad's head, its existence being a common folk belief.

Some Freudians have viewed the frog as symbolic of the penis. At first the penis is feared by a woman, they contend, but once she experiences sexual contact and pleasure, she realizes that the object of her fear is actually something desirable. This motif is supported in the Grimm folktale The Frog Prince. The theory is interesting, but in many variants of the tale the frog turns into a woman. Frenchmen have long been referred to as Frogs because of their ancient heraldic emblem, which was three frogs or toads.

See also: FROG AND THE OX, THE; GRIMM BROTHERS

*The Frog and the Ox*

1225

**Frog and the Ox, The**   Aesopic fable found in various European collections.

Some frogs had just had a harrowing experience down at the swampy meadow, and they came hopping home to report their adventure.

"Oh, Father," said one of the little frogs, all out of breath, "we have just seen the most terrible monster in all the world. It was enormous, with horns on its head and a long tail and hooves—."

"Why, child, that was no monster. That was only an ox. He isn't so big! If I really put my mind to it, I could make myself as big as an ox.

Just watch me!" So the old frog blew himself up. "Was he as big as I am now?" he asked.

"Oh, Father, much bigger," cried the little frogs. Again the father frog blew himself up and asked his children if the ox could be as big as that.

"Bigger, Father, a great deal bigger," chorused the little frogs. "If you blew yourself up until you burst, you could not be as big as the monster we saw in the swampy meadow."

Provoked at being outdone, the old frog made one more attempt. He blew and blew and swelled and swelled until something went *pop*. The old frog had burst.

Moral: *Self-conceit leads to self-destruction.*

The fable is told by Horace in his *Satires* (book 2), as well as by Thomas Carlyle in his *Miscellanies*, from a German variant. Thackeray uses it in the Prologue to his novel *The Newcomers*.

See also: AESOPIC FABLES

1226
**Froh**   In Norse mythology, an ancient god and all-father, whose worship was supplanted by Odin's cult. He appears in Wagner's *Der Ring des Nibelungen*.

See also: ODIN; *RING DES NIBELUNGEN, DER*

1227
**Frolka Stay-at-Home**   In Russian folklore, a hero who rescued three princesses who had been kidnapped. The first was held by a five-headed dragon, the second by a seven-headed dragon, and the third by a 12-headed dragon. Frolka, aided by a nameless soldier and a man called Erema, defeated all three monsters.

1228
**Fu Daishi**   Japanese name for Chinese Buddhist priest credited with the invention of the revolving bookcase, containing the 6,771 sacred books of Buddhism. It is believed that if the bookcase is revolved, three times more merit will be obtained than if one read all of the volumes.

1229
**Fuji Hime**   In Japanese mythology, Princess Fuji, who inhabits Fuji Yama, the most famous mountain in Japan. Called Ko-no-hana-saku-ya-hime (princess who causes the blossoms of trees to flower), she is portrayed in Japanese art with a large sun hat and a twig of wisteria in her hand.

1230
**Fujiyama**   In Japanese mythology, the sacred spirit of Mount Fuji and the guardian spirit of the nation. The mountain can only be climbed after ritual purification, but each July thousands of pilgrims climb to the summit. A Shinto legend describes the appearance of the mountain. Many years ago an old man who cultivated bamboo on the slopes found an infant girl and named her Kaguya-hime. She was considered the most beautiful girl in all of the land and became a princess of the emperor. Seven years after they were married, the princess told the emperor that she was not mortal and wanted to return to her celestial home. As a parting gift she gave the emperor a magical mirror in which he could always see her image. She then disappeared. The emperor tried to follow her to heaven by ascending Mount Fuji with the mirror in his hands. On the summit he could not find any trace of his princess, and his love for her caused his breast to break open, and the fiery passion set the mirror ablaze. Ever since smoke has risen from the top of the mountain.

1231
**Fulgora** (lightning)   In Roman mythology, goddess who protected houses against violent storms.

1232
**Furina** (thief)   In Roman mythology, goddess of robbers, worshiped at a sacred grove in Rome. In some ancient texts she is identified with the Furies. Her festivals were called Furinelia.

1233

**Fushi Ikazuchi**   In Japanese mythology, one of the Ikazuchi, the eight gods of thunder.

See also: IKAZUCHI

1234

**Futen**   In Japanese Buddhist mythology, god of the winds, derived from the Hindu wind god, Vayu. He is portrayed as an old man, bare-headed, with flowing beard and garments, walking and holding in his left hand a banner blown by the wind. He is one of the Jiu No O, 12 Japanese Buddhist gods and goddesses adopted from Hindu mythology.

See also: JIU NO O; VAYU

1235

**Fylgia** (follower)   In Norwegian folklore, a guardian spirit, or one's double or soul. Often the *fylgia* appears in dreams in animal form. If one sees the *fylgia* when awake, it indicates one's death. When a person dies, the *fylgia* passes on to another member of the family.

# G

**Gabriel** (man of God)    In Jewish, Christian, and Islamic mythology, archangel. Feast: 18 March in the Western church.

Gabriel plays a prominent role in the Bible as a messenger of God. He first announces to Daniel the return of the Jews from their captivity (Dan. 8:16) and explains the vision of the various nations (Dan. 9:21). In the New Testament Gabriel announces to Zacharias the coming birth of John the Baptist (Luke 1:19) and to the Virgin Mary that she will be the mother of Jesus (Luke 1:26). In Islam the Koran credits Gabriel, who is called Jiburili (Jibril), with dictating from the perfect copy in heaven the earthly copy of the Koran.

Milton, in *Paradise Lost* (book 4:550), calls Gabriel the "Chief of the angelic guards," recalling a Jewish belief. In his musical *Anything Goes* Cole Porter has a brilliant song, "Blow, Gabriel, Blow," which credits the angel with a magnificent trumpet and the task of announcing the end of the world. (The song was introduced by Ethel Merman.)

In Western Christian art Gabriel is usually portrayed as the messenger to the Virgin Mary announcing the coming birth of Jesus. He is often shown kneeling before her, holding a scroll with the words *Ave Maria, gratia plena* (Hail Mary, full of grace). In Greek and Byzantine por-

1236

trayals Gabriel is usually shown standing, not kneeling.

See also: DANIEL; JOHN THE BAPTIST, ST.; KORAN, THE; VIRGIN MARY; ZACHARIAS

1237

**Gada**    In Hindu mythology, the younger brother of Krishna (an incarnation of the god Vishnu).

See also: KRISHNA; VISHNU

1238

**Gaea** (Ge, Gaia) (earth)    In Greek mythology, Mother Earth; daughter of Chaos with Eros and Tartarus; called Terra or Tellus by the Romans. After the rule of Chaos (one of the infernal deities), Gaea appeared and gave birth to Uranus (the upper regions covering the earth). Then after having sexual intercourse with Uranus, she bore Cronus, Pallas, Oceanus, the Clyclopes, and the Titans. From the spilled blood and semen of Uranus she gave birth to the Erinyes, the giants, the Meliae, and Aurora. From the severed genitals of Uranus she became the mother of Aphrodite. An affair with Hephaestus produced Erichthonius; by Oceanus she bore Ceto, Crius, Eurybia, Nereus, Phorcys, and Thaumas; by Poseidon she bore Ogyges, Charybdis, and Antaeus. She is also the mother of Cecrops, Cranaus, Echo, Palaechthon, Rumor, Arion, and the serpent that guarded the Golden Fleece. Gaea appears in Hesiod's *Theogony* (116 ff.), the Homeric Hymns (not by Homer), and Vergil's *Aeneid.*

See also: ANTAEUS; APHRODITE; AURORA; ECHO; ERICHTHONIUS; GOLDEN FLEECE; HEPHAESTUS; HESIOD; OCEANUS; PALLAS; TITANS; URANUS

**1239**
**Gagavitz** (hill of fire)    In the mythology of the Cakchiquels, a branch of the Mayan Indians, progenitor and culture hero. The myths of Gagavitz are related in *The Annals of the Cakchiquels* (16th century), along with their legendary history. Early in the book, Gagvitz's companion Zactecauh (white mountain, hill of snow) is killed trying to cross a ravine, leaving Gagavitz alone. The hero arrives at Gagxanul (the naked volcano), now called Santa Maria, and is asked by the Indians there to help them capture fire. One Indian, Zakitzunún (white sparrow), offered to help. Gagavitz descended into the volcano while Zakitzunún threw water mixed with green stems of corn into the hole. Gagavitz stayed for some time, and the people were fearful he had been killed, but he emerged, bringing fire. The two were called heroes. Later Gagavitz sent warriors to capture Tolgom, then changed himself into a serpent and died, leaving two sons, Caynoh and Gaybatz.

**1240**
**Galahad** (hawk of battle)    In Arthurian legend, the purest and noblest knight, son of Lancelot and Elaine, who seeks the Holy Grail. He was described by Walter Map in his *Quest of the San Graal.* When the Round Table was founded, one seat, the Siege Perilous, was left unoccupied and could be used only by the knight who would succeed in the quest for the Holy Grail. All others who had attempted to sit in the seat had been swallowed up by the earth. When Sir Galahad sat in the seat, he was unharmed. Galahad went in search of the Holy Grail, even "took the Lord's body between his hands," and then died. Sud-

*Sir Galahad*

denly, according to one medieval source, "a great multitude of angels did bear his soul up to heaven" and "since then was never no man that could say he had seen the Holy Grail."

See also: ELAINE; HOLY GRAIL; LANCELOT OF THE LAKE; ROUND TABLE

**1241**
**Galanthis** (weasel)    In Greek mythology, Alcmena's maid. She aided her mistress during the birth of Heracles when Hera sent the childbirth goddess, Ilithyia, to retard Alcmena's labor with magic incantations. Galanthis fooled Ilithyia by pretending that Alcmena had already delivered. Caught off guard, Ilithyia's spell was broken, and Alcmena immediately delivered Heracles. In a fury Ilithyia transformed Galanthis into a weasel.

Ovid's *Metamorphoses* (book 9) tells of her transformation.

See also: ALCMENA; HERA; HERACLES; OVID; WEASEL

1242

**Galatea** (milk-white)   In Greek mythology, a Nereid, one of the 50 daughters of Nereus and Doris; sister of Thetis and Amphitrite. Galatea loved the handsome youth Acis, and the Cyclops Polyphemus loved Galatea. When Polyphemus saw Galatea and Acis alone, he killed Acis by hurling a rock at him. The stream of blood from Acis's mangled body was transformed by the gods into an inexhaustible stream of limpid water, which runs down to the sea to join Galatea. Theocritus's *Idylls* (11) and Ovid's *Metamorphoses* (book 13) tell of the myth, as does Handel's opera *Acis and Galatea* (1721) with a libretto by John Gay. The name Galatea also is given to the statue by Pygmalion that was turned into a live woman by Aphrodite. Pygmalion and Galatea became the parents of Paphos. This myth is told in Ovid's *Metamorphoses* (book 10).

See also: AMPHITRITE; DORIS; NEREIDS; OVID; POLYPHEMUS; THETIS

1243

**Gama Sennin**   In Japanese folklore, a deified mortal portrayed holding a frog, sometimes three-legged, in his hand, or with the animal climbing over his clothes or shoulder. Various folktales account for the iconography connected with Gama Sennin. One version tells how Gama Sennin went to bathe and was followed by a man named Bagen, who assumed the form of a frog to observe him. In a variant tale Gama Sennin took the form of a frog whenever he went near the water. In still another, Gama Sennin sold a drug to Bagen that made Bagen live 100 years. This incident is portrayed with Gama Sennin giving the pill to a frog, who is Bagen.

1244

**Gandharvas**   In Hindu mythology, celestial musicians who sing on mountaintops, under the god Varuna. Sometimes they are dangerous at twilight. Originally, there was only one Gandharva, mentioned in the sacred collection of hymns, the Rig-Veda; he guarded the sacred Soma juice. In present-day Hinduism the Gandharvas watch over marriage and protect virgins. One of their homes is in Alaka, located on the sacred mountain Meru. An aerial city, Vismapana (astounding), which appears and disappears, also is said to be one of their homes. It is often called Gandharva-nagana (capital city of the Gandharvas). In post-Vedic Hinduism and in Buddhism, Vismapana is a synonym for a mirage.

See also: MERU; RIG-VEDA; SOMA; VARUNA; VEDAS

1245

**Ganelon**   In the Charlemagne cycle of legends, a traitor. He was the count of Mayence (Mainz) and one of Charlemagne's paladins. Jealousy of Roland made him betray them all. He planned his evil deed with Marsillus, the Moorish king, and was successful. The Christians were defeated at the Battle of Roncesvalles, which forms one of the main episodes of *The Song of Roland*. Ganelon was 6½ feet tall, with large glaring eyes and fiery red hair. He was taciturn and morose. In European legend his name became a byword for a false and faithless friend. He appears in Dante's *The Divine Comedy* (Inferno) and is grouped by Chaucer with Judas, the betrayer of Jesus, in the Nun's Priest's Tale in *The Canterbury Tales*.

See also: CHARLEMAGNE; CHAUCER; JUDAS ISCARIOT; PALADINS, THE TWELVE; ROLAND

1246

**Ganesha** (Ganesa, Gunesh, Gunputty) (lord of hosts)   In Hindu mythology, the elephant-headed god of wisdom and good fortune. Ganesha is one of the most popular gods in present-day Hinduism. All sacrifices and religious

*Ganesha*

his son lose his head. To replace the head Indra used the head from his elephant mount.

Elephant-headed Ganesha, however, has only one tusk. The loss of the other tusk is accounted for in various myths. One says Ganesha used one of his tusks to transcribe the epic poem *The Mahabharata* and then lost it. In another myth his belly burst open from overeating, and the moon laughed at him, so Ganesha broke off his tusk and threw it at the moon, which slowly darkened as a result. In either case Ganesha is called Eka-danta (the single-tusked). Ganesha is leader of the Gana Devatas (troops of lesser gods), who attend his father Shiva.

One Hindu sect, the Ganapatyas, regarded Ganesha as the supreme being or god. In the *Ganapati Upanishad* he is thus addressed:

Praise to thee, O Ganesha! Thou art manifestly the truth; thou art undoubtedly the creator, Preserver, and Destroyer, the supreme Brahma, the eternal spirit.

In Indian art Ganesha is portrayed as a short fat man with a big belly, four hands, and, of course, his elephant head. In one hand he holds a conch shell, in another a discus, in the third a club or goad, and in the fourth a lotus. Sometimes he is seen riding on a mouse or attended by one, indicating, according to some accounts, his conquest of demonic forces symbolized by the rodent.

Ganesha has many epithets, among them Kari-mikha (elephant-faced), Heramba (boastful), Lamba-karna (long-eared), Lambodara (pendent-bellied), Dwi-deha (double-bodies), Vighna-hara (remover of obstacles), and Dwaimatura (having two mothers), an allusion to another birth myth that he was born from the sweat of his mother Parvati's body.

See also: *MAHABHARATA, THE*; SHIVA

ceremonies, all literary and musical compositions, and all worldly affairs (except funerals) are begun with an invocation to Ganesha. Most Hindu texts open with a "reverence to Ganesha" or "salutation to Ganesha."

There are a variety of myths accounting for his elephant head and human body. One is that his mother, Parvati, wife of the god Shiva, was so proud of her offspring that she asked Sani (Saturn) to look at the child. Sani looked on Ganesha, and the child's head was immediately burned to ashes. The god Brahma told Parvati to replace the head with the first head she could find—it was an elephant's head.

A variant myth tells how Parvati went to bathe and told her son Ganesha to watch the door so that no one would disturb her. Shiva, her husband, wished to enter. Ganesha tried to stop his father, and Shiva cut the lad's head off. To pacify Parvati, Shiva replaced the head with the first one he could acquire, which was an elephant's head. Another variant tells how Parvati formed Ganesha's head to suit her own desire, and yet another myth tells how Shiva was cursed for slaying Aditya (the sun) and was punished by having

1247

**Ganges** (going strongly or swiftly)  In India, sacred river and goddess whose waters are believed to have the power of cleansing one of past, present, and future sins.

According to Hindu mythology the Viyadganga (heavenly Ganges) flowed from the toe of the god Vishnu (some texts say Shiva) and was brought to earth by the prayers of Bhagirathi, a holy man. Bhagirathi called down the river to cleanse the ashes of the 100 sons of King Sagara; they had been burned to death by the sage Kapila after they had accused Kapila of stealing a horse that was to be sacrificed. The sage, having his devotions interrupted, "looked upon them for an instant, and they were reduced to ashes by the flames that darted from his person," according to one account. Some texts identify Kapila with the firegod Agni. Though Bhagirathi called the river down to earth, Ganga (who is also a goddess) was caught by the god Shiva on his brow, and her fall was checked by his matted locks. From this action, Shiva gained the epithet Ganga-dhara (upholder or controller of the Ganges). The river descended from Shiva's brow in several streams: four in some accounts, ten in others, seven being the generally accepted number. Another name for the river is Sapta-sindhava (the seven rivers).

See also: SHIVA; VISHNU

1248

**Ganymede** (rejoicing in virility)  In Greek mythology, a beautiful Trojan boy, son of Tros and Callirrhoë; brother of Assaracus, Cleopatra, and Ilus; mispronounced as Catamitus by the Romans, hence the English word *catamite*. Zeus, in the form of an eagle, seduced Ganymede and brought him to Olympus to be his cupbearer. Hera, Zeus's wife, hated the boy, whom Zeus loved. In an earlier version of the myth Ganymede was the son of King Tros and was carried off by Zeus in exchange for some horses. In the *Hymn to Aphrodite*, one of the hymns attributed to Homer but not by him, Ganymede is carried to heaven by a storm wind, but in Vergil's *Aeneid* (book 5) he was snatched up by an eagle or, according to Ovid's *Metamorphoses* (book 10), by

*Ganymede on Zeus' eagle*

Zeus himself. In some accounts of the myth the eagle was turned into the constellation Aquila and Ganymede into Aquarius. In Greek art Ganymede is portrayed as a beautiful youth. On one fifth-century B.C.E. red-figure mixing bowl he is shown holding a hoop and cock, favorite gifts from older men to young men. Ganymede's myth is used in Aristophanes' play *Peace*, and Plato uses it in his dialogue *Phaedrus* to explain Socrates' love for his male pupils. During the Christian Middle Ages, Ganymede became a term for a homosexual. Marlowe's play *The Tragedy of Dido, Queen of Carthage* (1594) opens with a scene between Jupiter and Ganymede. Ganymede asks Jupiter a favor, and in return Jupiter says, "I will spend my time in thy bright arms." Ganymede has been painted by Corregio, Rubens, and Rembrandt.

See also: *AENEID, THE*; CALLIRRHOË; HERA; ZEUS

1249

**Garboncias**  In Hungarian folklore, a supernatural being, born with all of his teeth or with extra fingers. The being exercises magical powers when in a trance. It often carries a big black book and begs for milk. Garboncias is similar to Tatlos, another supernatural being with magical powers in Hungarian folklore.

**Garden of the Hesperides**　　In Greek mythology, a garden owned by Atlas that contained a tree with Golden Apples guarded by the Hesperides and Ladon, a dragon. The tree was a gift to Hera when she married Zeus. Heracles 11th labor was to obtain the apples. He killed the dragon and took the apples, but they could exist only in the magic garden, so they were given to Athena, who returned them. Paris presented one of the Golden Apples to Aphrodite when he chose her in the Judgment of Paris. Hesiod's *Theogony*, Ovid's *Metamorphoses* (book 4), and Tennyson's *The Hesperides* deal with the myth.

See also: APHRODITE; ATLAS; HESIOD; HESPERIDES; LADON; OVID; PARIS; ZEUS

**Gareth** (gentle)　　In Arthurian legend, the youngest son of King Lot of Orkney and Margawse, Arthur's half sister. Gareth's mother did not want her son to be at Arthur's court and jestingly said she would consent to his going there only if he concealed his name and went as a scullion for 12 months. Gareth agreed. Sir Kay, the king's steward, named him Beaumains because his hands were extremely large. At the end of a year Gareth was knighted. He aided Lynette by freeing her sister, Liones (Lyonors), who was being held prisoner by Sir Ironside at Castle Perilous. At first Lynette treated Gareth with scorn, calling him a dishwasher and a kitchen boy. After Gareth overthrew five knights and freed her sister, she changed her opinion of him. Tennyson retells the tale in "Gareth and Lynette," part of his *Idylls of the King*. He changed the medieval legend and has Gareth marry Lynette instead of her sister, Liones.

See also: ARTHUR; LOT, KING

**Gargantua** (gullet)　　In medieval European (perhaps Celtic?) folklore, a giant famous for his enormous appetite. He appears in Rabelais's *Gargantua and Pantagruel*, in which he is the father of Pantagruel. One of his most famous exploits is to swallow five pilgrims in a salad. The name probably derives from Spanish *garganta*, meaning gullet, but Rabelais says that when Gargantua was born he was so large that one of his parents cried out *Que grand tu as!* (how large you are!), which sounds like "Gargantua." In *As You Like It* Shakespeare has a character say: "You must borrow me Gargantua's mouth first: 'tis a word too great for any mouth of this age's size."

**Garide Bird**　　In Siberian mythology, a fantastic bird who defeated the evil giant snake Losy. He was a form of the creator god Otshirvani and is a variant of the Garuda bird in Hindu mythology.

See also: GARUDA; LOSY; OTSHIRVANI

**Garlic**　　A strong-flavored spice. In European folklore, garlic was supposed to keep vampires away and was worn in a small bag around the neck. It is used extensively in folk medicine. According to legend, garlic can destroy the magnetic power of a loadstone.

**Garm** (Garmr) (barking)　　In Norse mythology, the hound of the underworld, chained in Gnipahellir, the cave at the entrance to Niflheim. Garm will break loose at Ragnarok (the end of the world) and kill the god Tyr and in turn be killed by Tyr. The name seems to have the meaning of one who destroys and appears as a base word in kennings. For example, fire is called "Garm of wood." Garm appears to be identical with Fenrir and appears in the *Prose Edda* and the *Poetic Edda*.

See also: FENRIR; KENNING; NIFLHEIM; *POETIC EDDA*; *PROSE EDDA*; RAGNAROK; TYR

*Garuda*

1256

**Garuda** (the devourer)   In Hindu mythology, a fantastic bird on which the god Vishnu rides. Garuda is the enemy of all serpents and the king of all birds, having inherited his hatred for serpents from his mother, Vinata, who had quarreled with Kadru, the mother of serpents. When Garuda was born, he was mistaken for Agni, the fire god, because of his brilliance. (He is identified in some texts with fire and the sun.)

Once Garuda stole the Amrita, the water of life, from the gods in order to purchase with it the freedom of his mother, Vinata, who was under the control of the evil Kadru. Indra discovered the theft and fought a fierce battle with Garuda, in which the Amrita was recovered but Indra's thunderbolt was smashed.

One legend in the epic poem *The Mahabharata* tells how Garuda's parents gave him permission to eat any evil man but not to touch any priest. Once, however, Garuda swallowed a Brahman and his wife, but the Brahman so

burned Garuda's throat that he disgorged both the priest and his wife.

In Indian art Garuda is portrayed as having the head, wings, talons, and back of an eagle and the body and limbs of a man. His face is white, his wings are red, and his body is golden; or he may be green.

Garuda has many epithets, among them Garutman (chief of birds), Pannaga-nasana (destroyer of serpents), Sarparati (enemy of serpents), Taraswin (the swift), and Vishnu-ratha (vehicle of Vishnu), in reference to his being the god's mount. Sometimes Garuda takes the form of Tarkshya, a fantastic figure who appears in some myths as a horse or bird. In variants Tarkshya is called the father of Garuda. Garuda is also called Aksha in some texts.

See also: AGNI; AMRITA; BRAHMAN; *MAHABHARATA, THE*; SOMA; VISHNU

1257

**Gasparilla, José Gaspar**   d. 1821. In American history and folklore, king of the pirates who established the kingdom of Gasparilla Island on the Florida Gulf Coast. He would capture a ship, kill all of the men, and take all the women into his harem. When he was finally captured by an American ship, he tied a cabin chain around his waist and jumped overboard, drowning himself.

Every February unruly plunderers take over the city of Tampa, Florida, in honor of the legendary pirate José Gaspar. The "Gasparilla Pirate Fest" begins when the world's only fully-rigged pirate ship sails into Tampa Bay, flanked by hundreds of pleasure craft and vessels of all shapes and sizes. The black-hulled *Jose Gasparilla* measures 165 feet in length and is topped by three masts that rise 100 feet above deck. Tugboats tow the craft and its crew of 700 pirates with flags flying and cannons booming as the vessel makes its way into the bay. The Tampa bay professional football team is called the "Pirates."

**1258**

**Gasterocheires** (bellies with hands)   In Greek mythology, the seven Cyclopes who built the walls of Tiryns.

**1259**

**Gayomart** (Gaiumart, Gaya-Maretan, Gayo-Maratan, Gayomard, Gayumarth, Kaiomarts, Kaiumers, Kayumard, Kayumurs) (dying life) In Persian mythology, primeval man and culture hero, created by the good god, Ahura Mazda. Gayomart existed as a spirit for 3,000 years before he assumed corporeal form as a handsome youth. After living 30 years he was poisoned by the evil spirit, Ahriman, at the instigation of Jeh, "the whore."

Gayomart appears in the Persian epic poem *Shah Namah*, by Firdusi, as the first king in the world. He lived in the mountains and dressed in animal skins. The animals "assembled round his throne, and did him homage." He had a son, Siyamek, whom he dearly loved, but a demon slew the lad. Later the demon himself was slain by Husheng, the son of Siyamek. Firdusi found Gayomart in Persian mythology, which tells how he was created along with the Celestial Bull. The evil Ahriman, however, "fell . . . upon the Bull and Gayomart: and slew them both." The seed of Gayomart fell to the ground, as did the seed of the Celestial Bull. From Gayomart's seed a rhubarb plant sprung up, which produced the first human couple, Mashye and Mashyane; from the Celestial Bull's seed all kinds of animals arose.

In Persian art Gayomart often appears dressed in animal skins teaching his people the arts of civilization. Sometimes his robes are more elaborate, with only a hint of the animal-skin origin.

See also: AHRIMAN; AHURA MAZDA; HUSHENG; *SHAH NAMAH*

**1260**

**Geb** (Keb, Qeb, Seb) (earth)   In Egyptian mythology, god who personified the earth's surface; the brother-husband of the sky goddess Nut. According to one myth, Geb was separated from Nut by the god Shu at the request of the sun god Ra, who was angered over their sexual embrace. Thus, the sky above and the earth below were created. The separation, however, left Geb inconsolable, and he cried so fiercely his wailing could be heard day and night, and his tears filled the oceans and seas.

Geb was often portrayed in Egyptian art in grief, lying under the feet of Shu, his head raised on one arm and one knee bent. He is identified in some myths as the father of Osiris, Isis, Nephthys, Set, and Horus, and as such he was known as "father of the gods" or "chief of the gods." It was also common to regard Geb as the appointed "heir of the gods" and the leader of the great Ennead. Geb also was portrayed as a man wearing on his head a goose, which is the hieroglyph of his name. The animal was also sacred to him, Geb being called Kenken-ur (the great cackler), referring to the belief expressed in some myths that he laid the egg from which the world sprang. In classical Greek times Geb was identified with Cronus, who was the father of the great Olympian deities.

See also: ENNEAD; HORUS; ISIS; NEPHTHYS; NUT; OSIRIS; RA; SET; SHU

**1261**

**Geirrod and Agnar** (Geirroth) (spear thrower) In Norse mythology, sons of King Hrauding; one evil, the other good; watched over by the god Odin and his wife Frigga. One day, when the two boys were eight and ten years old, they went fishing. Suddenly a storm arose, and their boat drifted far out to sea. It was finally stranded on an island inhabited by an old couple, Odin and Frigga in disguise. The boys were warmly welcomed and kindly treated, Odin choosing Geirrod as his favorite and teaching him the use of arms, while Frigga chose Agnar as her favorite. The boys stayed on the island for the winter. When spring came, they left for home on a boat that Odin provided. As the boat neared the shore, Geirrod quickly sprang out and shoved it far into the water, bidding his brother sail away. The wind veered, and Agnar was carried off, while Geirrod hurried home. He was joyfully received by his father, King Hrauding, and in time succeeded him on the throne.

Years later Odin taunted his wife, Frigga, about the outcome of the boys—his favorite had become king, whereas her favorite had married a giantess. Frigga replied that Agnar had a kind heart, but Geirrod was evil and lacked hospitality, mistreating his guests. Odin said he would prove that the charge was not true. Assuming the guise of a wanderer, wearing his cloud-colored cloak and slouch hat and carrying his pilgrim staff, Odin set out. But Frigga, to outwit him, sent Geirrod a secret warning to beware of a man in a wide mantle and broad-brimmed hat, saying he was a wicked enchanter who would destroy Geirrod.

As soon as Odin arrived, he was arrested and chained between two fires, which, however, did not destroy him. Eight days passed, and he was given no food, except for some ale that Agnar, who was a menial servant in his brother's palace, gave him. At the end of the eighth day Odin began to sing, first softly, then louder, a prophecy that the king would die by his own sword. As the last notes of the prophecy ended, the chains fell, the flames went out, and Odin appeared in his godlike form. Geirrod drew his sword to kill Odin but tripped and fell on the blade. Agnar then was made king by Odin. In some accounts Agnar is said to have been the son of Geirrod, not his brother.

See also: FRIGGA; ODIN

**Genius** (guardian spirit)  <sup>1262</sup> In Roman religion, a spirit who presided over the birth of a person, a place, or a thing, determining character and destiny. Genius is related to the Greek concept of the Daemon. A person's genius came into being at his birth and accompanied him throughout life, becoming his other living soul after death. Often a personal genius was portrayed as a per-

*Genius*

son, but a genius of a place was portrayed as a serpent. In Shakespeare's *Comedy of Errors* the Duke says of the twins Antipholi and Dromios:

One of these men is genius to the other;
And so of these. Which is the natural man
And which the spirit (5.1.332–4).

Spenser cites genius as a god of generation in both his *Epithalamion* (398–9) and *The Faerie Queene* (3.6.31–2). Milton's *Ode on the Morning of Christ's Nativity* (184–6) uses the word to refer to departing pagan gods.

See also: DAEMON

**George, St.** (tiller of the ground)  <sup>1263</sup> Third century. In Christian legend, patron saint of England, Germany, and Venice; also of soldiers and armorers. Greek Christians gave the title Great Martyr to St. George and venerated him as one of the most important saints in the Eastern church. Feast, 23 April.

In western Europe St. George's fame was established during the Crusades when Western and Eastern churches came into contact with one another. His cult was brought to England in the 14th century by Edward III, who chose him as patron of England and of the Order of the Garter. There are many versions of the saint's life, the most popular being the one in *The Golden Legend* by Jacobus de Voragine. St. George was a knight born in Cappadocia. In one of its cities a dragon molested the population. To appease it, lots were cast for either a young man or woman to feed to it so that it would not destroy the entire population. One day the lot fell to the daughter of the king. The king tried to stall the event, but the young girl finally had to offer herself to the dragon. Just as the dragon was about to attack the girl, St. George appeared on his horse and "drew out his sword and garnished him with the sign of the cross" and then attacked the dragon, which fell to the ground. George then took the young girl's girdle and placed it around the dragon's neck, and the "dragon followed her as if it had been a meek beast and debonair."

St. George is a favorite subject with artists, offering an allegorical expression of the Christian hero defeating evil. Other saints are also depicted as slaying dragons, such as St. Michael, St. Margaret, St. Silvester, and St. Martha. Among those who painted St. George are Mantegna, Jan Van Eyck, Rubens, Raphael, Tintoretto, and Dante G. Rossetti. He appears in an old ballad in Percy's *Reliques* and in Spenser's *The Faerie Queene*.

See also: DRAGON; *GOLDEN LEGEND, THE*

1264
**Gerda** (Gerdr, Gerd) (fence enclosing tilled land)　In Norse mythology, wife of Frey; "the most beautiful of women," according to the *Prose Edda*. She was the daughter of Gymir and the giantess Aurboda and was wooed by the god Frey, whom she at first refused. She finally accepted numerous gifts from the god.

See also: FREY; *PROSE EDDA*

1265
**Germanicus Caesar**　15 B.C.E.–19 C.E. In Roman history and legend, general, nephew, and adopted son of the Emperor Tiberius. According to legend, he was poisoned through black magic by Cnaeus Calpurnius Piso, governor of Syria.

Poussin's *The Death of Germanicus* pictures his death.

1266
**Geronimo**　1829–1909. In American history and western folklore, popular name of Goyathlay (one who yawns), a warrior who caused havoc on the Mexico-U.S. border for some 14 years, finally being captured by General George Crook. He was a Bedonkohe Apache (grandson of Mahko) by birth and a Net'na during his youth and early manhood. Some say that, as leader of the Apaches at Arispe in Sonora, he performed such daring feats that the Mexicans singled him out with the sobriquet Geronimo (Spanish for "Jerome"). Some attributed his numerous raiding successes to powers conferred by supernatural beings, including a reputed invulnerability to bullets. He appears in numerous Western tales as the symbol of Indian resistance to the white man. At the end of his life he dictated *Geronimo's Story of His Life*. His legend was filmed twice by Hollywood under the title *Geronimo*, in 1939 and in 1962.

1267
**Geryon** (crane)　In Greek mythology, a monster with three heads or three bodies and wings, son of Chrysaor and Callirrhoë, whose flocks were guarded by Orthus, a two-headed dog, and Eurytion, a shepherd. Heracles' tenth labor was to steal the flocks and drive them back to Greece. The hero killed the shepherd, the dog, and Geryon. Dante's *Divine Comedy* (Inferno) uses Geryon as a symbol of fraud. Geryon is the guardian of the Eighth Circle of Hell; he carries Vergil and Dante to its lowest region. William Blake depicted Geryon in his illustrations of Dante's epic.

See also: CALLIRRHOË; EURYTION; HERACLES

1268
**Gesar Khan**　Mongolian epic poem on the life of a fifth-century C.E. hero. The poem was made

available to Europe in a German translation by I. J. Schmidt in 1925 that was based on one printed from woodblocks in Beijing in 1716. In the work Gesar Khan is born with a divine mission: to bring peace and rule the world. As a small boy he is persecuted by his uncle, but in the poem he overcomes not only his uncle but demons, evil kings, and giants, rescues his mother from the underworld, and brings peace to China. Temples to Gesar Khan are found throughout Tibet, where he is a national hero. In China he is identified with the god of war, Kuan-yu. Full name: Gesar Ling of Khrom, which is apparently a Tibetan transliteration of "Emperor Caesar of Rome."

**1269**

**Ghost Riders**   In American folklore a legend and a popular song tell of a ghostly herd of cattle moving across a stormy sky. In Europe, especially in German-speaking countries, the legend of the Wild Hunt also tells of a horde moving unseen over the trees and across the sky.

See also: WILD HUNT

**1270**

**Ghoul**   In Arabic legend, demonic being who feeds on human bodies. A ghoul may be either male (ghul) or female (ghulah). Ghouls eat corpses of young children, often taking bodies from graves. If no graveyard is available, they will pursue live victims. Considered the offspring of Iblis, the Islamic Satan, ghouls can appear in various animal forms. Islamic tradition says Muhammad denied that any such beings exist, though some of his followers said he only denied that ghouls could assume various shapes. The term is now applied to certain types of sadists. Krafft-Ebing in *Psychopathia Sexualis* tells of Sergeant Bertrand, who stole bodies from Paris cemeteries in 1848 and was dubbed a ghoul by the popular press.

See also: IBLIS; MUHAMMAD

**1271**

**Gideon** (he who cuts down)   12th century B.C.E. In the Bible, O.T. (Judges), fifth of the judges of Israel. Gideon, a farmer, was threshing corn in a winepress to hide it from the Midianites when an angel appeared to him, telling him he was to deliver Israel (Judg. 6:11–40) from bondage. When Gideon asked the angel for proof of his identity, the angel touched Gideon's bread and meat with his staff, and they burst into flames. Convinced that the angel was from God, Gideon prepared to battle the Midianites. He then tested his army of 10,000 men by observing them when they stopped at a stream to drink water. Most of the men bent down and placed their faces in the water, but 300 of the men scooped the water into their hands to drink. Gideon determined that these 300 were his best soldiers because by not putting their faces into the water they remained constantly alert. He dismissed all but the 300 soldiers and staged a surprise attack against the Midianites, convincing the enemy that they were outnumbered by having his men blow trumpets and carry torches concealed in pitchers. When the trumpets were blown and the pitchers broken, revealing the torches, the Midianites fled. Gideon's attribute in Western art is the broken pitcher (Judg. 7:2–23). In the New Testament Epistle to the Hebrews Gideon is cited as a great man of faith.

**1272**

**Gidja**   In Australian mythology, one of the names of the moon, a male god who created the first woman by castrating Yalungur, the Eagle Hawk.

See also: DEERT; KOOPOO; NAJARA

**1273**

**Gikuyu (Kikuyu), Masai, and Kamba**   In African mythology (Kenya), the three sons of God. Each of the sons became the father of a tribe named after him.

One myth explains how God, who lived on top of Mount Kenya, gave a choice to his sons.

They were each to choose one from among three possible gifts. Gikuyu chose the digging stick, and his people became farmers. Kamba chose the bow, and his people became hunters. Masai chose the spear, and his people tended herds. In a variant myth God took Gikuyu to a high place, showing him all that God had made. In the center of creation was a special area selected for Gikuyu, where fig trees grew. God also gave Gikuyu a wife, Moombi, who bore him nine daughters. Gikuyu yearned for sons and went to God, who explained to him what he had to do in order to have sons. Gikuyu did as God told him, and when he returned home, nine young men were waiting there for him. Gikuyu permitted them to marry his daughters after they agreed to live in his household according to matrilineal descent and promised that property would be divided equally among the daughters on their parents' death.

In time, each of the daughters founded a clan that bore her name. Women were permitted to engage in polyandry, that is, they could each marry several husbands. The men, however, grew tired of sharing their wives with other men and planned a revolt. They agreed to make love to their respective wives at the same time in the hope that the women would become pregnant and therefore less able to put down the insurrection planned by the men. The plan worked, and the group changed its name from Moombi to Gikuyu. Polygamy was instituted, allowing men to have several wives. The women, however, on threat of killing all of the male children, won the right to retain the original female names for the clans.

1274

**Giles, St.** (young goat)    Died c. 712. In Christian legend, patron of beggars, blacksmiths, and cripples; one of the Holy Helpers. Venerated at St. Gilles, Provence. Feast, 1 September.

The legend of St. Giles, one of the most popular saints of the Middle Ages, is found in *The Golden Legend* by Jacobus de Voragine, a col-

lection of saints' lives written in the 13th century. Giles was born in Athens of royal blood. He was instructed in Bible studies from his youth. One day when he was on his way to mass, he met a sick man who asked him for alms. Giles gave him his cloak. When the cloak was placed on the crippled man, he was restored to health. Some time later Giles's parents died, leaving him heir, and he offered his wealth to the church.

One day as he was returning from church, he met a man who had been bitten by a serpent. Giles prayed over the man, and instantly the poison came out; the man's health was restored. At another time a man who was possessed by a devil was cured by Giles. These miracles, however, did not make Giles proud. Giles's fame reached King Charles (in some accounts said to be Charlemagne), who invited him to court and would often seek his advice. The king told Giles that he suffered from a secret sin that he could not even tell the saint. One Sunday, while Giles was saying mass, an angel came down with a paper on which was written the king's sin, a prayer for Giles to recite, and God's pardon. The paper was shown to the king, who then repented.

St. Giles was widely venerated in Europe. In England alone some 160 churches are dedicated to him. The name Giles is the English form of the Latin Aegidius, one of the most common names of the Middle Ages.

See also: CHARLEMAGNE; FOURTEEN HOLY HELPERS; *GOLDEN LEGEND, THE*

1275

**Gilgamesh** (Gilgamos, Gisdhubar, Gistubar, Izubar) (hero, father)    In Near Eastern mythology, hero king of Uruk in Mesopotamia who appears in a cycle of legends and myths, many incorporated into *The Epic of Gilgamesh*. Some Near Eastern scholars believe Gilgamesh to have been a historical person, the fifth king of Uruk, around whom a group of myths and legends evolved over the centuries. In some ancient accounts not part of the Gilgamesh epic, Gilgamesh's father is said to have been a *lilla*, which may mean an ignorant person or a fool; other accounts say his father was a priest of Kullab; and still others say Gilgamesh was the son of Lugulbanda, a shepherd god, who appears in the epic poem.

*The Epic of Gilgamesh*, told more than 4,000 years ago, predates the Hebrew scriptures and the Homeric epics. Relating Gilgamesh's quest for immortality, the epic speaks to us today in deeply moving human terms about our mortality. Numerous variant versions of the epic poem emerged throughout ancient Near Eastern history, indicating the extreme popularity of Gilgamesh. The most celebrated version, though incomplete, is preserved on 12 clay tablets from the library at Nineveh of Ashurnasirpal (seventh century B.C.E.). The tablets were discovered in the 19th century and subsequently installed at the British Museum in London as one of its prize possessions. When the gods created Gilgamesh, they endowed him with superhuman gifts and powers. His body was stronger and his courage greater than those of any other man. As a child Gilgamesh had dreamed of a being like himself, strong and handsome. He told his mother, Ninsun, about the dreams and how he longed for a companion equal to himself, but his mother was unable to help him, so he grew up unique and alone. Gilgamesh was proud of his godlike powers and used them to oppress his people with harsh laws, unjust taxes, and forced labor in building Uruk's mighty walls. No man or woman was safe from Gilgamesh. Maidens, wives, and even young men were taken by Gilgamesh to satisfy his lust. After many years of suffering, the people called on the gods to come to their aid. In response the goddess Aruru created Enkidu, a rival for Gilgamesh. Although as strong and courageous as Gilgamesh, Enkidu's body was covered with matted hair like that of a wild animal. The hair on his head was long like a woman's. Knowing nothing of civilization or the ways of men and women, Enkidu lived among the wild animals and was their companion. One day a young hunter spotted Enkidu freeing a trapped animal. Terrified by Enkidu's primitive appearance, the young man hid. When Enkidu departed, the hunter ran home to tell his father what he had seen. His father advised him to go to Uruk and tell Gilgamesh. When Gilgamesh heard about Enkidu, his proud nature was deeply offended. He told the hunter to go back with a temple prostitute to seduce the wild man. The woman exposed herself, and Enkidu became inflamed with sexual desire. The two lay together for six days and seven nights. Having exhausted himself with the woman, Enkidu returned to his animal companions, but they all fled from him. "Enkidu," said the woman, "now you are like a god because you have experienced sexual desire. Come with me to Uruk to meet the great King Gilgamesh."

When the two arrived in the city, they saw the people celebrating a coming marriage. But Gilgamesh came to the assembly hall to take the bride to his bed, as was his right as king. When Enkidu saw Gilgamesh approach the assembly hall, he stepped out of the crowd and blocked the way. The two men grappled with one another like two bulls. After Gilgamesh threw Enkidu to the ground, Gilgamesh's furor ceased. He stared at Enkidu, recognizing the friend and companion of his dreams. "There's not another man like you," Enkidu said to Gilgamesh. "You are favored by the gods, for your strength surpasses that of all men." Gilgamesh bent over and helped Enkidu to his feet. The two then embraced and kissed one another, sealing their friendship. Gilgamesh brought Enkidu to the palace to introduce him to his mother, Ninsun. When Ninsun realized that Enkidu was the man who had appeared in Gilgamesh's dreams, she adopted him as her own son. Because of Enkidu's tender love, Gilgamesh softened toward his people and was no longer oppressive. He established justice and peace in Uruk.

But beyond Uruk's protective walls was a forest inhabited by Humbaba, a fierce monster who guarded the Cedar Tree, sacred to the earth god Enlil. No man ever returned alive from Humbaba's mysterious domain. Gilgamesh and Enkidu went to the cedar forest to battle Humbaba.

Both men attacked the monster, and with the aid of Shamash, the god who protected Gilgamesh, the monster was defeated. Enkidu, clutching Gilgamesh's sword, slashed off Humbaba's massive head, which crashed loudly to the ground. Cries from the trees erupted throughout the forest. Even the sacred Cedar Tree cried out, "Why have you done this evil deed?" The two men then cut down the sacred tree.

The goddess Ishtar was so impressed with Gilgamesh's daring that she asked him to become her lover. Gilgamesh refused, however, remembering how she had destroyed all of her previous lovers. Determined that Gilgamesh should be punished for insulting her, Ishtar appealed to her father, Anu, to create Gudanna, or Alu (the strong), a majestic Bull of Heaven. But Gilgamesh and Enkidu also destroyed the Bull of Heaven. "You'll suffer, Gilgamesh, for scorning me and killing the Bull of Heaven," Ishtar cried out. To add to the insult, Enkidu challenged the goddess by throwing the bull into her face.

A council of the gods was held, and it was decided that Enkidu had to die. Enkidu's body began to waste away. On the 12th day of his suffering he cried out to Gilgamesh, "The great gods have cursed me. They have no pity. I must die this shameful death, denied the glory of dying heroically in battle." Enkidu then passed into a deep sleep that led to death. "Enkidu, Enkidu, my beloved friend and brother," Gilgamesh cried out in anguish. "Enkidu, I weep for you like a wailing woman. You were the ax by my side, the sword in my belt, the shield before me. And now you've been taken from me by the jealous gods." For seven days and seven nights Gilgamesh cried over his friend's body.

After Enkidu's burial Gilgamesh left Uruk and roamed from place to place. But he could find neither rest nor peace of mind. His thoughts were constantly on Enkidu and on his own mortality: "I'll also die and worms will feast on my flesh. I now fear death and have lost all my courage." Gilgamesh then made the arduous journey to the land of Utnapishtim, the hero of the Great Flood, to seek the secret of immortal life possessed by Utnapishtim and his wife. Though they told him he could not be immortal, they also gave him the location of a plant that would renew his youth. Gilgamesh found the plant, but when he rested it was stolen by a snake. Sadly Gilgamesh returned to Uruk, and Enkidu's spirit appeared to him. When he realized that death was the lot of all, he resigned himself to his mortality.

Near Eastern mythology accorded Gilgamesh the status of a minor god, as it did to his beloved Enkidu. Gilgamesh was invoked as an underworld deity and was associated with Tammuz, another man who descended to the land of the dead. He had control over the souls of heroes, whom he released from their prison house of death for nine days during the months of July and August.

Bohusalav Martinu's cantata for soloists, chorus, and orchestra, *The Epic of Gilgamesh*, is based on R. Campbell Thompson's English version of the poem. Ross Alexander's *Gilgamesh: A Primitive Ritual* tells the epic in dramatic form.

See also: ANU; ARURU; ENKIDU; ENLIL; ISHTAR; SHAMASH; TAMMUZ; UTNAPISHTIM

---

1276

**Gil Morice**   A Scottish ballad, included in Percy's *Reliques*, that tells of a natural son of an earl and the wife of Lord Barnard. He is brought up "in the gude grene wode." Lord Barnard, thinking Gil Morice to be his wife's lover, killed him with a broadsword, setting his head on a spear.

See also: *RELIQUES*

---

1277

**Ginnungagap** (gaping chaos filled with magic powers)   In Norse mythology, the primeval abyss between Muspell and Niflheim where the primeval giant Ymir was born and where he was slain by the gods Odin, Vili, and Ve. From Ymir's body the earth was formed. One of the roots of Yggdrasil runs down to where the Ginnungagap used to be. In the *Prose Edda* it is described in the following way: "When those rivers which are called Elivagar came so far from their source that the yeasty venom accompanying them hardened like slag, it turned into ice. Then when that ice formed and was firm, a drizzling rain that arose from the venom poured over it and cooled it into rime, and one layer of ice formed on top of the other throughout Ginnungagap."

See also: MUSPELL; NIFELHEIM; *PROSE EDDA*; YGGDRASIL; YMIR

1278

**Ginseng**    A root somewhat resembling a human body, used mainly in folk medicine. In Oriental folk medicine ginseng has long been regarded as a miracle cure, credited with healing epilepsy, insomnia, coughing, mental disorders, and digestive and respiratory illnesses, as well as epidemic illnesses such as cholera, measles, dysentery, malaria, typhoid, influenza, and other diseases. It was also an antidote to impotence and a sexual stimulant. In Korean legend a 15-year-old boy named Kim lived in a rundown hut with his father, Kang-won-do, who was dying. Kim prayed every day to the mountain spirit. One day he fell asleep during prayer, and the mountain spirit appeared and led him to the place where ginseng was growing. Directed by the spirit, he prepared a drink from the root of the ginseng and gave it to his father, who recovered. In another Oriental legend a poor man discovered some ginseng and tried to sell it in his village at an exorbitant price. The man was arrested for greed but managed to hide the ginseng inside his jacket. When the judge demanded the ginseng be presented as evidence, the man took out the root and ate it. The root made him so strong he was able to kill the guards and escape. Ginseng is not to be confused with the strong alcoholic drink named gin-sling, made of gin and lemon juice.

1279

**Girdle of Venus**    In Greek and Roman mythology, the girdle of Aphrodite, a magic girdle that evoked sexual passion in men and gods. Aphrodite used it and often lent it out. Once she lent it to Hera, Zeus's wife, who wanted to beguile the god and take his mind off aiding the Trojans in the war, giving the Greeks, whom Hera favored, a chance in battle.

See also: APHRODITE; HERA; VENUS; ZEUS

1280

**Gjallar-horn** (shrieking horn)    In Norse mythology, the horn of the god Heimdall, which will sound to announce the frost giants' attack on the gods when the giants pass the bridge Bifrost at Ragnarok, the end of the world. The *Poetic Edda*, in the poem *Voluspa* (the Sooth Saying of Vala), describes the scene:

To battle the gods are called By the ancient Gjallar-horn. Loud blows Heimdall, His sound is in the air.

Gjallar-horn was either hung on a branch of Yggdrasill, the world tree, or placed in the waters of Mimir's well as a drinking horn, where the lost eye of Odin lay.

See also: BIFROST; HEIMDALL; MIMIR; ODIN; *POETIC EDDA*; RAGNAROK; YGGDRASIL

1281

**Glastonbury**    In Arthurian legend, the place where Joseph of Arimathea planted his staff. It took root and burst into leaf every Christmas Eve, and the tree is called the Glastonbury Thorn. Glastonbury is a town in Somerset in southwestern England, dating from Roman times. King Arthur's wife, Guinever, is said to have been buried there.

See also: ARTHUR; GUINEVER; JOSEPH OF ARIMATHEA

1282

**Glaucus** (gray-green)    In Greek mythology, the name of various men. One was the son of Sisyphus and father of Bellerophon. He refused to let his mares breed, which so angered Aphrodite, goddess of sexual love, that she drove the mares mad. They tore Glaucus to pieces at the funeral games of Pelias. Another Glaucus was the grandson of Bellerophon. He fought on the side of the Trojans, but when he met Diomedes in battle, he laid down his spear and exchanged his gold armor for Diomedes' bronze armor on learning the two had family ties. Glaucus appears in Homer's *Iliad* (book 6) and Vergil's *Aeneid* (book 6). Another Glaucus was an Argonaut and fisherman who wished to live in the ocean. He was transformed into a sea god by Oceanus. His story is in Ovid's *Metamorphoses* (book 13).

See also: *AENEID, THE;* APHRODITE; BELLERO-PHON; DIOMEDES; *ILIAD, THE;* SISYPHUS

1283

**Gluskap and Malsum** (Glooscap, Glooska, Gluskabe)    In North American Indian mythology (Abnaki), twin brothers; Gluskap, a creator god, culture hero, and trickster killed his evil brother Malsum.

Gluskap and Malsum discussed their birth while still in their mother's womb. "I will be born as others are born," said Gluskap. But Malsum, being evil, said it was not proper that he should be born as others were. He wished to have an extraordinary birth. Gluskap was born first in the natural manner, but Malsum forced his way out of his mother's armpit, killing her as a result.

The two brothers grew up together. One day Malsum asked Gluskap how he would be killed, since Gluskap, as well as Malsum, possessed a charmed life. Gluskap, remembering how Malsum had caused the death of their mother, told a lie.

"I can be killed by the stroke of an owl's feather," he told Malsum.

"I can die only by a blow from a large fern root," replied Malsum.

One day Malsum decided he would kill his brother. He took his bow and arrow and shot Ko-ko-khas, the owl, and with one of his feathers struck Gluskap while he was asleep. Gluskap awoke suddenly and said it was not by an owl's feather that he would die, but by a blow from a pine root.

The next day Malsum led Gluskap into the deep forest to hunt. After the hunt, while Gluskap slept, Malsum hit him on the head with a pine root. Gluskap awoke and in anger chased Malsum deeper into the woods. Gluskap then came to a brook and said to himself, "Malsum does not know, but only a flowering rush can kill me."

Beaver, who was hidden among the reeds, heard Gluskap, and rushed to Malsum to tell him the secret. In return for the secret Malsum promised to give Beaver whatever he wanted. When Beaver asked for wings like a pigeon, Malsum laughed at him, and Beaver left in anger. Beaver then went to Gluskap and told him what had happened. Gluskap took a large-footed fern and killed Malsum, driving his evil magic below the earth. Malsum then became an evil wolf.

With Malsum out of the way and evil underground, Gluskap created the world from the body of his dead mother. He then took his bow and arrows and shot at ash trees, and people came out of the bark. Gluskap then made all of the animals and taught humankind the arts. But people were not grateful to Gluskap. This saddened him until he could no longer endure it. One day he made a feast by the shore. All of the beasts came to it. When the feast was over he boarded a great canoe and left. The beasts could hear him sing, but his voice grew fainter as the canoe moved on. Then a deep silence fell on the animals. Until then they could all understand one another's language, but from that time they could not, so each fled to his home. One day

Gluskap will return to restore the earth and make people and animals live together once more in peace and love.

See also: ATAENSIC; IOUSKEHA AND TAWIS-CARON

---

1284

**Gnosticism**   During the first six centuries of the Christian era, various sects attempted to align Christianity with the speculations of Greek philosophers. They considered themselves to be "knowers" rather than "believers." For them knowledge and not faith was the key to salvation. Thus, Christ was looked upon as a divine attribute that had been personified and the stories associated with his life as reflections of this attitude.

See also: ABRAXAS; FLIGHT INTO EGYPT; HEAVEN AND HELL

---

1285

**Goat**   A hollow-horned ruminant related to the sheep family, the goat was sacred to Hera, wife of Zeus in Greek mythology. Hera was closely identified with the she-goat at Largos, a center of her worship. There youths threw spears at a she-goat during a religious festival in honor of Hera. This rite was supposed to punish the goat for revealing the hiding place of Hera when once she fled to the woods to escape Zeus's anger.

The goat was also associated with Dionysus, a son of Zeus and Semele. To protect his son from Hera, Zeus transformed Dionysus into a black goat, thereby making the animal sacred to Dionysus, who was called "the Kid" or "one of the black goatskin." Dionysus' followers would tear to pieces a live goat and devour its raw flesh. Euripides' *The Bacchae* captures their joy and ecstasy. In one section the god's followers cry out: "Look, he comes. . . . He hunts the wild goat, killing it and tearing its raw flesh for food." Other Greek gods who shared the goat as a symbol are Pan and Silenus, as well as satyrs and fauns.

When one calls a man an "old goat," it still refers to the animal's supposed lecherous nature. In Hebrew mythology a goat was sacrificed to Yahweh and called the scapegoat. Jesus in the New Testament says God will separate the sheep from the goats, meaning the good from the evil, at the last judgment. The Nordic god Thor had his wagon drawn by goats. Later medieval belief often identified the goat with the devil. An old superstition in England says that a goat is never seen for a full 24 hours, because once a day he visits the devil to have his beard combed. There are numerous motifs associated with goats in the *Motif Index of Folk Literature*.

See also: DIONYSUS; HERA; PAN; THOR; YAHWEH; ZEUS

---

1286

**God and the Rising Waters**   Jewish fable found in the Midrash.

Once the waters on the earth kept rising, reaching almost to God's throne. The Almighty said, "Be still."

But the waters cried out: "We are the mightiest of all creation. Let us flood the earth."

God became angry, saying, "I will send sand on the earth and it will make a barrier to contain you."

When the waters saw the sand, they laughed. "How can such tiny grains contain us?" the waters said.

The sand grains, hearing the waters, became frightened. "How are we to survive?" they asked.

Their leader said, "Have no fear. True, we are small and each one of us is insignificant. But if we remain united, then the waters will see how strong we are."

When the sand grains heard this, they rose up in mounds, hills and mountains, forming a huge barrier against the waters. When the waters saw how great an army the sand was, they became frightened and retreated.

See also: MIDRASH

1287

**Godiva, Lady** (gift of God)   In English medieval legend, patroness of Coventry. In 1040 Leofric, earl of Mercia and lord of Coventry, imposed certain taxes on his tenants. His wife did not think the taxes were just. Leofric said he would not remove them unless she rode naked through the town at midday. Lady Godiva accepted his challenge and rode through the streets naked. Out of respect, everyone stayed indoors, but a certain tailor peeped through his window to see the lady pass and was struck blind. He was then called "Peeping Tom of Coventry." Leofric removed the taxes as a result of his wife's ride. Tennyson's poem "Godiva" treats the subject.

1288

**Gog and Magog**   In medieval British mythology, two giants, the sole survivors of a monstrous brood of children born to the 33 daughters of the evil Roman emperor Diocletian. The women murdered their husbands. Gog and Magog were set adrift on a ship and reached Albion (England), where they became friends of a group of demons. Their children were a race of giants who fought the hero Brut and his companions. All were destroyed except for Gog and Magog, who were brought to London in chains. They were made slaves and forced to act as porters at the royal palace, on the site of the London Guildhall. Statues of them can still be seen in London today. In the Bible Gog and Magog (Rev. 20:8) symbolize all of the future enemies of the Kingdom of God. Gogmagog hill, southeast of Cambridge, received its name from a giant who fell in love with the nymph Granta. She would have nothing to do with him and changed him into a hill.

See also: ALBION; BRUT

1289

**Goin**   In Australian mythology, an evil spirit in the form of an old man with claws like an eagle hawk and feet like an alligator.

See also: BUNYIP

1290

**Golden Age**   In Greek and Roman mythology, the first of the Four Ages of Man, the others being Silver, Bronze, and Iron. The Golden Age first appears in Hesiod's *Works and Days* and was later developed by the Roman poets Horace, Vergil, and Ovid. In Ovid's *Metamorphoses* (book 1) a description that influenced later literature is given of the Four Ages of Man. In English literature, Chaucer, Shakespeare, and Spenser cite the Golden Age. Shelley's poem "Hellas" says: "The world's great age begins anew / The golden years return. . . ."

See also: CHAUCER; HESIOD; OVID

1291

**Golden Apples of the Hesperides**   In Greek mythology, Golden Apples guarded by the Hesperides, daughters of Atlas and a dragon, Ladon. The Golden Apples grew on a tree that was a gift to Hera when she married Zeus. Heracles' 11th labor was to fetch the apples. When he did, the apples were given to Athena, who returned them to the Hesperides because they could not survive outside the magic garden. Hesiod's *Theogony*, Ovid's *Metamorphoses* (book 4), and Tennyson's poem *The Hesperides* recounts the myth.

See also: ATHENA; ATLAS; HERA; HESIOD; HESPERIDES; LADON; OVID; ZEUS

1292

**Golden Bough**   In Roman mythology, a bough that the Trojan hero Aeneas obtains as a passport to the underworld. In Vergil's *Aeneid* (book 6) Aeneas is told by the Cumaean Sybil that he cannot enter the underworld until he has found and broken off a golden bough and offered it as a gift to Proserpine, queen of the dead. The bough, identified as the mistletoe, was associated with Diana at Aricia, near Rome. According to some accounts, the golden bough had to be broken off a sacred tree by a slave, who then killed the priest-king guarding the tree and took his place, eventually to be killed in the same manner. This interpretation, given by Servius (fourth century C.E.) in his commentary on Vergil's *Aeneid*, inspired the monumental 12-volume study *The Golden Bough* by Sir James Frazer. Frazer opens his work with the ritual surrounding the slaying of the priest-king of Diana in a grove near Nemi and then goes on to explain ancient rituals, beliefs, and customs relating to magic, kingship, divinity, tree worship, taboos, totemism, rain, fire, and so on. Frazer's basic assumption is that all peoples have gone through the same cultural development and thus react in the same way. (This aspect of his work is now debated.) Frazer's chapters dealing with the Dying God had great influence on early 20th-century thinking and art. Among classical scholars, Gilbert Murray and Jane Harrison are in his debt. Creative artists such as T. S. Eliot and D. H. Lawrence also were influenced by his ideas, as was Freud in his *Totem and Tabu*. Other works by Frazer are *Totemism and Exogamy*, *The Belief in Immortality and the Worship of the Dead*, *Folklore in the Old Testament*, *The Worship of Nature*, *Myths of the Origin of Fire*, and *The Fear of the Dead in Primitive Religion*.

See also: AENEAS; *AENEID, THE*; DIANA; MISTLETOE

1293
**Golden Cockerel, Tale of the** Literary folk verse tale by Alexander Pushkin, published in 1833. Pushkin's verse uses the forms of Russian folk poetry to create a satirical folktale. An astrologer gave Czar Dodon a golden cockerel that had the gift of prophecy. When the bird crowed, it was a sign that danger was near. One day the Golden Cockerel crowed as the astrologer came to ask payment for the magical bird. King Dodon, responding to the bird's warning, killed the astrologer. Dodon, however, was then killed by the Golden Cockerel.

Pushkin's satirical verse tale was believed to have been based on a Russian folktale, and numerous anthologies that include the poet's work contain a note to that effect. However, in 1933 the source for Pushkin's tale was found in Washington Irving's well-known book *The Legends of the Alhambra*, which Pushkin read in a French translation published in the same year as the English original. The poet took the tales "The House of the Weathercock" and "The Legend of the Arabian Astrologer" as the bases for his poem. Pushkin's poem was used by the Russian composer Rimsky-Korsakov for his opera *Le coq d'or* (*The Golden Cockerel*).

1294
**Golden Fleece** In Greek mythology, the fleece of the winged ram stolen by the hero Jason with the aid of his mistress, Medea. The myth tells how Nephele, wife of King Athamas of Boeotia, convinced the king that his son Phrixus was responsible for a famine and had to be sacrificed to the gods. Phrixus, learning of the plan, fled with his sister Helle on the golden-winged ram. During the flight Helle fell in the water and drowned, but Phrixus reached Colchis. He married Chalciope, daughter of Aetës, and sacrificed the ram. Its fleece was then hung in a sacred grove in Colchis and guarded by a dragon. Jason, with Medea's aid, later stole the Golden Fleece. Apollonius's *Argonautica* tells the tale of Jason, Medea, and the quest, as does William Morris's *Life and Death of Jason*, a long narrative poem, and Nathaniel Hawthorne's "Golden Fleece" in his children's book *Tanglewood Tales*.

See also: APOLLONIUS; JASON; MEDEA

1295
***Golden Legend, The*** (*Legenda Aurea*) In medieval Christianity, collection of saints' lives and stories associated with the Christian year; compiled and written by Jacobus de Voragine, archbishop of Genoa (1230–1298). From earliest Christian times the compiling of saints' lives has been one of the main sources of Christian art and legends. The primary works include martyrologies (lists of martyred saints), passions, calendars, biographies, prose and verse compositions, and liturgical texts. One of the first collections of

saints' lives was compiled by Eusebius (c. 260–340), the church historian. His work, however, was lost. In the 10th century Symeon the Metaphrast rewrote, in elegant and refined Greek, a series of saints' lives based on earlier sources. In 1660 the *Martyr's Mirror* included hundreds of stories of Anabaptist martyrs. The most influential work, however, was and remains *The Golden Legend*. There are more than 500 manuscripts of the work in existence. The first century of printing produced more than 150 editions and translations. William Caxton, the first English printer, produced an English version in the 15th century. The popularity of *The Golden Legend* diminished during the Renaissance and Reformation, because the humanists disliked its "gutter Latin," and Protestants objected to its acceptance of fantasy.

1296

**Golden Stool, The**    In African cult, a symbol sacred to the Ashanti of Ghana. During the 18th century Osei Tutu, one of the rulers of the Ashanti, united his people and formed a powerful nation. Previously, they had been dominated by a neighboring tribe. Anokye, a ruler of that tribe, offended his king and left the country. He came to the Ashanti, saying that the god Onyame had sent him to them so that they would become a great nation. With great fanfare Anokye brought down from the heavens a stool covered with gold, which came to rest on Osei Tutu's knees. The king was so pleased with it that he had four bells made to hang from its corners. Anokye said that the stool was a physical manifestation of the soul of the Ashanti people. A magic potion, made of the hairs and fingernails of members of the Ashanti royalty, was drunk, and what remained was poured over the stool. No one was permitted to sit on the stool, although the king might pretend to and even rest his arm on it. Once a year the stool was carried through the streets under large ceremonial umbrellas in a great procession. Over the years

golden items were added to the stool to commemorate very special events.

In 1896 the Ashanti feared that the British, who since 1750 had held a monopoly over the Gold Coast, would destroy the golden stool. When Sir Frederic Hodgon demanded that the stool be brought to him so that he might sit on it, a bloody revolt ensued. The stool disappeared and was not seen again until 1921. While building a road, some men came upon the spot where the stool was hidden, and it was moved to a new location. Thieves discovered it and stole the gold from the stool, but when they tried to sell it, they were caught and jailed. They had to be guarded very carefully lest they be seized and killed. The authorities, recognizing the significance of the stool, restored it to the royal palace in Kumasi.

1297

**Goldfinch**    A bird with a yellow patch on each wing; in medieval Christian symbolism, the Passion of Christ. According to medieval Christian belief the goldfinch eats thistles and thorns, two symbols of Christ's Passion. In Renaissance paintings one often finds the Christ child holding a goldfinch, indicating his future suffering and death.

1298

**Golem** (shapeless mass)    In medieval Jewish folklore, a form given life when the mystical name of God was placed upon it. One medieval legend tells how the poet and philosopher Solomon Ibn Gabirol of Valencia created a golem maid. When the Christian king heard of the creature, he ordered Solomon killed for practicing black magic. However, the poet-philosopher proved that the creature was harmless by removing the name of God from it and having it then turn to dust. In a later tale, *The Golem of Chem*, the creature proves too much for its creator, Rabbi Elijah, who removed the magical name of God from the monster when it went on a destructive rampage. In later reworkings of the legends, such as *The Golem of Prague*, the monster becomes a defender of the Jews. In Yiddish, however, the word golem is used for a stupid person. The term *golem* appears in the Hebrew Scriptures in Psalm 139:16: "Thine eyed did see mine golem [shapeless mass]." The Jewish Publications translation of 1917 renders the term as "unformed substance."

**Goliath** (an exile)   In the Bible, O.T., a Philistine giant who was slain by the stripling David. Goliath was nine feet, nine inches tall (1 Sam. 17: 23–54). In Islamic legend Goliath is called Jalut and cited in the Koran (sura 2). In Western art Goliath is often shown decapitated at David's feet or being held by the young David.

1299

**Gollveig** (gold might)   In Norse mythology, a Vanir goddess. She came to the Aesir gods and was mistreated by them, but the exact details are not known. Gollveig was in part responsible for a war between the Vanir and the Aesir deities. In some accounts her name is given as Heid.

See also: AESIR; AESIR-VANIR WAR; VANIR

1300

**González, Conde Fernán**   c. 930–970. In medieval Spanish legend, count of Burgos who made Castile independent of the state of León. He is the subject of numerous heroic ballads and the 13th-century narrative poem *El poema de Fernán González.*

Both González and his wife, Sancha, often appear in Spanish ballads. According to various legends, Sancha rescued the count twice at the risk of her own life. The count had asked her hand in marriage from her father, Garcias, king of Navarre. On his way to join his bride the count was ambushed by men of the queen of León, who was the sister of the king of Navarre and opposed the match. The count was taken to a castle and imprisoned. Then a "pilgrim knight of Normandy," riding through Navarre, came to the

1301

castle where the count was imprisoned and later told his intended wife, Sancha, of the deep love the count held for her. In the ballad *The Escape of Count Fernán González* the knight says:

González loves thee, lady,—he loved thee long ago,—
Arise, let love with love be paid, and set González free (John Gibson Lockhart translation).

Sancha, moved by his words, bribed the jailer and fled with the count to Castile. Many years later, according to another legend, the count was again freed by his wife after he was ambushed by the men of the queen of León. This time Sancha, feigning a pilgrimage to Compostela to visit the tomb of St. James the Greater, passed the night in the castle where her husband was being held prisoner. She exchanged her clothes for his, and he escaped.

*El Poema de Fernán González*, believed to have been written by a monk of the Castilian monastery of San Pedro de Aslanza in the 13th century, recounts the history of Spain up to the birth of Fernán González and then relates the exploits of the hero.

See also: BALLAD

1302

**Go-oh**   In North American Indian mythology (Iroquois), the spirit of the winds who lives in the north sky. He controls all four winds; the bear, north wind; the panther, west wind; the moose, east wind; and the fawn, south wind. When the north wind blows, the Iroquois say, "The bear is prowling in the sky." If the west wind is violent, they say, "The panther is whining." When the east wind chills with its rain, they say, "The moose is spreading his breath," and when the south wind wafts soft breezes, they say, "The fawn is returning to its doe."

**Goonnear**    In Australian mythology, the evil carpet snake. He is the opposite of the wombat snake, Biggarro, who aids man to the spirit land, the Land of Perfection.

See also: BIGGARRO

**1304**
**Goose**    Large web-footed bird, connected with numerous deities in world mythology as a symbol of fertility, watchfulness, war, love, autumn, and the sun. The goose is sacred to various Egyptian deities such as Amun-Ra, Isis, Geb, Osis, Osiris, and Horus. Amun-Ra is sometimes called "The Great Grackler" in reference to his role as creator of the world when he laid the Cosmic Egg. In Greek mythology, the goose is sacred to Hera as queen of heaven, to Apollo as sun god, Ares as war god, and Eros as god of love and sex. According to Roman legend, when Rome was being invaded, the sacred geese in Juno's temple began to cackle when they spotted the enemy. They were killed by enemy soldiers but not before the Romans had been warned of the invasion. Later a golden goose was carried in procession in honor of the geese. The goose is sacred not only to Juno but to Mars as war god and Priapus as fertility god.

In Chinese mythology the goose is the bird of heaven, symbol of Yang, the male principle. In Japanese mythology the goose is a symbol of autumn, associated with the autumn moon. Wild geese are sacred to Brahma in Hindu mythology; he is often shown riding a magnificent gander.

In European Christian folklore, the English custom of eating the goose on St. Michael's Day is sometimes said to have originated in the time of Elizabeth I, who on St. Michael's Day received news of the defeat of the Spanish Armada while she was eating goose. But the story is apocryphal because the custom of eating goose can be traced back to the 15th century in England, when Edward IV ate the fat goose to augur the termination of the rainy and wintry season. Perhaps the best-known Aesop fable about a goose is

"The Goose That Laid the Golden Egg," which has given rise to the saying, "kill the goose that lays the golden egg," whenever people's greed alienates those who are generous to them. Another expression, "cook a person's goose," refers to the European legend of Eric, king of Sweden, who approached an enemy city and found a dead goose hung over one of its walls in derision of his invasion. As he set the town to torch, he is reported to have said, "I'm cooking the goose." There are numerous motifs associated with the goose in the *Motif Index of Folk Literature*.

See also: AESOPIC FABLES; APOLLO; ARES; BRAHMA; EROS; GEB; GOOSE THAT LAID THE GOLDEN EGG, THE; HERA; HORUS; JUNO; ISIS; OSIRIS; PRIAPUS; YANG

**1305**
**Goose That Laid the Golden Eggs, The**    Aesopic fable that appears in many European and Oriental sources, probably originally Indian because it appears in the *Jatakas, or Birth-Stories of the Former Lives of the Buddha*.

A farmer went to the nest of his goose to see whether she had laid an egg. To his surprise he found, instead of an ordinary goose egg, an egg of solid gold. Seizing the golden egg, he rushed to the house in great excitement to show it to his wife.

Every day thereafter the goose laid an egg of pure gold. But as the farmer grew rich, he grew greedy. And thinking that if he killed the goose he could have all of her treasure at once, he cut her open, only to find nothing at all.

Moral: *The greedy who want more, lose all.*
See also: AESOPIC FABLES; *JATAKA*

**1306**
**Gorboduc**    In British mythology, a king, father of Ferrex and Porrex; he divided his kingdom between them. Ferrex was driven out of the land by his brother; when he attempted to return, he was killed. Porrex was later murdered by his mother, who had favored Ferrex. *Gorboduc,*

written by Thomas Norton and Thomas Sackville, is the first English historical drama.

**1307**
**Gordian Knot** In Greek and Roman legend, a knot tied by a peasant named Gordius, the father of Midas, who became king of Phrygia. The knot was so complex that no one could unravel it nor even find the ends of the cord entwined within the knot. Gordius had dedicated his oxcart or chariot to Zeus, with the yoke tied to the pole in a knot. An oracle decreed that anyone who could unravel it would rule Asia. Alexander the Great cut it with his sword, fulfilling the oracle. Purcell's incidental music to *The Gordian Knot Untied* was written for a play now lost.

See also: ALEXANDER THE GREAT; MIDAS; ZEUS

**1308**
**Gore** (misery) In Slavic folklore, personification of misery and misfortune. Gore is described in one Russian folktale as a "wretched little man, with a miserable face and little thin legs and arms." According to the folktale, a merchant who had lost all his property because of Gore decided to do away with him. He asked Gore if he could make himself small enough to fit into the hub of a wheel. Angry at being challenged, Gore popped into the hole of the hub, and the merchant instantly shut Gore inside. (This kind of trickery is a common motif in folktales.) The merchant then took the wheel to the river and drowned Gore. With Gore's death, the merchant was restored to his former prosperity.

See also: TRICKSTER

**1309**
**Gorgons** (grim ones) In Greek mythology, three women monsters, the Euryae; daughters of Ceto and Phorcys, they are Euryale, Stheno, and Medusa. They had women's bodies, wings, brazen claws, and snakes for hair. They were sisters to the Graeae, three gray-haired old women who acted as their sentries. Euryale and Stheno were

*A Gorgon*

immortal and could not die, but Medusa was not and was beheaded by the hero Perseus. Her head was on the aegis or cloak of Zeus and Athena, and the sight of it could turn a person into stone. In Shakespeare's *Macbeth* (2.3) at the discovery of Duncan's murder, Macduff says: "Approach the chamber, and destroy your sight / with a new Gorgon."

See also: ATHENA; GRAEAE; PERSEUS; ZEUS

*Medusa*

**Gotham, Wise Men of**   In British medieval legend, a term for "wise fools." King John, on his way to Lyme Regis, intended to pass through Gotham in Nottinghamshire with his army. To prepare he sent heralds to announce he was coming. The men of Gotham did not want to see the king or his army because it meant that the land would be devastated and they would be forced to provide quarters for the soldiers. They decided to play fools. Some pretended to rake the moon out of a pond, some made a ring to hedge in a bird, and so on. When the king learned of their actions, he abandoned his intention of stopping in the village. One wise man remarked, "We ween there are more fools pass through Gotham than remain in it." A collection of popular tales called *Merie tales of the Mad Men of Gotam* was published during the reign of Henry VIII. Washington Irving gave the name Gotham to New York City in his *Salmagundi Papers*. There are localities around the world where fools are to be found: Phrygia in Asia Minor, Boeotia in Greece, Nazareth for the Jews, and Swabia and the East Frisian islands in modern Germany.

1311

**Govannon** (smithy)   In Celtic mythology, the British god of smithery, son of Don, brother of Gwydion. Govannon made weapons for the gods and brewed ale. He is best remembered as the uncle who kills his nephew Dylan. Ancient Roman writers equated him with their god Vulcan. In later medieval legend he appears as Gobhan Saer, an architect of magic power who is credited with building many towers and churches in Ireland.

See also: DYLAN; VULCAN

1312

**Go-vardhana**   In Hindu mythology, a sacred mountain on which Krishna (an incarnation of the god Vishnu) ordered the cowherds to worship him instead of Indra, the storm god. This so enraged Indra that he sent a deluge to wash away the mountain as well as the people. Krishna, however, held up the mountain with his little finger for seven days to shelter the people. Indra left baffled and afterward did homage to Krishna, who was called Go-vardhana Dhara (upholder of Go-vardhana).

See also: KRISHNA; VISHNU

1313

**Gracchi** (grackles)   In Roman mythology, the name given in Vergil's *Aeneid* (book 6) to the spirits or souls of unborn Roman heroes. In Roman history, above all they are two brothers named Tiberius and Gaius Sempronius Gracchus who instigated social and political reforms in the 130s and 120s B.C.E., as a result of which they were each killed; they were usually portrayed as symbols of catering to the mob, but sometimes of genuine reform.

See also: *AENEID, THE*

1314

**Graeae** (gray ones)   In Greek mythology, daughters of Phorcys and Cero; sisters of the Gorgons. The Graeae were Dino, Enyo, and Pephredo. They had only one tooth and one eye to share among themselves. The eye was stolen by the hero Perseus as they passed it from one to another. He would not give it back to them until they told him where Medusa was hiding.

See also: GORGONS; PERSEUS

1315

**Grand Bois d'Ilet**   In Haitian voodoo, lord of the night and night forests.

1316

**Gran Maître**   In Haitian voodoo, the creator god, distinct from the loas, who are deified spirits of the dead and looked upon as gods.

See also: LOA

1317

**Grannos**   In Celtic mythology, a god of healing worshiped by the continental Celts. Ancient Roman writers equated Grannos with either Aesculapius, their god of medicine, or Apollo. Several localities in France are named after Grannos, such as Aix-la-Chapelle (Aquae Granni), Graux, and Eaux Graunnes.

See also: AESCULAPIUS; APOLLO

1318

**Grape**   A berry used for making wine. In Greek mythology, the grape was associated with Dionysus, whose worship involved sexual rites assisted by wine as an intoxicant. In the Old Testament, Noah is credited with inventing wine and getting drunk (Gen. 9:20–21). In the New Testament, Jesus used wine as part of the ritual around the Holy Eucharist, the other element being bread. Jesus drank wine (Matt. 11:19), and at the marriage feast at Cana (John 2:1–11), his first recorded miracle, he turned water into wine to replenish the supply for the feast. In Christian art the Holy Eucharist is sometimes symbolized by bunches of grapes with ears of wheat.

See also: DIONYSUS; NOAH

1319

**Grasshopper**   Any of numerous insects having hind legs used for leaping. In Egyptian mythology the grasshopper was associated with happiness. In *The Book of the Dead* the deceased is to say: "I have rested in the field of grasshoppers." Another ancient Egyptian text tells how the pharaoh will "arrive in heaven like the grasshopper of Ra," the sun god. In ancient Hebrew belief the grasshopper symbolizes a scourge. In Aesop's fable "The Ant and Grasshopper," the creature is depicted as a fool who does not plan for his life, thus symbolizing irresponsibility. But in Greek belief the creature also symbolized nobility. In Chinese folk belief, abundance, good luck, and numerous sons are symbolized by the grasshopper.

See also: AESOPIC FABLES; ANT AND THE GRASSHOPPER, THE; *BOOK OF THE DEAD*; PHARAOH; RA

1320

**Great Carbuncle**   In American folklore, a large, magnificent stone with extraordinary brightness and power. Nathaniel Hawthorne's "The Great Carbuncle," included in *Twice Told Tales*, is based on the legend, which the author says is founded on "Indian tradition." In Hawthorne's telling, an alchemist, a merchant, and a cynic go in pursuit of the gem, only to be frustrated. A young couple also go in pursuit of the magnificent stone but come to realize what happiness they have and reject it. When they do, the author says the splendor of the gem waned. The motif of an incandescent jewel is widely found in folk literature.

See also: MOTIF

1321

**Great Goddess/Great Mother Goddess** Prehistoric female deity. Numerous goddesses are recognized through figurines from Stone Age Europe and from 7th and 6th millennia Anatolia. Fertility attributes include large hips, protruding bellies, and pendulous breasts, with some emphasizing sexual characteristics rather than pregnancy. A near-universal cult of the Mother Goddess declined when urban civilization developed. The divine figure may have had its beginning in ancient Anatolia and is often portrayed with various felines, leopards and lions in particular. Her male partner is portrayed as a bull. Throughout the Near East many goddesses may have evolved from this earlier figure.

See also: ARURU; DAMKINA; DEVI; ETANA; INANNA; KALI; KUMARA-SAMBHAVA; SATI; SHIVA; TAMMUZ; TELEPINUS; YONI

1322
**Great Stone Face, The**  In American folklore, a mountain that resembles a face, said by the Indians to be that of Manitou, one of their main gods; according to white settlers, the New Hampshire mountain is the face of Daniel Webster. Its power is displayed in Hawthorne's short story, "The Great Stone Face," in *The Snow Image and Other Twice-Told Tales*.

1323
**Grede**  In Haitian voodoo, god of the dead, who is lord of life as well. In the chamber dedicated to his worship a sculptured phallus lies next to a gravedigger's tools. His symbol is the cross.

1324
**Gregory the Great, St.** (watchman)  Died 604. In Christian legend, pope, Doctor of the Church. Patron saint of fringe makers, masons, musicians, scholars, singers, students, and teachers. Invoked against gout, plague, and sterility. Feast, 12 March.

Gregory, the first monk to be made pope, was noted for his learning, kindness, and charity. He sent St. Augustine (not to be confused with the St. Augustine who wrote the *Confessions*) to Canterbury to convert the English. He reformed church music and wrote numerous works on sacred subjects. The Gregorian chant, which he was popularly believed to have originated, was named in his honor.

*St. Gregory*

He appears in numerous legends from the Middle Ages. One legend tells how John the Deacon, his secretary and biographer, saw the Holy Ghost in the form of a dove perched on the shoulder of Gregory whenever he dictated his sermons or books. Another legend tells how the Archangel Michael, responding to the prayers of St. Gregory, stopped a plague that was threatening to destroy Rome. The legend of the Supper of St. Gregory tells how 12 poor men came to dine every evening with Gregory. One evening a 13th appeared. After dinner Gregory asked the man who he was. The man replied, "I am the poor man whom thou didst formerly relieve, but my name is Wonderful, and through me thou shall obtain whatever thou shalt ask of God." Gregory then knew that he had been visited by an angel.

The Mass of St. Gregory is the name given to the most famous legend associated with the saint. Once there was a man who doubted that Christ was present at the altar during the Mass. When St. Gregory heard this, he prayed that Christ would make known to the man his real presence at the altar. Suddenly, Christ appeared with the instruments of his Passion on the altar. In another account, when Gregory elevated the sacred Host, it began to bleed, convincing the man that truly this was the body of Christ.

The miracle of the Brandeum, similar in some ways to the previous miracle, concerns a relic of St. John the Evangelist, the Brandeum, or consecrated cloth. It was sent to the empress Constantia and was rejected by her with contempt. To show her that faith was more important than relics, St. Gregory laid the Brandeum on the altar. After praying, he took up a knife and pierced it, and blood flowed from it as if it were a living body.

Another legend in medieval folklore tells of the prayers of the saint for the soul of the pagan emperor Trajan. As told by Brunetto Latini, the teacher of Dante, the legend maintains that by Gregory's prayers the pagen emperor entered heaven.

In *The Divine Comedy* (Purgatory, canto 10) Dante makes reference to this legend and says that the soul of the emperor was placed in the heaven of Jupiter among the spirits of those who loved and exercised justice.

See also: AUGUSTINE, ST.; JOHN THE EVANGELIST, ST.

**Gremlins**    In American folklore of World War II, elves about 20 inches tall who wear green breeches, red jackets with ruffles, and top hats and spats and who cause mischief on aircraft. U.S. airmen used the term to account for any mechanical difficulty. The phrase was coined by an R.A.F. squadron command serving in India. It is compounded from Grimms' *Fairy Tales*, the only book available to the flyers, and Fremlin, the only beer available. It appears for the first time in print in Charles Graves's *Thin Blue Line* (1941), a documentary of the war years.

*Grettir the Strong*    Medieval Icelandic saga, believed to have been written in the 11th century. Grettir was the second son of Asmund and Asdis. His mother favored the boy, but his father took a dislike to him, since he constantly got into trouble. After Grettir slew Skegg in a quarrel about a lost meal bag, he was ordered into three years' banishment. He was given a sword by his mother and placed on a boat, *Haflidi*, which was wrecked on the island of Havamsey. Here Grettir remained for some time with its chief, Thorfinn. One evening he saw a fire break out from a mound, and believing that the mound concealed some treasure, he went the next morning to dig. The mound was known as the grave of Old Karr, Thorfinn's father. Working all day and night, he finally came to the treasure and was about to take it when the dead body of Old Karr awoke. A fight began, and Grettir cut off Karr's head and made sure it was laid at the thigh of the dead man so that he could not come to life again. He took the treasure and gave all of it except for a short sword

to Thorfinn, until he had done some great deed. In a short time he accomplished the deed by killing at Christmas a group of thieves who had come to rob Thorfinn.

After numerous other adventures and murders, Grettir became an outlaw. He was finally killed by a man named Thorbiorn Angle, who found Grettir in a hut asleep after having been wounded by the witch Thurid. Thorbiorn, after a battle with Grettir, seized his short sword and cut off his head. Later Thorbiorn Angle was killed by Grettir's brother, Thorstein Dromond.

*Griffin*

**Griffin** (Gryphon)    In European and Near Eastern mythology and folklore, a fantastic animal with the head and wings of an eagle, the body of a lion, and sometimes the tail of a serpent. Griffins drew the chariots of Zeus, called the Hounds of Zeus, and those of Apollo and Nemesis. They guarded the gold and fought with the Arimaspians, a Scythian people who had only one eye. In the Bible, the Cherubim who guard the gate to the Garden of Eden were griffinlike beings as well as those that guarded the Ark of the Covenant. During the Christian Middle Ages numerous legends about griffins concerned the magical properties inherent in their claws. So-called griffin claws, usually antelope horns, were made into drinking cups in the belief that they would change color in the presence of poison. In an Italian medieval bestiary the griffin is symbolic of the devil, but in general the griffin was seen as a symbol of Christ, who was like a lion because he reigned as king and like an eagle because of his Resurrection. Most Dante scholars see the griffin in Dante's *Divine Comedy* (Purgatory, canto 29) as a symbol of Christ.

See also: APOLLO; ARISMASPI; ARK OF THE COVENANT; CHERUBIM; ZEUS

1328

**Grimhild**   In Norse mythology, wife of Giuki; queen of the Nibelungs, or Burgundians. She used a magic potion to make Sigurd (Siegfried) fall in love with her daughter Gudrun. Grimhild appears in the *Volsunga Saga*, and in Richard Wagner's *Der Ring des Nibelungen* she is the mother of Gunther and Gutrune by King Giuki and mother of Hagen by Alberich, the evil dwarf.

See also: ALBERICH; HAGEN; NIBELUNGS; *RING DES NIBELUNGEN, DER*; SIGURD

1329

**Grisilda** (stone heroine, gray battlemaid)   In medieval European legend, a symbol of patience and obedience. She is often referred to as "Patient Grisel." Grisilda, the daughter of a charcoal burner, married Walter, marquis of Saluzzo. Her husband spent most of his time testing his wife to see if she would obey him and be faithful. He took away her two children and told her they were murdered. Then he divorced her and sent her home, saying he was about to marry another woman. Finally, he stopped the cruel joking. The tale is told by Chaucer in *The Canterbury*

*Tales* as "The Clerk's Tale." Chaucer based it on Boccaccio's version in *The Decameron*. Boccaccio's source was a French folk tale.

See also: CHAUCER

1330

**Gu**   In African mythology (Fon of Benin), god of metal; patron of blacksmiths, inventor of all crafts, identified with iron, and guardian of hunters and warriors. In some accounts Gu is conceived of as a metal weapon wielded by the bisexual creator god, Mawu Lisa, to clear the earth and make it habitable for humankind.

See also: OGUN ONIRE; MAWU LISA

1331

**Guagugiana** (Guaguyona, Vagoniona)   In the mythology of the Taino Indians of Cuba at the time of Columbus, a trickster hero. Guagugiana was taught the use of magic amulets by Guabonito, a woman who arose from the sea. Guaguiana's servant, or friend (depending on which way the various accounts are read), was Giadruvava, who was taken up to heaven and transformed into a bird.

See also: TRICKSTER

1332

**Guallipen** (Huallepen)   In the folklore of the Araucanian Indians of Chile, a fantastic amphibious animal. It has the head of a calf and the body of a sheep. If a pregnant woman sees, hears, or dreams of a *guallipen* on three successive nights, her child will be born deformed. Often the *guallipen* will rape ewes or cows, though the offspring will occasionally look like the mother, with only the feet or muzzle deformed.

1333

**Guatavita Lake**   In the mythology of the Chibcha Indians of Colombia, site of the temple of a serpent god who received offerings from the people. A certain chief of Guatavita discovered that his favorite wife was unfaithful to him. He had her lover impaled and then forced his wife to eat her lover's penis and testicles. Overcome with shame, the wife threw herself and her daughter into Guatavita Lake. The chief then asked his magician to bring the two back, as he still loved his wife. The magician went down to the bottom of the lake and found that the wife and child were living in an enchanted kingdom ruled over by a dragon. The chief insisted that they be brought to the surface. The magician again went down and came up with the little girl's dead body, but the dragon had eaten her eyes.

See also: DRAGON; EL DORADO

**1334**
**Guayavacuni** (Guayarakunny)   In the mythology of the Tehuelcho Indians of the Patagonian pampas in South America, supreme being and beneficent spirit.

**1335**
**Gucumatz** (plumed serpent)   In Mayan mythology, hero in the Mayan sacred book *Popol Vuh*, who could transform himself into an eagle, serpent, or tiger, among other animals. Along with the creator Tepeu, he consulted Hurukán to determine how they might make men and glorify the gods. The three then made the earth, and Gucumatz and Tepeu created the animals and mankind.

See also: *POPOL VUH*

**1336**
**Gudatrigakwitl** (old man above)   In North American Indian mythology (Wiyot), creator god who brought about his creation by joining his hands and spreading them out over the primordial vacuum.

**1337**
**Gudrun**   Name of several different women appearing in Norse and Germanic mythology. In the Norse *Volsunga Saga* Gudrun is the wife of Sigurd. He fell in love with and married her after being given a magic potion. After his death she married Atli but later killed him and his two sons. She appears as Kriemhild in the Germanic epic the *Nibelungenlied* and as Gutrune in Wagner's *Der Ring des Nibelungen*.

Gudrun is also the name of the heroine of the Icelandic *Laxdala Saga*, in which she is a selfish woman who marries successively Thorwald, Thord, and Bolli, though she loves Kjartan, whose death she brings about.

A German epic poem of the 13th century is titled *Gudrun*. The first part tells of Hagen, king of Ireland; the second part recounts Hetel's courtship of Hagen's daughter Hilden; and the third part tells of Gudrun, their daughter. Gudrun is engaged to Herwig of Zealand but is stolen by Hartmut of Normandy. She refuses to marry her abductor and for 13 years is forced to do servant's work. At last Herwig, accompanied by Gudrun's brother, rescues her. William Morris's *The Lovers of Gudrun*, part of *The Earthly Paradise*, retells the tale. Gudrun (Gutrune) appears in Arthur Rackham's illustrations for Wagner's Ring Cycle.

See also: ATLI; HAGEN; *NIBELUNGENLIED*; *RING DES NIBELUNGEN, DER*

**1338**
**Guecubus** (Guecufu, Huecuvu)   In the folklore of the Araucanian Indians of Chile, demonic beings capable of assuming animal and human forms. They sow the fields with caterpillars, weaken animals with disease, quake the earth, and devour the fish in rivers and lakes.

**1339**
**Guinechen** (master of men?)   In the mythology of the Araucanian Indians of Chile, supreme god. Guinechen controlled the forces of nature, giving life to people and animals. He was also called Guinemapun, "master of the land," and saved mankind when there was a flood by raising the mountains so that the people could escape the waters.

*Guinever (A. Beardsley)*

1340

**Guinever** (Ganor, Ganora, Generua, Ginevra, Genievre, Guenever, Guanhumara, Guanhumar, and Guinevere, as Tennyson spells it) (fair and yielding)    In Arthurian legend, the wife of King Arthur. Her name in Welsh is Gwenhywvar (the white ghost). According to Malory in *Morte d'Arthur* (he spells her name Guenever), she was the daughter of Leodegraunce, king of the land of Cameliard. She loved Lancelot of the Lake, one of the knights of the Round Table, and had a long love affair with him. When King Arthur went to war against Leo, king of the Romans, Guinever was seduced by Mordred, her husband's nephew (his son in some accounts). Arthur hurried back and Guinever fled. A desperate battle followed between Arthur and Mordred, in which Mordred was slain and Arthur mortally wounded. Guinever then took the nun's veil at Almesbury, where later she died. She was said to be buried at Glastonbury. In Tennyson's *Idylls of the King* she is guilty only of passion for Lancelot and takes no part in Mordred's treachery.

See also: ARTHUR; GLASTONBURY; LANCELOT OF THE LAKE; ROUND TABLE

1341

**Guirivilo** (Neguruvilu)    In the folklore of the Araucanian Indians of Chile, a catlike monster. Guirivilo is armed with a claw-pointed tail and lives in the water, coming out to devour people.

1342

**Gula**    In Near Eastern mythology (Babylonian), goddess of healing, life-giver, the great physician who preserved the body in health and who removed sickness and disease by the touch of her hand. She was married to Ninib, with whom she shared her powers. She not only did good works but was invoked to bring down punishment on one's enemies. She was also the intermediary between the gods of the living and the gods of the dead.

See also: NINIB

1343

***Gulistan, The*** (rose garden)    A collection of didactic fables in rhymed prose with interspersed verses by the Persian poet Sadi, written in 1258.

*The Gulistan* is made up of eight chapters or divisions, each one treating a different subject. They are "The Manners of Kings," "The Morals of Dervishes," "On the Excellence of Contentment," "On the Advantages of Silence," "On Love and Youth," "On Weakness and Old Age," "On the Effects of Education," and "On Rules for Conduct of Life."

The fables, which are brilliant gems of terse writing, have short verses interspersed with them to summarize the fables and point out the morals. Often, however, the result is ambiguous. Many of the moral questions brought up by the tales are answered in a Machiavellian manner. One of the English translators of the book in the last century told his readers to skip over these "as some of our queasy clergy do in reading the morning and evening lessons." Yet no less a moralist than Ralph Waldo Emerson wrote that Sadi's *Gulistan* "speaks to all nations, and like Homer, Shakespeare, Cervantes, and Montaigne, is perpetually modern." Emerson found in the book "the universality of moral law."

The first translation of *The Gulistan* into a Western language, Latin, was made in 1651. It soon was a popular book among the 18th-century Enlightenment philosophers such as Voltaire. One of the problems encountered by the book's English translators was Sadi's continual reference to lovemaking among boys, which the poet considered perfectly normal. James Rose, who translated the book in 1823, changed the male gender to the female and decided on "the process of leaving out of the translation a few words of the Persian text." A complete translation, with all of the sexual references, was made by Edward Rehatsek in 1888.

1344

**Gunlod** (inviter to battle)   In Norse mythology, a giantess, daughter of Suttung; mother of the god Bragi. She possessed the mead of inspiration, which was stolen from her by Odin, who seduced her. Gunlod appears in the *Poetic Edda* and the *Prose Edda*.

See also: BAUGI; BRAGI; SUTTUNG

1345

**Guy of Warwick** (wit, wide, wood)   In medieval British legend, hero whose exploits were first written down by an anonymous Anglo-Norman poet in the 12th century.

Guy, son of Syward of Wallingford, steward of the earl of Warwick, fell in love with Felice la Belle, the earl's daughter. At first Felice rejected Guy's love but later changed her mind and said she would accept him when he became a famous knight. Knighted by the earl, Guy went to sea, seeking adventures that would make him famous. After a year he returned to England to be honored by King Aethelstan. However, Felice feared

that if she married him he would lose all interest in his knighthood. She promised to marry him if he became the most famous knight in the whole world. Still in love, Guy returned to his life of adventure. His greatest achievement was the deliverance of the emperor of Constantinople from the Saracens. His reward for his mighty deeds was half of the emperor's kingdom as well as the emperor's daughter in marriage. At the altar Guy remembered Felice and fainted. The marriage was postponed, and under a pretext Guy left Constantinople.

Returning through Germany, Guy rescued two lovers, Sir Tirri and Gisel. Back in England, he heard that a dragon was ravaging Northumbria; he hastened there and after a violent battle killed the dragon. When he returned home, he found that his father had died. At Warwick he was welcomed as a hero, and he then married Felice.

After a month of marriage Guy thought of all of the time he had spent winning Felice's love and how little of his life he had given to Jesus. He vowed to expiate his sins by becoming a pilgrim. Felice attempted to stop him, telling him that she was pregnant. Guy told her that when the child was born she should give it to his former master and companion in arms, Sir Haraud of Ardern, to be educated. Felice gave Guy a ring as a parting gift. For many years, through many lands, Guy the Pilgrim "with a glad chere" pursued his way.

Once in the East he put aside his pilgrim's garb to fight the Saracen giant Amourant on behalf of Christian prisoners. Then, returning again to Germany, he helped Sir Tirri once more. Finally, as an old man he returned to England. The land had been invaded by the Danes under Anlaf, and King Aethelstan, directed by angels, begged the pilgrim (he did not know it was Guy) to aid them in their fight against the giant Colbrand. After a desperate fight near Winchester, Guy killed the giant. Leaving Winchester, Guy journeyed to a neighborhood near Warwick and settled in a place where a hermit had once lived. Soon after, Guy fell ill. It was revealed to him in a dream that he would die in a week's time. On the seventh day he found a messenger to carry to Felice the ring that she had given him at parting, so that she might know that he had come back.

The messenger took the ring to Felice, and she begged him for news of Guy. He told her that Guy had been living as a hermit in the woods among wild beasts, eating herbs and roots, and that Guy was near death.

Felice mounted her horse and rode to the woods to find Guy. When she entered his cell, Guy raised his eyes and hands toward her, as though asking her pardon for the sorrow he had caused her. She bent and kissed him, and he died.

After his death his body gave forth a sweet spicelike odor. Sick persons were cured of their diseases when they smelled it. It lasted until the day of his burial, which took place in the hermitage, for no man was able to remove the body from the cell, even though 30 knights attempted it. Felice then moved into Guy's cell and died there 40 days later.

1346
**Gwain** (little hawk)    In Arthurian legend, nephew to King Arthur, and probably the original hero in the quest for the Holy Grail. He appears in the Welsh *Mabinogion* as Gwalchmei. Gwain was known as "the courteous." In the Middle English poem *Sir Gawain and the Green Knight* (c. 1360), Gwain beheads the Green Knight in combat after having promised to meet him for a return stroke 12 motnhs later at the Green Chapel. On the appointed day Gwain and the Green Knight both arrive. Gwain's honor is then tested by the knight's wife, and Gwain proves himself pure. He escapes unharmed.

See also: ARTHUR; *MABINOGION, THE*

1347
**Gwaten**    In Japanese Buddhist mythology, moon goddess, derived from the Hindu god Soma. She is portrayed as a woman holding in her right hand a disk, symbol of the moon. She is

one of the Jiu No O, 12 Japanese Buddhist gods and goddesses adopted from Hindu mythology.

See also: JIU NO O; SOMA

1348
**Gwydion** (Gwidion) (to say poetry)    In Celtic mythology, a magician, king of the British Celts, son of Don, brother of Amgethon, Gilvaethwy, and Govannon, brother and lover of Arianrhod. Gwydion was noted for the arts of poetry, divination, and prophecy. Many of the myths attached to his name were transferred during the Middle Ages to King Arthur.

See also: ARIANRHOD; ARTHUR, KING; GOVAN-NON

1349
**Gwynn** (Gwynwas) (fair, blessed)    In Celtic mythology, a god of the underworld, son of Nudd. Gwynn was at first a war god who hunted men's souls, leading them to Annwn, the land of the dead, over which he ruled. In later Welsh legend he is the king of the Tylwyth Teg, the Welsh fairies, and chief of the Ellyllon, a band of fairy dogs similar to brownies. Often Gwynn is accompanied by an owl, indicating his earlier role as god of the underworld.

See also: BROWNIES; NUDD

1350
**Gyges** (earth-born)    In Greek mythology, one of the three giants, Hecatoncheires, sons of Uranus and Gaea; the others were Briareus and Cottus. Gyges is also the name of a shepherd (c. 685–657 B.C.E.) who killed the Lydian king and married his widow. He was aided in this feat, according to legend recorded in Plato's *Republic* (book 2), by a magic ring that made him invisible.

See also: GAEA; URANUS

# H

**Habid al-Nadjdjar**   In Islamic legend, saint identified with Agabus, a Christian prophet mentioned in the New Testament. In Acts (11:28) Agabus predicts a famine that is to take place during the reign of the emperor Claudius Caesar. The historian Josephus does mention a famine that depopulated the country of Judea. According to Acts (21:10), Agabus met St. Paul some time after this event.

In the Islamic account Habid al-Nadjdjar (the carpenter) is converted by two Apostles of Jesus and runs to tell the people of the city to follow them. The people are unmoved by his arguments and kill him, telling Habid to "enter into Paradise" (Koran, sura 36). In one legend Habid (who is not directly named in the Koran) was decapitated. He took his head and walked with it for three days, when it cried out: "How gracious Allah hath been to me, and that He hath made me one of His honored ones." This statement is recorded in the Koran (sura 36), although the decapitation is not mentioned. Sura 36 also reports that Allah sent the archangel Gabriel to the people: "And lo! they were extinct." The destruction of the people may stem back to the famine that is part of the Christian legend.

See also: ALLAH; GABRIEL; KORAN, THE; PAUL, ST.

**Hacavitz**   In Mayan Indian mythology, a mountain god, as well as the mountain where the god was worshiped. The Mayan book *Title of the Lord of Totonicapán* (16th century) says that Hacavitz was the god of Mahucutah, who "went up the height and breadth of Hacavitz itself." Giving the same name to a mountain and a god who dwells on it is quite common in mythology.

**Hactcin**   In North American Indian mythology (Jicarilla Apache), supernatural personification of objects and natural forces, creator of all things.

**Haddingjar**   In northern mythology, twin brothers named among the early kings of Norway or Sweden. They are believed by some scholars to have been twin heroic or godly figures, much like Castor and Pollux, Hengist and Horsa, and Romulus and Remus.

See also: CASTOR AND POLYDEUCES; HENGIST AND HORSA; ROMULUS AND REMUS

**Hades** (hidden, sightless)   In Greek and Roman mythology, god of the underworld, son of

*Hades*

Cronus and Rhea; brother of Demeter, Hera, Hestia, Zeus, and Poseidon. When he was born, Hades was swallowed by his father and later disgorged when Zeus, with the help of Metis, tricked Cronus. When Cronus was defeated by his rebel sons, Zeus, Poseidon, and Hades, the three gods drew lots on which part of the universe each would rule. The underworld fell to Hades. The god fell in love with Persephone, whom he abducted and made his wife, though she never bore him any children. No temples were dedicated to the god. The cypress and narcissus were sacred to him. In ancient art he was portrayed in a manner similar to his brothers Zeus and Poseidon, bearing a staff, symbol of authority. Sometimes he was accompanied by his wife, Persephone, and the three-headed dog Cerebrus. Among the many names in Greek and Roman mythology borne by the god are Ades, Aides, Aidoneus, Dis, Orcus, Pluto, and Pluton.

See also: DEMETER; HERA; HESTIA; METIS; PERSEPHONE; POSEIDON; ZEUS

1356

**Hadith**    In Islam, traditional sayings ascribed to Muhammad, which supplement the Koran. The compilation was made in the 10th century by the Muslim jurists Moshin and Bokhari. The Hadith was originally not allowed to be written down, but because there was danger of the traditions being forgotten or perverted, they were eventually written. They help clarify points of law or ceremonial observance on which the Koran is silent or does not provide enough information. Hadith also deal with the life of Muhammad and the circumstances attending the revelations made to him. Although Muslim authorities have been very strict in the canons laid down for the reception or rejection of these traditions, a great deal of uncertainty exists as to the authenticity of many inclusions in the Hadith. The laws embodied in the traditions are called the Sunnah. In addition to the Koran and Hadith, the Isma (consensus) of Muslim authorities covers points not explicit in the other works.

See also: MUHAMMAD

1357

**Haemus** (skillful?)    In Greek mythology, king of Thrace; son of Boreas and Orithyia; brother of Calais, Chione, Cleopatra, and Zetes; husband of Rhodope. Haemus and Rhodope were so pleased with themselves that they called themselves Zeus and Hera. For this sacrilege they were transformed into mountains (the Balkans, once called the Haemus range and today called the Rhodope Mountains). Ovid's *Metamorphoses* (book 6) tells the tale.

See also: OVID

1358

**Hafaza**    In Islamic mythology, angels who protect people from djinn; two are assigned to a person for the daytime and two for the night. They keep a register of all of one's actions: the one who stands on a man's right keeps a record of his good deeds, and the angel who stands on his left records all of his evil acts. Sometimes the angel on the right tries to persuade his angelic companion not to write down the evil deeds but to give the person at least six or seven hours to repent. The most dangerous time for a person is when the angelic guards are changing shifts, which takes place at the rising and the setting of the sun. The djinn are most active at this time because they know a person's angelic protection is at its weakest.

**Hagen** 1359
In the *Nibelungenlied* and in Wagner's *Der Ring des Nibelungen*, the slayer of the hero Siegfried. He is called Hagni in the earlier *Volsunga Saga*. Hagen is portrayed in Arthur Rackham's illustrations for Wagner's Ring Cycle.

See also: *NIBELUNGENLIED*; *RING DES NIBELUNGEN, DER*; *SIEGFRIED*; *VOLSUNGA SAGA*

*The Trinity*

**Hagia Sophia** (holy wisdom) 1360
In Christianity, second person of the Christian Trinity, Jesus Christ. The church dedicated to Hagia Sophia at Constantinople was built by Emperor Justinian between 532 and 537. When the Turks took Constantinople in 1453, the building was turned into a mosque.

**Hai K'ang** 1361
In Chinese legend, one of the seven Chu-lin Ch'i-Hsien (Seven Immortals). He was a student of the black arts, which he practiced under a willow tree. In Japanese legend he is called Riurei.

See also: CHU-LIN CH'I-HSIEN

**Haitsi-aibed** 1362
In African mythology (Hottentot), resurrected hero, born of a cow and the miraculous grass it had eaten; patron of hunters and a superb fighter. Haitsi-aibed's most famous battle was with Gaunab (thrower down), a monster who would sit at the edge of a deep pit and dare passersby to hurl a stone at him. The stone always rebounded, hitting the person and causing him to fall into the pit. When Haitsi-aibed accepted the challenge of Gaunab, he made sure to divert the monster, and then he hurled the stone so as to hit him under his ear, causing Gaunab to fall into the pit. In some variant accounts Gaunab falls into the pit three times, escaping twice but dying after the third fall. Other tales tell how Haitsi-aibed died and was resurrected. Even today many caves and cairns in South Africa are called Haitsi-aibed graves in reference to the tales.

**Halirrhothius** (roaring sea) 1363
In Greek mythology, son of Poseidon and Euryte. He raped Ares' daughter Alcippe. Ares in turn killed Halirrhothius and was brought to the Areopagus trial by Poseidon and acquitted.

See also: ARES; POSEIDON

**Haltia** (familiar spirit) 1364
In Finno-Ugric mythology, tutelary genius of a person. Each person

has his own *haltia*, which goes before him. If the *haltia* is a very potent one, it arrives home before the person does, announcing its presence by a crash. The *haltia* is believed to become a reality three days after birth, and it is considered dangerous for a baby to be alone before that time. The *haltia* is sometimes blamed for a man's poor actions, with people saying, "It was not he, but his *haltia*." Sometimes the terms *saattaja* (guide) and *onni* (fortune) are used in reference to *haltia*.

**1365**

**Halwanli, Hiwanama, and Ourwanama**   In the mythology of the Surinam region (formerly Dutch Guiana) in South America, rival brothers. Halwanli was the oldest, the lord of all things inanimate and irrational. Ourwanama, the second brother, was a worker of the fields, a maker of liquor, and the husband of two wives. The youngest brother, Hiwanama, was a hunter.

One day Hiwanama came to the territory of Ourwanama and met his brother's two wives, who got him drunk and then seduced him. When Ourwanama discovered what had happened he exiled his brother. Their mother complained about the loss of her son; as a result the wives were transformed into a bird and a fish, and Ourwanama was drowned in the sea. Halwanli then went in search of Hiwanama and found him among the serpents and other reptiles of the lower world. When he brought him back, Hiwanama became one of the greatest *peaimen*, magician-priests similar to medicine men.

**1366**

**Hamlet** (Amleth) (home)   In medieval legend, a Danish hero, son of Gerutha and Horvendill. The legend of Hamlet, or Amleth, was first told by Saxo Grammaticus, a Danish chronicler, in his *Historia Danica*.

Hamlet's father, Horvendill, was killed by his brother Feng, who then married Gerutha, widow of Horvendill. Hamlet, fearful of being killed, pretended to go insane. Feng put him to various tests to see if the madness was real.

Among other things he sought to entangle Hamlet with a young girl, his foster sister, but Hamlet's cunning saved him. When Hamlet slew an eavesdropper hidden in his mother's room and then hid all traces of the murder, Feng decided Hamlet was not insane. He sent Hamlet off to England in the company of two attendants, who bore a letter to the king of England, telling him to put Hamlet to death. Hamlet secretly altered the letter, and the two attendants were put to death instead. He also changed the letter to say that the king should allow Hamlet to marry his daughter. After marrying the princess, Hamlet returned to Denmark, taking with him hollow sticks filled with gold. He arrived in time for a funeral feast held to celebrate his death. During the feast he plied the courtiers with wine and executed his vengeance during their drunken sleep. He covered them with the woolen hangings of the hall, fastened down with sharpened pegs, and then set fire to the palace. With the death of Feng the people proclaimed Hamlet king. He then returned to England for his wife.

Other adventures follow, none of which have left traces on the plays inspired by the legend. The most famous, of course, is Shakespeare's *Hamlet*, which inspired Lizst's symphonic poem *Hamlet*, Tchaikovsky's fantasy overture *Hamlet*, Ambrose Thomas's opera *Hamlet*, and Shostakovich's incidental music to the movie of the play. Hamlet has been depicted in film by such actors as Sir Laurence Olivier (1948), Richard Burton (1964), and Mel Gibson (1991).

**1367**

**Handaka Sonja**   In Japanese Buddhist mythology, one of the perfected disciples, or *arhats*, of the Buddha, often portrayed with a bowl from which issues a dragon or a rain cloud (both symbols of water). Handaka Sonja holds the bowl aloft with his left hand and with his right carries the sacred Tama. Sometimes he is portrayed seated on a rock with a crouching dragon at the side to protect the Tama. In Sanskrit, Handaka Sonja is called Panthaka.

See also: ARHAT

*Han Hsiang Tzu*

**1368**

**Han Hsiang Tzu**   Ninth century C.E. In Chinese Taoist legend, a deified mortal, one of the Pa-Hsien, the Eight Immortals. He is portrayed playing a flute or floating on a hollow tree trunk. Once he was carried to the top of a magic peach tree growing near a palace. The bough broke, and he entered into immortality as he fell. During his lifetime he was credited with magically filling an empty tub with wine, as well as having flowers grow out of an empty pot and having golden poems appear on leaves. In Japanese legend Han Hsiang Tzu is called Kanshoshi.

See also: PA-HSIEN; PEACH

**1369**

**Hannya**   In Japanese folklore, a female demon who eats children. She often appears in No dramas and is portrayed by a mask with horns, open mouth, and sharp fangs.

See also: NO

**1370**

**Hansel and Gretel**   German folktale found in the Grimms' collection of *Household Tales*. Hansel and Gretel are the children of a poor woodcutter, who remarries after the death of his wife. The stepmother hates the children and says there is not enough food for them to eat. The children are abandoned in the forest but find their way home. They are sent out a second time and become lost. They discover the house of a witch, who captures them and prepares to eat them. Each day the witch feeds them and feels their hands and arms to see if they have gained enough weight to make them fit to eat. Instead of putting out his arm, Hansel puts out a bone, and the nearsighted witch keeps postponing the day of doom. Finally, the witch angrily says she is ready to eat Hansel, thin or not. She asks Gretel to go inside the oven to see if it is hot enough. Gretel says she does not know how. The witch demonstrates for her and the children push her into the oven and close the door. The children then fill their pockets with jewels and eventually return home to find their father alive and their stepmother dead.

Hansel and Gretel is tale type 327/327a, "The Children and the Ogre." Humperdinck's opera *Hansel and Gretel* is the best-known treatment of the folktale, though it varies the tale somewhat.

See also: TALE TYPE

**1371**

**Hantu**   In Malayan mythology, generic name for demons ghosts, and spirits.

**1372**

**Hantu Ayer and Hantu Laut**   In Malayan mythology, water and sea spirits or demons.

**1373**

**Hantu B'rok**   In Malayan mythology, the baboon demon sometimes called the coconut monkey. He is believed to take possession of dancers and enable them to perform wonderful climbing feats.

1374

**Hantu Denej**   In Malayan mythology, the demon of wild beasts' tracks.

1375

**Hantu Kubor**   In Malayan mythology, grave demons who also prey on the living when given the opportunity. With them are the Hantu Orang Mati Di-Bunch, the spirits of murdered men.

1376

**Hantu Pemburu** (demon hunter)   In Malayan mythology, the wild huntsman or specter huntsman who causes havoc for man.

There was a man named Hantu Pemburu whose wife was pregnant. She was "seized with a violent longing for meat of the *pelandok*, or mouse deer." But it was no ordinary mouse deer the woman wanted. She insisted that it should be a doe, "big with male offspring." Her husband, obedient to his wife's wishes, went into the jungle to seek the *pelandok*, taking his weapons and his faithful dogs. Through a misunderstanding, the man hunted the buck *pelandok*, "big with male offspring," of course, an impossible quest.

Hantu Pemburu hunted day and night, slaying one mouse deer after another, which he discarded because he believed they did not fulfill his wife's requirements. He had sworn a solemn oath that he would not return home unless he was successful, and he became a regular denizen of the forest, eating the flesh and drinking the blood of the animals that he slew.

In time he covered the whole earth. "I have hunted the whole earth over without finding what I want," he said to himself. "It is now time to try the firmament." He "holloa'd on his dogs through the sky" while he continued on earth, bending back his neck to watch their progress. After a long time his head became fixed on his back as a result of constantly gazing upward. He was no longer able to look down at the earth. A leaf from the *si limbak* tree fell on his throat and took root, and a shoot grew upward in front of his face. In this state, Hantu Pemburu still hunts through the Malay forest, urging on his dogs as they hunt through the sky, with his gaze always turned upward.

His wife is not forgotten in the myth. She gave birth to two children, a boy and a girl. When the boy was of age, he went in search of his father. On his way he came upon a man who said that the boy's father had borrowed a chisel from him and he wanted it returned. When the son found his father in the forest, he told him about the man.

"I will eat his heart and drink his blood," responded Hantu Pemburu. "So shall he be rewarded." From that day forth Hantu Pemburu has afflicted humankind.

1377

**Hantu Songkei** (loosening demon)   In Malayan mythology, a demon who sets about untying the knots made by hunters in snares for wildfowl. He is invisible below the waist, and he has a nose of enormous length (a symbol of his penis) and eye sockets stretched sideways to such an extent that he can see all around him.

1378

**Hanukkah** (Chanukkah) (dedication)   In Judaism, an eight-day festival commemorating the dedication of the second Temple by Judas Maccabeus. The Old Testament Apocrypha book 1 Maccabees (4:59) states, "Moreover Judas and his brethren with the whole congregation of Israel ordained that the days of the dedication of the altar should be kept in their season from year to year by the space of eight days . . . with mirth and gladness." According to one account in the Talmud, the festival lasts eight days because the oil found in the Temple was sufficient for only one day, but it burned for eight. The main symbol of Hanukkah is the menorah, an eight-branch candlestick with a socket for a ninth candle. Also called the Feast of Dedication, it falls on the 25th day of the month Kislev (around 10 December).

See also: MENORAH; TALMUD

1379
**Hanuman** (Hanumat) (having large jaws)   In the Hindu epic poem *The Ramayana*, a monkey hero. Hanuman was the son of Vayu, the wind god, by a monkey mother, Vanar. He and his monkey allies assisted Rama in his war against the demon king Ravana. In one episode in *The Ramayana*, Hanuman jumps from India to Lanka (Sri Lanka) in one leap. However, he is caught in the city by Ravana's men, and his tail is greased and set on fire. Hanuman jumps around from building to building, burning the entire city. He later flies to the Himalayas and brings back medicinal herbs with which he heals the wounded. Still later, he helps Rama win back Sita, Rama's wife, from Ravana and receives the reward of perpetual life and youth.

*Hanuman*

Hanuman is described as "vast as a mountain and as tall as a gigantic tower. His complexion is

yellow and glowing like molten gold. His face is as red as the brightest ruby; while his enormous tail spreads out to an interminable length. He stands on a lofty rock and roars like thunder. He leaps into the air and flies among the clouds with a rushing noise, while the ocean waves are roaring and splashing below." A drama, *Hanumannataka*, treating Hanuman's adventures is said to have been written by the monkey hero himself.

See also: RAMA; RAVANA; *RAMAYANA, THE*; VAYU

1380
**Haoma**   In Persian mythology, sacred healing plant from which an intoxicating drink was made, similar to the Hindu sacred plant Soma.

Thrita, a hero in Persian myth, is called the preparer of Haoma, the third man who prepared the magic drink for the world. He prayed to Ahura Mazda, the good creator god, for a medicine that would withstand the pain, disease, infection, and death that the evil spirits were working against men. In answer to Thrita's prayers Ahura Mazda sent down various healing plants that grew around the Gaokerena tree, a magical tree that had within it the seeds of all plants and trees, among them the sacred Haoma. The Haoma was used in various rites and was believed to make the dead immortal if they tasted it, grant children to women, and give strong men to young girls as their husbands.

See also: AHURA MAZDA; SOMA

1381
**Hapi** (Hap, Happy)   In Egyptian mythology, god of the Nile, who became identified in some myths with all of the great primeval creative deities and eventually was believed to have been the creator of everything. At a very early period Hapi absorbed the attributes of Nun, the primeval watery mass from which the god Ra emerged on the first day of creation. As a result, Hapi was regarded as the father of all beings. He held a unique position in Egyptian religion, although he was not in any theological system developed by the priests.

The light of Ra brought life to men and animals, but without the waters of Hapi every living thing would perish. Some hymns credit Hapi with causing the Nile to flood every year, thus irrigating the fields of Egypt. The flood was said to come from two caverns made from the imprints of Hapi's sandals. The god Khnum was in charge of these "secret caverns of Hapi." Hapi is usually portrayed as a fat man with blue or green skin and the breasts of a woman to indicate his powers of fertility. When he represents both the south and north Nile, Hapi holds two plants, the papyrus and the lotus, or two vases from which he pours out water.

See also: EARTH DIVER; RA

**1382**

**Hare** A rodentlike mammal, related to but larger than the rabbit; the two are often confused in world mythology and folklore. It was believed that the hare was abnormally lustful, and the animal came to be a symbol of lust as portrayed by medieval artists and writers. Most medieval books cite the belief that the hare was capable of changing its sex. The female animal was also believed to be able to conceive without the aid of a male and to retain its virginity. When a hare appears in a painting of the Virgin Mary, it is symbolic of the triumph of chastity. The enemies of Queen Elizabeth I of England called her a hare because her devoted subjects called her the virgin queen. It was a common belief that the appearance of a hare presaged misfortune. It is still considered unlucky for a hare to cross one's path, because witches could transform themselves into hares. In many African-American tales from the Southeast, the rabbit is the trickster. There are numerous motifs associated with the hare/rabbit in the *Motif Index of Folk Literature*.

See also: BR'ER RABBIT; UNCLE REMUS; VIRGIN MARY

**1383**

**Harimau Kramat** In Malayan mythology, ghost tigers. Once there was a man named Nak-hoda Ragam traveling in a boat with his wife, the princess of Malacca. When the princess, for some reason not revealed in the legend, pricked her husband to death with a needle, his blood flooded the boat. Another boat was passing, and the master of that vessel asked, "What have you got in your boat?"

"Spinach juice," replied the princess. She then went on her way and landed at the foot of Jurga Hill, where she buried all that remained of her husband—one thigh (she had thrown most of his body overboard). She also took ashore her two cats, which were in the boat with her when she murdered her husband. The cats turned into Harimau Kramat, ghost tigers, and became the guardians of the shrine.

**1384**

**Haris-chandra** In Hindu mythology, a king noted for his suffering.

One day when Haris-chandra was hunting, he heard female voices "from the sciences, who were being mastered by the austerely fervid sage Viswamitra, and were crying out in alarm at his superiority." Haris-chandra, as defender of the distressed, went to the rescue. Viswamitra was so provoked by Haris-chandra's interference that the sciences were destroyed. Haris-chandra was placed under the complete control of Viswamitra. The sage demanded from Haris-chandra a sacrificial gift, and Haris-chandra offered Viswamitra whatever he wanted, "gold, his own son, wife, body, life, kingdom, good fortune." Viswamitra stripped Haris-chandra of his wealth and kingdom, leaving him with nothing but a garment of bark and his wife and son.

In this state Haris-chandra left his wife and son, only to have the two also demanded by Viswamitra. With bitter grief the two were sold, and later Haris-chandra, the former king, was carried off "bound, beaten and confused, and afflicted."

The gods finally took pity on his suffering and took him to heaven, but Haris-chandra boasted of his merits and was thrown out. As he was falling, he repented of his foolishness, and his fall was arrested. He now dwells in the aerial city, which can still be seen floating in midair, according to some.

See also: VISWAMITRA

---

**1385**

**Harmachis** (Horus who is on the horizon)  In Egyptian mythology, the Greek form of the Egyptian god Rehoarakhty. According to legend, the Pharaoh Tuthmosis IV, while still a prince, was hunting in the deserts near Giza and sought shelter from the noonday sun in the shadow of the Great Sphinx. He soon fell asleep, and in a dream the Sphinx, as Rehoarakhty, promised him the throne of Egypt if he would clear away the sands that had engulfed the Sphinx. The prince awoke, cleared away the sand, and was later crowned king of Egypt. A stele erected at the site of the Sphinx by Tuthmosis IV records the dream and its consequences.

---

**1386**

**Harmonia** (concord)  In Greek mythology, daughter of Ares and Aphrodite, wife of Cadmus, king of Thebes; mother of Agave, Autonoe, Ino, Polydorus, and Semele. When Harmonia was married to Cadmus, Zeus, who arranged the match, gave Harmonia a necklace made by Hephaestus that promised its possessor beauty. In variant accounts, the necklace was given to Cadmus, who gave it to his wife, or the gift was given by Zeus to his mistress Europa or by Aphrodite to Harmonia. Given at the same time to Harmonia was a robe by Athena, who, some variant accounts say, also gave the necklace. Both gifts brought disaster on the family and played an important part in the Seven against Thebes as well as the war of the Epigoni. Finally, to stop the bloodshed, the gifts were placed in the temple of Apollo at Delphi, where they remained until the fourth century B.C.E., when they were stolen. Harmonia and Cadmus were turned into serpents. Ovid's *Metamorphoses* (books 3, 4) tells the

story, and Milton's *Paradise Lost* (9.503–506) refers to the transformation.

See also: APHRODITE; APOLLO; AREA; ATHENA; CADMUS; DELPHI; HEPHAESTUS; OVID; ZEUS

---

**1387**

**Haroeris** (Horus the elder, Horus the great)  In Egyptian mythology, Greek name for Har Wer, who was worshiped at Letopolis. Some texts say he was the son of Geb, the earth god, and Nut, the sky goddess; others that he was the son of Ra, the sun god, and Hathor, the cow goddess. Haroeris was worshiped with his female counterpart, Ta-sent-nefert, and their son, P-neb-taui, forming a trinity. In Egyptian art Haroeris is portrayed as a man with the head of a hawk wearing the double crown of Upper and Lower Egypt.

See also: GEB; HATHOR; NUT; RA

---

**1388**

**Harpies** (snatcher)  In Greek mythology, winged monsters with women's faces and vulture bodies, daughters of Thaumas and Electra or of Poseidon and Gaea. Some accounts give their names as Aello, Celaeno, and Ocypete. Hesiod's *Theogony* names Aello and Ocypete; Homer names Podarge. In Vergil's *Aeneid* (book 3) they harass Aeneas's men as they are resting and eating on their way to Italy; Celaeno, however, delivers a crucial prophecy to Aeneas. In Spenser's *Faerie Queene* (2.12.36) they are "the hellish Harpies, prophets of sad destiny," and in Milton's *Paradise Regained* (book 2.403) the banquet created by Satan vanishes "with sound of Harpies wings, and Talons heard."

See also: *AENEID, THE*; ELECTRA; GAEA; HESIOD; POSEIDON

---

**1389**

**Harpokrates** (Horus the child, the infant Horus)  In Egyptian mythology, Greek name for the Egyptian Heru-p-khart, a form of the god Horus. He was often portrayed with the sidelock of youth and wearing the double crown of Upper and Lower Egypt. His index finger is held to his lips, which the Greeks misinterpreted as a symbol of his discretion. They called Harpokrates the god of silence as a result of this mistake. Sometimes Harpokrates is shown being suckled by his mother, Isis.

See also: HORUS; ISIS

**Harris, Eliza** In American history and folklore, a black slave woman who fled north with her two children. When she reached the Ohio River, it was winter, and the ice was breaking up. Her pursuers, with bloodhounds, were left helpless at the shore as Eliza, leading her children, crossed the river by jumping from one ice floe to another. John Van Zandt, a Methodist minister who believed there was no such person as a slave, was known to be a main conductor on the Underground Railroad. Eliza Harris was harbored by the Van Zandts on her trip to Canada. The house is known as the "Eliza House." Van Zandt was the model for John Van Trompe in Harriet Beecher Stowe's antislavery novel *Uncle Tom's Cabin* and uses the episode as does the ballet sequence in *The King and I* by Rodgers and Hammerstein.

**Harut and Marut** In Islamic mythology, two fallen angels who teach men sorcery and magic. They are the brothers of Iblis, the father of the djinn, who is the best-known fallen angel in Islam.

According to the Koran (sura 2), Harut and Marut teach men "how to cause division between husband and wife." The two can work their evil only by permission of Allah. A number of legends are connected with this passage in the Koran.

In one account, when the angels saw how sinful man was they spoke contemptuously of him to Allah. "If you were in his place," Allah replied, "you would do no better."

The angels did not agree with Allah, and two of them, Harut and Marut, were chosen to fly down to earth for an experiment to test the truth of the matter. Allah told them that they were to abstain from idolatry, whoredom, murder, and drinking of wine (all forbidden to Muslims). When the two came upon a beautiful woman, Zorba (or Zurah), they fell victim to her sexual charms. They were discovered in the act by a man, whom they killed, hoping no one would learn of their deed.

Allah, watching from heaven, saw all that happened. The angels were called to see what Harut and Marut had done. "In truth, Thou wast right," they said to Allah. Harut and Marut were then given the choice of suffering in this world or the next. They chose to suffer on earth and were thrown into a "well in the town of Babylon, where loaded with chains," they took up the business of teaching men magic and sorcery. (In Persian the word *harut* is used for a magician.)

See also: ALLAH; IBLIS; KORAN, THE

**Hatfields and McCoys** In American folklore, two feuding families separated by a few miles of wild mountain and by Tug Fort, a creek that forms a natural boundary between Kentucky and West Virginia. The exact cause of the feud is not known. Some accounts say it had to do with a stolen pig; others say the slaying of Asa Harmon McCoy was the defining event. Asa Harmon, brother of Randolph McCoy, was a slave owner, but he was also a keen observer of his times. He defied the general sympathies of the region and enlisted in the Union army in 1864. He served for 11 months until he was felled by a broken leg and discharged from the army on Christmas Eve. He returned home to a chilly reception. He was threatened by Jim Vance, the ruthless uncle of Devil Anse Hatfield. It was Vance who promised a visit from the Logan Wildcats, a local "home guard" group. Asa Harmon fled to the hills and found refuge in a cave. For several weeks, he hid there, visited only by his wife and his slave, Pete, who brought food and supplies. On the night of 7 January 1865, it was Pete who inadvertently revealed Asa Harmon. The Wildcats had simply followed Pete's tracks in the snow. Asa Harmon met his fate at the end of a rifle. The feud went on for some time, and the death toll ranged from 50 to 200.

*Hathor*

1393
**Hathor** (Athyr, Athor) (house of Horus)   In Egyptian mythology, ancient sky goddess, great mother goddess often portrayed as a cow or with the head of a cow. Hathor, according to one Egyptian myth, stood on the earth as a cow in such a way that her four legs were the pillars holding the sky, and her belly was the firmament. Each evening Horus, as the sun god, flew into Hathor's mouth in his hawk form, and each morning he appeared again, reborn. Consequently, Horus was said to be both her husband and her son.

Hathor was one of the oldest known goddesses of Egypt, considered to be the great mother, or cosmic goddess, who conceived, brought forth, and maintained all life. She not only nourished the living with her milk but was said to supply celestial food for the dead in Duat, the underworld. The goddess also was known for her destructive role. One myth tells how the sun god, who had grown old and wanted to punish mankind for plotting to do away with him, sent Hathor to slay mankind. Hathor enjoyed the

slaughter so much that the other deities flooded the fields with an intoxicating brew, causing her to become drunk and cease her slaughter. Hathor's main temple was at Dendera, where she was worshiped with Horus and their son Ihi, or Ahi, who was portrayed as an infant playing the sistrum at her side (the sistrum was believed to drive away evil spirits). Great festivals were celebrated in her temple, the most important being the festival of her birth, held at the new year, which ended with a drunken orgy. Her temple became known as a palace of enjoyment and a house of intoxication and gave rise to her reputation as mistress of merriment and dance, as well as her popularity as a goddess of love, which caused the Greeks to identify her with Aphrodite.

In late Egyptian belief Hathor became the representative of all of the great goddesses in Egypt. Shrines were erected in her honor throughout the land. In her beneficent aspect she was called Nehem Away (the one who takes care of the deprived), referring to those who have been robbed or plundered.

See also: APHRODITE; AUDHUMLA; DUAT; HORUS

1394
**Hathsepsut** (foremost in nobility)   1501–1447 B.C.E. In Egyptian history and legend, one of the first women to rule in her own right as pharaoh. At the death of Thuthmosis II, Thuthomosis III was too young to rule. The decision was made to name Hathsepsut as regent until the young prince came of age. The beginning of their joint reign was marked by peaceful cooperation. But Hathsepsut soon seized the throne and relegated Thuthmosis III to an insignificant administrative role. She turned her attention to rebuilding Egypt internally and credited her kingship to the god Amun, to whom she built many monuments. The obelisks she erected to Amun in the temples at Karnak were of extraordinary size and were quarried and erected in record time. Her architect, Senemut, erected for her a funerary tem-

ple at Dier el Bahari in which the scenes show her famous trading expedition to the legendary land of Punt to obtain incense for Amun's cult. It also shows her divine birth, the episodes of which include the courting of her mother Ahmose by the god Amun. When Hathsepsut died, Thuthmosis III assumed his rightful position as pharaoh. Shortly thereafter, many of the monuments of Hathsepsut were destroyed in an attempt to obliterate her name. Some contend that this destruction was ordered by Thuthmosis III.

See also: AMUN

**1395**

**Hatim** In a Moroccan Islamic legend, a princess who turned into an almond tree. Before the advent of Islam, Hatim was a young, generous princess of the Tai tribe. Her father objected to her dispensing his wealth as well as her own, so he offered to let her choose exile or death. She chose death, but Allah rewarded her for her generous deeds by transforming her into "a tree of great beauty—the almond tree which enhances our orchards."

Even today, as the almond tree, she "continues to distribute gifts; her flowers are the joy of spring; her fruit has a delightful taste; her oil is sweet and clean; she inspires peace and heals the troubled hearts of men."

**1396**

**Hattara Aonja** In Japanese Buddhist mythology, one of the perfected disciples, or *arhats*, of the Buddha, often portrayed with a white tiger crouching at his feet. He holds a *nloi*, a short wand, symbol of power, and is sometimes seated on a rock. In Sanskrit, Hattara Aonja is called Bhadra (auspicious).

See also: ARHAT

**1397**

**Hatto** 10th century. In medieval northern legends, archbishop of Mainz who was devoured by mice because of his greed.

In 970 there was a famine in Germany. It was known that Hatto had amassed vast stores of wheat in his granaries. When the people asked him for help, he appointed a day for them to receive grain. When the day arrived, the crowd filled the archbishop's barn to capacity. He then locked the door and set the barn on fire, burning all of the people inside to death.

After his murderous act he had a good dinner and a good night's sleep, as usual. The next morning he saw that his portrait had been eaten by rats. As the archbishop was surveying the previous night's destruction, a servant rushed in to tell him rats had also eaten the remainder of the stored wheat. No sooner had the servant told his tale than another appeared to inform the archbishop that rats were converging on the palace. Hatto, looking out the window, could see thousands of the creatures descending on the building.

In terror Hatto fled by boat to a private island, where he had earlier built a tower. His flight, however, was in vain; the rats pursued him, attacked his boat, and landed on the island. The archbishop managed to reach the tower, but the rats caught up with him and ate him alive. Robert Southey in his *Metrical Tales* tells the legend:

> They have whetted their teeth against the
>   stones,
> And now they pick the Bishop's bones;
> They gnaw'd the flesh from every limb,
> For they were sent to do judgment on him.

There is a medieval watchtower on the Rhine, near Bingen, called the Mouse Tower, and Hatto's legend is associated with it. The tower, however, was built by Bishop Siegfried some 200 years after Hatto; it was built as a tollhouse for collecting duties on all goods passing through.

1398

**Hatuibwari**    In Melanesian mythology, a bisexual creator god of the Arosi, sometimes portrayed as a winged serpent with a human head, four eyes, and four breasts to suckle the young. Hatuibwari's symbols are sometimes assigned to another bisexual creator god, Agunus.

1399

**Hatyani of Debrecen**    1718–1786. In Finno-Ugric legend, physician and philosopher whose experiments gained him a reputation for black magic. Tales told about him are generally based on literary, not folk, sources.

1400

**Haumea**    In Polynesian mythology, Hawaiian fertility goddess, mother of Pele, also said to be the first woman. In some myths Haumea is identified with the earth goddess Papa.

See also: ATEA AND PAPA; PELE

1401

**Havelok the Dane** (of the lake haven)    In medieval northern legends, hero whose exploits are recorded in many 13th-century works, including an English one, *Havelok the Dane* (c. 1280–1300).

When King Aethelwold of England was about to die he committed his only child, Goldborough, to Earl Godrich of Cornwall, who swore to protect the girl and give her in marriage to a strong and handsome man. In Denmark, when King Birkaybeyn was on his deathbed, he entrusted his son Havelok and his two girls to the care of Earl Godard. The evil earl, however, had the two girls killed, and Havelok was given to Grim, a fisherman, who was to kill the boy. But one night in his cottage Grim saw a flame come out of the mouth of the sleeping boy. He looked at the boy and discovered a "king's mark" on his shoulder. Knowing this meant that the boy would one day be a king, he escaped with Havelok and his own family to England.

When Havelok grew up he entered the service of the cook of Earl Godrich of Cornwall. He became known for his strength and kindness. When the earl heard of Havelok he decided the lad should marry Princess Goldborough. Havelok took his wife to Grimsby, but at night Goldborough cried because she had married below her station. Then she saw a bright light come out of the mouth of the sleeping Havelok. She saw a gold cross on his shoulder.

Suddenly an angel's voice said, "Goldborough, do not cry. Havelok is a king's son. He shall be king of England and Denmark, and you shall be his queen."

Happy that she now had a king for a husband, Goldborough sailed with Havelok for Denmark, where because of his magic flame Havelok was made king. Earl Godard was sentenced by the people, flayed, drawn, and hanged. After four years Havelok returned to England, conquered Godrich, and was crowned king of England in London.

1402

**Hawk**    A bird of prey with a hooked beak and powerful claws. The cult of the hawk or falcon is one of the oldest in Egypt, where the bird was was identified with various sky or sun gods, such as the Horus gods and Ra. The bird also was identified with Osiris, the god of the dead. The main center of worship was at Hieraconpolis (hawk city). According to Herodotus' *Historia* (book 2), the punishment for killing a hawk was death. In Egypt the hawk was also sacred to the Greek god Apollo in his role as diviner. One of the earliest Greek fables, told by Hesiod in his *Works and Days*, is titled "The Hawk and the Nightingale." In it the hawk is portrayed as a greedy, vicious bird.

See also: APOLLO; HAWK AND THE NIGHTINGALE, THE; HORUS; OSIRIS; RA

1403

**Hawk and the Nightingale, The**    Aesopic fable found in Hesiod's *Work and Days*, written in the eighth century B.C.E. and considered the earliest known example of the Greek fables.

A hawk caught a nightingale and was carrying it high in the sky. The nightingale cried out, but the hawk was unmoved. It said to the poor bird: "What's wrong with you? Why scream? I'm your master and can do with you what I want. If I like I can let you go free, or if I prefer, I can eat you for dinner."

Moral: *He is a fool who fights with someone who is stronger than he—he will not only lose the battle but will also be disgraced.*

See also: AESOPIC FABLES; HESIOD

1404

**Haya-griva** (horse-necked)  In Hindu mythology, a demon who stole the sacred books, the Vedas, as they slipped out of the mouth of the god Brahma while he was sleeping. Haya-griva, in one myth, was killed by the god Vishnu. In a variant account Vishnu took the form of Haya-griva, recovering the Vedas from two other demons.

See also: BHRAMA; VEDAS; VISHNU

1405

**Hayk**  In Armenian folklore, hero who freed his people from the tyranny of King Bel of Babylonia. Hayk was a handsome giant with fine limbs, curly hair, bright smiling eyes, and strong arms. The bow and the triangular arrow were his weapons. Hayk freed his people, who lived in the plain of Shinar, from the tyranny of King Bel and brought them to the mountains of Armenia. There, however, he placed the native population in subjugation. The forces of King Bel pursued Hayk, and the hero shot an arrow, piercing the chest of the king and causing his forces to disperse. Hayk's son was Armenak, another Armenian hero.

Hayk is used in Armenian as a term for a giant as well as "great beauty." St. Gregory of Narek called the Virgin Mary "Hayk-like."

See also: BEL

1406

**Hazel**  A small tree of the birch family; in Norse mythology, sacred to Thor, the thunder god, and believed to be the actual embodiment of lightning. Medieval German Christians would place hazel twigs in the form of a cross on windowsills during a storm in the hope of stilling it. During Halloween, sometimes called Nutcrack Night in Europe, hazel nuts are put on the fire to foretell the fate of lovers. This custom is alluded to in Thomas Gray's poem *Elegy in a Country Churchyard.* In European folklore it was the custom for the leader of a wedding party to carry a hazel wand to ensure many offspring for the marriage. One medieval German legend says that Herodias, the wife of King Herod, who killed John the Baptist, was in love with the prophet. When his head was brought to her, she tried to kiss it, but it drew back and blew hard at her. Herodias was whirled up to the top of a hazel tree, where she still sits from midnight to cockcrow, floating in the air the rest of the time.

See also: JOHN THE BAPTIST; THOR

1407

**Head and the Tail, The**  Jewish fable found in the Talmud. Once the tail of a snake said to its head, "How much longer will you lead the way and drag me behind? Let me lead and you follow." "Very well," the head replied, "you go first." So the tail led the way, and the head followed. Nearing a ditch filled with water, the tail fell in, dragging the head after him. At another place, filled with thorn bushes, the tail and the head became tangled, scratched, and finally wounded. Is not the head to blame for agreeing to be led by the tail?

See also: TALMUD

1408

**Heaven and Hell**  Medieval Judaism, Christianity, and Islam all believed in a place of reward for the souls of the just with God and his angels and a place of punishment for the wicked with the devils.

*Dives in Hell and Lazarus in Heaven*

Ancient Hebrew religion, as expressed in the Old Testament, does not have any concept of heaven for the just. All of the dead, both good and evil, are sent to Sheol, the underworld, a dim and hopeless place. Thus, King Saul, who was hated by God, and the prophet Samuel, who was loved by God, are both sent to Sheol. Some passages in the Old Testament suggest that God had no control over Sheol; he is concerned only with the living, not the dead. When Judaism came into more contact with pagan religions, such as that of the Persians, the idea of heaven and hell developed. This belief was passed on to the writers of the New Testament and thence to the Christian Middle Ages.

The clearest expression of the concept of heaven is found in *The Divine Comedy* of Dante, in which the poet is given a glimpse of the Divine. Dante based his work on 1,000 years of Christian and pagan folklore and religion. Islam also based its descriptions of heaven, or paradise, called *Djanna* (garden), on earlier Jewish, Christian, and pagan folklore and mythology.

Sura 47 of the Koran says of heaven that "therein are rivers of water, which corrupt not; rivers of milk, whose taste changeth not; and rivers of wine, delicious to those who quaff it; And Rivers of honey clarified: and therein are all kinds of fruit for them from their Lord!" In sura 55, the faithful shall lie "on couches with linings of brocade . . . and the fruit of the two gardens shall be within easy reach. . . . Therein shall be the damsels with retiring glances, whom man nor djinn hath touched before them."

In Islamic mythology Djanna (like Dante's *Paradiso*) consists of various divisions: Gannat al 'Huld, or The Garden of Eternity (sura 25), Dâr as Salâm, or The Abode of Peace (sura 6), Dâr al Qarâr, or The Abode of Rest (sura 40), Gannat Hadn, or The Garden of Eden (sura 9), Gannat al Mâwâ, or The Garden of Resort (sura 32), Gannat al Na'hîm, or The Garden of Pleasure (sura 6), Gannat al Hilliyûn, or The Garden of the Most High (sura 83), and Gannat al Pirdaus, or The Garden of Paradise (sura 18).

From the various descriptions in the Koran, heaven is the realization of all that a dweller in a hot, parched, and barren land could desire—shade, water, fruit, rest, pleasant women, young men, and alcohol (denied to Muslims during their lifetimes).

In later Islamic writings Djanna is represented as a pyramid, or cone, consisting of the eight divisions. At the top is the fabulous tree *sidret-el-mounteha*. In *The Ascension of Muhammad*, a work in which Muhammad describes his journey through the various heavens (Muhammad was not the author), he says:

We attained the *sidret-el-mounteha*. That which is thus called is a large tree, some of whose branches are of emerald, others of pearl, with foliage similar to elephants' ears. Its fruits are of considerable size. From the foot of the tree gush four springs which flow into as many canals. Two of these canals are open to the skies, but the two others are covered. . . . The water of these two rivers is whiter than milk and sweeter than honey.

Angels coming toward me, greeted me, and brought three goblets, which they presented to me. In one was milk, in another wine, and in the third was honey.

On the leaves of the tree are the names of all of the people in the world. After sunset on the night of the 15th of Ramadan each year the leaves with the names of those who are to die during the year fall from the tree.

Djanna also contains a fountain, Salsabil (sura 76), signifying water flowing gently down the throat. It may also refer to wine, since it will be lawful to drink wine in paradise, although it is forbidden Muslims on earth.

The Christian heaven makes no provision for animals, but the Islamic Djanna admits 10 animals into its quarters. They are Noah's dove; Abraham's ram, which was sacrificed in place of Isaac; Moses' ox; Balaam's ass; King Solomon's ant; the Queen of Sheba's lapwing Balkis; Jonah's whale; the Islamic prophet Saleh's she-camel; and Borak, the fabulous animal who took Muhammad to heaven.

Jewish, Christian, and Moslem concepts of hell are quite similar. In *The Divine Comedy* Dante gives an elaborate description of hell in which he is guided by Vergil, the ancient Roman poet who was believed to be a magician during the Middle Ages.

Dante's description of hell was inspired by 1,000 years of Christian myth and legend. In one early nonscriptural Christian work, St. Peter describes hell: "And I saw another place right opposite, rough and being the place of punishment. And those who are punished there and the punishing angels had their robes dark; as the color of the air of the place is also dark; and some people were hung up by their tongues: they were those who had blasphemed the path of righteousness; and underneath them a bright baneful fire was lit."

Descriptions of hell such as this were the source for the elaborate punishments meted out in Dante's *Inferno*. Another source that may have influenced Dante, since it also had its effects on

*Hell*

Christian legend, is found in the *Pistis Sophia*, a third-century work of Christian Gnostics. Gnosticism, which had many forms, taught that there are two gods, one good God (the father of Jesus) and one evil God (the creator God of the Old Testament). This heresy also held that the Divine Spark, the soul, had to escape from the body, since physical matter was evil because it was controlled by evil spirits. Only through the *gnosis* (knowledge) of the unknown god and the redeemer who comes to earth could one be saved, but this was limited to only a few.

The *Pistis Sophia* reveals all of the elaborate machinery of hell. In one of its sections Mary Magdalene asks Jesus to describe the various regions of hell. Jesus replies: "The outer darkness is a huge dragon, with its tail in its mouth; it is outside the world and surroundeth it completely. There are many regions of punishment therein, for there are in it twelve dungeons of horrible torment. In each dungeon there is a ruler."

These rulers are, according to the *Pistis Sophia*, various demons who are then named and given elaborate descriptions.

The medieval machinery of hell passed on to the Protestant reformers, and even though they rejected the doctrine of Purgatory, they accepted the "devil and all his works."

In Islam the name given hell is Jahannam or Djahannam, derived from the Hebrew valley of Hinnom (Josh. 15:8) in the Old Testament. In many translations of the Koran the word is translated as hell or Gehenna.

The Koran frequently mentions Jahannam, although its precise physical image is unclear. Sometimes it appears to be a monster, as when in sura 139 Allah says Jahannam "shall be brought nigh" on the Day of Judgment. According to Islamic tradition Jahannam walks on four legs, each of which is bound by 70,000 rings. On each of them are 70 thousand demons, every one of which is strong enough to destroy mountains. A moving Jahannam makes buzzing, groaning, rattling sounds. Sparks and smoke come out of its mouth. When it is still separated from mortals by 1,000 years, it will break loose from the demons and throw itself on the people assembled for the Last Judgment.

*Heaven and Hell*

Alongside this image of a monster hell, resembling in many ways the Christian concept of a dragon-mouthed hell popular during the Middle Ages, is the belief that Jahannam has seven gates (sura 39). Islamic tradition has elaborated on the Koranic statement. Accordingly, Jahannam is situated under the pedestal of the world, above the bull Kuyuta and the fish Bahamut (corresponding to the Behemoth and Leviathan in the Bible), who support the earth. Jahannam is composed of seven stories forming a vast crater, where sinners are punished according to the kind and importance of their deeds, as in Dante's *Inferno*. The seven divisions of Jahannam are Jahannam proper, or Gehenna (sura 19), Lathâ, or the Flaming Fire (sura 70), Hutamah, or the Raging Fire that splits everything to pieces (sura 104), Sa'hîr, or the Blaze (sura 4), Saqar, or the Scorching Fire (sura 54), Gahîm, or the Fierce Fire (sura 2), and Hâiyeh, or the Abyss (sura 51).

Above the vast crater of Jahannam is Al-Sirat (or Se-Sirat, Arabic for "the path"), the bridge leading to paradise, the entrance of which is guarded by the angel Ridwan. Al-Sirat is "stretched over the back of Jahannam, sharper than a sword and finer than a hair. The feet of unbelievers slip upon it, by the decrees of Allah, and fall with them into the fire. But the feet of the believers stand firm upon it, by the grace of Allah, and so they pass to Abiding Abode."

At the lowest stage of Jahannam is a tree called Zakkum, which has heads of demons for flowers; a caldron of boiling and stinking pitch; and a well that reaches to the bottom of all things.

The time of punishment allotted to sinners varies with the interpretation of some Koranic texts. Sura 11 says: "The damned shall be cast into the fire . . . they shall dwell there so long as the heavens and the earth shall last, unless Allah wills otherwise." Yet another passage in the Koran (sura 23) reads: "Those who have destroyed themselves in Jahannam . . . shall dwell there forever."

See also: ABRAHAM; BALAAM; GNOSTICISM; ISAAC; JONAH; MOSES; MUHAMMAD; NOAH; PETER, ST.; RAMADAN; SALEH; SAMUEL; SHEOL; SAUL

1409
**Hebe** (youth)    In Greek mythology, cupbearer of the gods, daughter of Zeus and Hera. She was replaced in the position by the handsome youth Ganymede, whom Zeus abducted and raped. Hebe is cited in Milton's "L'Allegro" (26–29), Spenser's *Ruines of Time* (384–385) and Keats's *Endymion* (4.415–9). Hebe is sometimes referred to as the wife of Heracles after he was deified.

See also: GANYMEDE; ZEUS

1410
**Hebrus**    In Greek mythology, a river in Thrace with sand of gold. Orpheus's head, dismembered body, and lyre were thrown into the Hebrus by the Bacchants after they tore him to pieces. The river received its name from Hebrus, son of Cassandra, and a king of Thrace, who was said to have drowned himself there. Vergil's *Aeneid* (book 4) and Ovid's *Metamorphoses* (book 11) tell of the river.

See also: *AENEID, THE;* CASSANDRA; ORPHEUS; OVID

1411
**Hecate** (she who works her will)    In Greek mythology, pre-Hellenic goddess of the underworld, later identified as a form of Artemis. In some accounts she is said to be the daughter of Perses and Asteria or of Zeus and Demeter. Hecate was worshiped at crossroads and portrayed as a three-headed or three-bodied woman. Her functions and powers are described in detail in Hesiod's *Theogony*. The heroine in Euripides' *Medea* invokes Hecate, who was noted for her black magic and sorcery. In Shakespeare's *Macbeth* (3.5) Hecate appears as queen of the witches. In *King Lear* (1.1.112) the old king says: "For, by

the sacred radiance of the sun, / The mysteries of Hecate, and the night." William Blake's watercolor illustrating *Macbeth* also portrays the dark goddess. Hecate's epithets were Enodia (the wayside goddess) and Trioditis (goddess of the meeting of three routes).

See also: ASTERIA; DEMETER; MEDEA; ZEUS

1412
**Hecatommithi** (hundred tales)    An Italian collection of tales by Giambattista Giraldi Cinthio (1504–1573) that contains many European folk motifs. The collection influenced the English collection *Palace of Pleasure* (1566), providing Shakespeare with plots for *Othello* and *Measure for Measure*.

See also: MOTIF

*Hector and Ajax (John Flaxman)*

1413
**Hector** (holding fast)    In Greek mythology, eldest son of King Priam of Troy and Hecuba; brother of Aesaus, Cassandra, Creusa, Deiphobus, Helenus, Paris, Polydorus, Polyxena, and Troilus; married to Andromache; father of Astyanax (Scamandrius). Hector is the Trojan hero of Homer's *Iliad*. He was killed by Achilles and his dead body dragged around the walls of Troy. King Priam asked for his son's body, and Hector's funeral ends Homer's epic. Numerous episodes from his life appear in art and literature: the slaying of Patroclus (Achilles' male lover); Hector's combat with Ajax; his farewell to King

Priam and Hecuba; his farewell to his wife, Andromache; his death; and King Priam begging Achilles for his son's body. Hector appears in Homer's *Iliad*, Vergil's *Aeneid* (book 1), Ovid's *Metamorphoses* (books 13, 14), and Shakespeare's bitter play *Troilus and Cressida*, which ends with "Hector is dead; there is no more to say."

See also: ACHILLES; ANDROMACHE; ASTYANAX; CASSANDRA; HECUBA; *ILIAD, THE*; OVID; PARIS; POLYXENA; PRIAM

*The meeting of Hector and Andromache*

1414
**Hecuba** (Hekabe) (moving far off)    In Greek mythology, second wife of King Priam of Troy, mother of 19 of his 50 sons and 12 of his daughters; daughter of Dymas of Phrygia and Evagora or Glaucippe, of the river god Cisseus, or of the river god Sangarius and Metope; sister of Asius. Among her children are Hector, Paris, Cassandra, Polydorus, and Polyxena. After the fall of Troy she was taken into captivity by the victorious Greeks. She witnessed the death of her daughter Polyxena and discovered that her son Polydorus had been treacherously murdered by the Thracian king Polymnestor. Insane with sorrow, Hecuba beguiled Polymnestor into a secret place and tore out his eyes. While she was railing at the Greeks, she was transformed into a bitch. Hecuba appears in Euripides' plays *The Trojan Woman* and *Hecabe* and Ovid's *Metamorphoses*

(book 13) and is frequently cited by Shakespeare in his plays.

See also: CASSANDRA; HECTOR; PARIS; POLYXENA; PRIAM; TROY

1415
**Hegira** (Hijra) (departure)    Term used in Islam for the migration from Mecca to Yathrib, later Medina, made by Muhammad. The day of his arrival at Medina is not precisely known—16 June in some accounts and 30 September in others. The year usually assigned to it is 622. All dates in Islam are reckoned from the Hegira.

See also: MUHAMMAD

1416
**Heidrun** (Heithron) (bright)    In Norse mythology, a she-goat who provides mead for Valhalla. According to the *Prose Edda*, she "feeds on the leaves of a very famous tree called Laerath, and from her teats flows mead in such great abundance that every day a caldron, large enough to hold more than would suffice for all the heroes, is filled with it."

See also: EINHERJAR; *PROSE EDDA*; VALHALLA

1417
*Heiki-Monogatari*    (tales of the Heike clan) 13th century. Japanese historical romance telling of the conflict between the Heike (Taira) and the Minamoto (Genji) families.

The work was one of the most popular in medieval Japan, recited by minstrel-priests. It tells how the Heike, an all-powerful family in Japan, are eventually brought low. The novel places heavy emphasis on Buddhist thought, particularly on the evanescence of worldly glory. Toward the close of the work the Cloistered Emperor states: "All these pleasures too were as fleeting as empty dreams of dreams and empty delusions of delusions. All is vanity, as evanescent as the eternal turning of the wheel. Sad are the Five Signs of Decay for celestial beings! How much more so should it be for us, the sentient beings of the world!" (Hiroshi Kitagawa and Bruce Tsuchida translation).

The influence of *Heike-Monogatari* on later Japanese literature was immense. Many of its episodes supplied plots for No plays and later drama. Two other works, the *Gempei Seishuiki* (Records of the Rise and Fall of the Minamoto and Taira Clans) and *Heiji Monogatari* (Tales of Heiji) deal with the same subject.

See also: NO

1418
**Heimdall** (world gleam)   In Norse mythology, one of the Aesir, the son of nine mothers, the god who acts as watchman for the gods; sometimes called Rig. He has nine lives. It is his job to announce with his horn, Gjallar-horn, the approach of the frost giants when they come to battle the gods at Ragnarok, the end of the world. Heimdall will be killed by the evil god Loki, who in turn will be killed in battle.

The *Prose Edda* describes Heimdall as a "powerful deity" who "requires less sleep than a bird and sees by night as well as by day, a hundred miles around him. So acute is his ear that no sound escapes him, for he can even hear the grass growing on the earth and the wool on a sheep's back." He sacrificed one of his ears in the well under Yggdrasil, just as Odin had sacrificed one eye.

In the *Poetic Edda* the poem *Rigsthula* (The Song of Rig) tells how Heimdall repopulated the earth after some disaster. He fathers serfs, freemen, earls, and kings. Heimdall lives in Himinbjorb (heaven's cliffs) at the end of Bifrost; his horse is called Gulltopp and his sword, Hofund (head).

See also: BIFROST; GJALLAR-HORN; LOKI; *POETIC EDDA*; *PROSE EDDA*; RAGNAROK

1419
**Heinrich von Aue** (home ruler)   In medieval northern legends, hero who appears in a 12th-century poem, *Der arme Heinrich*. Heinrich was a nobleman who was struck with leprosy. He was

told that only a virgin who would die in his place could restore his health. He did not believe that any such thing would happen, and he gave away all of his riches to the poor. He went to live with a poor tenant farmer who was one of his vassals. The daughter of the farmer learned of the remedy and offered to die in Heinrich's place. When this was known, Heinrich was cured. Longfellow, in his poetic drama *The Golden Legend* (not to be confused with the medieval collection of saints' lives) used the legend as the basis for his plot. In some medieval accounts Heinrich is called Prince Henry of Hoheneck.

*Hel (Johannes Gehrts)*

1420
**Hel** (Hela, Hell) (concealer)   In Norse mythology, goddess of death; daughter of the evil god Loki and the giantess Angurboda; sister of Fenris and the serpent Midgard. Hel ruled over Nifelheim, where Odin gave her power over nine worlds or regions. Hel originally meant "grave," with the personification coming later. She lives

under one root of Yggdrasil, the frost giants live under another, and humans live under a third root. The *Prose Edda* says "all who die through sickness or old age" are Hel's subjects. Matthew Arnold in his narrative poem *Balder Dead* writes:

Hela into Niflheim thou threw'st And gav'st her nine unlighted worlds to rule, A queen, and empire over all the dead.

Hel lived in the palace called Elvidner (misery); her dish was Hunger and her knife, Starvation. She fed on the brains and marrow of people. Hel was believed to leave her home occasionally to roam the earth on her three-legged white horse. In times of pestilence or famine she was said to be using a rake if a part of the population escaped death, and a broom when whole villages and provinces were depopulated, as during the Black Death of the Middle Ages. The English word *hell* comes from the name of the goddess.

See also: ANGURBODA; FENRIR; MIDGARD; NIFELHEIM; *PROSE EDDA*

*Invention of the Cross*

1421

**Helena, St.** (bright one) c. 255–330. In Christian legend, empress, mother of the emperor Constantine; patron saint of dyers, nailsmiths, and needle makers. Invoked against fire and thunder. Feast, 8 August.

The legend of St. Helena is bound up in the discovery of the true cross. According to the account in *The Golden Legend*, written in the 13th

*St. Helena (Dürer)*

century by Jacobus de Voragine, Helena was probably of British birth, though her parentage and place of birth are still disputed. She married Constantius Cholorus and was the mother of Constantine the Great. Her great desire was to find the actual cross on which Jesus had been crucified. She went to Jerusalem with an army and found three crosses at Calvary. To find out which one of the three was Jesus' cross, she had each cross touch the body of a dead man. When the true cross touched the dead body, the man came back to life. She gave part of the true cross to her son Constantine as well as the nails. Her finding of the true cross was celebrated by a Christian feast observed on 3 May called Invention of the Cross, from Latin *invenire*. The feast was abolished in 1960 by the Roman Catholic Church as having no historical foundation. St. Helena is often portrayed holding a large cross. She wears a crown and imperial robes. Paolo Veronese, Agnolo Gaddi, and Piero della Francesca all painted scenes from her life and legend.

The Island of St. Helena in the South Atlantic was discovered on St. Helena's Day in 1501 by the Portuguese. Napoleon was exiled to this island in 1815 and lived there until he died in 1821.

See also: CONSTANTINE THE GREAT; *GOLDEN LEGEND, THE*

*Aphrodite presenting Helen to Paris*

1422

**Helen of Troy**   In Greek mythology, the most beautiful woman in the world; daughter of Zeus and Leda; married to Menelaus; mother of Hermione, Pleisthenes, and Nicostratus.

Zeus, in the form of a swan, seduced Leda, who produced two eggs. From the first hatched Helen and her brother Polydeuces (or Pollux). From the second egg came Clytemnestra and Castor. (The second egg, according to some accounts, was fathered by Tyndareus, the king of Sparta and husband of Leda.) When Helen was a young girl she was abducted by Theseus and Pirithous and rescued by her brothers Castor and Polydeuces, the Dioscuri. In some accounts she was the mother of Iphigenia by Theseus. She was so beautiful that all the available princes in Greece wished to marry her. To calm the intense rivalry Odysseus had all of the suitors swear to support the husband whom Helen would choose and to avenge any wrong to the couple caused by the marriage. After the agreement Helen chose Menelaus, brother of Agamemnon, who was husband of her sister Clytemnestra. Helen and Menelaus seemed to live happily until the day Paris abducted her. (Paris had been promised Helen by Aphrodite as a reward for naming Aphrodite the "fairest" in the Judgment of Paris.) Some accounts say Helen accompanied Paris willingly to Troy; others say she was taken by force. In any event, Menelaus rallied all of Greece to his aid, and the result was the Trojan War.

While in Troy, Helen bore Paris many children, all of whom died in infancy. After Paris's death she was briefly married to Deiphobus. When Troy fell through the trick of the wooden horse, Helen was returned to her husband Menelaus, who took her back as if nothing had happened. She then lived with Menelaus until her death. But some accounts say Helen was hanged by the maids of Argive Polyxo to avenge the death of Tlepolemus at Troy.

Some scholars believe Helen was originally a pre-Greek goddess with a tree cult (one in which the goddess was hanged from a tree, which might account for one version of her death) who was worshiped in Laconia and Rhodes. In the Homeric epics, however, Helen is entirely human. Homer's *Iliad* mentions that the Trojans treated her kindly, and in the *Odyssey* she is described as a hospitable wife. A later myth not included in Homer, devised to save her reputation, says that a phantom, not the real Helen, went to Troy. This myth is cited in Plato's *Phaedrus* and is followed in Euripides' *Helen* and Richard Strauss's opera *Die Ägyptische Helena* (The Egyptian Helen) with a libretto by Hofmannsthal. In general, however, most poets take a judgmental view of her behavior, among them Ovid, Seneca, and Vergil. She appears in Euripides' *Helen*, Ovid's *Heroides* (16), Shakespeare's *Troilus and Cressida*, W. B. Yeats's "Leda and the Swan," Tennyson's "A Dream of Fair Women," Brooke's "Menelaus and Helen," and Lang's *Helen of Troy*. Dante (Hell, Second Circle) places Helen among those driven by lust. Ronsard's *Sonnets pour Hélène* were written for Hélène de Surgeres, his last love. In Goethe's *Faust* (Part 2) Faust marries Helen, who symbolizes all that is most beautiful in ancient Greek life. In Marlowe's play *Dr. Faustus* Helen also appears to Faust, and hers is "the face which launched a thousand ships." Homer never describes her features, and she has not frequently appeared in art, though David's *Paris and Helen* portrays the couple, and a work from the school of Fra Angelico portrays *The Rape of Helen*.

See also: AGAMEMNON; APHRODITE; CASTOR AND POLYDEUCES; DIOSCURI; *ILIAD, THE*; IPHIGENIA; LEDA; MENELAUS; ODYSSEUS; *ODYSSEY, THE*; PARIS; SWAN; TROY; ZEUS

1423
**Helenus** (of the moon?)   In Greek mythology, a Trojan soothsayer, king of Epirus; son of King Priam and Cassandra, his twin; married to Andromache after both had been given as slaves to Pyrrhus, father of Cestrinus. Helenus said Troy could not be taken by the Greeks unless the sacred Palladium (an image of Athena) was removed from it. He was the only one of Priam's children to survive the war, and he entertained Aeneas on his way from Troy to Italy. He gave Aeneas a plumed helmet. Homer's *Iliad* (book 6), Vergil's *Aeneid* (book 3), and Ovid's *Metamorphoses* (book 13) tell of Helenus.

See also: AENEAS; *AENEID, THE*; ANDROMACHE; ATHENA; CASSANDRA; *ILIAD, THE*; OVID; PRIAM

1424
**Heliades**   In Greek mythology, Aegiale, Aegle, and Aetheria, sisters of Phaethon and daughters of Apollo (or Helios) and Clymene. They grieved so much over Phaethon's death that they were transformed into poplars. Ovid's *Metamorphoses* (book 2) tell of their fate.

See also: APOLLO; OVID; PHAETHON

1425
**Helios** (sun)   In Greek mythology, a Titan sun god, son of the Titans Hyperion and Theia; brother of Eos and Selene; married to Perseis (Perse); father of Aëtes, Circe, Phaethon, Pasiphaë, and Perses, as well as of seven sons by Rhode and several daughters by Clymene and Naera. In classical mythology the Greeks identified Helios with Apollo or Hyperion. When Zeus divided the universe, Helios was either away or forgotten, and therefore he received no

part. To appease him Zeus gave Helios the island of Rhodes, his main cult center, where the Colossus at Rhodes was dedicated to his worship. Helios drove across the sky each day in his quadriga, a four-horse chariot. In Roman mythology he was also called Sol. Among his epithets are Acamas (untiring), Panderces (all-seeing), and Terpimbrotos (he who makes mortals rejoice). In his *Laws* Plato advocates a cult of Apollo and Helios, so as to combine ancient ritual and rational thought. Spenser's *Prothalamion* (4) and Robert Herrick's "Corinna's Going a-Maying" cite the god.

See also: APOLLO; COLOSSUS AT RHODES; EOS; HYPERION; PASIPHAË; PHAETHON; SELENE; TITANS; ZEUS

1426
**Heliotrope** (turn-to-sun)   A fragrant, flowered herb of the borage family. In Greek mythology, the sun god Apollo and his love, the water nymph Clytie, account for the heliotrope's origin. The nymph fell in love with the god and he with her, but in a short time Apollo grew tired of the girl. She then sat on a riverbank for nine days and nights, taking neither food nor water nor sleep, only watching the chariot of Apollo move across the heavens from sunrise to dusk. The gods, taking pity on her, turned her into a flower, a heliotrope. A bloodstone, green quartz with red veins, used to be called a heliotrope. When it was placed in water, it turned the sun's rays to blood color. The stone also had the power to render its bearer invisible.

See also: APOLLO

1427
**Hemera**   In Greek mythology, a name for Day, a daughter of Erebus and Nox (night). Hemera, along with Aether (Light), dethroned their parents and seized control.

See also: NOX

**1428**

**Heng-Ê** In Chinese mythology, goddess of the moon, married to the Divine Archer, Hou-I. She stole the drug, or dew, of immortality, fleeing to the moon. In some accounts she is said to have been changed into a frog or toad, though the moon in Chinese mythology is also inhabited by a hare. She is sometimes portrayed as a human figure riding a three-legged frog.

**1429**

**Hengist and Horsa** (stallion and horse) In Anglo-Saxon mythology, semilegendary leaders of the Jutes, who landed in England in 449. Horsa died in the battle of Aylesford c. 455, while Hengist ruled in Kent until his death in 488. Their cult may have sacrificed horses as part of their ritual. There were many twin legendary figures in antiquity, such as the Dioscuri Castor and Pollux, Romulus and Remus, and others.

See also: CASTOR AND POLYDEUCES; HADDING-JAR; ROMULUS AND REMUS

**1430**

**Henry, St.** (home ruler) 972–1024. In Christian legend, Emperor Henry II, husband of St. Cunegund. Feast, 15 July.

Elected emperor in 1002, Henry fought against the pagans of Poland and Franconia, aided by Sts. Lawrence, George, and Adrian. He married Cunegund, and both took vows of chastity. Once the devil convinced Henry that Cunegund had committed adultery with their bishop. Henry commanded his wife "to walk barefoot upon white-hot plowshares a distance of 15 feet." Cunegund called on Christ to vindicate her honor. In anger Henry struck her cheek, but a voice from heaven called out: "The Virgin Mary has delivered Cunegund who also is a virgin." At Henry's death a host of demons arrived to carry off his soul, but St. Lawrence brought a golden bowl and placed it on the balance scales in favor of Henry. The emperor's soul then fled to heaven. A year after his death, Cunegund became a nun.

Henry is portrayed in medieval art in complete armor with his imperial crown, sword, and orb. He is often shown bearing a model of Bamberg cathedral, which he founded.

See also: ADRIAN, ST.; GEORGE, ST.; LAWRENCE, ST.

*Thetis and Eurynome receiving the infant Hephaestus (John Flaxman)*

**1431**

**Hephaestus** (fiercely shining) In Greek mythology, smith and fire god, son of Zeus and Hera or possibly of Hera alone; brother of Ares, Arge, Discordia, Eleithyia, and Hebe; married to Aphrodite; father of Eros by Aphrodite, of Camillus by Cabeiro, of Erichthonius by himself or Gaea or Attis, of Olenus and Tullius by Ocrisia, of the two Palici volcanoes by Aetna; also father of Cercyon. Hephaestus was called Vulcan or Mulciber by the Romans. He was born lame and ugly or was made lame by Hera, who was ashamed of his ugliness and threw him out of heaven into the sea, where he landed on the volcanic island of Lemnos. In a variant account Hephaestus's lameness resulted when his father, Zeus, flung him out of heaven for intervening in a fight between Zeus and Hera. After being thrown out of heaven, he lived for nine years with Thetis and Eurynome, water nymphs. He made numerous metal works for them including a metal throne, which was used to trap his mother, Hera. No one could free her except Hephaestus. Dionysus was called on, got Hephaestus drunk, and brought him back to Olympus, where he freed his mother from the seat. Hephaestus then was married to Aphrodite, goddess of love. The goddess, however, preferred Ares for her sexual partner. Aphrodite and Ares were discovered by Helios, the Titan sun god, who reported their affair to Hephaestus. Hephaestus placed a net over the bed in which the two deities were making love. Then he called the gods to witness the two in sexual intercourse. Some accounts say Hephaestus created Pandora, the first woman, or that he created mankind. Among Hephaestus's most famous artworks are the arms for Achilles, the arms for Aeneas, the shield of Heracles, the necklace (or girdle) of Harmonia, and the scepter of Agamemnon.

Hephaestus appears in Homer's *Iliad* and *Odyssey*, Hesiod's *Theogony*, the Homeric Hymns, Vergil's *Aeneid*, and Milton's *Paradise Lost* (book 1.742–46), where the poet captures Hephaestus's fall from heaven. Milton says Hephaestus was the architect of Pandemonium, the council hall of hell. In Greek art Hephaestus is often portrayed helping Zeus give birth to Athena or delivering Achilles' arms to Thetis.

See also: *AENEID, THE*; APHRODITE; ARES; ARGE; EROS; GAEA; HARMONIA; HEBE; HELIOS; HERA; *ILIAD, THE*; *ODYSSEY, THE*; PANDORA; VULCAN; ZEUS

*Hera*

1432

**Hera** (lady)   In Greek mythology, pre-Hellenic goddess, later said to be the wife of Zeus; sister of Demeter, Hades, Hestia, Poseidon, and Zeus. In Roman mythology, she is called Juno. Her four children by Zeus are Hephaestus, Hebe, Ares, and Ilithyia (Eileithyia). She was the daughter of Cronus and Rhea, according to Hesiod's *Theogony* (454). Hera's main function was as goddess of marriage and the sexual life of women. In many Greek myths she always appears at odds with her wandering husband Zeus, constantly persecuting his numerous mistresses and their children. Like Zeus, she was swallowed at birth by her father, Cronus, and rescued by Zeus, who later, in the form of a cuckoo, seduced her. Hera is portrayed in Greek and Roman art as a large, majestic woman, fully clad, wearing a diadem (in Greek archaic art sometimes a *polos*). Among her attributes are the crow, the cuckoo, the peacock (because she set the 100 eyes of the all-seeing Argus in its tail), and the pomegranate (symbol of fruitfulness). Hera was worshiped throughout Greece. Her most famous temples were at the Heraeum at Nemea in the Argolid, the great temple on the island of Samos, and the temple at Olympia. At her Greek festival, the Heraia, a shield was given as the prize in an athletic contest. Her most common Homeric epithet is "ox-eyed," and she is also known as Parthenia, referring to her role as a bride. In Spenser's poem *Epithalamion* he asks for the goddess's blessing on his marriage. Hera also appears in Tennyson's *Oenone*.

See also: ARES; ARGUS; CUCKOO; DEMETER; HADES; HEBE; HEPHAESTUS; HESIOD: HESTIA; PEACOCK; POMEGRANATE; POSEIDON; ZEUS

*Heracles*

1433

**Heracles** (glory of Hera)   In Greek and Roman mythology, hero noted for his immense strength. The Roman spelling of his name, Hercules, is frequently encountered in English literature. He was the son of Zeus and Alcmena. Alcmena had been seduced by Zeus when he assumed the form of her husband, Amphitryon. Heracles was loved by his father, Zeus, but Hera, Zeus's ever-jealous wife, constantly sought Heracles' destruction. She sent two serpents to kill Heracles, but the child strangled them with his bare hands. When he was a youth, Heracles killed the Thespian lion that had been ravaging

Amphitryon's flocks. He then wore its skin as a cloak, with the lion's head forming a hood. At one point Hera caused Heracles to go mad, leading him to kill his wife, Megara, and their children. As penance he had to submit to 12 labors under Eurystheus. The first labor was to slay the Nemean lion. He drove it into a cave, strangled it, and then skinned it. The second labor was to slay the Lernaenan Hydra, a many-headed monster that grew a new head to replace each one decapitated. Heracles cut off each head while his charioteer, Iolaus, seared the stump with pitch so that another head could not grow. The third labor was to capture the Erymanthian boar alive. Heracles captured it and returned with it to Eurystheus, who jumped into a jar out of fright at the sight of it. The fourth labor was to capture alive the golden-horned Cerynean hind. He pursued it for a year and finally captured it at a stream as it was drinking. The fifth labor was to drive off the bronze-beaked, arrow-feathered birds infesting the Stymphalian marsh. Athena gave Heracles a bronze rattle that when shaken startled the birds. They rose in flight, and Heracles killed many with arrows. The rest fled to the Black Sea. The sixth labor was to clean, in one day, the dung of 3,000 cattle from the stables of King Augeas of Elis. The hero diverted the rivers Peneus and Alpheus from their regular courses and sent them to clean the stables. When Augeas refused to pay Heracles one-tenth of the herd, Heracles killed him. The seventh labor was to capture the mad Cretan bull. Heracles brought it back to Eurystheus, who let it loose to ravage the land. It was later killed by Theseus. The eighth labor was to kill the man-eating mares of King Diomedes of Thrace. Heracles caught the king and fed him to the mares. The ninth labor was to capture the girdle of the Amazons. Heracles went to Queen Hippolyta, who possessed the girdle and was willing to give it to him. Hera, still jealous, convinced the Amazons that their queen was going to be killed. They attacked Heracles; he defeated them and killed Hippolyta. He took the girdle along with Antiope, sister of Hippolyta, as captive. The girdle was given to Admente, and Antiope was married to Theseus. The tenth labor was to fetch the red cattle of Geryon. The monster Geryon, who had three bodies, lived at Gades. His cattle were guarded by the two-headed dog Orthus and a shepherd, both of whom were slain by Heracles. The eleventh labor was to gather the Golden Apples of the Hesperides. The Golden Apples were guarded by a dragon, which Heracles slew, but the apples were later returned by Athena to the garden because they were sacred and could not survive except in the garden. The twelfth labor was to fetch the dog Cerberus from the underworld. Purifying himself at the mysteries of Eleusis, Heracles, guided by Hermes and Athena, descended to Hades and captured the monster, which was later returned to the underworld.

*Nemean lion*

Other adventures in Heracles' life were his joining of the Argonaut expedition for a short time under Jason, his madness when he killed his male lover Iphitus, and his return to the Oracle at Delphi to seek a cure. When the priestess refused an answer, Heracles seized the sacred tripod, saying he would set up another oracle. Apollo rushed in, and Heracles fought the god, only to be stopped by a thunderbolt hurled by Zeus. The priestess then gave Heracles the oracle he wished. Heracles assisted the gods in their battle against the giants. He married Deianira, Meleager's sister, who bore him five children. Believing it would restore his love for her, she sent her husband a poisoned robe that burned his flesh. While the flames arose, a cloud descended, and Heracles was welcomed in heaven. Hera was then reconciled to the hero, who later married Hebe, goddess of youth and spring. Heracles was popular in Greek cult, where he was a demigod, and among the Romans as a hero who fought against evil.

Heracles appears in Sophocles' *Trachinian Women* and *Philoctetes*, Euripides' *Alcestis* and *The Madness of Heracles*, and Seneca's *Hercules Furens*. In the Middle Ages and the Renaissance, Heracles' myth inspired Chaucer's *Monk's Tale* and part of the incomplete *Canterbury Tales*, which gives a summary of his life and deeds. In art perhaps the most famous image of the hero is the Farnese Heracles, discovered in 1540 in the Baths of Caracalla in Rome. It portrays the hero leaning on a club after his 12 labors, and it is ascribed to the Athenian sculptor Glycon (first century B.C.E.). The myth of the Choice of Heracles, first written down by Xenophon in his *Memoirs of Socrates*, tells how the hero was approached by two beautiful women before his 12 labors. One woman offered Heracles pleasure and a life of ease, and the other offered him a life of duty and labor for humankind. Obviously, the hero chose duty, as portrayed in two cantatas called *The Choice of Heracles*, one by Bach and one by Handel.

See also: ALCMENA; AMPHITRYON; ATHENA; DIOMEDES; GOLDEN APPLES OF THE HESPERIDES; HADES; HESPERIDES; HERMES; HERA; ZEUS

1434

**Hermaphroditus**   In Greek and Roman mythology, son of Hermes and Aphrodite. He was a half-man, half-woman divinity, having been united with the nymph Salmacis to form a hermaphroditic being. Some scholars believe the myth is derived from some ancient marriage rites in which the couples exchanged clothing. The myth is told in Ovid's *Metamorphoses* (book 4). Many ancient statues portrayed Hermaphroditus. Bartholomeus Spranger's *Hermaphoditus and Salmacis* (c. 1581) portrays the two near the nymph's pool. After the two were united, the pool weakened all who drank from it. Spenser's *Faerie Queene* took the idea of the enfeebling pool from the ancient myth. Hermaphroditus is also called Atlantiades and Atlantius.

See also: APHRODITE; HERMES; NYMPHS; OVID

1435

**Hermes** (stone)   In Greek mythology, messenger of the gods, son of Zeus and Maia; called Mercury by the Romans. Among Hermes' mistresses (and the offspring produced) are Acacallis (Cydon, possibly); Alcidamea (Bubus); Antianeira (Eurytus, Echion); Aphrodite (Hermaphroditus, Peitho); Carmenta (Evander); Chione (Autolycus); Chthonophyle (Polybus); Clytie (Myrtilus); Eupolemia (Aethalids); Herse (Cephalus, Ceryx); Penelope or Dryope (Pan); and Phylodameia (Pharis). He was also the father of Abderus, Arabus, Chryses, Daphnis, Eurymedon, Hapalycus, Nephalion, Philocaus, and possibly Silenus. Hermes is a complex god, his cult representing various aspects of godly patronage such as death, thievery, commerce, wealth, manual skill, and oratory. After his birth Hermes almost immediately stole Apollo's cattle. He invented the lyre, which he then gave to Apollo, who in turn gave Hermes the caduceus.

Hermes appears in *Hymn to Hermes* (one of the Homeric Hymns ascribed to Homer but not by him), and in Homer's *Odyssey* he is sent by Zeus to tell Odysseus to leave Calypso's island. In Vergil's *Aeneid*, under the name Mercury, he

tells the hero Aeneas to leave Dido and continue on his journey. His name is associated with *herma* (stone heap), because of the sound of the words. The herms were used as boundary stones and distance markers in Greece but eventually became anthropomorphic: in many ancient artworks, Hermes is portrayed as a herm, an ithyphallic stone column with a phallus attached, or sometimes he was portrayed entirely in phallic form. Of ancient artworks Praxiteles' statue of the nude Hermes holding the infant Dionysus is among the most famous. Renaissance artworks often portrayed Hermes as a graceful, vigorous young man with wings on his sandals and on the crown of his broad-brimmed hat, which came to symbolize his speed. In Roman art the staff (caduceus) came to symbolize the physician as well as the herald. Hermes had many epithets, among them: Argiphontes (slayer of Argus), Cylleneius, Epimelios (guardian of flocks), Hodios (patron of travelers and wayfarers), Nomios, Oneiropompus (conductor of dreams), and Psychopompus (conductor of souls to the underworld).

See also: APHRODITE; APOLLO; CADUCEUS; DAPHNIS; DIDO; DIONYSUS; HERMAPHRODITUS; MAIA; MERCURY; *ODYSSEY, THE*; PAN; PENELOPE; ZEUS

*Hermes weighing the souls of Achilles and Hector*

1436

**Hermes Trismegistus** (Hermes, three times great or very, very great) In Egyptian mythology, the Greek name for the god Thoth, who was identified by the Greeks with their god Hermes. He was believed to be the first magician and to have left a series of magical books for his followers. Longfellow's poem *Hermes Trismegistus* deals with the deity.

See also: HERMES; THOTH

1437

**Hermod** (courage in battle) In Norse mythology, a son of Odin and Frigga. A handsome god, Hermod was the messenger of the gods. He loved to enter battles and was often called "the valiant in combat." Aside from his helmet and corselet Hermod had a magic wand or staff, Gambantein, which he carried wherever he went.

Once, oppressed by fear of the future, Odin called on Hermod to put on his armor, saddle Sleipnir (the horse Odin alone was allowed to ride), and hasten off to the land of the Finns to see Rossthiof (the horse thief) for an answer to Odin's fear. Hermod hurried off, carrying not his magic wand, Gambantein, but Odin's runic staff. Rossthiof conjured up monsters to hinder Hermod, but Hermod soon mastered Rossthiof, binding him hand and foot and saying he would be set free only when he answered Hermod's questions. Rossthiof, seeing there was no hope of escape, pledged himself to do all Hermod wished. As soon as he was free again, he began to mutter incantations, which made the sun hide behind the clouds, the earth tremble, and storm winds rise.

Pointing to the horizon, Rossthiof asked Hermod to look, and the god saw a great stream of blood redden all the ground. While he was gazing at this, a beautiful woman suddenly appeared, and a moment later a boy stood beside her. To Hermod's amazement the child grew to full height in a moment and was carrying a bow and arrows.

Rossthiof said the blood portended the murder of one of Odin's sons, but if Odin wooed and won Rinda in the land of the Ruthenes (Russia), she would bear him a son who would attain his full growth in a few hours and avenge his brother's death.

Hermod rushed home to Odin and informed him of what had happened. Odin consoled himself, knowing that when one son died, another would avenge the death. There is considerable evidence that Hernod may once have been a human hero and not a god. Hermod appears in the *Poetic Edda*, the *Prose Edda*, and Matthew Arnold's narrative poem *Balder Dead*.

See also: *POETIC EDDA*; *PROSE EDDA*; RINDA; SLEPNIR

*Hero and Leander*

1438

**Hero and Leander** In Greek mythology, two lovers. Hero was a priestess of Aphrodite at Sestos when Leander fell in love with her. Each night he would swim from his home at Abydos on the opposite side of Hellespont to meet Hero, who guided him with a lit torch in her tower. One stormy night, however, Leander drowned, and Hero killed herself. The myth is told in Vergil's *Georgics* (3) and in Ovid's *Herodides* (18, 19). The most famous treatment in English literature is Marlowe's narrative poem *Hero and Leander* (1598), completed by Chapman. Other English poets who have treated the subject are Byron (who swam the Hellespont), Keats, Tennyson, and Dante Gabriel Rosetti. Mancinelli's opera *Ero e Leandro* (1896) also deals with the myth, as does an 1879 opera by Bottesini.

See also: APHRODITE; OVID

1439

**Heron**   A long-legged, long-necked bird having a long bill and large wings. In Egyptian mythology the heron was believed to house the *ba*, or soul. In *The Book of the Dead* there is a spell to help a deceased person effect transformation into a heron.

See also: BA; *BOOK OF THE DEAD, THE*

1440

**Hesiod**   Eighth century B.C.E. Earliest Greek poet after Homer. Hesiod is known for his *Works and Days* and *Theogony*, both of which deal with Greek mythology. Hesiod lived at Ascra in Boeotia, where he had a small farm on the slopes of Mount Helicon. According to the poet, the Muses visited him and gave him the gift of song. In his *Works and Days* he includes the myths of Pandora (he disliked women) and that of the Golden Age. Included in the work is the earliest Greek fable, The Hawk and the Nightingale. His other major work, the *Theogony*, is an attempt to systematize the genealogy of the gods leading to the kingship of Zeus over his father, Cronus. In this work he portrays the more sinister aspects of Greek mythology, such as castration, incest, child-swallowing, witchcraft, and human sacrifice, which were minimized or eliminated by Homer and later Greek and Roman authors. Scholars now believe that the fragments of a *Shield of Heracles* and a *Catalogue of Famous*

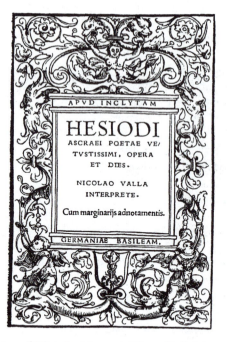

*Edition of Hesiod, title page (Hans Holbein)*

*Women* once ascribed to the poet are not by Hesiod.

See also: GOLDEN AGE; HOMER; MUSES; PANDORA

1441

**Hesione**   In Greek mythology, daughter of Laomedon, first king of Troy, and Strymo; sister of Astioche, Cilla, Clytius, Hicetaon, Lampus, Priam, and Tithonus; married to Telamon; mother of Teucer. Hesione was rescued from a sea monster by Heracles. When Heracles demanded payment, Laomedon refused, and the hero killed him and all of his sons except Priam. Hesione was then given by Heracles to his friend Telamon, and she was taken to Greece. Priam sent his son Paris to fetch her back, but Paris instead abducted Helen. Ovid's *Metamorphoses* (book 11) tells the tale.

See also: HELEN OF TROY; HERACLES; HESIONE; LAOMEDON; OVID; PARIS; PRIAM

1442

**Hesperides** (nymphs of the west)   In Greek mythology, guardians of the tree of Golden Apples in the garden at the world's end in the far west; daughters of Atlas and Hesperis. The Golden Apples were protected not only by the Hesperides, but also by a dragon, Ladon. For his twelfth labor Heracles, aided by Atlas, had to gather three of the Golden Apples. Heracles agreed to hold up the heavens in Atlas's place while Atlas took the apples. Vergil's *Aeneid* (book 4), Ovid's *Metamorphoses* (book 4), Milton's *Paradise Lost* (book 4), Pope's *Temple of Fame* (81), and William Morris's *Earthly Paradise* all cite the Apples of the Hesperides. Robert Herrick's *Hesperides*, a collection of Arcadian lyrics, was so named because it was written when he was the priest of a parish in the west of England. Shakespeare's *Love's Labour's Lost* (4.3.340–41) credits Heracles with gathering the apples: "For valour, is not Love a Hercules, / Still climbing trees in the Hesperides."

See also: *AENEID, THE*; ATLAS; GOLDEN APPLES OF THE HESPERIDES; HERACLES; HESPERIDES; LADON; OVID

*Hestia*

1443

**Hesperus** (evening)   In Greek and Roman mythology, the evening star, son of Astraeus and Eos, or Eos and Cephalius; father of Ceyx and grandfather of the Hesperides, who guarded the Golden Apples. Some Greek and Roman writers make Hesperus the morning star and use the name for the planet Venus. Homer's *Iliad* (book 22), Sappho's *Fragments* (95), Milton's *Paradise Lost* (book 4.605; book 9.49) and *Comus* (980–982), and Spenser's *Faerie Queene* (1.2.6) and *Epithalamion* (288) all refer to Hesperus, as well as others such as Shakespeare, Donne, and Jonson. The word *vesper* comes from Hesperus via Latin.

See also: ASTRAEUS; GOLDEN APPLES OF THE HESPERIDES; HESPERIDES; *ILIAD, THE*; VENUS

1444

**Hestia** (hearth)   In Greek mythology, one of the 12 Olympians; goddess of the hearth and home; firstborn of Cronus and Rhea; sister of Demeter, Hades, Hera, Poseidon, and Zeus. She was called Vesta by the Romans, and her shrine in Rome was kept by vestal virgins. There are no tales of her life, since she was a virgin who kept her vows.

See also: DEMETER; HADES; HERA; OLYMPIAN GODS; POSEIDON; VESTA; ZEUS

1445

**Hex** (six, witch)   In American folklore of the Pennsylvania Dutch, symbols and signs often found on Pennsylvania farm buildings, which are believed to protect animals from the Evil Eye and other spells. These symbols are also called barn art. The hex sign area includes all of Berks and Lehigh and portions of seven adjacent counties. The heaviest concentrations are found in the area of Old Route 22, called the "Hex Tour Highway." The Hex signs are drawn from a large repertoire of folk designs. The geometric patterns of quilts can easily be seen in the patterns of many hex signs.

1446

**Hex Chun Chan** (the dangerous one)   In Mayan mythology, a war god. In present-day folklore of the Mayans of Yucatán, he is a demonic spirit, greatly feared.

1447

**Hiawatha** (Haiowatha) (he makes rivers) 16th century? In North American Indian history and legend (Iroquois), founder of the League of Five, later Six, Nations, called the "League of the Long House": Mohawk, Oneida, Onondaga, Cayuga, Seneca, and Tuscarora, tribes occupying most of upstate New York.

According to Iroquois legend, Hiawatha was an Onondaga chieftain who sought the unity of various Indian tribes. At first he was violently opposed by the magician and war chief Atotarho, whose head was covered in snakes. Through his magic, Atotarho caused a gigantic white bird to kill Hiawatha's daughter. Hiawatha persisted with his crusade and converted the chief, Dekanawida (two river currents flowing together), and together they converted other tribes. Hiawatha then returned and converted Atotarho to the plan. Hiawatha combed the snakes out of Atotarho's hair, symbolizing his conversion. He then stepped into his white canoe and sailed away to the land of souls in the far west.

Henry Wadsworth Longfellow's narrative poem *The Song of Hiawatha* confused the historical Hiawatha with the god Manabozho, an Algonquian divinity, because his source, *Algic Researches* by H. R. Schoolcraft, was in error. Longfellow's poem has inspired many works, including parodies, beginning with Lewis Carroll's *Hiawatha Photographing*. A series of prints by

Currier & Ives deals with the poem. The work has been set to music and has inspired orchestral tone poems by Coerne, Delius, and Jong, among others. Samuel Coleridge-Taylor's *Scenes from the Song of Hiawatha* for chorus and orchestra is the best known.

See also: DEKANAWIDA; MANABOZHO

1448

**Hidari Jingoro** (Jingoro the left-handed) 1584–1634. Japanese sculptor.

According to legend, Jingoro once picked up a mirror that a girl had dropped in the street. On seeing the beautiful girl, he fell so deeply in love with her that he kept the mirror. He carved a wooden statue of her, and when the statue was completed he placed the mirror in a fold of its dress. Suddenly the statue came to life. For some time he was happy, but then his lord's daughter's head was demanded by an enemy of the lord or the enemy would destroy the princedom. Jingoro, an extremely loyal servant, cut off the living head of his statue. When the messenger who delivered the head to the enemy returned, he attacked Jingoro, thinking he had murdered the lord's daughter, and cut off Jingoro's right hand.

1449

**Hiisi** (Hisi, Lempo, Jutas) (dread place)   In the Finnish epic poem *The Kalevala*, the devil, sometimes called Juutas, from Judas, revealing the Christian influence on the final form of the epic. Hiisi is also used as a general term for demons who haunt Hittola (demon's domain), a dreary region with charred and burned heaths and hills, not far from Pohjola, the Northland.

*The Kalevala* (runes 13–14) tells of the Hiisi Elk, a magic elk created by Hiisi. The hero Lemminkainen had to subdue it to win the Maiden of Pohjola as his wife. Lemminkainen defeated the Hiisi Elk by the use of magic charms and prayers.

Hiisi originally referred to a sacred or sacrificial grove. In some parts of *The Kalevala* the term is used for dread or haunted places. Paha Mies (evil man) is another designation of the devil in

Finnish mythology. Paha Mies rules over Paha Valta, another name for hell.

See also: HITTOLA; JUDAS ISCARIOT; *KALEVALA, THE*; LEMMINKAINEN

**1450**

**Hikuleo**   In Polynesian mythology, Tongan god of the underworld, who lives in Pulotu, the land of the dead, believed to be an unseen island reached by boat.

**1451**

**Hilary of Poitiers, St.** (cheerful)   Fourth century. In Christian legend, Doctor of the Church. Patron of retarded children. Invoked against snakes. Feast, 14 January.

Hilary was bishop of Poitiers in France and author of numerous works dealing with Christian theology. One of the most fantastic elements in his legend is the "murder" of his daughter and wife, reported in *Les Petits Bolandistes* (vol. 1). St. Hilary had a daughter named Abra. When she reached marriageable age, the saint prayed that she might die, lest she should be corrupted by the world. His prayer was answered, and she died. His wife, "jealous of her daughter's happiness," asked her husband to pray that she might join her daughter. This he did, and his wife also died. One churchman, defending the saint's "murder" of his wife and daughter, wrote that the miracles were "more extraordinary than raising the dead to life." Brewer, however, in his *Dictionary of Miracles* writes that the saint "deliberately murdered both his victims."

Less gruesome than the deaths of his daughter and wife was the saint's power to drive serpents away in the manner of St. Patrick and his ability after death to rally forces against Alaric, the Arian king of the Goths, when he attacked Clovis, king of the Franks. The spirit of the saint appeared to Clovis and told him to "delay not, for as captain of the Lord's hosts am I come to thee this day, and the God of battles will deliver

the foe into thy hands." The saint's prediction proved true.

See also: PATRICK, ST.

**1452**

**Hilda, St.** (battle maid)   Seventh century. In Christian legend, abbess of Whitby Abbey. Feast, 17 November. Great granddaughter of King Edwin of Northumbria. Hilda could turn snakes into stone. When she died, her soul ascended to heaven in the company of angels. Medieval art portrays her with a royal crown at her feet or on her head to indicate her royal blood. She also holds a model of Whitby Abbey in her hand.

**1453**

**Hildebrandslied**   In German literary legend, a heroic lay in alliterative verse, recorded from oral sources around 800 C.E. The setting is the period of the Great Migrations (c. 350–500 C.E.), when a Germanic warrior named Hildebrand leaves his wife and young son to flee the Goth Odoacer's fury. He joins forces with Dietrich of Bern, king of the Ostrogoths, and only returns after many years. On a battlefield Hildebrand meets his own son, Hadubrand, who is also now a warrior. When Hildebrand asks his son who he is, telling him that he knows everyone in the clans, Hadubrand is immediately suspicious of the aging warrior. The father offers him rings of gold from around his arm, which he had earned in battles, but the son extends his spear to receive the gold, placing the spearhead in his father's face. A battle ensues, but the story breaks off before we know the ending. In at least two places in this ancient legend there are references that indicate that Christianity made an impact on the tale. Hildebrand speaks of "God . . . from heaven above," and a second time he says "Woe, almighty God, woeful fate." Most scholars see these statements as Christian overlay on an orally transmitted tale.

See also: DIETRICH OF BERN

**Hill, Joe**   1879–1915. In American history and folklore, folk hero of radical labor. Born in Sweden, Joel Hagglund came to the United States in 1902, where he first worked at a Bowery saloon in New York City. In 1910, he became a member of the Industrial Workers of the World, a labor organization also referred to as the Wobblies, and in 1911 he took part in the Mexican Revolution. He was charged with the murder of two men in Salt Lake City and later was shot by a firing squad. Some 30,000 people attended his funeral. On May Day of the same year they scattered his ashes in all states except Utah. He is the author of numerous labor songs, among them "The Union Scab," "The Tramp," and "Scissor Bill." His last telegram before his execution said: "Don't waste any time in mourning. Organize."

**Hino**   In North American Indian mythology (Iroquois), the thunderer. Armed with his mighty bow and flaming arrow, he was the eternal enemy of evil. Hino slew the great serpent of the waters, who was destroying the earth. Hino's wife is the rainbow, and his assistants are Oshadagea, the great dew eagle who lodges in the western sky and who carries a lake of dew in the hollow of his back, and Keneu, the golden eagle.

**Hinotama** (ball of fire)   During the internment of 19,000 Japanese Americans in Tule Lake, California, during World War II, stories common to rural Japan, but which had never been documented in the United States, began to appear in the camps. Stories of a ball of fire, interpreted as a ghost presaging death, were told along with stories of bewitchment, shape-shifters, omens, and so on. The graveyard area was considered especially dangerous, particularly during the period of citizenship renunciation.

One story of fireballs as bad omens near the latrine was recalled by an internee while walking to her apartment in Block 32: ". . . when something prompted her to look over her shoulder. She glanced up and was chilled by a strange glow hovering over the latrine roof. She shivered violently and hurried home to tell her mother, fully expecting her not to believe it. But her mother looked worried, opened the door, looked out but said nothing. The girl insisted on knowing what it was, and her mother told her she must have seen *hinotama*. A few days later an elderly bedridden block resident died."

See also: SHAPE-SHIFTER

**Hippogriff**   In Renaissance mythology, fantastic beast, half horse, half griffin, created by Ariosto in his epic *Orlando Furioso*. The hippogriff was sired by a griffin, and its mother was a mare. The beast had his father's feathers, wings, forelegs, head, and beak, but the rest was horse. Ariosto's imagination was stirred by Vergil's *Aeneid* with its poetic image to "cross griffins with horses," to signify something impossible.

See also: GRIFFIN

*Hippogriff*

**Hippolyte** (of stampeding horses)   In Greek mythology, the queen of the Amazons; daughter of Ares and Otrera; sister of Antiope and Penthesilea. Heracles' ninth labor was to obtain Hippolyte's magic girdle. According to one ancient account, Hippolyte was infatuated with Heracles and gave him her girdle, but when she came to deliver it to his ship, her women warriors thought she was being abducted. They attacked, and Heracles killed Hippolyte. Another account says Heracles gave her to Theseus in marriage, and she bore Hippolytus.

See also: AMAZONS; ANTIOPE; ARES; HIPPOLYTUS; PENTHESILEA; THESEUS

**Hippolytus** (of the stampeding horses)   In Greek mythology, son of King Theseus of Athens and Hippolyte, queen of the Amazons. Hippolytus was dedicated to chastity and worshiped the virgin goddess Artemis. Phaedra, his stepmother, fell madly in love with him, but he refused her advances. She then accused him of attempting to rape her. Theseus, convinced that Phaedra told the truth, prayed to his father, Poseidon, to kill Hippolytus as he drove from Athens to Troezen. Poseidon sent a sea monster, which frightened Hippolytus's horses, and he was flung from his chariot and dragged to his death. In Roman mythology Hippolytus is restored to life by Diana, the Roman counterpart of Artemis, and taken to her sacred grove in Aricia under the name Virbius. Hippolytus is the subject of Euripides' *Hippolytus*, Seneca's *Phaedra*, Racine's *Phèdre*, and Rameau's opera *Hippolyte et Aricie*, in which Hippolytus is restored to life.

See also: AMAZONS; ARTEMIS; DIANA; PHAEDRA; POSEIDON

**Hippolytus, St.** (horse destruction)   In Christian legend, patron saint of horses. Hippolytus was one of the jailers of St. Lawrence but was converted to Christianity by the saint. He helped bury the saint's body and was arrested as a result. The pagan judge "had Hippolytus tied by the feet to the necks of untamed horses, and dragged over thistles and thorns until he breathed his last," according to *The Golden Legend*, a book of saints' lives written in the 13th century by Jacobus de Voragine.

See also: GOLDEN LEGEND, THE; LAWRENCE, ST.

**Hippopotamus** (river horse)   A large mammal with a thick hairless body, found in and near rivers. In Egyptian mythology the hippopotamus had a dual role. Sometimes it was a beneficent being as symbol of the goddess Taurt, who aided women in childbirth. But it could also be a symbol of a demonic being as a form of the evil god Set. A form of Horus, called Her-tchema (Horus the piercer), referred to his role in spearing Set, who had assumed the form of a hippopotamus. Among Tutankhamen's treasures is a statue of a man, who may be the young Tut, holding a harpoon or lance pointed at an invisible foe, which may have originally been a figure of a hippopotamus, symbol of Set. In Edfu, a city sacred to Horus, harpooners were maintained whose duty it was to kill the animal. In the Old Testament the monster Behemoth is sometimes equated with the hippopotamus.

See also: HORUS; SET; TAURT; TUTANKHAMEN

**Hiru Ko no Kikoto** (Hirugo)   In Japanese mythology, eldest son of Izanagi and Izanami, the creator couple. He is sometimes credited with being the first fisherman.

See also: IZANAGI AND IZANAMI

**Hitomaru**   Seventh century C.E. In Japanese legend, deified poet invoked as the god of poetry. He was a foundling picked up at the foot of a persimmon tree by the warrior Abaye, who adopted him.

1464

*Hitopadesha* (book of good counsel)    Hindu collection of tales and fables, many of which are also found in the more popular collection *The Panchatantra*. Other stories were composed in Bengal between the 10th and the 13th centuries.

The setting for the collection of tales-within-a-tale is the court of King Sudarshana. One day the king discovered "that his sons were gaining no wisdom, nor reading the sacred Vedas, but were altogether going the wrong way." King Sudarshana decided to set his sons on the right path and chose a sage, Vishnu-Sharman, to instruct them. Vishnu-Sharman decided to enlighten the princes by telling them fables that would point out their duties. The book is divided into four sections: the winning of friends, the parting of friends, war, and peace. In his selection of the fables from the *Hitopadesha* included in *The Fables of India*, Joseph Gaer wrote: "The purpose of the book is to instruct. But the reason it survived through the centuries was not because it was so educational, but because it was so entertaining."

The tales bring out this point. The first, contained in part 1, is "The Jackal, Deer, and Crow."

Once there lived in a forest a deer, a crow, and a jackal. The deer and crow loved each other very much. One day the deer, roaming about, was seen by the jackal.

"Ho," thought the jackal on seeing how fat the deer was, "if I could but get this soft meat for a meal! It might be—if I can only win his confidence."

So the jackal went up to the deer. "Health be to you, dear friend," the jackal said to the deer.

"Who are you?" replied the deer.

"I'm Small-Wit, the jackal," he replied. "I live in the wood here, as the dead do, without a friend. But now that I have met you I feel as if I were beginning life again. Consider me your faithful servant."

"Very well," said the deer, and the two went off to the deer's house.

The crow, Sharpe-Sense, spotted the two and called out: "Who is this number two, friend deer?"

"It is the jackal," answered the deer, "that desires our acquaintance."

"You should not become friendly to a stranger without reason," said the crow. "Don't you know?

To folks by no one known house-room deny:
The vulture housed the cat, and thence did die."

The second tale, contained in part 2, is called "The Lion and the Old Hare," another fine example.

Once there was a lion, named Fierce-of-Heart, who made life very difficult for all of the animals because he massacred them all day long. It grew so bad that they all held a public meeting and drew up a respectful remonstrance to the lion.

"Wherefore should Your Majesty make carnage of us all?" they asked. "Let us daily furnish you with a beast for your meal."

"That arrangement is fine with me," the lion replied.

So each day the animals supplied the lion with one of themselves to eat. One day it was the old hare's turn to be eaten. He walked up to the lion at a very leisurely pace. The lion was very hungry and said, "How dare you take so long in coming?"

"Sire," relied the old hare, "I am not to blame. I was detained on the road by another lion, who exacted an oath from me to return when I should have informed Your Majesty."

"Go," replied the lion in a rage. "Show me instantly where this insolent villain of a lion lives."

The old hare took the lion to a place where there was a deep well and stopped. "Let my lord come hither," he said, "and behold the lion."

The lion approached the well and saw his own reflection in the water. He jumped into the well to attack what he believed to be another lion, and so he perished.

See also: FRAME TALE; *PANCHATANTRA, THE*; VEDAS

---

1465

**Hittola** (demon's domain)    In Finnish mythology, a dreary region with charred and burned heaths and hills, not far from Pohjola, the Northland. It is filled with demons.

---

1466

**Hkun Ai**    In Burmese mythology, a hero who married a Naga, a dragon woman, and fathered a king, Tung Hkam. Hkun Ai fell in love with a Naga princess and went to live in the kingdom of the Nagas. To make it easier for Hkun Ai, the king of the Nagas ordered all of the dragons to assume human form, which they did. At the time of the Nagas's water festival, however, they had to assume their dragon shapes. After seeing the Nagas sporting in the waters, Hkun Ai became gloomy and wanted to go home to his parents. His wish was granted. The Naga princess, however, said she would lay an egg from which a child would be hatched who could be fed with milk from Hkun Ai's little finger whenever he thought of her. A child was hatched from the egg and named Tung Hkam, or Golden Dead Leaves. When the boy grew up, he wanted to marry Princess Pappawadi, whose palace was surrounded by water and had to be reached without the use of bridge, boat, or raft. He called on his mother, who appeared and stretched her body from the shore to the palace on the island, and Tung Hkam walked over her to reach the princess, whom he married. Tung Hkam reigned for 72 years and was succeeded by two sons, Hkun Lu and after him Khun Lai.

See also: DRAGON; NAGA

---

1467

**Hlithskjolf** (Hlidskjalf) (watchtower)    In Norse mythology, the high seat of Odin chief of

the gods, in Valaskjalf from which he could overlook the nine worlds. Odin is referred to as the "Lord of Hlithskjolf."

See also: HUGIN AND MUNIN; ODIN

---

1468

**Hnossa** (jewel)    In Norse mythology, daughter of the goddess Freyja and Odur. According to the *Prose Edda*, she "is so very handsome that whatever is beautiful and precious is called by her name." The kenning for Freyja is "mother of Hnossa."

See also: FREYJA; KENNING; *PROSE EDDA*

---

1469

**Hodur** (Hod, Hoder) (battle)    In Norse mythology, a blind god, son of Odin and Frigga; twin brother of Baldur; tricked by the evil Loki, the fire god, into hurling mistletoe at Baldur, thus killing him. At Ragnarok, the end of the world, Hodur and Baldur will be reconciled when Hodur returns from death after being killed by Vali, and they will return to a purged cosmos.

See also: BALDUR; LOKI; RAGNAROK; VALI

---

1470

**Hoenir** (henlike)    In Norse mythology, an Aesir god, brother of Odin, who along with his other brother, Lodur, created Ask and Embla. Hoenir is called Vili (will) in the *Poetic Edda*. After the war between the Aesir and the Vanir, Hoenir went to live with the Vanir as part of an exchange of gods.

See also: AESIR-VANIR WAR; ANDVARI; ASK AND EMBLA

---

1471

**Hohodemi and Umi Sachi Hiko**    In Japanese mythology, rival brothers. Hohodemi was a great hunter and Umi Sachi Hiko was a great fisher. One day the two exchanged places, but Hohodemi lost the magical fishing hook of Umi Sachi Hiko, who then refused to return his magic bow and arrow. Hohodemi tried to propitiate his brother by making 500 new fishing hooks out of his sword, but Umi Sachi Hiko wanted his original hook. Hohodemi finally went down under the sea to Ryujin, the dragon king, who helped him find the lost hook, which was then returned to Umi Sachi Hiko. Ryujin also gave Hohodemi two jewels, one for the flowing and the other for the ebbing of the tides. With these magical jewels Hohodemi eventually became master of his brother.

1472

**Ho Ho Erh-Hsien** (the two immortals harmony and togetherness)    In Chinese mythology, patron gods of merchants, potters, and lime burners, portrayed as two short, fat, laughing men.

1473

**Ho Hsien-Ku** (the immortal lady Ho)    In Chinese Taoist mythology, one of the Pa-Hsien, the Eight Immortals. She achieved immortality after a course of lonely wandering among the hills, living on powdered mother-of-pearl and moonbeams. When called to court, she disappeared. She is portrayed with the lotus, her emblem, and invoked as the helper and guide to housekeepers.

See also: PA-HSIEN

*Ho Hsien-Ku*

1474

**Holy Grail**    In medieval Christian legend, talisman identified as the cup used by Jesus at the Last Supper and the object of a quest in many legends; often called the *Sangreal* (royal blood). The Grail is almost always associated with nourishment and can produce wished-for food or drink.

Although not all of the legends mention the origin of the sacred cup, a few trace it back to the creation of the world. They claim that, when Lucifer stood next to God the Father the other angels presented him with a beautiful crown, whose central jewel was a flawless emerald of great size.

When God the Father announced to his heavenly court that he was going to send his Son to earth, a war followed. Lucifer led the revolt against the Son and was cast out of heaven. During his fall to hell, the emerald dropped out of his crown and fell to earth. There it was fashioned into a cup or chalice used by Jesus at the Last Supper. When Jesus was dying on the cross, his side was pierced by the centurion Longinus, and Joseph of Arimathea caught a few drops of his blood, which flowed from his side into the cup. After the Crucifixion Joseph was locked in prison and was nourished by the Holy Cup, or Grail. He lingered some time in prison until Emperor Vespasian, hearing the tale of Christ, sent messengers to Palestine for relics, hoping to cure his son Titus of leprosy. Titus was cured by the magic handerchief of St. Veronica. Nevertheless, Titus searched out Joseph and freed him from prison. Fearful of being imprisoned again, Joseph embarked with his sister and his brother-in-law, Brons (derived from Bran, the name of the Celtic god), in a vessel bound for Marseilles. During their journey they had all of their needs supplied by the Holy Grail. On landing in France, Joseph was told by a heavenly messenger to construct a round table at which he and his companions could be seated, and the Holy Grail would supply each guest with the food he required. One seat at the table was to remain empty in memory of the traitor Judas. Only a sinless man could occupy the seat. Once a sinner attempted to sit in the seat and was swallowed up by the earth. Joseph was told that the enchanter Merlin would in time make a similar table, at which a descendant of Brons would have the honor of occupying this Siege Perilous.

From Marseilles the group slowly traveled to Glastonbury, England, with the Holy Grail. For some time it was visible to the people but then disappeared because of their sinful lives. It was borne off to Sarras, an island city (presumably located in the Mediterranean), where it was guarded, according to one legend, by King Evelake.

According to another medieval legend, a pilgrim knight laid a golden cross on the Holy Sepulcher, praying for a son. When his prayers were answered he named the boy Titurel and dedicated him to Christ. After Titurel had spent many years in warfare against the Saracens, an angel appeared to him and told him that he had been chosen to guard the Holy Grail, which was about to descend to earth once more and make its home at Montsalvatch. Impelled by this vision and led by a guiding cloud, Titurel set out on a quest for the holy mountain. After ascending the steep mountain, Titurel was given a glimpse of the Holy Grail. He was joined by a number of knights, who had been transported miraculously to the site. The knights, assisted by angels, erected a temple. As soon as it was completed the Holy Grail came down from heaven on a celestial beam of light and stayed in their midst.

Titurel, who was now fisher king and guardian of the sacred object, presided at the round table with the knights, who were miraculously fed by the Holy Grail. From time to time there appeared on the edge of the sacred cup, written in letters of fire, instructions bidding a knight to defend some innocent person or to right some wrong. The group was called the Knights of the Holy Grail. Guided by the Holy Grail, Titurel was told to marry. He chose a Spanish girl, by whom he had a son and daughter. The son, also marrying under divine guidance, had two sons and three daughters, one of whom became the mother of Perceval (Parzival).

Old and weary of kingship, Titurel resigned his office, first to his son, who was killed in war, and then to his grandson Amfortas. But Amfortas was restless and led a life of pleasure, neglecting his duties as keeper of the Holy Grail. Wounded by a thrust from a poisoned lance (in some accounts it is the lance of Longinus that wounded Jesus' side), Amfortas returned to Montsalvatch. His pain was intensified when he thought of his sins. One day he saw words on the rim of the cup that indicated his wound would be healed by a guileless fool.

The guileless fool was Perceval (Parzival), who after many adventures arrived at Montsalvatch. He was led into the banqueting hall and was awed by its splendor. Perceval noticed that his host, Amfortas, was suffering from some illness or wound. Then suddenly the doors opened wide, and a procession entered the hall. It circled the round table and went out again. In the procession were a servant who carried a lance, then some maidens who carried a stand for the Holy Grail, and finally the Holy Grail itself, brought in by Titurel's granddaughter.

After some time the knights were served food from the Holy Grail. When dinner was done, they left Perceval alone to ponder what the entire episode meant. Perceval ate and was taken to a room to sleep. When the next morning came, he found that the castle was deserted. The drawbridge opened as he left and closed after him, and he heard a voice cursing him but saw no one.

Perceval's sin was not asking Amfortas what ailed him. For this failing he had to do severe penance. After completing his penance he again arrived at the castle. Once more he entered the banqueting hall, and once more he beheld the procession. Strengthened by prayer, Perceval then asked the momentous question, whereupon Amfortas's wound was instantly healed, the aged Titurel was released from the pain of living, and Kundrie (the one who had cursed him earlier) was baptized. Perceval was then acclaimed the keeper of the Holy Grail.

Perceval's son Lohengrin, the Knight of the Swan, was another keeper of the Holy Grail, as was Galahad, the son of Lancelot of the Lake and Elaine. After Galahad's death, the Holy Grail returned to heaven. Originally, the Holy Grail had nothing to do with Christian legend. Some scholars connect it with the Celtic god Bran, who possessed a magic drinking horn in which "the drink and the food that one asked for, one received in it when one desired." When Christianity denied Bran's godhead, medieval folklore transformed him into an island king who possessed treasures and who sometimes fished from a boat in the river. One of his many treasures, sometimes assigned also to King Rhydderch of Strathclyde, who lived in the sixth century, was a platter on which "whatever food one wished thereon was instantly obtained," a cornucopia often found in Celtic legend. In popular lore a few objects have been associated with the Grail, such as a wooden cup in Wales and a green bowl in Genoa.

See also: AMFORTAS; ARTHUR; BRAN; ELAINE; GALAHAD; JOSEPH OF ARAMATHEA; JUDAS ISCARIOT; LANCELOT; LOHENGRIN; LUCIFER; PERCEVAL; TITUREL; VERONICA, ST.

**1475**
**Holy Innocents Day**    Christian feast celebrated 28 December remembering the children of Bethlehem "from two years old and under" who were slaughtered by the order of King Herod in his attempt to kill the infant Jesus (Matt. 2:16–18). In medieval English usage the name given to the day is Childermass (child's mass).

**1476**
**Homshuk**    In Mayan mythology of the Indians of Veracruz, Mexico, the corn spirit. Homshuk was at first opposed by the god Hurakán, who later accepted and took care of him because corn is necessary to maintain life.

See also: HURAKÁN

**1477**
**Ho-no-Ikazuchi**    In Japanese mythology, one of the Ikazuchi, the eight gods of thunder.

See also: IKAZUCHI

**1478**
**Horae** (hours, seasons)    In Greek mythology, children of Zeus and Themis; goddesses of the seasons, later of justice. Hesiod's *Theogony* names three: Eunomia (lawfulness), Dice (justice), and Eirene (peace). At Athens, Thallo (bloom), Auxo (growth), and Carpo (fruit) were added to the list. The Horae, along with the Moirae (the Fates), governed all human actions. Ovid's *Metamorphoses* (book 2.118) and Milton's *Comus* (986) cite the Horae. In Italian Renaissance art they are used to represent the four seasons as in the four statues on the S. Trinità bridge in Florence.

See also: EIRENE; EUNOMIA; HESIOD; OVID; THEMIS; ZEUS

**1479**
**Horai** (Horaizan)    In Japanese mythology, one of the three mountains in the Fortunate Islands of Paradise. It is the home of everlasting life, where live the crane, the tortoise, and the stag and where the plum tree, the pine, the peach, and mushrooms grow in profusion beside a jeweled tree.

**1480**
**Horatii**    Seventh century B.C.E. In Roman history and legend, three brothers who fought the three Curiatii. According to Livy's *History of Rome* (book 1), two of the Horatii were killed, but the third killed all of the Curiatii on the Alban side. As the victor returned to Rome, he met his sister, who was crying because she was to marry one of the Curiatii who had been killed. Horatius stabbed his sister for sympathizing with the enemy and was tried for murder by Tullus Hostilius, the third king of Rome; although acquitted, Horatius had to pass beneath a wooden beam as a symbol of expiation, and this became

known as the "sister's beam." Corneille's tragedy *Horace* and David's painting *The Oath of the Horatii* deal with the legend.

**Horatius Cocles** (one-eyed)   In Roman history and legend, hero who held the Etruscans at bay on the wooden Sublician bridge. He held the bridge until it was cut down behind him, and then he swam across the Tiber to safety. The legend is told in Livy's *History of Rome*; it inspired Macaulay's poem in the *Lays of Ancient Rome* and a painting by Géricault.

See also: LIVY

**Horus** (that which is above)   In Egyptian mythology, the hawk, or falcon, god. Horus is a Latin form of a Greek word for the Egyptian name Heru, or Hor. Originally, Horus was a local god who was worshiped along the delta region of the Nile. Eventually, his cult spread throughout Egypt and was carried into Roman times, when he was worshiped along with his mother, Isis.

*Horus*

The falcon, or hawk, one of the first animals worshiped in Egypt, was said to be the personification of the god Heru, who made the sky. In predynastic times there arose several hawk deities, among the most important being the falcon god at Hierakonpolis in Upper Egypt, where Horus took on the form of a solar disk with wings. When the kings of the south moved into Lower Egypt, uniting the two lands, Horus became known as the Uniter of the South and North, or Upper and Lower Egypt.

He was sometimes said to be the son of the cow goddess Hathor, whose name literally means "house of Horus." Each evening he would fly into the goddess's mouth, and each morning he would emerge reborn. In the most famous myth associated with him, however, Horus is the son of the god Osiris and the goddess Isis, and he avenges his father's murder by defeating the demonic god Set in a series of battles. Thus, Osiris is identified with the dead king and Horus with the living king. Sometimes the living king was said to embody within himself both Horus, the spirit of light, and Set, the spirit of darkness, reflecting the eternal strife that is always present in the universe. In his role as defeater of Set, Horus is variously portrayed as a mounted warrior with the head of a falcon and as a falcon-headed man with a large pointed spear driven into some foe. In one version of the myth, Horus had his left eye, which signified the moon, wounded in his battle with Set, thus giving rise to one explanation for the moon's various phases. The eye was healed by the god Thoth, and the restored eye, known as the *udjat*, became a powerful amulet.

Various "Horus gods" also appear in Egyptian mythology. Originally, many of them were separate deities, but eventually they were all blended into one and were considered various aspects of the same god. Among them are Harpokrates, Harsiesis (Horus the son of Isis), Harmachis (Horus who is on the horizon), Haroeris (Horus the elder), Horus-Behdety (Horus of Behdet), Horus Khenty en Maathyu (Horus at the head of those who see not?, also called blind Horus), Horus Khenty Khat (Horus at the head of the belly?), and Horus Netcher Nedjeitef (Horus the god, he who avenges his father).

See also: HATHOR; ISIS; OSIRIS; SET; THOTH

1483

**Hotai**   In Japanese folklore, a being with a monkey's body and a human head with long hair.

1484

**Hotaru Hime**   In Japanese folklore, daughter of Hi O, king of the fireflies.

Hi O lived in the moat of the castle of Fukui in Echizen. His bright but coquettish daughter, Hotaru Hime, was courted by many lovers, among which were a golden beetle, a black bug, a scarlet dragonfly, and a hawk moth. For each wooer she set a task of bringing her fire. All tried to get it from lamps and were burned to death as a result, except for the hawk moth, which had more cunning and crawled inside the paper wick of a candle. The candle was snuffed out before he reached the flame, but he escaped with his life. Finally, Hi Maro, the firefly prince, heard of the offer and successfully wooed Hotaru Hime. As a result, when dead insects are seen around temple lamps in Japan, there is a saying: "Princess Hotaru must have had many lovers tonight."

1485

**Hotots**   In Armenian folklore, evil spirits who live in the rivers and swamps. When they appear, they are covered with mire. They entice men with dancing, jesting, and singing, luring them to the swamps, where they drown them. Their companions, the old hags, who have breasts resembling those of ewes, live in pools and swamps. They like to drown children, men, horses, oxen, and buffaloes.

See also: MELUSINA; UNDINE

1486

**Houri**   In Islamic mythology, black-eyed damsels who live with the blessed in paradise. The Koran (sura 55) says that men in paradise will en-

joy "damsels with retiring glances, whom no man nor djinn hath touched before them." These houri possess eternal youth and beauty, and their virginity is renewable. Every believer will have 72 of these women to satisfy his sexual needs. His intercourse with them always produces a child, if he wishes one. If an offspring is desired, it will be a fully grown child in one hour. The promise of houris in paradise is found almost exclusively in those suras of the Koran written when Muhammad had only one wife, who was 60 years old. Later writings in the Koran speak of the proper wives of the faithful accompanying their husbands into the Garden of Paradise.

See also: KORAN, THE; MUHAMMAD

1487

**Howe's Masquerade**   In American history and folklore of the Revolution, a masked ball held by the British general Sir William Howe (1729–1814), commander-in-chief of the British army in the American Revolution, while Boston lay under siege by colonial forces in 1776. To show his contempt for the colonials, Howe asked some of his guests to dress in costumes representing Washington and his generals. But as the party progressed, a funeral dirge was heard outside, and a procession passed through the ballroom. It consisted of figures from the colonial past and last of all a tall man whose face was cloaked. Howe, furious at the interruption of his ball, ran toward the cloaked figure, only to discover it was a caricature of him as the last royal governor. Hawthorne's short story "Howe's Masquerade," included in his *Twice Told Tales*, deals with the legend. According to tradition, the grim procession appears each year.

1488

**Hsiao Kung**   13th century. In Chinese legend, a deified mortal worshiped as the god of rivers.

**Hsieh p'ing-an** In Chinese folk ritual, a thanksgiving service to the gods for their gifts during the year.

1489

**Hsien** (immortal) In Chinese mythology, a deified mortal or a deity who has never been mortal. It is similar to the Chinese *shen*, another word for divinity, spirit, god, or deified mortal.
See also: SHEN

1490

**Hsi-Shen** In Chinese mythology, the god of joy, portrayed carrying a basket or sieve in which are planted three arrows made of peach wood. Pictures of the god are used as talismans by brides.

1491

**Hsi Wang Mu** (queen mother of the west) In Chinese mythology, a goddess whose garden contains a magical peach tree where peaches ripen only once in 3,000 years and bestow immortality. In Japanese mythology Hsi Wang Mu is called Seiobo.
See also: PEACH

1492

**Huaca** (Guaca) In Inca mythology, a term applied to anything believed to be sacred or possessed of a spirit, such as a totem stone, a grave, and the crest of a mountain. A special category of these sacred items were the Apachitas, piles of stones that were gathered and placed at dangerous spots along roads or on mountain passes. One Spanish account, written by Juan de Santa Cruz Pachacuti-Yamqui Salcamayhua, called *Account of the Antiquities of Peru*, says that after the natives were converted to Christianity they "destroyed and pulled down all the huacas and idols" and punished those who consulted them. Today the word is used as a synonym for treasure

1493

*Huaca*

because of the jewelry and gold objects frequently found near the sites of ancient *huacas*.

**Hua-Kuang Fo** In Chinese Buddhism, the Buddha of Hua-kuang, patron god of goldsmiths and silversmiths and guardian deity of temples.

1494

**Huathiacuri** In the mythology of the Huarochiri (Warachiri) Indians of the western side of the coastal cordillera of Peru, son of the hero god Pariacaca. Huathiacuri learned many arts from his father. He came to a land where a rich Indian pretended he was the creator god. According to Francisco de Ávila, a Roman Catholic priest of San Damian, a parish in the district of the Huarochiri, who wrote *A Narrative of the Error*,

1495

*False Gods, and Other Superstitions and Diabolical Rites . . [of] the Indians* (1608), the rich man's house was roofed with yellow and red birds' feathers, and he had llamas of a great number of colors, so it was unnecessary to dye the wool they produced. This rich man fell ill with a foul disease. As Huathiacuri was traveling toward the sea, he overheard a conversation between two foxes and learned the cause of the great man's illness: his wife had committed adultery, and two serpents were hovering over his house eating his life away while a two-headed toad was hiding under the grinding stone. Huathiacuri caused the wife to confess, the monsters were destroyed, the rich man recovered, and Huathiacuri married the daughter.

1496
**Hubert, St.** (mind-bright)    Died 727. Bishop of Liège, France; patron saint of huntsmen, metalworkers, mathematicians, and dogs. Feast, 3 November.

The legend of St. Hubert is similar to that of St. Eustace, and the two are often confused in art. Hubert was the son of a nobleman of Aquitaine. On one great church festival all of the faithful went to church, but Hubert decided he wanted to hunt instead. During the hunt a stag of "great beauty" showed itself to Hubert, who was astonished to see a crucifix between its antlers. Then a voice came from the stag, saying: "Hubert, Hubert, how long will you spend your time chasing beasts in the forest and neglecting the things that pertain to your soul? Do you suppose that God sent you into the world to hunt wild beasts, and not rather to know and honor thy Creator?" Hubert was stupefied on hearing these words; he dismounted from his horse, prostrated himself on the ground, and worshiped the cross the stag bore. He vowed to abandon the world and become a hermit.

After studying under St. Lambert, he was ordained a priest and finally became bishop of Liège. His descendants were said to have the power to cure the bite of mad dogs. Thirteen years after his death his body was disinterred and found entire, even his episcopal robes being without spot or stain from corruption. A century after his death his body was removed from Liège to the abbey church of the Benedictines of Ardennes.

See also: EUSTACE, ST.; FOURTEEN HOLY HELPERS

1497
**Hud**    In Islamic legend, a prophet mentioned in the Koran (suras 7, 11, 26, 46) who preached to a pagan tribe, the Ad, who refused to listen to the message of Allah.

There are numerous legends surrounding this mysterious prophet, who is said to have lived some 150 years. The major legend (sura 7) concerns his preaching to the Ad tribe. The tribe refused to listen to the prophet, and as a punishment Allah sent them three years of drought. The tribe then sent Kail Ebn Ithar and Morthed Ebn Saad, with 70 other men, to the temple at Mecca to ask for rain. Mecca was then in the hands of the tribe of Amalek, whose prince was Moâwiyah Ebn Becr. The men were entertained outside the city by Moâwiyah and for a time forgot their mission. Later Moâwiyah told them they could have rain only if they followed the prophet Hud and listened to his preaching.

Kail went into Mecca with some of the others and begged Allah to send rain. Three clouds appeared, a white one, a red one, and a black one. A voice from heaven ordered Kail to choose, and Kail chose the last cloud, thinking it was filled with rain. Suddenly, as the cloud passed over, a terrible storm arose, which destroyed all of them except Hud and his faithful followers.

See also: ALLAH; KORAN, THE

1498
**Huehueteotl**    In ancient Mexican mythology, fire god, believed to be the oldest of the gods.

1499

**Huemac** (strong hand)   In Aztec mythology, god of earthquakes, sometimes equated with Quetzalcoatl. He was the last secular ruler of the city of Tollan before it was destroyed.

See also: QUETZALCOATL

1500

**Hueytonantzin** (our great ancient mother)   In Aztec mythology, Great Mother goddess of the lords of the four directions: Hueytecptl (ancient flint stone), Ixcuin (he who had four faces), Nanactltzatzi (he who speaks when drunk), and Tentmic (lipstone that slays?). Each day the four sons of Hueytonantzin slew their mother and sacrificed her to the sun.

See also: GREAT GODDESS

1501

**Hugin and Munin** (Huginn, Muninn) (thought and mind)   In Norse mythology, two ravens who fly about the world, then sit on Odin's shoulders, telling him what they have seen. Snorri Sturluson says in the Prose Edda: "Two ravens sit on his [Odin's] shoulders and say into his ear everything they see or hear. Their names are Jugin and Munin. He dispatches them at daybreak to fly over all the world and they return at breakfast time. From this he becomes wise about many events, and thus he is called the Ravengod." They also appear in the *Poetic Edda* and the *Prose Edda*.

See also: HLITHSKJOLF; ODIN

1502

**Huitaca**   In the mythology of the Chibcha Indians of Colombia, evil goddess of indulgence, drunkenness, and license. Huitaca came to earth to destroy the good works of the culture hero Nemterequeteba and to teach men evil. In some accounts she is said to be the wife of the chief of the gods, Bochica; in others she is said to be Chibcho, the moon, wife of Zuhe, the sun, who is considered to be a form of Bochica. One myth

tells how she was transformed into an owl or into the moon.

See also: BOCHICA; NEMTEREQUETEBA

*Huitzilopochtli*

1503

**Huitzilopochtli** (blue hummingbird on the left) In Aztec mythology, a war god associated with the sun. Ritual human sacrifices of prisoners were made to him. Huitzilopochtli was the brother of Quetzalcoatl. His mother, Coatlicue, one day picked up a ball of bright feathers on her way to the temple of the sun god. She placed them in her bosom, and as a result she became pregnant. When her family discovered her pregnancy they wanted to kill her, but Huitzilopochtli was born fully armed and killed them instead. In a variant myth Huitzilopochtli was a man who was the leader of the Aztecs during their wanderings from home. On his death, or when he returned to heaven, his skull became an oracle and told them what to do. Bernal Díaz del Castillo, in his *Verdadera historia de la conquista de la Nueva España*, which gives an eyewitness account of the Spanish conquest, describes the shrine of Huitzilopochtli, in which "the walls of the oratory were black and dripping with gouts of blood" and the floor "stank horribly." D. H. Lawrence, in his novel *The Plumed Serpent*, which tells of the reintroduction of Aztec gods to modern Mexico to replace Christ, includes a series of poems in honor of Huitzilopochtli.

See also: COATLICUE; QUETZALCOATL

1504

**Humbaba** (Huwawa, Kumbaba)    In the Babylonian epic poem *Gilgamesh*, demon-spirit, guardian of the sacred Cedar Tree, killed by Gilgamesh and Enkidu. Originally Humbaba may have been a nature divinity who became associated with evil forces. In one ancient prayer he was called the "supporter of evil" and "the merciless demon." In Babylonian art Humbaba is often portrayed with a beard made of the entrails of animals. Demon masks were often hung on doors to ward off evil, in the belief that greater evil—namely, Humbaba—would defeat some minor evil spirit.

See also: ENKIDU; GILGAMESH

1505

**Hunab Ku** (the only god)    In Mayan mythology, incorporeal god, father of Itzamná, the sky and sun god. He married Ixazaluch, the goddess of water, with whom he had a son, Itzamná, a literate and cultured immortal. No images of Hunab Ku were made.

See also: ITZAMNÁ

1506

**Hunahpú and Xbalanqúe**    In Mayan mythology, twin hero gods in the *Popol Vuh*, the sacred book of the ancient Quiché Maya of Guatemala.

One day Hun-Hunahpú, the father of Hunahpú and Xbalanqúe, while playing ball with his brothers, came within the vicinity of Xibalba, the underworld in Mayan mythology. The lords of Xibalba challenged Hun-Hunahpú to a ball game, and eventually he and his brothers were tortured and killed. Hun-Hunahpú's head was placed on a tree, which instantly bore fruit. Some time later, Xquic (little blood or blood of a woman), the daughter of a lord named Cuchumaquic, went to pick the fruit from the tree. She reached up, and some spittle from the skull fell into her palm.

"In my saliva and spittle I have given you my descendants," the tree said to Xquic. The girl then gave birth to Hunahpú and Xbalanqúe. As their father had before them, they encountered the lords of Xibalba. When they arrived in the underworld, they were told to sit down.

"This is not a seat for us; it is only a hot stone," the two told the lords. They then were told to enter the House of Gloom, then the House of Knives, then the House of Jaguars, and the House of Bats, where they encountered the vampire-bat god, Camazotz.

To protect themselves, they hid inside a blowgun. All night bats flew around them but could not touch them. When morning came, Hunahpú went to see if it was light, and Camazotz cut off his head. Hunahpú's head was placed in the ball court by the Xibalbans while a turtle took its place. Eventually, however, his head was restored. The two heroes went on to defeat the lords of Xibalba by using many magic means. They would kill each other and then restore themselves to life. When the lords saw this wonder, they also wanted to be killed and brought back to life. The heroes obliged with the first part but did not bring the lords back to life.

See also: CAMAZOTZ; *POPOL VUH*

**Hunding**   In Norse mythology, a king defeated by Helgi. He appears in the *Volsunga Saga* and Richard Wagner's *Die Walküre*, the second opera of *Der Ring des Nibelungen*. Hunding is portrayed in Arthur Rackham's illustrations for Wagner's Ring Cycle.

See also: *RING DES NIBELUNGEN, DER*

**Hun-tun**   In Chinese Taoist mythology, Chaos, from whom emerged the world. Shû, the god of the Southern Ocean, and Hu, the god of the Northern Ocean, were continually meeting in the land of Hun-tun. He treated them very well. They consulted together how they might repay his kindness. "Men all have seven orifices for the purpose of seeing, hearing, eating, and breathing," they said, "while Hun-tun, has not one. Let us try and make them." So Shû and Hu placed one orifice in Hun-tun every day for seven days. At the end of the seventh day Hun-tun died. In Chinese, Shû-hu, the combined names of the two ocean gods, is the word for lightning. This perhaps indicates the belief that lightning was responsible for ordering the mass of Chaos. In other texts Hun-tun is said to be a large yellow baglike bird; or he is the son of Huang Ti, the Yellow Emperor, who sent his son into exile.

**Hurakán** (Huracán) (the one-legged)   In Mayan mythology, a creator god. In the beginning, according to the *Popol Vuh*, sacred book of the ancient Quiché Maya of Guatemala, there was the god Hurakán hovering in the dense and primeval gloom over a watery waste. Hurakán passed over the surface of the waters as a mighty wind, saying one word, "earth." In response to this utterance a solid mass rose slowly from the deep. The gods (there were many) then took counsel to see what should be done next. Among the gods were Hunahpú, Gucumatz, Xpiyacoc, and Xmucané. After some discussion, it was decided to create animals, which they did. Then the gods carved wooden mannequins and gave them life, but they were too puppetlike. Hurakán sent a great flood to destroy them. All were drowned except for a few handfuls, whose descendants are said to be "the little monkeys that live in the woods." Later Hurakán made four perfect men—Balam-Quitzé, Balam-Agag, Mahucutan, and Iqui-Balam. They are the ancestors of the Quiché.

See also: BALAM-QUITZÉ; EARTH DIVER; GUCUMATZ; HUNAHPÚ; *POPOL VUH*; XPIYACOC AND XMUCANÉ

**Hushedar, Hushedar-mar, and Soshyant** (Aushedar and Ukhahyadereta, Aushedar-mah and Ukhshyad-nemangh, Soshans, Soshyans, Saoshyant, Saoshyas, Saoshyos)   In Persian mythology, three saviors who will announce the end of the world and its rebirth.

Hushedar, the first savior, "will bring the creatures back to their proper state." He will be born of a virgin from the seed of the prophet Zarathustra, which has been preserved in a lake. To prove his mission the sun will stand still at its noontime position for 10 days. For three years men will live at peace and see a glimpse of the future happiness, then evil will again assert itself, and the second savior, Hushedar-mar, will come. The sun will then stand still for 20 days, men will no longer eat meat, and they will be even closer to the final victory of good over evil. But evil will again arise in the form of the demon Azhi Dahaka, who will break loose from his bonds in a cave in Mount Demavend. When Azhi Dahaka is killed by the hero Keresaspa, the third and final savior, Soshyant, will arrive, all disease and death will be overcome, and the final judgment will take place.

See also: AZHI DAHAKA; KERESASPA; ZARATHUSTRA

**1511**

**Husheng** (Hoshang, Hoshyang)    In Persian mythology, king, culture hero, and discoverer of fire, appearing in the epic poem *Shah Namah* by Firdusi.

Husheng began his reign by destroying a demon who had killed his father, King Siyamek. When peace was restored, he went about civilizing the world, spreading justice. Husheng ruled seven regions of the world. He had power not only over men but over demons, who obeyed his commands. The king discovered minerals, separated iron from stone, invented the art of the blacksmith, taught men how to cook food, helped them to irrigate the fields, and most important, discovered fire. Firdusi describes in his epic how the king, passing by a mountain, saw

Something in aspect terrible—its eyes
Fountains of blood; its dreadful mouth sent
    forth
Volumes of smoke that darkened all the air.
Fixing his gaze upon the hideous form,
He seized a stone, and with prodigious force
Hurling it, chanced to strike a jutting rock,
When sparks arose, and presently a fire
O'erspread the plain, in which the monster
    perished (James Atkinson translation).

Husheng reigned for some 40 years and was succeeded by his son Tahumers.

See also: *SHAH NAMAH*; TAHUMERS

**1512**

**Hyacinth**    A large fragrant flower of the lily family. In Greek mythology, the hyacinth is associated with the love of the god Apollo for the young boy Hyacinthus, who was killed by a discus sent by the wind, Zephyr, who was also in love with the lad. Hyacinthus's blood was turned into a flower in his honor, and Apollo decreed an annual three-day festival, Hyacinthia. On the first and third days sacrifices were offered to the dead youth, and his sad fate was recounted in songs. Wearing garlands was forbidden, and no

bread could be eaten or songs sung to Apollo. But on the second day joy and amusement reigned; hymns in honor of Apollo were intoned, and citizens kept open house for friends and relatives. According to variant accounts, it was from the blood of the hero Ajax that the flower bloomed, when he lost to Odysseus in a contest for the arms of Achilles. In Christian symbolism, the hyacinth stands for prudence, peace of mind, and desire for heaven.

See also: ACHILLES; AJAX; APOLLO; ODYSSEUS; ZEPHYR

**1513**

**Hyacinthus**    In Greek mythology, a young man loved by Apollo; son of Amyclas and Diomedes of Pierus and the Muse Clio. Hyacinthus was killed out of jealousy by Zephyrus, the West Wind, with a discus. Apollo created a flower named in Hyacinthus's honor with Apollo's cries of grief, "Ai, Ai," etched on its petals. Varieties of flowers identified with Hyacinthus are the hyacinth, iris, and gladiolus. The hyacinth has come to stand for mourning. Milton's *Lycidas* (106) calls it "that sanguine flower inscrib'd with woe." Originally, Hyacinthus was a pre-Hellenic god whose worship was absorbed by Apollo's cult. A three-day festival, the Hyacinthia, was held at Sparta in honor of the god, who was worshiped at Amyclae in Laconia. On the first day of the festival a sacrifice to the dead was offered at the grave of Hyacinthus, which was under a statue of Apollo in the temple. The following day the people rejoiced. Boys and girls, accompanied by flutes and harps, went to the temple of Apollo, where games, competitions, sacrifices, and entertainments took place. A robe woven by Spartan women was offered to Apollo. Pausanias's *Descriptions of Greece* records a statue of Hyacinthus that portrayed the god with a beard. The myth of Apollo and Hyacinthus is told in Ovid's *Metamorphoses* (book 10). One of Mozart's earliest works, *Apollo et Hyacinthus*, is set to a Latin text.

See also: APOLLO; DIOMEDES; MUSES; OVID; ZEPHYRUS

**Hyarekhshaeta, Khorshed, and Mitro** 1514 In Persian mythology, three spirits connected with the sun. Hyarekhshaeta is the "brilliant sun" as the eye of the good god, Ahura Mazda, and is drawn in a chariot of swift horses. Khorshed is the "undying, shining, swift-horsed sun," and Mitro is the angel or spirit of the sun's light, a personification of friendship and good faith. Mitro assists righteous souls in their passage to the other world and punishes those who break promises or are fraudulent.

See also: AHURA MAZDA

*Heracles killing Hydra*

**Hydra** (water creature) 1515 In Greek mythology, a huge serpent with 7, 9, or 50 heads (accounts vary) in Lake Lerna in Argolis; offspring of Ty-

phon and Echidna. If one head was chopped off, another two would grow in its place. Heracles' second labor was to kill the monster. With the aid of Iolaus he accomplished the feat. The venom of Hydra was poisonous. Arrows dipped in the venom killed Cheiron, Nessus, and Philoctetes. Eventually the poison was used on a garment that killed Heracles. Hesiod's *Theogony*, Vergil's *Aeneid* (book 6), and Ovid's *Metamorphoses* (book 9) all cite the myth.

See also: *AENEID, THE*; ECHIDNA; HERACLES; NESSUS; OVID; PHILOCTETES; TYPHOS

**Hyena** 1516 A nocturnal, doglike animal that feeds mainly on carrion. In Egyptian mythology it was said that a stone, the "hyaenia," was found in the eye of the creature, and when placed under the tongue it gave the gift of prophecy. In Greek and Roman folklore it was believed that the hyena changed its sex and that if you caught the animal while it was male and castrated it, you could use its testicles to make a fine powder that would cure cramps. In medieval Christian folklore it was believed that the hyena could imitate the sound of human voices, often fooling men and dogs, who were devoured when they responded to the call. The hyena was also believed to mate with the lion, producing the Crocote, which had no teeth or gums in its mouth; all of its teeth were of one piece, like a box lid. Medieval Christian symbolism saw the hyena as representing the devil, vice, impurity, and hypocrisy.

**Hygeia** (health) 1517 In Greek mythology, goddess of health, daughter of Asclepius and Epione; sister of Acesis, Aegle, Iaso, Janiscus, Machaon, Panacea, and Podalirius; called Salus by the Romans. She was worshiped along with her father, and her name follows after his in the Hippocratic oath.

See also: ASCLEPIUS

1518

**Hylas** (of the woods)   In Greek mythology, an Argonaut, male lover of Heracles; son of Theiodamas, king of the Dryope, and Menodice, a nymph. When Heracles killed Theiodamas (divine tamer) for refusing the gift of a plow ox, he spared his son Hylas, who became his lover. The two went on the voyage of the Argonauts in search of the Golden Fleece. They landed at Cios, and Hylas went to fetch water at a fountain. He was drowned there by a water nymph, Pegae or Dryope, who had fallen in love with the handsome youth. Heracles went in search of Hylas with his sister's son Polyphemus, leaving the Argonauts to go on without him. Failing to find Hylas, Heracles did not leave the island until he had taken hostages from the Mysians. He made them promise to produce Hylas, dead or alive. From that time on, the inhabitants of Cios made a ritual search for Hylas, sacrificed to him every year at the fountain, and called him by name three times. Apollonius Rhodius's short epic *Argonautica* (The Voyage of the Argo) tells the myth.

See also: ARGONAUTS; GOLDEN FLEECE; HERACLES; NYMPHS

1519

**Hymen** (skin)   In Greek mythology, god of marriage, son of either Dionysus and Aphrodite or of Apollo and one of the Muses, Urania, Calliope, or Terpsichore. According to one account Hymen was an Argive youth who loved a young Athenian girl but could not win the consent of her parents. Disguised as a girl, he followed her to the sacred feast of Demeter at Eleusis, where he and a group of girls were kidnapped. Hymen saved all of them by killing the abductors and became the protector of young women. At Greek weddings the guests would cry out, "Hymen O Hymeneaus!" Eventually, the call came to represent a god of marriage who was seen as a young man holding a marriage torch and wearing a wreath. Spenser's wedding poem *Epithalamion* (25–29) asks his bride to awake from her sleep for "Hymen is awake." He appears or is cited in numerous English marriage songs and masques of the 17th century. Hymen is also called Hymenaeus.

See also: APHRODITE; APOLLO; CALLIOPE; DEMETER; DIONYSUS; MUSES; TERPSICHORE

1520

**Hymir** (the dark one)   In Norse mythology, a sea giant who owned a large caldron that the gods wanted. Tyr and Thor went off to fetch it from the giant. In one telling of the myth Tyr eventually killed Hymir. In another version Thor knocked Hymir overboard from a ship, and he drowned. The myth is told in the poem *Hymigkuitha* in the *Poetic Edda* and in the *Prose Edda*. In another myth, Hymir and Thor went fishing together and ventured into uncharted waters. When Thor hooked the Midgard Serpent, Hymir cut the line and allowed the serpent to survive. The episode is often depicted in drawings and carvings, with Thor's feet protruding through the bottom of the boat while he has the serpent on his fishing line.

See also: MIDGARD SERPENT; *POETIC EDDA*; *PROSE EDDA*; THOR

1521

**Hyperboreans** (beyond-the-north-wind men)   In Greek mythology, a people who lived in everlasting springtime north of the great river Oceanus, or at the North Pole, or in Britain. They were worshipers of Apollo, who, according to their belief, spent the winter months with them when he left his shrine at Delphi. Herodotus's *History* (book 4) says the Hyperboreans sent wheat-straw offerings to Apollo's shrine at Delos. Heracles brought the first olive tree to Olympus from their land, according to some accounts.

See also: APOLLO; DELOS; DELPHI; HERACLES; OCEANUS

**Hyperion** (the one above)   In Greek mythology, a Titan, son of Uranus and Gaea; husband of his sister Theia; father of the Sun (Helios), the Dawn (Eos), and the Moon (Selene), according to Hesiod's *Theogony* (371 ff). Hyperion is sometimes used as the name of the sun itself. In some accounts Hyperion is said to be a son of Apollo. Keats's unfinished poem *Hyperion* (1818) tells how Hyperion, the last of the Titans, is about to be deposed by Apollo, the Olympian sun god.

See also: APOLLO; GAEA; HESIOD; SELENE; TITANS; URANUS

**Hypermnestra** (excessive wooing)   In Greek mythology, eldest of the 50 daughters of Danaus, and the only one of the Danaidae who did not murder her husband (Lynceus) on her wedding night. She and Lynceus were the parents of Abas, ancestor of the hero Perseus.

See also: DANAIDAE; DORIS; PERSEUS

**Hypnos** (sleep)   In Greek mythology, god of sleep, son of Nyx (Nox) and Erebus; brother of Thanatos (death), Aether (upper sky), Cer

(bane), Dreams, Hemeia, Momus (blame), Moros (portion), and Nemesis; married to Pasithea; father of Morpheus; called Somnus by the Romans. According to Hesiod's *Theogony* (211,756), Hypnos lived in the underworld, but Homer says he lived in Lemnos. Hypnos had a human figure during the day but was transformed into a bird at night. Vergil's *Aeneid* (book 6) pictures Hypnos as a winged youth who touches the tired with a magical branch. Homer's *Iliad* (book 14), Hesiod's *Theogony*, and Ovid's *Metamorphoses* (book 11) also picture the god.

See also: *AENEID, THE*; HYPNOS; *ILIAD, THE*; MORPHEUS; NEMESIS; NOX; OVID; THANATOS

**Hypsipyle** (high gate)   In Greek mythology, queen of Lemnos; daughter of Thoas and Myrina; wife of Jason; mother of Euneus (Evenus), Deipylus, Nebrophonus, and Thoas. Hypsipyle did not kill her father when all of the women on Lemnos killed all of the men. When the Argonauts came to the island, all of the women were raped, and Hypsipyle became the wife of Jason, who abandoned her. Later the women of Lemnos exiled Hypsipyle to Nemea. Ovid's *Heroides* (book 6) and Chaucer's *Legend of Good Women* report her sad fate.

See also: ARGONAUTS; CHAUCER; JASON; OVID

# I

**Iatiku** (Iyatiku) (bringing to life)   In North American Indian mythology (Acoma), creator goddess along with her sister Natsiti. Their children, the Katsinas, have the power to bring rain and food. Some sources give the names of the two goddesses as Utset and Nowutset. Iatiku watches over people and promotes their general welfare. She is often identified as the breath of life.

1526

**Ibis**   A large wading bird related to the heron, with a long, thin, downward-curved bill. In Egyptian mythology the ibis was associated with Thoth. The ancient Greeks believed it was the natural enemy of snakes.

See also: THOTH

1527

**Iblis** (slanderer)   Satan in Islamic folklore, originally an angel called Azazel or al-Haris; he is the father of the djinn. When Allah was forming man, he took clay and after shaping it left it to dry for some 40 days (or 40 years, according to some Islamic versions of the myth). All of the *malaika*, or angels, who were created from rays of light, came to see Allah's new creation. Iblis, one of Allah's most important angels, appeared among them. He looked at the new creation and,

1528

knowing that Allah intended to make it more important than any angel, kicked it with his foot until it resounded. Allah then called all of the angels to come and worship Adam. Iblis refused because, as the Koran (sura 2) phrases it, he "was puffed up with pride."

When Allah in anger cast Iblis out of heaven, the angel cried: "Allah, grant me time. Do not banish me to outer darkness yet. Let me tempt Adam and his sons. Then we will see if they have faith!"

"I will give you until the Day of Judgment," Allah replied. "When that day comes, you will regret your evil deeds and pay dearly for them. You will be cast into a dark pit, never again to harm any souls. Now, out! Leave heaven."

Since that day Iblis has been tempting the sons of Adam to sin against Allah. Iblis is the father of Teer (Tir), the demon who brings about calamities, injuries, and losses of various kinds; El-Aawar, who encourages men to live in debauchery; Sot (Sut), who gives men the desire to lie; Dasism, who causes husbands and wives to fight with one another. (Harut and Marut, the Brothers of Iblis, also cause division between husband and wife.) Iblis is also the father of Zeleboor (Zalambur), who hovers over places of traffic, causing accidents and mischief. Since the invention of the automobile this demon has been kept astonishingly busy. In Western literature

Iblis appears in William Beckford's novel *Vathek, an Arabian Tale*.

See also: AZAZEL; HARUT AND MARUT; SATAN

1529
**Ichabod Crane**   In American literary folklore, a creation of Washington Irving in "The Legend of Sleepy Hollow," included in *The Sketch Book*. Ichabod looks like "some scarecrow eloped from a corn-field," according to Irving. He is in love with Katrina Van Tassel, daughter of a rich Dutch farmer in Sleepy Hollow on the Hudson in the days before the American Revolution. But his rival, Brom Van Brunt, outwits the Yankee schoolteacher. One night at a party, Ichabod leaves, riding a borrowed plow horse. On his way he is frightened by a headless horseman that rides after him and throws a round object at the terrified schoolmaster. Ichabod leaves the village never to be seen again. The next day the round object is discovered to be a pumpkin. Brunt then marries Katrina. The tale was used as the basis of Max Maretzek's opera *Sleepy Hollow: or, The Headless Horseman*; Douglas Moore's one-act opera *The Headless Horseman: or, A Legend of Sleepy Hollow* with a libretto by Stephen Vincent Benét; and Walt Disney's cartoon feature *Ichabod and Mr. Toad*, in which Irving's legend is narrated by Basil Rathbone.

See also: MOTIF

1530
**Ichimokuren** (one-eye)   In Japanese mythology, one-eyed god invoked to obtain rain during periods of drought.

1531
***I Ching*** (the book of changes)   Chinese work ascribed to the legendary Emperor Fu Hsi. It is a book of cosmological hexagrams giving the laws by which things change, used to foretell the future. It is regarded as a practical book and was one of those, along with books on agriculture and medicine, that were not ordered burned by the first emperor of China in his effort to control thought by destroying philosophical books. The book was also regarded as full of wisdom. Confucius said, "If I could study the *I Ching* for many years, I should be faultless." He read his copy so often that the binding twice wore out. He is said to have written some appendices to it. In the Western world it has been regarded as an occult work.

See also: CONFUCIUS

1532
**Icon** (Greek *eikon*: image)   Term used in the Eastern Orthodox Church for pictures, low-relief sculptures, and mosaics of Christ, the Virgin Mary, and the saints. Icons became popular in the East in the fifth century. In style, icons are hieratic, idealized images. Tradition rather than self-expression is the aim of the artist painting an icon. During the eighth and ninth centuries there was a reaction against icons, called the Iconoclastic Controversy. The triumph of those who defended icons is still celebrated as the Feast of Orthodoxy in the Eastern Church. Icons are kissed, genuflected to, and incensed because they are believed to exercise powers such as healing. Numerous icons have had miracles credited to them in legends: for example, the Christ of Edessa, which is said "not to have been made with hands" but to have come from heaven. According to another legend, the icon of Our Lady of Iviron was thrown into the sea by iconoclasts at Constantinople and was washed onto the shore of Mount Athos years later. The Russian church commemorates Our Lady of Iviron on 13 October.

1533
**Ida**   In Hindu mythology, goddess of speech and, in some texts, the earth. In the Rig-Veda, an ancient collection of hymns to the gods, she is primarily food, refreshment, or a libation of milk. One myth says she sprang up when the first

man performed a sacrifice to obtain children. The two were then married and had children.

See also: RIG-VIDA

**1534**

**Idaten**   In Japanese Buddhist mythology, god of peace and contemplation. Portrayed as a young man of martial bearing, he carries a halberd. The loose parts of his garment are kept in place by his feet as a symbol of subdued sexuality. He also is sometimes portrayed with both hands resting on the pommel of his sword.

**1535**

**Idomeneus** (knowing one)   In Greek mythology, king of Crete, Leucus, son of Deucalion; brother of Crete; husband of Meda; father of Idamente. Idomeneus went to the Trojan War with 80 ships and achieved great fame as a warrior. On his way home a storm arose, and he vowed to Poseidon that he would sacrifice the first person he encountered on landing if the storm ceased. The sacrificial victim turned out to be his own son Idamante. Leucus, lover of Meda, banished Idomeneus to Italy for the murder. Mozart's opera *Idomeneo re di Creta, Ossia Ilia ed Adamante* (1781) deals with part of the myth.

See also: DEUCALION; POSEIDON

**1536**

**Iduna** (Idunn) (rejuvenation)   In Norse mythology, one of the Aesir; goddess of the golden apples of immortal youth, food of the gods; wife of the god Bragi. Loki, the fire-trickster god, was forced by the giant Thjassi to trick the goddess Iduna. Odin, Hoenir, and Loki were out traveling. They were unable to cook an ox they had killed. An eagle in the tree, actually the giant Thjassi, said he would cook it for them if he could have some too. When he took too much, Loki struck him with a staff that stuck to the eagle as he flew away, with Loki still holding on to the staff. He would only be freed if he agreed to bring Thjassi one of Iduna's apples. Loki then

lured Iduna into the forest and told her that he had found apples growing a short distance from her celestial residence that were of much better quality than her own, and he persuaded her to go and look at them. Deceived by Loki's words, Iduna took her apples and went with him into the forest. When they entered the forest, Thjassi, covered in his eagle plumage, swooped down and took Iduna and her apples into his claws and flew off to Jotunheim, the home of the giants. The gods, deprived of their magic apples, began to wrinkle and turn gray, old age creeping fast upon them. When they discovered that Loki had caused all the trouble they threatened to punish him unless he could get Iduna back. Loki borrowed the goddess Freyja's falcon plumage and flew to Jotunheim. Finding Thjassi out fishing, Loki lost no time in changing Iduna into a sparrow and flying off with her. When Thjassi returned and discovered what had happened, he put on his eagle plumage and gave chase. When the gods saw Loki approaching, holding Iduna transformed into a sparrow between his claws and Thjassi with his outspread eagle wings ready to overtake them, they placed on the wall of Asgard bundles of chips, which they set afire the instant Loki had flown over them. As Thjassi could not stop his flight, the fire caught his plumage; he fell and and was killed by the gods. The myth of Iduna is told in the *Prose Edda*.

See also: AESIR; JOTUNHEIM; LOKI; *PROSE EDDA*

**1537**

**Ifrits** (Afrit, Afriteh, Alfrit, Efreet, Ifriteh)   In Islamic mythology, spirits often evil but sometimes good. They are but one of the five classes of djinn, or devils. The Koran (sura 27) makes a brief mention of the "Ifrit, one of the djinn." In Egyptian Islamic folklore an Ifrit means the ghost of a murdered man or one who died a violent death. Yet the female version of the Ifrit, called the Ifriteh, mentioned in *The Thousand and One Nights*, is a benevolent djinn. In one tale, "Second Old Man's Story" (night 2), a pious woman is transformed into an Ifriteh and carries a hero to an island to save his life. In the morning she returns and says: "I have paid thee my debt, for it is I who bore thee up out of the sea and saved thee from death, by permission of Allah. Know that I am of the djinn who believe in Allah and his prophet." Thus, some Ifrits are good spirits, converted to Islam.

See also: DJINN; KORAN, THE; *THOUSAND AND ONE NIGHTS*

**Ignatius Loyola, St.** (fiery)   1491–1556. In Christian legend, founder of the Society of Jesus (S.J.), known as the Jesuits. Feast, 31 July.

1538

Born in Spain, Ignatius became a page at the court of King Ferdinand. He entered the army and was severely wounded in 1521. That changed his whole future life. After a period of penance and visions of Christ, he began to study in preparation for a career in preaching. While at Paris he formed a community with five associates, who bound themselves to preach and teach in any part of the world to which they might be sent. After some years the pope confirmed the name of the Society of Jesus. Ignatius became the first general of his order. His most famous work, *The Spiritual Exercises*, describes a retreat of several days during which the soul, removed from all intercourse with the world, is occupied with the "all important business of salvation" of one's soul.

St. Ignatius Loyola is portrayed in one of Rubens's masterpieces, *The Miracles of St. Ignatius Loyola*, in a magnificent cathedral, dramatically imploring God to exorcise demons from the sick and lame. He wears Mass vestments. Sometimes the saint is portrayed with the monogram IHS on his breast.

**Ignatius of Antioch, St.** (fiery?) c. 35–107. In Christian legend, martyr and bishop. Feast, 1 February.

1539

According to numerous early Christian legends, Ignatius was a friend of the early church-

man St. Polycarp, both being disciples of St. John the Evangelist. One early tradition says that when Ignatius was a child Christ "set him in the midst" of his disciples. Ignatius took holy orders and was made bishop of Antioch. When the Roman emperor Trajan came to the city, he ordered Ignatius to sacrifice to the Roman gods. Ignatius refused and was sentenced to be eaten by lions. After his death in 107 the name Jesus was found written on his heart in golden letters.

See also: JOHN THE EVANGELIST, ST.

**Igraine** (Igerna, Igerne, Ygerne)   In Arthurian legend, mother of King Arthur and wife of Gorlois, lord of Tintagel Castle in Cornwall. According to one account, King Uther Pendragon tried to seduce Igraine but failed. As a result Uther and Gorlois fought, and Gorlois was killed. Uther then attacked Tintagel and forced Igraine to become his wife. Nine months later, Uther died, and on the same day King Arthur was born. Tennyson calls her Ygerne.

1540

See also: ARTHUR: UTHER PENDRAGON

**Ikazuchi**   In Japanese mythology, the eight gods of thunder. They are O-Ikazuchi, Ho-no-Ikazuchi, Kuro-Ikazuchi, Saku-Ikazuchi, Waki-Ikazuchi, Tschui-Ikazuchi, Naru-Ikazuchi, and Fushi-Ikazuchi.

1541

See also: FUSHI-IKAZUCHI; HO-NO-IKAZUCHI; O-IKAZUCHI; SAKU-IKAZUCHI; WAKI-IKAZUCHI

**Ikiryo**   In Japanese folklore, the ghost of a living person, his double.

1542

**Iktomi** (Unktomi)   In North American Indian mythology (Dakota and Lakota), trickster who invented human speech.

1543

See also: TRICKSTER; UNKTOMI

**1544**

**Iku**  In African mythology (Yoruba of south-western Nigeria), the death spirit or god.

**1545**

**Ildefonso, St.**  657–667. In Christian legend, archbishop of Toledo, Spain, and patron saint of the city; also Doctor of the Church. Feast, 23 January.

Ildefonso was noted for his devotion to the Virgin Mary. She appeared to him one day and said, "You are my chaplain and faithful notary. Receive from me this chasuble [outer vestment] which my Son sends you from His treasury." Then the Virgin placed the chasuble on Ildefonso. From that time Ildefonso never sat in the bishop's throne nor wore the holy garment. After his death another bishop attempted to wear the chasuble and died as a result. El Greco painted St. Ildefonso.

See also: VIRGIN MARY

**1546**

**Ilé-Ifé** (house wide)  In African mythology (Yoruba of southwestern Nigeria), the place of creation. One Nigerian myth says that when the earth was created, God sent a chameleon to examine it. He found the earth to be wide enough but not dry enough. The place was called Ifé (wide); later Ilé (house) was added to show that from this "house" all things originated.

**1547**

**Ilmarinen** (maker of the sky?)  In the Finnish epic poem *The Kalevala*, the smith, forger of the magic sampo.

Ilmarinen constructed the magic sampo, a three-sided mill that ground out salt, grain, and money. It was intended for Vainamoinen to give Louhi, the evil mistress of Pohjola, the North-land, to woo her daughter, the Maiden of Pohjola. However, it was Ilmarinen, not Vainamoinen, who won the bride. After the Maiden of Pohjola was murdered, Ilmarinen set

out again to Pohjola to woo the sister of his former wife. When the girl refused him, he abducted her. She reviled Ilmarinen, who out of anger turned her into a seagull.

The hero then constructed a woman of gold and silver to replace his dead wife. All was fine, except there was no life in the creature. At night he lay beside his golden bride and awoke the next morning realizing that his wife was cold. He offered his golden bride to Vainamoinen, who rejected the offer, telling Ilmarinen to melt down his bride for gold.

One of Ilmarinen's last creative acts was to forge a new moon and sun after the evil mistress Louhi had locked up the sun and moon. But, as in the case of the golden bride, the new moon and sun did not shine or have life.

Ilmarinen originally may have been a god, but all traces of his divinity have disappeared from his life as told in *The Kalevala*.

See also: LOUHI; MAIDEN OF POHJOLA; *KALEVALA, THE*; SAMPO; VAINAMOINEN

*Ilya Muromets (I. Bilibin)*

**1548**

**Ilya Muromets** (Ilya of Murom, Ilia Murometz, Ilya-Muromyets)  In Russian folklore, hero of superhuman strength who appears in the *bylini*, the epic songs, as well as in numerous folktales.

Ilya Muromets was a *bogatyr*, an epic hero, who had been a sickly child and could not move until he was 33 years old. Then two passing pilgrims gave him a "honey draught" that made him powerful. He used his strength to defend Christianity against the "infidels" and invaders from outside Russia. He traveled great distances on his wondrous horse Sivushko. In one of the *bylini* Ilya destroyed "the monstrous pagan idol" that came to the city of Kiev "breathing threats, striving to inspire fear" in the people. Ilya cut the idol in two. The hero's end was sad, for he boasted of his deeds before God and as a result was turned into stone.

Ilya is a combination of various Russian legendary and mythological characters. Some see him as a pre-Christian Svyatogor, but recent scholarship does not support this. Some of his attributes, such as his miraculous bow, are similar to those of the pagan Slavic god Pyerun. With his bow he could bring down church cupolas and split oaks into thin slivers. There is some evidence that Ilya Muromets actually might have lived in the 12th century. The peasants of Murom, for instance, are noted for their strength and size to this day.

The Russian composer Reinhold Glière used Ilya Muromets' legends for his mammoth third symphony, titled *Ilya Muromets*.

See also: BYLINA; PYERUN; SVYATOGOR

1549
**Imana** (almighty)    In African mythology (Banyarwanda of Ruanda-Urundi), creator god who tried to save man from Death. Thought of in human form, Imana is believed to be a large person with very long arms. He is a beneficent deity who tried once to stop Death but failed. Imana ordered everyone to stay indoors while he hunted Death. But one woman went out, and Death asked her to hide him. She consented and opened her mouth. He jumped inside, and she swallowed him. This angered Imana, who then

allowed Death to have its way with humankind. Imana is also credited with creating the first man, Kazikamuntu (root of man), who had many children. Their continual fighting caused them to disperse, and that is why mankind is found in every part of the earth.

See also: ABUK AND GARANG; KALUMBA

1550
**Imhotep** (he who comes in peace)    In Egyptian history and legend, a god of knowledge and healing who lived at the court of King Zoser during the Third Dynasty (2635–2570 B.C.E.). His tomb in the desert near Memphis and the nearby temple, the Asklepion, became a place of pilgrimage for the sick and also for childless couples. He is said to have designed the Step Pyramid. An architect and artist, Imhotep was deified and was invoked by subsequent generations. He was said to be the son of the god Ptah and was worshiped in a triad of gods at Memphis. He is usually portrayed as a priest with a shaved head reading a scroll while seated. The Greeks identified him with Asclepius.

See also: ASCLEPIUS; PTAH

1551
**Imilozi** (whistlers)    In African mythology (Zulu), ancestral spirits who whistle when they speak to man.

1552
**Inanna** (lady of heaven)    In Near Eastern mythology (Sumerian), Great Mother goddess from whom Ishtar, the great Near Eastern goddess, is derived. Inanna was goddess of fertility. Although associated with many beneficent aspects of nature, she was also believed to be demonic, destroying her numerous male lovers. Her most famous lover was Dumuzi (the true, or faithful, one), a form of Tammuz, who presided over agriculture. Dumuzi was also god of the underworld and was called the shepherd and lord of the sheepfolds. In some myths, even though he

was Inanna's husband, she had him destroyed in order to save her life. Most of the myths associated with Inanna were adopted by Ishtar's cult.

See also: GREAT GODDESS; ISHTAR; TAMMUZ

**1553**

**Inapertwa** In Australian mythology, two sky gods who formed human beings with stone knives.

**1554**

**Inaras** In Near Eastern mythology (Hittite), goddess who helped slay the evil dragon Illuyankas. She made the dragon drunk with wine, and with the aid of her lover, Hupasiyas, she had the dragon trussed up with a cord and killed by the weather god. As a reward for helping her, Inaras had a house constructed for her lover Hupasiyas but told him never to look out the window or he would see his mortal wife and children. He disobeyed and was killed by Inaras.

**1555**

**Inari** In Japanese mythology, god of rice, often portrayed as a bearded old man sitting on a sack of rice, flanked on either side by a fox. The foxes are his messengers, but often they are confused with the god in popular imagination. Inari is also regarded as the god of prosperity and patron of tradesmen.

**1556**

**Indarapatra** In Philippine mythology, a hero who killed various monsters. His brother was Sulayman, who slew three monsters with his magic ring but was killed by Pah, a huge bird, when he attempted to kill the fourth. Indarapatra killed the fourth monster with the magic water of life. Later he rescued some women and was given one for a wife.

See also: WATER OF LIFE

**1557**

**Indigetes** (Indiges, singular) (indigenous) In Greek and Roman mythology, the epithet was given to deified heroes such as Achilles, Aeneas, Heracles, and Romulus. In Roman religion, Indigetes were local deities worshiped only in particular places. *Variant spelling*: Indiges (singular).

See also: ACHILLES; AENEAS; HERACLES; ROMULUS AND REMUS

*Indra*

**1558**

**Indra** In Hindu mythology, the storm god, who governs the weather and dispenses rain, sending lightning and thunder with his thunderbolt, Vajra.

Indra, whose mother was Nishtigri, is frequently mentioned in the Rig-Veda, the ancient collection of hymns to the gods, as being at war with Vritra, the demon of drought and inclement weather. One hymn cites a battle with Vritra (restrainer):

> I will declare the manly deeds of Indra the
> first that he achieved, the thunder-
> wielder.

He slew Vritra, then disclosed the waters,
And cleft the channels of the mountain
      torrents. . . .
Footless and handless still, Vritra challenged
      Indra, who smote him with his bolt
      between the shoulders.
Emasculate yet claiming manly vigor, thus
      Vritra lay with scattered limbs.

Another hymn in the collection calls Indra

Highest of Immortals light,
God of gods by lofty might,
He, before whose prowess high
Tremble earth and upper sky,
He is,—mortals, hear my verse,—
Indra, Lord of Universe!

The high position accorded Indra in the Rig-Veda is not mentioned in later Hindu mythology, where he is placed in the second rank of the gods. Indra is ruler of the atmosphere and of the east quarter of the compass. He reigns, with his wife, Indrani, in Swarga, Indra's heaven, located on Mount Meru. Sometimes Indra's capital is called Deva-pura (city of the gods) or Pusha-bhasa (sun splendor).

One later myth, recorded in the Hindu epic *The Ramayama*, indicates Indra's lesser position in the Hindu pantheon. Megha-nada, a demon who had the power of being invisible, used his magic gift to capture Indra and carried off the god to Lanka (Sri Lanka). The gods, headed by Brahma, called the demon Indra-jit (conqueror of Indra). The demon asked for the gift of immortality if the gods wished Indra freed. Brahma refused but finally gave in to the demand. In one version of *The Ramayana*, however, it says that Indra-jit was killed and his head cut off.

In Indian art Indra is portrayed as a man with four arms holding a lance and thunderbolt, or with two arms and eyes all over his body, giving him the epithet Sahasraksha (the thousand-eyed). Indra is usually shown riding the elephant Airavata, which was produced during the churning of the ocean when the gods and demons

fought for the Amrita, the water of life. Indra's horse is Uccaihsravas (neighing loudly, or long-eared).

Indra has many epithets and titles, among them Vritra-hatta (the destroyer of Vritra) and Vajra-pani (of the thunderbolt). His two weapons are the *chakra*, the wheel or discus that cuts off limbs with its sharp edge, and the *svastika* or *vajra* (thunderbolt), which can be a whirling thunderbolt. Other epithets are Megha-vahana (borne upon the clouds), Deva-pati (chief of the gods), Divas-pati (ruler of the atmosphere), Marutwan (lord of the winds), and Swarga-pate (lord of paradise). Indra's chariot is called Vimana; his charioteer, Matali; his bow (the rainbow), Sakradhanus; and his sword, Paran-ja.

See also: CHURNING OF THE OCEAN; INDRANI; *RAMAYANA, THE*; RIG-VEDA; UCCAIHSRAVAS; VRITRA

1559

**Indrani**   In Hindu mythology, wife of Indra, the storm god. In the Rig-Veda, a collection of hymns to the gods, Indrani is called the most fortunate of females, "for her husband shall never die of old age." Indra chose Indrani as his wife because of her sexual appeal. She was ravished by Indra, who killed her father to escape his curse. She was never held in high esteem as a goddess.

See also: INDRA; RIG-VEDA

1560

**Inéz de Castro, Doña**   Died 1355. In Portuguese history and legend, murdered mistress of King Pedro I of Portugal. In 1325 Alfonso IV, the Brave, came to the throne. His son, Dom Pedro, was married to Princess Constanza but was in love with her lady-in-waiting Doña Inéz de Castro, who bore Pedro four children. After Constanza's death, King Alfonso feared Doña Inéz's power over his son and had her murdered. Dom Pedro revolted against his father and was made king in 1357, when he issued a general pardon for the murderers. In 1360, however, he had two of them tortured to death. A legend arose that Pedro had the corpse of his beloved Inéz exhumed and crowned queen. Luiz de Camoes' epic poem *The Lusiads* (book 3) tells the legend. Doña Inéz is the subject of Juaquin Serra's ballet *Doña Inéz de Castro* and Thomas Pasatieri's opera *Inés de Castro*.

**1561**

**Inti**   In Inca mythology, the sun, from whom the Incas believed they were descended. Married to his sister Mama Quilla, the moon, Inti was portrayed as a human, his face represented by a disk of gold surrounded by rays of flames. Inti was also called Apu-Punchau (the head of day). Every night Inti plunged into the sea, swam under it through the night, and emerged refreshed in the morning.

See also: CATEQUIL; CHASCA; CUCHA; MAMA QUILLA

**1562**

**Inua**   In Eskimo mythology (Unalit peoples at Bering Strait), shade or soul of a person.

**1563**

**Io** (moon)   In Greek mythology, priestess of Hera and daughter of the river god Inachus and Melia, a priestess of Hera at Argos. Zeus seduced the young virgin Io. Afterward he transformed her into a heifer to protect her from the ever-jealous Hera. Other accounts say Hera transformed her as a punishment for submitting to Zeus. Hera chose Argus, a being with 100 eyes, to watch over Io. Her father, Inachus, looking for his daughter, discovered the heifer, who wrote out her name with her hoof, but Inachus could not help her. At last, Hermes lulled Argus to sleep with songs and stories, then cut off his head. Not giving up, Hera sent a gadfly to punish Io. Io wandered to Egypt, where she was restored to human shape and bore Epaphus, a son of Zeus. The Ionian Sea, according to some accounts, is named after Io, who swam across it after she was changed into a heifer. Ovid's *Metamorphoses* (book 1) tells the myth of Io, and she

appears in Aeschylus's *Prometheus Bound*. In Roman art she appears on the frescoes of the house of Livia on the Palatine in Rome. Correggio painted *Io and Jupiter* (Zeus).

See also: ARGUS; HERA; HERMES; OVID; ZEUS

**1564**

**Iocauna**   In the mythology of the Indians of the Antilles during the time of Columbus, one of the names of their supreme god. Although Iocauna was "one, eternal, omnipotent, and invisible," according to Peter Martyr d'Anghera's account in *De Orbe Novo* (1516), the Indians believed he had a mother, who was known by five names: Attabira (Atabex), Mamon, Guacarapita, Tella, and Guimazoa. Iocauna was also called Guamaonocon or Yochu Vagua Maorocoti.

**1565**

**Ion** (he who goes)   In Greek mythology, son of Apollo and Creusa; brother of Janus; married to Helice; father of Aegicores, Argades, Gelem, and Hoples. Ion was abandoned by his mother but was rescued by Apollo and sent to Delphi. He became the ancestor of the Ionians. Ion was killed in the Trojan War. Euripides' *Ion* deals with his myth.

See also: APOLLO; DELPHI; JANUS

**1566**

**Iouskeha and Tawiscaron** (Yoskeha and Tawiscara)   In North American Indian mythology (Iroquois), twin gods, one good, the other evil. The unborn twins began to quarrel in their mother's womb. After his birth, Tawiscaron killed his mother. But the goddess Ataensic, their grandmother, believed that Iouskeha was evil and Tawiscaron good. The two brothers were constantly in conflict with each other. Iouskeha created fruit trees and pleasant bushes and placed the sun and moon in their sphere of heaven; Tawiscaron created thorns and the Rocky Mountains. In the end, Iouskeha succeeded in imprisoning his evil brother underground.

See also: ATAENSIC; GLUSKAP AND MALSUM

1567

**Iphicles** (famous might)   In Greek mythology, twin brother of Heracles, son of Amphitryon and Alcmena. When the two babies were in the cradle, Hera, ever hateful toward Heracles, sent two large snakes to destroy them, but Heracles, only a year old, squeezed the snakes to death. This story is cited in some accounts as evidence that Heracles was fathered by Zeus and Iphicles by Amphitryon. Iphicles was the father of Iolaus, who helped Heracles conquer the Lernean Hydra by cauterizing the place where the head had been cut off.

See also: AMPHITRYON; HERA; HERACLES; HYDRA; ZEUS

1568

**Iphigenia** (mothering a strong race)   In Greek mythology, daughter of Agamemnon and Clytemnestra; sister of Electra, Chromythemis, and Orestes. When Agamemnon's ships were stilled at Aulis on their way to the Trojan War, the king sacrificed Iphigenia to placate the virgin goddess Artemis after Agamemnon had killed one of her stags. Knowing that Clytemnestra would never agree to the sacrifice, Agamemnon sent for Iphigenia under the pretext that she was to marry Achilles. In some accounts the sacrifice of Iphigenia was carried out to completion, and she died. Other ancient accounts say that while the sacrifice was being prepared, Artemis swept up Iphigenia and took her off to Tauris, where she became the goddess's priestess. Anyone who was shipwrecked on the island of Tauris was sacrificed to Artemis. Iphigenia's brother Orestes, in search of the sacred image of Artemis, was shipwrecked on the island. After discovering his identify, Iphigenia fled with him, taking the image of Artemis. In Homer's *Iliad* Iphigenia is called Chrysothemis. Aeschylus's *Agamemnon* follows the myth that says she was sacrificed, whereas Euripides' *Iphigenia in Aulis* and *Iphigenia in Tauris* follow the story that says she was saved. Gluck's operas *Iphigénie en Aulide* and *Iphigénie en Tauride* are based on Euripides' version. Racine's *Iphigénie* and Goethe's *Iphigenie auf Tauris* also tell the myth.

See also: AGAMEMNON; ARTEMIS; ELECTRA; *ILIAD, THE;* ORESTES

1569

**Iphimedia** (Iphimedeia) (strength of the genitals)   In Greek mythology, a daughter of Tropias, married to the giant Aloeus. Iphimedia fled from Aloeus and had two sons, Otus and Ephialtes, by Poseidon. Iphimedia is mentioned in Homer's *Odyssey* (book 11).

See also: *ODYSSEY, THE;* POSEIDON

1570

**Iphis** (strength)   In Greek and Roman mythology, daughter of Telethusa of Crete and Ligdus. Iphis was raised secretly as a boy by her mother because her father, Ligdus, wanted only male children and would have killed her had he known she was a girl. When Ianthe, a young girl, fell in love with Iphis, the goddess Isis changed Iphis into a man. Ovid's *Metamorphoses* (book 9) records the myth.

See also: OVID

*Iris conducting Aphrodite to Ares (John Flaxman)*

1571

**Iris** (rainbow)   In Greek mythology, goddess of the rainbow and messenger of the gods; daughter of the sea deities Thaumas and Electra.

Homer's *Iliad* (books 3, 5, 8) makes her the messenger of Zeus, though in much later mythology she appears as an aide to Hera, wife of Zeus. One of her functions was to cut the thread of life that detained the soul in the body when it was dying. Iris appears in Hesiod's *Theogony*, Ovid's *Metamorphoses* (book 1 et seq.), and Vergil's *Aeneid* (book 4). In English poetry she is cited in Milton's *Paradise Lost* (book 2.244) to describe the vestment of the archangel Michael with its airy color, like the rainbow. In Greek art she is portrayed as a young woman with wings carrying a messenger's wand, also used by Hermes. There are two statues of Iris among the Elgin Marbles. Iris survives as the English word for the colored portion of the eye, as well as the name of a family of flowers, including the gladiolus and crocus, which in Christian symbolism is often substituted for the lily in paintings portraying the Virgin Mary.

See also: ELECTRA; ELGIN MARBLES; HERA; HESIOD; *ILIAD, THE;* ZEUS

1572

**Iron Crown of Lombardy**    In medieval history and legend, crown of Agilulph, king of Lombardy in 591, said to have been given by Pope Gregory the Great. Charlemagne was crowned with it. It is called the Iron Crown because the inner fillet of iron is said to have been beaten out of a nail from the true cross of Christ, which was given to Emperor Constantine by his mother, St. Helena. The outer circlet is of beaten gold and set with precious stones. In 1805 Napoleon placed the crown on his head with his own hands.

See also: CHARLEMAGNE; CONSTANTINE; GREGORY THE GREAT; HELENA, ST.

1573

**Irra** (Dibbara, Girra, Iea, Ura)    In Near Eastern mythology (Babylonian-Assyrian), god of pestilence, the fearful slaughterer who laid waste the plains, taking delight in destroying both land and humankind.

One poetic myth narrates how Irra determined to destroy Babylon. Ishum, the fire god, is told by Irra:

In the city whither I send thee,
Thou shalt fear no one, nor have compassion.
Kill the young and old alike,
The tender suckling likewise—spare no one.
The treasures of Babylon carry off as booty.

After much discussion, Ishum makes Irra settle for some song of praise in the god's honor. Wherever a tablet with the song or incantation was hung or set up, that house would be free from the onslaughts of the god. The text ends:

He who glorifies my name will rule the
    world.
Who proclaims the glory of my power
Will be without a rival.
The singer who sings of my deeds will not die
    through pestilence. —.
Let the inhabitants of all places learn to
    glorify my name.

1574

**Iruwa**    In African mythology (Chaga of Kenya), sun god who forgave a man who attempted to murder him. Once a man decided to destroy the sun for killing his two sons. When the plot was discovered, Iruwa not only forgave the man but gave him more sons and even wealth.

1575

**Isaac** (laughter)    In the Bible, O.T., son of Abraham and Sarah, promised heir of Abraham, half-brother of Ishmael, married to Rebekah, father of Jacob and Esau.

The main events of Isaac's life are told in Genesis. The book tells how Abraham was visited by three men (angels) who predicted the birth of a child to the aged couple, Abraham and Sarah. When Sarah heard this, she laughed.

*Isaac*

When Yahweh, the Hebrew god, wished to test Abraham's faith, he ordered him to sacrifice his beloved son Isaac. However, seeing that Abraham was willing to kill his son, Yahweh intervened and stopped the sacrifice. Later Abraham sent a servant to find a wife for Isaac. The first girl who offered the servant water at a well was to be Isaac's wife. It was the daughter of Laban, Rebekah, by whom Isaac had two sons, Esau and Jacob. By a trick Rebekah secured Isaac's deathbed blessing and right of succession for her favorite, Jacob, by covering his arms and neck with goatskin to impersonate his hairy brother Esau. When Isaac discovered he had been tricked, he could not give Esau back his inheritance, for once a blessing was given it could not be recalled. But Isaac prevented strife between the two brothers, who later buried him in a cave when he died at the age of 108. In Islamic mythology Isaac is called Ishaq. He is mentioned in the Koran (sura 21). Isaac usually appears along with his father, Abraham, in many works titled *The Sacrifice of Isaac*. The scene appears on the Florence Baptistery doors by Lorenzo Ghiberti.

See also: ABRAHAM; ESAU; ISHMAEL; JACOB; REBEKAH; SARAH

1576

**Isaiah** (Yahweh is salvation)   In the Bible, O.T., one of the Major Prophets, also title of an Old Testament book. Isaiah lived in Judah in the latter part of the eighth century B.C.E. and is believed to have been descended from a royal family. The Book of Isaiah is now considered to be only partly his work: chapters 1 to 39 by Isaiah, chapters 40 to 50 by another hand (referred to as Second Isaiah), and chapters 56 to 66 by a third and unknown author. In the New Testament Jesus often quotes from the Book of Isaiah, citing passages believed to refer to the Messiah. Later Jewish legend, not recorded in the Bible, says that in his old age Isaiah was "sawn asunder in the trunk of a carob tree by order of King Manasseh."

In Christian art Isaiah is often depicted with a scroll inscribed with the Latin words *Ecce virgo concipiet et parium filium* (Behold a virgin shall conceive and bear a son) (Is. 7:15), which is a mistranslation of the Hebrew original. The word *virgin* is not used in the Hebrew, but *young woman*.

In Islamic legend the name given to Isaiah is Sha'ya. He is not mentioned in the Koran, though Islamic as well as Jewish and Christian legend says he was murdered.

See also: MANASSEH

1577

**Ishana Ten**   In Japanese Buddhist mythology, god derived from the Hindu god Shiva, portrayed as a fierce figure with three eyes, holding in his right hand a trident and in his left a shallow vessel containing clotted blood. He is one of the Jiu No O, 12 Japanese Buddhist gods and goddesses adopted from Hindu mythology.

See also: JIU NO O; SHIVA

1578

**Ishmael** (may God hear)   In the Bible, O.T., son of Abraham and his concubine Hagar; half-brother to Isaac. Ishamel was cast out of Abraham's house; he married and settled at Paran. The Arabs are said to be descended from his 12 sons. His name has come to mean any outcast and was used by Herman Melville in *Moby Dick* as the name of the narrator. His classic opening line reads simply: "Call me Ishmael."

See also: ABRAHAM

1579

**Ishtar** (Istar) In Near Eastern mythology, Semitic mother-goddess, in part derived from the Sumerian mother-goddess, Inanna.

Ishtar was both a beneficent goddess, the mother of humankind, and a demonic deity, a warrior goddess "clad in terror," who caused even the gods to tremble. Ishtar thus combined in her person and worship nearly all of the attributes, both good and evil, of many Near Eastern goddesses. As the great mother of the gods and the mother of men, she grieved over people's sorrows, being called in one hymn "she who loveth all men" and in another addressed as the goddess who "lookest mercifully upon a sinner." In this beneficent role Ishtar bestowed life, health, and prosperity with her "life-giving glance." She was the giver of vegetation and the creator of animals, wedlock, maternity, and all earthly blessings and moral laws for humankind.

But alongside her beneficent role Ishtar was also a demonic goddess. She was the warrior goddess. Part of a votive tablet placed for Hammurabi, the great ruler, reads: "Ishtar has given thee conflict and battle; what more can'st thou hope?" Ishtar was also a storm goddess, "the lofty one who causes the heavens to tremble, the earth to quake . . . who casts down the mountains like dead bodies."

Because Ishtar combined so many attributes of other goddesses, the myths surrounding her are often in conflict. In one account, for example, she is said to be the daughter of the moon god, Sin, and sister of the sun god, Shamash. In another account she is the daughter of Anu, the lord of heaven. Both accounts agree, however, that she is connected with the planet Venus. She is called "lady of resplendent light" in that role and is symbolized by an eight-pointed star, a symbol later associated with the Virgin Mary in Christianity.

Ishtar's most important role, however, was as goddess of sexual love. In this aspect she displayed an extremely despotic attitude. In the Babylonian epic poem *Gilgamesh*, for example, she is at first in love with the shepherd Tammuz, then with a bird, then a lion, then a horse, then a shepherd, then a gardener, and finally with Gilgamesh, the hero king. Gilgamesh, however, rejects Ishtar because she had killed so many of her lovers, which the hero enumerates to the goddess, the prime example being her husband, Tammuz. Their cruel sexual relationship is vividly described in another poem, *Ishtar's Descent into the Underworld*. The poem is known in many different versions in Near Eastern literature, and the name of the goddess is often changed. In one text the name is Inanna.

According to the poem, Ishtar once looked down from her home in heaven to the deep pit of the underworld. She decided she wanted to go down, but she told her minister, Ninshubar, that after she was gone he was to "beat a drum in the holy shrine" for her sake, telling the gods Enlil, Nanna, Eridu, and Enki that she was in the underworld.

Ishtar then went down and arrived at the gate of the underworld. Its chief keeper, Neti, asked her what she wanted. She lied, telling him she had come for the burial rites of Gugalanna, husband of Ereshkigal, the queen of the underworld. Ereshkigal was also the sister of Ishtar. Neti then went to Ereshkigal and told her that her sister Ishtar was at the gates and wished to enter. Ereshkigal told Neti that he was to let Ishtar in but to be certain that when each of the seven doors of the underworld was unlocked Ishtar followed the rite connected with passage through the gate. Ishtar then went from door to door. At each door she was divested of some symbol of her power—her Shugurra, her royal rod, her necklace, two stones that lay on her breast, her golden ring, her pectoral gems, and finally the robe of sovereignty that covered her body.

At the last door Ishtar dropped naked on her knees before her sister, Ereshkigal. The queen, in conjunction with seven judges, pronounced the sentence that Ishtar was to die. Immediately, the goddess died, and her corpse was hung on a pike. Three nights passed. Ninshubar, her faithful follower, then did as the goddess Ishtar had earlier instructed him. He called on the gods for help, but only Enki responded. (In the poem Enki is called Ishtar's father.) He formed two beings, the Kurgarru and the Kalaturru, giving the first the food of life and second the water of life. The two descended to hell asking for Ishtar's body. When they found it, they sprinkled the food and the water on the body, restoring it to life. But one problem remained—another dead body had to be substituted for the restored one of Ishtar. The cruel goddess offered her youthful husband Tammuz, who was then grabbed by seven demons, killed, and taken to hell, where his body replaced that of the resurrected goddess.

A variant poetic version of *Ishtar's Descent into the Underworld* was used by the French composer Vincent d'Indy for his *Istar*, a set of symphonic variations for orchestra. Instead of the main theme coming first, it appears only at the end to indicate the complete nakedness of the goddess before the last gate. In d'Indy's text Ishtar descends to the underworld to find her husband Tammuz. She brings him back to earth because the land is barren without him (he was the spirit, or god, of vegetation).

Ishtar had numerous temples throughout the Near East. The chief seat of her worship was at Erech; others were at Ashur, Babylon, Nineveh, and Ur. Ishtar was identified with numerous other Near Eastern goddesses, such as Anath, Anunit, Aruru, Ashdar, Asherah, Astarte, Ashtoreth, Athtar, Belit, Innimi, Kilili, Mah, Meni, Nana, Ninharsag, Ninlil, and Nintud. Therefore, her symbols were also many. Among them were a dove, an ear of wheat, a forked tree, a lion, a serpent, an ornamented cone, a pillar, and a tree stem. Sometimes she was portrayed as a woman nursing a child, similar to Egyptian works showing Isis nursing Horus or Christian portrayals of the Virgin Mary nursing the child Jesus.

See also: ANU; ANATH; ARURU; ASTARTE; ERESHKIGA; HORUS; INANNA; SHAMASH; SIN; TAMMUZ

1580
**Ishvara** (supreme soul)    In Buddhism, title of the Hindu god Shiva meaning independent existence and used for a transcendent or extramundane god, a personal deity. The Buddha rejected this concept. He said: "If Ishvara be the maker, all living things should have silently to submit to their maker's power. They would be like vessels formed by the potter's hand; and if it were so, how would it be possible to practice virtue? If the world had been made by Ishvara there should be no such thing as sorrow, or calamity, or sin; for both pure and impure deeds must come from him. If not, there would be another cause beside him, and he would not be the self-existent one. Thus, you see, the thought of Ishvara is overthrown." Buddhism teaches the interdependence of all things as at once the causes and effects of everything and does not require an uncaused cause to make the universe.

See also: BUDDHA, THE; SHIVA

1581
**Isidore of Seville, St.** (gift of Isis)    Seventh century. In Christian legend, bishop of Seville, Doctor of the Church. Feast, 4 April.

The brother of St. Leander, who preceded him in his bishopric, Isadore was noted for his writings, the most famous being his *Etymologies*, an encyclopedia of information on every subject then known to man. The saint based his work on previous books and did not verify any of the facts or stories. His support of the anti-Semitic canons enacted in Spain against the Jews who did not accept Christianity greatly diminished his reputation.

Numerous miracles are recorded about the saint: Once a man wanted to steal a relic of St. Isidore and hid in the church where the saint was buried. When all was quiet, he broke open the shrine and cut off one of Isidore's fingers. No sooner had he done this than he was turned to stone. He thought it best to return the finger, which, when he could move again, he did, thanking the saint for his mercy in not killing him.

Murillo's painting of St. Isidore and St. Leander portrays each enthroned and robed in white, wearing their bishops' miters.

1582

**Isidore the Ploughman, St.** (gift of Isis)   12th century. In Christian legend, patron saint of Madrid, Spain. Isidore was a poor workman who could neither read nor write. One day his master, Juan de Vargas, went into the fields to see if Isidore was working or, as he had heard from other servants, praying. As Vargas came near the field, he saw two angels guiding the plow while Isidore knelt in prayer. Another legend tells how when Vargas was thirsty Isidore struck a rock with his goad and pure water flowed out. The saint is portrayed dressed as a workman, sometimes with a spade in his hand.

*Isis*

1583

**Isis** (throne goddess)   In Egyptian mythology, the Greek form of the Egyptian name Ast or Eset, the sister-wife of Osiris and the mother of Horus; a great mother goddess. Isis was part of the fourth generation of the Ennead of Heliopo-

lis and became more widely worshiped than any other Egyptian deity. Like other creator deities, she was able to produce life without a partner. She stimulated the inertness of Osiris and took his seed into her body to conceive their child. Often Isis and the goddess Hathor are commingled because both were great mother goddesses. This merging of religious and cultic beliefs and practices is called syncretism. The term was used by the Greek writer Plutarch for the union of Greek, Roman, and Egyptian cultic deities and beliefs during his day.

Numerous passages in the ancient Pyramid Texts state that Osiris, Isis, Set, and Nephthys were deified members of a family of human beings Plutarch, in his short book *Isis and Osiris*, writes that when Set killed his brother Osiris and threw his coffin into a river, Isis found the coffin and hid it, but Set discovered the hiding place, cut up Osiris's body, and scattered the pieces throughout Egypt. Isis recovered the dismembered parts, and with the help of the god Thoth restored her brother-husband and had intercourse with him, conceiving a child who was called Horus. *The Book of the Dead* has many allusions to Isis's loving care of Osiris, but it says little of her devotion to her son Horus, whom she reared so that he would become the avenger of his father.

The Metternich Stele (found in Alexanderia in 1828 and given to Prince Metternich by Mohammed Ali) tells how the goddess in her wanderings and sorrows cried out, "I, even I, am Isis, and I came forth from the house wherein my brother Set has placed me." For Set was not content with murdering his brother Osiris but took further vengeance by shutting Isis up in a prison. While she was confined there, Thoth, the prince of law in both heaven and earth, came to her and gave her advice that would protect her unborn son. With Thoth's help she escaped and later exclaimed, "I came forth from the house at eventide, and there also came forth with me my seven scorpions, who were to accompany me, and to be my helpers. Two scorpions, Tefen and Befen, were behind me, two scorpions, Mestet and Mestetef, were by my side, and three scorpions, Petet, Thetet and Maatet, showed me the way."

The seven scorpion goddesses led Isis to a village near the papyrus swamps. Isis sought shelter from a rich woman, who closed the door in her face (just as Joseph and Mary were not given shelter in the Christian legend). Enraged at the treatment Isis received from the woman, one of the scorpion goddesses, Tefen, made her way under the door of the woman's house, stung her child to death, and set the house afire. Isis, taking pity on the woman's grief for her child, restored him to life, and a flood of rain extinguished the fire. Meanwhile a peasant woman invited Isis to her house, and the goddess stayed there, while the woman who had rejected Isis suffered agonies of remorse.

Soon after, Isis brought forth her child Horus on a bed of papyrus plants in the swamps. She hid the boy carefully, fearing that he might by stung by some venomous reptile. One day she set out for the city of Am to obtain provisions for her son. When she returned, she found him lying dead, foam on his lips, the ground around him soaked with tears from his eyes. In a moment she realized that Set, in the form of a scorpion, had killed Horus. Her cries brought out the neighbors, but none could help her. Nephthys, her sister, came to her aid, telling her to appeal to the sun god Ra. She cried to the god, and the sun stood still in heaven. Thoth (a form of Ra in the myth) descended to earth to comfort Isis, repeating to her a spell that would restore Horus to life.

Isis learned the magic words, and when she uttered them, the poison flowed from her son's body, air entered his lungs, sense and feeling returned to him, and he was restored to life. Thoth ascended to heaven, and the sun resumed his course amid great rejoicing.

When Horus grew up, he fought against Set in a battle that lasted three days and three nights. Horus had gained the advantage when Isis, who was also Set's sister, took pity on her brother and allowed him to escape. Horus, filled with anger at his mother, avenged himself by cutting off her head. However, Thoth intervened and transformed the severed head into the head of a cow and attached it to Isis.

It is evident from a number of passages in various Egyptian texts that Isis possessed great skill in magic. In the *Hymn to Osiris*, Isis's use of magic words helps restore Osiris to life, and in *The Book of the Dead* one entire chapter is devoted to the purpose of bestowing on the deceased some of the magical powers of the goddess.

Isis was worshiped throughout Egypt. She had numerous titles, such as "the divine one," "the greatest of all the gods and goddesses," "the queen of all gods," "the female Ra," "the female Horus," "the lady of the new year," "the maker of sunrise," "the lady of heaven," and "the light giver of heaven." Worship of Isis spread beyond Egypt. From various classical writers we find that she was revered in several places in western Europe, being identified with Persephone, Tethys, and Athene, just as her husband, Osiris, was identified with Hades, Dionysus, and other foreign gods. In her chief temple in Rome the goddess was called Isis Campensis. Apuleius in *The Golden Ass* gives a description of a festival of Isis that was held in Rome in the latter half of the second century C.E. The writer calls the goddess *regina coeli*, or "queen of heaven" (a title later used for the Virgin Mary) and identifies her with Ceres, Venus, and Persephone. The holiest of all her sanctuaries known to the Greeks was at Tithorea. Pausanias, in his *Description of Greece* (chapter 32), writes that a festival was held there in her honor twice a year, in spring and autumn.

Isis was also identified with many local Syrian goddesses, and the early Christians bestowed some of her attributes on the Virgin Mary. Several of the incidents of the wanderings of Mary with the Christ Child in Egypt as recorded in the apocryphal Gospels reflect scenes in the life of Isis as described in the texts found on the Metternich Stele.

Isis is usually portrayed wearing the vulture headdress and holding a papyrus scepter in one hand and the ankh, the symbol of life, in the other. Her most famous symbol is the *thet*, the knot or buckle of Isis, which is indicative of her power to bind and also serves as a symbol of blood and life. Sometimes Isis is portrayed suckling her infant son Horus.

Among the many epithets of the goddess are Khut, as light giver; Usert, as earth goddess; Thenenet, as great goddess of Duat, the underworld; Satis, who spread the life-giving waters of the Nile flood; Anukis, as the embracer of the land and the producer of fertility by her waters; Ankhet, as the producer and giver of life; Kekhet, as the goddess of cultivated land and fields; Renenet, as the goddess of the harvest; Tcheft, as the goddess of food that was offered to the gods; and Ament (hidden goddess), as the great lady of the underworld who assisted in restoring the bodies of the blessed dead to live in the kingdom of Osiris, the lord of the dead.

See also: ANKH; *BOOK OF THE DEAD, THE*; DUAT; ENNEAD; GREAT MOTHER; HATHOR; HORUS; NEPHTHYS; OSIRIS; PYRAMID TEXTS; RA; SET; THOTH

1584

**Israel** (God fights, God rules?)   In the Bible, O.T., name given to Jacob after he had wrestled with the angel (Gen. 32:28) and again by God at Bethel (Gen. 35:10). Israel is also the name given to the region inhabited by the Twelve Tribes fathered by Jacob.

See also: JACOB

1585

**Israfel** (serafim, the burning one)   Angel of music in Islamic mythology who will announce the Last Judgment, the end of the world. Although Israfel is not named directly in the Koran, he appears in Islamic tradition. He is said to be the archangel who for three years was the companion of Muhammad and trained him for his role as the prophet. Gabriel, who is called Jiburili in Islam, then took over the task and dictated the Koran to the prophet from the perfect copy in heaven.

Alexander the Great, an important figure in Islamic legend, met Israfel before arriving in the Land of Darkness. There the angel stood on a hill and blew his trumpet. His trumpet will announce the Day of Resurrection, when he will stand upon the Holy Rock in Jerusalem and give the signal that will bring the dead back to life.

Edgar Allan Poe, fascinated by the sound of the angel's name and his function in Islamic mythology, wrote a poem called "Israfel." In its preface Poe quotes: "And the angel Israfel, whose heart-strings are a lute, and who has the sweetest voice of all God's creatures.—Koran." Apparently Poe confused a footnote in the Koran with text, as Israfel is not mentioned in the holy book.

In Egypt today it is believed that Israfel's music will refresh the inhabitants of paradise, as he does in Poe's poem, which inspired the title of Harvey Allen's biography of the poet and Edwin Markham's poem in Poe's honor, *Our Israfel*.

See also: ANGEL; ARCHANGEL; GABRIEL; MUHAMMAD

1586

**Italapas**   In North American Indian mythology (Chinook), the name given Coyote, who appears in much Indian mythology. Italapas aided Ikanam, the creator, in forming mankind as well as teaching them the arts. He made the first prairie by pushing the sea back. He elaborated various taboos regarding hunting. His character is different from that of other coyotes in that he is not a mischievous being. In the accounts of the Indians of California, for example, Coyote always attempts to thwart creation.

See also: COYOTE

1587

**Itzamná** (Yzamana, Zamana)   In Mayan mythology, culture hero and sky god who taught the Indians how to grow corn. He was the son of Hunabhú. Itzamná's most frequent title was Kin-ich-ahau (lord of the sun's face or lord, the eye of day) in his role as the sun's disk. At Itzamal there was a temple dedicated to Itzamná as Kin-ich-kak-mo (the eye of the day, the bird of fire), which people came to in times of pestilence. An offering was placed on the altar at noon and consumed by fire. A temple at Campeche, dedicated to him as Kin-ich-ahau-haban (lord of the sun's face, the hunter), had blood sacrifices; at another temple he was worshiped as Kabil (he of the lucky hand) for cures. In Mayan art Itzamná is portrayed as an old man with toothless jaws and sunken cheeks. He was revered by the priesthood as the patron of writing and learning. Paul Schellhas, when classifying the gods of some Mayan codices, gave Itzamná the letter *D*, and the god is sometimes referred to as God D.

See also: HUNABHÚ

1588

**Ivaldi** (the mighty)   In Norse mythology, father of the craftsmen dwarfs or elves who constructed the ship Skithblathnir; Odin's spear, Gungnir; and the golden hair for Thor's wife, Sif, which had been cut off by the fire-trickster god, Loki, and had to be replaced.

See also: ALFHEIM; SIF

1589

**Ivan the Terrible** (Russian: Ivan Groznyi) 1530–1584. In Russian legend, Ivan IV, czar of Muscovy, noted for his extreme cruelty. He was the first ruler to call himself czar, Russian for Caesar.

In 1564, after the treason of one of his counselors, Ivan organized a personal bodyguard called the Oprichnik, who acted in a manner similar to the Nazi Gestapo. They terrorized the countryside and executed "offenders" against the czar. Ivan's evil reputation made an impact on Russian legend, poetry, and music.

In one *bylina*, or heroic song, the czar resolves to kill his son because of an alleged conspiracy. The son is to be executed, but his mother and uncle intervene. The uncle seeks out the conspirator and kills him. Even though the son survives in the *bylina*, he was in fact killed by his father in 1581.

Rimsky-Korsakov's opera *Ivan the Terrible*, sometimes called *The Maid of Pskov*, deals with a romantic legend of Ivan's secret daughter, Olga, and her lover, Tutcha, who are killed when defending Pskov against Ivan's lust. Tchaikovsky's opera *The Oprichnik* also has a romantic plot. Anton Rubinstein's opera *The Merchant of Kalashnikov* uses Lermontov's poem *A Song About Tsar Ivan Vasilyevich, the Young Opricknik, and the Merchant Kalashnikov* as the basis for the libretto. Sergei Eisenstein's film *Ivan the Terrible*, in two parts, has music by Serge Prokofiev.

1590

**Iwa**   In Polynesian mythology, Hawaiian trickster and master thief, who stole while he was in his mother's womb. Once he had a contest with other thieves to see who could completely fill up a house with stolen goods in one night. Iwa waited until the thieves had fallen asleep, then he stole all of the goods from their houses and placed them in his house. Possessing a magic paddle, Iwa was capable of rowing from one end of the Hawaiian islands to the other in four strokes.

See also: TRICKSTER

1591

**Ixchel**   In Mayan mythology, water goddess who presided over floods, the rainbow, pregnancy, and weaving; believed by some scholars to be the goddess of the moon. Ixchel is a demonic goddess, the personification of the destructive nature of water. In one Mayan artwork she is portrayed as an angry old woman destroying the world by flood. Although she is generally demonic, she is married to Itzamná and is thus regarded as the mother of the Mayan pantheon. In Mayan art she is usually portrayed surrounded by the symbols of death and destruction, with a serpent on her head and crossbones on her dress. When classifying the gods in some Mayan codices, Paul Schellhas gave Ixchel the letter *I*, and she is sometimes referred to as Goddess I.

See also: ITZAMNÁ

**Ix-huyne**   In Mayan mythology, goddess of
the moon, though sometimes Ixchel, the water
goddess, is given that role.

See also: IXCHEL

*Tantalus, Sisyphus, and Ixion*

**Ixion**   In Greek mythology, the first murderer;
king of the Lapiths in Thessaly; son of Antion
and Perimele (or Ares or Phlegyas); married to
Dia; father of Perithous and, by a cloud, father of
the centaurs and Amycus. Ixion killed his father-
in-law and tried to seduce Hera, the wife of Zeus.
Ixion was tricked by Zeus, who caused a cloud to
appear in the form of Hera. Ixion had sexual intercourse with the cloud, fathering a race of centaurs. Zeus then hurled a thunderbolt at Ixion
and had Hermes confine him to the underworld,
tied to a fiery wheel that constantly revolved and
was lashed by serpents. Ovid's *Metamorphoses*
(book 12) tells the story. Ovid's image was passed
on to European medieval tradition, which saw
Ixion as symbolic of lewdness or sensuality, as it
saw Sisyphus as pride and Tantalus as avarice. Ixion appears in Dante's *Divine Comedy* (Hell),
Spenser's *Faerie Queene* (1.5.35), Pope's *Rape of
the Lock*, and Robert Browning's *Ixion*, in which
the English poet has Ixion gain insight through
his suffering.

See also: ARES; CENTAURS; HERA; HERMES;
OVID; PHLEGYAS; SISYPHUS; TANTALUS; ZEUS

**Ixtab**   In Mayan mythology, goddess of suicide. According to Mayan belief, a suicide went
directly to paradise, as opposed to Christian belief, in which the soul was assigned to hell. In
Mayan art Ixtab is portrayed hanging from the
sky by a halter around her neck. Her eyes are
closed, and signs of decomposition appear on her
body.

**Ixtlilton** (Yxtlilton) (the little black one)   In
Aztec mythology, god of medicine, fasting, and
games, whose temple contained jars of water
known as *tlital* (black water), used to heal the
sick, particularly children. Fray Bernardino de
Sahagún, in his *Historia general de las cosas de
Nueva España* (1570–1582), writes that when a
child was cured, the parents would take into their
home a priest who impersonated the god. At the
house a feast was held that "consisted of dances
and songs." When the priest impersonating the
god later left the house, "they gave him rugs or
shawls."

**Izanagi and Izanami** (the male who invites and
the female who invites)   In Japanese mythology, primeval creator god and goddess, ancestors of many Shinto gods as well as of the
principal islands of Japan.

Their myth is told in the *Kojiki* (records of ancient matters), written in 712 C.E. They appeared
on the expanse of high heaven before the earth
had been created and were chosen by the gods to
create the earth.

In the beginning there was only chaos. From
the mire, in the form of a reed, grew *kunitoko-
tatchi*, "eternal land ruler," and two subordinate
deities. Izanagi and Izanami were their descendants. The couple was given a jeweled spear, and
standing on the Floating Bridge of Heaven, a
rainbow, they pushed down the spear and pulled
up brine. They piled up the brine and formed the
island of Onogoro.

Izanagi and Izanami then came down to the island of Onogoro but found it deserted. They were lonely, and after looking intently at one another, decided to marry.

"How is thy body formed?" Izanagi asked Izanami.

"My body is completely formed except for one part that is incomplete," she replied.

"My body is completely formed, and there is one part that is superfluous. Suppose that we supplement that which is incomplete in thee with that which is superfluous in me, and thereby procreate lands."

The two slept together. A child was born, but without legs, so they cast it adrift in a reed boat. Their second child was the Island Awa, but they refused it also. Izanagi and Izanami then went up to heaven to ask the gods what the trouble was. They were informed that when they made love Izanami spoke first, which was wrong. The man was to speak first. They again slept together and gave birth to the eight islands that became Japan. Thus, at a Shinto wedding ceremony the groom speaks first.

The couple continued producing islands and gods until Izanami died giving birth to the fire god. Then Izanagi descended to the underworld, the *yomotsu-kuni*, in search of his wife. He lit a tooth of the comb that held his hair to illuminate his passage. Finding only the decaying corpse of his wife, he fled in horror. Reaching earth again, he hastened to bathe and purify himself in the river. From every garment he threw off and from every part of his body, from his feet to his nose, a fresh god was born, such as the Sun goddess, the Moon god, and Susano, the storm god.

See also: EARTH DIVER; *KOJIKI*; BIFROST; SUSANO

1597

**Iztaccihuatl** (white woman)    In Aztec mythology, mountain goddess described by Fray Diego Durán in his *Book of the Gods and Rites* (c. 1576), which deals with Aztec mythology, as a young woman "wearing clipped man's hair on the forehead and hanging down to the shoulders on the sides. Her cheeks were always painted with color." Ixtaccihuatl is also the name of a mountain in Mexico some 16,000 feet high, which, according to some commentators, resembles a woman lying down in a white shroud.

# J

*Jack and the Beanstalk (Arthur Rackham)*

butcher for some colored beans. When he returns home, his mother, angry at his stupidity, tosses the beans out a window. The next morning a large beanstalk is seen to have sprouted. Jack climbs the stalk and finds a giant's castle. He hides as he hears the giant sing, "Fee-fi-fo-fum / I smell the blood of an Englishman / Be he live or be he dead / I'll grind his bones to make my bread." Jack sees the giant's wife prepare a big dinner for the giant and watches as a little red hen lays a golden egg. When the giant falls asleep, Jack steals the hen. The next day he climbs the stalk again and this time steals bags of gold. Finally, the third time he steals the giant's harp, which cries out for help. The giant chases Jack down the beanstalk, but Jack cuts down the stalk and the giant is killed. Jack and the Beanstalk is incorporated into a story with other folktale characters in the musical *Into the Woods*.

1599

**Jacob** (supplanter)  In the Bible, O.T., the second son of Isaac and Rebekah, twin brother of Esau. Jacob was later renamed Israel by Yahweh, the Hebrew god.

Jacob's story is found in the Book of Genesis (chaps. 25–50). He was an agriculturalist, and his brother Esau was a hunter. Once when Esau was out hunting, he returned home very hungry and asked Jacob for some food. Jacob, a very wily

1598

**Jack and the Beanstalk**  English folktale popular in the British Isles and the United States. Jack, a rather simple boy, is sent by his mother, a widow, to sell their cow. Jack sells the cow to a

*Jacob*

man, would not give the food unless Esau sold him his birthright, which Esau did for "a pottage of lentils" (Gen. 25:34). In order to claim this birthright Jacob had to obtain a blessing from his father. He knew that his father would give the birthright only to Esau. When his father was old and blind, Jacob, with the help of his mother, Rebekah, disguised himself as Esau by wrapping his arms in goatskin. When his father touched the goatskin, he took Jacob to be Esau, because, as Jacob had said, "Esau my brother is a hairy man, and I am a smooth man" (Gen. 27:11). Isaac became suspicious when he heard Jacob speak. Isaac then said, "The voice is Jacob's voice, but the hands are the hands of Esau" (Gen. 27:22). Nevertheless, he gave his blessing—and Esau's birthright—to Jacob. Esau was so enraged that Jacob fled to his uncle in Haran. On his way Jacob stopped at night and lay down to sleep, using stones (fetish figures of gods) for a pillow. "And he dreamed, and behold a ladder set up on the earth, and the top of it reached to heaven: and behold the angels of God ascending and descending on it. And behold, the Lord [Yahweh] stood above it, and said, 'I am the Lord God of Abraham thy father, and the God of Isaac: the land whereon thou liest, to thee will I give it, and to thy seed.'" When Jacob awoke, he realized that Yahweh had been with him, and he took the stones of his pillow and erected a shrine, pouring oil on it and calling it Bethel (the house of God).

When Jacob arrived at Haran, he met Laban's beautiful daughter Rachel coming to water the sheep. Jacob rolled away the stone from the well, watered the sheep, kissed Rachel, and told her he was her kinsman. He then worked for his uncle for seven years to obtain Rachel, but Laban tricked him and had his daughter Leah slipped into the marriage bed instead of Rachel. When Jacob discovered he had married Leah instead of Rachel, Laban explained to him that it was not possible to give away his youngest daughter before the eldest was married. Jacob then agreed to work another seven years to obtain Rachel as his wife. It was Rachel who Jacob loved, but it was Leah who bore most of his children, as Rachel was barren until later in life.

After some 20 years, Jacob left with his wives and children for Hebron, the home of his father. Laban pursued him but eventually made peace. Approaching Seir, where Esau lived, Jacob sent many gifts ahead, fearful that his brother would kill him and his family. One night Jacob wrestled with and captured an angel, who begged to be released. Jacob consented on condition that the angel give him a blessing. "And he said, 'Thy name shall be called no more Jacob, but Israel: for as a prince hast thou power with God and with men, and hast prevailed'" (Gen. 32). (Angel is often a term for Yahweh in the Old Testament.) Jacob's most famous son was Joseph. In Islam Jacob is called Ya'qub.

In 1296 Edward I brought the stone on which the kings of Scotland were crowned to Westminster Abbey. British monarchs are seated on this stone during the coronation ceremony. The monk claimed that this was the very stone "pillow" that Jacob rested his head on when he had the vision of the ladder. Scenes from his life are frequently found in Western art. Gerbrandt van den Eeckhout's *Isaac Blessing Jacob* is one of the best known.

See also: ESAU; ISAAC; LEAH; LENTIL; REBEKAH; YAHWEH

1600

**Jagan-Natha** (Lord of the World)   In Hindu mythology, a form of Krishna and brother to Balarama. While Krishna is usually depicted as a handsome youth, Jagan-Natha's image is repulsively ugly. One myth that explains this difference says that Krishna was killed by a hunter, and his body was left to rot under a tree. His remains were found, and the bones were placed in a box. Then Vishnu directed King Indradyumna to make an image of Jagan-Natha and to put the bones in it. Vishvakarman, the architect of the gods, said that he would make the image, but he must not be disturbed until it was finished. After 15 days the king could not wait any longer, so Vishvakarman left the image unfinished, with no arms or legs.

See also: JUGGERNAUT; KALI; KRISHNA; SUBHADRA; VISHNU

1601

**Jahi**   In Persian mythology, demoness of debauchery. Jahi is called a malicious fiend and a harlot in the sacred ancient Persian book *Avesta*.

See also: *AVESTA*

1602

**Jambavat**   In the Hindu epic poem *The Ramayana*, the king of the bears, who aids Rama in his invasion of Lanka (Sri Lanka). Jambavat came into possession of a magic gem that protected its owner if he remained good but brought ruin on any evil person who had it. The magic gem came to Jambavat after its owner, Prasena, was killed by a lion for his evil life. The lion was in turn killed by Jambavat, who took the gem. Krishna (an incarnation of the god Vishnu) then came in search of the gem and fought Jambavat for 21 days. At the end of the battle Jambavat not only gave Krishna the gem but also offered his daughter, Jambavati. Later Jambavat joined in the war against the demon Ravana, who had abducted Rama's wife, Sita.

See also: KRISHNA; RAMA; *RAMAYANA, THE*; RAVANA; VISHNU

1603

**James, Jesse**   1847–1882. In American history and folklore, killer-bandit who, according to legend, stole from the rich to give to the poor. Born in Clay County, Missouri, the son of a preacher, Jesse and his brother Frank led a band of thieves throughout the 1870s. Popular sentiment was in James's favor, as expressed in the following folktale: One day he and his brother Frank were given a meal by a poor widow who was waiting for her landlord to collect an $800 mortgage. Jesse said the woman reminded him of his mother, and he would lend her the money needed. All she had to do was make sure the landlord gave her a receipt for the amount before he left. Jesse and Frank then left, and the landlord arrived. Taking the widow's money, he gave her the requested receipt and rode off. But he did not get too far before some masked men held him up and took the $800. James was later killed by one of his gang, Robert Ford. His brother Frank became a respectable farmer in later life. The American ballad "Jesse James" opens with:

Jesse James was a lad that killed many a man.
He robbed the Danville train.
But that dirty little coward that shot Mr.
    Howard [Jesse]
He laid poor Jesse in the grave.
It was Robert Ford, that dirty little coward,
I wonder how he does feel:
For he ate of Jesse's bread and slept in Jesse's
    bed
And laid poor Jesse in the grave.

Among the Hollywood movies about him are *Jesse James* (1939), *The Return of Frank James* (1940), and *The True Story of Jesse James* (1957); all are more legend than history.

See also: BELLE STARR

1604

**James the Greater, St.** (St. James Major) (Greek form of Jacob, one who takes by the heel, the supplanter)   First century. In the Bible,

*St. James the Greater (Dürer)*

N.T., Apostle; patron of Spain, pilgrims, and furriers. Feast, 25 July.

James, along with Peter and John, was present at the Transfiguration of Christ and the agony in the garden (Mark 5:37; 9:2; 14:33). After Christ's Ascension James was put to death by the sword at the command of Herod Agrippa (Acts 12:2).

The scant information on James in the New Testament was supplemented by medieval Spanish legend in which he was turned into St. Jago or Santiago, the military patron saint of Spain. According to Spanish legend, James was the son of Zebedee, an illustrious baron of Galilee, who, as the proprietor of ships, was accustomed to fish along the shores of a certain lake called Gennesareth solely for good pleasure and recreation. Having James be the son of a well-to-do family, and not a fisherman as in Scripture, accorded more with Spanish concepts of class distinction. In *The Divine Comedy* (Paradise 25:17) Dante calls St. James "the baron," alluding to the medieval belief.

According to legend, after Christ's Ascension, James preached the Gospel in Judea, then traveled over much of the world, and at last arrived in Spain, where he made few converts. One day, as he stood with his disciples on the banks of the river Ebro, the Virgin Mary appeared to him seated on the top of a pilar of jasper and surrounded by a choir of angels. James threw himself on his face. The Virgin then commanded him to build on that spot a chapel for her worship, assuring him that all this province of Saragossa, though now pagan, would at a future time be devoted to her. James did as he was told, and the church was called Nuestra Señora del Pilar (Our Lady of the Pillar). James then went back to Judea after a contest with a magician, Hermogenes, who not only renounced his evil ways but became a follower of James, who gave him his staff as the most effective means of defense against demons. James met his death at the command of Herod Agrippa. His body was carried to Joppa and conducted miraculously on an unmanned boat with sails to Spain, where a church was built in his honor by Queen Lupa after the evil woman had been converted to Christianity by a miracle. When Spain was overrun by the Moors, the shrine of the saint was forgotten, but in 800 the burial spot was found by a friar. The saint's body was moved to Compostela, where it brought about many miracles. In nearby Padron a huge stone is said to be the boat that brought him back to Spain.

Spanish historians number some 38 apparitions of the saint in which he helped the Spanish defeat their enemies. In one account St. James, mounted on a milk-white charger and waving aloft a white standard, led the Christians against the Moors, leaving some 60,000 Moors dead on the field. The battle cry from that engagement at Clavijo was "Santiago," the war cry of the Spaniards for centuries. In art works he is presented with the sword by which he was beheaded or with his cloak covered with seashells.

See also: APOSTLE; JOHN, ST.; PETER, ST.

1605

**James the Less, St.** (St. James Minor) (Greek form of Jacob, one who takes by the heel, the supplanter)    First century. In the Bible, N.T., Apostle, son of Alphaeus (Matt. 10:3) and of Mary (not to be confused with the Virgin Mary), mentioned in Mark (16:1). He is called "the Less" in the King James Bible and "the Younger" in the Revised Standard Version. Feast, 1 May. According to early Christian tradition, he was the first bishop of Jerusalem and was martyred when he was flung down from a terrace or parapet of the temple and the mob beat his brains out with a fuller's club (which is his symbol).

1606

**Janaka** (begetting)   In Hindu mythology, the father of Sita, Rama's wife. His daughter sprang up from the furrow when he was ploughing the earth for a sacrifice. Janaka was noted for his wisdom as well as for his opposition to the Brahmans. The *Brahmanas*, sacred writings, say: "He refused to submit to the hierarchical pretensions of the Brahamans, and asserted his right of performing sacrifices without the intervention of priests." However, Janaka eventually became a Brahman. In Hindu mythology Janaka is also the name of the king of Mithila, who was born from the dead body of his father.

See also: BRAHMAN; RAMA

1607

**Jan-Teng Fo**   In Chinese Buddhism, the Lamp Bearing Buddha, or Buddha of Fixed Light. According to one legend, a woman offered a few coins to burn oil before an image on Buddha's altar. The lamp she lit never had to be replenished. It was then prophesied that she would be born as a future Buddha, which, in a later life, she achieved.

1608

**Januarius, St.**   Fourth century? In Christian legend, bishop of Benevento, Italy; patron saint of goldsmiths. Invoked against eruptions of Mount Vesuvius. Feast, 19 September.

Januarius was beheaded for being a Christian; his body was taken to Naples and buried in the cathedral. Just before his removal, Mount Vesuvius was erupting and threatening to de-

stroy the entire city. No sooner had the body of Januarius entered Naples than the volcano became utterly extinct, "quenched by the merits and patronage of the saint," according to Edward Kinesman's *Lives of the Saints*. When the volcano erupted again in 1631, St. Januarius was invoked, and again the eruption ceased. The most famous feat of the saint, however, concerns the liquefaction of his own blood. The saint's blood is kept in two glass vials in the Church of San Gennaro (Januarius) in Naples. "When either vial, held in the right hand, is presented to the head of the saint," according to Kinesman's account, "the congealed blood first melts, and then goes on apparently to boil." The feat still takes place each year, though scientists give no satisfactory explanation. Each year a major feast is held in Little Italy, in New York City, in honor of San Gennaro. Luca Gordano painted the *Martyrdom of St. Januarius*, and Cosimo Fanzaga did a statue of the saint now in the Duomo, Naples.

1609

**Janus** (passage)   In Roman mythology, ancient Italian god of beginning, opening, doorways, entrances, and endings; husband of the spring nymph Juturna (or Cardea); father of Fontus (Fons). The month of January is named after Janus. In Rome it was the king who sacrificed to Janus, and in later times it was the *rex sacorum*. At each sacrifice Janus was mentioned first in every prayer, even before Jupiter. In early Italian mythology, Janus was connected with the sun as god of light, opening the heavens in the morning and closing them at the end of the day. As god of beginnings, Janus was worshiped at the beginning of the day, the month, and the year. According to Ovid's *Fasti* (book 1), when people greeted one another at the beginning of the year, they were to speak only words of good omen and give gifts of sweetmeats. In private worship Janus was invoked each morning as *pater matutinus*. He was invoked before any important undertaking, such as harvest, marriage, or birth. His most important worship was connected with the Roman

Forum. There the hearth fire of the Roman state was kept in the temple of Vesta, and there, symbolically, the people went out to war through the door of the state. The House of Janus (or Arch of Janus) was a small square building of bronze with doors at each end. Between them was a statue of Janus with two faces, facing in two different directions. The building was called *Jani gemini portoe*. This building, according to Vergil's *Aeneid* (book 7), was supposed to be opened with a formal ceremony before a war and was to remain open as long as the army was in the field. Janus's main feast was the Agonalia held 9 January.

Janus is cited in Milton's *Paradise Lost* where the cherubim are described as: "Four faces each / Had, like a double Janus. . . ." (book 2.128–9), and by Shakespeare in *The Merchant of Venice*: "Now, by two-headed Janus, / Nature hath fram'd strange fellows in her time. . . ." (1.1.50–1). Jonathan Swift's *To Janus on New Year's Day* (1729) opens with "Two-fac'd Janus, God of Time," and W. H. Auden's "New Year Letter" uses "the Janus of a joke."

Because of his two faces, or double-two, Janus was sometimes known as Bifrons (two-faced) or Quadrifrons (four-faced). The English word *janitor* comes from one of the meanings of Janus's name, door. In Roman art he was usually represented as a porter with a staff and key in his hands and with two bearded faces placed back to back and looking in opposite directions. In late Roman art he is portrayed both bearded and unbearded. Instead of a key and staff, the fingers of his right hand exhibit the number 300 (CCC), his left hand the number of the remaining days of the year (LXV).

See also: *AENEID, THE*; OVID

---

1610

**Jara-sandha**   In Hindu mythology, an enemy of Krishna (an incarnation of the god Vishnu). Jara-sandha was born from two mothers who produced half boys; they were united by the demon Jara. He was an ardent worshiper of the god

Shiva and opposed Krishna. In the Hindu epic poem *The Mahabharata* he is killed by Bhima.

See also: BHIMA; KRISHNA; *MAHABHARATA, THE*; SHIVA; VISHNU

---

1611

**Jarnvidjur** (ironwood)   In Norse mythology, the race of witches who lived east of Midgard in a place called Jarnvid.

See also: MIDGARD

---

1612

**Jason** (healer)   In Greek mythology, a hero, son of King Aeson of Thessaly and Alcimede (mighty cunning) or Polymede; brother of Promachus. When Pelias seized Aeson's throne, Jason was hidden and was brought up by the centaur Chiron. Reaching manhood, Jason returned to Thessaly to claim the throne. He arrived wearing only one sandal, having lost the other while helping an old hag (the goddess Hera in disguise). Having been warned of his coming, Pelias said he would gladly give up the throne to Jason, provided he first capture the Golden Fleece of King Aeëtes at Colchis. Gathering men for the journey (which Pelias hoped would end in Jason's death), the hero built the largest (and first) ship, called the *Argo*, and set sail. The Argonauts reached Colchis, and Jason found the Golden Fleece fastened to a sacred oak guarded by a dragon who never slept. Athena and Aphrodite came to Jason's aid by having Medea, King Aeëtes' daughter, fall in love with him. She helped him capture the fleece by her skill in magic and sorcery. Medea then fled with Jason, taking her young brother Apsyrtus with her. When they were pursued by Aeëtes, she cut up her brother and flung the pieces of his body into the sea, knowing her father would stop to retrieve them. They then arrived at Circe's island (she was aunt to Medea), where they were purified of the murder by pig's blood. When the Colchians caught up with Jason, he quickly married Medea, so they could not take her back to her father. Finally, they reached King Pelias and presented the Golden Fleece, which was hung in Zeus's temple. Pelias murdered Jason's brother, and Medea, again using her witchcraft, killed Pelias by persuading his daughters that he would be restored to youth if they cut up his body and put it into a boiling caldron. Jason did not take the throne but gave it to Pelias's son and returned to Corinth. After 10 years of marriage to Medea, he decided to marry Creusa, King Creon's daughter. Seeking revenge for her betrayal, Medea presented Jason's new bride with a beautiful garment that burned her to death when she put it on. Medea then killed her own children, saying to Jason, in the words of Robinson Jeffers's play *Medea*, "because I hated you more than I loved them." She then fled in a chariot to Athens, where she married Aegeus, father of Theseus. Jason died when part of the beached *Argo* fell on him.

The myth of Jason inspired Apollonius Rhodius's epic *Argonautica*, Ovid's *Metamorphoses* (book 7), Euripides' *Medea*, and operas based on it. Part of Chaucer's *Legend of Good Women*, Corneille's play, Robinson Jeffers's play, and William Morris's narrative poem *The Life and Death of Jason*, as well as works by Robert Graves and Jean Anouilh, are based on the Euripides version of the myth.

See also: AEGEUS; APHRODITE; ARGO; ARGONAUTS; ATHENA; CENTAUR; CHAUCER; GOLDEN FLEECE; HERA; MEDEA; THESEUS; ZEUS

One day a great uproar arose in the eating room of the monastery. The Buddha, having sent to inquire the reason, learned that Dabha Mulla, whose office it was to distribute to each person his portion of rice, had given great dissatisfaction by his method of distribution; hence the disturbance. The Buddha ordered Dabha Mulla to come before him, dismissed him from his employment, and then related the *Tandulanali-Jataka*. "In days of old a certain foolish officer, whose duty it was to fix value upon everything, was tempted by a bribe to value the city of Bararais and all it contained at a single measure of rice, in consequence of which he was dismissed with disgrace, and in his place a wise minister was appointed, whose valuations were always fair and equitable. The Buddha in a former state of existence was that officer."

The influence of the Jataka on Buddhist art is immense. In Ajanta, an ancient Buddhist monastery located near Aurangabad in the state of Manarashtra, India, for example, numerous frescoes depicting the episodes from the Jatakas are found. All Buddhist countries have their versions of the tales, which are used for elementary teaching, especially to children. The states have been reorganized since independence.

### 1613

**Jataka** (birth story)  Buddhist fables and folktales of the former lives of the Buddha, collected about 400 C.E. The Pali collection contains 547 tales in which Buddha often appears in animal or human form. These stories have little to do with the basic teachings of Buddhism. They are concerned rather with general moral virtues and the laws of Karma. Each tale follows a formula. A short example is number five, *Tandulanali-Jataka* (the measure of rice tale):

### 1614

**Javerzaharses and Kaches**  In Armenian folklore, patron guardians of marriage and childbirth who love to attend weddings. According to Armenian Christian writers, the Kaches, who are the husbands, are used by God as evil spirits to punish the wicked, a belief stemming perhaps from the legend that the wicked Armenian king Edward built a temple to worship the Kaches.

*The Jay and the Peacock*

**Jay and the Peacock, The**    1615    Aesopic fable found in various collections throughout the world.

One day a jay found some feathers a peacock had shed. Sticking them among his own rusty black ones, he began to strut about, ignoring and despising his old friends and companions. Dressed in his borrowed plumage, he very cockily sought out a flock of peacocks who were walking on the park lawn. Instantly detecting the true identity of the intruder, they stripped him of his finery and, falling on him with their sharp beaks, they drove him away.

The bedraggled jay, sadder but wiser, went to his former companions. He would have been satisfied to associate with them again. But the jays, remembering how obnoxious he had been with his airs and his vanity, drummed him out of their society. One of those whom he had so lately despised offered him the following advice: "Be contented with what nature made you and you will avoid the contempt of your peers and the punishment of your betters."

Moral: *Happiness is not to be found in borrowed finery.*

Horace, in his *Epistles* (book 1), alludes to the fable when he accuses one writer of borrowing the writings of another and says he will be found out "like the wretched crow when stripped of her stolen hues." Benedict of Oxford, in his Hebrew version of the fables, makes the bird a raven, although most English versions call it a jackdaw. Thackeray included the fable in the Prologue to his novel *The Newcomers*.

See also: AESOPIC FABLES

**Jayanti** (conquering)    1616    In Hindu mythology, the daughter of Indra, the storm god.

See also: INDRA

**Jemshid** (Jamshid)    1617    In Persian mythology, a culture hero and proud king, appearing in the epic poem *Shah Namah* by Firdusi.

Jemshid is a later form of the earlier divine hero Yima in Persian mythology. Firdusi took some of the exploits of the earlier mythological personage and used them in his epic. During Jemshid's reign, according to Firdusi, the first manufacture of iron weapons took place, as well as the making of linen and silk clothing, work in precious stones, and the invention of perfume and the art of medicine.

One day Jemshid ordered the demons who were under his power to lift him into the air so that he could see everything and be moved anywhere he wanted to go. All of this power and honor made the king too proud. He said to his learned men and ministers: "Tell me if there exists, or ever existed, in all the world, a king of such magnificence and power as I am?"

"Thou art alone, the mightiest, the most victorious. There is no equal to thee," the frightened ministers replied.

Allah saw how foolish the king was in what he said and punished him by throwing his empire into chaos. Jemshid's reign lasted for some 700 years. He was killed by the evil king, Zahhak, who captured him. Zahhak ordered two planks to be brought and fastened Jemshid down between them. His body was then sawed in two.

See also: *SHAH NAMAH*; YIMA; ZAHHAK

*Jephthah and his daughter*

1618

**Jephthah** (he sets free)   In the Bible, O.T., one of the judges of Israel, whose daughter went out to greet him on his return home from victory over the Ammonites, unaware that her father had vowed to offer up as a sacrifice to Yahweh, the Hebrew god, the first thing he met on returning home. The tale is told in the book of Judges (11:1–12:7). Jephthah's daughter appears in one of the ballads included in Percy's *Reliques*, titled "Jephtah Judge of Israel," which is quoted by Hamlet (act 1, sc. 2, line 400). She also appers in Alfred Lord Tennyson's poem "Dream of Fair Women," and Handel's oratorio *Jephthah* deals with the legend.

See also: *RELIQUES*; YAHWEH

1619

**Jeremiah** (whom Yahweh appoints)   In the Bible, O.T., one of the Major Prophets and title of an Old Testament book. Jeremiah is sometimes called the "weeping prophet" because he foretold the destruction of Jerusalem. In later Jewish legend, not recorded in the Bible, Jeremiah was taken to Egypt and stoned to death because of his gloomy predictions. Tradition credited him with the authorship of the Book of Lamentations in the Old Testament, though no present-day scholar accepts this. Our word *jeremiad*, a pitiful tale or, a tale of woe, is derived from the prophet's name. Rembrandt's *Jeremiah* is one of the best paintings portraying the prophet.

1620

**Jerome, St.** (sacred name)   c. 342–420. In Christian legend, one of the Four Latin Doctors of the Church. Translator of the Latin Bible called the Vulgate, which was the Bible of the Middle Ages. Patron of scholars. Feast, 30 September.

Eusebius Hieronymus Sophronius, or Jerome, was born at Strido near Aquileia. After a life of study and debate he left for Bethlehem in 385 to devote his time to retranslating the Latin Bible from the original languages because most of the current translations were flawed. Jerome was helped with his translations from the Hebrew Bible by Jews as well as by a group of women, the most notable being St. Paula.

*St. Jerome*

Jerome was noted for his sharp wit and his bitter attacks on his enemies. He often was at variance with St. Augustine; they wrote polite letters to one another filled with venom. But St.

Jerome's most famous letter deals with being a Christian virgin. Its merits for a woman, he writes, are far above marriage; wedlock only gives women "pregnancy, a crying baby, the tortures of jealousy, the cares of household management and the cutting short by death of all its fancied blessings."

The legend most associated with the saint concerns a lion. One day Jerome was reading with some monks when a lion entered the study. Though the lion was lame and limping, the monks were so frightened by the beast that they all ran away. St. Jerome stayed in the room, and the lion came up to him. The lion lifted its paw into the saint's hand, showing how it was bleeding from a thorn. Jerome extracted the thorn and bandaged the paw. When the lion was able to use its paw, Jerome set it to work for the monastery. Each day the lion would fetch food with the help of a donkey. One day the donkey was stolen by some traders, and the lion was accused of eating him, so Jerome forced the lion to do the work of the donkey. After some time the merchants returned, led by the stolen donkey, who was recognized by the lion. The lion chased the merchants and brought back the donkey.

St. Jerome is often portrayed with a lion nearby. Sometimes a large cat takes its place. He is also shown doing penance in a desert with a lion nearby. Sometimes a cardinal's hat is shown, though there is no historical authority for Jerome having been a cardinal.

See also: AUGUSTINE, ST.; DOCTORS OF THE CHURCH; LION

1621

**Jesus Christ** (Greek, Joshua, "Yahweh saves," and annointed one, the Messiah)   In Christianity, the Messiah, the Son of God, second person of the Holy Trinity made up of God the Father, God the Son, and God the Holy Spirit. In Islam, Jesus is not God's son but is considered a prophet. Numerous incidents of his life are given in the Koran.

*Flight into Egypt*

Details of the life of Jesus are presented in the four Gospels of the Christian New Testament. In the first three, those of St. Matthew, St. Mark, and St. Luke, many of the same incidents are narrated, earning them the title of the Synoptic Gospels, though they differ in details. The last Gospel, that of St. John, differs radically from the first three. In John's Gospel Jesus speaks in Gnostic terms, stressing the difference between those who have the Light and those who are in Darkness. Most modern scholars agree that it is impossible to reconstruct the "historical Jesus," since all of the documents are written from a Christian bias—the beliefs of the early Christian church—to prove that Jesus was the Messiah and the Son of God. No record of Jesus' existence is found in other contemporary sources.

Though the character of Jesus varies in the Gospels, the early church began to stress certain aspects of his person. St. Paul, writing in the New Testament, saw Jesus as the mediator between God and man. From Paul's epistles, or letters, it is clear that he does not place Jesus on a plane with God. For Paul, Jesus stopped the righteous anger of God against mankind by his sacrifice on the cross.

Further development in the person of Christ is found in the writings of the early Church outside of the New Testament. St. Ignatius, bishop of Antioch (first century), writes on the Incarnation (the term used for God being made into man): "There is one physician, fleshly and spiritual, begotten and unbegotten, God in man, true life in death, both of Mary and of God, first passable then impassable, Jesus Christ Our Lord."

When St. Irenaeus (c. 130–c. 200) writes on the person of Jesus, we have the belief, also found in St. John's Gospel, but not in the other three, that Jesus existed as God with God before the world began: "We have shown that the Son of God did not then begin to exist. He existed with the Father always; but when he was incarnate and made man, he recapitulated in himself the long line of the human race, procuring for us salvation thus summarily, so that what we had lost in Adam, that is, being in the image and likeness of God, that we should regain in Christ Jesus." However, these statements are those of the church that survived down to the Middle Ages, since the early Christian heresies were wiped out. From them, we have a much different concept of the person of Jesus. Certain heresies stressed that Jesus was only God and assumed human form, but not human nature along with it. Others said only a mirage of Jesus died on the cross. The view that finally dominated was that Jesus was fully man as well as fully God. This is found in the statement of the Council of Chalcedon (act V) held in 451.

Therefore, following the holy fathers, we all with one accord teach men to acknowledge one and the same Son, our Lord Jesus Christ, at once complete in Godhead and complete in manhood, truly God and truly man, consisting also of a reasonable soul and body; of one substance with the Father as regards his Godhead, and at the same time of one substance with us as regards his manhood; like us in all respects, apart from sin; as begotten for us men and for our salvation, of Mary the Virgin, the God-bearer (*Theotokos*); one and the same Christ, Son, Lord, Only-begotten, recognized in two natures without confusion, without change, without division, without separation; the distinction of natures

being in no way annulled by the union, but rather the characteristics of each nature preserved and coming together to form one person and substance, not as parted or separated into two persons, but one and the same Son and Only-begotten God the Word, Lord Jesus Christ; even as the prophets from earliest times spoke of him, and our Lord Jesus Christ himself taught us, and the creed of the Fathers has handed down to us.

*Jesus on the Cross*

Jesus not only appears in the New Testament but also in Islamic legends, in which he is accorded the status of a prophet. The Koran, the sacred book of Islam, calls Jesus: Isa (Jesus), Isa the Maryam (Jesus the son of Mary), Al-Masih (The Messiah), Kalimatu'llah (The Word of Allah), Qaulu 'l-Haqq (The Word of Truth), Ruhum min Allah (A Spirit from Allah), Rasulu 'llah (The Messenger of Allah), Abdu'llah (The Servant of Allah), Nabiyu'llah (The

Prophet of Allah), Wajihun fi 'd-dunya wa 'l-akhirah (Illustrious in this World and in the Next). Episodes from the life of Jesus are found scattered throughout the Koran. Most of them are believed to be derived from early Christian legends and writings, but not the New Testament, since they often contradict the New Testament and agree with various Christian heresies that existed at the time of Muhammad. He may have heard most of the tales orally. Jesus' birth of a virgin mother is believed in Islam. The Annunciation to the Virgin and his birth is narrated in Sura 19. Muhammad believed, as did some heretical Christians, that Jesus was not crucified at all, but that Judas took his place on the cross, or that there was only Jesus' likeness on the cross. Sura 4 of the Koran says: "Yet they slew him not, and they crucified him not, but they had only his likeness. And they who differed about him were in doubt concerning him; No sure knowledge had they about him, but followed only an opinion, and they really did not slay him, but God took him up to Himself. And God is Mighty, Wise." Though Jesus is highly praised in Islam, the Koran makes it quite clear that he is not God when it states in Sura 19: "Allah could not take to Himself a son." And in Sura 5: "The Messiah, the son of Mary, is only a prophet." The Christian belief in the Trinity seems to have been misunderstood by Muhammad, who may have thought it consisted of the Father, the Son, and the Virgin Mary.

The main events in the life of Jesus, as recorded in the Gospels are birth of John the Baptist foretold (Luke 1:5–13), Annunciation (Luke 1:26–31, Matt. 1:18-23), birth and naming of John (Luke 1:57–63), birth of Jesus (Luke 2:1–14), circumcision and naming of Jesus (Luke 2:21), presentation in the temple (Luke 2:22), coming of the Magi (Matt. 2:1), flight to and return from Egypt (Matt. 2:13–23), Jesus in the temple (Luke 2:41–50), baptism of Jesus (Matt. 3:13–17, Mark 1:9–10, Luke 3:21–22), temptation of Jesus (Matt. 4:1–11, Mark 1:12, Luke 4:1–13), call of first disciples (Matt. 4:18–22,

*The Resurrection of Christ*

Mark 1:16–20, Luke 5:1–11, John 1:35–51), Sermon on the Mount (Matt chaps. 5–7, Luke 6:17–49), first miracle (John 2:1–11), Nicodemus visits Jesus (John 3:1–15), John the Baptist's death (Matt. 14:1–12, Mark 6:14–29), the transfiguration (Matt. 17:1–8, Mark 9:2–8, Luke (:28–36), raising of Lazarus (John 11:1–44), Jesus enters Jerusalem (Matt. 21:1–11, Mark 11:1–11, Luke 19:28–44), cleansing of the temple (Matt. 21:12–16, Mark 11:15–19, Luke 19:45–48), the Last Supper (Matt. 26:20–29, Mark 14:22–25, Luke 22:14– 21), Jesus washes his disciples' feet (John 13:3–14), Jesus' agony (Matt. 26:36–46, Mark 14:32–42, Luke 22:39–46, John 18:1), betrayal and arrest (Matt. 26:47–56, Mark 14:43–50, Luke 22:47–54, John 18:2), Peter's denials (Matt. 26:69–75, Mark 14:66–72, Luke 22:54–62, John 18:15), Jesus before Pilate (Matt. 27:3, 11–26, Mark 15:1–15, Luke 23:1–25, John 18:28–40), Jesus mocked (Matt. 27:27–31, Mark 15:16–20, John 19:2), crucifixion, death, and burial (Matt. 27:35–66, Mark 15:24–47, Luke 23:33–56, John 19:18–42), resurrection (Matt. 28:1, Mark 16:1, Luke 24:1, John 20:1). The parables recorded in the Gospels are The Builders (Matt 7:24–27, Luke 6:47–49), The Sower (Matt. 13:3, Mark 4:1, Luke 8:4), The Wheat and the Tares (Matt. 13:24–30), The Mustard Seed (Matt. 13:31, Mark 4:30, Luke 13:18), The Leaven (Matt. 13:33, Luke 13:20), The Pearl of Great Price (Matt. 13:45), The Unmerciful Servant (Matt. 18:23–35), The Laborers in the Vineyard (Matt. 20:1–16), The Two Sons (Matt. 21:28–32), The Wicked Husbandmen (Matt. 21:33–56, Luke 20:9–18), The Marriage Feast (Matt. 22:1–14), The Fig Tree (Matt. 24:32), The Ten Virgins (Matt. 25:1–13), The Talents (Matt. 25:14–30), The Good Samaritan (Luke 10:25– 37), The Rich Fool (Luke 12:13–21), The Dishonest Steward (Luke 16:1– 14), The Rich Man and Lazarus (Luke 16:19–31).

See also: APOSTLE; GNOSTIC; IGNATIUS, ST.; MUHAMMAD; VIRGIN MARY ; KORAN, THE

1622

**Jezebel** (prince, exalted, i.e., Baal)   In the Bible, O.T., Phoenician wife of King Ahab of the northern kingdom of Israel in the ninth century B.C.E., symbol of an evil woman. Jezebel was the foe of the prophet Elijah, who prophesied her doom, saying, "The dogs shall eat Jezebel by the wall of Jezreel" (1 Kings 21:23). Eventually, she was killed when Jeru entered her city and had two eunuchs throw her out of her window. Jeru's horses trampled her body. After he had dined, Jeru ordered his soldiers to bury Jezebel's body, but the dogs had eaten it, leaving the skull, feet, and palms of her hands (2 Kings 9:35). A "painted Jezebel" refers to a woman of bold spirit and loose morals.

See also: ELIJAH

1623

**Jigoku**   In Japanese Buddhist mythology, hell located underneath the earth's surface. Jigoku consists of eight hells of fire and eight of ice. Each of the eight is then divided into sixteen distinct hells. The ruler of Jigoku is Emma-hoo, portrayed with a ferocious expression and dressed as a Chinese judge wearing a cap. In the paintings and prints of Jigoku that portray Emma-hoo there are heads on either side of him, each on a supporting stand. One is a female head, Miru-me, who can see all sinners' actions and from whom nothing can be hidden. The other head is Kagu-hana (the nose that smells), who can detect the smallest sin. A demon will take a sinner before a magic mirror, where his or her sins are revealed. Prayers by the living, through a Buddhist priest, may eventually save the sinner.

1624

**Jim Bludso**   1838–1905. In American folklore, a Mississippi steamboat engineer who was burned to death while saving his passengers from fire. He appears in John Hay's *Pike County Ballads*.

1625

**Jim Bridger**   1804–1881. In American folklore, a frontiersman, discoverer of the Great Salt Lake in 1824, of South Pass in 1827, of Yellowstone Park in 1830 (44 years before it was "officially" discovered), and founder of Fort Bridger on the Oregon Trail in 1843. Bridger was known for his sense of humor, and he loved to shock tenderfeet and easterners with his tall tales. He told of glass mountains and "peetrified" birds singing "peetrified" songs, and reminisced about the days when Pikes Peak was just a hole in the ground. His stories were related in such a serious manner as to fool even skeptics into believing them, making Jim's laughter all the louder when his ruse was revealed. When he passed over a precipice through a petrified mountain in Yellowstone with his horse, he said that gravity itself had become petrified.

**Jimmu Tenno**   660–585 B.C.E.? According to Shinto belief, first emperor of Japan, descended from the sun goddess, Amaterasu. The period before the advent of Jimmu Tenno is called *jindai* (the age of the kami) or *taiko* (remote antiquity).

See also: AMATERASU OMIKAMI

**Jina**   In Buddhism and Jainism, Sanskrit title meaning conqueror; often used for the Buddha in Buddhism and in Jainism for its leaders.

**Jingo Kogo**   170–269 C.E. In Japanese legend, empress who set out to conquer Korea.

The gods twice ordered her husband, the emperor Chuai, to conquer Korea, but the monarch paid no attention to the deities. After his death the empress, under the guidance of the gods, decided to undertake the conquest of Korea. Setting out, she stopped to fish at Matsura Gawa with three grains of rice as bait (the catching of fish was believed to be a lucky omen). She also prayed that if she was to succeed in her venture her hair would part as she was bathing, and this happened. All of the gods are said to have come to her aid, with the exception of Izora, the god of the seashore, who came clad in mud. However, the empress was served by Ryujin, the king of the sea. When a storm arose, large fish came to the surface of the sea to support the boats and prevent them from foundering. Hearing of this, the king of Korea promptly sent 80 boats laden with gold, silver, and cloth as tribute. He repeated the practice each year.

Jingo Kogo had set out while she was pregnant, but she delayed the birth by attaching a heavy stone to her waist. When she returned to Japan, her son Ojin was born. She did not ascend the throne again but served as Ojin's regent for 69 years.

In Japanese art Jingo Kogo is often portrayed writing the words *Koku O* (ruler of state) on a rock. She often is shown with a wide band around her forehead.

**Jingu-ji**   In Japan, a Buddhist temple within the compound of a Shinto shrine.

**Jiten**   In Japanese Buddhist mythology, earth goddess, derived from the Hindu goddess Prithivi. She is portrayed as a woman holding in her right hand a basket of peonies. She is one of the Jiu No O, 12 Japanese Buddhist gods and goddesses adopted from Hindu mythology.

See also: JIU NO O

**Jiu No O** (Jiu ni Ten)   In Japanese Buddhist mythology, 12 gods and goddesses derived from Hindu mythology. They are Jiten, Gwaten, Bishamon, Futen, Suiten, Rasetsu Ten, Bonten, Nitten, Ishana Ten, Taishaku Ten, Kwaten, and Emma Ten.

See also: BISHAMON; BONTEN; EMMA TEN; FUTEN; GWATEN; ISHANA TEN, KWATEN; JITEN; NITTEN; RASETSU; SUITEN; TAISHAKU TEN

**Jizo Bosatsu**   In Japanese Buddhist mythology, the name of the Sanskrit Bodhisattva, Kshitigarbha (earth womb), consoler of the dead, protector of women and children; called Ti-Tsang in China. As Jizo Bosatsu he is portrayed in the robes of a Buddhist monk, holding a monk's staff in one hand and a precious jewel in the other. This is his most popular form in Japan, though he also appears as Shogun Jizo (Jizo of the victorious armies), a war god mounted on horseback, and as Roku Juzo (the sixth Jizo), referring to his multiplication of himself into six beings to help save the world. The number six refers to the six realms of rebirth; also associated with roads and mountains.

See also: BODHISATTVA

**Jo and Uba**   In Japanese mythology, two spirits of pine trees. They are portrayed as an old wrinkled couple gathering pine needles, Jo with a rake, Uba with a broom and a fan. The two are usually accompanied by the crane and tortoise, symbols of longevity.

1634

**Joan of Arc, St.** (form of John, "Yahweh has been gracious") 1412–1431. In Christian legend, patron of France. Feast, 30 May.

At 13 years old Joan had visions that she later identified as the voices of St. Michael, St. Catherine, and St. Margaret. When Henry VI of England began the siege of Orleans in 1428, Joan, convinced that God had chosen her to remove the English from French soil, set out. She told the dauphin (later Charles VII) of her mission and, in male dress, led the French troops to victory in May and June of 1429. She stood beside Charles VII at his coronation in July. Not having sufficient numbers of troops to continue her campaign, however, she was taken prisoner in May 1430 by the Burgundians, who sold her to the English. She was tried on 12 charges of sorcery, wantonness in cutting her hair, and wearing male attire. While she was in jail, an English lord tried to rape her. A physical examination showed that Joan was a virgin, though the results were falsified by Bishop Cauchon, who sat at her trial. At first she gave in and signed a recantation of her claim to have been guided by Divine Providence, but in the following days she resumed her male attire and repudiated her recantation. She said, "If I were to be condemned and saw the fire lit and the wood prepared and the executioner who was to burn me ready to cast me into the fire, still in the fire would I not say anything other than I have said, and I will maintain what I have said until death."

*The Trial of Joan of Arc: Being the verbatim report of the proceedings from the Orleans Manuscript*, translated by W. S. Scott (1956), recounts that after the sentence was read, the bishop, the in-

quisitor, and many of the judges went away, leaving Joan on the scaffold. The order to burn her was given by an Englishman. "When Jeanne heard this order given, she began to weep and lament in such a way that all the people present were themselves moved to tears." The fire was lighted and Joan was "martyred tragically," according to the account.

St. Joan was canonized in 1920 and has been a favorite subject in music and literature. In Shakespeare's *Henry VI*, she is called a witch and seen as an impostor. Voltaire in his *La Purcelle* ridiculed Joan, making her visions part of her madness. Schiller, however, in his poetic tragedy *Die Jungfrau von Orleans*, looked at Joan with a romantic and heroic cast of mind. She is not burned at the end of the play but dies in battle. Mark Twain wrote *Personal Recollections of Joan of Arc*, in which he looks with kindly eyes upon the girl, whereas Anatole France's *Life of Joan of Arc* presents a more skeptical approach to the subject. Perhaps the most touching play is G. B. Shaw's *Saint Joan*, in which both sides, Joan's and the church's, are presented in a good light, in contradiction to history. Shaw did not wish to pick sides but merely to depict the clash of different ideologies. Jean Anouilh's *L'Alouette*, translated by Christopher Fry as *The Lark*, presented a different Joan, one more poetic and less convincing as a human being.

In films the legend of Joan of Arc has been told several times. Geraldine Farrar played her in *Joan the Woman*. Dreyer's *The Passion of Joan of Arc* is considered the classic treatment of the subject on film, though other versions have appeared. Ingrid Bergman's *Joan of Arc* is a very stiff Hollywood treatment of the subject. *Saint Joan*, with Jean Seberg, based on the Shaw play, was a box office failure. Hedy Lamarr made a short appearance as Joan in the *Story of Mankind*, and Robert Bresson did *The Trial of Joan of Arc* with Florence Carrez. Two recent films featured Leelee Sobieski (1999) and Milla Jovovich (1999) in the role of Joan.

Opera composers also have found Joan of Arc's legend of interest, with more than 25 works devoted to her, though only two are still performed. Verdi composed a *Giovanni d'Arco*, and Tchaikovsky rejected the unhistorical ending of Schiller and instead has Joan die at the stake in his opera *The Maid of Orleans*.

Though Joan of Arc has fared well in literature, movies, and opera, there are few noteworthy paintings of the saint. Ingres' *Joan of Arc at the Coronation of Charles VII* is in the rather stiff, mechanical style that Ingres developed to perfection.

See also: CATHERINE OF ALEXANDRIA, ST.; MARGARET, ST.

1635

**Job** (inveterate foe)    In the Bible, O.T., name of a hero and title of a book. The biblical Job is believed to be based on a figure in Near Eastern legend as well as on two Babylonian works, *The Poem of the Righteous Sufferer* and the *Acrostic Dialogue on Theodicy*. The Book of Job is largely in the form of poetry, though parts of it, the introduction and epilogue, are in prose and indicate that the work is based on a folktale. Job was a good man who worshiped God. In return God rewarded Job with many children and with material prosperity. Satan, the Adversary, who was part of God's court, taunted God, saying Job was good only because God took such good care of him. Remove his wealth and Job would curse God, Satan contended. God took up the challange. Job lost his children and his wealth, and finally he was afflicted with a horrible skin disease. Three friends, Bilad, Eliphaz, and Zophar, his "comforters," came to discuss why God had afflicted Job. They contended that Job must have sinned and that God was punishing him for his sin. This belief of reward for good in this life and punishment for evil are central to most Old Testament thought and had a great influence on Puritan and Fundamentalist beliefs. Job, however, would not accept his guilt. He argued with his friends, saying that although God was punishing him, he was innocent. Finally, God revealed himself to Job in all of his splendor. The question "Why do the innocent suffer?" is not answered. Instead Job is awed by God and accepts all. The Book of Job concludes with a prose folk tale in which Job's goods and health are restored, a contradiction of the main poetic theme of the book.

Some critics consider Job the greatest book in the Bible. Martin Luther called it "magnificent and sublime as no other book of the Scripture," and Alfred Lord Tennyson believed it to be "the greatest poem of ancient and modern times." Major art works inspired by Job include a series of etchings by William Blake and a symphonic score, *Job, a Masque for Dancing*, based on the Book of Job and the Blake etchings, by the English composer Ralph Vaughn Williams. In Islamic legend Job is called Aiyub and is cited in the Koran (sura 21): "And remember Job: When he cried to his Lord."

See also: SATAN

1636

**Jocasta** (Iocaste) (shining moon)    In Greek mythology, both mother and wife of Oedipus, whom she married not knowing he was her son; mother of Eteocles, Polynices, Antigone, and Ismene; daughter of Menoeceus. When Jocasta learned she was Oedipus' mother, she killed herself by hanging. Jocasta appears in Homer's *Odyssey* (book 11), where she is seen in the underworld by Odysseus. Homer calls her Epicaste. Sophocles' *Oedipus Tyrannus*, often called *Oedipus Rex*, and Euripides' *Phoenician Women* also feature Jocasta, as do modern versions of the Oedipus myth by Cocteau and Gide.

See also: ANTIGONE; ETEOCLES; POLYNICES; *ODYSSEY, THE*; OEDIPUS

1637

**Joe Baldwin**    In American folklore, a train conductor who was decapitated when his train was rammed by another train. The story dates back to 1867. In that year Joe Baldwin was a conductor for the Atlantic Coast Railroad line, and his job involved riding in the last car of the train.

One night, as the train was steaming along, he realized that his car seemed to be slowing down. He realized that it had become uncoupled and there was another train following behind. He was sure he would crash into the slowly moving car. Joe ran out onto the rear platform of the car and started wildly waving his signal lantern, trying to get the attention of the engineer of the train behind him. The engineer failed to see the lantern and continued on, finally crashing into the car where Joe had remained at his post. The coach was completely demolished, and Joe was killed, his head severed from his body. A witness reported that Joe stayed where he was, waving the lantern, through the entire wreck. Just seconds before the engine collided with the car, Joe's lantern was hurled away as if by some unseen but mighty force. It hit the ground and rolled over and over again, finally coming to rest in a perfectly upright position. His lantern is said to still glow on certain nights, preventing train disasters. It is locally called the Maco Railroad Light (Maco, North Carolina).

See also: CASEY JONES

**1638**
**Joe Magarac** (jackass)   In American literary folklore, a superhuman steelworker and folk hero of the Pittsburgh area steel mills, invented by Owen Francis, who published his Joe Magarac tales in 1931. Joe, born inside an ore mountain, was seven feet tall and made of steel. He worked day and night, only taking time out to eat five meals a day. He ended his life when he melted down his body to make steel for a new mill. He explains his name when he says: "Dat's me. All I do is eatit and workit same lak jackass donkey."

See also: FAKELORE; PAUL BUNYAN; PECOS BILL; MIKE FINK

**1639**
**John Barleycorn**   In English and Scottish folklore, personification of barley, the grain used to produce liquors.

**1640**
**John Chrysostom, St.** (Yahweh is gracious, golden-mouthed)   c. 347–407. In Christian legend, one of the Four Greek Doctors of the church. Invoked against epilepsy. Feast, 30 March.

Born in Antioch, he was ordained in 363 and soon was recognized for his eloquence, which obtained for him the name Chrysostom or Golden Mouth. In 403 at the Synod of the Oak, John's enemies—and they were many since he was rather violent and provocative in his language—got him banished from his see. He was recalled, but then he angered the empress Eudoxia and was exiled to Armenia. He was to be moved from there to Pytius in Colchis but died at Comana.

Gibbon in his *Decline and Fall of the Roman Empire* writes that "his relics, thirty years after his death, were transported from their obscure sepulcher to the royal city. The Emperor Theodosius advanced to receive them as far as Chalcedon, and falling prostrate on the coffin, implored, in the name of his guilty parents, Arcadius and Eudosia, the forgiveness of the injured saint."

See also: DOCTORS OF THE CHURCH

**1641**
**John Henry**   In American folklore, a black hero, born in Black River Country "where the sun don't never shine." When John Henry was born, he weighed 44 pounds. His mother said he had a "bass voice like a preacher," and his father said "He got shoulders like a cotton-rollin' rousterabout." When John Henry finished his first meal, he went out in search of work. Eventually he found his way to the Chesapeake & Ohio Railroad, which at that time was laying track and driving (digging) tunnels. The major episode in his legend tells of his contest with a steam drill. John Henry drove faster than the steam drill but died "with a hammer in his hand" from the exertion, according to one John Henry ballad. In another account he died during the

night from a burst blood vessel. Other accounts say John Henry died on the gallows for murdering a man.

He appears in Roark Bradford's novel *John Henry*, as well as in numerous American ballads that were collected by Guy B. Johnson in *John Henry: Tracking Down a Negro Legend*. Guy Johnson's research indicated that the earliest John Henry ballads originated in the oral tradition of hammer songs in the 1870s and evolved over time into the ballads with which we are familiar today. Alan Lomax recorded several variants of the song in his *Prison Songs, Volume II*. In some accounts John Henry is said to be white, not black.

**Johnny Appleseed**    1642    1774–1847. In American history and folklore, popular name of John Chapman, Massachusetts-born orchardist, who planted fruit trees in Pennsylvania, Ohio, Indiana, and Illinois. Johnny Appleseed was a hermit and a wanderer who was welcomed wherever he went in the Ohio territory. Everyone loved him, in spite of his unkempt appearance. He always carried a sack full of apple seeds to plant, and walked barefoot all year round. He knew the frontier woods better than anyone. Even the Indians respected Johnny Appleseed for his courage. He appears in numerous legends, a combination St. Francis and Yankee peddler, going from place to place, unharmed by the Indians, carrying his tools and a Bible. He appears in Vachel Lindsay's free-verse poem "In Praise of Johnny Appleseed" and in the pageant *The Return of Johnny Appleseed* by Charles Allen Smart.

**John the Baptist, St.**    1643    (Yahweh is gracious) First century. Patron of farriers and tailors. Forerunner of Christ. Feast, 24 June.

His life is narrated in the New Testament, where he is the son of Elizabeth, a relation of the Virgin Mary. John lived in Judea and preached on repentance for the forgiveness of sin. Thou-

*St. John the Baptist*

sands came to be baptized by him, including Jesus. John reproved King Herod for living in adultery with Herodias, his brother Philip's wife. One day Salome (not named in the New Testament), the daughter of Herodias, so pleased the king by her dancing that he vowed he would give her whatever she chose, even half his kingdom. Her mother told her to ask for the head of John the Baptist. The king, unable to take back an oath, sent the executioner to cut off the prophet's head.

St. Jerome writes that the disciples of John the Baptist buried the headless body in Sebaste, in Samaria, where many miracles took place at the tomb of the saint. Julian the Apostate was so annoyed by all of the miracles, according to the *Ecclesiastical History* of Ruffinus, that he had the body disinterred and burned to ashes. Some Christians, however, saved some of the bones.

The head of the saint was buried, according to the same source, by Herodias in the palace of

King Herod. It remained hidden until St. John the Baptist appeared to some men and told them where it was hidden. They stole the head and wrapped it in camel's hair. For centuries, however, two churches vied with each other, each claiming it had the head of the saint.

In Christian art St. John the Baptist is one of the most frequently portrayed saints. Narrations of his life usually include the following incidents culled from the New Testament: the annunciation to Zacharias (Luke 1:5–32) of John's coming birth; the birth and naming of St. John (Luke 1:57–64); St. John in the wilderness (Luke 1:8); baptizing (Matt. 3:5–6); rebuking King Herod for his evil life (Mark 6:17–20); the banquet of Herod at which Salome danced for his head (Mark 6:21–28); beheading, or decollation, and the presentation of the head to Herodias. The burning of the saint's bones by Julian the Apostate sometimes also appears, as in the medieval art of northern Europe. The saint has been painted by such artists as Tintoretto, Raphael, Titian, Fra Angelico, Da Vinci, and Caravaggio, who in 1595 portrayed the saint playfully embracing a lamb or sheep and again in 1610. In both instances the models seem to have been male favorites of the artist, who was noted for his male lovers.

In the Islamic legend, Yahyu is the name given John the Baptist. He is mentioned three times in the Koran.

See also: JEROME, ST.; SALOME; VIRGIN MARY; ZACHARIAS

1644

**John the Bear**   In European folktales, hero who is the son of a bear. He is also called Juan el Oso, Juan del Oso, and Ivanko the Bear's Son in various European folktales.

1645

**John the Evangelist, St.** (Yahweh is gracious) First century. Evangelist and Apostle, credited with the authorship of the Gospel that bears his name and three short general epistles in the New Testament. Christian tradition also credits John with the authorship of the Book of Revelation. Feast, 27 December.

John was the son of Zebedee, a Galilean fisherman, and the brother of James. Their mother, Salome (not to be confused with the woman who danced for the head of John the Baptist), might have been the sister of the Virgin Mary. John was one of the first disciples called by Jesus. Both John and his brother James were called "sons of thunder" or "sons of anger" by Jesus.

From earliest Christian times John has been identified as the "beloved disciple" named in the Gospel. He was present at the Last Supper, where he leaned his head on Jesus' breast. He stood at the cross when Jesus was crucified, and he was the first disciple to reach the tomb on Easter Day.

*St. John the Evangelist*

According to Christian legend, after the death of the Virgin Mary, who had been placed in his care by Jesus when he was on the cross, John preached in Judea with St. Peter. He then traveled to Asia Minor, where he founded the Seven Churches and remained principally at Ephesus. During the persecution of the Christians under the Roman emperor Domitian he was sent in chains to Rome and cast into a caldron of boiling oil. He was miraculously preserved and "came out of it as out of a refreshing bath." He was then accused of being a magician and exiled to Patmos in the Aegean, where he wrote the Book of Revelation.

Another legend says that while John was in Rome an attempt was made on his life. A poisoned chalice was given him, but before he could drink, a serpent appeared in the cup, and the hired killer who had poisoned the cup fell down dead at the saint's feet.

In a variant of the tale, the poisoned cup was administered by order of the emperor Domitian. In still another variant, Aristodemus, the high priest of the goddess Diana at Ephesus, defied John to drink from a poisoned cup. John did, and Aristodemus fell dead at his feet.

John is the only Apostle who, according to legend, did not die but fell asleep waiting for the Second Coming of Christ.

See also: APOSTLE; DIANA; PETER, ST.; VIRGIN MARY

**Jok** (creator)   In African mythology (Alur of Uganda and Congo), creator and rain god who presides over birth as Jok Odudu. Offerings of black goats are made to the god for rainfall. The Alur view the world as full of spirits and believe that their ancestors manifest themselves in the form of snakes or large rocks.
<!-- 1646 -->

**Jonah** (dove)   In the Bible, one of the Minor Prophets and title of a book of the Old Testament. Instructed by Yahweh, the Hebrew god, to preach repentance to the great but wicked city of Nineveh, the Hebrew prophet Jonah fled in a
<!-- 1647 -->

ship bound for the Phoenician city of Tarsish. When a storm arose, the sailors cast lots to see who was responsible for their trouble. The lot fell on Jonah, who confessed that Yahweh was displeased with him. Thrown overboard, Jonah was swallowed by "a great fish" (later folklore and the New Testament turn it into a whale) in which he stayed for three days before he was vomited out on dry land. Jonah then went to Nineveh and convinced its king and people that they must repent or be destroyed within 40 days. Yahweh saved the city, but Jonah was angry. Outside the city he built himself a shelter for shade. Yahweh made a gourd grow up to give Jonah additional protection from the burning sun, but at night Yahweh made a worm destroy the plant. Jonah was sorry for the gourd, and Yahweh taught Jonah a lesson, saying: "Thou hast had pity on the gourd, for which thou hast not laboured, neither madest it to grow; which came up in a night, and perished in a night: And should not I spare Nineveh, that great city, wherein are more than sixscore thousand persons that cannot discern between their right hand and their left hand; and also much cattle?" (Jon. 4:10–11).

Christian writers saw the tale of Jonah as foreshadowing certain incidents in the life of Christ. Matthew's Gospel has Jesus say: "For as Jonas [N.T. spelling] was three days and three nights in the whale's body; so shall the Son of Man be three days and three nights in the heart of the earth [tomb] (Matt. 12:40). Jonah is a symbol of the Resurrenction, and he frequently appears in early Christian art.

See also: YAHWEH

**Jonathan** (Yahweh has given)   In the Bible, O.T. (1 and 2 Samuel), the oldest son of King Saul and male companion to David. He took David's side when David disputed with Jonathan's father, King Saul. When Jonathan and Saul were killed, David lamented his death, saying: "The beauty of Israel is slain upon thy high places: now
<!-- 1648 -->

are the mighty fallen! . . . I am distressed for thee, my brother Jonathan: very pleasant hast thou been unto me: thy love to me was wonderful, passing the love of women" (2 Sam. 1:19, 26). The relationship between David and Jonathan is one of the strongest examples of male bonding in ancient Near Eastern legends, its only rival being Gilgamesh and Enkidu.

See also: DAVID; ENKIDU; GILGAMESH; SAUL

**1649**
**Jonathan Moulton**  In American New England folklore, a general who sold his soul to the devil in return for a gold coin placed in his boots once a month. He is sometimes referred to as the "New Hampshire Faust" or the "Yankee Faust." Once he put his boots on top of a chimney, and the devil started to drop down the gold coins. Since he had removed the bottom soles, the devil had to fill up the whole fireplace and chimney, but that night the house burned to the ground and no gold was found. At his death his friends opened Moulton's coffin to see if he had taken the gold with him, but they found nothing.

See also: FAUST

**1650**
**Jones, John Paul**  1747–1792. In American history and folklore of the Revolution, naval hero. Given command of the *Bon Homme Richard* and two other vessels, Jones attacked two British envoy ships, *Serapis* and *Countess of Scarborough*. During the battle Jones was asked by the British commander, "Have you struck?"

According to legend, he replied, "Sir, I have not yet begun to fight." After an intense naval battle the *Serapis* surrendered.

Jones's earliest biographer, Alexander S. Mackenzie, writing in 1841, said: "No hero ever sounded his own trumpet more unremittingly or with a louder blast." Jones wrote his *Memoirs* and appears in numerous American novels, such as James Fenimore Cooper's *The Pilot*, Herman Melville's *Israel Potter*, and Winston Churchill's *Richard Carvel*. Hollywood took up the hero in

*John Paul Jones* (1959), starring Robert Stack as the naval hero and Bette Davis as Catherine the Great of Russia.

**1651**
**Jord** (Jordh, Fyorgyn, Hloldyn, Iord) (earth)  In Norse mythology, primeval earth goddess, perhaps a giantess in the beginning; first wife of Odin; mother of the god Thor. A kenning for Thor is the "son of Jord." She was the daughter of Nott (night) and a dwarf. Jord was worshiped on high mountains. In Germanic mythology and in Richard Wagner's *Der Ring des Nibelungen* she is called Erda.

See also: KENNING; NOTT; *RING DES NIBELUNGEN, DER*; THOR

**1652**
**Jorkemo** (Yurkemi, Yorkami) (may Yahu establish?)  In Jewish folklore, angel of hail. In the Old Testament the Book of Daniel tells how King Nebuchadnezzar placed Shadrach, Meshach, and Abednego in a furnace for not worshiping his god. When the king looked into the furnace, he saw the three men and a fourth "like the Son of God" (Dan. 3:25). The three men were left unharmed by the flames. Jewish folklore identifies the fourth as Jorkemo. The angel wanted to quench the flames but lacked the power, so he asked the archangel Gabriel to cool the flames.

See also: GABRIEL; NEBUCHADNEZZAR

**1653**
**Joro Kumo** (courtesan spider)  In Japanese folklore, a ghost resembling a spider woman, who lures men to their death.

**1654**
**Joseph** (may he add, i.e., Yahweh)  In the Bible, O.T. (Gen. 37–50), hero, 11th son of Jacob and Rachel; brother of Benjamin, who brought the Hebrews to Egypt.

*Joseph sold into Egypt*

When Joseph was 17 years old, he took care of his father's sheep and goats with his half brothers, sons of the concubines Bilhah and Zilpah. Jacob loved Joseph more than any of his other sons because Joseph was born to him in his old age. Jacob had made for Joseph a robe with long sleeves (inaccurately translated in the King James Version as a coat of many colors). When Joseph's brothers saw his robe, they grew to hate him. He would tell them his dreams, which indicated that he would rule over them. One day while the brothers were at Dothan, they decided to kill Joseph. "Here comes that dreamer. Come on now, let's kill him and throw his body into one of the dry wells. We can say that a wild animal killed him. Then we will see what becomes of his dreams" (Gen. 37:19–20, Today's English Version). But Reuben heard them and tried to save Joseph, saying they should not kill him but just throw him in a dry well. He planned to come back and save Joseph. But Judah instead persuaded his brothers to sell Joseph to a group of Ishmaelites or Midianites (the sources vary in the biblical text). This they did and then told Jacob that Joseph had been killed by a wild animal. The boy was sold in Egypt to Potiphar, one of the pharaoh's officers, who was captain of the palace guard. Joseph prospered with Potiphar, who trusted him with all of his affairs. "Joseph was well built and good looking, and after awhile his master's wife began to desire Joseph and asked him to go to bed with her" (Gen. 39:7–7, Today's English Version). Joseph refused her sexual advances, Potiphar's wife accused him of attempted rape, and Joseph was cast into prison. There he interpreted the dreams of two prisoners; one was the pharaoh's chief baker and the other his wine steward. Joseph told the wine steward he would be free in three days but that the baker would be executed. It happened just as Joseph had predicted, so when the pharaoh had a dream that none of the Egyptian magicians could interpret, the wine steward told him of Joseph the Hebrew who could interpret dreams. Joseph was brought to the court and interpreted the pharaoh's dream as signifying that there would be seven years of plentiful harvest, then seven years of famine. When he heard this, Pharaoh appointed Joseph to take charge of stockpiling grain. Joseph was then called Zaphenath Paneah (revealer of secrets). After the seven years of plenty, the famine was so severe that Joseph's brothers went down to Egypt to get grain so that they would not starve. When Joseph saw them he recognized them, but they did not know him. He put them through various tests to see if they had learned any compassion since the time they attempted to kill him. When he realized they were sorry for what they had done and showed love for Benjamin and Jacob, he revealed himself to them. He then had his father, Jacob, and all of his family settle in Goshen. Before Jacob died, Joseph asked him to bless Joseph's two sons, Manasseh and Ephraim, by Asenath, the daughter of Potiphera, a priest of Heliopolis. Jacob blessed Ephraim, the younger son, but not Manasseh, the older. When Joseph died, he was embalmed and buried in Egypt. At the Exodus his body was taken by the Hebrews.

Thomas Mann's novel *Joseph and His Brothers* deals with the legend. Rembrandt's *Joseph and Potiphar's Wife* portrays one episode from the legend, and Handel's oratorio *Joseph and His Brothers* deals with the legend.

See also: ASENATH; BENJAMIN; ISHMAEL; JACOB; MANASTIPHERA

*St. Joseph and Jesus*

1655

**Joseph, St.** (may he add)   First century. In the Bible, N.T., husband of the Virgin Mary. Patron of carpenters, confectioners, the dying, engineers, the family, married couples, house hunters, pioneers, and travelers. Invoked in doubt and hesitation. Feast, 19 March.

Little is said of Joseph in the New Testament. He was of the House of David and accepted Jesus as his son when the angel told him "that which is conceived in her womb is of the Holy Ghost" (Matt. 1:20). Joseph died before Jesus began his public ministry.

During the Middle Ages St. Joseph was often referred to as a cuckold by Christians, who neglected his cult in favor of his wife, Mary. But in the 16th century his cult spread throughout the Roman church. According to medieval beliefs, St. Joseph's girdle was kept at Notre Dame, Joinville sur Marne, in the diocese of Langres. His walking stick was preserved in the Monastery of Angels in Florence and another stick and his hammer in the Church of St. Anastasia in Rome. The cloak with which St. Joseph covered Jesus in the stable also was preserved in the church.

1656

**Joseph of Arimathea** (may he add)   First century. In the Bible, N.T., the man who begged for the body of Jesus and laid it in his own tomb (Matt. 27:57–60). Medieval legend says he was imprisoned for years and kept alive by the Holy Grail, the cup Christ used at the Last Supper. He later brought the Holy Grail to Glastonbury in England.

See also: HOLY GRAIL

1657

**Joshua** (Yahweh is salvation)   In the Bible, O.T., successor of Moses and a leader of the Israelites during the Exodus and the settlement of Canaan. Joshua was the son of Nun and Ephraimite and was appointed by Moses as his successor. Three days after Moses' death, Joshua got ready for the invasion of Canaan. He sent out spies and moved camp up to the river Jordan. In one assault after another, he reduced the fortified towns on the opposite banks, the most famous being Jericho. Joshua under the guidance of Yahweh, the Hebrew god, marched his army around the walls for six days bearing the Ark of the Covenant (which some scholars believe contained a fetish or Hebrew snake god). On the seventh day they circled seven times; the priests blew their trumpets, and Joshua ordered the people to shout. As the shouts went up, the walls of Jericho fell down, and the Israelites conquered the city (Josh. 6:1–25). In another battle, Joshua ordered the sun to stand still so that his enemies could not escape at night (Josh. 10:13). Most of his legend is told in the Book of Joshua in the Old Testament. In Islam Joshua is called Yusha, though he is not named directly in the Koran.

Joshua appears in Dante's *The Divine Comedy* (Purgatory, canto 20; Paradise, cantos 9, 18). Handel's oratorio *Joshua* and the folk song *Joshua Fit the Battle of Jericho* tell of how God guided the Hebrews to victory over their enemies.

See also: ARK OF THE COVENANT; MOSES; YAHWEH

**Jotunheim** (Jotunnheim, Jotunheimr) (home of the giants)   In Norse mythology, the land of the frost giants, located under one of the tree roots of the cosmic or world tree, Yggdrasill, in the far northwest where the ocean joined the world's edge. Its capital was Utgard (outer place).

See also: UTGARD; YGGDRASILL

1659

**Jotunn** (devourers)   In Norse mythology, the giants who ruled before the Aesir gods, such as Odin; among them were the Hrimthursar (frost giants). Most of them were violent and wicked. They had heads of stone and feet of ice. Often they could transform themselves into eagles or wolves. Among the most famous were Kari (tempest) and his three sons: Beli (storm); Thiassi (ice), with his daughter, Skadi (winter); and Thrym (frost). Others were Johul (glacier), Frosti (cold), Snoer (snow), and Orifta (snowdrift). The god Thor married a giantess, Iarnsafa (ironstone), who bore him two sons, Magni (strength) and Modi (courage). It was believed that a battle between the gods and frost giants would bring about Ragnarok, the destruction of the world, and then its renewal.

See also: AESIR; RAGNAROK

1660

**Joukahainen** (Youkahainen) (genius of ice and snow?)   In the Finnish epic poem *The Kalevala*, an evil youth who entered into a contest with Vainamoinen and was defeated.

Hearing that the culture hero Vainamoinen was noted for his magic songs, Joukahainen, against his parents' wishes, challenged him to a singing contest. They questioned one another, asking who was present at the creation of the world. Joukahainen answered that he had been. Vainamoinen replied that Joukahainen was a liar. This so enraged the youth that he challenged Vainamoinen to a fight, but the culture hero sang magic songs that made Joukahainen sink into a swamp. Fearing he would die, Joukahainen offered Vainamoinen his sister Aino as a wife, and the hero released him.

Joukahainen returned home to his farm angry, telling Joukola, his mother, what had happened, but she was pleased that her daughter was to wed Vainamoinen. Joukahainen, however, continued to nurture a hatred against Vainamoinen. Once he lay in wait for him on his journey to Pohjola, the Northland, and shot at him, killing Vainamoinen's horse. Vainamoinen fell into the water and was driven out to sea by a tempest. Joukahainen rejoiced, thinking he at last had overcome Vainamoinen. However, the culture hero was not destroyed.

Joukahainen is often called Jouko, a shortened form of his name.

See also: AINOI; *KALEVALA, THE*; VAINAMOINEN

1661

**Jove** (sky, in the open air)   In Roman mythology, ancient Italian god identified with the Greek god Zeus; called Jupiter by the Romans, Jove is an Anglicized version of one the Latin forms of Jupiter's name.

See also: JUPITER; ZEUS

1662

**Juan Chi**   275–210 B.C.E. In Chinese legend, one of the seven Chu-lin Ch'i-Hsien (Seven Immortals). He is depicted with a boy attendant and his nephew, Juan Hsien, with fan and staff. In Japanese legend he is called Genshiki.

See also: CHU-LIN CH'I-HSIEN

1663

**Judas Iscariot** (Judas, man from Kerloth) First century. In the Bible, N.T., one of the Twelve Apostles, who betrayed Jesus to the chief priests in exchange for 30 pieces of silver.

Nothing is said in the New Testament regarding the calling of Judas to be one of Jesus' Twelve Apostles, nor is anything known of his early life. Judas was the Apostles' treasurer and handled the moneybag (John 13:29). When at the Last Supper Jesus announced that one of the Twelve would betray him, all asked, "Is it I?" The motivation for Judas's betrayal may have been more than greed for the 30 pieces of silver. He may have borne a grudge against Jesus after Jesus rebuked him for his criticism of Mary's (the sister of Lazarus) extravagance in using expensive oil from the alabaster box to anoint Jesus. Judas had complained that the oil could be sold and the money used to help the poor. St. John's Gospel (12:6) says of Judas's complaint, "This he said, not that he cared for the poor; but because he was a thief, and had the [money]bag, and bare [carried] what was put therein."

To fulfill his pact with the high priests Judas kissed Jesus in the garden as a signal to the soldiers to arrest Jesus (Mark 14:43–45). Shakespeare says: "So Judas kissed his Master, and cried, 'all hail!' whenas he meant *all harm*" (*Henry VI*, III, V, vii). After the arrest the traitor Judas tried to give back the blood money (Matt. 27:3–4), but it was refused by the priests, who mocked him saying, "What is that to us?" Judas then went to the Temple area and threw the silver on the floor and later hanged himself (Matt. 27:5). The Acts of the Apostles (1:18), however, gives a different account of Judas's death, saying "this man purchased a field with the reward of iniquity; and falling headlong, he burst asunder in the midst, and all his bowels gushed out." According to Christian tradition the "bursting asunder" was considered a special judgment, in order that his soul should escape from his bowels and not be breathed out through his lips since they had betrayed Jesus with a kiss. In Islamic legend it is believed that Judas was crucified in the manner of Christ while Christ was rising to heaven. Judas appears always as the archbetrayer. Dante's *The Divine Comedy* (Inferno) has the traitor chewed in the mouth of Satan.

See also: APOSTLE; CAIN AND ABEL; JOHN THE EVANGELIST, ST.; LAZARUS

1664

**Jude Thaddeus and Simon Zealot, Sts.** (praise and snub-nosed)     First century. In the Bible, N.T., Apostles. Jude is the traditional author of the epistle that bears his name in the New Testament. He is invoked in desperate situations. Feast for both, 28 October.

Jude may have been one of the brethren (Mark 6:3) of Jesus, being either the son of Mary and Joseph (one tradition held that Jesus had brothers and sisters) or the son of Joseph by a former marriage (another tradition, invoked to protect the virginity of Mary). Both Jude and Simon, according to tradition, preached the Gospel in Syria and Mesopotamia and were martyred in Persia. Jude was said to have been killed by a halberd (his symbol), and Simon was sawn asunder.

See also: APOSTLE

1665

**Judgment of Paris**     In Greek mythology, one of the principal myths regarding the origin of the Trojan War. The Judgment involved Paris in a dispute among the goddesses Hera, Athena, and Aphrodite. When Eris, goddess of discord, was not invited to the wedding banquet of Peleus and Thetis, she threw a golden apple marked, "for the fairest" into the gathering. Hera, Athena, and Aphrodite all competed for the apple, and each asked Zeus to award her the prize. To avoid making the choice, Zeus told the three goddesses to go to Mount Ida, where a handsome youth, Paris, was tending sheep. They were to ask him to make the judgment. (Paris had become a shepherd because his father, King Priam of Troy, had been warned that the lad would bring disaster upon Troy.) Each of the three goddesses sought Paris's favor. Hera offered him power, Athena offered wisdom, and Aphrodite promised him the most beautiful woman in the world, Helen. He chose Helen, and Aphrodite sent Paris to Sparta, where he seduced Helen, wife of King Menelaus, and fled with her to Troy. Menelaus followed with a host of Greeks under the command of Agamemnon, Menelaus's brother, and the Trojan War began.

The myth has been frequently retold and painted. The Judgment of Paris is either retold or cited in Vergil's *Aeneid* (book 1); Ovid's *Heroides*, which gives an elaborate description; Lucian, who made the apple golden and magic; the medieval retelling, *The Tale of Troy*; and Tennyson's *Dream of Four Women* and *Oenone*. The subject was painted by, among others, Cranach, Rubens, Watteau, Renoir, and Dali.

See also: AGAMEMNON; APHRODITE; ATHENA; HELEN OF TROY; HERA; PELEUS; THESIS; TROY; PRIAM

*Judith giving the head of Holofernes to her servant*

1666

**Judith** (Jewess)    In the Bible, Apocrypha, a heroine who helps save her city of Bethulia by cutting off the head of Holofernes, general of the Assyrian king Nebuchadnezzar. Judith was a young and beautiful widow of Manasseh and strictly followed the Mosaic law. Her city, Bethulia, had its water supply cut off by Holofernes, who wished to destroy the Jews for not aiding his king in the war against Arphaxad, king of the Medes. When the people began to despair and were ready to surrender, Judith told their chief priest, Ozias, that she would deliver the city. Putting off her widow's garments, she went with her maid to the enemy camp, pretending to have deserted her people. As she had planned, Holofernes fell in love with her and gave a feast in her honor. Holofernes got very drunk at the feast, and when he at last got Judith alone, thinking he was going to sleep with her, she cut off his head with two blows of a sword. She wrapped his head in a bag and left with her maid, pretending to go out to pray. When she returned to her city, she stood on its walls and showed the decapitated head of Holofernes to his army, which fled in terror. She then sang a hymn of praise to the Lord for delivering her people. In the Roman Catholic breviary her song is a hymn to be sung at Lauds.

Judith's tale inspired numerous paintings, such as those by Matteo di Giovanni and Paolo Veronese (c. 1528–1588). Racine's *Judith*, Friedrich Hebbel's *Judith*, and Jean Giraudoux's *Judith* all use the legend, as do Vivaldi and Mozart in oratorios, both titled *Bethulia Liberata*.

See also: MANASSEH; NEBUCHADNEZZAR

1667

**Juggernaut** (Jagganth, Jagan-natha, Jagan-nath) (lord of the world)    In Hinduism, a sacred image of Krishna, an incarnation of the god Vishnu.

When Krishna was accidentally killed by the hunter Jaras (old age), his body was left to rot under a tree. Some people found the bones and placed them in a box. Vishnu then appeared to Indra-dyumna, a holy king, and told him to make an image of Krishna called Juggernaut and to place the bones of Krishna inside. Viswakarma, the architect of the gods, undertook the commission on the condition that he be left undisturbed till the work was completed. After 15 days the king was impatient and went to Viswakarma to see how the work was progressing. Viswakarma was angry and left the statue unfinished—it had no hands or feet, only stumps. Indra-dyumna prayed to the god Brahma, who promised the king to make the image of the Juggernaut one of the most sacred in the world. Brahma gave the image eyes and a soul and acted as high priest at its consecration.

There is, however, a variant account of the origin of the image. A Brahman was once sent to look for a site for a new temple. The Brahman wandered about for many days. He then saw a crow dive into the water. The bird honored the water as if it were some god, and the Brahman chose the site as the one near which the temple should be erected. While the temple was being constructed, King Indra-dyumna was told in a dream: "On a certain day cast thine eyes on the seashore, when there will arise from the water a piece of wood 52 inches long and 18 inches broad; this is the true form of the deity; take it up and keep it hidden in thine house for seven days, and in whatever shape it shall then appear, place it in the temple and worship it."

The image of Juggernaut is located at Puri, a town in the Orissa state of northeast India on the Bay of Bengal. Each summer the images of Juggernaut and his brother and sister are carried on a large cart, dragged by pilgrims to their summer home. Though some worshipers have thrown themselves under the cart, this act is not part of the cult, though it has supplied the English language with the term *juggernaut* for "customs, institutions, etc., beneath which people are ruthlessly and unnecessarily crushed."

See also: BRAHMA; BRAHMAN; KRISHNA; VISHNU

**1668**
**Julana** In Australian mythology, son of Njirana among the Jumu in western Australia, who is in constant pursuit of women with his gigantic penis.

**1669**
**Julian Hospitaller, St.** (descended from Jove) In Christian legend, patron of boatmen, ferrymen, innkeepers, musicians, travelers, and wandering singers. Feast, 12 February.

Julian's life is found in *The Golden Legend*, a 13th-century book of the lives of the saints by Jacobus de Voragine. There is no factual information on the saint aside from the legend.

Julian was a young man who while hunting came upon a stag that told him he would kill his parents. Horrified at the news, Julian fled to another kingdom, where he became a knight and was given a rich widow as his wife. Meanwhile his parents searched for their son. One day they came to the castle where Julian lived and were received by Julian's wife. When they told their story, she knew that Julian was their son and offered them her own bed to rest the night. When Julian returned to his wife's bed, he saw two figures asleep beneath the blankets. Without a word he drew his sword and killed the couple. Discovering his evil deed, Julian and his wife fled. They lived for years near a shore and ferried people across. One night Julian ferried an aged leper who was so ill that Julian took him home and put him in his own bed. In the morning the leper revealed himself as an angel, saying God had forgiven Julian's murder of his parents.

The legend is illustrated in a series of stained-glass windows in the cathedral of Rouen, presented to the church by some boatmen. Flaubert wrote *The Legend of St. Julian the Hospitaller* based on the windows.

See also: GOLDEN LEGEND, THE

**1670**
**Jumala** (god) In Finnish mythology, a semiabstract term for the supreme being, mother of all things. The oak tree is her symbol. She bears similarity to Mother Earth, but she is greater. In some areas Jumala is a male deity. Jumala was sometimes called Kuoja (creator). He was later replaced by Ukko, the Finnish sky god.

See also: UKKO

1671

**Juniper**  An evergreen shrub. In European folklore, the juniper was regarded as a life-giving tree, as reflected in the *Tale of the Juniper Tree* by the Grimm brothers. The juniper berry is used in folk medicine in America as well as in Germany. The Hopi Indians used the boiled greens of the juniper to relieve sore throat, sour stomach, earache, and constipation. The berries were used to cure snakebite, plague, rheumatism, and venereal disease.

See also: ALMOND

*Juno*

1672

**Juno** (youth)  In Roman mythology, ancient Italian goddess, sister and wife of Jove (Jupiter). The Roman goddess, like her Greek counterpart, Hera, was the queen of heaven, Regina. As such, she was supreme among all of the goddesses and watched over women and marriage. Juno differs from Hera in that she is closely connected with the moon. The Calends were sacred to Juno Lucina, or Lucretia (goddess of childbirth), as the Ides were sacred to her husband, Jupiter. Every woman had her own protecting *juno* whom she worshiped on her birthday, just as every man had his *genius*. As Pronuba Juno, she presided over betrothal. Juno Juga yoked together the husband and wife in marriage. Juno Domiduea was worshiped as the couple was escorted to their new home, and its doorposts were anointed in honor of Juno Unixia. The most important festival of married women was the Matronalia, celebrated on 1 March, both at the temple of Juno Lucina and in the home. It was Juno Lucina, as well as Juno Sospita (Juno the savior), who watched over childbirth, protecting mother and child from harm. Juno's main temple was at the Capitol in Rome, close to the temple of Jupiter. In it were kept geese, animals sacred to her because they were prolific and domestic. There was also a temple on the Capitol dedicated to Juno Moneta (warner, admonisher; the admonisher or goddess of money). The use of symbolic money was sanctioned by the goddess and the temple of Juno Moneta was an early mint. The epithet Moneta, however, derives from the legend that the citadel was once saved against a secret assault by warning honks from Juno's sacred geese. One of her other feasts, celebrated on 7 July, was the Caprotina. Female slaves took part in the Caprotina, reenacting the legend that they once helped save the Romans from defeat.

Most references in English use Juno not only for the Roman goddess but for her Greek counterpart, Hera. Juno appears in or is cited in Shakespeare's *Cymbeline* (5.4.32) as wife, in Spenser's *Faerie Queene* (1.4.17) as Queen of Heaven, and in Milton's *Paradise Lost* (9.18) as a war goddess.

See also: GENIUS; HERA; JOVE; LUCRETIA

1673

**Juno and the Peacock**  Aesopic fable found in various European collections.

A peacock once placed a petition before the goddess Juno asking for the voice of a nightingale. Juno refused his request; when the bird persisted and said that he was the goddess's favorite bird, she replied: "Be content with your lot."

Moral: *One cannot be first in everything.*

Sean O'Casey's play *Juno and the Paycock* has the antihero, Jack Boyle, called Captain Jack, portrayed as a strutting "paycock." His wife, Juno, however, sees through her husband's poses and defections.

See also: AESOPIC FABLES; JUNO

**1674**

**Juok**    In African mythology (Shilluk of the Sudan), supreme god who divided the earth, represented as two divine loaves sent from heaven, with the river Nile. His helper is Nyikang, an ancient king who is the ancestor of the Shilluk and invoked as intermediary between them and Juok. Nyikang may represent the supreme deity of the earthly loaf.

**1675**

**Jurawadbad**    In Australian mythology, snake man, married to a woman who refused to have sexual relations with him. In anger he turned himself into a snake and hid inside a hollow log. When his wife peered into the log, he bit her and she died.

**1676**

**Jurupari**    In mythology of the Uapes Indians of Brazil, chief god, born of a virgin after she drank some *cachari*, a native beer. His cult was associated with male initiation rites from which women were excluded. If by accident a woman witnessed even a part of the rite, she was poisoned as a punishment.

**1677**

**Justa and Rufina, Sts.**    Third century. In Christian legend, patron saints of Seville, Spain. Feast, 19 July.

The two girls sold earthenware in a shop. One day a pagan woman came in to buy some for use in the worship of Venus, the goddess of love. Justa and Rufina refused to sell the goods, so the woman started to wreck the shop. Soon a crowd gathered and the two girls were accused of being Christians. They were arrested, but before they were taken, they destroyed a statue to Venus.

Both were condemned to death. Justa was put on a rack and cooked. Rufina was strangled to death.

See also: VENUS

**1678**

**Justina of Antioch, St.** (just)    Fourth century. In Christian legend, virgin martyr. Feast, 26 September.

The saint's life is told in *The Golden Legend*, a collection of saints' lives written in the 13th century by Jacobus de Voragine. Justina was the daughter of a pagan priest. One day as she sat at her window she heard the Gospel read by Proculus, a deacon of the church. She was so moved by his reading that she became a Christian. At night her parents had a vision of Jesus and his angels, and the next day they too became Christians.

Justina, however, was loved by a pagan magician, Cyprian, who had dedicated himself to the devil. He approached the girl with the devil, but the fiend fled when Justina covered her whole body with signs of the cross. Cyprian then invoked another devil, but again his seduction failed. Finally, he invoked the Prince of Demons, who came to Justina's chamber, pounced on her bed, and embraced her. As Justina made the sign of the cross, the demon melted away. Cyprian realized that there was no hope of seducing Justina and converted to Christianity. The two were arrested for being Christians; Justina was put in a boiling caldron, and Cyprian was burned to death. Some accounts say they were beheaded. St. Justina's symbols are a unicorn for virginity and a palm for martyrdom.

See also: GOLDEN LEGEND, THE

**1679**

**Juventas** (youth)    In Roman mythology, patron goddess of youth; mother of Alexiares and Anticetus by Heracles; equivalent to the Greek goddess Ganymede (Hebe). Juventas was portrayed as a beautiful woman dressed in variegated garments.

See also: GANYMEDE; HERACLES

# K

**Ka** (double)    In Egyptian mythology, the vital essence or abstract personality of a person. The *ka* was free to move from place to place and could separate itself from or unite itself to the body at will. The preserving of a dead man's *ka* was necessary if his body was to become everlasting. Funeral offerings, including meats, cakes, wines, and unguents, were made to a person's *ka*, and when food was not available, offerings were painted on the walls and were accompanied by specific prayers. In early Egypt tombs had special chambers where the *ka* was worshiped and received its offerings. The priesthood included a group called "priests of ka," who performed services in its honor. The *ka* is closely associated with the *ba*, the soul; the *ib*, the heart; the *khaibit*, the shadow of a man, and the *khat*, the whole body of a person.

See also: BA

1681

**Kaaba** (Ka'ba, Kaabeh, Caaba) (cube)    In Islam, a cube-shaped shrine located at Mecca. It contains Al-hajar al-aswad, the Black Stone, which may be a meteorite. The stone was located in the shrine before Muhammad destroyed the idols there when he captured the city. An Arabic historian recorded the worship of a four-sided stone, called allat or alilat, in the Assyrio-Bablylonian kingdom of Nabataea. The pagan Arabs used to worship the Black Stone, and Muhammad accommodated them by making it part of the sacred site.

According to some Islamic legends, the site was chosen because of its connection with the prophet Abraham. Abraham was led to Arabia by a stormy wind sent by Allah. The storm was in the shape of two heads (in one account, it had the head of a snake). Allah told Abraham to build a shrine at a site to which the storm would direct him. When the wind reached the site of the Kaaba, it wound itself around and said: "Build on me."

When Abraham was constructing the building, he stood on one of its stones, and his footprint, *Makam Ibrahim*, is shown to pilgrims to this day. The Black Stone in the shrine was once white but, according to Islamic legend, turned black because of the sins of man. It had been brought to the shrine by the archangel Gabriel.

In another, entirely different Islamic legend regarding the foundation of the Kaaba, it was Adam, not Abraham, who was responsible. After the Fall Adam went to Mecca. The archangel Gabriel with his massive wings uncovered a foundation. Angels then threw blocks on it from various places until the ground was level. Allah sent from paradise a tent of red jacinth in which Adam was to live. The tent, which was an angel, later became the Black Stone. When Adam made a covenant with men, they signed it on paper, and it was fed to the Black Stone, which ate it up. At the end of the world the Black Stone will sprout a tongue and name all of the good men and all of the sinners.

The Black Stone has been damaged several times. In the 11th century a man was sent by al-Hakim, Fatimid caliph in Egypt, to destroy it, but he succeeded only in splintering it slightly. The Black Stone is now in a silver casing about 10 feet across. The practice of kissing the stone is inherited from pagan times, although Muslims deny that any worship is paid to the stone.

See also: ABRAHAM; ALLAH; ARCHANGEL; GABRIEL; MUHAMMAD

1682

**Kabandha**    In Hindu mythology, an evil goblin slain by Rama. Originally, Kabandha was a good spirit or Gandharva, in the service of the storm god Indra. One day, however, Indra cast a thunderbolt at Kabandha, driving his head and thighs into his body. Kabandha was then "covered with hair, vast as a mountain, without head or neck, having a mouth armed with immense teeth in the middle of his belly, arms a league long, and one enormous eye in his breast." In his new form Kabandha became an evil goblin who fought against the hero Rama. When Rama defeated Kabandha the goblin asked the hero to have his body burned. When this was done, Kabandha came out of the fire restored to his original shape as a Gandharva before Indra's thunderbolt had struck him. He then aided Rama in his war against the demon king Ravana. Kabandha is sometimes called Danu.

See also: GANDHARVA; INDRA; RAMA

1683

**Kacha**    In the Hindu epic poem *The Mahabharata*, a man who wanted the power to restore the dead to life. Kacha studied with the sage Sukra (Usanas), who had the power of restoring the dead to life. Sukra, however, was a priest in the service of demons and did not wish to pass on

his magic powers to Kacha. So instead he killed his student. But each time he was killed, Kacha was restored to life by Sukra, who repented. The third time Kacha was killed, the demons burned his body and mixed the ashes with Sukra's wine. When Devayani, Sukra's daughter, who loved Kacha, asked her father to restore Kacha to life again, he performed his magic feats but heard the voice of Kacha coming from his own stomach. To save his own life Sukra taught Kacha the charm. He then allowed himself to be ripped open, and Kacha, on coming out, performed the magic rite and restored Sukra to life. Kacha, however, was not in love with Devayani. She therefore cursed him, saying that his magic charms would have no power, and he in turn cursed her, saying she would marry a member of a lower caste instead of a priest.

See also: *MAHABHARATA, THE*

1684

**Kachina**    In North American Indian mythology (Hopi and other Pueblo Indians), the spiritual, inner form of reality manifested by masked dancers. The term *kachina* is also used for small painted wooden dolls. Kachinas may be understood as spirits of the dead. Two kinds of kachinas are recognized: Mon kachinas never dance in groups, while ordinary kachinas do.

1685

**Kadaklan**    In Philippine mythology, creator god of the Tinguian Islands. Creator of the earth, sun, moon, and stars, Kadaklan is married to Agemem and has two sons, Adam and Balujen. His dog is Kimat, the lightning. During a storm Kadaklan beats on his drum to amuse himself.

1686

**Kae**    In Polynesian mythology, an old wicked priest who was killed and eaten. Tinirau, the sea god, invited Kae to a special ceremony in which his son was to be named. The priest was fed a piece of meat from Tutunui, the pet whale of

Tinirau, who remained alive. Kae so liked the taste of whalemeat that he asked his host if he might ride home on the whale's back. Tinirau agreed, saying Kae had to dismount the whale when they reached shallow water or the animal would die. Kae deliberately let the whale die, took it home, and ate it. The winds carried the scent of the whalemeat back to Tinirau, who sent 40 dancing girls to investigate the matter. Kae, they were told, could be identified by his large crooked teeth. The girls started to dance and sing, causing the people to laugh. But Kae kept his mouth shut so as not to reveal his large teeth. Finally, however, he could not restrain himself, and he laughed, revealing his large teeth. Seeing him, the girls cast a spell over the crowd. While Kae slept, they took him back to Tinirau, who had him killed and eaten. The natives say that is why there is cannibalism. In a variant of the myth Kae is married to Hina, a goddess, and their son rides the whale.

See also: TINIRAU

1687

**Kakebotoke** In Japanese Buddhism, a round copper or wooden plaque on which Buddhist images are carved in relief.

1688

**Kakurezator** In Japanese folklore, an evil spirit who carries the souls of sinners to hell. He is portrayed as a blind old man with a knotted staff.

1689

**Kala** (time) In Hindu mythology, an epithet applied to Yama, god of death, as well as to the creator god, Brahma.

See also: BRAHMA; YAMA

1690

**Kalanemi** (rim of the wheel of time) In Hindu mythology, an archdemon. Kalanemi took the form of a holy hermit and offered poisoned food to the monkey hero Hanuman. Hanuman, however, refused the food. He went instead to bathe at a nearby pond and was seized by a crocodile. Hanuman dragged it out of the water and killed it. From the crocodile's body arose a beautiful nymph who had earlier been forced by a curse to live in the crocodile's body until Hanuman would free her. The nymph told Hanuman that the holy hermit was the archdemon Kalanemi in disguise. Hearing this, Hanuman went back to Kalanemi, grabbed him by the feet, and hurled him through the air until he landed in Lanka (Sri Lanka) at the feet of the demon king Ravana. Later Krishna (an incarnation of the god Vishnu) killed Kalanemi, but the demon became incarnate again in the evil king Kamsa, the enemy of Krishna, and in Kaliya, a demon snake.

See also: HANUMAN; KALANEMI; KALIYA; KRISHNA; RAVANA; VISHNU

1691

***Kalevala, The*** (the land of heroes) Finnish epic poem compiled by Elias Lönnrot from oral traditions in Karelia, now part of Russia. The first edition contained 12,078 lines, the second, 22,795.

The word *Kalevala* is derived from Kaleva, a mythical hero. Kaleva, however, never appears in the epic poem, though his daughter Kalvevatoar and his descendant Kalevalainen are mentioned. *The Kalevala* consists of 50 runes (poems or songs, sometimes called cantos; the term appended to each section varies with different English translations) varying in length but all in unrhymed alliterative trochaic tetrameter. Here is an example from W. F. Kirby's translation, which also displays the use of "echo" lines:

> Vainamoinen, old and steadfast,
> Now resolved upon a journey
> To the cold and dreary regions
> Of the gloomy land of Pohjola.

The use of a set verse form helps unify the epic, since the sources, from diverse oral traditions, were various folksingers of different ages. *The Kalevala* is the only modern European epic compiled from songs actually existing among the people. Lönnrot visited the most remote regions of the land and with skillful editing produced the epic. He added a prologue of approximately 100 lines as well as some connecting links to unify the epic.

The first part of the epic (runes 1–10) narrates the birth and adventures of one of the main characters in the poem, Vainamoinen, the son of Luonnotar, daughter of the air. Vainamoinen is a magician, perhaps derived from a shaman in real life, who can work magic through his songs. Shortly after his birth (in the poem he is always portrayed as old) he was challenged to a singing contest by the evil Laplander Joukahainen. The challenge was taken up, and Joukahainen was defeated and plunged into a swamp. To save himself from drowning, Joukahainen promised his sister Aino to Vainamoinen as his wife. Vainamoinen accepted the offer, but Aino did not. She drowned herself to avoid marrying the old culture hero. Not giving up, Vainamoinen went in pursuit of Aino in the river, finding her in the form of a fish. Even in this condition the girl refused and fled back into the water. Vainamoinen then went to Pohjola, the Northland, in search of a wife. While journeying there he was shot at by Joukahainen but escaped with wounds. Vainamoinen reached the land of Pohjola, ruled by the evil mistress Louhi, who told Vainamoinen that she would give him her daughter, the Maiden of Pohjola (the girl's name is never given in the poem), as a wife if he could construct a magic sampo, a mill that produced grain, salt, and money.

Unable to construct the sampo by his magic songs alone, Vainamoinen called in the smith Ilmarinen (another hero of the poem) to aid him. Ilmarinen consented and produced the magic sampo. As a result, Ilmarinen was given the Maiden of Pohjola as a wife.

The next section of the epic (runes 11–15) narrates the adventures of Lemminkainen, the Don Juan figure in the epic poem. He married Kyllikki but soon discovered that she was unfaithful to him. He divorced her and went to the land of Pohjola to find a new wife. On his way Lemminkainen was murdered by Markahattu, a partly blind cattle herder whom he had insulted. However, the hero was restored to life by the magic spells of his mother (Lemminkainen's mother remains nameless in the poem).

The next main division (runes 16–25) tells of the marriage of Ilmarinen to the Maiden of Pohjola after performing a series of tasks imposed on him by Louhi, the girl's mother. The next section (runes 26–30) tells of Lemminkainen's coming to the wedding, to which he had not been invited. He entered the castle by force, insulted the guests, killed Louhi's husband, and fled to the island of Sarri. While on the island he slept with all of the women while their husbands were away. Lemminkainen fled the island when the husbands returned. He then set out for Pohjola with his companion-in-arms Kurra (Tiera), but they were defeated in their attempt to destroy the land.

The poem then takes on a tragic cast with the tale of Kullervo (runes 31–36). Kullervo is a tragic hero who raped his sister and then committed suicide. Before he killed himself, however, he murdered the Maiden of Pohjola. The next section (runes 37–49) tells how Vainamoinen, Ilmarinen, and Lemminkainen journeyed to Pohjola to steal the magic sampo. In this adventure the sampo was lost in a lake. A battle then ensued between Louhi's men and the three heroes, in which the final victory was given to Vainamoinen.

The last rune (50) tells how Marjatta, similar to the Virgin Mary, bore a son who became king of Karelia. Vainamoinen then departed the land. The last rune displays a good deal of Christian legendary material, which also is scattered throughout other sections of the poem, though the epic as a whole is certainly not Christian.

*The Kalevala* had tremendous influence on the national identity of the Finns, coming at a time of political and cultural upheaval against Russian domination. It appeared at one of the high points of European Romanticism, when each national group was seeking heroes in its past history and legend. The two most influential Finnish artists who have been deeply moved by the splendid epic are Jean Sibelius, one of the major composers of the early part of the twentieth century, and Akseli Gallen-Kallela, a painter who illustrated many of the scenes of the epic poem. The American poet Longfellow read a German translation of the poem that inspired the verse form of his *Song of Hiawatha*. The American poet not only used the *Kalevala* verse form but also recast some of its episodes, such as the departure of Hiawatha, modeled on the departure of Vainamoinen in the Finnish work.

See also: AINO; HIAWATHA; JOUKAHAINEN; KULLERVO; KURRA; LÖNNROT, ELIAS; ILMARINEN; LEMMINKAINEN; LOUHI; LUONNOTAR; MARJATTA; SAMPO; VAINAMOINEN

1692
**Kalidasa** (Kali's slave)    Hindu poet and dramatist of the fifth century. Numerous legends surround the poet. According to one account, Kalidasa was a Brahman's son. At the age of six months he was left an orphan and was adopted by an ox driver. He grew up without any formal education, but he was remarkably handsome and had graceful manners. Once it happened that the princess of Benares, who rejected one suitor after another because they failed to reach her standard as scholars and poets, rejected a counselor of her father. The counselor planned revenge. He took Kalidasa from the street and gave him the garments of a rich man and a retinue of learned doctors. He then introduced him to the princess, after warning Kalidasa that under no circumstances was he to speak. The princess was struck with Kalidasa's beauty and moved by his silence, which she took to be profound wisdom. She decided to marry him. After the marriage she discovered the trick, but Kalidasa begged her to forgive him. She told her husband to pray to the goddess Kali (a form of the goddess Devi) for wisdom.

The prayer was granted. Knowledge and poetical power descended miraculously upon Kalidasa, who in gratitude assumed the name that means Kali's slave. Feeling he owed this happy change to his wife, he swore that he would treat her only with respect, as his teacher, but without any familiarity (no sexual intercourse). This only angered the princess. She cursed Kalidasa, saying he would meet his death at the hands of a woman. At a later date, the legend continues, the curse was fulfilled. A certain king had written half of a stanza of verse. He offered a large sum of money to any poet who could worthily complete it. Kalidasa completed the stanza, but a woman whom he loved discovered the lines, and greedy for the reward herself, killed Kalidasa and passed off the couplet as hers.

Kalidasa's most important work is the drama *Shakuntala*, based on an episode of the Hindu epic poem *The Mahabharata*.

See also: BRAHMAN; DEVI; *MAHABHARATA, THE*

1693
**Kaliya** (black)    In Hindu mythology, a serpent king subdued by Krishna, an incarnation of the god Vishnu.

Kaliya lived in a pool that he poisoned with venom from his five heads. All the surrounding countryside was being destroyed by his fire and smoke. One day the boy Krishna went to the pool and was trapped by Kaliya in his coils. Kaliya, however, could not hold the boy, whose body miraculously expanded, causing the snake to lose his hold. Krishna then performed a dance of death on the heads of the serpent, causing blood to flow "copiously from his mouths." After this, Kaliya surrendered and worshiped Krishna, who did not kill him but merely sent him to another river to live. Kaliya is an incarnation of the archdemon Kalanemi, who had been earlier killed by Krishna.

See also: KALANEMI; KRISHNA; VISHNU

*Kalki*

1694

**Kalki** (impure, sinful)    In Hindu mythology, the last avatar of the god Vishnu, which has not yet occurred. Vishnu is to appear at the end of the world cycle seated on a white horse, with drawn sword blazing like a comet, for the final destruction of the wicked, the renewal of creation, and the restoration of purity. Gore Vidal's novel *Kalki* uses the Hindu myth.

See also: AVATAR; VISHNU

1695

**Kalmasha-pada** (spotted feet)    In Hindu mythology, a king condemned to eat human flesh.

One day King Kalmasha-pada went out to hunt and found two tigers. He killed one, but as it died it turned into an evil spirit. The other tiger disappeared, threatening vengeance. Kalmasha-pada returned to his palace and celebrated a sacrifice, at which the sage Vashishtha officiated. When the sacrifice was over, Vashishtha went out, and the evil spirit of the tiger assumed his form and told Kalmasha-pada to serve the food. The evil spirit then turned into a cook, preparing human flesh and serving it to Vashishtha when

he returned. When the sage discovered that the flesh was human, he cursed Kalmasha-pada, saying his appetite should only be excited by similar food. When Vashishtha discovered that it was not Kalmasha-pada's fault, however, he reduced the sentence to 12 years. The angry king, in turn, took water in his hands and was about to cast it at Vashishtha, when Kalmasha-pada's wife dissuaded him. "Unwilling to cast the water on the ground, lest it should wither up the grain, and equally reluctant to throw it up into the air, lest it should blast the clouds and dry up their contents, he threw it on their own feet," and they were scalded by it, becoming spotted black and white.

1696

**Kalumba**    In African mythology (Luba of Congo), creator god who attempted to stop Death. One day Kalumba told a goat and dog to watch the roadside because Death and Life were going to pass by. Life was to be allowed to pass, but Death was to be stopped. So the two animals watched, but in a short time they began to argue, and the goat left the dog alone. In no time the dog fell asleep, and Death, covered in a grass-cloth and tied to a pole, as if for burial, quietly passed by. Next day the goat returned and stationed himself. Life then came by and was attacked by the goat. That is how death came into the world, according to the Luba people.

See also: IMANA

1697

**Kama** (Kandarpa) (desire)    In Hindu mythology, the god of love, whose wife is Rati (love play). Kama is lord of the Apsaras, heavenly nymphs. In Indian art he is portrayed armed with a bow and arrow. The bow is of sugar cane, the bowstring a line of bees, and each arrow is tipped with a flower. Kama usually is shown as young and handsome, riding on a parrot and attended by the Apsaras. One of them carries a banner displaying the Makara, a fantastic sea animal, or a fish, on a red ground. From the banner Kama is sometimes called Makara-ketu, and from the flowers, Pushpa-ketana. Other epithets are Kusma-yudha (armed with flowers), Pushpa-dhanus (whose bow is flowers), Pushpa-sara (whose arrows are flowers), and Madana (the maddener).

See also: MAKARA; RATI

1698

**Kambel** In Melanesian mythology, a sky god. According to the beliefs of the Keraki Papuans, Kambel cut down a palm tree and heard sounds issuing from it. Within the tree were people. At night Kambel tried to catch hold of a shining white object that moved upward from the palm tree. It slipped away from him and became the moon.

In another tale Kambel sent several lizards out in search of fire. It was the smallest lizard that succeeded in bringing it back. Kambel cooked the pith of a palm over the fire, and by casting it into the sky, he caused the clouds to be created. It was said that these clouds caused the sky to be pushed up, separating it from the the earth.

Kambel is mentioned in another myth involving the concept of incest. A man became aware of an incestuous relationship occurring between his wife and his son. The father killed his son, and the boy's dog reproached the man for having committed such an awful act. Kambel put the feather of a cassowary in the dog's mouth to prevent the mother from learning how her son had died. Ever since that event dogs have lost the power of speech.

See also: OEDIPUS

1699

**Kami** (above, superior?) In Japanese Shinto mythology, generic term for deities or spirits. Everything, animate or inanimate, has a kami. It is also used as an honorific title for all that is held sacred, mysterious, powerful, and fearsome, such as wind, thunder, sun, rivers, trees, and rocks, as well as for qualities of growth, fertility, and reproduction.

1700

**Kana** In Polynesian mythology, Hawaiian trickster, born in the form of a rope, raised by his grandmother Uli. Once Kana went to rescue a girl who had been abducted and placed on an island hill. Each time he stretched himself to reach the girl, the hill grew taller, moving the girl farther and farther away. He then went to his grandmother Uli to eat because he had grown very thin in stretching himself. Uli fed Kana and told him that the island was really a gigantic turtle whose stretching power lay in its flippers. Kana returned to the island, broke off the turtle flippers, and saved the girl.

See also: TRICKSTER

1701

**Kananesky Amaiyehi** In North American Indian mythology (Cherokee), the water spider who brought back fire to the animals. In the beginning there was no fire, and the entire earth was cold. Using a flash of lightning, the Thunderers put fire into the bottom of a sycamore tree, but no animals were able to go near the tree and get the fire. After many attempts to get the fire, Kananesky Amaiyehi, the water spider, who had downy hair and red stripes on her bottom, volunteered to try. But the problem was, how was she to carry the fire? "I'll manage that," she said as she spun a thread from her body and wove it into a *tusti* bowl, which she fastened on her back. Then she crossed over to the island where the tree was located. She put one little coal of fire into her bowl and came back with it. Ever since, animals have had fire, and the water spider still keeps her *tusti* bowl.

1702

**Kanthaka** In Buddhist legend, the steed of the Buddha.

See also: BUDDHA, THE

*Kappa*

**Kappa**    In Japanese folklore, a river demon with the body of a tortoise, the limbs of a frog, and the head of a monkey. His head has a hollow at the top containing a strength-giving fluid. He lives in the water and comes out in the evening to eat. He sucks the blood of horses and cows through their anuses. He also drags humans into the water and sucks out their blood through their anuses. Humans can outwit him by being civil to him and bowing. This act forces Kappa to return the bow; his life fluid spills from his head and he loses his strength. He can also be placated by throwing cucumbers with the names and ages of family members into the water where he lives. If a human is challenged to single combat with a kappa, it is essential to accept and hope that it will not be able to keep its head erect during the encounter. The human can then extract a prom-

ise from the kappa while it is in its weakened state.

**Karadzich, Vuk Stefanovich**    1787–1864. Pioneer Serbian folklorist, linguist, collector, and ethnographer. He reformed Serbian and Croatian orthography and created the modern Serbo-Croatian literary tongue by switching from Church Slavonic traditional patterns to the Serbo-Croatian spoken dialect. Vuk was the first to collect and publish traditional Serbo-Croatian folklore that had been transmitted orally for generations during the Ottoman domination. His voluminous collection includes folksongs, ballads, heroic epics (including those featuring Marko [Kraljevich], the Prince), proverbs, and descriptions of folk life and customs. He was among the first folklorists to preserve variants, use the language as it was spoken, and identify informants.

See also: KRALJEVICH, MARKO

**Karashishi**    Stone lions often found in front of Buddhist temples in Japan.

**Karasu Tengu** (crow Tengu)    In Japanese folklore, a trickster spirit.

See also: TRICKSTER

**Karshipta**    In Persian mythology, a bird who brought the laws of the creator god, Ahura Mazda, to the underground cavern where Yima, the first man, had stored men and animals to save them from a winter that destroyed the earth. Karshipta recited the sacred *Avesta* in the language of birds.

See also: AHURA MAZDA; *AVESTA*; YIMA

1708

**Karu and Rairu**   In the mythology of the Mundurucu Indians of Brazil, father and son creator gods. Karusakahiby and his son Rairu emerged out of chaos. Rairu stumbled on a bowl-shaped stone, which he picked up, placing it on his head. It began to grow until it formed the heavens. He then knelt down before his father. The older god was jealous of his son, because he believed Rairu was too clever and therefore might contrive a scheme to overthrow him. When Rairu realized his father wished to kill him, he fled, but Karusakahiby discovered where he was hiding. When Karusakahiby was about to strike his son, Rairu cried out: "Do not hit me, for in the hollow of the earth I have found people, who will come forth and labor for us." The first people were then brought out from their underground home. They were separated into tribes, the laziest becoming birds, bats, pigs, and butterflies.

1709

**Kashyapa** (one who swallowed light)   In Buddhism, Buddha, the Keeper of Light, who lived on earth for some 20,000 years and converted 20,000 people. His mount is the lion, his right hand is in the pose of "charity," and his left hand holds a monastic garment. In Tibet he is called Hod-srun and in China Chia-yeh. Also the name of a principal disciple of Shakyamuni Buddha.

1710

**Kasogonga**   In the mythology of the Chaco Indians of central South America, a rain goddess.

1711

**Kasyapa**   In Hindu mythology, a sage who is quite obscure. In the *Mahabharata* Kasyapa was given 13 of Daksha's daughters as wives, representing the 13 months of the lunar year. One of the wives was Aditi, with whom he fathered 12 Adityas, representing the solar year.
   See also: ADITI; DAKSHA; DANAVAS; DITI

1712

**Kate Shelley**   In American folklore, Kate Shelley was a young girl who lived in Iowa near a railroad bridge that crossed over a river far below. On one stormy night the bridge collapsed and sent an engine crashing down into the river. Kate, hearing the sound of the train wreck, even over the sounds of the thunder and lightning, rushed out with her lantern and down the tracks to warn an oncoming passenger train of the danger just ahead. She was successful, and many lives were thus saved. The legend has moved from the little town of Moingona, where it supposedly took place, over to the town of Boone. Outside of Boone there is a very high railroad trestle, nearly 200 feet high, that has been renamed the Kate Shelley Bridge. During "Pufferbilly Days" in Boone, the Boone and Scenic Valley Railroad still takes passengers over this bridge, and on each trip the story of Kate Shelley is told.

1713

**Kaumodaki**   In Hindu mythology, the mace of Krishna (an incarnation of the god Vishnu), given to him by Agni, the fire god, when the two battled Indra, the storm god.
   See also: AGNI; INDRA; KRISHNA; VISHNU

1714

**Kaundinya**   Fifth century B.C.E. In Buddhist legend, the first disciple of the Buddha. According to Buddhist texts, Kaundinya "had thoroughly grasped the doctrine of the Holy One, and the Buddha, looking into his heart, said, 'Truly Kaundinya has understood the truth.'" Hence Kaundinya was called Ajnata-Kaundinya (Kaundinya has understood the teaching; Kaundinya has no more to learn).
   See also: BUDDHA, THE

1715

**Kavah**   Blacksmith in the Persian epic poem *Shah Namah* by Firdusi who refused to sacrifice his children to the evil king, Zahhak.

Kavah was a strong and brave blacksmith who had a large family. One day the lot fell to two of his sons to be sacrificed to feed the serpents that came out of the neck of King Zahhak. (The serpents had been placed there by the evil spirit, Ahriman.) Kavah went to the king and protested:

Why give the brains of my beloved children
As serpent-food, and talk of doing justice
 (James Atkinson translation).

Zahhak, taken aback by such boldness, ordered Kavah's sons to be released but placed Kavah's name on the list in their place.

"Are you then men, or what?" cried the blacksmith to the assembled court. "You have made a pact with this devil."

Kavah then tore the register, threw it under his foot, and left the court, taking his two sons with him. After he had left, the nobles complained to the king that such behavior should not be tolerated. Zahhak replied that he did not know what had overcome him in the presence of Kavah. The blacksmith then joined the forces of the hero Faridun, who was fighting against Zahhak and eventually defeated the king.

In the poem Kavah is credited with making the mace used by Faridun in battle. It resembled a cow's head, probably symbolic of fertility and thus strength.

See also: AHRIMAN; *SHAH NAMAH*; ZAHHAK

1716
**Kelpie** (Kelpy) ( heifer, colt)   In Celtic mythology, a Scottish spirit of lakes and rivers who caused travelers to drown. His tail strikes the water with thunder, and he disappears in a flash of lightning. Sometimes he appears as a horse who lures victims into mounting him and then rides off, plunging into a river and drowning the rider. Thus, to see a kelpie is a sign of impending death. There are numerous motifs associated with the kelpie: magic horse from water world; river says, "the time has come but not the man."

1717
**Kemp Morgan**   In American folklore, comic oil-digging hero, who could smell oil underground. He had a tremendous appetite and had a full-time cook, Bull Cook Morrison of Snackover, Oklahoma. Once he dug a well so deep that it came out in Brazil. Another time he dug a well that shot oil up to heaven, causing the clouds to slide. The angels complained, and Kemp put a cap on the well.

See also: FAKELORE

1718
**Kenelm, St.** (brave helmet)   Died 819. In Christian legend, saint venerated in Gloucester, Winchcombe, England. Feast, 17 July. Kenelm was the son of King Kenwulf of Wessex. When he was seven years old he was murdered on orders of his sister. The crime was reported to Rome by a white dove, which alighted on the altar of St. Peter's, bearing the following couplet:

In Clent cow pasture, under a thorn
Of head bereft, lies Kenelm king-born.

1719
**Kenning**   In Norse mythology, a word or phrase that consists of a base word and a modifer. The base word *Aegir* and the modifier *horse* combine to produce a kenning for a ship, "Aegir's horse." Kennings are common in written eddic poetry but they are also found in other Germanic languages. In skaldic poetry they are of particular importance because they refer to other myths and heroic legends and can only be understood if the listener to these tales also knows the story that is being referred to by the kenning. The kenning for poetry is "Dvalin's drink" because the mead of poetry was in the possession of the dwarf Dvalin.

See also: AEGIR; BYLEIPT; DVALIN; LOKI; *POETIC EDDA*; *PROSE EDDA*; SKALD

**Ken-ro-ji-jin**   In Japanese mythology, earth god, usually portrayed with a bowl in one hand and a spear in the other.

1720

**Kentigern, St.** (chief lord?)   Sixth or seventh century. In Christian legend, patron saint of Glasgow, Scotland. Feast, 14 January.

1721

St. Kentigern is credited with the founding of Glasgow Cathedral. The most famous medieval legend associated with the saint deals with Queen Langoureth, who had been unfaithful to her husband, King Roderich. The king had given his wife a ring, and she in turn gave it to her lover. Knowing this, the king stole up on the lover one night and took the ring from his finger without waking him. The next day Roderich asked his wife for the ring. Frightened at what she had done, the queen went to St. Kentigern for help. Kentigern prayed and then went to the Clyde River, where the king had thrown the ring and caught a salmon. He opened up the fish, extracted the ring, which the fish had swallowed, and gave it to the queen, who showed it to the king. The arms of Glasgow portray a salmon with a ring in its mouth, as well as an oak tree and bell, alluding to the legend that the saint called pagans to worship the Christian God by hanging a bell on an oak tree and ringing it. St. Kentigern is also called St. Mungo (dearest).

See also: DRUIDS; OAK

**Keresaspa** (Keresasp, Keresaspo, Garshasp)   In Persian mythology, hero who will slay the archdemon Azhi Dahaka at the end of the world.

1722

Keresaspa was a beautiful youth. He carried a club with which he slew the golden-heeled monster, Gandarewa, and he fought the giant bird, Kamak, which hovered over the earth with its gigantic wings so that no rain could fall. Once Keresaspa fought the horned dragon who ate men and horses. Keresaspa climbed on the monster's back and started to cook lunch, stewing some meat in a kettle. The monster got very hot, began to perspire, and darted forward, causing the hot water and meat to fall. Keresaspa fled in terror.

Though not always successful, Keresaspa will come again at the end of the world and with his club slay the monster Azhi Dahaka when the archdemon escapes from his prison in Mount Demavend to cause havoc in the world.

See also: AZHI DAHAKA

**Keri and Kame**   In the mythology of the Bakairi Indians of central Brazil, twin culture heroes. Keri and Kame were the sons of Oka, the jaguar, and his wife, who were originally made of wood. Oka's wife had become pregnant when she swallowed two finger bones. Her mother-in-law, Mero, hated her and murdered her. But before she died, a cesarean operation was performed by the twins' uncle Kuara, and the twin culture heroes were born. When they grew up, they killed their evil grandmother by setting a forest fire in which she burned to death. During the conflagration Kame also was burned, but Keri blew on him and restored him to life. In the process Keri was burned himself but also was restored to life. In their new forms Keri and Kame chose to take human shapes. They ordered the sun and moon in the heavens, separated the heavens from the earth, created fire from the fox's eye and water from the Great Serpent, and then the brothers went their separate ways.

1723

**Kerki**   In Finno-Ugric mythology, a spirit who promotes the growth of cattle. His feast was held 1 November, the Feast of All Saints in the Christian calendar. Closely connected with the dead, Kerki was honored by having a feast spread for him as well as by having the bathhouse heated. A straw doll representing Kerki was often set up in the corner near the stove.

1724

See also: ALL SAINTS' DAY

1725

**Kevin, St.** (handsome at birth)    Sixth century. In Christian legend, abbot of Glendalough (Wicklow, Ireland). Also known as St. Coegmen. Feast, 3 June.

One Lent, according to medieval legend, St. Kevin "fled the company of men to a certain solitude." He chose a small hut on an island, where he prayed and read. Every day it was his custom to pray for many hours with his hand outstretched through the window of the hut. Once a blackbird settled on his open hand and began building a nest, then sat in the nest and laid an egg. The saint was so moved by the bird that he did not withdraw his hand until the young birds were hatched. Another legend tells that Kevin would not allow women on his island retreat. One day he was followed to his hut by a woman named Kathleen. In anger the saint hurled Kathleen from a rock. From that day forth her ghost never left the place where St. Kevin lived.

1726

**Keyne, St.**    Fifth century. In Christian legend, a female hermit. Feast, 8 October. St. Keyne was the daughter of King Brycham of Brecknock. When she died, angels came and removed her hairshirt and replaced it with a white robe. Her well, located near Liskeard, Cornwall, is believed to give drinkers of its waters power over their wives or husbands. The trick is to get to the well before one's spouse.

1727

**Kezef**    In Jewish folklore, an angel of death who fought against Moses in Horeb. Kezef was seized by the high priest Aaron and imprisoned in the Holy Tabernacle. The incidents are not recorded in the Bible, however, but supplied by Jewish nonscriptural writings.

See also: AARON; MOSES

1728

**Kezer-Tshingis-Kaira-Khan**    In Siberian mythology, the hero of the flood myth as told by the Soyots. He saved his family on a raft when the flood came and re-created everything when the waters subsided. He is credited with the invention of wine, as is Noah in the Old Testament.

See also: NOAH

1729

**Khadau and Mamaldi**    In Siberian mythology, the first man and woman in myths told by the Amur. The myths vary: some say Khadau and Mamaldi created the earth or that they were the first parents of the shamans or that they were shamans themselves. Mamaldi created the Asian continent and the Island of Sakhalin and was then murdered by her husband, Khadau. Before she was killed, she gave her husband the souls of future shamans who had been created earlier.

See also: ABUK AND GARANG; ADAM AND EVE; ASK AND EMBLA

1730

**Khadijah**    In Islamic history and legend, first wife of the prophet Muhammad. She is one of the four perfect women in Islam, the others being Fatima, the prophet's daughter; Mary, daughter of Imran; and Asia, wife of the pharaoh drowned in the Red Sea.

See also: FATIMA; MUHAMMAD

1731

**Khen-Pa**    In Tibetan folklore, the Old Man or master of the sky, who is portrayed as an old man with snow-white hair, dressed in white robes, and riding on the white dog of the sky. In his hand he carries a crystal wand.

See also: KHON-MA

1732

**Khepera** (Khepri, Kheprer, Chepera) (created himself)    In Egyptian mythology, god who

*Scarab*

represented the rising or morning sun and was closely associated with the scarab, a beetle sacred in ancient Egypt.

Khepera was one of the original creation gods. He was said to have been self-created, born of his own substance. In one myth he copulated with his own shadow, and from his semen came Shu, the air, and Tefnut, moisture. From the union of Shu and Tefnut came Geb, the earth, and Nut, the sky; they in turn bore the great deities Osiris, Isis, Set, and Nephthys. This group of nine deities was worshiped in a cosmological system known as the ennead, or Company of Nine Gods. In another creation myth, the sun god Ra was said to have created himself in primeval time in the form of the god Khepera.

Khepera was portrayed in Egyptian art as a beetle-headed man or as a man with a beetle surmounting his head, or simply as a beetle. The scarab beetle pushing a large ball of dung was seen as an image of a giant beetle pushing the sun across the sky. Young beetles are hatched from buried dung balls, and this perhaps gave rise to the idea that Khepera was also self-generated and emerged from the ground.

Since it was believed that the beetle was the incarnation of Khepera, beetle amulets were worn to attract the power of the god and secure his protection. In Egyptian funerary practice beetles or beetle amulets, often inscribed with texts from *The Book of the Dead*, were buried with the mummies to help ensure their resurrection.

Roman soldiers in battle wore the likeness of the beetle on a ring.

See also: *BOOK OF THE DEAD, THE*; ENNEAD; GEB; ISIS; NEPHTHYS; NUT; OSIRIS; SHU; TEFNUT

1733

**Khnum** (Khnemu, Chnum) (molder)    In Egyptian mythology, a creator god who resided at Elephantine, the region the ancient Egyptians also believed to be the source of the river Nile, personified as the god Hapi. Egyptian views concerning Khnum changed during the course of their long history, but various ancient texts show that Khnum always held an exalted position among the Egyptian deities. He even appears on gnostic gems and papyri for some 200 or 300 years after the birth of Christ. Khnum was believed to have molded on his potter's wheel the great cosmic egg that contained the sun. He was also known as the potter who fashioned humankind and the gods. As a ram-headed deity, Khnum is often depicted at a potter's wheel fashioning from clay both the *ba* and *ka* of the ruler. The episodes depicting the birth of Hathsepsut

*Khnum*

at Dier el Bahari contain one vignette in which this scene is portrayed. Among Khnum's epithets are Khnum Nehep (Khnum the creator), Khnum Per-Ankh (Khnum, governor of the house of life), Khnum Khenti-Taui (Khnum, governor of the two lands), Khnum Neb (Khnum, lord), Khnum-Neb-Ta-Ankhtet (Khnum, lord of the land of life), and Khnum Khenti Netchem-Tchem Ankhet (Khnum, lord of the house of the sweet life).

See also: BA; GNOSTICISM; HAPI; HATHSEPSUT; KA

1734

**Kholumolumo**   In African mythology (Sotho of South Africa), a monster who swallowed all of the people and animals except for one pregnant woman. When the woman gave birth she named her son Moshanyana. He later attacked the monster and easily killed it because it could not move. Then Moshanyana opened up its stomach, letting out all of the people and animals. Though most were pleased, some men eventually grew envious of Moshanyana and plotted his death. He escaped three times but was killed on the fourth attempt.

1735

**Khon-Ma**   In Tibetan folklore, the Old Mother, who rides on a ram and is dressed in golden-yellow robes. In her hand she holds a golden noose, and her face contains 80 wrinkles. Her personal attendant is called Sa-thel-nag-po.

See also: KHEN-PA

1736

**Khonsu** (Chons, Chunsu, Khons) (navigator, he who crosses the sky in a boat)   In Egyptian mythology, a moon god whose cult center was at Karnak, where he, his father, Amun, and his mother, Mut, formed a holy triad. In the north he was said to be the son of Ptah and Sekhmet. In the triad Khonsu is represented as an unclad youth with the side lock of hair depicting youth

in Egyptian art. On his head are the representations of the full and crescent moon. Early references to Khonsu depict him as a terrifying figure, the "angry one of the gods," who strangled lesser deities and ate their hearts. It was for these ferocious qualities that he was invoked in spells against powerful demons. Khonsu was also a god of healing and aided both women and cattle to become fertile and conceive. One ancient myth tells how he saved a young princess from demonic possession. Once the king of Thebes prayed to a statue of Khonsu on behalf of the daughter of the prince of Bekhten. The god listened to the king's plea, nodded his head (the statue of Khonsu was provided with a movable head, which the priests manipulated), and promised to give his divine power to the statue that was to be sent to the city of the sick princess. The statue arrived in Bekhten, and its magical powers exorcised the princess of the demon that possessed her. The demon then spoke to Khonsu and acknowledged the god's superior power. Khonsu, the demon, and the prince spent a happy day together, after which the demon returned to his own dwelling place, and Khonsu returned to his home in the form of a hawk.

See also: AMUN; MUT

1737

**Khonvum**   In African mythology (Pygmy), supreme god, who makes contact with humans through an animal intermediary, usually a chameleon. He renews the sun each day by throwing broken pieces of stars, gathered during the night, at it.

See also: EFÉ

1738

**Kibuka**   In African mythology (Buganda of Uganda), a war god, brother of the demigod Mukasa. Kibuka assisted the Buganda army by hovering above the battlefield in the clouds and shooting arrows down at their enemies. During one battle some women were taken prisoners. Despite a warning not to have sexual relations with any of the women, Kibuka brought one of them to his hut. As a result, in the next battle he was mortally wounded on top of a tree and later died.

See also: MUKASA

**Kied Kie Jubmel**    In Lapland mythology, a stone god worshiped as late as the 17th century. The images of stone gods usually were extremely crude, making it difficult to decipher whether a man or animal or some composite figure was represented. In ritual connected with Kied Kie Jubmel, a male reindeer was selected for sacrifice. The reindeer's right ear was pierced and a red thread run through it; its blood was then preserved in a barrel. A priest took the blood, some of the fat, the antlers, the bones of the head and neck, and the feet and hooves; he anointed the idol with the fat and blood. The antlers were placed behind the stone image—the right horn with the penis of the animal attached to it, the left horn bearing an amulet of tin and silver worked together with the red thread. The elaborate ritual was performed to guarantee the worshiper good hunting and fishing. Kied Kie Jubmel was called Storjunka (the great lord) in Swedish. The term is sometimes generically applied to stone gods.

1739

**Kikimora** (tormenting spirit)    In Russian folklore, female house spirit who lives behind the oven, said in some accounts to be the wife of Domovoi, the male house spirit; sometimes said to be a *mora*, a person with two souls.

Kikimora appears in numerous folktales, though no precise image emerges. She looks after poultry and sometimes takes part in household tasks if the wife herself is diligent; if not, she causes havoc by making noises in the night and waking those asleep. Sometimes she causes women to tangle their spinning if they arise from their spinning wheels without making the sign of the cross. Anatol Liadov's symphonic

1740

poem *Kikimora* captures the capricious nature of the spirit. Ivan Bilibin's sketch shows a composite animal made up of chicken legs, semihuman hands, furry ears, horns, and a beaked face and wearing a peasant costume.

See also: DOMOVOI; MORA

**K'ilin** (Chi-len)    In Chinese mythology, a unicornlike creature. The male, *k'i*, and the female, *lin*, are combined into a compound word. The k'ilin has the body of a deer, the legs and hoofs of a horse; its head is like that of a horse or dragon, its tail like an ox or lion, and its horn is fleshy. Some Chinese works depict the animal as scaly, others as hairy. The k'ilin is a paragon of virtue and filial love. It walks so lightly as to produce no sound and does not hurt anyone. In Chinese legend the birth of Confucius was announced by the appearance of a k'ilin, and so was the philosopher's death. In Japanese the creature is called a kirin.

See also: CONFUCIUS

1741

**Kimon** (demon gate)    In Japan, gate placed on the north side of a garden; through it the spirits of evil are supposed to pass. A Shinto shrine is erected in front of the gate.

1742

**King Hal**    In American southern folklore, an escaped slave who ruled a kingdom near the fork of the Alabama and Tombigbee rivers. His kingdom was destroyed when one of his subjects, another runaway slave, went back to his white master and reported where Hal and his subjects lived.

1743

**Kinharingan**    In the mythology of Borneo, creator of the world and humankind, along with his wife Munsumundok. According to one myth, Kinharingan and his wife emerged from a rock in

1744

the middle of the ocean. They walked on the waters until they came to the house of Bisagit, the spirit of smallpox. He gave them some earth, and the couple proceeded to create land, sun, moon, stars and people. In exchange for the earth, however, Bisagit demanded that half of the people created by Kinharingan would have to die of smallpox. So every 40 years Bisagit comes to claim his due. In a variant myth, Kinharingan and his wife killed one of their children, cut it into small pieces, and planted the pieces in the earth; from it sprang all plants and animals.

1745

**Kintu and Nambi**  In African mythology (Buganda of Uganda), the first man and woman. Death did not want Kintu and Nambi, the first man and woman, to leave heaven for earth. Gulu, the sky god and father of Nambi, warned the couple of Death's wish, suggesting that they leave as soon as possible and not return to heaven for any reason. Nambi, however, returned to heaven to ask her father, Gulu, for some grain to feed her fowl. Death, who was Nambi's brother, took this opportunity to follow his sister to earth. Kintu became very angry when his wife came back to earth accompanied by Death, but Nambi told Kintu to wait and see if anything would happen. For a while both Kintu and Nambi lived very happily. They had many children. Eventually, Death came to their home and asked for one of Kintu's children to serve as his cook. After being turned down, Death asked a second time, but still Kintu refused, saying that Gulu would not be pleased to see his grandchild working as Death's cook. Death then threatened to kill the child if Kintu would not agree to give him up. Kintu did not agree, and the child died. In time more of Kintu's children died, so he turned to Gulu to find out what, if anything, could be done to stop Death's rampage. Gulu reminded Kintu of the warning he had given earlier, but nevertheless he sent Kaizuki, brother of Death and Nambi, to aid the couple. Kaizuki fought with Death but could not overcome him. Death went to hide in the ground, and Kaizuki could not get him to come out. Since then Death has lived underground and is always present.

In a variant myth Kintu lived alone with only one cow. Nambi came to visit him one day and fell in love with him. Before long, however, she had to return to her father, Gulu, the sky god. Nambi's relatives disliked Kintu because all he drank was milk, and they objected to her marriage. Gulu then decided to test Kintu and removed his cow, forcing Kintu to eat grass and leaves. Nambi, however, let Kintu know that his cow had been taken to heaven. Various tests were given by Gulu to Kintu, and in each one he succeeded. Finally, Kintu was allowed to marry Nambi. He was asked by Gulu to pick the cow that was his from among three large herds of cows that all looked alike. A bee came and told Kintu not only which cow to pick but which calves had been born to the cow while it was in heaven.

See also: ABUK AND GARANG; ADAM AND EVE; ASK AND EMBLA

1746

**Kirata-n-te-rerei** (the most beautiful of men) In Micronesian mythology, ancestor of the people of the Gilbert Islands. The son of Te-ariki-n-tarawa, a hero, and Na Te-reere, a tree goddess, Kirata-n-te-rerei was so handsome that a woman could conceive a child by just looking at his handsome body.

1747

**Kisagan-Tengri**  In Siberian mythology, a war god worshiped by the Mongols. He protected the army, helped them locate the enemy, and then brought them victory.

1748

**Kishimojin**  In Japanese mythology, goddess of women in childbirth, prayed to for offspring; protector of the Buddhist world and of children in particular.

Originally, Kishimojin was a cannibal woman in Hindu mythology, mother of 1,000 children. One child, Bingara, was converted by the Buddha, and later Kishimojin also was converted. In one myth she was condemned to give birth to 500 children to pay for her evil deeds, earning for herself the title Mother of Demons. In a variation she was sent to hell and was reborn in the shape of a ghoul to give birth to 500 devils, of whom she was to eat one a day because in life she had sworn to devour all of the children in one village.

She was converted by the Buddha in her second existence.

See also: BUDDHA, THE

1749

**Kitamba** In African mythology (Mbundu of Angola), a king who ordered all of his subjects to join him in a state of perpetual mourning when his wife died. No one was permitted to speak or make any noise in public. Despite the fact that the lesser chiefs objected strenuously to the king's proclamation, Kitamba continued the mourning. A council of elders appointed a doctor to help resolve the matter. The doctor and his little son dug a grave in the floor of their home in their effort to reach the underworld to see the king's wife. Each day they dug deeper, and at last they succeeded in reaching the king's wife, who explained to them that no one once dead could return to the realm of the living. She gave the doctor her armlet so that Kitamba would know that the doctor had succeeded in reaching her. When Kitamba saw the armlet, he finally permitted the mourning to end.

1750

**Kit Carson** 1809–1868. In American history and folklore, popular name of Christopher Houston, a frontiersman and guide who appears as a hero in many legends. One of Carson's contemporaries said that "Kit Carson's word was as sure as the sun comin' up" and "Kit never cussed more'n was necessary," making Carson a perfect subject for legend. Kit Carson appears in Willa Cather's novel *Death Comes to the Archbishop* and Joaquin Miller's literary ballad, "Kit Carson's Ride," included in his *Songs of the Sierras*.

See also: BUFFALO BILL

1751

**Kitpusiagana** (born by cesarean operation, taken from guts) In North American Indian mythology (Micmac), culture hero, second in power only to Gluskap.

See also: GLUSKAP AND MALSUM

1752

**Kitshi Manitou** (master of life, great mystery) In North American Indian mythology (Chippewa/Ojibwa), the great spirit, fullness of power.

See also: MANITOU

1753

**Kitsune** (fox) In Japanese folklore, a character who appears in many folktales and folk beliefs.

See also: FOX

1754

**Kiyohime** In Japanese legend, a woman who destroyed the monk Anchin when he refused her sexual advances.

Kiyohime was the daughter of an innkeeper at Masago at whose house Anchin, of the monastery of Dojoji, used to stay when on pilgrimage to Kumano. The monk petted the child, giving her a rosary and some charms, never thinking that her childish affection would one day develop into fiery love. However, the young girl's immodest advances soon became the bane of Anchin's life. As a result, her love turned to hatred, and Kiyohime called on the gods of the underworld to aid her in the destruction of Anchin.

Once Kiyohime pursued Anchin into the temple, and he fled and hid in the great bell, which was ten feet high and weighed so much that 100 men could not move it. Approaching the bell, Kiyohime lashed herself into a frenzy. As she nearly touched it, the superstructure of the bell suddenly gave way, and the bell fell with a dull sound over the monk, imprisoning him. At the same moment the figure of Kiyohime began to change. Her body became covered with scales, and her legs joined and grew into a dragon's tail. She wrapped herself around the bell, striking it with a T-shaped stick, and emitted flames from all parts of her body. Her blows rained on the bell until it became red hot and finally melted. Kiyohime fell into the molten mass, and only a handful of white ash could be found, the remains of the monk. The legend is used in a No play.

See also: NO

1755
**Knaninja**   In Australian mythology, name for totem ancestors who live in the sky as spirits.

1756
**Knecht Ruprecht** (servant Rupert)   In German folklore, the knight or servant of Jesus Christ at Christmastime. In Germany until the 19th century Knecht Ruprecht was impersonated by a man wearing high boots, a white robe, a yellow wig, and a mask. He would knock at the door on Christmas Eve or St. Nicholas Eve or Day (5 or 6 December) and say he had been sent by Jesus Christ to bring gifts to the children. Parents would then be asked if the children had been good. If the answer was yes, Knecht Ruprecht would give a gift to the children (provided earlier by the parents). If the children had been bad, he would give a whip or rod and tell the parents to use it on their children. He has many other names, including St. Nicholas.

See also: NICHOLAS, ST.

1757
**Knights Templar, Order of**   In French history and legend, nine knights who, at the beginning of the 12th century, assumed the responsibility of protecting pilgrims on their journey to the Holy Land. The name Templar was given to them because they kept their arms in a building given to them by an abbot of the convent on the site of the old Temple of Solomon in Jerusalem. They wore long white mantles with a bright red cross on the left shoulder. Their seal shows two knights riding on a single horse, the story being that they were so poor they had to share the horse.

See also: BAPHOMET; SOLOMON

1758
**Kobold**   In German folklore, a house spirit who likes to play pranks and make noise, but who also watches over the household. The Kobold warns the inhabitants about thieves, gives good advice, takes care of the cattle, and carries out certain household chores, but he must be rewarded for this work or else he will play a prank. In modern German, a young girl who quickly takes care of her housework is said to have her own Kobold. The same is said if someone becomes rich quickly.

See also: DOMOVOI; KIKIMORA

1759
**Kohin**   In Australian mythology, god dwelling in the Milky Way who sends thunder and lightning. He was once a warrior.

1760
**Koi**   In Australian mythology, generic name for the spirit of the bush.

1761
*Kojiki*   (records of ancient matters)   Book of Japanese Shinto mythology, written in Chinese characters, presented to the Japanese court in 712 C.E.

The *Kojiki* is the oldest Japanese book. It was commissioned by the emperor Temmu (673–686), who wished to preserve native Shinto beliefs under the growing strength of Buddhism, which was taking root in Japan. The emperor wished to avoid future corruptions of the "exact truth" and to ensure that future generations would understand the story of the creation of Japan and the divine ancestry of the monarch. The book is one of the basic sources for the study of Shinto mythology and belief.

The *Nihongi* or *Nihonshoki* (Chronicles of Japan), completed in 720, is the second most important text for Shinto, being twice the length of the *Kojiki*. It contains many of the myths of the earlier work, often giving variants. Many of the gods appear under different names. It traces myth, legend, and history up to 697.

See also: *NIHONGI*

**Kojin** In Japanese Shinto mythology, god of the hearth, sometimes portrayed with three faces and six arms, carrying a bow, arrows, sword, lance, saw, and bell. His shrine is usually located near a fireplace or stove in the kitchen. When his statue is placed in a garden, he is called Ji-Kojin (ground kojin). Sometimes he is portrayed by three thin plates of stone.

**Komdei-Mirgan** In Siberian mythology, a hero in a Tartar myth whose head was cut off and restored. One day Komdei-Mirgan went to hunt the black fox and in doing so broke his leg. He did not know that the black fox was the daughter of Erlik-Khan, the lord of the dead. While Komdei-Mirgan was trying to get up, Yelbegen, a monster with nine heads riding a 40-horned ox, came and cut off his head. Yelbegen then brought the head to the land of the dead. Kubaiko, the sister of Komdei-Mirgan, went in search of the head in the land of the dead. After numerous adventures she succeeded in getting the Water of Life from God, which restored her brother to life.

See also: ERLIK; WATER OF LIFE

**Kompira** In Japanese mythology, god of sailors and bringer of prosperity. He is portrayed as a fat man sitting down with his legs crossed, a purse in one hand.

**Konsei dai-myojin** (root of life great shining god) In Japanese Shinto belief, word for natural stones that have phallic shapes. The term also is applied to a stone carved in the shape of a phallus.

**Kookinberrook and Berrokborn** In Australian mythology, the first men created, made by the god Pundjel. They married Kunewarra and Kuurook.

See also: PUNDJEL

**Koopoo** In Australian mythology, the redplain kangaroo responsible for cats having spots. One day Koopoo met Jabbor, the cat who lived in the area Koopoo was traveling through. Jabbor asked Koopoo to divulge to him half of the secret ceremonies of the kangaroos. Koopoo, of course, refused, saying that the corroborees—big dances—belonged only to kangaroos. Jabbor wanted to fight for the secrets, but Koopoo called on other kangaroos, who threw spears at the cat. This act resulted in many cats having spots, for each spot represents a place where a spear entered Jabbor's body. As the cat lay dying, Deert, the moon god, came by and told Jabbor to drink a special kind of water that would permit him to come back to life. The other cats, however, prevented Jabbor from getting to the water. Deert grew angry and declared that because of this act all things would have to die. Only he, Deert, would be able to die and return to life again.

See also: DEERT; GIDJA; NAJARA

**Ko Pala**  In Burmese mythology, a king who returned to life as a crab. Ko Pala was chosen king when the ruler of the valley dwellers died with no heir to succeed him. The future king was brought in a basket and placed in the former king's house during the night. The people were so exhausted by the funeral ceremonies for the dead king that they accepted Ko Pala as the new king without any resistance. His reign, however, did not satisfy the people who had put him in the basket, so they placed him on an island and let him starve to death. After many reincarnations he returned as a crab when the entire land was flooded. He stayed until the waters had receded and then went to Loi Pu Kao (hill that the crab entered) and died.

**Koran, The** (The Qur'an) (the recitation)  Sacred scriptures of Islam, consisting of material given as revelation to Muhammad, the prophet of Islam, during the seventh century C.E., and gathered together for publication by his followers. It contains not only the religious but also the social, civil, commercial, military, and legal codes of Islam.

Muslims believe that the Koran has existed in heaven from all eternity in a form called *Umm alkitab*. A copy of this perfect text, which is part of the essence of Allah, was made on paper in heaven, bound in silk, and ornamented with gold and the precious stones of paradise. This sacred text was then given to the archangel Gabriel, who revealed it to Muhammad piecemeal, but he allowed the prophet to see the complete version of the book once a year. The night on which the complete Koran came down to the lowest heaven, where Gabriel could then reveal it to Muhammad, is called *Al Kadr*.

The Koran contains 114 suras, or chapters (literally, rows or series), estimated to contain about 6,225 *âyât*, or verses (literally, signs), which in most cases mark a pause in rhythm. The suras are not homogeneous but are unsystematic clusters of fragmented text. Muhammad directed that each fresh revelation that was given to him by the angel Gabriel be "entered into such and such a sura." The final arrangement of the book consists of the longest sura first and proceeds to the shortest last, thus not following the chronology of revelation.

Suras are called either "Meccan" or "Medinan," meaning they belong to the period before or after the Hegira, the immigration of Muhammad from Mecca to Medina (Yathrib) in 622—the year 1 in Islamic reckoning. A sura often contains material from both periods, and scholars have produced various editions and chronological arrangements of the contents of the Koran.

The material of the Koran is highly varied. There are many praises to Allah that equal the majesty of the Old Testament. In many places the heroes of the Hebrew scripture appear in the Koran in legends rendered differently from the accounts in the Old Testament. Jesus and John the Baptist also appear, as well as the Virgin Mary, but here the legends stem not from the New Testament but from many apocryphal writings of the early Church. Although scholars still debate the question, it is generally believed that Muhammad could not read or write, so all of his tales that are similar to tales in the Old and New Testaments are thought to have been gathered from oral sources.

The Koran begins with the following sura, in which Allah is entreated as the God of compassion and of mercy (*Rahman*):

Praise be to Allah, Lord of the worlds!
The Compassionate, the Merciful!
King on the day of reckoning!

A modern Muslim, Muhammad Zafrulla Khan, in his edition of the Koran, writes that "the Quran is verbal revelation and thus literally the Word of Allah. The reader needs to keep in mind that it is Allah speaking. . . . The Quran is extremely concise and is a masterpiece of condensation. It leaves a great deal to the intelligence of the reader, urges reflection and appeals constantly to the understanding." Of course, Western commentaries (especially those written prior to the present century) have not necessarily seen the suras of the Koran in the same light.

The earliest English translation was made in 1647 by Alexander Ross from a French version. Ross's attitude toward the sacred text can be gleaned from his "needful caveat" addressed to the Christian reader:

> Good Reader, the great Arabian Impostor now at last after a thousand years is by way of France arrived in England, and his *Alcoran* or Gallimaufry of Errors . . . hath learned to speak English.

The translator then goes on to condemn the prophet, who caused "silly people to believe that in his falling sickness . . . he had conference with the angel Gabriel." Thomas Carlyle, writing in the 19th century, tried to find a *via media* to Muhammad and the religion he preached. Carlyle found the Koran "toilsome reading," yet at the same time he found merit in the "primary character of the Koran . . . its *genuineness* . . . sincerity, in all senses."

Whatever the Western view of the Koran, it continues as perhaps the most widely read book in the world, surpassing the Bible in its readership. Sura 56, speaking of the Koran, says "Only the purified shall touch it." The act of reading the Koran is called *Tadjwid*, and a good Muslim must be ritually pure before embarking on reading or even touching a copy of the sacred text.

There are numerous variant romanized spellings of the Koran, among them Al-Koran, Alcoran, Al-Kur'an, Al-Kuron, the Qur'an. Sometimes the Koran is called Al-Kitab (the book) or Al-Furgân, from the root word "to separate" or "distinguish." The Koran helps separate or distinguish truth from falsehood in religious doctrine.

See also: ALLAH; GABRIEL; HEGIRA; JESUS; JOHN THE BAPTIST, ST.; MUHAMMAD; VIRGIN MARY

1770

**Korka-Murt and Korka-Kuzo** (man of the house, house ruler)    In Russian-Lapland folklore, household spirits who often take the form of the master of the house when they appear. They watch over the family, but if they are angry, they can bring nightmares or tangle the hair of those in the house. Since they are variable in their natures, a child is not left alone in the house because Korka-Murt and Korka-Kuzo might allow it to be kidnapped and replaced by a changeling. Sacrifices of black sheep often were made to the house spirits to appease them when they were angry. Other household spirits are Gid-Kuzo (cattleyard man), a spirit who looks after cattle, protecting them from beasts of prey; Domovoi, master of the house; Kikimora, a tormenting spirit; and Murt's So-Muret (bathhouse ruler), a spirit who lives in a dark corner of the bathhouse and resembles a tall, middle-aged man dressed in white shirt with wooden shoes. Sometimes he has only one eye. He appears before any great misfortune is about to take place. Obin-Murt is a spirit who protects the barn from fire and storm.

See also: DOMOVOI; KIKIMORA

1771

**Korobona**    In North American Indian mythology (Warrau), heroine raped by a man-serpent who gave birth to a boy and girl. Korobona's brothers believed they had killed the boy but years later discovered that their sister had saved him. Angry, they killed the lad, cutting his body into pieces. They allowed their sister to bury the remains, and they returned home. Korobona collected her son's remains and placed leaves and red flowers over them. Then she noticed that the leaves began to move, and suddenly a fully grown man appeared, armed with bow and arrows. He was the first Carib warrior, who later terrorized the Warrau.

**Korupira** (Kurupira, Curupira)   In the folklore of the Tupi Indians of Brazil, a forest demon. Korupira is often of a mischievous nature, but if he is in a good mood he will help hunters, teaching them the secrets of herbs. However, he does not like hunters to wound an animal, then leave it; each kill must be completed. Two folktales demonstrate the dual character of Korupira. Once, in return for some tobacco, Korupira helped a hunter. His only injunction was that the hunter not tell his wife of the transaction. The wife, sensing something was strange, followed her husband to the forest. As a result, she was killed by Korupira. A second folktale tells how Korupira was killed when a hunter tricked the demon into stabbing himself. After a month the hunter returned to get Korupira's blue teeth. When he struck the teeth, Korupira was restored to life. Not being especially angry, Korupira then gave the hunter a magic bow to hunt with, instructing him not to kill birds. The hunter disobeyed, and as punishment he was torn apart. But out of kindness Korupira replaced his torn flesh with wax, bringing the hunter back to life. Korupira then told the hunter not to eat hot foods. The hunter disobeyed and melted.

**Koshin**   In Japanese mythology, god of roads, portrayed with a fierce, scowling face and a third eye. He has either two, four, six, or eight arms. Two hands are folded in prayer. He is also portrayed with the sun and moon riding on clouds. Three monkeys, a cock, and hen are also sometimes included. The proverbial saying "Hear no evil, see no evil, speak no evil" came to be associated with monkeys when travelers to China and Japan saw three carved Koshin monkey deities on pedestals alongside the road, with their ears, eyes, and mouths covered up.

See also: ASS

**Kossuth, Lajos**   1802–1894. In Hungarian legend, freedom fighter in the war of independence. He was the minister of finance in the first independent national government and later became governor of Hungary. Following the collapse of the new government he had to flee the country and later died in exile. Hungarian folklore has made him a symbol of freedom. When he appeared, some peasants believed he was a reincarnation of Ferenc Rákóczi, an earlier fighter for Hungarian freedom, who was to come back when the country needed him. Some of the legends attached to Kossuth stem from those assigned to King Mátyás, another popular figure in Hungarian folklore.

See also: BARBAROSA; RÁKÓCZI, FERENC; MÁTYÁS

**Kostchei** (Koschey, Katschel)   In Russian folklore, a male aspect of Baba Yaga, an evil wizard whose soul is hidden in a duck's egg. Though often called deathless or immortal, Kostchei could die if one could find where the egg that contained his soul was hidden. If the egg was destroyed, Kostchei also would be destroyed. The egg is most often inside a duck, which is inside a rabbit, which is beneath an oak tree, on an island in the middle of the ocean. In Stravinksy's ballet *L'Oiseau de feu* (The Firebird) Ivan, the hero, finds the egg in the hollow of a tree and destroys it, causing Kostchei and his evil court to disappear forever. Kostchei appears in James Branch Cabell's novel *Jurgen*.

See also: BABA YAGA

**Koyan**   In Australian mythology, a tribal name for the good spirit. He is offered spears in worship.

**Kraken**   In Western European folklore, a fantastic sea monster or sea snake, also called the fish-mountain. Tales about the kraken seem to have originated during the Christian Middle Ages with numerous seamen's accounts of monsters haunting the deep. The kraken was described by Bishop Pontoppidan in his *Natural History of Norway* as being a mile and a half wide with tentacles that could capture ships and bring them down. There is a tale of a bishop returning by sea to his own country, who spotted what he believed to be an island. He went ashore and celebrated Mass. When he returned to his ship, he saw that it was not an island on which he had stood but a kraken afloat. Tennyson's early poem "The Kraken" deals with the fantastic being.

See also: WHALE

**Kraljevich, Marko**   1335?–1394. In Serbian legend, a historical figure of legendary proportions. Marko Kraljevich (Marko, the Prince), is featured in hundreds of Serbian epic-ballads and folk narratives that date to the 14th century. A fighter for the Orthodox Christian faith, Marko achieved prominence during the Ottoman period as a great Serbian folk hero even though he was, in historical fact, a Turkish vassal. The ballads, popular in Bulgaria and Romania as well, tell of his courage and incredible feats while fighting for freedom. His kind and just heart, physical prowess, strategic cleverness, and loyalty to his piebald steed, Sharatz, are identifying traits of his legend. Collections and translations of his adventures abound, beginning with those published in the early nineteenth century by Vuk Stefanovich Karadzich to recent comprehensive translations and analyses of the Marko heroic tale cycle.

See also: CULTURE HERO; VUK KARADZICH

**Kralyevich Marko**   1335?–1394. In Serbian legend, a hero believed to have lived for 300 years; he appears in Bulgarian and Rumanian legends as well. He is described as an upright man with a kind heart, even gaining the respect of the enemy Turks. One Serbian heroic ballad tells how he helped a Turkish princess, daughter of the sultan Bayazeth, and was thereafter called "my foster son" by the sultan, while he called the sultan "my foster father."

**Kratti** (spirit)   A Finno-Ugric guardian spirit who watches the property of the house owner.

**Kravyad**   In Hindu folklore, a flesh-eating goblin or any carnivorous animal. The term comes from *Kravyad*, the fire that consumes bodies on a funeral pyre.

**Kriemhild** (Krimhild)   In the *Nibelungenlied*, sister of Gunther; wife of Siegfried. Siegfried gave her a girdle and the Nibelungs' gold. She later avenged his murder, then was killed herself. In the Norse version of the legend in the *Volsunga Saga* she is called Gudrun, and Siegfried is called Sigurd.

See also: *NIBELUNGENLIED*; SIEGFRIED; *VOLSUNGA SAGA*

**Krishna** (the dark one)   In Hindu mythology, the eighth avatar or incarnation of the god Vishnu.

Krishna was sent to earth to rid it of evil spirits who committed "great crimes in the world." His birth accounts vary somewhat in Hindu texts. The major myth tells how Krishna escaped from the slaughter ordered by his evil uncle King Kamsa (brass) of Bhoja. The king heard that his cousin Devaki would have a child who one day would destroy him, so he ordered that Devaki be killed. Devaki, however, convinced Kamsa that

*Krishna*

she would deliver to him all of her children. Taken in by the promise, Kamsa let Devaki live.

In the meantime in heaven, Vishnu knew what was to happen and went to the subterranean watery hell. He brought back six embryos (which were actually six demons) and placed them in Devaki's womb. He then placed there another embryo, which would be his brother Balarama. (There are variant accounts of the birth of Balarama.) Kamsa killed each of the first six offspring. When it was time for the seventh birth, Devaki seemed to have a miscarriage, though in actuality while she was asleep, the embryo of Balarama was transferred to the womb of Rohini (red, red cow), the wife of the sage Vasudeva. Thus, Balarama was born from Rohini, and Kamsa was no wiser. Devaki, however, thought all seven of her offspring were lost. When she was pregnant for the eighth time, with Krishna, she carefully guarded herself. At the same time Yasoda (conferring fame) also became pregnant. The two gave birth on the same night, Devaki to Krishna and Yasoda to a girl. The sage Yasudeva, in order to save the boy, switched the children, placing Krishna in Yasoda's crib. When King Kamsa came and saw a girl in Devaki's crib, he was relieved. But he was still filled with anger and took the child "by the foot and whirled her around vigorously and dashed her violently to the stone floor." Miraculously the child "flew to heaven, unbruised."

Krishna's childhood was filled with wonders. Once Krishna and his brother Balarama were playing with some calves. Yasoda, Krishna's foster mother, became angry. To stop Krishna she tied him to a heavy wooden mortar in which corn is threshed and went on with her work. Krishna, trying to free himself, dragged it until it became wedged fast between two trees, which were then uprooted. The trees were two sons of the god of riches, Kubera, who had been trapped into the trees and were now free.

Kamsa, the evil uncle, once sent a demon after Krishna when he was wandering with cattle in the woods. The boy, seeing through the demon's disguise, seized him by the foot, swung him around his head, and dashed him against the ground. The next day another demon, in the form of a crane, attacked Krishna, locking him in its bill. Krishna became so hot that the crane released him, and then Krishna crushed its beak under his foot.

On another occasion Krishna challenged Indra, the storm god. Seeing the cowherds preparing to pray to Indra for rain, Krishna told them to worship the mountain instead because it provided food for their cattle, which in turn supplied them with milk. Acting on Krishna's advice, the cowherds presented to the mountain "curds, milk and flesh." This scheme was really intended to honor Krishna, for upon the summit of the mountain Krishna appeared, saying, "I am the mountain." Indra became so angry that he attempted to drown the people with a rainstorm, but Krishna lifted the mountain and sheltered his worshipers. Indra, defeated, later visited Krishna and praised him for saving the people, and Indrani, wife of Indra, asked Krishna to be a friend of their son, the hero Arjuna, who appears in the Hindu epic poem *The Mahabharata*.

In *The Mahabharata*, Krishna appears as the charioteer of Arjuna, reciting to Arjuna the Bhagavad-Gita (which forms part of the epic): "All the Universe has been created by me; all things exist in me." Arjuna addresses Krishna as "the Supreme Universal Spirit, the Supreme Dwelling, the Eternal Person, Divine, prior to all the gods, unborn, omnipresent." In the poem Krishna possesses a weapon, Sata-ghru (slaying hundreds), which is described as a stone set with iron spikes.

Krishna is highly honored as a great lover by the Indians. The love affairs between the *gopis*, girl cowherds, and Krishna are told of in the *Gita-Govinda*, an erotic love poem by Jayadeva, written about 1200. In the poem Krishna is portrayed as an extremely passionate lover of all the *gopis*. His main love, however, is for Radha, a married woman. (In some accounts Radha is said to be an incarnation of Lakshmi, the wife of Narayana, another incarnation of Vishnu.) When Radha's sister-in-law discovered the liaison she rushed to tell her brother Ayanagosha of his wife's infidelity. When Ayanagosha appears, however, Krishna transforms himself into the goddess Kali (a form of the great goddess, Devi), and Ayanagosha thinks his wife is worshiping the goddess. The *Gita-Govinda* in many ways resembles the Hebrew Song of Songs. As with the biblical work, Hindus have given this frankly erotic work a mystical interpretation. An Indian dance, Manipuri, originating in Manipur in northern India, narrates the loves of Krishna and the *gopis*. A ballet, *Radha and Krishna*, by Uday Shan-Kar also tells of the love affair.

On another occasion, when Krishna was dancing with a woman, the demon Arishata appeared in the form of a bull, attacking the party. Krishna seized Arishata by the horns, wrung his neck as if it had been a piece of wet cloth, and at last tore off his horns and beat Arishata to death with them.

Though a god, Krishna met death at the hands of a hunter, Jaraas (old age), who shot him with an arrow in the ankle, his only vulnerable spot. When he died, his spirit went to Goloka, his paradise. Dwaraka (the city of gates), which was holy to Krishna and was one of the seven sacred cities in Hinduism, submerged into the ocean seven days after his death. (The city is sometimes called Abdhi-nagari.)

The concept of Krishna as supreme god came late in Hinduism. Because Krishna is Vishnu, he is also called Hari, a title of Vishnu. The form *Hare* in Hare Krishna is the vocative.

See also: ARJUNA; AVATAR; BALARAMA; DEVI; INDRA; INDRANI; KUBERA; LAKSHMI; *MAHABHARATA, THE*; VISHNU

1784
**Kriss Kringle** (little Christ Child)   In Germanic folklore a corruption of the German *Christkindl*, who was said to walk through the streets on Christmas Eve. Children would leave a candle in the window to light the way and hope the Christ Child would bring gifts. Now Kriss Kringle is identified with St. Nicholas or Santa Claus, not the Christ Child.

See also: NICHOLAS, ST.

1785
**Krum-ku-dart-boneit**   In Australian mythology, evil spirits who wake men at night, take control of their bodies, and force them to hop until they die of exhaustion.

1786
**Kshandada-chara** (night walkers)   In Hindu mythology, evil spirits and ghosts who appear at night.

1787
**Kuang Ch'eng-Tzu**   In Chinese legend, a deified sage, credited with the power of controlling evil spirits and giving victory in war. He is portrayed standing with his face turned up and his arms folded, holding a medallion bearing trigrams from the *I Ching*.

See also: *I CHING*

*Kuang Ch'eng-Tzu*

**1788**

**Kuan Ti**  In Chinese mythology, a deified general, Chang Sheng, worshiped as a god of war and of literature. He was a native of Shansi who fled his province after killing an official for sexually abusing someone. He was joined by Chang Fei, a butcher, and Liu Pei, a peddler of straw sandals. Eventually, Kuan Ti was captured and executed. In 1594 the emperor Wan Li conferred on Kuan Ti the title "Supporter of Heaven, Protector of the Realm." Kuan Ti is invoked to avert war, not to encourage it.

**1789**

**Kuan-Yin** (one who hears sounds, prayers) **or Kuan Shih-Yin** (regarder of the world's sounds) In Chinese and Japanese Buddhism, spirit of mercy, patron of children. Kuan-Yin is a Buddhist entity that manifests itself in whatever form is suitable to rescue human beings from physical and spiritual danger. Some forms are male, some are female. Thirty-three forms are commonly described, but the number is said to be infinite. Kuan-Yin is the Sino-Japanese version of the Bodhisattva Avalokiteshvara (a name of uncertain meaning), who is sometimes worshiped as the chief minister of Amitabha Buddha and sometimes worshiped independently. As the minister of Amitabha, Kuan-Yin is shown as a man, often kneeling toward the worshiper and offering a lotus, in which the worshiper will be reborn in the Western Paradise. As an independent figure, Kuan-Yin is most commonly depicted as a male with 11 heads and 1,000 arms (all-seeing and all-helping) or as a female holding a lotus, symbol of purity, a jar of healing water, or a wishing jewel. She may be accompanied by a child, whom she will give to a woman who prays to her for offspring.

According to one Chinese myth, Kuan-Yin was the daughter of an Indian prince. Her name was Miao Shan, and she was a devoted follower of the Buddha. In order to convert her blind father, she visited him disguised as a stranger and informed him that if he swallowed an eyeball of one of his children he would have his sight restored. None of his children, when told, would consent to lose an eye. Miao Shan then miraculously created an eye, which she fed to her father, restoring his sight. She then persuaded her father to become a Buddhist by pointing out the folly of a world where a child would not sacrifice an eye for a parent.

In another myth Kuan-Yin was on her way to enter Nirvana when she paused on its threshold to listen to the cry of the world. She decided to stay in the world to teach mankind compassion and mercy.

An image of Kuan-Yin plays an important part in the plot of the movie *Three Strangers*, in which a sweepstakes ticket is placed under the image of Kuan-Yin to bring good luck. The ticket wins, and each of the three partners attempts to get all of the winnings—one even kills another. In the end no one wins.

In Japanese, Kuan-Yin is known as Kwannon or Kannon, and in various forms is known as Sho (the holy), Juichimen (11-faced), Senju

(1,000-handed), bato (horse-headed), and Nyoi-rin (she of the wishing wheel).

See also: AMITABHA; AVALOKITESHVARA; BOD-HISATTVA; BUDDHA, THE; LOTUS; NIRVANA

### 1790

**Kubera** (ugly body?) In Hindu mythology, god of wealth and guardian of the north; married to Riddhi (prosperity). Kubera was the brother of the demon king Ravana and once possessed Lanka (Sri Lanka). However, his evil brother, Ravana, ousted Kubera and took control. After Kubera had done severe penance, he was given the gift of immortality by Brahma, who appointed him god of wealth. Brahma also gave Kubera a magic aerial car called Pushapaka (that of flowers), which contained within it a city or a palace. It was stolen by Ravana but recaptured by the hero Rama and used by him to carry his wife, Sita, back to their native city, Ayodhya. Later Pushapaka was returned to Kubera. Pushapaka is also known as Ratna-varshuka (that rains jewels).

In Indian art Kubera is portrayed as a white man, having eight teeth, a deformed body, and three legs. His body is covered with various ornaments. He receives no worship in Hinduism but is worshiped in Japanese Buddhism. In Hindu belief Kubera rules over the Yakshas, semidivine beings, sometimes good and sometimes evil, as well as the Guhyakas (hidden beings), minor spirits who are guardians of hidden treasures.

See also: BRAHMA; BUDDHISM; RAMA; RAVANA

### 1791

**Kuda Sembrani** In Malayan mythology, a magic horse able to swim through water as well as fly through the air.

### 1792

**K'uei Hsing** In Chinese mythology, a deified mortal worshiped as a god of literature. He is portrayed as an ugly man with a sea dragon, symbol of wisdom.

### 1793

**Kuinyo** In Australian mythology, an evil death spirit who gives forth a repulsive odor.

### 1794

**Kukulcán** (Cuculcán, Kukulkán) (the god of the mighty speech, a serpent adorned with feathers?) In the mythology of the Toltecs, an ancient Nahuatl people of central and southern Mexico whose culture flourished about 1000 C.E., culture hero and god.

One account of Kukulcán's life was written by Bartolomé de Las Casas, a Roman Catholic bishop, in his *Historia apologética de las Indias Occidentales*, in an attempt to explain Indian religious belief vis-á-vis Christianity. According to Las Casas, Kukulcán was a "great Lord" who arrived at the city of Chichén Itzá from the west with 19 attendants, all bareheaded and wearing long robes and sandals. They ordered the people to "confess and fast," which the people then did ritually on Friday. The bishop seems to be trying to show the similarity between Indian beliefs and Christian ones, and in his work he stresses the superiority of the latter.

In another account of Kukulcán's life, found in an Indian work, the *Books of Chilam Balam*, it is reported that the city of Chichén Itzá was settled by four brothers who came from the four cardinal points. They lived "chastely and righteously" until one left (or died). Two of the brothers then quarreled and were killed by the people, leaving only the last, who was Kukulcán. He calmed the people and helped them build the city.

After he finished his work in Chichén Itzá, he founded and named the great city of Mayapán, which was to become the capital of the confederacy of the Mayas. In that city a temple was built in his honor. After completing his work Kukulcán journeyed westward to Mexico, or to some other spot where the sun set. The people said he had been taken into the heavens, where he watched over them and from which he answered their prayers. In Mayan art he is portrayed with a serpent's body, a quetzal's plumes, a jaguar's teeth, and a human head in his jaws. He is usually seated on the cross-shaped symbol of the compass.

**1795**
**Kukumatz and Tochipa**   In North American Indian mythology (Mojave), creators, twin brothers. Born of earth (woman) and sky (man), the two needed more room and raised the sky. Then they set the cardinal points and created the first people. In a variant myth, Mustamho, the son of a second generation of earth and sky, created the first people. In a myth told by the Walapai, part of the Yuman group that includes the Mojave, the name of the twins are Hokomata and Tochopa. In their myth the two brothers quarrel. Hokomata, jealous of his brother, who brought the arts to humankind, taught men the arts of war. In a rage Hokomata caused a flood that destroyed the earth, saving only his daughter, Pukeheh, in a hollow log, from which she emerged after the flood. She then gave birth to a boy whose father was the sun and to a girl whose father was the waterfall. From these two the earth was repopulated. In the Mojave variant of the myth, Mustambho took some people in his arms and saved them from the flood waters.

**1796**
**Kulhwch and Olwen**   Medieval Welsh tale included in *The Mabinogion*. It tells of the hero Kulhwch's love for Olwen, the daughter of the giant Yabaddaden. The giant assigns tasks for Kulhwch to complete before he will consent to give him his daughter in marriage. Kulhwch is aided by King Arthur. The work is one of the first Arthurian romances.

See also: ARTHUR; *MABINOGION, THE*

**1797**
**Kullervo** (gold, dear one)   In the Finnish epic poem *The Kalevala* (runes 31–36), a tragic hero who unknowingly raped his sister, then in remorse committed suicide.

Kullervo was the son of Kalervo, who had been slain by his brother Untamo. Only one pregnant woman of the Kalervo clan survived, bearing Kullervo at Untamola (Untamo's farm). While he was still in the cradle, Kullervo planned vengeance on his uncle for the slaughter of his father and family. Kullervo grew up strong but stupid. His uncle sent the youth to the smith Ilmarinen, whose wife, the Maiden of Pohjola, immediately took a dislike to him. She gave Kullervo a loaf of bread with a stone in it. In revenge he had her killed by wild beasts.

Escaping from Ilmarinen's farm, Kullervo wandered through the forest, where he met the Old Woman of the Forest, who informed him that his father, mother, brothers and sisters were still living. Following her directions, he found them on the border of Lapland. His mother told him that she had long supposed him dead and that his sister, her eldest daughter, had been lost while gathering berries. The lad then attempted to do different kinds of work for his mother but succeeded only in spoiling everything he touched, so he was sent to pay the land dues. On his way home Kullervo met his sister (he did not, however, know it was she). He dragged her into his sledge and raped her. Afterward, when his sister learned who he was, she threw herself into a torrent. Kullervo rushed home to tell his mother of the tragedy. She dissuaded him from suicide, telling him to retire to a retreat where he could recover from his remorse. But Kullervo resolved to avenge himself on Untamo, who had murdered his father, and prepared for war. He left home to joyous farewells, for no one but his mother was sorry that he was going to his death. He came to Untamola and laid waste the whole district, burning the homestead. On returning home he found his house deserted and no living thing about the place but an old black dog, which accompanied him into the forest where he went to shoot game for food. While traversing the forest, he arrived at the place where he had raped his sister. The memory of his deed came back to him, and he then killed himself.

The tragic legend of Kullervo inspired one of Sibelius's greatest symphonic works, the Kullervo Symphony, written when the composer was 27 years old. Scored for soprano, baritone, male chorus, and orchestra, it consists of five movements: (1) an orchestral introduction; (2) "Kullervo's Youth"; (3) "Kullervo and His Sister," for chorus, soprano, and baritone, portraying the seduction and rape; (4) "Kullervo Goes to Battle," another orchestral section; and (5) "Kullervo's Death," for chorus. The symphony uses the text of *The Kalevala*. It was Sibelius's wish that after 1893 his Kullervo Symphony should not be performed. It was not played again until 1958, after Sibelius's death in 1957, and was first recorded in 1971, taking its place among the most creative and imaginative late Romantic symphonic works.

See also: ILMARINEN; *KALEVALA, THE*; MAIDEN OF POHJOLA

1798

**Kumara-sambhava** (Kumara's occasioning) In Hindu mythology, an erotic poem by Kalidasa usually translated as *The Birth of the War God*, about the love of the god Shiva and his wife Parvati (a form of the great goddess Devi) and the subsequent birth of their son Kumara. Some sections contain explicit sexual descriptions, and prudish editors have cut them out of their translations.

See also: DEVI; SHIVA

1799

**Kumokums** In North American Indian mythology (Modoc) creator god. One day Kumokums found himself sitting by Tule Lake (in northern California) all alone. There was no land. So Kumokums reached down to the bottom of the lake and pulled up some mud and began to form land and the earth. When he finished that, he created life. Then, growing tired, Kumokums dug a hole and went to sleep inside. But it is believed he will awake one day.

See also: EARTH DIVER

1800

**Kumu-honua and Lalo-honua** (earth source and earth below) In Polynesian mythology, Hawaiian first man and woman according to some traditions.

See also: ADAM AND EVE

1801

**Kunapipi** In Australian mythology, the Great Mother goddess who formed the land from her body, produced children, animals, and plants, and taught humankind the gift of language. She is also called Waramurungundju and Imberombera.

1802

**Kuninwa-wattalo** In Australian mythology, evil spirits who attack at night, strangling their victims with a cord.

1803

**Kuo Tzu-i** Seventh century C.E. In Chinese mythology, a deified mortal worshiped as the god of happiness, often portrayed in blue official robes leading his small son, Kuo-ai, to court.

1804

**Kupalo** In Slavic mythology, god of peace, magic, water, and herbs. After the introduction of Christianity, Kupalo's attributes were combined with those of St. John the Baptist, whose festival was celebrated on the same day as the pagan god's, 24 June.

Both water and fire were closely connected with Kupalo's worship, which continued after the coming of Christianity. A straw doll of the god, dressed in a woman's gown and decked out with ribbons and other female ornaments, was carried in elaborate procession to a river, where it was bathed or drowned or in some cases burned. In addition to the god's role as a water deity there were rites connecting him to the worship of trees, herbs, and flowers. Among the Baltic Slavs, women would cut down a birch tree, remove its lower branches, dress it with garlands and flowers, and then sacrifice a cock to it. No men were allowed to take part in the ritual.

The fire-flower fern was the god's main sacred herb and was believed to control demons, bring good luck, and make one attractive to beautiful women. The only problem was that the fire-flower was guarded by demons and could be procured only in the forest at midnight, the hour when the magical flower appeared. When it appeared, it climbed up the stalk and burst into flames. If a person then seized the flower and avoided the demons (who would appear as monsters), the flower would belong to the venturesome person. This all took place on Kupalo's Night, when trees could move from place to place and hold conversations. However, only if one possessed the fire-flower could one understand the language of the trees.

See also: COCK; JOHN THE BAPTIST, ST.; LADO AND LADA

**1805**
**Kurra**   In the Finnish epic poem *The Kalevala* (rune 30), companion of the hero Lemminkainen.

When Lemminkainen wooed the Maiden of Pohjola, he asked his former comrade-in-arms, Kurra, to join him in an expedition against Pohjola, the Northland. However, Louhi, the evil mistress of Pohjola, sent her son Pakkanen (Jack Frost) to freeze the hero's boat in the lake. The two heroes almost froze to death, but Lemminkainen, with his powerful charms and invocations, overpowered Jack Frost, throwing him into a fire. Lemminkainen and Kurra then walked across the ice to the shore, wandered about in the waste for a long time, and at last made their way home.

Tiera, another name for Kurra in *The Kalevala*, is a Finnish word for snow caked up under a horse's hoof or on a person's shoe.

See also: *KALEVALA, THE*; LOUHI; MAIDEN OF POHJOLA

**1806**
**Kurriwilban**   In Australian mythology, a cannibalistic female monster, wife of Yaho. She has an upright horn on each shoulder for piercing her victims, who are always men. Her husband, Yaho, kills women.

See also: YAHO

**1807**
**Kururumany**   In the mythology of the Arawak Indians of the Guianas, a creator god. Kururumany created man and all goodness, while Kulimina created woman. One day Kururumany came down to earth to view his creation but was displeased to see that mankind had become corrupt and wicked. As punishment he took back the gift of eternal life and gave it to the serpents, lizards, and other vermin. Though Kururumany was a creator god, another deity, Aluberi, was preeminent over him. Aluberi, however, took no interest in the affairs of man. Kururumany was married to Wurekaddo (she who works in the dark) and Emisiwaddo (she who bored through the earth, perhaps suggesting that she was the cushi-ant).

**1808**
**Kvasir** (Kvaser) (spittle)   In Norse mythology, the wisest of men; born from spittle when the Aesir and Vanir gods spit into a caldron. He was so wise that there was no question he could not answer. He was killed by the dwarfs Fjalar and Galar, who wanted his magic powers. After Kvasir's death his blood was distilled in the Odhrerir, the magic caldron, and gave wisdom and the art of poetry to any who drank it. The kenning for poetry is "Kvasir's blood."

See also: AESIR-VANIR WAR; KENNING; ODHRERIR

**1809**
**Kwannon** (Kwanyin)   In Japanese mythology, the name for the Chinese goddess Kuan-Yin,

who in turn is derived from the Mahayana Buddhist being of mercy, Avalokiteshvara.

See also: KUAN-YIN; MAHAYANA

1810

**Kwaten** In Japanese Buddhist mythology, fire god derived from the Hindu god of fire, Agni, portrayed as a bearded old man with four arms. He holds a bamboo twig with a few leaves attached, a water vessel, and a flaming triangle, and he stands on a large flame. Sometimes he is dressed in flowing robes or is clad in a tiger skin.

He is one of the Jiu No O, 12 Japanese Buddhist gods and goddesses adopted from Hindu mythology.

See also: AGNI; JIU NO O

1811

**Kwoiam** In Melanesian mythology, an ugly child who killed his blind mother when she cursed him for lifting a loop of her hair. He then killed his relatives and numerous other people, taking their skulls and decorating them. Eventually, he grew tired of murder and was turned into stone.

# L

**Lacedaemon** (lake demon)    In Greek mythology, son of Zeus and Taygeta, the daughter of Atlas; married to Sparta, the daughter of Eruotas, by whom he had Amyclas and Eurydice, the wife of Acrisius. Lacedaemon introduced the worship of the Graces in Laconia and built a temple in their honor.

See also: ATLAS; EURYDICE; ZEUS

1812

**Lachesis** (measurer)    In Greek mythology, one of the three Morae (Fates), the others being Atropos and Clotho. Lachesis measured out the yarn that represented the span of life.

1813

*Clotho, Atropos, and Lachesis*

**Lado and Lada**    In Slavic mythology, male and female deities who personified marriage, mirth, pleasure, and happiness. The divine twins Lado and Lada are one aspect of a quadruple fertility deity. The others are Kupalo (water), Kostromo-Kostrobunko (grain), and Iarilo (sun). Each aspect has a feminine counterpart. Slavic folklore, under the influence of Christianity, later equated Lada with the Virgin Mary. Lada is also the name for Cinderella in a Slavic version of the folktale, in which she is portrayed as a princess with a golden star on her broom.

See also: CINDERELLA; KUPALO; VIRGIN MARY

1814

**Ladon** (cutter or laurel)    In Greek mythology, a hundred-headed dragon who guarded the Golden Apples of the Hesperides; son of Phorcys (or Typhon) and Ceto. Ladon was killed by Heracles when the hero went to fetch the Golden Apples.

See also: GOLDEN APPLES OF THE HESPERIDES; HERACLES; HESPERIDES; LADON

1815

**Lady of Shalott, The**    In Arthurian legend, a maiden who fell in love with Lancelot of the Lake and died because he did not return the love.

1816

Tennyson's poem "The Lady of Shalott" tells the tale.

See also: ARTHUR; LANCELOT OF THE LAKE

*Lady of the Lake (A. Beardsley)*

**1817**

**Lady of the Lake**   In Arthurian legend, an enchantress identified with Nimuë or Viviane (Vivien), the mistress of Merlin. She is responsible for the imprisonment of Merlin in a tree, for giving the magic sword to King Arthur, and for rearing Lancelot as a child. She lived in a castle in the midst of a lake that was impossible to pass. Lancelot was given to her as a child, and she plunged him into the magic lake with her. He was then called Lancelot of the Lake. She appears in Tennyson's *Idylls of the King*, James Branch Cabell's novel *Jurgen*, E. A. Robinson's poem *Lancelot*, and T. H. White's novel *The Once and Future King*.

See also: ARTHUR; LANCELOT OF THE LAKE; MERLIN; VIVIANE

**1818**

**Laertes** (ant, wasp)   In Greek mythology, the father (or foster father) of Odysseus; king of Ithaca; married to Anticlea, daughter of Autolycus. According to some accounts, Anticlea was pregnant by Sisyphus when she married Laertes. Her son was Odysseus. Eventually, Laertes retired, and Odysseus became king. Laertes was still alive when Odysseus returned from his wanderings after the Trojan War. He joyously received his son and aided Odysseus in dealing with the relatives of the slain suitors. Homer's *Odyssey* (book 11) and Ovid's *Metamorphoses* (book 13) feature Laertes.

See also: AUTOLYCUS; ODYSSEUS; *ODYSSEY, THE*; SISYPHUS

**1819**

**Laestrygones** (begetters of forgetfulness?)   In Greek mythology, cannibal giants who sank 11 of Odysseus's 12 ships and ate the men. According to Homer's *Odyssey*, the land where the Laestrygones lived had very short nights, so short that the shepherd driving his flock home would meet another shepherd driving his flock to pasture. The major city was Telepylus, founded by Lamus, and their king was Antiphates. The land has been located in Sicily and at Formiae in central Italy. The land of the Laestrygones is mentioned in Homer's *Odyssey* (books 9, 10), Ovid's *Metamorphoses* (book 14), and Horace's *Odes* (3.16.34) and is portrayed in a series of Roman wall paintings. The eight landscapes were found in 1848 and are now in the Vatican Library.

See also: ODYSSEUS; *ODYSSEY, THE*; OVID

**1820**

**La Fontaine, Jean de**   1621–1695. French author of fables, many based on Aesopic sources. The first volume of *Fables* was published in 1668 and added to until 1694. Witty and elegant, La Fontaine's fables are a mainstay of French literature. He was elected to the French Academy in 1683. He also wrote *Contes et novelles* (1664–1674), a collection of bawdy verse tales based on popular *fabliaux* from France and other parts of Europe.

See also: AESOPIC FABLES

1821
**Lahash** (flaming?)   In Jewish folklore, demonic angel who attempted to snatch away a prayer of Moses before it could ascend to God. As punishment Lahash and other angels who helped him were cast away from the Divine Presence and bound with fiery chains.

See also: MOSES

1822
**Laindjung**   In Australian mythology, ancestral figure, father of Banaidja. He rose out of the sea at Blue Mud Bay, his face foam-stained and his body covered with salt water marks.

See also: BANAIDJA

1823
**Laius** (thrush or man of the people or left-handed one)   In Greek mythology, king of Thebes; father of Oedipus; husband of Jocasta; son of Labdacus. An oracle had warned Laius that he would be put to death by his son, so when Oedipus was born, he ordered him killed. A compassionate nurse, unable to kill Oedipus, exposed him instead, and he was rescued and reached manhood. One day Oedipus encountered Laius on the road, not knowing Laius was his father. An altercation ensued over the right-of-way, and Oedipus killed Laius. The king was buried at the crossroads at the foot of Mount Parnassus, the place of his murder, by Damisistratus, king of Plataea.

See also: JOCASTA; OEDIPUS

1824
**Lakshamana** (endowed with lucky signs)   In the Hindu epic poem *The Ramayana*, a half brother of the hero Rama and his constant companion. When Rama was to die, Lakshamana took his place and drowned himself by walking

into the waters of the Sarayu River. The gods rained flowers on him and took him to heaven. Lakshmana's twin brother was Satru-ghna (destroyer of foes).

See also: *RAMAYANA, THE*

*Lakshmi*

1825
**Lakshmi** (good fortune)   In Hindu mythology, wife of the god Narayana (an incarnation of Vishnu), mother of Kama, and goddess of good fortune and beauty. Lakshmi is said to have four arms, but since she is representative of beauty, she is usually portrayed with only two. In one hand she holds a lotus. In the epic poem *The Ramayana*, Lakshmi is called "the mistress of the worlds . . . born by her own will, in a beautiful field opened up by the plough." Lakshmi is also known as Jaladhija (ocean born); Lola (the fickle), goddess of fortune and therefore especially worshiped by shopkeepers; and Loka-mata (mother of the world). The heroine in Delibes's opera *Lakmé* is named after the goddess.

See also: KAMA; *RAMAYANA, THE*; VISHNU

1826

**La Llorona** (weeping woman)   In American and Mexican folklore, the legend of a woman who weeps for her lost children may have existed since Aztec times. Bernardino de Sahagún points out a connection between the Weeping Woman and the Aztec goddess named Civacoatl, Chalmecaciuatl, or Tonantzin, who is described as wearing a white dress with a cradle on her shoulders as though she were carrying a child. When the goddess mixed among the Aztec women, she abandoned the cradle. In it was an arrowhead shaped like an Aztec sacrificial knife. At nightfall the goddess then went through the streets of the city shrieking and weeping and then disappeared into the waters of lakes or rivers.

In the legend in the Southwest of the United States two people, sometimes men and sometimes women, who are out late at night notice an attractive woman walking near them, usually near a river or a lake. They decide to follow her, do so for quite a while, but can never catch up. When they get close, she suddenly seems to be about a half block ahead of them, but when they decide to give up and start to turn toward home, the attractive woman herself turns around. She has the face of a horse and long, shiny, metallic fingernails. She then gives a long, piercing cry and disappears, revealing herself to be La Llorona out looking for her lost children who had been murdered or who had drowned in the water of the stream or lake.

See also: CHALMECACIUATL; COATLICUE

1827

**Lamb**   A young sheep. In the ancient Near East the lamb was often a sacrificial animal, appearing in both the Old and New Testaments as such. Jesus is called the Lamb of God (John 1:29) because he was sacrificed. In early Christian art the 12 Apostles are sometimes portrayed as 12 lambs. The Book of Revelation (7:9–17) shows the adoration of the lamb. It is somewhat ironic

that a church synod of Trullo held in 692 forbade the use of the lamb as a symbol of Christ.

See also: AGNES, ST.; APOSTLE; BIBLE (REVELATION); JOHN THE BAPTIST, ST.

1828

**Lamech** (wild man)   In the Bible, O.T., fifth descendant of Cain; husband of Adah and Ziilah; father of Jabal, Jubal, and Tubal-cain, inventors of musical instruments, animal husbandry, and bronze and iron weapons (Gen. 4:19–22).

See also: CAIN AND ABEL; NOAH

1829

**Lamia** (gluttonous, lecherous)   In Greek mythology, a fantastic being that sucked blood and ate human flesh; often in the form of a serpent with a woman's head; daughter of Belus and Libya. Lamia was a beautiful woman and a mistress of Zeus, whose children she bore. When Hera, Zeus's wife, discovered this, she killed all the children except for Scylla. In revenge Lamia decided to become a child-killer, and as a result of her evil she became a monster with the ability to remove her eyes at will. Keats's poem *Lamia* is based on a story he found in Burton's *Anatomy of Melancholy*, which in turn came from Philostratus (c. 170–240 B.C.E.) and tells of a young man, Lycius, who falls in love with Lamia. When Lycius discovers she is a serpent, she flees and he dies. Originally, Lamia may have been a Libyan goddess who was debunked by the Achaeans. Closely connected with Lamia, the Empusae had sexual intercourse with young men and sucked their blood while they slept.

See also: HERA; ZEUS

1830

**Lammas** (loaf-mass)   In British folklore, Christian feast held 1 August in which loaves made from the first harvest were blessed. The feast became confused with the Feast of St. Peter in Chains (1 August), when lambs were taken to church to be blessed, many believing that it was a "lamb-mass" not a "loaf-mass." In some parts of Scotland, menstrual blood was sprinkled on cows and on the floors of houses on Lammas Day to protect against evil. Lleu Law Gyffes' death on the first Sunday in August was celebrated with a feast called Lugh-mass, sometimes confused with Lammas.

See also: LLEU LAW GYFFES; PETER, ST.

*Lancelot in combat (Louis Rhead)*

1831
**Lancelot of the Lake** (lance, weaver's shuttle?) In Arthurian legend, one of the noblest knights of the Round Table, lover of Queen Guinever. Legends do not agree about Lancelot. In most medieval tales he is the son of King Ban of Benwick and was called Lancelot du Lac (Lancelot of the Lake) because the enchantress Lady of the Lake had plunged him into her magic lake when he was a child. In almost all tales Lancelot is a great champion who went in search of the Holy Grail, and twice he caught sight of it. He was also the lover of Queen Guinever, the wife of King Arthur. He became the father of Galahad by Elaine, after he had been deceived into thinking he was sleeping with Guinever. When King Arthur discovered his relationship with Guinever their two armies fought. Peace was finally made when Lancelot killed Sir Gwain. Lancelot came back to court to discover King Arthur dead and Queen Guinever a nun. He then became a monk and died. Lancelot appears in Chrétien de Troyes's *Lancelot*, Malory's *Morte d'Arthur*, Tennyson's *Idylls of the King*, E. A. Robinson's long narrative poem *Lancelot*, and T. H. White's *The Once and Future King*.

See also: ARTHUR; ELAINE; GALAHAD; GUINEVER; GWAIN; LADY OF THE LAKE; ROUND TABLE

1832
**Langsuyar** (Langhui)   In Malayan mythology, a female demon believed to be the spirit of a woman who died in childbirth. The original *langsuyar* was a beautiful woman whose child was stillborn. When she was told that the baby had become a *potianak*, or *nati-anak*, a demon in the form of an owl, she clapped her hands and without further warning "flew whinnying away to a tree, upon which she perched."

She is recognized by her green robe, her long tapering nails (considered a sign of beauty), and her long jet-black hair, which she lets hang down to her ankles. She wears her hair long to cover the hole in the back of her neck through which she sucks the blood of children. Her vampirelike proclivities can be successfully stopped if you can cut short her nails and hair and stuff them into the hole in her neck. Then she will become tame and act like an ordinary woman. Some legends report *langsuyars* who have married and had children. But they revert to their ghastly form and fly off at once into the dark forest if they see their children dance at a village festival.

To prevent a dead mother from becoming a *langsuyar*, glass beads are placed in the mouth of the corpse, a hen's egg under each armpit, and needles in the palms. If this is done, the dead woman cannot open her mouth to shriek, or wave her arms as wings, or open and shut her hands to assist in her flight from the grave in her night-owl form.

See also: LA LLORONA; VAMPIRE

1833
**Lan Ts'ai-ho**   In Chinese Taoist mythology, one of the Pa- Hsien, the Eight Immortals. She often is portrayed in a blue dress with one foot

*Lan Ts'ai-ho*

shod and the other bare. She is the patron of flower sellers and sometimes is shown holding a basket of flowers.

See also: PA-HSIEN

---

**1834**

**Lan-yein and A-mong**   In Burmese mythology, a brother and sister who possessed a magic drum. The two were happy for a while until one day Lan-yein, beating the magic drum, got a porcupine and served it for dinner. A-mong was wounded by the quills and believed her brother had intended to kill her. In revenge she destroyed the magic drum. She left for a village, where she married one of the local men. Lan-yein traveled to China, where he became "very powerful and very famous, and in the course of time was chosen Udibwa, or emperor of China."

---

**1835**

**Laocoön** (very perceptive)   In Greek and Roman mythology, priest of Apollo and Poseidon at Troy; son of Priam and Hecuba. Laocoön offended Apollo by marrying and profaning the god's image. In the last year of the Trojan War he was chosen priest to appease Poseidon because the Trojans had slain an earlier priest of the god. When the wooden horse was brought into Troy, Laocoön hurled a spear at it, warning the Trojans not to accept the Greek gift. Laocoön said: "I fear the Greeks, especially when they bring gifts." But the Trojans paid no attention to his warning. While Laocoön was sacrificing to Poseidon, Apollo (or Athena) sent a massive serpent that crushed Laocoön and his two sons, Antiphas and Thymbraeus, to death. The Trojans believed it was because he had hurled the spear at the wooden horse, and they therefore accepted it into their city. Vergil's *Aeneid* (book 2) tells the tale. An ancient statue group, carved in Rhodes about 25 B.C.E. and found in the ruins of the Baths of Titus in 1506, was bought by Pope Julius II for the Vatican Museum. The work was admired by Michelangelo, Bernini, Titian, and Rubens. El Greco's *Laocoön* (c. 1601) portrays the scene with a view of Toledo in the background.

See also: *AENEID, THE*; APOLLO; ATHENA; HECUBA; POSEIDON; PRIAM; TROY

---

**1836**

**Laodameia** (tamer of people)   In Greek mythology, a heroine; daughter of Acastus and Astydameia; sister of Sthemele, Sterope, and some unnamed brothers; wife of Protesilaus, the first Greek killed immediately on landing at Troy. In her grief Laodameia had a wooden statue made of her husband and slept with it every night. At first it was believed she had a lover, but when the truth was discovered, her father, Iphiculus, had the statue burned, and Laodameia cast herself into the flames and died. Laodameia appears in Homer's *Iliad* (book 2), Vergil's *Aeneid* (book 6), and Ovid's *Heroides* (which influenced Chaucer), where she is the symbol of a faithful lover. Wordsworth's poem "Laodamia" (1814) changes the tale by making her husband Protesilaus rail against his wife's passion and call for "reason," "self-government," and "fortitude."

See also: ACASTUS; *ILIAD, THE*;

---

**1837**

**Laodice** (justice of the people)   In Greek mythology, daughter of King Priam and

Hecuba. Laodice fell in love with Acamas, son of the Greek hero Theseus, when he came to Troy with Diomedes and an embassy to demand the return of Helen. Laodice contrived to meet Acamas at the house of Philebia, wife of the governor of the small town of Troas, which the Greek embassy visited. Laodice had a son by Acamas, whom she called Munitus. Afterward she married Helicaon, son of Antenor and Telephus, king of Mysia. When Troy was being destroyed, she threw herself from the top of a tower, or was swallowed up by the earth. In some ancient accounts her name is given as Astyoche. In Homer's *Iliad* (book 9) Laodice is the name used for Electra, daughter of Agamemnon.

See also: ACAMAS; AGAMEMNON; ELECTRA; HECUBA; *ILIAD, THE*; PRIAM; TELEPHUS

---

1838

**Lao Lang**   In Chinese mythology, the deified mortal Chuang Taung, worshiped as the god of actors. He is portrayed wearing a dragon crown and dressed in imperial robes. He is worshiped by actors before a performance because his patronage permits them to perform well.

---

1839

**Laomedon** (ruler of the people)   In Greek mythology, first king of Troy; son of Ilus and Eurydice; brother of Themiste; married Rhoeo or Strymo; father of Astyoche, Cilla, Clytius, Hesione, Hicetaon, Lampus, Priam, and Tithonus; also father of Bucolion by Calybe, a nymph. Zeus sent Apollo and Poseidon to build the walls of Troy as a punishment for infringing on his royal rights. They did so, but Laomedon refused to pay the gods, so Apollo and Poseidon sent a sea monster to ravage the land. Laomedon then called on Heracles to help save Troy and promised to pay him if he killed the monster. Heracles killed the monster, but again Laomedon refused to pay. So Heracles took 18 ships to Troy and destroyed Laomedon and all his sons except Priam. The father and sons were buried in a tomb outside the Scaen gate. It was believed

that as long as the tomb remained intact, Troy would not fall. Homer's *Iliad* (book 21), Vergil's *Aeneid* (books, 2, 9), and Ovid's *Metamorphoses* (book 12) all allude to the tale.

See also: *AENEID, THE*; APOLLO; EURYDICE; HERACLES; *ILIAD, THE*; NYMPHUS; OVID; POSEIDON; PRIAM

*Meeting of Confucius and Lao Tzu*

---

1840

**Lao Tzu** (old philosopher)   fl. c. 570 B.C.E. Chinese philosopher, traditionally considered founder of Taoism, the philosophy of the Tao (the way), worshiped as a deity.

Lao Tzu is believed to have been a contemporary of Confucius. He was the son of a high-ranking family, working for some time as an imperial archivist in Lo-Yang, but he left his position to lead a life of solitude. Many legends have grown up around his name. He had no human father, and his mother is said to have carried him in her womb for 72 years before he emerged from her left armpit, able to talk.

Lao Tzu's meeting with Confucius is frequently encountered in Chinese art. After the meeting Confucius was quite bewildered by the mystical Lao Tzu. He said, "I know how the birds fly, how the fishes swim, how animals run. But there is a dragon. I cannot tell how it mounts on the wind through the clouds and flies through the heavens. Today I have seen Lao Tzu, and I can only compare him with the dragon."

What most upset Confucius about Lao Tzu was his remark to repay "injury with kindness." Confucius' reply was that you give good for good, and justice for evil. But Lao Tzu said: "To those who are good to me, I am good, and to those who are not good to me, I am also good. And thus all get to be good. To those who are sincere to me, I am sincere; and to those who are not sincere with me, I am also sincere. And thus all get to be sincere."

According to legend, Lao Tzu planned to leave society. On the border, a customs official asked him to write a book before he retired from the world. So the sage wrote about "the proper way to live," the *Tao-te Ching* (Book of the Tao and Te).

See also: CONFUCIUS

1841

**Lapiths** (Lapithae) (flint chippers)    In Greek mythology, a mountain tribe in Thessaly related to the centaurs through descent from Ixion. The Lapiths came to symbolize civilization, the centaurs, barbarism. Ovid's *Metamorphoses* (book 12) gives a rich description of the battle between the Lapiths under their king, Pirithous, and the centaurs at the marriage feast of Hippodameia. The scene of the battle was featured in the frieze on the metopes (the section between the columns and the roof) of the Parthenon on the west pediment of the temple of Zeus at Olympia, and in the frieze of Apollo's temple at Bassae. Michelangelo did a sculptured relief of the battle, and Piero di Cosimo painted the scene.

See also: CENTAUR; OVID

1842

**Lara, Infantes de** (princes of Lara)    10th century. In Spanish history and legend, seven brothers who were killed by their uncle Ruy Valásquez in 986. The murder was arranged by Doña Lambra, Ruy's wife; she had the Moors perform the deed. The father of the boys, Gonzalo Gustos, was then invited to the hall of King Almanzor, the Moorish leader, to view his seven dead sons. The Spanish ballad *The Seven Heads* relates how the father, seeing the horrible sight, attacks Almanzor and his men and kills 13 of them before

being killed himself. Another Spanish ballad, *The Vengeance of Mudara*, tells how Mudara, the son of Gonzalez, the youngest of the seven brothers, avenges the death of his father by slaying Ruy Valásquez and having Doña Lambra stoned to death. Juan de la Cueva's play *Tragedia de los Infantes de Lara* and Angel de Saavedra's *El Moro Exposito* (the Moor in danger) deal with the legend.

See also: BALLAD

1843

**Lares**    In Roman mythology, spirits of the dead, worshiped at crossroads and in homes; children of Acca Larentia. Originally, the Romans buried their dead in their own houses until it was forbidden by the laws of the Twelve Tables. Every house had a *Lar familiaris* who was the tutelary spirit of the family. His chief care was to prevent the family from dying out. The Lares' image, dressed in a toga, was kept in the family. The Romans greeted the Lares with morning prayer and an offering from the table. At the chief meal a portion was left on the fire of the hearth for the family spirits. Regular sacrifices were offered on the calends, nones, and ides of every month and at all important family functions, such as the birthday of the father of the family. On such occasions the Lares were covered with garlands, and cakes and honey were placed before them. Wine, incense, and animals also were offered up to them. Outdoors the Lares were honored as tutelary spirits. At the crossroads (*compita*) there were always two *lares compitales* or *vicorum*, one for each of the intersecting roads. They were honored by a popular festival called Compitalia, held four times a year. The emperor Augustus added the *Genius Augusti*, and commanded that two feasts be held in honor of these divinities in May and August. In addition, there were the *Lares proestites*, belonging to the whole city. They were invoked with the mother of the Lares and called Lara, Larunda, or Mania. They had an altar and temple in Rome. The Lares were invoked as protectors on a journey, in the country, in war, and on the sea, and they were associated with the Penates, guardians of the household stores. In contrast to the good Lares were the evil spirits, the Larvae.

See also: PENATES

**1844**
**Latimikaik**   In Micronesian mythology, creator goddess who arose from a wave-beaten rock along with her husband, Tpereakl.

**1845**
**Latinus**   In Greek and Roman mythology, king of the Latini in Italy; son of Odysseus and Circe, according to Hesiod's *Theogony*, or son of Faunus and Marica, according to Vergil's *Aeneid* (books 7–11). In Vergil's account Latinus takes no part in the war between Aeneas and Turnus, though he arranges for a duel between the two to see who will marry his daughter Lavinia. Latinus also appears in Ovid's *Metamorphoses* (book 13) and Livy's *History of Rome*.

See also: *AENEID, THE*; FAUNUS; HESIOD; ODYSSEUS

**1846**
**Laurel**   An evergreen tree or shrub encompassing many varieties such as sassafras and cinnamon. In Greek mythology, the nymph Daphne, who refused Apollo's love, was transformed into a laurel tree. The tree was sacred to Apollo and his priestesses at Delphi; they chewed the leaves to bring on their oracular powers, or placed them under the pillow to acquire inspiration. Champions at the Pythian games, held in honor of Apollo's victory over the monster Python, were crowned with laurel wreaths. In Christianity the laurel is associated with triumph, eternity, and chastity and is a symbol of the Virgin Mary. St. Gudule carries a laurel crown. In English folklore, if two lovers pluck a

laurel twig and break it in half, each keeping a piece, they will always be lovers.

See also: APOLLO; DAPHNE; VIRGIN MARY

**1847**
**Laverna**   In Roman mythology, goddess of thieves and dishonest Romans; her altar was at the gate of Laverna in Rome. She was generally portrayed as a head without a body.

**1848**
**Lavinia**   In Roman mythology, second wife of Aeneas; daughter of King Latinus and Amata. She was betrothed to her relative Turnus, but an oracle had said she was to marry a foreign prince. When Aeneas killed Turnus, Lavinia's father gave her to Aeneas. After Aeneas's death, she fled the tyranny of Ascanius, her son-in-law, and gave birth to a son, Aeneas Sylvius. Lavinia appears in Vergil's *Aeneid* (books 6, 7) and in Ovid's *Metamorphoses* (book 14).

See also: AENEAS; *AENEID, THE*; LATINUS; OVID

*St. Lawrence (Dürer)*

**1849**
**Lawrence, St.** (from Laurentium, a city in Latium, a few miles from Rome)   Third cen-

tury. In Christian legend, patron saint of brewers, confectioners, cooks, schoolboys, students, washerwomen, and glaziers; patron of Nuremberg and Genoa. Feast, 10 August.

Lawrence was a deacon of the church who gave away its "treasures" to the poor. He was arrested by the pagan Romans, and when asked where the treasures were, he refused to answer and was "stretched out upon a gridiron . . . burning coals under, and held . . . with forks of iron," according to *The Golden Legend*, a collection of saints' lives written in the 13th century by Jacobus de Voragine. Lawrence is often portrayed dressed in a deacon's vestment, either standing or holding the gridiron, with a censor, palm, or book in the other hand. The phrase "lazy as Lawrence" is said to have originated when Lawrence was being roasted over a slow fire and asked to be turned, "for that side is quite done." His torturers interpreted this as the height of laziness.

See also: *GOLDEN LEGEND, THE*

1850
***Lay of Igor's Army, The***   Anonymous Russian epic in rhythmic prose believed to have been written in the 12th century.

*The Lay of Igor's Army* is considered one of the monuments of early Russian literature and is placed beside such world epics as the German *Nibelungenlied* and the French *Chanson de Roland*, though it is closer in feeling to the Finnish epic poem *The Kalevala*. The 16th-century manuscript of the work was first published in 1800 with a translation into modern Russian, but the manuscript was destroyed in the burning of Moscow during Napoleon's invasion in 1812. Some scholars doubt that the poem is a genuine work of the Middle Ages, assigning it to some clever forger, though the majority of scholars now accept it as genuine. The lay tells of an unsuccessful invasion by Prince Igor against the Polovtzi, or Cumanians, and combines references to both Christian and pagan elements. The epic reflects the political atmosphere at a time

when the people were calling for curbing the autocratic powers of their rulers.

Another Russian medieval work, generally called the *Zadonshchina*, celebrates the 1380 defeat of Russia's Tartar overlords by the armies of Dmitri Donskoy, grand prince of Moscow, and quotes passages from *The Lay of Igor's Army*, implying that Dmitri's victory avenges Igor's earlier defeat.

Alexander Borodin, one of the "Mighty Five" of Russian music, composed an opera, *Prince Igor*, based on the epic. The famous *Polovtzian Dances*, which are often performed in concert, are from the second act of the opera. They were also used for a ballet, *Prince Igor*, by Michel Fokine. Borodin's score was never completed, and Rimsky-Korsakov and Alexander Glazunov prepared the work for production. Anatol Liadov's symphonic poem *Ballad, In Old Days* was inspired by the epic.

In Russian *The Lay of Igor's Army* is called *Slovo o polku Igoreve* and may be variously translated as The Lay of Igor's Campaign, The Lay of Igor's Host, and The Lay of the Host of Igor. The novelist Vladimir Nabokov published an English translation, *The Song of Igor's Campaign*.

See also: *CHANSON DE ROLAND*; *KALEVALA, THE*; *NIBELUNGENLIED*

1851
**Lazarus** (God my help)   In the Bible, N.T., the name of the beggar in the parable of the Rich Man and Lazarus (Luke 16:19–31) and the name of the brother of Mary and Martha of Bethany and a good friend of Jesus. When he died, Jesus brought him back to life (John 11:1–57). In medieval Christian legend Lazarus went with Mary, his sister, to Gaul after the Crucifixion and became the first bishop of Marseilles, where he was later martyred. He is believed by some to have been the first bishop of Kition in Cyprus.

1852
**Leah** (wild cow)   In the Bible, O.T., "tender-eyed" oldest daughter of Laban; sister of Rachel;

wife of Jacob; mother of Reuben, Simeon, Levi, Judah, Issachar, and Zebulun. Through deceit by Laban, Leah was substituted in Jacob's marriage bed in place of Rachel, whom Jacob wanted to marry. For justification Laban explained to Jacob that Rachel was younger than Leah and could not be given in marriage before her older sister. Though Jacob loved Rachel best, it was Leah who bore most of his children, Rachel being barren until later in life.

See also: JACOB

1853

**Leanhaun Shee** (fairy lover)    In Irish folklore, the fairy mistress who seeks the love of mortals. If they refuse, she becomes their slave; if they consent, they are hers and can escape only by finding another to take their place. The Leanhaun Shee leeches her captives like a vampire, and the mortals waste away. Death is no escape from her. According to William Butler Yeats in *Irish Folk Stories and Fairy Tales*, "She is the Gaelic muse, for she gives inspiration to those she persecutes. The Gaelic poets die young, for she is restless, and will not let them remain long on earth—this malignant phantom."

See also: MELUSINE; VAMPIRE

1854

**Lear, King** (Leir, Lir)    In medieval British mythology, king of Britain, son of Bladud; his legend is told in Geoffrey of Monmouth's *History of the Kings of Britain*. In this version of the legend, Lear was not defeated by his evil daughters and sons-in-law. Instead "Lear led the assembled host together with Aganippus and his daughter [Cordelia] into Britain, fought a battle with his son-in-law, and won the victory, again bringing them all under his own dominions. In the third year thereafter he died, and Aganippus died also, and Cordelia, now mistress of the helm of state in Britain, buried her father in a certain underground chamber." Cordelia ruled the kingdom for some five years, and then two sons of her sisters attacked and imprisoned her, and she com-

mitted suicide. Shakespeare's *King Lear* is believed to be based on Holinshed's *Chronicles*, which varies the tale, as does Shakespeare's play, to bring out the drama. Jane Smiley's novel *A Thousand Acres* (1994) places the story of Lear on a farm in Iowa, where the father is king over his daughters, with whom he commits incest.

1855

**Lebe**    In African mythology (Dogon of the Republic of Mali), first ancestor to die. The Dogon have two categories of ancestors: those who lived before Death entered the world and thus are immortal, and those who came after Death appeared and are thus mortal.

When Amma, the creator god, finished the creation of the eight basic families, he then turned his attention to the organization of man's existence on earth. Lebe was required to feign death, and orders were given for him to be buried with his head pointing toward the north. The seventh ancestor, taking the form of a snake, swallowed his body and then vomited stones that fell into a pattern representing a human body. This arrangement of stones was believed to determine the nature of social relationships, especially marriages. The stones are regarded as a manifestation of the covenant between Amma and Lebe, who although not truly dead, pretended to be so that man might be given a life force. The shape of the Dogon home is symbolic. The door opens to the north, the direction in which Lebe's head pointed. Various features of the home are fraught with sexual implications: the ceiling, for example, is seen as male and the large central room as female. The flat roof is representative of heaven, and the earthen floor's significance is that Lebe was both buried and restored to life in the earth. The relationship of the ceiling to the floor is symbolic of the original union of god with earth.

1856

**Leda** (lady?)    In Greek mythology, an Aetolian princess, daughter of Thestius and Eurythemis;

later queen of Sparta; wife of Tyndareus; mother of Clytemnestra, Helen, Castor, and Polydeuces (the Dioscuri). The best-known version of her myth says that Zeus, in the form of a swan, seduced Leda, who hatched Helen and Polydeuces from an egg, Castor and Clytemnestra having been fathered by Tyndareus. Leda and the Swan was a popular motif in both ancient and modern times. Homer's *Odyssey* (book 11), Euripides' *Helen*, Ovid's *Metamorphoses* (book 6), Spenser's *Faerie Queene* (111.11.32) and *Prothalamium* (41), Keats's *Endymion* (1.157), Yeats's "Leda and the Swan," Aldous Huxley's *Leda*, and Rilke's "Leda" are some of the works that have dealt with the subject. Painters who have treated Leda are Michelangelo, Leonardo da Vinci, Raphael, Tintoretto, and Correggio.

See also: CASTOR AND POLYDEUCES; DISCOURI; HELEN OF TROY; *ODYSSEY, THE*; OVID; ZEUS

**1857**

**Leek**   An onionlike vegetable. The ancient Egyptians considered the leek sacred, viewing it as a symbol of the universe, each successive layer or skin of the vegetable corresponding to the layers of heaven and hell. The Hebrews in their Exodus from Egypt, mentioned leeks among the foods they missed (Num. 11:5). In Roman belief, the leek was a symbol of virtue and sacred to Apollo, whose mother, Latona, longed for leeks. In Welsh legend, St. David, a sixth-century bishop, ordered his men to put leeks on their heads to distinguish themselves from their Saxon enemies during a decisive battle. The Welsh won and credited the victory to the saint's move. In Welsh tradition, it was the custom before plowing for the workers to share a common meal in which each had contributed a leek. In Shakespeare's *Henry V* (IV,vii) Pistol ridicules the custom and is then forced to "eat the leek," a term that has come to mean to eat one's words.

See also: APOLLO; DAVID, ST.

**1858**

**Le-eyo**   In African mythology (Masai of Kenya), ancestor who lost the gift of immortality for humankind. Le-eye was told by God that when a child was being buried he was to repeat: "Man dies but returns to life; the moon dies but does not return to life." This, God told Le-eye, would ensure the rebirth of a person after death. When a child's body was being buried, Le-eye rushed to say the words, but in his confusion he said: "Man dies but does not return to life; the moon dies but returns to life." When his own child died, he tried to use the correct charm, but he had forfeited the chance to restore his child to life.

**1859**

**Legba** (Leba, Legua, Liba)   In African mythology (Fon of Benin), trickster of entrances and crossroads, the youngest son of the creator, often portrayed as the cosmic phallus or pictured looking at his genitals. One myth tells how Legba and God, his father, lived on earth together in the beginning of time. Legba did only what God told him to do, but the people blamed Legba when something bad occurred and credited God for the good things that happened in life. Legba felt that this was an unfair situation. Why should he be blamed for evil? But God said that was how it had to be. One day Legba tricked God by wearing his father's sandals while stealing yams from God's garden. When a search for the thief was conducted, Legba suggested that God must have taken the yams in his sleep. God knew that Legba was trying to deceive him, so he went into the sky, telling Legba to visit him at night and describe what happened each day on earth.

In a variant myth Legba directed an old woman to throw her dirty wash water into the sky. This angered God, who went back to heaven, leaving Legba on earth to report to him the activities of man.

Legba is associated with the oracle of Fa. Each morning Legba climbed into a palm tree and opened Fa's eyes. A system was developed whereby Legba knew if Fa wanted only one or both of his eyes opened. God eventually told Legba to teach men the method of Fa divination so that they could consult the oracle on their own and in this way come to know their destinies.

Worship of Legba is also found in Suriname, Brazil, Trinidad, and Cuba and in the voodoo, or *voudun*, cult in Haiti and New Orleans. In Haitian voodoo mythology Legba is a "principle of life," and his symbol indicates both masculine and feminine attributes, making him a sign of totality. He is the guardian of the sacred gateway, the Grand Chemin, the road leading from the finite world to the spiritual one, and he is often addressed in rites thus: "Papa Legba, open the gate . . . open the gates so that we may pass through." Some sects called the red sects, the voodoo cult representing the demonic forces in the world, believe that Legba was actually Jesus. Legba was hung on a cross, they contend, to serve as an edible human sacrifice—which, they point out, is what is meant by the words used in the Catholic Mass: "This is my Body. . . . This is my Blood." Priests on the island of Haiti, however, use the name Legba as an equivalent for the devil.

See also: FA; TRICKSTER; VOODOO

**1860**

**Leib-olmai** In Lapland mythology, bear spirit worshiped by the Scandinavian Lapps. Leib-olmai protected the bear, who was a holy animal, during the hunt. Only if proper prayers were made to him by the hunters would he allow them to catch the animal.

**1861**

**Leif Ericsson** c. 970–1020. In American history and legend, son of Eric the Red, who, according to some accounts, discovered part of North America. According to one account, given in the *Saga of Eric the Red*, Leif Ericsson was blown off his course during a voyage from Norway to Greenland and landed in a place called Vinland. Legend has it that Thorfinn Karlsefni

and his wife, Gudrid, also sailed to Vinland and resided in Leif's house. While they lived there, Gudrid gave birth to a son, and they named him Snorri. He was the first European child to be born in the New World.

During the 19th century there was a movement among Americans to prove that the saga and other accounts established that the Vikings landed on American soil before Columbus. Many scholars today believe that Leif landed on some part of the North American coast, but there is no agreement as to what part. In 1974 Yale University, owner of the Vinland Map, which indicated that Leif Ericsson discovered America, announced that the map was a fake. Longfellow's literary ballad *The Skeleton in Armor* about a mysterious tower in Touro Park, Newport, Rhode Island, accepts the structure as having been made by the Vikings. This belief is now generally discredited. Edison Marshall's novel *The Viking* is based on Longfellow's ballad. Gerard Tonning's opera *Leif Erikson* is in Norwegian.

*Lei Kung*

**1862**

**Lei Kung** In Chinese mythology, a thunder god portrayed as an ugly, black, bat-winged demon with clawed feet, a monkey head, and an eagle beak. He holds a steel chisel in one hand and a hammer in the other.

### 1863

**Leippya**   In Burmese mythology, the soul materializing as a butterfly that hovers about the body of the dead. During life, if the soul leaves the body, a person will become sick and die. Sickness is believed to be caused by wandering souls under the control of some evil person or witch. If a mother dies, she may come back as a spirit and attempt to steal the soul of her child. To avoid this, a mirror is placed near the child, and a film of cotton is draped on it. If the film slips down into a kerchief placed below the mirror, it is then laid on the child's breast, and the soul of the child is saved from its evil mother. The soul of King Mindon Min, who died in 1878, lived in a small, flat, heart-shaped piece of gold that was suspended over his body until burial.

### 1864

**Lemminkainen** (lover boy)   In the Finnish epic poem *The Kalevala*, handsome hero noted for his romantic and heroic exploits.

Lemminkainen's love life forms a good deal of the narrative in *The Kalevala*. One of Lemminkainen's first feats was to find a wife among the women on the island of Saari. At first they mocked him, so Lemminkainen, in anger, carried off Kyllikki to be his wife. She, obviously a woman who liked to have a good time, reproached him for his fighting, and he reproached her for her loose life. The two agreed, however, that he would not go to war and she would not go to the village dances. Howeer, Kyllikki forgot her promise. Lemminkainen then left her and went in search of another wife.

Lemminkainen went to the land of Pohjola, the Northland, where he wooed the Maiden of Pohjola. Her mother, Louhi, the evil mistress of Pohjola, set tasks for the hero. He accomplished all of them, except for killing the swan floating on the River of Death. While he was attempting to kill the swan, a partly blind cattle herder, Markahattu, murdered Lemminkainen because earlier the hero had insulted him. Lemminkainen's body was cut into pieces by the son of Tuoni (Death).

Lemminkainen's mother learned of her son's death when his comb began to bleed. She hastened to Pohjola, asking Louhi what had happened. Louhi told her the tasks she had set Lemminkainen. Paiva (the sun) then told her how Lemminkainen had died. She went with a long rake in her hand under the cataract in the River of Death and raked the water till she had collected all of the fragments of her son's body. She then joined them together through magic charms and salves.

The Maiden of Pohjola was then given to the smith hero, Ilmarinen, who had forged the magic sampo for Louhi. Enraged at not being invited to the marriage, the resurrected Lemminkainen went to Pohjola and entered the castle by force, killing the husband of Louhi.

When he returned to his home, he discovered his house burned down by raiders from Pohjola, though his mother was still alive. Lemminkainen again went to Pohjola with his companion, Kurra, though they were defeated by the cold. He joined Vainamoinen and Ilmarinen on their adventure to steal the magical sampo, which, however, was lost in the lake, with only fragments coming to the top of the water.

Lemminkainen is often called Lieto (reckless) and Kaukomieli (handsome man with a far-roving mind). He is also called Ahto, the name of the sea god in *The Kalevala*, perhaps indicating that once he was a god.

These adventures appealed to Sibelius, who composed *Four Legends for Orchestra* based on Lemminkainen's romantic and heroic exploits. The symphonic suite consists of four movements: (1) "Lemminkainen and the Maidens of Saari," dealing with Lemminkainen's seduction of all of the women on the island; (2) "The Swan of Tuonela," which captures the majestic swan floating on the River of Death; (3) "Lemminkainen in Tuonela," the hero's mother restoring her son to life after his murder; and (4) "Lemminkainen's Homeward Journey." Sibelius also composed three piano pieces called *Kyllikki*, evoking the legend of Lemminkainen's marriage to Kyllikki.

See also: *KALEVALA, THE*; KURRA; LOUHI; MAIDEN OF POHJOLA; SAMPO; SWAN; TUONI

1865
**Lempi** (erotic)   In Finnish mythology, personification of erotic love; father of the hero Lemminkainen in the Finnish epic poem *The Kalevala*. In the epic the mythical bay Lemmenlahti (rune 18) is a combination of *Lempi* and *lahti* (bay), suggesting that it was a trysting place for lovers. Lempi's wife, the mother of Lemminkainen, is not named in the epic.

Though Lempi was originally a man's name, it is usually given to women today. The female counterpart of Lempi is Sukkamielli (frenzied love).

See also: *KALEVALA, THE*; LEMMINKAINEN

1866
**Lemures** (ghosts)   In Roman mythology, evil spirits of the dead who often appeared as skeletons and were known to strike the living with madness. To expel them from the house, expiatory rites were held on 9, 11, and 13 May. This three-day period was called Lemuria or Lemuralia. According to Roman belief, the feast was first instituted by Romulus to appease the ghost of his murdered brother Remus and was called Remuria, later corrupted to Lemuria. During the three days of the rites the temples were closed and marriages prohibited. It was the custom for the people to throw black beans on the graves of the dead or to burn the beans, as the smell of the burning beans was believed to make the ghosts flee. Ovid's *Fasti* (book 5) tells of the various customs associated with the feast.

See also: OVID; ROMULUS AND REMUS

1867
**Lentil**   Leguminous plant with edible seeds, an ancient food. The Hebrew Book of Genesis (25:29–34) tells how Esau sold his birthright to his brother Jacob for a bowl of lentil pottage. In one of the many versions of *Cinderella*, a folktale found throughout the world, Cinderella is often portrayed as having to pick lentils out of the ashes. In India there is a saying: "Rice is good, but lentils are life."

See also: CINDERELLA; ESAU; JACOB

1868
**Leonard, St.** (strong as a lion)   Sixth century. In Christian legend, patron saint of prisoners, captives, slaves, cattle, and domestic animals. Feast, 6 November.

Popular during the Middle Ages, Leonard's life is told in *The Golden Legend*, a collection of saints' lives written in the 13th century by Jacobus de Voragine. Leonard was a favorite of the king of France. Whenever he visited, he would ask the king to release a prisoner, and the king always complied. Becoming dissatisfied with court life, Leonard went to preach in the forest. One day the king came through the area, accompanied by his pregnant queen. Suddenly the queen began to have labor pains. When Leonard heard her voice, he prayed to God to ease her delivery. The king was so pleased that he offered "many gifts of gold and silver," but Leonard "refused them all, and exhorted the king to give them to the poor." The king then offered him the whole forest, but Leonard chose just enough land to build a monastery on. He called it Nobiliacum because it "had been given by a noble king."

It was once believed that any prisoner who invoked the name of Leonard would immediately find himself free. He is usually depicted in art as a deacon holding chains or broken fetters in his hands.

See also: *GOLDEN LEGEND, THE*; LION

1869
**Leopard**  A large, ferocious, spotted carnivore of the cat family, usually having a tawny color with black markings. In Greek and Roman mythology the leopard was associated with Dionysus and Bacchus, the god having his chariot drawn by the animal. In his poem "Ode to a Nightingale" Keats says he prefers to be carried on the "viewless wings of Poesy" rather than be "charioted by Bacchus and his pards."

In medieval Christian folklore and symbolism the leopard represented cruelty, sin, lust, luxury, the devil, or the Antichrist, depending on the context. In one massive medieval mural of the Last Judgment the leopard is shown devouring the bodies of the damned. Often in Renaissance paintings the leopard is portrayed accompanying the Magi, who have come to honor the Christ child, as a symbol of the chained devil, eventually destroyed by Christ. In Dante's *The Divine Comedy* (Hell, canto 1) the poet is met by a leopard as he attempts to climb the hill of enlightenment. Most commentators on Dante see the animal as a symbol of his lust or luxury.

The panther, a black leopard, was one symbol of Christ in the Christian Middle Ages because it was believed the animal slept for three days and then emerged from its den with a roar. It was also believed that the panther's breath enticed all animals except the dragon. The dragon would flee to its den and fall asleep. The panther's sweet breath was seen as a symbol of the Holy Spirit, which came forth from Christ. This gift pleased the whole world except the dragon, who was the devil, and therefore he fled to hell.

See also: BACCHUS; DIONYSUS; DRAGON; MAGI

1870
**Leprechaun** (Leprecaun, Luchorpain) (small body?)  In Irish folklore, a small roguish elf. The leprechaun is noted for his knowledge of hidden treasure and his work on shoes. William Allingham, in his poem "The Leprecaun, or, Fairy Shoemaker," tells how he came upon a le-

prechaun working on a pair of shoes. The leprechaun was:

A wrinkled, wizen'd, and bearded Elf,
Spectacles stuck on his pointed nose,
Silver buckles on his hose,
Leather apron—shoe in his lap

Just when the poet appears to have captured the leprechaun, the elf offers a pinch from his snuffbox and then flings the dust in the poet's face; the poet sneezes while the leprechaun escapes. The American musical *Finian's Rainbow* (1947) features leprechauns.

See also: BROWNIE; CLURICANE; FAR DARRIA

1871
**Leshy** (Lesiy, Lesiye, Lesovik) (forest spirit)  In Slavic folklore, a mischievous forest spirit who can assume any shape. His skin is tinged with blue because of his blue blood, and it is as rough as tree bark. Sometimes he is depicted with horns and cloven hooves. He always wears his shoes on the wrong feet, and he casts no shadow. Said to be the offspring of a demon and a woman, a *leshy* will sometimes seduce a girl and take her to the forest, where he rapes her. Occasionally, a *leshy* will substitute an ugly spirit child for a real one. At the beginning of October the *leshies* disappear, indicating that they have died or gone into some type of hibernation, to reappear the next spring. Some Slavic folktales say the *leshy* marries. His wife is called Leshachikha and his children, *keshonki*. Béla Bartók's ballet *The Wooden Prince* uses some of the Slavic beliefs about *leshies* in its plot.

1872
**Lessing, Gotthold Ephraim**  1729–1781. German playwright who also wrote and published a collection of fables in 1759. Like his contemporary Christian Fürchtegott Gellert, Lessing produced fables in verse that were intended for the bedside table. Their sources were

Aesopic fables as well as those of other German writers of the genre.

See also: AESOPIC FABLES

### 1873

**Lethe** (forgetfulness)  In Greek and Roman mythology, river of forgetfulness in Hades (the underworld). In Vergil's *Aeneid* (book 6) the souls of the dead gather there to drink before they are reborn. Ovid's *Metamorphoses* (book 11) mentions Lethe as a river flowing around the Cave of Sleep, where its murmuring induces drowsiness. This passage in Ovid influenced Chaucer in his *Book of the Duchess* as well as Spenser's description of Morpheus in *The Faerie Queene* (book 1). In *The Divine Comedy* Dante says drinking the water of the river frees the souls from remembrance of their past sins. This image is used by Shakespeare in *Henry IV* when the new King Henry says: "May this be wash'd in Lethe and forgotten?" (Part II 5.2.72). Keats twice uses Lethe to mean death of the senses, in "Ode to a Nightingale" and "Ode to Melancholy."

See also: *AENEID, THE;* CHAUCER; HADES

### 1874

**Leto**  In Greek mythology, mother of Apollo and Artemis by Zeus; daughter of the Titans Coeus and Phoebe. Leto was called Latona by the Romans. According to Hesiod's *Theogony* (406), Leto was the "dark-robed and ever mild and gentle" wife of Zeus before he was wedded to Hera. But according to a later account, Leto was the mistress of Zeus after he was married to Hera. The Homeric *Hymn to Apollo* (attributed to Homer but not by him) tells how the goddess was pursued by the hatred of Hera but finally, with the aid of Poseidon, gave birth to her twins, Apollo and Artemis, on the island of Delos, which had been a floating island until that time but was thereafter permanently anchored in honor of the nativity of the twins. When Niobe said her children were more beautiful than Leto's, the goddess had Apollo and Artemis destroy all of Niobe's children. When the giant

Tityus attempted to rape Leto, he was cast into the underworld forever. Leto also appears in Homer's *Iliad* (book 21) and Ovid's *Metamorphoses* (book 6).

See also: APOLLO; ARTEMIS; DELOS; HERA; NIOBE; OVID; POSEIDON; TITANS; ZEUS

### 1875

**Lettuce**  Salad vegetable with edible leaves; in European folklore, believed to cause sterility. In some parts of England a head of lettuce in the kitchen was thought to render the woman of the house childless. Lettuce also was believed to alleviate lung disease. Its leaf, similar in shape to a lung, was considered beneficial in sympathetic medicine. To eat a head of lettuce before or during a sea voyage would prevent seasickness and ward off storms. In North American Indian belief, lettuce tea was given to a woman after childbirth to increase the flow of milk in her breast. Lettuce was eaten by the Egyptian god Set to make him potent; he kept a lettuce garden, from which he ate every day. In the Grimms' tale Rapunzel, the father is guilty of stealing a kind of lettuce called Rapunzel.

See also: SET

### 1876

**Leucippus** (white stallion)  In Greek mythology, king of Messenia, son of Perieres and Gorgophone. His daughters, Hilaera and Phoebe, called Leueippides, were abducted by Castor and Pollux. Idas and Lycceus, brothers of the two girls, fought to rescue them. Castor was killed, but Polydeuces (Pollux) was allowed by the gods to stand proxy for him in the underworld on alternate days. The myth is told in Pindar's *Nemean Ode 10.* Rubens's painting *The Rape of the Daughters of Leucippus* illustrates the myth. Leucippus is also the name of a son of Oenomaus and Euarete, brother of Hippodameia. He dressed as a woman to get closer to Daphne, whom Apollo loved. Daphne and her followers, on discovering the trick, killed Leucippus with Apollo's darts.

See also: APOLLO; CASTOR AND POLYDEUCES; DAPHNE; LEUCIPPUS

1877

**Leucothea** (white goddess)   In Greek mythology, the sea goddess Ino (she who makes sinewy), daughter of Cadmus; wife of Athamas and Harmmia; sister of Agave, Autonoë, Polydorus, and Semele. When her husband Athamas, king of Orchomenus, was driven insane by Hera, he thought that Ino was a lioness and that his sons Learchus and Melicertes were whelps. Ino fled with her son Melicertes, jumped into the sea, and was transformed by Zeus into a sea goddess. Melicertes became a minor sea god. Ovid's *Metamorphoses* (book 4) tells her tale. In Homer's *Odyssey* (book 5) Leucothea rises from the sea in the form of a sea mew when Odysseus's ship breaks up. She gives the hero her veil to tie around his waist so that he can swim through the sea to the island of Phaeacia. Milton's *Comus* mentions the goddess in relation to her son Palaemon, a minor sea god.

See also: ATHAMAS; CADMUS; HERA; *ODYSSEY, THE*; OVID; ZEUS

1878

**Leve** (the high-up one)   In African mythology (Mende of Sierra Leone), the sky god, often called Ngewo. At first Leve gave humankind all of its material desires. But soon Leve realized that greed was a large part of man's nature. "If I continue to give the people all they want, they will never leave me alone," he said. So one day Leve left mankind so that people would be less dependent on his gifts and would have to work to satisfy their needs.

1879

**Leza** (the one who besets)   In African mythology (central African peoples), sky god, creator of the world, and culture hero. Known to various African peoples, Leza is seen as creator and culture hero of various tribes. In one story he summoned a honey bird and gave it three sealed gourds. The bird was instructed to take the gourds to the first humans. Two of the gourds could be opened, but not the third. Overcome with curiosity, the bird opened all three. Two held seeds but the third held death, sickness, beasts of prey, and dangerous reptiles. These creatures could not be captured and put back in the gourds.

In another myth of the Basubiya, a Bantu people, Leza leaves for his sky home by a spider's thread after teaching the people various arts and how to worship him. When the people attempt to follow him by by climbing his web, it breaks and they fall back to earth.

Another myth told by the Ila of Zambia, Leza is responsible for death. Once Leza caused the brothers, sisters, and parents of a small girl to die. In time all of the girl's relatives died. Left an orphan, she eventually married, but before long her husband died. After her children gave birth to their children, they also died. Leza then caused the aging woman's grandchildren to die, too. To the woman's great surprise, however, each day she seemed to grow younger instead of older. She decided to build a ladder to the sky to ask Leza why he was doing these things. But the ladder crumbled before she could reach the sky, so she tried to find a road that would lead to Leza. She asked everyone she met where the road might be and told her sad story to all of the people along the way. They explained to her that all people were put into the world to suffer and that she was no exception. The woman never found the road to Leza, and like all others she died.

1880

**Libanza**   In African mythology (Upotos of the Congo), sky god and god of the dead. Libanza, though chief god, was not the first god. He was born of the union of his father, Lotenge, and Ntsombobelle, his mother. Before Ntsombobelle gave birth to Libanza, she brought forth thousands of serpents, mosquitoes, and other vermin, all of them armed with spears and shields. Libanza roamed the earth after his birth. He married several wives and had one son. He fought many people, killed his brother, and fought his aunt. Sometimes he even restored people to life after he had killed them. His disposition, however, caused his mother and his sister, Ntsongo, to hate him. His mother abandoned him and his sister said to him: "You killed your elder brother and you very nearly killed your own father. Do you imagine that I do not hate you? No, I hate you, and I should be glad to see you die." Earlier, his sister had asked Libanza to pick some palm nuts from a tree. He began to climb the tree, which grew taller and taller, until he reached the heavens, where he found his dead aunt, his murdered brother, and Lombo, king of the air. He fought Lombo and gained complete victory over the sky.

Now Libanza lives in the east, while his sister, Ntsongo, inhabits the west. On the day when he goes to see her in the west, everyone will fall ill and many people will die. The day will come when the sky will collapse and fall on all people. This would have happened already had it not been for the *molimons*, the souls of the dead, who have begged and prayed Libanza not to let the sky fall. The moon is a huge boat that sails across the whole earth, picking up the souls of the dead and bringing them to Libanza. The stars are lit by the souls of the dead, who sleep by day.

Libanza is responsible for death. One day he summoned all the people of the moon and the people of the earth. The people of the moon came promptly and were rewarded by Libanza. He said, "Because you have come at once when I called you, you shall never die. You shall be dead for only two days a month, and that will be to rest; thereafter, you shall return more splendid than before." But when the people of the earth arrived, he said, "Because you did not come at once when I called you, you shall die one day and you shall not return to life except to come to me." This is the reason the moon dies once a month and comes to life after two days, and why men, when they die, do not return, but go to Libanza in the sky.

**Libayé**    In North American Indian mythology (Mescalero Apache), clown, first of the Gahe, mountain gods, to step forward and sing and dance himself into creation.

1882

**Libitina**    In Roman mythology, a goddess who presided over death rites. Servius Tullius had a temple built in her honor, where everything needed for a funeral was sold. Lists of the dead were also kept in the temple. Originally, Libitina was an Italian goddess of voluptuous delight and of gardens, vineyards, and vintages. She was also associated with Venus and called Venus Libitina.

See also: VENUS

1883

**Lieh-tzu**    In Chinese history and legend a semi-legendary sage. He "dwelt on a vegetable plot for forty years, and no man knew him for what he was." He rode on the wind, and he took his pleasure from the sayings of Taoist philosophy. His message to his disciples was "Saying nothing and knowing nothing, there is in reality nothing that a man does not say, nothing that a man does not know."

1884

**Lif and Lifthrasir** (life and eager for life?)    In Norse mythology, man and woman from whom the new human race will spring after Ragnarok, the destruction of the world, the gods, and the frost giants. The myth is told in the *Prose Edda*.

See also: *PROSE EDDA*

1885

**Ligeia** (shrill)    In Greek mythology, one of the three Sirens; daughter of Achelous and Calliope;

*A Siren (C. Corvinus)*

sister of Leucosia and Parthenope. Her name is used by Edgar Allan Poe as the title of a poem and a short story.

See also: ACHELOUS; CALLIOPE; PARTHENOPE

1886

**Likho** (evil)   In Russian folklore, personification of evil, the demonic aspect of Dolya (fate) portrayed as a poorly dressed woman.

In a beneficent mood Dolya protects the family, but if in an evil mood, she is called Likho and brings disaster. According to one Russian folktale, "The One-Eyed Evil," Likho is described as a tall woman, scrawny, crooked, and with one eye. According to the tale, a blacksmith and a tailor went in search of Likho, since they had never seen her. A short time after they arrived at Likho's house she killed the tailor and served him to the blacksmith for dinner. To save himself, the blacksmith told Likho that he could restore her lost eye if only she would let him tie her with some ropes, because he would have to hammer the eye in and any sudden movement would be disastrous. Likho agreed and was easily

tied up, but just as easily she broke her bonds. A stronger rope was brought. She was again tied and this time was held fast as the blacksmith took out her other eye with a red-hot poker from the fire, making her completely blind. The blacksmith escaped by donning a sheepskin. He was nearly caught when his hand stuck to a golden ax in a tree. To free himself he had to cut off his hand because Likho, although blinded, was close behind him. When he arrived at his village, he told everyone what had happened: he had seen Likho, who not only left him with just one hand but also ate his companion.

1887

**Lilith** (storm goddess)   In Jewish, Christian, and Islamic mythology, female demon. She is said to haunt the wilderness in stormy weather. She is especially dangerous to children and pregnant women. In Jewish belief she was the first wife of Adam before Eve but was cast into the air for refusing to obey her husband. It was a medieval custom to place four coins on the Jewish marriage bed, which was to say "Adam and Eve" and "Avaunt thee, Lilith!" In the Old Testament Lilith is referred to as "the screech-owl" in Isaiah (34:14), "the night monster" in the Revised Version. Islamic folklore says she is the wife of Iblis, the devil, and the mother of all evil spirits. She appears in Goethe's *Faust* and Dante Gabriel Rossetti's *Eden Bower*.

See also: ADAM AND EVE; FAUST; IBLIS

1888

**Lily**   A large funnel-shaped flower. In ancient Egyptian symbolism, the lily was sometimes interchangeable with the lotus; it was the symbol for Upper Egypt. In Greek mythology, Zeus and Hera used lilies as part of their marriage couch. In Roman mythology, Venus was associated with the lily. In European folklore, lilies are used as protection against witches. In Christian symbolism, the lily is associated with the Virgin Mary and often portrayed in paintings of the Annunciation. St. Joseph, husband of the Virgin

*Lily (Walter Crane)*

Mary, often is portrayed holding a lily as a sign of chastity. The lily of the valley also is assigned to the Virgin Mary in Christian symbolism. This identification stems from an interpretation of a verse in the Song of Songs or Song of Solomon (2:1): "I am the rose of Sharon, and the lily of the valleys." In Japanese mythology, lilies stand for peace and tiger lilies for war. The white Easter lily given in America during the Holy Week is a symbol of death in Europe and is commonly found on gravestones.

See also: HERA; LOTUS; VENUS; VIRGIN MARY; ZEUS

**Lincoln, Abraham** 1809–1865. In American history and folklore, 16th president of the United States (1861–1865), called Honest Abe, the Rail Splitter, the Great Emancipator, and Great Martyr. He was born in a log cabin in Hardin (now Larue) County, Kentucky. His mother, Nancy Hanks, died in 1818. Lincoln settled in New Salem, Illinois, where he studied law and worked as a storekeeper, postmaster, and surveyor. Becoming a lawyer in 1836, he served in the state legislature from 1834 to 1841. He fell in love with Ann Rutledge (1816–1835), and their supposed love affair has become part of Lincoln's legend. In 1842 he married Mary Todd. Lincoln served as president during the Civil War and was assassinated on Good Friday, just a week after the conflict had ended. He became for many Americans a Christlike figure. Emerson wrote that Lincoln had "become mythological in a very few years."

It is often difficult to separate the historical man from the legendary one. Some of the main legends surrounding Lincoln follow. He was, from early life, a keen reader, spending hours near the fireside reading. As a store clerk, he was credited with great honesty. One day a woman ame into the store and purchased many goods, which Abe totaled at $2.26. Later he again added the prices and discovered he had made a mistake. He went in search of the woman and returned the difference, earning for himself the name Honest Abe. Because he was also more than six feet tall and strong, he was also known as the Rail Splitter. As a young man he was often called on to fight the town bully. Once Lincoln prayed at the bedside of a young Confederate soldier who was dying. The two repeated the well-known prayer, "Now I lay me down to sleep. . . ." Lincoln's religious faith formed the basis for many legends, but he was not connected with any religious organization or church. Many legends deal with his death. According to some, the president had dreams of his impending death. His ghost is said to inhabit the White House.

His life and legends have inspired many works, among them Walt Whitman's "O Captain My Captain" and "When Lilacs Last in the Dooryard Bloom'd," Robert E. Sherwood's play *Abe Lincoln in Illinois*, Carl Sandburg's six-volume *Abraham Lincoln*, Aaron Copland's work for voice narrator and orchestra, *A Lincoln Portrait*, and various movies, including *Abraham Lincoln* (1925); *Abraham Lincoln* (1930), starring Walter Huston; *Young Mr. Lincoln* (1939), starring Henry Fonda; and *Abe Lincoln in Illinois* (1939), starring Raymond Massey.

1890

**Lingam** (Linga) (penis)    In Hinduism, the sacred phallus of the god Shiva. Various myths account for the origin of phallus worship in India. According to one myth, after Shiva's wife had immolated herself to prove her love, the god was taunted by a beautiful girl, whom he then raped. Her husband cursed Shiva, saying the god should not be worshiped in his own form but only by the instrument of his violence, the phallus.

In a variant myth, Shiva was wandering naked, and the wives of holy men, excited by his physical appearance, had intercourse with him. The holy men cursed Shiva so that his penis fell off. As it fell to the earth, it grew to an immense size, reaching into the heavens and into the deepest earth. The gods Vishnu and Brahma decided to find out how long Shiva's phallus was. Vishnu descended into the earth and Brahma ascended to the heavens. When the two met, Vishnu said he could not discover the beginning of the phallus, but Brahma lied and said he had touched the top. When Shiva appeared, he called Brahma a liar. In another variant myth, Shiva had intercourse in front of Vishnu and Brahma and, out of shame, cut off his penis. *Lingam* worship in India takes many forms. Various metals, stones, and woods are used to construct the phallus. There are even portable *lingam* made of cow dung, butter, sandalwood, grass, and flowers. The *lingam* is normally set in the pan-shaped *yoni* (vagina) to express the union of opposites in Shiva. Members of the Hindu sect called Lingayat, in south India, wear *lingam* around their necks, as a Christian would wear a cross. One of the marriage customs of the Hindus was to have a bride deflowered in Shiva's temple by a carved *lingam* of the deity, thus making the child to be born a son or daughter of the god.

See also: BRAHMA; SHIVA; VISHNU; YONI

1891

**Ling-pai** (spirit white)    In Chinese folk belief, a white paper or cloth streamer used in rites to call the souls of the dead back from the hells.

1892

**Lion**    A large and powerful carnivorous cat. In Egyptian mythology the lion or lioness was a symbol of the war goddess Sekhmet. In Greek mythology the lion or lioness was associated with Phoebus, Artemis, Cybele, and Dionysus. In Roman mythology the animal was associated with Juno and Fortuna. In Hindu mythology Narasinha, the fourth avatar of Vishnu, is portrayed as half man, half lion. In Near Eastern mythology the lion or lioness is associated with various manifestations of the great Mother Goddess, as well as the gods Marduk, Ninib, and Nergal.

In the Old Testament the lion is a symbol of Judah, and in the New Testament it is a symbol of Jesus Christ, "the lion of the tribe of Juda, the Root of David" (Rev. 5:5), as well as a symbol in Christian art for the Gospel according to St. Mark, patron saint of Venice. In medieval Christian symbolism the lion could also stand for the devil (1 Peter 5:8). In the requiem Mass St. Michael was called on to deliver the souls of the faithful "from the mouth of the lion, lest the jaws of the pit swallow them." In medieval folklore it was believed that lion cubs were born dead and given life by their father when he breathed on them.

Though the lion was considered king of beasts, medieval folklore said the animal was afraid of creaking wheels, scorpions, fires, snake poison, and most of all, the cock. As a ruler the lion was known for kindness and mercy. Shakespeare in *Troilus and Cressida* (5.3) has Troilus say:

Brother, you have a vice of mercy in you
Which better fits a lion than a man.

The lion's kindness is found in such tales as Androcles and the Lion, as well as in Aesop's fables. There are numerous motifs associated with lions in the *Motif Index of Folk Literature*.

See also: AESOPIC FABLES; ARTEMIS; AVATAR; DIONYSUS; FORTUNA; JUNO; MARDUK; MARK, ST.; MICHAEL, ST.; NERGAL; SEKHMET; VISHNU

*The Lion and the Mouse*

### Lion and the Mouse, The

Aesopic fable found in various collections throughout the world.

A lion was asleep in his den one day when a mouse ran across his outstretched paw and up the royal nose of the king of beasts, awakening him from his nap. The mighty beast clapped his paw on the now thoroughly frightened little creature and would have made an end of him.

"Please," squealed the mouse, "don't kill me. Forgive me this time, O King, and I shall never forget it. A day may come, who knows, when I may do you a good turn to repay your kindness."

The lion, smiling at his little prisoner's fright and amused by the thought that so small a creature ever could be of assistance to the king of beasts, let him go.

Not long afterward the lion, while ranging the forest for his prey, was caught in a net hunters had set to catch him. He let out a roar that echoed throughout the forest. Even the mouse heard it and, recognizing the voice of his benefactor, ran to the spot where the lion lay tangled in the net of ropes.

"Well, Your Majesty," said the mouse, "I know you did not believe me once when I said I would return a kindness, but here is my chance." And he set to work to nibble with his sharp little teeth at the ropes that bound the lion. Soon the lion was able to crawl out of the hunter's snare to freedom.

Moral: *No act of kindness, no matter how small, is ever wasted.*

In the Indian version the lion is replaced by an elephant, as elephants were often tied to trees as a preliminary to taming them. The Greek form of the fable reached Egyptian literature about 200 C.E. The German composer Werner Egk set the fable for narrator, chorus, and orchestra in 1931 for a radio program.

See also: AESOPIC FABLES

### Lion in Love, The

Aesopic fable found in various European collections.

A lion fell in love with the beautiful daughter of a woodman. One day he came to ask the girl's hand in marriage. It was only natural that the woodman was not greatly pleased with the lion's offer and declined the honor of so dangerous an alliance.

The lion threatened the parents of the girl with his royal displeasure. The poor father did not know what to do. Finally, he said: "We are greatly flattered by your proposal. But you see, our daughter is a tender child, and her mother and I fear that in expressing your affection for her you may do her an injury. Would Your Majesty consent to have your claws removed and your teeth extracted before becoming a bridegroom?"

So deeply was the lion in love that he permitted the operation to take place. But when he came again to the woodman's home to claim the girl, the father, no longer afraid of the tamed and disarmed king of the beasts, seized a stout club and drove the unhappy suitor from his door.

Moral: *Even the wildest can be tamed by love.*

The fable was told by Eumenes to warn the Macedonians against the schemes of Antigonus, called the One-Eyed. When the empire of Alexander the Great was divided at his death, Antigonus received Phrygia, Lycia, and Pamphylia. He eventually acquired the whole of Asia Minor.

He was defeated and slain at Ipsus by allied forces in 301 B.C.E.

See also: AESOPIC FABLES; ALEXANDER THE GREAT

*The Lion's Share (Arthur Rackham)*

**Lion's Share, The**   Aesopic fable found in various collections throughout the world.

The lion preferred to hunt alone, but now and then he would invite other beasts to accompany him. On one such occasion the hunters cornered and killed a fat stag.

Taking a commanding position before the dead stag, the lion roared: "Beasts, it is time to divide the spoils. I demand that it be quartered. The first quarter shall fall to me as king of the beasts. The second is mine as arbiter. A third quarter is due me for my part in the chase. Now, as for the fourth part"—and here the lion gave an ominous growl—"let him take it who dares!"

Moral: *Many may share in the labors but not in the spoils.*

The companions of the lion in the Greek version of Phaedrus are a cow, a goat, and a sheep. In the medieval versions of Marie de France and Benedict of Oxford (whose tales are in Hebrew) the lion's partners are carnivorous, which seems appropriate to the setting.

See also: AESOPIC FABLES; LION; *HITOPADESH*

**Lir (Llyr, Lear, Ler, Leir) (sea)**   In Celtic mythology, a sea god, one of the Tuatha de Danann, who was deeply devoted to his four chil-

dren—Fionguala, a daughter; Aed, or Hugh; and Conn and Fiachra, twin boys—by his first wife, Aebh. His second wife, Aeife, became jealous and resolved to destroy the children. She took the children to King Borve the Red, a neighboring ruler, and through magic transformed them into swans. Because of her evil King Borve turned Aeife into a demon of the air. Then Lir and Borve set out to find the children, which they did, but they could not disenchant them. The period of transformation lasted 900 years. When they were finally released from their swan form by a Christian monk, they were old and withered. The monk, seeing that the angel of death would soon claim them, sprinkled each of them with water, baptizing them as they died.

The tale is told in the Irish *Fate of the Children of Lir*, which dates, according to some scholars, to the 18th century. Some believe that Lir is the original for Shakespeare's King Lear. The tale is also cited by James Joyce in his novel *Ulysses*.

See also: LEAR, KING; TUATHA DE DANANN

*Li T'ien-kuai*

**Li T'ien-kuai**   13th century? In Chinese Taoist mythology, one of the Pa-Hsien, the Eight Immortals. Li was a very handsome man. One day, as he was going up into the sky in his spirit form (after having mastered the Tao), he told his disciple that if his spirit did not return to his body in seven days, his body should be put in the fire. Six days passed, and the disciple had to go to see his sick mother. He left the body of Li unguarded. When the spirit of Li returned, it could not enter its own body but instead had to go into that of an old beggar. In art Li is portrayed as an old beggar with an ugly face, blowing his spirit into space in the form of a small human figure riding on a staff, horse, or frog. In Japanese legend Li T'ien-kuai is called Ri-Tekkai.

See also: PA-HSIEN

### 1898

**Little Red Riding Hood**   Popular European folktale found in many collections, among them Perrault's *Petit chaperon rouge* and the Grimms' *Rotkäppchen*. Believed by most scholars to be based on both oral and literary sources, the tale tells how Little Red Riding Hood is eaten by a wolf masquerading as her grandmother, or in some accounts, as her mother. Perrault ends his tale with Little Red Riding Hood's death and a short verse warning young girls to avoid wolves. It was most likely Perrault who added the red cap (cape) to the story as an indication of the social standing of the young girl. In the Grimms' version a hunter appears who kills the wolf and slits open its belly, which allows the grandmother to reappear. In some variants the hunter kills the wolf before it has eaten Little Red Riding Hood.

Little Red Riding Hood is tale type 333, the "Glutton," and is known in China, Korea, and Japan as "Grandaunt Tiger." In most of the oral sources in Europe and in Asia there are additional elements to the story: nakedness (the wolf tells the girl to take off her clothes for she won't be needing them), cannibalism (the girl is instructed to eat the bones and drink the blood of her slain grandmother), and defecation (which the girls uses to escape the wolf). None of these elements made their way into the published sources and are only found in field-collected variants. In 1985 Angela Landsbury played the

grandmother in a film version called *The Company of Wolves.*

See also: BROTHERS GRIMM; TALE TYPE; VARIANT

### 1899

**Liu Ling**   300–221 B.C.E. In Chinese legend, one of the seven Chu-lin Ch'i-Hsien (Seven Immortals). He was followed by a servant who carried a flask of wine in case he wanted a drink and a shovel in case he fell dead, so he could be buried where he fell. He is portrayed carrying a book. In Japanese legend he is called Keiko.

See also: CHU-LIN CH'I-HSIEN

### 1900

**Livy**   59 B.C.E.–17 C.E. Titus Livius, Roman historian, whose *History of Rome*, originally in 142 books (of which 35 still exist) tells many Roman legends, such as that of Romulus and Remus, Lucretia, the expulsion of the kings by Brutus, and the heroics of Camillus. During the Middle Ages Livy's work was highly respected. Dante gave him high praise, and the Renaissance political thinker Machiavelli wrote a commentary on some of Livy's work.

See also: CAMILLUS; ROMULUS AND REMUS

### 1901

**Lleu Law Gyffes** (he of the steady hand?)   In Celtic mythology, a culture hero among the British, often identified with the Irish culture hero Lugh, who was also a sun god. Lleu Law Gyffes was worshiped in Gaul and was the mythical founder of Lyons (Lugdunum), where he was known as Lugus. His father was Arianrhod and his mother was Math. Gwydion, Arianrhod's brother abducts and raises him as a child. When Gwydion gives the still unnamed child to his mother, she is embarrassed, which many have interpreted as a case of incest. Arianrhod is furious at the sight of the child, accusing Gwydion of "pursuing her [Math's] shame." His mother thus curses the child three times: he will have no other name than the one she gives him, he shall bear no arms unless she give them to him, and he will have no wife of the race of the earth. Gwydion overcomes each of these obstacles, the third by creating the beautiful Blouderwedd from flowers. She proves to be a bad wife and plots to kill him. When Lleu Law Gyffes is wounded, he turns into an eagle and flies to a magic oak tree. Gwydion finds him and returns him to his human shape. He then shames Blouderwedd and turns her into an owl.

See also: ARIANRHOD; BLATHNAT

**1902**

**Loa** (laws)   In Haitian voodoo, deified spirit of the dead who is looked upon as a god. The multitude of loas derives from the West African Dahomey people. Native Haitian loas are less numerous, but include the Petra Loa. The voodoo gods, called loas, *mystères*, or *voudoun*, are called forth from their other abode by the Houn'gan or Mam'bo (priest or priestess). They may enter a govi (special jar) or mount (take possession of) a voodoo follower. A loa that takes possession of a person completely controls all of the actions of that person, and the possessed loses all consciousness of self. The possessed person, called the *cheval* (horse) because he or she has been mounted by the loa, may prophesy, dance, and perform magic, none of which is recalled when the possessed awakens. A young girl, for instance, who is mounted by an old loa will become as feeble and practically as speechless as an old woman. Yet if an old man is mounted by a vigorous young loa, he will act like a young man. The sick who normally are unable to walk will dance and leap about. Generally, the entire personality of the mounted person is erased during the loa crisis.

The loas have sensitive feelings and are hurt by disrespect and sometimes cry when they feel neglected by the living. The word *loa* is believed to be derived from the French *lois* (laws), indicating a connection between man and the laws of creation.

**1903**

**Loch Ness Monster**   A lake monster said to inhabit Loch Ness in Scotland. In April 1933 a motorist driving along the shore of Loch Ness "saw" a fantastic animal some 30 feet long with a long neck and two flippers at about the middle of its body. It was also "seen" and described by others and made newspaper headlines. It is still one of the main attractions to the area. Does the Loch Ness monster really exist? The question still causes debate in Scottish taverns as well as in other English-speaking countries. Reports of the monster would seem to show that under the proper psychological and naturalistic conditions even our science-oriented age can conjure up a monster that can hold its own against fantastic beasts of ancient mythology.

**1904**

**Loco and Ayizan**   In Haitian voodoo, two healing loas believed to have been the first houn'gan and mam'bo (priest and priestess). Loco acts as a doctor who heals and repairs the body, and Ayizan protects against malevolent magic.

See also: LOA

**1905**

**Lohengrin**   In medieval German legend, the Knight of the Swan, son of Perceval (Parzival) and Conduiramour, defender of Else, the princess of Brabant, who was falsely charged with murder. Brought up with the Knights of the Holy Grail, Lohengrin was one day called to defend an innocent victim. He was told he would be conveyed to his destination by a swan. Perceval reminded his son that as a servant of the Holy Grail he must never reveal his name or origin unless asked to do so and that, having once made himself known, he was bound to return without delay. Guided by the swan, Lohengrin arrived as Else, charged with the murder of her brother, was waiting for a champion to defend her in a judicial duel. Lohengrin won the battle against Frederick, who had accused Else. Else then consented to become Lohengrin's wife without knowing his true name. The wedding took place at Antwerp, where the emperor, Henry the Fowler, came to celebrate with them. Lohengrin had cautioned Else that she must never ask him his name. But Else wished to know who her husband really was and finally asked the question. Lohengrin led her into the great hall, where in the presence of the assembled knights he told her that he was Lohengrin, son of Perceval, the guardian of the Holy Grail. Then, embracing her tenderly, he told her that "love cannot live without faith" and that he must now leave her and return to the Holy Mountain. After he had blown his horn three times, the swan boat appeared, and Lohengrin sprang into it and vanished. Some variants of the legend say that Else soon died; others say she lived on.

Wolfram von Eschenbach wrote his *Parzival* in 1210, in which Lohengrin plays a major role. The legend was used by Wagner in his opera *Lohengrin* (1847).

See also: HOLY GRAIL; PERCEVAL

### 1906

**Lokaloka** (a world and no world)   In Hindu mythology, a belt of mountains bounding the outermost of the seven seas and dividing the visible world from the regions of darkness. Lokaloka is also called Chakra-vada or Chakra-vala.

### 1907

**Lokapalas** (world protectors)   In Hindu mythology, the four guardians of the quarters of the earth: Yama, Kubera, Varuna, and Indra. Sometimes four other gods are listed: Agni, Vayu, Soma, and Surya. They in turn are assisted by the Diggajas (elephants of the directions): Airavata, Pundarika, Vana, Kumuda, Anjana, Pushapadanta, Sarvabhauma, and Supratika. The Diggajas are also called Dikpala (lord of the directions).

See also: AGNI; INDRA; KUBERA; SOMA; SUPRATIKA; SURYA; VARUNA; YAMA

*Loki's Punishment (Aubrey Beardsley)*

### 1908

**Loki** (fire, flame)   In Norse mythology, evil fire-trickster god; son of the giant Farbauti and the giantess Laufey, or Nal. Loki's wife was Siguna; Vali and Nari were his children. He became foster brother to the god Odin and was also counted among the Aesir, though he was not one of them. He was really a giant. Loki, or Loptur, is called Loge in Germanic mythology and in Richard Wagner's *Der Ring des Nibelungen*.

The *Prose Edda* describes Loki as "the calumniator of the gods, the contriver of all fraud and mischief, and the disgrace of gods and men. . . . Loki is handsome and well made, but of a very fickle mood and most evil disposition. He surpasses all beings in those arts called Cunning and Perfidy. Many a time has he exposed the gods to great perils, and often extricated them again by his artifices."

Loki was responsible for the death of the good and fair god Baldur. When the gods discovered Loki's part in Baldur's death, they threatened him with punishment, so he hid himself in the mountains. He built a house with four doors in order to see everything that passed around him. Often he assumed the likeness of a salmon and hid himself under the waters of a cascade called Franangursfors.

One day he took flax and yarn and worked them into a net, but learning that the gods were approaching his dwelling, he threw the net into the fire and fled to the river. When the gods entered Loki's house, Kvasir, who was known for his quickness and knowledge, traced out in the hot embers the vestiges of the burned net and told Odin that it must be an invention to catch fish. The gods then wove another net, following the model that was imprinted in the ashes. They threw the new net into the river in which Loki had hidden himself. Thor held one end of the net, and the rest of the gods held the other, but they failed to catch Loki. The evil god had leaped over the net into the waterfall. The gods divided themselves into two bands: Thor, wading midstream, followed the net, while the others dragged it along toward the sea. Loki knew then that he had only two chances to escape, either to swim out to sea or to leap over the net. He chose the latter, but as he took a tremendous leap, Thor caught him in his hand. Being extremely slippery, Loki would have escaped had not Thor held him fast by the tail, and according to the *Prose Edda*, "this is the reason why salmons have had their tails ever since so fine and thin." The *Prose Edda* continues:

The gods having thus captured Loki, dragged him without commiseration into a cavern, wherein they placed three sharp-pointed rocks, boring a hole through each of them. Having also seized Loki's children, Vali and Nari, they changed the former into a wolf, and in this likeness he tore his brother to pieces and devoured him. The gods then made cords of his intestines, with which they bound Loki on the points of the rocks, one cord passing under his shoulders, another under his loins, and a third under his hams, and afterwards transformed these cords into thongs of iron. Skadi then suspended a serpent over him in such a manner that the venom should fall on his face, drop by drop. But Siguna, his wife, stands by him and receives the drops as they fall in a cup, which she empties as often as it is filled. But while she is doing this, venom falls upon Loki, which makes him howl with horror, and twist his body about so violently that the whole earth shakes, and this produces what men call

earthquakes. There will Loki lie until Ragnarok (Blackwell translation).

In Wagner's music drama *Die Walküre*, Wotan, who corresponds to Odin, calls on Loge (Loki) to surround Brünnhilde with flames until a hero, Siegfried, frees her. Loki (spelled Lok) also appears in Matthew Arnold's narrative poem *Balder Dead*. Loki (Loge) is portrayed in Arthur Rackham's illustrations for Wagner's Ring Cycle.

See also: AESIR; ANGURBODA; BALDUR; FREYJA; HEIMDALL; KVASIR; *PROSE EDDA*; RAGNAROK; *RING DES NIBELUNGEN, DER*

1909
**Lokman** (Luqman, Lukman)  In Islamic legend, Arabian sage and author of fables. In the Koran (sura 31) Lokman is credited with great wisdom given him by Allah. Muhammad honored him as the author of proverbs, some of which are recorded in the Koran. A few centuries after Muhammad's death Lokman was also credited with the authorship of numerous fables.

The life of Lokman resembles that of Aesop. He was a slave, ugly and deformed, who was offered by God the choice of wisdom or prophecy and chose wisdom. In one legend Lokman's master offered him a bitter melon to eat. After Lokman ate the entire fruit, his master asked how he could eat such unpleasant food. Lokman replied that he should take the unpleasant with the pleasant from his master.

The first collection of Lokman's fables appeared in the late 13th century and consisted of some 40 fables. Although derived mainly from a Syriac collection of Sophos, or Aesopus, there is one fable in the collection that has not yet been traced to another source. A thornbush asks a gardener to tend it so that it may delight kings with its flowers and fruits. The gardener waters the bush every day, and it eventually overruns the garden. The fable somewhat resembles the one told by Jotham in Judges (9:7–15) in its depiction of the thornbush's cruel nature.

Some scholars have believed that *Lokman* is a corruption of King Solomon's name.

See also: AESOPIC FABLES; ALLAH; KORAN, THE; MUHAMMAD; SOLOMON

**1910**
**Longinus, St.**    First century. In Christian legend, name given to the centurion who pierced the side of Christ when he was on the cross (Matt. 27:54). The lance became a cult object during the Middle Ages, with numerous churches claiming to possess it. Feast, 15 March. In medieval Christian art St. Longinus is usually portrayed as a knight in full armor, in later Renaissance art as a Roman soldier with a spear or lance.

**1911**
**Long Juju**    In African legend, a prophet who lived in Nigeria during the period of the slave trade. Many people believed in his powers and therefore greatly feared him. He would sit at the entrance of a cave while visitors stood in the waters of a small river that ran alongside it and asked him questions, which he answered in a mysterious, nasal tone. He claimed to have the ability to tell which men were guilty of crimes and which were innocent. Those whom he declared guilty were sold into slavery.

**1912**
**Lönnrot, Elias**    1802–1884. Finnish folklorist and compiler of *The Kalevala*, the national Finnish epic poem. The son of a poor country tailor, Lönnrot studied to be a doctor at the University of Helsinki, becoming a district medical officer at Kajaani in eastern Finland. Inspired by the works of the Grimm Brothers, he made extensive collections of traditional oral folk poetry among the Lapps, Estonians, and Finns in Karelia and northwest Russia. He first published *The Kalevala* in 1835 and expanded it in 1849. Aside from this monumental work, Lönnrot edited *Kantelator*, a collection of Finnish folk poetry

consisting of 652 poems. Among the ballads are many that show similarity to those of central and western Europe, as well as Finnish versions of Christian legends. Through his efforts for a Finnish national identity, Lönnrot became one of the leaders of the nationalist movement, though more in the nature of a patriarch than a revolutionary.

See also: GRIMM BROTHERS; *KALEVALA, THE*

**1913**
**Lord of Misrule**    In medieval European folk custom, a person who directed the festivities of the holiday season during Christmas, from the feast of Christmas to Ephiphany, the Twelve Days of Christmas. He was sometimes called the King of Misrule, King of the Bean, the Abbas Stultorum, the Boy Bishop, Abbot of Unreason, Abbot of Misrule, or Bon Accord. During his rule he was furnished with hobby horses, dragons, and musicians, and he was allowed to tell his "subjects" to do nearly any deed.

**1914**
**Lorlei** (Loreley, Lurlei)    In German literary folklore and in local legend, an enchantress with long blond hair who sits on a cliff 133 meters above the Rhine river. She combs her hair and sings a song that bewitches the captains of ships down below, causing them to drive their vessels into the rocky crags and to lose their lives. While the literary versions by Clemens Brentano and particularly by Heinrich Heine in the early 19th century are well known, according to local legend the same spot on the Rhine is said to be the location of the Nibelungen horde.

See also: NIBELUNGENLIED

**1915**
**Losy**    In Siberian mythology, an evil giant snake defeated by the creator god Otshirvani, who took the form of a gigantic bird. In many Central Asian myths, Losy is called Abyrga.

See also: GARIDE BIRD; OTSHIRVANI

**1916**

**Lot, King** (covering)   In Arthurian legend, king of Orkney, defeated by King Arthur. In Malory's *Morte d'Arthur* Lot is the father of Gwain, Agravaine, Gaheris, and Gareth by his wife, Margawse, who was Arthur's sister.

See also: ARTHUR; GARETH; GWAIN; MARGAWSE

**1917**

**Lotis**   In Greek mythology, a nymph, daughter of Poseidon. She fled from Priapus's lust and was transformed into a lotus tree. Ovid's *Metamorphoses* (book 9) tells her tale.

See also: LOTUS; OVID; POSEIDON; PRIAPUS

**1918**

**Lotophagi** (lotus eaters)   In Greek mythology, a fantastic people of coastal Africa who lived on lotus fruit. They were visited by Odysseus on his homeward journey after the Trojan War, according to Homer's *Odyssey* (book 9). Herodotus's *Histories* says the Lotophagi lived in western Libya. The fruit has been identified as the *Cordia myxa* (sour plum) by some writers such as Pliny in his *Natural History*. Whatever the fruit, it produced forgetfulness, making one lose desire for home. Tennyson's "The Lotus-Eaters" deals with the myth.

See also: LOTUS; ODYSSEUS; *ODYSSEY, THE*

**1919**

**Lotus**   A water flower; in Egyptian mythology, associated with Osiris and his sister-wife Isis as a sign of life and resurrection. One Egyptian work portrays Isis emerging from a lotus flower. Egyptian mummies often held a lotus in their hands as a symbol of new life. In Hindu mythology, Vishnu and Brahma are associated with the lotus. Brahma is called "lotus-born" and often portrayed as a giant lotus sprouting from the navel of the god Vishnu, the "lotus-naveled." According to Buddhist legend, whenever the Buddha walked abroad, he left not footprints but the mark of the lotus, the "fairest flower" of the East. In one myth he is said to have first appeared floating on a lotus.

See also: BRAHMA; BUDDHA; ISIS: LILY; OIRIS; VISHNU

**1920**

**Louhi** (witch of the wind?)   In the Finnish epic poem *The Kalevala*, evil gap-toothed mistress of Pohjola, the Northland.

Louhi had two daughters, the lovelier being the Maiden of Pohjola, who was wooed by all three heroes in the epic: Vainamoinen, Ilmarinen, and Lemminkainen. Finally, after Ilmarinen forged the magic sampo for Louhi, he was given the bride. The sampo made Pohjola prosperous, and Vainamoinen decided to steal it for his land. He succeeded but was pursued by Louhi and her men. A great battle ensued in which the sampo was lost in the lake, with only a few pieces left floating on the waters. Louhi, angered because her land became barren after the loss of the sampo, sent a plague to Vainamoinen's land, but the hero healed his people by the use of magic. Not satisfied, the evil mistress then sent a great bear to ravish the herds, but Vainamoinen was again victorious. Finally, out of desperation, Louhi stole the sun and moon as well as fire from all of the hearths in Vainamoinen's land, but new fire was kindled by a thunderbolt from Ukko, the sky god. Ilmarinen then forged chains for Louhi, and out of fear Louhi released the sun and moon.

See also: ILMARINEN; *KALEVALA, THE*; LEMMINKAINEN; MAIDEN OF POHJOLA; SAMPO; UKKO; VAINAMOINEN

**1921**

**Louis, St.** (famous in battle)   1214–1270. In Christian legend, king of France. Commissioned La Sainte Chapelle in honor of relics of the true cross he obtained in the Holy Land. Feast, 25 August.

Louis was born at Poissy and came to the French throne when he was 11 years old. He defeated King Henry III of England in 1242 and twice made trips to the Holy Land. His life was

*St. Louis*

recorded by his personal friend Jean Joinville (1225–1317) in his *Historie de Saint Louis*. The work deals primarily with the first crusade of St. Louis and Joinville's relationship with the king. When the saint wished to make his second crusade to the Holy Land, Joinville writes that "those who recommended this voyage to the king sinned grievously." He therefore excused himself from the journey. Louis died of typhus at Tunis, and his bones and heart were taken back to France and enshrined in the abbey church of St. Denis. They were lost during the French Revolution. Another portion of his relics was taken to Palermo and placed in the cathedral of Monreale.

St. Louis is pictured as a king crowned, with fleurs-de-lis on his mantle and scepter. Often a crown of thorns is also shown. El Greco painted the saint with his page (1585–1590). He was canonized in 1297.

See also: DENIS, ST.

**1922**
**Lowa** (Loa)   In Micronesian mythology, creator god from whose leg the first man and woman, Wulleb and Limdunanij, emerged. The first couple had two children, one of whom tried to kill his father, Wulleb. Fleeing his murderous son, Wulleb descended to earth, and from his leg two more sons were born, the younger of whom, Edao, became a great magician.

See also: ADAM AND EVE

**1923**
**Luchtaine** (Lud)   In Celtic mythology, a woodworker god who made weapons for the Tuatha de Danann (the people of the goddess Danu) when they fought and defeated the Fomorians. He was particularly adept at making spears and shields.

See also: DANU; FOMORIANS; TUATHA DE DE-NANN

**1924**
**Lucifer** (light bearer)   In Christian mythology, name often given to Satan, though originally it probably referred to the morning star.

In Isaiah (14:4,12) the name Lucifer is figuratively applied to Nebuchadnezzar: "Take up this proverb against the King of Babylon.... How art thou fallen from heaven O Lucifer, son of the morning." St. Jerome, writing in the fourth century, as well as other Doctors of the Church, used the name Lucifer for Satan when commenting, "I beheld Satan as lightning fell from heaven" (Luke 10:18). In Christopher Marlowe's play *Doctor Faustus* and Dante's *The Divine Comedy* Lucifer is the king of hell. John Milton, in his epic poem *Paradise Lost*, gives this name to Satan, the demon of "sinful pride" before the Fall. A massive epic play, *Lucifer*, by Joost van den Vondel, the celebrated Dutch poet of the 17th century, has Lucifer as its main protagonist. George Meredith's poem *Lucifer in Starlight* treats Lucifer and his fall in a work tinged with skepticism.

See also: DOCTORS OF THE CHURCH; JEROME, ST.; SATAN

**1925**
**Lucretia**   In Roman legend, daughter of Lucretius and wife of the Tarquinius Collatinus, a relative of the king Tarquinius. She was raped by one of King Tarquinius's sons, Sextus. Lucretia informed her husband and her father of the deed and then killed herself. Her rape so inflamed the people that they overthrew the monarchy and established a republic. Her husband, who joined

the rebellion, was elected one of the new magistrates but abdicated because no one named Tarquinius should rule at Rome again. The legend is told in Livy's *History of Rome*, Ovid's *Fasti*, Chaucer's *Legend of Good Women*, and Shakespeare's long poem *The Rape of Lucrece*, which forms the basis for Benjamin Britten's opera *The Rape of Lucretia* (1946). The subject has been painted by Botticelli, Filippino Lippi, Titian, Tintoretto, Cranach, and Veronese.

See also: CHAUCER; OVID

1926
**Lucretius**   c. 95–c. 55 B.C.E. Roman poet, Titus Lucretius Carus, author of *De rerum natura* (On the Nature of Things), which, in six books, is an exposition of the materialistic and hedonistic Epicurean philosophy in poetic form. The argument suggests that the gods are unconcerned with human affairs but describes a tight connection between the physical laws that govern the material world and their implications for an ethical life. Despite the rejection of divine interference, mythological scenes are used frequently. Book 1 opens with a magnificent address to Venus as goddess of creation, and the evils of religious fanaticism are exposed by the tale of the sacrifice of Iphigenia at Aulis. Parts of *De rerum natura* were translated into English heroic verse by John Dryden. According to a medieval legend first stated by St. Jerome, Lucretius committed suicide after being poisoned by a love philter. Tennyson's *Lucretius* deals with the poet's death.

See also: IPHIGENIA; VENUS

1927
**Lucy of Syracuse, St.** (light)   Third century. In Christian legend, patron saint of eyes, cutlers, glaziers, notaries, peddlers, saddlers, servant girls, scribes, tailors, and weavers. Invoked against blindness, fire, infection, hemorrhage, and sore throat. Feast, 13 December.

Vowed to chastity, Lucy was arrested for being a Christian and ordered to sacrifice to the pagan gods. She refused and was placed in a whorehouse by the governor Paschasius.

"Here you will lose your chastity," said the governor to the girl. He then ordered some young men to "defoul her, and labor her so much till she be dead," according to *The Golden Legend*, a collection of saints' lives written in the 13th century by Jacobus de Voragine.

The men tried to rape the saint, but the Holy Spirit made her so "heavy that in no wise might they move her from the place." Paschasius became so enraged that he ordered a servant to pierce her throat with a poniard. She died on the spot.

The legend connecting her with the loss of eyesight is a later medieval legend. A young man fell in love with Lucy because of her beautiful eyes. She plucked them out and sent them to him in a dish, saying "now let me live to God." The man became a Christian, and God later restored Lucy's eyes. She is depicted in art carrying a palm branch and a platter with two eyes on it.

See also: *GOLDEN LEGEND, THE*

1928
**Lud**   In Finno-Ugric ritual, a sacred grove where the spirits of ancient heroes were worshiped. Each family had its own Lud, though children and women were not allowed into the sacred grove. The Lud spirit who lived in the grove usually demanded a blood offering. A foal was generally the victim, but sometimes it was a black sheep. Before beginning the sacrifice the people ascertained whether the Lud spirit would accept the offering by pouring fresh water and twigs over the sacrificial animal as they recited prayers. If the animal shivered, it indicated that the sacrifice was acceptable to the Lud spirit.

1929
**Ludd**   In Celtic mythology, Welsh sea god, believed equivalent to Nudd (Lludd), a god and king of the Tuatha de Danann. Ludd is the legendary founder of London. His temple in London was located near St. Paul's Cathedral, and

Ludgate Hill is named after the god. He was called Llawereint (silver handed) because a silver artificial hand replaced one of his hands that had been cut off. In later Celtic mythology, Ludd is the name of a British king, founder of London, buried at Ludgate. The later version is probably a mortal form of the earlier god.

See also: NUDD; TUATHA DE DANANN

*St. Luke painting the Madonna*

---

**1930**

**Ludki** (little people)   In Slavic folklore, dwarfs who originally inhabited Serbia but left when Christianity arrived because they could not stand the sound of church bells. They were small, with large heads and big protruding eyes, and they wore large red hats. They taught mankind how to build homes, and they were fond of music and singing. Gifted with the art of prophecy, they often helped human beings but found it difficult to get along with one another. When one died, his body was burned and his ashes put in a vessel that was buried in the earth. The tears shed at the funeral were collected in small jars and placed in ancient cemeteries. In Poland the dwarfs are called *krasnoludi* or *krasnoludki*; in Hungary, *lutky*.

**1931**

**Lugulbanda**   In Near Eastern mythology (Babylonian-Assyrian), shepherd god who appears as a protector and father of the hero in the epic poem *Gilgamesh*. Some myths say that Lugulbanda slew the monster bird, Zu, who had stolen the tablets of fate from the gods. He was most likely a deified Sumerian king and hero.

See also: GILGAMESH; ZU

**1932**

**Luke, St.** (from Lucama, a district in southern Italy)   First century. Evangelist, author of the Gospel that bears his name and the Acts of the Apostles in the New Testament. Patron saint of artists and physicians. Feast, 18 October.

Luke was the beloved physician (Col. 4:14) of St. Paul in many of his missionary journeys. He accompanied Paul to Rome, where he remained with his master and teacher until Paul's martyrdom, according to Christian legend not included in the New Testament. After the death of St. Peter and St. Paul (who were both executed on the same day, according to legend) Luke preached the gospel in Greece and Egypt. There are two traditions regarding his death. In the Greek church he is believed to have died a natural death; in the Western church he is believed to have been crucified at Patras with St. Andrew.

The belief that St. Luke was a painter comes from a Greek legend of the 10th century. A picture of the Virgin Mary was found in the catacombs with an inscription "One of the seven painted by Luca." It was assumed that "Luca" of the inscription was St. Luke, but the artist was probably St. Luke the Greek hermit. Legend expanded the identification: the Evangelist always carried two portraits with him, one of Christ and another of the Virgin Mary, which he had painted from life.

Numerous medieval European churches displayed "Black Madonnas" that were ascribed to St. Luke because of their age. They are usually black from the smoke of the burning candles that has encrusted the works. Numerous medieval Christian artworks portray St. Luke in the process of painting the Madonna and Child. When St. Luke is portrayed as an Evangelist, an ox (winged or unwinged) is often shown with him or made to symbolize the saint.

See also: ANDREW, ST.; PAUL, ST.; PETER, ST.; VIRGIN MARY

1933

**Luna** (the moon)   In Roman mythology, ancient Italian moon goddess; identified by the Romans with the Greek goddess Artemis, who was also associated with the moon. Luna had an ancient sanctuary in Rome on the Aventine, in which as goddess ruling the month she received worship on the last day of March, which was the first month of the old Roman year. As Noctiluca (lamps of the night) Luna had a temple on the Palatine that was lit at night.

See also: ARTEMIS

1934

**Lung-rta** (wind horse)   In Tibetan Buddhism, fantastic horse often found on flags, symbolizing the wind. According to L. Austine Waddell in *The Buddhism of Tibet, or Lamaism*: "The symbol is avowedly a luck-commanding talisman for enhancing the grandeur of the votary."

1935

**Lung Wang** (dragon king)   In Chinese mythology, a general word for a dragon. Dragons control waters and especially rain.

See also: DRAGON

1936

**Luonnotar** (Ilnatar)   In Finnish mythology, creator goddess, daughter of air or the heavens in the epic poem *The Kalevala*, who brought about creation.

The opening of *The Kalevala* tells how Luonnotar had spent her life "all alone in the vast emptiness of space." She descended from the heavens, and the waves carried her for 700 years. "The breath of the wind caressed her bosom and the sea made her fertile" as she was tossed by the waves. Then a gull, teal, eagle, or duck (the animal is not exactly identified) came "flying from the horizon," and Luonnotar "lifted her knees from the waves, and on it the bird made her nest and began to hatch her eggs." The girl became excited and felt heat "till she thought her knee was burning" and her "veins were melting." She jerked her knees, and the eggs rolled into the water and were shattered. From the lower fragments of the eggs the solid earth was fashioned, and the cracked eggs' upper fragments became the "lofty arch of heaven." The egg yolks became the sun; the whites, the gleaming moon. The spotted fragments became the stars and the black fragments were the clouds. Luonnotar went on to create capes, bays, seashores, and the depths and shallows of the oceans. Now the water mother, she gave birth to Vainamoinen, the culture hero and demigod in the epic poem.

Sibelius set part of *The Kalevala* text of the creation to music for female soloist and orchestra, calling the work *Luonnotar*.

See also: *KALEVALA, THE*

1937

**Lu Pan**   In Chinese mythology, a deified mortal worshiped as the god of carpenters and artisans.

1938

**Lutin**   In Haitian voodoo, the ghost of an unbaptized child, which wanders about never finding rest.

*Lu Tung-pin*

1939
**Lu Tung-pin**   Eighth century C.E. In Chinese Taoist mythology, one of the Pa-Hsien, the Eight Immortals. A scholar and recluse, he attained immortality at the age of 50. He is a patron of barbers, and the sick invoke him. In art he holds a Taoist fly brush and sword, which he uses to fight monsters. He was given the sword after he was tempted 10 times and overcame evil.

See also: PA-HSIEN

1940
**Lycaon** (wolf)   In Greek mythology, a wolf-man, king of Arcadia; son of Pelasgus; father of Callisto and 50 sons. Accounts of Lycaon vary. In some myths he appears as impious, in others as a culture hero. According to one myth, Lycaon's sons were evil, having slain their brother Nyctimus and offering the child in a soup to Zeus (who had disguised himself as a poor laborer). In anger Zeus slew all of the sons with a thunderbolt, restored Nyctimus to life, and transformed Lycaon into a wolf. In a variant account Lycaon himself offered the human flesh to test whether Zeus was really a god. In disgust Zeus sent a flood to destroy the earth; only Deucalion and his wife, Pyrrha, were saved. In yet another variant, Lycaon was a priest of Zeus Lycaeus and was spared death, though his children were killed. Some scholars believe that the myth is related to the cannibalism that was part of the cult of Zeus Lycaeus, in which it was believed that those who ate human flesh were turned into wolves and wandered in the wild for eight or 10 years before being able to return to human form—and then only if they did not eat any more human flesh. Ovid's *Metamorphoses* (book 1) and Vergil's *Georgics* (1.138) deal with the myth.

See also: ARCADIA; DEUCALION; WEREWOLF; ZEUS

1941
**Lynx**   A wildcat, half dog and half panther, having long limbs, tufted ears, and a short tail. In Egyptian mythology the lynx was called Maftet and regarded as a friend of the dead. In ancient Greek folklore it was believed that the lynx could see through walls or even a mountain. In medieval Christian belief the animal was a symbol of the omniscience and vigilance of Christ because of the belief in its magical sight. But it was also a symbol of avarice. Its urine was believed to harden into precious stones, which the greedy beast buried in the earth so no one could enjoy its treasure.